JN299241

ビジネス時事英和辞典

Dictionary of
Contemporary Business English

菊地義明 ▶著

三省堂

© 2010 菊地義明

DICTIONARY OF CONTEMPORARY BUSINESS ENGLISH

ビジネス時事英和辞典

Printed in Japan

装幀・組版設計 ─────────── 宗利淳一

組版 ─────────────── 原島康晴(エディマン)

はじめに

　時事英語関連用語辞典として，この『ビジネス時事英和辞典』には，新聞・雑誌等で取り上げられた過去10年の国内外の社会事象や，多用される時事英語特有の表現，新語，固有名詞，略語，関連語句などを含めて2万5,000語ほど収録されています。

　その収録分野は，政治，経済，国際関係，社会から金融，財政，産業，ビジネス，法律等にいたるまで多岐にわたっています。そのため，スポーツや文化など本書の限られた紙面で削除せざるをえない分野や用例もありますが，一般の英字新聞や経済誌，ビジネス専門誌の記事を読み解く上で役に立つものばかりです。

　また，これまでの時事英語辞典の見出し語は名詞中心のものがほとんどですが，本書の特長として，名詞以外に頻繁に使用される形容詞や基本的な動詞，動詞句も多数盛り込まれています。このほか時事英語の読解力を高めるため，関連情報として，用語の解説・説明も適宜，付してあるのも本書の特長です。

　ほぼ瞬時に変わる社会情勢のなかで，ニュース報道に使われる言葉や表現も目まぐるしく変化します。その意味で「この1冊で十分」とは言えませんので，時事英語については今後ともとりわけ最新用語に目を向けて取り組んで行く方針です。

　なお，本書を利用するにあたって，既刊の実用ビジネス用語英和辞典シリーズ『財務情報英和辞典』(三省堂刊)と『ビジネス実務総合英和辞典』(同)との併用をお薦めいたします。

20010年6月
菊地義明

目次

はじめに ─────────────────────────── iii

凡例 ──────────────────────────── iv–v

A—Z ─────────────────────────── 001–550

和英索引 ────────────────────────── 551–632

凡例

1. 見出し語
単一の語のほかに，2語以上からなる語句（分離複合語）も重要なものは見出し語として立てた。同じつづりで語源が異なるもの，複数の品詞を持つもののうち重要なものはそれぞれを見出し語としたが，番号などで区別することはしていない。

1.1 配列
見出し語の配列は原則としてアルファベット順としたが，分離複合語およびハイフンで結合された複合語は，構成要素の最初の語を基準としてひとまとまりで示した。数字は，アルファベットとは別種の文字として扱い，アルファベットよりも前に昇順で置いた。

1.2 品詞
単一の語には品詞を略記した。
- 名 名詞
- 形 形容詞
- 動 動詞
- 他動 他動詞
- 自動 自動詞
- 副 副詞
- 前 前置詞
- 接 接続詞
- 接頭 接頭辞

2. 語義
語義の区分はカンマで示した。

2.1 括弧類
括弧類を次の原則に基づいて使用した。
- （ ）注記，参照，略語の成り立ちなどを示す。
- 〈 〉他動詞の目的語や語の内包的意味を補助的に示す。
- 〔 〕用法面での注記を補助的に示す。
- ［ ］交換可能であることを示す。
- 《 》《略 》の形で略語を示す。

2.2 その他記号類
- ＝ ほぼ同義で用いられる語句を示す。
- ⇒ 当該の見出し語を含む例文が参照先に存在することを表す。

3. 副見出し
分離複合語および文の形をとっていない用例を副見出しとして示した。
配列と語義の書式は見出し語と同様の規則に基づく。

4. 用例
用例は原則として完全文の形で示した。見出し部分を斜字体で示した。

A

a

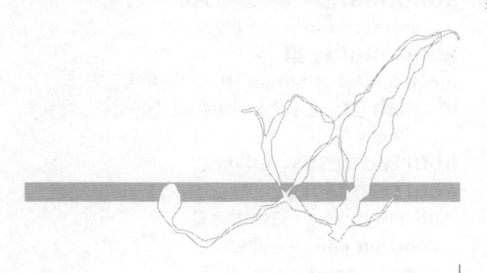

A- 原子力の，原子力を使う，原子力で動く，原子の，原子に関する （＝atomic）
 A-bomb blast 原爆の爆風
 A-bomb illness 原爆症
 A-bomb radiation 原爆放射能
 A-bomb sufferers [victims] 被爆者

abandon 動 廃止する，中断する，中止する，断念する，〈権利や財産を〉放棄する，廃棄する，遺棄する，除却する，〈船舶や積み荷を〉委付する，〈訴訟を〉取り下げる
 ▶ The minimum regulatory capital requirements were *abandoned*. （会社設立時の）最低必要資本金制度は，廃止された。

abandonment 名 廃止，中断，中止，放棄，廃棄，遺棄，除却，引渡し，委付，保険委付，委付保険，〈訴訟の〉取下げ
 abandonment of application 〈特許などの〉出願放棄
 equipment abandonment 設備の廃却
 property abandonment 財産放棄

abate 動 緩和する，軽減する，無効にする，弱まる，和らぐ，衰える，減少する，低下する
 abated currency inflows 資金流入の減少
 abated inflationary pressures インフレ圧力の低下
 ▶ There have been no signs of a rebound in the amount of outstanding loans, which continues on an *abated* decline. このところ引き続き減少傾向にある銀行の貸出残高に，反転の兆しは見えない。

abdominal 形 腹部の
 abdominal girth 腹囲

abduct 動 誘拐する，かどわかす，拉致する （⇒agent）
abductee 名 拉致被害者，拉致による行方不明者
abduction 名 拉致
 abduction issue 名 拉致問題
 abductions 名 拉致事件，拉致
abend 名 〈コンピュータ・プログラム実行中の〉異常終了，〈コンピュータ自体の〉異常停止，アベンド （＝abnormal end）
ability 名 能力，技能，技術，…力，アビリティ
 ability and skill 技能
 ability test 技能試験，技術テスト
 ability to access the market 市場での調達能力
 business needs for ability 能力重視の経営上の必要
 debt ability 借入能力，債務能力
 earnings ability 収益力
 economic ability 経済的能力
 entrepreneurial ability 企業家能力
 executive ability 経営能力
 financial [pecuniary] ability 資力，財力
 lending ability 貸出能力
 management's ability 経営陣[経営者]の能力，経営陣の手腕
 potential growth ability 潜在成長力
 productive ability 生産能力
ABM 弾道弾迎撃ミサイル（**antiballistic missile** の略）
 ABM treaty 弾道弾迎撃ミサイル制限条約，ABM

制限条約
abnormal 形 異常な, 変則な
　abnormal prions 異常プリオン
abnormality 名 異常
　congenital abnormalities 先天性異常
abolish 動 廃止する, 撤廃する (scrap), 放棄する, 廃絶する
aborted fetus 中絶胎児
abortion 名 妊娠中絶, 堕胎
　abortion drug 妊娠中絶薬
　abortion pill 中絶用ピル
　right to abortion 中絶権
about-face 名 方向転換, 〈態度や政策などの〉180度転換［転向, 転回］, 急転換, 回れ右（= about-turn; ⇒contender)
　do an about-face 180度転換する, 回れ右をする, 態度を一変させる
　do an about-face in economic policies 経済政策を180度転換する
abrupt 形 突然の, 急な
　abrupt announcement 突然の発表
absence 名 不在, 欠如, 欠勤
　absence rate 欠勤率
absentee 名 欠勤, 不在, 欠勤者, 不在者
　absentee ballot 不在者投票
　absentee director 不在重役
　absentee rate 欠勤率（= absence rate, absenteeism rate)
　absentee vote 郵送による投票 (postal vote), 不在投票
absolute 形 絶対の, 完全な, 純粋な, 無条件の, 絶対的な, 全面的な
absorb 動 吸収する, 吸収合併する, 配賦する, 填補する, 〈税金などを〉負担する, 解消する
▶ All assets of the company being *absorbed* are taken over by the surviving firm at book value. 吸収される会社（消滅会社）の資産は, すべて存続会社が簿価で引き継ぐ。
abstain (from) 動 棄権する, 遠慮する, 慎む, 差し控える, 控える, 禁酒する
abuse 動 悪用する, 乱用［濫用］する, 不正使用する, 虐待する, ののしる, 悪口をいう, 〈イメージなどを〉損なう
　abuse drugs 麻薬を乱用する
　abuse one's official powers …の公職の権力を濫用する
　be sexually abused 性的虐待を受ける
abuse 名 虐待, 酷使, 不正使用, 乱用, 過剰摂取, 飲みすぎ, 弊害, 悪習, 悪態, 毒舌, 悪口, 人身攻撃
　abuse of authority 職権［権力］の乱用［濫用］
　abuse of public office for personal gains 地位利用
　abuse of office 職権濫用
　abuse of rights 権利の濫用
　child abuse 児童虐待
　computer abuse コンピュータの悪用, コンピュータの不正使用
　drug abuse 麻薬乱用
academic 形 大学の, 学問の, 学業の
　academic controversy 学問上の論争
　academic record 学歴
　academic skills [ability] 学力
　academic year 学年
Academy Awards [Academy awards] アカデミー賞, オスカー（= AMPAS Awards, Oscar：米国の映画芸術科学アカデミー（the Academy of Motion Picture Arts and Science）が毎年3月に授与する映画賞）

主要アカデミー賞

best actor award	主演男優賞
best actress award	主演女優賞
best director award	監督賞
best picture award	最優秀作品賞
best supporting actor award	助演男優賞
best supporting actress award	助演女優賞

▶ The late Jennifer Jones was nominated for *Academy Awards* five times. 最近亡くなった女優のジェニファー・ジョーンズは, アカデミー賞に5回ノミネートされた。
accelerate 動 加速する, 加速させる, 促進する, 推進する, 拍車をかける
▶ The decline in China's exports *accelerated* in February as a slump in global demand worsened. 世界的な需要冷え込みの悪化で, 中国の2月の輸出減少は加速した。
accelerated 形 加速した, 促進された, 拍車がかかった
　accelerated amortization 加速償却, 加速減価償却, 加速なし崩し償却
　accelerated cost recovery system 加速原価回収制度［回収法］, 加速償却制度, 加速償却法, エイカーズ《略 ACRS》
　accelerated depreciation 相場下落の加速, 加速償却, 加速減価償却, 加速償却法

accelerated disposal of bad loans 不良債権処理の加速 （＝speeding up the disposal of nonperforming loans）
accelerated growth 加速的成長
accelerated inflation インフレの加速
accelerated method 加速償却法 （＝accelerated depreciation method）
accelerated price decline 価格下落の加速
accelerated restructuring efforts リストラ策の加速
accentuate 動 強調する，目立たせる
accept 動 承諾する，受諾する，受け入れる，同意する，〈手形や注文などを〉引き受ける，認める，容認する
acceptable 形 一般に認められている，公正妥当と認められている，認められている，許容できる，容認できる，許容範囲の，採択可能な
acceptance 名 〈申し込み［オファー］に対する〉承諾，承認，〈商品の〉受領，検収
　acceptance speech 〈米大統領，副大統領の〉受諾演説，大統領候補指名受諾演説
access 動 接続する，利用する，データを検索する，閲覧する，入手する，参加する，参入する，加入する，立ち入る，接近する
　access cash 資金を調達する
　access external sources of cash 外部から資金調達する （＝access external sources of funding, access external funding sources）
　access foreign technology 海外技術を導入する
　access information on …の情報を入手する
　access the capital markets 資本市場で資金を調達する，資本市場で調達する
　access the market 起債する，市場で資金を調達する
access 名 参入，参入機会，市場アクセス，加入，参加，利用，閲覧，〈コンピュータ・システムやネットワークへの〉接続，アクセス
　access line 加入回線，接続回線，端末回線，アクセス回線
　access right 参照権，アクセス権（端末，中央処理装置，データ，OSやファイルの利用権などがある）
　access route 進入路
　access to assets 資産の取扱い
　access to capital 資金調達，資金調達力
　access to funding [financing] 資金調達，資金源の確保
　access to information 情報の入手，情報の閲覧
　access to markets on an unsecured basis 無担保ベースでの資金調達
　access to records and books of account 会計記録と会計帳簿の閲覧
　access to the market 市場への参入，市場への参入機会，市場進出，市場アクセス，市場へのアクセス （＝market access）
　have access to …に立ち入る，…に面会する，…に参加する，…を入手する，…が利用できる，…を閲覧できる，…に接することができる （＝get access to）
　market access 市場への参入，市場への参入機会，市場進出，市場アクセス，市場へのアクセス （＝access to the market）
　market-access barriers 市場参入障壁
▶ It is a matter of urgency for future newcomers to have *access* to sufficient landing slots and adequate airport facilities. 発着枠の十分な確保と十分な空港施設の利用は，今後新規に参入する企業にとって急務となっている。
accommodate 動 …に金などを融通する，…の借金返済を猶予する，調停する，和解させる
accommodation 名 便宜，恩恵，調停，和解，割引，貸付金，融通手形，宿泊設備
accord 名 合意，同意，合意書，合意文書，協定，意見の一致，和解，代物弁済
account 名 口座，預金，勘定，勘定書，計算，計算書，収支，決算，決算書，会計，取引関係，取引先，説明，報告，記述，供述，理由，考慮，重要性
　a blow-by-blow account of …を逐一伝える報告，こと細かく述べた報告
　account books 会計帳簿，決算書 （＝accounting books, books of account, financial books）
　account holder 口座名義人
　account payable 買掛金，未払い金，支払い勘定，支払い債務，買入れ債務，購入債務，仕入債務
　account receivable 売掛金，未収金，未収入金，受取勘定，売掛債権，売上債権，受取債権 （＝account due, sales credit）
　call ... to account …に釈明を求める，…に責任を問う
　eyewitness account 目撃者の供述，目撃証言
　general account budget 一般会計予算
　global account management グローバル顧客管理

account balance

- **key account management** 主要顧客管理
- **non-interest-bearing account for individuals** 個人向け無利子の預金
- **off-the-book account** 簿外口座
- **open account** 当座預金, 当座勘定, 交互計算
- **open an account** 口座を開設する
- **ordinary account** 普通口座
- **personal account** 個人口座, 個人用口座, パーソナル・アカウント
- **savings account** 普通預金, 貯蓄性預金, 貯蓄預金
- **services account** 貿易外収支
- **special account** 特別会計, 特別取引先
- **specified account** 特定口座
- **trade account** 貿易収支
- **two sets of account books** 二重帳簿

account balance 差引残高, 勘定残高, 銀行口座の残高, 口座残高
▶ The 2009 condensed consolidated balance sheet reflects full consolidation of ABCD's *account balances*.　2009年度の要約連結貸借対照表は, ABCD社の勘定残高の完全連結を反映しています。

account settlement 決算 （＝settlement of accounts）
- **account settlement term ending in March** 3月決算期, 3月期

accountability 名　説明責任, 報告責任, 会社責任, 企業責任, 責任, 義務, アカウンタビリティ
- **accountability to customers** 顧客への説明責任
- **accountability to voters** 有権者への説明責任
- **administrative accountability** 行政の説明責任
- **corporate accountability** 企業の説明責任
- **management accountability** 経営の説明責任, 経営の説明責任能力
- **stewardship accountability** 受託責任
- **transparency and accountability of business management** 経営の透明性と説明責任

accountable 形　責任がある, 責任能力がある
- **be held accountable for** …の責任を問われる, …について責任がある
- **hold a person accountable for** 人に…の責任を持たせる, …の責任は人にある

▶ The company will reduce its capital by 99.7 percent to ¥100 million to make shareholders *accountable* for its financial difficulties.　経営不振［経営危機］に対する株主責任を明確にするため, 同社は1億円に99.7％の減資を実施する［99.7％の減資を実施して資本金を1億円とする］。

accountant 名　会計士, 会計［経理］担当者, 会計専門家, 監査人

accounting 名　会計, 会計処理, 会計処理方法, 会計学, 経理, 計算, 算定
- **accounting documents** 経理書類
- **accounting error** 経理ミス（＝accounting mistake）
- **accounting firm** 会計事務所, 会計士事務所, 監査法人
- **accounting fraud** 会計操作, 不正会計処理, 粉飾決算（＝accounting manipulation）
- **accounting irregularities** 不正経理
- **accounting malpractice** 不正会計
- **accounting manipulation** 会計操作（＝accounting fraud）
- **accounting method** 会計処理方法, 会計方法
- **accounting organization** 会計事務組織, 会計執行組織, 会計組織
- **accounting principle** 会計原則, 会計基準, 会計処理基準, 会計処理の方法
- **accounting rule** 会計規則
- **accounting scandal** 〈不正経理や粉飾決算などの〉企業会計疑惑, 会計疑惑, 会計処理疑惑, 会計不祥事, 会計スキャンダル, 不正会計事件
- **accounting standards** 会計基準, 会計原則（＝accounting criteria）

accounting period 会計期間, 会計年度, 事業年度, 計上時期
- **the accounting period ending March 31** 3月31日終了会計年度, 3月期決算
- **the latest accounting period** 当事業年度, 当期

accounts 名　財務書類, 財務諸表, 計算書類（＝financial statements）
- **accounts receivable** 売掛債権, 売掛金
- **accounts settlement ending in March** 3月期決算
- **annual accounts** 年次財務諸表
- **book of accounts** 会計帳簿, 財務帳簿（＝accounts book）
- **closing of accounts** 決算（＝closing of books）
- **consolidated accounts** 連結財務書類, 連結財務諸表（group accounts）
- **external accounts** 対外収支
- **final accounts** 決算報告書, 決算, 年次財務書

類、年次財務諸表
group accounts グループ財務書類、連結財務書類（＝consolidated accounts）
income and expenditure accounts 収支計算書
interim accounts 中間財務諸表、中間財務書類、半期財務書類（＝interim financial statements, interim statements）
midyear accounts 中間決算
profit and loss accounts 損益計算書
statement of accounts 決算、決算報告、決算報告書
the half-year closing of fiscal 2010 accounts 2010年度中間決算
the last period of settlement of accounts 最終決算期

accumulate 動 集める、蓄積する、累積する、積み上げる、積み増す、築く
accumulate basic data 基礎データを集める
accumulate financial assets 金融資産を積み増す
accumulated and accrued plan benefits 累積年金給付債務額
accumulated deficit 累積赤字（＝accumulative deficit）
accumulated dividend 累積配当、累積利益配当、累積未払い配当
accumulated depreciation (and amortization) 減価償却累計額、減価償却引当金（＝accrued depreciation, allowance [reserve] for depreciation）
accumulated earnings 利益剰余金、留保利益、累積利益、積立利益（＝accumulated income, accumulated profit, earned surplus, retained earnings）
accumulated plan benefits 年金未支給額、年金給付累積額、累積給付額、累積給付債務額
accumulated postretirement benefit obligation 累積退職後給付債務
accumulated profit 利益剰余金、留保利益（＝accumulated income）
accumulated total 累計額
▶ The *accumulated* total of Japanese investment in China exceeds $30 billion. 日本の対中投資［対中直接投資］の累計額は、300億ドルを超えている。

accumulation 名 蓄積、累積、積立て、蓄財、利殖、アキュムレーション
accumulation fund 蓄積資金、蓄積基金

accumulation method アキュムレーション法
accumulation plan 積立てプラン
accumulation trust 蓄財信託
asset accumulation 資産蓄積、年金保険
asset accumulation product 年金商品、貯蓄性商品
capital accumulation 資本蓄積（＝accumulation of capital）
capitalist accumulation 資本主義的蓄積
debt accumulation 累積債務、債務累積
degree of industrial accumulation 工業集積度
group asset accumulation 団体年金保険
individual asset accumulation 個人年金保険
inventory [stock] accumulation 在庫の増加、在庫増、在庫の積み増し、在庫蓄積、在庫累積、滞貨
involuntary accumulation 売れ残り
savings accumulation 貯蓄の増加

accuse 動 告発する、告訴する、起訴する、訴える、非難する、責める、指摘する

acid rain 酸性雨

acid test 厳しい検査、最終的な厳しい考査、厳しい試験、酸性試験、吟味、厳しい試練、試金石、正念場（＝severe test）

acquire 動 取得する、購入する、引き受ける、買収する（＝buy, purchase）
acquire a company via a share swap 株式交換で会社を買収する
acquire the company's shares through a takeover bid 株式公開買付け（TOB）で同社株を取得する
acquired business 買収した事業、非買収事業
acquired company 被買収会社、被買収企業（＝acquiree company, acquired firm）
use shares of the parent to acquire a Japanese company 親会社の株を用いて日本企業を買収する
year acquired 取得年度

acquirer 名 買収会社、買収企業、買収者、取得者、購入者、買取り手
corporate acquirer 企業買収者、買収企業
friendly acquirer 友好的買収者（⇒unfriendly takeover）
potential acquirer 買収者候補
would-be acquirer 買収希望者、買収側

acquisition 名 取得、購入、買取り、買付け、買収(takeover)、企業取得、企業買収、事業買収

acquisition offer 買収の申込み, 買収提案
acquisition price 取得価格, 買付け価格, 取得原価, 買収価格
acquisition proposal 買収提案 (＝acquisition offer)
acquisition talks 買収交渉

acreage 名 面積, 作付け面積, 坪数, エーカー数
▶The average *acreage* cultivated in Japan is 1.6 hectares per household. 日本の平均耕地面積は, 1戸当たり1.6ヘクタールだ。

across-the-board 形 一括の, 一律の, 全面的, 総括的, 全業種一律の, 全社的
across-the-board compliance 法令[規則]の全社的順守
across-the-board cuts in social security spending 社会保障費の一律カット
across-the-board drop 全面安
across-the-board selling 売り一色
across-the-board tax cut 一律減税
across-the-board wage hike 一律値上げ

across the board 全面的に, 全般的に, 軒並み, 一括して, すべてに公平に
appreciate across the board 全面高となる
improve across the board 全面高となる
plunge across the board 全面安となる
retreat across the board 全面安となる (＝fall across the board)
soar across the board 全面高となる (＝go up across the board)
tumble across the board 全面安となる
widen across the board 全面的に拡大する

act 動 行動する, 行動を起こす, 動く, 活動する, 役割を果たす, 作用する, 効果を発揮する, 出演する, 舞台に立つ, 演技する, 演じる
act as …を務める, …として働く, …として行為する, …の要因になる
act as the chairman of the arbitration panel 仲裁機関の議長を務める
act as a go-between 仲介者としての役割を果たす
act for …の代理を務める
act on …に効く, …に作用する
act quickly to put the matters right 事態を収拾するために素早く動く[行動する]

act 名 行為, 行動, 法律, 条令, 制定法
Act Against Unfair Competition 不正競争防止法
act of bankruptcy 破産行為
Act of Congress 〈米〉連邦議会制定法, 連邦の法律
act of indemnity 免責法
act of insolvency 〈銀行の〉支払い不能状態を示す行為 (手形の支払い拒絶や預金の払戻し拒否など)
act of law 法の作用, 裁判所の行為
Act of Parliament 〈英国の〉国会制定法
act of providence 神の行為, 不可抗力, 自然現象 (＝act of God)
act of sale 〈公式の〉売買記録
Clean Air Act 大気汚染防止法, 大気浄化法, 排ガス規制法 (Muskie Act (マスキー法) ともいう)
Community reinvestment Act 地域社会再投資法
completion of act 法案の成立
Consolidation Act 統合法
Consumer Credit Protection Act 消費者信用保護法
Equal Employment Opportunity Act 平等雇用機会法
Export Administration Act 〈米〉輸出管理法
judicial act 法律行為
Restrictive Trade Practices Act 制限的取引慣行法
Section 301 of the Trade Act of 1974 米通商法301条
Taft-Hartley Act タフト・ハートレー法 (Labor Management Relations Act of 1947 (1947年労使関係法) の通称)
Trust by act of law 法定信託
Uniform Sales Act 統一売買法

action 名 行動, 活動, 実行, 動き, 動向, 行政上の処分, 措置, 対応, 決議, 決定, 訴え, 訴訟, 裁判の判決, 行為, 作為, アクション (⇒blanket action)
action holiday 報償休暇
action level 限界水準
action plan 行動計画, 実行計画, アクション・プラン (＝action program)
action point 行動提案
administrative action 行政処分
affirmative action 積極的優遇措置, 積極的是正措置, 差別修正措置, 差別撤廃措置, 少数民族の優遇措置, アファーマティブ・アクション
blanket action 一斉摘発
business action 業務行為
class action 集団訴訟, 集団代表訴訟

disciplinary actions 懲戒処分
industrial action 争議行為, 労働争議, ストライキ
line of action 行動方針
price action 値動き
rating action 格付け見直し, 格付け変更
unofficial action 非公認活動, 非公式活動

activate 動 活性化する, 活発にする, 促進する, 作動させる, 起動させる, 活動させる, 行動させる, 実行に移す, 行使する, 戦時編成する, 戦闘配備する, 浄化する, 作動する, 始動する
activate the domestic demand 内需を活性化する
activate the facility 借入れを実行に移す
activate the option オプションを行使する
activated carbon [charcoal] 活性炭
activated sludge 活性スラッジ, 下水浄化泥

activation 名 活性化, 促進, 作動, 始動, 就職活動, 活性化対策, 浄化, 放射能

active 形 活発な, 活動的な, 活況を呈している, 取引量の多い, 積極的な, 現役の, 現職の, 勤続中の, 使用可能な状態にある, 動作中[動作状態]にある, アクティブ
active account 活動口座, 活動勘定
active aircraft 現役航空機, 現用航空機, 現用機
Active Army 米現役陸軍
active assets 活動資産, 生産活動資産, 生産資産, 生産資本
active bad debt account 回収可能性のある不良資産
active balance 黒字バランス
active balance of payments 国際収支の黒字
active ballistic missile defense 対弾道弾積極的防御[防護]
active bond 花形債券, 利付き公債
active buying 買い進み
active capital 活動資本
active capital goods 生産財
active circulation 〈貨幣の〉現在流通高, 銀行券流通高
active commerce [trade] 自主貿易, 直接貿易
active debt 利付き貸付け, 能動的公債
active deposit 流動預金, 活動預金
active discussion 白熱した議論
active employment policy 積極的雇用政策
active file 活動ファイル
active investor 能動的投資家
active job-opening ratio 有効求人倍率

active life fund 在職者基金
active management 積極的運用, アクティブ運用, 積極的な経営陣
active manpower policy 積極的労働力政策, 積極的マンパワー政策
active market 活発な市況, 活況市場, 好況市場, 好況市況, 好況
active money 活動現金, 取引貨幣, 金融活発
Active Movie Streaming Format 音声や画像をインターネットで即時送信するストリーミング技術の規格
active National Guard 米現役州兵
active noise control 能動的騒音抑制, アクティブ・ノイズ・コントロール
active partner 〈合名会社(partnership)の〉業務担当社員
active plan participant 勤続中の[現役の]制度加入者
active planning 実行計画, 活動計画
active policy 積極方針
active program 現在使用中のプログラム, 動作中[作動中]のプログラム
active reserve 活動積立金
active satellite 能動衛星
active securities 花形証券, 人気証券
active service 現役勤務, 現役
active service user 使用頻度の高い顧客
active smoking 能動喫煙(受動喫煙=passive smoking)
active state 動作状態
active stock 人気株, 花形株 (=active real share)
active stock market 活発な株式市場, 株式市場の活況
active system アクティブ・システム(コンピュータを組み込んだハイファイ装置)
active title 出版目録に載っている絶版以外の本 (=active list)
active trade balance 貿易収支の黒字
active trading 活発な取引
active vision 能動的ビジョン
pro-active moves 早めの対応
ratio of sufficiencies to active openings 労働力充足率

activity 名 活動, 動き, 働き, 活動範囲, 活動度, 操業, 事業, 業務, 業務活動, 取引, 活気, 活況, 景気, 好景気
acquisition activities 企業買収活動

banking activities　銀行業務
business activities　事業活動
commercial activities　商業活動, 営業活動
core activities　中核事業, 主力事業　(＝main activities)
economic activity　経済活動, 景気, 経済動向
financing activities　財務活動, 資金調達活動, 金融活動, 資金調達と返済に関する活動
hedging activities　ヘッジ取引
investing activities　投資活動
local citizenship activities　社会貢献活動
operating activities　営業活動
pick-up in activity　景気回復
quality control activity　QC運動
regional activity　地域活動
statement of activity　営業報告書, 活動報告書
trading activities　業務展開

actual 形　実際の, 実地の, 現実的, 現実の, 実質的, 事実上の, 現行の
actual achievement　実績
actual cost　実際原価, 取得原価
actual demand　実需
actual exchange rate　直物レート
actual expense　実際経費, 実費
actual growth rate　現実成長率
actual hour　実際発生時間
actual inflation　実際のインフレ率
actual losses　実際の損失額, 実損
actual market　顕在市場
actual margin　実効証拠金率
actual money rate　実際の金利
actual rate of interest　実際金利, 実質利子率　(＝actual interest rate)
actual transaction　実際取引
actual volume　実際操業度

acute 形　鋭い, 鋭利な, 激しい, 急性の
acute liver disorders　急性肝障害

ad hoc　特別の目的のための, 臨時の, 臨機応変の, 応急の
ad hoc committee [commission]　特別委員会
ad hoc headquarters　特別本部
ad hoc measure　臨時の措置, 応急措置
on an ad hoc basis　その場かぎりの判断に基づいて

ad hocracy [adhocracy]　臨機応変的経営
ADB　アジア開発銀行　(Asian Development Bankの略)
add 動　加える, 追加する, 加算する, 合計する, 付加する, 付け加える, 増す, 強化する, 高める, 押し上げる
add in　…を算入する, …を含める, …を加える
add on　付け足す, 加える, 追加する, 建て増す, 増築する
add synergy　相乗効果を高める
add to　…を増す, …を増大させる
add up　…を考慮する
add up to　合計して…になる, 結局…になる, 押し上げる
add value to　…の付加価値を高める
to add to　…に加えて

add-on 名　追加, 付属品, 付加装置, アタッチメント, 〈法案などの〉追加条項, アドオン
add-on CPU board　アドオンCPUボード
add-on equipment　追加機器, 付属機器, 付属設備, アタッチメント
add-on rate　アドオン金利(当初元本に基づいて利息を計算)
add-on software　アドオン・ソフト　(＝add-in software：既存のアプリケーション・ソフトに組み込んで, さらに別の機能を加えることができるユーティリティ・ソフト)
add-on telephone　アドオン電話

added value　付加価値
added value analysis　付加価値分析
added value goods　付加価値製品
added value per employee　従業員1人当たりの付加価値額(人材の余剰度合いを示す経営指標)
added value tax　付加価値税　(＝value-added tax：日本の消費税に相当)

additional 形　追加の, 付加的な, 特別の
additional assessment　追徴金
additional budget　追加予算, 補正予算
additional capex　設備投資の追加
additional easing　一層の金融緩和, 追加金融緩和
additional investment　追加投資
additional loan　追加融資
additional monetary easing measure　追加金融緩和策
additional order　追加注文
additional tax penalty　追徴税額
additional taxation　追徴課税
additional taxes　追徴税, 加算税, 増税

additionality 名　追加性
address 動　取り組む, 取り扱う, 処理する, 対応す

る，応対する，調整する，提出する，話しかける，呼びかける，演説［講演］する，声明を発表する，…にあて名を書く，〈注意などを〉…に向ける［注ぐ］，申し込む，委託する，託送する，請願［嘆願］する，…の解任請求をする
address a warning to …に警告を発する
address market risk 市場リスクに対応する
address oneself to …に専念する，…に着手する，…に話しかける，…に向かって発言する，…に請願する
address the audience 聴衆に呼びかける，聴衆に話しかける
address the conference 会議の出席者に講演を行う
address the meeting 集会の出席者に講演を行う
address 名 取組み，取扱い，処理，対応，〈処理の〉手際よさ，手早さ，敏速，話しぶり，提出，演説，講演，式辞，あいさつ，住所，あて名，あて先，解任請求，アドレス
address book アドレス帳，住所録
address unknown あて先不明
billing address 請求先住所
deliver [give, make] an opening address 開会の辞を述べる
domain address ドメイン（ネットワーク上のコンピュータの識別符号）
e-mail address メール・アドレス，Eメール・アドレス
farewell address お別れ演説
forwarding address 転送先
give [deliver, make] an address 演説する，講演をする
home address 自宅住所
inaugural address 就任演説，就任のあいさつ，就任の辞
Internet protocol address IPアドレス（＝IP address）
network address ネットワーク・アドレス
notification of change of address 住所変更届け
of no fixed address 住所不定の
office address 勤務先の住所
permanent address 連絡先，定住所，本籍
policy address [speech] 〈首相の〉所信表明演説
shipping address 配送先住所
subnet address サブネット・アドレス

television address テレビ演説
title and form [mode, style] of address 肩書きと呼び名［敬称］
virtual email address バーチャル・メールアドレス
adhere 動 付着する，支持する，固守する，固執する
adjacent 形 近くの，近隣の，隣接する
adjourn 動 延期する，休会とする，散会する
adjust 動 修正する，調整する，調節する，是正する，補正する，織り込む
adjust to the rise in inflation インフレ率上昇率を織り込む
adjust trade balance 貿易不均衡を是正する
adjusted current earnings 調整後当期利益《略 ACE》
adjusted earnings per share 調整後1株当たり利益
adjusted for inflation and taxes インフレと税金修正後の
be adjusted downward 下方修正される
in seasonally adjusted dollar terms 季節調整済みのドル表示額で
in seasonally adjusted GDP 季節調整済みGDPの
not seasonally adjusted 季節調整前の
risk-adjusted yield [returns] リスク調整後の利回り
seasonally adjusted annual rate 季節調整済み年率
adjustment 名 調整，修正，照合，整理，査定，精算
adjustment for taxable income 税務調整，申告調整
capital adjustment 資本修正
downward adjustment 下方修正，減額修正，下方調整
exchange rate adjustment 為替レートの調整
inventory adjustment 在庫調整
loss adjustment expense 損害査定費
prior period adjustment 過年度修正，過年度損益修正，前期損益修正
production adjustment 生産調整
seasonal adjustment 季節調整
structural adjustment 構造調整
upward adjustment 上方修正，増額修正
administration 名 経営，経営管理，経営陣，理事会，執行部，管理，運営，運用，統括，監督，事

務, 事務管理, 業務, 執行, 執務, 実行, 実施, 政権, 政府, 行政, 政府部局, 行政当局, 政権運営, 政権担当期間, 任期, 投薬, 投与, 治療
administration cost 一般管理費 (＝administration expense, administration overhead)
administration process 社内手続き, 事務手続き
business administration 企業経営, 商工経営, 経営管理, 経営学 (＝business management)
capital and administration 資本と経営
department administration 部門管理
financial administration 財務管理, 財政
general administration cost 一般管理費
human resources and administration department 人事・総務部
personnel administration 人事管理
the administration of shares 株式事務
the Barack Obama administration オバマ政権 (＝the Obama administration)
the board of administration 理事会
the Farmers Home Administration 農業住宅局
the Federal Housing Administration 〈米〉連邦住宅局
the Food and Drug Administration 〈米〉食品医薬局
the General Services Administration 調達庁
the incoming U.S. administration 次期米政権
the U.S. administration 米政府, 米政権
wage administration 賃金管理
administrative 形 経営管理上の, 経営上の, 運営上の, 管理上の, 管理的, 行政の
administrative ability 経営能力, 経営手腕, 管理能力, 行政手腕
administrative and maintenance expenses 維持管理費, 維持管理費用
administrative and selling expenses 一般管理費および販売費
Administrative Appeal Law 行政不服審査法
administrative control 管理統制, 業務統制, 運営管理コントロール, 行政管理
administrative cycles 管理サイクル
administrative expenses 一般管理費, 管理費, 経費 (＝administration costs, administration overhead, administrative and general expense)
administrative guidance 行政指導
administrative policy 業務方針
administrative process 運用過程
administrative reform 行政改革
administrative services 行政サービス
adopt 動 採用する, 採択する, 選出する, 指名する
ADR 米国預託証券 (American Depository Receipt の略)
ads 名 広告 (⇒advertising)
ads in the trains 車内広告
classified ads 求人広告 (＝classifieds)
newspaper ads 新聞広告
want ads 求人広告 (＝classified ads)
ADSL 非対称デジタル加入者回線, 非対称デジタル加入者線(asymmetric digital subscriber line の略)
adultery 名 不倫, 不貞, 不義, 密通, 姦通
commit adultery 不倫する, 不倫をする, 不貞を働く
double adultery 重姦通(既婚者同士の不倫)
advance 動 進歩する, 発展する, 前進する, 進出する, 増加する, 上昇する, 向上する, 値上がりする, 進める, 促進する, 〈提出する予定を〉繰り上げる, 前渡しする, 前払いする, 提供する
advance funds 資金を提供する
advance strongly 力強く伸びる, 力強く値上がりする, 大幅に伸びる, 大幅な伸びを示す, 力強い伸びを示す
advance 名 進歩, 発展, 進展, 革新, 前進, 進出, 増加, 上昇, 騰貴, 向上, 値上がり, 前払い, 前渡し, 前貸し, 融資, 借入れ, 前払い金, 前渡し金, 前貸し金, 前受金, 前金, 仮払い金, 借入金
advance copy 予定原稿, 新刊見本, アドバンス・コピー
advance-decline line 騰落株線 (＝A-D line)
advance in profits 増益
advance in productivity 生産性の伸び, 生産性の向上
advance man 先乗り要員, 先発員, 先遣隊員, 遊説準備隊員
advance notice 事前通告
advance of funds 資金の提供
advance sales 予約販売, 前売り
bank advance 銀行貸出
cash advance 頭金
economic advance 経済進展
generate a strong advance 業績を大幅に伸ばす

make a liquidity advance 資金を提供する, 流動性を供与する
royalty advance 〈著作権, 特許権などの〉前払い使用料
strong advance 力強い伸び, 大幅な伸び
technical advances 技術革新, 技術の進歩（＝advances in technology）
advanced 形 進んだ, 進歩［発展］した, 先端の, 最新の, 最新鋭の, 高度な, 高等の, 上級レベルの, 前渡しの, 期限前の, 繰上げの
advanced age 高齢
advanced ballistic re-entry system 新型弾道（大気圏）再突入システム
Advanced Communications Technology Satellite 実験通信衛星《略 ACTS》
advanced composite airframe program 先進複合材料体構造計画
advanced composite material 先端複合材料, 先進複合材料《略 ACM》
advanced concept technology demonstration 先進概念技術実証
advanced country 先進国（＝advanced nation）
advanced credit 既習単位
advanced degree 博士号
advanced developing nation 先進開発途上国
advanced economy 先進経済
Advanced Energy Projects 米政府の先端エネルギー・プロジェクト《略 AEP》
advanced gas-cooled reactor 改良型ガス冷却炉
advanced GDP figures GDP速報値
advanced industrial economy 先進工業国
advanced industrial nation 先進工業国
advanced industrialized nation 先進国
advanced information communications society 高度情報通信社会
advanced information society 高度情報化社会, 高度情報社会
advanced materials 新素材
advanced piloting system 先進的操縦システム
Advanced Planning & Scheduling 先端プランニング・スケジューリング・システム《略 APS》
advanced processing 二次加工, 川下部門
advanced redemption 繰上げ償還（＝early redemption）
advanced safety vehicle 先進安全自動車
advanced technology bomber 高度先端技術
advanced telecommunications features 先端通信機能
advanced television 高品位テレビ
advanced thermal reactor 新型転換炉《略 ATR》
advanced traffic information system 高度交通情報システム
advanced turbo-prop 先進ターボプロップ《略 ATP》
advanced nation 先進国（＝advanced country）
advanced technology 最新技術, 先進技術, 先端技術, 高度技術（＝high technology, sophisticated technology, state-of-the-art technology）
advanced technology in the field of space communications 宇宙通信先端技術
advanced technology industry 先端技術産業, 先進技術産業
advantage 名 有利, 利点, 強み, メリット, 利益, 優勢, 優位, 優位性, 競争力, 優遇措置
advantage price 優位価格
clear and sustainable advantages 明確かつ持続可能な優位性
comparative advantage 比較優位, 比較優位性（＝relative advantage）
cost advantage コスト面での競争力
economic advantages 経済的優位
gross advantage 総利益
mutual advantage 相互利益
net advantage 正味利益
ownership advantage 所有上の優位
relative advantage 比較優位
tax advantages 税制上の優遇措置, 節税効果
trading advantage 取引上の優位性
advent 名 出現, 到来
adversary system 〈米国の〉対審制度
adverse 形 逆の, 反対の, 逆向きの, 不都合な, 不利な, 不利益な, 意に添わない, 不運な, 不幸な, 批判的な, 有害な
adverse balance 国際収支の赤字（＝adverse balance of payments）
adverse balance of trade 輸入超過（＝adverse trade balance）
adverse budget 赤字予算
adverse comment 非難, 批判
adverse conditions 悪条件

adverse current 逆流
adverse economic conditions 経済情勢の悪化
adverse effect 逆効果, 不利な影響, 悪影響, マイナス影響, 悪材料 （＝adverse impact, negative effect）
adverse environment 厳しい環境
adverse exchange 逆為替, 下げ相場
adverse factor 悪材料
adverse impact 悪影響, 不利な影響, マイナス影響, 悪材料 （＝adverse effect）
adverse opinion 不利な意見, 批判的な意見, 不適正意見, 反対意見
adverse selection 逆選択（保険事故発生の可能性が高いリスクほど契約者が進んで保険に入りたがる傾向をいう）
adverse situation 困難な状況
adverse times 逆境
be bond-adverse 債券相場に打撃を与える
be under adverse circumstances 逆境にある

advertisement 名 広告, 広告宣伝 （＝ads, advertising）

advertising 名 広告, 広告宣伝, 広告宣伝費 （＝ads, advertisement）
advertising agent 広告代理店, 広告代理人
advertising budget 広告予算
advertising jingle 宣伝文句, 宣伝のかけ声
advertising linage 広告行数
advertising revenue 広告収入
advertising-to-editorial ratio 広告紙面比率

adviser [advisor] 名 顧問, 顧問業務, 顧問業, 顧問会社, 諮問, 相談役, 助言者, 〈米〉大統領補佐官, アドバイザー
commodity trading adviser 商品取引顧問会社, 商品投資顧問会社
Council of Economic Advisers 経済諮問委員会
financial adviser 財務顧問, 資金調達のアドバイザー, フィナンシャル・アドバイザー
investment adviser 投資顧問, 投資顧問業
special advisor 特別顧問
supreme adviser 最高顧問

advisory 形 顧問の, 諮問の, 助言の, 勧告の, アドバイザリー
advisory body 諮問機関 （＝advisory organ, advisory panel）
advisory business 顧問業務, 顧問業, 投資顧問業 （＝advisory service）
advisory committee 諮問委員会
advisory contract アドバイザリー契約
advisory council 諮問評議会
advisory subpanel 諮問機関
management advisory service 経営助言サービス

advocacy 名 弁護, 擁護, 支持, 支援, 唱道, 弁護士の職務, 圧力団体
advocacy activities 擁護活動, 支援活動
advocacy advertising [ad] 意見広告, 政見放送, 意見広告放送
advocacy group 支持者グループ, 支援者グループ, 活動グループ, 市民団体, …を守る会, …を実現する会, …のための会
advocacy journalism 特定の立場を支持する報道機関
advocacy organization [group] 圧力団体, 支援団体

advocate 名 擁護者, 支持者, 支援者, 信奉者, 賛成者, 唱道者, 主唱者, 提唱者, 弁護士
abortion rights advocates 中絶権支持者［支持者グループ］
advocate of [for] disarmament 軍縮論者
advocate of gun control 銃規制論者
advocate of reform 改革主唱者
advocates for abuse victims 虐待被害者の支援者［支援者グループ］
Faculty of Advocates 弁護士会
judge advocate 法務官
Lord Advocate 検事総長
peace advocate 平和論者

Aegis-equipped destroyer [vessel] イージス艦

aerial 形 航空の, 空中の, 空気の
aerial bombardment 空爆
aerial cableway 空中ケーブル, ロープウェイ
aerial farming 航空農業
aerial inspection [reconnaissance, surveillance] 空中査察, 空中偵察
aerial navigation 航空術
aerial photograph 航空写真
aerial refueling 空中給油
aerial search 空からの捜索
aerial space 領空 （＝airspace）
aerial spraying 空中散布
aerial survey 航空観測, 航空測量
aerial wire アンテナ

affair 名 仕事, 業務, 事務, 事業, 事態, 情勢,

状況, 事柄, 問題, 事件, 出来事, 事項, 関心事, 関係, 恋愛[不倫]関係 (⇒internal affairs)
affairs entrusted 委任事項
affairs of sate 国事, 政務
as affairs stand 現状では
Associate Director for Program Affairs 〈米運輸省商業用宇宙輸送室の〉プログラム担当次長
business affairs 仕事, 業務, 商務, 企業事象
community affairs 社会事業
congressional and intergovernmental affairs 議会・政府間問題
consular affairs 領事事務
consumer affairs 消費者問題
current affairs 時事問題
economic and agricultural affairs 経済・農業問題
economic affairs 経済問題, 経済情勢
environmental affairs 環境問題
financial affairs 財務内容, 財務状態, 財務状況 (＝financial position)
foreign affairs 外交問題, 外交
get one's affairs straight 財務を整理する
human affairs 人事
human rights and humanitarian affairs 人権・人道的問題
international affairs 国際問題, 国際関係, 対外関係, 国際情勢
international security affairs 国家安全保障問題
Judicial Affairs Committee of the lower house 衆院法務委員会
legislative affairs 立法問題
love affair 不倫, 情事, 恋愛事件, 〈物事に対する〉熱意, 熱狂 (＝an affair of love)
Ministry of Foreign Affairs 〈日本の〉外務省
monetary affairs 財務, 金銭上の問題, 金銭問題
national security affairs 国家安全保障問題
official affairs 公務
on business affairs 商用で, 所用で (＝on business)
personal affairs 人事, 個人的な問題
politico-military affairs 政治軍事問題
public affairs 公務, 公報, 広報
romantic affairs 情事
security affair 系列証券会社
state of affairs 事態, 形勢, 情勢, 財政状態
statement of affairs 状況報告書

Watergate affair ウォーターゲート事件
wind up one's affairs 店じまいをする
world affairs 国際問題, 国際社会
affect 動 影響を及ぼす, …に影響する, 変化をもたらす, …を対象とする, 害を及ぼす
affect a stock price 株価に影響を与える
affect the market 相場に影響を与える
be affected adversely 逆風となる, 向かい風となる, 悪影響を受ける, 不利な影響を受ける, 〈投資家心理などが〉冷え込む (＝be adversely affected)
be affected by …により影響を被る, …の影響を受ける, …に心を動かされる, …を悲しむ, 残念に思う
affiliate 動 提携する, 合併する, 傘下入りする, 加入する, 加盟する, 友好関係を結ぶ, 提携させる, 合併させる, 系列[傘下]に置く, 加入させる
affiliated card 提携カード, 共用カード
affiliated loan 提携ローン
affiliated supermarket 系列スーパー
bank-affiliated credit card company 銀行系クレジット・カード会社, 銀行系カード会社
bank-affiliated securities subsidiary 銀行系証券子会社
foreign-affiliated company 外資系企業
government-affiliated financial institution 政府系金融機関
affiliate 名 関係会社, 関連会社, 系列会社, 子会社, 外郭団体, 関係者, 提携者, 加入者, 参加者, アフィリエイト (＝affiliate firm, affiliated company, associate)
affiliate program 提携プログラム, アフィリエイト・プログラム (＝associate program：販売促進の手段として広まっている成功報酬型広告の一種。インターネットの自分のホームページにネット広告を載せ, それを見た人が実際に商品を買ったら報酬が得られる)
consolidated affiliate 連結対象の関連会社, 連結対象の持ち分法適用会社
investment in affiliate [affiliated company] 関係会社への投資, 関係会社株式
unconsolidated affiliate 連結対象外関連会社
affiliated 形 系列の, 系列下の, 提携している, 加盟[加入]している, 支部の, 付属の
affiliated company 関係会社, 関連会社, 系列会社
affiliated group 関連グループ
affiliated loan 提携ローン

affiliated person 利害関係者
affiliated supermarket 系列スーパー
affiliation 名 系列, 系列化, 系列関係, 親密, 親善, 親善関係, 関係, 養子縁組, 縁組, 入籍, 父子関係の決定, 提携, 協力, 協力関係, 合併, 併合, 同盟, 入会, 加入, 参加, 加盟
　affiliation proceedings 父子鑑定検査（= paternity test）
　business affiliation 企業の系列[系列化]
　corporate affiliations 系列関係
　industrial affiliations 企業系列
　party affiliations 党派関係
　sister-city affiliation 姉妹都市の提携, 姉妹都市関係, 姉妹都市縁組
affluent 形 豊かな, 裕福な, 豊富な
Afghan 名 アフガニスタン人, アフガニスタン語, 形 アフガニスタンの, アフガニスタン人の, アフガニスタン語の
　Afghan reconstruction conference アフガニスタン復興支援会議
afloat 形 流通している,〈水面・空中に〉浮かんでいる, 不安定になっている, 借金しないでいる, 借金[負債]がない, 副 破産しないで, 経営破綻[破綻]しないで, 流通して, 浮動して
　keep [stay] afloat 借金しないでいる, 借金しないでやっていく
　keep the company afloat 同社の破綻を避ける, デフォルトを避ける
▶ The U.S. government refused to provide public funds to keep Lehman Brothers *afloat*. 米政府は, リーマン・ブラザーズの破綻を避けるための公的資金の注入[投入]を拒んだ。
afoot 形 進行中の,〈事が〉起こっている, 計画されている
▶ Price cuts are *afoot* in other convenience stores. 値下げは, 他のコンビニでも行われている。
after-hours trading 時間外取引（⇒off-hours trading）
aftermath 名〈事件・災害などの〉直後, 余波, 影響, 結果
　in the aftermath of …の影響で, …の直後, …に続いて, …のさめやらぬ頃
after tax 税引き後, 税引き後で
　after-tax loss 税引き後損失, 税引き後赤字
　after-tax profit 税引き後利益, 税引き後黒字
age 名 年数, 年齢, 経過期間, 経過年数, 耐用年数
　age discrimination 年齢制限
　age of globalization グローバル時代
　effective age 実効築後経過年数
　entry age cost method 加入年齢方式
　pensionable age 支給開始年齢
　remaining economic age 経済的残存耐用年数
　voting age 選挙年齢（⇒age of majority）
　weighted average loan age 加重平均ローン経過期間
age bracket [group] 年齢層
age of majority 成人年齢
age of people decline 人口減少社会
agenda 名 議題, 課題, 協議事項, 予定, 予定表, 予定案, 政策, 覚書, 備忘録
　be high on the agenda 重要議題に挙げられる, 最重要課題となる
　fiscal agenda 財政政策
　humanitarian agenda 人道的政策
　item on the agenda 議題
　lending agenda 融資案件
　on the agenda 議事日程に載っている
agent 名 代理店, 代理人, 代行業者, 仲介業者, 斡旋業者, 担当者, 保険外交員, セールスマン, 捜査官, 工作員, 手先, スパイ, 諜報機関員, 主因, 動因, 要因, 作用物質, 薬剤, エージェント
　agent bank 幹事銀行, エージェント行（= lead bank, lead manager）
　agent of disease 病原菌
　blood-clotting agents 血液凝固因子
　cancer-forming agent 発がん物質（= cancerous-causing agent）
　cleaning agent 洗剤
　double agent 二重スパイ
　FBI agent FBI（米連邦捜査局）捜査官
　insurance agent 保険外交員, 保険代理店
　intelligent agent 情報の代理店
　nerve agent 神経ガス
　North Korean agent 北朝鮮工作員
　real estate agent 不動産業者（= estate agent）
　sales agent 〈保険などの〉営業職員, 保険外交員
　secret agent スパイ
　shopping agent ショッピング・エージェント(オンライン・ショッピングの支援・代行業者)
　transfer agent 名義書換え代理人, 証券代行機関
　travel agent 旅行案内業者, 旅行業者
aggravate 動 悪くする, 悪化させる, 激化させ

る, 増幅させる, 〈罪や負担などを〉一層重くする, 怒らせる, 悩ませる
aggravate fears 恐怖心を増幅させる
aggravated breach of trust 特別背任
aggravated employment situation 雇用情勢の悪化, 雇用状況の悪化
feel [be] aggravated しゃくにさわる
▶ The financial crisis is *aggravating* housing-market correction in several European economies at a time when external demand is fading rapidly. 外需が急速に落ち込んでいるときに, 金融危機で, 住宅市場の調整が欧州の一部で負担増となっている.

aggressive 形 積極的な, 意欲的な, 精力的な, やる気のある, 攻撃的な, 好戦的な, 攻めの, 侵略的な, 押しの強い, 強引な, 強気の, 野心的な, 粗暴な, 乱暴な, 大幅な, 大型の, 破格の, 過剰な, アグレッシブ
  aggressive asset management strategy 積極的な資産運用戦略, 強気の資産運用
  aggressive business strategy 攻めの経営戦略, 攻めの事業［企業］戦略
  aggressive easing (of monetary policy) 積極的な金融緩和, 大幅な金融緩和
  aggressive cost cutting measures 積極的なコスト削減策
  aggressive (interest) rate cuts 大幅な利下げ
  aggressive investment 攻撃的投資
  aggressive mark-up inflation 攻撃的マークアップ・インフレ
  aggressive pricing strategy 強気の価格戦略, 積極的な価格戦略
  aggressive propensity to consume 過剰な消費性向
  aggressive sales tactics 強引な販売戦術, 強引な勧誘
  aggressive stimulus package 大型の財政出動
  aggressive wage-push inflation 攻撃的賃金プッシュ・インフレ（物価安定時の賃金引上げにより発生する物価上昇）

agile 形 機敏な, 敏捷な, 素早い, 身軽な, 小回りのきく, 頭が切れる, 回転が速い, 活発な, 生き生きとした

aging 名 高齢化, 加齢, 老化, 老朽, 老朽化, 熟成, エイジング, 形 年老いた, 高齢の, 老齢の
  aging and unproductive dairy cows 乳廃牛（＝older dairy cows：高齢で乳の出が悪くなった乳牛）
  aging society with a declining birthrate 少子高齢化社会, 少子高齢化
  an aging population 高齢化, 高齢化人口（＝a graying of the population, the graying of society）
  an aging society 高齢化
  an aging society and declining birthrate 少子高齢化
  rapid aging of the population 急速な高齢化
  the aging of society, coupled with the declining birthrate 少子高齢化, 少子高齢化社会
  the rapidly aging population and the diminishing number of children 急激な少子高齢化
  the trend of an aging population coupled with a declining birthrate 少子高齢化の傾向

agree 動 同意する, 合意する, 合意に達する, 承認する, 承諾する, 賛成する, 取り決める, 決定する
  agree a price 話し合いで価格を決める
  agree in writing 書面で同意する
  agree on [upon] …について合意に達する, …について合意する
  agree to …することに合意する, …することに同意する
  agree to disagree [differ] about 意見の違いを認め合う
  agreed framework 枠組み合意
  as agreed 合意に従って
  as previously agreed すでに取り決めたように
  be agreed on …に関して同意見である
  I couldn't agree (with you) less. 絶対反対です.
  I couldn't agree (with you) more. まったく同感です.
  mutually agree 相互に同意する, 合意する

agreement 名 契約, 契約書, 合意, 合意書, 合意事項, 同意, 同意書, 協定, 協約, 取決め, 了解, 〈意見などの〉一致
  agreement on disarmament 軍縮協定
  aim at reaching a broad agreement 大枠合意を目指す
  basic agreement 基本的合意, 基本合意, 大筋合意, 基本合意書, 基本契約, 基本契約書
  come to [arrive at, reach] de facto agreement on …に関して事実上の合意に達する
  general agreement that …という一般的な意見の一致

in agreement with …に同意して, …と一致して, …に従って
labor agreement 労働契約, 労使協約
loan agreement 借入契約, 融資契約, 貸付け契約
monetary agreement 通貨協定
negotiate an agreement 契約を取り決める
reach a tentative agreement with …と暫定協定で合意する, …と暫定協定を結ぶ, 暫定協定が成立する
tacit agreement 暗黙の了解
trade agreement 通商協定
union agreement 労働協約
verbal agreement 口頭による取決め, 口頭契約
win an agreement 合意を得る

agribusiness 名 農業関連産業, アグリビジネス
agricultural 形 農業の, 農産物に関する
  agricultural negotiations 農業交渉 (= farm talks)
  agricultural product 農産品
  agricultural sector 農業分野
agriculture 名 農業
Agriculture, Forestry and Fisheries Ministry 農林水産省
aid 名 援助, 支援, 応援, 救援, 救援物資, 協力, 手助け, 補助器具, 補助具, 助手
  additional aid 追加支援
  aid activist 支援活動家
  aid bond 補助公債
  aid effectiveness 援助効果
  aid fund 助成金, 助成基金, 支援資金, 援助資金
  aid giver 援助国, 援助供与国 (= aid giving [providing] nation)
  aid package 支援策, テコ入れ策
  aid policy 援助政策, 支援策
  aid programs 開発援助, 援助計画
  aid receipts 援助受取額
  aid recipient 被援助国, 援助受取国, 援助を受ける側 (= aid receiver, aid receiving nation)
  aid-reliant country 援助依存国
  aid society 共済組合
  aid supplies 救援物資
  aid to foreign countries 対外援助
  aid-tying ひも付き援助
  aid volume 援助額, 援助量
  aid worker 救援物資を運ぶ職員
  aids and appliances 補助器械具
  aids to beauty 化粧品
  audio-visual aids 視聴覚教具
  bilateral aid 2国間援助
  dealer aids 販売店援助
  deliver aid to refugees 難民に救援物資を送る
  development aid 開発援助
  economic aid 経済的援助, 経済援助
  emergency aid for the victims 被災者への緊急援助
  external aid 対外援助
  financial aid 財政援助, 財政支援, 金融支援, 金融援助
  first aid 緊急処置, 応急手当て
  food aid 食糧援助
  foreign aid 海外援助, 外国の援助, 対外援助
  foreign aid disbursement 外国からの援助実施額
  foreign aid program 対外援助計画
  grant aid 無償援助
  grant in aid 助成金
  hearing aid 補聴器
  humanitarian aid 人道支援
  medical aid 医師の手当て
  military aid 軍事援助
  multilateral aid 多国間援助
  mutual aid 相互扶助
  nonproject aid プロジェクト以外の援助
  non-tied aid アンタイド援助
  official aid 公的援助
  official foreign aid 政府開発援助《略 ODA》(= official development aid)
  overseas aid 海外支援, 海外援助, 対外援助
  project aid 計画援助
  scholarship aid 奨学金
  security supporting aid 安全保障確保のための援助《略 SSA》
  state aid 政府補助, 国家補助, 国庫補助, 国庫補助金
  strategic aid 戦略的援助
  teaching aids 補助教材
  technical aid 技術援助
  tied aid ひも付き援助, タイド援助, タイド・エイド
AID 米国際開発局 (Agency for International Developmentの略)
aide 名 補佐官, 側近, 顧問, 副官, 助手
  a few top aides 少数の側近
  aide-de-camp 副官
  aide-memoire 〈外交の〉覚書

close aide　側近, 補佐官, 顧問, 助手, 副官
former close aides　元側近
White House aide　米大統領補佐官
AIDS　エイズ, 後天性免疫不全症候群（acquired immune deficiency syndromeの略。⇒HIV）
AIDS patient　エイズ患者
ailing 形　経営不振の, 業績が悪化している, 経営が行き詰まった, 不調の, 不況の, 病める
ailing auto business　経営不振の自動車事業, 業績悪化の自動車事業部門
ailing business　経営難の事業, 経営不振の企業
ailing company　経営不振の会社, 経営不振企業
ailing economy　病める経済, 不況の経済
ailment 名　病気
aim 動　めざす, ねらう,〈銃を〉向ける, 名 目標, 目的, 意図, ねらい
air 名　空気, 大気, 放送, エア
air-cooling effects　冷却効果
Air Pollution Control Law　大気汚染防止法
air-to-ground bombing drills　空対地爆撃訓練
air traffic security　航空保安
aircraft 名　航空機
airline 名　航空路, 航空路線, 定期航空路, 航空会社
airport 名　空港, 飛行場
airport lounge　空港ロビー
airport terminal building　空港ターミナル・ビル
alarm 動　警報を発する, 名 警報, 警報機
albeit 接　…にもかかわらず, …だけれども（= although, though）
alert 動　警戒させる, 警報を出す, 名 警戒警報, 形 油断なく気を配っている
high alert　厳戒態勢
Al-Qaida [al Qaida]　〈国際テロ組織の〉アル・カーイダ
alias 名　別名, 偽名, 仮名
alien registration system　外国人登録システム, 外国人登録制度
all-in 形　制限なしの, 全費用込みの,〈レスリングで〉フリースタイルの
all-in fee　全費用込みの料金
all-in rates　絶対値
all-in-one 名　一体型パソコン（中央処理装置, 補助記憶装置, 入出力装置などの各装置を一体化した小型パソコン）, オール・イン・ワン, 形 一体型の
all-in-one box　一体型, オール・イン・ワン型

all-in-one printer　一体型プリンター
All Japan Prefectural and Municipal Workers' Union　全日本自治団体労働組合, 自治労
all-time high　過去最高, 過去最高値, 史上最高値, 市場最高値, 上場来の高値, 過去最多, 過去最悪
all-time low　市場最安値, 上場来の安値, 過去最低
allegation 名　申立て, 主張, 弁明, 申し開き, 容疑, 疑惑
allege 動　主張する, 断言する, 断定する, 宣言する, 指摘する, 証言する, 申し立てる, 引合いに出す
alleged 形　…とされる, …したとされている, 真偽の疑わしい, …疑惑の, 申し立てられた, …事件
alleged illegal transactions　仮装売買疑惑
an alleged criminal　容疑者
an alleged evidence　疑わしい証拠
allegedly 副　報道によれば, 伝えられるところでは, 調べによると, 申立てによれば申立てによると, …と言われている, …したとして, …容疑で, …疑惑で（= according to allegation）
allergies 名　アレルギー
alleviate 動　和らげる, 緩和する, 軽減する, 軽くする, 楽にする
alleviate debt burden　債務負担を軽くする[軽減する]
alleviate pain　苦痛[痛み]を和らげる, 痛みを楽にする
alleviate punishment　減刑する
alleviate the anxiety of sex crime victims　性犯罪被害者の不安を軽減する
alleviate the bankruptcy shock　破綻ショックを和らげる
alleviate the debt burden　債務負担を軽くする, 債務を削減する
alleviate the exchange risk　為替リスクを軽減する
alleviate world tensions　世界の緊張を緩和する
alleviation 名　軽減, 緩和
alliance 名　提携, 提携関係, 連携, 連合, 統合, 同盟, 同盟関係, 同盟国（= tie-up）
alliance partner　提携先, 提携相手
alliance strategy　提携戦略
business alliance　業務提携, 経済団体
capital and business alliance　資本・業務提携, 資本提携を含む業務提携

capital alliance 資本提携
comprehensive alliance 包括的提携, 包括提携 (＝broad alliance)
dissolve one's alliance with …との提携関係を解消する
equity alliance 資本提携関係
food supermarket alliance 食品スーパー連合
form a capital and business alliance 資本・業務提携を結ぶ
four-way alliance 4社提携
global airline alliance 世界的な航空企業連合
Japan–U.S. alliance 日米同盟, 日米同盟関係
maintain one's capital alliance with …との資本提携を維持する
military alliance 軍事同盟
producer-retailer alliance 製販同盟
retail business alliance 流通業連合, 流通グループ
strategic alliance 戦略提携, 戦略的提携
three-way alliance 3社提携

Alliance of Small Island States
小島嶼国連合《略 AOSIS》

allocate 動 割り当てる, 配分する, 配賦する, 割り振る (＝allot)
▶ Any related unrealized exchange gains and losses are *allocated* to currency translation adjustment. これに関連する未実現為替差損益は, すべて為替換算調整勘定に配賦されています.

allocation
名 割当て, 配分, 配賦, 割振り, 配当 (＝allotment)
allocation of new shares to a third party 第三者割当て, 第三者割当て増資 (＝third-party share allotment)
allocation of shares 株式割当て (＝share allocation)
asset allocation 資産配分, 資金の割当て
foreign exchange allocation 外貨割当て, 外貨資金割当て
fund allocation 資金配分
liquidity allocation 資金の供給
private allocation 縁故者割当て
resource allocation 資源配分

allotment
名 株式の割当て (＝allocation)
final allotments 最終割当額
over-allotment option 超過引受オプション
third-party allotment 第三者割当て (＝allotment to third parties)

ALT アシスタント・ランゲージ・ティーチャー (assistant language teacherの略)

alternative
名 代案, 代替策, 選択肢, 代わるべき手段, 形 二者択一の, 代替の
alternative demand 代替需要, 選択需要
alternative director 代理取締役
alternative energy source 代替エネルギー源
alternative fuels 代替燃料
alternative liquidity 代替流動性
alternative planning 代替計画, 代替案
alternative technology 代替技術

altitude 名 高度, 標高, 海抜

amass 動 集める, ためる, 蓄える, 蓄積する, 捻出する

ambassador
名 大使, 使節, 代表, 代理人 (⇒diplomat)
a goodwill ambassador 親善大使, 親善使節 (＝an ambassador of goodwill)
a noncareer ambassador 〈民間起用の〉非職業外交官大使
a roving ambassador 移動大使 (＝an ambassador at large)
act as another's ambassador in negotiations 交渉の代理をする, 交渉で…の代理人を務める
an ambassador at large 無任所大使, 特使
an ambassador extraordinary 特命大使, 特派大使
an ambassador extraordinary and plenipotentiary 特命全権大使
an ambassador-level conference 大使級会議
an ambassador of peace 平和使節
an ambassador plenipotentiary 全権大使
an ordinary [a resident] ambassador 弁理大使
arrive in Tokyo as U.S. Ambassador 米国大使として東京に着任する
be appointed ambassador to France 駐仏大使に任命される
His Excellency the U.S. Ambassador to France 駐仏米国大使閣下
the Ambassador in [at] Washington ワシントン駐在大使
the American [U.S.] ambassador in Tokyo 東京駐在米国大使
the Japanese Ambassador to Great Britain 駐英日本大使 (＝the Japanese Ambassador to the Court of St. James's)

the Japanese Ambassador to Washington　駐米日本大使
the Russian Ambassador to the U.N.　国連駐在ロシア大使, ロシアの国連大使
the U.S. [American] Ambassador to Japan　駐日アメリカ大使

ambushes　奇襲攻撃

amend 動　修正する, 改正する, 変更する, 改変する, 改良する

amendment 名　修正, 改正, 変更, 改変, 改良, 修正[改正]案, 修正条項
the amendment of the Constitution　憲法改正, 改憲
the First Amendment　合衆国憲法修正第1条

American Recovery and Reinvestment Act　米国再生・再投資法

America's Career InfoNet　求職者が全米および各州の労働市場や雇用動向, 給与, 学歴の条件などを知ることができるウェブ・サイト（www.acinet.org）

America's Job Bank　全米規模のコンピュータによる職業紹介ウェブ・サイト（www.ajb.org）

America's Learning Exchange　求職者, 雇用主向けに教育や職業訓練に関する情報を提供するウェブ・サイト（www.alx.org）

America's Talent Bank　求職者のための履歴書掲載ウェブ・サイト（www.atb.org）

ample 形　豊富な, 潤沢な, 大量の, 十分な, 広い
ample funds　潤沢な資金
ample liquidity　高い流動性, 流動性の高さ, 豊富な資金, 大量の資金, 潤沢な資金

analyst 名　分析家, 情勢分析家, 解説者, 専門家, アナリスト
analysts' earnings estimate　アナリスト収益予想
analysts' opinions　アナリスト評価
bond market analyst　債券アナリスト
credit analyst　信用アナリスト
current analysts' consensus estimates　最新アナリスト予想
economic analyst　経済アナリスト, 経済情勢分析家
equity analyst　証券アナリスト
Financial Analysts Federation　全米証券アナリスト協会
fundamental analyst　ファンダメンタル・アナリスト
industry analyst　業界アナリスト, 産業アナリスト
investment analyst　投資アナリスト
political risk analyst　政治的リスク測定の専門家
securities analyst　証券アナリスト
Society for Investment Analysts　証券アナリスト協会
stock analyst　株式アナリスト
technical analyst　テクニカル・アナリスト

anchor 名　〈ラジオ・テレビ番組の〉総合司会者, ニュース・キャスター（＝anchorman, anchorperson）

anemic [anaemic] 形　活気[生気]のない, 生気に欠ける, 弱々しい, 貧血の, 貧血症の, 無気力な

angel 名　ベンチャー企業への個人投資家, エンジェル（ベンチャー企業育成のため, こうした企業に個人投資家が投資をしやすくする税制を「エンジェル税制」という）

animosity 名　敵意, 憎しみ, 恨み, 憎悪, 対立

announce 動　発表する, 公表する, 表明する, 知らせる, 告げる

anniversary 名　記念日, 記念祭
celebrate [commemorate] the anniversary of　…の記念祭を祝う
golden wedding anniversary　金婚式の記念日
mark the anniversary of　…の記念を祝う, …記念にあたる, …を記念する

announcement 名　発表, 公表, 表明, 知らせ, 広告
announcement of business results　業績発表, 決算発表, 決算短信（＝results announcement）
dividend announcement　配当発表
earnings announcement　利益発表, 業績発表
official announcement　公式発表, 政府声明, 公示
results announcement　業績発表

annual 形　年間の, 年次の, 通期の, 年1回の, 毎年の, アニュアル
annual accounts settlement　年次決算
annual general meeting of shareholders　年次株主総会, 定例[定時]株主総会
annual growth rate　年成長率, 年間伸び率[成長率]
annual income　年収
annual loss　年間赤字, 通期での赤字
annual meeting　定時総会, 年次総会, 定時株主総会, 年次株主総会
annual paid holiday　年次有給休暇
annual production　年間生産台数

annual report 年次報告書, 年次決算報告書, 年次営業報告書, 有価証券報告書, 年報, アニュアル・レポート
annual report to stockholders [shareholders] 株主向け年次報告書, 年次報告書
annual results 通期決算, 通期業績, 年間業績, 年間成績
annual return 年次報告書, 年次届け出書(英国の会社が会社登記官に届け出る財務報告書)
annual salary system 年俸制
annual securities report 年次有価証券報告書
annualized [annualised] 形 年率換算の, 年換算の, 年率の
  annualized basis 年率換算, 年換算, 年率
  annualized growth 年率の伸び, 年率の伸び率
  annualized growth rate 年率換算の成長率
  annualized rate 年率
  annualized terms 年率換算, 年換算, 年率 (＝annualized basis)
  on an annualized basis 年率換算で, 年換算で, 年率で
  quarter on quarter annualized rate 前期比年率
  seasonally adjusted annualized rate 季節調整済み年率
annuity 名 年金, 年金保険制度, 年金受領権, 年賦金, 出資金, 掛け金
  amount of annuity 年金総額
  annuity scheme 年金制度
  fixed annuity 定額年金
  occupational annuity 企業年金
  present value of annuity 年金現価
  retirement annuity 退職年金
  variable annuity 変額年金
anoint 動 指名する, 選定する, 塗布する, 塗油する, 塗る, すりこむ
anonymity 名 匿名, 無名, 特徴のないこと, 没個性, 平凡
anonymous 形 匿名の
anorectic 名 食欲抑制剤, 拒食症患者 (＝anorexic)
  ▶ *Anorectics* are used only to make medicines. 食欲抑制剤は, 医薬品の製造にしか使用できない。
anorexia 名 拒食症
  anorexia and bulimia 拒食症と過食症
Antarctica 名 南極大陸
Antiballistic Missile Treaty 弾道弾迎撃ミサイル制限条約, ABM制限条約

antibody 名 抗体
  antibody drug 抗体医薬
anticancer drug 抗がん剤
anticipate 動 予想する, 見込む, 見越す, 期待する, 予定する, 期限前に支払う, 見越して手を打つ
  anticipate a payment 期限前に支払う, 支払いを早くする
  anticipate a rise in interest rate 金利上昇を見越す
  anticipated commencement date 予定開始日
  anticipated import 見込み輸入
  anticipated loss 見込み損失, 予想損失 (＝anticipatory loss)
  anticipated price 見込み価格
  anticipated profit 見込み利益, 予想利益, 期待利益 (＝anticipatory profit)
  anticipated shipping date 出荷予定日
  anticipated transaction 予定取引, 予想される取引
  be tougher than originally anticipated 当初予想より厳しい
  higher-than-anticipated ... 予想を上回る…
  lower-than-anticipated ... 予想を下回る…
anticipation 名 予想, 予期, 予測, 予見, 想定, 見込み, 見越し, 見通し, 期待, 予定, 先手, 先取り, 予防, 事前行為, 〈信託財産の〉期限前処分, 期限前返済, 予見性, 先行技術
  anticipation discount 期限前支払い割引
  anticipation of an advance 先高見通し
  anticipation of decrease 先細り予想
  anticipation of life 寿命の想定
  anticipation of tax 課税見越し, 課税見込み
  anticipation rate 前払い割引率
  anticipation survey 見通し調査
  bond anticipation note 債券見込み債, 長期債借換え予定証券
  grant anticipation note 補助金見込み債, 贈与見込み証券
  in anticipation of …を期待して, …を予想して, …を見込んで, …をにらんで
  multi-valued anticipation 多値的予想
  revenue anticipation note 歳入見込み証券
  tax anticipation bill 納税準備証券, 租税証券
  tax anticipation note 税収見込み債, 税収見込み証券
anticipatory 形 予想の, 予想しての, 見越しての, 予期の, 先行の, 先回りの, 先取りした, 仮の

anticipatory aspiration group 期待熱望集団
anticipatory breach (of contract) 期限前の契約違反, 期限前の契約不履行, 期前違反
anticipatory demand 仮需要
anticipatory group 先行集団
anticipatory investment 先行投資
anticipatory letter of credit 輸出前払い信用状
anticipatory payment 手形の満期日前払い
anticipatory repudiation 期限前の契約履行拒絶
anticipatory socialization 社会化の先取り
anti-corruption campaign 腐敗防止キャンペーン
anti-cyclical measures 景気対策（＝anti-cyclical policy）
anti-deflation [anti-deflationary] policy 反デフレ政策
anti-deflationary strategy 反デフレ戦略, 対デフレ戦略
anti-depression cartel 不況防止カルテル, 不況カルテル
anti-depression policy 不況防止政策
Anti-Domestic Violence Law DV防止法
antidumping 名 反ダンピング（不当廉売）, ダンピング防止, 不当廉売防止, アンチダンピング
　antidumping actions 反ダンピング措置
　antidumping duties 反ダンピング関税, ダンピング防止関税, 不当廉売防止関税 (⇒Byrd Amendment)
　antidumping investigation 反ダンピング調査
　antidumping law 反ダンピング法, ダンピング防止法, 不当廉売防止法
　antidumping measure 反ダンピング措置
　antidumping order 反ダンピング命令
　antidumping probe 反ダンピング調査
　antidumping procedures 反ダンピング手続き
　antidumping rule 反ダンピング・ルール
　antidumping tariff 反ダンピング関税（＝antidumping duties）
　apply an antidumping law 反ダンピング法を適用する
　implement antidumping measures 反ダンピング措置を発動する
　the 1916 U.S. Antidumping Act 米国の1916年反ダンピング法［ダンピング防止法］
antigen 名 抗原

anti-inflation 名 反インフレ, インフレ抑制
anti-inflation allowance インフレ手当
anti-inflation [anti-inflationary] measures 反インフレ政策, インフレ抑制策, インフレ対策
anti-inflation policy 反インフレ政策, インフレ抑制策, インフレ対策
anti-inflationary device インフレ抑制の手段
anti-inflationary strategy 反インフレ戦略, 対インフレ戦略
antimissile [anti-missile] 形 対ミサイルの, ミサイル迎撃の
antimissile defense system ミサイル迎撃防衛組織（米国の戦略防衛構想（SDI）のこと）
antimissile missile ミサイル迎撃用ミサイル, 迎撃用ミサイル《略 AMM》
Antimonopoly Law 独占禁止法
antioxidant 名 酸化防止剤
antipiracy bill 海賊対処法案
antiprotectionism 名 反保護主義
anti-secession law 反国家分裂法
anti-Semitism 名 反ユダヤ主義
antitakeover measure 買収防衛策, 買収への対抗措置
antitakeover method 買収防衛方式, 買収防衛策, 買収への対抗策
antiterrorism 名 反テロ行為, 反テロ, テロ対策
Antiterrorism Law テロ対策特別措置法
antitrust 形 独占禁止の, 反トラストの, トラスト反対の, トラスト禁止の
antitrust cooperation accord 独占禁止法協力協定
Antitrust Division 米司法省反トラスト局
antitrust immunity 独占禁止法の適用除外《略 ATI》
antitrust law 独占禁止法, 反トラスト法（米国の場合, 独占禁止法の基本法であるシャーマン法（Sherman Act）, クレイトン法（Clayton Act）連邦取引委員会法（Federal Trade Commission Act of 1914）とそれを補完・修正する法律からなる）
antitrust legislation 反トラスト立法, 反トラスト法
antitrust policy 独占禁止政策, 独禁政策, 反トラスト政策
antitrust regulation 反トラスト規制
antitrust suit 独占禁止法違反訴訟
Clayton Antitrust Act 米クレイトン法（＝Clayton Act : 米国の独占禁止法の基本法であ

るシャーマン法(Sherman Act)を補完する法律。1914年に制定)

antivirus software ウイルス対策ソフト, ウイルス駆除ソフト (＝virus protection software)

AOSIS 小島嶼国連合 (Alliance of Small Island Statesの略)

apartheid 名 人種隔離政策, アパルトヘイト

APEC アジア太平洋経済協力会議, エイペック (Asia-Pacific Economic Cooperationの略)

API アプリケーション・プログラム・インターフェイス (application program interfaceの略。特定のソフトウェアやデータベースをインターネット上で動かす技術仕様)

apparel 名 衣服, アパレル

appeal 動 異議を申し立てる, 控訴する, 上告する, 訴える, 抗議する
 appeal against the verdict 判決を不服として控訴する
 appeal one's case to a higher court 事件を上級裁判所に控訴する
 appeal to the Supreme Court 最高裁判所に上訴する[上告]する

appeal 名 異議申立て, 不服の申立て, 〈高等裁判所への〉控訴[抗告], 〈最高裁判所への〉上告[上訴]
 a court of appeals 控訴裁判所
 lodge [enter, file] an appeal with the Tokyo High Court 東京高裁に控訴する

appearance 名 外観, 外見, 見た目, 見かけ, 様子, 体裁, 体面, 出現, 登場, 現われること, 出演, 出場, 出版, 発刊, 現象, 〔複数形で〕形勢, 情況, 状況, 出頭
 appearances are against 形勢は…に不利だ
 appearances are in one's favor 形勢は…に有利だ
 appearance at the hearing 公聴会への出席
 appearance money 出演[出場]謝礼金
 celebrity appearance 有名人出演
 favorable appearances 有利な形勢, 有利な状況
 first appearance on the stage 初舞台
 independence in appearance 外見上の独立性
 judge by appearances 見かけで判断する
 keep up [save] appearances 体面を保つ, 体裁をつくろう
 make an [one's] appearance 現われる, 世に出る, 出版される
 make an appearance in court 法廷に現われる

 outward appearance 外観
 personal appearance 容貌, 風采
 product appearance 製品の外観
 public appearance 公衆の場[面前]に姿を現すこと, 人前に姿を現すこと
 put in [make] an appearance ちょっと顔を出す, ちょっと出席する
 put on the appearance of …らしく装う
 unfavorable appearances 不利な形勢, 不利な状況

appendicitis 名 虫垂炎

appendix 名 付属文書, 付属書類, 別紙, 付録, 補遺, 付属物

appetite 名 食欲, 意欲, 欲望, 欲求, 好み, 選好, 選好度, 需要
 appetite for goods 消費ブーム
 appetite for reading 読書欲
 appetite suppressant 食欲抑制剤
 investor appetite 投資家の意欲, 投資家の投資意欲, 投資家の需要
 risk appetite リスク選好, リスク選好度, リスク選好の度合い
 sexual appetite 性的欲求, 性欲

appliance 名 器具, 装置, 電気製品

applicable 形 適用される, 適用できる, 応用できる, 配賦可能な, 妥当な, 適当な, 適切な, 適格な, 対応する
 applicable fees 適用料金
 applicable income taxes 適用所得税, 当該所得税
 applicable law 適用法, 準拠法, 適用される法律
 applicable tax law 適用される税法
 applicable tax rate 適用税率

applicant 名 出願者, 志願者, 応募者, 申請者, 申込み者
 job applicant 求職者
 patent applicant 特許出願者

application 名 申込み, 申請, 出願, 申請者, 申込み者, 願書, 信用状開設依頼書, 運用, 適用, 応用, 使途, 配賦, 予定配賦, 割賦適用業務, アプリケーション・ソフト, 応用ソフト, 応用システム, 適用業務, アプリケーション
 application for registration 登録申請
 application form 申込み書, 申請書, 願書
 application of funds 資金運用, 資金の使途, 資金の適用
 application software 応用ソフト[ソフトウェ

ア］, 市販ソフト （＝application, application package, application program）
applications satellite 実用衛星
applications technology satellite 応用技術衛星
commercial application 商用化, 実用化, 商用アプリケーション
common application environment 共通アプリケーション環境
computer application コンピュータ利用技術
electronic patent application 電子特許出願, 電子出願
license application 免許申請
listing application 上場申請
preliminary application for listing 上場の仮申請

apply 動 適用する, 応用する, 利用する, あてはめる, 配賦する
　apply for protection from creditors 会社更生手続きを申請する, 破綻申請する, 資産保全を請求する （＝file for protection from creditors）
　apply for protection from creditors under the bankruptcy reform law 民事再生法の適用を申請する （＝file for protection from creditors under the Civil Rehabilitation Law）

appoint 名 指名する, 任命する, 選任する, 指定する
▶ In the proposal, the investment fund requests nine people be *appointed* board members. この提案で, 同投資ファンドは, 9人を取締役に選任するよう求めている。

appointment 名 任命, 指名, 指定, 役職, 官職, 地位, 予約, 約束, 取決め, アポイントメント

appraisal 名 評価, 査定, 鑑定, 見積り
　appraisal gain 含み益, 評価益 （＝appraisal profit, latent gain）
　appraisal loss 含み損, 評価損, 保有株の評価損を損失に計上する減損処理額 （＝latent loss, valuation loss）
　appraisal of asset 資産の鑑定
　appraisal profit 含み益, 評価益 （＝appraisal gain, latent profit）
　appraisal profits and losses 含み損益, 評価損益 （＝latent profits and losses, unrealized profits and losses）
　appraisal value 評価額, 評価価値, 鑑定評価額,

査定価値 （＝appraised value, assessed value）
　performance appraisal 業績評価

appreciate 動 上昇する, 騰貴する, 〈相場が〉上がる, 高く評価する, 好感する, 正しく評価［理解］する, 鑑賞する, 感謝する
　appreciate across the board 全面高となる
　appreciate against [relative to] the US$ 対米ドルで上昇する, 米ドルに対して上昇する, 米ドルと比べて, 米ドルに照らして
　appreciating yen 円高

appreciation 名 〈価格・相場の〉上昇, 騰貴, 急騰, 増価, 平価切上げ, 正当な評価
　appreciation of the yen 円高, 円の騰貴, 円為替相場の上昇 （＝the yen's appreciation）
　appreciation of the yen against the dollar 円高・ドル安
　benefits of the yen's appreciation 円高差益
　capital appreciation キャピタル・ゲイン
　equity appreciation 株価上昇
　sharp yen appreciation 急激な円高
　yen's appreciation against the dollar 円高・ドル安, ドルに対する円相場の上昇
　yen's excessive appreciation 行き過ぎた円高

approach 名 主義, 方法, 方式, 手法, 取組み, 取組み方, 姿勢, 政策, 路線, 研究, 研究法, 解決法, 進入, 接近, アプローチ
　account analysis approach 勘定科目精査法
　contribution profit approach 貢献利益法 （＝contribution approach）
　cost-benefit approach 費用便益法
　expenditure approach 支出接近法
　management approach 経営方法, 意思決定論的アプローチ
　marginal income approach 限界利益法
　mark-to-market approach 値洗い方式
　principle-based approach 原則主義
　rating approach 格付け方法

appropriation 名 充当, 充用, 配分, 処分, 収用, 利益処分, 剰余金処分, 充当金, 支出金, 積立金, 承認済み予算額, 割当予算額, 配分額, 歳出予算, 政府支出金
　additional appropriation 追加予算
　appropriation budget 割当予算
　appropriation for national defense 国防費
　appropriation of private property 私的財産の没収
　appropriations bill 歳出法案, 歳出予算案, 政

府支出案
Appropriations Committee 米予算委員会
appropriations for redemption of bonds 社債償還積立金
budgetary appropriation 予算の計上
budgetary appropriations 予算割当額
capital appropriations 資本処分, 資本準備金
federal appropriation 米政府予算の承認
lump sum appropriation 総括予算, 一括割当て
military appropriation 軍事費, 軍事支出金
negotiations for additional appropriations 復活要求
profit appropriation 利益の処分

approval 名 承認, 承諾, 是認, 賛成, 賛同, 同意, 支持, 許可, 認可 (⇒disapproval)
approval rating [rate] 支持率
approval system 許可制
Cabinet approval rating 内閣支持率
shareholder approval 株主の承認

approve 動 承認する, 認める, 承諾する, 賛成する, 賛同する, 同意する, 支持する, 認可する, 許可する

aquatic 形 水の, 水中の, 水上の, 水生の
aquatic creature 水生生物

arbiter 名 審判者, 決定者, 決定機関, 判定者, 判定機関, 採決者, 仲裁者, 仲裁人調停者, 〈ある分野の〉権威
▶ The U.S. business cycle *arbiter* declared that the U.S. economy slipped into recession in December 2007. 米国の景気循環の判定機関が, 米経済は2007年12月から景気後退局面 (リセッション) に入ったことを公表した。

archenemy 名 最大の敵
archfoe [arch-foe] 名 大敵
architect 名 建築家
archrival 名 最大の競争相手, 最大のライバル, 大敵

ARF 東南アジア諸国連合 (ASEAN) 地域フォーラム (Association of Southeast Asian Nations Regional Forumの略)

arena 名 舞台, 中央舞台, 活動の場, 競争の場, 場, 会場, 世界, …界, 範囲, 領域, 分野, 劇場, 競演場, 闘技場, 試合場, アリーナ
arena for bullfight 闘牛場
arena stage 円形舞台, 屋内競技場, 屋内球技場
arena theater 円形劇場, コマ劇場
boxing arena ボクシング競技場, ボクシング試合場
enter the political arena 政界に入る (= enter the arena of politics)
literary arena 文壇
political arena 政争の場, 政治の舞台, 政界 (= the arena of politics)
solve the issue in the UN arena 国連の場で問題を解決する
the arena for a political debate 政治討論の会場, 政治討論の場
the international economic arena 国際経済の舞台, 国際経済会議の場
the whole arena of foreign policy 外交政策の全範囲

arid 形 湿気のない, 不毛な
arid area 乾燥地域

arm 名 子会社, 部門, 部局, 支店, アーム
brokerage arm 証券子会社, 証券会社, 証券部門
consulting arm コンサルティング部門, コンサルティング会社
financial arm 金融子会社, 金融部門 (= finance arm, financing arm)
long-arm jurisdiction 域外適用管轄権
research arm 研究所, 研究部門
treasury arm 財務部門

armed 形 武器を持った, 武装した, 武力による
armed attack 武力攻撃, 軍事攻撃
armed conflict 武力紛争, 軍事紛争, 武力衝突, 戦闘
armed forces [services] 軍隊, 軍
armed forces intelligence 外国軍情報
Armed Forces Qualification Test 軍資格試験 《略 AFQT》
Armed Forces Radio Service 米軍放送 《略 AFRS》
armed forces reserve center 予備軍 [予備役] センター, 予備役軍訓練所
armed insurgents 武装グループ, 武装組織
armed intervention 武力介入, 武力干渉
armed invasion 軍事侵攻
armed neutrality 武装中立
armed offensive 武力攻勢
armed robbery 武装強盗
armed struggle 武力闘争
armed to the teeth 大量の武器を携えた
heavily [well] armed soldiers 重装備の兵士

armored cavalry 機甲部隊

arms 名 武器, 兵器, 武力, 軍備, 兵役, 戦闘, 交戦, 戦争, 紋章, アームズ
- **arms buildup** 軍備増強
- **arms control** 軍備制限, 軍備管理
- **arms control agreement** 軍備管理協定
- **arms control measure** 軍備管理手段
- **arms cut** 軍備削減, 軍縮
- **arms dealer** 兵器商人
- **arms depot** 兵器庫
- **arms embargo** 兵器の禁輸, 武器輸出禁止 (＝embargo on arms shipment)
- **arms fire** 砲火
- **arms limitation agreement** 戦略兵器制限協定, 兵器制限協定
- **arms manufacturer** 兵器製造業者
- **arms race** 軍拡競争, 軍備拡張競争, 軍備競争
- **arms reduction** 兵器削減, 軍備縮小
- **arms reduction talks** 戦略兵器削減交渉, 兵器削減交渉
- **arms strategy** 軍備戦略
- **arms talks** 軍縮会議
- **be called to arms** 軍隊に召集される
- **be up in arms** 激しく抗議している, 憤慨している, 反旗を翻す
- **bear arms** 武器を所有する, 武器を携える, 武装する, 兵役に服する
- **bred to arms** 軍人の教育を受けて
- **call to arms** 軍隊を動員する
- **carry arms** 武器を取る, 兵役に服する
- **fly to arms** あわてて武器を取る
- **international arms sales** 武器輸出
- **lay down arms** 武器を捨てる, 停戦する, 戦い［敵対行動］をやめる, 降伏する
- **men at arms** 戦士, 兵士
- **passage at arms** 論戦, 論争
- **resort to arms** 武力に訴える
- **rise in arms** 武器を取って立つ, 兵を挙げる
- **suspension of arms** 休戦
- **take [up] arms** 武器を取る, 武装する, 戦端を開く, 兵を挙げる
- **take up arms against** …と戦う
- **throw down arms** 降参する, 武装放棄する
- **under arms** 戦闘の準備が整った, 武装して, 武器を取って

around-the-clock 形 24時間ぶっ通しの, 丸1日ぶっ通しの, 24時間休みなしの, 24時間営業の, 副 24時間営業で, 24時間休みなしで
- **around-the-clock operation** 24時間営業, 24時間操業
- **around-the-clock watch** 24時間警戒態勢

arm's length [arm's-length] 公正な, 独立した, 独立当事者間の, 独立企業間の, 独立第三者間の, 第三者間取引にかかわる, 商業ベースの
- **arm's length bargaining** 公正な取引, 独立当事者間の取引
- **arm's length basis** 純然たる商業ベース, 商業ベース
- **arm's length sale** 独立企業間の売買, 対等の立場での販売
- **at arm's length** 少し距離を置いて, 腕を伸ばした［腕の届く］距離に, できるだけ遠ざけて
- **keep a person at arm's length** …を敬遠する, …を寄せ付けない, …によそよそしくする

arrange 動 手配する, 取り決める, 手はずを整える, 取りまとめる, 準備する, 打ち合わせる, 解決する, 同意する, アレンジする

arrangement 名 手配, 準備, 打合せ, 取決め, 協定, 合意, 契約, 取りまとめ, 調整, 解決
- **arrangement committee** 準備委員会
- **barter arrangement** バーター取引
- **borrowing arrangement** 借入協定
- **business arrangement** 業務協定, 業務契約, 業務提携
- **formal arrangement** 正式取決め
- **institutional arrangement** 制度的取決め
- **monetary arrangement** 通貨協定
- **provisional arrangement** 仮協定
- **reciprocal trade arrangement** 互恵通商協定
- **revolving credit arrangement** 回転信用契約
- **swap arrangement** スワップ協定

arrears 名 延滞, 遅滞, 延滞金, 滞納金, 未納金, 未払い金

arrest 動 逮捕する, 検挙する, 拘置する, 拘留する, 〈進行を〉止める, 阻む, 阻止する, 遅らせる, 停止させる, 歯止めをかける, 〈注意を〉引く, 名 逮捕, 検挙, 拘置, 拘留, 阻止, 停止
- **arrest warrant** 逮捕状
▶ The economic downturn seems to have been *arrested* thanks to international policy coordination. これまでの国際的な政策協調の効果で, 景気悪化に歯止めがかかってきたようだ。

ARS 金利入札証券, オークション・レート・セキュリティーズ (⇒auction-rate security)

arthritis 名 関節炎

article 名 記事, 論説, 論文, 〈契約などの〉条項, 箇条, 条文, …条, 項目, 定款, 規約, 物件, 物品,

品物, 物, 商品, 品目, 〈海事関係の〉雇用契約, 〈事務弁護士や会計士の〉実務研修
a choice article 精選品
a hand-made article 手作り品
an article of faith 信条, 信念, 基本理念
an editorial article 社説 (=a leader, a leading article, an editorial)
article titles 条項の表題, 条項の見出し
articles consigned 委託積送品
articles durable 耐久品 (=durable articles)
articles enumerated 〈税率票の〉列挙品
articles free 無税品
articles in custody 保管品
articles not for sale 非売品
articles of agreement 契約書, 契約覚書, 〈社団の〉規約, 協定規約, 基本定款
articles of amendment 修正条項
articles of association 〈米国の会社の〉基本定款 (=articles of incorporation), 〈英国の会社の〉通常定款 (英国会社の基本定款=memorandum of association), 団体規約
articles of company 〈英国の〉通常定款
articles of consolidation 合併届出書
articles of consumption 消耗品
articles of dissolution 解散届出書
articles of export 輸出品
articles of furniture 家具
articles of incorporation 会社の基本定款, 設立定款, 定款 (=articles of association: 会社の方針を定めたもの. 日本は単一定款制度をとっているのに対して, 欧米では基本定款(articles of association, articles of incorporation)と付属定款(bylaws)の二つの定款制度をとっている)
articles of luxury 贅沢品
articles of trade 商品
articles on order 注文品
articles subject to taxation 課税品
branded article 有標品
contraband articles 禁制品, 密輸品
domestic articles 家庭用品
free articles 無税品
gift articles 贈答品
home-made articles 国産品, 国内製品
Japanese Article Number 日本商品コード, JANコード
manufactured articles 加工品, 製品, 工業品
memorandum and articles 定款

memorandum articles 保険不用品
proprietary articles 専売品, 特許薬品
ship's articles 船員雇用契約書
similar articles 類似商品, 同類商品
staple articles 主要品目
stock articles 在庫品, 手持ち品
tax-exempt [tax-free] articles 免税品
the Article 301 of the Trade Act 米通商法第301条
toilet articles 化粧品
uncustomed articles 未通関品目
articulate 動 はっきり説明する, 明確に述べる[表明する], 整然と話す, 明示する, 明確化する
artillery 動 砲兵隊
as of …現在で, …の時点で, …現在の, …の日付で, …の日付に
▶Daiei had about ¥1.04 trillion of interest-bearing debts *as of* the end of August 2004. 2004年8月末時点で, ダイエーは約1兆400億円の有利子負債を抱えていた。
ASAT test 人工衛星破壊実験(ASATはanti-satelliteの略)
asbestos 名 石綿, アスベスト
ASEAN アセアン, 東南アジア諸国連合 (Association of South-East Asian Nationsの略)
ASEM アジア欧州会議, アジア欧州首脳会議 (Asia-Europe (summit) meetingの略。1996年3月, アジアと欧州の関係強化を目的としてバンコクで第一回首脳会議を開いて発足。日本, 中国, 韓国, 東南アジア7か国と欧州連合(EU), 欧州委員会が参加)
Asia-Pacific Economic Cooperation アジア太平洋経済協力会議, エイペック《略 APEC》
Asia-Pacific region アジア太平洋地域
ASP アプリケーション・サービス・プロバイダー (application service providerの略。インターネット経由で各種ソフトウェアを一定期間貸し出すサービスのこと)
assassination 名 暗殺, 中傷, 名誉毀損
assault 名 暴行, 猛攻撃, 急襲
assemble 動 組み立てる, 生産する
assembly 名 集会, 集会参加者[出席者], 会議, 議会, 〈米州議会の〉下院, 組立て, 組立部品, 組立作業, アセンブリ
assembly cost system 組立原価計算
assembly defect rate 製品不良率
assembly district 米州議会下院議員選挙区

assembly hall 集会場, 会議場, 講堂, 組立工場
assembly industry 組立工業, 組立産業
assembly input costs 製造コスト
assembly language アセンブリ言語（＝assembler language：アセンブリ言語で書いたソース・プログラムを機械語に変換することをassemblyという）
assembly line 組立ライン, 組立作業ライン, 流れ作業, 一貫作業
assembly line system 組立ライン方式, 流れ作業方式, 一貫作業方式
assembly order sheet 組立順位表
assembly parts 組立部品（＝assembling parts）
assembly plant 組立工場（＝assembling plant）
assembly process 組立工程
assembly production 組立生産（＝assembling production）
assembly (production) order 組立指図書
assembly program アセンブリ・プログラム
assembly room 集会室, 娯楽室, 組立工場
assembly service 集荷サービス（＝assembling service）
assembly shop 組立工場（＝assembly plant）
assembly work 組立作業
local assemblies 地方議会
school assembly 全校集会, 学校の朝礼
Tokyo Metropolitan Assembly election 東京都議選

assemblyman 名〈米州議会の〉下院議員（＝assembly member：女性下院議員はassemblywoman）

assertion 名 主張, 断言

assess 動 評価する, 査定する, 審査する, 算定する, 判断する

assessment 名 評価, 査定, 審査, 算定, 判断, アセスメント
　assessment of bank properties 銀行資産の査定
　assessment of economic conditions 景気判断
　assessment of the economy 景気判断, 景気の基調判断, 景気判断（＝assessment on the state of the economy, economic assessment）
　assessments receivable 受取追徴金
　environmental assessment 環境評価, 環境影響事前評価, 環境アセスメント
　rating assessment 格付け評価
　skills assessment 技能評価
　technology assessment 技術評価, 技術の事前評価, テクノロジー・アセスメント

asset 名 資産, 財産, アセット
　asset appraisal 資産査定, 資産評価
　asset assessment 資産査定, 資産評価（＝asset appraisal, asset evaluation）
　asset-backed securities 資産担保証券, 商業用不動産証券, アセットバック証券《略 **ABS**》（銀行の貸出債権や企業の売掛債権などを担保に発行される証券）
　asset base 資産基盤, 資産構成
　asset erosion 資産の目減り, 資産価額の低下
　asset evaluation 資産の査定（＝asset assessment）
　asset impairment accounting 減損会計（＝accounting for the impairment of assets）
　asset management 資産管理, 資産運用, 投資顧問（＝asset）
　asset management company 資産管理会社, 資産運用会社
　asset provision 資産評価損引当金, 資産評価損引当金繰入れ額
　asset sales 資産売却
　asset value 資産価値, 資産価格, 純資産
　capital assets 資本的資産, 固定資産
　current assets 流動資産（＝liquid assets）
　excess of liabilities over assets 債務超過
　external assets 対外資産
　fixed assets 固定資産
　foreign assets 対外資産, 海外資産
　freezing terrorist-related assets テロ関連資産の凍結
　hidden assets 含み資産
　intangible assets 無形資産, 無形固定資産
　out-of-book assets 簿外資産
　quick assets 当座資産
　real assets 不動産
　securitized assets 証券化資産, 証券化した資産
　tangible assets 有形資産, 有形固定資産
　total assets 総資産

assign 動 割り当てる, 任命する, 指定する, 与える, 譲渡する, 委託する

assignment 名 割当て, 割当量, 譲渡, 譲渡証書

assistance 名 支援, 援助, 助力, 協力, 助成,

扶助, 助け, 役に立つこと, 利点
adjustment assistance 調整援助
be of great assistance to …にとって大きな利点だ
capital assistance 資本支援, 資金協力
development assistance 開発援助
financial assistance 金融支援, 財政援助, 資金援助, 資金協力
foreign assistance 対外援助, 外国援助
foreign assistance policy 対外援助政策
financial assistance package 金融支援策
give technical assistance to …に技術支援[援助]を行う
governmental financial assistance 政府補助金, 政府助成金
humanitarian assistance 人道援助, 人道支援
international assistance 国際支援, 国際協力, 国際貢献
medical assistance 医療支援
monetary assistance 金融援助, 資金援助, 貨幣的援助
mutual assistance 相互援助, 相互協力, 相互扶助
offer economic assistance 経済援助を申し出る
overnight assistance rate 翌日物介入金利
overseas development assistance 政府開発援助, 海外経済協力
pecuniary assistance 金銭的援助
provide financial assistance to …に金融支援[資金援助]を行う
public assistance 生活保護, 公的扶助
reciprocal assistance 相互援助, 相互支援
social assistance 社会扶助
technological [technical] assistance plan 技術援助計画, 技術協力計画
associated company 関連会社, 関係会社, 系列会社, 同系会社, 半数所有会社, 持ち分法適用会社 (=affiliated company, associate)
accounting for associated companies 関連会社の会計
loans from associated companies 関連会社からの借入金
loans to associated companies 関連会社への貸付け金
association 图 社団, 団体, 協会, 組合, 連合, 連合体
Association of Consumer Affairs Profes-

sionals 米消費者関連専門家会議, エイキャップ《略 ACAP》
commercial and industrial association 商工組合
employers association 経営者団体, 事業者団体, 使用者団体
incorporated association 社団法人
industry association 業界団体
memorandum of association 定款, 〈イギリスの会社の〉基本定款
National Association of Manufacturers 全米製造業協会
professional association 職業団体
trade association 同業組合, 産業団体, 事業者団体, 同業者団体, 商工団体
Association of South-East [Southeast] Asian Nations アセアン, 東南アジア諸国連合,《略 ASEAN》
assuage 動 鎮める, 和らげる, 緩和する
assume 動 〈任務や義務・債務を〉引き受ける, 〈債務などを〉肩代わりする, 負担する, 就任する, 就く, 責任を負う, 責任をとる, 引き継ぐ, 継承する, 占有する, …と仮定する, 推定する, 想定する, 予想する, 予定する, 見込む, 考慮する
assume A to be B AをBとみなす, AをBと仮定する
assume liquidity risk 流動性リスクを負担する
assume office 就任する
assume responsibility for …の責任を負う, …の責任を取る
assume the risk リスクを負う, リスクを引き受ける
assumed bond 保証社債
assumed loans 債務の肩代わり
assumed rate of interest 予定利率
assumed trend rate 予想傾向値
assumed yield 予想利回り
asthma 图 喘息(ぜんそく)
astrogation 图 宇宙飛行 (astro (宇宙) とnavigation (航海・航空) の合成語)
astronaut 图 宇宙飛行士 (⇒cosmonaut, mission commander)
asylum 图 政治犯保護, 政治亡命, 避難所, 収容所, 保護施設
asylum seeker 亡命希望者, 避難民
at-home care 在宅介護
at large 逮捕されていない, 捕まっていない, 逃走中の
ATI 米独占禁止法の適用外 (antitrust immu-

ATM 現金自動預け払い機, 現金自動預入引出機 (**automated teller machine**の略で, automatic teller machineともいう)
　ATM card ATMカード, キャッシュ・カード
　ATM fraud ATM詐欺
atrocious 形 凶悪な, 残虐な, 残忍な
attach 動 取り付ける, 貼付する, 添付する, 付属させる, 所属させる
attack 名 攻撃, 襲撃, 暴力, 非難, 批判, 酷評, 発作, 罹病, 発病, 措置, 対策, 開始, 着手
　a blistering attack 痛烈な批判[非難]
　a bomb attack 爆撃
　a general attack 総攻撃
　a night attack 夜襲
　a political attack 政治的攻撃
　a terrorist attack テロ攻撃
　an attack of fever 発熱
　come under an open attack 公然と非難される
　come under speculative attacks 投機的な売りにさらされる
　have a heart attack 心臓発作を起こす
　launch a surprise attack 奇襲攻撃を開始する
　speculative attacks 投機的な売り, 投棄圧力, 投機筋の攻撃, 投機的な動き
attempt 名 企て, 企画, 計画, 策, 措置, 試み, 努力, 挑戦, 攻撃, 襲撃, 攻勢, 未遂
　a coup attempt クーデター未遂事件 (=attempted coup)
　a takeover attempt 買収劇, 買収攻勢
　an attempt at murder 殺人未遂 (=attempted murder)
　an attempt at suicide 自殺未遂 (=suicidal attempt, suicide attempt)
　an attempt on the world record 世界記録への挑戦
　an attempt to commit a crime 未遂行為
　fail in an attempt 計画が挫折する
　in an attempt to …しようとして, …するため
attestation 名 証明, 立証, 公証, 言明, 証言, 宣誓, 〈大臣などの〉認証, 証明書
▶ The new cabinet was inaugurated following an *attestation* ceremony at the Imperial Palace. 新内閣は, 皇居での認証式を経て発足した.
attention 名 注意, 注目, 興味, 関心, 焦点, 集中力, 好意, 配慮, 気配り, 世話, 治療, 修理, 修復, 手入れ, …宛
　add special attention to …に特に注意する

attention deficit 注意欠陥
attention deficit disorder 注意力欠如障害, 多動性障害《略 ADD》
attract considerable attention 多大の注目を集める
be all attention 全神経を集中している, 全神経を集中して聞いている
be the center [focus] of attention 関心の的となる
bring A to B's attention AをBに知らせる
call [draw, turn] a person's attention to …に人の注意を促す, …に人の関心を向けさせる
call away a person's attention 人の注意をそらす
catch the attention of …の目にとまる
consumer attention 消費者の注目
devote one's attention to …に熱中する
escape the attention of …に気づかれない
fix one's attention to …に注意する
get the attention of …の関心を引く
give full attention to …に細心の注意を払う, …に全神経を集中する
have a short attention span 集中力が続かない
investment attention 投資先, 投資の関心
keep [hold] one's attention …の関心を引きつけておく
medical attention 治療
pay courteous attention to …を丁重に取り扱う
pay one's attention to …に言い寄る, …にいろいろ優しくする
policy attention 政策の焦点
attitude 名 態度, 姿勢, 考え方, 見方, 意見, 主張, 判断 (=stance)
　attitude change 態度変容
　attitude measurement 態度調査, 態度評定
　hostile attitude 反抗的な態度
　labor [work] attitude 勤労態度
　lending attitude of financial institutions 金融機関の貸出態度
　longstanding attitudes of curbing labor costs 長年の人件費抑制姿勢
　managerial attitude 経営姿勢, 経営者の態度
　open-minded attitude 打ち解けた態度
　political attitude 政治の動向
　positive attitude 肯定的な態度
　risk averse attitude リスク回避的な態度

risk seeking attitude リスク選好的態度
wait-and-see attitude 様子見
weak attitude 弱腰

attorney 名 代理人, 法律家, 弁護士
  Attorney General 〈米国の〉司法長官,〈英国の〉法務長官

attract 動 引きつける,〈顧客などを〉取り込む,〈資金などを〉集める, 興味を持つ［引く］, 呼び寄せる, 誘引する, 誘致する
  attract a lot of interest 大きな関心を集める, 大きな関心を呼ぶ
  attract a person's attention 人の注目を引く, 人の注目を集める
  attract companies 企業を誘致する
  attract new customers 新規顧客を引きつける, 新規顧客を取り込む, 新規顧客を開拓する
  attract foreign capital 外国資本を誘致する, 外資を誘致する (＝attract foreign investment)
  attract investment 投資を促す

attribute 動 …に帰する, …のおかげとする, …のせいにする
  A is attributed to B Aの原因はBであるとされる, AをBのおかげと考える (＝attribute A to B)
  the plays attributed to …の作品と考えられる劇

attributable to …に起因する, …に帰属する, …による (＝be caused by, be due to, be traceable to, result from)
  AB is primarily attributable to CD ABは主にCDに起因する, ABの主な要因［主因］はCDである, ABは主にCDによる
  current cost profit attributable to shareholders 株主帰属現在原価利益
  income attributable to ordinary activity 経常損益（正常な営業活動から生じる損益）
  losses attributable to credit defaults 信用デフォルトに起因する損失
  losses attributable to dilution 減額による損失, 減額に起因する損失, 受取債権の減額による損失

auction 名 競売, 競り売り, 公売, 入札, 公募入札, オークション
  30 year auction 30年物入札
  auction business オークション事業, オークション・ビジネス
  auction event オークションの入札
  auction participant オークション参加者
  auction price 入札価格
  auction rules オークション規定
  auction site オークション・サイト, 競売サイト（売り手が出品した品物を, 買い手が落札するホームページのこと）
  competitive auction 競争入札
  e-auction eオークション
  Net auction ネット・オークション (＝Internet auction)
  online auction オンライン・オークション
  open auction 公開競売
  quarterly auction 四半期入札, 四半期ごとの入札
  reverse auction 逆オークション, リバース・オークション
  sell by auction 競売で売却する

auction-rate [auction rate] market 金利入札証券市場, ARS市場

auction-rate security 金利入札証券《略 ARS》(＝auction-rate debt：米国の地方自治体や美術館などの文化施設が資金調達のために発行する満期20年以上の長期債で, 定期的に行われる入札で金利が変わるのが特徴。⇒accord, liquid)

auctioneer 名 オークション業者, 競売人

audience 名 聴衆, 観客, 観衆,〈テレビの〉視聴者,〈ラジオの〉聴取者, 読者,〈国王, 天皇, 法王などの〉公式会見, 正式会見, 謁見, 支持者, 賛同者, 信奉者, 愛好家,〈訴えなどの〉聴聞の機会
  a farewell audience 告別の謁見
  a large audience 多数の観客
  an audience at a theater 劇場の観客
  an audience chamber 謁見室
  an audience to hear one's plan …の計画を聴聞する機会
  audience participation 視聴者参加
  audience rating テレビの視聴率
  be received in audience by …から拝謁［謁見］を賜る
  grant an audience to …に謁見を許す
  have an audience with …に謁見する
  seek an audience with …に会見を求める
  target audience 対象になる視聴者［聴取者］

audio 名 音声, 音, 音響, オーディオ, 形 音声の
  audio communications 音声通信
  audio equipment 音響機器

audiotape 名 録音テープ

audiovisual communication products AVC (音響・映像・情報) 機器
audit 動 監査する, 会計検査する, 名 監査, 会計検査
auditing 名 監査, 会計監査
  auditing company 監査法人 (＝auditing firm)
  auditing contract 監査契約 (＝audit engagement)
  auditing firm 監査法人 (＝audit corporation, audit firm, auditing house, auditor：「監査法人」は，5人以上の公認会計士が共同で設立する法人。会計基準などに照らして企業決算が適正かどうかを第三者の立場で審査して，監査証明書(監査報告書)を出す)
  auditing report 監査報告書
  auditing services 監査業務
  auditing standards 監査基準 (＝audit standards)
auditor 名 監査人, 監査法人, 監査役, 会計検査官
  external auditor 外部監査人
  independent auditor 独立監査人
  internal auditor 内部監査人
  outside auditor 社外監査人
  statutory auditor 法定監査人, 常勤監査役
augment 名 増大する, 増す
auspices 名 後援, 援助, 支援, 主催, 指導, 明るい見通し, 前兆, 吉兆
austere 形 緊縮の, 質素な, 切り詰めた
  austere fiscal policy 緊縮財政政策, 緊縮財政
austerity 名 緊縮, 引締め, 質素倹約, 厳しさ, 厳格さ
  austerities 耐乏生活, 禁欲生活
  austerity budget 緊縮予算
  austerity drive 緊縮政策
  austerity measures 緊縮政策, 引締め政策, 緊縮策
  austerity plans 緊縮政策
authentication 名 認証, オーセンティケーション
  authentication number 認証番号
authorities 名 当局, 政府当局, その筋
  authorities concerned 関係当局, 関係官庁, 当該官庁, その筋
  customs authorities 税関当局
  financial and monetary authorities 金融・通貨当局
  financial authorities 金融当局
  government [governmental] authorities 政府当局
  investigating [investigative] authorities 捜査当局
  law enforcement authorities 警察当局
  legal authorities 法務当局
  local authorities 地方当局
  military authorities 軍当局
  monetary authorities 金融当局, 通貨当局
  municipal authorities 市当局
  tax authorities 税務当局
  territorial authorities 連邦・地方政府
  U.S. authorities 米政府当局
authority 名 権限, 権力, 権能, 代理権, 職権, 権威, 威厳, 迫力, 公共機関, 公的機関, 関係組織, 当局, 権威者, 専門家, 許可, 先例
  abuse of authority 権力の濫用
  apparent authority 表見的代理権限
  authority and duties of officers 役員の権限と職責
  budgetary authority 予算限度額
  by the authority of …の権能で, …の許可を得て
  competent authority 権限ある機関
  decision making authority 意思決定権, 決定権
  delegation of authority 権限の委譲
  exceed one's authority 越権行為をする
  exemptive authority 適用除外権限
  express authority 明示の代理権限
  full authority 全権限
  implied authority 黙示の代理権限
  line authority ライン権限
  local authority 地方自治体, 地方行政機関, 地方当局
  local authority bond 地方債
  on one's (own) authority 独断で, …の職権で
  regulatory authority 規制機関
  statutory authority 法的権限
  superior authority 当局, 管轄官庁, 官憲
  tax authority 税務当局
  the Education Authority 教育機関
authorization [authorisation] 名 認可, 許可, 公認, 承認, 権限付与, 授権, 委任
autocracy 名 独裁政治, 専制政治, 独裁権
autocratic state 独裁国家
automaker 名 自動車メーカー, 自動車製造業

者 (=carmaker)
automated [automatic] teller machine 現金自動預け払い機《略 ATM》
automatic accounts transfer system 自動引落し制度
automatic layering technology 複合材料の自動積層技術
automation 名 自動化, 省力化, 自動操作, オートメ化, オートメーション
Automobile Recycling Law 自動車リサイクル法
automobile weight tax 自動車重量税
autonomy 名 自治, 自治体, 自治権, 自立, 自律性, 自主, 自主性, 主体性, 自発性, 独立国
auxiliary 形 補助の, 予備の, 補助的な, 補助機関付きの
auxiliary generator 自家発電装置
availability 名 有効性, 有用性, 効力, 可能性, 入手可能性, 利用可能度, 可用性, 可用度, 使用可能度, 提供可能性, 提供, 確保, 稼働率, アベイラビリティ
　availability period 資金引出し可能期間
　availability theory 入手可能性理論, アベイラビリティ理論
　capital availability 資本の利用可能性, 資本のアベイラビリティ
　credit availability 信用の利用可能性, クレジット利用
　job availability 雇用機会
　labor availability 労働利用可能性, 労働需給
　land availability 土地取得, 土地の確保
　oil availability 原油の供給
available 形 有効な, 役に立つ, 利用[使用, 採用]できる, 利用[使用]可能な, 処分可能な, 充当可能な, 入手可能な, 調達可能な, 手が空いている, 暇な, 有望な, 当選見込みのある
　available balance 利用可能残高
　available banking facility 銀行借入れ枠
　available candidate 有望な候補, 当選見込みが大きい候補者
　available cash 利用可能現金
　available energy 有効なエネルギー
　available evidence 入手可能な証拠
　available for sale 商品販売可能額
　available-for-sale securities 売却できる証券
　available list 有効リスト
　available surplus 利用可能剰余金
　available time 使用可能時間, 可用時間, 納品期間, 納期
　be available on the internet インターネット[ネット]で閲覧できる
　be commercially available 実用化される
　every means available to use 利用できるあらゆる手段
　have no available cash 手元資金がない
　make available to …に提供する
　money available to invest [for investment] 投資に運用可能な金[資金]
avenue 名 大通り, 大街路, 並木道, …への道, …獲得の道, 〈目的達成の〉手段, 方法
　every legal avenue あらゆる法的手段
　pursue all avenues あらゆる手段を追求する, あらゆる手段を使う
　the avenue to success 成功への道, 成功に近づく道, 成功に通じる道
average 動 …の平均をとる, …の平均値を出す, 平均して…になる, 相殺する, 合算する
　average out 平均して…になる, 横ばいを脱して…になる
　▶ Corporate profits will *average* out to positive growth. 企業収益は, 横ばいを脱して積極的な増加[プラス成長]に転じるだろう。
average common shares outstanding 発行済み普通株式の平均数, 発行済み普通株式の平均株式数
average daily balance 平均残高, 1日平均残高
　the average daily balance of bank lending 銀行貸出の平均残高, 銀行貸出の1日平均残高
　the average daily balance of domestic bank lending 国内銀行貸出の平均残高, 国内銀行貸出の1日平均残高
　the average daily balance of M2 plus certificates of deposit M2と譲渡性預金(CD)の1日平均残高
　the average daily balance of the monetary base マネタリー・ベース(貨幣流通高と日銀当座預金との合計)の1日平均残高
average number of listed stocks [shares] 平均上場株式数, 上場株式総数の平均(「平均上場株式数」は(期初の上場株式数+期末の上場株式数)÷2で算出する。⇒turnover ratio)
average propensity to consume 平均消費性向(消費者が所得のなかから消費する割合)《略 APC》

avert 動 防ぐ, 避ける, 回避する, そらす, 背ける
avian flu 鳥インフルエンザ（＝avian influenza, bird flu）
avian influenza 鳥インフルエンザ（＝avian flu, bird flu）
award 動 与える, 授与する, 裁定する, 査定する
awry 形副 曲がった, 歪(ゆが)んだ, ねじれた, ずれた, 誤って, 不首尾に
　be awry 歪んでいる, 曲がっている, ずれている
　go awry 予定通りいかない, うまくいかない, 失敗する, 不首尾に終わる,〈目標から〉それる, 目的から外れる
　think awry よこしまな考え方をする
ax [axe] 動 解雇する, 首にする, 削減する, 止める, 廃止する
ax [axe] 名 解雇, 首切り, 人員削減, 経費削減, 縮小
axis of evil 悪の枢軸

B

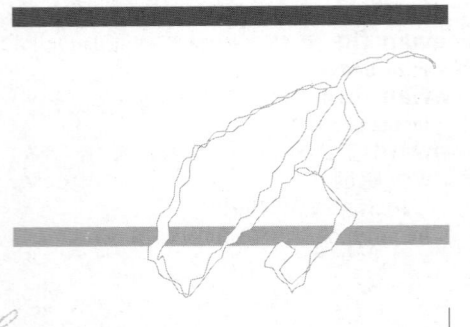

baby–boom generation 団塊の世代（＝baby boomers：第2次大戦後のベビー・ブームに生まれた人）
baby boomers ベビー・ブーマー，団塊の世代
babymoon 名 ベビームーン（出産を控えたカップルが二人きりの時間を過ごすこと。Honeymoonからの派生語で，動詞としても使われる）
back 動 支持する，支援する，後押しする，裏付ける，裏打ちする，〈金などを〉賭ける
 be backed by …を背景にしている，…を裏付ける，…に裏付けられる
 be backed by government guarantees 政府の保証が付いている
 credit card receivables–backed securities クレジット・カード証券
 Eximbank-backed financing 輸銀保証付き融資［融資案件］
 government-backed loans 政府保証融資額
 mortgage–backed bond モーゲージ担保債券，モーゲージ証券
 mortgage-backed securities モーゲージ担保証券，抵当証書担保付き証券
back 名 背，背中，後ろ，後部，奥，裏，裏側，裏面，背景，バック
 break the back of …を克服する，…を撃破［制圧］する，骨身を削る，一生懸命に頑張る，懸命に努力する，〈仕事などの〉最も難しい部分を片付ける（＝break one's back）
 cover one's back 責任回避策を取る，批判されないようにやる
 on the back of …を背景に，…を反映して，…に追随して，…を手がかりとした，…のために
 put one's back into …に最大限の努力をする
 ride on the back of …の助けを借りる，…にすがる
back–end cost バックエンド費用
back tax 追徴課税
back–to–back suicide bombings 連続自爆，連続自爆テロ
backbencher 名 新人議員，平議員
backburner [back burner] 名 後回し，二の次，棚上げ，棚上げ状態，保留，無視，〈料理用コンロ［レンジ］の奥の〉バーナー，形 重要でない，後回しの，棚上げにした
 put on the backburner 後回しにする，二の次にする，当分棚上げにする，先送りする，保留する，無視する
backchannel 形 裏ルートの，水面下の，名 裏ルート
 backchannel figures 裏ルートの重要人物
 backchannel talks 水面下の交渉［協議，話し合い］
backdrop 名 背景，事情，要因
 against the backdrop of …を背景にして，…を受けて
 against this backdrop こうした事情から，このような背景のもとに，これを受けて，こうした中で
 unfold against a backdrop of domestic unrest 内情不安を背景に展開する
backfire 動 裏目に出る，期待はずれに終わる，思わぬ悪い結果を生む，逆効果になる
backgrounder 名 〈政府の非公式な〉背景説

明, 非公式記者会見, 背景説明資料

backlash 名 強い反発, 激しい反動, 強いはね返り, 白人の反発, 反撃, 巻き返し運動
  a backlash vote 反発票
  a public backlash against …に対する国民の強い反発
  a widespread white backlash against …に対する白人の広範な反発
  produce a resentful backlash from …から激しい反発を招く, …から激しい反発を買う
  provoke a backlash 反発を引き起こす

backlog 名 未処理, 未処理部分, 残務, 仕事のやり残し, 在庫, 残高, 受注残高 (backlog figure), 注文残高, 手持ち注文, 予備貯蔵, 蓄積, 山積, 積み残した〈ソフトウエア開発の〉案件, バックログ (=backlogging)

backroom bickering 舞台裏の論争
backroom fixer 背後で糸を引く者, 黒幕 (=string-puller, wirepuller)

backsliding 名 逆戻り
backstage 形 舞台裏の, 裏方の, 秘密の, 内密の, 私生活の
  backstage crew 裏方の人々
  backstage deals 裏取引, 秘密の取決め
  backstage episodes 裏話
  backstage love affair 隠れた情事, 秘密の情事
  backstage manipulator 舞台裏で操る人, 黒幕
  backstage move 裏面工作

backstop 名 〈野球の〉バックネット, 捕手, 安全装置 (safeguard), 補強材, 補助材, 支え (support), 支持, 支援, 手助け, 補佐, 裏付け, 立証

bad assets 不良資産
bad bank バッド・バンク（金融危機の際に政府などが設立し, 公的資金を使って金融機関が抱える不良資産を, 帳簿に記載されている評価額で買い取る専門銀行 [資産管理会社]）

bad debt 不良債権, 不良貸付け, 貸倒れ, 焦げ付き, 貸倒れ損失 (=bad loan, nonperforming loan, uncollectible loan, unrecoverable loan)

bad loan 不良債権, 不良貸付け, 不良貸出, 不良融資, 貸倒れ (=bad debt, nonperforming loan, uncollectible loan)
  bad loan disposal 不良債権処理 (=disposal of bad loans, writing off bad loans)

Baghdad イラク政府, イラク, バグダッド
▶ A senior Iraqi official said that US allegations that *Baghdad* was producing weapons of mass destruction were baseless.　イラクの政府高官は, イラクが大量破壊兵器を製造中であるとする米国の主張には根拠がない, と語った。

bail 名 保釈, 保釈金
  accept [allow, take] bail 保釈を許す
  admit a person to bail 人に保釈を許す
  an application for bail 保釈願い
  bail bandit 保釈中に罪を犯す者
  be allowed bail 保釈になる
  be allowed out on bail 保釈金を積んで出所を許される
  be freed [liberated, released] on bail 保釈金で釈放される, 保釈金を払って釈放される, 保釈される
  be granted bail 保釈が許される
  be liberated on bail to the amount of ¥3 million 300万円の保釈金を積んで釈放される
  be (out) on bail 保釈中である, 保釈出所中である
  be under bail 保釈中である
  forfeit [jump, skip] bail 保釈中失踪する, 保釈中に行方をくらます, 保釈後出廷しない
  forfeit one's bail 保釈金を取り消される, 保釈金を没収される
  give [offer] bail 保釈金を積む
  go [put up, stand] bail for …の保釈保証人となる, …を保証する
  on bail 保釈金を積んで, 保釈金を出して
  post bail 保釈金を納める
  refuse bail 保釈を許さない
  save [surrender to] one's bail 〈出頭して〉保釈金没収を免れる, 〈被告が〉出廷する
  take [give] leg bail 逃亡する, ずらかる

bail out 動 救う, 救済する, 緊急援助する, 緊急の救済措置を取る, 金融支援する

bailout 名 救済, 緊急援助, 金融支援, 債務棚上げ, 救済措置
  bailout fund 救済資金
  bailout help 救済援助, 救済支援, 救済支援策
  bailout measure 救済措置
  bailout package [plan] 緊急援助策 [計画], 救済策 [計画], 金融支援策 [計画]
  U.S. federal bailouts 米連邦政府 [米政府] の救済措置, 米政府の救済策

bait-and-switch おとり商法
balance 動 …の釣合いをとる, …を均衡させる, …の均衡を図る, …の収支を合わせる, …の帳尻を合わせる, …で補う, 差し引く, 比較検討する, バランスをとる

balance opportunities with risks 機会とリスクを比較検討する
balance the profit and loss 損益を差し引く
balanced budget 均衡予算, 均衡財政, 財政均衡
balanced portfolio 均衡の取れた資産内容
be balanced out by …で相殺される

balance 图 収支, 差額, 残高, 勘定残高, 残金, 残り, 貸借勘定, 帳尻, 不足額, 繰越金残存価額, 均衡, 釣り合い, 貸借勘定, バランス
balance due 差引不足額, 支払うべき差引残高, 支払い金の差額
balance for the income account 所得収支 (=income balance)
balance of accounts 勘定残高
balance of capital account 資本収支
balance of current account 経常収支
balance of evidence 最有力な見方
balance of international payments 国際収支 (⇒balance of payments)
balance of invisible trade 貿易外収支 (保険, 船舶・航空運賃, 対外投資の利子・配当など, サービス取引の収支尻)
balance of power 勢力均衡
balance of revenue account 収益勘定残高
balance of terror 〈核保有国間の〉恐怖の均衡
balance of trade 貿易収支 (=trade balance : 製品類の輸出入取引の収支尻。⇒balance of payments)
balance of transfer account 移転収支 (政府の対外無償援助や個人の海外送金など, 対価を伴わない外国との一方的取引の収支尻のこと)
balance on services サービス収支
balance renewal バランス更新, 書換え, 再融資
cast the balance 形勢を一変する
fiscal balance 財政収支
hang [be, lie, tremble] in the balance 未解決である, 未定である, 見通しが立っていない, 不安定な状態にある, 崖っぷちの状態である, 瀬戸際にある, 危機にある, どっちつかずである, どうなるか分からない
invisible trade balance 貿易外収支
merchandise trade balance 貿易収支
on balance 全体としては, 結局のところ, すべてを考慮に入れて, 差し引きして
overall balance of payments 総合収支 (=overall balance)
service balance 貿易外収支
strike a balance はかりにかける, 清算する
strike a balance between …の間の均衡を図る [釣合いをとる, バランスを取る], …の間で妥協する, …の間の妥協点を探る
tip [swing, tilt] the balance against …に(形勢が)不利となる
total balance 総合収支
trade balance 貿易収支
uncollected balance 未収金

balance of payments 国際収支, 支払い差額, 支払い残高《略 BOP》(=balance of international payments; ⇒international balance of payments)
adjustment process of balance of payments 国際収支調整過程
balance of payments equilibrium 国際収支均衡
balance of payments, foreign trade and foreign exchange 国際収支

国際収支とは⊃ 国際収支は経常収支(balance of current account)と資本収支(balance of capital account)で構成され, この二つを合わせたものを総合収支(overall balance of payments)という。また, 経常収支は貿易収支(balance of trade)と貿易外収支(balance of invisible trade), 移転収支(balance of transfer account)から成り, 資本収支は長期資本収支(balance of long-term capital account)と短期資本収支(balance of short-term capital account)から成る。なお, 総合収支から短期資本収支を除いたものを基礎収支(basic balance of payments)という。

balance of current account 経常収支
balance of trade 貿易収支
balance of invisible trade 貿易外収支
balance of transfer account 移転収支
balance of capital account 資本収支
balance of long-term capital account 長期資本収支
balance of short-term capital account 短期資本収支
basic balance of payments 基礎収支(総合収支－短期資本収支＝基礎収支)
overall balance of payments 総合収支(経常収支＋資本収支＝総合収支)

balance sheet 貸借対照表, バランス・シート, 財務基盤, 財務体質, 財務内容, 財務状況, 財務状態, 財務, 資産《略 BS》(=B/S, position statement, statement of financial condition,

statement of financial position：「貸借対照表（バランス・シート）」は決算日現在の企業の財政状態を示すもので，総資産と負債および株主資本を記載した計算書)
balance sheet accounting バランス・シート会計
balance sheet information 貸借対照表情報
damaged balance sheet 資産の質の悪化
improve one's balance sheet 財務体質を改善[強化]する，資金ポジションを改善させる
strengthen one's balance sheet 財務体質を強化する
strong balance sheet 健全な財務内容，健全な財務状態
trim the balance sheet 資産を減らす

ballistic missile 弾道ミサイル，弾道弾
ballistic missile defense 弾道ミサイル防衛《略 BMD》
Ballistic Missile Early Warning System 弾道弾早期警戒システム《略 BMEWS》
long-range ballistic missile 長距離弾道ミサイル

balloon 動 膨らむ，かさむ，増大する，急増する，急騰する，高騰する，気球で飛行[上昇]する，値を上げる，膨らませる
ballooning cost コスト急増
go ballooning 熱気球で飛行する

balloon 名 風船，気球，バルーン融資，バルーン型返済，〈マンガのせりふの〉囲み[吹き出し]，丸いグラス，バルーン
advertising balloon アドバルーン
backed by balloons 満期元本増額支払い型[バルーン型]モーゲージを裏付けとする
balloon astronomy 気球天文学
balloon glass ブランデー・グラス
balloon loan [financing] バルーン融資
balloon maturity 元利合計満期払い，バルーン償還
balloon mortgage 満期元本増額支払い型モーゲージ，バルーン型モーゲージ
balloon note 風船手形（消費者の毎月の返済額を最終日だけ大きくするローン）
balloon payment 満期元本増額支払い，元利合計支払い，バルーン型返済，バルーン・ペイメント
balloon tire 低圧タイヤ
trial balloon 観測気球

ballooning 名 株価つり上げ（禁止されている株価操作の一種），株価膨らまし，急増，高騰

ballot 名 投票，新株割当抽選
absentee ballots 不在者投票
provisional ballot 暫定投票
strike ballot スト権投票

ban 動 禁止する，停止する

ban 名 禁止，停止，廃絶，禁止令 (⇒blanket ban)
import ban 輸入禁止，輸入停止 (＝ban on imports)
lift the ban on …を解禁する，…の禁止を解除する
put [impose, place] a ban on …を禁止する

bank 動 預金する，銀行に預ける，稼ぐ，積み上げる

bank 名 銀行
bank account 銀行口座，銀行預金口座，銀行勘定，預金
bank lending rate 銀行貸出金利
bank line of credit 銀行借入枠，銀行与信枠 (＝credit line)
bank loan [lending] 銀行貸付け，銀行融資，銀行貸付け金，銀行借入れ，銀行借入金，銀行間借款，銀行ローン，バンク・ローン
bank run 銀行の取付け騒ぎ，銀行取付け，取付け騒ぎ，取付け
bank service fee 銀行手数料
bank stocks 銀行株 (＝banks' shares)
bank-transfer scam 振り込め詐欺

Bank for International Settlements
国際決済銀行《略 BIS》

Bank of Japan 日本銀行，日銀《略 BOJ》
Bank of Japan [Japan's] Policy Board 日銀政策委員会
Bank of Japan's quarterly business confidence survey 日銀短観，企業短期経済観測調査

banking 名 銀行業，銀行業務，金融，預金，バンキング
banking group 銀行グループ，金融グループ，銀行・金融グループ
banking industry 銀行業，銀行業界，銀行界 (＝banking sector, banking world)

bankrupt 形 破産した，倒産した，経営破綻した，破綻した，支払い不能の，名 破産者，破綻者，破産宣告を受けた者，債務支払い不能者
go bankrupt 破産する，倒産する，破綻する，事業に失敗する (＝go bust, go under)

bankruptcy 名 倒産，破産，経営破綻，破産手

続き
bankruptcy cost 倒産コスト
bankruptcy notice 破産告知
bankruptcy proceedings [procedures] 破産手続き
bankruptcy protection 破産法の適用
Bankruptcy Reform Act 米連邦改正破産法, 連邦破産法
chain (reaction) bankruptcy 連鎖倒産
declaration of bankruptcy 破産宣告
file for [seek] a bankruptcy protection 破産法の適用を申請する
fraudulent bankruptcy 偽装倒産
personal bankruptcy 個人破産
petition of [in] bankruptcy 破産申請, 破産申立て（＝filing for bankruptcy）
referee in bankruptcy 破産審理人

bar 名 棒, じゃま物, 障壁, 障害, 被告席, 法廷, 弁護士, 弁護士業, 弁護士会, 法曹界, バー
bar chart 棒グラフ
bar code reader バーコード読取り装置, バーコード・リーダー
bar examination 司法試験
bar to promotion 昇進を妨げるもの
be called to the bar [Bar] 〈英国の〉法廷弁護士になる, 弁護士になる
be called within the Bar 〈英国の〉勅選弁護士になる
be chosen from the bar 弁護士のなかから選任される
behind bars 獄中[刑務所]で, 投獄中の, 服役中の
go to the bar 法廷弁護士になる
gold delivery bar 金地金
the bar of conscience 良心の審判

barbed wire 有刺鉄線

bare 形 裸の, 裸体の, 赤裸々な, ありのままの, 偽りのない, 公然の, むき出しの, 露骨な, 覆われていない, 木々のない, 緑のない, 空っぽの, 空の, ぎりぎりの, 最低限の, 最も基本的な, 単なる, ほんのわずかな,〈賠償用の〉保険をかけていない
a person bare of credit 信用のない人
at the bare mention of …と言っただけでも
bare accounts ありのままの説明
bare necessities of life 命をつなぐだけの必需品
be bare of cash 現金がない
by a bare majority ぎりぎりの過半数で, やっと過半数で
escape with bare life 命からがら逃げる
go bare 賠償責任保険なしで営業する
lay A bare [lay bare A] Aを暴露する［公にする, 公表する, 発表する, 明らかにする］, Aを打ち明ける
make a bare beginning on the subject その件で動きはじめる
the bare bones 要点, 骨子
the bare [barest] essentials 最低限必須のもの
the bare minimum 最低限の量
the bare necessities 最低限必要なもの
the bare truth of the matter 事の偽りのない真相

bargaining chip 交渉の切り札, 取引の切り札, 有利な取引材料
bargaining power 交渉力, 購買取引力, 買付け交渉力

barometer 名 尺度, 指標, 兆候, 気圧計, 晴雨計, バロメーター
business barometer 景気指標, 景気種数
coincidental barometer 景気の一致指標
economic barometer 経済指標
leading barometer 先行指標

barrel 名 バレル（石油の単位：米国では42ガロンで159リットル, 英国では42ガロンで191リットル）, 円筒形のもの, 政治資金, 運動資金, 多量
barrel per day 日量…バレル, 日産…バレル, 1日当たり…バレル《略 bpd》
in the barrel 無一文で
make barrels of money しこたま儲ける
on the barrel 即金で
per-barrel price 1バレル当たりの原油価格
scrape (the bottom of) the barrel 残りかすを使う, 最後の財源[方便]に頼る

barrier 名 障害, 障壁, 壁, 制約, 問題, バリア
barriers to entry 参入障壁
foreign trade barriers 外国貿易障壁
import barriers 輸入障壁
investment barriers 投資障壁
market barriers 市場障壁, 市場への参入障壁
nontariff barriers 非関税障壁
political barriers 政治的障壁
psychological barrier 心理的な壁
regulatory barriers 規制上の障壁, 規制上の障害
tariff barrier 関税障壁

trade barriers　貿易障壁

base 名　基準, 基本, 基礎, 基盤, 拠点, 基地, ベース
- **base lending rate**　基準貸出金利
- **base money**　ベースマネー, 基礎貨幣（= monetary base：ベースマネーは, 通貨供給の量を量るのに用いられる指標で, 現金と金融機関が中央銀行に預けている準備預金の合計）
- **base pay**　基本給（= base salary, basic pay）
- **base rate cuts in corporate taxes**　法人税の基本税率引下げ
- **base salary**　基本給, 本俸（= base pay）
- **base station**　基地局, ベース・ステーション
- **business base**　営業基盤, 経営基盤
- **earnings base**　収益基盤
- **funding base**　資金調達源
- **tax base**　課税基準, 課税標準, 税収基盤

based [–based] 形　…を（営業）基盤とする, …を基軸とする, …基準の, …に本部［本社・本店］を置く, …駐在の, …型の, …をベースにした, …に基づく, …主義の, …建ての, …密着型の
- **customer-based**　顧客基盤の
- **dollar-based investor**　ドル・ベースの投資家
- **IC-based card**　ICカード（= IC card）
- **market-based**　市場に基づく, 市場原理に基づく
- **merit- and achievement-based system**　能力・実績主義
- **narrow-based stock index**　業種別株価指数
- **performance-based**　成果主義の
- **performance-based pay**　能力給
- **technology-based company**　ハイテク関連企業

Basel Accord　〈1988年の〉バーゼル合意, バーゼル協定, BIS規制, BIS自己資本比率規制（= Basel Agreement, Basel Capital Accord）

baseline 名　基準, 基準線, 基準見通し, 指導基準（guideline）, 基調, 起点（測量の）基線, 遠近線, 〈野球のベース間を結ぶ〉塁線, 〈テニスやバレーボール, バドミントンなどの〉コートの両端を示す線, ベースライン
- **baseline budget**　基本予算, 基準になる予算, 予算の基準見通し
- **baseline budget deficit**　基準になる財政赤字
- **baseline play**　〔テニス〕ベースライン・プレー（ベースライン付近で打ち合うこと）

bashing 名　強打, ひどい打撃, 激しくたたくこと, 辛らつな非難, 厳しい批判, バッシング
- **Japan bashing**　日本たたき, ジャパン・バッシング

suffer a bashing　お灸をすえられる

basic agreement　基本的合意, 基本合意, 大筋合意, 基本合意書, 基本契約, 基本契約書
- **conclude a basic agreement**　基本契約を結ぶ, 基本契約を締結する
- **reach a basic agreement**　基本合意に達する, 基本合意する

basic pension　基礎年金

basis 名　方針, 基準, 根本原理, 主義, 方式, 基礎, 根拠, 論拠, 土台, 主成分, ベース
- **customs basis**　通関ベース
- **market price basis**　時価主義
- **on a consolidated [group] basis**　連結ベースで, 一括して
- **on a dollar denominated basis**　ドル表示で
- **on a full year basis**　通年で, 通期で
- **on a moment-to-moment basis**　瞬間瞬間ベースで
- **on a nominal basis**　名目で
- **on a same-store basis**　既存店ベースで
- **on an all-store basis**　全店舗ベースで
- **on an optional basis**　選択制で
- **on the basis of IMF formula**　IMF方式で
- **tax basis**　課税標準, 税法基準

▶GDP calculated on a nominal *basis* reflects economic conditions under deflation more accurately than real GDP.　〈物価変動の影響を除いた〉実質GDPより名目GDPのほうが, デフレ下の経済情勢を的確に反映している。

basis point　ベーシス・ポイント《略 **b.p.**》（為替・金利変動の基準単位で, 1ベーシス・ポイント＝0.01%, 100ベーシス・ポイント＝1%。⇒percentage point）

basket 名　かご, 集まり, 構成比率, 株式バスケット商品, バスケット
- **basket case**　経済破綻国, 手術で手足を切断された人, 正気を逸した人
- **basket category**　包括品目（同一関税率の品目）
- **basket clause**　〈契約などの〉包括的条項, バスケット条項
- **basket currency**　バスケット通貨
- **basket delivery**　バスケット方式
- **basket formula**　バスケット方式（複数国通貨の加重平均方式）
- **basket of currencies of major trading partners**　主要貿易相手国の通貨バスケット
- **basket purchase**　一括購入, 一括買取り（= lump-sum purchase）

basket transaction バスケット取引
cash baskets of stocks 株式の現物バスケット, 現物株式のバスケット
currency basket 通貨バスケット
standard basket (system) 標準バスケット方式 (=standard current basket system)

batter 動 乱打する, たたきのめす, 激しく打つ, 打ち壊す, 直撃する, 壊滅する, 砲撃する, へこませる, 使いつぶす
battered baby 被虐待児
battered child [baby] syndrome 幼児虐待 (=child abuse, child battering)
battered wife 虐待妻(夫から繰り返し暴力を受ける妻)
be battered by …をもろに受ける, 吹き付けられる, たたきつけられる, 定期的に虐待[家庭内暴力]を受ける

battle 動 戦う, 闘争する, …に取り組む
battle against inflation インフレと戦う
battle for control of …の経営権[支配権, 経営支配権]獲得のために戦う
battle with …と戦う
battle 名 戦い, 闘争, 戦闘, 競争, 一戦, 口論, 交渉, 戦争, バトル
a battle for power 権力闘争
a battle of wills 根くらべ
redraw the battle lines with …と一線を画す
the battle for deposits 預金獲得競争

battlefield 名 戦場, 戦闘区域, 対決場, 論争の的, 論争の場, 争い[闘争]の場 (=battle-ground)

bear down on …にどっと押し寄せる, …をのみ込む, …を圧迫する

bear market 弱気市場, 弱気相場, 下げ相場, 売り相場 (=bearish market)

bearing 名 関係, 関連, 関与, 影響, 面, 角度, 方向, 方位, 方角, 相対的位置, 立場, 忍耐, 忍耐力, 我慢, 態度, 振るまい, 出産, 収穫, 結実, ベアリング
ball bearings 玉軸受け
economic bearing 経済的関係
get one's bearings …を把握する
have little bearing on …にほとんど関係がない, …にほとんど関与していない
have some bearing on …に何かしら関係がある
interest bearing 利付き, 金利付き, 利子を生むこと

lose one's bearings 当惑する, 位置が分からなくなる
risk bearing 危険負担 (=bearing of risk)
take one's bearings …を確かめる
tax bearing 租税負担

be-all and end-all 最も大切なこと[物], 最も重要なこと, 何よりも大事なこと, 肝心なこと, 最高の目的, 精髄, 金科玉条

bearish 形 弱気の, 弱気含みの, 下落気味の, 下がり気味の, 見通しが暗い, 悲観的な見方の, 全面安の〈展開〉, 売り優勢の〈展開〉
bearish market 弱気市場, 弱気相場, 下げ相場, 売り相場, 株価低迷の局面 (=bear market)
bearish mood 先行き不安, 全面安の展開, 弱気の地合い, 弱気ムード (=bearish sentiment, bearish tone)

bedrock 名 根底, 基盤, 根本, 基本原則, 根本原理, 基本的原理, 基本的事実, 岩床, 岩盤, 形 基本的な, 根本的な
bedrock position 基本的立場
bedrock prices 底値
get [come] down to bedrock 本題に入る, 真相を究める

beef buyback scheme 牛肉買上げ制度 (=buyback scheme for beef)
beef products 牛肉製品
beef up 強化する, 増強する, 補強する, 拡充する, 向上させる, 食肉処理する (=strengthen)
beef-up 名 強化, 増強, 補強, 食肉処理
beeline 名 2地点間の最短距離, 一直線 (=bee-line)
make a beeline for …に一直線に向かう, …に真っすぐ向かう, …に直行する, …に一直線に進む

behavior [behaviour] 名 行動, 行為, 活動, 動向, 動き, 変動, 政策
behavior of inflation インフレ動向
behavior strategy 行動戦略
business behavior 企業行動
buying behavior 購買行動
consumer behavior 消費者行動, 消費者動向 (=consumer's behavior)
cost behavior 原価変動, 原価の動き
economic behavior 経済行為, 経済行動, 経済活動, 経済動向, 景気動向, 相場の動き (=behavior of the economy, economy's behavior)
Fed behavior FRB (米連邦準備制度理事会)の政策

interest rate behavior　金利動向　(＝behavior of the interest rates)
inventory behavior　在庫の動き
market behavior　市場行動, 市場動向, 市場の動き
noneconomic behavior　非経済的行為
optimal investment behavior　最適投資行動
optimizing behavior　最適化行動
price behavior　価格動向, 物価動向
producer's behavior　生産者行動
profit maximizing behavior　利益［利潤］最大化行動, 利益極大化行動
speculative behavior　投機的行動
spending behavior　消費行動, 消費パターン
supply behavior　供給行動
underlying behavior of the economy　景気の基調
yield behavior　利回りの動き

behind-closed-doors session　非公開の会談, 秘密裏の会談
behind-the-scenes 形　舞台裏の, 秘密裏の, 水面下の
behind-the-scenes concessions　舞台裏の譲歩, 水面下の歩み寄り
behind-the-scenes involvement　不明朗な関与, 舞台裏の関与
behind-the-scenes negotiations　舞台裏での交渉
behind-the-scenes preparatory sessions　水面下の事前折衝
behind-the-scenes talks　水面下の話し合い

Beige Book　米地区連銀景況報告書, 地区連銀景況報告, 地区連銀経済報告, ベージュ・ブック(＝tan book：米国の12の地区連銀(連邦準備銀行)が管轄する各地区の景気動向を分析して, 作成される経済情勢報告書。米連邦公開市場委員会(FOMC)の会議資料として用いられる)

Beijing 名　中国, 中国政府, 北京

beleaguered 形　包囲された, 窮地に追い込まれた, 困難［非難, 反対］にあっている, 非難にさらされている
be beleaguered with annoyance　いろいろ嫌な思いをさせられる
beleaguered president　窮地に追い込まれた大統領, 追い詰められた大統領, 非難にさらされている大統領

belie 動　〈期待などを〉裏切る, …に反する, …と矛盾する, 偽りであることを示す, 隠す, 誤って伝える

bellwether 名　先導者, 主導［指導］者, 〈市場動向の目安となる〉指標銘柄, 〈金利などの〉誘導目標
bellwether bond　債券指標銘柄
bellwether long bond　30年物指標銘柄(＝30-year bellwether bond)
bellwether stock　市場先導株

belt-tightening policy　緊縮政策

bench 名　判事席, 裁判官席, 裁判官, 判事, 法廷, 〈英議会の〉議席, 議員席, 議員
be raised [elevated] to the bench　裁判官に任命される［任じられる］
bench rate　標準金利, 基準金利
bench warmer [polisher]　補欠選手, 控え選手
bench warrant　〈裁判長発行［裁判所］の〉逮捕令状
sit [serve] on the bench　裁判官を務める, 審理中である
the back benches　一般議員席
the federal bench　米連邦判事
the front benches　与野党幹部席, 政党幹部席
the full bench　列席の全判事
the ministerial benches　政府与党議員席
the opposition benches　野党議員席

benchmark 名　基準, 尺度, 基準値, 測定基準, 基準指数, 基準銘柄, 指標, 指標銘柄, 政策金利(benchmark interest rate), ベンチマーク
benchmark bond　債券指標銘柄
benchmark corporate lending　基準法人貸出金利
benchmark five-year U.S. Treasury bonds　指標となる5年物財務省証券
benchmark interest rate　基準金利, 指標金利, 政策金利
benchmark issue　指標銘柄
benchmark Nikkei Stock Average　日経平均株価
benchmark price　基準価格
benchmark (interest) rate　基準金利, 指標金利, 政策金利
benchmark reserves　基準準備金
benchmark short-term interest rate　短期金利の誘導目標, 短期金利の指標
benchmark year　基準年
benchmark yield　指標銘柄利回り, 指標利回り
international benchmark　国際指標
seasonal benchmark　季節調整の基準

beneficiary 名　〈年金や保険金, 為替などの〉

benefit 動 利益を与える, …の利益になる, …のプラスになる, …に貢献する, 利益を得る, 恩恵を受ける, 利益が発生する
- benefit existing shareholders 株主の利益になる
- benefit from …から利益を得る, …の恩恵を受ける, …のメリットを受ける, …が追い風になる

benefit 名 利益, 利得, 便益, 利点, 効果, 給付, 給付金, 給付額, 退職金, 年金, 手当, 受益, 受益金, 税減額効果, ベネフィット
- benefit rate 手当の給付率
- cost-benefit analysis 費用便益分析《略 CBA》
- defined benefit plan 確定給付制度
- economic benefits 経済利益
- employee benefit plan 従業員給付制度, 従業員福利厚生制度
- fringe benefit 付加給付, 賃金外給付, 追加給付
- health care benefit 医療給付, 健康保険給付
- life insurance benefit 生命保険給付
- medical benefit 医療給付
- pension benefit 年金給付, 受取年金, 退職年金給付
- retirement benefit 退職給付, 退職給与
- social security benefit 社会保障給付
- vested benefit 受給権, 年金給付受給権, 受給権確定給付, 確定年金給付
- welfare benefit 福祉給付

benign 形 温和な, 慈悲深い, 低水準の, 良好な, 良性の, 見通しが明るい, 落ち着いている
- benign inflation 低いインフレ率, 低水準のインフレ, 低インフレ
- benign interest rate [rate] environment 良好な金利環境, 良好な金利動向
- benign neglect 善意の無策, 善意の無視政策, ビナイン・ネグレクト《悪意の無視=malign neglect》
- benign tumor 良性腫瘍
- policy of benign neglect 善意の無策の策, 善意の無視政策, ビナイン・ネグレクト政策

beset 動 悩ます, 悩ませる, 苦しめる, 取り巻く(surround), 取り囲む, 包囲する, 囲む, 閉じ込める, 襲う(assail), 付きまとう(harass), 飾る(ornament), ちりばめる(stud)
- be beset by [with] many difficulties 多くの困難 [難題] に悩まされる [苦しめられる]
- the issues besetting the two countries 両国が抱える問題

best 名 最高のもの, 最高の状態, 名士, ベスト
- get [have] the best of …を制する, …に勝つ, …を出し抜く
- go for the best 最後にうまくまとまる, 最も良い方向に向かう
- make the best of …を最大限に利用する, …を乗り切る, …を凌ぐ
- one's personal best …の自己最高記録, …の自己ベスト

bet 動 賭ける, 確信する, 断言する, 主張する, 予想する, 期待する
- be betting …を予想している, …を期待している
- bet on …を見越す, …に賭ける, …に投資する

bet 名 賭け, 掛け金, 賭けの対象, 予想, 見通し, 意見, 選択, 選択した行動, 選択の手段[方法], 確実な人物[こと, 物]
- a fair bet 正しい判断, 正しい選択
- a good bet 賢明な選択[判断, 行動], お薦め[お薦め品], 確実な人[こと, 物], 賭けの対象
- a reasonable bet 妥当な判断, 合理的な選択
- a safe [sure] bet 安全な選択, 安全な判断[行動], 安全な方法(…するのが)確実
- a sure bet 期待の星
- an even bet 五分五分の賭け
- hedge one's bets 両にらみで行く, どちらともとれる曖昧な言い方をする
- take [accept] an even bet 五分五分の賭けに応じる
- the [one's] best bet 第一にやるべきこと, お薦め[お薦め品], 最も賢明な選択, 最善の打つ手

bias 名 先入観, 偏見, ひいき, えこひいき, 偏り, 偏執, 歪み, 傾向, 地合い, 姿勢, スタンス, 才能, 技術, 興味, バイアス
- anti-American bias 反米思想
- bias distortion バイアスひずみ
- bias in measurement 測定上の偏り
- bias to easing policy 金融政策を緩和に傾ける姿勢
- bullish [positive] bias 強気の地合い
- conversion factor bias 変換係数の歪み
- downward bias 下降傾向, 景気の弱さ
- export bias 輸出偏向
- freedom from bias 不偏性
- have a bias against …に対して悪い先入観を持つ
- have a bias for [in favor of, toward] …をえこひいきする
- ideological bias イデオロギー的偏向

individual bias 個人の偏向
inflationary bias インフレ傾向, インフレ・バイアス
personal bias 個人的偏見
technological bias 技術的バイアス
tightening bias 金融引締めの姿勢, 金融政策を引締め方向に傾ける姿勢, 引締めぎみ
upward bias 上昇傾向

biased 形 偏った, 偏向した, 偏向的, 偏見を抱いた, 先入観を持った
biased coverage 偏向報道
biased growth 偏向的成長
biased question 誘導質問
import-biased technology innovation 輸入偏向的技術革新
pro-trade biased effect 親貿易［順貿易］偏向的効果
trade biased effect 貿易偏向効果
vote a directive biased toward firmness 〈金融政策を〉引締めに傾ける決定を下す

bickering 名 口論, 言い争い, いさかい, 内紛

bid for …に値を付ける, …に入札する, …の入札をする

bid 名 入札, 申込み, 〈入札の〉付け値, 落札価格, 競り, 提案, 買収提案, 買収案件, 買収, 株式公開買付け (TOB), 買い注文, 買い呼び値, 買い気配, 買い唱え (証券などの売買で買い手が希望する値段), 試み, 努力, 選挙への出馬, 立候補, ビッド
absentee bid 不在入札
bid bond 入札保証, 入札保証金
bid target 買収の標的
bid winner 落札業者, 受注業者, 落札予定会社
competitive bid 競争入札
high-stakes bid 一か八かの賭け, 大きな賭け
hostile bid 敵対的買収提案
make a bid for power 権力の座をねらう
make a successful bid 落札する, 受注する
minimum bid 最低入札価格
noncompetitive bid 非競争入札
possible winning bid 落札可能な価格
put in the highest bid 最高額の付け値をする
referential bid 参照入札
strong bids 強気の買い
submit bids 入札に応じる (=send in a bid)
the highest bid price 落札価格, 落札値
White House bid 米大統領選への出馬［立候補］, 米大統領をめざす政治活動
winning bid 獲得した買収条件

bid-fixing 名 談合行為
bid-rigging 名 談合, 入札談合, 不正入札, 不正工作
engage in bid-rigging 談合を行う
proactive involvement in the bid-rigging 談合への主体的関与
the law preventing bid-rigging involving government officials 官製談合防止法

bidder 名 入札者, 入札業者, 入札行, 競り手,〈参加などの〉申込み国

bidding 名 入札, 競り, 申込み, 命令 (=bid, tendering)

big-boned policy 骨太の方針 (=big-boned framework, big-boned guidelines)

Big Three 米国の3大自動車メーカー (GM, フォードとクライスラー), 3大国, ビッグスリー

big-ticket 形 高価な, 高額な, 高い値の付いた, 大型の
big-ticket item [product] 高額商品, 高価な商品, 大型商品, 目玉事業
big-ticket lease 高額リース物件
big-ticket purchase [spending] 高額商品の購入, 大型商品の購入 (=purchase of big-ticket items)

bigwig 名 実力者, 有力者, 重要人物, 大物, お偉方, 長老

bilateral 形 相互の, 双方の, 両者の, 相対の, 二者の, 二者間の, 二国間の, 左右相称の, 両側性の, 双務的な, 相互に義務を負う, 当事者双方が義務を負う, 当事者間の (⇒multilateral, trilateral, unilateral)
bilateral agreement 双務協定, 二国間協定, 双方の合意
bilateral aid 二国間援助
bilateral contract 双務契約, 双方的契約 (片務契約=unilateral contract)
bilateral credits 二国間信用供与
bilateral deal 二国間取引
bilateral deals 〈石油の〉直接取引 (=bilateral oil purchase deals)
bilateral double taxation treaty 二国間の二重課税防止条約
bilateral duopoly 双方複占
bilateral initiative 二国間交渉
bilateral line 相対取引, 相対ベース
bilateral loan 相対ローン, 相対ベースの融資
bilateral master agreement 当事者間の標準契約

bilateral mistake 当事者双方の錯誤, 共通的錯誤
bilateral monopoly 双方独占
bilateral nuclear disarmament 双務的核軍縮
bilateral oligopoly 双方寡占
bilateral relationship 二国間関係
bilateral settlement 双務決済
bilateral short-term advances 相対の短期貸出
bilateral summit 二国間首脳会談
bilateral talks 二国間協議, 二者会談
bilateral trade 二国間貿易, 双務貿易
bilateral trade agreement 二国間通商協定
bilateral trade friction 二国間の貿易摩擦
bilateral transaction 二国間取引, 双務取引, 双方的取引, 直接相対取引
bilateral treaty 二国間条約
negotiations on bilateral lines 相対ベースの交渉
on a bilateral basis 相対ベースで, 相対契約で
U.S-Japan Framework Talks on bilateral talks 日米包括経済協議

bilateralism 名 二国間交渉主義, 双務主義

bill 動 代金を請求する, 代価を請求する, 請求書を送る
▶ *Bill* us later. 後で当社に請求書を送ってください。

bill 名 手形, 為替手形, 証券, 米財務省短期証券, 証書, 紙幣, 札(さつ), 料金, 請求金額, 請求書, 勘定書, 〈クレジット・カードなどの〉利用明細書, 明細書, 訴状, 調書, 広告, ビラ, ポスター, ちらし, 表, リスト
a set of bills 組手形
acceptance of bill (of exchange) 手形引受け
agency bill 代理手形
banker's bill 銀行手形
bill at sight 一覧払い手形
bill of quantities 建築見積り書
bill of sale 売渡し証
blank bill 白紙の請求書
clean bill of health 完全健康証明書
collect a bill 集金する
domestic [home, inland] bill 内国為替
domiciled bill 他所払い手形
double name [named] bill 複名手形
duplicate bill 副為替手形
fit [fill] the bill 要求[条件]を満たす, 申し分ない, ぴったりだ
foot the bill for …の勘定をする, …の勘定を払う, …の費用を負担する, …の経費を持つ, …を合計する
gas bill ガス料金
honor a bill 手形の支払いをする
original bill 原手形
pay the bill for …の勘定を払う, …の付けを払う
security bill 証券担保為替手形
single name [named] bill 単名手形
sole bill 単独手形, 単独為替手形
top [head] the bill 主役を演じる
two-name bill 複名手形
unpaid bills 代金の踏み倒し
value bill 荷為替手形

bill 名 法案, 議案
bring a bill before the Senate 米上院に法案を送る
draft of bill 法案の草案
draw up a bill 議案を起草する
engrossed bill 清書された法案
enrolled bill 登録用法案
first regular appropriation bill 第一次通常歳出法案
introduce a bill into Parliament 法案を議会に提出する
original bill 法案の原文[原本]
original engrossed House bill 下院から回されてきた原法案
original enrolled bill 登録された法案の原本
pass a bill 法案を可決する
public bill 公共関係法案
reject [throw out] a bill 法案を否決する
shelve a bill 法案[議案]を棚上げする
veto a bill 法案に拒否権を発動する, 法案に拒否権を行使する
vetoed bill 米大統領に拒否された法案

binding 形 法律的に[法的に]拘束力のある, 法的に拘束する, 拘束力のある
binding agreement 法的に拘束力のある契約[合意], 拘束力のある合意
binding arbitration 法的に拘束力のある仲裁, 拘束力のある仲裁
binding force of laws 法の拘束力
binding obligation 拘束力のある義務
binding power 拘束力
▶ The main point of contention in court was whether this clause was legally *binding*. 法廷での主な争点は, この条項の法的拘束力の有無であった。

bio- 接頭 生物, 生命, 生物［生命］に関する
- **bio-arms** 生物兵器
- **biochips** 生物化学素子, バイオチップ（半導体素子に代わる電子計算機素子）
- **biocomputer** バイオコンピュータ
- **biodefense** 生物防衛
- **biodiversity** 生物多様性, 生物学的多様性
- **bioengineering** 生物工学, 生体工学
- **biofeedback** 生体自己制御
- **biofuel** バイオ燃料
- **biohazard** 生物災害, バイオハザード
- **bioindustry** 生物技術産業
- **bioinformatics** 生命情報科学, 生命情報工学, 生物情報学（分子生物学と情報科学が融合した学問分野）
- **biometric authentication [identification, recognition] system** 生体認証システム
- **bionics** 生体工学
- **bioplant** バイオ植物
- **biosensor** 生物感知器, 生体感応装置, バイオセンサー
- **biosphere** 生存権, バイオスフィア
- **biotechnology** 生物工学, 生命工学, 生命技術, バイオ技術, バイオテクノロジー
- **bioterrorism attack** 生物兵器テロ
- **biovegitable** バイオ野菜
- **bioweapon** 生物兵器

bioethanol vehicle バイオエタノール車
biological and chemical weapons 生物・化学兵器
biomass 名 生物資源, 量的生物資源, 生物量, 生物現存量, 生物体総量, バイオマス（石炭や石油などの化石燃料以外で, 木材や動物の糞尿, 生ゴミなど植物や動物から発生するエネルギー源）
biometrics 名 個人識別法, 本人証明技術, 生物統計［統計学］, バイオメトリクス
bioterrorist attack 生物テロ攻撃
biotoxin 名 動植物の毒, 生物毒性
bipartisan law 超党派立法
bird flu 鳥インフルエンザ（＝avian flu, avian influenza）
bird strike 鳥衝突, 鳥の衝突, バード・ストライク（航路上の鳥が飛行機の機体に衝突する事故のことで, とくにエンジンの空気吸入口に鳥が吸い込まれるケースが多い）
birth contract 代理出産契約
birth registration 出生届け
BIS 国際決済銀行 (Bank for International Settlementsの略。世界の金融監督当局や中央銀行で構成されている。⇒capital adequacy ratio)
BIS ratio 自己資本比率
BIS standard BIS基準

bite 動 かみつく, かむ, 刺す, …にかみ合う, 腐食する,〈好ましくない〉影響［効果］をもたらす, だます, 欺（あざむ）く
- **be bitten by [with]** …に夢中になる, …にとりつかれる, …にかまれる
- **bite into** …に食い込む, …に打撃を与える, …を腐食する, …を食べ始める
- **bite off more than one can chew** 自分の能力に余る仕事［がらにもないこと］を企てる, 自分の力以上のことをしようとする
- **bite on** …をよく考える［検討する］
- **bite on granite** 無駄骨を折る
- **bite the bullet** 苦しい状況に敢然と立ち向かう
- **bite the dust [ground]** 失敗する,〈機械などが〉動かなくなる
- **bite the hand that feeds you** 恩を仇で返す
- **bite the thumb at** …を馬鹿にする, …をからかう
- **bite the tongue** 舌をかむ, 沈黙する
- **get bitten in a swindle** 詐欺にひっかかる
- **once bitten twice shy** あつものに懲りてなますを吹く

black 名 黒字 (＝black figure; ⇒red)
black-and-white language 白黒をはっきりさせる論法, 白か黒かの単純に割り切った論法
black lung disease 黒肺病, じん肺 (＝pneumoconiosis; ⇒Pneumoconiosis Law)
black market ヤミ市, ヤミ市場, アングラ市場, ヤミ取引, ブラック・マーケット
Black Monday 世界的同時株安, 世界的株価暴落, ブラック・マンデー（1987年10月19日（月曜日）に記録したニューヨーク株式市場の株価の大暴落。ダウ平均株価（工業株30種）が, 1日で508.32ドル下落した）
blackmail 名 恐喝, ゆすり, ゆすり取った金, ブラックメール
blackout 名 停電, 空襲時の灯火管制, 報道管制, 緘口令, 一時的な通信途絶, 意識喪失, 記憶喪失
blacktop street アスファルト舗装道路
blanket action 一斉摘発
blanket ban 全面禁止
blanket testing 全頭検査
blast 動 激しく非難する, 強く批判する, 弾劾する,

攻撃する, 猛攻を加える, 爆破する, 吹き付ける, 大差で勝つ, 大敗させる
be blasted off toward …に向けて発射される
blast off 〈ロケットなどが〉発進する, 発射する, 離昇する, 打ち上げられる
blast 名 突風, 激しい非難, 強い批判, 弾劾, 攻撃, 猛攻, 銃撃, 爆破, 爆風, 爆発, 楽しい出来事, どんちゃん騒ぎ, 乱痴気パーティー
a blast from the past 懐かしのメロディー[ファッション]
at full blast 全力を挙げて, フル回転で, 最高の音量[強度, 速度]で
beer blasts ビール・パーティー
put [lay] the blast on …を非難する
suicide blast 自爆テロ
blastoff 名 〈ロケットなどの〉発射[打上げ]
blending 名 混合, 結合, 配合, 組合せ, 調和, 融合, 融和
blip 名 レーダー・スクリーン上の映像, 一時的な現象
blistering 形 痛烈な, 猛烈な, 焼け付くような
blitz 名 大宣伝, 大キャンペーン, 集中作戦, 電撃作戦, 急襲, 猛攻, 空襲
blitzkrieg 奇襲, 電撃戦, 電撃作戦, 迅速な集中攻撃
media blitz メディア・キャンペーン
bloated 形 膨れた, 膨れ上がった, 増大した, 肥大した, 巨大で効率が悪い, 過剰な
be bloated with pride 威張り腐っている
bloated inventory 増大した在庫, 過剰在庫, 在庫増
bloated profiteer 悪徳商人
bloc 名 …圏, …群, 団体, 連盟, 連合, 議員連合, 議員団, 地域, ブロック
Communist bloc 共産圏
core bloc コア通貨
dollar bloc ドル地域, ドル・ブロック
economic bloc 経済圏, 経済ブロック
farm bloc 〈米〉農民利益代表団, 農民議員団
former communist bloc nations 旧共産圏諸国
free trading bloc 自由貿易地域
monetary [currency] bloc 通貨圏, 通貨ブロック
opposition bloc 野党陣営, 野党側
regional economic bloc 地域経済ブロック, 地域経済圏
ruling bloc 与党陣営, 与党側, 与党

Western bloc 西欧圏, 西欧連合
yen (currency) bloc 円ブロック
block 動 閉鎖する, 封鎖する, 凍結する, 遮断する, 止める, …の流れを止める, 阻む, 阻止する, 防ぐ, 妨げる, 妨害する, ブロックする
block 名 市街の一区画, 区域, 塊, スランプ, 一時的な思考の停止, 相手を妨げる行為, ブロック
a block of shares 1取引単位の株式
a mental block 思考停止
annuity block 年金商品
block association 町内会, 隣組
block booking 〈券などの〉一括購入, 〈映画などの〉一括配給契約
block copy 版下
block grants 包括補助金, 定額交付金, 定額助成金, ブロック交付金
block insurance 包括保険
block investor 大口投資家
block offer 一括売出し, ブロック・オファー
block party 同一区域の住民による路上パーティ
block purchase ブロック買い
block release 社員研修一時休暇制度
block sale ブロック売り
block sales 大量販売, 大量売付け
block trade 大口取引, 大量取引
block patrol 自主的防犯パトロール
place a block order 大口注文を出す
blockade 名 封鎖, 閉塞, 経済封鎖, 海上封鎖, 道路[通信]封鎖, 交通遮断, 封鎖地域, 封鎖道路, 不通, 妨害, 障害, 障害物, 封鎖隊, 包囲軍
blockade against Japan 対日封鎖
blockade line 封鎖線
blockade policy 封鎖政策
blockade-running 封鎖破り
blockade zone 封鎖区域
break a blockade 封鎖を強行突破する, 封鎖を破る
economic blockade 経済封鎖
food blockade 食料封鎖
impose a blockade 封鎖を行う
lift [end, raise] a blockade 封鎖を解く, 封鎖を解除する
lift the arms blockade 武器封鎖を解く
naval [sea] blockade 海上封鎖
pacific blockade 平時封鎖
run a blockade 封鎖をかいくぐる
blockbuster 名 大型爆弾, 大当たり, 大成功, (大衆受けをねらった)大作, 大ヒット作品, 超ヒッ

ト商品，超ベストセラー，悪徳不動産屋［不動産業者］，影響力の大きい［強い］人，ブロックバスター
blockbuster deal 大型債
blockbuster success 大成功，大当たり
blog 名 ブログ （＝Web log：web（インターネット，ホームページ）とlog（記録）の合成造語であるweblogの略。手軽に開設できてだれでも書き込みが可能な日記風のホームページで，双方向の交流が可能）
blogger 名 ブログの書き手
Blood Law 血液法
blood product 血液製剤
blood transfusion 輸血 （⇒medical treatment, viral infection）
bloodless coup 無血クーデター
Bloomberg news agency 米ブルームバーグ通信社，ブルームバーグ通信
blow 名 打撃，衝撃，ショック
　deal a blow to …に打撃を与える，…に難問を抱えさせる
　strike a blow against …のために反対する，…に反抗する
　strike a blow for …のために努力する，…に加勢する
blow-out holiday 出産前の休暇 （＝last-hurrah breaks）
blue chip 優良株，主要銘柄
　blue-chip company [corporation, firm] 優良企業
　blue-chip issues [stocks] 優良銘柄，優良企業の銘柄
Blue House 青瓦（せいが）台，韓国の大統領官邸，韓国政府 （＝Chongwadae）
bluefin tuna 名 クロマグロ（ホンマグロ）
blueprint 名 詳細な計画，青図，青写真，青焼き，ブループリント
　a blueprint for fiscal reconstruction 財政建て直し［財政再建］の青写真
　a broad blueprint 大まかな青写真
　draw up a blueprint for …の詳細な計画を練る
blunder 名 しくじり，失敗，不覚，不手際，へま，大失策
　economic policy blunder 経済政策の失敗，経済失政
　make a blunder 大失敗をする，重大な誤りを犯す
Blu-ray standard ブルーレイ規格

board 名 取締役会（the board of directors），重役会，理事会，審議会，委員会，会議，省［庁，局，部］，掲示板，ボード
Big Board ニューヨーク証券取引所，ビッグ・ボード
board director 取締役，〈委員会などの〉理事 （＝board member）
board members' salaries 役員報酬
Chicago Board of Trade シカゴ商品取引所
fall across the board 全面安になる，全面的に下落する
Federal Home Loan Bank Board 米連邦住宅貸付銀行理事会
Federal Housing Finance Board 米連邦住宅金融理事会
Federal Reserve Board 米連邦準備制度理事会 《略 FRB》
Financial Accounting Standards Board 財務会計基準審議会
go on the board 上場する
Policy Board of the Bank of Japan 日銀政策委員会
Public Works Loan Board 英国の公共事業資金貸付委員会
Reserve Bank's board meeting 米連邦準備銀行理事会
rise across the board 全面高になる，全面的に上昇する
sit on the board 取締役を務める，役員［委員］を務める
special precinct board 特別委員会
board meeting 取締役会，取締役会会議，役員会，評議員会，理事会 （＝board of directors meeting）
extraordinary board meeting 臨時取締役会
regular board meeting 定例取締役会
▶ Members of the board of directors are selected at general shareholders meetings and are required to make the decisions on important matters as well as oversee the company president's performance by holding *board meetings*. 取締役は株主総会で選任され，取締役会を開いて重要事項の決定や代表取締役（会社社長）の職務執行の監視などを行う義務がある。
board member 取締役，役員，重役，理事，執行委員
board of directors 〈会社の〉取締役会，役員会，重役会，〈財団などの〉理事会 《略 BOD》
body language 身体言語，ボディ・ランゲージ

BoE イングランド銀行 (=the Bank of England)

bog 動 〈沼などに〉はまり込ませる, 身動きをとれなくする
- **be bogged down** 動きがとれない, 動きがとれなくなる
- **be bogged down in** …に陥っている
- **become [get] bogged down in** …にはまり込む, …を抜け出せない
- **bog down** 〈道路などが〉沈下する, 泥沼にはまり込む, 動きがとれなくなる
- **bog up** …を混乱させる

bogus 形 偽の, 虚偽の, 粉飾の, 模造の, 模倣の, 架空の (=fake)
- **bogus letter** ウソの文書
- **bogus cash card** 偽造キャッシュ・カード, 偽造カード
- **bogus product** 模倣品, 模造品, コピー商品

bolster 動 促進する, 伸ばす, 〈地位などを〉向上させる, 〈立場を〉強める, 強化する, 〈経済を〉増強する, 〈景気を〉浮揚させる, 〈ドルなどを〉支える, 支持する, 補強する, 救済する
- **bolster competitiveness** 競争力をつける
- **bolster the economy** 景気を浮揚させる
- **bolster the long-suffering housing market** 長期低迷の住宅市場を活性化させる
- **bolster the position** 地位を向上させる, 立場を強める
- **measures to bolster the economy** 景気浮揚策

bolt 動 逃げ出す, 飛び出す, 急増する, 急上昇する, 離党[脱党]する, 脱会する, 脱退する, 欠席する, 〈主義や主張を〉変える, 口走る, うっかりしゃべる

bolt 名 稲妻, 電光, 逃亡, 離党[脱党], 脱会, 脱退, 急増, 急上昇
- **a bolt from [out of] the blue** 青天の霹靂, 不意打ち, 思いがけない出来事[悲劇]
- **make a bolt for it** 逃げ出す
- **nuts and bolts** 基本, 土台, 基本的課題, 主眼点, 実際面, 実際
- **shoot one's bolt** 全力を尽くす

bond 名 債券, 社債, 公社債, 債務証書, 借用証書, 保証書, 支払い保証契約, 保証, 保証金, 保釈金
- **bond issuance [issue]** 社債発行, 債券発行
- **bond insurer** 金融保証専門会社, 金融保証会社, 〈米国の〉モノライン(債券など金融商品の保証を専門に行う米国の保険会社)
- **bond market** 債券市場, 公社債市場
- **bond price** 債券価格
- **collateral bond** 担保付き社債
- **convertible bond** 転換社債
- **debenture bond** 無担保社債
- **Euro bond** ユーロ債 (=Eurobond)
- **face value of bonds** 社債額面
- **foreign bond** 外債, 外国債券
- **government-guaranteed bond** 政府保証債
- **local government bond** 地方債
- **municipal bond** 市債, 地方債
- **passive bond** 無利子債券
- **power bond** 電力債
- **registered bond** 登録債
- **serial bond** 連続社債
- **special tax bond** 特定財源債
- **straight bond** 確定利付き社債, 普通社債
- **tax exempt bond** 免税債
- **time bond** 定期社債

bonus 名 手当, 賞与, 助成金, ボーナス

book 動 予約する(reserve), 記入する, 記帳する, 記録する(record), 調べる, (供述)調書を取る, 逮捕する, 計上する, 会計処理する, 帳簿に載せる, 積み増す
- **be booked for** …から逃れられない, …で調書を取られる
- **be booked out** 満員である
- **be booked up** 予約がいっぱいである, 予定がつまっている, 多忙である, 先約がある
- **be fully booked** 予約でいっぱいである, 予約[前売り券]が売れ切れである, 予約が満員[満席]である, 予定がつまっている (=be booked up)
- **book in** チェックインする, 宿泊手続きをする (=check in)
- **book out** 〈ホテルのフロントが〉チェックアウトを受け付ける
- **book through to** …までの通し切符を買う

book 名 本, 書籍, 書物, 著述, 著作, 帳面, …帳, 〈従業員などの〉名簿, 帳簿, 会計簿, ブック (⇒Beige Book)
- **bring someone to book** 人に行為の責任を取らせる
- **by the book** 正しい手続きに従って, 規則どおりに, 型どおりに, 杓子定規に
- **close the books** 終わらせる, 打ち切る, 止める, ピリオドを打つ, 帳簿を締め切る
- **cook books** 帳簿に手を加える, 帳簿をごまかす,

帳簿を改竄する, 粉飾する
off the books 記録されていない, 記入されていない
judge a book by its cover 見かけで判断する
on the books 記録されている, 記入されている, 予定［計画］されている

book value 簿価, 帳簿価額, 帳簿上の価格, 純資産額, 取得価格

booklet 名 小冊子, パンフレット（紙1枚のチラシはleaflet）

boom 動 急に沸く, 急に景気づく, 好況になる, 急騰する, 高騰する, 急増する, 上昇する, 大発展する, 急速に繁栄する, 急速に経済成長する, 鳴り響く, …の人気をあおる, …を景気づかせる
boom out a gun salute 礼砲を撃つ
booming economy 好景気
booming market 好景気市況, ブームに沸く市場
booming prices 急騰［高騰］している物価, 物価急騰［高騰］

boom 名 急騰, 高騰, 急成長, 急拡大, 急増, 景気, 好景気, 好況, 急開発, 大流行, ブーム
boom and bust 景気と不景気
boom baby ベビーブームの時に生まれた人
boom box 大型ラジカセ
boom-bust dividing line 景気不景気分割線, 景気判断の分かれ目（＝boom-or-bust line）
boom caused by a strong yen 円高景気（＝strong yen-caused boom）
boom prices 高騰した物価
borrowed [false] boom カラ景気
credit boom 借入れブーム
export boom 輸出の急拡大
housing boom 住宅建設ブーム, 住宅ブーム
investment boom 投資景気, 投資ブーム
population boom 人口の急増
sonic boom 衝撃音
spending boom 消費ブーム, 消費景気
temporary boom にわか景気, 中間景気
worldwide [world] boom 世界の好況, 世界的好景気, 世界的ブーム

boom-or-bust line [threshold] 景気判断の分かれ目, 景気の上向き・下向きの分かれ目（＝boom-bust dividing line, boom-bust threshold）
stay below the boom-or-bust line of 50 percent 景気判断の分かれ目となる50％を下回る
top the boom-or-bust line of 50 percent 景気判断の分かれ目となる50％を上回る

boost 動 推進する, 引き上げる, 増加させる, 拡大する, 押し上げる, 積み増す, 高める, 向上させる, 増強する, 強化する, 拡充する, 需要などを喚起する, 活気づかせる, 活性化する, 刺激する
boost demand 需要を喚起する, 需要を刺激する
boost domestic demand 内需を拡大する, 内需を喚起する, 内需を刺激する
boost growth 経済成長率を高める, 成長力を高める
boost productivity 生産性を高める, 生産性を向上させる
boost profitability 収益力［収益性］を高める, 利益率を高める
boost profits 利益を押し上げる

boost 名 押し上げ, 後押し, 増強, 活気づけ, 景気刺激, 発展, 向上, 増大, 急増, 上昇, 急上昇
boost in sales in the U.S. market 米国市場での販売急増
capital boost 増資
fiscal boost 財政面からの景気刺激策

bootstrap 形 自力での, 自分の努力による, 独力での, 独力で効果を上げる, 独立派の
bootstrap operation 自力作業
bootstrap program 援助計画

BOP ピラミッドの底辺（**bottom of the pyramid**の略。世界の人口を所得階層別に見た場合の底辺層のこと）
BOP business BOPビジネス（世界の人口の7割を占める年収3,000ドル未満の低所得者層をターゲットにしたビジネス）

borderless 形 国境のない, 境界線のない, ボーダレス

borrow 動 借り入れる, 融資を受ける, 資金を調達する, 借金する
borrow massive amounts of money 巨額の借入れをする
borrow money from a bank 銀行から資金を借り入れる
borrow money from depositors 預金者から資金を調達する, 預金者から金を預かる
borrowed capital 他人資本, 借入資本
borrowed money 借入金, 借金
borrowed security 借入有価証券
borrowed stock 借り株

borrower 名 借り手, 資金の借り手, 貸付け先, 貸出先, 融資先, 融資先企業, 債務者, 発行体, ボロワー

borrower of record 契約上の借入人
creditworthy borrower 信用力［信用度］が高い借り手, 優良貸出先
eligible borrower 適格融資先
heavy borrower 大口の借り手
noncommercial borrower 非営利的借り手
potential borrower 潜在的借り手
prime borrower 優良な借入人, 大口貸付け先, 大口融資先
problematic borrowers 問題融資先
shortage of borrowers 資金需要不足, 資金需要が少ないこと
sovereign borrower ソブリン発行体
top-notch borrower 超優良発行体
unrated borrower 無格付けの発行体

borrowing 图 借入れ, 資金調達, 借入金, 借金, 負債, 債務
borrowing capacity [power] 資金調達能力, 借入れによる資金調達能力, 借入能力
borrowing costs 資金調達コスト, 借入コスト, 借入費用 (⇒curb)
borrowing rate 借入金利
excessive borrowing 過剰借入れ
foreign borrowing 対外借入れ
name borrowing 名義借り
secured borrowing 担保付き借入れ
temporary borrowings 一時借入金

Botnet 图 ボットネット(パソコンをウイルス感染させてネットワーク化する手法。⇒cyber attack)

bottleneck 图 〈生産工程や進行過程などの〉障害, 妨げ, 隘路, 阻害要因, 遅れ, 問題, ネック, 交通渋滞地点, ボトルネック
bottleneck in a manufacturing process 生産工程上の障害［問題］, 生産工程のネック
bottleneck industry 隘路産業
bottleneck inflation 隘路インフレーション, 隘路インフレ, ボトルネック・インフレーション(資源や労働力など生産要素の不足が隘路となって, 波及的に生じる物価上昇)
cause a personnel bottleneck 人手不足を招く
create [cause, form, produce] a bottleneck 障害を生む, 障害を引き起こす
eliminate [reduce] a bottleneck in …のボトルネック［ネック］を解消する

bottom 图 底, 最低, 下限, 底値, 大底, 底入れ, 景気の谷, ボトム, 動 底に届く
be at the bottom of the list まったく重要視されていない
be at the rock bottom 底値を付ける, 〈士気などが〉低下する, どん底に落ち込む (＝hit the rock bottom)
be close to touching bottom 底入れが近い
buy at the bottom 底値で買いを入れる
bottom of the cycle 底入れ, 景気の谷
close at the bottom of the day's trading 安値引けとなる
double bottom 二番底 (＝second bottom)
first bottom 一番底
get to the bottom of …の真相を究明する
hit a five-year bottom 5年来の大底に落ち込む
hit bottom 底を打つ, 谷になる, 底固めする
hunt bargains at bottom 値頃買いをする
major bottom 大底
reach (the) bottom 底に達する, 底に届く, 底を打つ, 底入れする
reach the double bottom 二番底に至る
stand on one's own bottom 独立する, 自立する
the bottom falls [drops] out of …が底を割る, …が底をぬける, …が大底をつく, …が暴落する, …が大きな痛手を受ける［被る］, …が打撃を受ける
the bottom of the ladder 社会の下層部, 下積み仕事
touch (the) bottom 底入れする, 底をつく

bottom 形 底の, 最低の, 最下位の
bottom fishing 底値買い, 安値拾い, 安物あさり, 底値を拾う動き
bottom income 最低所得
bottom management 下部階層の管理職, 下位管理者層, 下級管理, ボトム・マネジメント (＝lower management)
bottom money なけなしの金
bottom price 底値
rock-bottom price 底値, 最低価格
rock-bottom salary 最低賃金
the bottom month of the recession 不況の底の月

bottom line 〈損益計算書の最終行の意味から〉純損益, 純利益, 利益, 当期利益, 純損失収益性, 取引の収支, 業績, 最終損益, 総決算, 最終結果・成果, 結論, 最終決定, 最重要事項, 要点, カギ, 問題の核心［カギ］, 肝心要(かなめ), ぎりぎりの線, 本音

bottom lines 業績, 収益
  contribute to the bottom line 利益［当期利益］に貢献する, 利益に寄与する
  enhance the bottom line 利益を押し上げる, 利益を増やす
  look at the bottom line 問題の核心に入る, 本題に入る
  sum up the bottom line 最終結果を要約する
  The bottom line is that ... 本当のことを言えば…である, 本音は…だ, 問題の核心［カギ］は…である, 肝心なのは…という点だ, …だけは譲ることができない, 結局…である, 要するに…ということだ
bottom out 底をつく, 底を打つ, 底入れする, 大底に達する, 底値に達する, 下げ止まる, 底打ちする, 最低レベルに達する, どん底まで下がる
bottoming out 底入れ, 下げ止まり, 底打ち, 底離れ
  sentiment of bottoming out 底入れ感, 底固め感
  signs of bottoming out 景気底入れの兆し
bottom-up 形 下位［下層］から上位［上層］への, 非階層的な
  bottom-up approach ボトムアップ方式, ボトムアップ・アプローチ
  bottom-up decentralization 下からの分権化, 下からの分権的組織
  bottom-up decision making 参加型の意思決定, 下からの意思決定
  bottom-up forecast ボトムアップ型予測
  bottom-up management 参加型経営, 下からの［下から上への］経営管理, ボトムアップ経営, ボトムアップ・マネジメント
  bottom-up society ボトムアップ社会（政治・経済の分野で下部が大きい役割を担う社会）
botulinum toxin ボツリヌス毒素
botulinus immune globulin ボツリヌス中毒免疫グロブリン《略 BIG》
bounce 名 はずみ, はね返り, 反発, 回復, 反騰, 増加, 弾力, 反発力, 追放, クビ
  a significant bounce in activity 景気の大幅回復
  earnings bounce 収益回復
bounce back 反発する, すぐに回復する［立ち直る］, 形勢を立て直す, 気を取り直す, はね返る, 影響がはね返ってくる
  bounce back in confidence 景況感が回復する
  bounce back significantly 大幅に増加する, 大幅に反発する
  bounce back slightly 小幅増加する, 小幅上昇する, 若干反発する
bourse 名 証券取引所, 取引所, 株式市況, 株式相場（＝securities exchange）
bovine spongiform encephalopathy 狂牛病《略 BSE》（＝mad cow disease）
box in 閉じ込める, 困難な立場に追い込む, 〈精神的に〉追い詰める
box office 興行収入, 切符売上金, 切符売り場
boycott 動 〈審議, 購買, 利用などを〉拒否する, 排斥する, ボイコットする, 不買同盟をする, 取引を拒絶する, 〈組織や人との〉関係を絶つ
  boycott Chinese products from food safety 食の安全から中国製品をボイコットする
  boycott a person 人を排斥する, 人を村八分にする
  boycott the vote on …の採決を拒否［ボイコット］する
boycott 名 拒否, 購買［利用, 参加］拒否, 棄権, 排斥, 取引拒絶, 不買［拒否, 排斥］運動, 不買同盟, ボイコット
  boycott of foreign goods 外国製品の不買運動, 外貨排斥
  declare a boycott against …に対して不買運動［参加拒否］を宣言する
  economic boycott 経済的不買同盟
  join the boycott of the Olympics オリンピックへの参加拒否に同調する
  launch [institute] a boycott 不買運動を始める, ボイコットを始める
bp [b.p.] ベーシス・ポイント（basis pointの略）
bpd 日量…バレル, 日産…バレル（barrel per dayの略）
brace 動 覚悟する, 備える, 支える, 安定させる, 補強する, 強化する, 強固にする, 〈心を〉引き締める
  brace oneself for …に対して覚悟する［備える］, 心の準備をする, …に対して気をしっかり持つ
  brace oneself to …する覚悟を決める
  brace up 元気を出す, 発奮する
bracket 名 階層, 層, グループ, 区分, 等級
  high income brackets 高所得者層
  highest wage brackets 最高賃金層
  middle or upper age brackets 中高年層
brain 名 脳, 頭脳, 知力, 知力の優れた人, 電子装置, ブレーン
  brain box 天才, 電子計算機, コンピュータ
  brain chemicals 脳内化学物質

brain child [brainchild] 創作品, 考案品, 発明品, 想像力の所産, 独創的な考え [発明, 計画]
brain computer 脳型コンピュータ
brain damage 脳損傷
brain death 脳死
brain drain 頭脳流出
brain gain 頭脳流入
brain industry 頭脳産業
brain infarct 脳梗塞
brain power index 総合的知能水準, ブレーンパワー指標《略 BPI》
brain reverse 頭脳回帰
brain scan 脳走査, 脳スキャン, 脳のCTスキャン, 脳診断レントゲン断層写真
brain scanner 脳診断レントゲン断層写真撮影装置
brain storm [brainstorm] 霊感, インスピレーション, 突然浮かぶ妙案 (=brain wave)
brain surgery 脳手術
brain-teaser 難問, なぞ, パズル
brain tissue 頭脳組織
brain [brains] trust 顧問, 専門顧問団, 専門家グループ
brain tumor 脳腫瘍
brain waves 脳波
brain writing ブレーン・ライティング《略 BW》
brains 知的指導者, 企画者, 黒幕, ブレーン
mechanical brain 人工頭脳

brainpower 名 思考力, 知力, 知能, ブレーン, 知力の優れた人

brainstorm 名 ひらめき, 思いつき, 名案, 素晴らしい考え (brainwave), インスピレーション, 突然の精神錯乱, 精神錯乱の発作, 動 ブレーンストーミングにかける, 意見 [考え] を出し合う

brainstorming [brain storming] 名 創造的集団思考法, 集団思考による問題解決法, ブレーンストーミング
brainstorming session [meeting] ブレーンストーミング形式の会議

brainware 名 ブレーンウエア (コンピュータの機械, 利用技術と利用分野を組み合わせて, コンピュータの有効な使い方を考え出す人)

brainwashing 名 洗脳, 強制的思想改造, 宣伝による説得

brainwork 名 頭脳労働, 精神労働, 頭脳作業
brainworker 名 頭脳労働者, 精神労働者
brake 名 制動装置, 歯止め, 抑制, 牽制, ブレーキ
act as a brake on [upon] …を抑制する働きをする, …にブレーキをかけることになる
apply brakes to …に牽制をかける
hit [slam on] the brakes ブレーキを踏む, ブレーキをかける
put on a brake [the brake, the brakes] on …にブレーキをかける, …を牽制する (=apply a brake on)
put the brakes [a brake] on …の進行を抑える, …に歯止めをかける, …の上昇を抑制する
take off the brake ブレーキを緩める, ブレーキをはずす

brand 動 烙印を押す, 汚名を着せる
brand 名 商標, 銘柄, 特定の銘柄品, ブランド, ブランド品, ブランド商品, ブランド店
brand value ブランド価値
brand name 商標名, 商品名, ブランド名, ブランド力, ブランド・ネーム

break away from …から離脱する [離れる], …から外れる, …から逃れる, …と袂を分かつ, …と関係を絶つ, …から政治的に独立する, …を急に改める, …を止める
break away from a prison 脱獄する
break away from bad practices 悪い慣行を止める
break away from the party 離党する

break down 故障する, 失敗する, 取り乱す, 自制できない, 精神的に参る

breakdown 名 〈機械の〉故障, 機能不全, 〈交渉の〉決裂, 挫折, 崩壊, 倒壊, 分析, 分解, 分類, 内訳, 構成, 健康悪化, 神経衰弱
a breakdown test 耐久試験
the breakdown of negotiations [talks] 交渉決裂
the breakdown of investment portfolio 投資ポートフォリオの内訳

breakneck changes 激変
breakneck speed 猛スピード
breakthrough 名 画期的な出来事, 輝かしい成果, 大きな成果, 難関突破, 突破, 突破口 [局面], 打開, 打破, 現状打破, 前進, 躍進, 飛躍的進歩, 急進展, 重大発見, 大発見

breakup 名 崩壊, 分裂, 決裂, 解散, 解体, 解消, 絶縁, 別離, 別れ, 仲たがい
breakup and privatization 分割民営化
breakup value 清算価値, 清算価額
marital breakup 結婚解消
party breakup 党の分裂

breathalyzer 名 飲酒検知器, 酒気帯検知器

(＝drunkometer)
▶ A *breathalyzer* reading indicated he had been drinking. 飲酒検知器の記録が,彼が酒を飲んでいたことを示した。

bribe 動 賄賂を贈る,買収する
bribe 名 賄賂,そでの下,誘惑物,えさ
  accept [receive, take] a bribe 賄賂を受け取る
  bribe-giver 贈賄者
  bribe-giving 贈賄
  bribe-taker 収賄者
  bribe-taking 収賄
  give [promise] a bribe 賄賂を使う,賄賂を贈る,贈賄する
  offer a bribe 賄賂を贈る[使う],賄賂を差し出す,贈収賄する
  pay ¥30 million as bribes 賄賂として3,000万円を支払う
  receive ten million yen in bribes 賄賂として1,000万円を受け取る
  take [accept, receive] a bribe 賄賂をもらう,賄賂を受け取る,収賄する

bribery 名 贈収賄,贈収賄行為,賄賂の授受,贈賄,収賄,汚職
  be proof against bribery 賄賂がきかない
  bribery case 賄賂事件,贈収賄事件,汚職事件(＝graft case)
  bribery of a public official 公務員の贈収賄
  bribery schemes 贈賄工作
  corrupt [influence] the judge by bribery [a bribe] 賄賂で裁判官を買収する
  practice bribery 賄賂を使う

bricks & mortar ブリック＆モルタル(「煉瓦と漆喰」の意味だが,ネット上でビジネスを行っていない実店舗だけの販売スタイルをとっている伝統的な企業を指す)

BRICs 有力新興国,ブリクス(高い経済成長を続けるBrazil (ブラジル), Russia (ロシア), India (インド)とChina (中国)の頭文字による造語)

bridge 動 つなぐ,〈溝や意見の違いなどを〉埋める,〈困難を〉乗り越える

brie 名 ブリーチーズ(柔らかい白色のチーズ)

brief 動 簡潔に報告する,経過報告する,概略[状況]を説明する, 名 要約,要約書,概要,概要書,要領書,準備書面

briefing 名 説明会,投資家向け説明会,投資家説明会,経過報告,概要報告,概況[状況]説明,背景説明,指示説明,戦況要約,要約書,セミナー

deep background briefing 〈ニュース・ソースを明かさないという条件での〉政府当局者の背景説明
general briefing 状況説明
off-the-record briefing オフレコ(報道しないという条件での)説明

bring 動 もたらす,持ってくる,連れてくる
  bring a person in guilty …に有罪の評決を下す
  bring about a big change 大変革をもたらす,大変革を成し遂げる
  bring down 打倒する,倒す,失脚させる,〈価格などを〉下げる,値段を下げさせる,撃墜する,着陸させる,〈名声や品位を〉落とす
  bring forth 生む,実を結ぶ,もたらす,〈提案などを〉出す,〈事実などを〉明らかにする,発表する,暴露する
  bring forward an opinion 意見を述べる
  bring in 〈収益や利益を〉もたらす,…を稼ぐ,…を持ち込む,導入する,〈議案などを〉提出する,…を連行する,〈陪審員が〉評決する
  bring in a verdict of "Not guilty" 「無罪」の評決を下す
  bring off うまく成し遂げる,うまくやってのける,救助する
  bring on …を引き起こす
  bring out 世に出す,明らかにする,出版する,引き出す
  bring the riot under control 暴動を鎮圧する
  bring the situation under control 事態を収拾する
  bring under 制圧する,鎮圧する
  bring up 育てる,告発する,〈議案などを〉提出する,〈問題を〉提起する
  bring upon oneself …に対して責任がある

bring forward 繰り上げる,早める,前倒しする,〈案や計画を〉提出する[示す],提示する,持ち出す,次期[次頁]へ繰り越す,提出期日を指定する

brinkmanship 名 瀬戸際政策,瀬戸際外交(＝brinksmanship)
  brinkmanship diplomacy 瀬戸際外交
  nuclear brinkmanship 核を使った瀬戸際政策

brisk 形 活発な,好調な,活気のある,活況の,繁盛している,急速に回復する
  brisk business 活発な取引
  brisk economic recovery 景気の急速な回復
  brisk exports 好調な輸出
  brisk performance 好業績

brisk sales 好調な売れ行き, 販売好調
broad 形 広い, 広大な, 幅の広い, 広範な, 一般的な, 広範囲に及ぶ, 広義の, 偏見のない, 大体の, 大ざっぱな, 大筋の, 明白な
 a broad agreement 大筋合意
 a broad experience 豊かな経験, 幅広い経験
 a broad index 広範囲な指数
 a broad line strategy 多品種供給戦略
 a broad rule 一般的な規準
 as broad as it is long 五十歩百歩の, 結局同じ
 broad-based stock index 総合株価指数
 broad facts 明白な事実
 broad liquidity 広義流動性
 broad market 大量取引高, 好況市場 (active market)
 broad money (M2+CDs) 広義のマネー (M2+CD), 広義の通貨 (M2+CD)
 broad money supply 広義の通貨供給量, 広義のマネー・サプライ
 have a broad back 簡単に処理できる
 take a broad view of …について偏見のない見解をとる, …を大観する
broadband communication 高速大容量通信, 広帯域通信, ブロードバンド通信 (=broadband)
broadband network 高速大容量通信網, 広帯域ネットワーク, 高速大容量通信ネットワーク, ブロードバンド・ネットワーク (=broadband communication network)
broadcast 動 放送する, 報道する, 番組に出演する
broadcast 名 放送, 放送番組, ブロードキャスト
 broadcast bond 放送債券
 broadcast communication 放送形通信
 broadcast media 放送メディア, 電波媒体 (=broadcasting media)
 broadcast satellite 放送衛星
 broadcast station 放送局
 Broadcast Technical Standard BTS規格
 live broadcast 生放送
broadcaster 名 放送会社, 放送局, 放送事業者, 放送者, 〈テレビの〉キャスター, 〈テレビ・ラジオの〉司会者, ブロードキャスター
 broadcaster's service area 放送区域, 放送サービス・エリア
 commercial broadcaster 一般放送事業者, 民放
broadcasting 名 放送, 放映, 番組制作

broadcasting interference 受信妨害 (=broadcast interference)
broadcasting satellite 放送衛星《略 BS》
broadcasting satellite service 衛星放送サービス, 放送衛星業務
broadcasting service 放送業務
broadcasting station 放送局
broadcasting via satellite 衛星放送
commercial broadcasting 商業放送
data broadcasting データ放送
digital broadcasting service デジタル放送サービス
ground-wave broadcasting 地上波放送
multichannel broadcasting 多チャンネル放送
private broadcasting corporation 民間放送局
spot broadcasting 現地放送
broader stock indicators 総合株価指数 (=broad-based stock index)
brokerage 名 証券業, 証券会社, 仲介, 仲介業, 仲買, 仲買業, 証券仲買会社, 仲介手数料, ブローカー
 brokerage experience 証券業の経験
 brokerage fee [commission] 委託手数料, 仲介手数料, 委託売買手数料
 brokerage house [firm] 証券会社 (=securities company)
 member brokerages of the Tokyo Stock Exchange 東証の会員証券会社, 東証の取引参加者
 retail brokerage 個人向け証券会社
 stock brokerage 株式委託売買, 株式の売買仲介業務, 証券仲介業
browse 動 閲覧する, 検索する, 拾い読みする, 目を通す (=retrieve)
browsing 名 閲覧, 検索, 拾い読み
brush off 無視する, 冷たくあしらう, 素っ気なく拒絶する, はねつける, 追い払う, 払い落とす, 払いのける
Brussels 欧州連合 (EU), 〈EU, NATOの本部があるベルギーの首都〉ブリュッセル
▶Washington and *Brussels* will conditionally accept a reduction of subsidies granted to U.S. and European Union farmers. 米国や欧州連合 (EU) は, それぞれ農業助成金 (農家に交付している助成金) の削減を条件付きで受け入れる方針だ.
BSE 牛海綿状脳症, 狂牛病 (**bovine spongiform encephalopathy**の略で, **mad cow disease**

のこと)
BSE-infected cow BSE感染牛
bubble 名 泡沫, バブル経済, バブル
  bubble economy バブル経済, バブル景気, バブル期, バブル
  the post-bubble economy バブル後
budget 動 予算に計上する, 予算を立てる, 予定を立てる
  budgeted activity [volume] 予算操業度
  budgeted cost 予算原価
  budgeted statements 見積財務諸表
budget 名 予算, 財政, 形 安い, 格安の, 予算の, 予算に合った
  austere [austerity] budget 緊縮予算
  balanced budget 均衡予算
  belt-tightening budget 緊縮型予算
  budget account 〈銀行の〉自動支払い口座, 自動引落し口座
  budget airline 格安航空会社
  budget allocation 予算配分
  budget appropriation 予算支出, 予算の割当て, 予算の計上, 予算の承認
  budget balance 財政収支
  budget compilation 予算編成
  budget constraint 予算的制約, 予算の制限
  budget cut 予算削減
  budget hotel ビジネス・ホテル, 格安のホテル
  budget implementation 予算の執行
  budget modification 予算修正
  budget numbers 財政収支の数字
  budget screening 事業仕分け
  budget surplus 財政黒字, 予算の黒字, 黒字財政
  draft budget 予算原案, 予算案
  expansionary budget 積極型予算
  extra budget 補正予算
  general account budget 一般会計予算
  provisional budget 暫定予算
  revised budget 補正予算 (＝additional budget, supplementary budget)
  second extra [supplementary] budget 第二次補正予算[予算案]
  under budget 予算以内で
budget deficit 財政赤字, 予算の赤字, 赤字財政 (＝budget gap)
  budget deficit reduction 財政赤字削減
Budget Message 予算教書 (＝budget documents, budget plan, spending plan：米

大統領が毎年1月に議会に提出する来年度予算のこと。一般教書(the State of the Union address), 経済報告(Economic Report of the President)と合わせて三大教書と呼ばれている)
budget year 会計年度 (⇒current budget year)
▶The U.S. government's 2010 *budget year* runs through Sept. 30. 米政府の2010会計年度は, (2009年10月から) 2010年9月までとなっている。
budgetary 形 予算の, 予算案の, 予算上の
  budgetary request 概算要求, 予算要求 (＝budgetary demand, initial budget request)
  budgetary request guidelines 概算要求基準 (＝ceiling on budgetary request)
buffer 名 緩衝装置, 緩衝器, 緩衝材,〈衝撃や苦痛を〉和らげるもの, クッション, 緩衝域, 破産防止手段, 調整, 調停役, バッファー
  buffer action 緩衝作用
  buffer against losses 損失を和らげるクッション
  buffer fund 緩衝基金
  buffer memory 緩衝記憶装置, バッファー・メモリ (＝buffer, buffer store)
  buffer state 緩衝国
  buffer stock [inventory] 緩衝在庫
  buffer zone 緩衝地帯, 非武装地帯
  capital buffer against …に備えるための資本増強
  foreign exchange buffer 外貨バッファー
  hit [run into] the buffers 失敗に帰す
  provide a buffer クッションになる
buffet 動 揺さぶる, 苦しめる, 痛めつける, 打ちのめす, 衝撃を与える, 翻弄する, 襲う,〈逆境などと〉戦う, 戦いながら進む
  be buffeted by …に翻弄される, …に痛めつけられる, …のショックを受ける, …が襲う
  buffet one's way into great waves 荒波を進む
  buffet one's way to riches and fame 苦労を重ねて富と名を成す
bug 名 バグ, 故障, 不良[欠陥]箇所(コンピュータのプログラムやシステムの誤り)
buildup 名 増加, 増大, 急増, 強化, 増強, 充実, 増進, 整備,〈新製品などの〉売込み, 売出し, 前宣伝, 宣伝,〈在庫などの〉積み増し, 準備作業, 準備期間, 準備を進めること, 蓄積, 発展, 盛り上がり
  buildup in foreign debt 対外債務の急増
  inventory buildup 在庫の積み増し, 在庫の増加
  military buildup 軍備増強

bulge 動 ふくらむ, 膨張する, 急増する
bull 名 強気筋, 強気, 買い方, 標的, 金的, 警官, 警察官, 雄牛, 無駄話, ブル
- buying bull 思惑買い
- Charging Bull ニューヨーク証券取引所前に置いてある「突進する雄牛」像
- dollar bulls ドルに強気な向き
- take the bull by the horns 〈困難などに〉勇敢に立ち向かう, 難局に立ち向かう, 英断的処置を取る

bull 形 強気の, 強気筋の, 上向きの, 買い方の
- bull account 強気筋
- bull–bear position 強気・弱気状態
- bull buying 強気買い
- Bull Moose 米革新党の支持者, 革新党の党員
- bull operation 強気筋の操作
- bull point 強み, 有利な点
- bull position 買い持ち, 強気状態
- bull session 〈主に男同士の〉グループ討論, ざっくばらんな討論, 放談会
- bull speculator 強気の投機家
- bull transaction 強気筋の取引

bull market 強気市場, 強気相場, 強気市況, 上げ相場, 上昇相場, 買い相場, 買い手市場（= strong market）
- be stable in the bull market 上げ相場で安定している
- make profits in the bull market 上昇相場［上げ相場］で利益を上げる
- the early return of a bull market 上げ相場の早期回復

bulldoze through 〈法案などを〉強引に通す, 無理に通す, 強行する
bullish 形 強気の, 上がり気味の, 見通しが明るい, 楽観的見方の, 積極的な
- be bullish on the domestic economy 国内景気に楽観的な見方をしている, 国内景気は見通しが明るい
- bullish factor 強気材料, 強材料, 好材料, 買い材料（= bullish influence, bullish support）
- bullish sentiment 強気の地合い
- bullish stock market 堅調な株式市場, 株式相場の上昇, 株高
- bullish tone 強気ムード
- make bullish predictions for …について強気の見方をする

bullying 名 いじめ, 弱いものいじめ（⇒workplace bullying）

bulwark 名 防波堤, 防御［防護］壁, 壁, 障壁, 支持者, 擁護者
bundle 動 束ねる, 包む, 〈ソフトウエアを〉同梱する, 名 束, 大金, 抱き合わせ販売, セット販売, 同梱ソフトウエア
bundler 名 献金集金人, バンドラー（米大統領選挙のカゲの立役者といわれる）
buoy 動 活気づかせる, 浮揚させる, 高める, 支える
- be buoyed by …で活気づく, …に支えられる
- buoy the economy 景気を浮揚させる

buoyant 形 活況の, 好調の, 上昇傾向の, 上がり気味の
- buoyant areas 好調な分野
- buoyant conditions 活況
- buoyant consumer spending 好調な消費支出, 消費支出の好調
- buoyant demand 需要の拡大, 需要の盛り上がり
- buoyant export 好調な輸出
- buoyant investment income 投資収益の増大
- buoyant market 市場の活況, 騰貴市場
- buoyant performance 好業績, 好決算（= brisk performance）

burden 動 …に重荷を負わせる, 〈義務, 責任を〉負わせる, …を悩ます, …を苦しめる
- be burdened with …を背負わされる, …を負わされる, …を背負っている, …を持っている, …に苦しめられる, …で苦しむ
- burden a nation [the people] with heavy taxes 国民に重税を背負わせる, 国民に重税を課す

burden 名 負担, 費用負担, 重荷, 間接費, 製造間接費, 経費
- burden of debt service 金利負担
- burden of disposing of bad loans 不良債権処理の負担, 不良債権処理損失
- burden of proof 立証責任
- debt burden 債務負担, 債務超過
- factory burden 製造間接費
- financial burden 金融負担, 財務面での負担, 財政負担, 経済負担
- public burden 国民負担

bureaucracy 名 官僚, 官僚政治, 官僚主義, 官僚制度, 官僚社会, 官庁の煩雑な手続き, お役所仕事, お役所の面倒な手続き
- bureaucracy and private sector 官民
- central government bureaucracy 中央官庁の官僚
- elite bureaucracy エリート主義の官僚

the collusion between the bureaucracy and the industry　官民癒着
union bureaucracy　組合官僚制

bureaucrat 名　官僚(government officer), 官吏, お役人, 公務員, 官僚政治家, 官僚主義者, お役所式の煩雑な事務手続き (⇒career bureaucrats)
bureaucrat-turned politician　官僚上がりの政治家
bureaucrats' collusive ties with businesses　官僚の業者との癒着, 官民癒着
business bureaucrat　企業官僚
excessive wining and dining of bureaucrats　官僚の過剰接待
high-ranking bureaucrat　高級官僚 (=high government official)
international bureaucrats　国際機関関係者
labor bureaucrat　労働官僚
minor bureaucrat　下級官僚 (=minor government official)
old-school bureaucrat　旧派の官僚主義者
scandals involving bureaucrats　公務員の不祥事問題
senior bureaucrat　高級官僚
the relationship between politicians and bureaucrats　政官関係
top bureaucrat　トップ官僚
top-level bureaucrat　キャリア官僚

bureaucratic 形　官僚政治の, 官僚主義の, 官僚的な, 官僚気質の, 手続きの煩雑な
be of bureaucratic origin　官僚の出, 官僚育ち
bureaucratic Cabinet [ministry]　官僚内閣
bureaucratic circles　官界, 官僚派
bureaucratic color　官僚的色彩
bureaucratic corruption　官僚汚職
bureaucratic decisions　官僚主義的な決め方
bureaucratic dogma　官僚独善
bureaucratic elite　官僚エリート
bureaucratic government　官僚政治
bureaucratic system　官僚制度, 官僚組織

burgeoning 形　急成長の, 急発展の, 急速に広がる, 新興の, 急増する
burgeoning foreign interest　活発な動きを見せる外資, 外資の活発な動き
burgeoning population　急成長の人口
burgeoning workforces　従業員の急増, 従業員の過剰
new burgeoning market　急成長の新市場

bushfire 名　山火事
business 名　事業, 商売, 商業, 取引, 営業, 業務, 業容, 職務, 職業, 実務, 実業, 実業界, 会社, 企業, 経営, 業績, ビジネス
business activity　経営活動, 事業活動, 景気
big business　大企業, 巨大企業
business accountability　独立採算
business alliance　業務提携 (=business tie-up), 経済団体
business boom　景気, 好景気, 好況, 景気上昇
business climate [environment]　事業環境, 企業環境, 経営環境, 企業風土, 経営風土, 企業の体質, 景況, 商況, 景気
business community [circles, world]　経済界, 財界, 産業界, 実業界
business integration　事業統合, 経営統合 (=integration of business, merger)
business integrity　商業道徳
business management　企業経営, 企業管理, 経営管理, 業務管理, 経営
business method　経営手法
business operating company [firm]　事業会社
business operation　業務運営, 企業運営, 企業経営, 経営, 営業活動, 営業運転, 業務, 事業, 業容
business partner　取引先企業, 取引先
business projection　業績見通し
business quarter　四半期
business registry system　営業登録制度
business results　営業成績, 企業業績, 業績, 決算 (=business performance, operating results)
business right　営業権
business soundness　経営の健全性
business ties　ビジネス関係, 事業上 [業務上] の関係, 取引関係 (=business relations)
core business　中核事業, 中核業務, 主力事業, コア・ビジネス
government-business cooperation　官民協調
niche business　得意分野
noncore business　非中核事業, 非主力事業
online business　オンライン業務, オンライン・ビジネス
solution business　問題解決型営業, ソリューション・ビジネス

business conditions　景気, 商況, 業況, 業況判断(DI), 景況判断, 業態, 事業環境, 経営の

実態

business confidence 景況感, 業況感, 業況判断, 企業マインド, 企業心理, ビジネス・コンフィデンス（＝business mind, business sentiment）

business cycle 景気循環, 景気（＝trade cycle）

business model ビジネス手法, 事業モデル, 事業計画, ビジネス・モデル

business model patent ビジネス・モデル特許（＝business method patent, patent for a business model）

> ビジネス・モデル特許 ⊃ IT（情報技術）を活用した新しい事業のやり方・仕組みに与えられる特許で, 1990年代の後半に米国で急速に発達した。その背景には, 知的財産権（知的所有権）を保護して産業の競争力を高める国家戦略があるといわれる。日本の場合, ビジネス・モデル特許の審査基準は, ITを用いた発明と, 専門家でも容易に思いつかないアイデアに限られている。

business sentiment 景況感, 企業の景況感, 企業の業況感, 業況判断, 企業マインド, 企業心理（＝business confidence, business mind）

business sentiment index 業況判断指数, 業況判断DI（＝diffusion index of business sentiment）

business term 事業期間, 決算期
  the business term ending in December 12月期決算, 12月に終了する事業期間
  the business term ending in late March 2011 2011年3月期, 2011年3月期決算, 2011年3月末に終了する事業期間, 2010年度

business tie-up 業務提携, 事業の提携（＝business alliance）
  conclude a business tie-up 業務提携する
  dissolve the business tie-up 業務提携を解消する
  form a business tie-up 業務提携する

business year 営業年度, 事業年度, 会計年度, 年度, 会計期間（＝accounting year, financial year, fiscal year）
  business year to March （来年）3月期, 今年度

businesspeople 名 ビジネスマン, ビジネスピープル

button-down 形 身なりのきちんとした, 都会風の, そつのない, 保守的な, 伝統的な, 伝統を地で行く, 型にはまった, 限られた, 認められた, ボタンダウン

buttress 動 支える, 支持する, 強化する

buy 動 買う, 購入する, 取得する, 買い取る, 買収する,〈株などを〉引き受ける（＝acquire, purchase）

Buy American 米製品の優先購入, 米製品の優先買付け［優先買付け政策］, バイ・アメリカン
  Buy American Act 米製品優先購入法, 米商品優先購入法, バイ・アメリカン法（大恐慌下の1933年に制定された。米政府が橋や道路建設などの公共事業の契約を企業と結ぶときは, 原則として米国製品を使うよう義務付けている）
  Buy American provision バイ・アメリカン条項

buy back 動 買い戻す, 買い取る（＝repurchase）

buy order 買い注文

buy time 時間稼ぎ

buyback 名 買戻し, 買取り, 買上げ, 自社株買戻し, 自社株買い, 自社株取得, 早期退職勧奨, 退職奨励金（＝buyout）
  buyback scheme for beef 牛肉買上げ制度（＝beef buyback system）
  share [stock] buyback 自社株買戻し, 自社株買い, 株式買戻し

buying 名 買い, 買付け, 購入, 購買, 仕入れ
  buying out 買取り, 買占め, 買収, 営業権の取得（＝buyout）
  buying period 仕入期間, 調達期間
  buying price 購入価格, 買付け価格, 買い値, 買価, 仕入値段, 仕入価格
  buying up 買収, 買占め
  central buying 集中仕入れ
  consumer buying 個人消費支出
  cooperative buying 共同仕入れ
  foreign investor buying 外国人買い, 外国人の買い（＝foreign buy）
  historical buying price 購入価格
  home buying 住宅購入
  impulse buying 衝動買い
  quantity [large-lot] buying 大量仕入れ
  selective buying 物色買い

buyout [buy-out] 名 買収, 会社［経営権］の買取り, 買占め, 乗っ取り, 株式の買付け, 金を払って引き取らせること, 金を払って退職させること（⇒management buyout）
  buyout firm 企業買収（M&A）専門会社
  buyout fund 買収ファンド
  employee [worker] buyout 従業員の会社買取り, 従業員の経営権買取り
  leveraged buyout レバレッジド・バイアウト《略

LBO》
management buyout マネジメント・バイアウト《略 MBO》(経営陣による自社株式の公開買付け)
strategic buyout 戦略的買収(経営戦略に基づいて行われる企業買収)

by the day 日毎に
by word of mouth 口コミで
Byrd Amendment 米バード修正法, バード法, 米国の反ダンピング(不当廉売)関税分配法(米政府がダンピング(不当廉売)と認定した輸入製品に対して課す関税の収入を, ダンピング被害を申し立てた企業に救済金として分配することを定めた法律。正式名称はContinued Dumping and Subsidy Offset Actで, 2000年10月に成立)

byte 名 バイト, 8ビット・バイト (**BinarY digiT Eight**の略。コンピュータのデータ単位で, 1バイト＝8ビット)
exabyte エクサバイト, Eバイト《略 EB》
gigabyte ギガバイト, Gバイト《略 GB》
kilobyte キロバイト, Kバイト《略 KB》
megabyte メガバイト, Mバイト《略 MB》
petabyte ペタバイト, Pバイト《略 PB》
terabyte テラバイト, Tバイト《略 TB》(1テラバイト＝1,000ギガバイト)

C

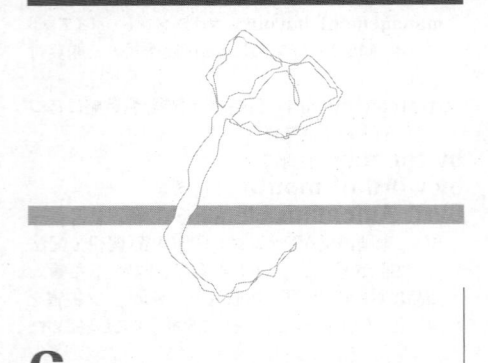

cabinet [**Cabinet**] 名　内閣, 閣議, 〈米〉大統領顧問団, 〈英国の〉閣議室
  all-nation cabinet　挙国一致内閣
  cabinet appointments　内閣人事
  cabinet approval　閣議の了承
  cabinet disapproval rating　内閣不支持率
  Cabinet-initiated policies　内閣主導の政策
  Cabinet Legislation Bureau　内閣法制局
  cabinet meeting [conference, council]　閣議
  Cabinet member [colleague, minister]　閣僚 (＝a member of the Cabinet)
  Cabinet posts　閣僚ポスト
  cabinet [Cabinet] reshuffle　内閣改造 (＝cabinet change)
  Cabinet Secretariat　内閣官房
  Cabinet Secretariat's classified fund　官房機密費
  cabinet's existence　内閣存立
  Chief Cabinet Secretary　内閣官房長官, 官房長官
  discord among Cabinet members　閣内不一致
  economic ministerial conference　経済閣僚懇談会
  form a Cabinet　組閣する, 内閣を組織する
  general resignation of the Cabinet　内閣総辞職
  key ministers of the Cabinet　主要閣僚
  meeting of Cabinet members in charge of economy-boosting measures　経済対策閣僚会議
  member of the President's Cabinet　閣僚
  non-cabinet partnership　閣外協力
  non-confidence vote against the Cabinet　内閣不信任案
  present cabinet　現内閣
  regular session of the Cabinet council　定例閣議
  shadow cabinet　影の内閣
Cabinet Office　内閣府
cadre 名　幹部, 幹部団, 幹部会, 指導者グループ, 中核, 中核グループ, 構造, 組織, 枠組み, 概要, 輪郭, 基礎, 基礎工事
Cesarean section　帝王切開
calamity 名　災難, 災禍, 惨禍, 惨劇, 惨事, 悲惨な事件, 不幸
CALEA　法執行のための通信援助法(Communications Assistance for Law Enforcement Actの略。捜査に必要と認定された通信傍受に通信業者が協力することを義務付ける法律)
calendar 名　暦, 暦法, スケジュール, 行事予定, 行事日程表, 法廷日程表, 審理事件表, 議会議事予定表, 議事日程, 目録, 一覧表, カレンダー
  calendar day　暦日(真夜中から翌日の真夜中まで)
  calendar half year　半暦年
  calendar month　暦月, 月数
  calendar number　日程番号
  Calendar of Business　〈米議会の〉議事日程
  Calendar of Motions to Discharge Committees　委員会審議解除動議日程
  calendar quarter period　暦四半期, 四半期

（＝calendar quarter, calendar quarter year）
Calendar Wednesday 水曜日程
calendar year 暦年，年度，12月期決算（「暦年」1月1日から12月31日までの1年で，a full calendar yearは1暦年，満1暦年を指す）
consent calendar 合意的議事日程
corporation calendar 会社の行事予定表
economic calendar 景気指標の発表
House Calendar 米下院議事日程，ハウス・カレンダー
new issues calendar 起債予定表
Private Calendar 私権法案議事日程，プライベート・カレンダー
Union Calendar 米連邦議事日程，ユニオン・カレンダー

call 動 〈会議などを〉招集する，呼び寄せる，呼ぶ，〈ストなどを〉指令する，償還する，〈貸付け金の〉返済［返還］を求める，電話をかける
call a special news conference 特別記者会見を召集する，特別記者会見を行う
call an ambulance 救急車を呼ぶ
call an election 選挙を行う
call at …にちょっと立ち寄る，…に停車する，…に寄港する
call back …を呼び戻す，電話をかけ直す，折り返し電話をする，再び訪問する
call down 叱りつける，降りてくるように言う，出頭させる
call off 〈ストなどの〉中止を指令［宣言］する，〈約束などを〉取り止める，中止する，中断する
call out 出動させる，呼び出す，動員する
call the existing bonds 既発債を償還する
call the loan 貸付け金の返済を請求する，ローンの償還を請求する
call for 要求する，求める，訴える，呼びかける，必要とする，予報する
call in 〈貸金［貸付け金，融資］を〉回収する，取り立てる，〈欠陥品などを〉回収する，〈助言や助けを〉求める，〈警察などに〉出動を要請する，要求する，〈苦情などの〉電話を入れる，電話で報告する
call in a doctor 医者に来てもらう，医師を呼ぶ
call in loans 貸付け金を回収する，貸出を回収する
call in off-duty nurses 非番の看護師に助けを求める，非番の看護師を招集する
call in the riot police 機動隊に出動を要請する，機動隊を投入する
call in the police 警察を呼ぶ

call in sick 電話で病気欠勤を届け出る
call market 短期市場，短期資金市場，コール市場（＝call money market）
calm down …を静める，穏やかにする，なだめる，静まる，落ち着く，治まる
camp 名 陣営，立場，野営，野営地，キャンプ場，〈強制労働〉収容所，収容施設，野営設備，野営テント，テント，仮設小屋，小屋，同志，グループ，仲間，キャンプ
aviation camp 航空隊
base camp 基地，ベース・キャンプ
be in camp 野営している
be in the same camp 志［主義］を同じくしている，同じ考えである，同意している
camp commander 収容所司令官
Camp David キャンプ・デービッド（米大統領の別荘）
camp follower シンパ（シンパサイザーの略），共鳴者
capitalist camp 資本主義陣営
conservative camp 保守陣営
day camp 昼間キャンプ
internment camp 強制収容所，捕虜収容所，敵性外国人収容所
makeshift camp 臨時収容施設
military camp 軍隊の野営地
prison [prisoner-of-war] camp 捕虜収容所
ruling camp 与党陣営，与党側，与党
socialist camp 社会主義陣営
summer camp 夏期キャンプ，臨海学校，林間学校
the East and West camps 東西両陣営

campaign 名 活動，動き，行動，運動（drive），販売促進運動，選挙運動，軍事行動，作戦，対策，計画，キャンペーン
advertising [ad] campaign 広告キャンペーン，広告・宣伝活動
anti-global warming campaign 地球温暖化防止運動，地球温暖化対策
buy-now campaign 即時購買運動
campaign against …反対運動，…撲滅運動
campaign chest 選挙資金，選挙運動資金
campaign club 選挙後援会
campaign finance law 選挙資金規制法
campaign for …賛成運動，…支持運動，…のための運動［活動］
campaign fund 選挙資金，選挙運動資金
campaign pledge 選挙公約（＝election

pledge)
campaign speaker 遊説員
campaign speech 選挙演説, 政見発表
campaign stop 選挙遊説
campaign to unilaterally control imports 一方的な輸入規制の動き
campaign tour [trip] 遊説旅行
campaign trail 地方遊説, 遊説
campaign van 選挙カー
carry on an election campaign 選挙運動をする
congressional election campaign 議会選挙戦, 議会選挙運動[活動]
fundraising campaign 募金運動
information campaign 広報活動
platform [oratorical] campaign 遊説
political campaign 政治運動
productivity campaign 生産性向上運動
run a campaign キャンペーンを実施する
campaigning 名 選挙戦
camphor injection カンフル剤の注入
cancel 動 取り消す, 白紙撤回する, 破棄する, 抹消する, 解除する, 解約する, 無効にする, 中止する, 運休にする, 〈株式を〉償却[消却]する, 〈契約を〉終結させる[解除する], 消印する
cancel a contract 契約を解除する, 解約する
cancel a coupon 利札に消印する
cancel dividend payment 無配に転落する
cancel out 相殺する, 棒引きにする, 消す, 償う
cancel the order 注文を取り消す
cancel the stock 株式を償却する
cancel with a stamp 消印する
canceled check 支払済み小切手, 用済み小切手, 無効小切手
cancelation [cancellation] 名 株式の消却[償却], 契約の解除, 解約, 免除, 破棄, 抹消, 中止
contract cancelation 解約, 契約の解除, 契約の打切り
debt cancelation 負債の帳消し, 負債の棒引き (=write-off)
mark down cancelation 値下げ取消高
mark up cancelation 値上げ取消高
policy cancelation 保険の解約
right of cancellation クーリング・オフ
▶ The company repurchased for *cancelation* its own common shares for an aggregate amount of $330 million. 同社は, 消却の目的で, 総額3億ドルの自社普通株式を買い戻した。

cancer 名 がん
advanced case of lung cancer 肺がんの進行期の症状
cancer-causing agent 発がん物質
cancer cell がん細胞
cancer check がん検診
cancer diagnostic center がん検診センター
cancer treatment drug 抗がん剤
cervical cancer 子宮頸部がん, 子宮頸がん
early case of breast cancer 乳がんの初期の症状
liver cancer 肝臓がん
rectal cancer すい臓がん
stomach cancer 胃がん
candidate 名 候補, 候補者, 立候補者, 志願者, 志望者, 応募者, 受験者, 有資格者, 候補地, …しそうな人, …になりそうな人
a candidate for an exam 受験志望者
a candidate for governor [governorship] 知事候補, 知事候補者, 知事立候補者
a candidate for mayor 市長候補, 市長候補者, 市長立候補者
a candidate for the scholarship 奨学金受給希望者, 奨学金希望者
a defeated candidate 落選候補
a doctoral candidate 博士論文提出有資格者[資格者]
a presidential [Presidential] candidate 大統領候補者, 大統領候補
a successful candidate 〈試験などの〉合格者, 〈選挙の〉当選者, 当選候補者
be a candidate for the next Presidency 次期大統領候補に立つ
be a prime candidate for …の公算が大きい[高い]
candidates running for the Lower House 衆議院立候補者
put up a candidate 候補を立てる
run a candidate 候補者を立てる
run candidate at …で立候補する, …で候補に立つ
stand as a candidate 立候補する (=offer oneself as a candidate)
support [back up, boost] a candidate 候補者を支援[後援]する
the nomination of a candidate 候補者指名
cannabis 名 大麻, カンナビス

cannabis user 大麻使用者

Canne film festival カンヌ映画祭

cap 動 上限を設ける[設定する, 定める], 抑制する, 〈上部を〉覆う, 保証する(cover), しのぐ, 勝る, 仕上げる, 完成する, …を締めくくる, 代表選手に選ぶ
  be capped for …の代表選手になる
  cap everything [the glove, the lot] あらゆるものの上に出る, 素晴らしい
  cap losses 損失を補償する, 損失をカバーする (⇒backstop)
  cap or limit the interest rate expense 金利経費に上限を設ける
  cap the climax 極限を超える, 上の上を行く, 度を越す, 極端に走る, 期待以上である, 期待以上のことをする, 意表を突く, 意表に出る
  cap the surge in oil prices 原油価格の上昇を抑制する
  cap to …に賛成する
  capped loan 上限のあるローン
  capped pawn チェス最大のハンディキャップ
  to cap it all さらに悪いことには, あげくの果てに

cap 名 上限, 最高限度, 最高, 上限金利, キャップ
  cap system キャップ制(政策分野別に歳出上限を定める制度)
  rate cap 金利キャップ (=interest rate cap)
  small cap stock 小型株
  spending cap 歳出上限
  the largest cap stock 時価総額が最大の銘柄
  volume cap 発行額の上限
  ▶The new law of California imposes a first-in-the-nation emissions *cap* on utilities, refineries and manufacturing plants. 米カリフォルニア州の新法は, 発電所[公共事業体]や製油所, 製造工場などの温室効果ガス排出量に米国内で初めて上限を設けている。

cap and trade キャップ・アンド・トレード(温室効果ガスの排出権取引の手法の一つ。政府が企業ごとに温室効果ガスの排出量枠(キャップ[排出量の上限])を割り当て, 排出量枠を超えた企業は枠を余らせた企業から超過分の排出権を買わなければならない仕組みのこと)

capability 名 能力, 可能性, 将来性, 才能, 素質, 潜在能力, 手腕
  bond placement capability 債券の販売能力
  generation capability 発電能力
  long-term capability 長期的能力
  nuclear deterrent capability 核抑止力
  operating capability 操業能力

  production capabilities 生産設備
  systems capability システムの力

capacity 名 能力, 資本, 資金, 設備, 生産能力, 操業度, 発電容量, 収容力, 収容能力, 地位, 資格, 立場, キャパシティ
  capacity building 人材開発
  capacity effect 能力効果, 生産能力効果
  capacity variance 操業度差異
  capacity utilization rate 設備稼動率
  capital capacity 資本生産能力
  cargo capacity 貨物積載力
  displacement capacity 〈船舶の〉排水量
  electrical capacity 発電容量
  equipment capacity 設備能力
  executive capacity 管理能力
  expand capacity 設備を拡張する, 生産能力を拡大する
  increase production capacity 生産能力を拡大する
  installed capacity 稼動発電能力
  manufacturing [production, productive] capacity 生産能力, 製造能力, 生産設備
  operate at full capacity フル稼働状態にある, フル稼働を維持する, フル操業する
  optimum capacity 最適操業度, 最適能力
  private capacity 個人の資格

capex 名 設備投資, 資本的支出, 資本支出 (=capital expenditure, capital investment, capital spending)

capital 名 資本, 資本金, 元金, 出資金, 〈保険会社の〉基金(株式会社の資本金に相当), 正味財産, 純資産
  bank capital requirements [standards] 銀行の自己資本比率規制
  capital alliance 資本提携 (=capital tie-up)
  capital and business links [alliances] 資本・業務提携
  capital boost plan 増資計画
  capital expenditure 設備投資, 固定資産投資, 資本支出, 資本的支出, 資本投資, 設備投資額, 固定資産投資額, 資本支出額, 資本投資額 (=capital investment)
  capital finance account 資本調達勘定
  capital goods 資本財
  capital loss 資本損失, 資産売却損, 資産譲渡損, 譲渡損失, キャピタル・ロス
  capital plan 資本計画, 資金計画
  equity capital 自己資本, 株主資本

flight capital 逃避資本
increase of capital 増資 (=capital increase)
large-capital stock 大型株
operating capital 経営資本
private capital 民間資本
reduction of [in] capital 減資
share capital 株式資本, 株式資本金
turnover rate [ratio] of capital 資本回転率
working capital 運転資金, 運転資本

capital adequacy ratio 自己資本比率 (=capital-asset ratio, capital-to-asset ratio, net worth ratio)

capital base 資本基盤, 自己資本, 資本金

capital gain 資本利得, 資産売却益, 資産譲渡益, 株式売買益, 譲渡所得, 値上り益, キャピタル・ゲイン

capital increase 増資, 資本増強, 〈保険会社の〉基金の積み増し[増額], 基金増資 (=capital expansion, capital increment, capital injection)

capital investment 設備投資, 資本投資, 資本投下, 出資, 出資金 (=capital expenditure, capital spending, investment in plant and other facilities)

capital market 資本市場, 長期金融市場, キャピタル・マーケット (⇒money market, securities market)

capital position 自己資本比率, 資本ポジション

capital spending 設備投資, 資本的支出 (=capex, capital investment; ⇒management plan)

capital standards 自己資本比率

capital tie-up 資本提携

capitalism 名 資本主義, キャピタリズム (⇒cybercapitalism)
　American capitalism 米国型の資本主義 (=American version of capitalism, U.S. style capitalism)
　commercial [mercantile] capitalism 商業資本主義
　corporate capitalism 株式会社資本主義
　crony capitalism 縁故資本主義
　finance [financial] capitalism 金融資本主義
　free market capitalism 資本主義市場経済
　guided capitalism 誘導的資本主義
　managerial capitalism 管理資本主義, 経営者資本主義
　modified capitalism 修正資本主義
　monopoly capitalism 独占資本主義

capitalist 名 資本家, 資本主義者, 資本主義, キャピタリスト
　capitalist camp 資本主義陣営
　capitalist competition 資本主義的競争
　capitalist economy 資本主義経済
　capitalist market economy 資本主義市場経済 (=free market capitalism)
　commercial capitalist 商業資本家
　factory capitalist 工場資本家
　mixed capitalist economy 混合資本主義経済

capitalization 名 資本構成, 資本総額, 資本化, 株式資本化, 資本調達, 収益の資本還元, 資本組入れ, 発行済み株式の時価総額, 長期資本, 資産計上, 資産化, 〈会社・事業などへの〉投資, 資本基盤 (=capitalisation; ⇒market capitalization)
　capitalization structure 資本構成
　capitalization issue 資本組入れ株式発行, 資本組入れ発行, 無償発行, 無償増資, 株式無償交付
　capitalization value 資本金額
　improve capitalization 資本基盤を強化する, 資本[資本基盤]を充実させる
　low [weak] capitalization 資本基盤が弱いこと, 弱い資本基盤, 資本基盤の弱さ, 脆弱な資本基盤
　minimum capitalization requirements 最低必要資本金額 (=minimum capital requirements)
　overall [total] market capitalization 市場の時価総額, 株式時価総額
　small capitalization stock 小型株
　strengthen capitalization 資本の充実化, 資本を充実させる, 資本基盤を強化する
　target capitalization 自己資本比率の目標

capitalize 動 資本化する, 資産化する, 資産に計上する, 資本として使用する, 資本に組み入れる, 現価計上する, 出資する, 投資する

capitalize on 利用する, 活用する, 生かす, つけ込む, 〈需要などを〉見越す
　capitalize on huge money flows 膨大な資金の流れを利用する
　capitalize on improved quality at production plants 生産拠点での品質向上を活用する

Capitol 名 〈米国の首都ワシントンの〉連邦議会

議事堂 (= the United States Capitol：州議会はthe state legislatureで、小文字のcapitolは州議会議事堂・州議事堂(Statehouse)を意味する)
Architect of the Capitol 議事堂建築監
Capitol Building 議会議事堂
Capitol Hill 連邦議会 (= Congress, the Hill)
Capitol police 議会衛視

captive 形 内製の, 専属の, 親会社専用の, 親会社に支配された, 支配下に置かれた, 支配下企業の, 企業おかかえの, 選択の自由のない, とりこになった, 魅せられた, 監禁された, 逮捕された, 捕獲された, つながれた, 係留された, 〈苦境などから〉抜け出せない
be captive to economic confusion 経済的混乱から抜け出せない
be taken captive 捕虜となる
captive audience 捕われの視聴者(広告や宣伝をいや応なしに聞かされ, 見せられる視聴者)
captive balloon 係留気球
captive bank 専属銀行
captive breeding 人口繁殖
captive field force 専属営業員
captive finance company 金融子会社
captive firing 〈ロケットの〉地上噴射, 静止燃焼試験
captive insurance 自家保険
captive insurance company [insurer] 専属保険会社
captive items 支配下企業の製品
captive market 専属市場(空港, ホテル, 鉄道駅, 大学構内の店舗など, 独立しているが他人に支配されている市場), 選択の余地のない消費者層
captive mine 自社鉱山, 自社炭鉱
captive shop 専属事務所, 自社店
captive store 自社直営店, 自社店
captive supplier 内製メーカー
captive test 〈ロケットの〉固定テスト, 静止[保持]試験

car 名 乗用車, 自動車, 車, カー
alternatively-fueled car 代替燃料車
car bomb 自動車爆弾
car card 車内広告
car carrier 自動車専用船
car hire [rental] company レンタカー会社
car inspection 車検
car navigation effect カーナビ効果(カーナビによる省エネ効果)
car navigation system 自動車経路誘導システム, カーナビ, カー・ナビゲーション・システム
car park 駐車場 (= parking lot)
car phone 自動車電話 (= carphone)
car pool 相乗り取決め, 自家用車相乗りグループ
car port 自動車置き場
car producer 自動車メーカー, 乗用車メーカー
clean car 低公害車, クリーン・カー
commercial car 商用車
compact car 小型車, コンパクト車, コンパクト・カー
estate car ステーション・ワゴン (= station wagon)
executive car リムジン, エグゼクティブ・カー
fuel-efficient car 低燃費車
full-size car 大型車, フルサイズ・カー
hydrogen fueled car 水素自動車
methanol fueled car メタノール車
mid-size car 中型車, ミッドサイズ・カー
new car sales 新車販売, 新車販売台数
passenger car 乗用車
patrol [squad] car パトカー
solar car ソーラー・カー (= solar powered car)
stock car レース用改造車, 家畜運搬車
subcompact car 小型大衆車, サブコンパクト車, サブコンパクト・カー
trade friction of cars 自動車摩擦
unmarked police car 覆面パトカー, 覆面警察車両
used [secondhand] car 中古車
car-share [sharing] scheme カーシェアリング制度, カーシェア制度

carbon 名 炭素, カーボン紙(carbon paper), カーボン
carbon copy 瓜二つ, 生き写し, カーボン紙を用いた写し
carbon cycle 炭素循環, 炭素サイクル
carbon dating 放射性炭素による年代測定 (= radio carbon dating)
carbon emissions 炭素排出量 (= carbon dioxide emissions)
carbon fiber 炭素繊維, カーボン・ファイバー
carbon sink 炭素吸収源
carbon steel 炭素鋼
carbon taxes 炭素税, 二酸化炭素税(二酸化炭素の排出量に応じて課税される)
carbon dioxide 二酸化炭素

carbon dioxide emissions 二酸化炭素排出量（＝carbon emissions）
carbon monoxide 一酸化炭素
　carbon monoxide poisoning 一酸化炭素中毒（＝CO poisoning）
carbon nanotube カーボンナノチューブ（超微細の炭素の管）
carcinogen 名 発がん物質（＝carcinogenic substance）
card 名 カード, クレジット・カード, キャッシュ・カード
cardholder 名 カード会員（＝card holder, card member）
cardiac 形 心臓の, 心臓病の
　acute cardiac insufficiency [dysfunction] 急性心不全
　cardiac arrest 心拍停止, 心臓麻痺
　cardiac failure 心臓麻痺
　cardiac infarction 心筋梗塞
care 名 注意, 注意義務, 配慮, 保護, 看護, 介護, 世話, 面倒, 医療, 医療保険, 関心事, ケア（⇒health care [healthcare], medical care）
　acute-care hospital 救急病院（＝emergency hospital）
　bathing care 訪問入浴
　emergency care 救急医療
　growing care units 継続保育室《略 GCU》
　health care benefits 健康保険給付, 医療保険給付
　home care 在宅医療, 在宅ケア
　managed care 管理医療, マネージド・ケア
　ordinary care 通常の注意
　perinatal medical care 周産期医療（出産前後の期間の医療）
　universal health care coverage 国民皆医療保険制度
career 名 経歴, 履歴, 職業, 専門的職業, 仕事, 生活手段, 生涯, 成功, 出世, 昇進, 全速力, キャリア（⇒mid-career [midcareer]）
　career break 育児などのための求職期間
　career bureaucrats キャリア官僚, キャリア組
　career change 転職
　career development program 社員の経歴開発計画, 職歴開発計画
　career-oriented society 学歴中心の社会
　career planning [plan] 経歴計画, 生涯計画, キャリア・プラン
　in full [mad] career 全速力で（＝at full speed）
　make a career 出世する, 成功する
　move up [climb] the career ladder 出世の階段を上る, 昇進する
　pursue a career in …の職業に進む
career-high 形 自己最多の, 自己最高の
caretaker 名 管理人, 世話人, 職務代行者, …代行
CARICOM カリブ共同体, カリコム（Caribbean Communityの略）
carrier 名 運送人, 運送業者, 航空［バス, トラック, 鉄道］会社, 持参人, 保険会社, 保険業者, 保険者, 通信業者, 通信事業者, 電気通信事業者, 保菌者, キャリア（⇒telecom carrier）
　aircraft carrier 航空母艦
　armored personnel carrier 装甲運搬車, 武装した兵員輸送車
　carrier bag 買い物袋
　carrier of germs 病原菌の媒介体
　carrier plane 艦載機
　carrier rocket 打上げロケット, 運搬ロケット
　disease carrier 病菌所有者
　flag [flagship] carrier 国を代表する航空会社, 国の代表的な航空会社
　international carrier 国際通信事業者
　nuclear carrier 原子力空母
　type I carrier 第一種電気通信事業者, 第一種事業者
carry 動 計上する, 算定する, 帳簿に記載しておく, 記帳する, 転記する,〈保険などを〉付ける, 設定する, 債務を負う
　be carried at cost 取得原価で計上される
　be carried at FIFO cost 先入れ先出し法で算定される
　be carried to …に転記される
　carried down 前期繰越し《略 C/D [c/d]》（＝brought down）
　carried forward 次期繰越し, 次頁繰越し《略 C/F [c/f]》（＝brought forward）
　carry a bank guarantee 銀行保証が付いている
　carry an allowance for doubtful accounts 貸倒れ引当金の設定を行う
　carry back 繰り戻す, 欠損［欠損金］を前期［前年度以前］に繰り戻す
　carry down 次期へ繰り越す
　carry forward 繰り越す, 欠損［欠損金］を次期［翌年度以降］に繰り越す（＝carry over）

carry the long-term debt　長期債務を負う
carry over　引き継ぐ, 持ち越す, 繰り越す (carry forward), 延期する
carry trade　キャリー取引, キャリー・トレード
cartel 名　企業連合, 党派連合, 密売組織, カルテル (価格形成やマーケット・シェア, 生産水準など競争を排除するために結ばれる協定や協定に基づく結合。⇒price cartel)
　cartel tariff　カルテル関税
　cocaine cartel　コカイン密売組織
　commissions cartel　売買手数料カルテル
　conditional cartel　条件［生産条件］付きカルテル
　export-import cartel　輸出入カルテル
　form [run] an international cartel　国際カルテルを結ぶ
　price fixing cartel　価格カルテル（＝pricing cartel）
　production cartel　生産カルテル, 生産連合
　profit-sharing cartel　利益配当カルテル
　purchasers' cartel　購買者カルテル
　quantity cartel　生産数量カルテル
　quotas cartel　割当カルテル
　rationalization cartel　合理化カルテル
　supply restriction cartel　供給制限カルテル
　trade cartel　貿易カルテル
carve out　〈道や運命などを〉切り開く, 開拓する, 作り上げる,〈名声などを〉努力して得る
　carve out a career　世に出る, 出世する, 名をあげる
case 名　事例, 問題, 事件, 件数, 見方, 論拠, 理由, 主張, 陳述, 申立て, 訴訟, 判例, 症例, 患者, 対象者, 受給者, 保護対象者, 場合, 実情, 真相, 事実, ケース
　a case in point　好例, 典型的な例
　appeal a case　上訴する
　bearish case　弱気の見方
　bullish case　強気の見方
　case agreed on　合意事実記載書
　case-based reasoning　事例に基づく推論《略 CBR》
　case history　事例史, 病歴
　case law　判例法
　case law precedent　判例法の先例
　case-lot wholesaler　小口卸売り業者
　case mark　荷印
　case method　事例研究法, 事例調査法
　case on appeal　上訴事実記載書
　case research　事例調査
　case stated　事実記載書, 訴訟事件摘要書
　case study　事例研究, ケース・スタディ
　case system　判例主義
　civil case　民事事件
　court case　裁判所の判例
　criminal case　刑事事件
　dismiss the case　訴訟を却下する
　divorce case　離婚訴訟
　drop a case　訴訟を取り下げる
　drug case　麻薬事件
　escape the worst case　最悪の事態を免れる
　file a case in a court　事件を法廷に持ち込む
　lay the case　申立てをする
　lose the case　訴訟に負ける, 敗訴する
　make a case against　…に反対の論拠を示す, …に反対論を唱える
　make a case for　…に賛成の論拠を示す, …の論拠を示す, …の擁護論を唱える
　make one's case　自分の言い分を述べる
　medical case　内科の患者
　on a case-by-case basis　個別ベースで, 個々の事例に従って, ケース・バイ・ケースで
　plead [put, state] one's case　事件を裁判する
　put the case　事情を説明する
　rest one's case　証拠提出を終える, 弁論を終える
　special case　例外
　the case for the prosecution　検察側の主張
　win [gain] the case　訴訟に勝つ, 勝訴する
cash 動　現金に換える, 換金する
　cash in　…を現金に換える, 換金する, うまく儲ける
　cash in on　…に付け込む［乗じる］, …を利用する, …でたんまり儲ける, …に付けこんで儲ける
　cash up [out]　売上を合計する, 清算する, 換金する, 現金化する
cash 名　現金, 預金, 現金預金, 現預金, 通貨, 資金, キャッシュ（「現金」とは会計上, 銀行預金のほかに小切手, 手形, 郵便為替なども含むが, 流動資産 (current assets) に含まれる cash は手元現金と銀行の要求払い預金を指す）
　cash burn　資金の枯渇, 手持ち資金の枯渇
　cash cow　金のなる木, ドル箱, 収入源, 資金源, 財産, 儲かる商品, 配当の良い優良株
　cash currency　現金通貨（＝cash currency in circulation, cash in circulation）
　cash handout　定額給付金支給
　cash transfer　送金（＝cash remittance）
　cash transport vehicle　現金輸送車

▶ Stock swaps allow the acquirer to purchase the company it wants to control without preparing a large sum of *cash*.　株式交換だと，買収企業は多額の現金を用意しなくても，相手先企業（経営権を握りたいと思う企業）を買収することができる。

cash flow　現金の収入と支出，現金収支，資金収支，資金の流出入，資金の運用・調達，資金繰り，現金資金，純収入，キャッシュ・フロー（現金収入と現金支出の総称）
 cash flow problems　資金難，資金繰り難，資金繰りの問題
 cash flow situation　資金繰り
 current cash flow　手元流動性
 face cash flow problems　資金繰りの問題に行き詰まる
 fixed cash flow　固定金利のキャッシュ・フロー
 floating cash flow　変動金利のキャッシュ・フロー
 statement of cash flows　資金収支表，資金収支計算書，資金フロー表，キャッシュ・フロー表

cash in circulation　貨幣流通高，現金通貨
▶ M2 consists of *cash in circulation*, demand deposits and quasi money.　M2は，現金通貨と要求払い預金［預金通貨：deposit money］と準通貨から成る。

cash-strapped 形　財政難の，財政難に陥った
cash tender offer　現金公開買付け，現金による株式公開買付け，キャッシュ・テンダー・オファー（買収先の会社の株式を現金で公開買付けする方法。⇒conversion of debt to equity）

casual 形　略式の，普段用の，普段着の，臨時の，一時的な，短期の，偶然の，偶発の，不定の，思いつきの，即席の，用意なしの，カジュアル
 casual clothes [wear]　普段着，スポーティーな服，カジュアル・ウエア
 casual cost control　原因別原価管理
 casual customer　ふりの客，時たまの訪問客
 casual employment　臨時採用，臨時雇用，一時雇用
 casual expenses　臨時出費，臨時支出
 casual hand [laborer, worker]　臨時工，臨時雇い，季節労働者　（=casual）
 casual [casualty] insurance　災害保険
 casual loss　偶発損失，臨時損失
 casual profit　偶発利益
 casual revenue　臨時収入
 casual unemployment　臨時工失業，季節労働者失業率
 casual work [labor]　臨時仕事

casual clothing　カジュアル衣料品，カジュアル衣料
 casual clothing retailer [store, shop]　カジュアル衣料量販店

casualty 名　災難，災害，偶発事故，人的損害，被害者，犠牲者，死傷者，死傷者数，犠牲者数
 casualty allowance　災害補償
 casualty and surety insurance　災害補償保険
 casualty insurance　災害保険，障害保険，損保保険
 casualty loss　災害損失，偶発損失，雑損
 casualty loss deduction　雑損控除　（=deduction for casualty loss）
 casualty profit　偶発利益
 casualty report service　〈ロイズの〉海難報告サービス
 commercial property and casualty　商業用損害保険
 property and casualty　損害保険
 property and casualty insurer　損害保険会社，損保会社

catapult 動　突然ある状態にする，勢いよく飛び出す，突然［一躍］…になる
 be catapulted out of [from]　…から放り出される，…から急に飛び出す
 catapult into [to]　突然…になる，…に突入する

catastrophe 名　災難，不幸，不幸な事態，不運（misfortune），大失敗，大災害，大惨事，災禍（disaster），大変動，悲劇的結末，大詰め，大団円，破局，破滅，破綻，カタストロフィ
 catastrophe insurance　巨大損害保険
 catastrophe loss　異常損失
 catastrophe risk　非常危険
 fiscal catastrophe　財政破綻

Catch-all or End-use Controls　キャッチオール規制　（=catch-all regulations）
catch quota　漁獲枠
caucus 名　党員集会（米大統領選候補者指名のための州ごとに行われる党員集会），〈米連邦議会での各党の〉幹部会，〈英国の政党の〉地方支部会，〈日本の〉両院議員総会

cause 名　原因，要因，理由，根拠，動機，主義，主張，大義（principle），運動，団体，目標，目的，訴訟事由［事実］，訴訟，〈議論の〉主題
 a cause for the crime　犯罪の動機
 a cause of action　訴因，訴訟原因
 a main [major] cause　主因，核心

bring one's cause before the court 提訴する

cause-and-effect relationship 因果関係

cause célèbre 大きな関心を引いた事件［訴訟事件］，悪名高い事件［裁判］

causes for inflationary concerns インフレの懸念材料

in the cause of world peace 世界平和のために

make common cause with …と共同戦線を張る，…と手を結ぶ，…と協力する

plead a [one's] cause 訴訟理由を申し立てる，言い分を申し立てる

potential causes of instability 不安定要因

show cause 申し開きをする，正当な理由を示す

show the cause 訴訟理由を提示する

the chain of cause and effect 因果のつながり

the day of cause 裁判の日

caution against ...ing …しないよう警告する
▶ Defense Secretary Donald H. Rumsfeld *cautioned against* viewing the missile defense plan as a foolproof means of defense. ラムズフェルド米国防長官は，ミサイル防衛計画を絶対安全な防衛手段と見ないよう警告した。

cautious 形 注意深い，用心深い，慎重な
 be cautious about [of, with] …に注意する，…について慎重である，…に用心している，…を警戒する
 cautious consumer spending 慎重な個人消費，消費者の買い控え
 take cautious stand against …に対して慎重な立場［スタンス］を取る

CBRN attacks 化学・生物・放射線物質・核兵器攻撃（CBRN＝chemical, biological, radiological and nuclearの略）

CCS 二酸化炭素の回収・貯留（技術）（**carbon dioxide capture and storage**の略。大気に放出される二酸化炭素を集め，地球や海水中に閉じ込めて固定する技術）

CD コンパクト・ディスク（**compact disc**の略）

CDO 債務担保証券（**collateralized debt obligation**の略。証券化商品で，社債やローン（貸出債権）などで構成される資産を担保にして発行される資産担保証券（asset-backed securities）の一種）

CDS クレジット・デフォルト・スワップ（金融機関を相手に，融資や証券化商品が焦げ付いた際に損失を肩代わりする金融派生商品。企業の破綻リスクを売買するもので，投資に対する保険効果を持つとされる。⇒credit default swap）

ceasefire 名 停戦，休戦，戦闘中止

cedar pollen スギ花粉

ceiling 名 限界，限度，上限，天井，最高，〈予算の〉概算要求基準，シーリング（下限＝floor）

celebration 名 祝い，祝賀，祝賀会，祝典，祭典，式典，式，賞賛，賛美，賛辞
 celebration banquet 祝宴
 hold a celebration 祝賀会を催す
 in celebration of …を祝って

celebrity 名 名士，〈映画，音楽，スポーツ界の〉有名人，著名人，タレント，人気者，名声（fame, renown)，評判，高名，知名度，セレブ（＝celeb）
 achieve celebrity status 有名人としての地位を築く
 gain [attain] celebrity 名声を博す，有名になる
 Hollywood celebrities ハリウッドのスターたち
 jump into celebrity 一躍有名になる
 regain celebrity 名声を取り戻す

cell phone 携帯電話（＝cellular phone, mobile phone; ⇒cloned cell phone）

censorship 名 検閲，検定，検閲制度，検閲官の職務［任務，任期］，潜在意識抑圧力
 censorship system 検閲制度，検定制度
 rigid [strict] press censorship 新聞の厳重な検閲

censure motion 問責決議案

center [centre] 動 中心［中央］に置く，集中させる，集中する，集まる
 be centered on …に集中する
 center on [around, at, in, round, upon] …に集中する，…を中心とする，…を中心に展開する，…を柱とする

center 名 中心，中央，中枢，中心地，中心点，拠点，本場，中心人物，花形，指導者，中間派，穏健派，重点地区，商業地区，繁華街，都市，総合施設，的，対象，センター（⇒child counseling center, distribution center）
 commercial distribution center 流通センター
 distribution center 物流センター，流通センター，配送センター（＝distribution facility）
 profit center 利益センター，利益中心点，利益責任単位，プロフィット・センター

center-left 名 中道左派，形 中道左派の（＝centre-left）
 center-left party 中道左派政党

center-right 名 中道右派, 形 中道右派の (=centre-right)
centerpiece 名 最重点項目, 最重要項目, 中心的な事項, 中核, 目玉, 呼び物
central bank 中央銀行(日本の場合は日本銀行を指す。⇒Bank of Japan)

> アメリカの中央銀行について ⊃ アメリカには単一の中央銀行が存在せず, 連邦準備制度(Federal Reserve System)のもと連邦準備区(Federal Reserve district)に設置された全米12の連邦準備銀行(Federal Reserve Bank)が実際の中央銀行業務をしている。ただし, the U.S. central bankといえば米連邦準備制度理事会を指す。

Central Council for Education 中央教育審議会
centralized processing 集中処理
centrifugal separator 遠心分離機
centrifuge 名 遠心分離機
centripetal force [power] 求心力(遠心力=centrifugal force)
centrism 名 中道主義
centrist 名 中道主義者, 中道派議員, 穏健派議員, 〈保守派と革新派の中間派の〉中道派(middle-of-the-roader), 穏健派
CEO 最高業務執行役員, 最高経営責任者, 最高業務執行理事 (=chief executive; chief executive officerの略)
ceremony 名 儀式, 式典, 式, 礼儀, 礼式, 作法, 虚礼, 形式ばること, セレモニー
　ceremony of launching a ship 進水式
　congratulatory ceremony 祝賀式
　graduation [commencement] ceremony 卒業式
　hold [have, observe, perform] a ceremony 式を挙げる, 式を行う
　master of ceremonies 司会者
　with all due ceremony きわめて厳粛に, 丁重に, ていねいに
　with ceremony 丁重に, 礼儀を尽くして, 仰々しく
　without ceremony 気軽に, 格式[儀式]ばらずに, 遠慮なく, 打ち解けて, 無造作に
certification 名 保証, 証明, 認可, 認定, 認証, 免許, 認定証, 証明[保証]書, 〈裁判所に対する〉意見確認
　certification mark 証明標章
　certification mark system 表示制度
　certification of audit 監査証明
　certification of contents 内容証明

certification of payment 支払い保証
certification of transfer 譲渡承認
certification proceedings 〈労働組合の〉交渉代表認証手続き
certification register 認証簿
export certification 輸出認証
pre-certification program 事前認可制度
self-certification loans 簡易審査型ローン
self-certification system 自己申告制
Certified Public Accountants Law 公認会計士法
certify 動 保証する, 証明する, 認可する, 認定する, 認証する, 確認する
　certified airmail 配達証明付き航空郵便
　certified check 支払い保証小切手, 銀行支払い保証小切手
　certified copy 認証謄本, 謄本, 認証付き写し
　certified extract 抄本
　certified financial statements 監査済み財務書類[財務諸表]
　certified invoice 領事証明付き送り状
　certified letter 公証書簡
　certified mail 配達証明, 配達証明郵便
　certified management accountant 公認管理会計士《略 CMA》
　certified minutes 会社の認証議事録
　certified transfer 証明書付き株式譲渡, 譲渡承認
　certified union 承認組合
CFTC 〈米〉商品先物取引委員会 (Commodity Futures Trading Commisionの略)
chain 名 系統, 連鎖, 連鎖店, チェーン・ストア, チェーン店, チェーン
chain reaction 連鎖反応
chairmanship 名 委員長のポスト, 委員長の地位
chalk up 動 収益[利益]をあげる, …を記録する, 計上する, 獲得する, 達成する
challenge 名 挑戦, 課題, 難題, 難問, 苦境, 試練, ハードル, 脅威, やりがいのある仕事, 任務, 要求, 要請, 請求, 〈競技などへの〉参加勧誘[参加呼びかけ], 〈試合などへの〉申込み, 挑戦状, 〈陪審員に対する〉拒否, 忌避, 異議, 異議申立て, チャレンジ
　a challenge to police 警察に対する挑戦
　a daunting technical challenge 技術的に難しいがやりがいのある仕事
　a host of challenge 多くの課題

a legal challenge　法的手段による抗議
accept [take up] a challenge　挑戦に応じる
be beyond challenge　文句がつけられない
challenge to the array [panel]　陪審員(候補)全員に対する忌避
give a challenge　挑戦する
issue [send] a challenge　戦いを挑む
meet [rise to] a challenge　試練に打ち勝つ，難局にうまく対処する，苦境を乗り切る
meet [respond to] the challenges　難題に対応する，難題に応える，要請に応じる
practical challenges　実践の場での課題
strategic challenge　戦略的な課題
the challenge in monetary policy for countries　各国の金融政策の課題

challenging 形　やりがいのある，意欲をそそる，興味をかきたてる，難しい，試練の，挑発的な，魅力的な，挑戦する，挑戦の

chamber 名　議院，議会，議場，会議室，会議所
audience chamber　接見室
both chambers of Congress　米議会の上下両院
Chamber　〈米連邦議会の〉本会議場
Chamber of Commerce and Industry Law　商工会議所法
Chamber of Commerce of the United States　〈米国〉商工会議所
House Chamber　〈米〉下院本会議
lower chamber　〈英〉下院(House of Commons)，〈日本の〉衆議院(House of Representatives)
upper chamber　〈英〉上院(House of Lords)，〈日本の〉参議院(House of Councilors)

champion 名　優勝者，選手権保持者，闘士，戦士，擁護者，支持者，チャンピオン

championship 名　選手権，選手権大会，擁護，優勝者の地位，〈権利などの〉擁護，弁護(defense)，支持
championship of women's rights　女性の権利の擁護
hold the tennis championship of the world　テニスの世界選手権[世界テニス選手権]を保持する
win [gain] the golf championship of the world　ゴルフの世界選手権[世界ゴルフ選手権]を獲得する

chancellor　〈ドイツの〉首相
German Chancellor　ドイツの首相

change 動　変える，変更する，変化させる，改める，改造する，替える，交換する，交替する，両替する，くずす(break)，現金に換える，自動 変わる，変化する，移行する
change a five-dollar bill　5ドル紙幣を両替する[くずす]
change from a manufacturing economy to a service economy　製造経済からサービス経済に移行する
change hands　政権を交代する，所有者[持ち主]が変わる，人手に渡る，変わる，更迭する，推移する，商品が売れる
change jobs with　…と交互に仕事をする
change one's mind　考えを変える

change 名　変動，変化，変革，変調，変更，改革，改正，増減，釣銭，小銭，チェンジ
cabinet change　内閣改造
change of government　政権交代（= change in political leadership）
change of guard　責任者や担当官の交代，多数党逆転，与野党逆転，衛兵交代
change of power　政権交代
changes in circumstances　環境の変化
cyclical changes　一時的な変化
high change　大変動
job change　転職（= job changing）
percentage change　百分率変化，変化率
personnel changes　人事刷新
political change　政治改革，政権交代
price-level change　物価変動
primary change　1次的な変化

Chapter 7 of the National Bankruptcy Act　米連邦破産法第7章，米破産法第7章（破綻した企業を再生させずに清算する手続きを定めた法律）

Chapter 10 of the National Bankruptcy Act　米連邦破産法第10章，米破産法第10章

Chapter 11　米連邦改正破産法第11章，米連邦破産法11章，チャプター・イレブン，会社更生手続き　(= Chapter 11 of the U.S. Bankruptcy Reform Act：企業の法的整理の一種で，日本の民事再生法に相当する。裁判所への申請と同時に，債権取立てが禁止され，経営体制を維持して事業を継続しながら経営再建を目指せる)
Chapter 11 bankruptcy　米連邦改正破産法，米連邦破産法11章
Chapter 11 bankruptcy protection　米連邦破産法11章の適用

charge 動 請求する, 課する, 要求する, 支払わせる, 負担させる, 借方に記入する, 借記する, 計上する, クレジット・カードで買う, 告発する, 摘発する, 充電する

- **be charged to income** 費用として計上される, 費用計上される (＝be charged to earnings)
- **be charged with** …の責任を負っている, …を担当している, …で告発［摘発］される
- **charge against** 費用として差し引く, 損失とみて差し引く

charge 名 費用, 料金, 税金, 課税金, 手数料, 代価, 代金, 請求金額, 借方記入, 借記, 負債, 借金, 責任, 義務, 任務, 担保, 担保権, 管理, 監督, 保管, 運営, 処理, 告発, 提訴, 〈陪審に対する裁判官の〉説示, 充電, チャージ

- **burden charge** 負担金
- **charge d'affaires** 臨時大使

charter 名 憲章, 宣言, 綱領, 使用契約, 特権, 特別免除［設立］認可書, 支店［支部］設置許可, チャーター

- **charter flight** チャーター便
- **charter member** 創立委員, 創立社員 (＝founder member)
- **charter party** 用船契約
- **corporate charter** 会社定款 (＝corporation charter)
- **the Charter of the United Nations** 国連憲章

chat 動 チャットする, 〈インターネット上で〉メッセージのやりとりをする, ネットで対話する

chat 名 チャット, 〈インターネット上での〉メッセージのやりとり, ネットでの対話, ネット上の書き込み (＝online talk)

> チャットとは ⇒ インターネットに接続したパソコンを使って, 不特定の人がおしゃべりをするようにネット上でメッセージのやりとりをすること. 専用ソフトを使うと, テレビ電話のように映像や音声のやりとりもできる. チャット参加者は, 多人数でも同時に会話ができ, 電子メールのようにアドレスを指定して送信する必要がない.

chatroom 名 チャットルーム
cheaper product 低価格品
checkbook diplomacy 小切手外交
checkup 健康診断, 精密検査, 〈機械などの〉点検, 検査

- **group medical checkups** 集団検診
- **health [medical, physical] checkup** 健康診断, 検査

chemical product 化学製品
chemical weapons 化学兵器
chemotherapy 名 〈がんなどの〉化学療法
chicken-and-egg argument 卵が先か鶏が先かの議論
chide 動 しかる, とがめる, 小言を言う, 非難する, 戒告処分にする, 戒告の懲戒処分にする
chief 形 主な, 主要な, 第一の, 最高位の, 最大の, 主任の, 主席の, チーフ

- **chief accountant** 会計課長, 会計係長, 会計責任者, 主任会計審査官
- **chief actuary** 保険計理人
- **chief competitor** 最大の競争相手, 最大のライバル
- **chief economist** 主任エコノミスト, チーフ・エコノミスト
- **Chief Executive** 米大統領 (chief executive＝州知事)
- **chief financial officer** 最高財務担当役員, 最高財務責任者 《略 CFO》
- **chief operating officer** 最高業務運営役員, 最高業務運営責任者, 業務執行役員, 最高執行責任者 《略 COO》
- **chief packager** 主幹事

chief executive 最高経営責任者(CEO), 企業のトップ, 〈米国の〉州知事(Chief Executive＝米大統領)

chief executive officer 最高業務執行役員, 最高経営責任者 《略 CEO》(経営戦略や経営ビジョンを決める企業のトップ. 米国では, CEOが会長を兼ねることが多い)

child abuse 児童虐待
- **Child Abuse Prevention Law** 児童虐待防止法

child care leave 育児休業, 保育休暇 (＝child-care leave, childcare leave)

child counseling center 児童相談所 (＝child consultation center)

child pornography 児童ポルノ
child prostitution 児童買春
Child-rearing and Nursing Care Leave Law 育児・介護休業法
chilled market 市場の冷え込み
China's Communist Party Congress 中国共産党大会
Chinese President 中国の国家主席
chip 名 珪素の記憶素子, 小型集積回路, パソコンの中央処理装置, 半導体, シリコン・チップ, チップ

- **bare chip** 裸の半導体チップ

biochip 生物化学素子, バイオチップ
chip set チップ・セット(複数のLSIチップをまとめたもの)
custom chips 特注IC
micro chip [microchip] マイクロチップ (＝silicon chip)
neuro chip ニューロ・チップ
silicon chip シリコン薄片, シリコン・チップ (＝IC chip)
violence chip Vチップ (＝V chip)

chipmaker [chip maker] 名 半導体メーカー, 半導体製造業者 (＝semiconductor manufacturer)

chock-full 形 ぎっしり詰まった, 満ち溢れている, 満ち満ちた, 盛りだくさんの

choke off 抑える, 抑制する, 妨げる, …の成長を阻止する, 〈議論や計画を〉止めさせる, 思いとどまらせる, 黙らせる, 意気消沈させる, 絞殺する, 窒息死させる

chronic 形 慢性の
chronic renal insufficiency 慢性腎不全

Chrysanthemum Throne 日本の皇位

CIA 米中央情報局 (Central Intelligence Agencyの略)

CIF 顧客記録 (customer information fileの略)

cinema complex 複合映画館, シネマ・コンプレックス, シネコン(一つの建物内に5〜6以上のスクリーンを持つ映画館)

circle 名 円, 輪, 一巡, 周期, 循環, 範囲, 圏, 全体, サークル
be beyond the circle of foretelling 予測がつかない
be trapped [get caught up] in a vicious circle 悪循環に陥る
come [go, turn] full circle 〈一周して〉振り出しに戻る, 元に戻る
go around [round] in circles 忙しいだけで進歩がない, 一向に先に進んでいない, 堂々めぐりをする
have a large circle of friends 交際の範囲が広い
in a domestic circle 家庭で, 内輪で
join [enter] the circle of …の仲間に入る
run circles around …よりはるかに勝る [ずっと上手である]
square the circle 不可能なことをやってみる, 不可能なことを企てる

circles 名 団体, グループ, …界, …社会, サークル
business circles 経済界, 産業界, 実業界, 業界 (＝business community, business world)
economic circles 経済界, 財界
financial circles 金融界, 財界 (＝financial sector)
official circles 官界
security circles 公安関係者
social circles 社交界, 交際の輪
upper [wellbred] circles 上流社会

circular sales transaction 循環取引(複数の企業間で商品を売買したように装い, 架空の売上を計上する不正取引)

circulate 動 配布する, 流通させる, 循環させる, 回覧する, 流通する, 広まる, 循環する, 出回る

circulation 名 配布, 流通, 循環, 回覧, 発行部数, サーキュレーション (⇒cash in circulation)
active circulation 紙幣流通高, 銀行券発行高
be in circulation 流通している, 出回っている, 使われている, 市販されている
be out of circulation 流通していない, 出回っていない, 使われていない
blood circulation 血液循環, 血行
circulation manager 販売部長
circulation market 流通市場
currency in circulation 通貨流通高
gross circulation 総発行部数
monetary circulation 通貨の流通, 流通通貨
passive circulation 未発行紙幣

circumstances 名 事情, 情状, 状況, 環境, 動向, 情勢, 状態, 事態, 場合, 出来事, 境遇, 暮らし向き, 身の上, 運命, 詳細
be in bad [needy, reduced] circumstances 困窮している, 逆境にある, 暮らしに困っている, 苦しい生活 [経営] 状態にある
economic circumstances 経済環境, 経済状況, 景気動向
extenuating circumstances 酌量すべき情状
one's private circumstances 内幕, 内情
price circumstances 物価動向, インフレ動向
the force of circumstances やむを得ない事情, 周囲のやむを得ない事情
the whole circumstances 事の一部始終
unforeseen circumstances 予見しなかった事情

cite 動 挙げる, 引用する, 引き合いに出す, 言及する, 特記する, 召喚する, 出頭を命じる, 表彰する,

顕彰する
CITES 絶滅の恐れのある動植物の国際取引に関する条約, ワシントン条約 (Convention on International Trade in Endangered Species of Wild Fauna and Flora)の略で, ワシントン条約の正式名称の略語
civil 形 市民の, 一般市民の, 民間の, 民事の
  civil action 民事訴訟
  Civil Aeronautics Board 米民間航空局《略 CAB》
  civil aviation 民間航空
  civil aviation negotiations 航空交渉
  civil case 民事事件
  civil code 民法, 民法典
  civil commotion 市民暴動, 暴動
  civil conflict 国内紛争
  civil court 民事法廷
  civil day 暦日 (＝calendar day)
  civil defense 民間防衛, 民間防衛体制
  civil defense corps 自警団
  civil disturbance 市民の暴動
  civil engineering project 土木工事
  civil fine 民事制裁金
  civil government 民政, 文民政府
  civil lawsuit [suit] 民事訴訟
  civil liability 民事責任
  Civil Liberties Association 人権擁護協会
  Civil List 英王室歳費（英議会が決定）
  civil penalty 民事罰, 制裁金, 過料
  civil procedure code 民事訴訟法
  civil rehabilitation law 民事再生法
  civil remedy 民事上の救済手段
  civil rights movement 公民権運動
  civil servant 公務員, 役人, 文官
  civil service system 公務員制度
  civil state 〈独身, 結婚, 離婚などの〉婚姻状態
  civil strife 内乱, 内戦
  civil trial 民事裁判
  civil unrest 国情不安
  civil war 国内紛争, 内乱, 内戦
civilian assistance 民生支援
CJD クロイツフェルト・ヤコブ病 (Creutzfeldt-Jakob Diseaseの略)
claim 動 〈権利を〉要求する, 請求する, 〈権利や事実を〉主張する, 自称する, 名乗る, 訴える, 〈責任などを〉認める, 〈地位や賞などを〉得る, 勝ち取る, 〈人命を〉奪う
  claim a place 地位を得る
  claim damages 損害賠償を請求する
  claim responsibility for …の犯行声明を出す
  claim the lives of …人の命を奪う, …人の死者が出る
claim 名 請求, 請求権, 請求事項, 特許請求の範囲, 信用, 債権, 債権の届出, 保険金, 権利, 権利の主張, 苦情, 苦情の申立て
  claims adjustment 損害査定
  claims for damages 損害賠償請求, 求償権
  claims process 保険金支払いプロセス
  collect claims 債権を回収する
  housing loan claim 住宅ローンの債権
  initial unemployment claims 新規失業保険申請件数
  policy claims 保険金請求, 保険金
  refund claim 還付申請書
clamp down on …を（厳しく）取り締まる, 差し止める, 弾圧する, 締め付ける
clarify 動 明らかにする, はっきりさせる, 分かりやすくする, 浄化する
clash 動 衝突する, ぶつかり合う, 対立する, 食い違う, 相反する, 対戦する, 激突する, 〈色が〉釣り合わない, 調和しない
  clash with cops 警官と衝突する
  clash with one's interests …の利害と相反する
clash 名 衝突, 争い, 対立, 〈意見などの〉不一致, 不調和, 対戦, 〈行事などの〉重なり, ぶつかり
  head-on clash 正面衝突
  military clash 軍事衝突
class action suit 集団代表訴訟, 集団訴訟 (＝class action, class action lawsuit)
classified 形 機密の, 極秘の
  classified diplomatic fund 外交機密費
  classified information 機密情報, 極秘情報, 高度の軍事機密情報
clause 名 〈法律や契約などの〉条項, 規定, 約款, 箇条, 項, 事項, 文言, 〈文法の〉節
  all risk clause オール・リスク（全危険）担保約款
  attestation clause 証明文言
  choice of law clause 準拠法指定条項
  contractual clause 契約条項
  emergency clause 緊急箇条
  enemy clause 敵国条項
  escape clause 免責条項, 例外規定
  force majeure clause 不可抗力条項
  incontestable clause 不可争条項
  insurance clause 保険約款

negative clause 担保留保条項
negligence clause 免責条項
penal clause 罰則
saving clause 留保条項, 但し書き
special clause 特別約款
standard clause 標準約款
waiver clause 免責条項, 放棄約款

clean 形 公正な, 瑕疵のない, 無条件の, 担保権が付いていない, 安全な, 清浄な, クリーン
 clean float 中央銀行が介入しない変動相場制, きれいな変動相場制, クリーン・フロート（中央銀行が介入する変動相場制を「dirty float（汚い変動相場制）」という）
 clean sweep 〈組織の〉全面的改革, 全勝
 come clean 本当のことを言う, 本音を吐く, 白状する, 罪を認める
 make a clean breast of …を白状する, …をすっかり打ち明ける, 真相を話す
 make a clean sweep of …を一掃する
 win the election by a clean sweep 選挙で完勝する

cleric 名 聖職者, 牧師
client 名 顧客, お得意, 得意先, 得意客, 取引先, 依頼人, 依頼者, 監査依頼会社, 被監査会社, クライアント（＝customer）
 attract clients 顧客を引きつける, 顧客を開拓する
 lure new clients 新規顧客を獲得する

climate 名 気候, 風土, 条件, 環境, 状況, 情勢, 傾向, 風潮, 思潮, 雰囲気, 空気, 地方, 地帯
 climate immigrant 気候移民
 climate refugees 気候難民
 the climate of opinion 世論

climate change 気候変動
 Climate Change Levy 気候変動税

climate-changing pollution 気候変動をもたらす汚染物質

climb 動 上昇する, 拡大する, 増加する, 昇進する, 出世する, 登る
 climb into the black 黒字に転じる
 climb out of recession 景気後退から抜け出す

climb-down 名 譲歩, 撤回

clinch 動 勝ち取る, 獲得する, …を決定的［確定的］にする, 固定する
 clinch a deal 取引［商談］をまとめる, 取引にかたをつける

clinical test 臨床試験, 治験（新薬の承認を受けるため, 動物実験のあと, 人を対象に有効性と安全性を調べる試験）

clinical training hospital 臨床研修病院
cloak-and-dagger 形 スパイ行為の, スパイ活動の, スパイものの, 諜報の, 陰謀の, 陰謀劇の
 cloak-and-dagger agents 諜報機関員, スパイ連中
 cloak-and-dagger services 秘密情報機関

clock ticking 秒読み, 秒読み段階
clone [clon] 動 コピー生物を作る, コピー生物を作製する, コピーする, 無性的に繁殖させる, 忠実になぞる
 cloned cattle クローン牛
 cloned cell phone クローン携帯（不正使用などの目的で, 1台ごとに携帯電話に割り振られた識別番号などを複製した携帯電話）
 cloned cow [dog, sheep] クローン牛［犬, 羊］
 cloning DNA クローン化したDNA, DNAの複製
 cloned humans with the same gene information 遺伝子情報が同一の複製（クローン）人間

clone 名 コピー人間, コピー生物, 複製品, 写し, 複写, まったく同じようなもの, ロボット, コンピュータの互換機, クローン

cloning 名 人口増殖, クローン作製術, コピー人間作製術, 分枝系, クローニング
 cloning procedures クローン作製技術
 cloning technology クローン技術

close 動 〈取引を〉終える, 引ける, 取り決める, 決める, 締め切る, 閉鎖する, 整理する, 清算する, 解散する
 close ranks 列を詰める, 結束する, 団結する
 close the [one's] books 〈決算などのために〉帳簿を締める, 株式名義の書換えを停止する

close 名 終値, 引け値, 引け, 終了
 at the close of business 営業終了時に, 営業時間の終了時に
 buy on close 引け値買い注文
 market on close 引け注文

closed-end 形 資本額固定の, 貸付け金額を固定した, 閉鎖式の, 多項選択式の, クローズド・エンド型の
 closed-end investment (trust) company 閉鎖式投資会社, 閉鎖式投資信託会社, クローズドエンド型投資会社
 closed-end management company クローズドエンド型投資会社
 closed-end mortgage 閉鎖担保, 閉鎖式抵当, クローズドエンド・モーゲージ（＝closed mort-

gage)

closed-end question 多項選択式質問, 限定選択肢質問

closing price 終値, 引け値 (⇒opening price)

closure 名 〈工場や店舗, 事業などの〉閉鎖, 封鎖, 閉幕, 閉会

cloud computing クラウド・コンピューティング

　クラウド・コンピューティングとは ⇒ インターネットを経由して, 手元のパソコンに取り込んでいない各種のソフトやデータを利用する仕組み。パソコン向けソフトのインストールや大規模なシステム更新の手間が省ける利点がある一方, 個人情報や企業経営に関するデータなどを事業者のサーバーに預ける必要がある。

clunker 名 オンボロ車[機械], ポンコツ車, さえないもの, 下手な人, 失敗, クランカー (=klunker)

　clunker rebates (program) 中古車下取り制度, 〈低燃費車への〉買替え助成制度 (⇒gas guzzler)

CMBS 〈米国の〉商業用不動産ローン担保証券, 商業用不動産担保証券 (commercial mortgage-backed securitiesの略)

coal burning 石炭消費量

coalition 名 連立政権, 連立, 連合, 合同, 一体化, 融合, 合体, 連携, 提携

　coalition against terrorism 対テロ連合
　coalition cabinet 連立内閣
　coalition forces 連合軍
　coalition government 連立政権 (=governing coalition)
　coalition of the willing 有志連合
　Coalition Provisional Authority イラクの連合国暫定当局 《略 CPA》

Coast Guard 米沿岸警備隊

cobalt-rich crusts コバルトリッチ・クラスト

coercion 名 強要, 強制, 強制力, 強迫, 抑圧, 威圧, 威力, 圧制, 専制, 弾圧政治

　external coercion 外部からの強制
　under coercion 強制されて

coffers 名 金庫, 資金, 財源, 資産, 国庫

　city's coffers 市の財源, 市の金庫, 市の財政
　government coffers 国庫
　the coffers of crime groups 暴力団の資金
　the coffers of the state 国庫, 国の財源, 国家財政 (=the state coffers)

co-finance 動 協調融資する

co-host 動 共同開催する

coincident indicator 景気一致指数, 一致指数 (=coincident index: 鉱工業生産指数, 百貨店販売額, 所定外労働時間指数など, 現状の景気の動きと同時期に並行して動く経済指標で, 景気の現状を示す)

cold shoulder 冷遇, 軽視, 冷たいあしらい, 冷淡な態度

Cold War 冷戦, 冷たい戦争

collaborative planning, forecasting and replenishment 需要予測と在庫補充のための共同事業 《略 CPFR》

collapse 動 経営破綻する(fail), 破綻する, 倒産する, 暴落する, 急減する, 崩壊する, 〈交渉などが〉決裂する

collapse 名 経営破綻, 破綻, 倒産, 崩壊, 倒壊, 決壊, 崩落, 暴落, 急落, 下落, 急減, 悪化, 〈計画などの〉挫折, 失敗, 頓挫, 〈神経などの〉衰弱, 虚脱, 虚脱状態

　a chain reaction of collapses 連鎖破綻
　collapse in demand 需要の急減, 需要の大幅落込み
　collapse in earnings 収益の落込み[急減], 大幅減益

collateral 名 担保, 担保物件, 担保品, 担保財産 (=mortgage, security), 形 副次的な, 付帯的な

　collateral company 傍系会社
　collateral damage 副次的被害, コラテラル・ダメージ(戦争やテロで発生する巻き添え被害)
　collateral export 見返り輸出(輸入の見返りとしてそれと同額の輸出をすること)
　collateral loan 担保貸付け, 抵当貸付け
　conditional collateral 付帯条件
　eligible collateral 適格担保
　import collateral 輸入担保
　maximal collateral 根抵当
　underlying collateral 担保物件, 裏付けとなる担保

collateralized debt obligation 債務担保証券 《略 CDO》

collect 動 集める, 収集する, 募集する, 〈債権や代金, 資源などを〉回収する, 〈年金や保険料, 税金などを〉徴収する, 〈預金などを〉獲得する, 支払いを受ける, 受け取る

collection 名 収集, 収集物, 収集品, 作品集, 〈債権や代金などの〉回収, 代金取立て, 集金, 募

集,〈年金や保険料,税金などの〉徴収,〈預金などの〉獲得,コレクション

collection place for ordinary large waste 粗大ゴミ置き場

collective 形 集団[団体]による,集団[団体]の,全体の,総合的な,包括的な,集産主義の
- **collective action** 集団行動
- **collective agreement** 〈労使間の〉団体協約
- **collective bargaining** 団体交渉
- **collective bargaining agreement** 労働協約,団体協約
- **collective decision** 集団意思決定
- **collective investment scheme** 集合投資計画,集合投資ファンド
- **collective self-defense right** 集団自衛権,集団的自衛権 (=the right to collective self-defense)
- **collective settlement** 集団和解
- **labor collective agreement** 労働協約

collusion 名 談合,不正,共謀,結託,癒着,なれ合い

collusive 形 共謀の,結託の,癒着した,もたれ合いの
- **collusive practices** 談合,なれ合いの関係,結託の関係,癒着構造
- **collusive ties** 癒着 (=collusive arrangements, collusive practices)

comb 動 徹底的に捜索する

combat 動 …と戦う,争う,…に反対する,反抗する,…を沈静化させる,…防止に努力する,…に対応する

combination 名 合併,連結,企業結合,企業連合,相互利益協定,結合,組合せ,関連性

combine 動 統合する,合併する,合算する,連結する,結合する,組み合わせる

combined 形 統合した,合併した,合算した,連結した,結合した,…の合算,…の合計[合計額]
- **combined operations** 事業統合
- **combined profits or losses** 損益の合算,損益の通算 (=combined profits and losses)
- **combined sales** 売上高の合計,全社合計の売上高,全社合わせての売上高

come clean about …についてすべてを明らかにする,すべてを打ち明ける,一切を自白する

come into force 実施される,発効する,法的実体を持つ

come out in favor of …賛成の態度を鮮明に打ち出す

come out with 発表する,公表する,打ち出す,出版する,製品化する,売り出す,出し抜けに…という

come up with …を提出する,提案する,打ち出す,出す,考え出す,見つける,思いつく,…を用意する,…に対応する,発表する,生産する

come-from-behind 形 逆転の,リードをひっくり返しての
- **come-from-behind win** 逆転勝ち
- **win a come-from-behind victory over** …に対して[…を相手に]逆転優勝する

comfort 名 やすらぎ,安心,安楽,快適,快適さ,心地よさ,不自由のない生活,慰め,慰安,便利な品
- **comfort letter** 財務内容に関する意見書,調査報告書,コンフォート・レター (=letter of comfort)
- **comfort letter for underwriter** 証券引受人への書簡,証券引受業者[幹事証券会社]に対する調査報告書 (=letter for underwriter)
- **comfort station** 公衆便所 (=public convenience)
- **comfort stop** 〈バス旅行の〉トイレ停車
- **comfort woman** 慰安婦,従軍慰安婦
- **the comfort of home** 家庭の便利な品,便利な家庭用品

coming year 来年度,来期,新年度

comment 名 意見,見解,論評,批評,解説,説明,解釈,注釈,〈…の〉反映,現われ,世評,うわさ,コメント
- **a matter of general comment** 一般のうわさの種
- **add comments or explanations** 注釈または説明を加える
- **closing comments** 締めくくりの意見
- **comment period** 意見公開期間
- **fair comment** もっともな意見
- **invite [arouse] comment** 人にとやかく言われる
- **letter of comment** 質問書
- **make outspoken comments on** …に対して遠慮なく論評する,…に対して率直に意見を言う,…に対して率直な意見を述べる
- **nice comments** 好意的な論評
- **positive comments** 肯定的な論評
- **suggestive comments** 示唆に富んだ解説

commerce 名 商取引,商業,通商,貿易,コマース

Commerce Department 〈米〉商務省

commercial 形 商業の, 商業上の, 商業的な, 商業ベースの, 通商の, 営利の, 民間の, 民放の, 大量生産型の, 量産的な, 市販の, 消費者向けの, 名 宣伝, 広告放送, コマーシャル

- **commercial bank** 商業銀行（米国の場合は, 連邦法または州法により認可を受けた銀行）, 都市銀行, 都銀, 市中銀行, 市銀, 銀行（商業銀行の主な業務は, 融資, 預金の受入れと外国為替）
- **Commercial Code** 商法
- **commercial flight** 民間航空機, 民間の定期航空便
- **commercial paper** 商業証券, 商業手形, コマーシャル・ペーパー《略 CP》
- **commercial trade** 商取引

commercialization 名 商品化, 製品化, 商業化, 実用化, 営利化

commercialize 動 商用化する, 商業化する, 実用化する, 営利化する, 商品化する, 産業化する

commission 動 権限を与える, 〈仕事などを〉委託する, 委任する, 任命する, 〈制作や執筆などを〉依頼する, 〈艦船などを〉就役させる

commission 名 手数料, 株式引受手数料, 報酬, 口銭, 委任, 委任状, 委託, 代理業務, 授与, 授権, 任命, 任命書, 委員会, 責務, 任務, 権限, 職権, 過失, 作為, 犯行, 〈犯罪などの〉実行, コミッション

- **brokerage commission** 株式委託売買手数料, 委託売買手数料, 委託手数料, 仲介手数料, ブローカー手数料（＝brokerage fee）
- **Commission on Civil Rights** 米公民権委員会
- **Commodity Futures Trading Commission** 米国の商品先物取引委員会
- **commission or omission** 作為または不作為
- **Consumer Product Safety Commission** 米消費製品安全委員会
- **Equal Employment Opportunity Commission** 米平等雇用機会委員会
- **Fair Trade Commission** 公正取引委員会
- **Federal Communications Commission** 米連邦通信委員会
- **Federal Election Commission** 米連邦選挙委員会
- **Federal Maritime Commission** 米連邦海運委員会
- **Federal Mine Safety and Health Review Commission** 米連邦鉱山安全・衛生審査委員会
- **Federal Trade Commission** 米連邦取引委員会
- **insurance commissions** 保険監督機関
- **Interamerican Association of Securities Commissions** 米州証券監督者協会
- **Interstate Commerce Commission** 米州際通商委員会
- **labor relations commission** 労働委員会
- **National Capital Planning Commission** 米首都計画委員会
- **Nuclear Regulatory Commission** 米原子力規制委員会
- **Occupational Safety and Health Review Commission** 米労働安全衛生審査委員会
- **Panama Canal Commission** 米パナマ運河委員会
- **Postal rate Commission** 米郵便料金委員会
- **United States International Trade Commission** 合衆国国際貿易委員会

commit 動 〈罪, 違法なことを〉行う, する, 犯す, 約束する, 公約する, 確約する, 取り組む, 関わる, 専念する, 全力を挙げる, 引き受ける, 委託する, 委任する, 付す, 〈法案や議案などを〉委員会に付託する, 〈刑務所, 精神病院などに〉送りこむ, 収容［収監］する, 〈…することを〉求める, 規定する, 〈時間や資金などを〉用いる, 支出する, 〈名声や立場などを〉危うくする

- **be committed for trial** 裁判にかけられる
- **be committed to** …する決意である, …すると誓う, …すると言明する, 〈主義, 主張に〉献身的である, 傾倒する, …に打ち込んでいる, …に尽力する, …に全力を挙げる（⇒committed to）
- **be commited to the cause of world peace [the peace of the world]** 世界平和のために貢献する
- **commit a bill** 法案を委員会に付託する, 法案［議案］を委員会の審議に付す
- **commit a crime** 罪を犯す, 犯罪行為をする
- **commit a lunatic to a mental hospital** 精神異常者を精神病院に収容する
- **commit a small amount of time to** …に時間を少し割く
- **commit a suspect (to prison)** 容疑者を拘留する
- **commit A to paper [writing]** Aを書き留める
- **commit lewd acts** みだらな［わいせつな］行為をする
- **commit oneself** 明確に意見を述べる, 明確に陳述する

commit oneself on …について自分[自己]の立場を明らかにする
commit oneself to …の立場を鮮明にする, …を明言する, …を引き受ける, 〈要求などを〉飲む, …を公約する, …する方針を定める, …に身を投ずる決意を固める, …に深く関与する[関わり合う]
commit oneself to a doctor's care 医者にかかる
commit oneself to a promise 確約する
commit to memory …を暗記する, 記憶にとどめる
commit troops to the front 部隊を前線に送り込む
repeatedly commit acts contrary to the public goods 公益に反する行為を繰り返して行う

commitment 名 姿勢, 参加, 取組, 関与, 献身, 熱心, 傾倒, 社会貢献, 約束, 言質, 確約, 約定, 公約, 誓約, 委任, 委託, 〈法案などの〉委員会付託, 立場の明確な表明, 協調融資団への参加意思表示, 融資参加の意向表明, 〈銀行の〉融資承認, 融資先, 売買約定, 売買契約, 取引契約, 契約債務, 契約義務, 未履行債務, 〈お金や時間などを特定の目的に〉利用する[使う]こと, 犯行, 拘留, 収監, 収監状, コミットメント
busy with commitments 用事で忙しい
get a commitment to …する約束を取り付ける
have a commitment to religion 宗教に傾倒している
have a financial commitment to …の支払いがある
make a commitment to one's jobs 仕事に真剣に取り組む
make substantial commitments to Asian markets アジア市場に本格的に進出する
strengthen commitment in the market 市場での足場を強化する

committed to …に取り組む, …に専念する, …に心する, …に入れ込む, …すると言明する, 明言する, …する決意である, …(の確保)に努める

committee 名 委員会, 協議会, 部会 (⇒House Standing Committees)
advisory committee 諮問委員会
audit committee 監査委員会
business conduct committee 業務委員会
committee on employee benefits 従業員待遇委員会
Committee on Government Operations 米政府活動委員会
Committee on House Administration 米下院管理委員会
committee on internal auditing 内部監査委員会
Committee on Rules 米議事運営委員会
Committee on the District of Columbia 米コロンビア特別区委員会
committee report 委員会報告
conference committee 米両院協議会, 米上下両院協議会
corporate value assessment special committee 企業価値評価特別委員会
executive committee 経営委員会, 執行委員会, 経営執行委員会
full committee 本委員会
internal audit and compliance committee 内部監査・法令遵守委員会
investigation committee 調査委員会
joint committee 合同委員会
majority committee table 米多数党委員会席
majority policy committee 米上院多数党政策委員会
management executive committee 経営執行委員会
managing committee 経営委員会
minority committee table 米少数党委員会席
Nomination and Compensation Committee 指名報酬委員会
operating committee 常務会
reference to committee 委員会に付託
select committee 特別委員会
social responsibility committee 社会的責任委員会
standing committee 常任委員会
standing joint committee 常任合同委員会
steering committee 運営委員会
subcommittee 小委員会
third party committee 第三者委員会
voluntary committee 任意の委員会

commodity 名 商品, 市況商品, 市況品, 日用品, 製品, 産品, 物品, 生産物, 財貨, 財
commodity exchange 商品取引, 商品取引所
commodity futures market 商品先物市場

common law コモンロー, 普通法, 英米法(英米においては, 判例法として形成されてきた慣習法体系を指す; ⇒equity law)
common-law husband [wife] 内縁の夫[妻]

common-law marriage 事実婚, 内縁関係
common share 普通株, 普通株式, 普通株資本金, 資本金 (＝common equity, common stock, ordinary share, ordinary stock:「普通株」は, 優先株(preferred share, preferred stock)や後配株(deferred share, deferred stock)のように特別の権利内容を持たない一般の株式のこと)
communication 名 通信, 伝達, 意思疎通, 相互理解, やり取り, 協議, 連絡, 手紙, コミュニケーション
 communication line 通信回線
 communication skills 自己表現能力, 自己表現技術
 communications privacy 通信の秘密
 executive communication 行政府書簡
 still picture communication 静止画像通信
 verbal communication 言葉による意思疎通, 言語コミュニケーション
 voice communication 音声通信
communique [**communiqué**] 名 声明, 公式発表, 公報, 声明書, コミュニケ
 issue [release] a joint communique 共同声明を発表する, 共同コミュニケを発表する
communism 名 共産主義, 共産主義体制
 anti-communism 反共産主義
communist 名 共産主義者, 共産党員, 形 共産主義の, 共産主義者の, 共産党の
 Communist [communist] bloc countries 共産圏諸国, 社会主義諸国
 Communist China 共産中国
community 名 地域, 地域社会, 地域共同体, 共同社会, 共同体, 社会, 一般社会, 団体, 業界, …界, 大衆, 一体感, 帰属意識, 共通性, 一致(財産などの)共有, コミュニティ (⇒international community)
 community affairs 地域社会の問題, 地域活動
 community antenna television 有線テレビ, ケーブル・テレビ《略 CATV》
 community care 地域保険医療制度
 community charge 地方負担金
 community college 地域短期大学, コミュニティ・カレッジ
 community home [house] 少年院, 感化院
 community media コミュニティ・メディア(地方紙やタウン誌, CATVなど地域社会を対象にしたメディア)
 community organization 社会事業団体
 community property 〈夫婦の〉共有財産
 community reception 共同受信 (＝community antenna reception)
 local community 地域社会, 地方公共団体, 地域住民
 rural [farming] community 農村共同体, 農村社会, 農村, 地方都市
 scientific community 科学界
 sense of community 連帯感
commuter 名 通勤者, 通学者, コミューター
 commuter belt 通勤圏, 通勤者居住地域, 近郊住宅街 (＝commuterland)
 commuter car 通勤用[通学用]自動車
 commuter pass 通勤・通学用定期券
 commuter ticket 定期券, 回数券
company 名 会社, 企業, 社団, カンパニー
 company contract 会社の定款
 company demand 自社需要
 company formation 会社設立, 会社創業
 statutory company 国策会社
comparable figures 比較可能数値 (＝corresponding figures)
compared to a year earlier 前年比で, 前期比で, 前年同期比で
compared with …と比べて, …に対して, …比で (＝compared to)
compatibility 名 互換性, 適合性, 両立性, 両立, 共存, コンパチビリティ
 forward compatibility 上位互換性, 上位互換 (＝upper compatibility, upward compatibility)
 full compatibility 完全互換性, 完全互換
 lower compatibility 下位互換性 (＝backward compatibility, downward compatibility)
compatible 形 互換性がある, 適合性がある, …対応の, コンパチブル[コンパティブル]
compensated dating 援助交際
compensation 名 報酬, 対価, 給与, 報償, 補償, 賠償, 代償, 報償金, 補償金, 賠償金, 慰謝料
 claim compensation from …に賠償金を請求する
 compensation for losses 損害補償, 損害賠償金
 seek compensation from …に補償を求める, …に賠償請求する (＝claim compensation from)
compensatory 形 補償の, 賠償の, 代償の, 埋め合わせの, 補整的

compensatory balances 歩積み両建て預金
compensatory budget 補正予算
compensatory damages 損害賠償, 補償的損害賠償(金), 填補損害賠償(金)
compensatory deposit 補償預金, 両建て預金, 歩積み(両建て)預金
compensatory error 相殺誤差
compensatory expenditure 補整的支出
compensatory finance 補整の財政, 補償融資
compensatory financing 補償融資, 補償融資制度
compensatory financing facility 補償融資, 輸出変動補償融資, 輸出変動補償融資制度
compensatory fiscal policy 補整的財政政策
compensatory goods 報奨物資
compensatory payment 補償金, 賠償金, 補償支払い
compensatory principle 〈税の〉受益者負担原則 (=benefit principle)
compensatory spending policy 補整的支出政策
compensatory stock option 補整的自社株購入権
compensatory tariff 相殺関税
compensatory tax policy 補整的租税政策
compensatory time 代休
compete 動 競争する, 競う, 争う, 張り合う, 渡り合う, 競合する
competing ideas 相容れない考え, 相反する考え
competition 名 競争, 競合, 競業, 競争相手, ライバル
　fair competition 適正な競争, 公正競争
　homogeneous competition 同質的競争
　oligopolistic competition 寡占的競争
　unfair competition 不正競争
competitive 形 競争力のある, 他社に負けない, 競争的, 競争上の, 安い, 低コストの (⇒cost-competitive)
　competitive auction [bid, bidding, tender] 競争入札
　competitive bid 競争入札 (=competitive bidding, competitive tender)
　competitive cost position コスト競争力
　competitive demand 競争的需要
　competitive depreciation 切下げ競争
　competitive edge 競争力, 競争上の優位, 競争上の優位性, 競争力での優位
　competitive environment 競争環境
　competitive factor 競争要因
　competitive financing 低コストの資金調達
　competitive firm 競争的企業
　competitive forces 競争原理
　competitive industry 競争的産業
　competitive market 競争的な市場
　competitive opportunities 競争の機会
　competitive pressure [threat] 競争圧力
　competitive price 競争価格, 競争値段, 低価格, 安い価格・値段
　competitive pricing strategy 競争力のある価格戦略
　competitive trends 競争環境
　price-competitive 価格競争力がある
competitive advantage 競争上の優位, 競争上の優位性, 競争力, 比較優位, 比較優位性, 競争有利性
　gain a greater competitive advantage 競争力を拡大する
　hold a competitive advantage 競争上の優位を保つ
　increase one's competitive advantage …の競争上の優位性を高める, …の競争上の優位を強化する
competitiveness 名 競争力, 競争 (⇒market competitiveness)
　competitiveness effect 競争力効果
　economic competitiveness 経済競争力
　gain competitiveness 競争力を獲得する, 競争力をつける, 競争力を増す
　global competitiveness 国際競争力 (=international competitiveness)
　increase competitiveness 競争力を高める, 競争力を強める (=enhance competitiveness, improve competitiveness)
　lose competitiveness 競争力を失う (=lose competitive edge)
　overseas price competitiveness 海外での価格競争力
　promote competitiveness 競争力を高める, 競争力を増進する
　reduce competitiveness 競争力を低下させる (=erode competitiveness)
　World Competitiveness Yearbook 世界競争力年鑑
competitor 名 競争相手, 競合他社, 同業者, ライバル企業, ライバル

compile 動 編集する, 編纂する, 作成する, 策定する, まとめる, 〈予算などを〉編成する, 集計する, 収集する, 機械語に翻訳する, コンパイルする, 得点を重ねる, 〈リードを〉広げる

complaint 名 苦情, 苦情の申立て, 不平, 不満, 抗議, クレーム, 告訴
- **cross-complaint** 逆提訴
- **file [lodge] a complaint with** …に苦情を申し立てる, …に告訴する, …に提訴する, …に訴えを起こす（＝make a complaint to）
- **file a criminal complaint against A with B** AについてBに告訴状を提出する, AをBに刑事告発する
- **lodge [make] a complaint A with B** AをBに告訴する

complementarity 名 相互補完性, 相互補足性, 補完性, 補足性

complementary 形 補完的な, 相互補完的な, 相互に補足し合う, 相補的な
- **commercial complementary loan** 商業補完ローン
- **complementary capital** 自己資本の補完的項目
- **complementary demand** 補完的需要, 相補的需要, 相互需要（＝reciprocal demand）
- **complementary economies** 相互補完関係にある経済, 経済の相互補完
- **complementary effect** 補完性効果（＝complementarity effect）
- **complementary factor** 補完的要因
- **complementary financing** 補完的融資, 補完融資
- **complementary goods** 補完財, 補完製品
- **complementary markets** 補完的市場
- **complementary pricing** 補完的価格設定
- **complementary product lines** 補完的製品ライン
- **complementary reinforcement** 補足的補強効果
- **complementary supply** 相互供給
- **complementary trade** 相補貿易

completion 名 完成, 完了, 完工, 達成, 成就, 成立, 満期
- **completion bond** 完成保証
- **completion ceremony** 落成式, 完工式
- **completion guarantee** 工事の完成保証
- **completion of a contract** 契約の成立
- **completion of the swap** スワップの満期
- **construction completion** 完工
- **home completion** 住宅の完工
- **job completion** 作業完了
- **percentage of completion** 完成割合, 進行, 工事進行

complex 名 複合体, 集合体, 施設群（facilities）, コンビナート, 複合ビル, 共同ビル, 大型ビル, 集合建築, 複合建築, 固定観念, 強迫観念, …恐怖症, 強い嫌悪感, コンプレックス
- **apartment complex** アパート団地, 団地
- **commercial complex** 複合商業施設
- **educational-industrial complex** 産学協同
- **factory complex** 工場群
- **housing complex** 団地
- **industrial complex** 工業団地, コングロマリット
- **inferiority complex** 劣等感
- **military-industrial complex** 軍産複合体
- **office complex** オフィスビル
- **persecution complex** 強迫観念
- **petrochemical complex** 石油化学コンビナート
- **residential complex** 住居用ビル（＝housing complex）
- **superiority complex** 優越感
- **training complex** 研修施設

compliance 名 承諾, 受諾, 遵守, 準拠性, 適合, 服従, コンプライアンス

compound 名 化合物, 合成物, 混合物, 複合体, 構内, 敷地, 居住区域, 壁などに囲まれた建物, 捕虜収容所
- **carbon compounds** 炭素化合物
- **ex customs compound** 通関渡し条件
- **organic compounds** 有機化合物
- **volatile compounds** 揮発性化合物

comprehensive 形 総合的な, 包括的な, 全面的な, 広範な, 幅広い
- **comprehensive antideflationary measures** 総合デフレ対策
- **comprehensive business tie-up** 包括的業務提携
- **comprehensive economic package plan** 総合経済対策
- **Comprehensive Employment and Training Act** 包括的雇用・訓練法《略 CETA》
- **comprehensive financial services** 総合金融サービス
- **comprehensive income** 包括利益, 包括的利益
- **Comprehensive Nuclear Test Ban Treaty** 核実験全面禁止条約《略 CTBT》
- **comprehensive package of economic mea-**

sures 包括的経済対策
comprehensive quantitative easing measures 全面的な量的緩和策
Comprehensive Test Ban Treaty 実験全面禁止条約《略 CTBT》

compromise 名 妥協, 譲り合い, 和解, 示談, 歩み寄り, 折衷, 妥協の結果, 妥協の産物, 妥協案, 折衷案, 中道, 中間, 中間物, どっちつかずのもの, 雑種, 〈名誉などを〉危うくすること, 損なうもの, 〈屈辱的な〉譲歩
  a compromise between a figure and a pictire 図案とも絵ともつかぬもの
  a compromise between Japanese and foreign styles 和洋折衷
  a compromise between two measures 折衷案
  a compromise of one's honor …の名誉を危うくする
  a compromise of principles 主義の譲歩
  a compromise plan 妥協案, 和解案
  a compromise tariff 妥協関税
  a happy compromise 円満解決
  a weak compromise 効果不十分な譲歩, 骨抜きの譲歩
  by compromise 妥協して
  effect a compromise between A and B AとBの間で示談を成立させる
  emerge as a compromise 妥協案として注目される, 和解案として浮上する, 妥協の産物である
  make [arrange] a compromise with …と妥協をする, …に歩み寄る
  make a compromise with one's principles …の主義を曲げる
  no room for compromise 妥協の余地がないこと
  political compromises 政治的妥協
  reach a compromise 妥協[和解]が成立する
  try to reach a compromise 妥協を得ようとする
  without compromise of one's dignity …の面目を損なわずに

computer 名 電算機, 電子計算機, コンピュータ
  computer chips 集積回路, 半導体, コンピュータ・チップ
  computer system コンピュータ・システム
  computer system's breakdown コンピュータ・システムの障害, システム障害（＝computer failure, computer malfunction)
  computer virus コンピュータ・ウイルス, ウイルス

computing 名 計算, 演算, コンピュータ処理, コンピュータ利用, コンピュータ, コンピューティング（⇒cloud computing）
  computing center 計算センター
  computing devices コンピュータ端末
  computing dictionary コンピュータ辞書
  computing power 総合的情報処理能力, コンピューティング能力
  computing solution service 業務処理・問題解決サービス
  computing speed 演算時間
  consumer computing 消費者によるコンピュータ利用
  distributed computing 分散処理, 分散コンピューティング

concealing income 所得隠し

concentrate 動 集中する, 集中させる, 全力を傾ける, 力を注ぐ, …に照準を合わせる, …に特化する

concentration 名 集中, 集中力, 専念, 専心, 精神集中, 集積, 集結, 濃縮, 濃度
  asset concentration 資産集中
  bank concentration 銀行集中
  business concentration 事業集中, 事業の集中度, 事業の統合
  capital concentration 資本集中, 資本の集積 （＝concentration of capital）
  concentration banking 銀行取引の集中化, 集中銀行制
  concentration camp 強制収容所
  concentration of industry 産業の集中
  concentration of ownership 所有権の集中
  concentration of wealth 富の集中
  concentration ratio 集中度, 集中率
  degree of seller concentration 売り手集中度
  economies of concentration 集積利益
  foreign exchange concentration clearing system 外国為替集中決済制度
  income concentration 所得集中
  industrial concentration 産業の集中, 工業集中
  market concentration 市場集中
  production concentration ratio 生産集中度, 生産集積度
  risk concentration management リスクの集中管理
  selection and concentration 選択と集中

urban concentration 都市集中
conception certificate 懐妊の証明書
concern 動 …に関係する, 利害関係がある, 影響を与える, 重要である
- **as concerns A** Aについては, Aに関しては, Aについて言えば, Aに言わせれば（＝where A is concerned）
- **be concerned about** …を心配している, …を懸念[心配]する, …に不安[懸念]を抱いている, …を警戒する, …を気遣う, …に配慮する
- **be concerned for** …に配慮する
- **be concerned to** …したいと思っている[願っている]
- **be concerned with [in]** …に関心を持っている[関心を示す, 関心を向ける], …に注意を注ぐ, …に関係がある
- **concerned parties** 利害関係人[関係者], 関係当事者, 影響を受けた当事者
- **so [as] far as A is concerned** Aに関するかぎり
- **the circles concerned** 関係方面
- **the concerned countries** 関係国
- **the parties concerned** 当事者, 利害関係者, 関係者

concern 名 関心, 関心事, 関係, 利害関係, 心配, 懸念, 懸念材料, 不安, 不安材料, 配慮, 問題, 会社, 企業, 企業体, 事業, 業務, 責務, 任務, 重要性
- **broader concerns such as the global financial crisis** 世界的な金融危機といった広域の懸念材料
- **consumer concerns** 消費者問題, 消費者のニーズ
- **credit concerns** 信用リスクに対する懸念, 信用リスク懸念, 信用力への懸念, 信用不安
- **have concern in** …に出資している
- **have no concern with** …とは何の関係もない
- **inflationary concern** インフレ懸念, インフレに対する懸念
- **internal concerns** 国内問題
- **political concerns** 政局不安, 政局に対する不安
- **primary concern** 最大の関心事
- **security concerns on the Korean peninsula** 朝鮮半島の安全保障上の懸念
- **serious concerns** 大きな懸念材料
- **strategic concerns** 戦略的観点

concert 名 一致, 協力, 協調, 提携, 音楽会, 演奏会, コンサート
- **charity [benefit] concert** 慈善コンサート
- **concert parties** 共謀行為者
- **concert tour** 演奏旅行
- **in concert with** …と協同で, …と協力して, …と提携して, …と協調して, …と歩調を合わせて, …の波に乗って

concerted 形 一致した, 一致協力した, 協調した, 協調的, 協力して行う, 共同による, 申し合わせた, 一斉の, 熱心な, 集中的な
- **concerted action** 協調行動, 共同行為
- **concerted (market) intervention** 協調介入, 協調市場介入
- **concerted raid on** …の一斉手入れ, …に対する一斉捜査
- **make a concerted effort** 一斉に進める
- **take concerted action with** …と協調行動を取る, …と一致した行動を取る

concession 名 権利, 特権, 免許, 許可, 認可, 譲歩, 割引, 割引料金, 売り場, 売店, 販売権, 営業権, 営業スペース, 利権, 権益
- **duty [tariff] concession** 関税譲許, 関税譲歩（＝concession of tariff）
- **oil field concessions** 油田の権益
- **pricing concession** 値下げ
- **reciprocal concession** 相互互恵
- **selling concession** 販売手数料
- **tax concession** 租税譲許, 税制優遇措置

condemn 動 非難する, 激しく非難する, 責める, 不治と宣告する, 見放す, 有罪の判決を出す, 有罪を宣告する, 宣言[宣告]する, 判定する, 〈公用に土地などを〉没収する[接収する]
- **be condemned for** …を激しく非難される, …を責められる
- **be condemned to** …するよう強いられる, …する運命にある
- **condemn ... for murder** …に殺人罪を宣告する
- **condemn ... to death** …に死刑を宣告する
- **line up to condemn** 一斉に非難する

condemnation 名 激しい非難, 非難, 非難声明, 非難の理由[根拠], 使用不適の申し渡し[認定], 治療不能の宣告, 有罪宣告, 有罪判決, 接収, 収用, 公用収用, 公用収用手続き, 廃棄
- **condemnation or dedication** 公用収用または公用地供与
- **condemnation proceeds** 収用補償金
- **official condemnation** 公式の非難声明

condition 名 条件, 状態, 状況, 情勢, 動向, 環境

business condition index 景気動向指数
economic conditions 経済状態, 経済状況, 経済情勢, 景気
income conditions 所得動向
labor conditions 労働条件 (＝working conditions)
operating conditions 事業環境
terms and conditions 条件
working conditions 労働条件, 働く環境

Condominium Ownership Law 建物区分所有法

conduct 名 行動, 行為, 行い, 態度, 振る舞い, 管理, 経営, 処理, 処置, 運営, 運営方法, 指導, 案内, 指針, 実施, 施行, 遂行
market conducts 市場行動
rules of conduct 行為規則, 紀律規則
unethical professional conduct 職業倫理違反行為

Confederation of Japan Automobile Workers' Union 全日本自動車産業労働組合総連合会, 自動車総連

conference 名 会議, 協議, 会談, 相談, 打合せ, 協議会, 両院協議会, 協議連盟, 運動団体連盟, 海運同盟 (＝conferencing)
conference call 電話会議, 電話による協議, 会議電話
conference committee 米両院協議会, 米上下両院協議会
Conference on Security and Cooperation in Europe 全欧安保協力会議《略 CSCE》(1995年, 欧州安保協力機構(Organization for Security and Cooperation in Europe)に改称)
conference procedure 米両院協議会手続き
conference report 米両院協議会の報告[報告書]
conference tariff 海運同盟運賃表
emergency conference call 緊急電話会議
European Conference 欧州会議
general conference 総会
group discussion conference 集団討議方式
have [hold] a conference with …と協議する
joint labor-management conference system 労使協議制
meet at the conference 会議の席につく
meet in conference 協議会を開く
news [press] conference 記者会見
shipping conference 海運同盟
sit in conference 協議する

Conference Board コンファレンス・ボード (米民間の代表的経済調査機関)
Conference Board [Board's] consumer confidence index コンファレンス・ボード消費者信頼感指数
Conference Board [Board's] survey of buying plan コンファレンス・ボードの購買計画指数

confidence 名 信頼, 信用, 信認, 信任, 信頼度, 自信, 消費者マインド, 企業心理, 景況感, 秘密, 内密, 秘密保持
public confidence in the Japanese financial system 日本の金融システムに対する国民の信頼
rise [increase] in confidence 消費者マインドの向上, 消費意欲の向上 (＝improvement in consumer confidence)
weak confidence 消費者マインドの冷え込み (＝depressed [lower] consumer confidence)

confidentiality of personal information 個人情報の秘密遵守

confiscate 動 押収する, 没収する, 〈財産を〉差し押さえる

conflict 名 〈利害・意見などの〉衝突, 争い, 争議, 論争, 紛争, 戦い, 戦闘, 対立, 矛盾, 不一致, 抵触, 葛藤, 板ばさみ
armed conflict 武力衝突, 軍事紛争
conflict of interest [interests] 利害の対立, 利害の不一致, 利害の抵触, 利害の衝突, 利益相反, 利益相反行為
conflict of laws 法の抵触, 抵触法, 衝突法, 国際私法, 州際私法
debt conflicts 債権問題
industrial conflicts 労使紛争, 労使闘争
trade conflict 貿易摩擦, 貿易紛争

conflicting 形 衝突する, 相争う, 矛盾する, 相反する, つじつまの合わない, 一致しない
conflicting interests 対立する利害, 利害の対立
conflicting parties 相争う政党, 相争う党派
conflicting reports 錯綜する報道, 入り乱れる報道, 矛盾する記事

confusion 名 混乱, 混乱状態, 騒動, 当惑, 混同, 取り違え
confusion in (the) financial markets 金融市場の混乱
confusion of debts 債務の混同
confusion of goods 物品の混和
the confusion of fact and fiction 事実と虚

構の混同, 事実と虚構の区別がつかないこと

congenital 形 先天的な, 先天性の, 生まれつきの

conglomerate 名 コングロマリット, 巨大複合企業, 複合企業, 複合企業体, 複合体, 多角化企業, 企業グループ (＝conglomerate company)
  conglomerate diversification コングロマリット的多角化 (＝vertical diversification)
  conglomerate integration 多角的統合, コングロマリット型統合, コングロマリット統合
  conglomerate merger 複合的合併, コングロマリット合併
  financial conglomerate 金融複合企業体, 金融複合体, 金融コングロマリット[複合体]

congress 名 会議, 学会, 大会, コングレス
  Congress of Industrial Organizations 米産業別労働組合会議《略 CIO》
  Congress of Racial Equality 人権平等会議
  medical congress 医学学会
  National People's Congress 〈中国の〉全国人民代表(者)大会, 全人代

Congress 名 〈米国の〉議会, 連邦議会, コングレス (⇒Diet, Parliament, Senate)

> 米議会 ⊃ 米国の議会は, 上院(the Senate)と下院(the House of Representatives)から成る。定員は上院が100名(各州2名)で, 下院は435名(各州の人口に応じて選出)。上院は条約の批准権, 大統領の感触任命に対する同意権を持ち, 下院は歳入法案の先議権を持つ。法案は, 上下両院を通過した後, 大統領が署名して法律となる。

  Acts of Congress 連邦法
  budget legislation through Congress 議会の予算審議
  call Congress together 議会を招集する
  Congress of the United States 米連邦議会
  each House of Congress 上院と下院
  Librarian of Congress 米議会図書館長
  Library of Congress 米議会図書館
  Republicans in Congress 議会共和党
  Third House of Congress 米議会の第三院(米上下両院協議会のこと)

congressional 形 米国議会の(Congressional), 国会の, 会議の
  congressional advisory committee 国会諮問委員会
  Congressional approval 議会の承認
  congressional budget 国会予算
  Congressional Budget Office 米議会予算局《略 CBO》
  Congressional delegation 米議会議員団
  Congressional district 米下院議員選挙区
  congressional-executive agreement 連邦議会承認の行政協定
  Congressional hearing 議会の聴聞会[公聴会]
  Congressional Information Service 議会情報サービス
  Congressional Leader 米議会指導者
  Congressional Record 議会議事録, 連邦議会議事録
  Congressional Republicans 米下院の共和党議員
  Congressional Research Service 議会調査部
  congressional staffer 米議会スタッフ(米上下両院議員の個人的スタッフ, 各種委員会の事務局スタッフなどを指す)
  Congressional support 議会の支持

Congressman [**congressman**] 名 〈米〉下院議員, 連邦議会委員 (＝member of the House of the Representatives: 女性はCongresswoman, congresswoman)

Congressperson [**congressperson**] 名 〈米〉下院議員

connection 名 関係, 関連, つながり, 脈絡, 前後関係, 縁故, 親戚, 縁故者, 人脈, コネ, 取引先, 取引業者, 接続, 連絡, 密輸組織, 秘密犯罪組織, 麻薬密売人
  business connection 取引関係
  causal connection 因果関係
  fiscal connection 財政連結
  government-business connection 官民一体
  trade connections 取引業者
  unregistered marriage connection 内縁関係

-conscious 形 …を意識した, …を重視した, …への意識[関心]が高い, …に敏感な, …に神経質な, …にこだわる
  beauty-conscious 美容に神経質な
  brand-conscious ブランドにこだわる, ブランド意識が強い
  credit-conscious 信用力を重視する
  environmentally-conscious 環境重視の, 環境のことを考えている
  money-conscious カネに敏感な
  self-conscious 自意識過剰の, 自己を気にする, 人前を気にする, 恥ずかしがる, 落ち着かない

consecutive 形 連続した, 通しの, 論理の一貫

した

consensus 名 合意, 総意, 同意, 一致した意見, 意見の一致, 大多数の意見, コンセンサス
 consensus building コンセンサス作り, 根回し
 consensus of opinions 意見の一致
 consensus of testimony 証言の一致
 general consensus 一般的な見方, 国民の合意
 national consensus 国民の合意, 国民的合意, ナショナル・コンセンサス
 reach [achieve] a consensus on …について意見の一致を見る, に関して合意に達する

consent 名 同意, 承諾, 承認, 合意, 意見の一致, 許可, 同意書, コンセント
 age of consent 承諾年齢
 by [with] one consent 満場一致で
 Consent Calendar 〈米議会の〉合意的議事日程
 consent dividend 見なし配当, コンセント配当
 consent letter 同意書簡, コンセント・レター (= consent statement in published prospectuses:1度発行した監査報告書の別の目的への使用を許可するときなどに使われる書簡)
 consent order 同意命令
 informed consent 十分な説明に基づく同意, 説明を受けた上での承諾[同意], 口頭でなく文書による同意, インフォームド・コンセント
 mutual consent 双方の同意, 相互的同意, 合意
 unanimous consent 全会一致, 全会一致の承認

conservation 名 保全, 保護, 管理, 節約, 天然資源保護, 自然保護
 conservation area 保全地区[地域], 保護地域[区域]
 conservation of nature 自然保護, 自然環境保全
 conservation works 自然保護事業
 energy conservation エネルギー節約, エネルギー保存, 省エネ
 environmental conservation 環境保護, 環境保全
 land conservation 国土保全
 oil conservation 石油節約
 river conservation 治水
 water conservation 水質管理, 水質保全

conservative 形 保守主義の, 保守的な, 保守党の, 右派の, 右翼の, 地味な, 控え目な, おとなしい, 慎重な, 手堅い, 内輪の, 古風な, 伝統的な, 名 保守主義者, 保守党員(Conservative), 保守派(conservatives) (⇒leftist)
 conservative accounting policy 保守的な会計方針
 conservative accounting practices 保守的な会計慣行
 conservative balance sheets 堅実な財務内容
 conservative estimate 控え目な見積り, 内輪の見積り, 控え目な推定
 conservative forces 保守勢力
 conservative gearing 低めの負債比率
 conservative government 保守政権
 conservative management 手堅い経営, 堅実な経営, 慎重な経営
 Conservative Party 〈英国の〉保守党
 conservative politician 保守党の政治家, 保守派の政治家
 conservative purchase 買い控え
 Energy Policy and Conservative Act 燃料規制法

consideration 名 対価, 代金, 手付け金, 〈契約の〉約因, 考慮
 consideration clause 対価条項
 consideration of tenders 入札の検討
 merger consideration 合併の対価
 political considerations 政治的配慮, 政治的な配慮

consistent with …と一致する, …と整合する, …と矛盾しない, …と一貫性がある

consolation prize 残念賞, 見返り

consolidate 動 整理統合する, 統合する, 合併する, 一元化する, 集約する, 整理する, 強化する, 連結する

consolidated 形 整理統合した, 統合した, 一本化した, 一元化した, 連結対象の, 連結した, 連結ベースの, 連結決算の
 consolidated affiliate 連結対象の関連会社, 連結対象の持ち分法適用会社
 consolidated basis 連結ベース (= group basis)
 consolidated tax return 連結納税申告, 連結納税申告書 (= consolidated return)

consolidation 名 統合, 企業統合, 新設合併, 整理, 再編, 強化, 地固め, 連結, 連結決算, 混載輸送
 budget consolidation 財政建て直し
 consolidation within the industry 業界再編, 業界の再編成
 economic consolidation 経済調整
 facility consolidation 工場統廃合

staff consolidation 人員整理
stock [share] consolidation 株式併合
consortium 名 共同事業体, 共同連合体, 国際借款団, 〈銀行の〉協調融資団, 債権国会議, コンソーシアム
conspiracy 名 陰謀, 共謀, 謀議, 共同謀議, 陰謀団
 a cloak and-dagger conspiracy スパイ活動の陰謀, スパイ作戦
 be charged with conspiracy to …する謀議で告訴される
 be in conspiracy to escape 共謀して逃げる
 conspiracy charges 共謀罪
 conspiracy of silence 沈黙の申し合わせ, 黙殺の申し合わせ
 conspiracy theory 陰謀説, 共謀説
 form a conspiracy against one's life …を殺そうと共謀する
 in conspiracy with …と共謀して
 on the conspiracy charges 共謀罪で
constitution 名 憲法, 構造, 構成, 組織
 Constitution Day 〈日本の〉憲法記念日
 Constitution of the United States アメリカ合衆国憲法(1789年3月4日に発効)
constitutional monarch 立憲君主
constraint 名 強制, 束縛, 圧迫, 制限, 制約, 限界, 拘束, 抑制, 締め付け, 阻害要因, 制約要因, 気がね, 遠慮
 act under constraint 強制されて行動する
 budget [budgetary] constraints 予算の制約, 予算の制限
 growth constraint 成長の阻害要因
 labor constraints 人手不足
 leverage constraints 借入制限, 借入制限条項
 skill constraint 技術的制約
 social constraints 社会的束縛, 社会の束縛, 社会的制約
 supply-side [supply] constraints 供給面の制約, 供給のボトルネック
construction 名 建設, 建築, 建造, 建設工事, 工事, 建造物, 構築物, 〈契約や条項の〉解釈(「解釈する」の意味 動 はconstrue)
 Construction and Transport Ministry 国土交通省
 construction contract 工事契約, 建設契約
 construction and performance 解釈と履行
consultancy 名 コンサルタント会社, コンサルタント業[機関], 相談, コンサルティング, 顧問医師の職[地位], 専門的意見[アドバイス]
consultation 名 相談, 諮問, 協議, コンサルティング・サービス, 審議, 協議会, 審議会, 会議, 参考, 参照, 調査, 診察, 〈弁護士の〉鑑定, コンサルテーション
 annual consultation 年次協議, 年次会議
 consultation body 協議機関, 諮問機関
 consultation papers 公開諮問文書
 joint consultation 労使協議
 legal consultation 訴訟協議
consulting firm コンサルタント会社
consume 動 消費する, 消耗する, 浪費する, 飲む, 食べる
 average propensity to consume 平均消費性向
 equilibrium propensity to consume 均衡消費性向
 marginal propensity to consume 限界消費性向
 private propensity to consume 民間消費性向
consumer 名 消費者, コンシューマー
 association of consumers 消費者組合
 consumer acceptance 消費者承認, 需要者承諾
 consumer characteristics 消費者特性
 consumer credit 消費者信用(分割払い, つけ, 短期ローンなど)
 consumer demand 消費者需要, 消費需要, 民間需要, 需要, 実需, 消費者ニーズ
 consumer electronics 家電, 家電製品, 情報家電, 民生用電子機器, 消費者向けエレクトロニクス[電子機器]
 consumer industry 消費財産業
 consumer market 消費者市場, 消費市場
 consumer movement 消費者運動
 consumer price survey 消費者物価調査
 consumer prices 消費者物価, 消費者物価指数
 Consumer Reports コンシューマー・リポート[レポート](米国の品質調査専門誌)
 consumer resistance 消費者の購買拒否 (= sales resistance)
 consumer sentiment 消費者心理(consumer's sentiment), 消費者マインド, 消費マインド, 消費意欲, 消費者態度指数(consumer sentiment index)
 low consumer mind 消費者信頼感が低いこと, 消費意欲が弱いこと

consumer confidence 消費者の信頼, 消費者信頼感, 消費者心理, 消費者マインド, 消費意欲
  consumer confidence index [data] 消費者信頼感指数, 消費者態度指数, 消費者マインド指数
  consumer confidence survey 消費者マインド調査, 消費者信頼感指数, 消費者マインド指数
consumer goods 消費財, 消費物資, 消費者用品 (＝consumers' goods, consumer product)
  consumer goods exports 消費財の輸出
  fast-moving consumer goods 高回転消費財《略 FMCG》
  finished consumer goods 完成消費財
  general consumer goods 一般消費財
consumer price index 消費者物価指数《略 CPI》(＝the key gauge of consumer prices)

米国の消費者物価指数

Consumer Price Index for All Urban Consumers	全都市消費者物価指数《略 CPI-U》
Consumer Price Index for Urban Wage Earners and Clerical Workers	都市賃金労働者消費者物価指数《略 CPI-W》

consumer product 消費者製品, 消費財, 民生用製品, 民生機器
  Consumer Product Safety Act 消費者製品安全法
  Consumer Product Safety Commission 消費者製品安全委員会
consumer spending 消費者支出, 個人消費, 家計部門の支出 (＝consumer expenditure, consumption expenditure)
  consumer spending growth 個人消費[消費支出]の伸び, 個人消費の拡大[増加] (＝growth in consumer spending, increased consumer spending)
  real consumer spending 実質消費支出
Consumers Union 全米消費者同盟
consumption 名 消費, 個人消費, 消費量, 消費高, 消費額, 消費支出, 消耗, 減耗, 肺結核
  collective consumption 共同消費
  consumption account 消費勘定
  consumption expenditure 消費支出
  consumption outlay 消費支出
  consumption plays 消費関連銘柄
  consumption structure 消費構造
  current consumption 経常消費, 現行消費
  family consumption 家計消費
  government consumption 政府消費
  gross domestic consumption 国内総消費
  household consumption 家計消費, 家計部門消費
  per capita consumption 1人当たり消費
  personal [individual, private] consumption 個人消費, 個人的消費
  public consumption 政府消費支出
  total consumption 総消費 (＝aggregate consumption)
consumption tax 消費税
  consumption tax rate 消費税率
  consumption transfer tax 消費譲渡税
  general consumption tax 一般消費税
contender 名 競争相手, 対抗馬, 競争チーム, 挑戦者, 論争者, 主張者, 候補者, ライバル
  contender to lead-manage the deal 主幹事候補
  leading contender 有力候補
content 名 〈情報・情報サービスの〉内容, 情報の中身, 情報, 趣旨, 要旨, 著作物, 〈ラジオやテレビの〉番組, 番組の内容, 事業, 収入源, 含有量, 容量, 容積, 体積, 面積, 広さ, 産出量, 満足, コンテンツ (⇒local content)
  content analysis 内容分析
  content-certified mail 内容証明郵便
  content production コンテンツ作成, コンテンツの制作 (＝production of content)
  contents note 包装の内容一覧表
  contents unknown clause 内容不知条項
  domestic content 国内部品調達比率, ドメスティック・コンテント
  export content 輸出含有量
  import content 輸入含有量
  job content 職務・仕事の内容
  labor content 労働価値, 加工価値
  loss content 回収不能, 信用損失
  loss content of assets 資産減価
  operative content 実効性
  regulation of illegal and harmful contents 違法有害コンテンツ規制
  resource content 資源含有量
contention 名 争い, 論争, 論点, 議論, 口論, 主張, 意見, 見方, 意見の対立, 競争, 〈通信の〉競合, コンテンション
  a bone of contention 争いのもと, 争いの種, 口論の原因, 不和の種
  in contention 論争中の, 競争中の

support the contention この見方を裏付ける
the main points of contention in court 法廷での主な争点
contentious 形 論争を引き起こす，議論を呼ぶ，論争好きな，論争的，異論のある，係争中の，訴訟の
continental shelf 大陸棚（海岸線から200カイリ（約370キロ・メートル）の排他的経済水域にある海底のこと。⇒U.N. Commission on the Limits of the Continental Shelf）
　Agreement of Continental Shelf of Japan and Republic of Korea 日韓大陸棚協定
contingency 名 偶発，偶発性，偶発事象［事項，事件］，不測の事態，緊急事態，非常事態，不慮の事故，臨時費用
　contingency fee 〈弁護士の〉成功報酬
　contingency fund 臨時費，偶発資金（＝contingent fund）
　Contingency Law 有事法
　contingency plan 非常事態計画，不慮の事故対策計画
contingent 名 派遣団，代表団，派遣部隊，分担，分担額，偶発事故
continue to 引き続き…する，継続して…する，今後とも…する，…を維持する
contraband 形 密輸による，輸出入禁止の，名 禁制品
　contraband goods 密輸品，輸出入禁制品
　contraband of import 輸入禁制品
　contraband of war 戦時禁制品
　non-contraband goods 輸出入非禁制品
contract 動 契約を結ぶ，契約する，請け負う，感染する，短縮する，縮小させる，減少させる，縮小する，減少する，収縮する，悪化する，マイナス成長となる，景気が悪化する，景気後退する
　contract in 正式に参加の契約をする
　contract out 正式に不参加を表明する，下請に仕事を出す
contract 名 契約，契約書，規約，協定，協定書，請負，契約商品，契約品，約定品
　interim contract 暫定契約
　reinsurance contract 再保険契約
　specialty contract 捺印契約
contract price 契約価格［価段］，契約値段，契約金額，協定価格，契約料，受注金額，落札価格（＝contract stipulated price）
contraction 名 縮小，収縮，減少，減退，後退，落込み，制限，節減，削減，マイナス成長，景気［業況］の悪化，景気縮小，景気後退，不況，短縮，短縮語，短縮形，〈負債を〉負うこと，〈病気などに〉かかること，契約を結ぶこと
　contraction coefficiency 収縮率
　contraction of the real economy 実体経済の景気後退
　contraction scale 縮尺
contractionary 形 縮小した，短縮した，悪化した，制限的，引締めの，デフレの
　contractionary economy 景気の悪化，景気収縮，景気後退（＝economic contraction）
　contractionary effect 引締め効果，縮小効果，デフレ効果
　contractionary factor デフレ要因
　contractionary gap デフレ・ギャップ（＝deflationary gap）
　contractionary impulse デフレ効果（＝deflationary impulse）
contradiction 名 逆転，矛盾，ねじれ，ねじれ現象
contribute 動 出資する，払い込む，納付する，拠出する，寄与する，貢献する，協力する，支援する，…に一役買う，…の要因になる
contribution 名 出資，拠出，寄与，貢献，寄付，協力，支援，寄付金，拠出金，負担金，掛け金，分担金，共同海損分担金，負担部分，求償権，保険料，納付金
control 動 支配する，掌握する，管理する，抑制する，操作する
control 名 支配，統制，管理，経営支配権，経営権，規制，抑制，制御，コントロール
　adaptive control 適応制御
　buy control of …の経営権［経営支配権］を取得する，…の経営権を買い取る
　capital control 資本規制，資本取引規制
　control brand コントロール・ブランド（＝double chop：メーカー名と流通業者名を併記したブランドのこと）
　maitain the control of …の支配権［経営支配権］を維持する，…の経営権を確保する
　sanitary controls 衛生管理
　separation of ownership and control 所有と経営の分離
　stock control 在庫管理，在庫調整
　take control of …の経営権を握る，…の経営権を掌握する，…の経営権を支配する，…の主導権を握る
　take full control of …の経営権を完全に掌握

する, …を完全子会社化する
tighten controls on futures trading 先物取引の規制を強化する
control-tower procedures 管制業務
controversial 形 論議[論争]の的となっている, 物議を醸している, 問題になっている, 議論の余地のある, 議論[異論]の多い, 賛否両論のある, 議論[論争]好きな
controversy 名 議論, 論争, 論議, 論戦, 口論, 紛争
  all disputes, controversies, or differences あらゆる紛争, 論争, または意見の相違
  be open to controversy 議論の余地がある
  enter into (a) controversy with …と論争を始める
  excite [stir] new controversy over …について新たな議論を呼び起こす
  the fact without [beyond, out of] controversy 議論の余地がない事実
convenience 名 便利, 便利さ, 利便, 利便性, 便宜, 打算, コンビニエンス
  convenience store コンビニエンス・ストア, コンビニ
convention 名 大会, 定期大会, 党大会, 集会, 会議, 総会, 約束事, 申し合わせ, 協定, 協約, 条約, 伝統的な手法[型], 決まり, しきたり, 慣例, 慣行, コンベンション （⇒national convention）
  annual convention 年次大会, 年次総会
  Convention Concerning the Protection of the World Cultural and Natural Heritage 世界の文化遺産及び自然遺産の保護に関する条約, 世界遺産
  Convention on International Trade in Endangered Species of Wild Fauna and Flora 絶滅のおそれのある野生動植物の国際取引に関する条約《略 CITES》
  Convention on the Law of the Seas 海洋法条約
  Convention on the Rights of the Child 子どもの権利条約
  Democratic [Democratic Party's] convention 民主党大会
  Geneva Convention ジュネーブ協定
  market convention 市場慣行
  military convention 軍事協定
  Ramsar Convention ラムサール条約, 国際湿地条約, 水鳥湿地保全条約
  rounding convention 四捨五入方法

tax [taxation] convention 租税条約
conversion of debt to equity 債務の株式化
conventional 形 従来の, 在来の, 従来型の, これまでの, 通常の, 伝統的な, 慣習的な, 型にはまった, 月並みの, 独創性のない, 核を使わない, 大会の, 会議の, コンベンショナル
  buck conventional wisdom 一般常識を覆す
  conventional bond 普通債
  conventional medicine 通常の医学
  conventional money rate 約定金利 （= conventional interest [interest rate]）
  conventional neutrality 協定中立
  conventional rate 協定運賃
  conventional tariff 協定関税, 協定税率
  conventional value 協定価格
  conventional weapons 通常兵器
  conventional wisdom 世間一般の通念, 一般通念, 世間知, 一般常識, 常識, 市場のコンセンサス
convert 動 転換する, 変える,〈公債などを〉切り替える, 換算する, 両替する
  convert bonds into shares 社債を株式に転換する
  convert profit into Japanese currency from dollars 利益をドルから円に換算する
convertible 形 転換可能な, 転換できる,〈通貨が〉兌換できる,〈通貨と〉交換できる
  be convertible into common shares 普通株式に転換できる
  convertible bond 転換社債 （=convertible debenture, convertible debt, convertible loan stock：社債として発行され, 途中で保有者の意思で株式に転換できる証券）
conveyor-belt sushi restaurant 回転ずし
conveyer [conveyor] belt system ベルトコンベヤー方式 （=conveyer system）
convict 動 〈…に〉有罪を宣告する, 有罪の判決を下す
  be convicted of …の［…で］有罪判決を受ける, …の判決を下される
  convict a person of 人に…の有罪判決を下す, 人を…で有罪の判決を下す
  have been previously convicted of theft 窃盗の前科がある
conviction 名 有罪判決, 確信, 信念, 説得, 説得力

a man with several previous convictions 前科数犯の男
make a conviction for a crime 犯罪に対して有罪の判決を下す

cookie-cutter 形 型にはまった, 月並みな (cookie cutter=クッキーの抜き型)

cooled 形 冷え込んだ, 冷やされた, 悪化した

cooling off 冷却期間, クーリング・オフ (＝cooling-off period: 消費者保護制度の一つで, 消費者が商品を購入する契約を結んでも, 契約後20日以内なら無条件で解約できる)

cooperation 名 協力, 協力関係, 協調, 協同, 協業, 提携, 交流, 提供, 援助, 共同経営, 協同組合
  capital cooperation 資本提携 (＝cooperation by holding capital)
  consumers' cooperation 消費者協同組合, 消費組合
  multi-economic cooperation 多国間経済協力

cooperative relationship 協力関係

coordinate 動 調整する, 協調する, 一元化する, 調和させる, 連携させる, 連携を取る, 連携する
  coordinated easing move 協調利下げ
  coordinated (interest) rate cuts 協調利下げ
  coordinated policy 政策協調
  coordinated terrorist attacks of Sept. 11, 2001 2001年9月11日の米同時テロ

coordination 名 調整, 調節, すり合わせ, 一元化, 統一, 協調, 連携, 整合, 足並み, 同等, 対等, 対等関係
  coordination action 協調行動
  coordination between the two groups 両グループ間の調整
  lack of coordination 足並みの乱れ
  policy coordination 政策協調, 政策調整
  policy coordination policy [efforts] 政策協調努力

COP 条約締約国会議 (Conference of the Partiesの略)
  COP 14 〈国連の〉気候変動枠組み条約第14回締約国会議 (＝the 14th Conference [Session of the Conference] of the Parties to the U.N. Framework Convention on Climate Change)

cope with …に対応する, …に対処する, …に対抗する, …に立ち向かう, …と張り合う, …を(うまく)処理する, …を切り抜ける, …を克服する

cope with a task 仕事を処理する
cope with corporate needs 企業のニーズに応える, 企業のニーズに対応する

co-principal 名 共同正犯

copyright 動 著作権を取得する, 版権を取得する, …の著作権を保護する
  copyrighted material 著作権のある著作物, 版権のある著作物, 著作権のある曲
  copyrighted music 著作権のある音楽

copyright 名 著作権, 版権, 形 著作権所有の, 版権所有の
  copyright-fee management contract 著作権料管理契約
  copyright holder 著作権所有者, 版権所有者, 著作者
  copyright protection 著作権保護
  copyright-related rights 著作隣接権
  copyright violation [infringement, piracy] 著作権侵害
  infringe the copyright 著作権を侵害する, 版権を侵害する
  out of copyright 著作権期限が切れた, 版権の期限が切れた

core 名 核, 中心, 中心部, 核心, 芯, 中核, 中枢, 主力, 主軸, 基本理念, 基本モデル, 基本設計, 〈原子炉の〉炉心, コア
  at the core 心の底では, 根底では, 芯は
  be rotten at the core 心が腐っている
  hard core 中核, 中核分子, 主要部分, 慢性失業者 (hard core unemployed), ハード・コア
  lie at the core of …の根底に深くひそむ
  magnetic core 鉄心, 発電子鉄心, 磁心
  to the core 心の底まで, 芯まで, 徹底的に, 根っから

core 形 核となる, 軸となる, 中心的な, 中核的な, 核心的な, 基本的な, 本業の
  core activities 主力事業, 中核事業, 主力業務
  core bank 主力銀行, 主力行
  core business 中核事業, 中核企業, 主力事業, 基幹事業, 根幹業務, 本業, コア・ビジネス (＝core business operation, core operation)
  core city 〈大都市圏の〉中核都市, 中心都市
  core competence 企業固有の競争力の核, コア・コンピテンス
  core consumer price index コア物価指数, 消費者物価指数のコア指数, コア指数
  core curriculum コア・カリキュラム
  core earnings 中核事業収益, 主力事業の収益,

コア収益
core inflation コア・インフレ率, 基礎インフレ率, コア指数 (＝core rate of inflation)
core machinery orders 船舶と電力を除く機械受注額［機械受注］
core memory 磁心記憶装置, 磁気コア
core nuclear reactor 〈原子炉の〉炉心
core operating profit 〈生命保険会社の本業のもうけに当たる〉基礎利益 (＝core profit)
core prices コア指数, コア物価指数 (＝core inflation)
core private machinery orders 民間需要の機械受注額（船舶・電力を除く）, 実質機械受注（船舶・電力を除く民需）
core private orders 船舶と電力を除く民需［民間需要］
core private-sector machinery orders 民間需要の機械受注額（船舶・電力を除く）
core producer prices 生産者物価のコア部分の指数, 生産者物価指数コア部分
core profit コア利益, 主力事業の利益, 生命保険会社の基礎利益
core store コア記憶装置
core strategy 基本戦略, 主力戦略, 中核戦略
core time コア・タイム（フレックスタイム制で, 必ず勤務することになっている時間帯）
core tube 〈粉末状の物質に挿入する〉見本抜取り管
non-core competence 非中核業務, ノンコア業務

cornerstone 名 基礎, 礎(いしずえ), すみ石, 土台, 礎石, 要(かなめ), 要石, 根拠
cornerstone laying ceremony 〈建築物の〉定礎式
lay the cornerstone of …の定礎式を行う, …の基礎を据える
the cornerstone of one's argument …の議論の根拠

corporate 名 形 企業(の), 会社(の), 法人(の), コーポレート
corporate body 企業体
corporate bond 社債 (＝corporate debenture)
corporate buyout [buy-out] 企業買収 (＝corporate acquisition)
corporate citizenship [citizen] 企業市民, 市民としての企業, コーポレート・シチズン (＝corporate citizenship)

corporate governance 会社の管理・運営, 会社管理法, 企業統治, 企業支配, 経営監視, コーポレート・ガバナンス
corporate governance reform bill 企業統治改革法案
corporate income 法人所得
corporate law 会社法
corporate raider 企業乗っ取り屋, 企業買収家（敵対的な方法で大量の株を買い集めて, 経営支配権をねらう者のこと）
corporate sector 企業部門, 企業
corporate sentiment 企業の心理, 企業の景況感, 企業の業況判断
corporate value 企業価値
corporate tax 法人税, 法人事業税（企業の利潤に対して課される国税）
Corporate Tax Law 法人税法
corporate tax on gross operating profit 外形標準課税, 業務粗利益への法人事業税［法人税］の課税

corporation 名 会社, 企業, 法人, 団体, コーポレーション
closed corporation 株式の非公開会社, 閉鎖会社 (＝closely held company)
corporation law 会社法 (＝corporate law)
Edge Act Corporation エッジ法会社, エッジ法人
family corporation 同族会社
Financing Corporation 米連邦調達公社
foreign corporation 州外法人, 国外法人, 外国企業
government corporation 公社
medical corporation 医療法人
Model Business Corporation Act 模範事業会社法《略 MBCA》
quasi-public corporation 第三セクター
surviving corporation 存続会社

correct 動 修正する, 訂正する, 是正する, 調整する
corrected documents 訂正文書
corrected financial statement 訂正有価証券報告書, 有価証券報告書の訂正

correction 名 修正, 訂正, 是正, 矯正, 反動, 調整, 調整局面, 添削, 校正
correction facility 刑務所
correction liquid 修正液
housing market correction 住宅市場の調整
inventory correction 在庫調整

correspondent

ongoing correction 今回の調整局面
temporary correction アヤ戻し（相場が下げ基調で，一時的に相場が高くなる場合のこと）
correspondent 名 特派員，通信員，取引先，文通者，コルレス先，為替取組先
　correspondent bank 取引銀行，コルレス銀行
　correspondent arrangement [agreement] コルレス契約
　war correspondent 従軍記者
corresponding 形 …に対応する，一致する，相当する，類似する，〈前に述べたことの〉結果として起こる
　compared with the corresponding month of last year 前年同月比で
corridor 名 回廊，回廊地帯，廊下，通路，ルート
　a corridors-of-power politician 舞台裏の政治家
　a corridor panel 通路壁の広告ポスター［広告掲示板］
　a humanitarian corridor 人道回廊，人道支援ルート，生活物資の輸送路
　the corridors of power 権力の回廊，〈政府高官などの〉上部階層（重要な政治決定の場）
　the Polish Corridor ポーランド回廊
corrupt 形 堕落した，不正の，汚職の，賄賂のきく
　corrupt practice 不正慣行
corruption 名 腐敗，堕落，退廃，汚職，贈賄，収賄，贈収賄，買収，改竄
cosmodrome 名 〈ロシアの〉宇宙ロケット発射基地，宇宙基地
cosplay 名 コスプレ（costume playの略。マンガやアニメなどの登場人物の衣装をまねて変装すること）
cost 名 原価，費用，経費，原価法，コスト（⇒push up costs）
　cost control 原価統制，原価管理，コスト管理，コスト削減，コスト・コントロール
　cost cut 経費削減，費用削減，コスト削減（= cost cutting）
　cost distribution 原価配分，費用配分，原価［費用］の配賦，費用［原価］の流れ（= cost allocation）
　cost improvement 原価改善，コスト改善，コスト削減
　cost of capital 資本費用，資本コスト，資本用役費，資本利子（= capital cost）
　cost of sales 売上原価（= cost of goods sold）
　estimated cost 見積り原価
　personnel costs 人件費（= staff cost）
　product cost 製品原価
　push up costs コストを押し上げる
　shoulder a portion of the costs 費用の一部を負担する
　unit cost 単位原価，個別原価
cost-competitive 価格競争力がある，価格競争力が高い，コスト競争力がある
cost cutting 経費削減，費用削減，コスト削減（= cost cut）
cost-effective [cost effective] 形 費用効果が高い，費用効率がよい，コスト効率がよい（= cost efficient）
cost effectiveness 費用効果，費用効率，コスト効率
cost-efficient 形 費用効率がよい，費用効率が高い，コスト効率がよい（= cost-effective）
cost reduction コスト削減，経費削減，費用削減，原価削減［低減］，原価引下げ，原価控除（= cost cutting）
　cost reduction competition コスト削減競争
　cost reduction efforts コスト削減努力，コスト削減策
Council of Economic Advisers 〈米大統領〉経済諮問委員会《略 CEA》（議会に提出する経済報告書の作成や経済動向の検討，経済政策に関する大統領への勧告などが主な任務）
count 名 〈起訴状の〉訴因，〈刑事訴訟の〉論点，問題点，容疑，計算，勘定，値（amount），総数，計数，統計，会計，決算，カウント
　be charged with two counts of murder 2件の殺人罪で告発される
　be indicted on three counts 三つの訴因で起訴される
　blood count 血球値，血球数
　cholesterol count コレステロール値
　hold a census count 人口調査を行う，国勢調査をする
　pollen count 花粉飛散数
　set no count on …を当てにしない，…を重視しない
　take count of …を重んじる，…を重視する，…を問題にする，…を数える
countdown 名 秒読み，秒読み段階，最終段階，最後の点検，カウントダウン
　complete the ten-countdown 10秒間のカウントダウンを終える

counter

stop the countdown 秒読みを中止する

counter 動 対抗する, …に反対する, 逆襲する, 反撃する, 阻止する, 抑制する, 対応する, 反論する, 反証をあげる

counter 形 逆の, 反対の, 副 逆に, 反対に
- counter argument 反対の議論, 反論
- counter cyclical policy 景気安定化政策 (= countercyclical policy)
- run [go, hunt] counter to …に反する, …に違反する, …に背く

counterculture 名 反体制文化, 対抗文化, カウンターカルチャー

counterfeit 動 偽造する, 模造する, 名 偽造品, 模造品, 偽物, 偽造通貨

counterfeit 形 偽の, 偽造の, 模造の
- counterfeit bank notes 偽造紙幣 (=counterfeit banknotes)
- counterfeit brand product 偽ブランド品

countermeasure 名 対策, 対応策, 対抗処置, 対抗手段, 対応手段, 報復手段
- countermeasures for terrorism テロ対策
- the preferred countermeasures against the financial crisis 金融危機への優先的な対応策

counterpart 名 同じ立場 [地位] にある人, 同等物, 同業者, 片方, 副本, 正副2通のうちの1通

counterproductive 形 逆効果の, 逆効果を生じる, 望ましくない結果を生む [引き起こす], 効果がない, 非生産的な

counterterrorism center テロ対策センター (=antiterror center)

countervailing tariff 相殺関税 (= countervailing duty：外国政府の輸出補助金や奨励金を受けた製品が, 不当に低い価格で輸入された場合に, 国内産業保護のためその報復措置としてかける関税)

coup 名 武力政変 (coup d'etat), クーデター, 大当たり, 大成功, 素晴らしい出来事 [行動], とっさの行動
- bloodless coup 無血クーデター
- coup d'etat [d'état] 武力政変, クーデター
- coup de grace 破壊行為, 破壊的な出来事, とどめの一撃

course 名 進路, 針路, 経路, 進行, 経過, 成り行き, 過程, 方向, 方針, 道, 講義, 講座, 教科課程, 修業期間, 一連の治療, コース
- course of exchange 外国為替相場表
- Courses of Study 学習指導要領
- due course of law 法の適正な過程 (=due process of law)
- during the course of of the current fiscal year 今期中, 今期
- holder in due course 正当な所持人, 善意の第三者, 善意取得者《略 H.D.C.》
- ordinary course of business 通常の商取引慣行, 通常の事業活動, 業務の通常の過程

court 名 裁判所, 法廷, 公判, 裁判, 裁判官, 判事, 役員会, 重役会, 委員会, 役員, 重役幹部, 王室, 宮殿, 宮廷, 御前会議, 宮中会議, 陳列場の一区画, ご機嫌とり, モーテル, コート
- appear in court 出廷する (=attend court)
- bankruptcy court 破産裁判所, 破産審査裁判所
- be taken to court 裁判にかけられる
- bring A before the court Aを裁判沙汰にする, Aを訴える
- civil court 民事法廷
- Claims Court 請求裁判所
- clear the court 傍聴人 (全員) を退廷させる
- Constitutional Court 〈タイの〉憲法裁判所
- contempt of court 法廷侮辱
- court above 〈上訴が行われたときの〉上訴裁判所
- court-appointed defense team 国選弁護団
- court below 〈上訴が行われたときの〉原審裁判所
- court case 法廷訴訟
- court for the trial of impeachment 弾劾裁判所
- court hearing 法廷審理
- court martial 軍法会議
- court of bankruptcy 破産裁判所
- court of domestic relations 家庭裁判所
- court of error 誤審裁判所
- court of first instance 第一審裁判所, 〈EUの〉初審裁判所
- court of general jurisdiction 一般的管轄裁判所
- court of justice [law] 裁判所, 法廷 (=law court)
- court of limited jurisdiction 制限的管轄裁判所
- court of nisi prius 巡回陪審裁判所
- court of record 記録裁判所, 正式記録裁判所
- court of sessions 〈米国の〉軽罪裁判所
- court protection from creditors 資産保全
- court reporter 法廷速記者, 訴訟手続き記録者
- Courts Act of 1971 〈英国の〉裁判所法

courtmartial — **create**

Courts of the United States 合衆国裁判所, 連邦裁判所
criminal court 刑事法廷
district court 地方裁判所
family court 家庭裁判所
go through the courts 法的処理をする, 法的処理を行う (⇒go through)
go to court 訴訟を起こす, 裁判沙汰にする
high court 高等裁判所
hold (a) court 開廷する, 裁判を開く, 裁判を行う
in court 裁判で, 法廷で
maritime court 海事裁判所
order the court (to be) cleared 傍聴人の退廷を命じる
out of court 法廷外で, 示談で, 審理なしで
out-of-court negotiations 示談交渉
settle out of court 示談にする, 示談で解決する
settle the case out of court 事件を示談で解決する
summary court 簡易裁判所
superior court 上位裁判所
take A to court Aを訴える, Aを裁判所[法廷]に訴える, Aを裁判沙汰にする
tax court 租税裁判所
territorial court 米準州裁判所, 連邦統治領裁判所
the Court of Admiralty 〈英国の〉海事裁判所
the Court of Appeal 〈英国の〉控訴院
the Court of Appeals 〈米国の〉控訴裁判所 (＝the federal appeals court)
the Court of Claims 〈米国の〉行政裁判所
the Court of Common Pleas 〈英国の〉民事訴訟裁判所
the court of directors 取締役会議, 取締役会
the High Court of Parliament 英国国会
the Judge Impeachment Court 裁判官弾劾裁判所
the Supreme Court 最高裁判所
The Tokyo District Court 東京地方裁判所, 東京地裁
wage a court battle 法廷闘争を展開する
courtmartial [court-martial] 名 軍法会議, 動 軍法会議にかける
cover 動 〈保険を〉かける[付ける], 〈費用や金額などを〉賄う, 〈損失の〉穴埋めをする, 〈損失などを〉補填する, …を抵当とする, …を担保に入れる, 〈問題などを〉取り扱う, …を対象とする, 含む, 表示する, 報道する, 取材する

cover up 隠蔽する, 隠匿する, 隠す, もみ消す
cover-up 名 もみ消し, もみ消し工作, 隠蔽, 隠蔽工作, 隠し立て, …隠し
coverage 名 報道(reporting), 報道記事, 取材, 取材範囲, 放送, 適用範囲, 〈保険の〉填補, 担保範囲, カバレッジ
building coverage 建蔽率
extended coverage 拡張担保
insurance coverage 保険担保, 保険の付保, 保険の担保範囲
press coverage 新聞報道, マスコミ報道
sales coverage 販売可能範囲, 販売対象範囲, 販売活動範囲, セールス・カバレッジ
universal health care coverage 国民皆医療保険制度
covert 形 人目につかない, 隠された, 秘密の, 裏の, 暗に示した, 〈女性が〉夫の保護下にある
covert operation 秘密工作, 裏工作
covert transaction 裏取引 (＝behind-the-scenes transaction)
CPA 連合国暫定当局 (Coalition Provisional Authorityの略)
CPFR 需要予測と在庫補充のための共同事業 (collaborative planning, forecasting and replenishmentの略)
CPI 消費者物価指数 (consumer price indexの略)
average CPI inflation CPIの平均上昇率
general CPI index 総合消費者物価指数
provisional CPI number 消費者物価指数速報値
crack down on …を厳しく[厳重に]取り締まる, …の摘発を強化する, …に対して断固たる措置を取る, …を弾圧する
crackdown 名 厳重取締り, 断固たる処置, 締め付け, 弾圧, 強化, 法律の厳重な施行
craft 動 〈巧みに, 精巧に, 丹念に〉作る, 策定する
cram education 詰め込み教育
cramming school 塾, 受験予備校
create 動 創造する, 創出する, 創作する, 作り出す, 開発する, 生み出す, 引き起こす, 発生させる, 〈会社などを〉設立する, 新設する, 設ける, 〈担保権などを〉設定する, 構築する, 伸ばす, 高める
create a market 市場を開拓する
create a portfolio of securities 証券ポートフォリオを構築する
create a security interest 担保権を設定する

create deals 案件を組成する
create jobs 雇用を創出する, 職場[仕事]を作る
create sales 売上を伸ばす
credibility 名 信頼, 信認, 信用力, 信頼性, 信頼度, 信憑性, 確実性, 真実性 (＝creditworthiness)
  anti-inflation credibility インフレ抑制姿勢に対する信認, インフレ抑制政策の信頼性
  credibility gap 言行不一致, 食い違い, 不信感, 信頼性不足
credit 名 信用, 与信, 債権, 貸方, 貸金, 融資, 預金, 利益, 信用状, 支払い猶予期間, 税額控除, 金融, クレジット
  credit contraction 信用収縮
  credit control 与信管理, 信用管理, 信用規制, 信用制限, 信用統制 (＝credit management)
  credit cost 与信費用, 債権処理費用, 不良債権処理額 (＝loan loss charge)
  credit crunch 貸し渋り, 信用危機, 信用逼迫, 信用不安, 信用規制, 信用収縮, 金融危機, 金融逼迫, 金融ピンチ, クレジット・クランチ (＝credit crisis)
  credit easing measures [steps] 金融緩和政策, 金融緩和措置
  credit freeze 信用凍結, 信用釘付け
  credit insecurity 信用不安
  credit line 貸出限度(額), 貸付け限度(額), 与信限度(額), 信用限度, 信用保証枠, 信用供与限度, 信用供与枠, 融資枠, 融資限度額, 利用限度額, クレジット・ライン (＝credit limit, line of credit)
  credit market 信用市場, 発行市場
  credit quality 信用の質, 信用度, 信用力
  credit rater 格付け機関 (＝credit rating agency)
  credit research agency 信用調査機関, 信用調査会社
  extend credit 信用を供与する
  investment credit 投資税額控除, 投資減税 (＝investment tax credit)
  raise credit 資金を調達する
  tax credit 税額控除
credit card クレジット・カード(顧客にとって利便性がもっとも高い決済手段で, B to C (B2C: 企業対消費者) の電子商取引では, 代引き, 銀行振込み, 郵便振替に次いで利用されている)
credit default swap クレジット・デフォルト・スワップ《略 CDS》(企業の破産や債務不履行に伴う損失から投資家を守るため, 債務不履行に陥った債券の元利を保証する金融派生商品)
credit rating 信用格付け, 企業の信用等級, 格付け評価, 格付け (＝rating)
  credit rating agency 格付け機関, 信用格付け機関 (＝credit agency, credit rater, rating agency)
  long-term credit ratings 長期格付け
credit risk 信用リスク
  credit risk transfer 信用リスク移転《略 CRT》
  credit risk transfer product 信用リスク移転商品 (＝CRT product)
creditor 名 債権者, 債権国, 債権保有者, 資金供与者, 取引銀行, 取引金融機関, 貸主, 貸方, 仕入先, クレディター
  creditor's [creditors'] meeting 債権者会議
  junior creditor 劣後債権者
  priority creditor 優先債権者
creditworthiness 名 信用度, 信用力, 信用の質
crescent of instability 不安定の弧(カリブ, アフリカ, 中東, 中央・南アジア・北朝鮮を結ぶ政情不安定な地域)
Creutzfeldt–Jakob Disease クロイツフェルト・ヤコブ病《略 CJD》(⇒mad cow disease)
crime 名 罪, 犯罪, 犯罪行為, 法律違反, 悪事, 愚行, 人道にはずれた行為, 恥ずべき行為, 残念なこと
  commit a crime 罪を犯す, 犯罪行為をする, 犯罪行為に及ぶ
  crime against humanity 人道に対する罪
  crime syndicate [gang] 暴力団, 組織暴力団
  white-collar crime ホワイトカラーの犯罪, 〈横領やコンピュータ犯罪など〉知能犯的な犯罪
criminal 名 犯罪者, 犯人
  hardened [habitual] criminal 常習犯
  war criminals 戦争犯罪人, 戦犯
criminal 形 罪の, 犯罪の, 罪を犯した, 刑事上の, 不面目な, ばかげた, 非常識な, ふらちな, 言語道断な, 間違った, 不誠実な
  criminal action 刑事訴訟, 刑事事件, 刑事手続き
  criminal case 刑事事件
  criminal charge 刑事責任, 刑事事件
  criminal code [law] 刑法
  criminal court 刑事裁判所
  criminal defendant 刑事被告人
  criminal (defense) attorney 刑事事件担当弁

護士
criminal forfeiture 刑事没収
Criminal Investigation Department 〈ロンドン警視庁〉犯罪捜査課《略 CID》
criminal law 刑法, 刑事法
criminal liability 刑事責任
criminal negligence 刑事過失, 刑事責任を問われる過失
Criminal Procedure Law 刑事訴訟法
criminal prosecution 刑事訴追, 刑事上の訴追
criminal responsibility 刑事責任, 刑事責任能力
face criminal charge 告発される（＝face prosecution）
file a criminal complaint with A against B Bを相手取ってAに刑事告訴する
prior [previous] criminal records 前科
crisis 名 危機, 経営危機, 重大局面, 難局, 重大な岐路, 分かれ目,〈重大事態の〉山場, 峠, 暴落, 恐慌, 不安, 不足, 問題, リスク
be in crisis 危機的状況にある
crisis management 危機管理
crisis preparedness 危機への備え
liquidity crisis 流動性危機, 資金繰りの悪化（＝crisis of liquidity）
critical 形 重大な, 枢要な, 決定的な, 危機の, 危急の, 危篤の, 批評の, 批評的な, 批判的な, 酷評する, 評論の, 評論家による, 鑑識眼のある, 臨界の
be critical of [about] …に批判的な, …のことをやかましく言う
be in (a) critical condition 瀕死の状態にある, 危篤である, 危機に臨んでいる
critical essay 評論
critical factor 決定的要因, 決定的な役割
critical period 臨界期, 危機の時代, 危機の時期, 危機
critical point 臨界点, 限界点, 重点項目
critical mass 最低限の経済規模, 採算の取れる規模, 望ましい成果を十分得るための確固たる基盤, 限界質量, 臨界質量, 限界量, 臨界量, 臨界, クリティカル・マス
critical path 危機経路, 最長時間経路, 問題経路, クリティカル・パス（プロジェクトを進める上で一番時間がかかる部分）
critical path analysis 危機[最長時間]経路分析, クリティカル・パス分析, CPA分析《略 CPA》
critical path method クリティカル・パス分析法, クリティカル・パス法《略 CPM》

criticality 名 臨界（原子炉内での反応に見られるように, 核分裂が持続的(自動継続的)に起こる状態のことをいう）
criticality accident [incident] 臨界事故
　臨界事故 ⊃ 核燃料の材料である濃縮ウランやプルトニウムが一か所に一定量集まって, 原子炉内の反応と同じように核分裂の連鎖反応を爆発的に起こしてしまう事故で, 強い放射線を放出し, 放射能レベルの高い核分裂生成物をも発生する。
criticism 名 非難, 非難の声, 批判, 攻撃, あら探し, 批評, 評論, 批評文
amid growing criticism 批判の高まるなか
arouse criticism 物議を醸す
defy every criticism どんな批評をも退ける, 批評の余地がない
receive severe [harsh] criticism 厳しい批判を受ける, 酷評を受ける（＝suffer harsh criticism）
crony 名 親友, 旧友, 盟友, 仲間, 取巻き
crony capitalism 縁故資本主義（＝cronyism）
crony families ファミリー企業（＝family companies）
cronyism 名 えこひいき, 身びいき, 縁故主義, クローニズム（⇒crony）
cross licensing [license] contract クロス・ライセンス契約, 交互実施許諾（＝cross licensing agreement）
cross shareholding 株式持ち合い（＝crossholding, cross-holding shares, interlocked shareholdings, interlocking shareholdings）
crossheld [cross-held] stocks 持ち合い株, 持ち合い株式（＝crossheld shares）
crowding-out 〈民間資金需要の〉締め出し, クラウディング・アウト
crowding-out effect 締め出し効果, クラウディング・アウト効果
crown jewel 最優良資産, 王冠の宝石, クラウン・ジュエル（買収される会社のとくに魅力のある重要資産）
crown jewel defense クラウン・ジュエル防衛, 有望資産売却戦略, 重要資産売却作戦（敵対的M&A（企業の合併・買収）への防衛策として, 買収を仕掛けられた企業が, 重要な資産や事業を外部に売却して企業価値を低下させ, 買収の意義を失わせること。scorched-earth defense（焦土作戦）とほぼ同じ意味で使われることが多い）

CRT product 信用リスク移転商品，CRTプロダクト（CRT＝credit risk transfer）
crude 名 原油（＝crude oil, crude petroleum）
 Brent crude ブレント原油
 Dubai crude ドバイ原油
 heavy crude 重質原油
 light crude 軽質原油
 marker crude 基準原油
crude 形 天然の，天然のままの，精製［加工］していない，処理されていない，補正されていない，粗雑な，粗末な，粗い，大雑把な，洗練されていない，未熟な，みだらな，名 原油
 crude futures 原油先物
 crude goods prices 原材料価格
 crude markets 原油相場
 crude materials 原材料
 crude ore 粗鉱
 crude palm oil パーム原油
 crude prices 原油価格
 crude production 原油生産
 crude productivity 粗生産性
 crude quantity 素材数量
 crude rubber 天然ゴム，生ゴム
 crude steel 粗鋼（⇒steel mill, steelworks）
crude oil 原油（＝crude）
 crude oil contract 原油先物
 crude oil price 原油価格（＝crude price）
crunch 名 危機，危機の状況，急場，土壇場，経済危機，〈経済上の〉引締め，財政難，クランチ
 liquidity crunch 流動性逼迫，信用逼迫
crux 名 核心，急所，ポイント，本質，要点，最重要点，肝心なところ，難問，難題，難点，なぞ
 crux of the matter [issue, problem] 問題の核心，問題の本質，問題の要点［最重要点］
 textual crux 本文の難解な箇所
CSF 主要成功要因（＝key success factor：critical success factorの略）
CSR 企業の社会的責任（corporate social responsibilityの略）
> 企業の社会的責任 ⊃ 消費者や従業員，社会に対する企業の責任で，法令遵守や環境への配慮，積極的な情報開示などを企業活動に取り入れる企業が増えている。投資家が投資先を選ぶ際の判断基準の一つにもなっている。

CT scan コンピュータ断層撮影画像，CT画像，CTスキャン（＝CT image）
CT scanner X線体軸層写真撮影装置，CTスキャナー
CTBT 包括的核実験禁止条約，核実験全面禁止条約（Comprehensive Nuclear Test Ban Treatyの略）
culprit 名 元凶，原因，誘因，犯人，刑事被告人，被告人
 the culprits for the financial crisis 金融危機の誘因，金融危機の背景にあるもの
cultivate 動 栽培する，養殖する，飼育する，培養する，耕作する，育てる，養成する，育成する，教化する，啓発する，開拓する，求める，形成する，高める，深める，磨く，養う，〈品質を〉改良する，促進する，奨励する
 cultivate a corporate image 企業イメージを高める
 cultivate a new market 新市場を開拓する
 cultivate one's mind 心を磨く
 cultivate oysters カキを養殖する
cultural 形 文化の，文化的，教養の
 cultural determinism 文化決定論
 cultural pluralism 文化の多元的共存
 cultural protectionism 文化保護主義
 Cultural Revolution 〈中国の〉文化大革命，文革
culture 名 文化，風土，体質，耕作，培養，養殖，教育，文明，文明社会，芸術［文化］活動，カルチャー
 cell culture 細胞培養
 corporate culture 企業文化，企業の体質，企業風土，社風，コーポレート・カルチャー
 credit cultures 与信の姿勢
 culture pearl 養殖真珠（＝cultured pearl）
 culture shock 文化的衝撃，文化の衝撃，文化ショック，カルチャー・ショック
 culture vulture 文化マニア，教養を身につけたがる人
 native cultures 土着の文化
 pop [popular] culture 大衆文化，ポップ・カルチャー
 risk-tolerance culture リスク許容度
 the two cultures 人文社会科学と自然科学［理工学］，文化と科学，二つの教養
 youth culture 若者文化
 water culture 水耕法
curb 動 抑える，制御する，抑制する，制限する，削減する，食い止める，防止する，束縛する，拘束する（＝kerb）
 curb credit expansion 信用拡大を抑える［抑

制する］
curb fiscal [government] spending 財政支出を抑える［抑制する］
curb inflation インフレを抑制する
curb 名 場外市場, 街頭株式取引所（＝curb market）
　curb broker 場外市場仲買人
　curb finance 場外金融
　curb market 場外取引市場, 場外市場（＝curbstone market）
　curb service 〈外食などの〉持ち運びサービス
curfew 名 夜間外出禁止令
currency 名 通貨, 為替, 為替相場, 流通, 流行, カレンシー
　common currency 共通通貨, 単一通貨
　currency authorities 通貨当局
　currency note 銀行券, 政府通貨, 政府紙幣
　currency swap deal 通貨［外貨］交換取引, 通貨スワップ取引, 通貨スワップ取引枠
　currency swings 為替変動（＝currency changes, currency fluctuation, currency movements, forex swings）
　hard currency 交換可能通貨, ハード・カレンシー（＝hard money: 米ドルや金と交換できる通貨）
　home currency 自国通貨
　key currency 基軸通貨, 国際通貨
　local currency 現地通貨(建て), 国内通貨(建て), 自国通貨(建て), ローカル・カレンシー
　soft currency 交換不能通貨, 軟貨, ソフト通貨, ソフト・カレンシー(米ドルやその他の主要通貨と直接交換できない通貨)
currency exchange rate 為替相場, 為替レート（＝exchange rate）
　exposure to changes in currency exchange rates 為替相場の変動によるリスク
　the recent instability of the currency exchange rate 最近の為替相場の不安定な動き
currency market 為替市場, 外国為替市場, 通貨市場, 為替相場（＝foreign exchange market）
　currency market intervention 為替市場への介入, 為替市場介入
　exposure to the currency markets 為替リスク
　forward currency market 為替予約市場
　Japanese currency market 円建て市場
　public intervention in the currency markets 為替市場への協調介入

current 形 現在の, 当座の, 当期の, 短期の, 臨時の, 経常的, 流動的, 名 流動, 流動性, 1年以内返済予定額, 当期分
　current budget year 今会計年度, 今年度
　current fiscal year 今年度, 今期（＝current business year, current year）
　current value accounting 現在価値会計, 時価主義会計《略 CVA》
current account 経常収支, 経常勘定, 当座預金
　current account [accounts] balance 経常収支
　current account deficit 経常赤字, 経常収支の赤字, 経常収支の赤字額
　current account deposit 当座預金（＝current deposit）
　current account profit 経常利益
　current account surplus 経常黒字, 経常収支の黒字, 経常収支の黒字額
curry favor with …の歓心を買う, …の機嫌をとる, …にへつらう
curtail 動 短縮する, 縮小する, 削減する, 節減する, 切り詰める, 弱める
curtailment 名 短縮, 縮小, 削減, 削減, 節減, 切り詰め
curtain 名 幕, 幕状のもの, 開幕, 開園, 終わり, 最後, 死, カーテン
　behind the curtain 陰で, 背後で, 幕裏で, ひそかに, こっそり
　bring [ring] down the curtain on …に結末をつける, …の幕を下ろす
　curtain fall 幕切れ, 終わり
　curtain raiser 前座の出し物, 開幕劇, 前狂言, 幕開けとなるもの, 前触れ, 先駆け, 小手調べ
　draw [drop, lower] the curtain on …を終わりにする［終わらせる］, …を秘密にする［秘密にしておく］, …を隠す
　drop the curtain 幕を下ろす, 閉幕する, 活動を終える
　raise [lift] the curtain on …を始める, …の活動を始める, …を知らせる, …を公表する, …を展開する, …の幕を上げる
　the curtain falls [comes down] on …が終わる
cushion 名 対策, 緩和策, 衝撃を和らげるもの, 緩衝材, マイナス効果［悪影響］を除くもの, 予備金, 準備金, 貯蓄, 資金援助, クッション
　capital cushion 資金力

cash cushion 資金力
cushion against loan loss 貸倒れ損失に対する準備金
cushion bond クッション・ボンド, クッション債券（値下りしにくい高クーポン債）
custody 名 保管, 管理, 保護, 保護預かり, 保護監督権, 監督, 養育権, 監禁, 禁固, 拘置, 拘留, 留置, カストディ
  be in custody 拘留される, 監禁される
  be in police custody on suspicion of …の容疑で警察に拘留される［拘置されている］
  custody account 保護預かり勘定, カストディ口座
  safe [safety] custody 保護預かり
  securities in custody 保管有価証券
custom-made 形 特別注文の, 注文仕立ての, あつらえの, オーダーメードの, 要求［目的］にぴったり合った（＝made-to-order, made-to-measure, tailor-made）
customer 名 顧客, 得意先, 得意客, 取引先, 需要家, 加入者, ユーザー
  customer base 顧客基盤, 顧客層
  customer complaint 顧客からの苦情, 顧客からのクレーム
  customer loyalty 顧客ロイヤルティ, 顧客の忠誠度, 顧客の忠誠心
  customer satisfaction 顧客の満足, 顧客満足度《略 CS》
  customer service 顧客サービス, 顧客への奉仕, 顧客へのサービス, 接客, カスタマー・サービス
  customer support 顧客支援
  customers' trust 顧客の信頼
customize 動 特別注文に応じて作り変える, 顧客の要求に応じて特注化する, 特注化する, 注文生産する, 変造する, 変更する, あつらえる, 個別化する
customized 形 特別注文に応じて作った, 顧客の要求に応じて特注化した, オーダーメードの, 特注の, 注文生産した
  customized manufacturing 特注化製造
customizing 名 特注化, 個別化（＝customization）
customs 名 関税, 税関
  customs authorities 関税当局
  Customs Tariff Law 関税定率法
cut 動 削減する, 切り詰める, 節減する, 縮小する, 減らす, 削除する,〈供給を〉止める, 引き下げる, 下げる, 無断で欠席する, 切り取る, 編集する, 製作する, 録音する, カットする

cut and paste カット・アンド・ペースト（文書の一部を切り取って別の場所［文書］に移動すること）
cut both ways もろ刃の剣である
cut corners 手を抜く
cut down on …を切り詰める, …を削減する
cut one's earnings estimate 業績予想を引き下げる, 収益予想を下方修正する
cut 名 削減, 節減, 縮小, 値引き, 引下げ, 切下げ, 配給停止, 中断, 停電,〈利益の〉取り分, 分け前, 傷口, カット
  cut in headline rate 利下げ（＝cut in interest rates, rate cut）
  dividend cut 配当引下げ, 減配
  Fed cut 米連邦準備制度理事会（FRB）による利下げ
  key rate cut 公定歩合の引下げ（＝discount rate cut, official discount rate cut）
  open cut 露天掘り
  parity cut 平価切下げ
  the latest cut 最新版
cut back 削減する, 切り詰める
▶ Consumers are *cutting back* spending on foods and daily necessities. 消費者は, 食品や日用品［日用必需品］への支出を切り詰めている。
cut back on …を削減［縮小］する, …を減らす, …を切り詰める, …を控える
cut into …を減らす, 下げる, …に割り込む, …を妨げる
cut short 途中で切り上げる
cutback 名 削減, 縮小, 圧縮, 短縮（複数形で使われることが多い）
  cutback in expenditure 支出削減
  cutback [cutbacks] in jobs 雇用削減
  cutback [cutbacks] in output 生産削減, 減産（＝production cutback）
  cutback in work hours 労働時間の短縮
  inventory cutback 在庫削減
  personnel cutbacks 人員削減, 人員整理
  power cutbacks 電力削減
  production cutback 生産削減
cutoff 名 供給の停止, 中止, 遮断, 最終期限, 締切り, 核分裂性物質生産禁止, カットオフ
  cutoff date 締切り日, 計算打切り日
  cutoff rate [point] 切捨て率, 棄却率
cutthroat 形 激烈な, 熾烈な, 激しい, 情け容赦ない, 壊滅的な, 死に物狂いの, 生き馬の目を抜く, 市場実勢を大きくはずれた, 出血サービスの, 凶

悪の, 人殺しの
cutthroat competition 激しい競争, 熾烈な[激烈な]競争, 首の締め合い
cutting edge 最前線, 最先端, 最新式, 最新型, 最新鋭, 先頭, 主導的地位, 鋭利な刃物（＝leading edge, sophisticated, state-of-the-art, top of the line）
cutting-edge 形 最前線の, 最先端の, 最新式の
cutting-edge technology 最先端技術, 最新技術, 先進技術
cyber 名 電脳空間, 人工知能, サイバー（⇒cyberspace, virtual space）
cyber- [cyber] 形 仮想…, 電子…, 電脳…, コンピュータ…, ネットワーク上の（コンピュータ・ネットワークと仮想現実に関する, という意味）
  Cyber Act サイバー法
  cyber blackmail サイバー恐喝
  cyber ethics 電脳倫理, サイバー・エシックス
  cyber police 網絡警察, サイバー・ポリス
  cyber shopping サイバー・ショッピング（インターネット上での電子マネーによる買い物）
cyberbuck サイバーバック（＝cybermoney, e-money）
cyberbusiness サイバービジネス（＝e-business : インターネットを使ってホームページを開設して, 消費者に直接販売するビジネス）
cybercash サイバーキャッシュ（＝digital cash, digital money, electronic money）
cybercensorship コンピュータ・ネットの情報検索
cybercrime ネット犯罪, サイバー犯罪, 電脳犯罪, コンピュータ犯罪, サイバークライム
cyberculture コンピュータ文化, サイバネーション文化, 電脳文化, 人工電脳化社会, サイバーカルチャー
cyberdemocracy サイバー民主主義, コンピュータ民主主義, サイバー・デモクラシー
cybermall 電子モール, 仮想商店街, サイバーモール（＝electronic mall, virtual mall）
cybermanners ネット・マナー, サイバーマナー（＝netiquette : インターネットやパソコン通信のマナー）
cybermarket サイバー市場, 電脳市場, ネットワーク上の市場, サイバーマーケット
cybermoney 電子マネー（＝cybercash, digital cash, digital money, electronic money）
cyberpublishing ネットワーク上での出版, サイバーパブリッシング
cybershop ネット・ショップ, サイバーショップ（＝Net shop）
cybersociety サイバー社会, 電脳社会, パソコン通信のネットワーク社会, サイバーソサイエティ
cyberworld サイバー世界, 電脳世界, サイバーワールド
cyber attack [**cyber-attack**] サイバー攻撃, サイバーテロ（＝cyberterrorist attack : インターネットを利用したテロ行為）
  anti-cyber-attack exercise 対サイバーテロ演習, 対サイバーテロ訓練
  cyber-terrorist attack サイバーテロ
cybercapitalism 名 サイバー資本主義
cyberspace 名 仮想の情報空間, サイバー空間, インターネット上の世界, ネットワーク世界, 電脳空間, インターネットの別名, サイバースペース（＝virtual space）
cyber-tactics 名 サイバー作戦
cyberterrorism 名 サイバーテロ（＝cyber terrorism : インターネットを利用したテロ行為）
cyberterrorist attack サイバーテロ（＝cyber terrorism, cyber-terrorist attack, cyberteroism）
cycle 名 周期, 循環, 動向, 景気, サイクル
  down cycle 景気悪化
  economic cycle 経済循環, 景気循環, 景気動向
  life cycle 生活循環, 製品寿命, 製品ライフサイクル, ライフサイクル
  ordering cycle 発注間隔
  output cycle 生産動向
  product life cycle 製品サイクル, 商品サイクル
  virtuous cycle 好循環
czar 名 権威, 権力者, 第一人者, 大家, 統括者, 帝政ロシア皇帝, 専制君主, 独裁者, ツァー（＝tsar, tzar）
  drug czar 麻薬王
  intelligence czar 情報機関の統括者

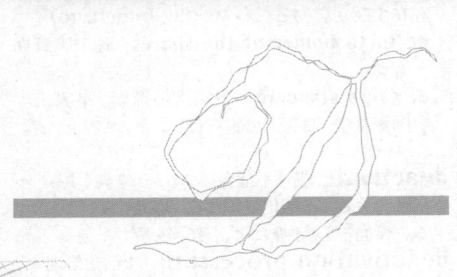

D

daily 形 毎日の, 日々の, 日常の, 1日当たりの, 日刊の
  daily average for the Nikkei index 日経平均の月中平均株価

damage 名 損害, 損害賠償, 被害(複数形には「損害賠償金, 損害賠償額, 損害額, 被害額」の意味もある)
  claim damages 損害賠償を求める
  compensation for damages 損害賠償
  damages lawsuit [suit] 損害賠償請求訴訟, 損害賠償訴訟
  demand damage compensation 損害賠償を請求する
  passive damages 逸失利益
  the amounts of damages from illegal withdrawals with bogus cards 偽造カードを使った不正な預金引出しによる被害額

dampen 動 弱める, 抑える, 抑制する, 鈍らせる, 鈍化させる, …を沈静化させる, …に水を差す, …の低迷を招く, …の気勢などをそぐ, 減退させる, 〈熱意などを〉くじく
  dampen demand 需要を抑制する
  dampen household spending 個人消費を抑える, 個人消費の低迷を招く
  dampen price fluctuations 価格変動を抑える
  dampen the world economy 世界経済の低迷を招く, 世界経済の足かせとなる
  dampening effect 抑制効果 (＝dampening influence)

data 名 情報, 文書, 資料, 指標, 統計, データ
  basic data 基礎資料, 基礎データ
  consumer data 消費指標
  data capture データの取り込み, 情報収集
  data center データ・センター (＝datacenter, Internet data center)
  data mining データ・マイニング (＝knowledge discovery in database)
  data on file 保管文書
  data retrieval 情報検索, データ検索
  employment data 雇用統計 (＝job data, labor data, labor market data)
  final data 確定値
  industrial production data 鉱工業生産指数
  key economic data 主要景気指標
  primary data 一次データ

dating Web site 出会い系サイト

Davos Conference [meeting] ダボス会議(世界経済フォーラム年次総会の通称。⇒World Economic Forum)

day care 就学前児童の保育, 高齢者や障害者の介護, 養護, デイケア
  corporate day-care 企業内保育
  corporate day-care center 企業内保育所, 企業内託児所, コーポレート・デイケア・センター
  day-care center 保育所

day service 日帰り介護, デイサービス

day trade デイ・トレード (＝day trading：インターネットでの株や債券などの取引のこと)

day trader デイ・トレーダー(定職を持たないで, パソコンを通じて1日中, 株取引などをするセミプロの個人投資家のこと)

daylight saving time サマータイム

de facto 事実上の, 実質的な, 実際に [事実上] 存在する, 現存する, ディファクト（＝defacto）
　de facto holder of the shares 株の実質保有者
　de facto standard 事実上の標準, 事実上の国際基準, 事実上の世界標準, デファクト・スタンダード
deactivate 動 不活発にする, …を鈍くする, 不活性化する, 不活化処理する, 爆発しないようにする,〈爆発物を〉不発にする, 任務を解く
deactivation processing 不活化処理
dead 形 死んだ, 枯れた, 稼動しない, 機能しない, 動かない, 使われていない, 不良の, 活気がない, 無感覚な, 無感動の, まったくの, 完全な, 絶対的な
　come to a dead end 行き詰まる
　dead cat bounce 〈株価などの大幅下落後の〉一時的回復
　dead duck 役に立たない人, 成功の見込みのない人 [物], 価値のない計画 [考え]
　dead freight 空荷（からに）運賃, 不積運賃
　dead loan 貸倒れ
　dead loss 丸損, まったくの損失
　dead stock [inventory] 不良在庫, 売れ残り品, 死蔵品, 農具, 活動のない地域, デッド・ストック
　dead storage 退蔵品, 死蔵品
　dead time 待ち時間, 非稼動時間, 休止時間
　dead wood 窓際族（dead woodは「枯れ枝」という意味）
　drop dead date 処分日
deadline 名 締切り, 期限, 回答期限, 最終期限, 原稿締切時間, 行動計画
　100-day deadline 100日行動計画
　bid deadline 入札締切り
　deadline of decision 意思決定の期限
　reply [response] deadline 回答期限
　set a deadline for …の期限 [最終期限] を決める
　work to the deadline 締切りに間に合わせる
deal 名 取引, 商売, 売買, 政策, 計画, 協定, 協約, 労使協約, 取決め, 合意, 契約, 協議, 協議書, 密約, 不正取引, 事件, 案件, 物, 一勝負, 取扱い, 扱い, 待遇, 仕打ち, ディール
　a big deal 一大事, 重大事件, 大したこと, 非常に重要なこと, 大きな取引, 大物
　agree a deal 取決めをまとめる
　cash deal 現金取引
　cold deal 人気のない銘柄
　cut a deal 協定を結ぶ
　do [make] a deal with …と取引する
　get a rough [raw] deal from …からひどい仕打ちを受ける
　give a fair [square] deal 公平に扱う
　seal a deal 契約を結ぶ, 取引契約に調印する
　structured deal 仕組み取引, 仕組み債
　deal a blow to …に打撃を加える, …に打撃を与える
deal with …を処理 [処置] する, 解決する, 取り扱う, 扱う, 取引する, 取引関係にある, 商う, 商売をする, …と密約を結ぶ, …と付き合う, …と会談する, …と折衝する, …に対処する, …に対応する
　deal badly with a person 人を冷遇する
　deal directly with …と直接取引する
　deal well with a person 人を優遇する
　deal with a crisis 危機に対処する, 難局に対処する
　deal with one's anger 怒りをコントロールする
　deal with the problem 問題に対処する, 問題に対応する, 問題を解決する
death 名 死, 死亡, 死者, 死亡者, 終わり, 終末, 絶滅, 消滅
　death blow 致命的な一撃
　death camp 強制収容所（＝concentration camp）
　death certificate 死亡診断書
　death-row inmate [convict] 死刑囚
　death sentence 死刑宣告
　death therapy 対死療法
　death toll 死亡者数, 総死亡者数, 死者数
　death with dignity 尊厳死
　sign one's own death warrant 自分で自分の首を締める
　sound [be] the death knell for [of] …の終焉を告げる
debacle 名 大失敗, 大惨事, 総崩れ, 混乱,〈市場の〉暴落, 崩壊, 瓦解, 大敗北, 大敗走, 完敗, 退散,〈河川の〉決壊, 大洪水, 山津波, 土石流
　debacles in the financial system 金融システムの崩壊, 金融システムの混乱
debate 名 議論, 討論, 討議, 討論会, 論議, 論争, 審議, ディベート
　policy debates 政治論争, 政策論議
　public debate 公開討論
debilitate 動 弱らせる, 衰弱させる, 弱体化させる
debt 名 債務, 負債, 借入れ, 借金, 債権, 借入金, 借入債務, 債務証券, 債券, 金銭債務, 金銭債

務訴訟, 金融債務, デット
clear debts 借金を返済する, 負債の返済に充てる
debt rating 債券格付け, 社債の格付け, 債務証書, 債務契約書 (＝bond rating)
debt restructuring 債務再編, 債務再構成
forgive debt 債務を免除する, 債権を放棄する
in debt 赤字の
outstanding debt 既発債, 借入金残高
unrecoverable debts 不良債権 (＝bad debts, nonperforming loans, uncollectible loans)

debt-for-equity swap 〈貸し手にとっての〉債権株式化, 〈借り手にとっての〉債務株式化, デット・エクイティ・スワップ (＝debt equity swap: 「債務の株式化」は, 金融機関に融資(借入金)を出資に振り替えてもらい, 株券を渡して増資すること)

debt-saddled 形 借金を背負っている, 負債 [債務, 赤字] を抱えた, 経営再建中の

debt security 債務証券, 債券, 債務証書 (＝debt, debt instrument:「債務証券」は, 一般に債券などの有価証券を指す)
 discount on the debt securities 社債発行差金
 issuance of debt and equity securities to the public 債券と株式の公募発行
 short-term debt and related securities 短期債務と関連証券
 underwrite debt securities 債務証券を引き受ける

debt servicing 債務返済, 債務の支払い, 利息払い (＝debt paying, debt service)
 debt-servicing capacity [capability] 債務返済能力
 debt servicing costs [expenditures] 国債費 (国債の償還とその利払いにあてる費用)

debut 動 発売する, 新規上場する, 上場する, 初登場する, 初舞台を踏む, デビューする
▶ Xinhua Finance was the first foreign firm to *debut* on the TSE Mothers market for start-ups. 新興企業向け市場の東証マザーズに上場したのは, 新華ファイナンス(中国の金融情報サービス会社)が外国企業としては初めてだ。

debut 名 発売, 新規上場, 上場, 初登場, 初舞台, 最初, 駆け出し, デビュー (＝initial public offering)

deceleration 名 低下, 減速, 鈍化, 鎮静化
decentralization 名 地方分権, 地方分散, 多極分散, 分権化, 非中央集権化, 集中排除
 decentralization of management 経営の分散化, 分散管理, 分権的管理
 economic decentralization 経済力集中排除
 industrial decentralization 産業分権化, 工業分権化

decide 動 決める, 決定する, 方針を固める, 解決する, 判断する, 決議する, 判定する, 判決[審判]を下す, 裁決する

decision 名 決定, 意思決定, 決断, 判断, 決議, 判定, 判決, 裁決
 business decision 経営判断, 企業の意思決定, 事業決定
 credit decision 融資判断, 与信判断, 信用判断
 decision accounting 意思決定会計
 market-driven decision 市場原理に基づく意思決定
 programed decision 定型的意思決定, 計画的決定 (＝programmed decision, programed decision making)
 subjective decision 主観的意思決定
 tactical decision 戦術的意思決定

decision making 意思決定, 政策決定, 経営判断
 decision-making forum 意思決定の場
 programed decision making 定型的意思決定 (＝programed decision, programmed decision making)
 short-run decision making 短期意思決定
 transparency in decision making 意思決定の透明性

decisive 形 決定的な, 決め手となる, 決定づける, 断固たる, 〈性格などが〉果断な, 果敢な, 決然とした, 決断力のある, 疑いの余地のない, 明白な, はっきりした
 be decisive of …を決定づける, …を決する, …の決め手となる, …を終局に導く
 decisive evidence [proof] 決定的証拠, 確証
 decisive manager 決断力のある経営者 [管理者, 監督]
 decisive measures 断固たる措置, 断固とした処置
 give a decisive answer きっぱり答える
 play a decisive role in …で決定的な役割を果たす [役割を演じる]

decommissioned aircraft carrier 退役空母, 退役航空母艦

declaration 名 宣言, 布告, 声明, 公表, 発表, 告白, 〈原告の〉供述 [訴答, 請求申立て], 〈証人の〉非宣誓供述, 申告, 宣告, 決議, 宣言書, 布告

文, 声明書, 声明文, 申告書
declaration forms　課税申告書, 収入申告書
declaration of import　輸入申告
declaration of political views　政見発表
declaration of the poll　選挙結果の公式発表
declaration of war　宣戦布告
duty of declaration　通知義務
import declaration system　輸入届け出制

declare 動　〈配当支払いなどを〉宣言する, 申告する, 計上する, 公表する, 発表する
be declared bankrupt　破産宣告を受ける
declare a cash dividend　現金配当を宣言する

decline 動　減少する, 低下する, 下落する, 落ち込む, 悪化する, 低迷する, 後退する, 衰退する, 縮小する, マイナスになる, 辞退する, 断る, 拒む

decline 名　減少, 低下, 下降, 下落, 悪化, 低迷, 後退, 衰退, 縮小, 落ち込み
back-to-back declines in two months　2か月連続の減少[下落]
buy on decline　押し目買い
credit decline　信用の質の低下, 信用の低下, 信用度の悪化（=decline in credit quality）
decline in capital expenditure　設備投資の減少
decline in inventories　在庫の減少
decline in refinancings　借換えの減少
earnings decline　利益[収益]の減少, 減益, 収益減（=decline in earnings, profit decline）
sharp decline in the business performance of export-related businesses　輸出関連業界[輸出関連企業]の急速な業績悪化
triple decline　トリプル安

declining 形　減少する, 低下する, 下落する, 低迷する, 傾く, 傾斜する, 斜陽の, …の低下, …の悪化

decode 動　解読する, 〈コードを〉復号する

decoupling 名　連動しないこと, 非連動, 非連動性, 脱同調化, デカップリング
decoupling theory　脱同調化理論, 非連動論, デカップリング論（世界景気は米国の景気と乖離して推移する, つまり米国の景気減速は中国やインドなど新興市場国の発展が続くので世界的な景気減速にはつながらない, という考え方）

decrease 動　減少させる, 引き下げる, 低下させる, 軽減する, 減少する, 低下する
decreased capital expenditures　設備投資の削減
decreased demand　需要減

decreased dividend　減配, 配当引下げ

dedication 名　献身, 専念, 専心, 除幕式, 献呈, 献辞

deduct 動　差し引く, 控除する, 引き落とす

deduction 名　差引, 控除, 控除項目, 差引額, 控除額, 減少額, 減額, 損金, 損金算入,〈送り状価格の〉引下げ, 演繹

deem 動　…と考える[思う, 見なす, 解釈する, 判断する]
deem highly of　…を尊敬する
deem lightly of　…を軽視する
deemed corporation　見なし法人
deemed issue　見なし発行
taxation on deemed dividend　見なし配当課税

deep 形　深い, 深層の, 深刻な, 複雑な, 難解な, 分かりにくい, 厄介な, ずるい, 腹黒い, 大量の, 大幅な, 大がかりな
deep cover　極秘にすること, 巧みに正体を隠すこと
deep discounter　超安売り店, 大幅割引店, ディープ・ディスカウンター（=hard discounter）
deep freeze　凍結, 凍結状態, 一時停止, 棚上げ, 急速冷凍, 冷凍冷蔵庫
deep recession　深刻なリセッション, 深刻な景気後退期, 深刻な不況（=severe recession）
deep-seated distrust　根深い不信
deep-set opposition　根強い反対
deep space　太陽系外宇宙空間, 深宇宙

deep six [deep-six, deepsix] 動　処分する, 廃棄する, 破壊する,〈水中に〉投棄する, 否決する,〈意見などを〉お払い箱にする, 名　処分, 廃棄, 投棄

deep throat　〈政府部内の〉内部告発者, 密告者, 情報源, ディープ・スロート（「ディープ・スロート」の名は, ニクソン米大統領を辞任に追い込んだ1972年6月のウォーターゲート事件当時, 話題を呼んだポルノ映画の題名からとられた）

deepen 動　深める,〈悲しみなどを〉増す, 深まる, 濃くなる, 悪化する, 深化する, 深刻化する
deepen ties with　…との関係を深める, …との関係を強化する

defamation 名　中傷, 誹謗, 悪口, 名誉毀損

default 動　履行しない, 実行しない, 出場しない, 欠場する, 欠席する, 裁判に欠席する, 欠席裁判を受ける, デフォルトになる, デフォルトに陥る, デフォルトを起こす
default on debt payments　債務返済でデフォ

ルトを起こす, 債務返済でデフォルトに陥る, 債務返済を実行しない
  default on one's obligations …の義務を履行しない, …の義務を実行しない
  default on the debt 債務を履行しない, 債務が不履行になる, 債務がデフォルトになる
  defaulted receivables 不履行債権, 不履行発生債権, デフォルトに陥った債権
default 名 債務不履行, 貸倒れ, 支払い停止, 滞納, 欠場, 不出場, 〈法廷への〉欠席, 〈コンピュータの〉既定値, 省略値, デフォルト値, デフォルト (=default of obligations)
  avoid [ward off] default on debt 債務不履行を避ける, 債務不履行を回避する
  be in danger of net capital deficiency, defaults of obligations and continued operating losses 債務超過や債務不履行, 継続的な営業損失などが発生する恐れがある
  be in default 〈義務・債務・契約などが〉不履行である
  declare default on national debt 国債の債務不履行を宣言する
  default premium 債務不履行プレミアム(約定利回りと期待利回りとの差)
  default risk 債務不履行リスク, 不履行リスク, 貸倒れリスク, デフォルト・リスク
  default setting 初期設定
  default value 初期値
  go into default 債務不履行になる
  judgment [judgement] by default 欠席裁判
  possible default on yen-denominated Argentine government bonds 予想される円建てアルゼンチン国債のデフォルト
  tax for default 加算税
defeat 動 破る, 負かす, 打ち負かす, 勝利を収める, 無効にする, 挫折させる, 覆す, 失敗させる, 〈提案などを〉否決する
defeat 名 負け, 敗北, 失敗, 挫折, 頓挫, 打倒, 打破
  crushing [massive] defeat 大敗
  suffer [meet, sustain] defeat 敗北を喫する
defect 名 欠陥, 瑕疵, 不具合, 欠点
  defects in the law 法の不備
  latent defect 隠れた欠陥, 隠れた瑕疵
defector 名 亡命者, 離党者, 〈他の会社やグループに〉移る人
defend 動 守る, 防ぐ, 防衛する, 防衛策をとる, 保護する, 擁護する, 弁護する

defendant 名 被告, 被告人
  a codefendant 共同被告
  a defendant's representative 被告代理人
defense [defence] 名 防衛, 国防, 防備, 防衛策, 防衛力, 防衛手段, 防衛施設, 防御物, 防御, 保護, 擁護, 弁護, 抗弁, 被告側, ディフェンス
  art [science] of defense 護身術
  defense against a takeover 買収防衛策
  defense attorney 弁護人, 被告側弁護士
  defense buildup 防衛力増強
  defense counsel 〈被告側〉弁護団, 弁護側
  Defense Intelligence Agency 〈米国防総省〉国防情報局
  defense lawyer 被告側の弁護士
  defense mechanism 防衛機制, 防衛機構
  defense-only policy 専守防衛の理念
  Defense Secretary 国防長官
  defense spending [expenditure, outlay] 国防費, 防衛支出
  dollar defense ドル防衛 (=defense of [for] the dollar)
  in defense of …を守って, …を防衛した, …を弁護して
  legal defense 正当防衛
  takeover defense 買収防衛手段, 防衛手段, 乗っ取り防衛手段, 買収防衛策
defensive 形 守りの, 防備の, 防御の, 守勢の, 自衛上の, 名 防衛, 守勢, 弁護
  defensive actions 防衛措置
  defensive consumer 消費に消極的な消費者
  defensive merger 防衛的合併(敵対的買収を防ぐ手段として, 独占禁止法などの法律に抵触する恐れのある同業他社や政府規制を受けている業種の会社などとあらかじめ合併してしまうこと)
  defensive view of the future 先行きについての慎重な見方
  on [onto] the defensive 守勢で, 防戦に努めて
defensive measure 防衛策, 防衛措置 (=corporate defensive measure, defense measure)
  adopt defensive measures against a hostile takeover 敵対的な買収[M&A]に対する防衛策を導入する
  defensive measures from hostile takeover 敵対的買収防衛策
deferred tax assets 繰延べ税金資産《略 DTAs》(=potential tax credits)
deficiency 名 不足, 欠損, 債務超過, 不足額,

損失金, 欠如, 欠乏, 欠陥, 欠点, 弱点, 不備
deficiency in assets 債務超過
deficiency of net assets 欠損金
deficiency payment 不足額の支払い, 不足払い, 赤字補填

deficit 名
損失, 欠損金, 損失金, 営業損失, 赤字, 不足, 不足額, 債務超過
accumulated deficit 累積赤字
current account deficit 経常赤字
deficit-covering bonds 赤字国債, 赤字地方債
deficit settlement of accounts 赤字決算
hit a record deficit 過去最悪の赤字となる, 過去最大の赤字となる
operate at a deficit 赤字経営をする
revenue deficit 歳入欠陥
twin deficits 双子の赤字
U.S. deficits 米国の財政赤字額, 米国の財政赤字 (=federal deficits)

deficit-ridden 形 赤字に悩む

define 動 明らかにする, 明確にする, 定義する, 示す, 規定する

defined 形 明確化した, 確定した, 限定された, 定義された, はっきりとした, 際立った
defined benefit plan 確定給付年金制度, 確定給付制度, 給付建て年金制度, 給付建て制度
defined contribution pension 確定拠出型年金(日本版401k), 確定拠出年金 (=defined contribution annuity：退職後の年金給付額が, 基金に対する掛金の額と基金の投資収益に基づいて算定される退職給付制度. 運用の成否で, 将来の年金額が増減する)

deflate 動 〈タイヤなどの〉空気を抜く, しぼませる, 〈インフレ安定のために通貨を〉収縮させる, 〈物価水準を〉引き下げる, 自信を失わせる, 鼻をへし折る, 〈記事などの〉間違いを指摘する, デフレ政策を取る
wages deflated by consumer prices 消費者物価指数を基準とする実質賃金

deflation 名 通貨収縮, 物価下落, 収縮, 下落, デフレ, デフレーション
counter [prevent, stop] deflation デフレを阻止する
creeping deflation 忍び寄るデフレ, 緩やかなデフレ (=mild deflation)
deflation of asset values 資産価格の下落, 資産デフレ
deflation policy デフレ政策, 収縮政策
hyper-deflation 超デフレーション

deflationary 形 通貨収縮の, 物価下落の, デフレの, デフレ的
deflationary gap デフレ・ギャップ
deflationary spiral デフレの悪循環, デフレ的循環, デフレ・スパイラル

deflator 名 デフレーター, 価格修正因子

deforestation 名 森林伐採

defraud 動 だまし取る, 詐取する, 〈財産などを〉巻き上げる
defraud customers of five million dollars 顧客から500万ドルを詐取する

defray 動 支払う(pay), 〈経費を〉支出する, 〈費用などを〉負担する

delay 名 遅延, 遅滞, 遅れ, 延期, 〈商品の〉延着, 猶予
delay in economic improvement 景気回復の遅れ (=delay in economic recovery)

delegation 名 代表団, 派遣団, 委任

deliberation 名 討議, 協議, 審議, 熟慮, 熟考, 慎重

delicatessen 名 調理済み食品販売店 (=deli)

delist 動 上場を廃止する, 上場を停止する

delisting 名 上場廃止, 上場停止

deliver 動 届ける, 配達する, 引き渡す, 渡す, 交付する, 送達する, 納入する, 提供する, 達成する, 実行する, 〈判定や評決などを〉行う, 〈判定を〉下す, 〈原油などを〉産出する

delivery 名 配達, 送達, 配送, 出荷, 納品, 納入, 完納, 引渡し, 受渡し, 交付, 意見の発表, 演説, 話し振り, 陳述, 解放, 救出, 分娩
buy for future delivery 先渡しで買う
cash on delivery sale 代金[現金]引換販売 (=COD sale, collect on delivery sale)
collect on delivery 代金引換渡し
door-to-door delivery service 宅配便 (=door-to-door parcel delivery service)
physical delivery 現物受渡し, 現渡し, 現引き

deluge 名 大洪水, 豪雨, 殺到, 氾濫, 動 〔受身形で〕殺到する, 押し寄せる, 〈場所を〉水浸しにする
a deluge of …の殺到, 大量の…
After us [me] the deluge! (わが亡き)後は野となれ山となれ.
be deluged with complaints 〈…に〉苦情が殺到する
have a deluge of offers 申し込みが殺到する

demand 動 要求する, 請求する, 求める, 要する, 必要とする

demand 名 需要, 要求, 請求, 催促, 申立て書,

デマンド
credit demand 信用需要, 資金需要
demand for arbitration 仲裁の請求, 仲裁申立て書
demand note 請求書, 一覧払い約束手形
final demand 最終需要
loan demand 借入需要 (＝demand for loans)
marginal demand 限界需要
meet [satisfy] demand 需要を満たす
sluggish [slack, slow] demand 需要の低迷, 需要不振
supply the demands for …の需要を満たす
demand-supply 形 需給の
　demand-supply adjustment 需給調整 (＝supply-demand adjustment)
　demand-supply gap 需給ギャップ
　demand-supply shortfall 需要不足
dementia 名 認知症
demilitarization 名 非武装化, 非軍事化
Demilitarised Zone 非武装地帯《略 DMZ》
democrat 名 民主主義者, 民政治論者, 米民主党員 (D., Dem., Democrat), 米民主党支持者
democratic 形 民主主義の, 民主制の, 民主政治の, 民主的な, 米民主党の (Democratic), 平等な, 庶民的な
　democratic centralism 民主集中制
　Democratic convention 〈米〉民主党大会
　democratic government 民主政治
　Democratic leaders 〈米〉民主党指導部
　Democratic National Convention 〈米〉民主党全国大会
　Democratic Party 〈米〉民主党
　Democratic Party of Japan 〈日本の〉民主党
　Democratic People's Republic of Korea 朝鮮民主主義人民共和国, 北朝鮮《略 DPRK》
democratization 名 民主化
Democrats 名 米民主党
demographic 形 人口動態に関する, 人口統計学の, 人口統計上の
　age-specific demographic structure 年齢別人口構成
　demographic change [shifts] 〈少子化, 高齢化などの〉人口動態変化, 人口統計の変化, 人口構成の変化
　demographic data 人口統計データ
　demographic statistics 人口動態統計, 人口統計

demographic structure 人口構成
demographic trend 人口動態
demonstration 名 デモ, デモ行進, 集団意思表示, 示威運動, 実物宣伝, 実演, 実演宣伝, 実演販売, 実証実験, 実証, 表示, 表明, 明示, 立証, 証明, 論証, 証拠, 例証, 実例, 陽動作戦, デモンストレーション
　demonstration expenses 実演宣伝費
　demonstration parade [march] デモ行進
　disperse a demonstration デモを解散させる
　mount a mass demonstration 大衆デモをやる
　put down a demonstration デモを鎮圧する
　stage [hold] a demonstration デモをやる
　Tiananmen [Tian An Men] demonstrations 天安門事件 (＝Tiananmen incident)
demonstrator 名 デモ参加者, デモ隊, 示威運動参加者, 実演販売員, 実演者, 実物宣伝用商品, 実地教授者, 立証者 [証明者, 論証者], 証拠となるもの
　crackdown on demonstrators 抗議デモ弾圧
-denominated 形 …建ての, …表示の, …ベースの
　dollar-denominated deal ドル建て案件
　dollar-denominated instrument ドル建て商品
　dollar-denominated new issuance ドル建て起債総額
　dollar-denominated receivables ドル建て債権
　in dollar-denominated terms ドル建てで, ドル表示で
　yen-denominated amounts 円ベースの総額
　yen-denominated bond 円建て債, 円債
　yen-denominated exports 円建て輸出
denomination 名 種類, 金種, 額面金額, 券面額, 貨幣金額, 〈金銭や重量などの〉単位 [名称], 表示
　currency denomination 通貨単位
　currency of denomination 表示通貨
　denominations of currency 金種
　minimum denomination 最低券面単位
denuclearization 名 非核化, 核放棄
denuclearize 動 非核化する, 核兵器を撤去する, 〈…の〉核武装を禁止 [解除] する
department 名 部門, 部, 課, 局, 省, 学部, 学科, 売り場, コーナー, 活動領域, 活動分野, 責任領域

Department for Education 〈英〉教育省
Department of Public Safety 〈米州の〉公安局
Department of Social Security 〈英〉社会福祉省
Department of the Environment 〈英〉環境保護局
New York Police Department ニューヨーク警察署
operating department 事業部門
purchasing department 購買部門

米国の主要政府政機関:

Department of Agriculture	農務省
Department of Commerce	商務省
Department of Defense	国防総省
Department of Education	教育相
Department of Energy	エネルギー省
Department of Health and Human Services	保健・福祉省, 保健社会福祉省
Department of Housing and Urban Development	住宅・都市開発省
Department of Justice	司法省
Department of Labor	労働省
Department of State	国務省
Department of the Interior	内務省
Department of Transportation	運輸省
Department of the Treasury	財務省
Department of Veterans Affairs	復員軍人省

dependence 名 依存, 依存状態, 依存度, 依存症, 依存関係, 常用癖, 信頼, 信用, 左右されること
　dependence on imports 輸入依存 (＝import dependence)
　dependence on specific market segments 特定市場への依存［依存度］
dependent 名 扶養家族, 被扶養者, 扶養親族
　allowances for dependents 扶養控除
　exemption for dependents 扶養控除
deploy 動 配備する, 実戦配備する, 配置する, 展開する, 装備する, 効果的に活用する
deployment 名 配備, 配置, 展開, 装備
　deployment of multinational forces 多国籍軍の配備
　forward deployment strategy 前方展開戦略
deportation order 国外退去命令
deposition 名 宣誓証言, 証言, 宣誓証書, 供述調書, 罷免, 免職, 堆積, 沈殿

depot 名 貯蔵所, 貯蔵施設, 補給所
depreciate 動 低下する, 下落する, 価値が下がる, 軟化する, 通貨を切り下げる, 減価償却する, 償却する
　depreciate over time 長期的に下落する
　depreciate the currency 通貨を切り下げる
depreciation 名 価値低下, 〈価格などの〉低下, 〈通貨の〉下落, 減価, 平価切下げ, 減価償却, 減価償却費, 償却, 償却費
　a moderate depreciation of the dollar 緩やかなドル安
　depreciation expense [cost] 減価償却費
　depreciation-inflation spiral 通貨切下げとインフレの悪循環
　depreciation of the real exchange rare 実質為替レートの下落
　depreciation period 減価償却期間, 耐用年数
　market value depreciation 市場価格の低下
　real depreciation in currencies 実質ベースでの通貨下落
depress 動 不景気にする, 不振にする, 低迷させる, 下落させる, 下落［縮小, 低迷］を招く, 押し下げる, 下げる, 圧迫する, 鈍化させる, 抑制する, 沈滞させる, 憂うつにする, 落胆［がっくり］させる, 意気消沈させる, 弱める, 衰えさせる
　depress economic activity 経済活動を沈滞させる
　depress economic growth 経済成長を鈍化させる
　depress interest rates 金利を引き下げる
　depress personal spending 個人支出の低迷を招く, 消費支出の低迷をもたらす, 個人消費の冷え込みをもたらす
depressed 形 不景気の, 不況の, 低迷した, 不振の, 貧困にあえぐ, 落胆した, 気落ちした, 体調を崩した
　depressed area [region] 不況地域, 貧困地区
　depressed classes 〈インドの〉最下層階級
　depressed consumer confidence 消費者マインドの冷え込み
　depressed economy 景気低迷
　depressed industry 不況産業, 産業不振
　depressed market 市場低迷, 沈滞市況, 相場の下落
　depressed sales 売上高の低下, 販売低迷, 販売不振
depressing effect 抑制効果, 下押し効果
depression 名 不況, 不況期, 不景気, 景気停

滞, 大恐慌, 低下, 停滞, 沈下, 減退, 衰弱, 意気消沈, うつ病, 低気圧
barometric depression 低気圧
the (Great) Depression 大恐慌, 世界大恐慌
world [global, worldwide] depression 世界的不況

DEPs ディーゼル排気微粒子 (**diesel exhaust particles**の略。ディーゼル排気に含まれる黒いすす状の粒子状物質で, 石油の不完全燃焼時に作られる。DEP中のポリフェノール化合物に活性酵素など反応性の高いラジカル化合物が含まれ, ぜんそくや肺がんなどの原因になっている。)

depth 名 深さ, 深度, 奥行き, 度合い, 〈市場などの〉厚み, 強さ, 力強さ, 濃さ, 激しさ, 奥底, 底, 深刻な時期, 〈問題などの〉難解さ, 分かりにくさ
depth charge [bomb] 〈潜水艦用〉爆雷
depth feasibility study 綿密な事業化調査
depth finder 水深測定器
depth gauge 測深器
depth interview 深層面接, 深層面接法, 深層テスト
in depth 徹底的に, 詳細に
in the depth(s) of …の最中に
management in depth 層の厚い経営
out of [beyond] one's depth 力 [能力] が及ばないで, 理解できないで, どうにもできないで
plumb the depths 極みに達する, どん底を経験する, 隠された部分を探す [見つける], どん底に沈む
sink to the depths ひどいことをする
the depth of despair 絶望のどん底
the depth of the recession 深刻な不況

deregulate 動 規制を緩和する, 規制を撤廃する, 自由化する, 市場開放する

deregulation 名 規制緩和, 規制撤廃, 自由化, 市場開放
deregulation of the civil aviation industry 民間航空産業の規制緩和, 空の規制緩和, 航空自由化
financial deregulation 金融の規制緩和 (= **deregulation of finance**)

derivative 名 派生商品, 金融派生商品, デリバティブ (= **derivative product**)
┌ **デリバティブとは** ⇒ 通貨や株式の現物取引でなく, 相場の変動を予測して行う先物取引や異なる通貨や金利を交換するスワップ取引, 株式や債券を売買する権利を取引するオプション取引など, 特殊な取引を組み合わせた金融派生商品。
credit derivatives 信用派生商品

derivative investment デリバティブ投資, 金融派生商品取引
derivative product 派生商品, 金融派生商品, デリバティブ (= **derivative**)
derivative transaction デリバティブ取引
equity derivatives 株式派生商品
financial derivatives 金融派生商品
mortgage derivatives モーゲージ派生商品

design 動 設計する, 計画する, 企画する, 整備する, 意匠を作る
▶ A stock split is a measure *designed* to enable investors, including those with only limited funds, to invest in a company by reducing the share purchase unit. 株式分割は, 株式の購入単位を小口化して, 少額の資金しかない投資家でも企業に投資できるようにするための手段 [資本政策] だ。

design 名 設計, 計画, 企画, 構想, 企て, もくろみ, 意図, 意匠, 模様, 図案, 下絵, 設計図, デザイン
cubic design 立体デザイン
design automation 設計自動化, デザイン・オートメーション《略 **DA**》
design, construction and testing 設計, 製作と実験
earthquake-proof design 耐震設計
experimental design 実験計画法
industrial design 工業デザイン, 工業意匠, インダストリアル・デザイン
industrial new design 実用新案
package design 包装デザイン, 包装意匠
process design プロセス設計
product design 製品のデザイン, 製品設計, 製品計画

designate 形 指名された, 指名を受けた, 内定の, 未就任の, 次期…, 新任命の
Council of Economic Advisers Director-designate 次期経済諮問委員会委員長
Premier-designate 次期首相, 新任命首相
treasury secretary-designate 次期米財務長官

desktop 形 卓上の, 卓上型, 卓上型, デスクトップ型, 名 デスクトップ型コンピュータ, コンピュータの画面, 画面の背景

destabilization 名 錯乱, 不安定化, 弱体化, 打倒

destabilize 動 錯乱する, 不安定にする, 弱体化させる, 動揺させる

destroy 動 破壊する, 壊す, 打ち砕く, 滅ぼす, 台なしにする, 〈文書などを〉無効にする, 〈動物などを〉

処分する, 殺す

destroyer 名 破壊者, 破壊するもの, 駆逐艦
detain 動 監禁[拘置, 留置, 拘留, 軟禁]する, 身柄を拘束する, 引き留める, 待たせる, 手間取らせる, 保留する
  be detained at a police station for questioning 取り調べのため警察署に拘留[留置]される
  be detained by an accident 事故で遅れる
  release [free] a detained American 拘束米国人を釈放する
  the police detain a person as a suspect 警察が人を容疑者として拘留[留置]する
detainee 名 抑留者, 身柄拘束者
  political detainees 政治的抑留者
  the handover of the detainees 身柄拘束者の引渡し
deteriorate 動 悪化する, 悪くなる, 深刻化する, 深刻になる, 低下する, 下落する, 減少する, 停滞する, 退化する, 老朽化する, 劣化する
  deteriorate further 一段と悪化する
  deteriorated earnings 業績の悪化
  deteriorated profitability 収益性の悪化
  deteriorating business 経営悪化
  deteriorating credit quality 信用の質の悪化, 信用度の悪化, 信用力の低下
  deteriorating employment situation 雇用環境の悪化, 雇用の悪化
  deteriorating subprime-loan market サブプライム・ローン(低所得者向け住宅融資)市場の悪化
deterioration 名 悪化, 低下, 減少, 停滞, 品質低下, 退化, 劣化, 老朽化
  business deterioration of borrowers 融資先の業績悪化
  credit [credit quality] deterioration 信用力[信用の質]の低下 (=deterioration in credit quality)
  deterioration in asset quality 資産の質の悪化
  earnings deterioration 収益の悪化, 業績の悪化
  profit deterioration 減益, 利益の減少
deterrence 名 抑止, 抑止力, 抑止効果
deterrent 名 抑止力, 抑止手段, 妨げるもの, 引留め役, 形 阻止する, 抑止力のある (⇒military deterrent, nuclear deterrent)
  deterrent capability 核抑止力

  deterrent effect 抑止効果
  deterrent potential 抑止力
  missile deterrent ミサイルによる抑止力
  nuclear deterrent 核抑止力
  war deterrent 戦争抑止力
  work as a deterrent 抑止力になる
detrimental 形 有害な, …に害[損失, 損害]を与える, 不利益な, マイナスの, 好ましくない
devastate 動 壊滅的打撃を与える, 完全に破壊する, 荒廃させる, 荒らす, 圧倒する, 圧勝する, 負かす, 唖然とさせる
develop 動 開発する, 整備する, 改善する, 改良する, 発展させる, 育成する, 土地などを造成する, 展開する, 現像する (=reve up)
developing 形 発展[発達]途上の, 開発途上の, 発展[開発]途上にある, 開発の
  advanced developing country 先進発展途上国, 先進開発途上国《略 ADC》
  developing areas 発展途上地域
  developing country exports 途上国輸出[輸出額]
  developing economies 新興国, 発展途上国 (=emerging economies)
  developing environments 発展途上国, 開発途上国
  developing fund 開発資金
  developing nation [country] 発展途上国, 開発途上国, 途上国
  developing world 発展途上世界, 第三世界 (=developing nations)
development 名 開発, 整備, 構築, 教育, 発展, 進歩, 進展, 展開, 推移, 動き, 情勢 (⇒sustainable development)
  application development system アプリケーション開発システム
  business development ビジネス開発, ビジネスの展開, 業務展開
  development assistance agency 開発援助機関
  development cost 開発費
  development fund 開発基金
  development project 開発計画, 開発事業, 開発プロジェクト
  economic development 経済開発, 経済発展, 経済成長, 景気動向
  end user development エンドユーザー開発
  full-scale development 本格開発
  infrastructure development インフラ開発, イ

ンフラ整備
joint development 共同開発
skills development スキル開発
device 名 装置, 周辺機器, 電気部品, 素子, 道具, 手段, 方策, 工夫, 考案, 操作, 計画, 図案, 模様, 意匠, デバイス
accounting device 会計上の操作
anti-inflationary device インフレ抑制の手段
charge coupled devices 電荷結合素子
electronic device 電子装置, 電子機器
input device 入力装置
magnetic memory device 磁気記憶装置
mobile devices 携帯機器
output device 出力装置
peripheral device 周辺装置, 周辺機器
portable device 移動端末
silicon on insulator device SOI素子
DI 景気動向指数, 業況判断指数 (**diffusion index**の略。⇒diffusion index, indicator)
business conditions DI 業況判断DI
coincident DI 一致指数DI
DI index 業況判断指数, 景気動向指数, DI指数
DI reading DIの数値
leading DI 先行指数DI
manufacturing DI 製造業の業況判断DI
overall financial conditions DI 資金繰り判断DI
price DI 価格判断DI
sentiment DI 業況判断DI
diabetes 名 糖尿病
dialogue [dialog] 名 対話, 対話体, 会話, 対談, 意見交換, 討論, 問答, 会議, 会談 (⇒framework of dialogue)
carry on a dialogue upon …について話し合う
enter into a dialogue with …と話し合いに入る
hold a dialogue together 話し合う
resume a dialogue with …との会談を再開する
solve the issue through a dialogue 対話で問題を解決する
dialysis 名 透析, 人工透析
DIC 預金保険機構 (**Deposit Insurance Corporation**の略)
dictatorial 形 独裁者の, 専制的な
dictatorial regime 独裁体制
dictatorial state 独裁体制の国
Diet 名 〈日本・ドイツ・デンマークなどの〉国会, 議会 (⇒Congress, Parliament)

a Diet guard 国会衛視
a Diet member 国会議員
a Diet record 国会議事録
a Diet seat 議席
an extraordinary Diet session 臨時国会
an ordinary Diet session 通常国会
both houses of the Diet 衆参両院
Diet deliberations 国会審議
the confidence of the Diet 国会の信任
the Diet Building 国会議事堂
diet aid ダイエット食品 (=weight-reducing food supplement)
difference 名 差, 差異, 違い, 区別, 意見の違い [食い違い], 意見の不一致, 意見の対立, 不和, 紛争, 格差, 差額, 不足分, 重大な変化 [影響]
a difference of opinion 意見の不一致, 意見の相違
a difference with one's superior 上役との不和, 上役との意見の違い
a distinction without a difference 不当な差別
class difference 階級的差別
clearest differences 決定的な違い
difference or dispute 意見の相違または紛争, 見解の相違または紛争
for all the difference it makes ほとんど違いがないことを考慮に入れて
important [striking] differences 大きな違い
iron out the differences 意見の対立の溝を埋める, 意見の違い [食い違い] を調整する
key [principal] difference 最大の違い
make a big [all the, great] difference 重大な相違を生じる, 決定的な違いを生じる, 重大な影響を持つ, 大きな関係がある, 大きな問題である, 大変なことになる, 大変重要である
make a difference 差をつける, 差異を生じる, 影響する, 重要である
make no difference 少しも重要でない, 変わりはない, どうでもいい
make up [settle] one's differences 不和 [紛争] を解決する
make up the difference 〈…で〉差額を埋め合わせする, 必要な金額の残りを出す
maximum difference 極大差
meet [pay] the difference 差額を支払う
regional difference index 地域差指数
sink [bury] one's differences 小異を捨てる
split the difference 妥協する, 歩み寄る, 折り

合う, 残りを均等に分ける[等分する], 差額の半分をとる
systematic differences 一貫した違い
with a difference 面白い, 珍しい, 一風変わった, 一味違った, 特別な, 並はずれた, 他のものとは違って, 特異なやり方で

differential 形 差別の, 差別的な, 区別の, 特異な, 相違[特性]を示す, 微分の, 名 格差, 賃金格差, 差額
  differential duties [tariff] 差別関税
  differential equation 微分方程式
  differential pricing 差別的価格設定, 差別価格
  interest rate differential 金利格差
  negative differential 長短逆転現象
  price differential 価格差
  yield differential 利回り格差
  wage differential 賃金格差
  widening price differentials 広がる価格格差

difficulties 名 困難, 問題, 苦境, 難局, 危機, 低迷, 悪化, 経営難
  balance of payments difficulties 国際収支の悪化
  financial difficulties 財政的困難, 経営危機, 資金繰りが困難な状況
  in-house difficulties 社内問題
  serious difficulties 深刻な経営難

diffusion index 景気動向指数, 業況判断指数《略 DI》(「業況判断指数」は, 日本銀行が景気の実態を把握するため3か月ごとに行う企業短期経済観測調査で, 企業の景況感を示す指数。⇒indicator)
  diffusion index of business sentiment [confidence] 業況判断指数《略 DI》
  diffusion index of retail prices 販売価格判断DI

dig in one's heels 頑として譲らない, 自らの立場を固守して譲らない

digestive internal department 消化器内科

digit 名 アラビア数字(0から9までの各数字), 数字, 桁
  double-digit increase rate 2桁の伸び率, 10%を超える伸び率
  hundred-digit number 100桁の数字
  significant digit 有効数字
  single-digit growth 1桁の成長, 1桁の経済成長, 10%を超える成長
  sum-of-the years digits method 等差級数法

  three digit inflation 3桁のインフレ

digital 形 デジタルの, デジタル技術の
  digital broadcasting service デジタル放送, デジタル放送サービス
  digital communication system デジタル通信システム
  digital consumer electronics デジタル家電, デジタル家電製品 (＝digital home appliances)
  digital divide 情報格差, 情報を持つ者と持たぬ者の断絶, インターネットを使える人と使えない人との格差, 情報化が生む経済格差, デジタル・デバイド
  digital electric appliances デジタル家電
  digital home appliances 情報家電, デジタル家電 (＝computerized appliances)
  digital household appliances デジタル家電
  digital information デジタル情報
  digital photography デジタル写真技術

dilemma 名 窮地, 難局, 板挟み, 難問, 深刻な問題, 両刀論法, ジレンマ
  a liquidity dilemma 流動性ジレンマ
  a moral dilemma 道徳的難問
  be in a dilemma about …でジレンマに陥っている, …で窮地に陥る
  be in an awkward dilemma 進退窮まる
  be on the horns of a dilemma 進退窮まる, 板挟みになる
  face [confront] a dilemma 板挟みにあう
  pose a dilemma 深刻な問題を引き起こす, 深刻な問題になる
  put a person in [into] a dilemma 人を窮地に陥らせる, 人を窮地に置く

dimension 名 寸法, サイズ, 大きさ, 容積, 面積, 次元, 規模, 範囲, 程度, 重要性, 様相, 面, 局面, 側面, 分野, 要素
  cultural dimension 文化的側面, 文化面
  nominal dimension 公称寸法
  take on dimensions 重要になる
  the dimensions of a problem 問題の範囲, 問題の大きさ, 問題の重要性
  the fourth dimension 4次元
  time dimension 時間次元

dip 動 一時的に下がる, 下落する, 低下する, 下降する, 減少する, 減退する, 下がる, 落ちる, 急降下する, 沈む
  dip below …を割り込む
  dip into currency reserves 外貨準備を使う,

外貨準備を取り崩す
dip into one's savings 貯金[貯蓄]を取り崩す, 貯金の一部を使う[利用する, 活用する]
dip into outright recession 完全な不況に落ち込む
dip to the lows 安値を付ける

dip 名 下落, 低下, 下降, 減少, 減退, 急降下, 沈下, 押し目（株価が下がることを「押し目, 押し, 下押し」と言い, 下げ幅が大きい場合を「深押し」と言う）
buy on dip [reaction] 押し目買い（押し目を狙って買うこと）
dip in profits 減益
dip on oil prices 原油価格の下落
double dip 〈一定期間内の〉2度の下降[下落], 〈景気の〉二番底, 二重払い, 二重取り, 二重の収入, ダブル・ディップ
enter into a genuine double dip recession 景気の本格的な二番底に突入する

diplomacy 名 外交, 外交交渉, 外交交渉術, 外交手腕, 外交術, 駆け引き（＝international politics）
armed diplomacy 武力外交（＝power diplomacy, power politics）
cowboy diplomacy カウボーイ外交, 軍事力偏重の外交（国際社会から批判を受けた8年間のブッシュ外交）
diplomacy on resources 資源外交
dollar diplomacy ドル外交, 金力外交
economic diplomacy 経済外交
equidistant diplomacy 等距離外交
Eurasia diplomacy ユーラシア外交
firm diplomacy 強硬外交
gunboat diplomacy 砲艦外交（大国が武力で小国を威圧して行う外交）
human rights diplomacy 人権外交
humiliating diplomacy 屈辱外交
independent diplomacy 独自外交
neutral diplomacy 中立外交
nonpartisan diplomacy 超党派外交
omnidirectional diplomacy 全方位外交
open diplomacy 公開外交
pound diplomacy ポンド外交
secret diplomacy 秘密外交
shuttle diplomacy 往復外交, シャトル外交
smart power diplomacy スマート・パワー外交（ハード・パワー（軍事）とソフト・パワーを組み合わせた外交）
spineless diplomacy 骨抜き外交
tightrope diplomacy 綱渡り外交
use diplomacy 外交手腕を振るう
warmongering diplomacy おどし外交
whirlwind diplomacy 駆け足外交

diplomat [diplomatist] 名 外交官, 外交手腕に優れた人, 外交家, 如才のない人, 駆け引きのうまい人, 人あしらいのうまい人（＝diplomatic official, foreign service officer）
a career diplomat 生え抜きの外交官, 職業外交官
a diplomat stationed [based] at …駐在の外交官
a student diplomat 外交官補
the top U.S. diplomat 米国務長官
top diplomat at the United Nations 国連大使

diplomatic 形 外交の, 外交上の, 外交関係の, 外交官の, 外交的な, 外交の手腕にすぐれた, 技巧的手腕のある, 人扱いがうまい, 気が利く, 如才ない, 駆け引きがうまい, 原文の
by diplomatic action [means] 外交的折衝によって
classified diplomatic funds 外交機密費
diplomatic bluebook 外交青書
diplomatic break [cessation] 外交断絶, 外交関係の断絶
diplomatic breakthrough 外交交渉の打開
diplomatic channel [trail] 外交ルート
diplomatic circles 外交界
diplomatic copy 原文の書写
diplomatic corps [body] 外交団
diplomatic courier 外交文書運搬者
diplomatic document [correspondence, note, paper] 外交文書
diplomatic enclave 在外公館の敷地
diplomatic evidence 文献上の証拠
diplomatic immunity 外交特権, 外交官免責特権, 外交官特権
diplomatic intercourse 国交
diplomatic isolation 外交的孤立, 外交関係の孤立
diplomatic issue [affair, problem, question] 外交問題
diplomatic language 外交用語（＝diplomatese, diplospeak）
diplomatic maneuvering 外交上の駆け引き
diplomatic mission 外交使節団

diplomatic notes 外交覚書
diplomatic offense [offensive] 外交攻勢
diplomatic official 外交官 (＝diplomat, diplomatist, foreign service officer)
diplomatic passport 外交旅券
diplomatic policy 外交政策, 外交方針
diplomatic pouch [bag] 外交用郵袋
diplomatic privilege 外交特権
diplomatic protection 外交的保護
diplomatic rhetoric [language] 外交辞令
diplomatic sense 外交感覚 (＝sense of diplomacy)
diplomatic service 外交, 外交官勤務, 外交官の職務, 大使[公使]館員 (＝foreign service)
diplomatic setback 外交の失敗
diplomatic skill [talent] 外交的手腕, 外交手腕, 外交術
diplomatic sources 外交筋
diplomatic stance 外交姿勢, 外交の姿勢
diplomatic ties 外交関係 (＝diplomatic relations)

diplomatic relations 外交関係, 国交
(＝diplomatic ties)
  establish [enter into] diplomatic relations [ties] with …との外交関係を樹立する
  restore full diplomatic relations 国交を正常化する
  revival [restoration] of diplomatic relations 外交の再開
  suspend diplomatic relations with …との外交関係を一時停止する

dire 緊急の, 急を要する, 差し迫った, 深刻な, 悲惨な, 恐ろしい, 極度の, ひどい

direct disbursement system 直接支払い制 (＝direct payment system)

direct investment 直接投資 (⇒foreign direct investment)
  direct overseas investment 海外直接投資
  external direct investment 対外直接投資
  inward direct investment 対内直接投資
  vertical direct investment 垂直的直接投資

direction 方向, 方向性, 方針, 指示, 先行き, 傾向, 動向, 流れ, トレンド, 方面, 範囲, 方角, 指示, 指図, 説明, 説明書, 説明書き, 指導, 指揮, 管理, 監督, 演出
  a clear sense of direction 明確な指針, 明確な方向性
  direction finder 方向探知機, 方位測定器
  direction indicator 〈車の〉方向指示器, 〈航空機の〉方向計, 定針儀
  export direction 輸出地域
  from all directions 各方面から
  in all directions 四方八方に
  in the opposition direction 反対方向に
  interest rate direction 金利の先行き, 金利動向 (＝the direction of interest rates)
  move in directions favorable to …に有利な方向に動く, …を優遇する方向に動く
  personal direction 個別指導
  productivity direction 生産力方向
  the directions of trade 貿易の流れ
  under the direction(s) of …の指導[指揮, 管理, 監督, 演出]の下に
  wait for direction 方向性を探る

directive 指令, 命令, 指図, 指令的, 命令的な, 指示的な, 指導的な, 支配的な
  budget directive 予算編成方針
  directive economy 指令経済
  directive interview 指示的面接
  rules directive of …を支配する法則
  Solvency Ratio Directive 自己資本比率指令
  unbiased directive 中立的な調節姿勢
  vote a directive biased toward firmness 金融政策引締めに傾ける決定を下す

director 取締役, 理事, 役員, 局長
  board director 取締役
  board of directors 取締役会, 役員会, 重役会, 理事会
  company director 会社役員, 役員
  executive director 業務執行取締役, 執行取締役, 専務[常務]取締役
  independent director 独立取締役
  inside director 社内取締役, 内部取締役, 内部重役
  meeting of board of directors 取締役会会議, 取締役会
  outside director 社外取締役, 外部取締役
  provisional director 一時取締役
  representative director 代表取締役
  senior managing director 専務, 専務取締役

disability 身体[精神]障害者, 障害, 疾患, 就業[労働]不能, 能力欠如, 無能, 無能力, 無資格
  children with severe disabilities 重度肢体不自由児
  chronic disability 慢性疾患
  development disability 発達障害

disability benefits 疾病給付
disability claims experience 疾病給付金請求件数
disability clause 災害特約
disability income insurance 疾病所得保険
disability insurance 傷病保険, 障害保険
disability pension 障害年金
disability plan 休業補償制度
disability retirement 就労不能退職
disability risk 所得補償リスク
industrial disability 労働不能
learning disability 学習障害
legal disability person 法的無能力者
multiple disability 複合障害
people with disabilities 障害者
permanent disability 永久的高度障害
presumed disability 推定高度障害
physical disability 体の欠陥
specified disability 特定高度障害

disadvantage 名 不利, 不利な立場, 劣位
absolute disadvantage 絶対劣位
competitive disadvantage 競争上の劣位性, 競争不利性, 競争上マイナス

disappointing 形 期待外れの, …の期待を裏切る, 予想を裏切った
disappointing news 悪材料
disappointing performance [results] 期待外れの業績, 期待を裏切る業績, 予想を裏切る業績

disapproval rating 不支持率
disarm 動 武装解除する
disarmament 名 武装解除, 軍備縮小, 軍縮, 軍備撤廃, 兵器処理
disarmament business 兵器処理ビジネス
disarmament conference 軍縮会議
nuclear disarmament 核軍縮

disarray 名 混乱, 無秩序, 乱雑, 乱脈, 乱れ, 不統一
be in disarray 混乱している, 混乱状態だ, 乱雑になっている, 乱れている
be thrown into disarray 波乱の展開となる
disarray in government 閣内不統一
economy in disarray 混乱している経済, 経済の混乱
policy disarray 政策の混乱

disaster 名 災害, 災難, 惨事, 事故, 障害 (fault), 不幸, 失敗, 大失敗, ディザスター
aircraft disaster 航空機事故
development disaster 開発災害

disaster area 被災地, 災害地, 災害指定地域
disaster assistance 災害地支援
disaster countermeasure headquarters 災害対策本部
disaster plan 危機管理マニュアル, ディザスター・プラン
disaster prevention 災害防止, 防災
disaster recovery 障害回復, 災害復興
disaster relief 災害救助, 災害復旧
disaster relief work 災害復旧工事
disaster site 災害の現場, 災害地, 事故現場
ecological disaster 生態系への大惨事
environmental disaster 環境災害
flood disaster 水害
industrial disaster 産業災害, 工場災害
major disaster 大災害, 大失敗
man-made disaster 人災
natural disaster 天災, 自然災害
total [complete] disaster 完全な失敗
worst disaster 最悪の事故

disband 動 解散する, 解体する
disc 名 ディスク (⇒disk)
disciplinary action 懲戒処分, 懲戒 (= disciplinary measures)

discipline 名 訓練, 鍛練, 修養, 規律, しつけ, 風紀, 統制, 抑制, 自制心, 忍耐力, 学習法, 学科, 学問分野, 分野, 懲罰, 懲戒, 制裁 (punishment), 苦行
a wide range of disciplines 幅広い分野
enforce discipline 規律を励行する
fiscal discipline 財政規律
keep discipline 規律を保つ
mental discipline 精神修養, 知的訓練
military discipline 軍規, 軍紀
moral discipline 道徳的規律, 道徳的修養[鍛練], 道徳のしつけ
party discipline committee 党紀委員会
scientific disciplines 科学分野
severe [strict] discipline 厳しい訓練, 厳しいしつけ, 厳しい規律
the lack of discipline 自制心の欠如

disclose 動 開示する, 公開する, 公表する, 発表する, 明示する

disclosure 名 企業内容の開示, 企業経営内容の公開, 企業情報の開示, 情報開示, 情報の公開, 事実の開示, 発明の開示, 開示, 公開, 公開性, 公表, 内容の特定, 告知, ディスクロージャー
adequate disclosure 適切な[十分な, 適正な]

開示, 適切な企業内容開示
disclosure obligation 企業情報開示義務
disclosure of official information 情報公開制度
fair disclosure 公正表示
financial disclosure 財務内容の開示
full disclosure 完全開示, 十分な開示, 完全表示, 完全公開性
global standard information disclosure 世界標準の情報開示
risk disclosure リスク開示
discount 動 割り引く, 割引する, 割り引いて売る［買う］, 織り込む, 調整する
▶ The stock price has already *discounted* recovery prospects. 株価は, すでに業績回復を織り込んでいる。
discount 名 割引, 割引率, 割引額, 割引料, ディスカウント
  cash discount 現金割引
  current discount 現行割引率
  discount consumer-electronics giant 大手量販店
  discount period 割引期間, 割引対象期間
  discount rate 公定歩合 （＝official discount sale)
  discount sales [sale, selling] 値下げセール, 割引販売, 割引売出し, ディスカウント・セール
  official discount rate 公定歩合 （＝discount rate)
  purchase discount 仕入れ割引
  quantity discount 数量割引
  sales discount 売上割引 （＝sales cash discount)
  subdistributor discount 二次代理店割引
  trade discount 卸売り割引, 仲間割引
  volume discount 大口割引, 数量割引, 回数割引
discretion 名 判断, 判断［選択, 行動］の自由, 自由裁量, 裁量, 裁量権, 決定, 自由決定権, 思慮分別, 慎重さ, 口がかたいこと
  age [years] of discretion 分別年齢, 識別年齢（刑法上の責任を持つ年齢で, 英米法では14歳）
  at one's discretion …の判断で, …の決定に従って, …の思いどおりに （＝at the discretion of)
  judicial discretion 法律上の裁量
  leave the matter [issue] to A's discretion 問題をAの判断［裁量］に任せる
  monetary discretion 金融政策
discretionary 形 自由裁量の, 任意の, 随意の, 選択的な
  discretionary account 売買一任勘定, 一任勘定
  discretionary administration 裁量行政
  discretionary consumption 選択的消費
  discretionary contract 随意契約
  discretionary education ゆとりある教育
  discretionary fiscal policy 自由裁量的財政政策
  discretionary fund management 一任勘定の投資運用
  discretionary hour 自由裁量時間
  discretionary income 自由裁量所得, 裁量所得, 純可処分所得
  discretionary investment management arm 一任勘定の投資運用子会社
  discretionary order 売買一任注文
  discretionary outlays 裁量的支出
  discretionary power 裁量権, 自由裁量権
  discretionary spending 裁量的経費, 随意支出, 選択的支出
  discretionary work 裁量労働, みなし労働
  discretionary working system 裁量労働制 （＝discretionary working-hour system)
discrimination 名 差別, 差別待遇, 区別, 識別, 識別力, 鑑識眼, 優遇, えこひいき
  card discrimination code カード識別コード
  ethnic discrimination 民族差別
  pay discrimination in jobs 仕事での給与差別
  price discrimination 価格差別
  sex discrimination 性差別
discussion 名 討議, 審議, 検討, 協議, 論議, 討論, 議論, 話し合い, 話題, 講義, 論文, 論考, ディスカッション
  be down for discussion 討議に持ち出される
  be under discussion in the Diet 国会で審議されている, 国会で審議中だ
  come up for discussion 話題に上る
  discussion memorandum 討議メモ, 討議資料（discussion paper)
  fruitless discussions 無益な論争, 水かけ論
  group discussion conference 集団討議方式
  have a lively discussion about [on] …について活発に話し合う
  invite discussion 是非の批評を乞う
  Management's discussion 経営者の検討［解

説]，経営者の概況説明
Management's Discussion and Analysis 経営者の分析・検討［検討・分析］，経営者の分析・解説，財務分析と説明，経営者による事業概況報告《略 MD&A》
meet for the discussion 一堂に会して議論する
panel discussion 公開討論会，代表討論会，討論会，パネル・ディスカッション
priority in budgetary discussion 予算先議権
the issues under discussion 議論されている問題
trade discussions 貿易協議

diseconomy 名 不経済，デメリット
diseconomies of scale 規模の不経済，規模の不経済性，スケール・デメリット
external diseconomies 外部不経済
internal diseconomies 内部不経済

dishonest businesses 悪徳商法

disk 名 磁気ディスク，磁気ディスク記憶装置，ディスク（＝disc）
blank disk 生ディスク
disk drive ディスク装置，ディスク・ドライブ
floppy disk フロッピー・ディスク（＝diskette, flexible disk）
hard disk 固定ディスク，ハード・ディスク
magnet-optical disk 光磁気ディスク
optical disk 光ディスク
shared disk 共有ディスク

dislocation 名 混乱(disruption)，狂うこと，〈岩石の〉断層，〈骨の〉脱臼
economic dislocation 経済の混乱，経済的混乱
political dislocation 政治の混乱，政治的混乱

dismiss 動 解雇する，解任する，罷免する，追放する，解散させる，却下する，棄却する

dismissal 名 解雇，免職，解任，罷免，追放，解散，却下，棄却，〈訴えの〉取下げ，退去，放校
disciplinary dismissal 懲戒免職
dismissal and nonsuit 訴訟却下
dismissal notice 解雇通知（＝pink slip）
dismissal pay [compensation, wage] 解雇手当（＝severance pay）
dismissal verdict 罷免判決
dismissal without prejudice 再訴可能な訴え却下
temporary dismissal 一時解雇
unfair [wrongful] dismissal 不当解雇

disorder 名 無秩序，混乱，乱雑，乱脈，騒乱，騒動，不調，異常，障害，病気
civil disorder 市民の騒乱
eating disorder 摂食障害
fall [throw] into disorder 大騒ぎになる，大騒ぎにする，秩序を乱す，秩序が乱れる
physical disorder 身体の不調
sleep disorder 睡眠障害

disparity 名 格差，開き，差，相違，差異，不一致，不均衡，不釣り合い，不平等
disparities between public and private sector pensions 年金の官民格差
disparity in technology 技術格差
economic disparities among workers 労働者間の経済格差
income disparity 所得格差（＝income divide, income gap）
public-private disparities 官民格差
societal disparity 社会的格差

dispatch 動 派遣する，〈文書などを〉発送する
dispatch 名 発送，派遣，迅速，速達便，特報，公文書，運送業者，運送店（＝despatch）
dispatch of engineers 技術者派遣
dispatch staff 派遣社員（＝dispatch worker）

disposable 形 自由に使える，自由に処分できる，自由になる，利用できる，使用できる，処分可能な，可処分の，使い捨てできる
disposable goods 使い捨て商品
disposable household income 家計の可処分所得
disposable personal income 個人可処分所得，可処分所得（＝personal disposable income）
disposable profit 処分可能利益

disposable income 可処分所得，税引き後所得，手取り給与(take-home pay)
national disposable income 国民可処分所得
nominal disposable income 名目可処分所得
personal disposable income 個人可処分所得
real disposable income 実質可処分所得
total disposable income 総可処分所得

disposal 名 処分，処理，売却，除却
disposal of a (business) segment 事業部門の処分
disposal of bad loans 不良債権処理（＝bad-loan disposal, disposal of nonperforming loans）
disposal of equipment 設備の処分，設備売却
disposal of industrial waste 産業廃棄物の処理

disposal of shares 株式の売却
loan disposal costs 債権処理費用, 不良債権処理費用
refuse disposal 廃棄物処理
sanitary disposal 衛生的処理
speedy disposal 即時処分
waste disposal 廃棄物処理
waste oil disposal 廃油処理
water disposal 水処理

dispute 名 紛争, 争い, 意見の相違, 論争, 係争, 争議, 議論, 討論, 討議
demarcation dispute 労組間紛争
dispute resolution [settlement] 紛争解決, 紛争処理
dispute settlement 紛争の解決, 紛争処理
dispute settlement procedures 紛争処理手続き
industrial dispute 労働争議, 労使紛争 (= industrial strife, trade dispute)
labor dispute 労働争議
pay dispute 賃金闘争
solidarity dispute 団結争議
tax dispute 税の異議申立て
trade dispute 貿易摩擦, 通商摩擦, 貿易紛争 (= trade conflict, trade friction)

disputed 形 議論[討議, 審議]されている, 論じられている, 〈信憑性, 真偽などが〉疑われている, 争われている, 係争中の, 論争[争議]中の, 未解決の, 紛争の対象となっている, …の論争[紛争], 疑惑の, …の不正疑惑, …疑惑
disputed bills 請求に関する紛争
disputed nuclear weapons 核戦争の論争
disputed presidential election 大統領選挙の不正疑惑
disputed territory 紛争地域

disruption 名 混乱, 中断, 停止, 分裂, 崩壊, 破壊, 遮断, 粉砕, 途絶, 継続[存続]不可能, 通信の途絶, 通信障害
disruption in the economy 経済の混乱 (= economic disruption)
disruption of energy supply エネルギー供給の中断
environmental disruption 環境破壊, 環境の悪化, 公害
labor disruptions 労働争議
market disruption 市場の混乱, 市場崩壊
systemic disruption システミック・リスク
temporary disruption of foreign aid 対外援助の一時停止[凍結]

dissident 名 反体制派, 反体制の人, 意見を異にする

dissolution 名 解散, 〈契約の〉解除, 解消, 取消し, 解体, 廃棄
the dissolution of the House of Representatives [lower house] 衆議院の解散
the dissolution of unprofitable operations 不採算事業の整理

dissolve 動 解散する, 契約を解除する, 解消する, 取り消す, 解体する, 廃棄する, 消滅する, 崩壊する

distort 動 歪める, 歪曲する, 曲げる, 誤り伝える
distort history 歴史を曲解する
distort the economy 経済を歪める

distortion 名 歪み, ねじれ, 偏向, 偏向度, 歪曲, 曲解, こじつけ, 後遺症
distortion index 偏向度指数
financial distortion 金融上の歪み
market distortion 市場の歪み
monopoly distortion 独占による歪み
price distortion 価格の歪み, 価格偏向
seasonal distortions 季節要因
statistical distortions 統計の歪み

distress 名 窮地, 苦境, 困窮, 貧困, 経営不振, 業績悪化, 経営難, 心痛, 苦痛, 苦悩, 悩みの種, 遭難, 動産差し押さえ, 差し押さえ動産[物件], 形 投げ売りの, 出血販売の
distress goods 投げ売り品
distress price 出血価格
distress sale [selling] 投げ売り, 狼狽売り
distress warrant 動産差し押さえ令状
economic distress 生活難
financial distress 金融不況, 経営難
show signs of distress 疲労[苦痛]の色を見せる

distribute 動 分配する, 分売する, 販売する, 供給する, 配給する, 配送する, 配布する, 流通させる, 配信する
distributed database 分散型データベース, 分散データベース
distributed network 分散型ネットワーク

distribution 名 流通, 物流, 配給, 配布, 配分, 供給, 頒布, 販売, 分売, 分配, 配当, 配信, 分布, 分類, 区別, ディストリビューション
commercial distribution 商品流通
distribution and marketing support company 物流・販売支援会社

distribution channel 流通経路, 流通チャネル, 配給経路, 販路 (=channel of distribution)
distribution company for companies 企業向けの物流会社[物流企業]
distribution industry 流通業界
distribution network 物流網, 流通網, 流通ネットワーク, 販売網
food distribution 食品流通
freight distribution 物流
frequency distribution 度数分布
income distribution 所得分配, 所得分布
international distribution of goods 国際物流
labor distribution 労働分布
market distribution 市場分配
news distribution ニュース配信
normal distribution 正規分布
optimum distribution of resources 資源の最適配分
physical distribution 物的流通, 物流
program distribution on the Net 番組のネット配信
quantity distribution 数量分布
wealth distribution 富の配分

distributor 名 販売店, 販売代理店, 代理店, 輸入代理店, 総輸入元, 流通業者, 流通業, 問屋, 卸売り業者, 配達人, ディストリビュータ

distrust 名 不信, 疑惑

disturbance 名 混乱, 騒ぎ, 騒動, 騒乱, 暴動, 動揺, 不安, 心配, 不調, 妨害, 障害, 障害物
balance of payments disturbance 国際収支不安
currency disturbance 通貨不安
digestive disturbance 胃障害
disturbance model 〈方程式の〉誤差模型, 誤差モデル
emotional disturbance 精神障害
monetary disturbance 金融不安, 金融混乱
racial disturbances 人種暴動
secular disturbance 長期的混乱

ditch 動 水上に不時着する, 不時着水させる, 溝へはまらせる, 見捨てる, 捨てる, 厄介払いする

ditch 名 溝, 堀, 水路, どぶ, 排水溝, 窮地
be driven to the last ditch 窮地に追い詰められる, 土壇場に追い込まれる
ditch digger [ditchdigger] 重労働者, 肉体労働者, 土方, 溝掘り機
irrigation ditch 灌漑用水路

dive 動 急落する, 暴落する, 急降下する, 飛び込む, ダイビングする, 潜水する, 没頭する
dive into …に乗り込む, 突っ込む, 飛び込む, 飛び降りる, 没頭する, 打ち込む, 深入りする
dive into a purse 財布に手を突っ込む
dive into losses 赤字に転落する, 損失に転落する
dive into policies 政策に没頭する
dive toward …に向かって急落する

dive 名 急落, 暴落, 急降下, 下落, 落ち込み, 飛び込み, ダイビング, 潜水
dive bomber 急降下爆撃機
make a dive for …に向かって突進する
take a dive 〈業績などが〉落ち込む, 暴落する, 急落する

divergence [divergency] 名 分岐, 逸脱, 脱線, 相違, 不一致, 開き, 乖離, 変動幅, 離散, 拡散, 分散
cyclical divergence 景気サイクルのずれ
divergence band 変動幅
divergence indicator 乖離指標
divergence of views 意見の相違
divergence theory 拡散理論
economic divergence 経済格差の拡大
equalizing divergence 格差均等化

diversification 名 多様化, 多角化, 多角経営, 経営多角化, 分散, 分散化, 分散投資, 変化
business diversification 事業の多角化 (=diversification of business)
commodity diversification 商品の多様化
diversification investment 分散投資
diversification of the portfolios ポートフォリオの分散, ポートフォリオの分散投資, ポートフォリオの多様化 (=portfolio diversification)
diversification of the product mix 製品構成の多様化, 製品構成の多角化
diversification plan 多角化計画
market diversification 市場多様化
product diversification policy 製品多様化政策
strategy of diversification 経営多角化戦略, 多角化戦略, 多様化戦略 (=diversification strategy)

diversify 動 多角化する, 多様化する, リスク,〈市場などを〉分散する, 拡大する
diversify investment sites 投資先を分散する (=diversify one's portfolio)
diversify products 製品を多様化する
diversify risks リスクを分散する

well-diversified assets 十分に分散化された資産

divest 動 〈資産などを〉整理する，売却する，手放す，取り除く，放棄する

divestiture 名 企業分割，〈資産の〉分割，〈事業や不採算店舗などの〉整理［売却］，再編成，〈権利などの〉剥奪 （＝divestment）

divestment 名 整理，売却 （＝divestiture）
- **divestment of equity into public hands** 株式の公開
- **divestment of subsidiaries** 子会社の売却

divide 名 格差，断絶，分水嶺，境界線，分岐点，分かれ目，分割，分裂
- **digital divide** 情報格差，情報を持つ者と持たぬ者との断絶，インターネットを使える人と使えない人との格差，情報化が生む経済格差，デジタル・デバイド
- **divide between gets and get-nots** 得た者と得なかった者［得られなかった者］との格差
- **divided Diet** ねじれ国会

dividend 名 配当，利益配当，配当金，分配金（米国では，一般に会社が四半期ごとに配当を支払う。生命保険の配当金は，主に保険料の運用収益が契約時の想定を上回った場合に，その差額が契約者に支払われる）
- **dividend payment on equity** 株式配当
- **dividend per share** 1株当たり配当，1株当たり配当金，1株当たり配当額 《略 **DPS**》
- **dividend ratio** 配当率 （＝dividend rate）
- **dividend yield** 配当利回り（1株の株価に対する配当金の割合。配当利回り（％）＝（1株当たり配当金÷株価）×100）

division 名 事業部，事業部門，部門，部・課，分野，分割，分配，不一致，分裂
- **accounting division** 経理部，経理課
- **business devision** 事業部門，事業分野
- **division manager** 部長
- **division of duties** 職務の分担，事務分掌
- **division of income** 所得の分担，所得の分割
- **division of labor** 分業
- **division of the economic pie** パイの分配
- **division organization [system]** 事業部制
- **operational administration division** 業務本部
- **perfect division of labor** 完全分業
- **social division of labor** 社会的分業
- **system of tripartite division** 3分割制

dlrs 名 ドル （**dollars**の略）

DNA 名 デオキシリボ核酸 （**deoxyribonucleic acid**の略。遺伝子を構成する分子化合物）
- **DNA fingerprinting** DNA指紋検査法 （＝genetic fingerprinting：遺伝子指紋法）
- **DNA profiling** DNA鑑定法（DNAによる個人識別法）
- **DNA sequencing technology** DNA配列決定技術
- **DNA test [testing]** DNA鑑定

do business 営業活動を行う，営業する，事業を行う，事業を展開する，ビジネス活動をする，取引する （＝operate）
- **doing business** 営業行為，商行為
- **the Livedoor way of doing business** ライブドア商法

doctor 動 不正に変更する，手入れをする，治療する

doctor's license 医師免許

doctrine 名 教義，主義，信条，〈政党などの〉政策，〈国家政策の〉公式宣言，理論，学説，ドクトリン
- **Bush Doctrine** ブッシュ・ドクトリン（脅威に対しては先制攻撃も辞さないという力の論理を全面に出したブッシュ（George W. Bush）米大統領の外交方針）
- **Carter Doctrine** カーター・ドクトリン（ペルシャ湾地域を支配しようとする外部勢力に対して，軍事力を含めてあらゆる手段を行使してそれを阻止するというカーター米大統領の方針）
- **doctrine of comparative advantage** 比較優位説，比較優位論 （＝theory of comparative advantage [costs]）
- **economic doctrine** 経済学説
- **military doctrine** 軍事ドクトリン（国防の長期的な指針を示す基本文書）
- **Monroe Doctrine** 相互不干渉主義，モンロー主義，モンロー・ドクトリン（ジェイムズ・モンロー米第5代大統領が1823年12月の大統領教書で発表した米国の外交政策の基本姿勢）
- **the doctrine of gravitation** 重力［引力］の原理

document 名 文書，書類，資料，文献，記録，ドキュメント
- **accounting documents** 経理書類，会計書類 （＝financial documents）
- **auditor-submitted documents** 監査人提出書類
- **document room** 〈米上下両院の〉文書室，文献室

dodge — **domino**

issue of document　書類の交付
loan document　借入証書
maritime document　海事書類
nonnegotiable documents　譲渡不能書類, 非流通書類
source document　原始書類
Superintendent of Documents　政府印刷局の文献部長
Weekly Compilation of Presidential Documents　〈米国の〉週刊大統領公式文書

dodge 動 逃れる, 巧みにそらす, 巧みにごまかす, さっと身をかわす, うまく避ける, 回避する, 名 言い抜け, ごまかし, 妙案, 策略, 身をかわすこと
barely dodge the attack　かろうじて攻撃をかわす[避ける]
dodge an investigation　調査をごまかす
dodge military service　徴兵を逃れる
dodge one's obligations　義務を回避する
dodge pursuit　追跡をかわす, 追跡をそらす
dodge tax payment　納税を逃れる, 納税を免れる, 脱税する
dodge the accusation　非難を回避する
dodge the question　質問をかわす, 質問をはぐらかす
make a quick dodge　さっと身をかわす
tax dodge　脱税, 税金を逃れるための手段, 税金逃れの手

Doha Round of multilateral trade talks　世界貿易機関(WTO)の新ラウンド(新多角的貿易交渉), ドーハ・ラウンド
Doha Round of WTO talks　世界貿易機関(WTO)の新多角的貿易交渉

doldrums 名 沈滞, 低迷, 不振, 不況, 不景気, 冷え込み, 中だるみ
be out of the doldrums　底を脱する
in the doldrums　不景気で, 不振の, 厳しい状況の, 意気消沈して
remain in the doldrums in most areas　ほぼ全域で冷え込みが続いている
the doldrums in the manufacturing industry　製造業の不振

dole 動 分配する, 配布する, 支給する, 少しずつ分け与える, 名 失業手当
be [go] on the dole　失業手当を受けている
dole out　分配する, 配布する, 支給する
the dole queue　失業者の列, 失業者数

dollar 名 ドル, ドル相場
be dollars to doughnuts　十中八九は確かだ, 実際確かだ
be priced in dollars　ドル建てである (=be dollar-based)
Canadian dollar　カナダ・ドル
dollar-defense measures　ドル防衛策
dollar-denominated exports　ドル建て輸出
dollar gap　ドル不足
dollar preference　ドル選好
dollar sign　ドル記号(dollar mark), 金を稼ぐチャンス
dollars and cents　金銭
firming of the dollar　ドルの強含み

domestic 形 国内の
domestic consumption　国内消費
domestic economy　国内経済, 国内景気, 日本経済
domestic demand　国内需要, 内需
boost domestic demand　内需を刺激する, 内需を喚起する
domestic demand-based growth　内需型成長
domestic-demand expansion policy　内需拡大策
fading domestic demand　需要の落込み
faltering domestic demand　内需の冷え込み
shrinking domestic demand　内需の低下
weak [weakened] domestic demand　内需の低迷, 内需が弱いこと

dominance 名 支配, 支配力, 統治, 権勢, 主導権, 優勢, 優越, 卓越, 圧倒的に強い立場
bureaucratic dominance　官僚主導の体制
come under the dominance of　…の統治下に入る

dominate 動 支配する, 制ές する, 威圧する, 優位に立つ, …に強い影響力を持つ, 占領する, 占める
dominate the market　市場を支配する, 市場を押さえる, 市場で圧倒的な力を持つ, 市場で圧倒的な地位を占める
family-dominated group　創業者一族が支配する企業グループ
male-dominated　男性優位の, 男性中心の

domination 名 支配, 統治, 優勢, 優位
be under the domination of　…の支配下にある
free oneself from foreign domination　外国の支配から独立する

domino 名 ドミノゲーム, ドミノ
domino effect　ドミノ効果, 将棋倒し(連鎖反応による累積的効果)

donate / Dow Jones

- **domino theory** ドミノ理論
- **domino liver transplant** ドミノ肝移植
- **donate** 動 寄付する，寄贈する，提供する，与える，拠出する
  - **donate blood** 献血する
  - **donate money to** …に献金する
- **donated** 形 寄付された，寄贈された，贈与された，拠出された
  - **donated blood** 献血，献血された血液
  - **donated capital** 受贈資本（＝donated surplus）
  - **donated property** 贈与財産
  - **donated surplus** 贈与剰余金（＝donated capital）
- **donation** 名 寄付，寄付金，献金，手当，贈与，贈与品，寄贈，寄贈品，提供
  - **accept a donation of organs** 臓器提供を受け入れる
  - **appeal for blood donation** 献血を求める
  - **charitable donation** 寄付金，慈善寄付
  - **donation tax** 贈与税
  - **large [handsome] donations** 多額の寄付金
  - **make a donation to charity** 慈善事業に寄付をする
  - **out-of-work donation** 離職手当
  - **small donations** 少額の寄付金
  - **tax credits for donations** 寄付金控除
- **donor** 名 寄付者，寄贈者，〈援助などの〉供与国，拠出国，〈臓器や血液などの〉提供者，ドナー
  - **donor card** ドナー・カード（脳死移植に不可欠な臓器提供意思表示カード）
  - **donor country** 援助国
- **door-to-door sales** 訪問販売
- **doping** 名 禁止薬物使用，ドーピング
- **dormant** 形 活動休止中の，休眠している，休眠中の，現在使われていない，潜在的な，潜伏中の，未開発の
  - **dormant account [accounting] system** 複会計制度
  - **dormant balance** 休止残高，不活動残高
  - **dormant claim** 眠った権利，長期間請求されていない権利
  - **dormant execution** 強制管理
  - **dormant funds** 眠れる資金，眠っている資金
  - **dormant judgment** 未発動の判決
  - **dormant partner** 匿名組合員，匿名のパートナー，匿名社員，弱小社員（＝secret partner, silent partner, sleeping partner）
  - **dormant partnership** 匿名組合
  - **dormant patent** 休眠特許
- **dossier** 名 書類一式，〈特定の事件などに関する〉一件書類
- **double** 動 2倍になる，倍増する，倍加する
- **double** 名 影武者，替え玉，分身，代役，そっくりの人［物］，スタントマン
- **double** 形 二重の，2桁の，2倍の，複式の
  - **double bottom** 二番底
  - **double-digit gain** 2桁の伸び（＝double-digit growth, double-digit increase）
  - **double shift** 2交代制
  - **double taxation relief** 二重課税の回避
  - **double withdrawal** 二重引落し
  - **represent a double blow** 二重の打撃になる
- **double digit** 名 2桁，2桁台
  - **double-digit growth** 2桁成長，2桁の伸び，10%を超える伸び
  - **double-digit increase** 2桁増
  - **double-digit inflation** 2桁インフレ，2桁の物価上昇，10%を超えるインフレ
- **double dip recession** 景気の二番底，景気の底割れ
  - **enter into a double dip recession** 景気が二番底に突入する
  - **sink into a double dip recession** 景気が底割れする
- **Dow** 名 ダウ平均，ダウ・ジョーンズ平均，ダウ工業株平均，ダウ（＝Dow Jones average）
  - **Dow theory** ダウ理論
  - **New York [NY] Dow** ダウ平均，ニューヨーク・ダウ
  - **the Dow** ダウ平均，ダウ工業株平均
- **Dow Jones** ダウ・ジョーンズ工業株平均，ダウ工業株平均，ダウ・ジョーンズ社
  - **Dow Jones average [Average]** ダウ・ジョーンズ平均，ダウ・ジョーンズ平均株価，株式ダウ価平均，ダウ平均
  - **Dow Jones Composite** ダウ・ジョーンズ総合65種平均株価
  - **Dow Jones Index** ダウ・ジョーンズ指数
  - **Dow Jones industrial average [Industrial Average]** ダウ工業株平均，ダウ工業株30種平均，ダウ平均株価（工業株30種），ダウ（工業株30種）平均，ダウ平均《略 DJIA》（＝Dow Jones industrials）
  - **Dow Jones industrials** ダウ平均株価（工業株30種）（＝Dow Jones industrial average）

downbeat 形 重苦しい, 悲観的な, (見通しが)暗い, 暗たんとした, 陰気な, 下降傾向の, 盛り上がりのない
　downbeat outlook 暗い見通し, 見通しの暗さ
　downbeat market sentiment 市場の暗い地合

downfall 名 没落, 凋落, 失脚, 〈人気などの〉急落, 転落, 破滅の原因, 大降り, どしゃ降り

downgrade 動 格下げする, 格付けを引き下げる, 下方修正する
　downgrade one's credit rating on …の信用格付けを引き下げる
　downgrade the firm's group operating profit forecast 同社の連結営業利益見通しを下方修正する

downgrade 名 格下げ
　review for possible downgrade 格下げの方向で検討する
　under review for possible downgrade 格下げの方向で検討中, 格下げの方向で格付けを見直し中

Downing Street 英国政府, 英国首相, ダウニング街, ダウニング・ストリート(この通りの10番地が英首相官邸, 11番地が大蔵大臣官邸)
　No. 10 Downing Street 英国蔵相官邸
　No. 11 Downing Street 英国首相官邸

download 動 〈情報を〉転送する, 受信する, 取り込む, ダウンロードする (⇒upload)

downside 名 〈株価などの〉下降傾向, 下落傾向, 下落, 下気味, 業績悪化, 現役, 不利, 不利益, 不利な点, デメリット, 悪い面, 否定的な側面 (⇒upside)
　downside potential 下落する可能性
　downside risk 下落する危険性, 価格下落の危険性, 下振れリスク, 下値リスク, 下値の余地, 業績悪化のリスク, 減益要因, 可能損失額, ダウンサイド・リスク
　downside risks to the economy 景気の下振れリスク, 景気が悪化するリスク
　downside support line 下値支持線 (= downside support)

downsize 動 規模を縮小する, 削減する, 人員削減する, 人員整理する, 経営を合理化する, リストラする, 小型化する, 軽量化する (=miniaturize, scale down)
　downsize drastically 大幅に縮小する
　downsize the workforce 人員を削減する
　downsize unprofitable sections 不採算部門を縮小する

downsizing 名 小型化, 規模の縮小化, 縮小, 合理化, 人員整理, リストラ, 脱大型コンピュータ現象, ダウンサイジング (=miniaturization, scaledown)
　downsizing of long-term auctions 長期債入札額減額
　downsizing target 合理化計画, 人員削減計画

downtown 名 都心部, 中心街, 繁華街, 商業地区, ビジネス街, 賑やかな盛り場, ダウンタウン

downturn 名 低迷, 減速, 悪化, 下落, 下降, 下降局面, 下振れ, 落込み, 景気の落込み, 冷え込み, 不況, 後退, 景気後退, 衰退, 不振
　business downturn 不景気, 景気後退 (= downturn in business)
　cyclical downturn 景気後退, 景気の悪化, 景気低迷
　downturn in foreign economies 海外経済の下振れ
　global downturn 世界不況, 世界同時不況, 世界的な景気後退 (=global economic downturn)
　growth downturn 成長下降点
　prolong a downturn 景気後退を長引かせる

downward 形 下向きの, 下方への, 減少の, 落ち目の, 下落する, 下降する, 低下する, 低落する, 衰退する, 副 下向きに, 減少へ, 低下して, 衰退して, 落ち目に, 〈上から〉下まですべてにわたって (⇒upward)
　downward movement of prices 物価下落[低落]の動き
　downward pressure 低下圧力, 引下げ圧力
　downward revision 下方修正
　downward risk 損失リスク
　downward sloping demand 右下がりの需要
　from the president downward 社長をはじめ全社員
　slight [modest] downward revision 小幅な下方修正
　downward trend 下落傾向, 下落基調, 下降傾向, 下降トレンド, 低下局面

DPRK 朝鮮民主主義人民共和国, 北朝鮮 (Democratic People's Republic of Koreaの略)

draft 動 設計する, 起草する, 〈下図を〉書く, 選抜する, 抜擢する, 徴兵[徴募, 召集]する, 移動する, 派遣する
　draft a bill 法案を起草する
　draft a contract 契約書を作成する

draft a person to a post 人をある地位に抜擢する
draft a plan 計画を立てる
draft a speech 講演の草稿を作る
draft new recruits 新兵を徴兵する
draft this year's budget 今年[今年度]の予算を編成する

draft [draught] 名 原案, 草案, 草稿, 下書き, 為替手形, 手形, 小切手, 通風, 通風装置, ドラフト
　demand draft 要求払い手形, 送金小切手《略 D/D》
　dollar draft ドル建て払い手形
　draft beer 生ビール
　draft bill 草案
　draft board 徴兵選抜民間委員会
　draft budget 予算案
　draft declaration 宣言案
　draft dodger 徴兵忌避者
　draft legislation 法案
　draft legislation regarding possible military attacks on the nation 有事関連法案, 有事法案
　draft resolution 決議草案
　make a rough draft of the article 記事の草稿を作る
　sight draft 一覧払い手形
　the first draft 初稿
　the last draft 最終稿
　unpaid draft 不渡り手形

drafting 名 案文策定, 起草, 計画立案
　drafting committee 起草委員会
　drafting work 起草作業

drag 名 〈景気などの〉押し下げ効果, 押し下げ要因, 減速効果, マイナス要因, 阻害要因, 邪魔物, 足かせ
　drag from inventory adjustment 在庫調整による景気押し下げ効果
　drag on the economy 景気押し下げ効果, 景気減速要因, 成長率の押し下げ要因, 経済成長の足を引っ張る要因
　fiscal drag 財政面からの景気押し下げ効果

drain 名 排水溝, 排水管, 放水路, 下水[排水]施設, 〈頭脳などの〉流出, 〈資源などの〉枯渇, 減少, 漸減, 消耗, 消失, 負担(burden), 金食い虫
　brain drain 頭脳流出
　cash drain 現金流出
　dollar drain 金の流出, 資金流出, ドル流出

down the drain 経営状態が悪化して, 非常に悪化[低下]して, 浪費されて, 無駄になって
　drain on liquidity 流動性の枯渇
　drain on one's energy 精力の消耗
　drain on resources 資源の無駄遣い
　economic drain 経済的消耗, 経済的負担
　enormous drain on the domestic economy 国内経済に対する莫大な負担
　internal drain 内部的枯渇
　liquidity drain 流動性の流出, 流動性の枯渇, 流動性の吸い上げ
　technology drain 技術流出

DRAM ダイナミックRAM, 動的RAM, 記憶保持動作が必要な随時書込み読出しメモリ (dynamic random access memoryの略。半導体メモリの一種で, パソコンなどの主要メモリに広く使われている。半導体チップの上に情報を何度も書き込んだり消したりできる反面, 電源を落とすと記憶情報が消えてしまう)

dramatic 形 劇的な, 急激な, 大幅な, ダイナミックな, 印象的な, めざましい, 注目に値する, 驚くような, 大げさな

drastic 形 思い切った, 大胆な, 抜本的な, 徹底した, 徹底的な, 大幅な, 急激な, 激烈な, 猛烈な, 大型の, 大規模な
　apply drastic remedies 荒療治を施す, 荒療法を施す
　drastic cut in …の思い切った節減[削減]
　drastic inventory reduction 在庫の大幅削減
　drastic policy 思い切った政策, 大胆な政策, 抜本的な政策[施策]
　drastic tax-reduction measures 大型減税策, 大型減税措置

draw 動 〈銀行などから金を〉引き出す, 〈給料などを〉受け取る, 〈手形・小切手を〉振り出す, 起草する, 起案する, 立案する, 作成する, 生む, 生じる, もたらす
　draw a check for ¥5 million on the bank 銀行に500万円の小切手を振り出す
　draw a draft at 30 d/s (days after sight) under a confirmed credit 確認信用状に基づいて一覧後30日払いの為替手形を振り出す
　draw down funds 資金を引き出す, 貸出を実行する
　draw interest on a savings account 銀行預金[普通預金]の利子が入る
　draw [draw out] money from a bank 銀行から金を引き出す

draw on the loan 資金を引き出す
draw the loan within 10 days 10日以内に融資を実行する
draw up 〈文書などを〉作成する，起草する，〈計画を〉立てる［立案する，策定する，作成する］，引き寄せる，引き上げる，〈車を〉止める，整列させる，並べる
draw up a blueprint for …の綿密な計画を策定する
draw up a document 文書を作成する
draw up a will 遺言書を作成する
draw up [make out] the draft of the treaty 条約を起草する
draw up the net 網を引き揚げる
drawer savings タンス預金
drilling technology 掘削技術
drive 動 運転する，…の原動力になる，…の牽引力となる，…を動かす，…をもたらす，…を喚起する，駆り立てる，無理に…させる
　be driven by …を原動力とする，…が追い風になる，…が大きな意味を持つ
　drive a wedge between …の間を離反させる，仲たがいさせる
　drive at …を意図する，…を言おうとしている
　drive customer demand 消費者需要を喚起する
　drive growth 成長をもたらす，成長の原動力となる
　drive out …を追い出す
　drive the markets 相場を動かす
　drive under the influence of alcohol 飲酒運転をする
drive 名 政策，路線，主導，動因，キャンペーン，取組み，組織的運動，募金運動，駆動装置，装置，気力，決意，意欲，志向，原動力，推進力，駆動力，ドライブ
　austerity drive 緊縮政策
　disk drive ディスク装置，ディスク駆動機構，ディスク・ドライブ
　dollar drive ドル貨獲得促進
　drive to promote a new product 新製品の販促キャンペーン
　efficiency drive 効率向上，効率性の向上
　productivity drive 生産性向上運動
　structural reform drive 構造改革路線
　technological drive 技術志向
-driven 形 …志向の，…主導の，…主導型の，…優先の，…中心の　（＝-led, led by）
　futures-driven 先物取引中心の
　market-driven 市場原理に基づく，市場志向の　（＝market-oriented）
　order-driven 注文主導型の
　profit-driven 利益志向の，利益志向の強い，利益追求型の　（＝profit-oriented）
　retail-driven 個人投資家主導の
　scale-driven 数量効果が大きい
　swap-driven スワップ主導型の
driver 名 原動力，推進力，牽引役，エンジン，主因，ドライバー　（＝cause, driving force）
　growth driver 成長の原動力
　key drivers 重要な原動力［推進力］，主要な原動力，主因
　main drivers 主因，主要エンジン　（＝key drivers）
driver's license 運転免許
driving force 原動力，推進力，牽引役，牽引車，主因　（＝driver, locomotive engine; ⇒locomotive）
　a driving force behind …の原動力，…の牽引役
　a driving force of the economic growth 経済成長の牽引役
drop 動 落とす，落下させる，下げる，降ろす，〈数，量を〉減らす，投下する，止める(call off, cancel, scrap)，〈計画などを〉断念する，中止する，〈関係を〉断つ，手を切る，〈訴訟を〉取り下げる，口にする，ほのめかす，解雇する，除名する，除外する，排除する，省略する，〈物を〉返す，返却する，〈麻薬などを〉飲む，自動 減少する，低下する，下落する，落ち込む　（＝decrease, fall）
　be dropped from the list of …のリストから外される［除外される］
　drop a full point 1％低下する
　drop a hint [remark] 意向をほのめかす，ヒントを与える，それとなくヒントを口にする，ヒントにおわす，ちょっとほのめかす，口をすべらす
　drop a subject 話題を打ち切る
　drop [discontinue] a suit 訴訟を取り下げる
　drop behind 落伍する
　drop below …を割り込む
　drop economic sanctions 経済制裁を止める
　drop money over the transaction 取引で損をする
　drop one's jaw 口をポカンと開ける
　drop the curtain 幕を降ろす
　drop to …まで落ち込む

drop 图 減少, 低下, 下落, 落ち込み, 低迷, 悪化
　drop in asset quality 資産内容の悪化
　drop in demand 需要の現象, 需要の落込み, 需要の減退
　drop in earnings 減益 (=drop in income, drop in profits)
　drop in output 生産低下, 生産の落込み
　drop in profits 減益
drop-off 图 減少, 下落, 低下
　drop-off in sales 販売低下, 売上の減少
　drop-off service 取次ぎサービス
drop out 脱落する, 落伍する, 落ちこぼれる, 〈体制から〉離脱する, 脱退する, 体制外で生きる, 中退する, 退学する, 逃避する, 〈競技から〉抜ける, なくなる, 消失する, ドロップアウトする
　drop out of English 英語では使われなくなる
　drop out of society 社会から逃避する
　drop out of the line 戦列から落伍する
drop shipping ドロップシッピング (サラリーマンや主婦の副業として人気がある新手のインターネット・ビジネス。メーカーなどが在庫として抱えている商品を, 個人が代わりにネット上で宣伝, 販売する商法で, 発送などは業者が請け負い, 卸値と販売価格の差額が個人の利益となる)
DRTS データ中継技術衛星 (Data Relay Test Satelliteの略)
drug 图 麻薬, 覚せい剤, 麻酔剤, 薬, 薬剤, 薬物, ドラッグ
　designer drug 合成抗生物質
　drug abuse [misuse] 薬物乱用, 麻薬乱用
　drug addict [abuser, offender] 麻薬常用者, 麻薬患者, 薬物中毒者
　drug addiction 薬物中毒, 麻薬中毒
　drug automatism 薬物自動症
　drug baron [lord] 麻薬組織のボス, 麻薬王
　drug bust 麻薬の手入れ
　drug buster 麻薬取締官
　drug czar [agent] 麻薬取締官
　drug dealer [peddler, pusher] 麻薬の売人, 麻薬密売人, 麻薬取引業者
　drug design 薬剤設計
　drug drop 麻薬受渡し所
　Drug Enforcement Administration 米麻薬取締局《略 **DEA**》
　drug information service 医薬品情報活動, DIサービス
　drug interaction 薬物相互作用
　drug runner [mule] 麻薬の運び屋
　drug squad 麻薬捜査課
　drug syndicate 麻薬密輸組織
　drug withdrawal 麻薬の禁断症状
　Drugs, Cosmetics and Medical Instruments Law 薬事法
　fiscal drug 財政の麻薬漬け, フィスカル・ドラッグ
　miracle drug 妙薬
　stimulant drugs 覚せい剤
drum 動 太鼓をたたく, ドラムを演奏する, たたく
　be drummed out of …から追い出される, …から追放する
　drum down …を沈黙させる
　drum into 叩き込む, 教え込む
　drum up 宣伝する, 勧誘して回る, …を獲得する, 〈人を〉呼び集める, 召集する, 〈商売などを〉活気づかせる
　drum up business for new products 新製品を売り込む, 新製品の取引獲得のために努力する
　drum up support for …への支持を取り付ける, …に対する支援を呼びかける
　drum up votes 票集めをする
dry 形 乾いた, 乾燥した, 水気がない, 干上がった, 枯渇した, 底をついた, 面白くない, 無味乾燥な, 退屈な, ありのままの, 偏見のない, 甘味のない, 辛口の
　dry answer にべもない返事, 冷淡な返事
　dry fact ありのままの事実
　dry (land) farming 乾地農法
　dry fight 無血闘争
　dry goods 反物類, 織物類
　dry groceries 固形食品類
　dry luncheon 禁酒[酒抜き]午餐会
　dry run for …の予行演習, 模擬試験, 試運転, 空砲射撃演習, リハーサル
　dry season 乾期, 渇水期
　dry spell 日照り続き
　dry state 禁酒州
　dry weather 干ばつ
　go dry 禁酒法を敷く, 禁酒する
dual-income family 共働き家庭, 共働き世帯
dual-list 動 重複上場する
dual-use items 軍事・民生両用の物資, 軍民両用物資
dub 動 …と呼ぶ, …と称する, あだ名を付ける, 〈他言語に〉吹き替える, 追加録音する, 音響効果を加える, 〈せりふや音楽を〉入れる, 〈複数の録音を〉合成録音する, 〈録音したものを〉複製[再録音]する, ダビングする

due 形 正当な, 正式の, 適切な, 適正な, 適法の, 合法の, 十分な, 相当の, 合理的な, 履行義務のある, 支払い義務のある, 支払い期日のきた, 満期の過ぎた, 当然支払われるべき, 予定されている

due date 支払い期日, 返済期日, 満期日, 満期, 社債の償還日, 履行期日, 期日, 納期 (= date of payment)

due diligence investigation 事業買収前のデュー・ディリジェンス調査, 事前精査, 資産査定 (「デュー・ディリジェンス調査」は, 事業買収希望者が譲渡側の協力を得て行う専門家による買収対象会社の資産, 債務, 財務内容や営業内容, 従業員などに関する調査. 買収額や増資の際に引き受ける株式の価格を判断する基準となる)

DUI 飲酒運転 (= driving while intoxicated: **driving under the influence of alcohol**の略)

dull 形 元気のない, 不活発な, 低迷した, 停滞した, 不振の, 軟調の, 〈商売が〉振るわない, 鈍い, さえない, 切れ味の悪い, 単調な, 面白くない, 飽き飽きする, 退屈な

  dull market 元気のない市場, 軟調な市場, 景気の悪い市場

  dull sales volume 販売数量の低迷

  dull trade 商況不振, 不活発な[停滞した]市況, 活気のない商況

Duma 名 ロシア連邦議会下院

dummy 名 模造品, マネキン人形, 人形, 操り人形, 手先, 傀儡(かいらい), ロボット, 替え玉, 〈ページの〉割付け, 束見本, ダミー, 形 模造の, 偽の, 架空の, 見せかけだけの, 名義だけの, 名ばかりの

  dummy company トンネル会社, 架空の会社, ダミー会社

  dummy variable regression ダミー変数を用いた回帰分析

  dummy warhead 模擬弾頭

dump 動 投げ売りする, 不当廉売する, 乱売する, ダンピングする, 投げ捨てる

dumping 名 投げ売り, 不当廉売, 乱売, たたき売り, 〈ゴミなどの〉投げ捨て, 〈廃棄物の〉投棄, ダンピング

  antidumping 反ダンピング, ダンピング防止

  antidumping duties ダンピング防止関税, 反ダンピング関税, ダンピング防止関税, ダンピング関税

  dumping ground ゴミ集積所

  dumping margin ダンピング率 (= dumping penalty margin)

  dumping petition ダンピング提訴

  file a dumping complaint against …をダンピング提訴する, …をダンピングで提訴する

  illegal dumping 不法投棄

  reversal dumping 逆ダンピング

durable goods 耐久財, 製造業耐久財 (= durable product)

  durable consumer [consumers'] goods 耐久消費財

  durable goods orders 耐久財新規受注高[受注額], 製造業耐久財新規受注高

  durable producer goods 耐久生産財

  new orders for durable goods 耐久財新規受注高, 耐久財新規受注額

  orders for durable goods 耐久財新規受注額

  spending on durable goods 耐久財への支出

duress 名 威嚇, 強要, 強制, 脅迫, 拘束(confinement), 監禁

  be held in duress 監禁されている

  be made under duress 脅迫されて行われる

  under duress 脅迫されて, 強要されて

duty 名 義務, 責任, 任務, 職務, 職責, 勤務, 関税

  ad valorem duties 従価税

  alternative duties 選択関税

  compensating duties 相殺関税

  countervailing duties 相殺関税

  division of duties 職務分担, 職務分掌

  duty appraiser 関税審査官

  duty concession 関税譲許

  duty cost 関税込みコスト

  duty officer 当直官

  entertainment duties 娯楽税, 興業税

  executive duties 経営執行職務, 経営職務

  general preferential duties 一般特恵関税

  mutual preferential duties 相互特恵関税

  night duty allowance 夜勤手当

  off duty 非番, 勤務外, 勤務時間外

  on duty 当番, 勤務中, 勤務時間中

  port duties 入港税

  prohibitive [prohibition] duties 禁止関税, 禁止的輸入税

  refund of duties 戻し税

  social duties 社会義務

  temporary duty 臨時職務

  specific duties 従量税

  transit duties 通過税

DV ドメスティック・バイオレンス, 配偶者による暴力 (**domestic violence**の略)

DVD デジタル多用途ディスク, デジタル・ビデオ・ディスク (=digital video disk：**digital versatile disk**の略)
DVD format DVD方式
DVD recorder デジタル多用途ディスク・レコーダー, DVDレコーダー
DVD recording function DVD録画機能
HD DVD format HD (高品位) DVD方式 (= High-Definition DVD format)
next-generation DVDs 次世代DVD, 次世代デジタル多用途ディスク
dwindle 動 次第に減る[減少する], だんだん小さくなる[少なくなる], 縮小する, やせ細る,〈名声, 勢力が〉衰える,〈質が〉低下する, 重要性を失う
　dwindle into a tropical depression 勢力が衰えて熱帯低気圧になる
　dwindle one's reputation to nothing …の名声を無にする
dwindling 形 減少[縮小, 衰退]している, 減少傾向にある
dynamic 形 活動的な, 精力的な, 活発な, 活力にあふれた, エネルギッシュな, 動学的な, 動態的な, ダイナミック

dynamic activities 精力的な活動, 活発な活動
dynamic adjustment 動態的調整, 動学的調整
dynamic analysis 動態分析
dynamic balance 動学的均衡, 動的釣り合い
dynamic budget 動態的予算
dynamic economics 動態経済学, 経済動学
dynamic economy 動態経済, ダイナミックな経済
dynamic engineering 機械工学
dynamic equilibrium 動態的均衡, 動的均衡
dynamic growth 動的成長, 動学的成長
dynamic model 動学モデル, 動態モデル
dynamic movement 動学的変動
dynamic programing [programming] 動的計画, 動的計画法, ダイナミック・プログラミング《略 DP》
dynamic ratio 動態比率
dynamic relocation 動的再配置
dynamic statistics 動態統計
dysfunction 名 機能障害, 機能不全, 機能異常
dysfunctional 形 機能障害の, 機能不全の, 機能異常の

E

E. coli 大腸菌
   E. coli O-157 病原性大腸菌O157
e-commerce site 電子商取引サイト
early 形 早い時期[時間]の, 早期の, 初期の, 当初の, 即時の, 期前の
   early adopter 初期採用者[導入者], 早期採用者
   early bird special 先着サービス
   early detection of cancer がんの早期発見
   early extinguishment of debt 負債の早期償却
   early forecast [projection] 当初予想
   early majority 初期追随者
   early monopoly 初期独占
   early payment 期前返済, 早期返済
   early phase [stages] 初期段階, 初期
   early redemption [pay-off] 繰上げ償還
   early repayment 期限前償還, 早期完済
   early retirement 早期退職, 希望対象, 期限前返済
   early retirement packages 早期退職プラン
   early retirement scheme [plan, program] 早期退職制度, 早期定年制, 希望退職, 期限前返済
   early termination 早期終了, 期限前解約
   early warning system 早期警戒制度, 早期警報システム（レーダー・システム）
   early withdrawal 期限前解約
earmark 動 予算を組む, 〈…の目的に資金などを〉当てる, 〈資金を〉投入する, 〈予算などを〉計上する, 指定する, …を区別する

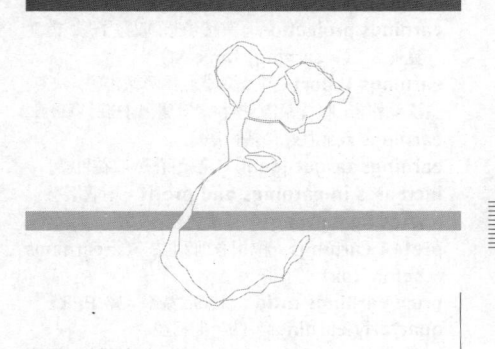

earn 動 稼ぐ, 稼得する, 利益を上げる, 〈報酬などを〉得る, 獲得する, 生む, もたらす
   earn a profit 利益を上げる
   earn above-average returns 市場平均を上回る利益を上げる
   earn interest 利息が付く
   pay-as-you-earn 源泉課税
   save-as-you-earn 天引き積立て
earner 名 稼ぎ手, 稼得者, 利益を生み出すもの, ドル箱, 儲かる仕事
   foreign exchange earner 外国為替取得者
   high wage earner 高給取り
   income earner 個人所得者, 俸給生活者, 所得稼得者
   low income earner 低所得者
   middle income earner 中所得者
   nice little earner 簡単に儲かる仕事
   salary earner 給料生活者
   small income earner 小額所得者
   two-earner family 共稼ぎ世帯
   upper income earner 高所得者
   wage earner 賃金労働者, 勤労者, 給料生活者
earnings 名 収益, 利益, 純利益, 利潤, 所得, 収入, 投資利益, 業績, 決算 (=gains, profits, returns)
   after-tax earnings 税引き後利益 (=earnings after tax)
   earnings estimate 業績予想, 収益予想 (=earnings forecast, earnings projection)
   earnings forecast 業績予想, 業績見通し, 収益予想, 利益予想 (=earnings estimate, earn-

earthquake / eclipse

ings projection, profit forecast)
earnings projection 業績予想, 収益予想, 業績見通し (=earnings forecast)
earnings report 業績報告, 業績報告書, 決算, 決算報告, 収益報告, 損益計算書, 財務計算書
earnings results 業績, 決算
earnings target [goal] 業績目標, 収益目標
increases in earnings and profit 増収増益
operating earnings 営業利益
pretax earnings 税引き前利益 (=earnings before tax)
price earnings ratio 株価収益率《略 PER》
quarterly earnings 四半期利益
reported earnings 計上利益, 公表利益, 決算報告上の利益, 財務報告上の利益
stagnant earnings 収益の悪化, 業績の低迷
statement of earnings 損益計算書
earthquake 名 地震
earthquake-proof design 耐震設計
ease 動 緩和する, 和らげる, 緩める, 軽くする, 軽減する, 引き下げる, 低下する
ease foreign exchange risks 為替リスクを軽減する
ease inflationary pressures インフレ圧力を低下させる
ease liquidity 流動性を高める
ease (monetary) policy 金融政策を緩和する, 金融政策を緩める, 金融を緩和する
ease restrictions on …への規制を緩和する, …への規制を緩める
ease slightly 小幅低下する
easing 名 緩和, 軽減, 引下げ, 低下, 金融緩和, 利下げ
additional easing 一層の金融緩和
aggressive easing 積極的な金融緩和, 大幅な金融緩和
easing in capacity 設備稼動率の低下
easing in inflation インフレ率の低下
easing of quantitative credit regulation 量的信用緩和
further easing in interest rates 一層の利下げ
further easing moves 一層の金融緩和の余地
monetary easing 金融政策の緩和, 金融緩和, 利下げ
East Asia free trade area 東アジア自由貿易[ビジネス]圏
East Asian community 東アジア共同体

eastward expansion 東方拡大
NATO東方拡大 ⊃ 西欧の安全を守る目的で1949年に12か国体制で設立された北大西洋条約機構 (NATO) が, 冷戦時代に共産圏に属していた中・東欧諸国を新規加盟国として迎え入れること。1999年にポーランド, チェコ, ハンガリーが加盟したのに続き, 2002年11月22日にチェコのプラハで開かれたNATO首脳会議で新たに旧ソ連圏7か国の2004年同時加盟が決定した。新規加盟国は, ルーマニア, ブルガリア, スロバキア, スロベニアと, 旧ソ連の一部だったエストニア, ラトビア, リトアニアのバルト3国。NATOは, この東方拡大で26か国体制となった。今後, アルバニアやクロアチアなども加盟を望んでいる。

easy 形 容易な, 簡単な, 楽な, 寛大な, 甘い, 緩やかな, 快適な, 快い, 豊かな, 裕福な, 〈商品供給や相場, 市況などが〉だぶついた
easy budget 予算緩和
easy credit 金融緩和, 信用緩和, 信用拡張
easy dollars 低利資金
easy life 豊かな生活
easy mark [game, prey, target, touch, victim] お人よし, お人よしのカモ
easy market 市場のだぶつき, 緩慢な市場
easy payment [installment] 分割払い
easy payment plan [system] 分割払い方式 (=easy purchase system)
easy terms 分割払い, 楽な条件, 低利借入れ
take the easy way out 安易[楽]な方法で難局を切り抜ける
easy monetary policy 金融緩和政策, 金融緩和策, 金融緩和 (=easy money policy, easy money step)
easy money 金融緩和, 低利の金, 不正に儲けた金, 悪銭
additional easy money step 追加金融緩和政策
easy money policy 金融緩和政策, 金融緩和策, 低金利政策
easy money step 金融緩和策
easy money times 金融緩和期
easy money with surplus budget 金融緩和と黒字予算
ECB 欧州中央銀行, 欧州中銀 (European Central Bankの略)
eclipse 名 〈太陽, 月の〉食, 衰退, 失墜, 喪失
a lunar eclipse 月食 (=an eclipse of the moon)
a partial eclipse 部分食

a total eclipse 皆既食
an eclipse of the sun 日食 (=a solar eclipse)
ECO 経済協力機構 (**Economic Cooperation Organization**の略)
eco- 形 環境の, 環境保護の, 環境対応の, 生態の, 生態学の, エコ
- **eco-activist** 環境運動家, 環境汚染防止運動家
- **eco-bank** エコ・バンク(環境保護意識の強い企業に融資する銀行)
- **eco-business** エコ・ビジネス
- **eco-car** エコカー (=environmentally-friendly car)
- **eco-conscious** 環境を意識した, 環境に敏感な, エココンシャス (=ecology conscious)
- **eco-energy city** エコ・エネルギー都市
- **eco-factory** [**ecofactory**] エコ・ファクトリー(地球環境問題を考慮しながら経済的利益も得られる生産工場)
- **eco-fair** 環境見本市, エコ・フェア
- **eco-friendly** 環境にやさしい, 生態にやさしい, 環境を破壊しない, 自然環境に合っている, 環境への負荷が少ない (=environment-friendly)
- **eco-friendly car** 環境対応車
- **eco-fund** エコファンド(環境問題に積極的に取り組む企業の株式などに投資する投資信託。生産過程での二酸化炭素の排出量や電機使用量の削減, 風力, 太陽光発電, 水処理などの取組みが評価される)
- **eco-guerrilla** エコ・ゲリラ(過激派の環境保護運動家)
- **eco-horror** 生態に与える影響
- **eco-labeling** エコ表示, 環境保全ラベル (=environmental labeling, green labeling)
- **eco-management** 環境管理, 環境経営
- **eco-management and audit scheme** エコ管理監査要項
- **eco-materials** エコ・マテリアル(環境保全と資源保護に役立つ製品の材料)
- **eco-station** エコ・ステーション
- **eco-tax** 環境税 (=environmental tax)

ecocentric management 環境中心経営, 環境経営, エコセントリック・マネジメント
ecocide 名 環境破壊, エコサイド(環境汚染などに起因する生態系の破壊)
ecocity 名 環境共生都市
ecodevelopment 名 環境維持開発 (=sustainable development)
ecodoom 名 大規模環境破壊 (=large-scale ecological destruction)
ecofreak 名 環境保護狂, 環境問題に異常なほど神経質な人 (=fervent environmentalist, ecology freak, pollution freak)
ecohouse 名 環境共生住宅
ecological 形 生態の, 生態学の, 生態学的な, 環境保護に関心のある, 環境保護意識を持った, 環境にやさしい, エコロジカル
- **ecological allergy** 生態エネルギー
- **ecological architecture** エコロジカル・アーキテクチャー
- **ecological art** 環境芸術, 生態学的芸術, 自然物利用の芸術, エコロジカル・アート
- **ecological balance** 生態学的バランス, 生態学的均衡
- **ecological biogeography** 生態生物地理学
- **ecological channel structure** 生態的経路構造
- **ecological competition** 生態的競争
- **ecological concept** 生態概念, 生態学的概念
- **ecological cycle** 生態循環
- **ecological destruction** 環境破壊
- **ecological drive** エコ・ドライブ
- **ecological efficiency** 生態効力
- **ecological environment** 生態的環境
- **ecological equilibrium** 生態系の均衡
- **ecological factor** 生態的要因
- **ecological footprint** 生態系に対する不変の影響
- **ecological map** 生態学的環境評価地図
- **ecological market segmentation** 生態学的市場細分化, 生態的市場細分化
- **ecological marketing** 生態的マーケティング論, エコロジカル・マーケティング
- **ecological model** 生態学モデル, 生態的モデル
- **ecological niche** 生態の地位
- **ecological order** 生物と環境との秩序
- **ecological organism** 生態の有機体
- **ecological process** 生態的過程
- **ecological pyramid** 生態的ピラミッド
- **ecological sanction** 生態的制裁
- **ecological science** 生態学 (=ecology)
- **ecological succession** 生態遷移
- **ecological system** 生態系, 生態学的システム, 生態的システム, エコロジカル・システム (=ecosys, ecosystem)

ecology 名 生態, 自然環境, 環境, 生態学, 社会生態学, 人間生態学, エコロジー

ecology fashion 自然志向のファッション, エコロジー・ファッション
human ecology 人間生態学
economic 形 経済の, 経済上の, 財政上の, 家計の, 経済学の, 実用上の, 実用的な, 実利的な, 有利な, 儲かる, 値段の安い
economic agent 経済主体, 経済行為者
economic assessment 景気判断, 景気の基調判断 (＝assessment of the economy)
economic behavior 経済行為, 経済活動, 経済行動
economic benefits 経済的利益, 経済効果
economic bloc 経済圏, 経済ブロック
economic choice 経済的動機
economic climate 経済環境, 経済情勢, 景況, 景気
economic contraction 景気の悪化, 景気収縮, 景気縮小, 景気後退, 不況, マイナス成長 (＝contractionary economy)
economic entity 経済実体, 経済的実体
Economic Espionage Act 〈米国の〉経済スパイ法
economic forecast [outlook] 経済予測, 経済見通し, 景気予測, 景気見通し, 経済展望
economic fundamentals 経済のファンダメンタルズ, 経済の基礎的条件, 景気のファンダメンタルズ (＝fundamentals of the economy)
economic leverage 経済的影響力
economic life 経済生活, 経済耐用年数, 経済寿命 (economic age)
economic motivators 経済的要因
economic special area 経済特区
economic stimulus measures 景気テコ入れ策, 景気浮揚策, 景気刺激策, 景気刺激対策景気対策, 経済対策
economic union 経済統合, 経済同盟
economic activity 経済活動, 経済動向, 経済情勢, 景気, 実体経済
market-defined economic activities 市場経済活動
national economic activity マクロ経済, 経済成長率
rebound in economic activity 景気回復, 景気が拡大基調に戻ること, 景気の勢いが回復してきたこと
regulate economic activities 経済活動を規制する
economic conditions 経済状態, 経済状況, 経済情勢, 景況, 景気
adverse economic conditions 経済情勢の悪化
decline in economic conditions 景気の悪化
improved economic conditions 経済状態の改善
poor [recessionary, sluggish] economic conditions 景気低迷, 景気の悪化
economic cycle 経済循環, 景気循環, 景気動向, 景気変動
better economic cycle 景気回復, 景気の上向き
economic up-cycle 景気回復
strengthening of the economic cycle 景気が勢いを増すこと
the momentum of economic cycles 景気の勢い
economic development 経済開発, 経済発展, 経済成長, 景気動向, 経済動向, 経済情勢
economic development program [plan] 経済開発計画
economic development zone 経済開発区
national economic development 国家経済開発, 全国経済開発
outward-looking economic development 開放路線による経済開発
economic downturn 経済［景気］減速, 景気後退, 景気の悪化, 景気低迷, 景気沈滞, 景気の下降局面, 不況, 不景気
mitigate economic downturns 景気後退を抑える
normal economic downturn 景気の一般的な下降局面
economic expansion 景気拡大, 景気回復, 経済成長, 経済拡張 (＝business expansion)
chalk off economic expansion 経済成長を抑える
sustained economic expansion 経済の持続的な成長
economic growth 経済成長, 経済発展, 景気浮揚, 経済成長率 (＝growth of the economy)
commit to economic growth 経済成長に全力を挙げる
encourage economic growth 景気浮揚を図る
facilitate economic growth 経済成長を促す
qualitative economic growth 質的経済成長, 質的成長

sustained economic growth　経済成長の持続
the prospects for economic growth　経済成長の見通し
zero economic growth　ゼロ成長

economic partnership　経済連携
economic partnership agreement　経済連携協定《略 EPA》(人と資本の交流を含む協定)
economic partnership talks　経済連携協議, 経済パートナーシップ協議
economic partnership treaty　経済連携協定

economic performance　景気, 景気動向, 経済実績, 経済活動, 経済成長率
improved economic performance　景気回復
pickup in economic performance　景気拡大, 景気回復

economic power　経済大国, 経済力 (= economic giant)
major economic power　経済大国
massive economic power　経済大国

economic recovery　景気回復 (= business recovery, economic improvement, economic revival, economic upturn)
block economic recovery　景気回復を妨げる
pace of economic recovery　景気回復の足取り
slow [sluggish] economic recovery　景気回復の足取りが重いこと
worldwide [global] economic recovery　世界的な景気回復

economic report　経済報告, 経済報告書, 経済白書, 経済教書
monthly economic report　月例経済報告
Economic Report of the President　経済報告, 米大統領経済報告, 経済教書
economic reports　景気指標 (= economic results)

economies 名　経済, 経済性, 経済地域, 経済群, 経済国, 国, 諸国, エコノミー
agglomeration economies　集積の経済
economies of network　連結の経済性(複数の企業や組織間で形成されるネットワークから生み出される経済性のこと)
economies of scale　規模の経済, 規模の経済性, 規模の拡大, 規模の利益, スケール・メリット, 数量効果, エコノミー・オブ・スケール (= economy of scale, scale merit：少品種大量生産の経済効率を意味する)
economies of scope　範囲の経済, 範囲の経済性, 多様化の経済, エコノミー・オブ・スコープ (= economy of scope：複数の製品を生産したほうが, 単一の製品を生産する場合よりも生産コストが安くなる現象のことで, 製品多様化・経営多角化の経済性を指す)
economies of speed　スピードの経済, スピードの経済性, エコノミー・オブ・スピード (= economy of speed)
emerging economies　新興国, 新興経済群, 新興経済地域, 新興経済国
external economies　外部経済
growing economies　新興経済地域
internal economies　内部経済
localization economies　地域特化の経済
non-dollar economies　非ドル通貨圏
oligopolistic economy　寡占経済
open-market economies　自由市場経済, 市場経済
regional economies　地域経済
size of the economies　経済規模
the Group of 20 major industrial and emerging economies　主要先進国と新興国の20か国・地域(G20)

economism 名　経済主義

economist 名　経済学者, 節約家, 倹約家, エコノミスト
business economist　経営学者, 経営経済学者, 企業経営専門家, ビジネス・エコノミスト
company economist　企業内エコノミスト, カンパニー・エコノミスト
home economist　家政学士, ホーム・エコノミスト
home economist in business　消費者問題担当者, ヒーブ《略 HEIB》
Street economist　ウォール街のエコノミスト, 市場エコノミスト (= Wall Street economist)

economy 名　経済, 経済性, 景気, 節約, 倹約, 効率的使用[利用], 経済機構, 経済組織, 経済国, 社会, 経済成長率, 成長率, エコノミー, 形 経済的な, 安価な, 割安な, 徳用の
boost the economy　景気を刺激する, 景気を活性化する
centrally planned economy　中央計画経済
command [controlled] economy　統制経済
discourage the economy　景気の足を引っ張る
drag on the economy　経済成長率を押し下げる要因
economy class　旅客機の普通席[割安席], エコノミー・クラス (= coach class, tourist class)
economy drive　経費削減運動, 経費節約運動

[運動期間]
economy fare エコノミー・クラスの料金
economy of truth ウソも方便
economy size 徳用サイズ, エコノミー・サイズ
Economy Watchers index 景気ウオッチャー指数
general economy 経済全体
new economy 新しい経済, ニューエコノミー (=digital economy, e-economy, IT economy, new economy)
old economy オールド・エコノミー (=t-economy, traditional economy)
political economy 政治経済学

ecosystem 名 生態系 (=ecological system, ecosys)

ecotop 名 生態環境

ecotourism 名 エコツーリズム
Ecotourism Promotion Law エコツーリズム推進法(2008年4月に施行)

edge 動 ゆっくり移動する, じりじり動く[進む], 少しずつ変動する, …を取り巻く, …を縁どる
edge down じりじり下がる[低下する], じり安になる, 少しずつ下がる
edge down a little 弱含む, 小幅ながら減少する
edge downwards [downward] じり安傾向にある
edge higher じりじりと上昇する, 小幅上昇する, 小幅ながら引き上げられる, 微増となる
edge lower じりじりと低下する, 小幅低下する, 小幅ながら引き下げられる, 微減となる
edge up じりじり上がる[増える], じり高になる, 少しずつ上がる, 小幅上昇する, 強含む
edge up a little 強含む, 小幅ながら増加する, 微増となる
edge up through 小幅上昇して…を突破する
edge upwards じり高傾向にある

edge 名 先端, 優位, 優位性, 優勢, 強み, 瀬戸際, 限界, 効果, 刃, 稜線, エッジ
competitive edge 競争上の優位(性), 競争力
cutting edge 鋭利な刃, 最前線, 最先端, 先頭, 主導的地位, 最新式 (=leading edge)
decisive edge 決定的優位
gain an edge on …に対して優位を勝ち取る
have an edge 優る, 優勢である, 優位に立つ
have the edge on [over] …より少し優れている, …より少し強みがある
leading edge 主導的地位, 最先端, 最前部, 最前線, 先頭, 最新式, トップ (=cutting edge)

take the edge off 弱める, そぐ, 鈍らせる
technological edge 技術的優位, 技術的優位性

edition 名 版, 刊, 号
electronic edition 電子版
enlarged edition 増補版
first edition 初版
limited edition 限定版

editor 名 編集者, 編集責任者, 〈新聞・雑誌の〉編集主任, 主筆, (担当)部長, 〈出版物の〉校訂者, 編纂者, 〈映画, ラジオ, テレビ番組の〉報道者, 編集プログラム, 文書編集ソフト, エディター
city editor 〈米・カナダ〉ローカル・ニュース編集主任, 〈英国〉財政ニュース編集主任
editor in chief 編集長, 編集責任者, 編集主幹
news editor ニュース記事担当部長
sports editor スポーツ欄担当の編集主任, スポーツ記事担当部長

editorial 名 社説(leading article), 論説, 形 編集の, 編集上の, 編集者の
editorial advisory board 編集諮問委員会
editorial board member 論説委員
editorial comment 論説
editorial policy 編集方針
editorial staff 編集スタッフ, 編集部員, 編集部
editorial writer 論説委員 (=editorialist)

education 名 教育, 教養, 学識
adult education 成人教育
compulsory education 義務教育
consumer education 消費者教育
life-long education 生涯教育
Ministry of Education, Science and Technology 文部科学省
paid education leave 有給学習休暇

EEZ 排他的経済水域 (⇒exclusive economic zone)

effect 名 影響, 影響額, 発効, 効力, 効果, 施行, 趣旨, 意味
adverse effect 逆効果, 不利な影響, 悪影響, 悪材料
backwash effect 逆流効果
competitiveness effort 競争力効果
currency effects 為替の影響
cyclical effects 景気循環要因
expansionary effect 景気刺激効果
knock-on effect 連鎖反応, 連鎖効果, ドミノ効果 (=domino effect)
legal effect 法的効力
leverage effect 他人資本効果, テコの効果, 梃

率効果, レバレッジ効果
liquidity effect 流動性効果
price effect 価格効果
productivity effect 生産力効果
psychological effect 心理効果
pump-priming effect 呼び水効果
ripple effect 波及効果 (＝repercussion effect)
secondary effect 二次的要因
tax effect 税効果

effective 形 有効な, 効果的な, 効率的な, 実施されている, 実施中の, 効力をもつ, 実効の, 事実上の, 実際の, 実働の
cost-effective コスト効率がよい, 費用効率がよい, 費用効果が高い
effective demand 有効需要
effective devaluation 実効為替切下げ
effective elasticity 有効弾力性
effective job offer ratio 有効求人倍率
effective job openings 有効求人数
effective labor supply 有効求職, 有効求職者数
effective net worth 有効正味資産, 有効純資産
effective power 有効電力
effective production 有効生産量
effective range 有効範囲, 有効性
effective rate of duty 実効税率
effective tariff 実効関税
effective tax 実効税額
effective yield 実効利回り
real effective exchange rate 実質実効為替レート

effectively 副 事実上, 実際(in effect), 実際に, 有効に, 効果的に

efficiency 名 効率, 効率性, 能率, 有効性, 能力 (⇒energy efficiency)
capital efficiency 資本効率
distribution efficiency 流通効率
economic efficiency 経済効率, 経済の効率性, 経済性
efficiency rating 勤務評定
efficiency variance 能率差異
energy efficiency エネルギー効率
investment efficiency 投資効率
labor efficiency 作業効率, 作業能率
market efficiency 市場の効率性
operating efficiency 営業効率, 事業効率

production efficiency 生産効率
efficient 形 効率的な, 効率のよい, 能率的な, 有能な, 有効な
cost-efficient コスト効率の高い, 低コストの
cost-efficient source of financing 低コストの資金調達源
efficient management 効率的経営, 経営の効率化
efficient market 効率的市場
fuel-efficient 燃費効率のよい, 低燃費の
labor-efficient 労働効率の高い
more efficient running 運営の効率化

effort 名 努力, 試み, 尽力, 取組み, 動き, 活動, 作業, 仕事, 運動, キャンペーン, 募集, 対策, 政策, 策, 努力の成果, 労作, 力作, 立派な演説
best efforts 最大限の努力, 最大努力, 最善の努力, 委託募集
collective effort 総力
cooperative efforts 協力関係
gap-closing efforts 赤字削減努力
in an effort to …しようとして, …しようと努力して, …するため, …を目指して, …を狙って
joint effort 提携関係
self-help efforts 自助努力
streamlining efforts リストラ努力, リストラ策, 合理化措置, 合理化への取組み

El Niño エル・ニーニョ現象, ペルー沖の異常海温・異常潮流現象 (⇒La Niña)

elect 動 選出する, 選任する, 選挙する, 選ぶ, 決める, 選択する
-elect [elect] 形 次期…, 当選した, 選ばれた, 選出された
the bride-elect いいなずけ
the chairperson-elect 議長当選者
the Elect of God 神の選民
the mayor-elect 市長当選者
the U.S. President-elect 米次期大統領

election 名 選挙, 選任, 当選, 票決, 投票, 選択
be defeated [unsuccessful] in an election 選挙に負ける, 落選する
be sure of election 当選確実
canvass for an election 選挙運動をする
Central Election Commission 中央選挙管理委員会
clean [honest] election 公正な選挙
commit oneself to election 出馬を表明する
election address 選挙演説 (＝election speech)

election administration [overseeing] committee 選挙管理委員会 (＝election board)
election by ascending 繰上げ当選
election bulletin 選挙公報
election campaign 選挙運動, 選挙戦
election committee 選挙委員会
election day 投票日, 選挙日
Election Day 〈米国の〉選挙日, 国民選挙日 (4年に1度, 米大統領・副大統領の選挙人(elector)を選挙する日。4で割り切れる年の11月第一火曜日で, ほとんどの州で法定休日 (legal holiday) になっている)
election district 選挙区
election irregularities [frauds] 選挙違反
election monitoring 選挙監視
election pledge 選挙公約 (＝campaign pledge, election promises)
election polling committee 選挙対策委員会
election rally 選挙相場
election results 選挙結果
election returns 開票結果 (＝election results)
federal election officials 連邦選管当局者
general election 総選挙
gubernatorial election 知事選挙, 知事選
hold [conduct, have] an election 選挙を行う
local [provincial] election 地方選挙
mayoral election 市長選
municipal election 地方選挙
national election 国政選挙
polling day 選挙日 (＝election day)
preliminary election 予備選挙
presidential election 大統領選挙, 総裁選挙
primary election 予備選挙 (＝primary)
run [stand] for election 立候補する, 選挙に出る
single-member election districts 小選挙区制
special election 補欠選挙 (＝by-election)
state election 州選挙
U.S. midterm elections 米中間選挙, 米国の中間選挙
win a close [hard-fought] election 接戦の末選挙に勝つ
win [carry] an election 当選する, 選挙に勝つ (＝win in an election)
electioneering 名 選挙運動 (＝election campaign)
elective 形 選択の(optional), 選択権のある, 随意に決められる, 随意選択の, 選挙の, 選挙で選ばれた, 〈手術が〉緊急に必要でない, 急を要しない
elective checkup 一般検診
elective monarchy 選挙君主政体
elective office 選挙による公職
elective position 選挙で決まる地位
elective subject 選択科目
elector 名 選挙人, 有権者, 米大統領[副大統領]選挙人
electoral 形 選挙の, 選挙人の, 選挙に関係する
electoral college [Electoral College] 米大統領[副大統領]選挙人団 (electoral collegeの1員をelectorという)
electoral district 選挙区 (＝election district)
electoral mandate 選挙民から与えられた権限
electoral rally 選挙集会
electoral roll [register] 有権者名簿
electoral vote 大統領選挙人団による選挙
electric 形 電気の, 電力の, 発電の (＝electrical)
electric appliance and material control law 電気用品取締法
electric capacity 発電容量
electric car [vehicle] 電気自動車
electric enterprise law 電気事業法
electric machinery firm [company] 電機メーカー (＝electrical machinery firm)
electric supply system 電力供給体制, 電力供給システム
electric utility 電気事業
electric power 名 電力, 電源
electric power capacity 発電能力
electric power company 電力会社
electric power cost 電力原価
electric power development 電源開発
electric power generating cost 発電原価
electric power generation 発電
electric power generation with refuse incineration ごみ焼却発電, ごみ発電
electric power industry 電力業界, 電気事業
electric power purchased 購入電力
electric power sold 販売電力量
electric power system 電力系統
electrical 形 電気の, 電機の, 電動の, 電気製品に関する, 電撃的な
electrical breakdown 電気の故障

electrical capacity 発電容量
electrical consumption 電力消費
electrical distribution 送配電網
electrical energy 電気エネルギー
electrical engineering 電気工学
electrical utilities 電力会社, 電力事業
electrical appliance 家庭用電気器具, 家電, 電気器具 (=electric appliance)
Electrical Appliances and Materials Safety Law 電気用品安全法, 電安法
electrical machinery 電機, 電気機械
electrical machinery and apparatus 電気機械器具
electrical machinery sector 電機業界 (=electric machinery sector)
electricity 名 電気, 電力, 電荷, 電流, 電気の供給, 送電, わくわくする感覚, 興奮
annual amount of electricity generated 年間発電電力量
annual amount of electricity sold 年間販売電力量
electricity blackout 停電
electricity company [firm] 電力会社
electricity consumption 電力消費
electricity demand 電力需要
Electricity Enterprise Act 電気事業法
electricity output 電気生産量
electricity rates 電気料金
electricity sector 電力業界
electricity trading 電力取引, 電気の売買
electricity trading market 電力取引市場
electricity usage 電気使用量
generate electricity 発電する, 電気を起こす
grid of electricity supply 配電網
hydraulic electricity 水力電気 (=waterpower electricity)
large-lot electricity demand 大口電力需要
machine run by electricity 電動機械
static electricity 静電気
supply electricity 電気を供給する, 電気を送る
supply of electricity 電力供給 (=electricity supply)
surplus electricity 余剰電気
electroluminescence 名 電界発光, エレクトロルミネッセンス
electronic 形 電子の, 電子工学の, コンピュータ化された, エレクトロニック
electronic application 電子出願

electronic authentication 電子認証
electronic calculator 電卓 (=pocket calculator)
electronic cash 電子キャッシュ, 電子マネー (=electronic money)
electronic certification 電子認証
electronic communication business 電気通信事業
electronic component 電子部品, エレクトロニクス部品
electronic conference 電子会議, 遠隔会議, 電信会議, テレコンファレンス (=teleconference, television conference, video conferencing)
electronic control 電子制御
electronic data processing system 電子データ処理システム, 電子情報処理システム, 電子情報処理方式
electronic device 電子装置
electronic government 電子政府 (=e-government)
electronic mail 電子メール, 電子郵便, Eメール (=email [e-mail])
electronic market 電子市場 (=e-market, electronic marketplace, Internet exchange)
electronic money 電子マネー, 電子貨幣, 擬似通貨, エレクトロニック・マネー (=cybermoney, digital cash, digital money)
electronic money business 電子マネー事業
electronic paper 電子ペーパー
electronic settlement 〈ネット・ショッピングなどの〉電子決済
electronic toll collection system ノンストップ自動車料金支払いシステム《略 ETC》
electronic voting 電子投票
electronic trading 電子取引, 電子商取引, 電子売買, コンピュータ取引, 電子トレーディング, システム売買 (=e-commerce, e-trading)
electronic voting 電子投票
electronics 名 電子機器, 電子製品, 電子工学, エレクトロニクス
consumer electronics products 家電製品
electronics company 家電メーカー, 電機企業
electronics components 電子部品
electronics industry 家電業界, エレクトロニクス産業
electronics manufacturing service 製造工程請負工場《略 EMS》(電機や通信機器メー

カーから商品の製造を請け負う専門企業のこと）
electronics products 電子製品
element 名 要素, 要因, 構成要素, 成分, 項目, エレメント
　cyclical element 景気循環要因
　elements of accounting 会計の基本要素
　elements of financial statements 財務諸表の構成要素, 財務諸表の要素
　essential element of the agreement 本契約の絶対条件
　grant element グラント・エレメント, 贈与要素, 援助条件, 緩和指数《略 GE》
　program element 計画要素
　risk element リスク要因
　speculative element 投機的要素
eleventh hour ぎりぎりのところ, ぎりぎりの段階, 土壇場, 最後ぎりぎりの瞬間, きわどい時
eligible 形 受給資格がある, 適格の
eliminate 動 撤廃する, 廃止する, 排除する, 削減する, 廃棄する, 除去する, 相殺消去する, なくす, 解消する, 敗退させる, 脱落させる, 失格させる, 殺す, 排泄する
　eliminate competitors 競争相手を退ける
　eliminate economic disadvantage 経済的な遅れを解消する
　eliminate nuclear weapons 核兵器を廃絶する
　eliminate oneself from …から手を引く
　eliminate racial discrimination 人種差別を排除する[なくす]
　eliminate side effects 副作用を除去する
　eliminate tax incentives 税制上の優遇措置を撤廃する
　eliminate the budget deficit 財政赤字をなくす
　eliminate the criminal 犯人を消す[殺す]
　eliminate the waste of overproduction 過剰生産の無駄を省く
elimination 名 撤廃, 廃止, 排除, 削除, 廃棄, 除去, 相殺消去, 解消, 〈競技などの〉予選, 敗退, 脱落
　the elimination of middleman 中間商人排除論, 問屋無用論
　the elimination of nuclear weapons 核兵器廃絶, 核廃絶
　the elimination of punitive duties 報復関税の撤廃
　the elimination of tariffs 関税撤廃
elite 名 選り抜きの人[人々], 選ばれた人[人々], 影響力[権限]を持つ人々, 精鋭, 幹部, 首脳, 特権

階級, 〈社会の〉中枢, エリート, 形 選り抜きの, 精鋭の, エリート主義の, エリートの
　the power elite 首脳, 首脳部
elitism 名 特権意識, エリート意識, エリート主義, エリートによる支配
elusive 形 うまく逃げる[かわす], 逃げをうつ, 捕らえにくい, とらえ所のない, 捕捉しがたい, 見つけにくい, 手に入れにくい, 達成しがたい, 理解しにくい, 思い出しにくい
　elusive argument つかみ所のない議論
　elusive dream なかなか実現しない夢
　elusive meaning 分かりにくい意味, 理解しがたい意味
embargo 名 通商禁止[停止], 通商禁止命令, 出入港禁止命令, 通商停止, 輸出[輸入]禁止, 禁輸, 禁輸政策, 貿易制限, 貿易禁止, 制限, 禁止, 禁止措置, 制裁
　be under an embargo 貿易が禁止されている, 輸出禁止になっている, 出入港禁止になっている, 出港停止中である, 停止されている
　ease the embargo 禁輸政策を緩和する
　embargo goods 禁輸品
　embargo of imports 輸入禁止
　gold embargo 金輸出禁止（＝embargo on gold）
　impose [lay, place, put] an oil embargo against …に対して石油［原油］輸出禁止を課す, …に対する石油輸出を禁止[停止]する
　oil embargo on Iran 対イラン石油全面禁輸措置
　lift the embargo 制裁を解除する
　lift [raise, remove, take off] the embargo on arms to …に対する武器輸出禁止を解除する, …に対する武器輸出禁止を解く
　U.N. embargo 国連経済制裁
embattled 形 多くの問題[困難]を抱えた, 経営不振の, 敵に包囲された, 陣容を整えた, 防備を固めた, 戦闘の準備を整えた
embedded derivative 組込みデリバティブ
embezzlement scandal 横領事件, 着服事件（＝misappropriation）
embryonic human stem cells ヒト胚性幹細胞
embryonic stem cells ES細胞, 胚性幹(ES)細胞, 万能細胞（＝embryonic stem cells, ES cells）
emcee [MC] 名 〈テレビ［ラジオ］の〉司会者 (master of ceremonies), 動 司会する

EMCF 欧州通貨協力基金 (European Monetary Cooperation Fundの略)

emerge 動 現われる, 出現する, 台頭する, 浮上する, 発生する, 生じる, 明らかになる, 知られる, 明白となる, 注目されるようになる, 抜け出す, 脱却する, 脱する

emergence 名 出現, 発生, 浮上, 開始, 台頭, 激化, 〈危機などからの〉脱出, 脱却

emergency 名 緊急, 有事, 緊急事態, 非常事態, 突発事故
- emergency advances 非常貸出
- emergency aid [assistance] 緊急援助, 緊急支援
- emergency amortization 緊急償却, 特別償却, 加速償却
- emergency call 緊急電話
- emergency case 急患, 救急箱
- emergency chute 緊急脱出装置
- emergency communication network 非常用通信ネットワーク
- emergency core cooling system 緊急炉心冷却装置
- emergency credit 緊急融資
- emergency dispute 緊急争議
- emergency doctor 救急医
- emergency duty 緊急関税 (＝emergency tariff)
- emergency economic measures 緊急経済対策
- emergency employment measures 緊急雇用対策
- emergency evacuation 緊急退去, 緊急避難, 緊急の撤退
- emergency facilities 緊急施設
- emergency facility 緊急資金
- emergency financing mechanism 緊急融資メカニズム
- emergency fund つなぎ資金, 非常資金, 非常準備金, 特別準備基金
- emergency funding rate 緊急貸出金利
- emergency hospital 救急病院
- emergency import curbs 緊急輸入制限
- emergency import restrictions 緊急輸入制限, 緊急輸入制限措置(セーフガード) (＝emergency import limits, emergency "safeguard" import restriction, safeguard)
- emergency landing 緊急着陸
- emergency legislation 緊急立法, 有事法制
- emergency loan 緊急融資, 救援融資, つなぎ融資
- emergency measures 緊急措置, 緊急関税制度
- emergency medical services 救急医療
- emergency medical system 救急医療体制
- emergency order 緊急注文
- emergency power 非常指揮権, 非常統治権
- emergency relief 緊急援助
- emergency reporting service 救急通報サービス
- emergency reserve 緊急準備金
- emergency room 救急治療室, 救急医療室, 救急病室《略 ER》
- emergency shareholders meeting 緊急株主総会, 臨時株主総会
- emergency squad 緊急要員
- emergency stairway [staircase] 非常階段
- emergency stockpile エネルギー備蓄
- emergency supplies 緊急援助物資
- emergency tariffs 緊急関税
- financial emergency 財政危機
- resort to emergency measures 緊急手段に訴える

emerging 形 新興の, 新生の, 最新の, 先端的な
- emerging company 新興企業, 成長企業, 新興のベンチャー企業
- emerging countries 新興国 (＝emerging economies [nations])
- emerging economic players 新興国 (＝emerging [countries, economies])
- emerging economies 新興経済国, 新興経済地域, 新興経済群, 新興国 (＝emerging economic players)
- emerging industry 先端産業, 先端業界
- Emerging Issues Task Force 緊急問題専門委員会
- emerging market 新興市場, 急成長市場, 新興成長市場, エマージング・マーケット
- emerging technology 先端技術, 新技術
- newly emerging competitors 新規参入者

emission 名 排気, 排出, 放出, 排ガス, 排気ガス, 放出量, 放出物, 排出物
- carbon dioxide emissions 二酸化炭素排出量
- emission control 排ガス規制, 排気ガス規制
- emission control standard 排ガス[排気ガス]規制基準
- emission credits 排出枠, 排出量, 排出権 (＝emission permits, emission rights)

emission filter 排ガス浄化装置
emission level 排ガス・レベル, 排出量
emission permits 排出権
emission quota trading 排出量取引, 排出権取引
emission reduction 排出量削減
emission rights 排出権
emission standards 排ガス基準
emissions from diesel-powered vehicles ディーゼル車の排ガス
emissions of carbon dioxide 二酸化炭素の排出量
emissions of greenhouse gases 温室効果ガスの排出量
gas emission regulations 排ガス規制
greenhouse gas emissions 温室効果ガス排出量
regulation of total emission 総量規制
toxic air emissions 毒性ガスの放出量
toxic emissions 有毒排気物
trade in CO2 emission credits 二酸化炭素の排出量[排出権]取引
vehicle emission standards 自動車排出ガス基準, 自動車排ガス基準

emission trading 排出量取引(温暖化ガスの排出削減が進んで余裕が出た国と, 逆に増加して温暖化ガス削減目標の達成が難しい国との間で,「排出枠」を売買する方式)
emission trading system 排出量取引制度

emitter of greenhouse gases 温暖化ガスの排出国

employ 動 雇用する, 雇う, 雇い入れる, 使用する, 利用する

employability 名 雇用適性, 雇用されうる能力, エンプロイアビリティ

employee 名 従業員, 社員, 職員, 被雇用者, 雇い人, 使用人
active employees 在籍従業員, 現従業員
career employee 常雇い従業員
company employee 会社員, 会社従業員
Employee Assistance Program 従業員支援制度, 従業員支援プログラム《略 EAP》
employee contributions 従業員の拠出金
employee house organ 社内報 (=employee magazine)
employee manual 従業員便覧
employee ownership scheme 従業員持ち株制度
employee rating 人事考課 (=merit rating)
Employee Retirement Income Security Act 1974年に制定された米国の従業員退職所得保障法, 1974年退職者年金保障法, 企業年金法, エリサ法《略 ERISA》
employee satisfaction 従業員満足, 従業員の満足, 企業内組織の満足《略 ES》
employee savings plan 従業員貯蓄制度, 従業員貯蓄計画
employee welfare fund 従業員福利厚生基金 (=employee benefit fund)
employees on loan 出向社員
employees' income 雇用者所得 (=income of employed persons)
full-time employee 正社員
government employee 国家公務員
hourly employee 時間給制の従業員
inactive employee 休職従業員
junior employee 準社員
managerial employee 管理職, 管理職従業員 (=management employee)
occupational employee 非管理職従業員
paid employee 遊休従業員
part-time employee パート社員, パートタイマー, パートタイム労働者
permanent employee 正社員, 常用雇用, 常用労働者 (=full-time employee, regular employee)
public employee 公務員 (=government employee)
rank-and-file employee 一般社員, 一般職員
regular employee 正社員 (=full-time employee)
retired employee 退職従業員
salaried employee 月給制の従業員, 定額給従業員, サラリーマン
temporary employee 臨時従業員, 派遣社員

employer 名 雇用主, 雇用者, 雇い主, 使用者, 事業主, 企業主, 企業
employer's liability to third party 使用者責任
employers' accounting 雇用主の会計処理
employers' contributions to social security schemes 社会保険雇い主負担
employers' income 雇用者所得
employers' organization 経営者団体
survey of employers 事業所調査

employment 名 雇用, 使用, 利用, 就労, 勤

め, 職
cases of employment 就職件数
continuous employment system 継続雇用制
deterioration in employment 雇用の悪化, 雇用情勢の悪化
employment adjustment 雇用調整
employment conditions 雇用情勢, 雇用環境, 雇用条件, 待遇 （＝employment situation）
employment cost 人件費
employment crisis 雇用危機
employment data 雇用統計 （＝employment figures）
employment environment 雇用環境
employment inequality 雇用の不平等
employment insurance program 雇用保険制度 （＝employment insurance system）
employment market 雇用市場, 労働市場
employment measures 雇用対策
employment opportunity 雇用機会, 就労機会
employment promotion 雇用促進
employment safety net 雇用の安全網, 雇用のセーフティ・ネット
Employment Service 〈英国の〉雇用サービス庁
employment service act 職業紹介事業法
employment situation 雇用環境, 雇用状況, 雇用情勢 （＝employment conditions）
employment stabilization 雇用安定 （＝stabilization of employment）
employment system 雇用制度
Equal Employment Opportunity Act 〈米国の〉雇用機会均等法, 平等雇用機会法
fixed-term employment 有期雇用
full employment 完全雇用
illegal employment 不法就労
increased employment 雇用の伸び, 雇用の拡大, 雇用の増大
measures to boost employment 雇用対策
over-employment 過剰就業, 人員過剰
public employment security office 公共職業安定所
temporary employment 一時雇用
emporium 名 商業の中心地(mercantile emporium), 中央市場, 大商店, 百貨店, 〈劇場やドライブインなどの〉大きい営業所, ギフト・ショップ
empower 動 権限を与える［付与する］, 権力［資格］を与える, 処理能力を与える, 自由裁量権を与える, 能力を高める, 〈…することを〉許す, 可能にする, …できるようにする

be empowered [entitled] to …することができる, …の権利を持つ
be empowered to veto a bill 法案を拒否する権限を与えられている
empowerment 名 権利の付与, 権限の付与, 権限責任付与, 能力向上, 能力を高めること, エンパワーメント
emulation 名 競争, 対処, 張り合い, 模倣, エミュレーション
en 前 …で, …に, …の中に, …を着た（語源はフランス語で英語の"in"に当たる）
en bloc ひとまとめにして, 一括して, 一括で （＝in a block）
en masse 全体として, ひとまとめにして, 全部一緒に, 一緒に, 一団となって, 集団で, 一斉に （＝in a mass）
en passant ついでに, ちなみに （＝by the way）
en rout (to, for) …への途中で （＝on the way (to, for)）
en suite 一続きの(in a series), 続いて(in succession), 一組［一揃い］で, 一揃いになって （＝in suite）
resign en bloc 総辞職する
enact 動 法律を制定する, 立法化する, 〈交渉などを〉まとめる, 上演する(perform), 演じる, …の役を演じる, 〈出来事や状況が〉繰り返して起こる, …を行う
be enacted …が行われる, …が成し遂げられる, …が繰り返して起こる
enact a bill 法案を法律化する
enact a budget deal 予算交渉をまとめる
enact a law 法律を制定する
enacted tax rate 法定税率
enactment 名 法律の制定, 立法, 立法化, 法律, 法令, 条令, 法規, 法律の規定［条項］, 〈演劇の〉上演(performance)
enactment of law 法律制定
enactment of legislation 立法［法律］の制定
encourage 動 促進する, 促す, 助長する, 奨励する, 勧める, 誘致する, 誘導する, 励ます, 勇気づける, 激励する, 刺激する
encourage economic growth 景気を刺激する, 景気浮揚を図る
encourage exports 輸出を促進する
encourage investment 投資を促す, 投資を誘致する
encourage savings 貯蓄を奨励する

encouragement 名 促進, 奨励, 勧告, 誘致, 激励, 勧奨, 刺激, 刺激効果, 援助, 支持
　encouragement of consumption 消費刺激, 消費刺激効果
　encouragement of new products 新商品［製品］の奨励
　encouragement of research and development 研究開発の奨励
　encouragement to retire 退職勧奨
　encouragement to save 貯蓄奨励
　offer words of encouragement to …に励ましの言葉を贈る

encouraging 形 元気づける, 勇気づける, 励みとなる, 刺激となる, 明るい, 好材料の
　be encouraging 好調である, 好材料だ
　encouraging economic figures 明るい経済指標
　encouraging letter 励ましの手紙
　encouraging sign 明るい兆し, 明るい兆候
　look encouraging 好材料に見える, 明るい材料のようだ, 好調なように見える

encroach on [upon] …を侵害する, 侵犯［侵入, 侵食］する, 制限する, 削ぐ

end 動 終わる, 終了する, 完了する, 済む, 止む, 停止する, …の結果になる, 終える, 終わりにする, 止める, 廃止する, …をしのぐ, …を凌駕する
　the year just ended 前期
　six months ended December 31, 2010 2010年12月31日に終了する［終了した］6か月（間）, 2010年7-12月期, 2010年下半期, 2010年後期

end 名 終わり, 終了, 満了, 終結, 最後, 結末, 末尾, 破滅, 滅亡, 終焉, 廃止, 端, 端部, 先端, 末端, つき当たり, 周辺部, 外縁部, はずれ, 郊外, 限界, 限度, 目的, 究極目的, 目標, 成果, 結果, 部門, 部分, 担当部分, 受け持ち部分, 期末, 年度末
　achieve one's end [ends] 目的を達成する
　balance at end of (the) year 期末残高
　cheap low end 低価格品
　discount the end of economic recovery 景気腰折れを織り込む
　end-of-period sale 冬季セール
　industrial end 工業最終使用者
　long end (of the market) 長期債, 長期物
　loose ends 未処理事項
　open end 限度がないこと, 無制限, 自由回答式, オープン・エンド
　opposite [other] end 対極
　regular year-end dividend 年度末配当
　short end 短期債, 短期物
　the end of recovery 景気腰折れ
　the sales end of the company 同社の販売部門
　the two ends of the market 市場の両極
　top end 上限
　upper end of the market 高級市場
　▶ The per-barrel price has been hovering around the lower *end* of the $110 level in recent weeks. 1バレル当たりの原油価格は, ここ数週間, 110ドル台前半で推移している。

end 形 最終の, 最終的, 末端の
　end consumer 最終消費者 (＝end user)
　end goal 最終目標
　end investor 最終投資家
　end item 最終品, 完成品, 最終品目
　end markets 末端市場
　end money 予備費
　end product 最終製品, 最終産物
　end result 最終結果
　end use 最終用途
　end value 最終価値

end to end 端末同士, 端末間, ユーザー同士, エンド・ツー・エンド
　end-to-end digital connection 全デジタル回線接続, 端末間のデジタル回線接続
　end-to-end fiber optics transmission 端末相互間の光ファイバー通信
　end-to-end network management 端末間ネットワークの管理

end user 最終使用者, 最終利用者, 最終投資家, 一般使用者, 端末利用者, エンド・ユーザー
　end user charge 最終利用者料金
　end user computing エンドユーザー・コンピューティング《略 EUC》(エンド・ユーザーにとって使いやすい形での情報システムの構築, 運用と管理を指す)
　end-user common line 市内外共用回線
　end user development エンド・ユーザー開発《略 EUD》

endangered species 絶滅のおそれのある種, 絶滅危惧種

endorsement 名 支持, 是認, 承認, 賛成, 推薦, 裏書き, 裏書条項 (＝indorsement)

endoscope 名 内視鏡

energy 名 精力, 活力, 気力, 活動力, 熱意, 決断力, 気迫, エネルギー

Agency of Natural Resources and Energy 資源エネルギー庁
alternative energy 代替エネルギー
energy conservation 省エネルギー, 省エネ, エネルギー節約, エネルギー保護, エネルギー保存
energy efficiency rate 熱効率比率《略 EER》
energy elasticity エネルギー弾性値
energy equivalent エネルギー換算
energy intensive エネルギー集約型
energy park エネルギー資源共同利用地
Energy Research and Development Administration 米エネルギー研究開発局《略 ERDA》
energy supply エネルギー供給
ex food and energy 食品とエネルギーを除くコア指数で (=CPI ex food and energy)
Federal Energy Regulatory Commission 米連邦エネルギー規制委員会
geothermal energy 地熱エネルギー
International Atomic Energy Agency 国際原子力機関《略 IAEA》
International Energy Agency 国際エネルギー機関《略 IEA》
Law Concerning Rational Use of Energy 省エネルギー法
National Energy Policy Act of 1992 1992年全米エネルギー政策法
ocean thermal energy 海洋熱エネルギー
primary energy 一次エネルギー
renewable energy 再生可能エネルギー, 自然エネルギー

energy saving エネルギー節約, 省エネルギー, 省エネ
energy-saving air-conditioner 省エネ冷暖房装置
energy saving efforts 省エネ努力, 省エネ活動, 省エネ対策
energy saving standard 省エネ基準
energy saving target 省エネ目標
energy saving technology 省エネ技術

energy source エネルギー源, エネルギー
alternative energy sources 代替エネルギー源
new environmentally friendly energy sources 環境に優しい新エネルギー
primary energy source 一次エネルギー源
renewable energy sources 恒久的エネルギー源

enfeeble 動 弱くする, 弱める, 弱らす, 弱体化する, 衰えさせる, 衰弱させる
▶ Public funds should be injected not only to buy up toxic assets, but also to boost the capital bases of *enfeebled* financial institutions.　公的資金は, 不良資産の買取りだけでなく, 弱体化した [体力の落ちた] 金融機関の資本増強にも注入すべきだ.

enforcement 名 施行, 実施, 実行, 権利行使, 強制, 強行, 執行, 〈判決の〉強制執行
accounting and audit enforcement 会計・監査執行
Budget Enforcement Act of 1990 1990年予算執行法
credit enforcement 信用補強
Drug Enforcement Administration 麻薬 [薬物] 取締局
enforcement of fiscal measures 財政出動
law enforcement 法執行
law enforcement authorities 警察当局
law enforcement officials 司法当局者, 警官
order of enforcement 執行命令
rights of enforcement 強制権

ENG 電子取材 (electronic news gathering の略)

engagement 名 合意, 約束, 取決め, 雇用, 従事

engine 名 原動力, 検索エンジン (searching engine), エンジン
engine displacement エンジン排気量
the engine for the overall economy 経済全体を引っ張る原動力
the engine of growth 成長の原動力
the engine of the Japanese economy 日本経済の原動力
the engine of the regional economy 地域経済の牽引役
the engine that boosts personal consumption 個人消費を押し上げる原動力

engineer 動 考え出す, 発案する, 演出する, 巧みに処理 [管理, 運営, 計画, 工作] する, 誘導する, 仕組む, 〈裏で〉工作する, 操る, 設計する, 建設する, 〈技師として〉携わる, 〈工事を〉監督する
engineer a bill through Congress 法案の議会通過を計る
engineer a plot 陰謀をめぐらす [たくらむ, 企てる], 計略をめぐらす
engineer the cover-up 隠蔽工作を発案する
design and engineer a project プロジェクトを設計する

engineered capacity　理想的生産能力
engineered cost　工学的管理可能原価, エンジニアド・コスト
engineered food　強化食品, 保存食品
engineered security　仕組み証券
engineered standard　工学的標準
engineered variable cost　技術的変動費
genetically engineered food　遺伝子組換え食品

engineering machinery maker　工学機器メーカー

engulf [ingʌlf] 動　飲み込む, 巻き込む, 取り囲む, 包む, 襲う

enhance 動　高める, 向上させる, 押し上げる, 増やす, 強化する, 補強する
enhance earnings　業績を伸ばす, 業績を向上させる, 業績を改善する
enhance financial health　財務体質［財務内容］を改善する, 財務の健全性を高める
enhance quality　品質を向上させる, 品質を改善する

enhancement 名　増加, 増大, 増進, 向上, 改善, 上昇, 騰貴, 強化, 整備, 補強, 拡張, 改良, 高度化
enhancement business　信用増強業務
enhancement of info-communications functions　情報通信機能の高度化
environmental enhancement　環境向上

enormous 形　巨大な, 莫大な, 膨大な, 大規模な, 巨額の, 大幅な, 豊富な, ものすごい, はなはだしい, 途方もない, 極悪な, 凶悪な, 無法な, 非道な
an enormous criminal　極悪犯人, 凶悪犯人
an enormous intervention　大規模介入
enormous investments in public infrastructure　インフラ整備［社会資本］への巨額の投資

enriched uranium　濃縮ウラン

enroll 動　入会させる, 登録する, 〈グループの〉一員にする, 加入する, 入会する, 記入する

enrollment 名　入会, 加入, 登録, 登記, 記録, 記載, 登録名簿, 入会者数, 登録者数
enrollment rate [ratio]　入学率, 就学率
health insurance enrollment　健康保険登録
open enrollment　オープン加入制度

ensure 動　確保する, 確実にする, 確実に…になるようにする, 確かなものにする, 保証する, 円滑に進める, 〈危険などから〉守る
ensure A against risk [danger]　危険からAを守る
ensure a post for [to] a person　人に地位を保証する（＝ensure a person a post）
ensure market position　市場での地位を維持する［強化する］
ensure oneself from harm　危害から身を守る
ensure protectionism　保護主義に傾斜する
ensure stable [uninterrupted] supplies of raw materials　原材料の安定供給を確保する
ensure sufficient money　十分な資金を確保する
ensure the timely payment　期限どおりの支払いを保証する

enter 動　〈市場などに〉参入する, 〈団体などに〉加入する, 加盟する, 入会する, 参加する, 参加登録する, 入る, 記入する, 記載する, 提起する, 申請する, 申し出る, 申し込む, 正式に記録にのせる, 〈判決などを〉正式に登録する, 契約を結ぶ, 〈コンピュータにデータなどを〉入力する, 立ち上げる, …にログインする, 〈土地に〉立ち入る, 占取する
enter a protest　異議を申し立てる
enter a recession　景気後退局面入りする
enter an action against　…に対する訴状を提出する, …を告訴する
enter into a double-dip recession　景気が二番底に突入する
enter into an agreement [a contract]　契約を結ぶ, 契約を締結する
enter into diplomatic relations with　…と外交関係を樹立する, …と国交を樹立する
enter into force　効力を生じる, 発効する
enter judgment　判決を裁判所の記録に正式に記録する
enter new markets abroad　海外の新市場に進出する
enter the bond market　債券を発行する
enter the debt market　起債する
enter the market　市場に参入する, 市場に進出する, 市場に加わる, 市場を利用する

enterprise 名　事業, 大事業, 事業体, 企業, 会社, 起業家マインド, 進取の気性, 企画, 企て
abortive enterprise　失敗に終わった事業
collective enterprise　集団的企業
corporate [incorporated] enterprise　法人企業
corporative enterprise　共同体企業
Electricity Enterprise Act　電気事業法
enterprise competition　企業競争
enterprise culture　企業文化, 企業社会, 起業

文化, 起業社会, 起業精神
enterprise differentiation 企業差別化
enterprise of middle standing 中堅企業 (=medium-sized enterprise)
enterprise union 企業別組合, 企業組合
enterprise zone 産業振興地域
financial enterprise 金融企業, 金融事業
foreign-backed enterprise 外資系企業
free enterprise 自由企業, 自由企業主義
government-owned [government-run] enterprise 国営企業
government sponsored enterprise 政府系機関
joint enterprise 共同事業
local public enterprise 地方公営企業
nongovernment enterprise 非政府企業
nonpublic enterprise 非公開企業
pilot enterprise 実験企業
profit of enterprise 企業者利得
regulated enterprise 規制対象企業
smaller enterprise 中小企業
spirit of enterprise 起業家マインド, 企業心, 進取の精神
world enterprise 世界企業

entertainment 名 接待, 歓待, 供応, もてなし, 交際
entertainment industry 娯楽産業 (=amusement industry, entertainment business)
excessive entertainment 過剰接待

entire fiscal year 通期, 事業年度全体 (=entire business year, the whole business year)

entity 名 事業体, 企業体, 組織体, 統一体, 法的存在者, 法主体, 事業単位, 単位
autonomous entity 独立企業
entity's legal power 企業の法的権限
foreign entity 海外企業体, 在外企業体, 外国企業
government entity 政府機関
government-related [government-sponsored] entity 政府系機関
issuing entity 発行者 (=borrowing entity)
local public entity 地方公共団体
political entity 政治的な単位
special purpose entity 特別目的会社
unconsolidated entity 非連結事業体

entrepreneur 名 企業家, 起業家, 経営者, 事業家, 事業主, プロモーター, 興行主, アントレプレナー
aggressive entrepreneur 攻撃的な起業家 [企業家]
auto-centered [ego-centered] entrepreneur 自己中心型企業家, 自己中心的企業家
business entrepreneur 企業経営者, 企業家
creative entrepreneur 創造的企業家
entrepreneur investment 企業家投資
entrepreneur shortage 企業家不足, 企業者不足
far-seeing entrepreneur 先見性のある起業家
founding entrepreneur 創業者
hard-driving entrepreneur 熱心な起業家
local entrepreneur 現地起業家
seasoned entrepreneur 経験豊かな経営者

entrepreneurial 形 企業家の, 起業家の, 経営の, 起業家精神が旺盛な, 企業の
entrepreneurial activity 起業活動
entrepreneurial business 起業家精神が旺盛な企業
entrepreneurial capital 企業家資本, 企業者資本
entrepreneurial education 企業者教育
entrepreneurial quality 企業者的資質
entrepreneurial role 企業者[企業家]の役割
highly entrepreneurial 起業家精神が旺盛な

entrepreneurship 名 起業, 企業家精神, 起業家精神

entrust 動 委託する, 委任する, …の管理を任せる
entrusted research 研究委託

entry 名 記入, 記帳, 記録, 登録, 登記, 記載, 記載事項, 参加, 参入, 入会, 入場, 入国, 参加者, 出品物, 〈土地への〉立入り, 通関手続き, 通関申告, 入力
book entry 帳簿記入
data entry データ入力
entry barriers 参入障壁 (=barriers to entry, entry problems)
entry-exit registration system 出入国登録制度
entry market 参入市場
entry permit 入国許可, 入国許可証
export entry 輸出手続き
import entry 輸入手続き
make an entry 記入する, 記帳する
single-entry bookkeeping 単式簿記

environment 名 環境, 情勢, 動向, 局面, 展開
bullish environment 強気市場

business environment 事業環境, 企業環境, 経営環境, ビジネス環境
environment-conscious materials エコマテリアル
environment tax 環境税 (=green tax)
livable environment 生活適性環境
marine environment protection 海洋環境の保護
physical environment 物理的環境, 物的環境
environmental 形 環境の, 周囲の, 環境保護に関する, 環境にやさしい, 環境を害さない
environmental contamination 環境汚染
environmental creation 環境創造
environmental crusade 環境改革運動
environmental impact assessment 環境影響評価《略 EIA》
environmental mutagens 環境変異原
environmental release 環境放出
environmental tax 環境税
environmental tobacco smoke 間接喫煙
environmental variable 環境変数
environmental protection 環境保護
Environmental Protection Agency 〈米〉環境保護局, 〈米〉環境保護庁《略 EPA》
environmental protection laws 環境保護関連諸法
environmental protection standards 環境保護基準
environmental quality 環境の質
Environmental Quality 〈米大統領の〉環境報告
environmental quality improvement 環境の質改善, 環境改善
environmental quality standard 環境基準 (=ambient environmental quality standard, environmental air quality standard)
environmentally friendly 環境にやさしい (=eco-friendly, environment-friendly)
envisage 動 明確に心に描く, 心に思い浮かべる, 思い描く, 予想する, 想像する, 予測する, 考察する, 見据える, 直視する, 見込む, 見る, …に直面する
envisage a plan 計画を立てる
envisage dangers 危険に直面する
envisage exit strategies 出口戦略を見据える
envisage realities 現実を直視する, 現実を見据える
envoy 名 (外交)使節, 使者, 代表, 公使, 特使
envoy extraordinary and minister plenipotentiary 特命全権公使

Imperial envoy 勅使
special envoy 特使
the top envoy 大使
U.N. envoy to Iraq 国連イラク特使
EPA 経済連携協定 (economic partnership accordの略)
EPA 米環境保護局 (Environmental Protection Agencyの略)
epicenter 名 震源地, 震央(震源の真上の地点), 爆心地, 中心点
epidemic 名 伝染病, 流行病, 流行, はやり, 普及, 伝播, 多くの発症, 集団発生, 多発, 続出, 頻発, 蔓延, 〈人々の間に〉急速に広がるもの, 形 流行性の, 流行の, はやりの, 〈人々の間に〉パッと広がる
an epidemic disease 流行病, 伝染病
an epidemic of influenza [flu] インフルエンザの流行
Equal Employment Opportunity Law 雇用機会均等法
equal opportunity 平等機会, 機会均等, 機会平等
equality 名 等しいこと, 等しい状態, 平等, 同等, 均等, 対等, 互角, 一様性, 均質性, 等式
be on an equality with …と対等である, …と対等の立場[地位]にある
equality in [of] value 価値が同じであること
equality of opportunity 機会均等 (=equal opportunity)
equality of reward 報酬の平等
equality of sacrifice 犠牲の平等
equality of status 地位の平等
equality sign 等号, イコール記号 (=sign of equality)
income equality 所得の均等
racial equality 人種的平等
sexual equality 男女平等 (=equality of [between] the sexes)
shareholder equality 株主平等
sovereign equality 主権平等
equilibrium 名 均衡, 均衡状態, 均衡水準, 均衡レート, つり合い, 平衡, 平衡状態, 平等
equipment 名 設備, 施設, 機器, 装置, 用品, 製品, エクイップメント
business equipment 事務機器, ビジネス機器
data terminal equipment データ端末装置《略 DTE》
digital equipment デジタル機器
electronic equipment 電子機器, 電子設備

industrial equipment 産業機械
office equipment オフィス機器
precision equipment 精密機器
production equipment 生産設備, 製造設備, 製造装置
semiconductor equipment 半導体装置
terminal equipment 端末機器, 端末装置
transmitting and receiving equipment 送信設備と受信設備, 送信・受信設備
► *Equipment* sales in our telecommunications industry typically tend to lag economic upturns. 通信業界の機器販売は, 景気回復より遅れるのが通常です[通信機器販売は通常, 景気回復に遅行する傾向があります]。

equity 名 株式, 持ち分, 持ち分権, 自己持ち分, 自己資本, 純資産, 純資産価値, 正味価額, 証券, エクイティ
  common equity 普通株
  equities businesses 証券部門
  equity accounting 持ち分会計
  equity buyback 株式の買戻し自社株の買戻し
  equity capital 自己資本, 株主資本, 株主の出資資本, 株主持ち分, 払込み資本, 株式資本
  equity capital to total assets 自己資本比率
  equity contribution 出資
  equity dividend 自己資本配当
  equity fund 株式ファンド, 投資ファンド
  equity holder 持ち分権者, 持ち分証券保有者
  equity holdings 株式保有, 株式所有, 保有株式, 持ち株, 出資比率 (=stock holdings)
  equity investment 株式投資, 直接投資, 出資 (=stock investment)
  equity issue 増資
  equity market 株式市場 (=stock market)
  equity of security holders 証券保有者持ち分
  equity participation 資本参加, 出資, 株式投資
  equity revaluation 持ち分評価替え
  equity securities 持ち分証券, 持ち分有価証券
  equity stake 持ち分, 株式持ち分, 出資比率
  raise equity 増資する
  return on equity 株主資本利益率《略 ROE》 (=rate of return on equity)
  shareholders' equity 株主持ち分, 株主資本, 資本の部 (=stockholders' equity)
  total liabilities and equity 負債資本合計

equivalent 名 同等物, 等価物, 相当額, 相当分, 換算, 換算額, 同意語, 形 同等の, 等価の
  annual equivalent 年換算
  bond equivalent basis 債券換算利回り
  energy equivalent エネルギー換算
  equivalent coefficient 等価係数
  equivalent form of value 等価形態
  equivalent index number 等価指数
  equivalent mass 等価質量
  equivalent performance 生産等量, 完成品換算数量
  equivalent period 同期
  equivalent production 生産等量, 完成品換算数量
  equivalent resistance 等価抵抗
  equivalent variation 等価的変化
  oil equivalent 石油換算
equivalent to …に相当する, …に当たる, …と同等[同価値, 同量]

ER 救急治療室 (emergency roomの略)

erode 動 減少させる, 低下させる, 低下をもたらす, 脅かす, 圧迫する, 浸食する, 悪化させる, 脅かす, 浸食される, 失われる, 目減りする
  erode competitiveness 競争力を低下させる
  erode confidence in …に対する信認を低下させる[信認の低下をもたらす]
  erode financial reserves 財政基盤を脅かす
  erode profitability 収益性を圧迫する
  erode sharply [rapidly] 急落する

erosion 名 減少, 低下, 下落, 目減り, 悪化, 圧迫, 浸食, 浸食作用, 腐食, 破壊
  asset erosion 資産の目減り, 資産価額の低下
  erosion of corporate ethics 企業倫理の低下, 企業倫理の欠如
  margin erosion 利益率の低下, 利ざやの縮小
  market share erosion 市場シェア[シェア]の低下, 市場占拠率の低下
  the erosion of core operations 主力事業の悪化, 中核事業[基幹事業]の悪化
  the erosion of tax bases 課税基準の浸食

errant 形 誤った, 不貞の, 道を踏み外した, 軌道[コース]からそれた, 遍歴する
  a huge errant sell order 大量の売り注文
  a knight-errant 武者修業の騎士 (=an errant knight)
  an errant husband 浮気な夫, 不貞な夫

ES cells 胚性幹細胞, ES細胞, 万能細胞 (embryonic stem cellsの略)

estimate 動 見積もる, 試算する, 推定する, 評価する

estimate 名 見積り, 推定, 推計, 予想, 予測,

概算, 試算, 推定値, 推定量, 評価, 判断, 見積り書, 概算書
earlier reported estimate 速報値
initial prospect 当初の予想, 当初予想
market consensus estimate 市場のコンセンサス予想
market estimates 市場予想
preliminary estimate 暫定推定値
profit estimate 利益予想, 損益予想, 業績予想 (=profit forecast)
the previous estimate 前回の予想, 前回予想
estimated 形 見積りの, 推定の, 概算の
estimated balance sheet 見積り貸借対照表
estimated costs 見積り費用, 見積り原価, 費用見積り (cost estimate), 原価見積り
estimated figure 推定値
estimated life 見積り有効期間, 見積り耐用年数
estimated premium 概算保険料
estimated price 予想価格
estimated usable period 見積り耐用年数 (=estimated useful life)
ETC system ノンストップ自動料金支払いシステム, ETCシステム (electronic toll collection systemの略)
ethics 名 倫理, 道徳, 倫理体系, 行動の規範
code of ethics 倫理綱領 (=business conduct code, code of conduct)
corporate [business] ethics 企業倫理
erosion of corporate ethics 企業倫理の低下, 企業倫理の欠如, モラル・ハザード
ethics charter 企業行動憲章 (=charter of ethics, corporate ethics charter, ethics code)
ethnic [ethnical] 形 人種の, 民族の, 民族的, 民族調の, 民族特有の, 民族色豊かな, 少数民族の, 民族学上の, …系の, 異教の, エスニック
ethnic Chinese 華僑
ethnic cleansing 民族浄化
ethnic communities 民族社会
ethnic concerns 民族問題
ethnic conflict 民族紛争, 民族的対立, 民族対立
ethnic costume [dress, outfit] 民族衣装
ethnic culture 民族文化
ethnic dance 民族舞踊
ethnic discrimination 民族差別
ethnic dispute 民族紛争
ethnic diversity 民族の多様性, 民族多様性

ethnic food エスニック料理, 民族特有の料理
ethnic friction 民族間の摩擦
ethnic group 少数民族集団, 少数民族, 民族, 種族, エスニック・グループ
ethnic heritage 民族遺産
ethnic makeup 民族構成
ethnic minority 少数民族
ethnic music 民族音楽
ethnic neighborhood 特定民族の居住区域
ethnic polarization 人種的対立化, 人種的分極化
ethnic purity 民族の同質性, 国家的同質性, 民族的純粋性
ethnic religion 種族宗教
ethnic slaughter 民族大虐殺
ethnic slur 特定民族に対する中傷
ethnic stew 人種のシチュー, 異人種[異民族]との共存
ethnic strife 民族紛争
ethnic tensions 民族間の緊張, 民族対立
ethnocentric firm 国内志向型企業
EU 欧州連合 (⇒European Union)
欧州統合の推移

1952年7月	欧州石炭鉄鋼共同体(ECSC)設立
1958年1月	欧州経済共同体(EEC), 欧州原子力共同体(EURATOM)設立
1967年7月	上記3共同体の統合で欧州共同体(EC)誕生
1993年11月	欧州連合(EU)誕生
1999年1月	欧州単一通貨のユーロ導入
2002年1月	ユーロ紙幣とユーロ硬貨の流通開始
2003年2月	ニース条約発効
2007年10月	リスボン条約案採択
2009年10月	アイルランド, 国民投票再投票でリスボン条約を批准。12月1日にリスボン条約発効

an expanded, 27-nation EU 27か国体制の拡大EU
anomaly in EU legislation EU規則の変則的規定
EU directive EU指令
EU member EU加盟国
EU trade EU域内貿易
EU Trade Commissioner EU通商担当委員
EU's fulltime president EUの欧州理事会常任議長(EU大統領)
EU's tariff policy EUの関税政策
the average economic growth rate of the new EU members EU新加盟国の平均経済

成長率
the economy of the 27-nation EU EU27か国全体の経済［経済成長率］
the enlargement of the EU 欧州連合(EU)の拡大
the EU's Constitution EU憲法（＝EU charter）
the EU's tariff policy EUの関税政策
the presidency of the EU EU議長国
the president of the EU 欧州連合(EU)委員長，EU大統領
the rotating presidency of the EU 輪番制の欧州連合(EU)議長国

EU constitution EU憲法 （＝EU charter：拡大EUの基本理念をうたった前文と448条の条文からなる。任期2年半の常任議長(EU大統領)と共通外交・安保政策推進のためのEU外相を新設する。2006年11月の発効を目標としていたが，発効には全加盟国批准が条件となっている。⇒EU [EU's] president)

EU [EU's] president EU大統領(欧州理事会常任議長) （＝EU's fulltime president：⇒Lisbon Treaty, president）

EU大統領（欧州理事会常任議長）：EUのトップ。2009年1月発効のEUの新基本条約「リスボン条約」で，EUの外務相にあたる新設の「対外活動庁」を率いる外交安保上級代表(foreign policy chief)とともに創設された。任期は2年半，1回改選が可能となっている。これに伴い，EUのトップは半年交代の輪番制から専従体制となった。EU首脳会議の議題の決定権を持つが，法案拒否権のような権限はない。

euro ユーロ （＝Euro：欧州単一通貨。1991年1月1日に導入された。独仏伊など11か国でスタートしたユーロ導入国は，2009年1月から16か国に拡大して，基軸通貨ドルに次ぐ「第二の通貨」としての存在感が高まっている）

euro area ユーロ圏，欧州圏 （＝euro zone, eurozone）
euro coins ユーロ硬貨(1，2ユーロ硬貨のほか，1, 2, 5, 10, 20, 50セント硬貨の計8種類がある)
euro notes [banknotes] ユーロ紙幣(5，10，20, 50, 100, 200, 500ユーロの計7種類がある)
euro zone countries ユーロ圏諸国，ユーロ圏各国，ユーロ圏
the 16 countries using the euro ユーロ圏16か国

European Central Bank 欧州中央銀行，欧州中銀《略 ECB》

European Commission 欧州委員会
European Court of First Instance 欧州第1審裁判所
European Union 欧州連合《略 EU》
欧州連合(EU)関連語句

Amsterdam Treaty	アムステルダム条約
Committee of Permanent Representatives	常駐代表委員会
European Commission	欧州委員会
European Council	欧州理事会
European Council headquarters	欧州理事会本部
European Parliament	欧州議会
European Union's head office	欧州連合(EU)本部，欧州連合(EU)欧州委員会
European Union's 27 member states	欧州連合(EU)加盟27か国
Presidency	議長国
Treaty of Maastricht	マーストリヒト条約

Eurostat 名 欧州連合(EU)統計局，ユーロスタット
eurozone 名 ユーロ圏，欧州圏 （＝euro zone）
euthanasia 名 安楽死 （＝mercy killing）
negative euthanasia 消極的安楽死
positive euthanasia 積極的安楽死
evacuation recommendations 避難勧告
evacuee 名 避難民，疎開者
evade 動 ごまかして避ける，逃れる，免れる，回避する，…しにくい，…を無駄にする
evasion 名 うまく逃げる［逃げる］こと，逃避，忌避，回避，ごまかし，言い逃れ，逃げ口上，口実，言い抜け
evasion of the laws 法の網［法網］をくぐる
income tax evasion 所得税の脱税
tax evasion 脱税，課税逃れ，税金逃れ （＝tax fraud）
event 名 動き，動向，事象，事態，出来事，事件，成り行き，結果，事由，事柄，事項，行事，催事，イベント
annual event 年中行事
coming events 予想される出来事，予定中の行事
current [present] events 時事
economic events 経済の動き，経済動向，景気動向，経済事象
event-driven fund イベント・ドリブン型ファンド（国際会議や要人の来日などの重要なイベントに合わせて株価変動の予測を立て，株式を売買する手法）

event management 催事管理, イベント管理
event planner イベント・プランナー（催事の企画, 演出, 運営などを専門に手がける者・会社）
fortuitous event 偶発的な事象
fund-raising event 資金集めの行事
future events 将来発生する事態
historical event 歴史上の事件, 歴史上の出来事
infrequent event 突発事象
leave the rest to the events それから先は成り行きに任せる
the course of events 事の成り行き, 事件の成り行き, 一連の事件
the sequence of events 事の次第
watch events with interest 成り行きを注視する

eventuate 動 結果が…となる(result in), …の結果になる, …に終わる,〈結果として〉起こる[生じる], 帰着する
eventuate from …から生じる, …から起こる
eventuate ill 不首尾に終わる
eventuate in a compromise 和解に達する
eventuate in a failure 失敗に終わる
eventuate in an agreement 合意に達する
eventuate well 好結果に終わる

eventuation 名 結末, 結果として生じること, 帰着

evidence 名 証拠, 根拠, 証拠資料, 証拠物件 (evidential matter), 証言, 証人, 指標, 兆候, 兆し, 形跡
available evidence 入手可能な証拠
bear [give, show] evidence of …の兆候[形跡]を示す
circumstantial evidence 状況証拠
conclusive evidence 決定的証拠
direct evidence 直接証拠
evidence-based crisis management 根拠に基づく危機管理
evidence of a pick-up in economic activity 景気回復の兆候, 景気が上向いていることを示す指標
evidence of bottoming inflation インフレが底を打った兆し
evidence to the contrary 反証
give evidence 証言する, 事情[状況]を説明する
in evidence 証拠として, 証人として, 目立って, はっきり見えて
internal evidence 内部証拠

material evidence 有力な物的証拠, 重要な物的証拠
objective evidence 客観的証拠
on the evidence of …の証言に基づいて
prima facie evidence 一応の証拠
physical supporting evidence 物的証拠
scientific evidence 科学的根拠

ex- 接頭 前の, 元の, 以前の, 元…, 前… (= former)
ex-administrative vice minister 元事務次官
ex-convict 前科者
ex-execs 旧経営陣, 元経営陣 (=former ex-ecutives)
ex-executive 元役員, 元管理職, 元経営者
ex-member 前[元]会員
ex-president 前[元]大統領, 前[元]社長

ex post fact 事後の[事後に], 過去にさかのぼった, 遡及的な[遡及的に], 遡及適用される (=after the fact)

exacerbate 動 悪化させる, 激化させる, 増大させる, 高める, 怒らせる
exacerbate the employment situation 雇用情勢を悪化させる
exacerbate the risks リスクを高める

exacerbation 名 悪化, 激化, 憤激

examination 名 調査, 検査, 監査, 試験, テスト, 検証, 考査, 考察, 審査, 審理, 診断, 診察, 尋問
competitive entrance examination 競争率の高い入学試験
cross-examination〈証人に対する弁護士の〉反対尋問
customs examination 税関審査
examination in chief 主尋問, 直接尋問
examination of a patient 患者の診察
examination of a witness 証人尋問, 証人の審問
examination paper 試験問題(examination question), 試験答案(test paper [sheet])
make a close [careful] examination of accounts 財務書類[会計記録, 帳簿]を念入りに調べる
make a full [thorough] examination of …を徹底的に調べる, …を詳細に検討[審査]する
make examinations in accordance with generally accepted auditing standards (GAAS) 一般に認められた監査基準[会計原則]に従って監査を行う

on examination 調査の上で, 調べてみると, 調査[試験, 検診]の結果では
under examination 審理[審査]中の, 調査[検査, 審査, 審理]中
undergo [have] a medical [physical] examination 健康診断を受ける

examine 動 調べる, 調査する, 検査する, 試験する, 試問する, 検証する, 検討する, 審査する, 審理する, 診断する, 診察する, 〈証人・被告を〉尋問する
examine risk factors リスク要因を検討する
examine serious crimes 重大犯罪を審理する
examine the company's financial statements 同社の財務書類[財務諸表]を監査する
examine the reconstruction plans of borrowers 融資先企業の再建計画を検証する

exceed 動 越える[超える], 上回る, …以上である, …に勝る

excellence 名 優秀, 優越, 卓越, 一流, 一流性, 長所, 美点, 優れた特性, 抜群の腕[腕前]
academic excellence 学業優秀 (=excellence in scholarship)
dispute excellence with …と肩を並べる
emulate the excellences 優秀さを競う
excellence in cooking 料理の腕前 (=excellence as a cook)
excellence in workmanship 仕上がり[技量・製作]が素晴らしいこと, 見事な仕上がり
moral excellence 道徳上の美点
prize foe excellence in design デザイン優秀賞
reach high excellence 優秀の域に達する
sense of excellence over others 他人に対する優越感
unequivocal excellence 超一流

excellent 形 優れた, 秀でた, 優秀な, 卓越した, 一流の, 並はずれた, 並々ならぬ, すばらしい, 見事な, 結構な, 良好な, 大量の
excellent company 超優良企業
excellent idea 優れたアイデア, すばらしいアイデア
excellent liquidity 流動性の高さ
excellent quality 優良品質, 優良品
excellent relationship 良好な関係

exception 名 例外, 除外, 限定, 特例, 除外事項, 限定事項, 異議, 不服, 反対, 異議申立て
exception [exceptions] clause 免責条項
make no exception(s) 例外を設けない, 特別扱いはしない
management by exception 例外管理
take exception to …に異議を申し立てる, …に(強く)反対する, …に腹を立てる

exceptional 形 特別の, 例外の, 桁外れの, 特別損益の, 特別項目の, 名 特別損益, 特別項目
exceptional gains 特別利益 (=exceptional profits)
exceptional provision 特別引当金
exceptionals 特別損益
operating profit before exceptional items 特別項目前の営業利益, 特別損益計上前の営業利益
pre-exceptional pretax profits 特別項目前の税引き前利益

excess 名 形 超過, 超過額, 過剰, 余剰, 過度
excess consumption 過剰消費
excess quotas for greenhouse gas emissions 温室効果ガスの削減分, 温室効果ガスの排出権
excess workers 過剰雇用者 (=surplus staff)

excessive 形 過度の, 極端な, 法外な, 不当な, 多すぎる, 過多の, 過剰な, 割高な
excessive action 行き過ぎた行動
excessive advertisement [advertising] 誇大広告
excessive borrowing 過剰借入れ
excessive competition 過当競争
excessive demand 不当な[法外な]要求, 要求の行き過ぎ, 過剰需要, 超過需要
excessive expense structure 過剰なコスト構造
excessive growth 過度の成長, 経済成長の行きすぎ
excessive investment in plant and equipment 過剰設備投資
excessive lending 過剰融資
excessive liabilities 過剰債務, 債務超過, 債務超過額
excessive packaging 過剰包装
excessive profit 不当利得, 暴利
excessive profits tax 超過利得税
excessive service 過剰サービス, サービス過剰
excessive speculation 過当投機
excessive spending 過剰消費, 過剰な財政支出
excessive trading 過当取引
excessive wining and dining 過剰接待

exchange 動 交換する, 取り替える, 両替する, やり取りする, 〈契約などを〉取り交わす, 〈契約書に〉サインする

exchange 名 交流, 交換, 意見交換, 会話, 議論, 両替, 為替, 為替相場,〈証券や商品の〉取引所, 取引, 交易, 電話交換所, 職業安定所
- **arbitration of exchange** 為替裁定取引
- **commodity exchange** 商品取引所
- **cultural exchange between the two countries** 両国間[二国間]の文化交流
- **currency exchange office** 両替所
- **economic exchange** 経済交流
- **exchange control** 為替管理
- **exchange depreciation** 為替の切下げ, 為替価値の下落[減少]
- **exchange dumping** 為替ダンピング(輸出品の競争力を高めるため自国通貨の為替相場を不当に切り下げること)
- **exchange gains** 為替差益
- **exchange-listed company [firm]** 証券取引所上場企業, 上場企業
- **exchange market** 為替市場, 取引市場, 為替相場
- **exchange of gunfires** 銃火の応酬
- **exchange of hostages** 人質交換
- **exchange of information** 情報交換
- **exchange of views** 意見の交換
- **exchange parity** 為替平価
- **exchange position** 〈為替銀行の〉為替の持ち高, 為替ポジション
- **exchange risk** 為替リスク
- **exchange speculation** 為替投機
- **exchange student** 交換留学生
- **floating exchange** 変動相場
- **foreign exchange** 外国為替
- **forward exchange** 先物為替
- **heated exchange** 白熱した議論
- **share exchange** 株式交換 (＝exchange of shares)
- **telephone exchange** 電話交換局

exchange offer エクスチェンジ・オファー(一種のスワップ。会社側が同社の発行済み証券(旧証券)と同社の新証券または新証券と現金の組合せとの交換を提案すること)

exchange rate 為替相場, 為替レート, 交換レート, 交換比率 (＝rate of exchange)
- **assumed exchange rate** 想定為替レート
- **average exchange rates prevailing during the year** 期中の実勢平均為替レート
- **exchange rate movements** 為替変動, 為替レートの変動 (＝exchange fluctuation, exchange rate changes [fluctuations, moves])
- **exchange rate policy** 為替政策
- **Exchange Surveillance Commission** 証券取引等監視委員会
- **stock-for-stock exchange rate** 株式交換の交換比率

exchange-traded fund 上場投資信託, 株価指数連動型上場投資信託《略 ETF》

exclusive economic zone 排他的経済水域《略 EEZ》(国連海洋法条約により, 沿岸国は200カイリ(約370キロ・メートル)まで排他的経済水域を設定することができ, この水域で沿岸国は海洋, 海底とその下で天然資源の開発, 探査, 管理や経済活動に関して主権的権利を持つとされる)

executive 名 経営者, 管理職, 重役, 会社役員, 役職員, 執行役員, 執行部, 執行機関, 行政部 (executive department), 行政官, エグゼクティブ
- **Chief Executive** 米大統領
- **chief executive** 企業などのトップ, 最高経営責任者(CEO), 理事長
- **government executives** 政府官僚
- **incumbent executives** 現経営陣, 現職の経営陣
- **subordinate executive** 従属役員,〈副社長などの〉副業務執行役員
- **top executive** 最高経営者, 最高執行部, 最高経営幹部, 経営首脳, 経営者

executive 形 執行権のある, 執行権をもった, 執行力のある, 行政上の, 管理者の, 経営者[陣]の, 経営上の, 幹部の, 経営陣のための, 高価で高品質の, 高価でぜいたくな
- **Deputy Assistant to the President and Executive Assistant to the Chief of Staff** 米大統領副補佐官・首席補佐官事務補佐官
- **executive ability** 経営能力, 管理能力, 実務の才能, 経営手腕
- **executive actions** 行政措置
- **executive agency** 行政機関, 執行機関
- **executive agreement** 〈米国の〉行政協定
- **executive aid** 秘書 (＝administrative assistant)
- **executive airplane** 重役専用機
- **executive and judicial bodies** 行政司法機関
- **executive board** 重役会, 役員会, 理事会, 上層部
- **executive board meeting** 役員会, 理事会, 執行委員会
- **executive body** 執行委員会, 実行委員会

executive branch 行政府
executive businessman 高級ビジネスマン
executive chairman 執行委員長
executive class エグゼクティブ・クラス (= business class：first classとeconomy classの中間)
executive clemency 〈米大統領[州知事]の既決囚に対する〉行政減刑処置
executive committee 執行委員会, 実行委員会, 業務執行委員会, 経営委員会, 経営執行委員会
executive committee meeting 経営委員会, 業務執行委員会, 中央執行委員会
executive compensation 役員報酬, 経営者報酬
executive council 執行委員会, 経営委員会
executive decision 管理的意思決定
executive department 行政部
executive development 経営者教育, 経営者啓発, 経営者育成 (＝management development)
executive director 執行取締役, 業務執行取締役, 専務[常務]取締役, 常務理事, 理事, 〈協会などの〉会長, 頭取, 事務局長
executive duties 業務執行職務, 経営執行職務, 経営職務
executive editor-in-chief 〈新聞社の〉代表取締役主筆
executive function 業務執行機能, 経営執行機能, 管理機能, 管理職能
executive job 管理事務, 管理業務, 管理職, 管理職務
executive management 経営管理
Executive Mansion 米大統領官邸(White House), 州知事官邸[公邸]
executive office 業務執行室
executive official 最高管理職員
executive order 行政命令, 政令, 米大統領命令[大統領令]
executive organ 執行機関
executive personnel 管理職員
executive position 管理職, 管理職位
executive power 執行権, 行政権
executive privilege 〈守秘事項に関する〉米大統領特権, 行政府特権
executive producer 〈映画の〉製作総指揮者
executive remuneration packages 執行役員の報酬

executive responsibility 管理責任
executive search 〈社長クラスの〉人材スカウト業
Executive Secretary for Cabinet Liaison 〈米〉内閣連絡担当事務秘書官
Executive Secretary, National Security Council 〈米〉国家安全保障会議担当事務秘書官
executive session 〈米上院の〉行政審議会, 〈米議会幹部の〉秘密会, 秘密会議, 非公開会議
executive suite 重役室
executive summary 概要
executive talent 実行力
executive unit 管理単位
executive vice president 業務執行副社長, 副社長, 専務[常務]《略 EVP》
executive work 管理業務
management executive committee 経営執行委員会

Executive Office
米大統領官邸 (=Executive Office Building, White House)

Executive Office Building 米大統領官邸, 行政府ビル《略 E.O.B.》(ホワイトハウスの別館)
Executive Office of the President 米大統領府, 米大統領行政府

米大統領補佐機関

Council of Economic Advisers	経済諮問委員会
Council on Environmental Quality	環境問題委員会
National Critical Materials Council	国家重要物資委員会, 戦略重要物資会議
National Security Council	国家安全保障会議
Office of Administration	管理局
Office of Management and Budget	行政管理予算庁, 行政管理予算局
Office of National Drug Control Policy	薬物取締政策局, 連邦薬物管理政策局
Office of Policy Development	政策開発局
Office of Science and Technology Policy	科学技術政策局
Office of the United States Trade Representative	合衆国通商代表部
Office of the Vice President of the United States	合衆国副大統領事務局
The White House Office	ホワイトハウス事務局

executive officer 〈企業の〉業務執行役員,

上席業務執行役員, 経営者, 幹部, 役員,〈機構の〉行政官,〈指揮官の〉副官,〈軍艦などの〉副長,〈連隊以下の〉副隊長

exemption 名 控除, 課税控除, 控除額, 義務の免除, 免責, 例外
- basic exemption 基礎控除
- exemption for dependents 扶養控除
- exemption for spouse 配偶者控除
- exemption of debt 債務免除
- export exemption 輸出免税
- tariff [duty] exemption 関税免除
- tax exemption 免税
- total exemption 全額免除

exercise nut エクササイズ狂
exercycle 名 エクササイクル(エクササイズ用の固定自転車)
exhaust heat 排熱
exhaustion 名 消耗, 疲労, 疲弊, 枯渇, 使い果たすこと, 底を突くこと
existing 形 存在する, 現存する, 存続している, 現行の, 既存の, 従来の, 現在の, 今回の, 実績ベースの, 既存店ベースの
- a company organized and existing under the laws of the State of California カリフォルニア州の法律に基づいて設立され現存する法人
- existing contract 現行契約, 現存契約
- existing customer [client] 既存の顧客, 既存顧客, 既顧客
- existing debt 既存の債務
- existing home sales 中古住宅販売, 中古住宅販売戸数 (=sales of existing homes)
- existing inflation 実績ベースのインフレ率
- existing issue 既発債
- existing law 現行法
- existing market 既存市場, 現存市場
- existing mortgage 現存抵当
- existing operations 既存の事業, 従来の事業, 現地企業
- existing product 既存製品
- existing right 既存の権利, 既存権利
- existing reserves 埋蔵資源
- existing store 既存店, 既存店舗

exit 動 去る, 退場する, 退出する, …から撤退する, 終了する, 終える
- barriers to exit 流出障壁, 撤退障壁
- exit the market 市場から撤退する
- exit the week 週を終える
- exit the word processor ワープロを終了する

exit 名 退場, 退出, 撤退, 出国, 出口, 流出, 売却
- current exit value 売却時価
- exit barrier 撤退障壁
- exit interview 退職者面接, 解任者面接
- exit poll 出口調査
- exit price [value] 売却価額
- exit strategy 出口戦略
- exit visa 出国ビザ

Exon–Florio provision of the 1988 trade law 1988年通商法のエクソン・フロリオ条項(米国の安全保障を損なう企業買収の禁止)

expand 動 拡大する, 拡張する, 広げる, 拡充する, 増やす, 引き上げる, 展開する, 成長する, 発展する, 上昇する, 膨張する, 改善する, …の内容を充実させる, 詳述する
- expand capacity 設備を拡張する, 生産能力を拡大する
- expand cultural exchange 文化交流を広げる
- expand infrastructure インフラを拡張する
- expand one's operating loss projection …の営業損失[営業赤字]予想額を引き上げる
- expand production 生産を拡大する
- expand the computer network コンピュータ・ネットワークを拡張する
- expanded lead manager 拡大主幹事
- expanded memory 拡張メモリ
- expanded NATO 拡大NATO
- expanded polystyrene 発泡スチロール

expansion 名 拡大, 拡張, 設備拡張, 景気拡大, 成長, 上昇, 多角化
- credit expansion 信用拡大, 信用拡張, 信用膨張, 貸出の伸び, 金融拡大, 金融緩和
- domestic [home] demand expansion 内需拡大 (=expansion of domestic demand)
- expansion effect 拡張効果, 拡大効果
- expansion investment 拡張投資
- expansion of job opportunities 雇用拡大
- expansion of money [the currency] 通貨の膨張
- expansion period 景気拡大局面
- horizontal expansion 水平的拡大
- market expansion 市場拡大, 市場拡張
- monetary expansion 金融拡大, 金融緩和, 通貨拡大[膨張]
- numerical expansion 量的拡大
- production [output] expansion 生産の増加, 生産の伸び, 生産拡大

productivity expansion 生産力拡充
quantitative expansion 量的拡大, 量的拡張
sustained economic expansion 持続的な経済成長, 経済の持続的な成長
trade expansion 通商拡大, 貿易拡大 (＝expansion of trade)

expansionary 形 拡大の, 拡張の, 膨張性の, 発展性の
adopt [pursue] an expansionary economic policy 経済拡大政策をとる
expansionary budget 積極型予算, 積極的予算
expansionary economy 拡張経済, 経済拡大
expansionary effect 景気押し上げ効果, 景気刺激効果
expansionary financial policy 拡張的金融政策
expansionary fiscal policy 財政出動による景気刺激策, 財政政策の緩和
expansionary monetary policy 金融政策の緩和, 金融の量的緩和策, 拡張的通貨政策
expansionary policy 景気刺激型の政策
expansionary production 拡張的生産
expansionary thrust of fiscal and monetary policy 景気刺激型の金融・財政政策

expatriate 動 国外に追放する, 名 海外駐在員, 海外移住者, 国籍離脱者
expatriate citizens 国外在住の国民

expect 動 期待する, 見込む, 予想する, 見積もる, 推定する, …するつもりである, …するだろうと思う, …と思う, 要求する, 求める
as might be [have been] expected 当然予想されたように, 思ったように, さすがは…だけあって, やっぱり(だめだった)
be expected to …することが予想[期待]される, …するものと考えられる, …と見込まれる, …になりそうだ, …する見込みである
be (only) to be expected 予想どおりである, 不思議ではない
expected amount of losses 予想される損失額
expected inflation (figures) 期待インフレ率, 予想インフレ率
expected profit 期待利益, 予想利益, 期待利潤
expected profitability 期待利益率, 予想利益率
expected return 期待収益, 予想収益, 期待収益率
expected value 期待値

expectation 名 期待, 予想, 見通し, 見積り, 推定, 期待値
come ahead of GDP expectations GDP (国内総生産) 予想を上回る
come on the high side of expectations 市場予測の平均を上回る
disappoint market expectations 市場の期待を裏切る
expectation gap 期待ギャップ
expectation of life 見積り耐用年数, 期待耐用年数 (＝expected life)
expectations for the year as a whole 通期予想, 通期見通し, 年間予想
growth expectations 成長率予測
inflation [inflationary] expectation インフレ期待, インフレ見通し
interest rate expectations 金利見通し
market expectations 市場の期待, 市場の予想, 市場予測
profit expectation 利益予想
short-term [near-term] expectation 短期見通し, 短期期待
the lowest end of expectations 予想範囲の下限

expedite 動 促進する, 早める, 急ぐ, 手早く片付ける, 発送する, 派遣する

expert 名 専門家, 熟練者, 有識者, 玄人, エキスパート
expert panel 有識者会議
expert power 専門家パワー
expert system 専門家システム, エキスパート・システム (＝knowledge-based system)

expertise 名 専門知識, 専門技術, 専門家の報告書, ノウハウ (＝knowhow)

external investigation committee 外部調査委員会

expire 動〈期間が〉満了する, 終了する, 満期になる,〈期限が〉切れる,〈時効が〉成立する

exploit 動 開発する, 開拓する, 利用する, 活用する, 搾取する, 食い物にする, 名 功績, 偉業, 業績, 手柄
exploit assets 資産を注ぎ込む
exploit demand 需要を利用する
exploit natural resources 天然資源を開発する
exploit overseas markets 海外市場を開拓[開発]する
exploit scale economies 規模の経済を活用する
exploit the high growth 成長の機会をつかむ

exploitation 名 開発, 開拓, 利用, 活用, 宣伝,〈販売などの〉促進, 搾取
  absolute exploitation　絶対的搾取
  capitalist exploitation　資本主義的搾取
  exploitation campaign　宣伝活動
  exploitation colony　搾取植民地
  exploitation cost　開発原価
  exploitation film　金もうけ映画
  intermediary exploitation　中間搾取
  labor exploitation　労働搾取
  market exploitation　市場開拓, 市場開発
  monopolistic exploitation　独占的搾取
  monopsonistic exploitation　需要独占的搾取
  relative exploitation　相対的搾取, 相対搾取
  resource exploitation　資源開発

exploration 名 探検, 探査, 踏査, 研究, 調査, 診察, 検診, 触診
  exploration of a possibility　可能性を探ること
  exploration of (outer) sapce　宇宙開発 (=space exploration)
  oil exploration　石油開発, 石油探査, 石油探鉱
  seismic exploration　地震探査
  voyage of exploration　探検航海

exploratory right　試掘権

explosive 形 爆発的な, 爆発性の, 爆発寸前の, 急激な, 一触触発の, 非常に危険な, 論議を呼ぶ, 強大な
  explosive device　爆破装置
  explosive factor　火種, 危険な要因
  explosive growth　急激な発展, 爆発的な成長, 急成長, 爆発的拡大, 急増, 激増
  explosive increase　爆発的な増加, 急増, 激増
  explosive issue　論議を呼ぶ問題, 議論の紛糾する問題
  explosive population growth　爆発的な人口増加, 急激な人口増加[人口の伸び]
  explosive situation　一触即発の状況

export 名 輸出, 輸出品, 輸出製品, 供給
  agricultural export　農産物輸出
  capital goods export　資本財の輸出
  consumer goods exports　消費財の輸出
  contraband of export　輸出禁制品
  degree of dependence on exports　輸出依存度
  elasticity of export　輸出弾力性
  Export Administration Regulations　米輸出管理規則[規制], 米輸出行政規則
  export agent　輸出代理店
  export and import index　輸出入物価指数 (=export and import price index)
  export ban　輸出禁止
  export bonus　輸出助成金, 輸出奨励金, 輸出補助金 (=export bounty)
  export clearance　輸出通関
  export competition　輸出競争
  export control system　輸出管理体制
  export drive　輸出ドライブ, 輸出拡大圧力, 輸出競争力
  export–import balance　輸出入バランス
  Export–Import Bank of the United States　米[合衆国]輸出入銀行 (=Eximbank)
  export incentive　輸出誘因, 輸出刺激
  export industry　輸出産業
  export inspection　輸出検査
  export–intensive industry　輸出集約産業
  export machine　輸出用機械
  export market　輸出市場
  export mentality　輸出志向
  export order　輸出注文, 輸出受注
  export orientation　輸出志向, 輸出主導型
  export–oriented industry　輸出志向産業
  export proceeds　輸出代金, 輸出売上高
  export processing zone　輸出加工区
  export restraint　輸出規制, 輸出制限 (=export restriction)
  export subsidies　輸出補助金, 輸出助成金, 輸出奨励金
  export supply　輸出供給
  export surplus　貿易収支の黒字
  export volume　輸出量, 輸出数量
  foreign export earnings　外貨獲得
  growth in exports　輸出の伸び
  increase in exports　輸出の増加, 輸出の伸び
  industrial exports　製品輸出, 工業製品輸出
  invisible export　貿易外輸出
  propensity to export　輸出性向
  real export　実質輸出額
  real net export　実質純輸出
  total exports　輸出全体
  unauthorized export　不正輸出
  U.S.–destined exports　対米輸出, 米国向け輸出

export–driven 形 輸出主導の, 輸出主導型の (=export-led)
  export–driven economic recovery　輸出主導の景気回復

export-driven growth 輸出主導の成長, 輸出主導型[先行型]成長, 輸出リード型成長
export-led 形 輸出主導の, 輸出主導型の (＝export-driven)
  export-led economic recovery 輸出頼みの景気回復, 輸出主導型の景気回復
  export-led economies 輸出主導型経済
  export-led growth 輸出主導の成長, 輸出主導型[先行型]成長, 輸出リード型成長
  export-led recovery 輸出主導の景気回復, 輸出主導型の景気[業績]回復
export-oriented 形 輸出志向の, 輸出中心の, 輸出重視の, 輸出主導型の
  export-oriented business 輸出指向型企業, 輸出企業
  export-oriented companies 輸出企業, 輸出産業, 輸出指向型企業
  export-oriented firms 輸出志向企業, 輸出型企業, 輸出企業 (＝export-oriented businesses [companies])
  export-oriented industry 輸出志向産業
  export-oriented manufacturer 輸出企業, 輸出メーカー, 輸出中心のメーカー
export-related businesses 輸出関連企業, 輸出関連業界
exported 形 輸出される, 輸出された, …の輸出
  exported capital 輸出資本
  exported goods 輸出品
  exported inflation 輸出インフレーション, 輸出インフレ
  exported item 輸出品目
exporters 名 輸出業者, 輸出企業, 輸出産業, 輸出国
exporting company 輸出企業
expose 動 〈危険に〉さらす, 暴露する, 公然と売り出す, 陳列する, 展示する, 摘発する, すっぱ抜く, 経験させる
  be exposed to credit risk 信用リスクを負う, 与信リスクを負う, 信用リスクにさらされる
  be exposed to interest rate risk 金利リスクにさらされる
  be exposed to losses 損失を被る
  expose goods for sale 販売商品を陳列する, 販売品を展示する
exposure 名 〈危険などに〉さらされること, 影響されること, 損失の危機に瀕していること, 暴露, 摘発, 発覚, 露顕, 露出, 〈商品の〉陳列, 〈テレビや新聞に〉取り上げられること, リスク, 危険度, 投資, 融資, リスク資産総額, 融資総額, 与信残高, 債権, 債権額, エクスポージャー
  credit exposure 与信リスク, 信用リスク
  economic exposure 経済リスク
  Exposure Draft 米財務会計基準審議会（FASB）などの討議資料, 公開草案《略 ED》
  exposure to changes in interest rates 金利変動リスク（＝exposure to interest rates）
  exposure to credit risk 信用リスク
  exposure to highly leveraged transactions 負債比率の高い取引（HLT）への融資《略 HLT融資》
  exposure to the weather 風雨にさらされること
  external exposure 対外債権残高
  financial exposure 資金負担, 金融リスク
  have a large exposure to …の運用比率が高い, …リスクが高い
  investment exposure 投資リスク, 投資
  radiation exposure 放射線[放射能]流出
  real estate exposure 不動産投資, 不動産融資
  reduce exposure to the risk of loss 損失リスクを減らす, 損失リスクを軽減する
  risk exposure リスク, リスク・エクスポージャー
  the exposure of a criminal 犯人の摘発
  the exposure of personal information 個人情報の暴露
  the exposure of the plot 陰謀の摘発
expressway 名 高速道路（＝limited access highway）
  Metropolitan Expressway 首都高速道路
extend 動 〈援助の手を〉差し伸べる, 〈援助などを〉与える[行う], 〈信用やローンなどを〉供与する, 提供する, 〈言葉や祝辞などを〉述べる, 時間を延長する, 延期する, 拡張する, 広げる
  extend credit 信用を供与する
  extend funds 資金を拠出する, 資金を提供する
  extend loans 融資する
  extend yen loans as part of Japan's ODA 日本の政府開発援助として円借款を供与する
  extended coverage endorsement 拡張担保特約
  extended fund facility 拡大信用供与制度
extent 名 程度, 範囲, 規模, 広さ, 大きさ, 限度, 限界, 差押え令状
  the extent of contractual relationship 契約関係の限度
  the extent of disclosure 開示の範囲
  the extent of reduction in prices 物価の下

げ幅
the extent of test 調査範囲
the extent of the contract 契約の範囲
the extent of the market 市場範囲
the nature, extent and terms of financial products 金融商品の性質, 範囲と条件
to some extent ある程度まで
to the extent of …の範囲[限界]まで
to the extent that …するほど, …という点で
to the fullest [maximum] extent 最大限に
extenuating circumstances 酌量すべき情状, 情状酌量, 軽減事由
extermination of rats ネズミの駆除
exterminator 名 害虫駆除業者
external 形 外部の, 対外的な, 国外の
external assets 対外資産, 対外資産残高（日本の政府や企業, 個人が海外に持っている資産）
external audit 外部監査 （＝external auditing）
external bond financing 外債発行による資金調達
external borrowing 対外借入れ
external debt 対外債務
external deficit 国際収支の赤字
external economic affairs 対外経済問題
external equilibrium 対外均衡
external financing 外部調達資金, 外部資金の調達, 外部金融 （＝external funding）
external funds 外部資金, 外部調達資金（銀行などからの借入れ, 株式や社債, 手形債務などにより外部から調達する資金）
external information 外部情報
external memory 外部記憶装置
external position 対外収支
external pressure 外圧
external surplus 国際収支の黒字
external trade 貿易収支
external transaction 外部取引

extradition 名 引渡し, 送還
extralegal measure 超法規措置
extraordinary 形 特別の, 臨時の, 異常な
extraordinary board of directors 臨時取締役会
extraordinary board of directors meeting 臨時取締役会
extraordinary gain 特別利益, 異常利得 （＝special gain）
extraordinary general meeting 臨時株主総会（原則として年1回開く定時株主総会とは別に, 定款変更など株主総会決議が必要な重要事項の決定を行うときに開く）
extraordinary loss 特別損失, 異常損失, 経常外損失 （＝special loss）
extraordinary profit 特別利益（保有株式の売却やメーカーの工場売却による利益）
extraordinary shareholders meeting 臨時株主総会
extraordinary meeting 臨時総会（アメリカではspecial meetingという）
extraordinary meeting of shareholders 臨時株主総会 （＝extraordinary general meeting）
extraordinary meeting of the board of the directors 臨時取締役会
extraterritorial area 治外法権区域
extremism 名 過激主義, 急進主義
extremist 名 急進主義者, 極端論の支持者
eye 動 注目する, 着目する, 計画する, もくろむ, 視野に入れる, 検討する, 考慮する, 見込む, 狙う, 関心を示す, 希望する
eye a management integration 経営統合を計画する
eye post as …の地位を狙う
eye tie-up with …との提携を計画する[もくろむ]

F

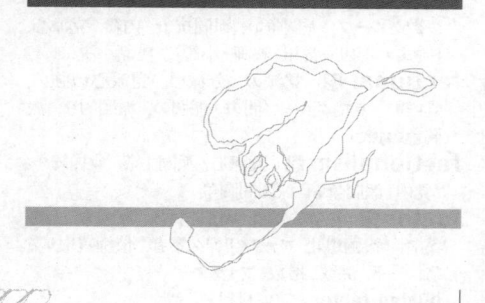

FAA 米連邦航空局（Federal Aviation Administrationの略）
fabricate 動 捏造する, 偽造する, でっち上げる, 改竄する, 組み立てる, 製作する, 製造する
  fabricated certificate 偽証明書（＝fake certificate）
  fabricated expenses 架空経費
  fabricated results 粉飾決算, 業績改竄
  fabricating cost 製造原価
face 動 …に直面する, …に見舞われる, …を仕掛けられる, …の対象になる, …を抱える, …に向かう, …に立ち向かう, …に耐える, …を直視する
  be faced with serious financial problems 深刻な金融問題に直面する
  face a loss 損失を抱える
  face competitive threats 競争圧力に直面する, 競争圧力にさらされる, 競争力で後れをとる
  face facts 事実を直視する
  face up to …を直視する, …を受け止める, …に決然と立ち向かう, …に対処する
  the challenges facing the world economy 世界経済が直面する課題, 世界経済が抱える課題
face-saving 形 顔を立てる, メンツを立てる, メンツを保つ
face-to-face 名 面と向かっての, 顔をつき合わせた, 膝を交えての, 差し向かいでの, 直接の, 直接体面した, 副 面と向かって, 顔をつき合わせて, 差し向かいで, 直接対面して
  face-to-face meeting 直接対話
  face-to-face talks 膝づめ談判
facilitate 動 助長する, 促進する, 進める, 円滑に進める, 容易にする, 後押しする, 楽にする, …の手助けをする, …を手伝う
  facilitate a conversation 話がとぎれないようにする
  facilitate market entry into …への参入を促進する
  facilitate secondary market trading 流通市場での売買を促進する
facility 名 融資枠, 融資, 信用供与, 信用枠, 手段, 便宜, 場所, 建物, 設備, 施設, 工場, 機関, 手洗い, トイレ, 制度, 適性, 才能, 腕前, 熟練, 流暢, 器用さ, ファシリティ
  communication facilities 通信機関（＝facilities for communication）
  credit facility 信用供与, 信用供与制度, 金融制度, クレジット・ファシリティ
  facilities for travel 交通の便, 交通機関
  financial facilities 金融機関（＝monetary facilities）
  give [afford] every facility for …に対してあらゆる便宜を図る[便宜を与える]
  guarantee facility 債務保証
  harbor facilities 港湾施設, 港湾設備
  have a natural facility for …の天性がある
  manufacturing facilities 生産拠点, 生産設備（＝production facilities）
  medical facilities 医療施設
  nuclear waste facility 核廃棄物処理場
  sewage treatment facilities 下水処理施設
  show [have] great facility in …に優れた才能を示す

faction 名 派, 党派, 分派, 派閥, 対立グループ, 少数グループ, 派閥争い, 派閥抗争, 内紛, 党派心, ドキュメンタリー番組［映画, 小説］, 実話小説

factional 形 党派の, 分派の, 党派心の強い, 党内の, 党内グループ間の, 派閥の, 派閥的な, 派閥色の強い

factionalism 名 党派心, 派閥主義, 党内紛争, 〈党内〉派閥争い, 派閥間闘争

factor 名 要素, 要因, 因子, 材料, 原動力, 金融業者, 金融機関, ファクタリング業者, 債権買取り業者, …率, 係数, 指数, ファクター
  buying factor 買い材料
  cost factor コスト要因, 原価要素
  load factor 負荷率, ロード・ファクター
  market factor 市場要因, 市場因子, 市場要素
  negative factor マイナス要因, 悪材料, 売り材料 (＝unfavorable factor)
  political factor 政治的要因, 政治的要素
  positive factor プラス要因, 好材料, 買い材料 (＝favorable factor)
  seasonal factor 季節要因

factory 名 工場, 生産設備, 製造業, メーカー, 在外［海外］代理店
  factory brand 生産工場独自の商標, ファクトリー・ブランド
  factory capacity 工場の生産能力, 生産設備能力
  factory closing [closure] 工場閉鎖
  factory demand 製造業新規受注高
  factory orders 製造業受注高, 製造業新規受注高, 製造業受注残高
  factory output 製造業生産高
  factory sector 製造業
  munitions factory 軍需工場
  obsolete factories 老朽化した生産設備
  pilot factory 実験工場
  subcontracting factory 下請工場

fail 動 経営破綻する, 破綻する, 倒産する, 破産する, 失敗する, …を怠る (＝collapse)

fail safe 絶対安全性, 障害時の安全性, フェール・セーフ（システムに異常・障害が生じても出力の安全性は維持されること）

fail to …できない, …しない, …することを怠る

failure 名 経営破綻, 破綻, 倒産, 破産, 〈債務や義務などの〉不履行, 失敗, 〈機械などの〉機能停止, 故障, 障害 (＝collapse)
  financial failures 金融破綻
  system failure システムの故障, システムのトラブル, システム障害

Fair Labor Standards Act 〈米国の〉公正労働基準法《略 FLSA》

fait accompli 既成事実

fake 動 偽造する, 模造する, 変造する, 改竄する, 捏造する, 複写する, 模写する, 隠す, 見せかける, …のふりをする, …に手を加える
  fake a traffic accident 交通事故と見せかける
  fake illness 仮病を使う, 病気を装う

fake 形 偽の, 偽造の, 改竄した, 偽装した, 偽物の, いかさまの, 狂言の (＝bogus, counterfeit, phony [phoney])
  fake certificate 偽証明書
  fake credit card 偽造クレジット・カード (＝counterfeit credit card)
  fake money 偽札 (＝fake bill)
  fake overtime payments カラ残業代, 実態に合わない超過勤務手当
  fake product コピー製品, 偽ブランド製品 (＝pirated product)
  fake transaction 偽装売買, 偽装取引

fall 動 下落する, 低下する, 減少する, 崩壊する, 失墜する, 〈手形の〉期限が来る
  fall below …を割り込む, …を割る
  fall flat 失敗する, 大失敗する, 成立しない, 不成立に終わる, 期待にこたえられない
  fall into recession 景気後退局面［景気後退］に入る
  fall off dramatically 急激に落ち込む, 急減する
  fall on [upon] …を襲う, …に殺到する, …の負担になる, …に課せられる, …をふと思いつく, …がふと思いあたる, …に出会う, …を経験する, …に向けられる, …に注がれる
  fall on hard times 困窮する
  fall out of the race 取り残される
  fall through 失敗する, 失敗に終わる, 実現しない, 無駄になる
  fall through the lower end of …の下限を下回る
  fall to new lows against …に対して史上最安値を更新する
  fall under …に分類される, …に該当する, …の分野［範囲, 部類］に入る, …の影響を受ける, …に取りつかれる

fall 名 下落, 低下, 減少, 崩壊, 滅亡, 脱落, 失墜, 陥落, 降水量
  earnings fall 減益

fall in interest rates 金利の低下 (=fall in rates)
fall in the value of the dollar ドル安
falls in GDP GDPのマイナス成長
sharp fall in money market rates 短期市場金利の急低下
the rate of fall in prices 物価の下落率

fall [get, lag] behind …に[…より, …が]遅れる, …に後れを取る, …から落伍する, …に先行される, …を滞納する
fall behind in global competitiveness 国際競争に遅れる, 国際競争から落伍する
fall behind in tax payments 納税が遅れる, 税金を滞納する, 税金が支払えない
fall behind in the development of …の開発で後れを取る
fall behind schedule 予定より遅れる
fall behind with one's payments 支払いが遅れる, 決済が遅れる

fall short of …を下回る, …に達しない, …を割る, …が欠乏[不足]する, …に不十分である (=come short of)

fallacy of composition 合成の誤謬(一個人, 一企業に妥当なことが社会全体にとっても妥当である, という前提から生じる誤謬)

fallback [fall-back] 形 代替の, 万一の時[緊急時]に働く, 不時の, 名 後退, 撤退, 代替品, 蓄え, 準備品, 予備品, 頼みの綱, 最後のよりどころ
fallback pay 出勤給
fallback plan 代替案
fallback position 代替策

falling 形 落ちる, 下がる, 低下する, 下降する, 下落する
falling backlog 受注残高の減少
falling deficit 財政赤字の縮小, 財政赤字の減少
falling demand 需要の低下, 需要の減少, 需要の落ち込み
falling funding costs 資金調達コストの低下
falling profit margin 利益率の低下
falling stock market [prices] 株価の下落, 株安 (=fall in stock prices)
falling tax rates 税率の低下

fallout 名 落伍[落後], 離脱, 脱落, 脱退, 後退, 撤退, つまずき, 失敗, 解散, 不測の結果[事態], 後遺症, 放射性物質の降下, 放射性降下物, 原子灰, 放射能塵, 死の灰
fallout from the collapse of the stock market 株式市場急落の後遺症, 株式値下りの後遺症
fallout from the global economic downturn 世界的な景気後退[景気減速]による不測の事態
fallout shelter 降下原子灰退避所

false 形 不正な, 不法な, 不正確な, 虚偽の, 偽造の, 偽の, 人造の
false accusation [charge] 冤罪
false financial statements 虚偽記載の有価証券報告書
false labeling [marking] 虚偽表示

falsification 名 偽造, 偽装, 改竄, 捏造, 変造, 詐称, 虚偽記載

falsify 動 偽造する, 偽装する, 改竄する, 捏造する, 変造する, 詐称する, 虚偽記載する
falsified financial documents 虚偽の財務書類
falsified financial statements 虚偽記載の有価証券報告書, 虚偽記載の財務書類
falsified stock option dealing 株式オプションの偽装売買, 偽装株式オプション取引

falter 動 低下する, 弱まる, 鈍化する, 低迷する, 伸び悩む, 冷え込む, ふらつく, つまずく
faltering capital spending 設備投資の低迷
faltering demand for new credit 新規借入需要の減退, 新規借入需要の落込み[冷え込み]
faltering economic recovery 足踏み状態の景気回復, 景気回復のふらつき
faltering regional economies 地域経済の低迷, 地域経済の冷え込み[伸び悩み]

family 名 家族, 一家, 一家全員, 世帯, 同族, 一族, 先祖, 家系, 家柄, 集団, ファミリー
family allowance 家族手当, 児童手当
family background 家族環境
family brand 統一ブランド, 代表商標, 共通ブランド, ファミリー・ブランド
family business 家業
family circle 内輪, 近親者たち, 一家の人たち, 〈劇場の〉家族席
family court 家庭裁判所
family credit 児童家族手当
family doctor かかりつけの医者, ホーム・ドクター, 一般開業医 (=family practitioner)
family feud お家騒動, 内紛
family hour [time] 家族視聴時間
family leave 家族休暇
family man マイホーム主義の男, 家庭生活を大

事にする男, 妻子持ちの男性（=family-oriented person）
family planning 家族計画, 産児制限
family practice 家庭医療
family register 戸籍
family therapy 家族療法
good families 名門の家柄
one-parent [single-parent] 母子［父子］家庭
two-income families 共働きの家庭
Fannie Mae 米連邦住宅抵当金庫［抵当公庫］, ファニー・メイ（Federal National Mortgage Associationの通称で, 米政府系住宅金融会社。フレディ・マック（米連邦住宅貸付抵当公社）の姉妹会社（sister company））
far 形 遠い, 遠いほうの, 最も遠い地点の, 奥の, 遠隔の, 極端な（extreme）
a far left party 極左政党
be a far cry from …から遠距離にある, …にはほど遠い, …とは別世界だ, …とは非常に異なる, …とは大きな違いだ, …とは別物［雲泥の差］だ, …とは似ても似つかない
be far behind 大きく遅れをとっている
be few and far between ごくまれだ, まれである
far month 期先物
the Far East 極東
the far left 極左, 極左陣営
the far right 極右, 極右陣営
far-right nationalist 極右民族主義者
far-right party 極右政党
fare 動 うまくやっていく, 暮らす, 行く, 旅行する, 食べる, 飲む
fare badly 下手にやる, やり方がまずい
fare forth 出かける
fare less well それほど成功を収めていない
fare well うまくやる, うまくいく,〈事が〉運ぶ, うまくやっていく, 成功を収める
fare 名 運賃, 料金, 乗客, 作品, 出し物, 飲食物, 料理
double fare 往復運賃
ocean freight fares 外洋貨物輸送費
return fare 帰りの料金［運賃］, 往復運賃
round-trip fare 往復運賃
single [one-way] fare 片道運賃
traditional fare 伝統的な料理, 伝統料理
farewell address お別れ演説
farm 名 農場, 農園, 農地, 農業, 飼育場, 養殖場, 託児所, …施設, …場, 貯蔵庫

family farm 家族農場, 家族農業経営
farm animal 家畜
Farm Belt 〈米中西部諸州の〉穀倉地帯
Farm Credit Administration 〈米〉農業信用局《略 FCA》
Farm Credit System 〈米国の〉農業信用制度
farm household 農家
farm income 農業収入（=revenue for farming）
farm inventories 農産物在庫
farm land 農地
farm output 農業生産高
farm subsidies 農業補助金
farm team [club] 〈米大リーグの〉二軍, 二軍チーム
Federal Farm Credit Bank 連邦農業信用銀行
fish farm 養魚場
organic farm products 有機農産物
sewage farm 下水利用農場
wind farm 風力発電所, 風力発電施設
farm out 下請に出す, 仕事を請け負わせる, 仕事を任せる, 丸投げする
farming 名 農業, 農場経営, 牧畜, 養殖
cooperative farming 農業共同経営
dairy farming 酪農業
diversified farming 複合農業経営
dry (land) farming 乾地農法
farming fisheries 栽培漁業
farming household 農家
fish farming 養殖漁業
group farming 農業生産組織
organic farming 有機農業
fast breeder nuclear reactor 高速増殖炉（=fast breeder, fast breeder reactor）
fast food providers 外食業界
fast-track 形 出世コースに乗った, 出世コースの, 出世が速い, ファスト・トラック
fast-track bill 無修正・一括審議法案
fault 名 過失, 過誤, 欠陥, 瑕疵, 欠点, 短所, 不備, 不完全, 故障, 障害, 断層, 亀裂, フォールト
active fault 活断層
be at fault for …に対して責任がある, …の責任がある
fault tree analysis 故障の木解析《略 FTA》
find fault with …のあらを捜す, …を批判する
free from defects or faults 瑕疵・欠陥がない
liability without fault 無過失責任
with all faults 売り手は責任を持たないという了

解で
favor [favour] 動 …を好む，…に好意を示す，…を歓迎する，…に賛成する，…を支持する，…をえこひいきする，…に有利になる，…を助ける，…を促進する
  be favored 買われる
  be favored with …に恵まれる
  favor A over B BよりAを優先する，AをBより高く評価する
  most-favored nation treatment 最恵国待遇
favor 名 好意，支持，賛意，賛成，引立て，便宜，便宜供与，利益供与，記念品
  curry favor with voters 選挙民の機嫌をとる
  establish an L/C in our favor 当社を受益者として信用状を開設する
  favor-taxes for land trade 陸運奨励関税
  move in favor of …に有利に動く
favorable [favourable] 形 有利な，好都合な，好ましい，良好な，好調な，明るい，追い風になる
  favorable balance of payments 国際収支の黒字
  favorable balance of trade 輸出超過
  favorable treatment to foreign companies 外資優遇，外資優遇策
  on favorable terms 有利な条件で
FBI 米連邦捜査局 (**Federal Bureau of Investigation** の略)
FDI 外国からの直接投資，対内直接投資，対外直接投資 (**foreign direct investment** の略)
FDIC 米連邦預金保険公社 (**Federal Deposit Insurance Corporation** の略)
fear 名 懸念，不安，警戒感，恐れ，疑念
  credit fear 信用不安 (=credit crisis, credit crunch)
  deflation fears デフレ懸念 (=deflationary concerns, deflationary fears, fears of deflation)
  fears over economic growth 景気の先行きへの懸念
  inflation fears インフレ懸念 (=fear of inflation, inflationary fears)
  prepayment fears 期限前償還に対する懸念，期限前償還懸念
feasibility 名 実行可能性，実現可能性，企業化可能性，採算性，フィージビリティ
feasibility study 実行可能性調査，実現可能性調査，実行可能性研究，企業化調査，企業化可能性調査，準備調査，採算性調査，フィージビリティ・スタディ
feature 動 特集する，記事にする，大きく取り上げる，呼び物にする，売り物にする，目玉商品にする，…を特色[特徴]にする，主演させる，主役を演じる，重要な役割を演じる
feature 名 特徴，特色，特性，製品特性，機能，形状，条項，措置，条項，特集記事，特別番組，呼び物，目玉商品，長編映画
  added features 機能の充実，付加機能
  common features 共通点
  demand features 要求払い条項
  performance, features and durability 性能，形状と耐久性
  protective features 保護措置
  security features 担保条項
  special feature coverage 特別報道番組
Fed 名 米連邦準備制度理事会，FRB (=Federal Reserve: Federal Reserve Boardの略称。米連邦準備銀行 (Federal Reserve Bank) や米連邦準備制度 (Federal Reserve System)，米連邦公開市場委員会 (Federal Open Market Committee) を意味するときもある)
  Fed Chairman [**chairman**] 米連邦準備制度理事会 (FRB) 議長，FRB議長 (=Fed chief, Federal Reserve Board Chairman [chairman])
  Fed regions 米地区連銀
federal 形 連邦の，連邦政府の，連邦制の，連邦組織の，アメリカ合衆国の
  federal district 連邦区
  federal district court 米連邦地裁
  Federal Election Campaign Act 米連邦選挙資金規正法 (米国の大統領選や連邦議員選挙の資金などを規制する法律)
  Federal Employers' Liability Act 連邦雇用者責任法
  federal grand jury 連邦大陪審
  Federal Trade Commission 米連邦取引委員会 《略 FTC》 (=U.S. federal antitrust regulators)
  Federal Unemployment Tax Act 米連邦失業保険税法
  federal unemployment taxes payable 米連邦失業保険税未払い金
Federal [**federal**] **funds** フェデラル・ファンド，米連邦準備制度の自由準備預金，政府資金，即日利用可能預金 《略 FF》 (アメリカの市中銀行が

連邦準備銀行(FRB)に預けている資金)
- **federal funds market** フェデラル・ファンド市場, ニューヨーク連邦資金市場
- **federal funds purchased** フェデラル・ファンド取り入れ, フェデラル・ファンド借入金
- **federal funds sold** フェデラル・ファンド放出, フェデラル・ファンドの貸出残高
- **Federal [federal] funds target rate** フェデラル・ファンド(FF)の誘導目標金利

Federal [federal] funds rate
短期金利, FFレート, FF金利, フェデラル・ファンド金利, フェデラル・ファンド適用金利, フェデラル・ファンド・レート (=Fed funds rate, key interest rate, key rate)

> FF金利と公定歩合 ⊃「FF金利」は短期金融市場の状況を最も敏感に反映する指標金利の一つで, 米国の民間銀行が翌日決済で相互に資金を貸し借りするときに適用する金利のこと。日銀の無担保コール翌日物金利に相当する。「公定歩合」は, FRB(米連邦準備制度理事会)が[最後の貸し手]として金融機関に貸し付けるときの金利で, 一般にFF金利より高めになる。

Federal Open Market Committee
米連邦公開市場委員会《略 **FOMC**》(=Federal Reserve Open Market Committee:米国の金融政策の最高意思決定機関で, 短期金融政策と公開市場操作に関する方針を決定する。連邦準備制度理事会の理事7人と地区連邦準備銀行の総裁5人(このうち1名はニューヨーク連銀総裁)で構成)

Federal Reserve
米連邦準備制度理事会 (=Federal Reserve Board:米連邦準備制度(Federal Reserve System)や連邦公開市場委員会(Federal Open Market Committee), 連邦準備銀行(Federal Reserve Bank)を意味することもある)
- **Federal Reserve Bank** 米連邦準備銀行《略 **FRB**》
- **Federal Reserve Bank of New York** ニューヨーク連銀
- **Federal Reserve Board Chairman [chairman]** 米連邦準備制度理事会(FRB)議長, FRB議長 (=Fed Chairman, Federal Reserve Chairman)
- **Federal Reserve System** 米連邦準備制度《略 **FRS**》(米国の中央銀行制度)

Federal Reserve Board
米連邦準備制度理事会, 米連邦準備理事会《略 **FRB**》(=Federal Reserve:米国の連邦準備制度(FRS)の統括機関で, 正式名称はBoard of Governors of the Federal Reserve System。理事は7人で上院の承認を経て大統領が任命し, 任期は14年)

Federal Reserve Districts
全米12の連邦準備区(全米12の連邦準備区に, 米国の連邦準備制度(Federal Reserve System)を構成する連邦準備銀行(Federal Reserve Bank)が1行ずつ設置されている)

Federal Reserve Open Market Committee
米連邦準備制度理事会(FRB)の連邦公開市場委員会

Federation Council
ロシア連邦議会の上院 (定数178議席, 議員の任期は4年)

Federation of Electric Power Companies
電気事業連合会

fee 名 料金, 入会金, 入場料, 納付金, 会費, 手数料, 使用料, 報酬, 謝礼, 実施料, 対価, フィー, 所有権, 相続財産権

feed 動 与える, 食事を与える, 餌をやる, 肥料をやる, 〈機械に〉原料を送る, 〈原料を〉機械に送り込む, 〈データを〉送る, 〈電算機にデータなどを〉入れる, 提供する, 供給する, 〈情報を〉伝える, 吹き込む, 〈感情を〉あおり立てる, 楽しませる, 満足させる
- **be fed up with** …にうんざりする, …にあきあきしている (=be fed up to the back teeth with)
- **feed a parking meter** パーキング・メーターに料金を入れる
- **feed one's anger** 怒りをあおる, 怒りをつのらせる
- **feed racial hostility** 人種的敵意をあおり立てる
- **feed the eyes** 目を楽しませる
- **feed the vanity** 虚栄心を満足させる, 虚栄心を満たす

feedback 名 反応, 反響, 声, 意見, 帰還, 自動制御機能, フィードバック
- **feedback from a consumer** 消費者からの声, 消費者からの意見
- **feedback inhibition** フィードバック制御
- **valuable feedback loop** 貴重な意見

feeler 名 打診, 探り, 事前調査, 〈動物の〉触覚, 触手, 感情的[感覚的]な人
- **put [send, throw] out feelers** 探りを入れる
- **put out feelers in** …に触手を伸ばす

fence 名 垣根, 柵, フェンス
- **fence-mending** 関係修復, 地盤固め
- **mend fences** 関係を修復する, 仲直りする
- **mend one's fence** …の地盤固めをする, …の立場を固める
- **sit on the fence** 形勢を見る, どちら側にも加担しない, 日和見をする

fenfluramine 名 フェンフルラミン(食欲抑制

剤；原発性肺高血圧症を引き起こすとして回収された）

fertility rate 出生率
fiasco 名 大失敗, 大失態, 不首尾,〈ローンの〉焦げ付き
fiber 名 繊維, ファイバー
 aramid fiber アラミド繊維
 artificial fiber 人造繊維, 化学繊維 （=man-made fiber）
 carbon fiber 炭素繊維
 cotton fiber 綿紡糸
 fiber cable 光ファイバー・ケーブル （=fiber optic cable, optical fiber cable）
 fiber glass ガラス繊維
 fiber optic lines 光ファイバー・ケーブル （=fiber optic lines）
 natural fiber 天然繊維
 optical fiber cable 光ファイバー・ケーブル
 spinning fiber 紡績繊維
 textile fiber 織物
fiber optic (cable) network 光ファイバー網, 光ファイバー通信ネットワーク
fiber optics 光ファイバー, ファイバー光学, 光学繊維, 光ファイバー技術 （=optical fiber）
 fiber optics communications equipment 光通信装置, 光学繊維通信装置
fiber optics network 光ファイバー網, 光ファイバー通信ネットワーク （=fiber network, fiber-optic cable network, fiber optic network）
fibrinogen 名 フィブリノゲン（血液凝固第一因子のこと）
fictitious 形 架空の, 偽の, 偽りの, うその, 虚構の（false）, 偽造の, 本物でない（not genuine）, 想像上の, 実体のない, 作り話の, 擬制の
 fictitious annual coupon 見なし利息
 fictitious asset 擬制資産, 架空財産
 fictitious bill [paper] 空手形
 fictitious capital 擬制資本
 fictitious demand [use] 仮需要, 偽りの需要
 fictitious name 偽名, 架空の名前, 架空名義
 fictitious payee 〈手形や小切手の〉架空の受取人
 fictitious person 法人 （=artificial person, corporate person）
 fictitious withholding tax 見なし源泉課税
fiduciary market 信託市場
field 動 うまく処理する, うまくさばく,〈候補者を〉立てる, 出す, 擁立する, 出場させる,〈軍隊などを〉配置する
field 名 田, 野原, 領域, 分野, 市場, 実地, 現場, 現地, 出先,〈天然資源の〉埋蔵地帯, 産出地帯, 競技場, グランド, 運動場, フィールド
 diamond field ダイヤモンド鉱地
 field audit 実地監査, 現場監査, 実物監査
 field marketing staff 第一線の営業員, 外交販売員, 外交員, 巡回営業担当社員 （=field sales force）
 field research 実地調査, 現場調査, 現地調査, フィールド・リサーチ
 field study 実地調査, 現地調査, 実地研究, フィールド・スタディ
 gain the field 市場を獲得する
 magnetic field 磁場
 oil field 油田
 other business fields 異業種
 playing field 事業環境, 競争条件
 scientific fields 科学分野
fierce competition 熾烈な競争, 激しい競争 （=cutthroat competition）
Fifth (Amendment) 黙秘権, 米国憲法修正第5条
 claim the Fifth (Amendment) 黙秘権を主張する
 take the Fifth (Amendment) 黙秘権を行使する, 証言を拒否する
fight 動 戦う, 争う, 立ち向かう, 抵抗する, 競争する, 努力する, 奮闘する, 口論する, 言い争う
 fight against inflation インフレと戦う
 fight back …に抵抗する, 反撃する
 fight down 抑える, …と争って勝つ, …をやっつける, …を圧倒する
 fight fire with fire 同じ手段で対抗する, 同じ論法を使う
 fight it out あくまで戦う, 決着がつくまで戦う
 fight off 撃退する, 打ち勝つ
 fight one's way 困難を排して進む, 奮闘して［頑張って］進む
 fight shy of …を避ける, …を嫌がる
 fight the case 訴訟で争う, 事件で争う
 fight the charges 告訴で争う
fight 名 戦い, 争い, 闘争, 奮闘, 運動, けんか, 抗争, 口論, 戦意, 闘志, 闘争心, ファイト
 a fight against crime 防犯運動
 a stand-up fight 正々堂々の戦い
figure 名 数字, 数値, 値, データ, 統計, 値段, 金額, 総額, 合計, 実績, 計算（figures）, 人物,〈人

の〉姿，…な人，人影，体型，スタイル，プロポーション，名士，大立て者，図形，…形，図案，イラスト
advanced GDP figures GDP速報値
corresponding figures 比較対応数値
CPI figure 消費者物価指数
double figures 2桁の数字
financial figures 財務実績，業績，決算
first quarter figures 第1四半期の実績，第1四半期決算
industrial production figures 鉱工業生産統計，鉱工業生産高
producer price figure 生産者物価指数
retail price figures 小売物価指数
round figure 円形
sales figures for new automobiles 新車販売台数
the government figures on prices and employment 政府の物価統計と雇用統計
trade figures 貿易統計

file 動 提出する，申請する，申し立てる，保管する，整理保管する
file a claim against …に損害賠償を請求する
file a complaint with …に提訴する，…に告訴する，…に告訴状を提出する
file a criminal complaint against …を刑事告発する
file a damages suit against …を相手取り損害賠償を求める訴訟を起こす
file a declaration of bankruptcy and a request for asset protection with …に破産宣告と財産保全の処分を申請する，…に破産宣告と財産保全の処分を申し立てる
file a lawsuit [suit] 提訴する，告訴する，訴えを起こす，訴訟を起こす
file a petition with …に提訴する
file a preliminary injunction 仮処分を申請する（＝file a provisional disposition）
file a provisional disposition 仮処分を申請する（＝apply for an [a provisional] injunction）
file a request with A for B Aに対してBを申請する
file a suit against A for B AをBで提訴する，AをBで訴える
file an indictment against …を起訴する，告発する
file final reports on income for this year 今年度の確定申告書を提出する

file for bankruptcy [insolvency] 破産を申し立てる，破産申請する，破産法を申請する，再生法を申請する
file for court protection from creditors 資産保全を申請する，破綻申請する，会社更生手続きを申請する（＝file for protection from creditors, seek court protection from creditors）

file 名 ファイル，資料，記録
file-sharing software [program] ファイル交換ソフト
file-sharing service ファイル交換サービス
file-swapping service ファイル交換サービス
file for 提出する，申請する，届け出る，申し込む，申し立てる，訴えを起こす，提訴する
file for bankruptcy 破産を申し立てる，破産申請する，破産法を申請する，破産法の適用を申請する，再生法を申請する（＝file for insolvency）
file for bankruptcy protection under the Corporate Rehabilitation Law 会社更生法の適用を申請する
file for court protection from creditors 資産保全を申請する，破綻申請する，会社更生手続きを申請する（＝file for protection from creditors, seek court protection from creditors）

final income tax return 確定申告（＝final tax return）

finanize 動 完結させる，最終処理をする，決着をつける
finalize a deal for …の最終調整をする，…の最終協議をする

finance 動 融資する，貸し付ける，出資する，資金を出す，資金を供給する，資金を調達する，〈赤字などを〉埋め合わせる，補填する，…の資金に充てる
be fully financed by …が100%出資する
finance capital needs 資金需要を賄う
finance mergers or acquisitions 合併や買収の資金調達をする
jointly finance 共同出資する（＝finance jointly）

finance 名 金融，財務，財務内容，財政，財力，財源，資金，資金調達，融資，ファイナンス
debt finance デット・ファイナンス，負債金融，負債による資金調達
direct finance 直接金融
equity finance エクイティ・ファイナンス，株式発

行による資金調達
finance ministers and central bank governors [chiefs] 財務相[蔵相]と中央銀行総裁, 財務相[蔵相]・中央銀行総裁
structured finance 仕組み金融
financial 形 金融の, 財務の, 財務上の, 金銭的, 金銭面での
financial aid package 金融支援策, 財政援助策 (=financial assistance package, financial rescue package)
financial asset 金融資産, 貨幣性資産
financial assets' deflated prices 資産デフレ, 金融資産の物価下落
financial authorities 金融当局
financial bailout bill 〈米国の〉緊急経済安定化法案(金融安定化法)
financial contribution 財政支援
financial flexibility 財務弾力性, 財務上の柔軟性, 不測の事態が生じたときの資金調達能力
Financial Function Early Strengthening Law 金融機能強化法
financial hemorrhaging [loss] 金融上の損失, 損失
financial instrument 金融商品, 金融資産, 金融手段, 金融証書 (=financial goods, financial product)
financial market 金融市場(「金融市場」は, 資金の供給者である貸し手と資金の需要者である借り手との間で資金取引が行われる場)
financial sanctions 金融制裁
financial assistance 金融支援, 資金援助 (=financial aid, financial backing, financial support)
 extend a financial assistance 金融支援を行う, 財政支援を行う
 offer ¥500 billion in financial assistance 5,000億円の財政支援[金融支援]を行う
financial condition 財政状態, 財政状況, 財務状態, 財務内容, 財務基盤, 金融情勢
 deteriorating financial condition 財政状態[財政状況]の悪化
 management's discussion and analysis of financial condition and results of operations 財政状態と経営成績の経営者による分析・検討
financial crisis 金融危機, 金融パニック, 金融恐慌, 経営危機, 経営難, 経営破綻 (=financial difficulties)

full-blown financial crisis 全面的な金融危機
financial health 財務の健全性, 財務内容, 財務状況, 財務体質, 経営の健全度[健全性] (=financial soundness)
 boost financial health 財務体質[財務状況]を強化する, 財務上の健全性を高める
 deteriorations in financial health 財務体質の悪化
financial institution 金融機関
 clean sweep of troubled financial institutions 問題のある金融機関の一掃, 経営難の金融機関の一掃, 経営破綻の金融機関の一掃
 governmental financial institution 政府系金融機関
 the early disposal of bad loans held by financial institutions 金融機関の不良債権の早期処理
 the realignment of financial institutions 金融機関の再編
financial regulation(s) 金融規制
 Report on Financial Structure and Regulation ハント報告
 stringent financial regulations 金融規制の強化
 tighter financial regulations 金融規制の強化
financial report 財務報告, 財務報告書, 業績報告, 有価証券報告書
 amended financial report 有価証券報告書の訂正
 falsified financial report 有価証券報告書[財務報告書]の虚偽記載
financial results 財務成績, 財務実績, 業績, 金融収支, 決算
 crooked financial results 不正決算, 不正会計
 financial results for the fiscal second-half 下半期[下期]の決算, 下半期の業績
 interim financial results 中間決算
financial services 金融サービス
 Financial Services Act of 1986 1986年金融サービス法
 Financial Services Agency 金融庁《略 FSA》
 Financial Services Agency Commissioner 金融庁長官
 Financial Services Committee 金融サービス委員会
financial stability 金融システムの安定, 金融の安定, 金融安定化
 Financial Stability Board 金融安定理事会,

金融安定理事会《略 FSB》(金融監督に関する国際基準を制定する機関の金融安定化フォーラム(FSF)に代わる新機関)
Financial Stability Forum 金融安定化フォーラム《略 FSF》(G-7主要先進国と発展途上国、国際通貨基金、世界銀行、国際証券監督者機構の各代表で構成される)

financial statement
財務報告書、財務報告、有価証券報告書(financial statementは、以下の関連語句に示すようにfinancial statements(財務書類・財務諸表)の形容詞として使われることもある)
  financial statement amounts 財務書類の数値
  financial statement misstatement 財務書類[財務諸表]の虚偽表示
  financial statement presentation 財務書類[財務諸表]の表示
  financial statements 財務諸表、財務書類、企業財務情報、決算書、経営分析、有価証券報告書

financial system
金融制度、金融システム
  Financial System Council 金融審議会

financially self-sustaining
資金を自ら賄う

financially troubled
経営危機に直面している、経営が悪化した、経営不振の、財政が逼迫した、財政難の、財政難に陥っている

financier 名
金融会社、金融業者、〈事業の〉資金供給者、投資家、資本家、銀行家、融資家、財務官、資本家
  act as financiers 資金を提供する
  government-affiliated financier 政府系金融会社
  government-affiliated mortgage financier 政府系住宅金融会社[金融公社]

financing 名
資金調達、資本調達、金融、融資、借入れ、ローン、財務、資金
  cash flows from financing activities 財務活動に伴う現金収支[資金収支]
  conditional financing ひもつき融資
  Financing Corporation 連邦調達公社
  financing requirements 資金需要、借入需要、資金調達必要額
  free financing ゼロ金利ローン (=zero financing, zero-percent financing)
  interim financing つなぎ融資
  mutual financing 無尽
  permanent financing 長期資本
  project financing プロジェクト金融、特定事業に対する金融、プロジェクト・ファイナンス (=project finance)
  straight financing 直接融資
  structured financing 仕組み金融

financing operations
金融活動、融資活動、金融事業、市場からの資金調達、財務活動、財務
  financing operations based on government policies 政策金融

fine 名
罰金、違約金、制裁金、課徴金、手数料、許可料
  civil fines 民事制裁金、民事の罰金
  criminal fines 刑事の罰金
  large fines 巨額の罰金

fire 動
首を切る、首にする、解雇する (=ax, axe, sack)

fire 名
火事、火災、火、砲火、射撃、発射、火責め、攻撃、集中攻撃、批判、非難、苦難、試練
  be on fire with …がブームになっている
  come under fire from …から非難[攻撃]を受ける
  draw fire for …で非難を浴びる
  draw fire from …から集中砲火を浴びる
  draw one's fire …の非難[批判、攻撃]の的になる、…の非難[敵意]を招く
  fire company 消防隊
  fire department 消防署
  fire drill 防火訓練、消防演習
  fire engine 消防車
  fire escape 火災避難設備
  fire exit 非常口
  fire policy 火災保険
  hang fire 遅れる、手間どる
  set the world on fire 世間をあっといわせる、大成功する

firebrand 名
扇動者、扇動家、政治的活動家、アジテーター

firewall [fire wall] 名
防禦壁、業務隔壁、情報隔壁、情報漏洩防止システム、ネット上のセキュリティ・システム、不正侵入防止機能[防止装置]、不正侵入防止ソフト、ファイアウォール(「情報隔壁」は、同グループの銀行と証券会社が顧客情報を共有することを禁止することをいう)

first 形
第一の、一番目の、真っ先の、最上の、一流の、主要な、最も重要な、首位の、最高幹部の、ファースト
  (at) first hand 直接に、じかに
  be accepted on a first come, first serve(d)

basis 先着順に受け付けられる
first aid (treatment) 応急手当て
First Amendment 米憲法修正第一条
first cause 第一原因, 原動力
First Couple 大統領夫妻
first family [First Family] 米大統領一家[家族], 米州知事[市長]一家
first fruits 最初の成果, 初物, 初穂
first lady 米大統領夫人(非公式の呼称), 米州知事[市長]夫人, ファースト・レディー
first language 母語
first mate [officer] 一等航海士
first offender 初犯者
first papers 第一書類(米国帰化の際に最初に提出する書類)
First Petty Bench 〈最高裁の〉第一小法廷
first reading 〈米議会での〉第一読会(議案を検討すべきかどうかを検討する)
first strike 先制攻撃, 第一撃
first-strike capability 先制攻撃力, 第一撃能力
first string 一軍選手
first water 〈宝石類の〉最上質
make the first move 先手を打つ, 先手を取る
fiscal 形 国庫の, 国庫収入の, 財政の, 財政上の, 会計の, 年度の
fiscal and monetary convergence 財政・金融収斂
fiscal deficit 財政赤字, 財政不足, 財政不足額
fiscal disbursement 財政出動
fiscal discipline 財政規律, 財政節度
fiscal investment and loan program 財政投融資計画《略 FILP》
fiscal practice 財政措置
fiscal preference 財政選好
fiscal reconstruction 財政再建, 財政の立て直し, 財政健全化 (=fiscal rehabilitation, fiscal restructuring)
fiscal stamp 収入印紙
fiscal stimulus 財政刺激策, 財政面からの刺激, 財政面からの景気刺激, 財政出動
fiscal stringency 緊縮財政
fiscal policy 財政政策
fiscal policy objective 財政政策目標
pro-growth fiscal policy 成長志向型財政政策
fiscal year 会計年度, 事業年度, 営業年度, 年度, 会計期間 (=business year, financial year, fiscal period)
the current fiscal year 今年度, 今期
the entire fiscal year 通期, 事業年度全体
the preceding fiscal year 前年度, 前期
Fitch Investors Service, Inc. フィッチ・インベスターズ・サービス, フィッチ(米国の代表的な格付け機関)
fitness 名 適合, 適合性, 適格, 健康, 健康状態, 健康づくり, 体力
fitness for any particular purpose 特定目的適合性, 特定目的への適合性
fitness instructor 美容健康指導員
physical fitness 体の健康
five-day school week system 学校週5日制
fix 名 苦境, 窮地, 〈一時的な〉解決策, 位置, 位置確認, 理解, 麻酔, 〈麻薬の〉注射, 不正, 買収, 八百長, 八百長試合, 〈コンピュータ・プログラムの〉修正
a quick fix 即効薬, 緊急措置, 〈当座の, 一時的な〉問題解決策, 安易な解決策
be in a fix 困っている, 窮地に陥っている, 板ばさみになる
get a fix on …を理解する
look for a quick fix その場しのぎの手段[解決策]を探す, 安易な解決策を探す
fixed 形 固定した, 固定式の, 固定型, 確定した, 変動しない, 一定の, 安定した
fixed capital formation 固定資本形成 (=fixed capital investment:設備など固定資本への投資)
fixed cost 固定費用, 固定費
fixed exchange rate system 固定為替相場制, 固定相場制
fixed line network 固定通信網
fixed pension system 確定給付型年金制度, 確定給付型年金
fixed rate 定率
fixed-rate income tax cut 定率減税 (=fixed-rate income tax reduction)
fixed-rate tax deductions 定率減税
flag-raising ceremony 国旗掲揚式典
flagging 形 衰えている, 低迷する, 低迷が続く, 下落傾向の, 弱い, 疲れた
flagging demand 需要低迷
flagging economic growth 失速気味の経済成長
flagship 名 主力商品, 主力製品, 目玉商品, 最重要製品, 目玉, 最も代表的なもの, 最も重要なも

の, 旗艦, 最高級船, 最大の船[航空機], 最上位機種, 主力機種
flagship carrier 代表的な航空会社
flagship operation 主力事業
flagship product 主力製品, 主力商品, 目玉商品
flagship store 旗艦店, 母店, 主力店, 主力店舗

flaming 名 〈ブログなどの〉炎上(インターネット上で公開されているブログなどの開設者に, 反感を持つ人からの批判や中傷が殺到する現象のこと)

flashpoint 名 発火点, 引火点, 一触即発の地域

flat 形 横ばい, 横ばい状態の, 伸び悩みの, 一律の, 均一の, 経過利子なし, フラット
flat glass 板ガラス
flat market 伸び悩み市場
flat price 均一価格
flat rate 均一料金, 均一運賃, 固定料金, 定額
flat yield 直接利回り
flat yield curve 横ばいイールド・カーブ

flat-lined 形 低迷する, 伸び悩みの

flat screen TV 薄型テレビ (＝flat-panel TV)

flaw 名 ひび, 割れ目, 傷, 欠陥, 瑕疵, 欠点, 短所, 弱点, 〈文書などの〉不備, 誤り, ミス
a design flaw 設計ミス
conceal [hide] the flaw 欠陥を隠す

Fleet Street 英国新聞界, フリート街

flexibility 名 柔軟性, 弾力性, 順応性, 適応性, 融通性, 伸縮性, 余地, 柔らかさ, フレキシビリティ
budget flexibility 予算伸縮性
built-in flexibility 自動伸縮性, 構造的伸縮性, ビルトイン・フレキシビリティ
flexibility of prices 物価の弾力性, 物価の伸縮性, 価格弾力性
formula flexibility 定式的伸縮性, フォーミュラ・フレキシビリティ
upward flexibility 上方伸縮性

flexible 形 柔軟な, 柔軟性のある, 曲げやすい, しなやかな, 伸縮自在の, 機動的な, 弾力性の, 順応性のある, 適応性がある, 適応性に富んだ, 融通のきく, 伸縮的な, 伸縮型の, フレキシブル
flexible benefits 弾力的付加給付
flexible budget 弾力性予算, 変動予算 (＝variable budget)
flexible charge account 伸縮型回転掛売り勘定 (＝all-purpose revolving account)
flexible exchange policy 柔軟な為替政策
flexible exchange rate 変動為替相場, 屈伸為替相場

flexible manufacturing system フレキシブル生産システム, フレキシブル生産ライン, 多品種少量自動生産システム 《略 FMS》
flexible money [monetary] policy 伸縮的通貨政策
flexible mortgage 根(ね)抵当
flexible price 伸縮価格
flexible pricing 伸縮的価格設定 (＝variable pricing)
flexible rate mortgage 変動金利抵当貸付け (＝adjustable rate mortgage)
flexible rate system 屈伸相場制
flexible tariff 伸縮関税
flexible time [hours] 自由勤務時間(制), フレックスタイム(制) (＝flextime, flexitime, gliding time)
flexible trust 管理型投資信託
flexible work [working] hours 裁量労働制, フレックスタイム制 (＝flexible time, flextime)
fully flexible 自由に選択できる

flight 名 飛行, 定期航空便, …便, …線, 航路, 移動, シフト, 逃避, 流出, 飛躍, フライト
capital flight 資本逃避, 他国への資本の流出, 資本の国外移転 (＝flight of capital)
connecting flight 乗り継ぎ便
flight capital 逃避資金, 逃避資本 (＝refugee capital)
flight class 座席等級(ビジネス・クラス(business class), エコノミー・クラス(economy class), ファースト・クラス(first class), ツーリスト・クラス(tourist class)などがある)
flight control 航空管制, 航空管制所
flight (data) recorder 飛行記録装置, フライト・レコーダー
flight-dependent training 特殊飛行訓練
flight-independent training 一般的飛行訓練
flight interruption manifest 一括運送委託書類
flight manifest 乗客名簿, 積み荷目録
flight to quality 質への逃避(価格変動リスクがある株式から安定性のある債券などへの資金の移動)
offer code-share flights 共同便を運航する

flip-flop [flip-flap] 名 とんぼ返り, 逆転, 〈政策や方針の〉180度転換, 〈180度〉方向転換, 〈意見や態度の〉急変, 花火, 爆竹, フリップ・フロップ, 動 方向転換する, 決定を変える, 方針を二転三

転させる
float 動 提案する，提示する，〈株や債券などを〉発行する，新規に発行する，株式公開する，〈会社を〉新規上場する，〈会社を〉設立する，〈通貨を〉変動相場制に移行する，変動相場制にする，〈小切手を〉不渡りにする，〈考えなどを〉広める，噂を流す，広がる，漂う，流れる
- allow the currencies to float 通貨を変動相場制にしておく
- float a bond issue 債券を発行する
- float a company 会社を設立する
- float an issue of stock 株式を発行する，株式を売り出す
- float bonds 社債を市場に売り出す
- float loans 起債する
- float on the stock exchange 証券取引所に上場する
- float rumor 噂を流す
- float the currency 変動相場制にする

float 名 〈証券の〉発行，〈通貨の〉変動，変動相場制，流通量，未決済小切手，取立て中の手形［小切手類］，浮動株数，小口現金，設立，フロート
- added float 追加発行
- clean float きれいな変動相場制
- controlled float 管理された変動相場制
- dirty float 汚い変動相場制
- free float 浮動株，浮動株式
- joint float 共同変動相場，共同フロート
- public float 公開株

floatation ⇒flotation

flood 動 氾濫させる，増水させる，あふれさせる，どっと押し寄せる，殺到する
- be flooded with …であふれる，…でいっぱいになる
- be flooded with sellers 大量の売りを浴びる，売り一辺倒になる
- flood the market 売り浴びせる，売り崩す（売り物を人為的に増やして相場の下落を促進すること），供給過剰を引き起こす

flood 名 洪水，氾濫，殺到
- a flood of information 情報の氾濫
- be destroyed by floods 洪水で破壊される

floor space 床面積

flotation 名 株式公開，新規発行，売出し，起債，上場（＝floatation, going public, IPO, listing）
- a new flotation of government bonds 新規発行国債
- bond flotation market 起債市場
- equity flotation 株式公開
- flotation cost 債券発行費，発行費
- flotation of a loan 起債，資金の募集
- flotation of a new company 新会社株式の売出し
- flotation of bonds 債券発行
- overseas flotation 海外起債
- registration statement for the flotation 株式上場の登録届け出書

flounder 動 低迷する，停滞する，難航する，苦労する，問題を抱える，まごつく，失敗する
- floundering cash flow 資金の動きの停滞
- floundering financial markets 低迷する金融市場

flow 名 流れ，流出，移動，フロー
- capital flows 資本移動，資本の流れ，資本流出，資本流入
- capital flows in 資本の流入
- capital flows out 資本の流出
- cash flow-through 資金の流れ
- circular flow 循環的流れ，循環
- commodity flow 財貨の流れ，財貨流通
- financial flow 金融の流れ，財務フロー，資金フロー，資本移動
- flow of funds 資金の流れ，資金移動，資金循環，資金フロー，マネー・フロー
- money flow 資金循環，マネー・フロー
- new coverage flows 新規保険契約の収益

flu 名 インフルエンザ（＝influenza）
- bird flu 鳥インフルエンザ
- flu shot インフルエンザの予防注射
- swine flu 豚インフルエンザ

fluctuate 動 変動する，上がり下がりする，乱高下する，動揺する
- fluctuate between A and B AとBの間を上下する
- fluctuate between hopes and fears [despairs] 一喜一憂する
- fluctuate sharply 乱高下する

fluctuation 名 変動，変化，上がり下がり，乱高下，騰落，動き
- cyclical fluctuation 景気変動，周期的景気変動，循環変動
- exchange fluctuation 為替変動，為替相場の変動，為替の騰落（＝foreign exchange fluctuation）
- fluctuation band 変動幅

seasonal fluctuation　季節変動
wild fluctuations in oil prices　原油価格の乱高下

fly in the face of　…を公然と無視する，…に食ってかかる

FMS　フレキシブル生産システム（flexible manufacturing systemの略。一般にNC工作機械，産業用ロボット，自動搬送システム，自動倉庫システム，自動保守・点検システム，コンピュータ中央管理システムで構成。フレキシブル生産ラインともいう）

focal point　焦点，注目の的，〈活動などの〉中心

focus 名　焦点，ピント，中心，軸，的，注目の的，集中，集中化，重点，力点，重視，重視の姿勢，志向，傾斜，目的，意図，意義，関心，関心事，課題，震源地，フォーカス
　business focus　事業の中心，事業範囲の絞り込み
　cost focus strategy　コスト集中戦略
　customer focus　顧客重視，顧客重視の姿勢，顧客志向，顧客の満足度重視，顧客の満足に力を入れる
　focus on service quality　サービスの質の重視
　focus on the bottom line　利益重視，利益を重視する姿勢

focus on　…に焦点を当てる，…に焦点を合わせる，…に焦点を置く，…に的を絞る，…を重視する，…を強調する，…を中核に据える，…を中核事業にする，…に力を注ぐ，…に注目する，…に執着する，…に結集する，…に専念する

follow suit　追随する，先例に従う，前例に倣う，人のまねをする

following 前　…の後に（after），…の結果として，…を受けて，名 信奉者，崇拝者，支持者，部下，ファン，形 次の，後に続く，以下の，次に述べる，次に掲げる

follow-up 名　追加的措置，追い討ち，追跡，追跡調査，事後検討，事後点検，継続治療，継続努力，続報，続編，第二弾，追い討ち，フォローアップ
　follow-up advertising　事後広告
　follow-up investigation　追跡調査
　follow-up notice　督促状

FOMC　米連邦公開市場委員会

food 名　食品，食料，食物，食べ物，フード
　dairy products　乳製品
　food additives　食品添加物
　food allergy　食品アレルギー（＝food intolerance）
　food & beverage control　食材・飲料管理，FBコントロール

Food and Agriculture Organization　国連食糧農業期機関《略 FAO》

Food and Drug Administration　米食品医薬品局《略 FDA》

food basket　穀倉地帯，食糧生産地帯
food chain　食物連鎖
food contamination　食品汚染
food court　レストラン街
food cycle　食物環
food for thought　考える材料，思考の糧
food irradiation　食品照射
food labeling system　食品表示制度
food miles　食品の輸送距離
food poisoning　食中毒
food processor　万能調理用具，フード・プロセッサー
food rations　食料配給
Food Recycling Law　食品リサイクル法
Food Sanitation Law　食品衛生法
food security　食糧安全保障
food self-support ratio　食料自給率（＝food-self sufficiency ratio）
food service industry　外食産業，外食業界
food, shelter and clothing　衣食住（＝food, clothing and shelter）
food to go　お持ち帰り食品
food value　栄養価，食品栄養価
food waste　食品廃棄物
fresh food　生鮮食品

food safety　食の安全，食品の安全性
　European Food Safety Authority　欧州食品安全局
　food safety administration　食品安全行政
　Food Safety Commission　食品安全委員会（2003年7月，食品安全基本法に基づいて内閣府に設置された）

foot 動　支払う，負担する，…の責任を負う，…を合計する，総計で…となる
　foot the bill　勘定を支払う，支払いをする，費用を負担する
　foot the bill for　…の勘定を支払う，…の責任を負う
　foot up an account　勘定書を絞める
　the receipts will foot up to　受取り金額は絞めて［合計で，総額で］…となる

foot 名　足，足取り，歩み，歩行，最下部，基部，台，底，下部，末席，最下位，フィート，フット
　find one's feet [legs]　新しい仕事に慣れる，初

めての環境に慣れる, 落ち着く, ひとり立ちする
get ... back on one's feet …を立ち直らせる, …を再生させる, …を再生する
get [start] off on the right foot 出だしが好調である, 出だしがうまく行く, 好調にスタートする
get [start] off on the wrong foot 出だしでつまずく, 出だしでうまく行かない, 出だしで失敗する
have [get] a foot in the door 〈…に〉うまく入り込む, 成功の見込みがある, (…の)きっかけ[端緒]をつかむ
have one's [both] feet on the ground 現実的[実際的]である, 地に足がついている, 分別のある行動をする
keep [have] a foot in both camps 対立する両陣営に通じている, 二股(ふたまた)をかける
miss one's foot 失脚する, 足を踏み外す
put one's best foot forward [foremost] 全力[ベスト]を尽くす, できるだけ急ぐ, 全速力で行く, できるだけよい印象を与える, 愛想よく振舞う, 精力的に振舞う
put one's foot down 断固とした態度を取る, 断固たる措置を取る, 決然と行動する, 譲歩しないで頑張る, アクセルを踏む (put one's foot to the floor)
put one's foot in it [one's mouth] 失言する, へまをやる, しくじる
shoot self [oneself] in the foot ばかなまねをする, 自殺行為である

footage 名 一連の画面, 映像, シーン, 映画フィルム, フィルムのフィート数, 全長

footing 名 合計, 合算, 突合せ, 合計検算, 締切り, 入会金, 立場, 足場, 足がかり, 地歩, 地盤, 基盤, 関係, 間柄
gain a footing in …に地歩を得る, …に足がかりを得る, …で地位を占める
keep one's footing …の地位を保つ
lose one's footing …の足場を踏み外す, 足場を失う, 失脚する
on an equal footing 対等の立場
stand on an equal footing 対等の立場に立つ

footstep 名 足跡, 足音, 足取り, 先例, 階段
follow the footsteps of …の足跡をたどる, …の先例[例]にならう, …の志を継ぐ

Forbidden City 紫禁城(中国北京市の中心部を占める旧清朝の帝居。現在は博物館で「故宮」と改称されている)

force 動 強制する, 強要する, 強いる, 押し付ける, 押し進める, 押し込む, 追い込む

be forced to …を余儀なくされる, …を強いられる, …せざるを得ない, …に追い込まれる, …を迫られる
forced currency 強制通貨
forced liquidation 強制破産 (=involuntary liquidation)
forced market 人為相場
forced sale [selling] 投げ売り, 強制売買, 株式の強制処分, 競争処分, 公売

force 名 力, 強さ, 威力, 暴力, 腕力, 猛威, 勢力, 影響力, 支配力, 効果, 効力, 意味, 真意, 有効性, 要因, 実施, 施行, 動き, 法的効力, 拘束力, 兵力, 軍隊, 軍, 部隊, 軍事力, 軍事行動, 風力, フォース
against the force of gravity 重力に逆らって
allied forces 同盟軍, 連合軍
be put into force 実施される, 施行される, 効力を発生する (=come into force)
bring ... into force …を実施する, 施行する
by [with] force and arms 暴力と武器で, 不法な手段で
by force of …の力で, …によって (=by means of)
by (the) force of the circumstances 環境の力で, 事情に迫られて, やむを得ず
come [be brought, enter] into force (and effect) 実施される, 施行される, 効力を発生する[生じる], 発効する
competitive forces 競争原理
conservative forces 保守勢力
conventional armed forces 通常戦力
driving force 原動力, 推進力
field sales force 外務員, 外交販売員
force and effect 効力, 有効
force majeure 不可抗力, 天災
fundamental force ファンダメンタルズ要因
ground forces 地上軍
guiding force 推進力, 指針
in force 実施中の, 施行されて, 有効で, 大勢で, 大挙して
Israeli forces イスラエル軍
join forces with …と協力する, …と力を合わせる, …と連携する, …と提携する, …と一丸となる
labor force 労働力, 全従業員
leave the force 退職する
life insurance in force 生命保険の保有契約高
market forces 市場の力, 市場諸力, 市場要因, 市場原理, 需給関係
military force 軍事力

multilateral force　多国籍軍
occupation forces　占領軍
of no force　効力がない，無効の
open-market forces　市場原理
paramilitary forces　軍事治安部隊
political force　政治力
potent force　実力者
productive force　販売力
public force　警察，警官隊
put [carry] into force　実施する，施行する
resort to force　力に訴える
sales force　販売員，販売要員，販売力
Self-Defense Force　自衛隊
task force　対策委員会，対策本部，専門委員会，専門調査団，特殊任務を持つ機動部隊，タスク・フォース
technical force　テクニカル要因
the force of economic events　経済力
the force of the law　法律の効力，法の拘束力
the original force of words　言葉の元来の意味
the third force　第三勢力
the use of force　武力行使，軍事力の行使，暴力の行使
turn out in force　団結する
underlying forces　構造的要因
U.S. Army forces　米陸軍
with all one's force　全力を尽くして，精一杯
work force　労働力，従業員，労働者，人員（＝workforce）

force out　辞職させる，立ち退かせる

Fordism　名　大量生産大量消費，フォーディズム（米フォードの創設者ヘンリー・フォードの経営理念で，大量生産・大量消費を可能にした生産システムのモデルのこと）

forecast　動　予測する，予想する，予見する

forecast　名　予測，見通し，予知，予見，予想，予報（＝forecasting）

bearish forecast　弱気の見通し
business forecast　景気予測，景気見通し，業績見通し，業績予測，経営予測
cash forecast　資金予測
central forecast　中心的予想（＝central tendency forecast）
consensus forecast　コンセンサス予想，コンセンサス予測，市場予想
demand forecast　需要予測
earlier forecast　当初予想，前回の予想

forecast of exchange rates　為替相場予測（＝forecast of foreign exchange rates）
forecast of prices　物価展望
group net profit forecast　連結純利益［税引き後利益］予想
group operating profit forecast for the current year　今年度の連結営業利益見通し
operating profit forecast　営業利益予想，営業利益見通し
profit forecast　利益予想，収益見通し，業績予想

foreclosure　名　差し押さえ，抵当流れ，質流れ，抵当権の請戻し権喪失，担保権実行，担保権行使，物的担保実行手続き

foreclosure proceedings　担保権実行手続き
home foreclosures　住宅の差し押さえ，住宅ローンの焦げ付き［貸倒れ］
in-substance foreclosure　実質的な担保権行使
mortgage foreclosure　抵当物の差し押さえ，住宅の差し押さえ，抵当流れ（＝foreclosure of a mortgage）

forefront　名　第一線，先頭，最前部，最前線，最先端，中心，重要部分

foreign　形　外国の，海外の，他国の，外国産の，外国行きの，外国人の，対外の，対外的な，対外…，管轄外の，法適用外の，無縁の，無関係の，異質な，有害な

foreign affairs　外交問題，外交
Foreign and Commonwealth Office　〈英国の〉外務省《略 FO》
foreign bank　外国銀行，外資系銀行，外銀，他店，他行
foreign borrowings　外貨建て債務，対外借入れ
foreign cash reserves　外貨準備高，外貨準備（＝foreign currency reserves, foreign reserves）
Foreign Corrupt Practices Act　〈米国の〉海外不正支払い防止法，海外不正行為防止法
foreign debt servicing　対外債務の返済，外貨債務の返済
Foreign Labor Certification　外国人労働者雇用許可
foreign liabilities　対外負債
Foreign Secretary　〈英国の〉外務大臣（＝the Secretary of State for Foreign and Commonwealth Affairs）
Foreign Service　〈英国の〉外交部

foreign assets 海外資産, 外国資産, 対外資産, 在外資産, 外貨建て資産（日本の対外資産は, 日本の政府, 企業, 個人が海外に持つ資産。この対外資産の金額から, 外国の政府, 企業, 個人が日本に持つ資産（対外負債）の金額を差し引くと, 「対外純資産」となる）
  cumulative ownership of foreign assets 対外資産の累計額
  net acquisition of foreign assets 対外資産の純増
  net foreign assets 対外純資産, 海外純資産, 国外資産
  SEC-required disclosure of foreign assets 国外資産に関するSEC（米証券取引委員会）の開示要求

foreign currency 外貨
  foreign currency bill 外貨手形
  foreign currency-denominated bond [securities] 外貨建て債券
  foreign currency deposit 外貨預金, 外貨預託（⇒guasi money）
  foreign currency deposit system 外貨預託制度
  foreign currency forward 為替先物予約
  foreign currency reserves 外貨準備高, 外貨準備（＝foreign cash reserves, foreign exchange reserves, foreign reserves, forex reserves：「外貨準備」は, 海外への支払いに備えて国や日銀が保有している外貨建て資産の金額）
  foreign currency transaction 外貨建て取引
  foreign currency wholesale deposits 外貨大口預金

foreign exchange 外国為替, 外国為替取引, 為替差損益（＝forex）
  Foreign Exchange and Foreign Trade Control Law 外為法
  Foreign Exchange and Foreign Trade Law 外国為替及び外国貿易法, 外為法
  foreign exchange fluctuations 為替変動, 為替相場の変動（＝foreign currency fluctuations）
  foreign exchange loss 為替差損
  foreign exchange margin trading 外国為替証拠金取引
  foreign exchange market 外国為替市場
  foreign exchange rate 為替相場, 外国為替相場, 為替レート
  foreign exchange reserves 外貨準備高（＝foreign currency reserves）

foreign policy 外交政策, 外交方針, 対外政策
  adherence to American foreign policy positions 米国の外交政策への追随
  foreign policy objective 外交目標
  foreign policy tool 外交手段
  independent foreign policy 独自の外交政策, 自主的外交政策
  omnidirectional foreign policy 全方位外交
  unilateral foreign policy 一国主義の外交政策, 一国主義の外交方針

foremost founding father 初代建国の父

forerunner 名 先駆, 先駆者, 前身, 予兆, 前兆, 先行指標, 先人, 先祖
  a forerunner of trends in capital spending 設備投資の先行指標
  the forerunner of national decline 国家［国民］衰亡の前兆

foreseeable 形 予知［予見, 予測］できる
  for the foreseeable future 当面, 当分の間, 近く
  foreseeable gain 予想利益
  foreseeable loss 予想損失
  in the foreseeable future 近い将来に, 間もなく

forestall 動 …を回避する, …を予防する, …を阻止する, …を未然に防ぐ, …の機先を制する, …を出し抜く, 〈計画の〉裏をかく, 〈商品を〉買い占める

forestry business 林業, 林業経営
forestry industry 林業

forex 名 為替, 外国為替（⇒foreign exchange）
  forex reserves 外貨準備高, 外貨準備（＝foreign currency reserves, foreign exchange reserves, foreign reserves）

forge 動 鍛える, 作り出す, 〈計画などを〉案出する［立てる］, 作成する, 築き上げる（form）, 築く, 強化する, 偽造する（counterfeit）, 変造する, 〈うそなどを〉捏造する, でっち上げる, 〈難事を〉成し遂げる
  forge a cheque [check] 小切手を偽造する
  forge a compromise 妥協する
  forge a document 文書［書類］を偽造する
  forge a plan [design, scheme] 計画を作る［立てる, 策定する］
  forge a report 報告書を作成する
  forge a signature 偽の署名をする
  forge a strong bond of cooperation 協力の強い絆を築く

forge ties [links, relationships] with …との関係を築く[強化する]
forged 形 偽の, 変造した, 偽造した, 捏造された
　forged bill [note] 偽札
　forged cash card 偽造[変造]キャッシュ・カード
　forged driver's license 偽造運転免許証
　forged information 偽情報
　forged passport 偽造パスポート
forgive 動 許す, 容赦する, 大目に見る, 〈債権などを〉放棄する, 〈債務を〉免除する
　forgive the entire debt 債務[借金]をすべて免除する
　forgive the entire loan 債権[貸付け]をすべて免除する
forgo [forego] 動 控える, 差し控える, 遠慮する, 止める, 見送る, 断念する, 放棄する
form 動 設立する, 組織する, 創設する, 組成する, 結成する, 構成する, 作り出す, 築く, 構築する, 形成する, 形づくる, 設定する, まとめる, …になる, …として機能する
form 名 書式, 様式, 形, 形式, 形態, 形状, 外形, 外観, 種類, 用紙, 申込み書, 決まり文句, 慣用文
　application form 申込み用紙, 申込み書式, 出願書式
　as a matter of form 形式上 （＝in form）
　fill in the form 書式に記入する
　in due form 正式に
　Lloyd's form ロイド[ロイズ]書式
　long form audit report 長文式監査報告書
　narrative form 記述式
　request form 請求書
　short form bill of lading 略式船荷証券
formal 形 形式的な, 形式ばった, 形の, 形態[形式, 外形]上の, うわべだけの, 実質を伴わない, 堅苦しい, 堅い, 公式の, 正式の, 本式の, 格式の高い, 儀礼的な, 秩序だった, 整然とした, 調和[釣り合い]のとれた, 規則正しい, 理論的な, 系統立った, 組織的な, 正規の, 伝統的な, 因習的な, 慣例による, フォーマル
　formal agreement 正式契約, 正式合意
　formal announcement 公式発表
　formal arrangement 正式の取決め
　formal authority 形式的権限
　formal authorization 正式の認可, 公認
　formal call 儀礼的訪問
　formal contract 正式契約, 方式契約, 要式契約
　formal lawsuit 本訴
　formal organization 制度的組織, 公式組織
　formal party 形式的当事者
　formal proposal 正式提案, 正式見積り書
　formal status 法律上の分類
formality 名 （公的）手続き, 形式的手続き, 正規の手続き, 形式的[儀礼的]行為, 儀式, 堅苦しさ, きちょうめんさ, 規則[手続き]を固守すること, 形式ばる[形式にこだわる]こと, 習慣的なこと, 因襲, 型どおり[紋切り型]のあいさつ
　customs formalities 通関手続き, 税関手続き
　formalities of judicial process 裁判の正式手続き
　legal formalities 法律上の手続き, 法的手続き
format 名 様式, 形式, 方式, 書式, 形態, ディスクの初期化, ディスクの記録方式, ファイル形式, フォーマット
　format check 書式検査
　format for accounts 財務諸表[財務書類]の様式
　logical format 論理的フォーマット （＝high level format）
　physical format 物理フォーマット （＝low level format）
　prescribed format 統一様式
　unified format 統一規格, 規格の統一
formation 名 形成, 生成, 組成, 策定, 決定, 設立, 創立, 創業, 構築, 編成, 樹立, 構成, 配列, 配置, 構造, 統合, 編隊, 隊形, 岩層, 植物群, フォーメーション
　capital formation 資本形成
　formation flying 編隊飛行
　formation of alliances 提携関係の構築
　formation of regional trade blocs 地域貿易ブロックの形成
　habit formation 習慣形成
　new formations 新語
　property formation 財産形成
　stock [inventory] formation 在庫形成
　the formation of a cabinet 組閣, 内閣の組織
　the formation of the heart 心臓の構造
　the formation of Vitamin C ビタミンCの生成
former 形 以前の, 元の, 前…, 元…（「現役の, 現職の, 現…」＝active）
formulate 動 策定する, 形成する, 立案する, 案出する, まとめる, 体系化する, 公式化[定式化]する, 〈製法に基づいて〉製造する
　formulate a plan 計画を策定する, 計画を立案する
　formulate a policy 政策を策定する, 政策[方

針]を打ち出す
formulate a strategy 戦略を形成する, 戦略を策定する, 戦略をまとめる
formulation 名 策定, 形成, 立案, 案出, まとめ, 体系化, 公式化, 表現の仕方, 〈薬などの〉調合, 成分, 薬剤, 化粧品
forum 名 会議, 公開討論会, 討論の機会, 討論の場, 交流の場, 交流広場, 広場, 裁判所, 法廷, 批判, 裁断, フォーラム
  hold [have] a forum on …のフォーラムを開催する
  Major Economies Forum 主要経済国フォーラム
  open forum 公開討論会
  regional economic forum 地域経済会議
  South Pacific Forum 南太平洋諸国会議
  the forum of conscience 良心の裁断
  the forum of public opinion 世論の批判
  the six-party forum 6か国協議
forward exchange contract 先物為替予約, 為替先物予約, 為替予約
forward-looking 形 将来を見越した, 将来を見据えた, 将来を見通した, 積極的な, 進歩的な, 前向きの, 未来志向の, 先見的な
  forward-looking information 将来情報, 先行きについての情報
  forward-looking investment 将来を見越した投資
  forward-looking posture over …に対する前向きの姿勢
fossil fuels 化石燃料
foundation 名 基金, 財団, 設立, 創立, 創業, 建国, 土台, 基礎, 基盤, いしずえ, 根拠, ファンデーション
  business foundation 事業基盤
  charitable foundation 慈善団体
  fiscal foundation 財政基盤
  foundation collateral 財団抵当
  foundation fund 〈保険会社の〉基金(株式会社の資本金に相当), 基本積立金
  foundation member 創立会員
  foundation of management 経営基盤
  foundation school 維持基金で運営されている学校, 財団設立の学校
  historical foundation 歴史的根拠
  incorporated foundation 財団法人
  nonprofit foundation 公益法人
  private foundation 私的財団
founder 名 創設者, 創業者, 創始者, 設立者, 発起人, 開祖
  founder chairman 創業者会長
founding family 創業家
fragile 形 壊れやすい, 傷つきやすい, もろい, 弱い, ひ弱な, 虚弱な, 脆弱な, 不十分な, はかない, 不安定な, 永続しない
  fragile consumer confidence 弱い消費意欲
  fragile economy 脆弱な経済, 弱い経済
  fragile evidence 不十分な証拠
  fragile excuse 見えすいた言い訳
  fragile goods こわれ物, 易損品
fragility 名 壊れやすさ, 傷つきやすさ, もろさ, 弱さ, ひ弱さ, 虚弱性, 脆弱性, はかなさ
  fragility of profit structures 収益構造のもろさ
  fragility of the financial markets 金融市場の脆弱性
framework 名 枠組み, 骨組み, 基本, 基本構造, 大枠, 体制, 構図, 関係, 体系, 制度, 仕組み, 環境, 場, フレームワーク
  agreed framework on new trade rules 新貿易ルールの枠組み合意 (＝framework agreement on new trade rules)
  economic framework 経済関係
  framework accord [agreement] 枠組み合意
  framework of dialogue 対話の枠組み
  institutional framework 制度的枠組み
  international supervisory framework for financial institutions 金融業界[金融機関]の国際的監視体制
  legal framework 法的枠組み
  new budgetary framework 新予算制度
  regulatory framework 規制の枠組み, 規制上の枠組み, 規制体系, 規制環境
  set up an official framework to engage in periodic talks 定期協議を行う正式の場を設ける
  the framework for tackling unemployment 失業対策の骨格
  within the framework of …の枠組みのなかで
  Third Conference of Parties to the United Nations Framework Convention on Climate Change 気候変動枠組み条約第三回締約国会議, 温暖化防止京都会議, 京都会議
  U.S.-Japan Frameworks Talks on bilateral trade 日米包括経済協議
fraternity 名 友愛, 友情, 連帯感, 同業者, 同業組合, 同業者仲間, 協同団体, 共済組合(benefit

society), 宗教団体(religious society), 信徒団体, 仲間, …連中, …界,〈男子大学生の〉社交クラブ, 友愛会
fraternity house 〈大学の〉学生クラブ会館, 友愛会会館
the legal fraternity 法曹界
the medical fraternity 医師会, 医師仲間

fraud 名 詐欺, 不正, 不正行為, 操作
accounting fraud 会計操作
cash card fraud キャッシュ・カード詐欺（= card fraud）
corporate fraud 企業詐欺, 企業の不正行為
fraud cases investigated and prosecuted by the SEC 米証券取引委員会(SEC)が調査・摘発した不正事件
fraud charges 詐欺罪
fraud sales かたり商法, 詐欺商法
'It's me' fraud おれおれ詐欺
management fraud 経営者の虚偽不正
mislabeling fraud 偽装工作
tax fraud 租税詐欺（書類を捏造するなどして税務当局を騙そうとした行為）

fraudulent 形 詐欺の, 詐欺行為の, 不正な, 欺瞞的な
fraudulent act 詐欺行為
fraudulent advertising 誇大広告
fraudulent ballots 不正票
fraudulent conveyance 詐害行為, 詐欺的譲渡
fraudulent financial reporting 不正な財務報告
fraudulent invoice 架空請求書（= fraudulent bill）

Freddie Mac 米連邦住宅貸付抵当公社, フレディ・マック(Federal Home Loan Mortgage Corporationの通称で, 米政府系住宅金融会社)

free 動 自由にする, 解放する, 釈放する,〈責任を〉軽減する,〈苦しみなどから〉救う, 取り除く
be freed from prison 刑務所から釈放される
be freed from shackles 束縛から解放される
free one's mind 心の荷を下ろす
free oneself from one's difficulties 難局を脱する
free oneself from trouble 悩みがなくなる
free the hostages 人質を解放する
–free 形 …のない, …を含まない, …を受けない, …に影響されない
barrier-free バリア・フリーの
duty-free 免税の

fault-free [defect-free] chips 欠陥のないチップ
interest-free 無利息の
nuclear-free zone 非核武装地帯, 非核地帯
risk-free asset 安全資産, 無リスク資産
tax-free income 非課税収入, 免税所得
visa-free visit ビザなし訪問

free-fall 動 暴落する, 急落する, 売り一色の展開になる
free fall [freefall] 名 急落, 暴落, 歯止めなき下落, 棒落ち, 棒下げ, 売り一色の展開, 自由落下
be in a free fall 下げ止まる兆しがない, 下げ止まりの兆しが見えない, 売り一色の展開だ
stock market free fall 株式市場の暴落, 株価暴落, 株価急落
trigger a free fall of the U.S. dollar ドル[米ドル]の暴落を引き起こす

free market 自由市場, 自由主義市場,〈外国通貨の〉実勢市場
free market economy 自由経済, 自由主義市場経済, 自由市場経済
free market price 市中相場
free market rate 市場相場

free-marketer 名 自由市場主義者

free trade 自由貿易, 自由貿易主義
free trade accord 自由貿易協定
free trade area 自由貿易地域, 自由貿易圏
free trade negotiations 自由貿易交渉
free trade imperialism 自由貿易帝国主義（= the imperialism of free trade）
free trade pact 自由貿易協定
free trade policy 自由貿易政策
free trade system 自由貿易体制
free trade talks [negotiations] 自由貿易交渉
free trade tariff 自由貿易関税
free trade zone 自由貿易圏, 自由貿易地域, 保税地域

free trade agreement 自由貿易協定《略 FTA》
bilateral free trade agreement 二国間貿易協定
multilateral free trade agreement 多国間の自由貿易協定
North American Free Trade Agreement 北米自由貿易協定
regional free trade agreement 地域的自由貿易協定
U.S.–Canada Free Trade Agreement 米加自

由貿易協定

freebies 名　販売促進用の景品（＝free samples, give-aways）

freedom 名　自由, 自主, 独立, 解放, 免除, 特権, 使用権, フリーダム
- freedom fighter　反体制活動家
- freedom from all taxes　免税
- freedom of association　結社の自由
- freedom of capital movement　資本移動の自由化
- freedom of choice　選択の自由
- freedom of conscience　良心の自由
- freedom of entry　新規参入の自由
- freedom of expression　表現の自由
- Freedom of Information Act　〈米国の〉情報の自由法, 情報公開法《略 FOIA》
- freedom of information system　情報公開制度
- freedom of speech　言論の自由
- freedom of the air　空の自由
- the freedom of the city　名誉市民権

freefall 名　底割れ, 売り一色
- go into (a) freefall　売り一色の展開となる, 買いの手が止まる
- send the market into freefall　市場［相場］が売り一色の展開となる
- share price freefall　株価の底割れ

freeze 動　凍結する, 据え置く

freeze 名　凍結, 据え置き
- asset freeze　資産の凍結
- credit freeze　信用凍結, 信用釘付け
- deep freeze　凍結, 凍結状態, 一時停止, 棚上げ
- freeze-in effect　凍結効果（＝lock-in effect）
- freeze on the implementation of the pay-off system　ペイオフ制度実施の凍結, ペイオフ制度の凍結, ペイオフ凍結
- pay freeze　賃金凍結, 給与凍結
- price freeze　価格凍結, 物価凍結（＝freeze on prices）
- wage freeze　賃金凍結

frenzy 名　熱狂, 過熱, 激しい興奮, 狂乱

fresh 形　新しい, 新規の, 新たな, 斬新な, 新着の, 追加の, 別の, 未使用の, 新鮮な, 生々しい, 生の
- be green and fresh to the job　仕事に慣れていない
- be [get] fresh with　…になれなれしくする
- break fresh ground　新天地を開拓する, 新分野を開拓する, 新事実を発見する
- fresh capital　新規資本, 新たな資金, 追加資本, 増資
- fresh complexion　健康な顔色, 若々しい顔色
- fresh data　生のデータ
- fresh election　出直し選挙
- fresh evidence　新たな証拠
- fresh ideas　斬新なアイデア, 斬新な考え
- fresh money　追加資本, 追加資金
- fresh signs　景気指標
- fresh supply　新規供給
- fresh water　真水, 淡水, 新鮮な水
- make a fresh start　再出発する, 新規まき直しを図る
- take a fresh look at the plan　計画を見直す

fresh frozen plasmas　新鮮凍結血漿（献血血液を分離したり, 成分献血で採取したりした血漿を, 止血などの働きをする成分が損なわれないように凍結させたもの）

freshman 名　1年生, 新人
- freshman congressman　米下院の1年生議員［新人議員］
- freshman senator　米上院の1年生議員［新人議員］

freshness date　品質保持期限, 品質保証期限, 賞味期限

friendly 形　友好的な, 好意的な, 親しい, 親善的な, 交戦状態にない, 敵対関係にない
- be friendly to one's proposition　…の提案を支持する
- be on friendly relation with　…と友好関係にある
- friendly acquisition　友好的買収（＝friendly takeover）
- friendly action　申し合わせ訴訟, 友誼的裁判
- friendly fire　友軍砲火（誤って味方を攻撃すること）
- friendly game [contest, match]　親善試合
- friendly offer　友好的買収
- friendly society　共済組合, 互助組合（＝benefit society）
- friendly stock price　高めの株価, 高めの株価水準
- friendly state [nation]　友好国
- friendly takeover　友好的買収（＝friendly acquisition）
- friendly takeover bid　友好的株式公開買付け, 友好的TOB, 株式公開買付けによる友好的買収,

友好的買収
friendly tender offer 友好的TOB（株式公開買付け）
friendly visit 親善訪問
friendly wind 順風, 追い風
–friendly 形 …に役に立つ, …に有利な, …にやさしい, …が使いやすい, …になじみやすい
bond–friendly news 債券相場にとっての好材料
customer–friendly market 顧客に有利な市場
eco–friendly 環境にやさしい, 自然環境にあった（＝environmentally friendly）
ecologically–friendly 環境にやさしい（＝eco–friendly, environment–friendly)
environment–friendly technology 環境にやさしい技術
investor–friendly 投資家になじみやすい
user–friendly ユーザーに使いやすい, ユーザーに分かりやすい, 使いやすい, 使い勝手がよい, 操作が簡単な

from a broader point of view 大局的に見ると
▶ *From a broader point of view*, the lowering of promised yields on premium investments would surely protect the benefits of policyholders. 大局的に見れば, 生保が保険契約者に約束した保険料投資の運用利回り（予定利率）を引き下げたほうが, 確かに保険契約者の利益を保護することになる。

from a year ago [earlier] 前年比［前期比］で, 前年比, 前年［前年度, 前期］に比べて, 前年から（＝from the previous year, from the year before）

front 名 〈新聞の〉第一面,〈本の〉冒頭部分, 扉, 活動の領域, 分野, 隠れみの, カムフラージュ, 側面, 前面, 正面, 前線, フロント
come to the front 有名になる, 頭角を表す, 全面に出る
on all fronts あらゆる分野で
on both the fiscal and monetary fronts 財政・金融両面で
on the economic front 経済面では, 経済活動の面では, 経済分野では
the popular front 人民戦線
up front 前金で, 明白に
front 形 前の, 前方の, 前部の, 正面の, 第一面の, 重要な, 顕著な, 表向きの, 表看板の, 名目上の
front bench 〈英下院の〉前列席
front company 幽霊会社, 名目会社, ペーパー・カンパニー, ダミー会社

front desk 受付,〈ホテルの〉フロント
front group 表向きの組織, 隠れみの
front line 最前線, 第一線
front–loading 前倒し, 前倒し実施, 前倒し執行
front man 表看板, 表向きの人物［代表者］, 顔, 番組司会者（presenter）,〈楽団の〉指揮者,〈バンドの〉リーダー, メイン・ボーカリスト
front money 前金, 前払い金
front office 経営陣, 幹部, 警察本部
front organization 名目上の組織
front page 〈新聞などの〉第一面
front rank 一流, 最高位
front burner 最優先事項, 優先考慮事項, 最重要事項, 優先事項, 最大の関心［関心事］, 重大な関心事
front burner issue 最優先問題
on the front burner 最優先で, 重要視されて
put on the front burner 最重視する, 最優先する, 優先する
front–load 動 前倒しする, 前倒しして実施する
front month 直近の月, 期近物（front monthは一番手前の月, 直近の月, つまり翌月を指す。期近物は, 石油先物取引では翌月から9か月の先物商品を指す）
front–runner [front runner, front-runner] 名 最有力候補［候補者］, 先頭走者, トップランナー, 優勝候補, トップ企業, 第一人者, フロント・ランナー
front–runner approach トップランナー方式（現時点で販売されている製品で最も省エネ性能が優れているものを目標とする方式）

frozen 形 冷凍の, 凍結した, 凍結された, 当面使用できない, 固定されている, 焦げ付いた, 釘付けにされた, 冷害を受けた, 冷淡な
frozen account 凍結勘定
frozen asset 凍結資産
frozen embryo 急速冷凍した受精胎児
frozen food 冷凍食品
frozen food manufacturer 冷凍食品メーカー
frozen frame 瞬間的静止画面, ストップ・モーション
frozen loan 貸付け金の焦げ付き, 焦げ付き貸金
frozen stock 滞留品

fruit 名 果物, 果実, 実, 結晶, 所産, 成果, 結果, 利益, 実績, 報酬, フルーツ
bear [produce] fruit 実を結ぶ, よい結果が出る, 効果を生む
enjoy the fruits of …のうまみを吸い取る

fruit cultivation 果樹栽培
fruit farming 果樹園芸
fruit machine スロット・マシーン (=slot machine)
the fruits of labor 労働の成果

fruitful 形 実りの多い, 実りがある, 多産[多作]の, 成果のある, 有利な, 有益な, 効果がある
a fruitful job 収入の多い仕事
fruitful talks 実りある会談[協議], 有益な会談

fruition 名 〈目標の〉達成, 成就, 実現, 結実, 成果, 結晶, 喜び, 楽しみ
bring one's plans to fruition …の計画を実現させる
come to fruition 実を結ぶ, 実現する, 成就する
have the fruition of …を楽しむ
the fruition of a good life よき生活の享受
the fruition of one's hopes …の希望の実現
the fruition of one's purpose …の目的の達成

fruitless 形 実を結ばない, 不毛の, 利益の出ない, 無益な, 効果がない, 無駄な
be fruitless of profit 利益にならない
▶The rescue efforts proved *fruitless*. 救済努力は実を結ばなかった[救済策は行き詰まった]。

frustrate 動 いらいらさせる, 失望させる, 期待にそむく, 欲求不満にさせる, 失敗[挫折]させる, 挫折感を与える, 台なしにする, 駄目にする, くじく, 邪魔する, 妨害する
be frustrated by [at] …に苦労する
be frustrated in one's ambition 野望をくじかれる
be frustrated in one's aspirations やる気をくじかれる
be frustrated in one's attempt 企てに失敗する, 企てをはばまれる
be [feel, get] frustrated with …でいらいらさせられる, …に不満を持っている
frustrate a plan 計画を挫折させる

frustration 名 不満, 苛立ち, 失望, 落胆, 挫折, 失敗, 目的達成不能, 履行不能, 無効にすること, 欲求不満, フラストレーション
anger and frustration at …に対する怒りと不満
experience a series of frustrations 一連の失敗を味わう
frustration of contract 契約の履行不能
frustration of purpose 契約目的の達成不能
sense of frustration 挫折感

FSB 金融安定化理事会, 金融安定理事会 (Financial Stability Boardの略)

FSF 金融安定化フォーラム (Financial Stability Forumの略。金融監督の国際協調強化のため, 1999年2月のG7で設立を決定。現在, G7各国と国際通貨基金(IMF), 世界銀行のほかにオランダ, スイス, オーストラリア, シンガポール, 香港の各代表者が参加)

FTA 自由貿易協定 (free trade adreementの略)

FTC 〈日本の〉公正取引委員会 (Fair Trade Commissionの略)

FTC 米連邦取引委員会 (Federal Trade Commissionの略)

fuel 動 給油する, 燃料を補給[供給]する, 活気づかせる, 勢いづかせる, 激化させる, 加速する, 悪化させる, あおる, あおり立てる, 刺激する, 支持する, …を支える要因となる, …に支えられる
be fueled by …で動く, …で勢いづく[拍車がかかる, 高まる, 激化する, 加速する], …が原動力となる
fuel domestic demand 国内需要を拡大する, 国内需要を喚起する[刺激する]
fuel inflation インフレを加速させる, インフレ再燃をもたらす
fuel inflationary sentiment インフレ心理をあおる

fuel 名 燃料, 核燃料, エネルギー, エネルギー源
alternative fuel 代替燃料
fossil fuel tax 炭素税
fossil fuels 化石燃料
fuel consumption 燃料消費, 燃料賞費量
fuel efficiency 燃料効率, 燃費効率, 燃費, 省エネ
fuel oil 燃料油, 燃料オイル, 重油
fuel rod 原子炉の燃料棒, 燃料管
fuel surcharge 燃油特別付加運賃, 燃料特別付加料金
fuel tax 燃料税
liquid fuel 液体燃料
motor fuel tax 自動車燃料税
nuclear fuel 核燃料, 原子燃料
residual fuel 残油
synthetic fuels 合成燃料

fuel cell 燃料電池
┌
│燃料電池とは◯ 水に電気を通して水素と酸素に分ける電気分解とは逆の原理で, 石油やガスなどから取り出した水素と, 空気中の酸素を化学反応させて電気を作る仕組み。大気汚染源の窒素酸化物や硫黄

酸化物が出ないため，究極のクリーン・エネルギーといわれる．
fuel-cell electric vehicle 燃料電池電気自動車《略 FCEV》
fuel-cell engine 燃料電池エンジン
fuel-cell vehicle 燃料電池自動車
molten carbonate fuel cell 溶解炭酸塩型燃料電池

fuel-efficient 形 燃費効率[燃料効率]がよい，燃費がよい，低燃費の
- **fuel-efficient car** 低燃費車，燃費効率がよい車
- **fuel-efficient engine** 低燃費エンジン

full-blown [full blown] 形 満開の，成熟しきった，本格的な，全面的な

full business year 通期（=full fiscal year）

full facilities closure 施設の全面閉鎖

full-fledged 形 本格的な，本腰を入れた，一人前の，ひとかどの，れっきとした，立派な，十分に訓練を積んだ，資格十分の，十分に発達[進展]した，羽毛が生え揃った
- **full-fledged multilateral trade system** 本格的な多角的自由貿易体制
- **full-fledged recovery in corporate investment in plant and equipment** 企業の設備投資の本格回復
- **full-fledged recovery in the real economy** 実体経済の本格的な回復
- **full-fledged recovery track** 本格回復の軌道
- **full-fledged threat** 現実的な脅威
- **full-fledged work on compiling the budget** 本格的な予算編成作業
- **make a full-fledged recovery** 本格的に回復する

full inventory of weapons program 兵器に関する完全なリスト

full line 全機種，全品種，全製品，全車種，フルライン
- **full line offering** 全品種提供，全品種供給
- **full line strategy** フルライン戦略

full recovery 本格回復，全面回復

full-scale 形 本格的な，総力を挙げての，全面的な，完全な，実物大の
- **full-scale probe** 徹底的な調査
- **full-scale recovery** 本格回復，本格的な回復，全面回復，全面的な回復（=full-fledged recovery, full recovery）
- **full-scale rehabilitation** 全面的立て直し

full-service brokerage フルサービス証券会社

full-time employee 正社員，正規の従業員，常勤従業員，常勤（=full-time worker, full-timer, regular employee）

full time payroll 正規雇用

full withdrawal 全面撤退，〈預金などの〉全額引出し

full-year 形 通期の
- **full-year earnings target** 通期の収益目標，通期の業績目標
- **full-year net income forecast [projection]** 通期純利益予想，通期の税引き後利益予想
- **full-year profit forecast** 通期の利益予想，通期の利益見通し，通期の損益予想（=full-year profit estimate）

function 動 機能する，作動する，動く，働く，職務[機能，役目]を果たす

function 名 機能，職能，職務，任務，業務，役目，役割，働き，部門，公式の行事，関数
- **consumption function** 消費関数
- **controlling function** 管理機能
- **departmental function** 部門機能
- **function of staff** スタッフ機能
- **head office functions such as planning and personnel management** 企画や人事管理などの本部機能
- **intermediary function** 仲介機能
- **production function** 生産関数，生産職能
- **supply function** 供給関数
- **synergy and closer coordination between the functions** 部門間の相乗効果と緊密な協調関係

fund 動 資金を調達する，積み立てる，資金を賄う，資金を提供する，拠出する，出資する，〈赤字などを〉補填する
- **amounts funded** 積立額
- **be fully funded** 十分積み立ててある
- **fund large public expenditures** 巨額の財政赤字を賄う
- **fund pension costs as accrued** 年金費用を発生時に積み立てる
- **fund through issuance of debt** 債券の発行で資金を調達する

fund 名 資金，基金，積立金，ファンド
- **additional funds** 追加資金
- **Asian Development Fund** アジア開発基金
- **buyout fund** 買収ファンド
- **development fund** 開発基金

fund collecting system　集金システム
fund deal　資金取引
fund raising　資金調達, 資本調達
fund transfer　資金移動, 資金のシフト, 口座振替え, 送金　(＝the movement of funds)
quick fund　当座資金
supply of funds　資金の供給
trust fund　信託基金

fund-of-funds　ファンド・オブ・ファンド(投資信託に投資する投資信託(「投信の投信」)で, 投資家から集めた資金の運用を, 別の複数の投資信託に再委託する仕組み)

fundamentals 名　基本, 原理, 根本原理, 基礎, 基礎的条件, 基本的指標(国の成長率, インフレ率, 財政収支, 金融情勢, 為替レート, 経常・貿易収支の六つ), 体質, ファンダメンタルズ
economic fundamentals　経済のファンダメンタルズ, 経済の基礎的条件, 景気のファンダメンタルズ, 経済の体質, 経済の実態　(＝fundamentals of the economy)
financial fundamentals　財務面のファンダメンタルズ, 財務体質
friendly fundamentals　ファンダメンタルズ面の強気材料
long-term credit fundamentals　長期的な信用のファンダメンタルズ

fundamentalism 名　原理主義
Islamic fundamentalism　イスラム原理主義
market fundamentalism　市場原理主義
Muslim fundamentalism　イスラム原理主義

funding 名　資金調達, 調達, 調達手段, 積立て, 資金化, 資金源, 長期債化, 〈長期国債の〉借換え, 基金設立, 融資, 拠出, 資金供与, 資金提供, 出資, 事業費, 財政援助
contribute funding to　…に資金を拠出する
funding contributions　年金積立額
funding costs　資金調達コスト　(＝costs of funding)

funding report　収支報告書
funding requirements　資金需要　(＝funding needs)
funding vehicle　資金調達手段

furlough 名　〈海外駐在の公務員や軍人の〉休暇, 一時解雇(temporary layoff), 一時帰休, レイオフ, **動** 休暇を与える, 一時解雇する, 一時帰休[一時休業]させる, 休業させる
▶Governmental subsidies like the one for firms *furloughing* workers should be further expanded.　従業員の一時休業を行う企業に対する助成金などのような政府助成金は, さらに拡充すべきだ。

further 動　促進する, 推進する, 助長する, 増進する, 助成する, 助ける

fuse 動　融合させる, 合併させる, **自動** 融合する, 一緒になる, 合併する

futures 名　先物, 先物取引, 先物契約, 先物為替
futures trader　先物取引業者

futures exchange　先物取引所, 先物取引
Hong Kong Futures Exchange　香港先物取引所
London International Financial Futures Exchange　ロンドン国際金融先物取引所
Manila International Futures Exchange　マニラ国際先物取引所
New York Futures Exchange　ニューヨーク先物取引所
Tokyo International Financial Futures Exchange　東京金融先物取引所

FX 名　外国為替　(＝foreign exchange, forex)
FX business　外国為替取引
FX margin trading　外国為替証拠金取引, FX取引(FX取引では, 一定額の現金を証拠金として差し入れ, それを担保にインターネットなどで外貨を売買できる)

FY　会計年度, 事業年度, 営業年度, 年度　(**fiscal year**の略)

G

G7 [**G-7**] 先進7か国財務相・中央銀行総裁会議, 先進7か国会議, 7か国蔵相会議, G7 (＝Group of Seven：日・米・英・独・仏・伊・加の7か国が参加。2003年からロシアが参加して, G8(Group of Eight)となる)
G-7 talks G7の協議

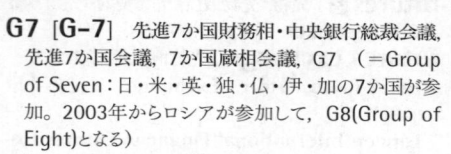

G8 [**G-8**] 主要8か国, 主要8か国首脳会議, 8か国蔵相会議, 中南米8か国グループ (＝Group of Eight)
G-8 environment ministerial meeting G8(主要8か国)環境相会議
G-8 leaders G8首脳 (＝Leaders of the Group of Eight)
G-8 nations 先進8か国, 主要8か国(日・米・英・独・仏・伊・加・露の8か国)
G-8 statement G8声明
G-8 summit 主要8か国首脳会議, G8サミット
the chair of the G-8 meeting G8議長国
with the G-8 leadership 主要8か国(G8)の主導で

G20 [**G-20**] 世界20か国・地域(G20), G20 (＝the Group of 20：G7(日米欧先進7か国), 新興国(中国, インド, 南アフリカ, サウジアラビアなど)12か国と欧州連合(EU)の財務相・中央銀行総裁による国際会議)

gaffe 名 〈外交上の〉失敗, しくじり, へま, 失言, 失態, 不手際, 非礼, 〈芝居の〉とちり

gain 動 獲得する, 得る, 入手する, 伸ばす, 拡大する, 増す, 上がる, 上昇する, 向上する, 得をする[得になる], 有利になる
gain an upper hand 優勢になる, 優勢な立場を確保する
gain currency 流行する
gain ground 確実に力をつける, 人気が上がる, 成功する, 徐々に広く知られるようになる
gain market share シェア[市場シェア]を獲得する, シェアを拡大する, シェアを伸ばす, シェアを奪う
gain on [**upon**] …に追いつく, …まで改善する, …を引き離す, …を浸食する
gain power 権力を得る
gain production scale 生産の規模を拡大する
gain substantial value 価値が大幅に上昇する
gain 名 利益, 利潤, 増加, 増大, 増進, 伸び, 拡大, 上昇, 向上, ゲイン
actuarial gains and losses 保険数理上の損益
capital gain 資本利得, 資産売却益, 資産譲渡益, 株式売買益, 譲渡所得
economic gain 経済拡大
efficiency gain 生産性の伸び, 生産性向上 (＝productivity gain)
employment gain 雇用の伸び, 雇用の増加
exchange gain 為替差益 (＝currency gain, foreign exchange gain, forex gain)
financial gain 利益の追求
gain from operations 営業利益
income gain 所得の伸び
market share gains マーケット・シェアの拡大, 市場シェアの拡大
paper gain 含み益
price gains 物価上昇, インフレ, インフレ率の上昇 (＝gains in prices)

sales gains 売上の伸び
small gain 小幅な［わずかな］伸び, 小幅利益
game 名 駆け引き, 計略, 策略, 遊び, 娯楽, 遊戯, 試合, 試合運び, 競技, 勝負, 狩猟, 獲物, 事業, 計画, 企て, 職業, 仕事, 商売, ゲーム
　bargaining game 交渉ゲーム
　game console ゲーム機
　game law 狩猟法
　game of choice 偶然を伴うゲーム
　game plan 戦略, 行動計画, 作戦計画, 慎重な計画, 予定の行動［方針］
　improve [raise] one's game …の腕を上げる
　war game 机上演習
　zero-sum game ゼロ和ゲーム
gamesmanship 名 駆け引き, きわどい戦術, 反則すれすれの頭脳プレー［戦法, 手段］
gamut 名 全範囲, 全領域, 全域, 全般, 全音域, 全音階
　run the gamut from A to B AからBまで多岐にわたる, AからBまでさまざまだ
　run the gamut of …の全域にわたる, 全範囲を経験する
　run the whole gamut 〈…から…までを〉すべて含む［示す, 表す, 経験する］
　the gamut of …の全域, …のすべての範囲, …のすべて, あらゆる…
　the gamut of suffering あらゆる苦難
　the whole gamut of あらゆる種類の…, あらゆる…
gap 名 格差, 隔たり, 開き, 差, 不一致, 相違点, 落差, 空白, ギャップ
　demand supply gap 需給ギャップ (＝gap between demand and supply)
　the gap in the market 市場参入の好機, 新製品開発の好機
　trade gap 貿易赤字
　wage gap 賃金格差
garner 動 〈票などを〉獲得する, 〈注目や支持を〉集める(collect, gather), 〈情報などを〉得る(acquire, get), 蓄える(store up), 蓄積する, 貯蔵する, 保管する, 〈利益を〉上げる
gas 名 ガソリン(gasoline, petrol), 気体, ガス, 〈自動車の〉アクセル, 麻酔ガス, 無駄話, ばか話
　compressed gas 圧縮ガス
　exhaust gas 排出ガス, 排ガス
　flue gas 排煙
　gas chamber ガス処刑室
　gas emissions 温室効果ガスの排出量 (＝emissions of greenhouse gases)
　gas field ガス田
　gas gauge 燃料計
　gas grids ガス・パイプライン網
　gas guzzler [gas-guzzler] 燃費の悪い大型車, 高燃費車, ガソリンをくう大型車 (＝gas-eater)
　gas main ガス本管, ガス輸送本管
　gas mileage 燃料効率, 燃料消費量, 燃費, 1ガロン当たりの走行マイル数
　gas pedal 〈自動車の〉アクセル
　gas-to-liquid (GTL) products GTL製品
　liquefied methane gas 液化メタンガス《略 LMG》
　liquefied petroleum gas 液化石油ガス《略 LPG》
　step on the gas スピードを速めていく
gasoline 名 ガソリン, 揮発油 (＝gas)
GATT 関税と貿易に関する一般協定, 関税貿易一般協定, ガット (General Agreement on Tariffs and Tradeの略)
gauge [gage] 動 判断する, 評価する, 測定する, 計測する, 算定する, 算出す
gauge 名 基準, 尺度, 指標 (＝gage)
　the gauge of trade in goods and services モノやサービスの取引を示す指標
　the key gauge of consumer prices 消費者物価指数
　the most closely watched gauge of money supply とくに注目されるマネー・サプライの指標, 代表的なマネー・サプライの指標
　the most watched gauge とくに注目される指標
Gaza Strip ガザ地区, パレスチナ・ガザ地区
GCC 湾岸協力会議 (Gulf Cooperation Councilの略)
GDP 国内総生産 (gross domestic productの略)
　advanced GDP figures GDP速報値
　annualized nominal GDP growth 年率換算での名目GDP成長率
　GDP revisions GDP改定値
　nominal GDP 名目GDP
　per capita GDP 人口1人当たりのGDP
　real GDP 実質GDP (国内経済がある一定の期間に生み出したモノやサービスを合計した金額から物価変動の要因を取り除いた額)
　real GDP growth (rate) 実質GDP成長率
GDP deflator GDPデフレーター
「GDPデフレーターとは ⊃ 消費者物価指数が店頭価

格の動向を示すのに対して，GDPデフレーターは，消費のほか投資なども含めた経済全体の物価動向を示す。物価変動を反映する名目GDPを，物価変動の影響を除く実質GDPで割って算出する。

gear 動 照準を合わせる，〈…を…に〉適合させる[合わせる]，適応させる(adapt), 調整する(adjust), 連動させる，〈…を…に〉切り換える，振り向ける，用意する(prepare), 提供する(supply), かみ合う，連動する
 be geared 負債比率を高める，ギアリングを高める
 be geared to [for] …向けだ，…に照準が合わせてある，…するようにしてある，…するようになっている
 be geared up for [to] …の準備ができている，…に順応する
 be highly geared 負債比率が高い，ギアリングが高い
 be low geared 負債比率が低い，ギアリングが低い
 gear up 促進する，速度を速める，高速ギアにする
 gear with …とかみ合う，…と適合する，…と連動する，…と調和する
gear 名 伝動装置，機械装置，装置，装備，道具，用具，設備一式，家庭用品，個人の所有物，身の回り品，持ち物，衣類，衣類，段階，ギア
 be in low gear 低調だ，低い
 be out of gear 調子が狂っている，ギアがかみ合わない
 be thrown out of gear 計画からはずれている
 come into gear 連動する
 get into gear 順調に動き出す，軌道に乗る
 go into full gear 本格化する
 in [into] high gear 全速力で，全力で
 medical gear 医療器具
 move into high gear 急ピッチで進む，全力で進む，本格化する
 move into top [full] gear 最高潮に達する
 shift gear ギアを変える，方向を変える，方法を変える
genco 名 電力会社 (＝generating company)
gender identity disorder [crisis] 性同一性障害
gene 名 遺伝子，遺伝因子，遺伝原質，ジーン
 dominant gene 優性遺伝子
 gene bank 遺伝子バンク，遺伝子銀行，遺伝子貯蔵所
 gene deletion 遺伝子削除，(不要な)遺伝子の除去

gene insertion 遺伝子挿入，欠けている遺伝子の挿入
gene mapping 遺伝子地図作り
gene mutation 遺伝子突然変異
gene pool 遺伝子プール，遺伝子供給源
gene recombination 遺伝子組換え
gene splicing 遺伝子組換え，遺伝子接合 (＝gene transplantation, recombinant DNA research)
gene therapy 遺伝子治療
recessive gene 劣性遺伝子
general 形 一般の，一般的な，全般的な，総合的，多岐にわたる，概略的な，概略の，通常の，総…
general account 一般会計
general account budget 一般会計予算
General Accounting Office 米議会会計検査院 《略 GAO》
General Agreement to Borrow 国際通貨基金(IMF)の一般借入取決め 《略 GAB》
General American 一般アメリカ英語
general anesthesia 全身麻酔
General Assembly 米州議会，国連総会
general cargo 一般貨物
general construction company 総合建設会社，総建築請負業者，ゼネコン (＝general contractor)
general counsel 〈米企業の〉顧問
general election 総選挙
General Election Day 総選挙日(4年毎の米大統領選挙日で11月の第一月曜日の次の火曜日)
general expenditures 一般歳出
general headquarters 総司令部
general meeting 総会，株主総会
general merchandise store 総合スーパー 《略 GMS》
general officer 将官
general opinion 世論
general practice 一般診療
general practitioner 一般開業医
General Secretary 書記長，幹事長，書記局長
General Secretary of the Communist Party of China 中国共産党総書記
general shareholders meeting 株主総会 (＝general meeting, general meeting of shareholders, general shareholders' meeting, shareholders' general meeting, stockholders' meeting)
general staff 管理スタッフ，参謀，幕僚，ゼネラ

ル・スタッフ
- **general strike** ゼネスト
- **general terms and conditions** 一般取引条項, 一般取引条件, 一般条項, 一般条件
- **the general good** 公益
- **the general public** 一般大衆, 公衆

generate 動 生み出す, 生成する, 引き起こす, …を占める, 発生する
- **funds generated from operations** 事業活動に伴って発生した資金
- **generate cash [cash flow]** キャッシュ・フローを生み出す, キャッシュ・フローを生成する
- **generate electricity** 発電する
- **generate profits** 利益を生み出す, 利益を稼ぐ
- **internally generated funds** 内部調達資金

generation 名 世代, 発生, 生成, 形成, 創出, 産出, 生産, 発電, ジェネレーション
- **capital generation** 資本創出
- **cash generation** キャッシュ・フロー, キャッシュ生成能力
- **cogeneration** コジェネレーション, 電気・熱併給, 熱併給発電
- **combined cycle generation** 複合サイクル発電, 複合発電 (＝power generation by combined cycle)
- **employment generation** 雇用創出, 雇用産出
- **from generation to generation** 世代から世代へ, 代々 (＝for generations)
- **generation capability** 発電能力
- **generation gap** 世代[世代間]のずれ, 世代の断絶, ジェネレーション・ギャップ
- **geothermal generation** 地熱発電 (＝geothermal power generation)
- **hydraulic generation** 水力発電
- **integrated gas combined cycle generation** 石炭ガス化複合サイクル発電
- **profit generation** 収益確保
- **pumped-power generation** 揚水発電 (＝pumping-up hydraulic power generation)
- **solar electric generation** 太陽光発電
- **solar thermal electric generation** 太陽熱発電 (＝solar thermal power generation)
- **trip generation** 発生交通量
- **wholesale generation** 卸電気事業者
- **wind generation** 風力発電 (＝wind power generation)

generator 名 発電機, 発生装置, 発生源, 供給源, 生み出すもの, 電力会社, 電気事業者, 〈コンピュータの〉生成プログラム (generating program)
- **cash generator** 資金源
- **generator of air pollution** 大気汚染源, 大気汚染の発生源
- **profit generator** 利益発生源, ドル箱
- **program generator** 生成プログラム, プログラム・ジェネレーター, ジェネレーター
- **wholesale generator** 卸し電気事業者

generic drug 後発医薬品, ジェネリック医薬品
genetic 形 遺伝子の, 遺伝子による, 遺伝学的な, 発生学的な
- **genetic alphabet** 遺伝子アルファベット (DNA (デオキシリボ核酸) 中の四つの塩基で, その組合せが遺伝コードを作る)
- **genetic code** 遺伝暗号, 遺伝コード, 遺伝情報
- **genetic copying** 遺伝子の人為的複製
- **genetic disease** 遺伝病
- **genetic drift** 遺伝的浮動
- **genetic engineering** 遺伝子工学
- **genetic fingerprint** 遺伝子指紋
- **genetic fingerprinting** 遺伝子指紋法
- **genetic load** 遺伝的負荷 (突然変異による有害な遺伝子の蓄積)
- **genetic makeup** 遺伝子の構造
- **genetic manipulation** 遺伝子操作, 生命操作
- **genetic map** 遺伝子地図, 遺伝地図
- **genetic marker** 遺伝標識
- **genetic material** 遺伝子試料
- **genetic mutation** 遺伝変種
- **genetic screening** 遺伝子スクリーニング

genetically altered food 遺伝子組換え食品 (＝GM food)
genetically modified [engineered] food 遺伝子組換え食品 (＝genetically altered food, GM food)
genetically modified seeds 遺伝子組換え種子
genocide 名 集団殺害, 集団虐殺, ジェノサイド
geopolitical risks 地政学的リスク
get down to business 仕事にとりかかる
get-out 名 脱出
get out of …から抜け出す, …から逃れる[逃げ出す], …を徐々に止める
- **get out of a deflationary trend** デフレ傾向から抜け出す
- **get out of a difficult situation** 難局を脱する
- **get out of an agreement** 契約を反故にする
- **get out of sight** 見えなくなる

get out of the car 車から降りる
gets and get-nots 得た者と得なかった者，得た者と得られなかった者
get-tough policy 強硬政策
giant 名 巨大企業，大企業，大国，巨匠，偉人，非凡な才能の人，巨人，形 巨大な，大手の，大型の
  banking giant 金融大手
  food giant 食品大手，食品業界の巨大企業
  giant capital stock 大型株
  giant merger 大型合併
ginseng root 朝鮮人参
gift reminder service ギフト・リマインダー・サービス(誕生日や結婚記念日など大切な日を登録しておくと，事前に知らせてお薦めギフトの提案を行うもの)
Gini Index ジニ係数 (＝Gini coefficient, Gini ratio)
Ginnie Mae ジニー・メイ(Government National Mortgage Association (政府住宅抵当金庫 [米政府系住宅金融公庫])の通称)
gist 名 要旨，要点，主旨，本質，骨子，急所，ポイント，〈訴訟の〉主要訴因
give in to …に屈する，…に屈服する
give oneself up 自首する，出頭する，降参する
given 形 与えられた，一定の，定められた，決められた，指定の，特定の，所定の，既定の，任意の，作成された(executed)，交付された，名 当然のこと
  be given to …の傾向がある，…の癖がある
  take A as given Aを真実であると考える
given 前 …があるとすれば，…と仮定すると，…とすると，…がある以上，…があれば，…から見て，…を考慮に入れると，…を考えると
  given that …を仮定すれば，…であるとすると，…である以上
  given the circumstances このような情勢の下
  given the fact that …という事実を考えると
  given the opportunity 機会があれば
glitch 名 突然の故障，障害，異常，誤作動，突発事故，欠陥，トラブル
global 形 全世界の，世界の，世界的規模の，国際的な，地球規模の，地球全体の，包括的，グローバルの，広範囲の，全体的な，全面的な，総合的な，包括的な
  global climate change 地球規模の気候変動
  global disarmament conference 世界軍縮会議
  Global Fund to Fight AIDS, Tuberculosis and Malaria (GFATM) 世界エイズ・結核・マラリア対策基金
  global information infrastructure グローバル情報基盤《略 GII》
  global issues initiative 地球規模問題イニシアティブ《略 GII》
  global positioning system 全地球測位システム，全地球位置把握システム，世界的位置決定システム，世界測位衛星システム《略 GPS》
  global workforce 世界の従業員，全世界の従業員
  on a global scale 地球規模で
global warming 地球温暖化 (＝the warming of the earth)
  global warming gases 地球温暖化ガス (＝greenhouse gases)
globalism 名 世界化，世界的関与主義，世界統合主義，汎地球主義，世界的干渉政策，グローバリズム
globalization 名 世界化，国際化，地球的規模化，全世界一体化，グローバル化，グローバリゼーション
  increasing globalization and a worldwide opening of markets グローバリゼーションの進展と世界的な市場開放
  market globalization 市場のグローバル化 (＝globalization of markets)
globalize 動 世界化する，国際化する，地球的規模にする，グローバル化する
glocal 形 グローバル化とローカル化の同時並行的，グローカル(グローバルとローカルの合成語)
  glocal action グローカル・アクション(環境問題について「地球的規模で考え，地球的に行動しよう(think global and act local)」という取組み)
  glocal firm グローカル企業
glocalization 名 グローカリゼーション(企業は地球規模で事業を展開する一方，各地域の地域性に適した方法を取るべきだ，という考え方)
gloomy 形 暗い，陰うつな，陰気な，憂うつな，悲観的な，期待の持てない，絶望的な
  gloomy income and employment situations 所得・雇用環境の悪化
  gloomy outlook [prospect] 暗い[暗澹たる]見通し，暗い前途，悲観的な先行き
  take a gloomy view of …を悲観的に見る，…について悲観的な見方をする
GLP 動物実験規範，非臨床試験基準 (**good laboratory practice**の略)

glut 名 供給過剰, 過度の供給, だぶつき (= oversupply)
　a global money glut 世界的な金余り (= a glut of global money)
　a glut on the global steel market 世界の鉄鋼市場の供給過剰

GM 遺伝子組換え(の) (**genetically modified**の略)
　GM labeling 遺伝子組換え食品の表示
　GM materials 遺伝名費組換え原料[原材料], GM原料
　non-GM materials 非GM原料
　Products with GM labels GM表示の食品

GMAT 米国のビジネス・スクールへの入学希望者のための統一試験 (**Graduate Management Admission Test**の略。米国の経営学修士号(MBA)を取得する第一歩となる)

GMP 医薬品製造品質管理基準 (**good manufacturing practice**の略)

GMQ [**g.m.q, G.M.Q**] 適商品質, 適商品質条件, 販売適性品質, 優良商品品質 (**good merchantable quality**の略)

GMS 総合スーパー, ゼネラル・マーチャンダイズ・ストア (**general merchandise store**の略。食品, 衣料品, 雑貨などの日用品を総合的にそろえた大規模小売店のこと)

go bankrupt 破産する, 倒産する, 破綻する, 事業に失敗する (= go bust, go under)

go belly-up 倒産する, 破綻する, 経営破綻する (= go bankrupt, go bust)

go electronic 電子化する (= go 'e')

go-go 形 急成長する, イケイケの, ゴーゴー
　go-go conglomerate ゴーゴー・コングロマリット (ベンチャー企業や成長分野の企業を買収して急成長するコングロマリット)
　go-go fund ゴーゴー・ファンド(格付けや知名度に関係なく値上がりしそうな株を取り入れて資産の増大を狙う投資信託)

go-it-alone administration 〈ブッシュ米大統領の〉「わが道を行く」政権

go private 株式を非公開化する, 非公開会社にする

go public 株式公開する, 株式を上場する, 秘密情報を公開する
　▶ Common shares in Google Inc. *went public* on the U.S. Nasdaq Stock Market in 2004. インターネット検索グーグルの普通株式は, 2004年に米国ナスダックに上場された。
　▶ Microsoft's annual revenue fell for the first time since the company *went public* in 1986. マイクロソフト社の通期の売上高は, 1986年の上場以来初めて, 前年比で減少した。

go sour 〈計画などが〉失敗する, 不調に終わる, だめになる, こじれる, 酸っぱくなる

go through 検討する, 念入りに調べる, 経験する, 味わう, …に直面する, 切り抜ける, やり通す, 通過する, 承認される, 〈取引などが〉成立する, 〈手続きなどを〉取る

go under 破産する, 倒産する, 破綻する, 事業に失敗する (= go bankrupt, go belly-up)

goal 名 目標, 目的, 目的地, ゴール
　goal of price setting 価格設定目標
　goal setting 目標設定
　interim goal 中間目標
　long-term goal 長期目標, 長期的目標
　profit goal 利益目標

going 名 状況, 状態, 進み具合, 形勢, 進行, 行方, 出発
　going long 思惑買い, 見込み買い, ロングにする (投資や投機を目的として有価証券を買うこと)
　going private 株式の非公開化, 非公開会社化
　going public 株式の新規公開, 株式公開, 機密情報の公開
　going short 思惑売り, 見込み売り, ショートにする (空売り(short sale)と同義で, 思惑で有価証券を売ること)
　hard going 難航, 難しい
　heavy going 骨が折れる, 難解だ
　rough going 難航, 難航している
　while the going is good 形勢が有利なうちに, 状況がよいうちに

going 形 現行の, 現在の, 一般に行われている, 運転中の, 稼動中の, 営業中の, 順調な, うまく行っている, 儲かっている
　going business 順調な事業, 順調な商売
　going price 現行価格, 時価
　going rate of interest 実勢金利
　going wages 現行賃金

golden pension ゴールデン・ペンション(企業買収交渉で, 買収先の会社の役員に対する報酬として, 買収する会社が年金の支払いを長期的に保証すること)

golden share 黄金株, 特権株(「黄金株」は, 株主総会での合併などの提案に拒否権を発動できる「拒否権付き株式(種類株式)」のこと)

good 形 好調な, 堅調な, 優良の, 優秀な, 良好

な, 好材料の, 強気の, 十分な, かなりの, 高い, 大幅な, 一流の, 親切な
good bargain 得な[割安な]買い物
good buy 特売品
good clinical practice 医薬品の臨床試験の実施に関する基準《略 GCP》
good crop [harvest] 豊作（＝rich harvest）
good delivery 完全受渡し, 適格受渡し, グッド・デリバリー
good loc [location] 場所良好, 環境良好
good merchantable quality 適商品質, 商品としての品質《略 GMQ》
good money 優良資金, 即利用可能な資金, 他で有効に使えた金, 苦労して得た金, 高賃金(high wages), 良貨
good name よい評判, 名誉
Good Neighbor Policy 善隣政策, 善隣外交政策(ルーズベルト米大統領が1933年に行った中南米との親善政策)
good news よい知らせ, 明るい材料, 好材料, 望ましい状況, 満足すべき状況, 楽しい人
good offices 斡旋, 尽力, 調停, 強制調停, 影響力
good risk 優良危険, グッド・リスク(損害の発生率が少なくて保険会社に有利なリスク. 不良危険＝bad risk)
good works 慈善行為, 善行
make good 成功する,〈損害の〉賠償をする,〈費用や賠償金などを〉支払う,〈目的を〉果たす[遂げる],〈約束を〉果たす[履行する],〈不足を〉補う[埋め合わせる], 立証する, 実証する,〈地位や立場を〉保持する[確保する]

goods 名 物品, 商品, 製品, 財貨, 財産, 財, 貨物, 動産, 有体動産
basic goods 生活必需品
brown goods 〈テレビ, ビデオ, オーディオなどの〉電子製品
consumer durable goods 耐久消費財（＝durable consumer goods）
consumer nondurable goods 非耐久消費財
convenience goods 最寄り品(消費者が小売店で少量ずつ買う商品)
finished goods 製品, 完成品, 加工品, 最終財
goods and services 商品とサービス, 財貨とサービス, 財貨・サービス, モノとサービス, 財貨と役務, 財貨と用役（＝services and goods）
goods in bond 保税貨物（＝bonded goods）
goods in transit 未着品, 輸送品

impulse goods 衝動買い商品, 衝動購買商品, 衝動品
industrial goods 生産財, 産業財, 工業品
public goods 公共財
semimanufactured [semi-processed] goods 半製品（＝semifinished goods）
shopping goods 買い回り品(ファッション関連や耐久消費財などの商品)
substitute goods 代替財
white goods 〈冷蔵庫や洗濯機などの〉大型家電製品,〈タオルやシーツなどの〉家庭用リンネル製品

goodwill 名 善意, 好意, 厚意, 親切, 親切心, 親善, 友好, 快諾, のれん, 営業権, 得意先, 顧客[顧客網], 信用, 信頼, 株
goodwill ambassador 親善大使
goodwill mission 親善使節団
goodwill visit 親善訪問
people of goodwill 善意の人々, 良識派

govern 動 支配する, 統治する, 治める, 管理する, 運営する, 管理運営する, 取り締まる, 制御する, 規定する, 決定する, 左右する, …に適用される, …の決定基準[原則]となる
be governed by Japanese laws 日本法を準拠法とする, 日本法に準拠する, 日本法が適用[採用]される

governability 名 統治能力, 運営能力, 自主能力

governance 名 統治, 支配, 管理, 監督, 管理法, 経営法, 運営法, 統治能力, ガバナンス
corporate governance reform bill 企業統治改革法案
governance style 統治スタイル
information governance 情報ガバナンス, 情報統治

governing 形 統治する, 支配する, 左右する, 統制する, 運営する, 管理する, 監督する, 主要な, 主導的な, 指導的な, 支配的な, …を規定する, …に関する
governing body 監督機関, 理事会
governing language 支配言語, 適用言語, 基準言語
governing law 準拠法, 適用法（＝applicable law）
governing party 政府与党, 与党
the governing concept 理念
the motives governing one's decision …の決定を左右する動機

government 名 政府, 政治, 政権, 行政

caretaker government 暫定政権, 暫定内閣, 選挙管理内閣
central government 中央政府, 国
coalition government 連立政権
federal government 連邦政府
government-aided financing 政策金融
government-backed financing operations 政策金融
government debt 国債, 政府の債務, 政府の財政赤字
government money 政府資金, 公的資金
government officials 政府当局者, 政府高官, 官僚, 政府当局, 公務員
government spending 歳出
local government 地方政府, 地方自治体, 公共団体, 地方
military government 軍事政権
municipal governments 市町村, 地方自治体
prefectural governments 都道府県
state government 州政府
government-affiliated 形 政府系の
government bond 国債, 政府債券
government bond issuance 国債発行
GPS 全地球測位システム (**global positioning system**の略)
grace period 猶予期間
gradation 名 段階的移行, 漸次的移行, 変化, 推移, 段階, 色調の濃淡, ぼかし
grade 名 等級, 階級, 段階, 程度, 過程, 評点, 成績, 評価, 格付け, 学年, 傾斜度, 勾配, グレード
Grade A 一級品の, 最高級の
grade crossing 平面交差点, 踏切
grade point 学業成績換算評点
grade separation 立体交差
grade teacher 小学校の先生
make the grade 基準[標準]に達する, 成功する, 合格する
graduate 名 卒業生, 学士, 大学院生
graduate school 大学院
new graduate 新卒生, 新卒
graduated 形 段階的な, 累進的な, 漸増の, 漸増型の
graduated deterrence 〈核兵器の〉段階的抑止戦略
graduated-payment mortgage (loan) 元利返済漸層型モーゲージ
graduated tax 累進税
Grammy Awards グラミー賞(米国レコード芸術科学アカデミー(National Academy of Recording Arts and Science)が優秀なレコード歌手, 演奏家に毎年授与する賞)
Grand 名 1,000ドル《略 G》
grand bargain 包括的取引, グランド・バーゲン
grand slam 圧勝, 完勝, 満塁ホームラン, タイトルの総獲得, グランドスラム
grant 動 与える, 付与する, 許諾する, 許可する, 承諾する, 認める, 譲渡する, 移転する
grant 名 〈政府の〉補助金, 助成金, 交付金, 無償資金, 無償給付, 研究助成金, 奨学金
categorical grants 使途別補助金
grant aid 無償資金協力
grant award 義援金
grant commitment 助成の約束
grant element 〈政府借款中の〉贈与比率, 贈与要素, 援助条件緩和指数, グラント・エレメント
grant-in-aid 無償援助, 補助金, 助成金, 交付金
graphite-moderated nuclear reactor 黒鉛減速炉
grapple with …に取り組む, …と(がっぷり)組み合う, …と取っ組み合い[つかみ合い]をする
grass roots 一般人, 一般庶民, 大衆, 有権者, 草の根
gratitude money 謝礼金
graying 形 高齢化 (= ageing, aging: 高齢化社会はaging society, graying society)
Great Cultural Revolution 中国の文化大革命, 文革
Great Depression 大恐慌, 世界大恐慌, 世界恐慌 (= Depression)
Great Hall of the People 〈北京の〉人民大会堂
Great Recession 大不況
green 形 環境の, 環境保護の, 環境にやさしい, 環境に配慮した, 許可された, 準備完了の, 予定通りに進んだ, グリーン
green audit 環境監査, 環境適合検査
green belt 緑地帯, 緑化地帯
Green Belt Movement グリーン・ベルト運動
green book 〈FRB(米連邦準備制度理事会)が作成する〉経済見通し
green business 環境事業, 環境ビジネス
green card 〈米国での〉労働許可証, 外国人永住許可証, 〈英国での〉国際自動車保険証
green collar グリーンカラー[グリーン・カラー]

(＝green-collar worker：再生可能なエネルギーやエネルギー効率化, 環境保全などの産業に従事する労働者のことで, ビジネスを通して環境問題に取り組む人や環境にやさしい働き方をする人なども指す)

green [greens] fee ゴルフ場使用料, プレー費用, グリーン・フィー

green jacket 緑のジャケット, 優勝

green labeling [labelling] 緑の表示, エコ表示

green light 青信号, 正式許可, 許可, 認可, ゴーサイン

Green Paper 緑書(英政府刊行の政策試案集)

green pea 大学新入生

green power 金, 金力, 財力, グリーン電力 (green electricity), グリーン・パワー

green product エコ製品, 環境[地球]にやさしい製品, 環境重視製品, グリーン・プロダクト

green productivity 環境にやさしい生産性, グリーン・プロダクティビティ

green revolution 緑の革命(品種改良などによる農産物の大増産), 穀物増産のための技術革新, 環境革命, 環境に対する関心の高まり

green room 主演者控え室

green shoots 景気回復の動き, 回復の兆し, 成長[発展, 復活]の兆し, 再生の動き

greenback 名 米ドル, 米ドル紙幣(米ドル紙幣の裏面がすべてグリーンなのでこう呼ばれている)

▶ The depreciation of the *greenback* will result in exchange losses on assets held in dollars. ドル安が進むと, 保有するドル建て資産に為替差損が生じる。

greenery 名 緑樹, 樹木, 草木, 青葉, 木立, 緑地, 温室(greenhouse)

greenery on a rooftop 屋上緑化

greenhouse 名 温室, 地球の大気, 温室効果ガス

greenhouse effect 温室効果, 地球温暖化の効果

greenhouse gas emissions 温室効果ガス排出量, 温室効果ガスの排出量, 地球温暖化ガスの排出量 (＝emissions of greenhouse gases, greenhouse gas discharge)

greenhouse gas reduction 温室効果ガス削減

greenhouse gases 温室効果ガス, 地球温暖化ガス, 温暖化ガス《略 **GHG**》(＝global warming gases)

greenmail 〈買収や高値での引取りを目的にした〉株式の大量買取り, 〈法外な価格での〉株の買戻し, グリーンメール, 動 株式を大量に買い取る, 法外な価格で株を買い戻す, グリーンメールを仕掛ける (greenbackとblackmailとの合成語)

grid 名 送電線網, 送電網, 〈ガス[水道管]の〉敷設網, 道路網, 放送局網, 碁盤の目, グリッド

electricity [electric] grid 送電線網, 送電系統, 電力網

power grid 配電網

smart grid スマート・グリッド(IT技術を利用して電力利用を最適化する次世代電力網)

gridlock 名 交通渋滞

grill 動 厳しく問い詰める, 詰問する, 厳しく尋問する, 取り調べる, 厳しく追及する, 網焼きにする, バーベキューにする

grip 動 しっかりつかむ, 理解する, 把握する, 深い影響を与える, 影響力[支配力]を持つ, 〈注意, 興味を〉引きつける, 心を奪う, 〈病気が〉襲う

be gripped by …に心を奪われる, …に引きつけられる, …の影響を受ける, …で動けなくなる

grip one's argument …の論旨を理解する

grip one's attention …の注意を引く

grip one's courage 勇気を奮い起こす

grip one's imagination 想像力をかきたてる

grip (the attention of) the audience 聴衆の心をつかむ, 観衆の心をとらえる

gripping book 感銘の深い本

grip 名 支配, 影響, 支配力, 影響力, 牽引力, 引きつける力, 理解力, 把握力, 処理能力, やる気, 撮影班の裏方, グリップ

be in [get into] the grip of …にとらえられる, …に見舞われている, …から深刻な影響を受けている, …にはまる

come [get] to grips with …に真剣に取り組む, …を理解[把握]する, …とけんかする

get [have, take] a grip on …をつかむ, …を支配する, …を理解[把握]する, …を認識する

grocery store 日用雑貨・食料品店, 食品スーパー

gross 名 合計, 総額, 総, 形 総計の, 全体の, 控除前の, 控除をしない, グロス

gross domestic product 国内総生産《略 **GDP**》(GNPから海外からの純所得を差し引いたもの)

gross margin 売上総利益, 売上利益, 粗利益, 売上利益率, 粗利益率 (＝gross margin percentage, gross margin ratio)

gross national product 国民総生産《略 **GNP**》(1年間の総生産額から中間生産物を差し引いたもの)

gross operating profit 業務粗利益
gross profit 売上総利益, 粗利益, 粗利, 差益 (=gross margin, gross profit margin, gross profit on sales：売上総利益＝純売上高－売上原価)
ground 名 地面, 地表, 地上, 土地, 用地, 土壌, 敷地［構内］（複数扱い）, 場所, …場, 領域, 分野, 範囲, 運動場, 競技場, 根拠, 理由, 原因, 動機, 立場, 見方, 見地, 意見, 基礎(basis), 基盤(foundation), 根源, 大本, 状況, 話題, 問題, グラウンド, 形 地面の, 地上の, 陸生の, 底性の, 海底の, 基礎的な
- **be burned to the ground** 全焼する, 焼失する, 灰燼に帰する
- **be on shaky ground** 論拠が不確かである
- **break fresh [new] ground** 新生面［新天地, 新領域］を開拓する, 新分野を開く, 新事業に挑戦する, 新事業［新企画］に乗り出す
- **break ground** くわ入れをする, 起工する, 着手する, 〈事業, 掘削などを〉始める, 開幕する, 掘る, 耕作する
- **breeding ground** 飼育場, 養殖場
- **come [go] to the ground** 負ける, 敗退する, 失敗する, 滅びる
- **common ground** 一致点, 共通点, 妥協の余地
- **cover much ground** 大いにはかどる, 広い範囲に及ぶ
- **down to the ground** 徹底的に
- **from the ground up** 最初から, 一から, 一から十まで, 完全に, 徹底的に
- **gain [gather, make, make up] ground** 前進する, 進歩する, …に追い付く, …を追い越す, 広まる, 普及する, 一般化する, 流行する, 受け入れられる, 優勢になる, 成功する, 評価［支持, 力］を得る, 影響力を増す, 〈病人が〉回復する
- **get in on the ground floor** 〈計画などに〉当初から参加する, 初期の段階から参画する［加わる］, 〈市場などに〉最初から参入する
- **get off the ground** 離陸する, 順調なスタートを切る, 〈仕事や会社などを〉軌道に乗せる, 〈事業を〉立ち上げる
- **give ground to** …に譲歩する, …まで後退する
- **go to ground** 様子見を決め込む
- **ground attack** 対地攻撃, 地上攻撃
- **ground ball** ［野球］ゴロ (=grounder)
- **ground-based radar** 地上基地レーダー
- **ground control** 地上管制, 地上管制員, 地上管制装置, 地上の測量規準
- **ground controlled approach** 着陸誘導管制《略 GCA》
- **ground controller** 地上管制官, 〈宇宙船の〉地上管制部
- **ground crew** 地上整備員, 地上勤務員
- **ground fighting** 地上戦 (=ground assault [battle, operation, warfare])
- **ground floor** 〈建物の〉1階, 〈事業などへの〉初期参加, 〈市場への〉初期参入
- **ground forces [troops]** 地上軍
- **ground handling** 地上業務
- **ground pollution** 土壌汚染
- **ground rules** 〈行動の〉基本原則, 基本原理, 大枠
- **Ground Self-Defense Force** 〈日本の〉陸上自衛隊《略 GSDF》
- **ground total** 単純集計
- **ground water** 地下水
- **ground wire** 避雷針, 接地線, アース
- **ground zero** 爆心地, 核爆発の真下あるいは真上の地面の点 (=center of an explosion, hypocenter)
- **happy hunting ground** 獲物が豊富な狩猟場, 宝の山, 天国
- **keep [have] both feet on the ground** 足に地がついている, 実際的である
- **lose a good deal of ground** 反落する
- **lose further ground** 続落する
- **lose ground** 勢力を失う, 影響力を失う, 人気を失う, 評価［支持］を失う, 失敗なる忘れられる, 衰える, 衰退する, 悪化する, 退却する, 譲歩する, 値崩れを起こす
- **lost ground** 下げ幅
- **maintain one's ground against** …に対して自己の立場を守る
- **off the ground** 飛行中, 進行中
- **on delicate ground** 微妙な立場に, 微妙な状態に
- **on good grounds** 相当の理由で
- **on humanitarian grounds** 人道的見地から, 人道上
- **on neutral ground** 中立の立場で, 対等の立場で
- **on the ground** 実地に, 現場で, 実用的に, 一般大衆［草の根］に
- **plowed ground** 耕地
- **prepare the ground for** …の下準備をする
- **recover the lost ground** 下げ幅を取り戻す

shift [change] one's ground　…の論拠[論旨]を変える，…の立場を変える，意図を変更する
stamping ground　よく行く場所
stand [hold, keep] one's ground　踏みとどまる，自分の立場[意見]を守り抜く，自分の主張を固守する，一歩も後へ引かない，がんとして譲らない，屈しない，〈現状を〉しっかり直視する，〈敵に〉背中を見せない
touch ground　本題に入る，〈船が〉水底に触れる

ground 形　すりつぶした，磨いた，ざらざらの（grindの過去形・過去分詞）
　ground beef　牛ひき肉
　ground finish　磨き仕上げ
　ground glass　すりガラス

ground-based 形　地上に配備された

group 動　…をグループとしてまとめる，傘下に…がある

group 名　企業集団，集団，団体，連結，企業グループ，グループ
　deprived group　恵まれない人々，貧困地域グループ
　group activity　団体活動
　group consumption　団体消費
　group discussion　団体討議
　group dynamics　集団力学，社会力学
　group insurance　団体保険
　group net income　連結純利益，連結税引き後利益（＝consolidated net income）
　group net loss　連結純損失，当期連結純損失，連結税引き後赤字（＝consolidated net loss：企業グループ全体の税引き後損失）
　group net profit　連結純利益，当期連結純利益，連結税引き後利益（＝consolidated net profit：企業グループ全体の税引き後利益）
　Group of Two　2大主要国，G2
　group representation　集団代表制
　group sales　連結売上高（＝consolidated revenues, consolidated sales）
　peer group　同業他社，仲間集団，仲間グループ，ピア・グループ
　pressure group　圧力団体

grow 動　増加する，増大する，拡大する，高まる，伸びる，成長する，発展する，向上する，栽培する，伸ばす
　fast-growing sector [segment]　急成長部門，急成長を遂げている部門
　grow earnings　利益を増やす，利益を伸ばす
　grow 5 percent over the previous year　前年同期比で5％増加する

growing 形　成長する，増大する，拡大する，伸びる
　fast-growing sector　急成長部門（＝rapidly growing sector）
　growing competition　競争の激化
　growing demand　需要の伸び，需要の拡大
　growing sales　販売の伸び

growth 名　成長，成長率，経済成長，伸び，伸び率，増加，増大，景気
　balance sheet growth　資産の増加
　balanced growth　均衡成長，均衡のとれた成長
　be a plus for growth　経済成長に寄与する
　equity growth　資本の増加
　export growth　輸出の伸び，輸出の増加，輸出の伸び率
　growth goal　成長目標
　growth in sales and profits　増収増益
　growth of the economy　経済成長率
　growth potential　成長潜在力，潜在成長力，成長余地，成長能力，成長力，成長ポテンシャル
　growth product　成長商品，成長製品
　high growth　高成長，高度成長，高度経済成長
　internal growth　内部成長，内部の成長（＝organic growth）
　lower economic growth　低成長，成長鈍化，経済成長率の低下（＝lower growth, slower growth）
　monetary growth　マネー・サプライ伸び率，通貨供給量伸び率（＝money supply growth）
　negative growth　マイナス成長
　output growth　生産の増加，生産の伸び[伸び率]
　potential growth　潜在成長率
　secular growth　長期的な発展，持続的成長
　slower economic growth　経済成長の減速，経済成長の鈍化，経済成長率の低下

growth path 名　成長経路，成長軌道，成長路線
　balanced growth path　均衡成長経路，均斉成長経路
　efficient growth path　有効成長経路
　equilibrium growth path　均衡成長経路
　full-capacity growth path　完全能力成長経路
　full-employment growth path　完全雇用成長経路
　moderate economic growth path　穏やかな成長軌道

optimal [optimum] growth path　最適成長経路
required growth path　必要成長経路
von Neumann balanced growth path　ノイマン均衡成長経路

GSE　政府系住宅金融機関, 政府支援機関, 政府系機関, 政府援助法人 (Government Sponsored Enterprisesの略. ファニー・メイ (Fannie Mae) やフレディ・マック (Freddie Mac) などの住宅関連や農業関連の政府後援企業のこと)

GSM　グローバル移動通信システム, 汎欧州デジタル携帯電話規格 (Global System for Mobile Communications)
GSM home base station　GSMホーム基地局
GSM network operator　GSMネットワーク運営会社
GSM operator　GSM事業者
GSM phone call　GSM通話
GSM roaming　GSMローミング
GSM subscriber　GSM加入者
GSM terminals　GSM端末, GSM (方式) 携帯電話

GTL　ガス・ツー・リキッド (gas to liquidの略)《略 GTL》(天然ガスを原料にして軽油やガソリン, 灯油などの液体燃料を生産すること. 1993年から商業化が進み, 世界各地の大型ガス田でGTL工場の建設計画が進められている)

GTL products　GTL製品
> GTL製品とは ⊃ GTLでできた燃料のこと. GTLでできた燃料は, 原油から作る場合と比べて硫黄分や窒素分などが少ない. このうちGTL軽油は, ディーゼル燃料として使うと燃費も向上でき, 二酸化炭素削減にもつながるとされる. また, GTL製品は, 燃料電池自動車向けとしても期待されている.

guaranteed yield　予定利率 (=promised yield: 生命保険会社が保険契約者に約束した運用利回りのこと)

guard against [from]　…に用心する, …を警戒する [警備する], …を […から] 守る, …を保護する, …に備える

guard 名　防護, 防衛, 防御, 警備, 警戒, 監視, 警戒心, 用心, 不信感, 安全装置, 保護装置, 守衛, 警備員, 監視員, 護衛, 守護隊, 警衛隊, 護衛隊, ガード
be caught [taken] off guard by　…により不意をつかれる, …により不意打ちされる
be off (one's) guard against　…に油断している
be on (one's) guard against　…に警戒している
catch [take] A off guard　Aの不意をつく, Aのすきをつく, Aの油断に乗じる
come off guard　非番になる
on guard　当番で (=on duty)
stand [keep, mount] guard　見張りをする, 歩哨に立つ, 監視体制を取る
stand on one's guard　警戒する, 用心する

guardian 名　保護者, 守護者, 後見人, 管理人, 保管者
guardian ad litem　訴訟後見人
Guardian Angels　ボランティア自警団
guardian of the law　法の番人
legal guardian　法的後見人
natural guardian　人として当然の後見人 (未成年者の父または母など)

Guardian Council　護憲評議会 (イランの選挙監督機関)

guerrilla [guerilla] 名　遊撃兵, ゲリラ兵, 不正規兵
anti-government guerrillas　反政府ゲリラ
guerrilla band　ゲリラ隊, 不正規軍
guerrilla operations [activities]　ゲリラ活動
guerrilla tactics　ゲリラ戦法
guerrilla theater [theatre]　街頭演劇
guerrilla warfare [war]　ゲリラ戦
Islamic guerrillas　イスラム・ゲリラ

guidance 名　案内, 指導, 生活指導, 進路指導, 手引き, 手本, 指針, 教え, 〈ミサイル, ロケットなどの〉誘導, ガイダンス
administrative guidance　行政指導
career guidance　進路案内, 進路指導
child guidance　児童相談
general guidance　一般的な指針
guidance counselor　進路 [生活] 指導担当カウンセラー
guidance policy finance　政策金融
guidance radar　ミサイル誘導レーダー
guidance system　〈ミサイルなどの〉誘導システム
implementation guidance　実施ガイド
Islamic guidance　イスラムの教え
Spiritual guidance　精神的な教え
technical guidance　技術指導, 専門的指導
under the guidance of　…の指導に基づいて, …の案内で
vocational [occupational] guidance　職業指導
window guidance　窓口指導, 窓口規制

guideline 名 基準, 指導基準, 運用基準, 指導, 指針, 指標, 上限, ガイドライン (⇒budgetary request guidelines)
　budgetary request guidelines　概算要求基準 (=ceiling on budgetary request)
guilty 形 有罪の, 罪悪感[罪の意識]がある, やましい, 〈罪や過失などを〉犯した, …に責任がある, 〈倫理的に〉罪深い, 非難すべき
　a guilty deed [act]　犯罪行為, 犯行
　a guilty intent [mind]　殺意
　a guilty verdict　〈陪審による〉有罪の評決
　be found guilty　〈陪審裁判で〉有罪と評決される
　be guilty of stealing [theft]　窃盗の罪[窃盗罪]を犯している
　find the defendant guilty of a crime as charged　訴えのとおり被告を有罪とする
　guilty feeling　罪悪感
　guilty party　加害者
　have a guilty conscience　気[良心]がとがめる, やましい心がある
　plead guilty to　…の罪を認める, …に対して有罪を認める
　plead guilty to (the charge of) murder　殺人(の訴え)を認める
　plead not guilty to　…に対して無罪を申し立てる, …を否認する
guinea pig　実験台, モルモット
Gulf States　〈米国の〉メキシコ湾岸諸州(フロリダ, アラバマ, ミシシッピー, ルイジアナの各州とテキサス州), ペルシャ湾岸諸国
Gulf War　湾岸戦争(1991年1月17日から2月28日までの)(イラク軍のクェート侵攻後, 米国中心の多国籍軍とイラク軍との間で行われた戦争)
　Gulf War crisis　湾岸危機
　Gulf War (veteran's) syndrome　湾岸戦争症候群, 湾岸戦争後遺症 (=desert fever, Desert Storm (Persian War) syndrome)
gunship 名 〈速射砲などを搭載した〉武装ヘリ[軍用機]
guru 名 カリスマ的指導者, 指導者, リーダー, 権威者, 助言者, ベテラン, 〈ヒンズー教の〉導師[尊師], グル
　hippie guru　ヒッピー族の精神的指導者
　homemaking guru　カリスマ主婦
gut 名 腸, 内臓, はらわた, 消化器[器官], 腹, 腹部, 根性, 勇気, 度胸(courage), 決断力(determination), 気力, 胆力, ガッツ, 感情, 直間, 本能, 本質, 重要な部分, 要点, 中身, 内容, 実質, 〈機械などの〉可動部分, 心臓部, 作動部, ガット
　gut course　単位の取りやすい課目, 楽勝課目
　gut disease　消化器疾患
　gut feeling　直感, 勘, 虫の知らせ
　gut reaction　本能的な反応
　gut-wrenching　断腸の思いの
　have [show] a lot of guts　すごく根性がある
　have [get] the guts to do　大胆にも…する, 勇気をもって…する
　slog [sweat, work] one's guts out　懸命に働く, 死にもの狂いで働く
gynecologist 名 婦人科医

H h

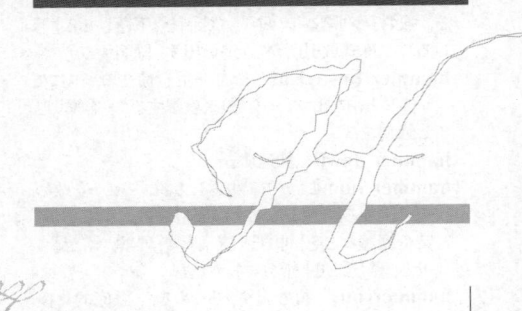

hack 動 不正にアクセスする, 名 コンピュータ・システムへの不正アクセス
hacker 名 ハッカー, 侵入・破壊者, コンピュータ侵害者, コンピュータ・システムへの不正行為者, コンピュータ・マニア, コンピュータ破り
hacking 名 不正アクセス, ハッキング
had best …するのが一番よい, …すべき
► Companies *had best* engage in fair competition that reflects the true cost of business. 企業は, 正当な業務コストを反映した適正な競争を行うべきだ。
hair-growth stimulant product 発毛剤
hair growth treatment 育毛トリートメント
half 名 中間, 半期, 半分, 2分の1, 半時間, 30分, 形 半分の, 不十分な, 中途半端な
　a ton and a half 1.5トン (=one and a half ton)
　half-and-half 半々の, 中途半端な
　half board 〈ホテルの〉1泊2食付きサービス
　half-landing 階段の踊り場
　half-life [halflife] 〈放射性物質の〉半減期, つかの間の繁栄期［最盛期］
　half measures 妥協策, 不十分な政策, 中途半端な［間に合わせの］手段
　half pay 給料の半分, 休職給
　half time [half-time] 半日労働, 半日勤務, 半日給, 中休み, ハーフタイム
　half truth [half-truth] 真実の一部しか伝えない説明［話］
half-baked 形 不十分な, 不完全な, 中途半端な, 生半可な, 未熟な, 常識のない, 愚かな, 常軌を逸した
　a half-baked scheme 不十分な計画, 不完全な計画
　a half-baked youth 青二才
half-mast 名 〈弔意・遭難信号を示す〉半旗の位置
half year 上半期, 半期, 中間
　half-year earnings report for the fiscal period up to September 9月中間決算, 上半期 (4-9月期)業績, 上半期決算
　half-year net profit forecast 半期純利益予想
halfway house 社会復帰施設, 更生施設, 妥協の産物, 宿泊所, 宿屋
hallmark 名 特徴, 特質, 目印, 看板, 品質保証, 太鼓判, 折り紙, 保証するもの, 純度検証印, 優良刻印
　bear the hallmark of …を保証する, …を証明する, …に折り紙をつける
　the hallmark of capacity 能力の証明, 能力を証明するもの
halo effect 後光効果, 光背効果, ハロー効果 (人事考課などで, 部分的な強い印象が全体の評価につながること)
halve 動 二等分する, 半分に分ける, 半分に減らす［引き下げる］, 半減させる, 50%引き下げる, 50%削減する, 半額にする, 〈試合を〉引き分ける, 半減する
Hamas 名 ハマス(イスラム原理主義組織)
hammer 動 まとめる, 考え出す, 大打撃を与える, 激しく攻撃［非難］する, 力説する, 叩く, 叩き込む,

hammer 叩きのめす, 完全に打ち負かす, 一方的にやっつける, 強く打つ[蹴る], 殴る, 〈株価を〉下落させる[下げる], 〈株式取引所から〉追い出す, 除名する
- **hammer (away) at** …を一生懸命やる, …にこつこつと精を出す, …を激しく攻撃する, …を繰り返し強調する
- **hammer down** 加速する
- **hammer home** …を繰り返し力説する, …を改めて強調する, 〈意見などを〉無理に押しつける, 〈考えや議論などを〉叩き込む, 認識[理解, 銘記]させる, 〈釘などを〉十分に打ち込む
- **hammer out** 打ち出す, まとめる, 〈徹底的に検討して〉考え出す, 案出する, 〈計画を〉立てる[練る], 〈議論して〉合意を打ち出す[解決する], 〈曲を〉弾く

hammer 图 槌, 金づち, 〈議長や裁判官, 競売人の〉木づち, 〈車の〉アクセル, 〈時計やゴングの〉打ち子, ハンマー
- **be due for the hammer** 解雇される運命にある
- **be [come, go] under the hammer** 競売に付される[かけられる], 競売で売られる
- **go [be] at it hammer and tongs** 口論する, 殴りあう, 激しく議論する, 猛烈に働く, 猛烈な勢いで取りかかる
- **hammer and sickle** ハンマーと鎌 (旧ソ連の国旗で共産主義のシンボル。ハンマーは労働者, 鎌は農民の象徴)

hand 图 手, 管理, 支配, 世話, 技量, 腕前, 人, 職人, 働き手, 人手, 誓約
- **a show of hands** 挙手による採決
- **change hands** 所有者[持ち主]が変わる, 株主が変わる, 人手に渡る, 政権を交替する, 更迭する
- **get [become] out of hand** 手に負えなくなる, 収拾がつかなくなる
- **give a helping hand to** …に救いの手を与える
- **hand in [and] glove with** …と極めて[非常に]親密で, …と関係を密にして, …とぐるになって[…とぐるで], …と共謀して, …と結託して
- **hand in hand** 手に手を取って, 一致協力して, 共に手を携えて
- **have a serious problem on one's hands** 解決すべき深刻な問題を抱えている
- **helping hand** 救いの手, 支援の手, 援助の手, 手助け
- **join hands with** …と提携する, …と手を組む
- **keep one's hands off** …に手を出さない, …に干渉しない
- **make money hand over fist** お金をどんどん儲ける
- **play one's own hand** 私利をはかる
- **put [set] one's hand to** …に着手する, …に署名する, …するよう努力する
- **receive [get] a big hand from** …から拍手喝采を受ける
- **show [reveal] one's hand** 手の内を見せる, 本心[真意]を明かす
- **sit on one's hands** 手をこまねいている, 傍観する, 何もしないで様子を見る, 拍手をしない, 賛同しない, 賛意を示さない
- **stay one's hand** 延期する, 延ばす
- **strike hands with** …と契約を交わす, …と契約する, …と協力を約束する, …と手を握り合う
- **take [have] a hand in** …に関係[関与]する, …に加担する, …を共にする
- **wash one's hands of** …から手を引く
- **weaken the hands of** …の気勢をそぐ

handcuff 動 手錠をかける, 拘束する, 縛る

handheld 形 手で持てる, 携帯型の, 携帯用の, 手のひらに乗る, ハンドヘルド

handling 图 取扱い, 操作, 操縦, 処理, 対応, 運用, 運営, 手法, 荷役, 運搬, 〈商品の〉出荷, 盗品の取引, ハンドリング
- **careful handling** 慎重な扱い[操作, 対応]
- **poor handling of the situation** 状況に対する対応のまずさ

handout 图 配布, 分配, 譲渡, 声明, 声明文, 情報, 発表文書, 新聞発表 (press [news] release), 配布資料, 宣伝用ビラ[パンフレット], 広告, ちらし, 試供品, 無料サンプル, 補助金, 給付金, 予算, ハンドアウト
- **flat-sum (cash) handouts** 定額給付金
- **government handouts** 政府予算, 政府補助金, 政府給付金

handset 图 〈電話の〉送受話器, 〈携帯電話や無線機の〉端末機, 携帯電話, ハンドセット
- **portable video game handset** 携帯ビデオゲーム機

hands-off 形 不干渉の, 干渉しない, 傍観の, 傍観主義の
- **hands-off attitude** 傍観主義の姿勢[態度]
- **hands-off economy** 自由放任経済 (=laissez-faire economy)
- **hands-off policy** 不干渉政策, 自由放任政策

hands-on 形 実地の, 実践的な, 実際的な, 実務的な, 直接関与する, 自ら先頭に立つ, 口出しする, 個人の参加をねらった, 手作業の, 手動の

hands-on learning environment 実践的な学習環境

hands-on management 経営幹部が事業の全レベルで直接関与する経営方式

hands-on manager 自ら実務に携わるマネージャー［経営者］

hands-on operation 実地の職業活動

hands-on training 実地訓練, 実地職業訓練, 実地研修

Hantaan virus ハンタウイルス（ネズミが媒介して急性腎障害を起こす）

harassment 名 嫌がらせ, ハラスメント

academic harassment アカデミック・ハラスメント, アカハラ

harassment at work 職場での嫌がらせ

power harassment 職権による人権侵害, 職場での上司による嫌がらせ, パワハラ, パワー・ハラスメント（職務上の権限や地位を背景に, 上司が部下の人格や尊厳を傷つける行為）

sexual harassment in the workplace 職場での性的嫌がらせ, 職場でのセクハラ

hard 形 固い［堅い, 硬い］, 堅固な, 難しい, 困難な, 苦しい, つらい, 力のいる, 骨の折れる, 厳しい, 厳格な, 過酷な, 強気の, 議論の余地のない, 高値安定の, 習慣性の, アルコール度の強い, ハード

hard-charging 出世志向の強い

hard coal 無煙炭

hard core 中核, 中核分子, 主要部分, 慢性失業者

hard currency 硬貨, 交換可能通貨, 米ドルや金と交換できる通貨（＝hard money）

hard discounter 超安売り店, ハード・ディスカウンター

hard drugs 〈コカインやヘロインなど〉習慣性のある麻薬

hard going 難航

hard hat [hardhat] 安全用ヘルメット, 保安帽, 建設労働者, 〈労働者階級の〉保守主義者, 保守反動家, 頭の固い愛国者

hard-hitting anti-inflation policy 積極的なインフレ対策

hard labor 重労働

hard-lining 強硬路線を主張する, 強硬方針をとる

hard look 厳しい目付き, 精細な検討

hard money 硬貨, ハード・マネー（連邦議会選挙の候補者への直接献金のこと）

hard nut 粘り強く積極的な人

hard-pressed 〈財政的に〉苦しんでいる, 苦境にある, 〈金や時間に〉追われている

hard science 自然科学（物理学, 化学, 地質学など）

hard time 困難, ひどい目

hard times 不景気, 不況, 不況時, 難局

hard word 難解な言葉, きつい言葉

hard-core 形 中核の, 中核をなす, 絶対的な, 無条件の, 本格的な, 筋金入りの, 非妥協的な, 頑固な, 徹底抗戦の, どぎつい, 露骨な, 慢性的な (chronic)

hard-core pornography どぎついポルノ, ハードポルノ（＝hard porn：性行為を露骨に描写するポルノ）

the hard-core rebels 徹底抗戦の反乱者

the hard-core unemployment 慢性失業者, 慢性失業者群

hard-disk [hard-disc] drive ハードディスク駆動装置《略 HDD》

hard-hit 形 ひどい打撃［痛手, 被害］を受けた, 被害が大きかった［ひどかった］

hard landing 強行着陸, 〈宇宙船やロケットなどの〉硬着陸, 景気拡大期に続く急激な下降, ハードランディング

hard-landing economic policy 強行着陸（ハードランディング）の経済路線

hard-landing policy 強硬路線

hard line [hardline] 強硬路線, 強気路線

hard-line approach 強硬姿勢（＝hard-line stance）

hard-line stance 強硬姿勢

take a hard line on [over] …に対して強硬路線をとる

hard-liner 名 強硬派, 強硬派の人, 強硬論者

criticism by hard-liners 強硬派の批判

hard-liners and moderates 強硬派と穏健派

hard power ハード・パワー（軍事力, 核戦力や経済力など他国を強制できる力のこと。とくに「核戦力」は, 米国のハード・パワーの象徴ともいわれている）

hardened criminal 常習犯

hardhattism 名 保守反動主義, 反対意見弾圧政策, 弾圧政策

hardship 名 苦難, 困難, 困苦, 辛苦, 辛酸, 苦境, 困窮, 窮乏, 苦労, 圧制, 虐待

endure [bear] many hardships 多く［幾多］の苦難に耐える, 多くの困苦に耐える

face many hardships 多くの困難［苦難］に立ち向かう

go through financial hardships 経済的苦難を乗り切る
suffer economic hardship 経済的困窮にあえぐ

Harris poll ハリス(米世論調査会社)の意識調査, ハリス・インタラクティブ社の世論調査

hatchet 名 手斧
　bury the hatchet 和解する, 和睦する, 仲直りする, 戦いをやめる
　hatchet job 悪意に満ちた中傷, 嫌味たっぷりの批評, 厳しい批判, 中傷
　hatchet man 〈雇われ〉殺し屋, 犯罪者, 嫌な仕事の代行人, 暴露記事を書くジャーナリスト

haunt 動 苦しめる, 悩ませる, …の脳裏を去らない, 絶えずつきまとう, よく訪れる, 足繁く通う, よく出入りする

have yet to まだ…していない, …をまだ果たしていない, まだ…でいる
　▶The company *has yet to* receive approval for the action at its shareholders meeting. 同社は, 株主総会でこの措置の承認をまだ得ていない.

havoc 名 大混乱, 大損害, 大破壊, 大きな影響, 無秩序, 荒廃

hay fever 花粉症, 枯れ草熱 (=pollen allergy, pollinosis)

hazard map 災害予測地図, ハザード・マップ

HCV C型肝炎ウイルス (**hepatitis C virus**の略)

head 動 進む, …に向かう, …を率いる, …を統括[指揮]する, 主導する, …の先頭に立つ, 〈会社を〉経営する
　be heading downwards 下降トレンドを描く
　head along 前進する
　head down 下げ相場になる
　head for bankruptcy 破産に向かう, 破産に傾く
　head into …に向かう
　head off …を防ぐ[防止する], …を遮る, …を回避する, …を食い止める, …させないようにする
　head off to …に向かう
　▶The company's business management and planning headquarters is *headed* by its representative director. 同社の経営企画管理本部は, 代表取締役が統括している.

head 名 責任者, 最高責任者, 指導者, 経営者, 社長, 党首, ファン, 麻薬常習者, ヘッド
　be [stand] head and shoulders above …よりはるかに優れている, …よりずば抜けている, …より抜きん出ている
　be over head and ears 〈借金などで〉首が回らない, 夢中になっている
　bury one's head in the sand 事実を見ようとしない, 現実を無視する
　head count 人口調査, 世論調査, 頭数, 雇用人数
　head hunter [headhunter] 人材スカウト会社, 人材スカウト業, 人材スカウト係, 雇用担当者
　head office 本社, 本店, 本部, 本拠 (=headquarters, home office)
　head shop マリファナ専門店, マリファナ用品店
　head trip 知的経験, 高揚感
　per head 1人当たり
　stick one's head in the sand 真相を認めようとしない, 現実から目をそらす

head-to-head 形 接戦の, 互角の勝負の

headline 名 〈新聞や雑誌などの〉見出し, 〈本の章などの〉表題, 欄外見出し(heading), 〈ページの〉柱, 〈ニュースの〉主な項目
　banner headline 〈新聞第一面トップの〉トップ抜き大見出し, 全段抜き大見出し, 全段大見出し
　hit [grab, make] (the) headlines 大きく報じられる[報道される], 重大ニュースになる, 大々的に[大きく]取り扱われる, 大々的に宣伝される
　news headlines ニュースの主な項目

headquartered 形 …に本社[本部, 本店]を置く, …に本社が設けられている

health 名 健康, 健康状態, 健全性, 保健, 医療
　corporate health 企業の健全性, 企業体質, 経営体質
　credit health 信用の健全性, 信用の質
　health examination 健康診断
　health facilities 保健施設
　health farm ヘルス・センター
　health-giving exercise 健康運動
　health hazard 健康に有害な物質
　health kicks 健康マニア
　health maintenance organization 健康医療団体, 健康医療組織, 医療友の会《略 HMO》
　health physics 保健物理学
　health resort 保養地
　health service 公共医療サービス
　health spa 減量道場, スポーツ・ジム, ヘルス・センター
　health supplements 健康補助食品
　health tips 健康に関するアドバイス
　health visitor 家庭巡回保健婦
　industrial health 産業衛生学, 労働衛生学
　mental health 心の健康
　Ministry of Health, Labour and Welfare

厚生労働省
National Health Service 国民医療制度
occupational health program 衛生管理制度
public health center 保健所
public health service 公衆衛生サービス
retiree health benefits 退職者健康保険

health care [healthcare] 健康医療, 健康管理, 医療, 医療保険, ヘルスケア
  health care expense 健康医療費, 医療費 (＝health care cost：米国の健康保険制度は, 国民皆保険ではなく, 民間保険会社が販売する医療保険が中心。そのため, 福利厚生の一環として, 米国の企業は従業員や退職者の医療保険への加入を支援している)
  health care industry 医療産業 (＝health care service)
  health care insurance program 医療保険制度, 医療制度
  health care (delivery) marketplace 医療サービス市場
  health care provider 医療機関
  health care reform 医療改革, 医療制度の改革
  health care sector 医療部門
  health care services 医療サービス
  health care system 医療制度
  home health-care business [service] 在宅医療サービス, 在宅ケア・サービス

health insurance 健康保険
  health insurance card 保険証
  health insurance society 健康保険組合
  health insurance system 健康保険制度, 医療保険制度 (＝health insurance plan)
  national health insurance 国民健康保険
  voluntary health insurance 任意健康保険

healthy 形 健康的な, 健全な, 好調な, 順調な, 堅調な, 活況の, 活力のある, 有益な, 相当な, かなりの, ヘルシー
  healthy balance sheet 健全な財務体質
  healthy diet 健康に良い食事
  healthy foreign demand 海外からの活発な引き合い, 堅調な外需
  healthy food 健康食品
  healthy growth 健全な成長, 順調な伸び
  healthy increase 好調な伸び, 順調な伸び, 堅調な伸び (＝healthy advance, healthy gain, healthy growth)
  healthy mind 健全な精神
  healthy profit かなりの利益, 大きな利益
  post a healthy gain [advance, growth, increase] 順調な伸びを示す, 好調な伸びを示す
  rise by a healthy margin 大幅に増加する

hearing 名 意見聴取, 公聴会, 聴聞会,〈裁判所の〉審理, 公判, 審問,〈委員会などの〉尋問[審判]
  congressional hearings 米連邦議会の公聴会
  FTC hearings 公正取引委員会(FTC)の審判
  hold a public hearing 公聴会を開く
  open hearing 公聴会
  preliminary hearing 予備審理
  private hearing 非公開の聴聞会
  public hearing 公聴会, 公判
  Senate hearing 米上院公聴会
  the first hearing of a trial 初公判

heartening 形 元気づけられる, 勇気づけられる, 励まされる, 心強い

heartland 名〈地方の〉中心部, 中心地, 中心地域, 心臓部, お膝元

heat island phenomenon ヒート・アイランド現象

heat-related ailments 熱中症
heat-resistant material 耐熱材
heat up 〈徐々に〉熱くなる, 激しくなる, 激化する,〈状況が〉悪化する, 緊迫する,〈議論が〉白熱する
heat wave 熱波, 炎暑
heavily indebted people 多重債務者
heavily indebted poor countries 重債務貧困国《略 HIPCs》

heavy 形 重い, 重質の, 大量の, 大規模の, 大型の, 多額の, 巨額の, 重大な, 活発な
  heavy advance [rise] 大暴騰
  heavy borrower 大口の借り手
  heavy capex 多額の設備投資, 大型の設備投資
  heavy decline [fall] 大暴落
  heavy handed action 手荒い行為
  heavy investment 大型設備投資, 多額[巨額]の設備投資 (＝heavy capex)
  heavy losses 巨額の損失
  heavy oil products 重油製品
  heavy order 大量注文
  heavy payment 巨額の支払い, 巨額の支出
  heavy user 大量利用者, 大口使用者[利用者], ヘビー・ユーザー

heavy penalty tax 重加算税 (＝heavy additional tax)

heel 名 かかと, かかと状のもの, 卑劣な奴, 信頼できない者, 後半, 最後の部分, ヒール
  at the heels of …のすぐ後に続いて, …の直後

hegemonism

に引き続いて
bring [call] a person to heel …を服従させる, …を従わせる, …を抑え込む
dig one's heels [feet, toes] in 頑固に拒否する, 自分の考え[主張]を貫く (＝in one's heels)
on [upon] the heels of …の直後に引き続いて, …のすぐ後に
tread on one's heels …のすぐ後の続く (＝tread on the heels of)
under the heel of …に(完全に)支配されて, …に踏みにじられて, …にしいたげられて
hegemonism 名 覇権主義
hegemony 名 覇権, 覇権主義(hegemonism), 支配, 支配力, 政治的支配権, 盟主権, 主導権, 実権, 指導権, 指導力(leadership), 優位, 優位性, 優勢, ヘゲモニー
　absolute hegemony in Asia アジアでの絶対的覇権, アジアでの絶対的優位性
　economic hegemony 経済的支配権
　hegemony of the globe 世界主導権
　hold [assume, have] the hegemony of …の覇権を掌握する[握る], …を支配する
　hold economic and political hegemony 経済と政治を支配する
　maritime hegemony 海洋覇権
　obtain the hegemony of …に対して覇権を獲得する
　political hegemony 政治的支配権
　struggle for commercial hegemony [supremacy] 商業上の覇権を競う
heighten 動 高める, 強める, 増す, 増大させる, 激化させる, 増す, 強まる
　heighten public awareness about …に対する一般の認識[意識]を高める, …に関する一般の知識を高める
　heightened competition 競争の激化
　heightened efficiency 効率向上
　heightened risk リスクの増大
heinous 形 極悪な, 凶悪な, 非道な, 恐るべき, 忌まわしい, 憎むべき, 法外な
heir apparent 後継者
Helicobacter pylori ヘリコバクター・ピロリ菌 (胃かいようの原因となる胃のバクテリア[細菌])
helm 名 指導的地位, 指揮権, 〈船の〉舵
　be at the helm of …の舵を握る, …を支配する, …を牛耳る, …を指導する立場にある
　take the helm 政権を取る, 政権を握る (＝take the helm of the nation)
　take the helm of …の舵を取る, …を指導する
help 動 支援する, 援助する, 後押しする, 助ける, 支える, 助長する, 促進する, 改善する, 活性化する, …の要因[一因]となる, …に貢献する, …に寄与する, 追い風になる, 〈病気などを〉治す, 和らげる
　help one's ruin 破滅を早める
　help to raise production 増産を促進する
　help to support the stock 株価を支える要因[一因]になる
help 名 支援, 援助, 助力, 助け, 役に立つこと, 後押し, 助長, 促進, 救助, 救済貢献, 寄与, 従業員, 雇い人, お手伝い, 救済手段, 治療法, 対処法, ヘルプ
　dealer helps 販売店援助
　domestic help 家事手伝い
　help desk 問い合わせ窓口, 顧客サービス担当部署
　Help for Sellers 販売者用ヘルプ
　help-wanted ad [advertisement] 求人広告
hemorrhage 動 出血する, 大量出血する, 〈巨額の〉資産を失う, 失う, 損失を出す, 急速に減少する
hemorrhage [hemorrhaging] 名 流出, 損失, 出血, 大量流出, 激減
　asset hemorrhage 資産の流出
　cerebral hemorrhage 脳出血
　financial hemorrhage 資金の流出, 金融上の損失, 損失
hepatic disorder 肝機能障害
hepatitis 名 肝炎
　hepatitis B virus B型肝炎ウイルス(HBV)
　hepatitis C virus C型肝炎ウイルス(HCV)
　hepatitis E virus E型肝炎ウイルス(HEV)
　hepatitis infection 肝炎感染
herald 動 予告する(foretell), 告げる(announce), 告知する, 布告する(proclaim), 案内する, 先触れ[前触れ]する
herald 名 予告, 告知, 前兆, 前触れ, 先触れ, 先駆者, 告知者, 伝達者, 報道者, ヘラルド
Heugens ホイヘンス(米航空宇宙局(NASA)と欧州宇宙機関(ESA)の土星探査機カッシーニから2004年12月24日に切り離され, 日本時間で1月14日夜, 土星最大の衛星タイタンに着陸. その後, 軌道を周回するカッシーニにタイタンの観測データを送信)
hierarchy 名 階級組織, 階級制度, 階層制度, 職制制, 序列, 上下関係, 上層部, 支配層, 組織化, 体系づけ, ヒエラルキー
　command hierarchies 命令系統
　established hierarchies 既存の上下関係

hierarchy of goals 目標の階層構造
hierarchy of needs 欲求階層（＝needs hierarchy）
hierarchu of responsibilities 責任の序列
management hierarchy 経営階層
occupational hierarchy 職業階層
organizational hierarchy 組織の階層, 組織の序列, 組織の上下関係
vertical hierarchy 垂直的段階組織

high 名 高値, 最高, 最高値, 最高記録, 新記録
all time high 過去最高, 史上最高値, 上場来の高値, 過去最多, 過去最悪
be near all-time highs 過去最高に近い水準にある
be through many highs and lows 多くの浮き沈みを経験する
historical high 過去最高, 過去最高の水準（＝historic high）
intraday high ざら場の高値, 取引時間中の高値
make a high of …の高値を付ける
reach a historical high of 過去最高の…に達する
reach a new historical high 過去最高を更新する
remain near a high 最高値近辺で推移する
set [hit] a new high 新記録を樹立する, 新高値をつける, 過去最高を更新する, 過去最高となる
strike new highs above …を上回る過去最高値をつける
the word from high on 天の声
week's high 週の高値
year high 年間最高値

high 形 高い, 高度な, 高水準の, 高級な, 強い, 大きな, 最重要な, 活発な
high alert 厳戒態勢
high arctic 極北の地
high atmospheric pressure 高気圧
high blood pressure 高血圧
high circles 上流社会
high command 〈軍の〉最高司令部, 最高幹部, 最高首脳部, 首脳部
high commission [High Commission] 高等弁務官事務所
High Commissioner 高等弁務官
High Court 〈米国の〉最高裁判所
high day 祝日, 祭日, 祝祭日
high domestic demand 内需拡大
high end 高級志向（low end＝大衆志向）

high fashion 最新流行, 最新のデザイン, 高級なデザイン, オートクチュール, 最新流行の高級服飾品
high finance 多額の金融取引［金融操作］, 多額の融資, 大規模な金融活動
high five 祝福
high foreign policy 高次の外交政策
high growth rate 高い伸び率, 高成長率
high horse 傲慢な態度
high life [living] 贅沢な生活, 派手な暮らし
high noon 正午, 真昼, 最盛時, 絶頂
high places 〈組織の〉重要ポスト, 上層部
high point 見せ場, 絶頂, ハイライト（＝high spot）
high polymer 高分子化合物
high posture 高姿勢（＝high profile）
high-priced product 高価格品, 高額商品
high priest 第一人者, 指導者, 大祭司, 祭司長
high profile 脚光を浴びること, 注目されること, 注目されている人, 派手に振舞う人, 高姿勢をとる人, 高姿勢, 明確な態度
high public prosecutor's office 高等検察庁
high resolution 高解像度, 高分解能, 高精度, 高精細度, ハイゾリューション
high road 幹線道路, 主要道路, 公道, 確実な道, 正道, 近道
high seas 公海, 外洋, 外海（＝the open seas）
high season 最盛期, 繁忙期（peak season）, 稼ぎ時, 書き入れ時
high sign 〈警告, 再確認の〉合図, 警告の身振り, 目配せ
high spirits 上機嫌, 陽気, 元気
high spot 最高潮, 楽しい瞬間, 見せ場, 絶頂, 頂点, 最も重要な部分, ハイライト（＝high point）
high street 大通り, 本通り, 目抜き通り
high style 拡張高い文体
high summer 真夏, 盛夏
high table 主賓席, 〈大学食堂の〉教官用食卓
high tide 高潮, 満潮, 満潮時, 絶頂, 最高潮, クライマックス
high time 好機, 潮時, 楽しいひととき, 愉快な時, 歓楽の時
high touch 〈握手などで〉体に触れること, 人間的感触
high treason 反逆, 大逆罪
high water 満潮, 高潮, 最高水位
high words 激論
higher earnings 増益, 高収益
higher education 高等教育, 大学教育

higher prices 値上げ, 物価上昇, 価格上昇
higher profits 増益, 高収益
higher turnover 売上高の増加, 取引の活発化
higher volume 販売数量の増加
higher yen 円高
highest common factor 最大公約数
high-definition 形 高鮮明度の, 高品位の, 高解像度の《略 HD》
  high-definition DVD player 高品位DVDドライブ
  high-definition television [TV] 高品位テレビ, 高解像度テレビ, 高精細度テレビ, ハイビジョンTV《略 HDTV》
high-end 形 高級志向の, 高級の, 超高速の, 高速型, 高度, 最高価格帯の, 高価なフル装備の, ハイエンド
  high-end cosmetics 高級化粧品
high frequency 高周波《略 HF [hf]》
  high-frequency communications 高周波通信
  high-frequency radio wave band 高周波数帯, 高無線周波数帯
high-level 形 高位高官の, トップクラスによる, 上層部による, 高所での, 高度の, 高水準の, 高レベルの, ハイレベルの
  high-level language 高級言語, 高水準言語, 高レベル言語
  high-level nuclear waste 高レベル核廃棄物
  high-level officials [personnel] 高官
  high-level radioactive waste 高レベル放射性廃棄物
  high-level talks ハイレベル協議
high-profile 形 脚光を浴びる, 世間の注目を集める, 人目を引く, 注目の, 著名な, 明確な, 鮮明な, 大型の
  high-profile issues 注目の銘柄, 注目を集めている銘柄
high-ranking 形 地位 [身分] の高い, 高官の, 上級の
high return 高収益, 高い収益率, 高い運用益, 高利回り, 高いリターン, ハイリターン
  high-risk high return ハイリスク・ハイリターン (危険性の高い金融資産で高い運用益が期待できること)
  higher return asset 利回りの高い資産
  provide high return 利回りが高い
high rise [high-rise, highrise] 高層ビル, 高層建築 (＝high-rise building, skyscraper)
high-speed 形 高速の, 高速度の
high-spirited 形 元気がいい, 威勢がよい, 血気盛んな, 上機嫌の, 盛大な
high-stakes 名 大ばくち, 大きな賭け, 形 大ばくちの, 大きな賭けの, 一か八かの
  high-stakes meeting 一か八かの会談, のるかそるかの会談 (＝make-or-break meeting)
high-tech 名 先端技術, 高度技術, 高度科学技術, ハイテク (＝high technology)
  high-tech capability 高い技術力
  high-tech industry 先端産業, 高度技術産業, ハイテク産業 (＝high technology industry)
high technology 高度先端技術, 高度技術, ハイテク, ハイテクノロジー (＝advanced technology, high-tech)
high yield 高利回り, 大きい利回り
higher-priced 形 値上りした
highlight 動 目立たせる, 強調する, 際立たせる, 浮き彫りにする, 取りあげる, 絞り込む, 象徴する
highlight 名 焦点, 目玉商品, 際立った特徴, 呼び物, 最重要事件, 最重要部分, 最も興味を引く部分, 最高潮の場面, 最も明るい部分, ハイライト
highly 副 高度に, 極度に, 極めて, 非常に, 大いに, 高く評価して, 好意的に
  highly-centralised government [state] 権力が極度に集中している国, 中央集権が徹底している国
  highly cyclical 景気循環色が強い, 景気循環の影響を大きく受ける
  highly descended 名門の出で
  highly enriched uranium 高濃縮ウラン《略 HEU》
  highly leveraged 負債比率が高い, 財務レバレッジが高い
  highly liquid investments 流動性の高い投資
  highly skilled business expert 高度専門職業人
  highly sophisticated microchips 高性能マイクロチップ
  speak highly of …を大いに賞賛する
  think highly of …を高く評価する
hijack [highjack] 動 〈飛行機などを〉乗っ取る, 〈輸送中の貨物を〉強奪する, 奪い取る, 襲う, 〈アイデアなどを〉盗用する, ハイジャックする
hijack 名 乗っ取り, 乗っ取り事件, 強奪, 盗用, 襲撃, ハイジャック (＝hijacking)
hijacker 名 ハイジャック犯, 乗っ取り犯, 輸送中

hike / holder

の貨物強奪犯

hike 動 引き上げる、上げる、積み増す
- **hike interest rates** 金利を引き上げる、利上げする
- **hike loan loss provisions** 貸倒れ引当金を積み増す

hike 名 引上げ、値上げ、値上がり、上昇
- **discout rate hike** 公定歩合の引上げ
- **fare hike** 料金引上げ、値上げ
- **further rate hike** もう一段の利上げ
- **hike in the consumption tax** 消費税の引上げ
- **price hike** 値上げ、価格引上げ、物価上昇
- **rate hike** 利上げ、金利の引上げ（=interest rate hike）
- **wage hike** 賃上げ、賃金引上げ

Hill 名 米連邦議会、米国議会（⇒Capitol）

hint 名 暗示、ほのめかし、気配、兆港、兆し、助言、有益な情報、ヒント

HIPCs 重債務貧困国（heavily indebted poor countriesの略）

hire 動 採用する、雇う、雇用する、賃貸しする、賃借りする、金を払う

hire 名 賃金、給料、使用料、賃借料、社員、新入社員

hiring 名 採用、雇用、新規雇用、雇用関係、雇用契約、新入社員、賃貸借
- **direct hiring** 直接雇用
- **hiring of a ship** 用船
- **hiring requirements** 雇用要件
- **marginal cost of hiring** 限界雇用費用

hit 動 打撃を与える、…に達する、記録する、打つ
- **be hard hit** ひどい目にあう、大きな打撃を受ける
- **hit a new high** 新高値をつける、過去最高値を記録する、過去最高値となる
- **hit a new low** 新安値を付ける、最安値を更新する
- **hit a snag** 思わぬ障害にぶつかる
- **hit an all-time high** 過去最高に達する、史上最高値を記録する、最高記録に達する
- **hit an all-time low** 過去最低に達する、史上最安値を記録する、最低記録に達する
- **hit bottom** 底を打つ、底をつく、底入れする、底固めする、谷になる（=bottom out）
- **hit the ground running** 熱心に力強く進めて行く、快進撃を続ける、上々の滑り出しをする
- **hit the market** 市場に登場する、発売される（=go on sale）

hit 名 打撃、大当たり、大成功、検索結果、検索項目の該当［該当項目］、〈ホームページなどの〉利用、〈サイトへの〉アクセス［アクセス件数］、ヒット
- **hit product** ヒット商品
- **make [score] a big hit** 大ヒットする、大当たりを取る
- **take a hit** 損失を出す、損をかぶる

HIV エイズウイルス、ヒト免疫不全ウイルス、エイズ（human immunodeficiency virusの略）
- **be infected with HIV** エイズウイルス（HIV）に感染する、エイズに感染する
- **HIV antibody** HIVの抗体
- **HIV carrier** エイズ感染者
- **HIV positive** HIV陽性の、エイズウイルス陽性の、HIV感染を示す陽性反応

Hizbollah guerrillas ヒズボラ（イスラム教シーア派組織）

hoarded stock タンス株（個人などが株券の形で保有し、証券保管振替機構に預託していない株式のこと）

hoax 名 狂言、捏造、人をかつぐこと、一杯食わせること、悪ふざけ、いたずら
- **bomb hoax** 狂言爆弾事件
- **make a hoax call** いたずら電話をする
- **play a hoax on** …にいたずらする

ho-hum 形 退屈な、つまらない、面白みのない、ありふれた（ho-humは、退屈なときに出す「アーア」などの発声を意味する間投詞として使われるときもある）

hold 名 把持、把握、掌握、勢力、支配力、影響力、威力、一時的停止［遅れ］、中止、延長、足場、船倉、〈飛行機の〉貨物室、ホールド
- **be on hold** 一時保留となる、延期される、待機している
- **be put on hold** 一時中止される、据え置かれる
- **get [catch, lay, seize, take] hold of** …をつかむ（grasp）、…を理解する、…を獲得する
- **hold back on** …を差し控える、…にしり込みする
- **hold out for** …をあくまで主張する、…をあくまで要求する、支持する
- **hold time** 〈ロケットなどの打上げ作業の〉遅れ
- **keep ... on hold** …を据え置く
- **lose one's hold against** …に対して威力［影響力］を失う
- **put ... on hold** …を一時中止する、一時棚上げにする
- **take hold** 定着する、確立する

holder 名 所有者、保有者、保持者、所持人、株主、契約者、会員、ホールダー（=owner）

holding

- de facto holder of the shares　株の実質保有者
- debenture [bond] holder　社債保持者, 債券保有者
- debt holder　債券保有者
- draft [bill] holder　手形所持人
- fund holder　年金制度の受託者,〈英国の〉公債所有者, 公債投資家
- loan holder　債権者
- portfolio holder　金融資産保有者, ポートフォリオ保有者
- total stock holders' equity　株主持ち分合計

holding 名　所有, 保有, 保持, 占有, 所有持ち分, 保有株, 持ち株比率, 子会社, 所有財産, 保有財産
- asset holding　資産保有
- bond cross holding　債券持ち合い
- holding period　所有期間, 保有期間, 投資期間
- lower one's holding in th company　同社の持ち株比率を引き下げる
- security holding　証券所有, 証券保有
- stock [share] holding　株式保有

holding company　持ち株会社 (=holding corporation：⇒management resources)

　持ち株会社 ⊃「持ち株会社」は, 他社の株式を所有してグループ企業を形成し, 傘下のグループ企業を統括してグループ全体の戦略を策定するほか, 投資・資金計画やトップ人事などを支配する。これに対して持ち株会社の「グループ企業」は, 独立会社として持ち株会社の計画・方針に基づき独自の計画を立てて事業活動を行うとともに, トップ以外の人事権なども持つとされる。

holdings 名　持ち株, 保有株, 保有高, 持ち株比率, 持ち株会社, 資産
- latent losses on holdings of stocks　保有株式の含み損
- liquidate one's holdings　持ち株[保有債券]を売却する
- long-term equity holdings　長期保有株式
- portfolio holdings　金融資産保有高, ポートフォリオ保有
- stock holdings　保有株式, 持ち株, 出資比率

holidaymakers 名　休日の行楽客 (=vacationers, vacationists)

hollow out　…に穴を開ける, …に空洞をつくる, …をくり抜く

hollowing-out 名　空洞化 (=hollowing, hollowing out, hollowization)

hollowization 名　空洞化 (=hollowing, hollowing out, hollowing-out)

hologram 名　ホログラム, レーザー写真

holy city　聖都, 聖地

home appliance　家電, 家庭用電気器具, 白物
- home appliance manufacturer　家電メーカー (=electrical appliance maker)

home-based worker　在宅就労者

home delivery service　宅配サービス, 宅配業務, 宅配事業

home education　家庭教育

home equity loan　ホーム・エクイティ・ローン (所有する住宅の市場価値から負債を差し引いた正味価値を担保にお金を借りる仕組み)

home foreclosure　住宅の差し押さえ, 住宅ローンの焦げ付き

home mortgage　住宅ローン (=home mortgage loan)
- home mortgage loan　住宅ローン

home page　⇒homepage

home shopping　ホーム・ショッピング, テレビ通販

Homeland Security Department　〈米〉国土安全省

homeless 形　家のない, 宿なしの, 飼い主のない, ホームレスの

homemaker 名　主婦

homepage 名　ホームページ (=home page, site, Web page, Web site, welcome page)

homicide 名　殺人
- homicide by negligence　業務上過失致死

homogeneous 形　均質の, 同種の, 等質の, 同質の

hook, line and sinker　まったく, 完全に, すっかり

hooligan 名　フーリガン

hopeful 名　前途有望な人, 候補者, 志願者, 期待される選手[チーム]
- gold-medal hopeful　有望な金メダル候補
- presidential hopeful　大統領候補

hospice 名　末期患者専門病院, 終末期医療施設, 末期患者の看護施設, ホスピス

host 動　主催する, 開催する,〈番組の〉司会をする,〈パーティーなどで〉主人役を務める, 歓待する

host 名　主催者, 開催国, 開催地, 議長国, 会場提供者,〈番組の〉司会者, 司会役,〈動植物の〉生息地, ホスト

host computer ホスト・コンピュータ, 大型汎用機, ホスト計算機, 多重アクセス・コンピュータ
hostage 名 人質
hostile 形 敵対的な
- **hostile mergers and acquisitions** 敵対的M&A（企業の合併・買収）, 敵対的M&A（⇒ mergers and acquisitions）
- **hostile takeover** 敵対的買収, 敵対的M&A（＝hostile acquisition, unsolicited takeover）
- **hostile takeover bid** 敵対的株式公開買付け, 敵対的TOB, 株式公開買付けによる敵対的買収, 敵対的買収（＝hostile bid）
- **hostile (takeover) bidder** 敵対的買収者（＝hostile acquirer, hostile bidder）

hot-button issue 重大な争点, 重大な問題, 強い関心を呼ぶ問題
house 名 商社, 商店, 会社, 業者, 取引所, 住宅, ハウス
- **acceptance [accepting] house** 手形引受商社, 引受商社, 手形引受業者
- **house arrest** 自宅軟禁
- **house [employee house] organ** 社内報
- **house renovator** 住宅リフォーム会社（＝housing renovation firm）
- **issuing house** 証券発行会社, 発行商社
- **securities [brokerage] house** 証券会社（＝stockbroking house）
- **trading house** 証券会社, 商社, 貿易会社

House 名 〈米国の〉下院（435議席で任期は2年）, 議事堂, 議会, ロンドン株式取引所
- **Bar of the House** 議場正面席
- **Clerk of the House** 米下院事務総長
- **Committee of the whole House on the State of the Union** 米連邦の現況に関する下院全院委員会
- **Committee on House Administration** 下院管理委員会
- **first-term House members** 下院の新人議員
- **hard line House bills** 強硬な下院案
- **House and Senate Office Buildings** 米上下両院議員会館
- **House and the Senate** 米上下両院
- **House Calendar** 米下院議事日程, ハウス・カレンダー
- **House Chamber** 米下院本会議
- **House Committee on Energy and Commerce** 米下院エネルギー・商業委員会
- **House Majority leader** 下院院内総務
- **House Manual** 下院便覧
- **House of Commons** 〈英国・カナダの〉下院
- **House of Councilors** 〈日本の〉参議院（＝米国のthe Senate）
- **House of Lords** 〈英国の〉上院
- **House resolution** 下院決議
- **House proposal** 下院案
- **House resolution** 下院決議
- **Law Revision Counsel** 米下院の法律改正顧問
- **Lower House [lower house]** 〈日本の〉衆議院（House of Representatives）, 〈英国の〉下院（House of Commons）
- **order of business of the House** 米下院の議事運営
- **original engrossed House bill** 下院から回されてきた原法案
- **report a bill favorably to the House** 下院本会議に上程する
- **the Speaker of the House** 米下院議長（＝the Speaker）
- **the speaker [Speaker] of the House of Commons** 英下院議長（＝House Speaker）
- **Upper House [upper house]** 〈2院制議会の〉上院（＝英国のthe House of Lords, 米国のthe Senate）

House of Representatives 〈日本の〉衆議院, 〈米国連邦議会の〉下院
- **Deschler's Procedure in the House of Representatives** デシュラーの下院手続き集
- **the House of Representatives election** 衆院選挙
- **the leader of the House of Representatives** 米下院幹部
- **the speaker of the House of Representatives** 衆議院議長, 米下院議長（＝the Speaker of the House）
- **the U.S. House of Representatives** 米議会下院
- **the U.S. House of Representatives Committee on Oversight and Government Reform** 米下院の監視・政府改革委員会

House Standing Committees 米下院常任委員会

Agriculture	農業委員会
Appropriations	歳出委員会
Armed Services	軍事委員会
Banking, Finance and Urban Affairs	銀行・金融・都市問題委員会

Budget	予算委員会
District of Columbia	コロンビア特別地区委員会
Education and Labor	教育・労働委員会
Energy and Commerce	エネルギー・商業委員会
Foreign Affairs	外交委員会
Government Operation	政府運営委員会
House Administration	下院管理委員会
Interior and Insular Affairs	内務・島嶼問題委員会
Judiciary	司法委員会
Merchant Marine and Fisheries	海運・漁業委員会
order of business of the House	下院の議事運営
Post Office and Civil Service	郵便・公務委員会
Public Works and Transportation	公共事業・運輸委員会
Rules	議事委員会
Science, Space and Technology	科学・宇宙・技術委員会
Small Business	中小企業委員会
Standards of Official Conduct	公職者倫理委員会
Veteran's Affairs	復員軍人委員会
Ways and Means	歳入委員会
Clerk	事務総長

houseclean 動 改革する, 行政改革する, 一新する, 粛清する, 人員整理する, 合理化する, 掃除する
household 名 家庭, 世帯, 所帯, 家計
 household assets 家計金融資産, 個人の金融資産
 household consumption 家計消費, 家計消費支出
 household deposit 個人預金高
 household financial assets 個人金融資産
 household income 家計所得
 household outlays 1世帯当たり消費支出, 家計支出, 個人消費 (=household spending)
 household passed 受信可能世帯
 household purchasing power 家計の購買力
 household survey 家計調査
 low income households 低所得者層
 non-salaried household 一般世帯
 non-workers household 非勤労者世帯
 wage-earning [workers] households サラリーマン世帯, 勤労者世帯
housing 名 住宅, 住宅市場
 housing area 住宅地
 housing supplier 住宅メーカー
housing loan 住宅金融, 住宅ローン
 housing loan claim 住宅ローンの債権
 housing loan tax break 住宅ローン減税, 住宅減税
housing starts 住宅着工, 住宅着工戸数, 住宅着工件数, 新設住宅着工戸数, 新規住宅着工件数
hover 動 さまよう, うろつく, うろうろする,〈ある水準に〉とどまる, 低迷する, 付きまとう,〈ヘリコプターなどが〉飛び舞う
 hover around 10 percent level 10％前後で推移する, 10％の水準で推移する
 hover at around …のあたりを低迷する
 hover between life and death 生死の境をさまよう
howitzer 名 りゅう弾砲, 曲射砲
HPV ヒトパピローマウイルス (**human papillomavirus**の略。100種類ほどあって, HPV16型とHPV18型は子宮頸部がんの原因ウイルスとして特定されている)
HSR Act ハート・スコット・ロディノ改正反トラスト法, HSR法 (**Hart-Scott-Rodino Antitrust Improvements Act**の略)
hub 名 中心, 中央部, 中軸, 中核, 中枢, 拠点, 重要拠点, 集線装置 (LANの複数のケーブルを束ねる装置), ハブ
 hub airport 拠点空港, ハブ空港 (各方面から国際線が集まって, 近隣国や国内の他空港に乗り継ぎできる拠点空港)
 the Hub 〈米マサチューセッツ州の〉ボストン市
 the hub of commerce 商業の中心
 the hub of the domestic airline industry 国内線の拠点空港
huge 形 大きな, 巨大な, 多大な, 莫大な (enormous), 大規模の, 大型の, 大幅な, 巨額の, 超有名な, ビッグな
 huge amounts of debt 巨額の負債
 huge current account deficits 巨額の経常赤字
 huge facilities 大規模施設, 大規模な生産拠点
 huge growth in demand 需要の大幅な伸び
 huge stimulus measures 大型の景気刺激策, 大型の経済対策
human 形 人間の, 人間的な, 人間らしい, ヒューマン, 名 人間
 human affairs 人事

human antibody ヒト抗体（人体に侵入した細菌やウイルスなどの異物にとりついて働きを奪う特殊なたんぱく質）
human assessment ヒューマン・アセスメント（経営管理技法の一つで，管理職の相互啓発訓練，マネジメント適制度診断，昇進候補者の選択などが含まれる）
human beta interferon ヒト・ベータ・インターフェロン
human capital 人的資本，人的資源，人材
human cells 人間の細胞
human chain 人間の鎖
human clones クローン人間
human cloning コピー人間作り，ヒトのクローン
human dry docking [dock] 人間ドック
human ecology 人間生態学，人間環境，ヒューマン・エコロジー
human embryonic stem cells ヒトES細胞，ヒト胚性幹細胞
human energy 人的エネルギー，人力
human engineering 人間工学，人間管理《略 HE》
human environment 人間環境
human error 人災，人為ミス，人的ミス
human factors engineering 人間要素工学
human genome 人間の遺伝子，人間の全遺伝情報，ヒトゲノム
human growth hormone ヒト成長ホルモン
human immunodeficiency virus ヒト免疫不全ウイルス《略 HIV》
human information processing 人間情報処理
human intelligence 人的情報収集，情報収集分析活動，スパイによる情報収集，電子機器による諜報活動《略 HUMINT [humint]》
human interest stories 三面記事
human interface コンピュータと人間との対話，人とコンピュータ・システムとの接点（またはその技術），ヒューマン・インターフェース（＝man-machine interface）
human investment 人的投資
human leucocyte antigen ヒト白血球抗原
Human Life Amendment 〈米国の〉人間の生命に関する合衆国憲法修正案
Human Life Statute 〈米国の〉人命尊重法
human motivation 人間動機付け
human nature 人間性，人情
human potentials movement 人間潜在能力開発運動
human power 人的資源
human relations 人間関係，対人関係，人的関係，人間関係論，人間企業論
human sciences 人間科学，人文科学
human services 人的サービス，福祉サービス
human shield 人間の盾
human skill 人的熟練
human trafficking 人身売買
human torpedo 人間魚雷
human waste し尿
human-wave tactics 人海戦術
human resources 人的資源，人材，人事部，人事［人材］管理部門，労務管理部門
human resources [resource] administration 人的資源管理
human resources [resource] management 人的資源管理，人材管理《略 HRM》（人事労務管理のこと）
human resources [resource] planning 人的資源計画，人事［人員］計画
human rights 人権
human rights abuses 人権侵害
human rights activist 人権運動家，人権保護活動家
human rights advocates 人権派
human rights monitors 人権監視団体，人権監視機関
human rights violation 人権侵害
humanitarian 形 人道主義的な，人道的な，人道的見地からの，博愛主義の，人間中心主義の
humanitarian aid 人道支援，人道的支援，人道主義的支援
humanitarian assistance 人道支援，人道主義的援助，人道的支援物資
humanitarian corridor 人道回廊
humanitarian intervention 人道的介入
humanitarian issues 人道上の諸問題
humanitarian operations 人道作戦，人道的活動
humanitarian relief 人道的支援（＝humanitarian assistance）
humanitarian situation 人道的状況
on humanitarian grounds 人道的見地から，人道上
hunger-stricken 形 飢えに苦しむ
hunker down …の構えをとる，隠れる，潜伏する，座り込む，腰を据えてかかる，…に腰を据えて取

り組む
hurdle 名 障害, 困難, 難関, 障害物, ハードル
　clear the first hurdle　最初の難関を突破する
　jump the hurdle　障害を飛び越える, 結婚する
　stumble at the first hurdle　第一歩からつまずく
hurt 動 損害を与える, 損なう, 打撃を与える, 悪影響を受ける, 妨害する
　be hurt by　…で損害を受ける, …により打撃を受ける
　hurt consumer prices　消費者物価が上昇する
　hurt exports　輸出が打撃を受ける
　hurt one's reputation　…の評判を損なう
　hurt the yen　円が下落する, 円安となる, 円が売られる
hush money　口止め料
hybrid 名 ガソリン電気自動車, ハイブリッド車, 〈ヒトと動物の〉融合動物, 雑種, 混血児, 混成語, ハイブリッド
　hybrid car　ハイブリッド車, ガソリン電気自動車（＝hybrid vehicle）
　hybrid ES [embryonic stem] cell　異種間融合胚, 異種間ES細胞, 異種間胚性幹細胞
hydrogen 名 水素
　hydrogen fuel-cell vehicle　水素燃料電池車, 水素による燃料電池車[自動車]
hyperactivity disorder　多動性障害

I

i

IAEA 国際原子力機関 (International Atomic Energy Agencyの略)
IAIS 保険監督者国際機構 (International Association of Insurance Supervisorsの略)
IASB 国際会計基準審議会 (International Accounting Standards Boardの略)
IC chips IC (集積回路)チップ
IC tag 電子荷札, ICタグ (=integrated circuit tag)
ICAO 国際民間航空機関, イカオ (International Civil Aviation Organizationの略)
ICC 国際刑事裁判所 (International Criminal Courtの略)
icon 名 絵文字, アイコン
ICT 情報通信技術 (international communication technologyの略。情報処理の技術と通信の技術)
ICU 集中治療室 (intensive care unitの略)
ID 発信者番号, 識別符号, 識別番号, 認証 (identificationの略)
　ID card 身分証明書, IDカード (=identity card)
　ID number ID番号, 識別番号, 納税者番号, 取引先番号 (=identification number)
　palm vein ID system 手のひら静脈認証システム
　social security ID number 社会保障番号
IDA 国際開発協会, 第二世界銀行 (International Development Associationの略。発展途上国のうち特に所得の低い貧困国を対象に, 主に無利子融資による支援を行う世界銀行グループの国際機関。1960年発足, 現在は162か国が加盟している)
IDC インターネット・データ・センター (Internet data centerの略)
idea 名 考え, 構想, 意見, 見解, 思いつき, 着想, 考え方, 概念, 観念, 思想, 目的, 意図, 計画, 狙い, 見当, 感じ, 予感, 印象, 漠然とした知識, アイデア
　exchange ideas with …と意見交換する
　fixed idea 固定観念
　fresh idea 斬新なアイデア
　general ideas 一般観念
　idea advertising 意見広告
　idea generation アイデア創造, アイデア発想
　outdated idea 時代遅れの考え方 [思想]
identification 名 本人 [身元] 確認, 身分証明 [証明書], 確認, 確定, 同定, 特定, 照合, 検証, 識別, 識別番号, 発信者番号, 鑑定, 一体感《略 ID》
　bird identification book 鳥類同定図鑑
　feel identification with …との一体感を感じる
　identification card 身分証明書, IDカード (=identity card)
　identification of the signature 署名の鑑定
　identification section 鑑識課
　identification tag [disk] 認識票
　job identification 職務識別
　just identification 合致識別
　management identification 企業意識
　organizational identification 組織への一体化
　party identification 政党帰属意識
　personal identification number 個人識別番

号，〈銀行カードの〉個人暗証番号, 暗証番号, パスワード《略 PIN》
receiver terminal identification 送信先確認表示

identification number
ID番号, 識別番号, 納税者番号, 取引先番号（＝ID number, identifier number）

identify 動 特定する, 認定する, 確認する, 識別する, 見分ける, 表示する, 明示する, 明記する, 実名を明かす
▶ The police could not *identify* the cause of the man's death. 警察は，この男性の死因を特定できなかった．

identity 名 身元, 正体, 素性, 身分証明, 本質, 本人, 自分自身, 己（おのれ）自身, 自己認識, 個性, 独自性, 性格, 主体性, 同一, 同一性, 自己同一性, 一致, 帰属意識, 意識, 伝統, 類似, 類似例, 民族性, 国民性, 一体性, 企業イメージ, 個人情報, 住所・氏名, 恒等式, 作風, 芸風, アイデンティティ
  a sense of identity 一体感
  accounting identity 会計恒等式
  close identity 結びつき
  conceal one's identity …の身元を隠す
  confirm the identity of customers 顧客の身元を確認する
  corporate identity 企業[会社]としての独自性, 社風, 企業認識, 企業の存在意義, 企業イメージ統合戦略, コーポレート・アイデンティティ《略 CI》(CI計画には，一般に企業理念の確立，社名のロゴタイプや社章, シンボルマーク, 社用封筒, 便箋, 名刺などの統一，企業理念に基づく企業活動などが含まれる)
  definitional identity 定義式
  disclose one's own identity …の身元を明かす
  establish a person's identity …の身元を確認する[確かめる], …が本人であることを確認する, …の正体が分かる
  ex ante identity 事前的恒等式
  ex post identity 事後的恒等式
  find out the identity of the stalker ストーカーの正体を見破る
  identity card IDカード, 身分証明書（＝ID card, identification card）
  identity crisis 自己喪失, 自己同一性認識の危機, 自己同一性危機, ノイローゼ, 自己認識の危機, アイデンティティ・クライシス
  identity of the prospective third party purchaser 予定される第三者購入者の住所・氏名
  identity parade 事件の容疑者確認のため[面通しのため]警察署に集められた人の列（＝identification parade, lineup）
  identity theft 個人情報泥棒
  lose one's identity 主体性[本性]を失う, 自己を見失う, アイデンティティを失う
  make one's identity public …の身分を公表する
  mistaken [false] identity 人違い
  national identity 民族性, 国民性, 民族意識, 民族的[国民的]一体性
  prove a person's identity …の身元を明らかにする, …の身元を確かめる
  recognize a person's identity …が当人であると認める
  the sense of identity 個人としての自覚, 自信

ideology 名 理念主義, 観念論, 抽象的思考, 空想, 空論, 観念形態, 観念学, イデオロギー
idle real estate 遊休不動産
IEA 国際エネルギー機関（International Energy Agencyの略）
IEC 国際電気標準会議（International Electrotechnical Commissionの略）
IFRS 国際財務報告基準（International Financial Reporting Standardsの略。2004年まで「国際会計基準(IAS)」と呼ばれていた）
IGCC 石炭ガス化複合発電（integrated gasification combined cycleの略）
ignite 動 …に点火する, 火をつける, 発火させる, 引き起こす, 燃やす, 燃え上がらせる, 焼く, 燃焼させる, …を引き起こす発端になる, …に火がつく, …に燃え移る
  ignite antiwar passions 反戦感情に火をつける
  ignite fears of inflation インフレ懸念を呼ぶ
illegal 形 違法な, 非合法な, 不法な
  illegal access 不正アクセス
  illegal bid 不正入札
  illegal confinement 不法監禁
  illegal copy 違法コピー
  illegal donations ヤミ献金, 違法献金
  illegal dumping 不法投棄
  illegal employment 不法就労
  illegal entrant [alien, immigrant] 不法入国者
  illegal image 違法画像
  illegal moneylender 違法金融業者, ヤミ金融業者（＝illicit moneylenders）
  illegal trafficking 不法売買

illicit

illicit 形 違法の, 不法の, 不正な, 禁制の, 許されない, 不義の
- **illicit gain** 不正利益
- **illicit love** 不倫
- **illicit production of drugs** 麻薬密造
- **illicit sale of drugs** 麻薬の密売

image 名 画像, 映像, 心像, イメージ
- **biometrics image** 生体認証画像
- **live-action images** 実写並の画像
- **moving image** 動画
- **still image** 静止画像

imbalance 名 不均衡, 差, アンバランス
- **balance of payments imbalance** 国際収支の不均衡 (＝payment imbalance)
- **basic imbalance** 基礎的不均衡
- **global imbalance** 世界的な国際収支の不均衡, グローバル・インバランス
- **inventory imbalance** 過剰在庫
- **macro imbalances** マクロ経済の不均衡
- **supply and demand imbalances** 需要と供給の不均衡, 需給不均衡 (＝imbalances between supply and demand)
- **workload imbalance** 作業負担量［仕事量］の不均衡, 労働力の不均衡

IMF 国際通貨基金 (International Monetary Fundの略)
- **IMF annual consultation** IMF年次協議, IMF年次会議
- **IMF credit** IMF借款
- **IMF Board of Governors** IMF総務会
- **IMF drawing [purchase]** IMF引出し
- **IMF gross fund position** IMFグロス・ファンド・ポジション ((各国出資額×2) IMFの各国通貨保有額＋一般借入額)
- **IMF interim committee** IMF暫定委員会
- **IMF managing director** IMF専務理事
- **IMF mission** IMF代表団
- **IMF par value** IMF平価
- **IMF position** IMFポジション
- **IMF quota** IMF割当額, IMFクォータ (IMFが加盟国に割り当てている拠出金［IMFの加盟国への出資割当額］)
- **IMF reserve position** IMF準備ポジション (IMF加盟国からの借入金総額で, IMFがいつでも返済することになっている)
- **IMF reserve tranche** IMFリザーブ・トランシュ (IMFから無条件で融資される部分で, IMF割当額とIMF自国保有額との差額)
- **IMF special drawing account** IMF特別引出し勘定
- **IMF special drawing rights** IMF特別引出し権 《略 SDR [SDRs]》
- **IMF standby agreement** IMF借入予約協定, IMFスタンドバイ取決め［契約］
- **IMF subscription** IMF出資
- **Trust Fund of IMF** IMF信託基金

immigration 名 移住, 移民, 移民者数, 出入国管理業務, 出国［入国］審査
- **illegal immigration** 不法入国
- **Immigration and Naturalization Service** 〈米〉入国帰化局, 移民帰化局 《略 INS》
- **immigration authorities** 入国管理当局
- **immigration control** 出入国管理, 入国審査
- **Immigration Control and Refugee Recognition Law** 入管難民法
- **immigration control office** 出入国管理事務所
- **immigration inspector** 入国審査官
- **immigration officer** 入国管理官

immune 形 免疫の, 免疫性の, 免疫体を含む, …から免れた, 免除された, …の影響を受けない
- **be immune frm criticism** 批判されない
- **be immune from taxation** 課税を免除されている
- **be immune to [from] the disease** その病気に対して免疫になっている
- **be immune to trends in the business cycle** 景気変動の影響を受けない
- **be not immune to [from]** …と無縁でない, …の例外ではない
- **immune system** 免疫組織

impact 名 影響, 影響力, 効果, 打撃, 衝撃, 衝撃力, ショック, 衝突, 刺激, 強い印象, インパクト
- **adverse impact** 悪影響, 悪材料
- **deflationary impact** デフレ効果
- **disinflationary impact** インフレ抑制効果
- **environmental impact assessment** 環境影響評価, 環境アセスメント 《略 EIA》
- **financial impact** 財務上の影響
- **forex impact** 為替による影響, 為替の影響 (＝foreign exchange impact)
- **impact aid** 米政府の財政的援助, 政府補助金 (政府機関の公務員の子弟が通う学区に社払われる)
- **impact day [date]** 発表日, インパクト・デー (株式や社債の新規発行条件の公表日)

impact effect 即時的効果, 衝撃効果
impact loan 外貨借款, インパクト・ローン(使途を限定しない外貨貸付け, 外貨借入れ])
impact on competitive position [moves] 競争力に与える影響
inflationary impact インフレ圧力
reflationary impact 景気刺激効果
side impact 副次的効果[結果]
tax impact 租税公課

impair 動 損なう, 弱める, 減じる, 劣化する, 制約する

impasse 名 袋小路, 行き詰まり, 行き悩み, 停頓, 窮地, 難局, 対立, 不振
a political impasse 政治的行き詰まり
be at an impasse 行き詰まる
reach an impasse 行き詰まる, 停頓する
sales impasse 売れ行き不振

impeachment 名 弾劾, 訴追, 告発, 告訴
Impeachment Court 弾劾裁判所
impeachment process 弾劾手続き
Judge Impeachment Court 裁判官弾劾裁判所

impede 動 妨げる, 邪魔する, 阻害する, 妨害する

implant 動〈臓器などを〉移植する,〈人工心臓などを〉埋め込む,〈受精卵を子宮壁に〉着床させる,〈思想などを〉植え付ける[吹き付ける]

implement 動 実施する, 実行する, 遂行する, 施行する, 適用する

implementation 名 実施, 実行, 遂行, 履行, 施行, 運用, 適用, 開発, 構築, 実現, 実装, インプリメンテーション

implicate 動 巻き込む, 連座[加担]させる, 関わり合わせる, 結びつける, 関連を持たせる, 関係[関連]があることを示す, 意味する, 包含する, ほのめかす, 影響を与える
be deeply implicated with …と深い関係がある
be implicated in …に関わっている, …に関与している, …に巻き込まれる, …に責任がある, …と深く結びついている
be implicated in a conspiracy 陰謀に巻き込まれる
be implicated in a crime 犯罪に連座する, 犯罪に巻き込まれる
be implicated in a pay-off scandal 贈収賄事件に関与[関係]している
implicate A as B AをBの原因として指摘する

implication 名 影響, 結果, かかわり合い, 密接な関係, 連座, 巻き添えにすること, 意味, 裏の意味, 意味合い, 要因, 材料, 含み, 含蓄, 暗示, 黙示, 黙示的表示, もつれ合い, 紛糾
by implication 暗に, 言外に
carry misleading implications 誤解を招く含み[意味合い]を持つ
credit implications 格付けへの影響
financial implications 財務上の影響
implication of law 法律の運用
negative implications マイナス要因, 悪材料
positive implications プラス要因, 好材料
tax implications 税務上の取扱い

import 動 輸入する, 導入する,〈データを〉転送する, 取り込む, 移動する
imported capital 資本の導入
imported inflation 輸入インフレ[インフレーション](=import inflation)
imported input content 輸入投入含有量
imported items 輸入品目, 輸入財

import 名 輸入, 輸入品, 輸入製品, 輸入額, 導入, 重要性, 意味, インポート
import agency 輸入代行業者
import control 輸入貿易管理
import cost 輸入物価
import growth 輸入の伸び, 輸入の増加
import inflow 輸入拡大
import levy 輸入課税, 輸入課徴金
import license bond rate 輸入担保率(=import deposit rate)
import of final goods 製品輸入
import of foreign capital 外資導入
import payment 輸入代金支払い, 輸入支払い
import quota system 輸入割当制度
import replacement industry 輸入代替産業
import saving 輸入節約
import settlement 輸入決済
import stability 輸入安定
import subsidy 輸入補助金, 輸入奨励金
import substitution 輸入代替
import supply 輸入供給
import surcharge 輸入課徴金(=import surtax)
import surplus 輸入超過, 貿易収支赤字
import usance 輸入代金の延べ払い, 輸入ユーザンス
import without (foreign) exchange 無為替輸入

import WPI 輸入物価指数
invisible export and import 貿易外収支
impose 動 課税する,〈税金などを〉課する,〈義務などを〉負わせる,〈危険などを〉与える,〈条件などを〉設ける, 売りつける, 押し付ける, 強いる
- **impose conditions on** …に条件を付ける, …に条件を設ける
- **impose economic austerity** 緊縮政策を遂行する
- **impose economic sanctions** 経済制裁に踏み切る, 経済制裁を科する
- **impose high tariffs on** …に高率の関税をかける
- **impose restrictions on** …を規制する, …を制限する
- **impose a tax on** …に課税する, …に税をかける

improve 動 改良する, 改善する, 整備する, 促進する, 推進する, 強化する, 向上させる, 拡大する
- **improved business performance** 業績改善
- **improved quality** 品質向上, 品質改善

improvement 名 改良, 改善, 促進, 推進, 向上, 増加, 伸び, 上昇, 拡大,〈景気などの〉回復, 好転, 改修工事, 整備
- **business improvement order** 業務改善命令
- **cost improvements** コスト削減
- **environmental improvement** 環境改善
- **harbor improvement** 港湾整備
- **improvement patent** 改良特許
- **improvement in profitability** 収益性の改善, 収益力の改善
- **improvement trade** 加工貿易
- **improvements to leased offices** 賃貸事務所改造費
- **inventions, improvements or developments** 発明, 改良または開発
- **market improvement** 上げ相場
- **operational improvement order** 業務改善命令
- **practice improvement** 業務改善
- **productivity improvement** 生産性向上
- **quality improvement** 品質向上, 品質の改善
- **standard improvements** 標準造作
- **trade (balance) improvement** 貿易収支の改善

in a bid to …するために, …をめざして, …しようと試みて, …しようとして
in a row 1列に, 連続して, 引き続いて, 続けて
in anticipation of …を見越して, …を期待して, …を予想して, …に先立ち
in compliance with …に準拠して, …に従って (=in accordance with)
in conjunction with …と連携して, …と協力して, …と組み合わせて, …と共に, …と一緒になって
in full swing 真っ最中の, 最盛期の, 最高潮に達した, 急ピッチで進んでいる, どんどん進んでいる,〈生産などが〉フル操業に入っている, フル稼働している, 整いつつある
in line with …に沿って, …と一致[調和]して, …に連動[同調]して, …に合わせて, …に従って, …に伴って, …に応じて, …を追いかける形で
in response これを受けて
in tandem with …と並んで, …と協力して, …と提携して
in terms of …では, …の点で, …に関して, …について, …の見地から
in the face of …に直面して, …に鑑(かんが)みて, …を考えると, …にもかかわらず
in the pay of …に雇われている, …に雇われた, …に使われている
in the wake of …に引き続いて, …に続いて, …の後, …を受けて, …の結果(として), …に従って, …に倣って, …として, …によって (=in one's wake)
in vitro fertilization 体外受精
inactivated polio vaccine 不活化ワクチン, ポリオ不活化ワクチン (=inactivated vaccine)
inaugural 形 就任の, 就任式の, 発足に当たっての, 発会[開会, 開場, 開通, 落成]の, 名〈米大統領の〉就任演説(inaugural address), 就任式(inaugural ceremony)
- **an inaugural address** 就任演説, 就任のあいさつ, 就任の辞
- **an inaugural ball** 米大統領就任
- **an inaugural ceremony** 就任[発会, 開会, 開場, 開通, 落成, 除幕]式
- **an inaugural function** 開館式
- **an inaugural gala** 大統領就任祝賀会
- **an inaugural meeting** 発会式, 創立の会合, 創立総会
- **an inaugural policy speech** 就任施政方針演説
- **the inaugural flight to China** 中国への第一便, 中国への初フライト[就航初フライト]
- **the inaugural number [issue]** 創刊号 (= the first issue, the first number, the initial

number)
the Presidential inaugural 大統領就任式
inaugurate 動 就任させる, 落成式を行う, 開会式を行う, 〈船などを〉就航させる, 〈仕事・事業を〉開始する, 発足する, 始める
inauguration 名 就任, 落成, 除幕, 開会, 発会, 開通, 就航, 開業, 創業, 開始, 発足, 就任式, 落成式, 除幕式, 開会式, 発会式, 開通式
 an inauguration advertising 慶祝広告
 an inauguration ceremony 就任式 (＝inaugural ceremony)
 the Inauguration Day 米大統領就任式の日（大統領選挙年(4で割り切れる数)の翌年の1月20日）
in-car audiovisual product 車載AV用品
incentive 名 刺激, 刺激策, 刺激剤, 誘因, 動機, やる気［気持ち］, 励み, 奨励, 促進策, 振興, 報奨, 報奨金, 販売促進金, 出来高払い, インセンティブ
 adaptation as incentive 刺激［誘因］としての適合
 an incentive to crime 犯罪の誘因, 犯罪を引き起こす誘因
 credit incentive 信用誘因
 financial [monetary] incentive 金銭的誘因, 特別手当
 incentive for buying 購買意欲, 購買動機
 incentive rate 割戻し率
 incentive regulation インセンティブ規制, インセンティブ方式の規制
 incentive system 輸出報奨制, 奨励給制, 刺激策
 incentive trip [tour] 報奨旅行, 報奨ツアー
 interest incentive effect 利子刺激効果
 incentives for exporters 輸出振興策 (＝export incentives)
 listing incentive 上場誘因
 price incentive 価格誘因
 refinancing incentive 借換えの利点
 sales incentives 販売奨励金, 販売促進策
 savings incentives 貯蓄奨励策
 shareholders incentives 株主優待, 株主優待制度
 tax incentives 税制上の優遇措置
incentive 形 刺激的な, 挑発的な, 誘発的な, 奨励的な, 奨励の, 励みとなる
 be incentive to industry 勤勉の励みになる
 incentive agency 報奨品取扱い代理業

incentive award 奨励報酬, 報奨金
incentive bonus 奨励特別手当
incentive compensation plan 奨励報償制度（会社が一定以上の利益をあげたとき, 経営者を対象に規定の報酬以外にボーナスを支払う制度）
incentive consumers' goods 刺激的消費財
incentive item 報奨品, 奨励品
incentive pay [wage] 能率給, 刺激給, 奨励給, 奨励金, 報奨金
incentive payment system 奨励給制度, 奨励急制
incentive pricing 誘発的価格設定
incentive program [plan, scheme] 報奨制度, 報奨金制度, 促進計画
incentive speech 刺激的な演説, 挑発的な演説, 激励演説
incentive stock option (plan) 奨励株式オプション制度, 奨励ストック・オプション制度《略 ISO》
inch 動 徐々に動く, 少しずつ動く［進む］, じりじり［じわじわ］動く
 inch down 徐々に下がる, 少しずつ下がる, じりじり下がる
 inch forward 徐々に前進する, 少しずつ前進する (＝inch one's way forward)
 inch up 徐々に上がる［上昇する］, 少しずつ上がる, じりじり上がる (＝inch higher)
 inch upward 徐々に上昇する
incipient recovery 景気回復の局面, 景気持ち直しの局面, 回復局面
include 動 含む, 算入する, 組み入れる, 盛り込む, 計上する, 処理する, 記載する, 表示する, 掲載する, 収録する
income 名 利益, 収益, 所得
 business income 企業利益, 企業収益, 事業所得
 consolidated net income 連結純利益, 連結当期純利益
 disparity in income 所得格差 (＝income disparity, income gap)
 earned income 給与所得, 勤労所得
 fixed income securities 確定利付き証券, 債務証券, 債券
 high income family 高所得世帯
 income account surplus 所得収支の黒字［黒字額］, 所得黒字 (＝income surplus)
 income after tax 税引き後利益 (＝after-tax income)

income before extraordinary items 経常利益
income disparity 所得格差（＝disparity in income）
income forecast 収益見通し, 収益予想
income from operations 営業利益
income indemnity system 所得補償制度, 農家に対する直接支払い制度
income not reported 申告漏れ額
income source 収入源
income surplus 所得収支の黒字［黒字額］（＝income account surplus）
investment income 投資収益
national income 国民所得
net income 純利益, 当期純利益
nonoperating income 営業外損益, 営業外収益
one-time income 一時所得
ordinary income 経常損益
premium income 収入保険料
real income 実質所得, 実質所得
income tax 所得税, 法人税, 法人所得税
income tax benefit 税額減少利益, 税務上の特典［恩典］
income tax benefit of loss [operating loss] carryforward 繰越し欠損金の税務上の特典［恩典］
income tax bracket 所得区分
income tax deduction for dependents 所得税の扶養控除
income tax effect 所得税効果, 税効果
income tax payable 未払い所得税
income tax rebates 所得税の還付, 戻し税
income tax reductions 所得税減税
incoming 次の, 次期の, 後任の, 後継の, 引き継ぐ, 入ってくる, 流入する, 到来する, 到着する, 新入りの,〈利子などが〉生じる, 付く
incoming calls かかってくる電話, 外からの電話
incoming cash flow 現金流入
incoming clearings 交換持帰り手形
incoming exchange 被仕向け為替
incoming goods [merchandise] 入荷, 入荷商品
incoming profits 収益, 利益金, 儲け
incoming tide 上げ潮
incomings and outgoings 収入と支出
incorporate 設立する, 会社［法人］組織にする, 法人化する, 組み込む, 組み入れる, 取り入れる, 織り込む, 受け入れる, 合併する, 契約の一部とする, 具体化する
be incorporated (as) a member of a group グループの一員になる
be incorporated into …に編入される
incorporate adjustments 調整を加える
incorporate expected changes 予想される変動を織り込む［盛り込む］
incorporate one's suggestions into the report …の提案を報告書に組み入れる
incorporated administrative accountant 英国の管理会計士
incorporated business [enterprise] 法人企業
incorporated city 合併でできた市
incorporated company [corporation] 有限責任会社, 有限会社
incorporated institution 法人組織
locally incorporated subsidiary 現地法人の子会社
incorporation 会社の設立, 法人格の付与, 法人組織, 会社, 合併, 編入, 組込み
capital incorporation 資本の組入れ
country of incorporation 居住国名
incorporation procedure 会社設立手続き
incorrect 正しくない, 適切でない, ふさわしくない, 不正確な, 間違った, 誤った, 不正解の, 事実に反する, 不作法な
incorrect acceptance 過誤採択
incorrect behavior 不作法
incorrect information 誤った情報, 間違った情報
incorrect rejection 過誤棄却
increase 増やす, 上昇させる, 引き上げる, 押し上げる, 拡大する, 高める, 伸ばす, 強化する, 増大する, 増加する, 増える, 伸びる, 激化する
increase capital strength 資本基盤を強化する
increase inhouse processing 内製比率を高める
increase one's capital 増資する, 資本金を増やす
increase one's equity ownership 持ち株比率を引き上げる
increase shareholders value 株主価値を高める, 株主の利益を高める
increased competition 競争の激化
increased dividends received 受取配当金の増加
increased investment 投資の拡大

increased productivity 生産性の向上, 生産性の伸び
increased quarterly dividend 四半期増配, 四半期配当の引上げ
increased sales 販売の増加, 販売の伸び, 売上［売上高］の伸び

increase 名 増加, 増大, 伸び, 上昇, 引上げ, 拡大, 高まり
   base rate increase 基準金利の引上げ
   cost increases コストの上昇
   dividend increase 増配, 配当引上げ （＝increase dividend）
   general capital increase 一般増資
   increase in exports 輸出拡大, 輸出の伸び
   increases in income and profit 増収増益
   increase in revenues and profits 増収増益, 収益と利益の増加
   increase of capital stock 増資（＝increase in capital stock, increase of capital）
   increase of sales 売上増加
   inventory increase 在庫の増加
   paid-in capital increase 有償増資
   post a healthy increase 好調な伸びを示す
   price increase 価格上昇, 価格の高騰, 値上がり, 値上がり率, インフレ率
   productivity increase 生産性の伸び
   rate increase 利上げ, 料金引上げ
   rating increase 格上げ
   supply increase 供給増
   tax increase 増税
   wage increase 賃上げ, 賃金引上げ, 賃金の上昇, ベース・アップ

incrementalism 名 漸進主義
incubation period 潜伏期間, 孵化期間
incubator 名 企業育成機関, 企業育成施設（＝business incubator, incubator facility）
incumbent 形 現職の, 在職の, 義務として課される
   incumbent executives 現経営陣, 現職の経営陣
   incumbent Republican congressman 現職の共和党議員
   the incumbent 現職者

incur 動 引き起こす, 発生させる, 招く,〈損失や損害を〉被る［受ける］, 負う, 負担する, 引き受ける, 負債に陥る, 怒りを買う
   immense bad loans incurred by banks 銀行が抱える莫大な不良債権
   incur a group net net loss 連結純損失, 連結税引き後赤字
   incur a significant loss 大きい損失を被る
   incur debts 負債を負う, 借金を背負い込む
   incur further damages さらに損害を受ける
   incur one's displeasure …の機嫌を損ねる
   incur responsibility 責任を負う
   incur the borrowing costs 借入［資金調達］コストを負担する
   incur the wrath of …の激しい怒りを買う
   incur unseen liabilities 不測の債務を負う, 不測の債務が発生する
   previously incurred liabilities 過去に発生した負債

independence 名 独立, 独立性, 自立, 自主性
independent 形 独立した, 自立した, 独立系, 個別の, 自主的な
   independent administrative institution 独立行政法人
   independent contractor 独立業務請負人, インディペンデント・コントラクター《略 IC》（個人として企業と契約して, 専門性の高いプロジェクトを請け負う人）
   independent director 独立取締役, 社外取締役
   independent power producer 独立系発電事業者《略 IPP》（卸電力事業を営む事業者）
   Independent System Operator organizations 独立系統運用機関（送電線の運用・管理にあたる非営利組織）

independent agency [establishment] 独立行政機関

米国の独立行政機関と公社：

Administrative Conference of the United States	合衆国行政協議会
African Development Foundation	アフリカ開発基金
Central Intelligence Agency	中央情報局《略 CIA》
Commission on Civil Rights	公民権委員会
Commodity Futures Trading Commission	商品先物取引委員会
Consumer Product Safety Commission	消費製品安全委員会
Defense Nuclear Facilities Safety Board	防衛関係原子力施設安全委員会
Environmental Protection Agency	環境保護庁《略 EPA》
Equal Employment Opportunity Commission	平等雇用機会委員会

Export-Import Bank of the United States	合衆国輸出入銀行
Farm Credit Administration	農業信用局
Federal Communications Commission	連邦通信委員会
Federal Deposit Insurance Corporation	連邦預金保険公社
Federal Election Commission	連邦選挙委員会
Federal Emergency Management Agency	連邦緊急管理庁
Federal Housing Finance Board	連邦住宅金融委員会
Federal Labor Relations Authority	連邦労働関係院
Federal; Maritime Commission	連邦海運委員会
Federal Mediation and Conciliation Service	連邦調停仲裁庁
Federal Mine Safety and Health Review Commission	連邦鉱山安全・衛生審査委員会
Federal Reserve System	連邦準備制度
Federal Retirement Thrift Investment Board	連邦職員退職貯蓄投資委員会
Federal Trade Commission	連邦取引委員会《略 FTC》
General Services Administration	共通役務庁
Inter-American Foundation	米州基金
Interstate Commerce Commission	州際通商委員会
Merit Systems Protection Board	メリット・システム保護委員会
National Aeronautics and Space Administration	航空宇宙局
National Archives and Records Administration	国立公文書・記録管理局
National Capital Planning Commission	首都計画委員会
National Credit Union Administration	信用組合庁
National Foundation on the Arts and the Humanities	芸術・人文科学基金
National Labor Relations Board	労働関係委員会
National Mediation Board	調停委員会（鉄道・航空労使調停委員会）
National Railroad Passenger Corporation (AMTRAK)	鉄道旅客公社（アムトラック）
National Science Foundation	科学基金
Nuclear Regulatory Commission	原子力規制委員会
Occupational Safety and Health Review Commission	労働安全衛生審査委員会
Office of Government Ethics	政府倫理局
Office of Personnel Management	人事管理庁
Oversight Board for the Resolution Trust Corporation	貯蓄機関決済信託公社監督委員会
Panama Canal Commission	パナマ運河委員会
Peace Corps	平和部隊
Pennsylvania Avenue Development Corporation	ペンシルバニア街開発公社
Pension Benefit Guaranty Corporation	年金給付保証公社
Postal Rate Commission	郵便料金委員会
Railroad Retirement Board	鉄道退職者委員会
Resolution Trust Corporation	貯蓄機関決済信託公社
Securities and Exchange Commission	証券取引委員会《略SEC》
Selective Service System	選抜徴兵制度
Small Business Administration	中小企業庁
Tennessee Valley Authority	テネシー渓谷開発公社
United States Arms Control and Disarmament Agency	合衆国武器規制・軍縮庁
United States Information Agency	合衆国情報庁
United States International Development Cooperation Agency	合衆国国際開発協力庁
United States International Trade Commission	合衆国国際貿易委員会
United States Office of Special Council	合衆国公務公正・適正確保特別顧問局
United States Postal Service	郵政公社

in-depth discussions 掘り下げた論議, 突っ込んだ議論

index 動 消費者物価指数にスライド［連動］させる, スライド［指数化］方式にする

index 名 指数, 指標, 指針, 索引, インデックス

coincident index 一致指数
commodity index 商品指数
composite index 景気総合指数《略 CI》
consumer price index 消費者物価指数《略 CPI》
cost of living index 生計費指数
DI index 業況判断指数, 景気動向指数, DI指数 (DI=diffusion index)
diffusion index 景気動向指数
Dow-Jones index ダウ平均株価指数
general index of retail prices 小売物価総合指数
index of business conditions 景況判断指数, 業況判断指数
index of industrial output 鉱工業生産指数, 工業生産指数 (=index of industrial production)
index of lagging indicators 遅行指数
index of leading economic indicators 景気先行指標総合指数, 景気先行指数, 先行指数（景気先行指数は, 景気の現状より約6か月先の景気の動きを示す指標）
index of output at mines and factories 鉱工業生産指数
industry-wide index of business conditions 景況判断指数（全産業）
lagging index 遅行指数
leading index 先行指数
retail price index 小売物価指数《略 RPI》
Nikkei Index 日経平均
stock price index 株価指数 (=stock index)

indication 名 表示, 兆し, 動き, 気配, 動向, 指標, 気配値, 条件の提示
  cyclical indication 景気指標
  grey market indication グレー・マーケットの気配値
  objective indications of intent 意図の客観的表示, 意図を客観的に示すもの
  preliminary indications 仮条件
  receive indications from …から条件の提示を受ける
  submit an indication 条件提示を行う, 条件を提示する
  ▶ Under the severe income and employment situations, personal consumption has yet to show *indications* of a full-fledged recovery. 厳しい所得・雇用環境の下で, 個人消費に本格的な復調の気配がまだ見えない。

indicator 名 指数, 指標, 指針, インディケーター
  coincident indicator 一致指数
  DI of the coincident indicators 景気一致指数 (DI)
  DI of the lagging indicators 景気遅行指数 (DI)
  DI of the leading indicators 景気先行指数 (DI)
  economic indicator 経済指標, 景気指標
  financial indicator 財務指標
  inflation indicator インフレ指標
  key economic indicators 主要経済指標
  labor market indicators 労働統計
  lagging indicator 遅行指数
  leading indicator 先行指標, 先行指数
  monetary indicators 金融指標
  numerical indicator 数値目標
  performance indicator 業績指数, 業績指標
  profitability indicator 収益性指標

indict 動 起訴する, 告発する

indictment 名 起訴, 告発, 起訴状
  be under indictment for …の罪で起訴されている, …のかどで起訴されている
  file a summary indictment against …を略式起訴する
  written indictment 起訴状

indiscriminate fishing 乱獲

individual 形 個人の, 個人的, 個別の, 個々の
  individual advantage 個人的利益
  individual audience rate 個人視聴率
  individual consumption 個人消費, 個人的消費
  individual demand 個別需要
  individual family 個別家計
  individual interview 個別面接
  individual investor 個人投資家
  individual life insurance 個人生命保険, 個人保険
  individual member 個別会員
  individual proprietor 自営業者
  individual savings 個人貯蓄
  individual stockholder [shareholder] 個人株主
  individual supply 個別供給

induced pluripotent stem cell 人工多能性幹細胞, 万能細胞, iPS細胞 (=iPS cell)

industrial 形 産業の, 工業の, 鉱工業の, 工業の発達した, 工業生産の, 産業[工業]用の, インダストリアル

industrial automation application 産業自動化アプリケーション
industrial competitiveness 産業競争力
industrial complex 工業団地, コングロマリット
industrial crops 工芸農作物
industrial espionage 産業スパイ (＝economic espionage)
industrial firms 製造業
industrial nations and territories 先進国と地域
industrial organization 産業組織
industrial policy 産業政策
industrial power 先進国, 工業力, 産業力
industrial production index 鉱工業生産指数, 工業生産指数 (＝index of industrial output, index of industrial production, industrial output data, industrial output index)
industrial property rights 工業所有権
industrial revitalization 産業活性化, 産業再生
Industrial Revitalization Corporation 産業再生機構《略 **IRC**》(＝Industrial Revitalization Corporation of Japan)
Industrial Revitalization Law 産業再生法
industrial robot 産業用ロボット
industrial structure changes 産業構造転換
industrial output 工業生産, 工業生産高, 鉱工業生産, 鉱工業生産高 (＝industrial production)
industrial output data 鉱工業生産指数
industrial output index 鉱工業生産指数, 工業生産指数
industrialist 名 実業家, 事業家, 企業家, 産業人, 産業資本家, 財界人
industrialization 名 工業化, 産業化
export-led industrialization 輸出主導型工業化, 輸出リード型工業化
export-oriented industrialization 輸出志向型工業化
import-substituting industrialization 輸入代替工業化
regional industrialization 地域工業化
industrialized country [economy, nation, power] 工業国, 工業先進国, 先進国
advanced industrialized countries 先進工業国
heavily industrialized country 重工業国
less industrialized country 後発工業国
newly industrialized countries 新興工業国群《略 **NICs [NICS]**》
newly industrialized country 新興工業国《略 **NIC**》(韓国, 香港, マレーシアなど)
newly industrialized economies 新興工業経済群, 新興工業経済地域《略 **NIEs [NIES]**》(＝newly industrializing economies)
industry 名 産業, 工業, 産業界, 工業会, 業界, …業, メーカー
basic material industry 素材産業
competitive industry 競争的産業(業界全体が完全競争の状況にある産業)
content industry コンテンツ(情報の内容)産業
downstream industry 川下産業
emerging industry 先端産業
financial industry 金融業界, 金融界, 金融産業
food service industry 外食産業
industry association 業界団体 (＝industry group)
industry-government alliance 官民協力, 官民共同
industry leader 業界リーダー, 業界最大手
industry output 鉱工業生産, 鉱工業生産指数 (＝industrial output)
industry segment 事業別セグメント, 産業別セグメント, 産業セグメント, 事業区分, 事業分野, 事業部門 (＝industrial segment)
industry standard 産業基準, 業界基準, 業界規格, 統一基準
key industry 基幹産業, 基礎産業, 重要産業
mining and manufacturing industries 鉱工業
nuclear power industry 原子力産業
reproductive industry 再生産業
steel industry 鉄鋼産業
sunrise industry 成長産業, サンライズ産業
sunset industry 斜陽産業, 衰退産業, サンセット産業
supporting industry すそ野産業
telecommunications and information industry 情報通信産業
tertiary industry 第三次産業(サービス産業とほぼ同じで, 商業, 運輸・通信業, 金融業, 公務・自由業, 有給の家事サービス業などのこと)
the collusion between the bureaucracy and the industry 官民癒着 (＝bureaucrats' collusive ties with businesses, collusive ties

inefficiency / **inflationary**

between the private and public sectors)
the hollowing out of (Japanese) industry 産業空洞化 （＝deindustrialization）
trigger industry トリガー産業（景気回復や革新の牽引役を果たす産業のこと）

inefficiency 名 非効率, 非能率, 効率の悪さ, 要領の悪さ, 無効果, 無能力
economic inefficiency 経済的非効率
inefficiency of the Japanese agricultural industry 日本の農業［農産物］の非効率性

inexpensive 形 費用［金］のかからない, 価格が安い, 安い, 低コストの, 高価でない, 値段の割に価値がある
appear inexpensive 割安感がある, 割高感がない
inexpensive election 金のかからない選挙
inexpensive goods 安い商品
inexpensive labor 安い労働力

infection 名 伝染, 感染, 汚染, 伝染病, 感染症, 感化, 影響［悪影響］
HIV infection エイズ・ウイルス感染, HIV感染
infection in hospitals 院内感染
massive infection 集団感染
prevent further infection 感染拡大を防ぐ
suffer from [develop] an infection 伝染病にかかる

infectious 形 感染症の, 感染性の
infectious disease 感染症
infectious gastroenteritis 感染性胃腸炎

infighting 名 内紛, 内輪もめ, 内ゲバ, 内部抗争, 接近戦 （＝internal strife, internal wrangling）

inflate 動 膨らませる, かさ上げする, 水増しする, 上乗せする,〈価格などを〉つり上げる, 上昇させる, 押し上げる, 誇張する

inflation 名 物価上昇, 物価上昇率, 物価高騰, 通貨膨張, インフレ, インフレ率, インフレーション
adjustments to restate costs for the effect of general inflation 一般物価水準変動の影響による修正表示
asset inflation 資産インフレ
consumer inflation 消費者物価の上昇
consumer (price) inflation 消費者物価の上昇, 消費者物価上昇率
core inflation 基礎インフレ率, コア・インフレ率
cost-push inflation 生産費の上昇によるインフレ, コストプッシュ・インフレ
creeping inflation 忍び寄るインフレ, 緩やかなインフレ （＝mild inflation：物価上昇率が2〜4％で持続する状態）
demand-pull inflation 需要インフレ, デマンドプル・インフレ（総需要に生産量が追いつかないで起こるインフレ）
expected inflation 期待インフレ率
higher inflation インフレ率上昇 （＝rising inflation）
inflation-adjusted real terms インフレ調整後の実質, 物価変動の影響を除いた実質
inflation-adjusted retail sales 実質小売り売上高
inflation fears インフレ懸念 （＝fears of inflation）
inflation gains and/or losses インフレ損益, インフレ利得および／または損失
inflation pressure インフレ圧力 （＝inflationary pressure）
inflation's performance インフレ動向
outlook for inflation インフレ見通し
outlook for the economy and inflation 経済・物価情勢の展望
producer price inflation 生産者物価上昇率
real return net of inflation インフレ調整後の実質利回り
resurging inflation インフレ再燃
retail price inflation 小売物価上昇率
service inflation サービス価格上昇率
stock price inflation 株価急騰
true inflation 真性インフレ
vicious inflation 悪性インフレ （＝malignant inflation）
wage inflation 賃金インフレ

inflation rate 物価上昇率, インフレ率
consumer price inflation rate 消費者物価指数上昇率
core inflation rate コア・インフレ率, 基礎インフレ率, 消費者物価指数コア指数の上昇率, コア指数
reduced inflation rate インフレ率の低下
underlying inflation rate 基礎インフレ率

inflation target インフレ目標, インフレ・ターゲット （＝inflationary target, target inflation rate）
inflation target policy インフレ目標政策

inflationary 形 インフレの, インフレを誘発する, インフレを引き起こす, インフレ要因になる
anti-inflationary strategy [measures] イン

フレ抑制策
inflationary climate [environment]　物価を取り巻く環境, インフレ環境, インフレ的雰囲気
inflationary concerns　インフレ懸念, インフレに対する懸念
inflationary credit creation　インフレ的信用創造
inflationary depression　インフレ不況
inflationary effect　インフレ効果
inflationary expectations　インフレ期待
inflationary finance [financing]　インフレ金融
inflationary force　インフレ要因, インフレ圧力
inflationary gain　インフレ利益
inflationary gap　インフレ・ギャップ (完全雇用の達成に必要な有効需要を上回る需要があること)
inflationary hedge　インフレ・ヘッジ (金・土地などへの投資など, インフレによる通貨価値の下落に伴う損失を防ぐために取る手段)
inflationary impact [impulses]　インフレ圧力 (=inflationary pressure)
inflationary influence　インフレ作用, インフレの影響
inflationary loss　インフレによる損失
inflationary mechanism　インフレ機構, インフレのメカニズム
inflationary momentum　インフレの勢い
inflationary period　インフレ期間
inflationary policy　インフレ政策
inflationary price movement　インフレ的物価変動
inflationary prices　物価高騰, 高騰した物価
inflationary process　インフレ過程
inflationary recession　インフレ不況
inflationary sentiment [mentality, psychology]　インフレ心理, インフレ・マインド
inflationary sign　インフレの兆候
inflationary spiral　悪性インフレ, インフレの悪循環
inflationary slowdown　インフレ率の低下
inflationary pressures　物価上昇圧力, 上昇圧力, インフレ圧力, インフレ誘発の圧力, インフレ懸念 (=inflationary impacts)
　constrain [deflate] inflationary pressures　インフレ圧力を抑える
　counter [relieve] inflationary pressures　インフレ圧力を抑制する
　decline in inflationary pressures　インフレ圧力の緩和
　ease inflationary pressures　インフレ圧力を抑制する, インフレ圧力を低下させる
　reduce inflationary pressures　インフレ圧力を低下させる, インフレ圧力を低減する
　offset inflationary pressures　インフレ圧力を相殺する
　releasing of inflationary pressures　インフレの再燃
　rise in inflationary pressures　インフレ圧力の高まり, インフレ圧力の上昇
　subdued inflationary pressures　インフレ圧力の鎮静化
　wage inflationary pressures　賃金インフレ圧力
　weakness of inflationary pressures　インフレ圧力の低下
inflict 動　与える, もたらす, 押し付ける, 課す, 負わせる
　be inflicted with [by]　…に苦しめられる, …に悩まされる
　inflict a blow on　…に一撃を加える
　inflict damages [losses] on　…に損害を与える, …に損害をもたらす
　inflict injury on　…に危害を加える
　inflict one's views on　自分の意見を…に押し付ける
　inflict punishment on　…を罰する
influence 名　影響, 波及, 影響力, 支配力, 勢力, 威光, 威信, 感化, 感化力, 作用, 効果, 要因
　dampening influence　抑制効果
　driving under the influence　飲酒運転
　exert enormous influence over　…に大きな影響を与える, …に大きな影響を及ぼす, …に強大な影響力を行使する
　horizontal influence　水平的影響
　inflationary influence　インフレ作用, インフレの影響
　influence buying　買収, 買収工作 (影響力を金で買うこと)
　influence effect　勢力効果
　influence peddler　政界仲介業者, 政界ブローカー, 地位利用者, 地位利用の汚職者
　influence peddling　口利き, 斡旋, 地位利用の汚職
　neutral influence　中立の作用, 中立的影響
　person of influence　実力者, 有力者
　Racketeers Influence and Corrupt Organizations Act　集団暴力腐敗組織法
　seasonal influence　季節的影響, 季節的要因

under the influence of …の影響を受けて, …に支配されて, …に左右されて, …に酔って
vertical influence 垂直的影響

influential 形 影響力の強い, 影響力[支配力]の大きい, 有力な, 顔がきく

influenza 名 インフルエンザ (⇒flu)
avian influenza H5N1 鳥インフルエンザ (H5N1)
influenza antiviral drugs インフルエンザ抗ウイルス薬
rampant influenza 猛威をふるうインフルエンザ
the new influenza virus 新型インフルエンザ・ウイルス
the new strain of type A influenza 新型インフルエンザ(A型)

influx 名 流入, 参入, 殺到, 流れ込み
an influx of complaints 苦情の殺到
influx of foreign funds 海外[国外]資金の流入, 海外[国外]からの資金流入

informant 名 情報提供者, 内部告発者, 密告者, インフォーマント

information 名 情報, 消息, 知識, ニュース, インフォメーション
accounting information 会計情報
authentic information 信頼に足る情報, 信頼すべき情報
classified information 機密情報, 極秘情報
confidential information 秘密情報, 機密情報
confidentiality of personal information 個人情報の秘密遵守
financial information 財務情報, 金融情報
general information 一般情報
information appliances 情報機器
information beacon 情報標識
information conduits 情報伝送路
information disclosure 情報開示, 情報公開
information governance 情報統治, 情報ガバナンス
information leak 情報漏洩, 情報漏らし
information movement and management 情報伝送処理
information processing 情報処理
information provider 情報提供者, 情報提供事業者, インフォメーション・プロバイダー《略 IP》
information transmitter 情報発信者, 発信者
inside information 内部情報, インサイダー情報, 未公開の重要情報, インサイド情報 (=insider information)
insurance information 保険情報, 保険に関する情報
internal information 内部情報
nonpublic information 非公開情報
operating information 運転情報
position information 位置情報
primary information 一次情報
public information 公開情報, 情報公開, 広報
supplementary information 補足情報
technical information 技術情報
technological information 技術情報, 専門情報, ノウハウ
trading information 取引情報

information technology 情報技術, 情報通信技術, 情報処理技術, 情報工学, 情報科学, インフォメーション・テクノロジー《略 IT》 (=Info technology, info-technology, infotech)
information technology agreement 情報技術協定《略 ITA》
information technology governance IT全般の統治能力, ITガバナンス, インフォメーション・テクノロジー・ガバナンス《略 ITG》
information technology industry 情報技術産業, IT産業, IT業界
information technology issues IT関連銘柄

informed 形 博識の, 見聞の広い, 消息通の, 事情によく通じた, 情報に通じた, 情報に基づく
an informed decision 情報に基づく決定[判断], ある程度状況を理解した上での判断
informed consent 十分な説明に基づく同意, 十分な情報提供に基づく同意, 説明を受けた上での承諾・同意, 口頭でなく文書による同意, 納得診察, インフォームド・コンセント
informed readers 博識の読者
informed sources [observers] 消息筋, 情報筋, 内部事情に通じた人々, 関係者
keep a person informed 人に新情報を常時提供する
well-informed 情報[事情]に通じている, 見聞の広い

informer 名 密告者, 情報提供者(informant), 通報者, たれ込み屋, 情報屋

inforsize 動 効率的に情報[情報源]にアクセスする

infotainment 名 報道娯楽番組(informationとentertainmentの合成語)

infotech 名 情報技術(informationとtechnologyの合成語)

infrastructure 名 〈経済・社会・産業の〉基盤, 社会的生産基盤, 基本施設[設備], 社会資本, 〈企業・組織の〉下部組織, 下部構造, インフラ整備, インフラ, インフラストラクチャー
- **basic infrastructure** 基本的インフラ
- **business infrastructure** 営業基盤
- **Defense Information Infrastructure** 防衛情報通信基盤《略 DII》
- **economic infrastructure** 経済的下部構造
- **global information infrastructure** 世界情報基盤, グローバル情報基盤
- **information infrastructure** 情報通信基盤, 情報インフラ
- **infrastructure facilities** 基礎的施設
- **infrastructure for the Internet** インターネットのインフラ
- **infrastructure program** インフラ整備計画
- **new infrastructure** 新社会資本
- **public key infrastructure** 公開鍵基盤《略 PKI》
- **social infrastructure** 社会的経済基盤, 社会資本, 社会資本整備, 社会的生産基盤, 社会のインフラ

infringe on 侵害する, 制限する

infringement 名 権利の侵害, 侵犯, 契約違反
- **infringement of copyright** 著作権の侵害
- **infringement of patents** 特許権侵害 (= patent infringement)
- **infringement of privacy** プライバシーの侵害
- **infringement of the law** 法律違反, 法令違反
- **patent infringement** 特許権侵害

inherit 動 引き継ぐ (take over), 受け継ぐ, 継承する, 相続する, 譲り受ける

inheritance 名 継承, 相続, 遺産, 相続財産, 文化的遺産, 伝統, 遺伝, 遺伝的形質
- **a dispute [quarrel] over an inheritance** 遺産をめぐる争い
- **estate of inheritance** 相続財産, 相続可能不動産物権
- **inheritance duty** 遺産取得税, 相続税
- **inheritance tax** 相続税
- **receive property by inheritance** 相続で財産を受け取る, 財産を相続する
- **right of inheritance** 相続権

in-house 形 内部の, 社内の
- **in-house investigation** 社内調査, 内部調査 (= in-house probe, internal investigation)
- **in-house report** 社内調査報告

inhuman 形 非人道的な, 残忍な, 冷酷な
- **inhuman acts** 非人道的行為

initial 形 最初の, 初めの, 初期の, 期首の, 当初の, 設立時の
- **initial development** 初期開発
- **initial establishment** 当初設定
- **initial estimate** 当初予想, 当初見積り, 当初見積り額
- **initial guarantee** 根保証 (= basic guarantee)
- **initial investigation** 予備的調査
- **initial investment** 初期投資, 初期投資額, 原始投資, 原初投資
- **initial numbers** 速報値
- **initial order** 初注文, 当初注文
- **initial placement** 募集業務
- **initial projection** 当初予想, 当初の見通し
- **initial salary** 初任給
- **initial price** 初値 (= initial share [stock] price)
- **initial public offering** 株式公開, 新規株式公開, 新規株式公募, 新規公募, 上場直前の公募, 第1回株式公募, 株式の公開公募, 上場《略 IPO》(= debut, initial public offer)
- **initial stages** 初期の段階
- **initial stock** 期首在庫, 期首在庫量[在庫高]
- **initial stock price** 初値 (= initial price, initial share price)

initiate 動 始める, 起こす, 創始する, 設立する, …に着手する, …に乗り出す, 創案する, 加入[入会, 入社]させる, 授ける, 伝える, 手ほどきをする, 初歩[コツ]を教える, 〈議案を〉提出する, 提案する, 発議する
- **bureaucrat-initiated policymaking** 官僚主導[官主導]の政策作り
- **initiate a downturn** 景気後退をもたらす
- **initiate a new method** 新方法を創案する
- **investor-initiated ratings** 投資家の依頼による格付け
- **politician-initiated policymaking mechanism** 政治家主導[政治主導]の政策作りの仕組み

initiative 名 独創力, 独自性, 自主性, 創意, 進取の気性, 企業心, 率先, 主導権, 主導, 自ら行動すること[行動する力], 議案提出権, 発議, 発案, 提案, 案, 政策, 計画, 構想, 方針, 戦略, 対策, イニシアチブ
- **energy saving initiatives** 省エネ対策, 省エネ

ルギー対策
individual initiative 個人の自主性
lose the initiative in …で主導権を失う
multilateral initiative 多国間交渉
peace initiative 和平案
policy initiatives 政府の政策, 政策効果
private initiatives 民間プロジェクト, 民間の発意
put forward an initiative 解決案を示す
social initiatives 社会政策
Structural Impediments Initiative 日米構造協議
take the initiative 主導権を握る, 先手を打つ
take the initiative in 率先して…する
taxpayer initiatives 住民の直接請求
the U.S. border security initiative 米国の国境警備戦略
under the initiative of …の主導のもとに
use one's (own) initiative 自ら決定し行動する

inject 動 注入する, 投入する, 供給する, 投資する, 導入する (=provide)
inject funds into markets 市場に資金を供給する
inject liquidity into the system 市中に流動性を供給する
inject public funds 公的資金を注入する, 公的資金を投入する

injection 名 注入, 投入, 供給, 導入, 注射, 〈人工衛星などを〉軌道に乗せること, 軌道に乗る時間[場所], 〈軌道などへの〉宇宙船(その他)の投入, インジェクション
additional capital injection 追加出資
capital injection 資本の注入, 資本の増強, 増資, 保険会社への基金拠出, 保険会社の基金増資 (=capital increase)
injection molding 射出成形, インジェクション成形
injection of equity 増資
injection of public funds 公的資金の注入, 公的資金の投入 (=public funds [fund] injection)
injection steelmaking インジェクション製鋼法
investment injection 投資注入
liquidity injection 流動性の供給

injunction 名 差止命令, 差止請求, 禁止命令, 仮処分
ex parte injunction 一方的差止命令
mandatory injunction 命令的差止命令, 作為命令的差止命令, 作為的差止命令
permanent injunction 本案的差止命令 (=perpetual injunction)
preliminary injunction 暫定的差止命令 (=interlocutory injunction, temporary injunction)
prohibitory injunction 禁止的差止命令
provisional injunction 仮処分, 暫定的差止命令 (=preliminary injunction)
quia timet injunction 事前差止命令, 予防的差止命令
structural injunction 制度改革的差止命令

in-kind donation 現物供与
inmate 名 〈病院の〉入院患者, 患者, 〈養老院の〉収容者, 〈刑務所の〉在監者[収容者], 囚人, 同室者, 同居人, 同宿者, 寄宿人
death-row inmate 死刑囚

innovation 名 革新, 革新性, 刷新, 斬新, 改革, 変革, 開発, 新制度, 〈新制度などの〉導入, 〈画期的な〉新製品, 新機軸, 新工夫, 新手法, 新発明, 技術革新, イノベーション
business innovation 経営革新
capital-saving innovation 資本節約的技術革新
capital-using innovation 資本使用的技術革新
economic innovation 経済的革新
factor-saving innovation 要素節約的技術革新
financial innovation 金融革新, 金融イノベーション, 新金融商品
imitative innovation 模倣的革新
innovation diffusion 技術革新の普及
innovation information system イノベーション情報システム《略 IIS》
innovation management 技術革新管理, イノベーション管理
innovation process 技術革新過程
intensity of innovation 技術進歩集約度
labor-intensive innovation 労働集約的技術革新
neutral technical innovation 中立的技術革新
product innovation 製品開発, 商品開発, 画期的な新製品, 製品イノベーション

innovative 形 革新的な, 斬新な, 新機軸の, 画期的な, 新しい, 最新の (=innovatory)
innovative efficiency 革新的効率
innovative imitation 技術革新の模倣, 革新的模倣

inoculation 名 予防接種, 接種, 種痘,〈思想などの〉植付け, 感化, 芽継ぎ, 接ぎ木, 土壌の改良
　administer the inoculation　予防接種を行う
　protective inoculation　予防接種
input 名 投入, 投入量, 投入物, 入力, 関与, インプット
　capital input　資本投入, 資本拠出, 資本投入量
　imported input　輸入投入量
　input goods　投入財
　input/output device [unit]　入出力装置, 入出力機器
　national input　国民投入量
　output/input ratio　産出・投入比率
　production inputs　原材料
　technology input　技術投入量
insect and pest control firm　害虫駆除会社
inside 形 内部の, 内側の, 屋内の, 社内の, 内勤の, 内々の, 秘密の, 内情[内幕]に通じた, 内部からの
　inside counsel　社内弁護士
　inside cover　〈本の〉扉
　inside director　社内取締役
　inside informant　内部告発者
　inside information　内部情報, 秘密情報, インサイダー情報, 未公開の重要情報, インサイド情報, 内部の消息（=insider information）
　inside job　内部犯行, 内部の者による犯行, 内部犯罪
　inside knowledge　内情
　inside man　内勤者, 内勤の従業員
　inside manipulation　内部操作
　inside market　場内市場
　inside selling　屋内販売
　inside skinny　秘密情報, マル秘情報,〈トラックの〉内側走路
　inside story　内幕話, 秘話
　inside track　有利な立場
insider 名 インサイダー, 内部者, 関係者（「インサイダー」は, 証券の投資判断に影響を及ぼす未公開の重要情報を知ることができる立場にいる公開会社の役員や取締役, 主要株主などをいう）
　industry insiders　業界関係者
　insider information　インサイダー情報
　insider lending　内部貸付け
　insider trading　インサイダー取引, 内部者取引（=insider dealing, insider stock trading：内部情報（insider information）を利用して証券取引を行うこと）
inspection 名 検査, 帳簿の閲覧, 査察, 視察, 点検, 実査, 査閲, 監査 (=investigation)
　an intrusive inspection　強制力を伴う査察
　car inspection　車検
　import inspection　輸入検査
　inspection sales technique　点検商法
　on-the-spot inspections　立ち入り検査
　physical inspection　実査
　random inspections　抜き打ち査察
　sampling inspection　抜き取り検査
　site inspection　現場検査
　surprise inspections　抜き打ち検査
　the inspection of cargo on ships　船舶の貨物検査
instability 名 不安, 動揺, 不安定, 不安定要因, 不安定性, 優柔不断
　currency instability　通貨不安
　instability of the currency exchange rate　為替相場の不安定な動き
　monetary instability　通貨不安
　political instability　政治的不安定, 支持不安
　potential causes of instability　不安定要因
instantaneous water heater　瞬間湯沸かし器
institution 名 機関, 公共機関, 金融機関, 組織, 法人, 企業, 会社, 施設, 制度, しきたり, 慣例, 慣行, 慣習, 設立, 設定, 制定
　academic institution　学術団体
　charitable institution　慈善団体
　economic institution　経済制度
　fiduciary institution　信用機関
　finance institution　金融制度, 金融機構
　financing institution　融資機関
　institution of laws　法律の制定
　lending institution　貸出機関, 金融機関
　nonprofit institution　非営利団体
　political institutions　政治制度
　premier institution　優良企業, 卓越した企業
　public institution　公共機関
　Smithsonian Institution　スミソニアン研究所
institutional 形 組織の, 組織的な, 故郷機関の, 施設の, 制度[制度上]の, 慣習[慣習上]の, 画一的な, 地味な, 企業イメージを高めるための
　institutional advertising　企業広告
　institutional approach　制度的研究
　institutional arrangement　制度的取決め
　institutional development　組織開発

institutional framework 制度的枠組み
institutional implement 制度的手段
institutional investment 機関投資
institutional investor 機関投資家 (=institutional lender：資産運用を専門とする銀行や保険会社，年金，投資顧問，各種団体・組合などの投資家の総称)
institutional setting 制度的背景

instruction 名 指示，通達，指図書き，指図書，〈機器の〉取扱い説明[説明書]，指令，命令，教授，訓練，教育，研修，知識，教訓，学問，インストラクション

actual instruction 実命令
follow the instructions 指示[指図]に従う，指示書きの手順に従う
instruction manual 取扱い説明書
instructions for use 使用上の指示[取扱い説明]
issue instructions 指示を出す，通達を出す
job instruction 職務指導
letter of instruction 指図書，信用指図書，手形買取り指図書
logical instruction 論理命令
on the instructions of …の指示に基づいて
reference instruction 参照命令
remittance instruction 送金通知書[案内書]
shipping instructions 船積み依頼書
under instruction 教育中，教育を受けている，研修中

instrument 名 証書，証券，有価証券，手段，支払い手段，商品，機器，機器

capital raising instrument 資金調達手段
electronic instruments 電子機器
instrument of ratification 批准書，批准文書
instrument of one's crime …の犯罪の手先
insurance instrument 保険商品 (=insurance product)
medical instruments 医療器械
musical instrument 楽器
optical instruments 光学器械
policy instruments 政策手段
precision instruments 精密機器
treasury instruments 米財務省証券

insurance 名 保険，保険契約，保険金額，保険料，保険条件

annuity insurance 年金保険
export insurance 輸出保険
fire insurance 火災保険
government-run nursing care insurance system 介護保険制度
insurance benefits 保険給付金，保険金
insurance company [firm] 保険会社 (=insurer)
insurance contract 保険契約
insurance fund 保険資金，保険基金，保険金，保険預り金
insurance policy cancellation 保険の解約，保険契約の解除
insurance policyholder 保険契約者
insurance premium 保険料
marine insurance 海上保険
medical insurance 医療保険
nonlife insurance 損害保険
pension insurance 年金保険
social insurance 社会保険
unemployment insurance 失業保険

insure 動 〈加入者が…に〉保険をかける，保険を付ける，付保する，〈保険業者が…について〉保険契約を結ぶ，保険契約する，保険を引き受ける，保険証券を発行する，保証する，補償する，請合う，確保する

insured amount 保険金額，保険契約金額 (=life insurance coverage)
the insured 被保険者，保険契約者

insurer 名 保険会社，保険業者，保険者，保証人 (=insurance company, insurance enterprise, insurance firm)

insurgency 名 反乱，反乱行為，反政府暴動

insurgent 名 〈政党内の〉反対分子，暴徒，反乱者，反乱軍の兵士，武装勢力

intake 名 摂取，摂取量，摂取物，受入れ，取入れ，導入，吸入，吸入量，通気孔，収入，売上高，採用人員，新規採用人員

capital intake 資本導入
cut water intake 取水を制限する
food intake 食物の摂取，食糧摂取量
salt intake 塩分摂取量
▶An excessive *intake* of vitamin A by pregnant woman increases the risk of congenital abnormalities in newborn babies. 妊婦がビタミンAを過剰に摂取すると，新生児の先天的異常の危険性が高まる。

integrate 動 統合する，一本化する，一元化する，一体化する，統一する，系列化する，一貫生産する，完成する，構成する，人種差別を撤廃する，形 総合的，部分から構成される，完全な

integrate business 経営統合する (=inte-

grate operations)
integrated circuit chip IC（集積回路）チップ
integrate management 経営統合する
integrated management 経営統合，一体的運用
integration 名 統合，一元化，統一，企業の系列化，集約権
  backward integration 後方統合
  currency integration 通貨統合
  economic integration 経済統合
  enterprise application integration 企業内アプリケーションの統合
  financial integration 金融統合
  forward integration 前方統合
  horizontal integration 水平統合
  integration efficiency 統合効果
  integration of affiliates 関連会社の統合
  integration of distribution system 流通系列化
  integration of physical distribution 物的流通の統合
  large scale integration 大規模集積回路《略 LSI》
  management [operational, business] integration 経営統合
  system integration architecture システム構築体系
  vertical integration 垂直統合
integrity 名 保全，領土保全，完全，無欠，無傷の状態，完全性，一体性，統一性，整合性，一致していること，誠実，清廉，潔白，信頼，信認
  business integrity 商業道徳
  credibility and integrity 信頼と信認
  integrity and reliability of the financial statements 財務書類の完全性と信頼性
  legal integrity 法的整合性，法律上の整合性
  market integrity 市場の整合性
  national integrity 自国の独立性，自国の独立
  territorial integrity 領土保全
intellectual asset 知的資産（「知的資産」には，特許や著作権などの知的財産のほかに，企業のノウハウやブランドなどが含まれる）
  ▶ Businesses in Japan and other industrial nations need to make more active use of patents, copyrights, brands and other *intellectual assets* to keep up with changes in the global economy. 日本などの先進国企業は，世界経済の変革に対応するため，特許や著作権，ブランドなどの知的資産を一段と積極的に活用する必要がある。

intellectual property 知的所有権，知的財産権（＝intellectual property right）
Intellectual Property High Court 知的財産高等裁判所
intellectual property right 知的所有権，知的財産権（＝intellectual property）
intelligence 名 情報，情報収集，情報機関，諜報，知能，知識，理解力，知性，機転，報道，通信
  Central Intelligence Agency 〈米国の〉中央情報局《略 CIA》
  far-seeing intelligence 先見の明
  intelligence activity 諜報活動，スパイ活動
  intelligence agency [bureau, office] 情報局，情報部
  intelligence agent 諜報員，スパイ
  intelligence analyst 情報分析家
  intelligence-gathering satellite 情報収集衛星
  intelligence network 情報網
  intelligence officer 情報当局者
  intelligence organ [service] 諜報機関，情報局
  intelligence quotient 知能指数《略 IQ》
  intelligence sources 情報筋，消息筋
  intelligence surveillance 情報監視
  intelligence test 知能検査
  intelligence war [warfare] 情報戦
intend to …する方針である，…する意向である，…する予定である，…を意図する，…を計画［企画］する，…する意思がある，…するつもりである
intensify 動 強める，高める，強化する，増強する，激化する，強くなる，深刻化する，高まる，活発になる
  intensified global competition グローバル競争の激化
  intensified price competition 価格競争の激化
intensity 名 激しさ，強さ，強度，集約度，震度
  capital intensity 資本集約度
  factor intensity 要素集約度
  labor intensity 労働集約度，労働強度
  skilled intensity 技術集約度
  trade intensity index 貿易結合度指数
intensive care unit 集中治療室《略 ICU》
intention 名 意志，意思，意向，意図，目的，狙い，意欲，考え，構想，計画
  buying intention survey 購買意向調査
  declaration of intention 意思表示

interactive / **interim**

- **foreign investment intentions** 外国からの投資申請件数
- **intention to buy [purchase]** 購買意図, 購入の意欲
- **investment intention** 投資意欲, 投資計画
- **with good intentions** 善意で, 誠意をもって

interactive 形 双方向の, 対話型, 対話式, 会話型, 対話処理, 対話性, 相互作用, 相互に情報を交換できる, インタラクティブ
- **interactive education** 対話型テレビ教育
- **interactive media** 対話型メディア, 双方向メディア
- **interactive processing** 対話型処理, インタラクティブ処理

inter-Korean dialogue 南北対話
inter-Korean relations 南北関係
intercept 動 迎撃する, 阻止する, 妨害する, 遮断する, 遮る, 横取りする, 奪う, 奪取する, 傍受する, 切り取る, 区切る
interception 名 迎撃, 阻止, 妨害, 遮断, 横取り, 奪取, 傍受
- **interception missile system** 迎撃ミサイル・システム
- **interception of radio communication** 無線通信の傍受
- **interception order** 迎撃命令, 破壊措置命令

interceptor 名 迎撃ミサイル, 迎撃戦闘機
- **interceptor missile** 迎撃ミサイル

interdependence 名 相互依存, 相互依存性, 相互依存関係, 持ちつ持たれつの関係, 助け合い

interest 名 利息, 利子, 金利, 株, 持ち分, 利益, 権益, 利権, 利害関係, 関係者, 同業者, 業界, 企業, …側
- **interest bearing liability** 有利子負債（= interest bearing debt）
- **interest burden** 金利負担
- **interest charged on the loan** 返済金利
- **Interest Limitation [Restriction] Law** 利息制限法
- **interest payment** 利払い, 金利の支払い, 利子支払い, 利息の返済, 支払い利息

interest bearing debt 有利子負債, 利付き債券（=interest-bearing liability）

> **有利子負債とは** ⊃ 金利をつけて返済しなければならない債務のこと。銀行などから借りた借入金のほか, 社債の発行などで市場から調達した資金の償還額なども有利子負債に加えられる。有利子負債の残高は, 企業の財務内容の健全性を測る指標の一つになって

いる。

interest rate 金利, 利息, 利子率, 利率
- **interest rate cut** 利下げ, 金利の引下げ
- **interest rate increase [hike]** 利上げ, 金利の引上げ

interfere 動 干渉する（intervene）, とやかく言う,〈余計な〉口出しをする, …に乗り出す, 仲裁する, 調停する, 妨げる, 妨害する, 邪魔する, 損なう, 害する, 性的いたずらをする,〈利害などが〉衝突する（clash）, 対立する,〈電波などが〉混信する
- **interfere in private concerns** 私事に口出しする, 私事におせっかいをやく
- **interfere in the internal affairs** 内政に干渉する
- **interfere with a woman** 女性に暴行する
- **interfere with cultural development** 文化的発展を妨げる
- **interfere with health** 健康を害する
- **interfere with rescue operations** 救助活動の邪魔をする

interference 名 干渉, 口出し, 介入, 仲裁, 調停, 邪魔, 妨害, 妨害行為, 衝突, 対立, 抵触, 抵触審査, 特許争い, 特許権争い, 同一発明の先発明者認定手続き, 受信障害害, 混信, インターフェアレンス
- **government interference** 政府の干渉, 政府の介入
- **interference in the nation's internal affairs** 同国の内政への干渉
- **interference pattern** 干渉パターン
- **interference with contract relations** 契約関係の妨害
- **interference with government officials in excercising their duties** 公務執行妨害
- **interference with market mechanisms** 市場原理との衝突
- **radio interference** 電波障害
- **run interference** 厄介な問題を事前処理する

intergenerational transfer of assets 世代間の資産移転
▶ To stimulate the economy, the promotion of *intergenerational transfer of assets* through the reduction of or exemption of gift tax was proposed. 景気刺激策として, 贈与税減免による世代間の資産移転促進が提言された。

Intergovernmental Panel on Climate Change 気候変動に関する政府間パネル《略 IPCC》

interim 形 中間の, 半期の, 期中の, 中間会計

期間の, 暫定的な, 一時的な, 仮の
interim aid 暫定援助, 中間援助
interim audit 期中監査, 中間監査
interim committee 暫定委員会
interim dividend 中間配当, 仮配当
interim earnings report 中間決算, 中間決算報告, 中間利益報告書 (＝interim financial results, interim results, midterm earnings report)
interim election 中間選挙
interim financial report 中間財務報告, 中間財務報告書 (＝interim report, interim financial information)
interim government 暫定政府, 暫定政権
interim net profit 中間期の純利益, 半期の純利益, 中間期の税引き後利益
interim order 暫定的命令
interim receipt 仮領収書
interim regime 暫定政権 (＝interim government)
interim ruling 中間判決
interim settlement of accounts 中間決算
issue [deliver] an interim report 中間報告を発表する
on an interim basis 一時的に, 暫定的に
pass an interim budget 暫定予算を可決する
interlocking directorate 兼任重役, 兼任役員
intermediary 名 仲介者, 仲介人, 仲介機関, 仲裁人, 仲裁者, 仲裁機関, 調停者, 媒介, 媒介の手段, 媒介物
business intermediaries 仲介の企業
financial intermediary 金融仲介機関, 金融仲介業者, 金融機関
market intermediary 証券会社
nonbank financial intermediary 銀行以外の金融仲介機関
nonmonetary intermediary 非貨幣的の仲介機関
private financial intermediary 民間金融仲介機関
risk intermediary リスク仲介機関
intermediary 形 仲介の, 中継の, 中間の, 媒介する
intermediary bank 仲介銀行, 受け皿銀行
intermediary bribery 斡旋収賄
intermediary business 仲介業
intermediary cost 中間コスト

intermediary exploitation 中間搾取
intermediary fee 仲介手数料
intermediary function 仲介機能
intermediary goods 中間財 (＝intermediate goods)
intermediary improvement trade 中継加工貿易
intermediary materials 中間財
intermediary role 仲介の役割
intermediary trade [commerce] 仲介貿易, 通過貿易, 3国間貿易
internal affairs 国内情勢[事情], 国内問題, 内政, 内部事情, 内部問題
internal control 内部統制, 社内管理, 内部チェック, 内部チェック体制(「内部統制」は, 粉飾決算や経営者の不正・ごまかしなど, 企業の不祥事を防ぐため, 社内の管理・点検体制を整え, 絶えずチェックすることをいう. 日本の上場企業は, 2008年度から内部統制に関する報告が義務付けられている)
internal control questionnaire 内部統制の質問書
internal control structure 内部統制機構, 内部統制構造
internal control system 内部統制組織, 内部統制機構
lax internal controls 甘い内部チェック体制
Internal Revenue Service 〈米国の〉内国歳入庁《略 IRS》
international 形 国際的, 国際間の, 国際上の, インターナショナル
achieve an international reputation 国際的名声を博す
international accounting standards 国際会計基準
international agreement 国際的合意, 国際合意, 国際協定
International Air Transport Association 国際航空運送協会《略 IATA》
international airfares 国際航空運賃
international arrest order 国際手配
International Atomic Energy Agency 国際原子力機関《略 IAEA》
International Chamber of Commerce 国際商業会議所
International Civil Aviation Organization 国際民間航空機関《略 ICAO》
International Commission for the Conser-

vation of Atlantic Tunas 大西洋まぐろ類保存国際委員会《略 ICCAT》
International Committee of the Red Cross 赤十字国際委員会
international consortium 国際共同事業体, 国際借款団, 国際融資団
International Convention for the Suppression of Acts of Nuclear Terrorism 核テロ防止条約
International Court of Justice 国際司法裁判所
International Criminal Court 国際刑事裁判所《略 ICC》
international division of manufacturing 国際分業
International Energy Agency 国際エネルギー機関《略 IEA》
international financing [finance] 国際金融
International Institute for Management Development 国際経営開発研究所
International Maritime Organization 国際海事機関《略 IMO》
International Mathematical Olympiad 国際数学オリンピック《略 IMO》
international migration of labor 国際労働移動
International Monetary Fund 国際通貨基金《略 IMF》
International money order 国際為替
international noose 国際包囲網
International Olympic Committee 国際オリンピック委員会《略 IOC》
International Panel on Climate Change 気候変動に関する政府間パネル《略 IPCC》
International Security Assistance Force 国際治安支援部隊《略 ISAF》(アフガニスタンで2001年に活動開始)
international space station 国際宇宙ステーション《略 ISS》
international standard 国際基準
International Thermonuclear Experimental Reactor 国際熱核融合実験炉《略 ITER》
International Trade Commission 〈米〉国際貿易委員会《略 ITC》
International Trade Organization 国際貿易機構《略 ITO》
international tribunal 国際裁判所
International Tribunal for the Law of the Sea 国際海洋法裁判所
international waters 公海 (=high seas)
International Whaling Commission 国際捕鯨委員会

International Accounting Standards
〈国際会計基準審議会(IASB)が作成している〉国際会計基準《略 IAS》(2005年1月1日から新しい呼び名として「国際財務報告基準(International Financial Reporting Standards)」に改められた。⇒IFRS)

international balance of payments
国際収支

国際収支関連用語:

basic balance	基礎収支
capital balance	資本収支
current account balance	経常収支 (=current balance)
foreign reserves	外貨準備
goods & services balance	貿易・サービス収支
income balance	所得収支
investment balance	投資収支
invisible balance	貿易外収支
long-term capital balance	長期資本収支
overall balance	総合収支
services balance	サービス収支
short-term capital balance	短期資本収支
trade balance	貿易収支
transfer balance	移転収支

internationalise 動 国際化する, 国際管理下に置く

Internet 名 インターネット, ネット (=internet, Net)
　create an Internet-based bank ネット専業銀行を設立する
　distribute television programs via the Internet テレビ番組をネット配信する
　have access to Internet services インターネットにアクセスする
　Internet-based commerce ネット商取引, ネット取引 (=e-business, e-commerce, electronic commerce, Internet commerce)
　Internet protocol インターネットの通信規約, インターネット・プロトコル《略 IP》

internship 名 就業体験, 就労体験, インターンシップ(学生が一定期間, 企業の職場で就労体験をする制度)

Interpol 名 国際刑事警察機構, インターポール (International Criminal Police Organization (ICPO)の略称)

intervene 動 間にある[入る, 起こる], 介入する, 介在する, 仲裁[調停]する, 〈内政などに〉干渉する, 口を出す, 〈会話に〉割り込む, 邪魔に入る, 〈第三者が〉訴訟に参加する
　intervene between A and B　AとBの仲裁に入る
　intervene in defense of the dollar　ドル防衛のために介入する
　intervene in the currency market　為替市場に介入する
　intervene in the dispute　紛争の仲裁をする, 紛争の調停をする
　intervene in (the) internal affairs　内政に干渉する
　intervene in the New York foreign exchange market　ニューヨーク外国為替市場に介入する
　intervene to avoid currency volatility　為替相場の乱高下[極端な変動]を防ぐために介入する
　militarily intervene in　…に軍事的に介入する

intervention 名 介入, 市場介入, 協調介入, 干渉, 口出し, 介在, 仲裁, 調停
　armed intervention　武力介入, 武力干渉
　conduct yen-selling intervention　円売り介入を実施する
　coordinated intervention　協調介入
　currency market intervention　為替市場への介入, 為替市場介入 (＝foreign exchange intervention, forex intervention)
　dollar-supporting market intervention　ドルの下支えを図る市場介入
　forex intervention　為替介入
　intervention currency　介入通貨
　intervention in management　経営介入, 経営への口出し
　intervention in the currency market　為替市場への介入, 通貨市場への介入
　intervention rate　市場介入金利
　military intervention　軍事介入
　three-way intervention　三極の市場介入
　yen-selling, dollar-buying intervention　円売り・ドル買い介入

interview 名 会見, 記者会見, 会談, 取材訪問, 面接, 面談, 診察, インタビュー
　depth interview　深層面接, 深層面接法
　exclusive interview　単独会見, 単独インタビュー, 独占インタビュー
　group interview　集団面接法, グループ面接法
　interview survey　面接調査
　job interview　就職面接 (＝interview for a job)

intifada 名 インティファーダ(イスラエル占領地域(ヨルダン川西岸とガザ地区)でのパレスチナ人の対イスラエル抵抗闘争)

intraday trading　取引時間中の取引, ざら場の取引

intraparty conflict　党内抗争

intrasquad game　〔野球〕紅白戦

introduce 動 導入する, 持ち込む, 使用を開始する, 始める, 発売する, 売り出す, 公開する, 上場する, 〈法案を議会に〉提出する, 紹介する, …の始まりとなる
　introduce a bill to Congress　法案を議会に提出する
　introduce a new product　新製品[新商品]を発売する
　introduce a nonconfidence vote against the Cabinet　内閣不信任案を提出する
　introduce an early retirement scheme　早期退職制度を導入する
　introduce various regulation measures　各種の規制措置を導入する
　introduced capital　出資金 (＝capital introduced)
　introduced stock [share]　公開株

introduction 名 導入, 新規導入, 新規導入品, 使用開始, 輸入, 伝来, 伝来品, 発売, 公開, 上場, 〈核兵器などの〉持ち込み, 注入, 挿入, 紹介, 序論, 序説, 概論, 入門書
　foreign investment [capital] introduction　外資導入 (＝introduction of foreign capital, introduction of foreign investment)
　introduction of an inflationary target　インフレ目標の導入
　introduction of stock [share]　株式公開
　worldwide simultaneous introduction of cheaper models　低価格機種の世界同時発売

inundate 動 浸水させる, 水浸しにする, 氾濫する, 押し寄せる, 殺到する

inundation 名 浸水, 冠水, 洪水, 氾濫, 〈注文などの〉殺到, 充満

invent 動 発明する, 考案する, 創案する, 創出する, 創作する, 開発する, でっち上げる, 捏造する

invention / **investment**

invent a new idea 新しいアイデア［考え］を生み出す
invent an alibi アリバイをでっち上げる
invent an excuse 口実を作る, 言い訳をでっち上げる

invention 名 発明, 発明品, 発明力, 発明の才 (inventiveness), 考案, 新案, 創作, 創案, 新案品, 創作品, 創案品, 作り話, でっち上げ, 捏造
constitution of the invention 発明の構成
detailed description of the invention 発明の詳細な説明
effect of the invention 発明の効果
finding [identifying] of a claimed invention 発明の認定
invention in service 職務発明
invention information 発明情報
invention of process 方法の発明
sole invention 単独発明
unity of invention 発明の単一性
utilization of inventions 発明の利用

inventory 名 在庫, 在庫品, 棚卸し, 棚卸し品, 棚卸し資産, 棚卸し高, 棚卸し表, 財産目録, 目録, 保有数
carry inventory 在庫を抱える
inventory finance 在庫金融
inventory index 在庫指数
inventory investment 在庫投資
inventory reduction 在庫削減, 在庫圧縮, 在庫調整, 在庫整理 (=cuts in inventory)
liquidate inventories 在庫を削減する, 在庫を取り崩す
make [take] an inventory of …の目録を作る, …の棚卸し表を作る
rebuild inventories 在庫を積み増す

invest 動 投資する, 投下する, 投入する, 運用する
invest to build 市場構築投資, 構築投資
invest to enter 市場参入投資, 参入投資
invest to rebuild 市場再構築投資, 再構築投資
invested amount 投資額
invested assets 運用資産
invested fund 投下資本, 投資資金

invest in …に投資する, 出資する, 投じる
invest in a joint venture 合弁会社に投資する
invest in common stocks 普通株式に投資する
invest in R&D 研究開発に投資する
invest in real estate 不動産に投資する

investigate 動 調査する, 究明する, 研究する, 取り調べる, 捜査する

investigation 名 調査, 検査, 審査, 監査, 査察, 研究, 究明, 取調べ, 捜査, 調査［研究］報告, 調書, 調査書, 研究論文
antidumping investigation アンチダンピング調査
credit investigation 信用調査
family budget investigation 家計調査
forcible investigation 強制調査
internal investigation 内部調査, 社内調査 (=in-house investigation)
judicial investigation power 司法調査権
investigation on fiscal operations 財政監査

investigators 捜査当局 (=investigating authorities)

investment 名 投資, 出資, 運用, 投資額, 投資物, 投資事業, 投資資産, 投資勘定, 資金投下, 証券, インベストメント (=investing)
attract investment 投資を誘致する, 投資を呼び込む
diversified investment 分散投資
equipment investment 設備投資
equity investment 株式投資
fixed asset investment 固定資産投資
investment advisory unit 投資顧問会社, 投資顧問業
investment capital 投資資本(投資に充当する資金)
investment conditions [environment] 投資環境
investment decision 投資判断, 投資の意思決定, 投資決定
Investment Deposit and Interest Rate Control Law 出資法(出資の受入れ, 預り金及び金利等の取締りに関する法律)
investment fund 投資ファンド, 投資資金
investment grade 投資適格格付け (=investment-grade, investment-grade rating)
investment-grade securities 投資適格債
investment opportunity 投資機会, 投資対象, 運用先
investment performance 運用実績, 投資実績, 投資成績
investment policy 投資方針, 投資政策, 運用方針
investment portfolio 投資ポートフォリオ, 投資資産, 投資資本構成, 投資の内容
investment scheme 投資形態, 投資ファンド, 投資計画, 投資システム

investment spending 投資支出
investment target 投資対象, 投資目標
less investment in plant and equipment 設備投資の抑制
investment trust 投資信託, 投信(一般投資家から資金を集め, 集めた金を専門家が株や債券などに投資して, その運用益を投資家に還元する金融商品)
portfolio investment 証券投資, 株式・債券投資, ポートフォリオ投資
quoted investment 上場証券
return on investment 投資利益率, 投資収益率, 投資利回り《略 ROI》
stock investments 株式投資, 保有株

investment bank 投資銀行, 証券会社(「投資銀行」の主な業務は, 証券引受け(underwriting), 新規株式公開(IPO)とM&A(企業合併・買収)の仲介)

investment banking operations 投資銀行業務 (=investment banking business)

investor 名 投資家, 投資者, 投資会社, 出資者, 出資企業, 資本主, 投資側, 投資国, 権利などの授与者, インベスター
  foreign [overseas] investors 外国人投資家, 海外投資家, 外資
  individual investor 個人投資家
  institutional investor 機関投資家
  investor confidence 投資家の信頼
  investors sentiment 投資家の意識
  major investor 大手の投資家
  retail investor 小口投資家, 個人投資家, 最終投資家
  small investor 個人投資家, 小口投資家
  wholesale investor 機関投資家

investor [investors] relations 投資家向け広報, 投資家向け広報活動, 投資家向け情報公開, 財務広報, 証券広報, 戦略的財務広報, 対投資家関係, IR活動, インベスター・リレーションズ《略 IR》(株主や投資家に対して投資判断に必要な情報を提供することがインベスター・リレーションズで, 一般にIR(アイアールと呼ばれている。有価証券報告書や決算短信だけでなく, 決算説明会や工場見学会などの自主的な開示も含まれ, 最近はインターネットを利用した活動が盛ん)

invisible 形 目に見えない, 無形の, 隠れた, 貿易外の
  invisible balance 貿易外収支 (=invisible account, balance of [on] invisible trade, invisible trade balance)
  invisible capital 無形資本
  invisible current item 貿易外経常項目
  invisible current transaction 貿易外経常取引
  invisible earnings 貿易外収入
  invisible exports and imports 貿易外輸出入, 無形の輸出入, 貿易外収支
  invisible goods 無形財
  invisible hand 見えざる手
  invisible payment 貿易外支払い
  invisible supply 市場外供給, 未出荷高
  invisible trade deficit 貿易外取引の赤字
  invisible trade surplus 貿易外取引の黒字

invite 動 招待する, 招く, 依頼する, 要請する
invoke 動 〈助け, 保護などを〉求める, 〈力や法に〉訴える, 実施する, 発動する, 行使する, …を連想させる
involve 動 参加させる, 参入させる, 関与させる, 関わらせる, 巻き込む, 巻き添えにする, 含む, 包含する, 包む, 伴う, 必要とする, 意味する, もたらす, 熱中させる, 夢中にさせる, 没頭させる, …に影響を与える, …に関わる, 難局に追い込む, 困難な立場に立たせる
  be involved in …に参加する, …に参入する, …を行う, …に関与する, …に関わる, …に巻き込まれる, …に依存している, …に協力する, …に夢中になる, …に熱中している
  be involved with …に関連している, …に関わる, …と絡み合っている

involvement 名 参加, 参入, 関与, 関わり, 関わり合い, 掛かり合い, 介入, 財政困難, 包含
  direct involvement 直接関与
  market involvement 市場への参入, 市場参入の度合い
  military involvement 軍事面での関与

in-work benefits 就労者への給付, 仕事に就いている者への給付

IOC 国際オリンピック委員会 (International Olympic Committeeの略)

IOSCO 証券監督者国際機構, 国際証券監督機構 (International Organization of Securities Commissionの略)

IP インターネットの通信規約, インターネット・プロトコル (internet protocolの略)
  IP address IPアドレス(インターネットへの接続の際, コンピューターに割り当てられる認識番号)
  IP call service IP電話サービス (=Internet Protocol call service)

IP phone service IP電話サービス（＝Internet Protocol telephone service）
IP telephone IP電話（家庭や企業が引いたブロードバンド（高速大容量通信）回線を利用して，音声信号を細切れのデータにしてインターネット網でやりとりし，通話する仕組み）
IPCC 気候変動に関する政府間パネル（International Panel on Climate Changeの略）
IPE ロンドン国際石油取引所（International Petroleum Exchangeの略）
IPO 株式公開，新規株式公開，新規株式公募，公開公募，新規公募，上場（**initial public offering**の略。会社が一般投資家に株式を初めて売り出すこと）
iPS cell 万能細胞，iPS細胞（⇒induced pluripotent stem cell）
IR アイアール，投資家向け広報，投資家向け広報活動，財務広報，インベスター・リレーションズ
IRC 産業再生機構（＝Industrial Revitalization Corporation of Japan：**Industrial Revitalization Corporation**の略）
Iraq war イラク戦争
Iraqi 形 イラクの，イラク人の
　Iraqi Governing Council イラク統治評議会
irk 動 困らせる，悩ます，怒らせる，うんざりさせる，じりじりさせる，いらいらさせる
iron 名 鉄，鉄分，鉄剤，アイロン，鉄製器具，強固［冷酷］なこと
　have many irons in the fire 一度に多くの仕事に手を出す
　iron and steel industry 鉄鋼業
　iron deficiency anemia 鉄欠乏性貧血
　iron foundry 鋳鉄工場，製鉄所
　iron hand [fist] 鉄のムチ，強硬，強権政治，厳しい支配，ワンマン体制，厳しい内面
　rule ... with a rod of iron …を鉄のムチで治める，圧制を行う，強権政治で…を支配する（＝rule with an iron hand [fist]）
iron out 円滑に行くようにする（smooth out），〈傷害などを〉取り除く，調整する，解消する，解決する，処理する，片付ける，和らげる（harmonize），調和させる，アイロンをかける
　iron out important issues 重要な問題を片付ける［処理する，解決する］
　iron out misunderstandings 誤解を解く，誤解を取り除く
irregularity 名 不正行為，不法行為，乱脈経営，乱脈融資，不祥事，不品行，不規則性，変則，誤記
　irregularities such as influence-wielding, bid-rigging and subcontracting entire public works contracts 口利きや談合，公共事業の丸投げなどの不正行為
　trading irregularities 不正取引
ISAF 国際治安支援部隊（International Security Assistance Forceの略）
Islamic 形 イスラムの，イスラム教の，イスラム教徒の，ムスリムの
　Islamic Conference Organization イスラム諸国会議機構
　Islamic Development Bank イスラム開発銀行《略 IDB》
　Islamic extremists イスラム過激派
　Islamic fundamentalism イスラム原理主義（＝Islam fundamentalism）
　Islamic Jihad イスラム聖戦機構，イスラム聖戦（＝Islamic Holy War：イスラム教シーア派の過激派を中心に組織されたテロ活動グループ）
　Islamic legal system イスラム法系
　Islamic militants イスラム武装勢力，イスラム過激派
　Islamic militants of Hamas イスラム原理主義組織ハマスの武装要員
　Islamic Republic News Agency イスラム共和国通信社《略 IRNA》（イランの国営通信社）
　Islamic Republican Party 〈イランの〉イスラム共和党
　Islamic Resistance Movement イスラム抵抗運動
　Islamic Revolutionary Movement イスラム革命運動《略 IRM》
　Islamic theocracy イスラム国家の神権政治
　Moro Islamic Liberation Front 〈フィリピンの〉モロ・イスラム解放戦線《略 MILF》
　Organization of the Islamic Conference イスラム諸国会議機構《略 OIC》
Islamist groups イスラム原理主義組織
Islamization 名 イスラム化政策（Islamization drive），イスラム化
island nations [countries] 島国諸国
ISO 国際標準化機構（正式名称はInternational Organization for Standardizationで，International Standards Organizationともいう）
ISS 国際宇宙ステーション（**international space station**の略）
issuance 名 発行，支給，配給，刊行，入札

issuance of new shares 新株発行, 増資
issuance of the arrest, search and seizure order 逮捕・捜査・押収令状の発行
issue 動 〈証券などを〉発行する, 売り出す, 起債する, 〈手形を〉振り出す, 配当を行う, 発表する, 公表する
issue new shares 新株を発行する
issue 名 証券, 株, 銘柄, 発行, 発行債, 発行部数, 交付, 〈手形の〉振出し, 問題, 問題点, 争点, 論点, 成り行き, 結果, 結末
- **authorized issue** 授権発行数
- **bank of issue** 発券銀行
- **be at issue with** …と論争中［係争中］である, …と意見が合わない
- **bond issue** 社債発行, 公債発行
- **bring a case to an issue** 事件に決着をつける
- **critical issue** 深刻な問題
- **current issue** 指標銘柄
- **deal with the issue** 問題に対処する
- **equity issue** 増資, 出資証券
- **face the issue** 事実を事実と認めて対処する
- **implementation issues** 実務上の問題
- **in the issue** 結局は, 要するに
- **issue market** 発行市場
- **issue of fact** 事実上の問題点
- **issue of law** 法律上の問題点, 法律上の争点
- **join issue** 双方が争点を提起して裁決を求める, 論争する (take issue), 対立する
- **key issue** 重要課題
- **labor issue** 労働問題
- **make an issue of** …を問題にする, …について騒ぐ
- **moral issue** 倫理上の問題
- **outstanding issues** 懸案事項
- **par isuue** 額面発行
- **public issue** 公募, 公募債
- **real issues** 切実な問題
- **regulatory issues** 規制上の問題
- **senior issue** 上位証券
- **settle the issue** 問題を解決する
- **take [join] issue with** …と論争［議論］する, …と対立する, …と意見が合わない, …に異議を唱える
- **the amount of public bond issues** 公債発行額
- **the daily issue of a newspaper** 新聞の毎日の発行部数
- **the latest issue of a magazine** 雑誌の最新号

issued shares 発行済み株式, 発行済み株式数, 発行株式数 (=issued stocks: 会社の授権株式(会社が発行できる株式の上限数)のうち, すでに発行された株式の総数)

IT bubble ITバブル, IT投資バブル, ネット株バブル (=the bubble in IT investments, the information technology bubble, Net bubble)

item 名 項目, 品目, 種目, 細目, 事項, 商品, 用品, 品物, アイテム
- **abnormal item** 異常項目
- **adjustment item** 修正項目, 調整項目
- **balance sheet item** 貸借対照表項目
- **balancing item** 調整項目
- **base item** 基本項目
- **big item** 目玉商品
- **big-ticket item** 高額商品, 高価な商品
- **cash item** 現金項目
- **corporate items** 本社事項
- **fungible items** 汎用品
- **infrequent item** 突発事項
- **item control** 単品管理
- **Item Response Theory** 項目反応理論
- **line item** 勘定科目
- **operating item** 営業項目, 営業品目
- **popular item** 売れ筋商品, 売れ筋, 人気商品 (=hot item)
- **prior period item** 前期修正項目
- **sensitive item** 輸入要注意品目
- **unusual item** 特別損益項目

ITER 国際熱核融合実験炉 (International Thermonuclear Experimental Reactorの略)

ITU 国際電気通信連合 (International Telecommunication Unionの略)

IWC 国際捕鯨委員会 (International Whaling Commissionの略)

J j

Japan Aerospace Exploration Agency 宇宙航空研究開発機構
Japan Association of Corporate Executives 経済同友会
Japan-bashing 名 日本たたき, 日本いじめ, ジャパン・バッシング
Japan Business Federat-on 日本経済団体連合会, 日本経団連《略 JBF》
Japan Chamber of Commerce and Industry 日本商工会議所
Japan Coast Guard 海上保安庁
Japan Consumers' Association 日本消費者協会
Japan External Trade Organization 日本貿易振興機構(ジェトロ)
Japan Federation of Bar Associations 日本弁護士連合会
Japan Inc. 日本株式会社, 日本企業
Japan Independent Stores Association 日本商店連盟, 日商連
Japan Medical Association 日本医師会
Japan money ジャパン・マネー (日本企業の海外投資資金・資本)
Japan-passing 名 日本無視, ジャパン・パッシング
Japan Teachers' Union 日教組
Japan–U.S. alliance 日米同盟
Japan–U.S. Business Conference 日米財界人会議
Japan–U.S. Joint Committee 日米合同委員会
Japan–U.S. security alliance 日米同盟
Japan–U.S. security treaty 日米安保条約
Japan–U.S. Status of Forces Agreement 日米地位協定
Japan–U.S. structural impediments initiative talks 日米構造協議
Japan–U.S. summit meeting 日米首脳会談
Japanese Agricultural Standards Law 日本農林規格法, JAS法
Japanese Association of Corporate Executives 経済同友会
Japanese Institute of Certified Public Accountants 日本公認会計士協会
Japanese management 日本型経営, ジャパニーズ・マネジメント(一般に, 欧米の企業との対比で, 終身雇用制や年功序列制, 企業内組合など日本独自の経営方式のこと)
Japanese Society for Rights of Authors, Composers and Publishers 日本音楽著作権協会《略 JASRAC》
Japanese spouses of North Koreans 日本人配偶者, 日本人妻
Jasdaq ジャスダック (Japan Securities Dealer's Association Quotationの略。日本の新興企業向け株式店頭市場。2004年12月13日, 店頭市場から証券取引所(Jasdaq Securities Exchange)に移行して取引を開始)
jaws 名 瀬戸際, 崖っぷち
in the jaws of …の状態に陥る

out of the jaws of　…の状態を脱する
the jaws of　ほとんど…も同然，ほぼ確実な…，…の入口，…の狭い入口
throw oneself into the jaws of death　窮地に陥る，死地に陥る
JEITA　電子情報技術産業協会（Japan Electronics and Information Technology Industries Associationの略）
Jemaah Islamiyah　ジェマア・イスラミア（東南アジアのテロ組織）
jeopardize 動　危険にさらす，危険［危機］に陥れる，危うくする，損なう，ダメージを与える
jettison 動　放棄する，撤廃する，廃棄する，破棄する，処分する，見捨てる，投げ捨てる，投棄する，投下する，射出する，切り離す，投げ荷［打ち荷］する，名 放棄，撤廃，廃棄，破棄，処分，投げ荷，打ち荷
jettison a large portion of deck cargo　甲板積み荷の大部分を投げ捨てる［投棄する］
jettison a loss-making department　不採算部門を切り離す
jettison underperforming operations　不採算事業を切り離す
jettison seat　射出座席
JICA　国際協力機構（Japan International Cooperation Agencyの略）
Jihad [Jehad]　聖戦，〈思想，主義のための〉戦い，ジハード（＝holy war）
job 名　職，職場，職務，任務，業務，雇用，就職口，働き口，仕事，作業，責務，勤めめ，役目，難事，問題，事態，厄介なこと，困ったこと，強盗，犯罪，不正，汚職，美容整形，整形［美容整形］手術，形成外科手術，ジョブ
bad job　困った事態
be out of a job　失業している，失業中だ
be paid by the job　一仕事いくらで支払われる
by the job　請負で，仕事単位で，仕事単位の契約で，一仕事いくらで
closed job cost sheet　締切り個別原価計算表
do a job　罪を犯す
do a job on　…に危害を加える，…を台なしにする，…をやっつける，…を壊す
do the job　目的を達する，効果がある，うまく機能する，うまくいく
fall down on the job　失敗する，しくじる，務めを果たせない
get a job with　…に就職する
have a job to　…するのに苦労する

inside job　内部［内部の者］の犯行，屋内の仕事
job action　順法闘争，スローダウン（slowdown：故意の減産・操業短縮，のろのろ戦術，怠業），組織的抗議行動（＝industrial action）
job applicant　求職者
job application　求職
job assignment　職務割当て
job background　職務経歴
job bank　人材銀行，国営職業斡旋所（＝job-center）
job category　職務
job change　転職（＝job hopping）
job classification　職務分類，職階，職階制
job content　職務内容
job creation　雇用創出
job depth　職務深度
job description　職務記述書，職務分掌規定，職務内容説明書（職位の権限と責任事項を記載したもの）
job design　職務設計
job discrimination　仕事上の差別
job enlargement　職務拡大
job enrichment　職務充実，職務充実化
job evaluation　職務評価，職務査定
job experience　職務経験
job holder　就業者，定職に就いている者，政府職員（＝jobholder）
job-hopper　転職者，職を転々と変える人
job hopping　転職（＝job change）
job-hopping part-time worker　フリーター
job hunter　求職者（＝job seeker）
job hunting　求職，求職活動，就職活動，仕事探し，職探し（＝job seeking）
job improvement　職務改善
job interview　就職面接，求職面接
job knowledge　職務知識
job leaver　離職者
job loser　失職者，失業者
job lot　規格はずれ品，不揃い商品，大口商品，端株，作業ロット，小口取引，ロット
job management　ジョブ管理
job market　労働市場，雇用市場，求人市場，雇用情勢，雇用
job opening　欠員，求人，求職
job opportunity　雇用機会，就労機会，就業機会，就業のチャンス，求人
job-oriented terminal　特定業務用端末装置
job performance　職務遂行，職務能力，仕事

ぶり

job placement 就職斡旋, 就職紹介 (job introduction), 労働者派遣
job placement office 職業安定所
job rate 職務給
job rating 職務評価
job redesign 職務再設計
job-related accommodation 社宅
job requirement 職務資格
job rotation 職務配置, 職務転換, 配置転換, 計画的異動, 職務歴任制, 職場輪番制, ジョブ・ローテーション
job satisfaction 職務満足, 職務充足, 仕事の満足感, 仕事のやりがい
job search 求職活動, 求職, 職探し (＝job hunting)
job sharing 仕事分担, ジョブ・シェアリング
job shortage 就職難 (＝harsh employment)
job situation 雇用情勢, 雇用状況, 雇用環境
job specialty 専門職種
job specifications 職務明細書
job standard 作業標準, 課業, 職務基準
job step ジョブの構成単位, ジョブ・ステップ
job study 作業研究, 職務研究
job tax credit 雇用促進税額控除
job title 職階
job transfer 転勤
job vacancy 求人
job work 請負仕事, 注文仕事
jobs for the boys えこひいきの人事
just the job ちょうど望みどおりのもの, うってつけの物[人]
key job 基準職務
know one's job …の仕事に精通している, よく心得ている
make a bad job …に失敗する
make a (good) job of it うまくやってのける
make a (good) job on …を立派にやってのける
make the best of a bad job 不利な状況で最善をつくす
man for the job 適任者
more than one's job's worth …の権限外である
odd jobs 半端な仕事, 臨時の仕事
off the job 非番で, 仕事を休んで
on the job 仕事[作業, 勤務]中の, 仕事に精を出して, 〈機械などが〉作動中で, 油断なく, 警戒して

outside job 外部[外部の者]の犯行, 屋外の仕事
provide jobs 雇用を創出する
pull a bank job 銀行強盗をする
sellers' job market 求人の売り手市場
service jobs サービス部門の雇用
skilled job 熟練労働, 熟練度の高い職
the job at hand 当面の仕事
unskilled job 単純労働, 熟練度の低い職

job loss 失職, 失業
　job loss recovery 雇用を失う回復, ジョブ・ロス・リカバリー
　job losses 雇用者数の減少, 雇用の減少

job offer 求人
　job offers 求人, 求人数, 有効求人数
　provisional [informal] job offers 内定
　the ratio of job offers to job seekers 有効求人倍率 (＝the job offers to applicants ratio, the ratio of job openings to registered job applicants)
　the seasonally adjusted job offer to job seeker ratio 有効求人倍率(季節調整値)

job opening 欠員, 求人, 求職
　job openings 新規雇用, 新規求人, 新規雇用数, 求人数
　job openings per job seeker 有効求人倍率, 求人倍率

job security 職務保証, 雇用保障, 雇用維持, 雇用の安定, 職の安全
　job security accord 雇用維持協定

job seeker 求職者 (＝job hunter, jobseeker)
　the job seeker-job opening ratio 有効求人倍率
　the ratio of job offers to job seekers 有効求人倍率

job training 職業訓練
　Job Training Partnership Act of 1982 1982年職業訓練協力法《略 **JTPA**》
　off-the-job training 職場外訓練, 職場外教育訓練, 集合教育, オフJT (＝off-JT)
　on-the-job training 職場内訓練, 職場内教育訓練, 職場研修《略 **OJT**》 (＝on-JT)

jobless 形 失業中の, 仕事のない, 名 失業者
　jobless claims 失業保険新規受給申請者数, 失業保険新規申請件数
　jobless people 失業者 (＝the jobless)
　jobless rate 失業率, 完全失業率 (＝unemployment rate)

jobless recovery 雇用なき経済回復, 雇用の回復なき景気回復, ジョブレス・リカバリー

joblessness 名 失業, 失業率 (＝unemployment)
▶ Increase in corporate failures and *joblessness* in the United States will be another blow to the U.S. economy. 米国で企業倒産や失業が増大すれば、米国経済に再び打撃を与えることになろう。

jobseeker 名 求職者 (＝job seeker)
　Jobseeker's Agreement 求職者協定, 求職者合意制度
　jobseeker's allowance 求職者給付

jockey 動 (だまして)手に入れる, 巻き上げる
　jockey for position 策を弄して優位な地位を得る, 優位な地位を得ようと画策する, 優位に立とうとする

join 動 参加する, 資本参加する, 加わる, 入る, 協力する, 協同する, 提携する, 入会する, 入社する, …に入る, 加盟する, 合流する, 始める
　join a company 入社する
　join a syndication シ団に参加する
　join forces 連携する, 提携する, 力を合わせる, 協力する, 手を組む, 手を結ぶ, 勢力を結集する, 統一会派を組む
　join hands 連携する, 提携する, 手を結ぶ, 手を組む, 協力する, 力を合わせる, 勢力を結集する, 支援する (＝join forces)
　join the board 取締役会に加わる, 取締役に就任する, 取締役に選任される
　join the deal 案件に参加する, 同案件に参加する
　join with [up] …に協力する, …と提携する

joint 形 共同の, 合同の, 連帯の, 連合の, 合弁の, 共有の, 共通の, ジョイント
　joint account 〈主に夫婦名義の〉共同預金口座, 共同勘定
　joint action 協調行動, 共同行為
　joint ballot 連記投票
　Joint Chiefs of Staff 〈米国防総省の〉統合参謀本部《略 JCS》
　joint committee 〈米〉両院合同委員会, 両院協議会
　Joint Committee on the Economic Report 〈米〉合同経済委員会, 〈米〉経済合同委員会
　joint communique [statement] 共同声明, 共同文書
　joint consultation 労使協議
　joint convention 米両院合同会議
　joint custody 連帯親権, 連帯保護義務
　joint debt 連帯債務
　joint decision 共同決定, 共同決定事項
　Joint Declaration on Denuclearization of the Korean Peninsula 朝鮮半島非核化共同宣言
　Joint Direct Attack Munition 衛星誘導のジェイダム弾《略 JDAM》
　joint efforts 一致した努力[協力]
　joint exercises 合同演習
　Joint FAO/WHO FAO/WHO合同食品規格委員会
　joint fare 共同運賃
　joint firm [company] 合弁会社, 共同運営会社
　joint float 共同変動相場制, 変動相場制への共同移行
　joint holding company [firm] 共同持ち株会社
　joint inquiry 共同調査, 合同調査
　joint intervention 協調介入, 協調市場介入 (＝coordinated intervention, joint market intervention)
　joint investigation team 合同捜査チーム, 合同捜査班
　joint management 共同経営(joint operation), 共同管理
　joint management company 共同運営会社, 合弁による運営会社
　joint market intervention 協調介入, 協調市場介入
　joint military exercises 合同軍事演習, 合同軍事訓練
　joint names 連名
　joint offense 共犯
　joint owners 共有者, 共同所有者
　joint project [enterprise] 共同[合同]事業, 共同プロジェクト
　joint property 共有財産
　joint public-private company 第三セクター
　joint purchase 共同購入, 共同仕入れ
　joint resolution 〈米上下両院の〉合同決議, 共同決議, 両院決議
　joint responsibility [liability] 共同責任, 連帯責任, 連座制
　joint session of Congress 米議会の上下両院合同会議
　joint signature 連署
　joint stake 共同出資, 共同出資比率
　joint stock company 株式会社 (＝joint stock corporation)

joint study [research] 共同研究
joint use of fiber-optic networks 光ファイバー網の共同利用
joint venture 合弁会社, 合弁事業, 合弁, 共同企業, 共同企業体, 共同事業, 共同事業体, 共同出資会社, 共同出資事業, ジョイント・ベンチャー《略 JV》 (＝corporate joint venture, joint business, joint venture company)
 corporate joint venture 合弁会社, 共同事業会社 (＝joint venture company)
 fifty-fifty joint venture 折半出資の合弁会社 (＝50-50 joint venture, 50% joint venture)
 form [set up] a joint venture with …と共同出資会社を設立する, …と合弁会社を設立する
 joint venture company 合弁会社, 共同事業会社 (＝corporate joint venture)
 risk-averse joint venture リスク回避型の合弁企業
 set up a 50% joint venture 折半出資の合弁会社を設立する
jointly 共同で, 合同で, 連合して, 連帯して
 be sponsored jointly by …の共同主催である, …が共同主催する
 jointly develop 共同開発する (＝work together to develop [invent])
 jointly own 共同所有する, 共同出資する (＝equally own)
jolt 揺り動かす, 震動させる, 衝撃[ショック]を与える, …に動揺を与える, …を驚かせる, …に干渉する
jolt 揺れ, 震動, 衝撃, ショック, 動揺
journal 専門誌, 雑誌(magazine, periodical), 定期刊行物(periodical), 日刊紙(daily newspaper), 週刊誌, 日記, 日誌, 議事録, 国会議事録, 取引記録, 仕訳, 仕訳帳, 航海日誌(log, logbook), ジャーナル
 cash receipt [receipts] journal 現金収納帳
 general journal 一般仕訳帳
 Journals 英国国会議事録
 medical journal 医学雑誌, 医学誌, 医学専門誌
 monthly journal 月間雑誌, 月刊誌
 quarterly journal 季刊雑誌, 季刊誌
 summary journal 総合仕訳帳
journalism 報道機関, 新聞雑誌類, 新聞雑誌界, 新聞雑誌の記事, 大衆向けの記事, 文筆業, ジャーナリズム
judge 判断する, 考える, 評価する, 批評する, 非難する, 批判する, 推定する, 見積もる, 裁判する, 審理する, 裁く, 判決を下す

judge 裁判官, 判事, 裁判長, 治安判事, 審判員, 審判, 審査員, 目利き, 鑑定家, ジャッジ
 a chief judge 裁判長
 a citizen judge 市民の裁判員
 a federal judge 連邦判事
 a High Court judge 〈英国の〉高等法院判事, 最高裁判所判事
 a judge a quo 原審裁判官
 a judge ad quem 上訴審裁判官
 a judge advocate 〈陸・空・海の〉法務官
 a judge of a speech contest 弁論大会の審査員
 a judge's bench 判事席
 a preliminary [an examining] judge 予審判事
 a presiding judge 裁判長, 首席判事
 a side judge 次席判事
 an administrative law judge 行政法審判官
 an assistant judge 判事補
 an associate [puisne] judge 陪席裁判官[判事], 〈主席裁判官以外の〉普通裁判官, 平裁判官
 the chief judge of the Tokyo High Court 東京高裁長官
 the Impeachment of Judges Act 裁判官弾劾法
 the Judge Impeachment Court 裁判官弾劾裁判所 (＝Court of Impeachment of Judges)
 the panel of judges 審査員団
 the Tenure of Judges' Office Act 裁判官分限法
judgment [judgement] 判断, 判定, 判決, 裁判, 審判, 意見, 考え, 見解, 見識, 思慮分別, 判断力, 非難, 批判, 天罰, 神罰, 報い
 a judgment of acquittal 無罪判決
 a judgment of conviction 有罪判決
 against one's better judgment 不本意ながら
 default judgment 欠席裁判 (＝judgment by default)
 form an independent judgment on …について独自の意見[考え]を述べる
 in one's judgment …の考えでは
 judgment call 審判判定, 個人的判断
 lose one's judgment …の判断力を失う
 pass [give, make] judgment on …に判決を下す, …を判断[判定, 評価]する, …について意

見を述べる, …を批判する
reserve judgment 判断を保留する, 差し控える
sit in judgment over [on, upon] …を裁く, …を非難する, …を批判する
judicial 形 司法の(judiciary), 裁判の, 裁判による, 裁決による, 裁判官の, 賢明な, 判断力[識別力]のある, 批判的な, 公正な, 公平な
judicial act 法律行為
judicial admission 法廷での事実承認, 法廷での自白
judicial assassination 〈死刑など〉司法による暗殺
judicial authorities 司法当局
Judicial Conference of the United States 合衆国司法会議
Judicial confession 裁判上の自白
judicial definition 判例
judicial discretion 裁判所の裁量, 法律上の裁量
judicial immunity 裁判官の免責
judicial inquiry 司法調査
judicial investigation power 司法調査権
judicial legislation 裁判官立法, 司法による立法
judicial murder 法による殺人, 不当と考えられる死刑宣告
judicial notice 裁判所による通知
judicial police 司法警察
judicial power [powers] 司法権, 裁判権
judicial precedent 判例, 判決例
judicial procedures 裁判手続き
judicial proceedings 裁判手続き, 訴訟手続き, 司法手続き
judicial process 司法手続き, 司法
judicial records 裁判手続きの記録
judicial review 司法審査[審査権], 違憲審査, 違憲立法審査[審査権], 〈主に英国の〉司法審査手続き
judicial ruling 判例
judicial sale 司法上の売却
judicial scrivener 司法書士
judicial separation 裁判別居, 判決に基づく夫婦の別居 (＝legal separation)
judicial supremacy 司法権の独立, 司法権の優越
judicial system 司法制度
outside the judicial process 司法手続きによらないで
right of judicial review 法令審査権, 司法審査権
judiciary 形 司法の, 裁判の, 裁判所の, 裁判官の
Judiciary Act of 1789 1789年裁判所法
Judiciary Committee 法務委員会 (＝Committee on Judiciary Affairs)
judiciary legislation 司法部に関する立法
judiciary proceedings 裁判手続き
Senate Judiciary Subcommittee 米上院司法小委員会
jump 動 跳ね上がる, 急増する, 急上昇する, 上昇する, 大幅に上がる, 飛ぶ, 飛躍する, 〈異例の〉昇進をする, 出世する
jump 名 急騰, 暴騰, 跳ね上がり, 急増, 急上昇, 急転, 飛躍, 急激な進歩, 画面の飛び, 省略, ジャンプ
jump in prices 価格の上昇, 物価高騰
sharp jump in exports 輸出急増
▶ Wholesale prices rose 1.3 percent from the previous year, reflecting a *jump* in prices of steel and oil products. 企業物価(日本の旧卸売り物価)指数は, 鉄鋼や石油製品の価格の上昇を反映して, 前年比で1.3％上昇した。
jump-start 動 活発化させる, 急発進させる, 始動させる, …に活を入れる
juncture 名 事態, 危急の事態, 重大時期, 重大な情勢[局面], 危機, 時期, 時点, 正念場, 危機, 接合, 接続, 接合点, 継ぎ目, 連結, 連絡地
at this juncture この重大時期[重大事]に, この危急の事態に際して, この際
reach a juncture 危機に達する
junk 名 投資不適格, ジャンク債, ジャンク
junk bond ジャンク債, くず債券, 格付けの低い[投資不適格の, 信用度の低い]債券, 高利回り債, 不良債券, ジャンク・ボンド
junk territory [status] 投資不適格レベル
junta 名 〈クーデター後の〉暫定政府, 軍事政権
jurisdiction 名 裁判管轄, 裁判管轄権, 裁判権, 管轄権, 管轄区域, 法域, 権限, 司法権, 司法行政, 司法権, 行政権や徴税権などを行使できる国家や地方自治体
jury 名 陪審, 審査団, 審査委員会, 評決
grand jury 大陪審, 起訴陪審
petty [petit] jury 小陪審
▶ The *jury* is still out. 評決は, まだ下されていない[結論は, まだ出ていない]。
just-in-time かんばん方式, ジャストインタイム, ジット《略 JIT》(＝JIT, JIT system, just-in-

time system, "Kanban" system：トヨタ自動車の生産管理方式で，部品の在庫ゼロをめざして，必要なときに必要な量だけ部品を納入させる方式)

justice 名 公正, 公平, 正義, 正当, 正当性, 裁判, 裁き, 司法, 裁判官, 判事, 治安判事,〈英国の〉最高法院判事, 処罰, 当然の報い
  bring A to justice Aを裁判にかける, Aを法廷に引き出す
  Chief Justice of the United States 米最高裁判所長官
  court of justice 法廷, 裁判所
  criminal justice system 刑事司法制度
  Department of Justice 米司法省
  do justice to …に正当な扱いをする, …を公平に扱う[評価する], …をよく表している
  escape justice 処罰を免れる
  Justice of the Peace 治安判事
  rough justice 不当な扱い
  Supreme Court Justice [justice] 米最高裁判所判事

K

kaleidoscope 名　万華鏡, 千変万化, 目まぐるしく変化するもの［景色, 状況, 模様］, カレイドスコープ
kangaroo 名　カンガルー
 kangaroo closure　カンガルー式討論終結法（修正案だけに絞って討論する方法）
 kangaroo court　リンチ, つるし上げ, 人民［私的］裁判, 不当裁判, 不正規裁判, でっち上げ
 kangaroo system　トラックと鉄道による複合一貫輸送, カンガルー方式
 kangaroo ticket　カンガルー・チケット
KBM　知識ベース・マシン（knowledge based machineの略）
KEDO　朝鮮半島エネルギー開発機構（Korean Peninsula Development Organizationの略）
keep out　…を締め出す, …を排除する, …を防ぐ, 立ち入らない, 中に入らない
keep pace with　…と足並みを揃える, …と歩調を合わせる［揃える］, …に遅れないようについて行く, …に比例する, …に合わせて変わる
 keep pace with inflation　インフレと足並みを揃える
 keep pace with the rate of change　変化のペースについて行く
keep up with　…に遅れないでついて行く, …と歩調を合わせる, …に対応する, …に屈しない, …の情報に通じている, …と交際する, …をやり続ける
 keep up with [on] international relations　国際関係についての情報に明るい
 keep up with the changing times　時代の変化に対応する
 keep up with the plan　この計画について行く
 make investments to keep up with growth　成長に見合った投資を進める
keep ... under wraps　…を隠しておく, …を非公開にする, …を秘密にしておく
key 名　鍵, 要（かなめ）, 手がかり, 重要地点, 要所, 重要人物, キー
 hold the key to　…の鍵を握る
 the key to revitalizing the economy　景気浮揚への鍵
 the key to success　成功の秘訣［鍵］, 成功にとって重要なこと
key 形　重要な, 主要な, 枢要な, 最大の, 基幹の, 中心の, 中核の, 基軸の, キー
 break through key resistance (level)　主要な抵抗線を突き抜ける［突破する］
 close below key support　主要な支持線を割り込んで引ける
 key account　主要得意先, 上得意先
 key areas　中核業務, 主要部門, 主要セクター
 key arteries　主要幹線道路
 key aspect　重要な局面
 key buying influence　主要な購買影響者《略 KBI》
 key currency　基軸通貨, 国際通貨, キー・カレンシー（＝international currency, reserve currency）
 key determinant　最大の要因, 主要要因
 key economic data　主要景気指標, 主要経済指標（＝key economic indicators, key economic series）
 key factor　重要な要因, 主要要因, 主な要因

key figure 中心人物
key hardware 主要設備
key indicator 主要指標, 指標
key industry 基幹産業, 主要産業
key issue [question] 重要問題, 最大の問題
key locations 主要国, 主要都市
key money 基軸通貨 （＝key currency）, 保証金, 手付け金, 礼金, 権利金
key official [officer] 幹部
key policy instrument 政策の柱
key resistance 主要な抵抗線
key short-term bank lending rate 短期銀行貸出金利の誘導目標
key statistics 主要経済指標
key tenant 核テナント, 核店舗, キー・テナント
play a key role 重要な役割を果たす

key-capture software キーキャプチャー・ソフト（打ったキーを自動的に記録するソフトウェア）

key gauge 指数, 指標, 重要［主要］な基準［尺度］
　a key gauge of the current state of the economy 景気の現状を示す主要基準（景気一致指数）
　the key gauge of consumer prices 消費者物価指数

key interest rate 政策金利, 主要政策金利, 基準金利, 指標金利, 金利の誘導目標, FF金利（＝benchmark rate, key rate）
　boost [raise] a key interest rate to the highest level 政策金利［フェデラル・ファンド金利］を最高水準まで引き上げる
　leave one's key interest rate unchanged 政策金利を据え置く
　raise the key interest rate by a quarter of a percentage 政策金利を0.25％引き上げる
　slash [cut, reduce] one's key interest rate 政策金利を引き下げる

key rate 政策金利, 基準金利, 指標金利 （＝key interest rate：米国の場合, a key rateはフェデラル・ファンド（FF）金利を指し, key rates（複数形）は公定歩合（official discount rate）とフェデラル・ファンド（FF）金利の誘導目標の二つを指す。なお, 日銀の「公定歩合」は2006年8月11日から「基準割引率および基準貸付利率」に変更された。）⇒key interest rate, official discount rate）

keynote 基調, 要旨, 基本方針, 基本政策
　keynote address [speech] 基調演説, 基調講演, 基本方針演説

keynote speaker 基本方針発表者 （＝keynoter）

kick in 効果が出始める, 動き出す, 作動し始める, 〈感情が〉出てくる, 湧く, 〈金を〉寄付する, 献金する, 決済する, 死ぬ

kick off 始める, 開始する, 始まる, 開幕する

kickback 不当な手数料, 割戻し金, バック・リベート, 裏金, リベート, 賄賂, 〈従業員の給料の〉ぴんはね, 予想外の反発, 盗品の返却, キックバック
　kickback from a subcontractor 下請業者からの裏金［リベート］
　kickback of duty 戻し関税
　pay kickbacks to …にリベートを支払う
　receive kickbacks from trade connections 取引業者からリベートを取る

kidnap 誘拐する, 拉致する
kidney transplant 腎臓移植, 腎移植
killer app 究極のソフト, 新技術導入の動機［決め手］, 決定版, 特長, キラー・アップ（app＝application）
killer bees 敵対的買収を防ぐための専門家集団, 殺し屋ミツバチ, 兵隊バチ, キラー・ビーズ
killer content キラー・コンテンツ（大衆に人気の高いソフトウエアや番組のこと）
kilobyte キロバイト （＝K, KB, Kbyte：情報量の単位で, 1,024バイト）
kilter 調子, 状態, 好調, 整った状態
　out of [off] kilter 不調で

kingmaker 陰の実力者, 〈政界などの〉黒幕, 米政党の選挙組織（machine）をとりしきる者, 立候補指名者, 国王擁立者, キングメーカー
　behind-the-scenes kingmaker 陰の実力者

knee-jerk 反射的な, 自動的な, とっさの, 反射的に反応する, 型にはまった, 型どおりの反応を示す
　in a knee-jerk manner 型どおりに, 型にはまったやり方で
　knee-jerk reaction 自動的［反射的］反応

knell 鐘の音, 弔いの鐘, 弔鐘, 不吉な前兆, 凶兆
　ring [sound, toll] the knell of …の終わりを告げる, …の消滅を告げる［知らせる］, …の廃止を知らせる
　toll the death knell of …の終わりを告げる, …の弔鐘を鳴らす

Knesset クネソト（イスラエル国会）

knockdown 格安の, 廉価な, 特価の, 最低の, 組立方式［組立式］の, 現地組立方式の, 折りた

たみ式式の, 圧倒的な, 強烈な, ノックダウン方式の, ノックダウン
knockdown blow 大打撃, 必殺打
knockdown brawl 激論
knockdown export 現地組立輸出, ノックダウン輸出 (部品を輸出して現地で組み立ててから販売する方法)
knockdown import 国内組立輸入, ノックダウン輸入
knockdown plan 組立[現地]方式, ノックダウン方式 (＝knockdown system)
knockdown price 最低価格, 最安値, 格安値, 底値
knockdown table 組立式[折りたたみ式]のテーブル
knockoff 名 にせブランド品[商品], 模造品, イミテーション
knock-on effect 連鎖反応, 連鎖効果, ドミノ効果, 将棋倒し
knowhow [know-how] 名 ノウハウ, 技術情報, 技術知識, 専門知識, 専門技術, 製造技術, 技術秘密, 技術秘訣, 手法, 秘伝, 奥義, 秘訣, コツ (＝expertise)
　confidential knowhow 秘密ノウハウ
　conveyance of knowhow ノウハウの供与
　industrial knowhow 産業技術
　knowhow transfer ノウハウ譲渡, ノウハウの移転
　management knowhow 経営のノウハウ, 経営の専門知識
　production knowhow 生産技術のノウハウ
　technical knowhow 技術専門知識, 技術的専門知識, 技術ノウハウ
　transfer of knowhow and technical assistance ノウハウの移転と技術援助
knowledge 名 知識, 知的資産, 認識, 理解, 承知, 精通, 熟知, 情報, 知りうる範囲, ナレッジ
　common knowledge 周知の事実
　exclusive knowledge 専門知識
　explicit knowledge 形式知
　knowledge acquisition 知識獲得
　knowledge base system 知識ベース・システム (＝expert system, knowledge-based system)
　knowledge-based facility 知識ベース機能
　knowledge discovery in database データベースによる知識発見《略 KDD》(＝data mining)
　knowledge engineer 知識エンジニア, ナレッジ・エンジニア《略 KE》(人工知能を応用したシステムの分析設計を行うソフトウエア・エンジニア)
　knowledge engineering 知識工学
　knowledge industry 知識産業, 情報産業
　knowledge intensive [knowledge-intensive] industry 知識集約型産業
　knowledge management 知識管理, 知的資産管理, 知識経営, ナレッジ経営, ナレッジ・マネジメント《略 KM》
　knowledge representation 知識表現
　knowledge system 知識システム, 知識ベース, 人工知能システム, エキスパート・システム (常識, 経験則, 事実, 対処法などをデータベース化したもの)
　knowledge worker 知的労働者, 知識労働者, ナレッジ・ワーカー
　prior knowledge 予備知識
　public knowledge 公知
　tacit knowledge 暗黙知
known 形 有名な, 著名な, 名の通っている, 既知の, 周知の, 公知の
　a known criminal 前科のある犯罪者, 名うての犯罪者
　a known fact 周知の事実
　a known quantity 有名人, よく知られた人, 一般に認められた人[物], 既知の事柄
　a less-known issuer 知名度の低い発行体
　a less-known name 無名の銘柄
　known or unknown 既知のまたは未知の
　known to the public 公知の
Korean Armistice Agreement 朝鮮戦争休戦協定
Korean Peninsula Energy Development Organization 朝鮮半島エネルギー開発機構《略 KEDO》(1994年の米朝枠組み合意に基づいて, 95年3月に設立された国際共同事業体。核兵器の原料となるプルトニウムの抽出が容易な黒鉛減速炉の運転を北朝鮮が凍結する代わりに, プルトニウムの抽出が困難な軽水炉を建設する)
krypton 85 クリプトン85 (原子番号36の気体。天然には存在せず, 原子炉のなかで核燃料ウランが分裂して作られる)
Kyoto mechanism 京都メカニズム (途上国の二酸化炭素など温室効果ガス排出量の削減分を先進国が購入できる仕組み)
Kyoto Protocol 京都議定書 (＝the Kyoto pact, the global climate pact)

L

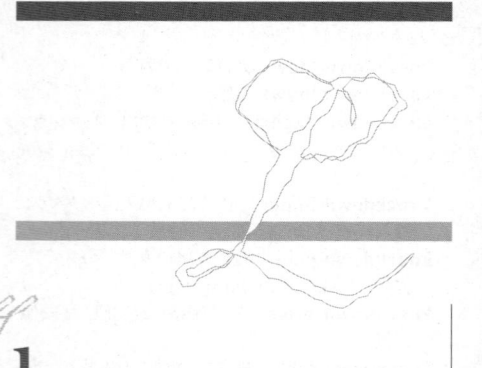

La Niña ラ・ニーニャ現象（台風の多発，集中豪雨，高温・少雨などの現象を引き起こす。⇒El Niño）
labeling 名 表示，分類，ラベル表示，ラベルの貼付，ラベリング（＝label）
  best before date labeling 賞味期限の表示
  false labeling of food 食品の偽装表示，食品偽装
  grade labeling 等級ラベル表示
  ingredient labeling 成分表示
labor [labour] 名 労働，労務，労働力，労働者，労働者側，仕事，骨折り，苦心，苦しみ，苦悩，陣痛，産みの苦しみ，分娩
  administration of labor 労働行政
  agricultural labor 農業労働
  amount of labor supplied 労働供給量
  brain labor 頭脳労働
  capital and labor 労使，労働者と資本家
  career labor 専門職労働
  child labor 児童就労，児童労働
  collective labor agreement 労働協約（＝labor agreement）
  common labor 肉体労働，不熟練労働
  dispute between capital and labor 労使間紛争
  forced labor 強制労働
  industrial labor force 産業労働力，工業労働力
  intellectual labor 知的労働，精神的労働
  International Labor Organization 国際労働機関《略 ILO》
  Knights of Labor 〈米〉労働者権利擁護組合，労働騎士団
labor affairs section 労務課
labor agreement 労使協約，労働協約（＝collective agreement, collective bargaining agreement, labor collective agreement, trade agreement）
labor arbitration 労働仲裁
labor camp 強制収容所
labor conditions 労働条件
labor contract 労働契約
Labor Department 〈米〉労働省
labor dispute 労働争議
labor distribution rate 労働分配率
labor force 労働力，労働人口，労働力人口（＝work force）
labor force participation rate 労働力率，労働力の就業率
labor-hearing system 労働審判制度（労使双方の幹部やOBが，審判員として裁判官と対等の立場で審理に加わる制度。書面ではなく口頭での審理が中心で，審判員として経営者側と労働者側からそれぞれ1人参加する）
labor hearings 労働審判
labor-intensive firm 労働集約型企業，労働集約的企業
labor leader 組合の幹部
labor of Hercules 困難な大仕事
labor of love 篤志事業，自分の好みでする事業，楽しんでやる仕事
labor offensive 労働攻勢
labor organization 労働組織，労働団体，労働

機関
labor saving investment 省力化投資
labor shortage 人手不足, 労働力不足, 労働者不足
labor spy 〈経営者側の〉労働スパイ
Labor Standards Bureau 労働基準局
labor standards inspection office 労働基準監督署
Labor Standards Law 労働基準法
labor supply 労働力供給, 労働需給
labor time variance 労働時間差異, 作業時間差異 (＝labor hour variance)
labor turnover 労働力の移動, 雇用・解雇による労働者の動き
labor union 労働組合, 労組, 労働団体 (＝trade union)
Labour Party 英労働党(保守党(Conservative Party)と並ぶ英2大政党の一つ)
lost labor 無駄骨折り, 無駄骨, 徒労
manual [hand] labor 手仕事, 肉体労働[労働者]
mechanical labor 筋肉労働
organized labor 組織労働者
seasonal labor 季節的労働
simple labor 単純労働
spring labor offensive 春闘
sweated labor 低賃金労働
wage labor 賃金労働

labor cost 人件費, 労働コスト, 労務費, 雇用コスト
labor cost advantage 労働コスト面での競争力
labor cost budget 労務費予算
labor cost per hour 1時間当たりの労働コスト
labor cost theory 労働価値説 (＝labor cost theory of money)
labor cost variance 直接労務費差異
labor costs 雇用コスト指数

labor management 労務管理, 労使
joint labor–management conference system 労使協議制
labor–management cooperation 労使協調 (＝labor management harmony)
labor–management dispute 労使紛争, 労使対決
labor–management negotiation [talks] 労使交渉
labor–management relations 労使関係 (＝labor relations)

Labor–Management Relations Act of 1947 1947年労使関係法(通称「タフト・ハートレー(Taft-Hartley)法」)

labor market 労働市場, 労働需給
labor market conditions 労働需給 (＝labor market situation, supply and demand on the labor market)
labor market data 雇用統計 (＝labor market statistics)
labor market environment [situation] 雇用情勢
liquidation of labor markets 労働市場の流動化

lack 名 不足, 欠乏, 欠如, 不備, (十分に)ないこと, 不足しているもの
a lack of communication 十分な意思の疎通の不足
for lack of …がないために
lack of ability 能力不足
lack of alternation 雇用機会の欠如
lack of coordination in …の足の乱れ
lack of demand 需要不足
lack of experience 経験不足
lack of funds 資金不足
lack of infrastructure インフラの不備
lack of job security 雇用不安
lack of oxygen 酸欠, 酸素欠乏
lack of supply 供給不足

lackluster [lacklustre] 形 精彩がない, 活気がない[乏しい], 不活発な, 生気がない, 輝きのない, ぱっとしない, さえない, あまり目立たない, つまらない, 不振の, 低迷している, 停滞している, 動きが鈍い, 足取りが鈍い, 伸び悩みの (＝sluggish)
lackluster economy 景気停滞, 経済の低迷, 景気低迷
lackluster growth 伸び悩み, 伸びの低迷
lackluster market condition 活気がない市場, さえない市場
lackluster performance さえない成績, ぱっとしない業績[成績], 業績低迷[不振]
lackluster trading 薄商い

ladder 名 はしご, 階段, 道, 段階, 序列, 階層, 階級, 地位, 出世街道, 出世階段, 手段, 方法, 〈ストッキングなどの〉伝線(run)
be at the top of the ladder 最高の地位にある
be high on the political ladder 政治的地位

が高い

begin from the bottom of the ladder 裸一貫から身を起こす

climb (up) a corporate ladder 企業の昇進階段を上る, 企業で出世する

climb (up) the ladder of estimation 高い評価を得る, 評価が高くなる

climb (up) the ladder of success 出世の階段を上る

get one's foot on the ladder in …の道に入る, …を始める

get up [climb] the ladder はしごを上る, 絞首刑に処せられる（＝be hanged）

ladder of advancement 昇進階段, 出世階段

ladder truck 〈消防用の〉はしご車

see through a ladder わかりきっている

step ladder distribution (method) 階梯式配賦法

step ladder sheet 階梯式配賦表

the ladder of success 出世の階段, 成功の手段, 成功への道

lag 動 出遅れる, 遅行する, 予定通り進行しない, …に追いつかない, …についていけない, 下回る

lag behind …から取り残される, …より遅れる, …を下回る

lagged adjustment 遅れを伴う調整, 調整の遅れ

lagged effect 遅行効果

lagged supply adjustment 遅れを伴う供給の調整

lagging 形 遅い, 遅れる, 遅行する, 時間の遅れを伴う, 景気停滞の

lagging economy 遅行経済

lagging employment upturn 雇用市場［労働市場］の回復の遅れ

lagging series 遅行系列

lagging signal 遅行指標

lagging indicator 遅行指標（＝lagging index：現状の景気の動きに遅れて動く（景気の動きに半年から1年遅れる）経済指標）

lame duck 名 死に体, 指導力の弱化した現職指導者, 再選に失敗して残任期間を務めている議員, 無力な人, 役立たずの人, レームダック

lame-duck 形 役に立たなくなった, 任期が残り少なくなった, 死に体の, 死に体となった

LAN 狭域通信網, 域内通信網, 企業内情報通信網, 構内通信網, ローカル・エリア・ネットワーク, ラン（local area networkの略）

land 名 土地, 用地, 農地, 農耕地, 陸, 陸地, 地帯, 場所, 所有地, 国土, 国民, ランド

green land 牧草地

land agent 土地売買周旋業者, 不動産業者, 土地管理人

land bank 不動産銀行

land development 土地開発

land force(s) 陸軍, 陸上部隊

land freeze 土地売買凍結, 土地譲渡凍結

land grab 〈政府などによる〉土地の収奪

land grant 無償土地払い下げ

land holding tax 地価税（＝land price tax）

land holdings 保有地

land-lease payments 土地使用料

land mine 地雷, パラシュート爆弾

land office 公有地管理事務所

land ownership right 土地所有権

land registry 土地登記所

land shark 地上げ屋（＝land speculator）

land sharking 地上げ, 地上げ行為

land subsidence 地盤沈下（＝ground subsidence）

land tax [taxation] system 土地税制（＝land-related tax）

land transfer tax 土地譲渡益課税, 土地譲渡税

land value tax 地価税

the promised land 理想の場所

work the land 農作物を作る

land price 土地価格, 地価

falling land prices 地価の下落

the average land price for commercial areas 商業地の全国平均の地価

landfall 名 上陸

make landfall 上陸する

landfill site 埋め立て地

landline 名 陸上回線, 固定電話

landmark 名 標識, 目標, 目印, 画期的な事件, ランドマーク

landslide victory 圧勝, 地滑り的大勝利, 圧倒的大勝利

languish 動 活力［元気］がなくなる, 減退する, 低迷する, 停滞する, 次第に衰える, 弱る

large-scale en bloc casting technology 大型一体鋳造技術

largest shareholder 筆頭株主, 大株主

laser 名 レーザー（light amplification by stimulated emission of radiation）（刺激された放射線放出による光波増幅）の略）

blue lasers 青色レーザー
laser angioplasty レーザーによる血管形成手術
laser beam レーザー光線
laser device レーザー発光素子
laser diode 半導体レーザー
laser material processing レーザー加工（＝laser processing）
laser ranging レーザー距離測定法
laser scanner レーザー・スキャナー
red lasers 赤色レーザー

lash out at …を激しくののしる, 激しく非難する, 激しく打つ

lassitude 名 倦怠感, 疲労感, 脱力感, 無気力, 気乗りのなさ, 無関心

last-ditch 形 最後の望みをかけた, 最後のチャンスをかけた, 死力を尽くした, ぎりぎりの最後の, 後に引けない, 絶体絶命の, 土壇場の, 必死の, 懸命の
  a last-ditch effort ぎりぎりの努力, 懸命の努力
  a last-ditch resistance 最後の抵抗
  fight a last-ditch stand 最後の抵抗をする, 背水の陣をしく
  try a last-ditch play 最後ぎりぎりの手を試みる

last-hurrah breaks 出産前の休暇（＝blow-out holiday）

latecomer 名 新規参入者, 遅れて参入した企業, 最近参入した会社, 後発, 新入り, 新参者, 遅刻者（⇒newcomer）

latent 形 潜在的な, 表面に出ない, 潜伏している, 潜伏性の, 含みを持つ（企業保有資産の現在価値［市場価値］が帳簿上の価格を上回っている場合に「含みを持つ」という）
  latent analysis 潜在性分析
  latent asset 含み資産（企業保有資産の現在価値［市場価値］が, 帳簿上の表示価格より大きい場合の差額）
  latent defect 隠れた欠陥, 隠れた瑕疵
  latent demand 潜在需要
  latent gain 含み益, 評価益（＝appraisal gain, latent profit, unrealized gain）
  latent loss 含み損, 評価損（＝appraisal loss, unrealized loss）
  latent period [stage] 〈病気の〉潜伏期
  latent profit 含み益, 評価益（＝appraisal profit, latent gain, unrealized profit）
  latent resources 潜在資源
  latent unemployed 潜在失業者
  latent value 含み益

latest 形 最新の, 最先端の, 今回の, 今年度の, 最終の, 前回の
  at the latest 遅くとも（早くとも＝at the earliest）
  the latest fiscal first half 今年度上半期, 今年度上期, 今年度中間決算
  the latest installment 最新作

latitude 名 自由, 裁量, 裁量権, 許容範囲, 許容度, ゆとり, 余地, 地方, 地帯, 地域, 緯度
  cold latitudes 寒帯地方
  education with latitude ゆとりある教育
  high latitudes 高緯度地方
  latitude for judicial discretion 法律上の裁量の余地
  low latitudes 低緯度地方
  temperate [warm] latitudes 温帯地方

latter term 下半期, 下期, 後期（＝the latter half）

laugh off 笑い飛ばす, 一笑に付す, 笑って一掃する, 笑ってごまかす

launch 動 開始する, 着手する, 発売する, 売り出す, 市場に出す, 導入する, 投入する, 上場する, 〈コンピュータ・プログラムを〉立ち上げる［起動する］, 〈ロケットなどを〉打ち上げる［発射する］, 〈船を〉進水させる
  launch a discount store ディスカウント店を出店する
  launch a hostile takeover bid 敵対的株式公開買付けを実施する, 敵対的買収を仕掛ける
  launch cell phone services 携帯電話サービスを開始する
  launch funds ファンドを設定する
  launch futures on stocks 株式先物を上場する

launch 名 発表, 起債発表, 開始, 着手, 〈新製品の〉発売, 新発売, 上市, 導入, 実施, 〈大型船・ロケットの〉打上げ［発射］, 〈船の〉進水, ローンチ（＝launching）
  launch control 発射管制, 発射管制センター
  launch crew 〈ロケットの〉打上げ要員
  launch operations 打上げ作業
  launch [launching] pad 発射台, 出発拠点, 出発点（＝launchpad）
  launch site 発射場, 発射基地, 発射台（launch pad）, 打上げ基地, ミサイル基地
  launch vehicle 打上げ用ロケット
  launch window 最適打上げ時間帯, 打上げ可能時間帯（＝window）

launch-on-warning system 核の警戒態勢

launder 動 不正資金を洗浄する, 不正資金の出所を隠す, 合法的に偽装する, マネー・ロンダリングをする
　laundered funds 洗浄資金, 洗浄された資金, 資金の洗浄

laundering 名 不正資金の洗浄, 不正資金の出所偽装工作, 犯罪資金の洗濯, 資金洗浄, マネー・ロンダリング（＝money laundering）
　crime organization's money-laundering operations 犯罪組織[暴力団]のマネー・ロンダリング活動
　the laundering of illegally earned profits 違法収益の洗浄, 違法収益の出所偽装工作

laundry list 〈ホテルなどの〉洗濯物記入表, 細部にわたる長々としたリスト
　a laundry-list of きわめて広範囲の…

laureate 名 受賞者, 桂冠詩人
　Nobel laureate ノーベル賞受賞者
　Poet Laureate 桂冠詩人

law 名 法律, 法令, 規則, 法, 法則, 手法, 規則（rule）, 規定, 慣習, 戒律, 法的手段, 訴訟
　administrative law 行政法
　Amended Usury Law 改正出資法
　applicable law 適用法, 準拠法（＝governing law, law applicable）
　at [in] law 法律に従って
　attorney at law 弁護士, 事務弁護士
　be at law 訴訟中である
　be in trouble with the law 警察沙汰になる
　break [violate] the law 法を犯す
　choice of law 準拠法[適用法]の指定
　civil law 民法
　commercial law 商法
　common law 慣習法, 判例法, 普通法, 不文法, 英米法, コモン・ロー
　conflict of laws 抵触法, 国際私法, 州際私法, 法の抵触, 衝突法（＝private international law）
　constitutional law 憲法
　copyright law 著作権法
　criminal law 刑法
　enter the law 法曹界に入る
　equality before the law 法の前の平等
　go to law 告訴する, (…を)訴える
　governing law 準拠法（＝applicable law, law to control, proper law）
　guardian of the law 法の番人
　international law 国際法（＝law of nations, public international law）
　law-abiding nation 法治国家
　law agent 事務弁護士（＝solicitor）
　law and order 法と秩序, 公安
　law court 法廷, 裁判所
　law degree 法律学位
　law firm 法律事務所
　law of averages 世の習い, 世の常, 事の常
　law of nations 国際法
　law of nature 自然の法則
　law officer 法務官
　law school 法科大学院, ロースクール
　law term 裁判開廷期
　local law 現地法, 地域的個別法律, 実質法地域法
　military law 軍法
　practice [the] law 弁護士になる, 弁護士をする, 法律を業とする（＝follow the law）
　resort to law 法律に訴える, 法的手段に訴える
　statutory law 制定法
　tax law 税法
　the law 法曹界, 法律関係の職業, 警察官, 警官, 警察
　the spirit of the law 法の精神
　the substantive laws of the State of California, U.S.A. 米国カリフォルニア州の実体法
　unwritten law 不文法
　within the law 法の範囲内で
　written law 成文法

law-abiding spirit 順法精神
law enforcement 法の執行
　law enforcement agency 法執行機関
　law-enforcement authorities 警察当局
　law-enforcement officer [agent] 法執行官（警察官や保安官など）

lawmaker 名 議員, 立法者（＝law maker, legislator）

lawmaker-sponsored 形 議員立法の
▶ A *lawmaker-sponsored* relief bill for atomic-bomb sufferers was passed by the upper house and sent to the lower house. 議員立法である原爆症救済法案が参議院で可決され, 衆議院に送付された.

lawsuit 名 訴訟, 民事訴訟（＝suit）
　class action lawsuit 集団代表訴訟
　derivative lawsuit 株主代表訴訟
　enter [bring in] a lawsuit against …に対して訴訟を起こす

file a lawsuit with …に提訴する
formal [plenary] lawsuit 本訴
lawsuit claims 訴訟による請求権
pending lawsuit 係争中の訴訟
withdraw a lawsuit against …に対する訴訟を取り下げる

lawyer 图 弁護士, 弁護人, 法律家, 法律通
defense lawyer 被告側弁護人
practicing lawyer 開業弁護士
pragmatic lawyer 実務家の弁護士
shyster lawyer 悪徳弁護士

lay judge 一般人による裁判員, 裁判員
lay judge candidate 裁判員候補者
lay judge system 裁判員制度, 一般人による裁判員制度
supplementary lay judge 補充裁判員

lay labor judge 一般市民の労働裁判員

lay off 解雇する, 削減する, 低減する, 雇用調整する, 解消する, 回避する, レイオフを進める
laid-off worker 解雇された労働者, 解雇された従業員
lay off workers [employees] 従業員を解雇する

layoff 图 解雇, 削減, 低減, 人員削減, 一時解雇, 一時帰休, 雇用調整, 休養期間, 休暇, レイオフ (＝lay-off, redundancy)

LBO 借入資金による企業買収 (leveraged buy-outの略)

LCC 格安航空会社 (low-cost carrierの略)

LCD 液晶表示装置, 液晶ディスプレー (liquid crystal displayの略)

LCD TV 液晶テレビ

lead 動 導く, 誘導する, 先導する, 案内する, 指導する, …を率いる, …の主導権を握る, …の先頭に立って指揮をとる, …の先頭に立つ, …の首位に立つ, …の首位を占める, 先行する, …の最初にある, …の一番[トップ]である, トップ記事になる, 追い込む, 至らせる, 誘導尋問する, …の主席弁護人となる, リードする
lead a case 訴訟事件の主席弁護人として働く
lead a discussion 議論の口火を切る
lead a flank movement 側面運動を指揮する
lead nowhere 何の成果も得られない, 何の結果も得られない, うまくいかない, らちが明かない
lead on to the subject 話をその問題に向ける, 話をその問題に持っていく
lead off …を始める, …の口火を切る, …から始まる, …から伸びている, 〈野球の回の〉先頭打者となる
lead the market 消費者をリードする
lead the output cycle by five months 生産動向に5か月先行する
lead the pack 先頭に立つ, トップを行く (＝be ahead of the pack)
lead the rebound 景気回復を主導する
lead the way 道案内をする, 先導する, リードする, トップを走る, 率先する
lead up to 結局…になる, …の糸口となる, …を引き起こす, …に徐々に話を持っていく, 話題を…に向ける, 〈期間が〉…に先立つ

lead 图 首位, トップ, 先頭, 優位, 優勢, 主導権, 指揮, 指示, イニシアチブ, 差, 主役, 主演俳優, 〈新聞記事の〉書き出し, トップ記事, 冒頭の部分, 前文, 前例, 先例, 手本, 見本, 模範, 手がかり, かぎ, 糸口, 鉱脈, リード
be under the lead of a person …の指導を受けている
follow the lead of …の例にならう, …の手本に従う, …の指示に従う
give a lead 手本を示す, 模範を示す
have a lead of more than 100 votes over …に100票以上の差をつける
retain a lead over …で優位に立ち続ける
take over the lead of …の主導権を握る
take the lead 先頭に立つ, 首位に立つ, 率先する, 音頭を取る, 他より先に行う, 他に先駆けて行う, リードする

lead 形 先頭の(first), 先導の, 中心の, 主役の, 最も重要な, 主要の, 第一の, 主任の, トップの
lead analyst 主任アナリスト
lead bank 主要銀行, 幹事銀行, 主幹事行 (＝lead manager)
lead story トップ記事, トップ・ニュース
lead time 先行期間, 準備期間, 生産準備期間, 企画段階から生産開始までの所要時間, 発注から納品までの期間, 調達期間, 入荷期間, 納期, リード・タイム

lead to …を引き起こす, …をもたらす, …を招く, 〈結果として〉…になる, …に発展する, …に達する, …に通じる, …につながる, …に注ぎ込む

leader 图 経営者, 経営陣, 首脳, 首脳陣, 指導者, 指導部, 党首, 〈米議会〉院内総務, 最大手, おとり商品, 目玉商品, 特売品, 主力株, 一流株, 社説, 〈新聞の〉トップ見出し, リーダー
deputy leader ナンバー2
floor leader 院内総務

House Majority Leader 下院院内総務
leader merchandising おとり商品政策, おとり商品戦略
leader offering おとり商品の提供
leader price 指導価格
leader pricing おとり価格設定
leaders 主力株, 首脳陣, 首脳, 経営陣, 指導部, 指導者
loss leader おとり商品, 特価品, 目玉商品, おとり政策
Majority Leader 多数党院内総務
market leader 主導株, 先導株, マーケット・リーダー
Minority leader 少数党院内総務
price leader 価格先導者, 価格指導者, 目玉商品, プライス・リーダー
Senate leaders 上院指導部
wartime leader 戦時指導者
world leaders 各国首脳

leadership 名 指導, 指揮, リーダーの地位, 指導者の地位, 指導者の資質, 指導力, 統率力, 指導性, 先導制, リーダー性, 指導者グループ, 〈政党などの〉執行部, 首脳部, 指導部, 最高幹部, 幹部, 体制, 政権, リーダーシップ
follow the leadership of …の指揮に従う
lack of leadership 指導力不足
leadership position 主導的地位 (＝leading position)
leadership role リーダーの役割, 指導的役割
lose the leadership of …の主導権を失う
new leadership 新体制
political leadership 政権, 政治的指導力, 政治指導者
price leadership 価格先導制, 価格指導力, 価格指導性(「価格先導制」は, 指導的企業が発表した価格を, 他社が受け入れること)
strong leadership 強い統率力
take over the leadership 主導権を引き継ぐ, 政権を引き継ぐ
take [assume] the leadership of …を指揮する, …の司会をする
under one's leadership …の主導の下に, …の指導[指揮]の下に, …の体制で

leading 形 主要な, 最重要な, 一流の, 大手の, 有力な, 主力の, 首位の, 主導的
leading actor 主演男優
leading article 〈新聞の〉社説, 論説, 〈定期刊行物の〉主要記事, トップ記事
leading authority 最高権威者, 最高権威
leading case 先例となる判決, 指導的判決
leading commodity 主力商品
leading economic indicators 景気先行指数, 景気先行指標総合指数 (＝leading index, leading indicators)
leading expert 第一人者
leading index 先行指数, 景気先行指数, 景気先行指標総合指数 (＝leading indicator, the index of leading economic indicators)
leading indicator 先行指標, 先行指数 (＝leading index：鉱工業生産財在庫率指数, 耐久消費財出荷指数など, 現状の景気の動きに先立って動く経済指標)
leading light 影響力のある人物, 重要人物, 大家, 導燈
leading (market) position 主導的地位
leading motive 主要な動機
leading nations [countries] 主要国, 先進国
leading question 誘導尋問

leading edge 主導的地位, 最先端, 最前部, 最前線, 先頭, 最新式, 最新型, 最新鋭, トップ (＝cutting edge, sophisticated, state-of-the-art, top of the line)
leading-edge technology 先端技術, 最先端技術, 最新技術
leading edges of innovation 技術革新の最先端

leadoff 名 開始, 形 先頭の, 一番手の
leadoff issue 最初の問題, 最初に取り組むべき[最初に手がけるべき]問題
leadoff hitter 一番手, 先頭打者, 最有力者
leadoff interpellator 〈議会などでの〉質問のトップバッター

leak 動 漏らす, 流出させる, リークする, 漏れる, 流出する, 名 漏れ, 漏洩, 漏れ口, 漏電
leaked personal data [information] 流出した個人情報, 個人情報の流出

leakage 名 漏れ, 漏洩, 流出
leakage of capital outflows 資本の国外流出
radiation leakage 放射能漏れ

leapfrog 名 かえる跳び, 馬跳び, 他に追随して賃上げ[値上げ]すること, 〈交戦中の〉交互躍進

learning curve 学習曲線, 習熟曲線
learning rate 学習率, 習熟率

lease 動 賃貸しする, 賃借りする, 貸し出す, 借り上げる, リースする
►The company *leases* its products to customers

under sales-type leases. 同社は，同社製品を販売型リースで顧客にリースしている．

lease 名 賃貸借，賃貸借契約（書），借地［借家］契約，〈鉱物資源の〉開発契約，リース，リース契約

least developed countries 後発開発途上国，後発発展途上国《略 LDC [LDCs]》

least less-developed country 後発発展途上国，後発途上国，後発開発途上国，最貧国《略 LLDC》

lecture circuit 講演行脚

LED 発光ダイオード（light-emitting diodeの略）
  blue LEDs 青色発光ダイオード

-led 形 …主導の，…主導の，…主導型，…先行型，…の指導による，…による，…中心の（=-driven, led by, -oriented）
  deflation-led economic slowdown デフレ不況
  demand-led recovery 需要主導型の（業績［景気］）回復
  export-led economic recovery 輸出主導の景気回復，輸出頼みの景気回復
  export-led economies 輸出主導型経済
  export-led growth 輸出先行型成長，輸出主導型成長，輸出リード型成長
  export-led industrialization 輸出主導型工業化，輸出リード型工業化
  Shiite-led government シーア派主導の政府

left-of-center 形 中道左派の（⇒right-of-center）

left-wing [leftwing] 形 左派の，左翼の，左翼政党の

left-winger [leftwinger] 名 左派の人，左翼主義者，左派，左翼（⇒rightist）

leftism 名 左翼思想

leftist 名 左派，急進党員，急進主義者，過激主義者（=left-winger; ⇒rightist）
  group of violent extreme leftists 極左暴力集団
  leftist infantilism 左翼小児病
  leftist radicals 極左分子（=radical leftists）

leftmost 形 極左の，最も左の

legal 形 法律の，法律上の，法定の，法的な，合法的な，適法の，司法の場での，リーガル
  legal act 合法的行為
  legal advice 法律に基づく助言
  legal adviser 法律顧問，顧問弁護士
  legal affairs bureau 〈日本の〉法務局
  legal age for …の法定年齢，…できる成人年齢

［法定年齢］
  legal aid 司法扶助，法的扶助，法律扶助
  legal alien 合法的外国人居住者
  legal amendment 法改正，法律の改正
  legal avenue 法的手段
  legal basis for …の法的根拠
  legal capital 法定資本
  legal ceiling 法定金利の上限（=legal cap, legal interest rate ceiling）
  legal claim 法的請求権
  legal consultation 訴訟協議
  legal contract 適法契約
  legal date 支払い期日，満期
  legal detriment 法的不利益
  legal device 法的手段
  legal duty [obligation] 法的義務
  legal enforceability 法的強制力
  legal entity 法人，法的主体，法的実体
  legal ethics 弁護士の倫理，法曹倫理
  legal expense 法廷費用，訴訟費用
  legal fee 弁護士費用，法定手数料
  legal hours 法定労働時間
  legal industry 弁護士業界，法曹界（=legal circles）
  legal instrument 法定投資
  legal interest 法定利息
  legal interest rate 法定金利，法定利率
  legal investment 適法投資
  legal knowledge 法的知識，法律の知識，法律的知識
  legal language 法律用語
  legal liability 法的責任
  legal list rule 法定銘柄原則
  legal means 法的手段
  legal monopoly 法定独占，合法的独占
  legal mortgage 法定抵当，普通法上の譲渡抵当
  legal name 正式氏名，氏名
  legal notification 法定公告
  legal obligation 法的義務
  legal offense 法律上の罪
  legal opinion 法律意見書，リーガル・オピニオン
  legal pad 法律用箋，リーガル・パッド
  legal person 法人
  legal power 法的権限
  legal proceedings 訴訟手続き，訴訟，法的手続き，裁判手続き
  legal process 法の過程，法の手続き，合法的手続き

legal profession 法律専門家, 弁護士業, 法専門職, 法曹, 法曹界
legal remedies 法的救済措置
legal representative 法務担当者, 法律上の代表者, 法定代理人, 遺産管理人, 遺言執行人
legal reserves 法定準備金 (=legal capital reserves, legally required reserves)
legal right 法的権利, 法律上の権利, 法が認めた権利
legal separation 法定別居, 法的別居
Legal Services Corporation 〈米国の〉法律扶助機構
legal standing 法的根拠
legal status 法的地位
legal stock 法定資本
legal system 法律制度, 法制, 法体系, 法系
legal tariff 法定関税
legal tender 法定貨幣, 法貨, 本位貨幣
legal title 所有権, 法律上の所有権
legal trust 適法トラスト
legal action 法的措置, 法的手続き, 法律上の訴え, 訴訟
　take a legal action against …を相手取って訴訟を起こす
　take legal actions 法的措置を取る
legality 名 合法性, 適法性
legally required reserves 法定準備金 (=legal capital reserves, legal reserves)
legislation 名 立法, 法律制定, 法案, 法律, 規則
　budget legislation 予算審議
　Cabinet Legislation Bureau 〈日本の〉内閣法制局
　company legislation 会社法
　draft legislation 法案 (=proposed legislation)
　enactment of legislation 法律[立法]の制定
　enabling legislation 設立法
　EU legislation EU規則
　legislation investigation 〈議会による〉国勢調査
　monetary legislation 金融立法
　protectionist legislation 保護貿易法, 保護貿易立法
　protective legislation 貿易保護法
　reform of financial legislation 金融制度改革
　seek legislation 立法を求める
　send the U.S. Congress legislation seeking to 米議会に…を求める法案を提出する
　tax legislation 税法
legislative 形 立法権のある, 立法の, 立法上の, 立法府の, 法律を制定する, 法律に定められた, 名 立法府[立法部] (legislative body [branch], legislature)
legislative act 立法行為, 議会制定法
legislative action 法的措置
legislative apportionment 議席配分
legislative assembly 立法議会, 〈米一部の州の〉州議会
legislative body 立法府
legislative branch 立法部門
legislative control 法的統制
Legislative Counsel 立法顧問
legislative council 〈米国の州〉立法審議会, 〈英国の二院制議会の〉上院
Legislative Council 〈日本の〉法制審議会
legislative day 議会開会中の毎日
legislative history 〈法律の〉制定史
legislative jurisdiction 立法部の権限に属する事項
legislative measures 法的手段, 法的措置
legislative number 立法番号
legislative officer 議員
legislative power 立法権
legislative proceedings 立法手続き
legislative proposal 法案, 法案提出
legislative reapportionment 選挙区割り変更, 選挙区再編成, 議員定数変更
legislative recess 立法府の休会期間
Legislative Reorganization Act 立法再組織法
legislative remedy 法的救済手続き
Legislative Reorganization Act 立法再組織法
legislative ruling 立法府の決定
legislator 名 立法者 (lawgiver), 法律制定者, 〈国会・議会の〉議員
legislature 名 立法機関, 立法府[立法部], 議会 (米国ではCongress, 英国ではParliament, 日本ではDietという)
　a two-house legislature 二院制の立法部
　both chambers of the legislature 〈日本の〉衆参両院
　Congress and state legislatures 米連邦議会と州議会
　provisional legislature 臨時議会
　state legislature 州議会
legitimacy 名 合法性, 正統性

lend 動 貸し出す, 貸し付ける, 融資する
lender 名 貸し手, 貸主, 金融機関, 銀行, 融資行, 貸出行, 融資者, 資金の出し手, 貸金業者, レンダー
  bank lender 融資銀行, 融資行, 取引銀行
  consumer lender 消費者金融会社 (＝consumer loan lender)
  mortgage lender 住宅ローンの貸し手
  private lender 民間金融機関
  regional lender 地方銀行, 地銀
  the lender of (the) last resort 最後の貸し手, 最後の手段としての貸し手(中央銀行のこと)
lending 名 貸出, 貸付け, 融資, 貸借
  bank lending 銀行貸出, 銀行融資
  consumer lending 消費者金融, 消費者ローン
  corporate lending 企業向け貸出, 企業向け貸付け, 企業向け融資
  excessive lending 過剰融資
  lending business 貸出業務, 融資業務 (＝lending operation)
  lending (interest) rate 貸出金利
  less lending 融資抑制
  Lombard lending ロンバード貸出
  minimum lending rate 最低貸出金利
  name lending 名義貸し
  prime lending rate 一流企業向け最優遇貸出金利, 一流企業に対する短期貸付け金利, プライム・レート (＝prime rate)
  restricted lending 貸し渋り
  stock lending 証券貸借
  unsecured lending 無担保融資, 無担保貸付け
lesser of two evils 次善の策
lesson 名 学課, 授業, 授業時間, 習い事, けいこ, 教訓, 苦い経験, 経験, 教え, 戒め, 見せしめ, レッスン
  a bitter lesson 苦い経験
  a valuable lesson 貴重な経験
  learn one's lesson 教訓を学ぶ, 失敗の教訓に学ぶ
lethargic 形 だるい, 無気力な, 不活発な, 不振の, 鈍感な, 無感動の
leukemia 名 白血病
level 名 水準, 標準, 程度, 数値, 高さ, 段階, 面, 観点, 幅, 水位, レベル
  at local level 地方レベルで
  at national level 全国レベルで, 全国的に
  at the net level 当期利益で, 当期利益レベルで, 当期損益レベルで
  at the operating level 営業利益で
  be at near record low levels 過去最低に近い水準にある
  borrowing level 資金調達コストの水準
  consumption level 消費水準
  current level of earnings 現在の収益水準
  debt level 負債[債務]水準
  emission level 排ガス・レベル, 排出レベル, 排出量
  historical level of loss 過去の損失率
  inventory level 在庫水準
  middle management level 中間管理層
  net level 当期利益ベース
  new levels of sophistication 一段と高い水準
  on a practical level 実務面では
  on the level 正直に[正直な], 公明正大に[公明正大な]
  performance level 業績水準
  remain at about the same level ほぼ同水準にとどまる
  remain at high levels 高水準で推移する
  savings level 貯蓄率
  share price level 株価水準 (＝stock market level)
  stay at a high level 高水準で推移する, 高水準を維持する
  stock market level 株価水準
  volume level 操業度
level 形 平らな, 平坦な, 水平の, 共通の, …と同等[同位, 同程度]の, 冷静な, 落ち着いた, バランスのとれた, 一様な, 変化のない
  be level with …と同じ高さである, …と同水準にある
  cabinet level talks 閣僚級会談, 閣僚レベル会談 (＝talks at cabinet level)
  do one's level best 最善を尽くす, 全力を尽くす
  keep [have] a level head 冷静さを保つ, 正しい判断ができる
  keep level and calm 沈着冷静である
  level farmland 平坦な農地
  level pegging with …と力が互角の, …と平等の, …と同点の, …と実力伯仲の
  level playing field 共通の土俵, 同じ土俵, 平等の競争条件, 平等な立場
  level-headed [levelheaded] 良識のある, 思慮分別のある, 〈判断が〉冷静な
  level race 互角の競走[レース]
  speak in level tones 落ち着いた話し方をする

level off 横ばい状態になる, 成長が止まる, 伸び悩む, 水平になる, 水平飛行をする, 平均化する (=level out)

leveling off [**leveling-off**] 横ばい, 横ばい状態, 踊り場 (=leveling out)

level out 横ばい状態になる, 成長が止まる, 伸び悩む, 水平になる, 水平飛行をする, 平均化する (=level off)

leverage 動 借入金で投機をする, …を利用する, 生かす, 借入金で〈企業などを〉買い取る

leverage 名 借入れ, 借金, 借入比率, 借入余力, 負債, 負債比率, 借入資本, 財務レバレッジ, テコ, テコの作用, 手段, 影響力, 力, 有利な立場, レバレッジ(「レバレッジ」は投資額に対する借入金の割合で, 「財務レバレッジ」は資本金に対する負債の割合(debt-to-equity ratio: 負債自己資本比率, 外部負債比率)の高さを示す)
 bargaining leverage 交渉力
 diplomatic leverage 外交的な働きかけ
 economic leverage 経済的影響力
 financial leverage 財務レバレッジ, 借入比率, 負債比率
 leverage effect 梃率効果, テコの効果, レバレッジ効果, 他人資本効果
 leverage ratio 負債比率, レバレッジ・レシオ, レバレッジ比率 (=leverage test)

levy 動 徴収する, 課する, 課税する, 賦課する, 割り当てる, 取り立てる, 差し押さえる, 押収する, 召集する
 levy one's property …の財産を差し押さえる
 levy taxes on …に課税する, …に税を課する
 levy the tax on accrued interest 経過利息に課税する

levy 名 徴収, 課税, 徴税, 徴収額, 強制割当て, 取立て, 差押え, 押収, 召集
 capital levy 資本課税, 資本課徴
 corporation levy 法人税割
 import levy 輸入課税
 industrial levy 産業賦課金
 levy en masse 国民召集
 levy in kind 物品課税, 物税, 現物徴税
 levy of attachment 財産差押え
 levy of execution 強制執行
 retroactive levy foe delinquent charge 遅延損害金の遡及徴収
 taxes and levies 税金と公課

LGBT 性的少数者 (**lesbian, gay, bisexual, and transgender**の略)

liabilities 名 債務, 負債, 借金, 賠償責任
 amount of liabilities 負債金額
 contingent liabilities 偶発債務
 current liabilities 流動負債
 external liabilities 対外負債, 外部負債
 net liabilities 正味負債, 債務超過額
 off-the-book liabilities 簿外債務 (=off-the-book debts)

liaison 名 連絡, 連絡事務, 渉外, 渉外係, 接触, 密通, 不倫, 不倫行為
 liaison council of ministries and agencies concerned 関係省庁連絡会議
 liaison office 連絡事務所, 駐在員事務所
 liaison officer 連絡将校, 連絡官

Lib Dems 〈英国の〉自由民主党 (**Liberal Democrats**の略)

libel 名 名誉毀損罪, 侮辱, 侮辱するもの, 不名誉となるもの, 誹謗文書, 〈原告の〉陳述書
 a libel action [case, suit] 名誉毀損訴訟
 a libel on human nature 人間性を侮辱するもの
 file a libel against …を相手取り名誉毀損訴訟を起こす
 file a libel suit with A against B Bを相手取ってAに名誉毀損の訴えを起こす
 publish a libel against …の名誉毀損になる文書を発行する
 spread libels against …に対する誹謗文書をばらまく

liberal 形 自由な, 自由思想の, 自由主義の, 進歩的な, 気前のいい, 寛大な, 大まかな, 古い習慣にとらわれない, 豊富な
 liberal arts 教養科目, 人文社会
 liberal democracy 自由民主主義, 自由民主主義国家
 Liberal Democrats 〈英国の〉自由民主党
 liberal economic policy 自由主義的経済政策, 自由経済政策
 liberal education 一般教育, 高等普通教育
 liberal thinker 自由主義思想家

liberalism 名 自由主義, 放任主義, リベラリズム
 classical liberalism 古典的自由主義
 economic liberalism 経済的自由主義
 neo-liberalism [**neoliberalism**] 新自由主義

liberalization 名 自由化, 規制緩和, 開放, 国際化
 capital liberalization 資本の自由化 (=liberalization of capital)

exchange liberalization 為替自由化（＝liberalization of exchange, liberalization of exchange control, liberalization of foreign exchange）
financial liberalization package 金融自由化案, 金融の規制緩和案[緩和策]
import liberalization 輸入の自由化
liberalization of capital transactions 資本取引の自由化, 資本自由化
liberalization of interest rates 金利の自由化
liberalization of the electricity market 電力市場の自由化, 電力自由化, 電力市場の規制緩和（＝power liberalization）
liberalization of the financial industry 金融自由化, 金融の規制緩和（＝financial deregulation, financial liberalization）
liberalization of the labor market 労働市場の開放
liberalization of the yen 円の国際化
market liberalization 市場の自由化, 市場開放, 市場の規制緩和
partial liberalization 一部自由化, 部分開放
rate of liberalization 自由化率（＝liberalization rate）
total liberalization of brokerage commissions 委託手数料の完全自由化
trade liberalization 貿易自由化
liberalize 動 自由化する, 規制緩和する, 開放する, 解禁する
liberation front 解放戦線
license [licence] 名 営業免許権, 許可, 認可, 免許, 特許, 許諾, 実施許諾,〈商標やソフトウエアなどの〉使用許諾, 実施権, 使用権, 鉱業権,〈不動産の〉立入り権, 許可書, 免許状, ライセンス
  application for export license 輸出承認申請書
  blanket license 包括許可
  business license 営業免許（＝license of business）
  grant of license 実施権の許諾, 実施許諾
  import license 輸入許可, 輸入承認
  import license bond rate 輸入担保率
  import license statistics 輸入承認統計
  letter of license 支払い期日延期状, 債務履行猶予契約[契約書]
  license agreement 実施権許諾契約, 特許権実施契約, 実施権契約, 技術援助契約, ライセンス契約
  license application 免許申請
  license registration 登録免許
  license tax 免許税, 事業免許税, 特許税
  patent license 特許ライセンス, 特許実施権
  revoke one's license 免許を取り消す
  right to license 許諾権
  technical license 技術実施権, 技術ライセンス, テクニカル・ライセンス
  trademark license 商標使用許諾
licensing 名 実施許諾, 使用許諾, 認可, 免許, 許認可, ライセンス供与, ライセンス契約, ライセンシング
  export licensing 輸出許可
  film licensing 映画上映権
  industrial licensing system [regime] 産業活動許可制度
  licensing of technology 技術供与
  licensing standards 許認可基準
  licensing system 免許制
lie detector ウソ発見器
lie-down [lie-in] 名 集団座り込み
lieutenant governor 〈米州の〉副知事
life and environmental science 生命環境科学
life expectancy 平均寿命, 平均余命
life insurance 生命保険
  life insurance benefits 生命保険給付, 生命保険給付金, 生命保険の保険金
  life insurance company [firm] 生命保険会社（＝life insurer）
  life insurance industry [sector] 生命保険業界, 生保業界
life insurer 生命保険会社（＝life insurance company, life insurance firm）
life support 生命維持装置
life-sustaining measures 延命措置
lifeline 名 生命線, 命綱, 生活物資補給路, 物資補給路,〈人生相談を受ける〉命の電話, ライフライン
lifelong education 生涯教育
lifelong learning facility 生涯学習施設
lifestyle [life style] 名 生活様式, 生き方, 暮らしぶり, ライフスタイル
  lifestyle ailments 生活習慣病
  Lifestyles Of Health And Sustainability 健康と環境重視の生活様式, ロハス（健康と環境を重視し, 持続可能な社会のあり方を求める生活様式のこと）
lifetime employment system 終身雇

用制度

lift 動　持ち上げる, 上げる, 高める, 引き上げる, 増やす, 移動する, 輸送する, 空輸する, 解禁する, 〈制限や禁止などを〉解く, 解除する, 廃止する, 盗む, 万引きする, 掘る, 掘り上げる
lift a hedge　ヘッジを外す
lift oil prices　原油価格を引き上げる
lift output　増産する
lift restrictions [regulations] on　…に対する制限 [規制] を撤廃する
lift spending　消費を押し上げる, 消費を拡大する
lift the night curfew　夜間外出禁止令を解除する
lift the government's full-deposit guarantee　政府の預金全額保護 (ペイオフ) の凍結を解除する
lift the import ban　輸入禁止を解く
liftoff [lift-off] 名　〈ロケットなどの〉打上げ, 発射, 〈ヘリコプターなどの〉離昇, 垂直離陸
light 名　光, 明かり, 電灯, 照明, イルミネーション, 信号機, 光源, 光明, 啓発, 見方, 見地, 観点, ライト
by the light of nature　自然に, 直感的に
cast [shed, throw] light on　…に解明の光をあてる, …について新情報を与える
come [be brought] to light　明るみに出る, 発覚する
in a bad light　不利に, 不利な見方で
in a good light　有利に, 有利な見方で
in (the) light of　…に照らして, …を考慮して, …に鑑みて, …の見地から
see the light (of day)　生まれる, 公開される, 出版される, 日の目を見る, 存在が知られる, 初めて実施される, 理解するようになる
stand in one's light　…の出世を妨げる, …の邪魔をする
light electrical equipment　軽電機
light industry　軽工業
light-emitting diode　発光ダイオード《略 LED》(電流を光に変換する半導体で, 携帯電話の表示装置や大型スクリーンなどに使われる)
light-water reactor　軽水炉, 軽水型原子炉《略 LWR》(=light-water nuclear reactor)
lighting technology　発光技術
like-for-like 形　既存店ベースの, 同一条件の, 同種の, 同等の
likely 形　有望な, 見込みのある, 有力とされる, 予想される, 見込まれる, 必死である, 副　たぶん, おそらく

be highly likely　公算が大きい, 可能性が高い
be likely to　…する見通しだ, …する見込みだ, …する模様だ, …しそうだ, …の可能性が大きい
most likely scenario　標準的シナリオ
limit 名　限度, 極度, 限界, 制限, 限度額, リミット
borrower limit　与信限度
credit limit　信用限度, 与信限度, 信用貸出限度
daily price limit　値幅制限　(=price limit)
lending limit　貸出限度
lower limit　値幅制限の下限, 下限
oil output limits　原油生産枠
order without limit　成り行き注文
policyholder limits　保険契約者に対する与信限度
price limit　値幅制限, ストップ値段
stock-buying limit　株式買入れ枠
stop limit　ストップ・リミット
stop limit order　指し値注文
trading limit　取引制限
upper limit　上限
linchpin 名　主軸, 要 (かなめ), 不可欠のもの
line 名　〈商品の〉種類, 機種, 事業部門, 組立工程, 路線, 進路, 経路, 方向, 方針, 方法, 考え方, 主義, 姿勢, 手段, 〈損益計算書の〉経常利益 [当期純利益], 電話線, 伝送路, 通信回線, 回線, 職業, 商売, 仕事, 職種, 家系, 血統, 境界線, 国境線, 境目, 限界, 限度, 列, 行列, 航路, 運送会社, 輸送会社, ライン
above the line　標準以上で
above the line profit　経常利益
assembly line　組立ライン, 流れ作業, アセンブリ・ライン
bank line　銀行与信枠
be in line with　…と一致する, …と変わらぬ水準 [同水準] にある, …と連動する, …に沿っている, …を反映している
be in one's line　…の得意分野である
below the line　異常損益項目, 範囲外
bottom line　利益, 収益性
common line of trade　商売仲間
draw a line between A and B　AとBの間に一線を画す
draw the line　限度を設ける
fixed-phone line　固定電話回線
front line　前線
full line　全機種, 全製品, 全品種, フルライン
go on wrong lines　方針を誤る
indicative dividing line between expansion

and contraction signals 景気拡大と景気後退の判断の分かれ目
International Date Line 日付変更線
line and staff organization ライン・アンド・スタッフ組織, ライン・スタッフ組織, 直系参謀組織
line authority 管理者の権限, ライン権限
line department ライン部門（製造業の生産部門・販売部門, 販売業の総務, 人事, 経理, 調査, 企画などのスタッフ部門に対して, 販売部門など直接売上げにかかわる部門をライン部門という）
line drawing 線画
line feed 改行, 行送り
line manager 直属の上司, 製造・販売部門の意思決定者
line of business 事業部門, 事業の種類, 営業項目
line of control 実効支配線
line of credit 与信限度, 与信[貸付け]限度額, 与信限度枠, 信用供与枠, クレジット・ライン（= credit line）
line of work 職種
line officer 戦闘部隊担当将校
merchandise line 商品構成
off line 〈端末などが〉接続されていない状態で, 作動していない, 活動休止中の
on line コンピュータ回線で, 回線接続中の, コンピュータ回線を使って, 作業[活動]中の
on the line 危険にさらして, 危険にさらされて, 失われる可能性がある, 電話に出て, ただちに
on the same lines 同一方針で
product line 製品構成, 製品系列, 製品ライン
product line control 製品別管理
production line 生産ライン
pro-United States line 親米路線
reach the end of the line 行き詰まる, 難局に至る
take a cautious line 慎重路線を取る
take a firm [hard, strict] line about [on, over, with] …について厳しい処置を取る
take a tough line on …に強硬手段を取る, 強硬路線を取る, 強硬策を取る
toe the line [mark] 指示どおりに行動する, 方針に従う, 規律などに従う
top of the line 最高機種
trend line 趨勢線
with only pride on the line プライドだけを賭けて

lineup 名 顔ぶれ, 陣容, 編成, 布陣, 品揃え, 商品構成, 機種構成, 車種構成, 製品一覧表, 番組編成, テレビ番組編成予定表, ラインアップ
product lineup 品揃え, 商品数
starting lineup 発足時の陣容

lingering 形 長引く, 遅々として進まない, ぐずつく, なかなか消えない, なかなかすたれない, はかどらない
lingering arbitration 遅々として進まない調停, 長引く調停
lingering effects 後遺症
lingering negotiations 長引く交渉, 遅々として進まない交渉
lingering recession 長引く不況

link 動 つなぐ, 結びつける, 連結する, 関係[関連]づける, 連動させる, リンクさせる, 結びつく, 結合する, 一体化する, 接続する, 提携する, 連合する, リンクする

link 名 結びつき, つながり, 関係, 関連, 因果関係, 提携, 連結,〈鎖の〉輪, 環

linkage 名 結合, 連結, 連鎖, 連関, 関連, つながり, 二国間外交交渉, リンケージ

lion 名 勇者, 名士, 花形, 人気者, 名所, 名物, 獅子, ライオン
a lion in the way [path] 前途の難関
put [place] one's head in the lion's mouth 好んで危険を冒す
the lion's share 最大の比率, 最大のシェア, 最大の部分, 大きい取り分, 大部分, 一番おいしいところ
twist the lion's tail 英国の悪口を言う, 英国の悪口を書く

lionize 動 特別扱いする, 重要人物として扱う

liquefaction 名 液化, 液状化現象

liquefied natural gas 液化天然ガス《略 LNG》

liquid 形 流動性がある, 流動性の高い, 現金に換えやすい, 換金性が高い, 融通が利く
liquid asset balances 流動資産残高
liquid capital goods 流動資本財
liquid cargo 液体貨物
liquid fuel 液体燃料
liquid fund 流動資金
liquid gas 液化ガス
liquid market 流動性の高い市場
liquid net worth 流動純資産
liquid petroleum 鉱油
liquid propellant 液体燃料
liquid refreshment 飲み物

liquid reserve　流動準備金

liquid crystal　液晶
liquid crystal display　液晶表示装置, 液晶ディスプレー《略 LCD》
liquid crystal polymer　高分子液晶
liquid crystal screen TV　液晶テレビ（＝liquid crystal display television）

liquidate 動　〈借金や負債を〉弁済する［返済する, 支払う］, 決済する, 清算する, 処分する, 処理する, 〈証券や資産などを〉売却［現金化］する, 在庫を削減する, 〈会社などを〉整理する, 解散する, 破産する

liquidation 名　流動性, 流動化, 決済, 清算, 処分, 処理, 整理, 解散, 破産, 売却, 現金化, 換金（「流動化」は, 保有資産の支配権を第三者に移転して資金調達すること）
asset liquidation　資産売却
compulsory liquidation　強制清算
corporate liquidation　会社整理
creditors' voluntary liquidation　和議
forced liquidation　強制破産
go into liquidation　破産する, 清算を開始する, 清算する, 解散する
income at liquidation　清算所得（＝liquidation income）
inventory liquidation　在庫削減, 在庫整理, 在庫取り崩し
involuntary liquidation　強制破産, 強制整理（＝compulsory liquidation, forced liquidation）
legal liquidation　法的整理
liquidation dividend　清算配当
liquidation of government bonds　国債の流動化
liquidation preference　残余財産分配優先権
liquidation risk　流動性リスク
liquidation value　清算価格
voluntary liquidation　任意清算, 任意整理, 自主解散, 自主清算

liquidity 名　流動性, 流動資産の換金性, 流動資産の換金能力, 流動性の高さ, 資金繰り, 資金

> 流動性とは ⊃ 流動性は, 一般に株式や債券などの流通性のことで, marketability（市場性: 市場で容易に売買できること）とほぼ同じ意味を持つ。このほかに, 自己資産を現金化する能力を意味する場合もある。

ample liquidity　高い流動性, 流動性の高さ, 豊富な資金, 大量の資金, 潤沢な資金

broad liquidity　広義流動性（＝broadly-defined liquidity）
ease liquidity　流動性を高める
increase liquidity in the monetary system　市中に流動性を供給する
inject liquidity into the banking system　市中に流動性を供給する
liquidity advance　資金提供
liquidity crisis　資金繰りの悪化, 流動性危機
liquidity crunch　信用逼迫, 流動性逼迫
liquidity dilemma　流動性ジレンマ
liquidity facility　信用供与枠, 流動性枠, 流動性ファシリティ
liquidity injection　流動性の供給
liquidity property　流動性資産
liquidity risk　流動性リスク
liquidity shortage [scarcity]　流動性の不足
liquidity sources　資金源
liquidity surplus　流動性過剰
liquidity target　流動性目標
manage liquidity　流動性を抑える
market liquidity　市場流動性
provide ample liquidity to financial markets　金融市場に大量の資金を供給する
provide liquidity　流動性を提供する, 流動性を供給する
pump liquidity in the system　市中に流動性を供給する
tightened liquidity　資金繰りの悪化
withdraw [remove, squeeze out] liquidity from the money markets　短期金融市場から資金［流動性］を吸い上げる

liquidity trap　流動性の罠, 流動性トラップ, 流動性の落し穴（市場金利がゼロ％近くになって, それ以上の金融緩和ができず, 中央銀行による通常の金融政策が効かない状態のこと）
be stuck in a Keynesian liquidity trap　ケインズのいう流動性の罠に陥っている
fall into a liquidity trap　流動性の罠に陥る

Lisbon Treaty　リスボン条約

> リスボン条約 ⊃ EUの新基本条約。未発効に終わった欧州憲法を簡素化した条約で, EU加盟27か国が2007年12月にポルトガルの首都リスボンで調印し, 2009年12月1日に発効。欧州理事会常任議長（EU大統領）や外交安保上級代表（EU外相）の創設を定めたリスボン条約の狙いは, EUの組織運営の効率化と, EUを米・中・露に比肩する大国の地位に押し上げることにある。

list 動 上場する, 上場される, 表示する, 表記する, 記載する, 掲載する, 記録する, 計上する, 名を挙げる, 指定する

list 名 表, 名簿, 一覧表, 目録, 明細書, リスト

listed 形 リスト［表］に記載された, 上場された

  companies listed on stock exchanges 証券取引所に上場されている企業

  listed building 重要文化財建築, 保存指定建築物

  listed company 上場会社, 上場企業, 公開会社, 公開企業 （＝listed corporation, listed enterprise, listed firm）

  listed land prices 公示地価 （＝listed prices of land, posted prices of land）

  listed price 表示価格, 定価, カタログ記載値段 （＝list price）

  listed security 上場証券, 上場有価証券

  listed share 上場株式, 上場株 （＝listed stock）

listing 名 上場, 不動産仲介, 不動産仲介契約, 名簿, 表, 表の作成

literacy 名 操作能力, 読み書き能力, 教養, リテラシー

  computer literacy コンピュータ・リテラシー（コンピュータの使用・操作能力）

  information literacy 情報リテラシー（情報の処理・利用能力）

  Internet literacy インターネット・リテラシー（＝network literacy：インターネットを使いこなす能力）

  media literacy メディア・リテラシー（新聞・雑誌・テレビ・映画, インターネットなど, 各種メディアが何を伝えているのかを視聴者が主体的に分析, 評価して, 使いこなす能力, つまり自己発信していく能力）

  network literacy ネットワーク・リテラシー（インターネットなどを使って情報を収集・発信する能力）

lithium-ion [lithium ion] battery リチウムイオン電池

litigation 名 訴訟, 論争, 紛争

  a litigation initiated against …に対して提起される［提起された］訴訟

  litigation costs [expenses] 訴訟費用

  litigation, proceeding or controversy 訴訟, 訴訟行為または紛争

live up to …を守る, …を実行する, …に従って行動する, 〈義務や責任などを〉果たす, 〈期待などに〉沿う

live-virus vaccine 生ワクチン（生きたウイルスを使ったワクチン）

livestock industry 畜産業界

LNG 液化天然ガス （**liquefied natural gas**の略）

load factor 〈航空機などの〉搭乗率, 利用率

load-shedding 局地的送電停止

loan 動 融資する, 貸し出す, 貸し付ける

loan 名 貸付け, 貸出, 融資, 借入れ, 債権, 貸出債権, 債務, 借款, 債券発行, 貸付金, 借入金, ローン

  loan shark 高利貸し, サラ金, サラ金業者, ヤミ金融業者

  loan sharking 高利貸し業, ヤミ金融, ヤミ金融業

  loan waiver 債権放棄

  loan write-off 債権放棄, 債務免除 （＝debt forgiveness, loan forgiveness, loan waiver）

loan loss provisions 貸倒れ引当金, 貸倒れ準備金 （＝loan loss reserves）

loan loss reserves 貸倒れ引当金, 貸倒れ準備金 （＝loan loss provisions, reserves for bad loans, reserves for loan losses, reserves for possible loan losses：「貸倒れ引当金」は, 融資などの債権から担保などを差し引いた金額に対して, 貸出先企業が倒産して回収できない確率を考慮して計上する。経営状況が悪い企業向けの債権ほど, 引当率は高くなる）

loanword 名 借用語, 外来語

lobby 動 〈議員に〉運動する, 陳情する, ロビー活動をする, 〈法案通過に〉圧力をかける, 〈法案の〉裏面工作をする, 法律改正の圧力をかける, 〈…するよう〉働きかける

  lobby a bill through ロビー活動によって法案を通す

  lobby Congress to …するよう議会に働きかける

  lobby for continued support 支援の継続を陳情する

lobby 名 圧力団体, ロビー団体, 院外団, 陳情団, 〈英国議会の〉控え室, 投票者用控え廊下（division lobby）, ロビー

  a lobby correspondent 議会詰め記者

  a lobby-fodder 陳情者の要求に奉仕する議員

  lobby group 圧力団体, 政治的圧力団体, ロビー団体, ロビー活動団体 （＝lobbying group）

lobbying 名 ロビー活動, 院外活動, 議会工作, 陳情運動, 請願運動, ロビーイング

  Administration lobbying 議会工作

gun lobbying 銃砲規制反対派
lobbying campaign ロビー活動（＝lobbying effort）
lobbying group ロビー活動団体, 圧力団体（＝lobby group）
lobbyism 名 陳情運動, 院外活動, 法案通過[法案否決]運動, 議会工作, ロビイズム
lobbyist 名 院外工作者, 法案通過[法案否決]運動者, 陳情者, ロビイスト
lobbyist politician 族議員
local 形 地元の, 土地の, 現地の, 地方[地域]の, 地域的な, 局部的な, 狭い, 偏狭な, 市内の, 同一区内の, ローカル, 名 〈労働組合などの〉支部, 地元住民, 地方記事, 地方弁護士, 局部麻酔, 普通列車
local affairs 地方問題
local anesthesia 局所麻酔
local area network 狭域通信網, 構内[企業内]情報通信網《略 LAN》
local assemblies 地方議会
local assembly capacity 現地生産能力（＝local output capacity）
local authority 地方自治体, 地方公共団体, 地方官庁, 地方当局
local autonomy 地方自治
Local Autonomy Law 地方自治法
local bond 地方債
local brand 地方商標（＝regional brand）
local businesses [companies] 地元企業, 地場産業, 国内企業, 国内業界
local call rate 市内通話料金, 市内電話料金（＝local call charges, local telephone rate）
local celebrities 地元名士
local center 地方の中心都市, 地域センター
local city 地方都市
local color [colour] 地方色, 郷土色
local community 地域社会, 地方社会
local computer ローカル・コンピュータ（他のコンピュータと接続しないで単体で運用するコンピュータ）
local corporate tax 法人事業税（企業活動に対して課される地方税）
local corporate tax formula based on business size 外形標準課税
local cost 現地コスト
local economic zone 局地経済圏
local economy 国内経済, 地元の経済
local election 地方選挙
local employment 限定勤務地制度

local exports 地場輸出
local finance 地方財政
local improvements 地域的公共事業, 地域改良
local interests 地元企業
local manufacture 現地生産
local markets 現地市場, 地元市場
local maximum 極大
local minimum 極小
local municipalities 地方自治体
local number 市内番号
local office 現地事務所
local opinion 偏狭な見解
local option 地方選択権, 地方的選択権
local pain 局部的な痛み
local paper [rag] 地方紙
local partner 現地パートナー
local police 地元警察
local production 現地生産, 国内生産（＝local assembly, local output）
local public servant [worker] 地方公務員
local radio ローカル（ラジオ）放送[放送局]
local residents [people] 地方住民, 地元住民, 現地人
local society 現地社会
local standard 地域的基準
local taxes 地方税
local telecommunications facilities 地域通信設備
local telephone service 市内電話サービス, 地域電話サービス
local time 現地時間
local train 普通列車
person of local ideas 視野の狭い人
local content 現地調達, 現地調達率, ローカル・コンテント
Local Content Act 自動車部品国内調達法, ローカル・コンテント法, 現地調達率規制[条項], ローカル・コンテント規制[条項]
local content rate 現地調達率, 現地部品[現地物資]調達率, 国産化率
local content requirements [provisions] 現地調達率規制[条項], 国産化率規制, ローカル・コンテント条項
local government 地方政府, 地方行政, 地方自治体, 地方自治制, 地方公共団体, 地方
local government bond 地方債
local government current revenue 地方政

府経常収入
local government-run universities 公立大学
locality 名 場所, 地域, 区域, 近辺, 現場, 現地, 居所, 所在地, 方向感覚, 土地勘
　the locality of a lawsuit 裁判地, 裁判籍
　the locality of a mineral 鉱物の産地
　the locality of residence 居住地
　the locality of the crime 犯罪の現場
localization 名 地域特化, 地域的集中, 局地［局部］化, 局所限定, 局限, 地方化, 地方分権, 現地採用, 位置測定, 配置, ローカリゼーション（国や地域に応じてソフトウエアやハードウエアの仕様を変更すること）
　localization economies 地域特化の経済
　localization of industry 産業の地域的集中
　personnel localization 人材の現地採用
localized 形 地方に限定した, 局地的な, 局所的な, 局部的な
　localized downpours 集中豪雨
　localized swelling 局部的な腫れ上がり
　localized warfare 局地戦
location 名 立地, 立地条件, 場所, 位置, 配置, 所在地, 拠点, 用地, 敷地, 〈商品の〉置き場所, 〈データの〉記憶場所, 野外撮影場, ロケーション
　degree of location 集積度
　fixed location 固定ロケーション（商品を置く場所の固定化）
　free location フリー・ロケーション（商品などを置く場所の自由化）
　geographical location 地理的位置
　industrial location 産業立地, 工業立地, 産業配置 （＝location of industry）
　location decision 立地決定
　location factor 立地要因 （＝location force）
　location of industry 産業立地, 工業立地
　manufacturing location 工業立地
　offshore locations 海外拠点
　plant location 工場所在地, 工場立地
　prime location 一等地
　store location 店舗立地, 商業立地
lock horns with …と激しく衝突する, …と激しくやりあう
lock in 〈利益や価格を〉確定する, 〈コストを〉固定する, 確保する
lock-in 名 監禁, 占拠, 乗っ取り, ロックイン
lock-on 名 〈レーダーによる〉攻撃物体の自動追跡

locker-room language ひわいな言葉
lockout 名 工場閉鎖, 建物への立入り禁止, 締め出し, ロックアウト
lockstep 名 型にはまったやり方, がんじがらめの配列, 〈前の人と間隔を詰めて歩調を合わせる〉密接行進法
lockup [lock-up] 名 監禁, 戸締り, 門限, 留置所, 刑務所, 貸し店舗, 〈約束手形, 債務などの〉期限延長, 塩漬け, 塩漬け株, 資本の固定, 固定資本, 損益の確定, 転売禁止, ロックアップ（企業買収交渉で, 買収成立から一切の処理が済むまでのあいだ第三者による買収の脅威をなくすため, 買収する会社と被買収会社が取り交わす取決めのことも「ロックアップ」という）
locomotive 名 原動力, 推進力, 牽引役, 牽引車, 機関車, 主因, 刺激剤 （＝driver, driving force, locomotive engine）
　locomotive effect 経済成長を促進する効果, 景気刺激効果
　locomotive engine 牽引力, 牽引役, 原動力, 推進力, 機関車 （＝driver, driving force, locomotive）
locus 名 軌跡, 軌道, 場所(place), 所在地
　constant returns locus 一定収穫軌道
　constant variance locus 分散軌跡
　consumption locus 消費軌跡
　locus classicus 〈引用された〉名句
　locus contractus 契約地
　locus criminis 犯罪地
　locus delicti 不法行為地
　locus sigilli 捺印箇所 （＝the place of the seal）
　optimal locus 最適軌跡
locust years 苦難の時代, 苦難の年月
lodge 動 正式に申し出る, 提出する, 訴える, 告訴する, …を持ち込む, 収用する, 保管する
　lodge a complaint with …に苦情を申し出る
　lodge a murder complaint against …を殺人で告訴する
　lodge a protest with …に異議申立てを行う
　lodge important documents with a bank 重要書類を銀行に保管する［預ける］
log 動 〈文書に〉記録する, 記入する, 航行する, 飛行する, 〈材木などを〉切り出す
　log in 接続する, アクセスする, 利用する （＝access, log on）
　log onto …に接続する, …にアクセスする, …を利用する

log 名 記録, 航海日誌, 航空日誌, 〈インターネットなどの〉接続記録, アクセス記録, 利用記録, 〈サーバーの〉通信記録, 〈船の〉速度測定器, ログ
  business log 業務日誌, 業務記録
  flight log 航空日誌
  log file ログ・ファイル(コンピューター内に残された実行履歴ファイル)
  log-in ログイン (＝log-on：コンピュータ・システムの使用開始)
  log-in ID [name] ログインID, ユーザー名 (＝user ID, username)
  log-out [logout] ログアウト (＝log-off：コンピュータ・システムの使用終了)

loggerhead 名 不恰好な頭, 頭, ばか, 間抜け
  at loggerheads over …をめぐり争っている, …のことで争う
  at loggerheads with …と言い争って, …と争って, …と論争して, …とけんかして
  fall [go] to loggerheads けんかを始める, 殴り合いを始める
  join [lay] loggerheads together 額を集めて協議する

logging 名 森林伐採, 木材伐採, 伐採搬出

logjam 名 行き詰まり, 停止, 停滞, 渋滞, 阻止, 妨害, 封鎖(blockade)
  be caught in a logjam 行き詰まってしまう
  break the logjam 局面を打開する, 行き詰まりを打破する[打ち破る, 打開する]

logistic support 後方支援

Lohas ロハス, 健康と環境に配慮したライフスタイル (Lifestyles Of Health And Sustainabilityの略)

long 形 長い, 長期の, 買い持ちの, 強気の, 見込み薄の, 危険な, ロング
  long-awaited 長い間待ち望んでいた, 待望の, 待ちに待った
  long-cherished desire 宿願
  long-dated 長期の
  long-drawn speech 長たらしい演説
  long-expected 待ちこがれた
  long haul 長距離, 長期間, 長距離輸送
  long-headed 先見の明のある(far-seeing), 賢明な
  long-life [longlife] 長持ちする, 日持ちする
  long-lived asset 長期保有資産, 長期性[長期]資産, 固定資産 (＝capital asset, fixed asset, long term asset, plant and equipment, property)
  long odds 低い可能性
  long position 買い持ち, 買い建て, ロング・ポジション
  long run 長期
  long shot 遠写し, やってみる価値のある試み, 〈一か八かの〉賭け, 確率の低い賭け, ロング・ショット
  long-sighted 遠視の, 先見の明のある
  long-stay patient 長期入院患者
  long suit 長所, 得手, 得意とするところ
  long ton 英トン《略 L/T》(2,240ポンド(約1,016Kg)に相当)
  long tongue 多弁, おしゃべり
  long-winded 長たらしい, 冗長[冗漫]な, くどい, 息の長く続く

long-established 形 設立されて長い, 歴史の古い
  long-established company 伝統企業, 老舗

long range 長期, 長距離
  long-range budget 長期予算
  long-range business planning 長期経営計画
  long-range cash forecast 長期資金予測
  long-range cost 長期の費用, 長期費用, 長期原価 (＝long-run cost)
  long-range fund [cash] planning 長期資金計画
  long-range management planning 長期経営計画 (＝long range planning)
  long-range profit planning 長期利益計画

long-run [long-running] 形 長期の, 長く続いている
  long-run cost 長期的費用, 長期費用, 長期原価
  long-run forces 長期的動向, 長期動向
  long-run trend 長期傾向, 長期的動向, 長期トレンド

long-standing [longstanding] 形 長年の, 積年の, 長期にわたる
  long-standing corporate structure 長年[積年]の企業体質, 長年の企業構造

long-term contract 長期契約, 長期請負契約, 長期工事契約
  long-term contract balances 長期請負契約支出金
  long-term contract work 長期請負
  long-term contract work in progress 長期請負契約, 長期未完成請負工事 (＝long term contract)

long-term debt 長期債務, 長期負債, 長期

借入金, 長期借入債務, 固定負債 （＝long-term borrowings, long-term obligation）

long-term employment 長期雇用
long-term government bonds 長期国債
long-term interest rate 長期金利

> 長期金利とは ⇒ 期間1年以上の金利で, 新規発行された10年物国債（長期国債）の流通利回りを指標に使う。国債価格が上がれば長期金利が下がる関係にある。企業向け貸出や住宅ローン金利にも影響する。景気が悪いと経済活動が停滞し, 長期金利も下がる。

loom 動 次第に迫ってくる, 不気味に迫る, 不気味に浮かび上がる, 立ちはだかる, 待ち受ける, ぼんやりと現われる［姿を見せる］, 非常に重大に思える
- **loom in sight** かすかに見える, ぼんやり見える
- **loom large** 立ちはだかる, 非常に気にかかる, 大きく広がる
- **loom up ahead** 前方にぼんやりと現われる

loophole 名 抜け穴, 抜け道, 逃げ道, 盲点, 小窓,〈壁の〉小さい穴, 銃眼, ループホール
- **a tax loophole** 租税の抜け穴
- **close a legal loophole** 法の抜け穴［抜け道］をふさぐ
- **exploit loopholes in the Non-Proliferation Treaty** 核拡散防止条約（NPT）の抜け穴を利用する
- **seek legal loopholes** 法の抜け穴［抜け道］を探す

loosening of monetary policy 金融政策の緩和

lopsided 形 一方に片寄った, 一方に傾いた, 一方的な, 一方が重すぎる［大きすぎる］, 不均衡な, 左右不均衡の, 釣り合いの取れない, いびつな, アンバランスな
- **lopsided trade** 片貿易, アンバランスな貿易
- **lopsided victory** 一方的な大勝利

lose 動 赤字を出す, 損失を被る, 失う,〈競争などに〉負ける, 下落する
- **lose competitiveness** 競争力を失う （＝lose competitive edge）
- **lose money** 損失を出す, 赤字を出す, 損失を被る
- **lose some ground** 値を下げる

loser 名 敗者, 負け犬, 負け組, 成功しない人, 失敗者, 被害を被る人［物］, 値下がり銘柄, 値下がり株 （⇒winner）
- **a bad loser** 負け惜しみの強い人, 往生際の悪い人
- **a born loser** 何をやってもうまくいかない人, いつも負けてばかりいる人
- **a good loser** 素直に負けを認める人
- **a three-time loser** 前科3犯の者
- **losers** 負け組, 負け組企業, 値下がり銘柄, 値下がり銘柄数
- **weak-yen losers** 円安の打撃を受ける企業

loss 名 損失, 欠損, 欠損金, 赤字, 赤字額, 損失, 損害額, 減損, ロス
- **loss in production** 生産の減少, 減産, 減産分
- **loss of coordination disorder** 統合失調症
- **loss projections** 損失予想額, 予想損失額
- **loss-sharing system** ロス・シェアリング方式, 損失分担方式（国と営業譲渡先が損失を分担する方式）

loss-making [lossmaking] 形 赤字続きの, 赤字の, 採算が合わない
- **loss-making area** 不採算部門 （＝lossmaking）
- **loss-making business results** 赤字決算
- **loss-making department** 不採算部門
- **loss-making outlet** 赤字店舗 （＝money-losing outlet）

lost decade 失われた十年

low 名 安値, 底値, 最低, 底, 最安値, 最低値, 最低記録, 低水準
- **a closing low** 終値での最安値
- **a new low** 新安値, 最安値の更新
- **all time lows** 過去最低の水準 （＝historic lows）
- **an all time low** 過去最低, 史上最安値, 最安値, 上場来の安値, 過去最良
- **an intraday low** 取引時間中の安値, ざら場の安値
- **cyclical low** サイクルの底
- **fall to new lows** 史上最安値を更新する （＝set new all-time lows）
- **historic lows** 過去最低水準
- **hit a 20-year low** 20年ぶりの低水準となる

low 形 低い, 安い, 低水準の, 低級な, 劣った, 悪い, ロー
- **all-time low** 最低記録, 過去最低, 史上最安値
- **hit a low point** 底を打つ
- **low birthrate** 少子化
- **low carbon society** 低炭素社会
- **low comedy** どたばた喜劇
- **low dividend** 低配当
- **low fuel consumption car** 低燃費車

low growth　低成長
low growth path　低成長軌道
low income　低所得
low-income earners　低所得者, 低所得者層
low inflation　低インフレ, インフレ率低下
low inflation policy　インフレ抑制政策
low interest rate policy　低金利政策
low-level radioactive waste　低レベル放射性廃棄物
low-lying coastal countries　海岸沿いの低地国
low margin　薄利
low price　安い値段, 安価, 安値, 低価格
low price policy　低物価政策
low spirits　落胆, 意気消沈
Low Sunday　復活祭の次の日曜日
low technology　低技術, ローテク
low tide　干潮, 干潮時
low value added　低付加価値
remain low　低水準にとどまる

low cost　低コスト, 低費用, 低原価, 低利, 低賃金
low-cost countries　低コスト国
low-cost funds　低利の資金, 低利の資金調達
low-cost labor　低コスト労働力, 低賃金の労働力
low-cost loan　低金利ローン, 低費用融資, 低利融資
low-cost strategy　低コスト戦略, 低費用戦略
low-cost structure　低コスト構造
low-cost technology　低コスト技術　(＝appropriate technology)

lower 動　引き下げる, 押し下げる, 低減する, 低下させる, 抑える, 下げる, 減らす, 安くする, 下方修正する
lower borrowing costs　資金調達コストを低減する
lower one's profit forecasts　業績予想［業績見通し］を下方修正する　(＝slash one's profit forecasts)

lower 形　下の, 下部の, 下層の, 下級の, 下流の
a lower court　下級裁判所
the lower classes　下層階級
the lower forty-eight　〈アラスカ・ハワイを除く〉米国本土48州　(＝the Lower 48)
the Lower House　〈2院制議会の〉下院,〈日本の〉衆議院

lower house　〈日本の〉衆議院, 衆院,〈英国の〉下院
Lower House Budget Committee　衆議院予算委員会
Lower House plenary session　衆議院本会議
Lower House Speaker　衆議院議長

Loya Jirga　〈アフガニスタンの〉国民大会議, ロヤ・ジルガ
loyalist 名　支持者, 体制擁護者
loyalty 名　忠実性, 忠実度, 忠誠心, 信頼度
lucrative 形　利益が得られる, 儲かる, 大変金になる, 利益の大きい, 有利な　(＝profitable)
lucrative business　儲かる商売, 有利な事業
lucrative investment　有利な投資
lucrative upstream division　利益の大きい原油採掘［原油生産］部門

lump sum　一括払い, 大金, 合計金額
lump sum payment　一括払い, 一時金
lump sum purchase　一括購入
lump sum repayment　一括返済
lump sum sale　一括売却
pay in a lump sum　一括払いで支払う　(＝make a lump sum payment)
provide a lump sum　資金を一括供与する

lunar 形　月の, 月に関する, 月面で用いられる
lunar base　月面基地
lunar (excursion) module　月着陸船　(＝lunar lander)
lunar landing　月面着陸
lunar orbit　月周回軌道
lunar rover　月面移動車

lurch 名　不意の傾斜, 傾き, 傾向, よろめき, 千鳥足
downward lurch　急落
upward lurch　急上昇, 急騰

lure 動　勧誘する, 誘い込む, 引きつける, 誘致する, 導入する　(＝attract)
lure customers　顧客を勧誘する, 顧客を取り込む
lure foreign companies　外資を導入する, 外国企業を誘致する

luxury brand　高級ブランド
LWR　軽水炉　(**light water reactor**の略)

M

m

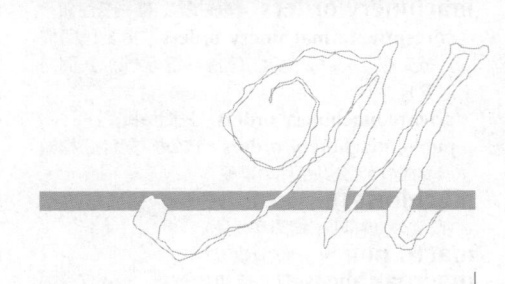

M 通貨供給量, マネー・サプライ（money supplyの略。市場に流通している通貨量（currency in circulation：通貨流通高）のこと）

M1 マネー・サプライM1, エム・ワン, M1（＝M one：M1＝預金通貨＋現金通貨）

M2 マネー・サプライM2, エム・ツー, M2（＝M two：M2＝預金通貨＋現金通貨＋定期性預金が中心の準通貨。「準通貨」は, 定期性預金のほかに, 外貨預金や非居住者の円預金など即時に換金できない銀行預金のこと）

M3 マネー・サプライM3, エム・スリー, M3（＝M three：M2に譲渡性預金(CD)とゆうちょ銀行, 農協, 信用金庫などの預貯金や信用元本などを加えたもの）

M & A 企業の吸収合併, 合併・買収, 企業取得と合併（merger and acquisition [mergers and acquisitions]の略）
   financial M&A 財務的M&A（財務上の利益を上げることが目的のM&A）
   friendly M&A 友好的M&A
   hostile M&A 敵対的M&A
   M&A advisory firm M&A（企業の合併・買収）助言会社
   M&A bid 企業の合併・買収提案, M&Aの提案
   M&A deal M&A取引, M&A案件（＝M&A transaction）
   M&A market 企業の合併・買収(M&A)市場
   strategic M&A 戦略的M&A（事業の再構築を目的とするM&A）

m to m EC マーケット同士の取引[電子商取引]（＝M2M：market to market ECの略）

machination 名 陰謀, 策謀, 企み
machine 名 機械, 機器, 機構, 組織, ミシン, 自動車, コンピュータ,〈米政党の〉選挙組織,〈組織の〉幹部集団, マシン
   answering machine 留守番電話
   machine gun 機関銃
   machine language 機械語（＝machine code）
   machine shop 機械工場, 組立[修理]工場
   machine tool 工作機械
   machine toolmaker 工作機械メーカー
   machine translation 機械翻訳, コンピュータによる自動翻訳
   military machine 軍事機構
   party machine 党執行部, 政党執行部
   washing machine 洗濯機

machine-readable 形 機械可読式の, 機械読取り式の
   machine-readable passport 機械読取り式旅券
   machine-readable works 機械読取り可能な著作物

machinery 名 機械, 機械類, 機械装置, 機器, 機構, 組織, 機構, 機関, 体制, 勢力, 分子
   farm machinery 農業機械
   heavy machinery 重機械
   industrial machinery 産業機械, 産業用機械
   machinery and equipments 機械設備, 機械・設備, 機械装置, 機械および装置
   the complaints machinery 不満分子
   the machinery of government 政治機構
   transportation machinery 輸送機器, 輸送用

機械

machinery orders 機械受注, 機械受注額
 core private machinery orders　実質民間機械受注, 実質機械受注（船舶・電力を除く民間需要）
 private machinery orders　民間機械受注
 public machinery orders　官公機械受注, 機械受注のうち公共部門の需要
machinist 名　機械工, 修理工, 機械運転者, 〈政党の〉幹部員, 機関兵曹長
macro policy　マクロ政策
macroanalysis 名　巨視的分析, マクロ分析（国民経済を大きく全体としてとらえ, 物価, 不況, 失業, 国際収支などを考えるもの）
macroeconomic [macro-economic] 形　巨視的経済の, マクロ経済的, 経済全体の（⇒microeconomic）
 macroeconomic adjustment　マクロ経済的調整
 macroeconomic analysis　マクロ経済分析
 macroeconomic background　マクロ経済環境
 macroeconomic behavior [behaviour]　マクロ経済的行動
 macroeconomic environment　マクロ経済環境
 macroeconomic management　マクロ経済的管理, マクロ経済管理
 macroeconomic model　巨視的経済モデル, マクロ経済モデル, マクロ・モデル
 macroeconomic phenomenon　巨視的経済現象
 macroeconomic planning　巨視的経済計画
 macroeconomic policy　巨視的経済政策, マクロ経済政策
 macroeconomic recovery　マクロの景気回復
 macroeconomic restraint　マクロ経済面の自制
 macroeconomic situation　マクロ経済状況
 macroeconomic theory　巨視的経済理論, マクロ経済理論
 macroeconomic variables　マクロ経済変数
 macroeconomic volatility　マクロ経済の変動性
macroeconomics 名　巨視的経済学, マクロ経済学
macroengineering [macro-engineering] 名　マクロ工学技術, マクロエンジニアリング
macroforecasting [macro-forecasting] 名　マクロ予測
macrophage activating factor　マクロファージ活性化因子《略 MAF》
mad cow disease　狂牛病（＝bovine spongiform encephalopathy, BSE）
Mad Hatter's disease　水銀中毒症
made-to-order [made-to-measure] 形　注文で作った, あつらえの, おおつらえ向きの, オーダーメードの（＝made-to-measure）
Mafia [Maffia] 名　犯罪秘密結社, 腹心の部下, マフィア
mafia 名　秘密集団, 暴力組織, 〈影響力のある〉集団, 有力者集団, 閥, 側近の支持者グループ, 側近グループ
 the California Mafia　レーガン大統領側近グループ
 the Irish mafia　ケネディ大統領側近グループ
Mafioso 名　マフィアの構成員
magic bullet　魔法の弾丸, 無害［無副作用］薬剤, 特効薬, 解決手段, 解決
maglev 名　磁気浮上式超高速列車, 磁気浮力推進システム, リニア（リニア・モーターカーの一種で, magnetic levitationの略）
magnetic information　磁気情報
magnitude 名　大きさ, 大小, 規模, 重要性, 重大さ, 量, 多量, 広大, 振幅, 〈人格の〉偉大さ, 光度, 等級, 震度, マグニチュード
 a decision of great magnitude　極めて重要な決定
 a magnitude 8 earthquake　マグニチュード8の地震
 an order of magnitude　大規模, 10倍の数量
 coverage and magnitude　対象と規模
 economic magnitude　経済量
 magnitude of demand　需要の大きさ
 magnitude of the cycle　景気循環の振幅
 magnitude of the year-on-year [year-over-year] change　前年同月比伸び率
 measured magnitude　計測量
 of the first magnitude　第一級の, 一流の, 最も［極めて］重要な, 1等星の
maiden 形　初めての, 初回の, 未婚の, 処女…
 maiden flight　処女飛行, 初飛行
 maiden horse　未勝利馬
 maiden name　〈既婚女性の〉旧姓
 maiden speech　〈初当選後の議会での〉処女演説, 就任演説
 maiden voyage　処女航海, 初航海
Mail Law　郵便法

mail order 通信販売, 通販, 通信販売の注文
main 形 主力の, 主要な, 主な
- **main business** 主力事業, 本業（＝core business, main operation）
- **main creditor banks** 主要取引銀行, 主力取引銀行, 主力銀行（＝main banks, main financing banks）
- **main [major] currencies** 主要通貨
- **main operation** 主力事業, 中核事業, 中核業務（＝core business）
- **Main Street** 保守的な社会,〈小都市特有の〉因習的文化, 普通の人,〈小都市の〉大通り, 目抜き通り（high street）, 中心街, 国内産業

Mainland China 中華人民共和国, 中国本土, 中国大陸

mainstay 名 主力, 主力商品, 支え, 支柱, 大黒柱, 頼みの綱, 拠り所
- **mainstay business** 主力事業（＝core business, main business, main operation）
- **mainstay export item** 輸出の主力製品［商品, 品目］
- **mainstay issues** 主力銘柄
- **mainstay operation** 主力事業（＝core business, main operation, mainstay business）
- **mainstay products** 主力製品, 主力商品

mainstream 名 主流, 本流, 主潮（「非主流」＝nonmainstream）
- **mainstream economics** 主流経済学

maintain 動 保つ, 維持する, 持続する, 続ける, 進める, 据え置く, 整備する, 保守する, 保全する, 手入れをする,〈家族などを〉養う, 支える, 支持する, 主張する
- **maintain a negative outlook** ネガティブ（弱含み）の見通しを据え置く
- **maintain a steady hand** 金融政策を据え置く
- **maintain a tight monetary policy stance** 金融引締めのスタンスを維持する
- **maintain diversification** 多角化を進める
- **maintain good relations with** …と良好な関係を保つ
- **maintain international price competitiveness** 国際価格競争力を維持する
- **maintain one's high margins** 高い利ざやを確保する
- **maintain one's silence** 沈黙を守る

maintenance 名 維持, 保守, 保全, 整備, 維持管理, 修理点検, 扶養, 支持, 擁護, 主張, メンテナンス
- **breakdown maintenance** 事後保全
- **capital maintenance** 資本維持
- **central maintenance** 集中保全
- **corrective maintenance** 修理保守
- **industrial maintenance** 産業扶助
- **income maintenance** 所得維持
- **maintenance contract** 保守契約
- **maintenance float** 補充予備在庫, 補充用の予備在庫
- **maintenance free** メンテナンス不要, メンテナンス・フリー
- **preventive maintenance** 予防保全, 予防的保守, 定期保守
- **price maintenance** 価格維持
- **productive maintenance** 生産保全《略 PM》
- **scheduled [routine] maintenance** 定期保守
- **separate maintenance** 別居手当
- **supplementary maintenance** 補充保守

major 名 成人, 成年者, 専攻科目, …専攻学生, 少佐, 国際石油資本, 大手メーカー, メジャー
- **chemical majors** 大手化学メーカー
- **international oil majors** 国際石油資本, メジャー（＝major oil companies, majors）
- **majors** 国際石油資本（major oil companies, oil majors）, 大手メーカー

major 形 主要な, 重大な, 大手の, 大口の, 大規模な, 大型の, 大きいほうの, 大部分の, 過半数の, 多数の, メジャー（⇒minor）
- **build a major position** 大きな地位［確固とした基盤］を築く
- **major acquisition** 大型買収
- **major barrier** 大きな障害
- **major (business) cycle** 主循環（＝Juglar cycle, Juglar wave）
- **major cause** 大きな原動力, 主因
- **major grain companies** 穀物メジャー
- **major importer** 輸入大国, 主要輸入国
- **major leagues** 先進工業国
- **Major Leagues** 大リーグ, メジャー・リーグ
- **major litigation** 大型訴訟, 主要な訴訟
- **major market** 主要輸出先, 主要輸出国市場
- **major market top** 大天井
- **major movement** 大勢（＝major swing, major trend）
- **major oil companies** 国際石油資本, メジャー
- **major player** 大手企業, 大手, 主流, 大口の買い手
- **major peak** 大天井

majority | makeup

major power　主要国, 大国
major total　最終合計, 大計
major trading partners　主要な貿易相手国
majority　名　過半数, 大多数, 多数, 多数派, 多数党, 大半, 大部分, 得票差, 成年, 成人
a majority of creditors　大半の債権者
absolute [overall] majority　絶対多数
by a small majority　僅かの差で, 僅差で
decision by majority　多数決 (＝majority decision)
early majority　初期追随者（イノベーションの普及過程で初期採用者の後に続く者）
gain a majority　過半数を獲得する
House majority leader　〈米〉下院院内総務
late majority　後期追随者（イノベーションの普及過程で初期追随者の後に続く者）
majority committee table　多数党委員会席
majority control　過半数支配, 過半数所有支配
majority decision　多数決
majority interest　過半数持ち分, 多数株主持ち分 (＝consolidated equity：連結持ち分, 親会社持ち分)
majority leader　院内総務, 多数党院内総務, 与党院内総務（米上下両院の多数党の院内活動責任者）
majority owned company　過半数所有会社, 過半数子会社 (＝majority owned subsidiary：社外議決権株式の50％超を他の会社に所有されている会社・子会社)
majority owner　過半数株主
majority ownership　過半数所有
majority policy committee　上院多数党政策委員会
majority rule　多数決, 多数決原理
majority share　過半数の株式 (＝majority stake)
majority shareholder [stockholder]　過半数株主, 支配株主
majority stake　過半数株式
majority support　賛成多数
majority verdict　多数票決, 過半数票決
majority vote　多数投票
majority voting　多数決による票決
majority whip　〈米議会の〉院内副総務, 多数党院内幹事
outright majority　単独過半数
overwhelming majority　圧倒的多数
principle [rule] of majority decision　多数決の原理[ルール], 多数決 (＝majority rule)
Senate majority leader　上院院内総務
simple majority　単独過半数, 単純多数
the age of majority　成人年齢
vote down by a majority vote　多数決で否決する
win the election by [with] a majority of fifty　50票差で選挙に勝つ
with majority support from　…の賛成多数で
make for　…となる, …を示す, …を生み出す, …の代用をする, …を助長する, …を助成する, …に寄与する, …の役に立つ, …に便利である, …に向かう[接近する], …に近づく, …を襲う,〈意見などを〉固める, 強める
make good　〈約束などを〉果たす, 遂行する, 履行する,〈損害を〉弁償する, 償う,〈費用などを〉支払う, 返金する,〈立場などを〉保持する, 確保する, 強化する, 立証する, 実証する, 修理する, 修復する
make good in the business　事業で成功する
make good on　…を果たす, …を遂行する
make good one's promise　約束を果たす[履行する]
make landfall　上陸する
make or break [make-or-break]　運命を左右する, 成否をかけた, …の成否を決める, 一か八かの, のるかそるかの, 成功か失敗か
make-or-buy decision　自製か購入かの選択, 自製か購入かの意思決定, 自製・購入選択, 自製か購入の決定
make-to-order　名　注文生産, 受注生産
make up　作り上げる, でっちあげる, かさ上げする, 埋め合わせる
make up for　…を補填する, …の穴埋めをする, …を埋め合わせる, 帳消しにする
makeover　名　イメージ・チェンジ, 模様替え, お色直し, 改良, 改造, 改装, 改築, 改善, 練り直し, 変身
makeshift　形　間に合わせの, 一時しのぎの, 急場しのぎの, 代用の, 臨時の, 仮の, 仮設の,　名　代用品, 当座しのぎの策, 間に合わせのもの
makeshift causeway　仮設道路
makeshift measures　一時しのぎの策, 急場しのぎの措置, 場当たり的な対応, 姑息な手段
makeshift shelter　仮設避難所
makeup　名　組織, 構造, 構成, 組立て, 陣容,〈新聞の〉割付け, 気質, 性格, 化粧, 化粧品,〈大学の〉追試験, 再試験, 補講
makeup men　〈新聞社の〉整理記者

makeup of government bond issuance 国債発行の構成
the genetic makeup 遺伝子構成

making 名 製造, 製作, 形成, 作る過程, 成立, 発達［発展, 成長, 成功］の原因［理由］, 原料, 素質, 要素
  be the making of …を成長［発展, 発達］させるものとなる
  budget making 予算査定
  decision making 意思決定, 政策決定
  goods making 財貨生産
  have the makings of …の素質がある
  in the making 発生［発達］過程にある, 発展中の, 製作中の, 編纂中の, 完成前に
  of one's own making 自分で招いた
  policy making 政策決定, 政策立案（＝policymaking）
  steel making 製鋼
  the making of a nuclear weapon 核兵器の原料

maladaptation 名 不適応, 順応不良
maladministration 名 失政, 処理の誤り, 運用の誤り, 不始末
malaise 名 不定愁訴,〈体の〉不調, 不快, 不快感, 不安, 沈滞, 低迷
Malcolm Baldrige National Quality Award マルコム・ボルドリッジ全米品質賞
malfeasance 名 (公務員の)背任行為, 不法［違法］行為, 不当［不正］行為, 汚職（＝malpractice）
malfunction 名 機能障害, 機能不全, 故障, 誤作動, 不調
  a computer malfunction コンピュータのシステム障害
  the malfunction of a new computer system 新コンピュータ・システムの故障［障害］
malicious act 悪質な行為
malpractice 名 不正, 不正［違法, 不法］行為, 背任行為, 失態, 汚職, 業務過誤, 医療過誤, 医療ミス, 不当処置（＝malfeasance）
  malpractice insurance 業務過誤保険
  professional malpractice 職業専門家の業務懈怠(けたい)
mama and papa store 小売零細店, 零細小売店, 家族経営の小型店, パパママ店（＝ma-and-pa store, mama and pop store）
man-machine communication マン・マシン通信

man-machine interface マンマシン・インターフェース《略 MMI》（＝human interface, human-machine interface：人とコンピュータが意思疎通を図るための設計思想, 技術または装置）
man-machine system 人間機械系, マンマシン・システム（＝human-machine system）
manage 動 管理する, 経営する, 統括する, 統率する, 監督する, 幹事を務める, 運用する, 運営する, 運用管理する, うまく処理する, 対処する, 取り扱う, 使いこなす,〈困難などを〉乗り切る, 切り抜ける
  manage future events 将来発生する事態に対応［対処］する
  manage liquidity 流動性を抑える
  manage the business 事業を統括する
  managed assets 管理資産
  managed care 管理医療
  managed currency [money] 管理通貨
  managed economy 管理経済, 経済運営
  managed floating exchange 管理変動為替
  managed trade 管理貿易
management 名 経営, 管理, 運用, 運営, 取扱い, 業務執行, 経営管理, 経営陣, 経営側, 経営者側, マネジメント
  asset (and) liability management 資産負債総合管理, 資産負債管理, バランス・シート管理《略 ALM》
  bottom-up management 参加型経営, 下からの経営管理, ボトムアップ経営, ボトムアップ・マネジメント
  business management 企業管理, 企業経営, 経営管理
  capital management 資本管理
  centralized management 集中管理, 集中的管理, 集権管理
  configuration management 環境設定管理, 構成管理, コンフィギュレーション管理
  cooperative management 共同管理（＝joint management）
  cost management 原価管理, コスト管理, コスト・マネジメント
  crisis management 危機管理
  current management 現経営陣
  data resource management データ資源管理
  decentralized management 分権的管理
  demand side management 需要管理, デマンド・サイド・マネジメント
  diversified management 多角経営
  Japanese management 日本型経営（＝Jap-

anese style management)
liability management 負債管理
lower management 下級管理層
management accountability 経営の説明責任, 経営の説明責任能力
management accounting 管理会計 (= managerial accounting)
management by exception 例外管理
management by objectives 目標管理, 目標管理制度 《略 MBO》
management competency 経営者の資質
management conditions 経営状態, 経営状況
management decision 経営者の意思決定, 経営意思決定, 経営判断 (=managerial decision)
management development 経営教育, 経営者教育, 経営者啓発, 経営幹部教育, 経営幹部育成 (=executive development)
management foundation 経営基盤
management integration 経営統合 (= business integration)
management-level worker 管理職
management merger 経営統合
management philosophy 経営理念, 経営方針, 経営哲学 (=management creed)
management plan 経営計画 (=management planning)
management policy 経営方針, 経営路線, 経営政策
management reform panel 経営改革委員会
management resources 経営資源
management responsibility 経営責任 (= the responsibility of management)
management risk 経営リスク, 経営者リスク, マネジメント・リスク (=managerial risk)
management strategy 経営戦略
management system 経営体制, 経営システム, 管理システム, 経営者組織, マネジメント・システム
management team 経営陣, マネジメント・チーム (=management profiles)
middle management 中間管理層, 中間管理者層, 中間管理職, ミドル・マネジメント
money market management 金融調節
product design management 製品設計管理 《略 PDM》
relationship management 取引先総合管理 《略 RM》
right of management 経営権 (=management right)
stock management 株の運用, 株式運用

management buyout [buy-out] 経営者による自社買収, 経営陣による自社株式の公開買付け, 経営者による営業権取得, 経営陣による企業買収, マネジメント・バイアウト

> MBOとは ⇒ 企業の経営者が, 一般株主や親会社などから自社株を買い取って, 企業や事業部門の経営権を買い取ること。一般に, 敵対的買収の防衛や子会社が独立する際に用いられるM&A (合併・買収) の手法。上場企業の場合は, 経営陣が買収を実施する会社を別に設立し, 自社の資産を担保にして投資会社や金融機関から融資を受け, その資金でTOB (株式公開買付け) を行い, 一般株主から株式を広く買い集めることが多い。最近は, 非上場にすることを目的に実施する例が目立っている。その背景には, 敵対的買収への防衛策のほかに, 株式持ち合いが崩れて年金基金のような「物言う株主」が増えてきたことなどの要因があるといわれる。親会社から自社株を買って子会社が独立する際の利点としては, 社内体制が変わらないことや, 親会社との関係が比較的良好に保たれる点が挙げられる。

manager 名 経営者, 管理者, 幹部, 幹部社員, 部長, 理事, 〈銀行の〉支店長, 幹事 (引受会社), 投資顧問, 支配人, 責任者, 管財人, マネージャー
acting manager 部長代理, 支配人代理
advertising manager 宣伝部長
departmental manager 部門管理者
financial manager 財務管理者
lower manager 下級管理者
money manager 資金運用者
personnel manager 人事担当重役
purchasing manager 購買部長
risk manager リスク管理者
sales manager 販売部長, 営業部長, 販売責任者
store manager 店長
team of bond managers 債券運用チーム

managerial 形 経営 [管理, 操作, 処理] の, 経営上の, 経営者の
managerial decision 経営の意思決定, 経営判断 (=management decision)
managerial philosophy 経営理念
managerial policy 経営方針

mandate 動 義務付ける, 強制する, 命じる, 権限を与える, …の統治を委任する, マンデートを獲得する
federally-mandated services 米連邦から委託されたサービス

IMF-mandated interest rate hike IMFの条件を受け入れた利上げ
mandated group マンデートを獲得したグループ
original mandated amount 調達予定額
mandate 名 権限, 権能, 要求, 命令, 指令, 委託, 委任, 委任契約, 委任統治, 植民地, 〈選挙民の〉信任, 〈手形や小切手の〉支払い委託, 無償のサービス契約, 〈社債発行者からの主幹事に対する〉引受業務の依頼［委任］, マンデート
bank mandate 銀行委任書
competition for the mandate マンデート獲得競争, マンデート争奪戦, 主幹事争い
have a mandate to …する権限がある
mandate letter 委任状, マンデート・レター (=letter of mandate)
seek a mandate for …への支持を求める
verbal mandate 口頭のマンデート
mandatory 形 義務的な, 強制的な (compulsory), 必修の (obligatory), 命令的な, 命令の, 指令の, 委任の, 委託の
Immediate Response Mandatory 折り返し返事が必要
mandatory administration [rule] 委任統治
mandatory dividend 義務的配当
mandatory import quotas 強制的な輸入割当量
mandatory labeling 義務表示
mandatory power 委任統治国
mandatory redemption 強制償還
mandatory requirements 強制要件
mandatory retirement age 定年退職年齢, 定年
mandatory retirement system 定年制
mandatory spending 義務的経費
mandatory vocational training 必修科目としての職業訓練
manhunt 名 犯人追跡, 犯人捜査, 捜索
maneuver [manoeuvre] 名 操縦, 巧みな誘導, 駆け引き, 策略, 計略, 企み, 工作, 巧みに処理すること, 〈軍隊などの〉作戦行動, 軍事大演習, 演習, 軍事訓練
behind-the-scenes maneuver 舞台裏工作
room for maneuver 変更の余地
try various maneuvers あの手この手を試みる
manic depression 躁うつ病
manifesto 名 宣言, 声明, 宣言書, 声明書, 政策綱領, 政権公約, マニフェスト
manipulation 名 操作, 不正操作, 市場操作, 相場操縦
accounting manipulation 会計操作
currency manipulation 通貨操作
earnings manipulation 利益の不正操作
financial manipulation 経理操作
income manipulation 利益操作
market manipulation 市場操作, 株価操作, 相場操縦
stock (price) manipulation 株価操縦, 株価操作
manned 形 有人の, 乗組員を乗せた
manned expedition 有人探査
manned flight 有人飛行
manned maneuvering unit 有人移動ユニット, 人間操縦装置［ユニット］, 背負い式推進装置, 船外活動用操縦装置, 船外活動装置《略 MMU》
manned mission 有人飛行 (=manned flight)
manned-orbital station 有人宇宙ステーション
manned space station 有人宇宙ステーション《略 MSS》
manned spacecraft 有人宇宙船
Manned-Spacecraft Center 有人宇宙飛行センター《略 MSC》
manned submersible 有人潜水艇［潜水船］, 有人潜水装置
manpower 名 労働力, 労力, 人的資源, 人材, 人手, 労働人員, 人員, 従業員, マンパワー
manufacture 動 製造する, 生産する, 製作する, 作る, 作り出す, 捏造する, でっち上げる
manufacture 名 製造, 生産, 製作, 製品
craft manufacture 工芸製品
export manufacture 輸出製品
local manufacture 現地生産 (=local manufacturing)
manufacture order 製造指図書
nondurable manufactures 非耐久財製造
outside manufacture 外注製品
manufactured 形 製造された［製造される］, 生産された, 製作された, 捏造された, 自製の, …の製造［生産, 製作］
cost of goods manufactured 製造原価
manufactured evidence 証拠の捏造
manufactured exports 製品輸出, 工業製品輸出, 輸出工業製品
manufactured material 自製材料
total manufactured product 製造業生産高
manufacturer 名 製造業者, 製造会社, 製造

者, 製造元, 製作者, メーカー, 工場主 （=maker）
chemicals manufacturer 化学品メーカー
headline business conditions diffusion index of manufacturers 製造業の業況判断DI
index reading for manufacturers' sentiment 製造業の景況感
manufacturer's inventories 製造業在庫
manufacturers' suggested retail prices メーカー希望小売価格
non-manufacturers 非製造業
manufacturing 名 製造, 生産, 加工, 製作, 生産拠点, マニュファクチュアリング
　computer-aided manufacturing コンピュータ支援［援用］製造
　flexible manufacturing system フレキシブル生産システム
　full scale manufacturing 一貫製造
　infant manufacturing industry 幼稚製造業
　integrated manufacturing 一貫生産
　labor-intensive manufacturing 労働集約型製造業
　mass manufacturing 大量生産
　original equipment manufacturing 相手方ブランド製造業者, 相手先商標製品［製造］《略 OEM》
　petty manufacturing 小規模製造
　rebound in manufacturing (activity) 製造業の回復
　set up manufacturing 生産拠点を設ける
　shift manufacturing offshore 海外に生産拠点を移す
manufacturing 形 製造の, 生産の, 製造過程の, 製造業の
　manufacturing bases 製造拠点 （=manufacturing facilities）
　manufacturing capacity 生産能力, 製造能力
　manufacturing cost 製造費, 製造原価, 製造コスト, 生産コスト
　manufacturing department 製造部門
　manufacturing expertise 製造技術
　manufacturing facilities 生産拠点, 製造拠点, 生産設備 （=production facilities）
　manufacturing jobs 製造業の雇用
　manufacturing lead time 製造期間
　manufacturing location 工業立地
　manufacturing order 製造指図書
　manufacturing output [production] 製造業の生産, 工業生産, 製造業生産高
　manufacturing overhead 製造間接費
　manufacturing resource planning 製造資源計画《略 MRP》
　manufacturing sources 下請け
　manufacturing specification 製造仕様書
　manufacturing statement 製造原価報告書, 製造原価明細書
　manufacturing subsidiary 製造業子会社
　manufacturing supplies 製造用消耗品
　move manufacturing capacities to …に生産設備を移す［移転する］
map out 詳細な計画を立てる, 綿密に計画する, 計画する, まとめる, 策定する, 詳細に示す
　map out concrete measures 具体策をまとめる
　map out monetary policy 金融政策を決める
　map out rules for promoting free trade 自由貿易推進の新ルールを策定する
　map out the basic plan 基本計画をまとめる, 基本計画を立てる
marathon talks 長時間に及ぶ会談, 長時間にわたる協議
margin 名 開き, 幅, 差, 票差, 得点差, 余裕, 余地, 売上総利益, 利益率, 利ざや, 証拠金, 委託証拠金, 委託保証金, 担保金, 手付け金, マージン
　additional margin 追加証拠金
　after-tax margin 税引き後利益率
　by a wide margin 大差で
　gross margin 売上総利益, 売上利益率, 粗利益率 （=gross margin percentage）
　margin improvement 利益率改善
　margin of error 誤差
　margin of fluctuation 変動幅
　margin of safety 安全余裕率
　margin percentage 利益率
　margin requirement 証拠金, 証拠金率
　margin trading 信用取引 （=margin transaction）
　net margin 純販売利益, 純売買差益, 純利益
　net profit margin 売上高利益率
　operating income margin 営業利益率 （=operating margin）
　product margins 製品利益率
　profit margin on sales 売上高利益率
　retail margins 小売マージン
marine resources 海洋資源
maritime 形 海の, 海上の, 海に関する, 海洋の, 沿海の
　maritime hegemony 海洋覇権

maritime police action 海上警備行動
maritime protection and indemnity insurance 船主責任保険, PI保険
Maritime Provinces 沿海諸州(カナダ最東端の3州)
Maritime Self-Defense Force 海上自衛隊
maritime survey 海洋調査
maritime traffic 海上交通
mark 動 …に印をつける, …を表す, …の位置を示す, …を示す, 物語る, 特徴づける, 目立たせる, 際立たせる, 記念する, 祝う, 記録する, 点数[評価]をつける, 採点する, …に注意を払う
　be marked by …で際立っている, …が目立つ, …が印象的だ
　be marked out for promotion 出世は間違いない, 抜擢されて昇進する
　mark down 値下げする, …を書きとめる, …のノートを取る
　mark off …を区別する, 区分する, 区画する
　mark out …を仕切る, …を設計する, …の計画を立てる, …を目立たせる
　mark the boundary with a dotted line 境界を点線で示す
　mark the 10th anniversary of the foundation of the company 会社の創立10周年記念にあたる[10周年記念を祝う]
　mark time 足踏みする, 様子を見る, 成り行きを見守る
　mark up 値上げする, …を書き加える, …に高い点をつける
mark 名 水準, 標準, …台, …の大台, 記号, 符号, 標識, 標的, 目標, 成績, 評価, マーク
　be wide of the mark 的を外れている, 見当違いである, 要領を得ない (=be beside [off] the mark)
　fall short of the mark 標準に達しない
　get off the mark スタートを切る, 物事を始める
　hit the mark 的を当てる, 的中する, ピタリと当たる, 図星である, 成功を収める, 目的を達する
　make one's mark 成功する, 希望を達する, 有名になる, 名を挙げる, 署名する
　of mark 重要な, 著名な
　off the mark 不正確な, 見当違いの, 的外れな
　on the mark 正確な, 当を得た
　up to the mark 標準に達している, 体の調子がよい, 元気で
　within the mark 失敗ではない
mark to market 評価替えする, 時価で評価する
mark-to-market accounting system 時価会計制度
markdown 名 値下げ
market 動 販売する, 売り出す, 市場に出す
market 名 市場, 市中, 相場, 市況, 売買, 販路, マーケット (=marketplace, mart)
　active market 活況市場
　aftermarket 販売後市場, 有価証券の流通市場, 補修部品市場, 関連ハードウエア/ソフトウエア/周辺装置の市場, アフター・マーケット (=after market, aftermath market)
　appear on the market 上場する
　bear market 弱気市場, 下げ相場, 売り相場
　bull market 強気市場, 上げ相場, 買い相場
　capture the market シェアを獲得する
　corner the market 市場を買い占める
　credit market 金融市場, 信用市場, 発行市場
　enter the market 市場に参入する, 市場に進出する, 市場を利用する, 市場に加わる
　exchange market 為替市場
　exploit the market 市場を開拓する
　hyper market ハイパー・マーケット (=hypermarket, superstore：都市郊外に広大な売場もち, ワン・フロアの倉庫式店舗で, 食料品, 非食料品(衣料品, 電気器具, 家具, 家庭用品, 園芸用品, 建材など)を幅広く品揃えし, 可能なかぎりの安売りを売り物にしてセルフサービス方式を採用した大型スーパー)
　intervene in the market 市場に介入する, 市場介入に踏み切る
　issue market 発行市場 (=investment market)
　make a market マーケット・メークを行う, 市場を形成する, 値付け業務を行う, マーケット・メーキング (=market making)
　make inroads in the market 市場に参入する
　market fundamentalism 市場万能主義, 市場原理主義
　market interest rate 市中金利 (=open market rate)
　market leader 商品購入決定者, 商品購入影響者, 消費者, 主導株, 先導株, 業界トップ, マーケット・リーダー
　market liquidity 市場流動性,〈金融商品市場で株式や債券などを売買するための〉豊富な資金
　market maker 市場開拓者, 市場を形成する消費者, 証券業者, 証券ディーラー, 値付け業者,

マーケット・メーカー（「値付け業者」は，株や債券などの流通市場で，価格形成を行う証券業者のこと）

market opening 市場開放

market opportunity 市場機会，ビジネス機会，事業機会

market participant 市場参加者，市場参入企業，市場関係者（＝market player）

market player 市場関係者，市場参加者，市場筋，マーケット・プレーヤー（＝market participant）

market quotes 市場相場価額

market rate 市場金利，市場相場，市場レート，銀行間相場

primary market for securities 証券の発行市場

put ... on the market …を売りに出す，…を発売する，…を市販する

security market 証券市場

sensitive market 不安市況，不安定市場

shares on the market 流通している株式

strong market 強気市場，強気市況

tap the market 市場に登場する，市場で調達する

time the market 市場の好機を選ぶ，市場のタイミングをとらえる，市場のタイミングを判断する，市場のタイミングに合わせる，市場のタイミングを図る

trading market 流通市場，トレーディング・マーケット

weak [soft] market 軟弱市況，軟調市況

withdraw from the Japanese market 日本市場から撤退する

market-based 形 市場に基づく，市場原理に基づく（＝market-driven）

market-based currency system [regime] 市場原理に基づく通貨制度

market-based economies 市場経済

market capitalization 株式の時価総額（＝market capitalization value, market valuation：株式の外部発行済み株式総数に株式の時価を掛けた額）⇒market valuation）

market economy 市場経済，市場型経済

market economy model 市場経済モデル

move to a market economy 市場経済への移行

open market economies 自由市場経済，市場経済

market forces 市場の力，市場諸力，市場要因，市場原理，需給関係

respond to market forces 市場の力に任せる，市場原理に反応する

market-oriented 形 市場原理に基づく，市場重視型，市場志向型の，市場型の，市場中心の，市場に重点を置く

market-oriented economy 市場型経済，市場経済

market-oriented sector selective 市場重視型個別協議

market price 市場価格，市価，時価，売価，相場，実勢価格

market price basis 時価主義（＝market principle）

market price convertible system 時価転換方式

market price method 時価主義，時価方式，時価法

the latest market price 最新の実勢価格

market share 市場占拠率，市場占有率，市場シェア，マーケット・シェア，シェア（＝share）

market valuation 時価総額（＝aggregate market value, market capitalization, total market value; ⇒market capitalization）

> 時価総額 ⊃ 株価による企業の価値を示す「時価総額」は，株価に発行済み株式数を掛けて算出する。時価総額が大きいほど，企業の信用度が高く，資金を証券市場から集めやすい。また，時価総額が小さいと，買収の対象になりやすい。

market value 市場価値，市場価格，市価，時価，時価評価額（＝market price）

aggregate market value 時価総額（＝market valuation, total market value）

current [present] market value 市場の実勢価格，現在の市場価格，現在の市場価値，現行の市場価格，時価（＝current market price）

fair market value 公正市場価格［価額］，公正市価，時価

implied market value 売却可能価格

market value accounting system 時価会計制度，時価主義会計制度

market value depreciation 市場価格の低下

market value of assets 資産の市場価値，資産の時価

mid-market value 中値

open market value 公開市場価値

then-market value その時点の市場価格

marketing 名 市場取引，市販，販売，売買，流

通, 配給, 分配, 公開, マーケティング(「マーケティング」は, 優れた製品を適正な価格で, 最適な販売チャネルを通じて消費者に提供するための活動のこと)
  marketing channel 販売チャネル, 販売経路, 流通チャネル, マーケティング・チャネル(ある商品・サービスがメーカーから最終消費者に渡るまでの取引の流れの経路。主に, メーカーの営業所, 卸売り業者, 小売業者, 配送業者などによって構成される)
  marketing strategy マーケティング戦略(マーケティング目標を達成するための活動で, 具体的にはターゲットを設定し, それに向けて最も効果的なマーケティング・ミックス(商品, 価格, プロモーション・チャネルなど)を構築すること)
markoff 名 値下げ
markon [mark-on] 名 値入れ, 値入れ額, 値入れ率 (=markup)
markup 名 値上げ, 値入れ, 値入れ額, 値入れ率 (商品の原価と売価の差), マークアップ
  markup cancellation 値上げ取消し, 値入れ取消し, 値入れ訂正, 値入れ戻し
  markup percentage 値入れ率
  markup pricing 値入れ法, マークアップによる価格設定(コストに一定の金額を加えて販売価格を設定する方法)
  markup reduction planning 値下げ計画
marriage 名 結婚, 婚姻, 結婚生活, 結合, 融合, 合体, 調和, 一致
  civil marriage 届出結婚
  common-law marriage 事実婚, 同棲
  marriage license [licence] 結婚許可書 (=marriage lines)
  marriage of theory and practice 理論と実践の合致[一致]
  marriage settlement 夫婦財産契約, 夫婦間の財産獲得の取決め
marshal 動 整理する, 整頓する, 〈戦力を〉整える, まとめる, 配置する, 〈人や物を〉集める, 導く, 育成する, 先導する, 案内する
mart 名 市場 (=market, marketplace)
martial law 戒厳令, 軍政の法
martyrdom 名 殉教, 殉死, 殉難, 苦難, 受難, 苦悩
mass 形 大量の, 多量の, 大衆の, 集団の, 多数の, マス
  mass consumption 大量消費
  mass market outlet 量販用販路
  mass marketer 量販市場を志向する会社[メーカー]
  mass transit 大量輸送, 大量輸送交通機関, 都市交通網, マス・トランジット
  mass treatment 一括処理
mass-produce 動 量産する, 大量生産する
  mass-produced electric vehicles 量産型電気自動車
  mass-produced goods 大量生産品, 量産品
massive 形 巨額の, 多額の, 巨大な, 大量の, 多量の, 多大の, 大規模な, 大々的な, 大がかりな, 大幅な, スケールの大きい, 大きい, 大型の, 極端な, 旺盛な, 活発な, 強力な, 充実した, 有名な
  massive intervention 巨額の介入, 大型介入
  massive investment 大規模投資, 大がかりな投資, 巨額の投資
mastermind 動 陰で指揮する, 首謀者として指揮する, 背後で操る, 主導する
mastermind 名 首謀者, 黒幕, 指導者, 主導者, 〈計画の〉立案者, 傑出した知性[知能], 優れた知性[知能]の持ち主
match-fixing scandal 八百長疑惑
matching system マッチング方式(研修医の研修先の決定方法)
matchmaking 名 結婚仲介
matchup 名 組み合わせ, 対決, 比較
material 名 材料, 原材料, 材質, 原料, 資材, 素材, 物質, 構成物質, 服地
  advanced materials 新素材
  hazardous materials 有害物質
  intermediate materials 中間財
  material [materials] control 材料管理
  material costing 材料費計算
  material evidence 物証, 物的証拠
  material instrument 有形資産
  material price variance 材料価格差異
  material storage cost 材料保管費
  materials handling 資材運搬, 運搬管理, マテハン
  materials industry 素材産業
  raw materials 原材料, 原料, 素材, 資材, 天然資源
  related materials 関連資料
maternal 形 母の, 母体の, 母胎の
  maternal fetal intensive care units 母体・胎児集中治療管理室《略 MFICU》
matter 名 問題, 主題, 対象, 内容, 事項, 議題, 事情, 事態, 情況, 事柄, 主要事実, 重要, 重大さ, 厄介なこと, 難儀, 故障, 物質, 物体

a matter of …の問題, およそ[約]…, 数…(a few), わずか
a matter of life and [or] death 死活問題, 重大事
a matter of opinion 意見の相違
a matter of record 〈法廷での〉記録事項
a matter of time 時間の問題
all matters relating hereto 本契約に関連する一切の事項
as a matter of course [routine] もちろん, 当然, 当然のことながら, 当然のこととして
as a matter of fact 実は, 実際のところは, 実を言うと, 実際
as a matter of policy 主義として
as (the) matter stands 現状では
organic matter 有機物
go straight to the heart [crux] of the matter 問題の核心にずばり迫る
improve matters 事態を改善する
in a matter of hours 数時間で, 数時間くらい[程度]で
key corporate matters 重要な経営事項
let the matter drop [rest] それ以上事態[事]を荒立てないことにする, 心配するのを止める
postal matter 郵便物
printed matter 印刷物
reading matter 読み物
solid matter 固体
subject matter of insurance 保険の目的
take matters into one's own hands 自ら行動を起こす
the matter in hand 当面の問題
within a matter of seconds あっという間に

mausoleum 名 壮大な墓, 霊廟, 陵

maximization 名 最大化, 極大化
expected utility maximization 期待効用極大化
output maximization 産出量の最大化, 産出量極大化
wealth maximization 富の極大化

maximize 動 〈…を〉最大にする, 最大限にする, 最大限に増やす, 極限まで拡大[強化]する, 最大化する, 極大化する
maximize access to market capital 市場から資金を最大限に調達する
maximize profits 利益を最大にする, 利益を最大限に伸ばす, 利益を追求する
maximize shareholders' value 株主の価値の最大化を図る, 株主の資産価値を極大化する
maximize yields 利回りの最大化を図る, 利回りを最大限に高める

MBA 経営管理学修士, 経営学修士号 (Master of Business Administrationの略。ビジネス・スクール(経営学大学院)の修士課程修了者に与えられる学位。実務家養成のため, 会計・法務などのカリキュラムを実践的に学ぶのが特徴)

MBM 肉骨粉 (meat-and-bone mealの略)

MBS 住宅ローン担保証券, 住宅ローン証券 (mortgage-backed securitiesの略)

me-too product 類似製品

meager 形 不十分な, 貧弱な, 粗末な, 乏しい, やせた, やせ細った, 無味乾燥な, 精彩のない
a meager salary 安月給
meager price increases 物価上昇率の鈍化

meal kits キット食品

mean 動 意味する, 表す, 意図する, …するつもりである, …しようと思う, 〈ある目的に〉予定する, 計画する, 当てる, …の重要性[意味]を持つ, …を本気で言う, …する結果になる, …の前兆である
be meant to …しなければならない, …することになっている, 〈…の〉狙いは…にある
mean business 真剣である, 冗談ではない
mean nothing to …に理解できない, …に馴染みがない
mean something [anything] to …に馴染みがある, …がよく知っている
mean well 悪意はない, 良かれと思って行動する

measure 動 測定する, 計る, 寸法をとる, 評価する, 見積もる, 十分考慮する, 慎重に選ぶ

measure [measures] 名 対策, 措置, 対応, 政策, 施策, 方策, 策, 手段, 比率, 指標, 尺度, 基準測定値, 測度
administrative measures 行政措置
antideflationary measures デフレ対策, デフレからの脱却策
counter measures 対抗措置, 対抗手段, 対策
debt measures 債務比率
fiscal measures 財政政策, 財政措置
inflation measures インフレ指標
liberalization measures 自由化措置, 規制緩和措置
measure of risk aversion リスク回避度
punitive measures 制裁措置, 報復措置
reflationary measures 通貨調節策, リフレ対策
temporary measure 時限措置
workable measures 実行可能な施策

measured 形 測った，測定[計測，実測]された，算定された，調整された，従量制の，慎重な，慎重で注意深い，動きが規則的な，安定的な，一様な (uniform)，リズミカルな
  measured concrete steps 慎重な具体策，安定的な具体策，それに応じた具体的な措置
  measured equity levels 融資比率
  measured magnitude 測定量，計測量
  measured service 従量制サービス
  measured variable 実測された変数
meat processor 食肉加工業者，食肉加工会社
meatpacking plant 食肉加工工場
MEBO 経営陣と従業員による企業買収（management employee buyoutの略。買収対象会社の経営陣と従業員が，金融投資家と共同で買収対象会社の株式を買収する取引を，マネジメント・エンプロイー・バイアウト（MEBO）という）
mecenat 名 文化活動への貢献[寄与]，芸術・科学支援活動，文化支援，文化支援事業，メセナ
mechanism 名 機構，構造，仕組み，制度，方式，方法，機械装置，メカニズム
  adjustment mechanism 調整機構
  control mechanism 制御機構，制御メカニズム，統制機構
  cost pass-through mechanism 価格転嫁メカニズム
  decision-making mechanism 意思決定機構，政策決定機構
  financial mechanism 金融メカニズム
  financial support mechanisms 金融支援の仕組み
  inducement mechanism 誘発機構
  market [market-based] mechanisms 市場原理，市場機構，市場のメカニズム
  price mechanism 価格機構，価格メカニズム
  self-regulating mechanism 自己調整機構
meddling 名 干渉，お節介
media 名 媒体，商品，マスコミ，報道機関，メディア
  advertising media 広告媒体，広告メディア
  communication media コミュニケーション媒体
  grab the media spotlight マスコミの脚光を浴びる
  interactive media 対話型メディア
  mass media マス・メディア，マスコミ
  media allocation 媒体配分
  media blitz 大規模なテレビ宣伝
  media board 電子黒板
  media coverage マスコミに取り上げられた時間[紙面]の量
  media event マスコミ操作による事件，マスコミが作り上げた事件，マスコミ界の大事件，マスコミに誇大宣伝された事件，マスコミが注目している出来事[催し]，マスコミの取材を狙って催す行事，〈テレビの〉特別番組
  media hype マスコミ宣伝
  media kit メディア・キット（＝press kit：マスコミ向けの会社の宣伝資料）
  Media Laboratory メディア・ラボ（米マサチューセッツ工科大学（MIT）の研究機関）
  media literacy メディア・リテラシー（コンピュータ・ネットワークを使いこなす能力）
  media mix 媒体ミックス，広告媒体の組合せ，メディア・ミックス
  media packet ニュース媒体向けPR資料
  media planning 媒体計画
  media-shy マスコミ恐怖症の，マスコミ嫌いの
  mediaspeak マスコミ語，メディア語
  mixed media 混合媒体，複合素材芸術
  news media ニュース報道，報道機関，マスコミ
  physical media 物理的媒体
  print media 印刷媒体
  savings media 貯蓄商品
mediacracy 名 メディアクラシー（情報社会を背景にマスコミが絶大な力をもつようになった傾向）
mediagenic 形 マスコミ向きの，マスコミ受けのする
medialand 名 マスコミの世界
mediaman [mediaperson] 名 通信員，マスコミの記者，報道関係者
mediamorphosis 名 マスコミによる事実の曲解，曲解報道，歪曲報道（＝media metamorphosis）
median 形 中央の，中間の，中位の，中心の，名 中央値，中位数，中線，メディアン[メジアン]
  median chart 管理図
  median duration of unemployment 失業期間の中位数
  median estimate 予測の中央値
  median family 中位の家族，メディアン世帯
  median household メディアン世帯，メディアン家計
  median point 中点，重心
  median price 中心価格，価格の中央値
  median rate 中心相場（medial rate），仲値（売

り相場と買い相場の平均値）
median value 価格の中央値
national median 全国中央値
peer group median 同業他社の中央値
population median 母中央値
sample median 標本中央値

mediate 動 調停する, 仲裁する, 和解させる, 取り次ぐ

mediation 名 〈紛争の〉調停, 仲裁, 調整, 事態収拾, 解決, 口利き
mediation plan 調停案
mediation practices 口利きの慣行, 口利きの行為
voluntary mediation 任意調停

medical 形 医療の, 医用の, 医学の, 内科の, メディカル
medical adviser 医者
medical and health insurance 医療健康保険
medical assistance 医療支援
medical benefit 医療給付
medical bulletin 病状発表
medical certificate 診断書
medical checkup [examination] 健康診断, 人間ドック
medical costs [fees] 医療費
medical engineering 医用工学, メディカル・エンジニアリング
medical equipment 医療機器
medical examination 健康診断, 診査
medical examiner 会社の診察医, 検死官
medical expenses 医療費
medical history 既往症, 病歴
medical institution 医療機関, 医療施設
medical jurisprudence 法医学
medical malpractice 医療過誤
medical officer 診療所医, 診療所員, 保健所員, 保健所長
medical practitioner 開業医
Medical Practitioners Law 医師法
medical profession 医療専門家, 医療従事者
medical reformatory 医療少年院
medical representative 医薬情報担当者
medical supplies 救急医薬品
national medical expenditure 国民医療費

medical care 医療, 保健医療, メディカル・ケア
medical care provider 医療従事者
medical care system for the elderly 高齢者医療制度

perinatal medical care 周産期医療（出産前後の期間の医療）

medical insurance 医療保険
medical insurance premium 医療保険費
medical insurance system [plan, program, scheme] 医療保険制度
medical insurance system [plan] for the elderly 高齢者医療保険制度

Medicaid 名 国民医療扶助, 低所得者・身体障害者医療費補助制度, メディケイド（65歳未満の低所得者, 身体障害者が対象）

Medicare 名 高齢者医療保障制度, 高齢者医療保険, メディケア

meet 動 〈要求や基準などを〉満たす, 〈要望や期待に〉応える, 応じる, 対応する, 〈費用などを〉支払う, 返済する, 賄う
meet customer needs 顧客のニーズに応える[対応する], 顧客のニーズにマッチする, 顧客のニーズを満たす
meet demand 需要を賄う, 需要に応える, 需要増に追いつく
meet the obligations 債務を返済する, 債務を履行する（＝meet debt commitments）
meet the requirements 要件［必要条件, 条件］を満たす, 条件に合致する, 基準に適合する, 基準を満たす, 要求に応じる
meet the target range 目標を達成する

meeting 名 会議, 会, 総会, 大会, 理事会, 場, ミーティング
annual general meeting 年次総会, 年次株主総会
board meeting 取締役会会議, 取締役会
creditor's meeting 債権者会議
IR meeting 投資家説明会, IRミーティング
one-on-one meeting 投資家との個別ミーティング（＝one-to-one meeting）
ordinary council meeting 定例理事会（＝regular council meeting）
regular general meeting 定例総会, 定例株主総会（＝ordinary general meeting）
stockholders [shareholders] meeting 株主総会（＝shareholders' meeting, stockholders' meeting）
trilateral meeting 3者会議, 3か国会議

MEF 〈エネルギーと気候に関する〉主要経済国フォーラム（**Major Economies Forum**の略）

megabank 名 巨大銀行, 超巨大銀行, 巨大銀行グループ, メガバンク

megamerger 名 超大型合併, 超巨大合併
- **megamerger campaign** 大合併運動, 超大型合併運動

megastore 名 超大型チェーン店, 超大型小売店, メガストア

megatechnics 名 大規模機械化

mega-trendy 形 最新流行の, 最先端を行く

me-ism 名 自分主義, 自己中心的な考え方, ミーイズム

melon 名 利益, 所得, 余剰利益, 特別配当, 多額の利益配当
- **cut [carve, split] a melon** 特別配当をする, 利益を分ける, もうけを山分けする
- **cutting a melon** 特別配当
- **nice melon** 多額の利益配当

meltdown 名 〈株価の〉暴落, 急落, 下落, 経営破綻, 崩壊, 炉心溶解, 原子炉溶解, メルトダウン
- **housing mortgage meltdown** 住宅ローン市場の崩壊
- **market meltdown** 市場崩壊

melting 形 心を和ませる, ほろりとさせる, 同情をさそう
- **be in the [a] melting pot** 再考中である, 思案中 [討論] 中である
- **go into the melting pot** 大変革される, 改革される, 〈感情などが〉和らぐ
- **in the melting pot** 流動的な, 流動的で
- **melting point** 融点, 融解店
- **melting pot** るつぼ, 人種のるつぼ (melting pot of races), 人種・文化の交じり合った国 [地域], アメリカの別称
- **put [cast, throw] A into the melting pot** Aを根本的に改める

member 名 会員, 構成員, 社員, 部員, 加盟国, 参加国, メンバー
- **board member** 役員, 取締役
- **corporation member** 法人会員
- **full member** 正会員 (=regular member)
- **grass-roots members of the Labour Party** 英労働党の一般党員
- **member firm** 会員企業, 会員会社, 加盟企業
- **Member of Congress** 米下院議員
- **Member of Parliament** 英下院議員

membership 名 会員の資格, 会員の身分 [地位], 会員, 構成員, 会員数, 会員権, 全会員
- **associated membership** 準会員
- **membership card** 会員証
- **membership dues** 会費, 会員負担金

memorandum of understanding 基本合意書, 予備的合意書, 意思表明状, 了解覚書

mental 形 精神の, 心の, 知的な, 知力の
- **have a mental block about** …を生理的に受け付けない
- **make [take] a mental note of** …を覚えておく
- **mental ability** 知能
- **mental arithmetic** 暗算
- **mental association** 連想
- **mental breakdown** 精神衰弱
- **mental competency test** 精神鑑定
- **mental depression** うつ病
- **mental development** 知能の発達
- **mental disorder [ailment, disease, illness]** 精神疾患, 精神錯乱, 精神異常, 精神病, 精神障害
- **mental disturbance** 精神的動揺
- **mental illness** 心の病気, 心の病, 精神障害, 精神病
- **mental image** 心象
- **mental reservation** 心中留保

mentee 名 メンターの支援の受け手, メンティー (⇒mentor)

mentor 名 良き指導者 [助言者], メンター (後輩の相談相手になる直属の上司以外の先輩社員が「メンター」で, 仕事の進め方や今後のキャリア形成などについて助言する。メンターの支援の受け手を「メンティー」という。⇒mentee)

mentoring 名 メンターによる支援, メンター制度 (メンター制度は, 新入社員の離職を防ぎ, 人材育成にもつながる制度として導入する企業が増えている)

mercantile 形 商業の, 商人の, 商売の, 貿易の, 重商主義の, 報酬目当ての, 欲得ずくの
- **mercantile (credit) agency** 商業興信所, 興信所, 信用調査機関 (=commercial agency, commercial enquiry office, credit bureau)
- **mercantile bill** 商業手形
- **mercantile bookkeeping** 商業簿記
- **mercantile burglary insurance** 商品盗難保険
- **mercantile capital** 商業資本
- **mercantile credit** 商業信用, 企業間信用, 商業信用貸し
- **mercantile emporium** 商業の中心地, 貿易の中心地
- **mercantile law** 商事法, 商法 (=commercial law, law merchant)
- **mercantile marine** 商船, 商船隊, 海運力

mercantile open stock burglary policy　商業財盗難保険
mercantile paper　商業証券, 商業手形, 売買手形, 為替手形, 約束手形
mercantile partnership　商事組合, 商会
mercantile report　商業興信報告
mercantile risk　商業危険, 商品危険, 商品リスク
mercantile school　重商主義派
mercantile society　商業主義的［商業主義的, 営利主義的］社会
Mercantile Stores　マーカンタイル・ストアーズ（米国の百貨店チェーン）
mercantile system　重商主義, 商業体系（= mercantilism）
mercantile trade [trading, transaction]　商取引
mercantile exchange　商業取引所, マーカンタイル取引所, 商品取引
　Chicago Mercantile Exchange　シカゴ・マーカンタイル取引所《略 CME》
　New York Mercantile Exchange　ニューヨーク商業取引所《略 NYMEX [Nymex]》
mercantilism 名　重商主義, 商業主義, 営利主義, 商業本位, 商人気質（commercialism）, 商人根性
merchandise 名　商品, 物品, 品物, 製品, モノ
merchandise trade　モノの貿易, モノの取引, 商品貿易, 財の輸出入, 貿易取引
　merchandise trade gap　モノの貿易赤字, 財の貿易赤字, 貿易収支の赤字額, 商品貿易の赤字, 貿易赤字（= merchandise trade deficit）
　merchandise trade surplus　モノの貿易黒字, 財の貿易黒字, 貿易収支の黒字額, 商品貿易の黒字, 貿易黒字
merchant 名　小売商, 小売商人, 商人, 商業者, 業者, 貿易商, 加盟店, 取引先, 顧客, マーチャント
　call sales merchant　訪問販売業者
　futures commission merchant　先物取引業者, 先物ブローカー
　merchants' risk　荷主危険負担, 荷主危険持ち
　merchants' rule　商人計算法
　wholesale merchant　卸商, 卸売商, 問屋
merchant 形　外販の, 商人の, 商売の, 貿易の, マーチャント
　go merchant　外販を始める
　merchant adventurer　貿易商
　merchant agent　販売代理人
　merchant association　商業組合

merchant bank　投資銀行, 商業銀行, マーチャント・バンク（証券引受業務のほか, 企業の合併・買収の斡旋, 貿易手形の引受け, 保険業務や金の取引など多種多様な業務を展開している）
merchant banking　マーチャント・バンキング業務, マーチャント・バンキング
merchant banking firm　企業金融会社
merchant bill　商業為替手形
merchant carrier　商人船主（船舶を保有して運送人のほかに貿易取引を行う商人）
merchant category code　加盟店業種コード
merchant control　加盟店管理
merchant fee　加盟店手数料
merchant law　商事法
merchant manufacturer　商人企業家
merchant marine　商船隊, 全商船, 商船
Merchant Marine Act　海運法
merchant middleman　中間商人, 中間業者, 中間商業者, 差益商人
merchant qualification standard　加盟店資格基準
merchant rate　対顧客相場
merchant service　海上貿易
merchant ship　商船（= merchant vessel, trading ship）
merchant trade　仲介貿易（= merchanting trade）
merchant trader　商品取引業者, 仲介貿易業者
merchant system　マーチャント・システム（インターネットで大規模な買い物のサービスを提供するシステム）
merchant wholesaler　卸売業者, 所有権卸売業者, 危険負担卸売業者
merchantability 名　商品性, 市販可能性, 市販性, 市場性（= merchantable quality）
mercy killing　安楽死（= euthanasia）
merge 動　合併する, 吸収合併する, 経営統合する
　merge operations　経営統合する（= integrate operations）
merger 名　合併, 経営統合, 事業統合, 統合, 吸収合併, 併合
　conglomerate merger　複合的合併, 複合企業型合併, コングロマリット合併
　debt-financed merger　借入れによる合併
　defensive merger　防衛的合併
　downstream merger　逆吸収合併（子会社による親会社の吸収のこと）
　horizontal merger　水平的合併, 同業他社との

合併

merger agreement [deal] 経営統合の合意書，経営統合の契約[契約書]，合併協議書

merger negotiations [talks] 合併交渉，経営統合交渉

merger on an equal basis 対等合併

multi-merger 多角的合併

outright merger 友好的合併

stock-for-stock merger 株式交換による合併

vertical merger 垂直的合併

merger and acquisition
企業の吸収合併，合併・買収，企業取得と合併《略 M&A》（＝mergers and acquisitions）

merger and acquisition activities 合併・買収（M&A）業務

M&A関連用語

black knight	暗黒の騎士，敵対的買収者，企業乗っ取り屋，ブラック・ナイト
corporate raider	企業買収の仕掛け人，乗っ取り屋，買占め屋
defensive merger	防衛的合併
golden parachute	黄金の落下傘，ゴールデン・パラシュート
greenmail	法外な価格での株の買戻し，グリーンメール
greenmailer	グリーンメールで金儲けをする人，グリーンメーラー
junk bond	ジャンク債，くず債券，投資不適格の信用度の低い債券
leveraged buyout	借入金による企業買収，レバレッジド・バイアウト《略 LBO》
Pac-Man defense	パックマン防衛，逆転攻撃，パックマン・ディフェンス
poison pill defense	ポイズン・ピル防衛，毒薬条項防衛，毒入り避妊薬
scorched-earth tactic	焦土作戦（敵対的買収に備えて，会社の最優良資産などを売却して会社の価値を減少させること）
shark repellent	サメ駆除剤（敵対的買収に備えて，定款を改正したり転換優先株などを発行して買収コストを高めたりすること）
shark watcher	サメ監視人（企業買収の動きを専門に監視する会社）
white knight	白馬の騎士，友好的買収者，ホワイト・ナイト
white squire	純白の従者，ホワイト・スクワイア

mergers and acquisitions
企業の合併・買収《略 M&A》（＝merger and acquisition）

merit 名
長所，美点，とりえ，手柄，功績，功労，勲功，価値，値打ち，賞罰，功罪，真価，理非，是非，〈訴訟の〉本案

a man of merit 立派な人

a matter of merit 手柄とすべきこと

according to one's merits …の功ľ労に応じて

artistic merit 芸術的価値

decide a case on its merits 事件を理非によって判決する

make a merit of …を手柄にする，…を自慢する

merit-based pay plan 業績連動報酬制度，業績連動型の報酬制度，成果主義型の報酬制度，成果主義型賃金制度（＝merit-based pay system：「成果主義」は，本人の能力や業績に対する貢献度などを基準にして待遇を決める人事制度）

merit goods メリット財

merit rating 成績評価，人事考課

merit system 能力給制度，実力本位制度，実力登用制度，能力主義任用制度，メリット・システム

Merit Systems Protection Board 米メリット・システム保護委員会

merit wants 価値欲求，メリット・ウォンツ

on one's merit …の功績[真価]によって

the Order of Merit 〈英国の〉功労勲章(位)《略 O.M.》

meritocracy 名
能力主義，能力主義社会，実力主義，実力[能力]社会，実力主義制度，成績重視主義，知的エリート階級，エリート支配

meritocrat 名
実力者，知的エリート，英才，秀才

mess 名
混乱，混乱状態，散乱，散乱状態，乱雑，紛糾事態，困った事態[立場]，苦境，窮境，窮地，困難，問題，へま，失敗，取り散らかしたもの，汚いもの，ごみの山，会食仲間，会食室，食堂

a mess of 多くの…（＝a lot of）

a mess of pottage 目先の小利，犠牲の大きすぎる小利，高い犠牲を払って得た物質的快楽

be at mess 会食中である

get into a mess 困ったことになる，窮地に陥る

make a mess of …を台なしにする，…をめちゃめちゃにする，…をぶち壊す

make a mess of it へまをする

mess hall 〈軍隊の〉食堂

mess kit 食器セット

sell one's birthright for a mess of pottage 目先の小利にこだわって大利を失う

message 名
通信文，伝言，言付け，文面，〈電子メールでの〉通信情報[伝達事項]，通達，声明書，〈大統領の〉教書，〈商業放送の〉コマーシャル，伝

えようとする一番重要なこと, 狙い, 要旨, 意図, 教訓, 使い, 使命, 買い物, メッセージ
Budget Message 〈米大統領の〉予算教書
commercial message コマーシャル, 広告文, 宣伝文句《略 CM》
email message 電子メール
get the message 真意が分かる, 真意を理解する
go on a message 使いに行く
keep to the message 党の狙い［考え］をはっきり打ち出す, 党の考えを強調する
off message 政党の公式見解を述べずに
on message 政党の公式見解を述べて
send a message of congratulations to …に祝電を送る
presidential message 大統領教書（＝President's Message）
Special Message 〈米大統領の〉特別教書
State of the State Message 〈米州知事の〉施政方針演説
State of the Union Message [Address] 〈米大統領の〉一般教書
State of the World Message 〈米大統領の〉外交教書
the President's message to Congress 〈米大統領の〉議会への教書
metabolic syndrome メタボリック症候群, メタボリック・シンドローム（内臓脂肪型肥満（内臓肥満・腹部肥満）に高血糖・高血圧・高脂血症のうち2つ以上を合併した状態をいう）
diagnostic criteria for metabolic syndrome メタボリック症候群の診断基準
metastability 名 準安定性
methane gas メタンガス
methane hydrate メタンハイドレート（天然ガスの主成分のメタンが低温高圧下で水に溶けたもので, 石油や天然ガスに代わる新天然資源として注目されている。その形状から,「燃える氷」ともいわれる）
method 名 方法, 手法, 方式, 手順, 順序, 筋道, 基準, 主義, メソッド
accrued method 発生主義
Delphi method デルファイ法
equity method 持ち分法
fixed rate method 定率法
market price method 時価主義
percentage of completion method 工事進行基準
production sharing method 生産物分与方式, PS方式
production unit method 生産高比例法
Metropolitan Expressway Public Corporation 首都高速道路公団
microanalysis 名 微視的分析, ミクロ分析
microchip 名 マイクロチップ（＝silicon chip（シリコン・チップ）：コンピュータの製造に使われる超小型の半導体片）
microeconomic 形 微視的経済の, ミクロ経済的（⇒macroeconomic）
microeconomic behavior [behaviour] ミクロ経済的行動, ミクロ経済学的行動
microeconomic foundation 微視経済的基礎, ミクロ経済学的基礎
microeconomic policy 微視的経済政策, ミクロ経済政策
microeconomics 名 微視的経済学, ミクロ経済学
microorganism 名 微生物
microprocessor 名 マイクロプロセッサー（マイクロコンピュータの中央演算処理装置の部分）
mid–career [midcareer] 形 中途の, 昇進停滞の, ミッドキャリアの
midcareer employment 中途採用
midcareer personnel 中途社員, 中堅社員
mid–career plateau 昇進停滞点, 昇進停滞段階
mid–career recruiting 中途採用
middle–aged and elderly workers 中高年労働者
Middle Class Bill of Rights 中間層の権利章典, 中間層の権利宣言
Middle East crisis 中東危機
Middle East peace process 中東和平プロセス
middle manager 中間管理職, 中堅管理職, 中堅幹部
middleman 名 仲買人, 仲卸業者, 仲介者
midsize 名 形 中規模の
midsize companies 中小企業
midsize general contractor 中堅ゼネコン, 準大手ゼネコン
midterm 名 中間, 中期（＝medium term）
midterm business plan 中期経営計画, 中期事業計画, 中期経営構想, 中期経営プラン
midterm earnings report 中間決算, 中間決算報告（＝interim earnings report, midterm financial report）
midterm goal 中期目標

midterm report 中間決算, 中間決算報告, 半期報告, 中間報告 (=interim report, midterm business report, midterm earnings report)
midterm results 中間決算, 半期の業績
midterm settlement of accounts 中間決算 (=interim settlement of accounts)
midterm [interim, off-year] election 米中間選挙(4年ごとの大統領選挙の中間年の11月に行われる。米上院議員の3分の1と下院議員の全員(435人)の選挙のほか, 州知事, 州議会その他の地方選挙と住民投票などが実施される)
migraine 名 偏頭痛
migrant worker 移民労働者
migration worker 出稼ぎ労働者, 移動労働者, 季節労働者
mileage [milage] 名 総マイル数, 総走行[飛行]マイル数, 走行距離, 〈旅費の〉マイル計算, マイル計算運賃, 〈1ガロン[リッター]当たりの〉燃費, 利益, 有用性, 恩恵
　food mileage フード・マイレージ(輸入食料の重さに輸送距離をかけた数値で, トン・キロメートルの単位で表す。食卓から近い所でとれた食材のほう[輸入品より国産品を買うほう]が, 環境に優しいという考え方)
　mileage allowance マイル当たりの旅費(社用に車を使って1マイル当たりに支給される旅費)
　mileage point マイレージ・ポイント
　mileage service マイレージ・サービス(搭乗距離に応じて無料航空券などの特典がつく航空会社のサービス)
　mileage sign 道路標識
　mileage ticket 〈一定マイル数乗車できる〉マイル数切符
milestone 名 里程標, マイル標石, 一里塚, 重要な段階, 画期的な事件[出来事, 段階, 局面, 時期], 節目, 大目標, マイルストーン
militant 名 戦士, 兵士, 闘士, ゲリラ(の一員), 交戦者, 形 戦闘中の, 交戦中の, 闘争的な, 戦闘的な, 攻撃的な, 好戦的な, けんか好きの
　Islamic militants イスラム武装勢力, イスラム過激派
　militant group 武装グループ, 過激派グループ, 戦闘的な集団
　militant militia 好戦的な武装組織
　militant mullahs イスラム教徒の法学者
　militant network 軍事網
　militants 武装勢力, 過激派
　Taliban militants タリバン兵士

military 名 軍, 軍人, 軍隊, 軍部, 将校
　arrogance of the military 軍部の横暴
　serve in the military 軍隊に入っている
military 形 軍の, 軍隊の, 軍式の, 軍人の, 軍事の, 軍事上の, 軍事面での, 陸軍の
Military Academy 〈米〉陸軍士官学校《略 MA》
military action 軍事行動
military administration 軍事行政, 軍政 (=military government)
military age 徴兵年齢
military appropriation 軍事支出金, 軍事費
military authorities 軍当局, 軍部
military base 軍事基地
military borderline 軍事境界線
military campaign 軍事作戦, 軍事行動
military capability 軍事力, 武力, 兵力 (=military force)
military civilian 軍属
military coup 軍事クーデター
military deterrent 軍事的抑止力
military discipline 軍紀, 軍律
military establishment 軍事体制, 軍事常備兵力, 軍部, 軍用[軍事]基地
military exercise 軍事演習
military fatigues 軍隊の作業服
military government 軍事政権, 軍政, 軍政府
military honors 軍葬の礼
military hygiene 軍隊衛生
military industrial 軍事産業労働者
military-industrial complex 軍産複合体, 産軍複合体《略 MIC》
military intelligence 軍事情報, 軍事機密, 軍事諜報, 軍事諜報局《略 MI》
military jurisdiction 軍事裁判権
military law 軍法
military operations 軍事作戦, 軍事行動
military personnel 軍人
military police 憲兵隊《略 MP》
military postures 軍事態勢, 軍事政策
military strike 軍事攻撃
military supplies [stores] 軍用品, 軍需品
military trial 軍事裁判
military tribunal 軍事法廷, 軍事裁判所
military force [might] 軍事力, 武力, 兵力
　deployment of military forces abroad 海外派兵
　multilateral military force 多国籍軍
　projection of military forces 軍事力の行使

unilateral projection [deployment] of military force overseas　海外への単独派兵
unilateral use of military force　単独での海外派兵
militia　名　民兵, 州兵, ミリシア（白人優越主義などを主張する米国の民間武装組織）
militia group　民兵組織
mill　名　〈紡績, 製紙, 製鋼などの〉工場, 製作所, 製鉄所, 製造所, 工作機械, 粉砕器, 装置類, 機械類, ミル(grinder)
go [put] through the mill　苦労する, つらい目にあう
mill base system　工場基点価格制
mill ends　工場残品
mill hand [millhand]　職工, 紡績工, 製粉工
mill net price　工場正味価格, 工場手取り価格
mill-run order　ミル・ラン（特別操業に十分な数量の）注文
run of the mill [run-of-the-mill]　ありふれた, 並の
–minded　形　…志向の, …に熱心な, …好きの, …に強い関心がある, …重視の, …優先の（＝-oriented, single-minded）
education-minded　教育に熱心な
independence-minded　独立志向の
like-minded　考え方を共有する, 似た考え方の, 気質が同じな, 同意見の
money-minded　金に執着する, 金儲けへの執着心が強い
performance-minded　実績重視の
mindset [mind-set]　名　考え方, 物の見方, 発想, 思考, 思考様式, 心的態度, 姿勢
mine-clearing work　地雷撤去作業
mini [mini-]　形　小型の, 軽微の, ミニ…
mini communication　ミニコミ
mini-cycle in growth　景気のミニサイクル
mini-max [minimax] bond　ミニマックス債（＝minimax）
mini-max principle　ミニマックス原理［原則］（＝minimax：予想される最悪の結果のうち, 最小の損失をもたらす行動を選択すべきである, とする戦略理論）
upleg of the mini-cycle　ミニサイクルの上昇局面
miniaturization　名　小型化（＝downsizing, scaledown）
minibudget　名　小型補正予算
minimization　名　最小化, 極小化, 軽減

cost minimization　費用［コスト］極小化（＝minimization of cost）
income tax minimization　所得税の軽減
risk minimization　リスク極小化
minimize　動　最小限に抑える［とどめる］, 最小限にする, 最小限に減らす, 最小限に評価する, 軽く見る, 軽視する, 見くびる, 〈画面などを〉小さくする
minimize adverse effects on the stock market　株式市場への悪影響を最小限に抑える
minimize capital investment [outlay]　設備投資を最小限に抑える
minimize noise　騒音を最小限に抑える
minimize the risk of　…の危険性［リスク］を最小限にする, …のリスクを最小限に抑える
minimum　名　最低, 最小, 最小限, 最小値, ミニマム, 形　最小の, 最小限の
minimum access　最低輸入量, 最低輸入義務, 最低輸入枠, ミニマム・アクセス
minimum capital　最低資本金, 最低自己資本
minimum capital requirements　最低必要資本金額, 会社設立時に必要な最低資本金
minimum wage　最低賃金
mining　名　採掘, 採鉱, 鉱山業, 鉱業, 資源開発, 地雷敷設, 機雷敷設
coal mining　採炭, 石炭採掘, 炭鉱業
index of mining and manufacturing production　鉱工業生産指数
mining damage　鉱害
mining industry　鉱業
mining lease　採鉱権
mining right　採掘権, 鉱業権
mining tax　鉱業税
minister　名　大臣, 閣僚, 公使, 牧師
administrative vice-minister　事務次官
Council of Ministers　閣僚理事会
minister of state　〈大臣を補佐する英国の〉次官
minister plenipotentiary　全権使節
Minister without Portfolio　無任所大臣
Prime Minister　総理, 首相
ministerial　形　大臣の, 内閣の, 閣僚の, 閣僚レベルの, 政府の, 政府側の, 行政上の, 聖職者［牧師］の, 補助の, …の助けとなる, …に役立つ
assume the ministerial post　閣僚ポストにつく
ministerial clearance　政府の許可, 当局の許可
ministerial-level meeting [talks]　閣僚級会議
ministerial meeting　閣僚級会議, 閣僚級の会合, 閣僚会議（＝ministerial conference, ministerial-level talks）

ministerial position 閣僚ポスト
talks at (the) ministerial meeting level 閣僚級会議, 閣僚級[大臣級]の会談（＝ministerial-level talks）
ministry 名 〈英国, 日本の〉省, 内閣, 閣僚, 大臣の職務[任期]
ministries concerned 関係省庁
the Economy, Trade and Industry Ministry 経済産業省（＝the Ministry of Economy, Trade and Industry）
the Finance Ministry 財務省（＝the Ministry of Finance）
the Foreign Ministry 外務省（＝the Ministry of Foreign Affairs）
the Ministry 内閣
the Ministry of Defence 〈英国の〉国防省
minor 形 さほど大きくない, 小規模な, 比較的重要[重大]でない, 影が薄い, 軽微な, 割と軽い, 二流の, 二流以下の, 未成年の, 年下の, 短音階の, 短調の, マイナー（⇒major）
in a minor key 沈んだ調子で
minor activities 小規模事業
minor (business) cycle 小循環
minor offense 軽犯罪
minor planet 小惑星（＝asteroid）
minor player 二流[二流以下の]選手, 中小企業[組織, 団体]
minor swing 小波動
minor total 小計
suffer minor injuries 軽傷を負う
minority 名 少数, 少数派, 少数集団, 少数民族, 未成年
be in a minority of one 孤立無援である
be in the [a] minority 少数派である
buyout of minorities 少数株主持ち分の買取り（＝minority buyout）
ethnic minority 少数民族
policies in favor of minorities 少数民族の優遇政策
minority 形 少数の, 少数派の, 少数民族の
minority buyout 少数持ち分の買取り
minority committee table 少数党委員会席
minority control 少数支配
minority equity 少数株主持ち分, 少数株主権
minority government 少数党政府
minority group 少数派, 少数集団, 少数民族, 少数グループ
minority leader 〈米上下両院の少数派政党の〉院内総務, 野党院内総務, 少数党指導者
minority ownership 少数者所有
minority report 少数派報告, 少数意見
minority shareholder [stockholder] 少数株主
Minority Whip [minority whip] 少数党院内幹事, 少数党副院内総務
minority interest 少数株主持ち分, 少数株主損益, 少数株主持ち分利益, 少数利益, 過半数以下の出資, 少数株主権（「少数株主持ち分」は, 子会社の資本額のうち親会社の持ち分に属さない部分で, 少数株主に帰属する部分）
minus territory マイナス, マイナス基調（＝negative territory）
▶The government downgraded its forecast for Japan's real gross domestic product in fiscal 2009 to *minus territory*. 政府は, 2009年度の実質国内総生産（GDP）の予想をマイナスに下方修正した。
mirror 動 反映する, 映し出す, 映す, …とよく似ている
▶The firm's growth has *mirrored* its cost-cutting efforts. 同社のこれまでの成長は, 同社のコスト削減努力を反映している。
mirror 名 鏡, 反射鏡, ミラー
mirror neuron 鏡神経細胞, ミラー・ニューロン
mirror swap 反対スワップ
mirror symmetry 鏡面対称, 左右対称
mirror transaction [trade] 反対取引
MIRV 各個誘導多核弾頭（multiple independently targeted reentry vehicleの略）
misappropriation 名 流用, 不正流用, 不正目的使用, 悪用, 着服, 横領, 使い込み
fund misappropriation 資金の流用, 資金の着服
misappropriation of any copyrights, trademarks or trade secrets 著作権, 商標または営業秘密の不正使用
misappropriation of company assets 会社資産の横領, 会社資産の流用
miscarriage of justice 誤審
misconduct 名 不正行為, 違法行為, 職権乱用, ずさんな管理[運営]
misery index 経済不快指数
misgiving 名 不安, 懸念, 心配, 疑念, 疑い, 疑惑, 不信の念
mislabeling 名 不当表示, 不正表示, 偽装表示
mislabeling fraud 偽装工作
misleading 形 紛らわしい, 誤解を招く, 虚偽の

misleading advertisement 紛らわしい広告, 誤解を招きやすい広告, 虚偽の広告
misleading information 虚偽の情報
mismanagement 名 失政, ずさんな管理[経営], 管理の誤り, 経営の失敗, 不始末, やりそこない
mismatch 名 ミスマッチ (＝mismatching)
missing in action 戦闘中の行方不明兵《略 MIA》
missile 名 ミサイル
  cruise missile 巡航ミサイル
  ground-guided missile 地上誘導弾《略 GM》
  ground-launched cruise missile 地上発射巡航ミサイル《略 GLCM》
  interceptor missile 迎撃ミサイル (＝interceptor)
  intercontinental ballistic missile 大陸間弾道弾《略 ICBM》
  intermediate-range ballistic missile 中距離弾道ミサイル
  missile defense ミサイル防衛《略 MD》
  Missile Technology Control Regime ミサイル関連技術輸出規制《略 MTCR》
  Standard Missile-3 スタンダード・ミサイル3《略 SM-3》
  Theater Missile Defense 戦域ミサイル防衛《略 TMD》
mission 名 任務, 任務飛行, 飛行任務,〈特殊〉宇宙飛行, 使命, 活動, 代表団, 派遣団, 使節団, 伝導, 布教, 布教施設, 伝導本部, ミッション
  carry out one's mission 任務を果たす
  economic mission 経済使節団
  error of mission 脱漏の誤謬
  mission accomplished 任務完了
  mission commander 〈宇宙の〉船長
  mission control (center) 地上管制センター, 宇宙管制センター
  mission specialist 搭乗専門[搭乗運用, 宇宙船運用]技術者, 宇宙船科学研究員, スペース・シャトルの乗員, ミッション・スペシャリスト《略 MS》
  mission statement 基本規約, 企業目標の提示, 企業目標
  peacekeeping missions 平和維持活動
  refueling mission in the Indian Ocean インド洋での給油活動
misstatement 名 虚偽表示, 虚偽記載, 不実表示 (＝misrepresentation)
▶ Freddie Mac revealed its *misstatement* of earnings. フレディ・マック(米連邦住宅貸付抵当公社)が, 利益の不実表示をしていたことを明らかにした。
misstep 名 つまずき, 踏み誤り, 踏み外し,〈判断などの〉誤り, 過失, しくじり, 失策
mistake 名 過ち, 間違い, 誤解, 失策, 失敗, 愚行, ミス
  error of mistake in writing 誤記による誤謬
  fatal mistake 致命的なミス
misuse 名 誤用する, 悪用する, 乱用する, 不正流用する
mix 名 構成, 組合せ, 混合, 比率, 内容, 中身, ミックス
  asset mix 資産構成, 資産配分
  business mix 事業構成, 事業内容
  export mix 輸出攻勢
  portfolio mix ポートフォリオの構成, 有価証券の中身, ポートフォリオ・ミックス
  product mix 商品構成, 製品構成, 製品組合せ, プロダクト・ミックス
mixed economy 混合経済
mobile 形 移動式の, 携帯用の
  mobile launch pad 移動式発射台
  Mobile Number Portability (MNP) system 携帯電話の番号持ち運び制度
mobile phone 携帯電話
  mobile phone handset 携帯電話機, 携帯電話端末機
mobility 名 移動, 移動性, 機動性, 機動力, 流動, 流動性, 動き, 動きやすさ, 可動性, 移り気, 気まぐれ, モビリティ
  capital mobility 資本移動, 資本の移動性 (＝mobility of capital)
  factor mobility 生産要素の移動性, 要素移動性
  horizontal mobility 水平移動, 水平的移動
  job mobility 転職の機会
  labor mobility 転職, 労働[労働力の]移動性, 労働力の移動
  mobility allowance 交通手当
  social mobility 社会的移動, 社会的移動性
  vertical mobility 垂直移動, 垂直的移動
mobilize 動 動員する, 結集する, …を戦時体制にする, 流通させる
mode 名 方法, やり方, 方式, 様式, 流儀, あり方, 型, 形態, 流行, 風潮, 慣行, スタンス, 姿勢, 方向, 最頻値, 気分, 鉱物組成, モード
  a mode of thinking 考え方
  a new mode of life 新生活様式
  all modes of mass transit あらゆる大量交通手段 (⇒mass transit)

batch mode 一括処理方式
be all the mode 大流行である
be in an easing mode 金融緩和のスタンス[姿勢]を続けている
be in holiday mode 休み気分だ
compatible mode 互換モード
enhanced mode 拡張モード
follow the mode 流行を追う
in mode 流行して
interactive mode 対話モード
out of mode 流行遅れで, すたれて
real time mode 即時処理方式
repeat mode リピート機能
return to a tightening mode 引締めのスタンス[姿勢]に戻る
the latest mode 最新の流行

model 名 モデル, 模型, 型, 型式, 車種, 機種, 新案, 模範
buying behavior model 購買行動モデル
consumer behavior model 消費者行動モデル
decision model 意思決定モデル
econometric model 計量経済モデル
Model Business Corporation Act 〈米国の〉模範事業会社法
performance model 業績モデル
pricing model 価格決定モデル
role model 手本, 理想像, 理想の姿, 雛型, 模範生, 優等生
stock valuation model 株式評価モデル
utility model 実用新案
valuation model 評価モデル

moderate 動 縮小する, 低下する, 下がる, 鈍化する, 減速する, 抑える, 和らげる弱める, 低下させる, …の司会をする, …の進行役をする, 点検する, 監査する
continue to moderate 鈍化傾向が続く
moderate a debate 討論会の司会をする
moderate competitive threat 競争圧力を弱める
moderate demands 要求を和らげる
moderate profitability 収益性を低下させる

moderate 形 手頃な, 適度の, 程よい, 適当な, 並みの, 普通の, 中くらいの, 中程度の, 僅かの (slight), 小幅の, 軽度な, 穏健な, 穏健派の, 穏和な, 穏やかな
at a moderate price 手頃な価格[値段]で, 格安料金[値段]で
moderate demand 需要薄

moderate discount 緩やかな証券発行差金
moderate supply 供給薄
moderate wage 低賃金

modernize 動 近代化する, 現代化する, 現代風にする

modest 形 緩やかな, 穏やかな, 小幅の, 適度な, 穏当な, 控え目な, ささやかな, 大きくない
modest demands 控え目な要求
modest economic recovery [expansion, rebound] 穏やかな景気回復
modest improvement 小幅改善, 緩やかな改善
modest income 適度の収入
modest increase [gain] 小幅な伸び[増加], 緩やかな伸び
modest rally 穏やかな上昇局面
modest upward path 穏やかな上昇軌道

molding [moulding] 名 鋳造, 塑造, 金型 (かながた)
molding technology 金型技術

molecular 名 分子
molecular target drugs 分子標的薬

molestation 名 痴漢行為, 性的いたずら, 性的虐待, 児童虐待

mom-and-pop 形 零細の, 家族経営の, 小規模の (=mama and papa, mama and pop; ⇒mama and papa store)

moment 名 瞬間, 短時間, 時, 時期, 機会, 場合, 重大性, 重要性
at this moment in time 現時点では, 今は
defining moment 決定的瞬間
for the moment [present] 当面, 当座は, 今は, 差し当たり
moment of truth 決定的瞬間, 決定的な時,〈のるかそるかの〉正念場, 危機的瞬間, 最後の審判の瞬間

momentum 名 はずみ, 勢い, 余波, 惰性, 契機, 要素
add [spur] momentum to …に拍車をかける, …にはずみをつける
begin to lose momentum 減速傾向が出る
earnings momentum 収益力
gain cyclical momentum for a recovery 景気回復の循環にはずみをつける
gain momentum 弾みをつける, 勢いを増す, 拡大する, 加速する
gather momentum 勢いを増す, 勢いがつく, 加速する, 拡大する, 本格化する, 上向きになる (=gain momentum)

inflationary momentum インフレの勢い
lose momentum 失速する, 減速する, 勢いがなくなる, 息切れする, 下向きになる
upward momentum 上昇の勢い, 上値の勢い
Monday morning quarterback 事が済んでから助言をする人, 後からとやかく批判する人, 結果論で他人を批判する人
monetarism 名 通貨主義, マネタリズム (景気対策の中心に通貨供給量の調節や金利の操作などを置く理論)
monetary 形 金融の, 通貨の, 貨幣の, 財政上の, 金銭の, マネタリー
  International Monetary Market 国際通貨市場《略 IMM》
  monetary adjustment 金融調節 (＝monetary administration, monetary control)
  monetary aggregate 量的金融指標, マネー・サプライ
  monetary assets 金融資産 (financial assets), 貨幣資産 (「金融資産」は銀行券, 預金, 売掛金, 公社債, 株式, 受取手形などを指し, 「貨幣資産」は会計学では現金, 当座預金, 受取手形, 売掛金, 市場性有価証券などをいう)
  monetary authorities 金融当局, 通貨当局
  monetary conditions 金融情勢
  monetary crisis 通貨危機, 金融危機, 貨幣恐慌
  monetary device 金融調節手段
  monetary easing policy 金融緩和政策, 金融緩和策 (＝monetary ease, monetary expansion, monetary relaxation)
  monetary expansion 金融緩和, 通貨拡大 (＝monetary easing, monetary relaxation)
  monetary facilities 金融機関
  monetary growth マネー・サプライの伸び率
  monetary indicators 金融指標
  monetary integration 通貨統合
  monetary items in the balance sheet 貸借対照表の貨幣性項目
  monetary management 金融操作, 金融的管理, 通貨管理
  monetary relaxation 金融緩和
  monetary reward 金銭的報酬
  monetary stability 金融の安定, 通貨安定
  monetary stabilization 通貨安定化, 通貨安定政策
  monetary statistics マネー・サプライ統計
  monetary stimulus 金融緩和
  monetary union 通貨統合, 通貨同盟
  monetary unit 貨幣単位, 金額単位
monetary base マネタリー・ベース, 貨幣的ベース (＝high-powered money base, money base：日本銀行券発行高, 貨幣流通高と日銀当座預金 (民間金融機関の中央銀行預け金) の合計で, 日銀が金融市場に供給している資金の残高を示す)
  monetary base balance マネタリー・ベースの残高
monetary policy 金融政策, 通貨政策 (＝money policy)
  easing of monetary policy 金融政策の緩和, 金融緩和 (＝easier monetary policy, monetary easing, monetary policy easing)
  monetary policy decision 金融政策の決断
  monetary policy makers 金融政策当局
  tightening in monetary policy 利上げ
  tightening of monetary policy 金融政策の引締め (＝monetary tightening)
money 名 金, 金銭, 通貨, 貨幣, 資金, 金融, マネー
  borrowed money 借入金
  call money コール借入金, 短期資金, 銀行相互間の当座借入金, コール・マネー
  call money rate コール・レート
  easy money 金融緩和, 低利の金, 低金利
  hard money 硬貨
  hot money 短期資金, 投機資金, ホット・マネー
  hush money 口止め料
  key money 権利金, 保証金, 礼金
  lose money 赤字を出す, 損失を出す, 損失を被る
  make money 利益を生み出す, 利益を上げる, 利益を得る, 資金を稼ぐ
  money easing 金融緩和
  money game 投機的取引, マネー・ゲーム
  money inflow 資金流入
  money laundering 不正資金の洗浄, 資金洗浄, マネー・ロンダリング (犯罪で得た資金の出所や所有者を隠す行為。⇒laundering)
  money-losing company 赤字企業, 赤字会社 (＝loss-making company, red-ink firm)
  money rate 金利, 市中金利
  money resources 財源
  money stock 通貨供給量, マネー・ストック (＝money supply)
  money transfer 振替え, 口座振替え, 現金振込み, 代金振込み, 振込み, 資金の移動, 送金
  money wages 実際に支払われた賃金, 貨幣賃金
  raise money 資金を調達する

ready money 手持ち現金
short-term money rate 短期金利
tight money 金融引締め, 金融逼迫, 資金需給の逼迫
tight money policy 金融引締め政策, 高金利政策

money flow 資金循環, 資金の流れ, 送金 (money transfer), マネー・フロー
money flow table 資金循環表, マネー・フロー表
money flows 送金 (=money transfers)

money market 金融市場, 短期金融市場, マネー・マーケット (長期金融市場はcapital market。「短期金融市場」は, 短期の金融資産であるコール, 手形, 譲渡性預金(DC), 現先などの資金取引が行われる金融市場のこと)
long-term money market 長期金融市場
money market instruments 短期金融市場証券, 短期金融商品
money market management 金融調節
short-term money market 短期金融市場
tighten the money market 金融を引き締める

money supply 通貨供給量, 資金供給, マネー・サプライ (=money stock: 中央銀行と市中金融機関が民間に供給する通貨の量で, 通貨にはM2 (現金, 要求払い預金, 定期性預金)のほかにCD (譲渡性預金)が含まれる)

moneykeeping tool 資金管理手段
moneylender 名 金貸し, 貸金業者, 金融業者
moneylending 名 金貸し, 貸金
　Moneylending Control Law 貸金業規制法
　moneylending business sector [industry] 貸金業界
moneymaking 名 金儲け, 利殖, 利益を上げること, 貨幣利得, 造幣
　moneymaking instruments 利殖手段
moneyman 名 投資家, 後援者, パトロン
monitor 動 監視する, 管理する, 調査する, チェックする, 評価する, 把握する, 分析する, モニターする
　closely monitor the market 市場の動向に十分注意する, 市場の動きを注意深く監視する
　monitor insurers' capital positions 保険会社の自己資本の状態を監視する
monitor 名 外電受信者, 監視者, 監視モニター, モニター装置, 監視装置, ディスプレー, 学級委員, …係, モニター
　blood pressure monitor 血圧計
　professional-use monitor 業務用のモニター
　the UN monitors 国連監視員, 国連監視チーム

monitoring 名 監視, 監視活動, 監理, 管理, モニタリング
　monitoring post 監理ポスト, 監視ポスト
　monitoring range 目標水準, 目標圏, 監視レンジ
　monitoring survey 追跡調査
　portfolio monitoring ポートフォリオ管理, ポートフォリオの評価基準
　practice monitoring 業務監視
　risk monitoring リスク管理
　the United Nations cease-fire monitoring group 国連停戦監視団

monoline 名 単一の事業, 金融保証保険会社, 金融保証会社, 金融保証専門会社, モノライン (=bond insurer:「モノライン」は, 債券など金融商品の保証を専門に行う米国の保険会社で, 倒産などで社債購入者に元本と利息を支払えない場合に会社に代わってその支払いを保証する。生命保険や自動車保険, 火災保険などの各種保険を手がける保険会社を「マルチライン (multiline)」という)
　monoline bond insurer 債券専門保険会社
　monoline health insurer 健康保険専門会社

monolith 名 一枚岩, 一枚岩に統制された組織, 一枚岩の組織, モノリス
monolithic 形 一枚岩の, 完全に [一本に] 統制された, 巨大な, どっしりとした, 単一の, モノリシック
　monolithic circuit 集積回路, モノリシック回路
　monolithic IC 半導体集積回路, モノリシック集積回路

monopolization 名 独占, 専売
monopolize 動 独占する
monopoly 名 独占, 売り手独占, 供給独占, 独占権, 独占事業体, 独占企業体, 独占体, 専売, 専売公社
　monopoly goodwill 独占的営業権, 特許的営業権
　monopoly on information 情報の独占
　monopoly price 独占価格
　monopoly provider 独占企業

month-on-month 名 形 副 前月比 (=month-on-month figure)
monthly 名 月例の, 毎月の
　monthly economic report 月例経済報告
mood 名 気分, 気持ち, 機嫌, 怒り, 不機嫌, むら気, 感情, 雰囲気, 地合い, 心理, ムード
　be in a mood 機嫌が悪い
　bearish mood 弱気の地合い
　defensive mood 警戒ムード

favorable mood 好調な地合い
mood conditioning 気分調整
mood disorder 気分障害
mood swings 〈突然の〉気分変動
speculative mood 思惑気分
Moody's Investors Service Inc. ムーディーズ・インベスターズ・サービス, ムーディーズ（米国の代表的格付け機関）
moon 名 月, 衛星, ムーン
moon buggy [crawler, jeep, rover] 月面車
moon probe 月探測機, 月探査宇宙船
moon prospector 月探測機
moon roving vehicle 月面車《略 MRV》
mooncraft 名 月旅行宇宙船
moonflight 名 月旅行, 月飛行
moonlet 名 小衛星
moonscape 名 月面風景, 月面の眺め, 月面写真, 荒涼とした眺め
moonship 名 月探測船, 月旅行用宇宙船
moonshot 名 月への打上げ, 月ロケット
moonstation 名 月ステーション
moonstroll 名 月面歩行
moonwalk 名 月面歩行, 〈ダンスの〉ムーンウォーク
moonwalker 名 月面歩行者, 月面車
moonwatcher 名 人工衛星の観測者
moonwork 名 月面作業
Moon Trade 〈株などの〉時間外取引, 時間外サービス, ムーン・トレード（＝after-hours service, after-hours trading）
Moore's Law ムーアの法則（コンピュータの処理能力は18か月毎に2倍の割合で増加するという経験則）
moot 形 議論の余地のある, 未決定[未解決]の, 論争中の, 実際的価値[意味]のない, 動 討議する, 議題にのせる, 議題にする, 議論に持ち出す
be mooted 議題として提出される
moot court 模擬法廷
moot point 論争点, 未解決点
moot question 議論の余地のある問題, 未解決の問題
mop-up operations 掃討作戦
moral 名 道徳, 倫理, 品行, モラル
moral 形 道徳の, 道徳上[道義上]の, 道徳的[倫理的]な, 教訓的な, 品行方正な, 精神的な
moral character 徳性, 品位
moral consciousness 道徳意識
moral hazard 倫理観[責任感]の欠如, 道徳的危険, モラル・ハザード
moral law 道徳律
moral obligation 道徳的義務
moral philosophy [science] 倫理学, 道徳哲学
moral suasion 道徳的説得（moral persuasion）, 口先介入
moral support 精神的支援, 暗黙の支援
morale 名 労働意欲, 勤労意欲, 勤労意識, 士気, モラール
morality 名 道徳, 倫理, 道義, 行動の善悪, 道徳性, 倫理性, 道義性, 倫理体系, 風紀, 品行方正, 教訓, モラル
commercial morality 商業道徳
political morality 政治倫理
public morality 公衆道徳
morass 名 困難, 困難な立場, 難局, 苦境, 泥沼
moratorium 名 〈活動の〉一時停止[一時禁止], 支払い停止, 支払い猶予期間, 返済猶予, 返済延期, 凍結, モラトリアム
debt moratorium 債務返済停止, 債務返済の凍結, 債務の返済猶予
debt-servicing moratorium 債務返済の停止, 債務返済の凍結, 債務返済のモラトリアム
interest payment moratorium 利払い停止, 利払いの延期, 利払いの凍結
lift the overseas borrowing moratorium 海外での資金調達の凍結を解く
lifting the moratorium on a deposit payoff system 預金ペイオフ制度の凍結解除
moratorium on missile tests ミサイル実験凍結
reduction or moratorium on interest payment 金利減免
repayment moratorium 債務の返済猶予, 債務返済の延長, 債務返済の凍結
moribund 形 死にかけている, 瀕死の, 消滅[絶滅]しかけている, 滅亡寸前の, 低迷状態の
revive a moribund economy 瀕死の経済をよみがえらせる
mortgage 名 抵当, 担保, 担保不動産, 譲渡抵当, 抵当権, 抵当権設定, 抵当証書, 担保付き融資, 住宅ローン, モーゲージ
adjustable mortgage [mortgage loan] 変動金利モーゲージ（＝adjustable-rate mortgage, adjustable-rate mortgage loan）
credits for mortgage payments 住宅取得控除
first mortgage bond 第1順位抵当権付き債券
home mortgage 住宅ローン

mortgage-backed bond モーゲージ担保債券, モーゲージ担保債

mortgage bank 住宅金融会社, 住宅金融専門機関 （＝mortgage banker）

mortgage debenture 担保付き社債

mortgage debt 担保付き長期債務, 抵当借り

mortgage deed 担保証券

mortgage foreclosure 住宅ローンの焦げ付き, 抵当流れ, 抵当権［抵当権］の行使［実行］, 譲渡抵当実行手続き, 物的担保実行手続き, 譲渡抵当受戻し権喪失手続き

mortgage loan 抵当貸し, 担保付き貸付け金 （＝mortgage receivable, secured loan）, 住宅ローン

mortgage note 担保付き長期手形

mortgage-related securities モーゲージ関連証券

mortgages payable 担保［抵当］付き借入金

mortgages receivable 担保［抵当］付き貸付け金

stripped mortgage securities 分離型モーゲージ証券

mortgage-backed securities
住宅ローン担保証券, 住宅ローン証券, モーゲージ証券《略 MBS》（＝mortgage-backed product, mortgage-backeds）

Moscow 名 ロシア, ロシア政府, 〈ロシア連邦の首都〉モスクワ

Mossad 名 モサド（イスラエル情報機関）

Mothers 名 マザーズ（東京証券取引所のベンチャー企業向け市場で, 1999年11月に開設した）

mothball 動 〈計画などを〉棚上げにする, 〈使用しないで〉しまい込む, 保存する, 〈艦船などを〉予備役に入れる

mothball 名 〈ナフタリンなどの〉防虫剤の玉, モスボール

 in mothballs 予備の, 引退の, 第一線から退いて, 棚上げにされて, しまい込んで, 長い間使用していない, 問題にならないと退けられて

 mothball fleet 予備艦隊

motion 名 提議, 提案, 動議, 発議, 申し立て, 運動, 移動, 動き, 運ず, 動作, 身振り, モーション

 carry [adopt, pass] the motion overwhelmingly 発議を圧倒的多数で可決する

 censure motion against the prime minister 首相問責決議案

 confidence motion 信任決議案

 linear motion 線運動

 Motion carried! 動議可決!

 motion of the highest privilege 最優先動議

 motion sickness 乗り物酔い, 宇宙酔い

 motion study 動作研究

 motion to adjourn 散会の動議

 motion video 動画

 no-confidence motion against the Cabinet 内閣不信任決議案

 put forward [propose] a motion 動議を提出する

 set the wheels in motion 手を打つ, 手はずを整える

motivate 動 動機［刺激］を与える, 動機づける, 意欲［興味］を起こさせる, 意欲を高める, やる気を引き出す

motivation
名 動機づけ, 刺激誘因, 意欲, 購買動機, 学習意欲, モチベーション

 buying motivation 購買動機 （＝motivation of purchase）

 economic motivation 経済的動機づけ

 extrinsic motivation 外的動機づけ

 intrinsic motivation 内的動機づけ

 motivation control 動機づけ管理

 motivation research 動機調査, 購買動機調査, モチベーション・リサーチ《略 MR》（＝motivational research）

 motivation to spend 消費意欲

 profit motivation 利潤動機, 利潤志向

mount 他動 登る, 上がる, 乗る, 据え付ける, 取り付ける, 載せる, 搭載する, 配置する, 貼る, 固定する, 開始する, 始める, 着手する, 取りかかる, 〈運動などを〉起こす, 〈デモなどを〉組織する, 〈劇を〉上演［公演］する, 〈攻撃を〉仕掛ける, 自動 高まる, 増大［増加］する, 強まる

 mount a campaign [drive] 運動を起こす, 運動を始める, 運動を実施する

 mount a counterattack against …に反撃［反論, 逆襲］する

 mounting criticism 高まる批判, 批判の高まり

 mounting losses 損失の増大

move 動 動かす, 移す, 移動させる, 移転する, …する気にさせる, 提議する, 動議を出す［提出する］, 提案する, 売る, さばく, 動く, 行動する, 措置を取る, 移動する, 移行する, 進行する, 経過する

 move against …に対抗する

 move an amendment to the bill 法案の修正を提出する

 move into profit 黒字に転換する

move the stock 在庫をさばく
move to a new all-time high 過去最高に達する
move 名 動き, 動向, 変動, 移動, 移行, 行動, 運動, 進展, 処置, 措置, 対応, 対策, 政策, 手段, 異動, 移転, 引っ越し
 best moves 最善の動き, 最善の措置, 最善の対応
 competitive moves 競争力
 credit-tightening move 金融引締め策
 in a move to …する動きとして, …する動きの中で
 limit move 値幅制限
 make a preemptive move 先手を打つ
 market move 市場の動き, 市場動向
 seasonal moves 季節要因
movement 名 動き, 行動, 活動, 運動, 移動, 動向, 流れ, 進展, 進行, 変化, 変動
 capital movement 資本移動
 consumer movement 消費者運動
 environmental movement 環境保護運動
 interest rate movement 金利動向, 金利変動 (=interest rate move)
 price movement 価格変動, 物価動向
 price movement restriction 値幅制限
 zero defects movements 無欠陥運動, 無欠点運動, ZD運動
mover 名 発起人, 発議者, 動議提出者, 発動力, 主唱者, 移転者, 引っ越し業者, 売れる[売れ筋の]商品, 株が大量に買われたり売られたりしている会社
 mover and shaker 有力者, 実力者, 大物, お偉方(複数形=movers and shakers)
 the chief mover 主唱者, 原動力 (=prime mover)
 the prime [first] mover 原動力, 発動機[原動機], 主唱者, 発起人, 動議提出者
moving strike convertible bond 転換社債型新株予約権付き社債《略 MSCB》
MOX fuel プルトニウムとウランの混合酸化物(MOX)燃料, MOX燃料
MRI 磁気共鳴映像法 (magnetic resonance imagingの略)
much-heralded 形 前評判の高い, 鳴り物入りの, 大々的に発表された
mull 動 検討する, 討議する, 熟考する, 思案する, …についてあれこれ考える, …に頭を絞る, …を台なしにする, …についてへまをやる
multichannel television 多チャンネル・テレビ, マルチチャンネル・テレビ

multilateral 形 多国間の, 多国間主義の, 多国籍の, 多数国参加の, 多角的な, 多面的な, 多元的な, 多辺の
 multilateral accord 多国間合意
 multilateral agreement 多数当事者の合意, 多国間協定, 多辺的協定, 多角協定
 multilateral barter 多角バーター貿易
 multilateral clearing agreement 多角的清算協定
 multilateral compensation 多角相殺
 multilateral cooperation 多国間協力, 多角的協力
 multilateral currency realignment 多角的通貨調整, 多角的平価調整, 多国間通貨調整
 multilateral documentation 標準取引の契約書
 multilateral format 多国間の形式
 multilateral initiative 多国間交渉
 multilateral institution 国際機関
 multilateral management 多角経営
 multilateral (military) force 多国籍軍
 multilateral monetary compensation 多角的通貨相殺
 multilateral payment agreement 多角的支払い協定, 多角的決済協定
 multilateral security guarantees 多国間の安全保証
 multilateral settlement 多角決済
 multilateral surveillance 多角的監視, 多角的共同審議
 multilateral trade 多角貿易, 多角的貿易, 多角的通商, 求償貿易, バーター貿易
 multilateral trade agreement 多角的貿易協定
 multilateral trade negotiations 多角的貿易交渉, 多角的通商交渉, 多国間貿易交渉《略 MTN》
 multilateral trade talks 多角的貿易交渉, 多国間貿易交渉 (=multilateral trade negotiations)
 multilateral treaty 多国間条約
 new round of multilateral trade negotiations 新多角的貿易交渉(新ラウンド)
multilateralism 名 多角主義, 多国間主義
multilateralization 名 多角化, 多辺化
 multilateralization of position 対外準備の多角化
multilayered trade policy 重層的な通商政策

multilingual audio-text translation system 多言語音声自動翻訳システム

multimedia 名 複合メディア, マルチメディア（数値データや文字データなど既存の情報媒体のほかに, 音声や画像のデータをコンピュータで一括管理して管理・コントロールすること）
  multimedia multiplexer マルチメディア多重化装置

multinational 形 多国籍の
  multinational company [firm] 多国籍企業（＝multinational corporation, multinational enterprise, multinational firm）
  multinational force 多国籍軍（＝intl force）

multiple 名 倍数, 倍率, 株価収益率, チェーン・ストア[チェーン店]
  cash multiples キャッシュ・フロー倍率
  earnings multiple 株価収益率
  price cash earnings (P/CE) multiple 株価キャッシュ・フロー倍率

multiple 形 複合の, 複合的な, 複式の, 多重の, 多種多様な, チェーン店の, マルチプル
  multiple access 多元接続
  multiple activity chart 複合活動図表, 複合作業分析図表
  multiple application 多重申込み, 重複申込み
  multiple brand entries 複数ブランド参入
  multiple car crash 玉突き衝突, 多重衝突
  multiple channel 複合経路
  multiple choice 多肢選択, 多肢選択方式, 多項目選択法
  multiple-choice questions 多項選択法, 多岐選択質問
  multiple correlation 重相関, 多重相関, 多元相関
  multiple cropping 多毛作
  multiple currency standard 多数通貨本位制
  multiple debtor 多重債務者（＝multiple loan borrower）
  multiple employer plan 複合事業主制度
  multiple exchange rate (system) 複数為替相場, 複数為替相場制
  multiple fracture 複雑骨折
  multiple growth model 多段階成長モデル
  multiple line insurance [policy] 多種目保険
  multiple line law 〈米国の〉兼営法
  multiple listing 同時上場, 不動産の共同斡旋
  multiple objective linear programming [programming] 多目的線型計画法

Multiple Orbit Bombardment System 多数軌道爆撃システム《略 FOBS》
  multiple organ failure 多臓器不全
  multiple pricing 複数価格設定
  multiple reentry vehicle 多弾頭再突入ミサイル, 複数弾頭《略 MRV》
  multiple regression analysis 重回帰分析, 多重回帰分析
  multiple sales 重複販売
  multiple sclerosis 多発性硬化症《略 MS》
  multiple shift 多交替, 多交替制
  multiple sourcepurchasing 複数仕入先方式, 重複仕入先方式
  multiple standard 多元的本位
  multiple step form 区分式
  multiple-step income statement 区分損益計算書
  multiple store [shop] チェーン店, チェーン・ストア
  multiple story warehouse 多層式倉庫
  multiple target market 複数標的市場
  multiple tariff system 複数関税率制度
  multiple trading 同時売買
  multiple unit packaging 複数単位包装
  multiple unit price 複数単位価格
  multiple unit pricing 複数単位価格表示制
  multiple warhead 多弾頭, 複合弾頭

multiplex broadcasting 音声多重放送（＝multichannel broadcasting）

multipolar 形 多極の, 多極的な, 多極性の, 分散の
  multipolar world 多極構造の世界, 多極化界, 多極的勢力均衡の世界
  the age of multipolar balance of power 多極的勢力均衡の時代

multipolarity [multi-polarity] 名 多極化, 多極化現象

multipurpose 形 多目的の, 多用途の, 複数の目的に使用される, 汎用の, マルチパーパス
  multipurpose card 汎用カード
  multipurpose information 多目的情報
  multipurpose project 多目的計画, 総合計画

multislice computer tomography (CT) scanner マルチスライスCTスキャナー, マルチスライス・コンピュータ断層撮影装置

munition 名 軍需品, 軍用品, 軍用資材, 武器・弾薬, 必需品, 資金
  munition depot 武器庫, 軍需品補給所
  munition dump 軍需品臨時集積場

munition factory [plant] 軍需工場 （=munitions plant)
munitions company 軍需企業
munitions for an election campaign 選挙運動資金
munitions industry 軍需産業
munitions of war 軍需品
multitiered 形 重層的な
municipal 形 地方自治の, 地方自治体の, 市政の, 市[町]の, 市営[町営]の, 内政の, 国内の
municipal authorities 市当局, 町当局
municipal bankruptcy 地方自治体の財政破綻, 市町村の財政破綻
municipal board of education 市教育委員会
municipal bond 地方債, 市債券, 市債
municipal corporation 地方公共団体, 地方自治体, 私有公社
municipal court 市裁判所
municipal enterprise 地方公営事業, 地方公営企業
municipal general obligation bond 地方一般財源債
municipal government 地方自治体, 市当局, 市政
municipal lease 公共リース
municipal management 市の管理[経営], 市営
municipal office 市役所, 町役場
municipal official 市役所職員
municipal property tax 固定資産税
municipal revenue bond 地方特定財源債
municipal securities 地方債
municipal tax 市町村税
municipal undertaking 市営事業
municipal waste 都市廃棄物
municipality 名 自治体, 地方自治体, 公共団体, 市[町]当局, 市行政, 市民
loans to municipalities 公共団体貸付け, 公共団体貸付け金
local municipality 地方自治体
obligations of municipalities 地方自治体の債券
muscle 名 力, 腕力, 圧力, 強制力, 勢力, 影響力, 筋肉, 筋(きん), 用心棒, 護衛, ボディガード, 殺し屋, 刺客, 必要なもの, 肝要な[基本的な, 本質的な]

diplomatic muscle 外交的影響力
financial muscle 財力
flex one's muscle(s) 力を誇示する, 力のあるところを見せつける, 腕を振るう, 影響力を行使する
heart muscle 心筋
legal muscle 法的影響力
military muscle 軍事力, 武力
muscle pill 筋肉増強剤 （=anabolic steroid)
muscle relaxant 筋弛緩剤
political muscle 政治的影響力
put military muscle into foreign policies 力による強圧的外交政策をとる
music distribution 音楽配信
Muslim 名 イスラム教徒, ムスリム, 形 イスラム教の, イスラム教徒の, イスラム文化の
Black Muslim ブラック・ムスリム(白人との分離を主張する米国のイスラム教徒)
Muslim Brotherhood ムスリム同胞団
Muslim extremist イスラム過激派
must 名 必須の条件, 絶対必要な物[事], マスト
a must book 必読の書
a must-have かならず手に入れるべき物
a must-win game どうしても勝たなければならない試合
must-have items どうしても欲しい商品
mutual 形 相互の, 共通の, 共同の, 共有する, ミューチュアル
mutual aid association 共済組合
mutual company 相互会社
mutual defense agreement 相互防衛協定
mutual dependence 相互依存, 相互依存関係
mutual fund 投資信託, 株式投資信託, 投資信託会社, ミューチュアル・ファンド
mutual insurance 相互保険
mutual manufacture of products 製品の相互供給
mutual recognition agreement 相互承認協定
Mutual Security Act 相互安全保障協定
mutual security treaty 相互安全保障条約
MVNO 仮想移動体通信事業者 （mobile virtual network operatorの略。無線局を自ら開設しないで, 免許を受けた既存の移動通信事業者から通信回線を借りて携帯電話サービスを行う通信事業者のこと)

N n

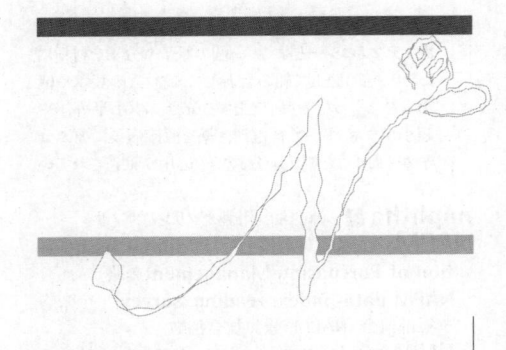

N- 形 核の, 核兵器の, 原子力の (nuclearの略)
 N-program 核計画, 核開発計画, 核兵器開発計画 (＝nuclear arms program, nuclear arms development program)
 N-security summit 核安全保障サミット, 核安保サミット (＝nuclear security summit)
 N-umbrella 核の傘
NAFTA 北米自由貿易協定 (**North American Free Trade Agreement**の略)
name 動 指名する, 任命する, 選ぶ, 選出する, 指定する, 命名する, …の名前を挙げる, 公表する, 決め
▶ Sony Corp. *named* Vice Chairman Howard Stringer as the company's new chairman and group chief executive officer. ソニーは, ハワード・ストリンガー副会長を, 同社の新会長兼グループ最高経営責任者 (CEO) に任命した。
▶ The investment fund is not *named* on the firm's list of shareholders. この投資ファンドの名は, 同社の株主名簿には記載されていない。
name 名 名称, 呼称, 名義, 名目, 評判, 名声, 名士, 有名人, 大物, 家門, 一門, 一族, 銘柄, ネーム, 形 有名な, 一流の, 名の通った, 広く知られた, 定評のある
 a big name 有名人
 a man of name 名士, 有名人
 a man of no name 無名の人
 American names 米国勢
 assume a false name 偽名を使う
 clear one's name 汚名を晴らす
 firm name 照合, 屋号
 gain [get, make] a name as …として名をなす
 get a bad name 評判を落とす
 good quality name 優良銘柄
 have a good name for …の評判が高い
 have a name for …で知られている, …で名を挙げる
 in all but name 事実上, 実質上
 in name 名目上
 in one's name [in the name of] …の名義で, …という名前で, …の名の下に
 lend one's name to …を支援する, …に名義を貸す
 maiden name 結婚前の姓
 make one's name as …としての名声を得る
 name credit 優良貸出先
 name designer 一流デザイナー
 name lending 名義貸し
 name recognition 知名度
 name university 有名大学, 一流大学
 proprietary name 特許登録名, 特許商品名
 the name of the game 肝心なこと, 最も大事 [重要] なこと, 最も重要な側面, 本質, 究極の目的 [狙い, 目標], 真相
–name 形 …の名をもつ, …の名声を持つ
 a big-name sportsman 大物スポーツマン
 brand-name clothes 有名ブランド服
nanometer 名 ナノ・メートル (1ナノ・メートルは10億分の1メートル)
nanotech product 超微細化技術の製品, ナノテク製品
nanotechnology 名 超微細加工技術, 超微細加工・計測技術, 超微小技術, ナノ技術, ナノテ

ク, ナノテクノロジー
　ナノテクノロジーとは ⊃ 一個の原子や分子を材料にしたり, 部品として組み合わせてミクロ大の装置や機械などを作ったり, 研究をする分野。極小半導体や超小型ロボット, 燃料電池, 薬を直接病巣に運ぶ分子カプセルなど幅広い分野での応用が期待されている。

naphtha 名　揮発油, 粗製ガソリン, ナフサ
NAPM　全米購買部協会 (National Association of Purchasing Managementの略)
　NAPM data [index, reading, survey]　全米購買部協会 (NAPM) 景気総合指数
　NAPM employment index　全米購買部協会の雇用指数
　NAPM index of manufacturing activity　全米購買部協会景気総合指数
　NAPM survey balance on prices　全米購買部協会の価格指数 (＝NAPM price index)
　NAPM's index of industrial activity　全米購買部協会景気総合指数
　NAPM's monthly index of new orders　全米購買部協会の月次受注指数
narrow 動　狭める, 縮める, 縮小させる, 限定する, 狭まる, 狭くなる, 縮小する
　narrow the supply/demand gap　需給ギャップを縮小する [縮める], 需給の格差を縮小する
　narrowed [narrowing] operating margins　営業利益率の縮小
　narrowed [narrowing] yield spread　利回り格差の縮小
narrow down　〈範囲を〉絞り込む, 〈範囲を〉絞る, …に限定する
　narrow down the choice to　選択の範囲を…に絞る
　narrow down the list to　リストを…に絞り込む
NASA　米航空宇宙局 (National Aeronautics and Space Administrationの略)
NASD　全米証券業協会 (National Association of Securities Dealersの略)
NASDAQ　ナスダック, 米店頭株式市場, 全国店頭銘柄気配自動通報システム, 全国店頭銘柄建値自動通報システム, 店頭銘柄自動通報システム (National Association of Securities Dealers Automated Quotations Systemsの略)
　Nasdaq composite index　ナスダック総合株価指数, ナスダック店頭市場の総合指数, ナスダックの総合指数
nation 名　国, 国家, 国民, 民族, 種族, 部族, ネーション
　Article 8 nation of IMF　IMF8条国
　most-favored nation　最恵国
　nation state　民族国家
　sovereign nations　各国政府, ソブリン発行体
　the law of nations　国際法
　the president's speech to the whole nation　全国民への大統領演説 [スピーチ]
national 形　国民の, 国家の, 全国的な, 国立の, 国有の, ナショナル
　gross national demand　国民総需要
　gross national expenditure　国民総支出
　gross national supply　国民総供給
　national anthem　国歌
　National Archives and Records Administration　米国立公文書・記録管理局
　National Association of Purchasing Management's (NAPM) survey　全米購買部協会景気報告
　National Association of Realtors　全米不動産協会
　National Association of Securities Dealers　全米証券業協会
　national bank　連邦法銀行, 国法銀行, 全国銀行
　National Bank Act of 1864　1864年連邦法銀行法
　National Bureau of Economic Research　全米経済研究所《略 NBER》(経済学者が米国の景気循環を中立的な立場で判定する民間の非営利団体)
　National Business Hall of Fame　アメリカ経営者の殿堂
　national capital　国民資本
　national convention　全国大会, 全国党大会
　national economic activity　マクロ経済
　National Economic Council　米国家経済会議《略 NEC》
　national economic stability　国民経済の安定
　national economy　国民経済, 国の経済
　National Federation of the Agricultural Co-operative Association　全国農業協同組合連合会, 全農
　national forest　国有林
　National Guard　〈米〉州兵 (州内の治安維持や災害救助などに出動する)
　national health insurance card　国民健康保険証
　National Institute for Environmental Stud-

ies　国立環境研究所
National Institute of Science and Technology　科学技術政策研究所
National Labor Relations Act　〈米国の〉全国労働関係法
National Medal of Honor　国民栄誉賞
national median　全国中央値
national outlay　国民支出
national pension plan　国民年金, 国民年金制度　（＝national pension program, national pension system)
national pension premiums　国民年金保険料
National People's Congress　〈中国の〉全国人民代表大会, 全人代　（＝China's figurehead parliament：中国の国会）
National Personnel Authority　人事院
national referendum　国民投票
National Referendum Law　国民投票法
national regulations　国内規制
national resident registry network system　住民基本台帳ネットワーク・システム
national savings　国民貯蓄
National Space Development Agency of Japan　宇宙開発事業団《略 NASDA》
National Tax Administration Agency　国税庁
national unity government　挙国一致政府
national wealth　国富

national income　国民所得
circulation of national income　国民所得循環
full-employment level of national income　完全雇用国民所得水準
national income accounting　国民所得計算
national income accounts　国民所得勘定
national income at constant prices　実質国民所得
national income basis　国民経済計算ベース
national income policy　国民所得政策
national income statistics quick estimation　国民所得統計速報
net national income　国民純所得

National Security Council　米国家安全保障会議
米国家安全保障会議のメンバー：

The President	大統領
The Vice President	副大統領
The Secretary of State	国務長官
The Secretary of Defense	国防長官
Statutory Advisers	法定顧問
Director of Central Intelligence Agency	中央情報局長官
Chairman, Joint Chiefs of Staff	統合参謀本部議長

Nationality Law　国籍法
nationalization 名　国有化, 国営化, 国営, 全国拡大, 全国展開
nationalize 動　国有化［国営化］する, 国営にする, 全国に拡大する, 全国展開する
nationwide 形　全国的な, 全国の, 全国規模の, 全国に及ぶ
NATO　北大西洋条約機構（North Atlantic Treaty Organizationの略）
natural 形　自然の, 自然界の, 天然の, 生まれつきの, 自然発生的な, 当然の, もっともな, 生き写しの, 実物そっくりの, 真に迫った
　have a natural talent [ability] for　…の天賦の才能
　natural attrition　自然減
　natural calamity [disaster]　自然災害, 天災
　natural childbirth　自然分娩
　natural disaster relief　自然災害救助, 災害救助
　natural enemy　天敵
　natural heritage　自然遺産
　natural increase　自然増（＝natural growth）
　natural law　自然法, 自然法則
　natural life　寿命, 天寿
　natural representation　真に迫った描写
　natural resources　天然資源
　natural result　当然の結果
　natural rights　生得の権利
　natural science　自然科学
　natural selection　自然淘汰
　natural wastage　自然減

natural gas　天然ガス
liquefied natural gas　液化天然ガス《略 LNG》
natural gas distribution　天然ガスの配給
natural gas field　天然ガス田
natural gas hydrate　天然ガス・ハイドレート《略 NGH》
natural gas liquid　液体天然ガス, 天然ガス液, 天然ガソリン《略 NGL》
natural gas output　天然ガスの産出
natural gas reserves　天然ガス埋蔵量
production of natural gas　天然ガスの生産

solidified natural gas　固形化天然ガス

navigation 名　航行，航海，航海術，航空，航空術，ナビゲーション
- aerial navigation　航空術，航空学
- car navigation system　カーナビ，自動車経路誘導システム，カー・ナビゲーション・システム
- inland [internal] navigation　内陸航行
- Navigation Acts　航海条令
- navigation satellite　航行衛星
- navigation system　自動航行システム，ナビゲーション・システム
- satellite navigation system　衛星航行システム，衛星運行システム
- Treaty of Commerce and Navigation between Japan and the USA　日米通商航海条約

neck and neck [neck-and-neck] 副　互角に，負けず劣らず，接戦で，五分五分で，競り合って
- run neck and neck　接戦を演じる

needs 名　必要，必要性，必要量，必要額，要求，欲求，需要，必需品，課題，ニーズ
- achieving needs　達成欲求
- basic needs　基本的ニーズ，基本的要求，一次的［基礎的］欲求，最低生活費
- borrowing needs　借入需要，資金調達需要，調達額
- capital needs　資金需要，資本必要額，必要資本
- common needs　共通の要求
- credit needs　信用のニーズ
- customer needs　顧客のニーズ
- daily needs　日常必需品
- development needs　開発のニーズ
- financing needs　資金調達需要，資金ニーズ，調達額
- investment needs　投資ニーズ
- labor needs　労働必要量，労働需要
- meet [satisfy] customer needs　顧客のニーズに応える，顧客のニーズに対応する，顧客のニーズにマッチする，顧客のニーズを満たす，顧客のニーズを満足させる
- short-term financing needs　短期資金ニーズ
- structure of needs　欲求構造
- working capital needs　運転資金の必要額，運転資金のニーズ

NEET　無業者，ニート（Not in Education, Employment or Trainingの略。1990年代末のイギリスで生まれたことばで，「学校にも行かず，働いてもいないし，職業訓練にも参加していない」若者のこと）

negative 形　マイナスの，負の，逆の，赤字の，反対の，弱含みの，弱気の，消極的な，悪影響を与える，有害な，否定的な，悲観的な，成果が上がらない，ネガティブ，名　弱気材料，悪材料，マイナス要因（⇒positive）
- cast the negative vote for　…に反対票を投じる
- negative campaign [campaigning]　負の選挙運動，非難・中傷合戦，ネガティブ・キャンペーン
- negative correlation　負の相関，逆相関
- negative currency effects　為替差損
- negative effect [impact]　悪影響，悪材料，マイナス影響，マイナス効果，負の効果，負の側面
- negative equity　負の資産（資産の時価がそれを担保とする未払いの抵当権の価値を下回ること）
- negative evidence [instance]　反証
- negative goodwill　消極のれん，消極的のれん，負ののれん，マイナスの営業権
- negative growth　マイナス成長
- negative implications　悪材料，マイナス要因，格下げの方向
- negative (income) tax　負の所得税，逆所得税（低所得者に国が与える社会保障給付）
- negative list　残存輸入制限品目リスト，承認が必要な輸入品目リスト
- negative marketing　絞りの戦略，ネガティブ・マーケティング
- negative net gearing　純負債比率
- negative option　消極的選択権（通信販売で頼みもしない商品が送られてきたときに，その代金を支払うか商品を送り返すかの選択権）
- negative outlook　ネガティブ（弱含み）の見通し
- negative spread　逆ざや（＝negative yield：運用利回りが保険契約者に約束した予定利率を下回ること）
- negative territory　マイナス，マイナス基調（＝minus territory）
- negative vote　反対投票
- negative wealth effect　逆資産効果（土地や株その他の資産価格の下落）
- negative yield　逆イールド，逆ざや（＝negative spread）

negative net worth　債務超過，債務超過額，税引き後利益の赤字，赤字
- develop [have] a negative net worth　債務超過になる
- fall into a negative net worth　債務超過に

陥る
recover one's negative net worth …の債務超過を解消する

negligence 名 過失, 怠慢, 不注意, 手抜かり, 手抜き
- **medical negligence** 医療過失
- **negligence of duty** 職務怠慢
- **negligence resulting in death** 過失致死
- **negligence tax** 過少申告加算税
- **professional negligence** 業務上過失

negotiate 動 交渉する, 〈交渉して〉取り決める, 協議する, 協定する, 商議する, 話し合う, 〈手形, 小切手などを〉譲渡する, 換金する
- **be on a strong [good] negotiating position** 交渉上有利な立場にある
- **negotiate a new deal with** …と新規契約を結ぶ
- **negotiate the deal** 取決めを結ぶ
- **negotiated price** 協議価格
- **negotiated transaction** 交渉案件, 相対売買
- **negotiated underwriting** 協議引受け, 協議引受方式

negotiation 名 交渉, 協議, 商談, 取引, 流通, 権利の移転, 譲渡, 〈輸出地の取引銀行による〉荷為替手形の買取り, ネゴシエーション
- **competitive negotiation** 競争的交渉
- **enter into final negotiations with** …と最終調整に入る
- **first-round negotiations** 初協議, 第一回協議
- **integrative negotiation** 統合的交渉
- **negotiation by draft** 取立て為替
- **negotiation charge** 手形買取り手数料, 買取り手数料(手形取組み時に銀行が請求する手数料)
- **negotiation credit** 手形買取銀行無指定信用状, ネゴシエーション信用状
- **negotiation of export bill** 輸出手形の買取り
- **sectoral negotiation** 分野別交渉
- **trust merger negotiations** 信託部門の経営統合交渉

negotiator 名 交渉者, 交渉担当者, 交渉員, 協議者, 〈小切手などの〉譲渡人, 裏書人
- **debt negotiator** 債務交渉担当者
- **Special Trade Negotiator** 米大統領通商交渉特別代表

neoliberalism 名 新自由主義
nepotism 名 縁故主義, 身内びいき, 同族登用
nerve agent 神経ガス
Net [net] 名 インターネット, ネット (= Internet, net, internet)
Net shopping ネット・ショッピング (= electronic commerce, Internet shopping, online shopping)
Net user ネット利用者, ネット・ユーザー (= Internet user, netter)
net 形 基本的な, 最終的な, 結局の, 正味の, 掛け値のない, 純粋の, 税引き後の
- **net asset** 純資産, 正味資産(総資産から総負債を差し引いた資産残高)
- **net asset value per share** 1株当たり純資産価値, 普通株式1株当たり純資産価値(book value per share (1株当たり純資産, 1株当たり簿価)あるいはnet tangible assets per share (1株当たり純有形資産価値)ともいう。会社が解散した場合, 株主は持ち株数に応じて残った財産が分配されるが, そのときの1株当たり資産が「1株当たり純資産」で, 解散価値ともいわれている)
- **net buying** 株の買い越し, 買い越し額 (= buying on balance, on-balance buying: 一定期間に有価証券を売った量と買った量を比較して, 買った量が多い場合に買い越しとなる)
- **net creditor position** 対外純資産残高
- **net exports** 純輸出(純輸出=輸出−輸入)
- **net external assets** 対外純資産(対外純資産=日本の政府, 企業, 個人が海外に持つ資産(対外資産: external assets)−海外の政府, 企業, 個人が日本に持つ資産(対外負債: external debts, external liabilities)。net foreign assetsともいう)
- **net income** 純利益, 当期純利益, 税引き後利益, 純所得, 純収入, 日銀の剰余金 (= net profit, profit after tax)
- **net loss** 純損失, 当期純損失, 税引き後赤字, 最終赤字, 赤字決算
- **net premium revenues** 正味収入保険料, 正味保険料収入(正味収入保険料は, 非金融機関の売上高に当たる)
- **net profit** 純利益, 当期純利益, 税引き後利益, 最終黒字
- **net profit per share** 1株当たり純利益
- **net selling** 売り越し

net operating profit 純営業利益, 営業純利益, 金融機関の業務純益

> 業務純益とは ⊃ 銀行の「本業によるもうけ」を, 業務純益という。これは, 貸出金と預金の利息の差から生じる「資金利益」, 手数料などの「役務取引等利益」, 債券の売買益などの「その他業務利益」の合計

から，経費を差し引いて算出する。

net worth 自己資本, 資本, 自己資金, 株主持ち分, 純資産, 正味資産, 正味財産
- high net worth customers 資産家, 富裕層, 富裕な顧客 （＝high net worth clients）
- negative net worth 債務超過
- net worth ratio 自己資本比率 （＝capital adequacy ratio, capital-asset ratio）
- ratio of liabilities to net worth 負債比率
- return on net worth 株主資本利益率
- total liabilities and net worth 総資本

network 名 網状組織, 関連組織, 連絡網, 通信網, 回線網, 回路網, 網, 通信ネットワーク, ネットワーク
- interbank network 銀行間ネットワーク
- nationwide network 全国ネットワーク
- network appliance ネットワーク家電
- network configuration ネットワーク構成
- neural network 神経回路網, 神経回線網, ニューラル・ネットワーク
- wide area network 広域通信網, 広域ネットワーク《略 WAN》

netbook 名 ネットブック（小型・軽量・安価で機能を絞ったパソコン）

neurotoxin 名 神経毒

neurotransmitter 名 神経伝達物質
- neurotransmitter dopamine 神経伝達物質ドーパミン

neutral 形 中立の, 中性の, 灰色の, ニュートラル
- neutral budget 中立予算, 均衡予算
- neutral equilibrium effect 中立的均衡効果
- neutral policy 中立的政策（景気に影響を与えない政策）
- neutral shift 中立的移行
- neutral stance 〈引締めと緩和の両にらみの〉中立の姿勢
- return to neutral 中立に戻る
- switch the monetary policy from tighter to neutral 金融政策を引締め気味から中立に転換［変更］する
- take a neutral stance on …について中立の姿勢［スタンス］を取る

neutrino 名 ニュートリノ
- neutrino astronomy ニュートリノ天文学
- neutrino detector ニュートリノ観測装置, 素粒子観測装置

new 形 新規の, 新しい, 人に知られていない, 不案内の, 新任の, 珍しい, 不慣れな, ニュー

- new broom 新任の改革推進者, 改革に意欲的な新任者, 新任者, ニュー・リーダー
- New China News Agency 新華社通信 （＝Xinhua）
- New Civil Rights Act 新公民権法
- new deal market 発行市場
- new high 新高値, 過去最高値, 空前の高値, 過去最高, 最高記録, 新最高記録
- new international economic order 新国際経済秩序《略 NIEO》
- new issuance of government bonds 国債の新規発行, 国債の新規発行額
- new low 新安値, 安値, 最低記録, 空前の安値, 過去最低
- new middleman ニュー・ミドルマン（顧客の購買代理店の役割を果たすビジネスで, 顧客の特定のニーズに関連する商品や情報を集めて提供し, その購入を支援するビジネスのこと）
- new wave 新しい波, 新思潮, 新傾向, ヌーベル・バーグ, ニュー・ウェーブ （＝nouvelle vague）

New Deal 革新政策, ニュー・ディール政策, ニュー・ディール（1933年の世界的不況の際にとられたルーズベルト大統領の経済復興と社会保障を柱とした経済再建政策）
- Green New Deal グリーン・ニューディール（環境やエネルギー分野への重点的な投資で, 景気刺激や雇用創出を実現する政策）

New Dealer ニュー・ディール政策支持者［推進者］

New Dealish ニュー・ディールにふさわしい, ニュー・ディールに適した

New Dealism ニュー・ディール的政策, ニュー・ディール支持

new economy 新しい経済, ニューエコノミー（＝digital economy, e-economy：インターネットを使った新しい経済システム。自動車, 建設, 不動産, 繊維, 流通などの成熟産業を指すオールドエコノミーに対して, インターネット・ベンチャーやドットコム企業, IT関連の産業や企業を指す）

new-fangled [newfangled] 形 新型の, 最新式の, はやりの, 新奇な, 新しがりやの

New York 〈米〉ニューヨーク市（New York City, NYC）, ニューヨーク州（New York State, NY）, ニューヨーク（愛称はニューヨーク市がthe (Big) Apple, Fun City, Empire Cityで, ニューヨーク州がthe Empire State）
- Federal Reserve Bank of New York ニューヨーク連邦準備銀行

New York capital market ニューヨーク資本市場
New York Commodity Exchange ニューヨーク商品取引所《略 Comex》
New York Daily News ニューヨーク・デイリー・ニューズ（米国の大衆誌）
New York Dow ニューヨーク・ダウ（ダウ・ジョーンズ社の修正平均株価）
New York Fed ニューヨーク連銀
New York foreign exchange market ニューヨーク為替市場
New York Mercantile Exchange ニューヨーク商業取引所, ニューヨーク・マーカンタイル取引所《略 NYMEX [Nymex]》
New York money market ニューヨーク金融市場
New York Stock Exchange ニューヨーク証券取引所《略 NYSE》（＝Big Board）
New York Times ニューヨーク・タイムズ（米国の代表的日刊紙）

newcomer [new comer] 图 新規参入企業, 新規参入組, 新規参入者, 新規参入業者, 新規事業者, 新任, 新人, 新入社員, 新メンバー, 初心者, ずぶの素人, 新たに台頭・出現してきたもの（⇒latecomer）

newly 副 新たに, 新しく, 最近, 近頃
  newly developing Big Five 新ビッグ5, 新ビッグ・ファイブ（開発途上国のなかの経済大国。中国, インドネシア, ブラジル, インド, ロシアの5か国）
  newly industrializing economies 新興工業国, 新興工業経済群《略 NIEs [NIES]》（＝newly industrialized economies, newly industrializing countries：アジアの韓国, 台湾, 香港, シンガポール, 中南米のアルゼンチン, メキシコ, ブラジルなどを指す。）
  newly rated issuer 新規格付け発行体

news 图 情報, 知らせ, 便り, 近況, 消息, 報道, 報道情報, 記事, ニュース番組, 真新しいこと, 材料, 統計, 指標, ニュース
  economic news 景気指標, 経済指標
  disappointing news 悪材料
  disturbing news 弱気材料
  friendly news 好材料
  news account ニュース記事
  news advisory ニュースねたの提供
  news agency 通信社（＝news service, wire service）
  news agent 新聞［雑誌］販売業者（＝news-agent, newsdealer）
  news analyst ニュース解説者, ニュース解説委員
  news anchor ニュース番組司会者
  news blackout 報道管制
  news broadcast ニュース放送
  news bulletin 〈短い〉ニュース放送, ニュース速報
  news commentary 時事解説
  news commentator 時事解説者
  news conference [briefing] 記者会見（＝press conference）
  news coverage 新聞報道, 取材
  news flash ニュース速報, ニュース特報, ニュース・フラッシュ（＝newsflash）
  news hole 記事用紙面, 記事用誌面, 記事面, 記事スペース（新聞広告以外のスペース）
  news hound 新聞記者
  news on inflation インフレ指標
  news peg ニュース・ペグ（ニュース・リリースのうち特にニュース性のある重要な要因）
  news [press] release ニュース配信, ニュース発表, ニュース・リリース
  news report ニュース報道
  news reporter 報道番組レポーター
  news room ニュース編集室, 新聞［雑誌］閲覧室（＝newsroom）
  news service 通信社（＝news agency, wire service）
  news show ニュース番組（＝news program）
  news sources 情報源
  news story 報道記事
  on the news これを受けて, この報道を受けて, このニュースを受けて
  price news 物価統計

newsagent 图 新聞販売業者, 雑誌販売業者（＝news agent, newsdealer）
newsbeat 图 〈新聞記者の〉取材担当区域, 持ち場（＝beat）
newsbrief 图 ニュース短信
newscast 图 ニュース放送, ニュース放送番組
newscaster 图 ニュース番組放送者（newsreader）, 新聞記者, 報道記者（＝newsman）
newsdealer 图 新聞販売人［販売業者］, 雑誌販売人［販売業者］（＝newsagent）
newsflash 图 ニュース速報, 緊急重大ニュース（＝news flash）
news-gatherer 图 ニュース記事収集者, ニュース記事取材者

newsgroup 名 ニューズグループ（共通の関心を持つインターネット加入者同士の情報交換グループで，NetNewsのグループ）

newshound 名 新聞記者，報道記者，事件記者，記者（＝newshawk）

newsletter 名 社報，公報，回報，回報，PR誌，年報，月報，報告書，時事開設，時事通信，ニューズレター（＝news-sheet）

newsmagazine 名 時事週刊誌，週刊情報誌，ニュース雑誌

newsmaker 名 時の人，ニュースに登場する人，ニュース種になる人，報道価値のある事件［人］，話題の出来事

newsman 名 新聞記者(reporter)，報道記者，ジャーナリスト，新聞売り子［配達人］（＝newscaster）

newsmonger 名 ゴシップ屋，うわさ好き

newspaper 名 新聞，新聞紙，新聞社
- **newspaper advertising ethical code** 新聞広告倫理綱領
- **newspaper drop** 新聞回収箱
- **Newspaper in Education** 「教育に新聞を」，エヌ・アイ・イー（⇒NIE）
- **special-interest newspaper** 特殊新聞，業界新聞

newspaperman 名 新聞記者，新聞編集者，新聞経営者，ジャーナリスト

newsperson 名 報道記者，ニュース報道記者，レポーター，ニュース報道に携わる人ニュース担当者，ニュース・キャスター（複数形＝newspeople）

newsprint 名 新聞印刷用紙，新聞用紙

newsreader 名 ニュース番組放送者，ニュース放送担当者，ニュース・アナウンサー（＝newscaster）

newsreel 名 ニュース映画

newsroom 名 ニュース編集室

newsstand 名 新聞［雑誌］売店，新聞売り場，新聞販売店，キオスク

newstime 名 ニュース時間

newsworthy 名 話題の，報道価値のある，ニュース・バリューのある，ニュースになる

newsy 形 話題の豊富な，ニュースの豊富な，話好きな，うわさ好きな，名 新聞売り，新聞配達人

NEXI 日本貿易保険（Nippon Export and Investment Insuranceの略）

next generation 次世代
- **next generation medicine** 次世代新薬

NGH 天然ガス・ハイドレート（natural gas hydrateの略）
▶ *NGH* stabilizes as a solid at around minus 20 C. 天然ガス・ハイドレート(NGH)は，マイナス20度前後で固形状態が安定する。

NGO 民間活動団体，非政府組織，非政府機関，非政府団体（non-governmental [nongovernmental] organizationの略）

NHTSA 米全国高速道路交通安全局，米全国高速道路安全局，米全国高速道路交通安全局（National Highway Traffic Safety Administrationの略）

NICU 新生児集中治療室（neonatal intensive care unitの略。保育器や人工呼吸器，輸血・点滴器具などを備えて，早産による超未熟児や重病を持った新生児を集中的に治療する病棟）

niche 名 特定分野［領域］，分野，領域，すき間，適所，適した場所［地位］，ふさわしい地位，ニッチ
- **niche business** 得意分野
- **niche industry** すき間産業，ニッチ産業
- **niche market** ニッチ市場，市場の特定分野，すき間市場
- **niche marketing** すき間市場販売戦略，ニッチ・マーケティング（未開発のすき間市場・ニッチ市場への適応をめざすマーケティング）
- **niche strategy** ニッチ戦略
- **specialized niche** 得意分野

NICs [NICS] 新興工業国［工業群］，中進工業国（newly industrialized [industrializing] countriesの略）

NIE エヌ・アイ・イー，「教育に新聞を」（Newspaper in Educationの略。新聞各社から新聞の提供を受け，新聞を学習教材として活用する学習活動のこと）

Nielsen research ニールセン調査

NIEs [NIES] 新興工業経済地域，新興工業経済群（newly industrializing [industrialized] economiesの略）

night 名 夜，夜間，夜中，夕べ，宿泊，暗黒，ナイト
- **night duty [shift]** 夜勤
- **night duty allowance** 夜勤手当
- **night fighter** 夜間迎撃機
- **night latch [lock]** 防犯錠
- **night mart** 株の夜間市場，夜間取引市場（＝night market, nighttime market, nighttime marketplace）
- **night safe [depository]** 夜間金庫（＝night deposit safe）
- **night shift bonus** 夜勤手当

night spot ナイトクラブ, ナイトスポット
night trading [session] 夜間取引
night watch 夜警
night watchman 夜警員
nightmare 名 悪夢, 恐ろしい経験［状況, 出来事］, 厄介なこと
　have a nightmare うなされる, 悪夢を見る, 恐ろしい経験をする
　nightmare scenario 悪夢のシナリオ, 最悪のシナリオ
Nikkei index 日経平均 （=Nikkei Index）
Nikkei Stock Average 日経平均株価, 日経株価平均, 日経平均 （=the benchmark Nikkei index）

> 日経平均株価とは ⊃ 株式相場全体の動きを示す指標の一つ。東証一部上場の代表的な225社の株価合計を, 一定の除数で割って算出する。除数は調整値で, 株式分割や銘柄入れ替えのときに変更する。東証株価指数（TOPIX）が銀行株など時価総額の大きい株価の動きに敏感なのに対して, 日経平均はハイテク株の組入れ比重が高く, ハイテク株の動きに左右されやすい。

nine-figure 形 9桁の数字の, 億単位の, 数億ドルの
nip 動 妨げる, 阻止する, …の腰を折る, 摘み取る, ひったくる, 盗む, 辛勝する, 小差で敵を破る
　nip ... in (the) bud …をつぼみのうちに摘み取る, …を未然に防ぐ, …を徹底的に阻止する
　nip in with a smart question すかさず気のきいた質問をする
　nip one's plot …の陰謀を阻む
nip and tuck 五分五分で（neck and neck）, 互角で, 負けず劣らずの, 整形手術（plastic surgery）
Nippon Export and Investment Insurance 日本貿易保険 《略 NEXI》（独立行政法人）
nitrogen oxides 窒素酸化物 《略 NOx》
nitty-gritty 名 本質, 核心, 肝心なこと, 基本, 基本的事実, 厳しい現実, 厳然たる真実
　get down [come] to the nitty-gritty 核心に触れる, 核心に入る, 事実［実情］を直視する, 根本問題に迫る
nix 動 否決する, 否認する, 否定する, 拒絶する, 禁止する, 名 無（nothing）, 皆無, 拒否, 拒絶
No. 10 [Number Ten] Downing Street ダウニング街10番地, 英国首相官邸, 英国政府 （=Number Ten）
no-holds-barred 形 制限のない, 束縛のない, 無制限の, やりたい放題の, 遠慮のない, どんな手を使っても構わない, 型破りの
Nobel 名 〈ダイナマイト発明者の〉アルフレッド・ベルンハルト・ノーベル, ノーベル賞, ノーベル（ノーベル賞は, 物理学, 化学, 生理学・医学, 経済学, 文学, 平和の各部門で功績のあった人物・組織に対して毎年贈られる）
　Nobel laureate ノーベル賞受賞者
　Nobel Committee ノーベル賞委員会
　Nobel Memorial Prize in Economic Science ノーベル経済学賞
　Nobel Peace Prize ノーベル平和賞
　Nobel prize [award] ノーベル賞
　Nobel Prize for Peace ノーベル平和賞 （=Nobel peace prize）
　Nobel Prize in Chemistry ノーベル化学賞
　Nobel Prize in Economics ノーベル経済学賞
　Nobel Prize in Literature ノーベル文学賞
　Nobel Prize in [for] Medicine ノーベル医学賞
　Nobel Prize in Physics ノーベル物理学賞
　Nobel Prize in Physiology ノーベル生理学賞
　Nobel Prize in Physiology or Medicine ノーベル生理学・医学賞
Nobelist 名 ノーベル賞受賞者
nominal 形 名目の, 名目上の, 名目ベースの, 名義上の
　nominal capital 公称資本, 名目資本 （=authorized capital, nominal share capital）
　nominal GDP 名目GDP（国内総生産）, 名目GDP成長率
　nominal gross domestic product 名目国内総生産（GDP）, 名目GDP
　nominal growth 名目成長率
　nominal growth rate 名目成長率 （=nominal growth）
　nominal interest rate 表面利率, 名目金利 （=nominal interest, nominal rate of interest）
nominal terms 名目, 名目ベース（実質=real terms）
　in nominal terms 名目で, 名目ベースで
　the GDP growth in nominal terms 名目GDPの成長率
nominate 動 指名する, 推薦する, 指名推薦する, 推挙する, 任命する（appoint）, ノミネートする
　be nominated for a best actress award 最優秀女優賞［主演女優賞］にノミネートされる, 最

優秀女優賞[主演女優賞]候補に指名される
- **be nominated for president [the Presidency]** 大統領候補に推薦される
- **nominate a person to [for] a public office** …を公職に任命する

nominee 名 米大統領候補, 米大統領候補被指名者, 公認候補者, 候補者
- **nominees for the Grammy Awards** グラミー賞候補者
- **presidential nominee** 大統領候補, 大統領候補被指名者

nonaggression treaty 不可侵条約 (= nonaggression pact)

nonagricultural products 非農産品 (= nonfarm products)

nonaligned [non-aligned] 形 非同盟の, 中立の
- **nonaligned countries** 非同盟諸国
- **nonaligned countries [nations] summit** 非同盟諸国首脳会議
- **nonaligned states** 非同盟国家

nonalignment 名 非同盟

noncandidacy 名 立候補不表明, 不出馬表明, 不出場

noncombat troop 非戦闘部隊

noncombatant 名 非戦闘員

noncompetitive contract 随意契約

nonconfidence 名 不信任
- **noconfidence motion** 不信任案 (nonconfidence bill), 不信任決議案
- **noconfidence vote** 不信任決議案の投票

nonconformist 名 反体制の人, 反体制派, 非協力者

noncontributory plan 非拠出年金制度, 非拠出型退職金制度

noncore business 非中核事業, 非主力事業

nonelite bureaucrats ノンキャリア

nonexistent 形 実在しない, 存在しない, 架空の
- **nonexistent address** 実在しないアドレス
- **nonexistent phone number** 架空電話番号

nonfast-track 形 ノンキャリアの

nonfinancial 形 金融以外の, 非金融, 金融を除く
- **nonfinancial company** 非金融会社, 金融以外の会社, 金融を除く会社
- **nonfinancial entity** 非金融事業体
- **nonfinancial institution** 非金融機関, 金融機関以外の企業, 金融機関を除く企業

nonlethal weapon 殺傷までには至らない武器

nonlife insurance company 損害保険会社, 損保会社 (= casualty insurance company, nonlife insurance firm, nonlife insurer)

nonlife insurance policy 損害保険証券, 損害保険, 損保

nonlife insurer 損害保険会社, 損保会社, 損保 (= nonlife insurance company)

nonmanagerial employee 一般社員, 非管理職

nonmanufacturer 名 非製造業, 非製造業者 (= nonmanufacturing business)

nonmanufacturing business 非製造業 (= nonmanufacturer)

nonmanufacturing sector 非製造業, 非製造部門, 非製造業セクター (= nonmanufacturing businesses)

nonnuclear 形 非核の, 核兵器ぬきの, 核兵器[核エネルギー]を使わない
- **three nonnuclear principles of not producing, possessing or introducing nuclear weapons** 核兵器を作らず, 持たず, 持ち込ませずの非核3原則

nonpartisan [nonpartizan] 名 党派に属さない[無所属の]人, 超党派の人, 超党派

nonpayment of insurance benefits [claims, money] 保険金の不払い

nonperforming loans 不良債権, 不良貸付け, 貸倒れ (= bad debts, uncollectible loans)

nonpermanent member of the U.N. Security Council 国連安全保障理事会の非常任理事国

nonprescription drugs 市販薬, 一般用医薬品

nonprofit corporation 非営利法人

nonprofit foundation 公益法人 (= public interest corporation, public service corporation, public utilities corporation)

nonproliferation 名 拡散防止, 不拡散
- **nonproliferation regime** 拡散防止体制
- **nonproliferation strategy** 拡散防止戦略
- **Non-Proliferation Treaty** 核拡散防止条約, 核不拡散条約《略 NPT》

nonrefundable agreement 不返還特約

nonregular employee 非正規雇用者

nonregular worker 非正規労働者, 非正規

社員（⇒regular worker）

nonresident investor 外国人投資家, 海外投資家, 非居住者投資家（「外国人投資家」は, 年金基金や資産運用会社, ヘッジ・ファンドなど, 欧米の機関投資家の総称として使われる）

nonsterilization 名 非不胎化

nontariff [non-tariff] 形 非関税の
 nontariff barrier 非関税障壁（= nontariff trade barrier）
 nontariff items 非関税商品, 非関税品目
 nontariff trade barrier 非関税貿易障壁《略 NTB》

nontaxable 形 非課税の, 課税対象とならない, 課税対象外の, 免税の
 nontaxable goods 非課税品
 nontaxable income 非課税所得
 nontaxable investment 免税投資
 nontaxable revenue 非課税収益
 nontaxable securities 非課税有価証券, 免税有価証券
 nontaxable write-off 無税償却
 nontaxable write-off of bad loans 不良債権の無税償却（= tax-free disposal of bad loans）

nonworking labor force 非労働力人口（= nonworking population）

nonworking population 非労働力人口

norm 名 基準, 規範, 規準, 標準(standard), 一般標準, 水準, 模範, 典型, 標準的な方式［やり方］, 平均, 平均学力, 達成基準, 要求水準, 基準労働量, ノルマ, 責任量, 責任生産量
 above [beyond] the norm of …の平均以上
 behavioral norms 行動規範, 社会通念
 cultural norms 文化的規範, 社会規範
 industry-wide norm 業界標準
 production norms 責任生産量, 生産ノルマ
 solvency norms 支払い能力規制

normal trade relations 正常通商関係

normalization 名 正常化, 標準化, 規格化, 正規化, 共通基準値決定
 financial normalization 金融正常化
 normalization negotiations 正常化交渉（= normalization talks）
 normalization of bilateral ties 国交正常化, 二国間関係の正常化
 normalization of diplomatic relations [ties] 外交関係の正常化, 国交正常化
 normalization talks 正常化交渉, 国交正常化

交渉

normalize 動 正常化する, 平常化する
 normalizing relations 関係正常化

norovirus 名 ノロウイルス
> ノロウイルス ⇒ 口から入り, 人間の腸で増えて下痢や腹痛, 嘔吐を起こす。カキなどの貝類を生食した場合の食中毒が知られるが, 患者の吐瀉物などを通じて感染する場合が多い。かつて「小型球形ウイルス」と呼ばれていたが, 2002年から国際的に「ノロウイルス」に名称が統一された。

North American Securities Administrators Association 北米証券行政官協会

North Atlantic Treaty Organization 北大西洋条約機構《略 NATO》

nosedive 動 急減する, 急落する, 暴落する, 急速に悪化する, 名 暴落, 急落

nosocomial (hospital) infection 院内感染

notch 動 記録する, 樹立する, 収める, 得る, 獲得する
 notch the benchmark rate lower 政策金利を引き下げる

notch 名 段階, 級, 程度, 順位, ノッチ
▶ The unemployment rate dipped down a *notch* to 5.5 percent last month, from 5.6 percent in June. 先月の失業率は, 6月の5.6%から5.5%に1ノッチ(0.1ポイント)減少した。

note 名 手形, 約束手形, 証券, 債券, 債権表示証書, 紙幣, 通知書, 文書, 書類, 伝票, 覚書, 注釈, 注記, 解説, 注意, 注意事項, 注意書き, 但し書き, 原稿, 手記, 短信, 書き置き, 音符, 音色, 調子, 印象, 特徴, 特色, ノート(証券の「ノート」は一般に中期の債務証券を指すが, 米財務省証券に対して使うときは, 償還期限が1年超10年以内の中期証券のことをいう)
 auditing for note receivable 受取手形監査
 cautionary note 注意書き
 compare notes 意見を交換する, 印象［経験］を話し合う
 contract note 契約書
 delivery note 配達証明書
 diplomatic note 外交文書
 explanatory notes 内容解説
 hit [strike] the right note 適切な意見を述べる
 loan on note 手形貸付け
 note of resignation 辞職届
 original notes 原作者による注釈

notice — **nuclear**

premium note　保険料支払い約束手形
private note　私募債
savings note　貯蓄債券
secured note　担保付き手形
sick note　傷病診断書
sight note　一覧払い約束手形, 一覧払い手形
speak without notes　原稿なしで話す
take note of　…に注意［注目, 留意］する
ten-year note auction　米国債10年物の入札
unpaid note　不渡り手形
warrant-attached note　ワラント債
worthy of note　注目に値する

notice 名　通知, 通告, 予告, 警告, 掲示, ビラ, 紙上紹介, 批評, 寸評
assessment notice　課税通知書
at short notice　即刻, すぐ, ほとんど予告なしで
bankruptcy notice　破産告知
dismissal notice　解雇通知
legal notice　法的通知
notice board　掲示板
public notice　公告
take notice of　…に注意を払う, …に基づいて行動する

ウェブ上の法的通知（legal notice）の種類：

copy right	著作権
disclaimer	権利放棄条項, 免責条項
privacy policy	プライバシー規定
registered trademark	商標権
terms of use	利用規約

noticeable 形　人目を引く, 目に付く, 目立つ, 注目に値する, 顕著な, 著しい, 重大な, 明確な, 明快な

notification 名　通知, 通知書, 通報, 通告, 届け出, 告示, 公告, 告知, 催告
legal notification　法定公告
notification period　告示期間
notification of statute　設立文書

novel 形　新規な, 奇抜な, 斬新な, 革新的な, 新手の

no-win situation　勝ち目のない状況, 成功しそうにない状況, 絶望的状況

NPT　核拡散防止条約（**Nuclear Nonproliferation Treaty**の略）

NSC　米国家安全保障会議（**National Security Council**の略）

nuclear 形　核の, 核に関する, 核兵器の, 核燃料の, 原子力の, 原子力利用の, 名 核エネルギー

go nuclear　核兵器保有国となる, 核兵器を保有［使用］するようになる, 核武装する
nuclear abolition　核廃絶
nuclear accident　原子力事故（＝N-accident）
nuclear activities　核開発活動, 核活動
nuclear armament　核武装
nuclear arms　核兵器（＝nuclear weapon）
nuclear arsenal　核兵器, 核兵器の備蓄, 核兵器貯蔵施設, 核兵器保有量
nuclear attack　核攻撃
nuclear base　核兵器基地, 核兵器発射基地
nuclear bomb　核爆弾
nuclear button　核攻撃開始命令のボタン
nuclear capacity　核兵器保有数量
nuclear chain reaction　核連鎖反応
nuclear club　核クラブ, 核兵器保有国グループ（米・露・英・仏・中など）
nuclear deterrent　核抑止力（＝nuclear deterrent capability）
nuclear deterrent capabilities　核抑止力
nuclear development program　核開発計画
nuclear device　核爆弾
Nuclear Electro-Magnetic Pulse　核電磁パルス《略 NEMP》
Nuclear Emergency Search Team　〈米エネルギー省の〉放射性物質緊急探査班, 核緊急捜索チーム
nuclear energy　核エネルギー, 原子力（＝atomic energy）
nuclear engineering　原子工学
nuclear fallout　死の灰, 核爆発による放射性降下物
nuclear family　核家族
nuclear fusion reactor　核融合炉
nuclear grapeshot　小型戦術核兵器
Nuclear Industry Radioactive Waste Executive　〈英国の〉核廃棄物処理監視機関《略 NIREX》
nuclear inspection　核査察
nuclear magnetic resonance　核磁気共鳴装置《略 MMR》
nuclear medicine　核医学, 放射線治療
nuclear molecule　原子核分子
nuclear non-proliferation　核不拡散, 核核酸防止《略 NNP》
Nuclear Nonproliferation Treaty　核拡散防止条約《略 NPT》(米国, ロシア(旧ソ連), 英国,

フランス，中国の5カ国以外が核兵器を持つことを禁じた条約で，1970年に発効。現在，188カ国が加盟している。インド，パキスタンやイスラエルは未加盟》
nuclear physics 核物理学
Nuclear Posture Review 〈米国の〉核戦力体制見直し《略 NPR》
nuclear proliferation 核拡散
nuclear-propelled 原子力推進の
nuclear-propelled cruiser 原子力巡洋艦
nuclear propulsion 原子力推進, 原子力推進装置
nuclear reaction 核反応
nuclear reactor 原子炉(旧称：atomic pile)
Nuclear Regulatory Commission 米原子力規制委員会《略 NRC》
nuclear resonance 核共鳴
nuclear strike 核攻撃
nuclear supplies group 原子力供給国グループ《略 NSG》
nuclear terrorism 核テロ
nuclear umbrella 核の傘, 核による拡大抑止《核保有国が，同盟国への武力による威嚇攻撃に核兵器で報復する意志と能力を示して，同盟国への威嚇や攻撃を未然に防ぐ仕組み》
nuclear warfare [war] 核戦争
nuclear warhead 核弾頭
nuclear waste 核廃棄物 (＝radioactive waste)
nuclear watchdog agency 核監視機関
nuclear winter 核の冬, 核戦争後の地球規模の寒冷化現象

nuclear fission
nuclear fission chain reaction 核分裂の連鎖反応, 臨界反応
nuclear fission compounds 核分裂生成物

nuclear-free 形
核のない (＝nuke-free)
Nuclear-Free Independent Pacific 非核独立太平洋《略 NFIP》
nuclear-free zone 核保有禁止区域, 非核地帯, 非核武装地帯, 核兵器[原子力]使用禁止地帯

nuclear fuel 核燃料
nuclear fuel cycle 核燃料サイクル
nuclear fuel reprocessing 核燃料の再処理, 使用済み核燃料再処理
nuclear fuel reprocessing plant 核燃料再処理施設, 核燃料再処理工場

nuclear power 原子力, 核エネルギー, 原子力発電, 核保有国 (＝atomic power)
nuclear power generation 原子力発電
nuclear power plant [station] 原子力発電所
nuclear power plant arm 米原発子会社

nuclear-powered 形 原子力を利用した
nuclear-powered ship 原子力船 (＝nuclear ship)
nuclear-powered submarine 原子力潜水艦

nuclear weapon 核兵器 (＝atomic weapon)
HEU-type nuclear weapon HEU（高濃縮ウラン）型核兵器（HEU＝highly enriched uranium）

nucleic acid amplification test 核酸増幅検査, NAT検査（HIVの抗体を検出する）

nuisance 名
迷惑な人[もの], 厄介, 生活妨害, ニューサンス
nuisance e-mail 迷惑メール

nuke 名 核兵器, 原子力発電所
nuke-free world 核のない世界, 核兵器のない世界

number 名
数, 数字, 数値, 統計, 番号, 番地, 度数, 指数, 総数, 件数, 人数, 曲目, 演目, 好ましい物[商品], 好ましい状況[事態, 仕事], ナンバー
a number of three figures 3桁の数
box number 私書箱番号
cardinal number 基数
do a number on …に危害を与える, …をあざ笑う, …を口汚くののしる
economic numbers 景気指標
even number 偶数
inflation numbers インフレ統計
integral number 整数
number one 主要人物, 中心人物, 実力者, 最高実力者
number portability system 〈携帯電話の〉番号持ち運び制度 (＝mobile number portability system, MNP system)
number two 2番目の実力者
numbers 多数, 多数派, 多勢
numbers-juggling 数字合わせ (＝numbers game)
Number Ten 英首相官邸, 英国政府 (⇒No. 10 [Number Ten] Downing Street)
odd number 奇数
one's number …の仲間, 集団, グループ
payroll numbers 雇用統計
PIN [personal identification] number 個人暗証番号

    preliminary number　速報値
    price numbers　物価指数
    random number　乱数
    real [actual] number　実数
    round number　概数
    serial number　通し番号
    the index number of prices　物価指数
    the number of open positions　求人数
    trade numbers　貿易統計
numerical 形　数の, 数に関する
    numerical target　数値目標
numeronym 名　数略語, ヌメロニム（長い英単語を数字で省略して表現する語; i18n＝internationalization, d11n＝documentationなど）
nursing 名　看護
    nursing facilities　保育施設
    nursing home　特別擁護老人ホーム, 老人ホーム, 療養所,〈私営の〉個人病院
    nursing leave system　介護休業制度（＝the holiday for nurse system）
    nursing mother　乳母, 養母
    nursing officer　〈病院の〉婦長
nursing care　介護
    nursing care at home　在宅介護（＝at-home nursing care）
    nursing care benefits　介護給付
    nursing care business　介護事業
    nursing care insurance system　介護保険制度, 介護保険（＝nursing care system）
    nursing care service　介護サービス（＝nursing services）
    nursing-care taxi service　介護タクシー
    nursing care worker　介護福祉士
nurture 動　育てる, 育む, 養育する, 教育する, しつける, 養成する, 育成する, 助長する, 促進する, …を心に抱く, …に栄養物を与える
    nurture public distrust in　…に対する国民の不信を助長する
    nurture senior management　経営陣を育成する
nutritional balance　栄養のバランス
nuts and bolts　基本, 本質, 土台, 大枠, 基本的問題, 仕組み,〈機械の〉作動部分, 可動部, 主眼点, 詳細な段取り, 実務面での細部, 実際, 実際面, 実地細目
    the nuts and bolts of corporate management　企業経営の実際
nuts-and-bolts 形　基本的な, 主要な, 主眼の, 実際的な, 実践的な
NYMEX　ニューヨーク・マーカンタイル取引所, ニューヨーク商業取引所（⇒New York Mercantile Exchange）
NYSE　ニューヨーク証券取引所（＝Big Board: New York Stock Exchangeの略）
    NYSE Composite Index　NYSE総合株価指数, ニューヨーク証券取引所総合株価指数（＝NYSE composite index）
NYSE Euronext　NYSEユーロネクスト（ニューヨーク証券取引所を運営するNYSEグループと, パリ, オランダなど欧州の取引所を統括するユーロネクストが合併して設立された持ち株会社）

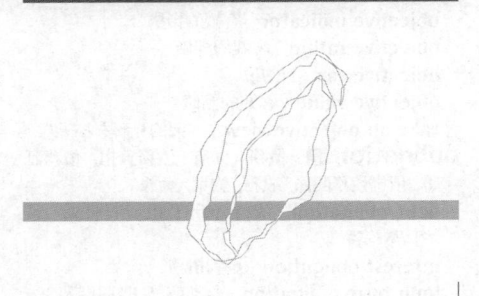

O

OAPEC アラブ石油輸出国機構, オアペック (Organization of Arab Petroleum Exporting Countriesの略)
OAS 米州機構 (Organization of American Statesの略)
oasis 名 憩い[くつろぎ, 気晴らし, 慰め]の場, 憩いの時, オアシス
oath 名 誓い, 宣誓
 a false oath 偽誓
 an official oath 就任時の宣誓 (=an oath of office)
 break [violate] the oath 誓いを破る
 on [under, upon] oath 誓って, 誓いを立てて, 宣誓して, 宣誓の上
 swear [make, take] an oath 誓う, 誓いを立てる, 宣誓する
 swear an oath of allegiance to …に忠誠を誓う
 take [recite] the oath 宣誓を行う
 take the (official) oath of office as the 44th president of the United States 第44代米国大統領就任の宣誓をする
 testimony under oath 宣誓証言
 the mayor's oath of office 市長就任の宣誓
 the oath of a juror 陪審員の宣誓
OAU アフリカ統一機構 (Organization of African Unityの略)
obesity 名 肥満
obituary 名 死亡記事, 死亡記事広告, 訃報 (=obit)
 obituary column 死亡記事欄, 死亡欄 (=obit column)
 obituary notices 死亡記事, 死亡広告 (=death notices)
object 名 物体, 固体, 対象, 目的, 目標, ねらい, オブジェクト
 attain one's object …の目的[目標]を達成する
 barter object 物々交換の対象[対象物]
 object lesson 〈教訓の〉よい実例, 実物教育
 object of taxation 課税の対象, 課税物件
 object of the exercise 実際の目的, 隠された目的
 object-oriented concept オブジェクト指向[志向]概念
 policy object 政策目標
 sex object 性的対象
objective 名 目標, 目的, 対象, 目的地
 economic policy objective 経済政策目標
 financial policy objective 金融政策目標
 fiscal policy objective 財政政策目標
 international policy objective 対外政策目標
 intertemporal objective 異時的目標
 medium-term objective 中期目標
 objective of financial reporting 財務報告の目的
 short-term objective 短期目標, 目先の目標
objective 形 客観的な, 客観的目標に基づく, 個人的な感情を交えない(impartial), 事実に基づく, 実在の, 本当の, 目的の, 目標の
 objective commercial act 営業的行為
 objective determinant 客観的決定要因, 客観的決定因

obligation

- objective factor 客観的要因
- objective indicator 客観的指標
- objective rating 客観的評価
- objective tax 目的税
- objective value 客観的価値
- take an objective view 客観的見解をとる

obligation 图 債務, 負債, 債務負担, 債務証書, 債権債務関係, 義務, 約束, 金銭
- debt obligation 債務, 債務負担, 債務証書, 債務契約書
- interest obligation 金利債務
- long term obligation 長期債務, 長期借入金
- obligation to secrecy 守秘義務
- obligations hereunder 本契約に基づく義務, 本契約上の義務(hereunder＝under this agreement)
- payment obligation 支払い債務, 支払い義務
- pension obligation 年金債務
- waiver of obligation 債務免除

observer 图 観測筋, 市場観測者, 消息筋, 評論家, 傍聴者, 立会人, 目撃者, 航空偵察員, 機上観測員, 監視員, 国連派遣団員, 〈法律や習慣を〉守る人, 遵法者, オブザーバー
- industry observer 業界筋
- international observers from the United Nations 国連からの国際監視団

obsession 图 頭から離れない人[こと], 強迫観念, 固定観念, 執念, 執着, 妄想

obstetric hospital 産科医院

obstruction 图 妨害, じゃま, 妨げ, 障害, 支障, 妨害行為, 障害物, 詰まり, 議事妨害, 〈道路の〉遮断, 腸閉塞, オブストラクション
- a bowel obstruction 腸閉塞
- an obstruction to progress 進行の妨げ
- the obstruction of justice 裁判の妨害

obstructionism 图 議事妨害, 議事妨害行為

obstructive tactics 妨害戦術

obtain 動 取得する, 調達する, 入手する, 獲得する（＝acquire）
▶ External funds required to meet the additional cash requirements of at least $300 million in 2010 are expected to be *obtained* by offering debt securities in the market. 2010年には外部調達資金として少なくとも3億ドルの追加資金必要額が発生しますが, この資金は市場で債券を募集発行して調達する予定です。

OCC 米財務省通貨監督局 (**Office of the Comptroller of the Currency**の略)

occasion 图 時, 場合, 理由, 根拠, 理由付け, 原因, 引き金, 機会, 好機, 絶好[最適]の時期, 催し, 行事, イベント, 儀式
- an occasion for fear 恐怖の原因
- be equal to the occasion 困難な事態にうまく対処する, 臨機応変の処置をとる, 機に臨んで立派な働きを見せる
- choose one's occasion 好機を選ぶ
- for the occasion 臨時に
- give occasion to …を引き起こす
- if the occasion arises [should arise] 機会があれば, 必要が起きたら, いざという場合には
- improve the occasion 機会を利用する
- on great occasions 大祝典の日に
- on the first occasion 機会のあり次第
- on the occasion of …という大切な日に, …という重要な行事で, …の折に
- rise to the occasion 難局に対処する, 困難な事態にうまく対処する
- take [seize] (the) occasion to 機会を利用して…する, 機に乗じて…する, …する好機をとらえる

occupancy 图 占有, 現実の所有, 実際の居住, 占有期間, 所有期間
- occupancy rate 搭乗率, 利用率

occupation 图 職業, 仕事, 職, 業種, 〈仕事などに〉従事すること, 占領, 占拠, 制圧, 支配, 〈地位などの〉保有, 暇つぶし, 娯楽, 余暇の過ごし方
- business occupation 営利業務
- during one's occupation of office 在職中に
- intellectual occupation 知的職業
- occupation army [force] 占領軍
- occupation census 職業統計調査
- occupation disease 職業病
- occupation road 〈私設の〉専用道路
- occupation structure 就業構造 (＝structure of occupation)
- professional occupation system 専門職制度
- regular occupation 定職
- seek occupation 職を求める
- skilled occupation 熟練を要する仕事

occupational 形 職業の, 職業上の, 占領の
- occupational disease 職業病 (＝industrial disease)
- occupational hazard 職業上の危険
- Occupational Safety and Health Review Commission 米労働安全衛生審査委員会
- occupational therapy 作業療法

occupy 動 占領する, 占有する, 〈空間, 場所を〉

占める[使用する], 〈注意などを〉引く, 〈時間を〉費やす
be occupied in …で忙しい
occupy an important position 重要な地位につく, 重要な地位を占める
occupy oneself with …に専念する, …に没頭する, …に一生懸命だ

ocean 名 海, 海洋, 大海原, …洋, …海, オーシャン
ocean bottom 海底
ocean current 海流
ocean disposal of waste 廃棄物海洋投棄
ocean engineering 海洋工学
ocean greyhound 快速汽船
ocean lane [route] 海洋航路, 遠洋航路
ocean liner 遠洋定期船, 大洋航路船, 大洋航路定期船
ocean resources 海洋資源
ocean tramp 遠洋不定期船
oceans of trouble 多くの困難

oceanic 形 大洋の, 海洋の, 外洋域の, 遠洋の, 海底の, 広々とした, 大洋州の
oceanic climate 海洋性気候, 海洋気候
oceanic resources 海底資源

ODA 政府開発援助 (**official development assistance**の略)
net disbursements of ODA ODAの純支出額
ODA donee ODA被供与国, ODA被援助国
ODA donor 政府開発援助供与国, ODA供与国, ODA援助国
ODA recipient ODA受入れ国

odd-even allocation 奇数偶数番方式配給制

odds 名 不平等, 不均等, 優劣, 有利な条件, ハンディキャップ, 見込み, 可能性, 確率, 公算, 勝ち目, 勝算, 勝てる度合い, 歩(ぶ), 賭け率, 優勢, 争い, 不和, 強敵, オッズ
a bit over odds 法外に, とてつもなく, ちょっとありそうにない
against (all) the odds ありそうにない[不可能な]ように見えるにもかかわらず, 非常な困難にもかかわらず
at odds of 10-3 10対3の賭け率で, 10対3の確率で
be at odds with …とけんかしている, …と争っている, …と対立する, …と戦う, …と意見が合わない
be odds over …をめぐって対立している[争っている], …で反目している

beat the odds 強敵を打ち負かす
by (all, long) odds はるかに, 断然, 確かに, 疑いもなく, あらゆる点で, 十中八九は
charge over the odds 法外な金を請求する
even odds 五分五分のチャンス, 五分五分の確率
great odds 大変な困難
heavy [great, terrible] odds 恐ろしい敵
lay [give] odds 有利な条件を与える, ハンディキャップを与える
long odds 勝ち目が薄い確率, 大差の確率, まったく起こりそうにないこと, 見込みがほとんどないこと, 強敵, 強い相手
make no odds 釣り合っている
odds and ends がらくた(bits and pieces), くず物, 半端物, 残り物
odds of survival 生存率
odds-on 五分以上勝ち目のある
odds-on candidate 当選確実の候補者
odds-on favorite 本命馬, 優勝候補者, 有力な本命馬
over the odds 予想以上に高く
pay over the odds 法外な金を支払う
rise against the odds 優勢な敵を相手に立ち向かう
short odds 勝ち目のある確率, 小差の確率, 起こりそうなこと
shorten the odds 実現に近づける
take [receive] odds 有利な条件を得る, ハンディキャップを付けてもらう
win against long odds 強敵に勝つ
within the odds 見込みがありそうな, どうやら見込みがある

OECD 経済協力開発機構 (**Organization for Economic Cooperation and Development**の略)

OEM 相手先ブランドによる生産方式, 相手先ブランド製造業者, 相手先商標製造業者 (**original equipment manufacturer**の略)

off-brand 名 有名ブランドでない商品, 無銘品

off-budget spending 予算外支出, オフ・バジェット予算

off-camera 形 カメラに向かない[撮影されない]ときの, 日常生活の, 私生活の

off-color jokes きわどいジョーク

off-hours trading 時間外取引 (⇒after-hours trading)
off-hours trading system 時間外取引制度, 時間外取引

off-market trading 取引所外取引, 市場外取引 (=off-market transactions)
off-the-book 形 帳簿外の, 簿外の, 記録されていない
  off-the-book account 簿外口座
  off-the-book deal 簿外取引
  off-the-book debts 簿外債務 (=off-the-book liabilities)
  off-the-book funds 簿外資金, 裏金
  off-the-book property 含み資産
  off-the-book transaction 簿外取引 (=off-the-book deal)
off-the-cuff 形 とっさの, 準備なしの, ぶっつけ本番の, にわかの, 即席の
off-the-record 形 非公式の, 記録にとどめない, 内密の, オフレコの (取材源の名前を伏せることを前提に取材する方法を「オフレコ」という)
off year 名 米大統領選挙の行われない年, 中間選挙年, 不振の年, 外れ年
offending enterprise 加害企業
offense [offence] 名 罪, 犯罪, 違法行為, 侵害, 違反, 立腹, 憤慨, 侮辱, 攻撃
  capital offense 死罪
  commit an offense against the law 法を犯す
  criminal offense 刑事犯, 刑事犯罪
  first offense 初犯
  impeachable offense 告発されるべき犯罪
  launch a massive offense against …に対して大攻勢を開始する
  offense against good taste 悪趣味
  previous offense 前科
  second offense 再犯
  serious offense 重犯
  sex offenses 性犯罪
  speeding offenses スピード違反
  sex offense 性犯罪
  traffic offense 交通違反
offensive 名 攻勢, 攻撃, 攻撃的態度
  all-out offensive 全面攻勢
  be on the offensive 攻勢に出ている, 攻撃中である
  get on [get over to, take] the offensive 攻勢に出る
  ground offensive 地上攻撃
  peace offensive 平和攻勢
  spring (labor) offensive 春闘 (=spring wage negotiations, spring wage offensive)
  take [act on, go on, go over to] the offensive against …に対して攻勢に出る
offensive 形 攻勢の, 積極的な, 攻撃の, 攻撃的な, 攻撃用の, 腹立たしい, 不愉快な, 不快な, 嫌な, 目障りな, 失礼な, 無礼な, 侮辱的な
  offensive air 攻撃航空部隊
  offensive missile 攻撃用ミサイル
  offensive movements 攻勢, 攻撃的な行動
  offensive sounds 耳障りな音
  offensive strength 攻撃力
  offensive weapons 攻撃用武器, 攻撃用兵器
offer 動 申し込む, 提供する, 販売する, 〈金利などを〉提示する, 〈買収などの〉提案をする, 〈株式などを〉発行する, 〈株式を〉売り出す
  offer a bid to …に対して買収提案をする
  offer the stock at ¥250,000 a share in the initial public offering 新規株式公開で同株を1株25万円で売り出す
  offer to sign 署名する意向を示す
offer 名 申込み, 売申込み, 申し出, 提案, 提示, 提示額, 申請額, 取引希望価格, 付け値, 売呼び値, 割引, 値引き, オファー
  at the price on offer 提示価格で, 大安売り中
  be open to offers 値段交渉に応じる用意がある
  be under offer 契約済みである, 売約済みである
  buying offer 買い申込み, 買いオファー
  buyout offer 買収の申込み, 買収提案 (=acquisition offer)
  demand and offer curve 需要・オファー (提供) 曲線
  foreign capital offer 外資攻勢
  offer by subscription 予約募集
  offer by tender 〈株式の〉入札発行
  offer for sale 募集売出し, 売出発行, 売出し
  offer of credit 信用供与の申し入れ
  offer of work [employment, jobs] 求人, 求人数
  offer price 募集価格, 発行価額, 売出価格, 買付け価格, 買取り価格, 提示価格, TOB (株式公開買付け) 価格
  offers to existing shareholders 割当て発行
  on offer 申込み受付け中, 募集中, 販売中, 売りに出されている, 提供中
  take advantage of special offers 特別割引を利用する
  wage offer 賃金提示額
  what's on offer 特売品
offering 名 募集, 売出し, 〈株式などの〉発行,

株の公開[上場], 入札, 贈り物, 進物,〈教会などへの〉献金, 提供, 提供品, 販売, 売却, 売り物, 提案, 案件(募集=primary distribution, primary offering, 売出し=secondary distribution, secondary offering:⇒ IPO)
equity offering 株式発行, 株式公募
initial public offering 新規公募《略 IPO》
initial stock offering 新規株式公開, 新規株式公募
management offering 経営者割当て発行
noncompetitive offering 非競争入札
offering circular 分売案内書, 募集案内書, 目論見書
offering date 募集取扱日
offering memorandum 募集覚書, 目論見書
offering price 公募価格, 募集価格, 売出価格
offering size 入札総額
offering statement 募集届け出書, 発行目論見書
primary offering 募集(新規発行される有価証券の取得申込みを勧誘すること)
public offering 公募, 株式公開(募集の場合も売出しの場合も, 両者区別なく public offering と呼ばれる)
public offering bond 公募債
public stock offering 株式公募, 株式公開, 株式上場, 公募増資 (=public equity offering, public offering, stock offering)
rights offering 株主割当て発行
security offering 有価証券の募集
shelf offering 一括募集
stock offering 株式発行, 株式公開, 株式公募
terms of the offering 発行条件
underwrite the offering 売出しを引き受ける

office 图 事務所, 営業所, 会社, 勤め先, 仕事場, 店舗, 診療室, 研究室, 省[庁, 課], 官職, 公職, 職務, 仕事, 任務, 役目, 責任ある地位, 要職,〈政党の〉政権担当,〈複数形で〉尽力, 好意, 便宜, 世話, オフィス
admissions office 入試事務局
assume [take] office 就任する
back office バック・オフィス, 事務部門, 事務処理, 後方部門, ディーリング管理業務
be [remain] in office 在職している, 在任中, 政権を担当している, 要職に就いている
be out of office 在職していない, 政権を担当していない
box office 切符売り場,〈映画などの〉売上

branch office 支社, 支店, 支所, 支部
do the office of …の役目をする
Executive Office of the President 〈米〉大統領府
field office 営業所
Foreign and Commonwealth Office 〈英〉外務省
good offices 便宜, 好意, 援助, 尽力
head office 本社, 本店, 本部, 本拠
hold office 職に就いている, 政権[官職]に就いている
hold office as …を務める
Home Office 〈英〉内務省
inter-office account 本支店勘定
leave [go out of] office 退任する, 辞職する, 政権を離れる, 下野する
marketing office cost 営業事務費
offer one's good offices to …に便宜を供与する
office block [building] オフィス・ビル
office equipment 事務機器, オフィス機器
office hours 執務時間, 営業[開店]時間, 勤務[診療]時間, 学生指導時間
Office of Administration 〈米〉管理局
Office of Business Economics 〈米〉企業経済局
Office of Government Ethics 〈米〉政府倫理局
Office of Management and Budget 〈米〉行政管理予算庁[予算局] (=Bureau of the Budget)
Office of National Drug Control Policy 〈米〉薬物取締政策局
Office of Personnel Management 〈米〉人事管理庁
Office of Policy Development 〈米〉政策開発局
Office of Science and Technology Policy 〈米〉科学技術政策局
Office of the United Nations High Commissioner for Refugees 国連難民高等弁務官事務所
Office of the United States Trade Representative 〈米〉通商代表部
Office of the Special Representative for Trade and Negotiations 〈米〉通商交渉特別代表部
office supplies 事務用品, オフィス事務用品

office work　事務
office worker　事務職員, 事務員, 会社員, サラリーマン
principal office　本社事務所, 本店事務所, 主たる事務所, 本社, 本店, 本部
registered office　登記上の本社[本店], 登録事務所
representative office　駐在員事務所, 在外公館
resign [leave] office　辞任する
take [enter upon] office　就任する
take the oath of office　就任の宣誓をする, 就任宣誓する
term of office　任期, 在職期間（＝office term）
the whole office　全職員, 全社員, 全従業員
through [by, thanks to] the good offices of　…の好意で, …の世話で, …の援助で

officer 名　公務員, 官公吏, 職員, 会社役員, 役員, 業務執行役員, 士官, 将校, オフィサー
chief executive officer　最高業務執行役員, 最高経営責任者, 最高業務執行理事《略 CEO》
chief financial officer　最高財務担当役員, 最高財務責任者《略 CFO》
commanding officer　指揮官, 部隊長
commissioned officer　将校, 士官
compliance officer　業務監査役, 法令・規則遵守担当役員, コンプライアンス・オフィサー
corporate officer　株式会社の役員, 会社役員
customs officer　税関吏（＝custom house officer）
executive officer　業務執行役員, 上席業務執行役員, 執行役員, 業務執行理事
First Officer　一等航海士
intelligence officer　情報当局者, 情報将校
military officer　陸軍将校
naval officer　海軍将校
officer of the day　当番将校, 日直将校
police officer　警官, 巡査（＝officer of the law）
probation officer　保護監察官
public officer　公務員
retired Army officer　退役陸軍将校
returning officer　選挙管理委員
senior executive officer　常務執行役員, 上席業務執行役員
serve as an officer　将校を務める, 将校として務める

official 名　役員, 経営者, 公務員, 職員, 当局者, 担当者, 関係者
current and former officials　現役職員とOB
finance official　財務当局者
financial market officials　金融市場関係者, 金融関係者
government officials　政府当局者, 政府高官, 官僚, 政府当局, 公務員
high official　高官
high-ranking officials　上層部, 幹部
middle-ranked official　中堅幹部
police officials　官憲

official 形　公の, 公的な, 公式の, 正式の, 公認の, 公示の, 公用の, 公務上の, 表向きの, 一般に公開されていない
file an official complaint　正式に苦情申立てをする
official barriers　法律上の制約, 法的な障壁
official development assistance　政府開発援助《略 ODA》
official duties　公務
official exchange rate　公定レート
official gazette　官報
official interest rate　政策金利（＝official rate）
official land prices　公示地価
official pledge　公約
official receiver　破産管財人
official report　正式な報告
official retail price　公定小売価格
Official Score Certificate　公式認定証
Official Secrets Act　〈英国の〉国家機密保護法
official telecommunications equipment supplier　公認通信機器納入業者

official discount rate　公定歩合（＝bank rate, discount rate, official bank rate）

offset 動　相殺する, 埋め合わせをする, 帳消しにする, 吸収する, 吸い上げる, 解消する, 打ち消す, 〈リスクなどを〉カバーする, 名　相殺, 相殺額, 差引勘定, 埋め合わせ
be partially offset by　…で一部相殺される, …で部分的に相殺される
more than offset　十分相殺する, かなり相殺する
offset an account payable against an account receivable　買掛金を売掛金と相殺する
offset market risk　市場リスクを吸収する, 市場リスクを相殺する, 市場リスクをカバーする
offset the loss　損失の穴埋めをする, 損失をカ

バーする
offshoot 名 派生物, 分派, 分家, 横枝, 支流
off-year election 〈米〉中間選挙 (=midterm election)
OFHEO 米連邦住宅公社監督局 (Office of Federal Housing Enterprise Oversightの略)
oil 名 石油, 原油, オイル
 oil cake 油かす
 oil crisis [crunch, shock] 石油危機, 石油逼迫, 石油ショック, オイル・ショック
 oil demand 石油需要, 原油需要
 oil deposit 石油鉱床
 oil distributor 石油元売り
 oil dollars オイル・ダラー (=petrodollars：石油の輸出や利権で獲得したドル)
 oil (drilling) rig 石油掘削装置 (=oilrig)
 oil drum 〈石油の〉ドラムカン
 oil embargo 石油輸出禁止
 oil field 油田
 oil field concession 油田採掘権, 油田の権益
 oil-for-food program 石油・食糧交換プログラム (イラクの人道援助物資購入のための国連の措置)
 oil glut 石油供給過剰
 oil industry complex 石油コンビナート
 oil infrastructure 原油の関連設備
 oil inventory 原油在庫
 oil lease 油井借地権
 oil lump 油塊
 oil majors 国際石油資本, 石油メジャー, 石油資本
 oil money オイル・マネー (石油産出国が保有する資金)
 oil palm 油ヤシ
 oil platform [rig] 石油採掘装置, 海底石油掘削用足場
 oil pressure 油圧
 oil producer 産油国
 oil prospecting 石油試掘, 石油探査
 oil refiner-distributor 石油元売り会社
 oil refinery 製油所
 oil refining 石油精製
 oil refining capacity 石油精製能力
 oil reserve 石油備蓄
 oil shock 石油危機, 石油ショック, オイル・ショック
 oil slick 流出原油, 海面の油, 油膜
 oil sludge 油泥
 oil strike 石油の発見, 石油の掘り当て

 oil tanker 原油タンカー, 油送船, オイル・タンカー (=oiler)
 oil weapon 石油兵器, 石油攻勢, 石油を武器にした脅迫的外交手段
 oil well 油井
 oil wholesalers 石油元売り各社, 元売り各社
 pour oil on troubled waters 怒りを静める, 暴動を鎮める
 strike oil 石油を掘り当てる, 大発見する, 大成功する
 oil price 原油価格, 石油価格
 runup in oil prices 原油価格の急騰, 原油価格の上昇
 softness in oil prices 原油価格の下落
 spot oil prices 原油のスポット価格
oilberg 名 超マンモス・タンカー
oiler 名 原油タンカー, 油送船, オイル・タンカー (=oil tanker)
oiling 名 石油汚染
oilman 名 石油会社の経営者 (oil company executive), 石油企業家, 石油業者, 製油業者, 油井所有者, 油井操作技師, 石油関連産業で働く人
old economy オールドエコノミー (=t-economy：IT関連の産業や企業を指すニューエコノミーに対して, 自動車, 建設, 不動産, 繊維, 流通などの成熟産業を指す)
olive branch 友好, 和平, 和解, 和平・和解策, オリーブの枝
 hold out [extend, offer] an [the] olive branch 和平[和解, 和議]を申し入れる[申し出る]
 the wife and olive branches of …の妻子
ombudsman 名 〈新聞社などの〉苦情処理係, 苦情調査官, 記事審査係, 行政監査官, 行政監査専門委員, 行政監察委員, オンブズマン
omnibus 形 包括的な, 総括的な, 多項目の, 多くのものを扱う, オムニバスの
 omnibus bill 総括的法案, 包括法, 一括法案, オムニバス法案 (=omnibus legislation)
 Omnibus Budget Reconciliation Act 包括財政調整法
 omnibus opinion 包括意見, 各種意見
 omnibus surveys 多項目調査
 Omnibus Trade and Competitiveness Act of 1988 1988年包括通商・競争力法
omnidirectional diplomacy 全方位外交 (=omnidirectional foreign policy)
on a real-term basis 実質, 実質ベースで

on-again, off-again [on-again or off-again] **negotiations** 断続的な交渉，たびたび中断する交渉

on-camera 形 カメラの前で，テレビ画面で

on and off 断続的に

on condition of anonymity 匿名を条件に

on tenterhooks 気をもんで，やきもきして，気がかりで，心配して

on the back of …に加えて，…に引き続いて，…に伴って，…の後に

on the drawing board 構想中の，構想段階の，計画段階の

on the heels of …に続いて，…のすぐ後に続いて

on the job [on-the-job] **training** 職場内訓練，職場研修，社内の職業訓練《略 OJT》

on-the-job union work 勤務時間中の組合活動，ヤミ専従

on-the-record 形 公式の，記録された，公にされている，オンレコの（録音や撮影を認められ，取材源を明らかにして発言内容をすべて報道できる取材方法を「オンレコ」という。⇒off-the-record）

on the Richter scale マグニチュードで

on-the-spot inspection 立入り検査，立入り考査，立入り調査（＝on-site inspection）

on the strength of …を根拠にして，…に基づいて，…を頼りにして，…の力で，…の影響で，…の勧めで

on track 軌道に乗って，順調に進んで

once-in-a-century crisis 100年に1度の危機

one-child policy 一人っ子政策

one-eight hundred number 米国のフリーダイヤルの電話番号（＝1-800 number）

one-liner 名 短い冗談，気の利いたことば，寸評，1文ジョーク

one-off losses 特別損失，1回限りの損失

one on one [one-on-one] 名 1対1(one to one)，〈1対1の〉対決，マンツーマン，マンツーマンのスポーツ［ゲーム］

one percenter 暴走族（バイク使用者の100人に1人は暴走族といわれる）

One Seg ワンセグ（ワンセグは，「1セグメント放送(one segment broadcasting)」の略称。移動端末向けにテレビ番組を放送することができる新しい地上デジタル放送サービス）

one-stop 形 1か所ですべて揃う，ワンストップ

one-stop center ワンストップ・センター

one-stop service ワンストップ・サービス（消費者のニーズを満たすため，主力商品と関連商品をすべて一つのサイトで提供するサービスのこと）

one-stop service of administration ワンストップ行政サービス（国民の各種申請や届け出など，政府の国民向けサービスの窓口を一つにして一括して行うもの）

one-stop shopping 1か所での同時まとめ買い，1か所ですべて済ませる買い物，一点集中購買，関連購買，ワンストップ・ショッピング

one-up 動 …を出し抜く，…に一歩先んじる，…の一歩先を行く，名 一歩先んじること，一歩先を行くこと，一歩追い抜くこと

Oneworld ワンワールド（世界を代表する航空会社11社で構成される国際航空連合。⇒SkyTeam）

one way or the other いずれにせよ

ongoing 形 進行中の，進行している，進展中の，進展している，継続中の，継続している，継続して行われる，今回の

ongoing alliance projects 現在進行中の業務提携プロジェクト

ongoing concern 継続企業（＝going concern）

ongoing deflation デフレの進行

ongoing negotiations 現在進行中の交渉

oniomania 名 強迫的買い物症候群

online [on-line] 形 副 オンライン，オンライン式，直結，回線接続中，コンピュータ回線で，コンピュータ回線を使って，コンピュータのネットワークで，インターネットで，ネット上で，ネットで《略 OL》

online clearing オンライン決済

online debit service インターネット即時決済サービス，オンライン即時決済サービス

online drug sales 医薬品ネット販売，ネット医薬品販売

online fraud オンライン詐欺

online grocery ネット・スーパー（インターネットで注文を受け付け，生鮮食品や雑貨類を宅配するサービス）

online retailer ネット販売業者，ネット・ショッピング業者

online shopper ネット・ショッパー，オンライン・ショッピング利用者（＝Net shopper, Net shopping user）

online shopping ネット・ショッピング，オンライン・ショッピング（＝Internet shopping：インターネットやパソコン通信サービスで行われている

通信販売）

online shopping mall 電子商店街，仮想商店街（＝virtual mall）

online stock brokerage ネット証券会社（＝online brokerage, online securities brokerage）

online survey ネット調査，インターネットでの調査

online trading ネット取引，ネット専業取引，オンライン取引（＝Internet trading, Net trading）

▶ The firm is scheduled to bring a new plant *online* in 2010. 同社は，2010年から新工場を稼働させる予定だ．

OPEC 太平洋地域経済協力機構（Organization of Pacific Economic Cooperationの略）

OPEC 石油輸出国機構，オペック（Organization of Petroleum Exporting Countriesの略）

op–ed 名 社説対向面，解説記事面，署名入り寄稿欄のページ（＝Op-Ed）

open 他動 開く，開ける，開設する，出店する，開店する，営業を始める，暴露する，〈市場などを〉開放する，初値を付ける，始める，開始する，〈事件の〉冒頭陳述をする，〈再審理のために判決などを〉取り消す，自動 始まる，開演する，〈ファイルなどが〉開く，〈道路などが〉開通する，開店する，〈景色が〉開ける，展開する，〈映画などが〉初公開される，封切りになる，オープンする

open a border [frontier] to …に門戸を開く

open an account with …に口座を開く，…に口座を開設する

open fire 銃を撃ち始める，発砲する，射撃を始める，火ぶたを切る

open fire on demonstrators デモ参加者に向かって発砲する

open for …の前座をつとめる

open the possibility of …の可能性に道を開く

open the public debt markets 公募債市場を開放する，公募債市場を自由化する

open the road to …への道筋をつける

open up to public ownership 株式を公開する

open 形 開かれた，開放的な，制限のない，自由な，公開の，周知の，営業中の，開会中の，未決定の，未解決の，未決算の，非武装の，無防備の，オープン

open bidding [bid] 公開入札，一般競争入札（＝open tendering）

open college 成人教育大学

open collar worker 在宅勤務者

open date 賞味期限（＝harmless period of food）

open–door policy 門戸開放政策，機会均等政策，ドア開放政策，自由入室制度

open enrollment [admission] 大学全入方式

open–list system 非拘束名簿方式

open market operations 公開市場操作

open question 未解決の問題

open rate 基本料金

open sea 公海

open season 解禁日

open session 公開協議

open skies agreement 航空自由化協定，オープンスカイ協定

open source オープン・ソース（ソースコードを公開して，そのソフトウエアを改良したり再配布したりすることができるようにすること）

open bank assistance オープン・バンク・アシスタンス（銀行の経営が破綻する前に政府支援で銀行の事業譲渡をする手法．早期支援すれば預金保険制度への負担が最小で済むと判断される場合や，銀行倒産が金融システムの安定性に悪影響を与えると予想される場合に発動される）

open–end 形 限度のない，無制限の，開放式の，自由回答式の，オープン式の，オープン・エンド型の

open–end contract 数量不確定契約，不定契約

open–end credit オープンエンド・クレジット（消費者対象の回転信用）

open–end fund オープン・エンド型投資信託

open–end management company オープンエンド型投資会社

open–end mortgage 開放担保，開放式抵当，オープンエンド・モーゲージ

open–end [open–ended] question 自由回答式質問

opening 名 開始，開会，開会式，開通，開幕，開店，開場，冒頭，序盤，初日，寄り付き，期首，就職口，求人，空席，空き，欠員，定員，機会，好機，〈弁護人の〉冒頭陳述，オープニング

opening price 新規株式公開(IPO)銘柄の公開価格，寄り付き価格，寄り付き

> **公開価格とは** ⇨ 証券会社が引き受けた新規公開株式を投資家に売り出すときの1株当たり価格のこと．これに対して，株式市場に上場したときに最初についた値段を初値という．

operate 動 経営する，運営する，操作する，事業を展開する，営業する，操業する

be operated under a holding company 持ち株会社の下に運営される, 持ち株会社の傘下で運営される
continue to operate 営業を続ける, 運営を続ける, 操業を続ける
operate at capacity フル稼働を維持する
operate businesses 各種事業を展開する, 事業を進める
operate diverse businesses 多様な業務を展開する
operate in the red 赤字運営する

operating 形 経営上の, 営業上の, 業務の
operating costs 営業費, 営業コスト, 営業上の費用, 営業費用, 営業経費, 業務費, 創業費, 運営費 (＝operating expenses)
operating deficit 営業赤字
operating earnings 営業利益
operating expense 営業費用, 営業費, 経常経費 (＝operating cost)
operating funds 運転資金, 営業資金 (＝operating capital, working capital, working funds)
operating loss 営業損失, 事業損失, 営業赤字, 営業欠損金, 欠損金 (＝operational loss)
operating performance 営業成績, 経営成績, 営業業績, 業績
operating profit 営業利益, 営業収益, 営業黒字,〈金融機関の〉業務純益 (＝income from operations, operating income：売上高から販売・管理費を差し引いた収益で, 本業のもうけを示す)
operating real estate 事業用不動産
operating revenue 営業収益, 営業収入, 売上高
operating system 基本ソフトウエア, 基本ソフト, システム・ソフト, オペレーティング・システム《略 OS》

operation 名 営業, 営業活動, 事業, 業務, 経営, 活動, 操作, 運転, 運行, 稼動, 機能, 作用, 公開市場操作, 介入操作, オペ, オペレーション
buying operation 買い操作, 買いオペ, 買いオペレーション
discontinued operations 廃止事業
domestic sales operations 国内営業部門
full operation 本格稼動, 完全操業, フル稼働
go into operation 操業を開始する
income from operations 営業利益
integrate operations 経営統合する, 事業を統合する
lending operation 融資業務, 貸出業務
market operations 市場操作
merge operations 経営統合する (＝integrate operations)
operation improvement plan 業務改善計画
Operation Nudge オペレーション・ナッジ
operation of a pension plan 年金制度の運用
operation study 作業研究
Operation Twist オペレーション・ツイスト (＝Operation Nudge：短期金利引上げと長期金利引下げの操作で景気調整を行う方法)
reduction of operation 操業短縮
retail operation 小売業, 小売事業
safe operation 安全操業
selling operation 売り操作, 売りオペ, 売りオペレーション
swap operation スワップ操作
take over operations 経営を受け継ぐ
transfer operation 振替操作
treasury operation 財務運用
yen-selling, dollar-buying operation 円売り・ドル買い介入操作

operational 形 操作［運転］上の, 運用［運用上］の, 経営［経営上］の, 業務上の, 営業［営業上］の, 戦略［作戦］上の, 機能している, 使用できる
operational efficiency 経営効率, 業務効率, 業務［作業］の効率性
operational integration 経営統合 (＝business integration, management integration)
operational manual 取扱い説明書, 操作の手引き
operational research 作戦研究, 業務調査, オペレーションズ・リサーチ《略 OR》 (＝operations research)

operator 名 運営者, 経営者, 事業主, 事業者, 事業会社, 運営会社, 会社, 電気通信事業者, 電話交換手, 交換取扱い者, コンピュータを操作する人, 運転者, 株の相場師, 仕手, 演算子, 演算記号, オペレータ
auction site operator オークション・サイト運営会社, 競売サイト運営業者
mobile phone operator 携帯電話事業会社
operator's agent 船会社代理店
seasoned operator 株の玄人筋
stock market operators 証券取引所［株式市場］で業務を行う者
tour operator 旅行会社

opinion 名 意見, 考え, 考え方, 信念, 見解, 持論, 監査意見, 意見表明, 判断, 所見, 鑑定, 評価, 〈弁護士の〉意見書, オピニオン
- a difference of opinion　見解の相違
- a matter of opinion　議論の余地のある問題
- a second opinion about　…についてのもう一つの判断
- act up to one's opinions　…の信念によって行動する
- ask for a second opinion　他の医者の所見を求める
- business opinion　景況感
- collective opinion　統一意見
- credit opinion　格付け見解（＝rating opinion）
- have a low [bad] opinion of　…に対する評価が低い, …を悪く思う
- have no opinion of　…をよいと思わない
- legal opinion　法的見解, 弁護士意見書
- medical opinion　医者の意見
- opinion advertising　意見広告
- opinion leader [maker]　世論形成者, オピニオン・リーダー（世論の形成や表明で主導的役割を果たす人）
- opinion of counsel　弁護士の意見
- opinion poll　世論調査（＝poll, public opinion poll, public opinion survey）
- political opinion　政見
- professional opinion　職業専門家の意見
- public opinion　世論
- the general opinion　世間一般の考え

opponent 名 相手, 反対者, 敵対者, 反対論者, 反対勢力, 対抗勢力, 敵, ライバル

opportunity 名 機会, 事業機会, 好機, 場, 環境, 可能性, ビジネス・チャンス, チャンス
- business opportunity　ビジネス機会, 事業機会, 商機会, ビジネス・チャンス（＝business chance）
- capitalize on a market opportunity　市場の機会をとらえる, 市場の機会を生かす
- creation of job opportunities　雇用機会［就労機会］の創出
- merit-based opportunity　実力主義
- opportunity assessment　市場機会の分析［評価］, オポチュニティ・アセスメント
- opportunity cost　機会原価
- opportunity of advancement　昇進の機会
- take advantage of opportunities　機会をとらえる, 機会をつかむ, 機会を利用する
- window of opportunity　機会の窓, 機会の手段, 瞬時の好機, 好機

opposition 名 反対, 対立, 抵抗, 抗議, 反発, 反感, 反撃, 野党, 野党の立場, 反対党, 反対派, 反対者, 批判者, 批判勢力, 相手, 相手チーム, 敵対者, ライバル, 対照, 対比
- congressional opposition to　…に対する議会の反対
- have an opposition to　…に反対する, …に反対である
- in opposition to　…に反対して, …に対立して
- meet [meet with, run into] opposition　反対を受ける, 抵抗に会う
- offer armed opposition　武力抵抗の構えを見せる, 武力で対抗する, 武力抵抗する
- offer opposition to　…に反対［抵抗］する
- opposition leader　反対派［批判勢力］の指導者, 反対勢力指導者, 野党党首
- opposition pressures　野党の圧力
- opposition to society page　社会対抗面
- sales opposition　販売［売買］拒否
- the [His, Her] Majesty's loyal Opposition　〈英国〉在野党
- the main opposition party　最大野党
- the opposition benches　〈英議会の〉在野党席
- the opposition whip　野党の院内幹事（与党の院内幹事＝government whip）
- union opposition　組合の反対［拒否, 抵抗］

optical fiber　光ファイバー
- optical fiber cable　光ファイバー・ケーブル
- optical fiber submarine cable　光ファイバー海底ケーブル

optical magnetic disk　光磁気ディスク（＝magneto-optical disk, MO disk）

optimism 名 楽観的な見通し, 楽観的なスタンス, 楽観的雰囲気, 楽観主義, オプティミズム
- export [trade] optimism　楽観的な輸出見通し, 輸出楽観論, 輸出楽観主義
- financial optimism　金融楽観主義
- measure of consumer optimism　消費者マインドの指標

optimistic 形 楽天的な, 楽観的な, 楽天主義の, 甘い
- optimistic expectations　楽観的な見通し
- optimistic outlook　楽観的な見通し, 甘い見通し
- optimistic sentiment　楽観論, 楽観ムード
- over-optimistic　楽観的すぎる, 甘すぎる

option 名 選択, 取るべき道, 選ぶべき方法[手段], 選択肢, 選択手段, 選択の余地, 選択科目, 選択権, 優先的選択権, 購入選択権, 売買選択権, 〈商品の〉有料付属品, 付加的機能, オプション取引, オプション
- **at one's option** …の選択で
- **call option** 買付け選択権, コール・オプション
- **equity option** 株式オプション
- **exercise of option** オプションの行使
- **funding option** 資金調達の選択肢, 調達手段の選択肢
- **futures and options market** 金融先物市場, 先物・オプション市場
- **index option** 株価指数オプション, 指数オプション
- **option holder** オプション保有者, オプションの買い手
- **option price** オプション価格
- **option trading** オプション取引（＝option transaction：あらかじめ決められた期日に株を売買する権利(オプション)を売買する取引）
- **options assumed in merger with** …との合併による引継ぎオプション
- **options exercisable** 行使可能オプション
- **options outstanding** 未行使オプション, オプション残高
- **over-the-counter option** 店頭オプション
- **put option** 売付け選択権, 売る権利, プット・オプション
- **renewal option** 更新選択権
- **spot option** 現物オプション
- **stock option plan** 株式購入選択権制度, 株式選択権制度
- **trade option** 約定オプション, 上場オプション

optional 形 選択の, 任意の, 随意の
- **optional identification number system for taxpayers** 選択制納税者番号, 金融番号

oral contraceptive 経口避妊薬（＝pill, birth control pill）

Orange Book オレンジ・ブック（情報システムのセキュリティ・レベルのガイドラインで, 米政府が作成。正式名称はDepartment of Defense Trusted Computer System Evaluation Criteria）

Orange Revolution オレンジ革命（2004年ウクライナ大統領選挙の結果に対する抗議運動とそれに関する政治運動のこと。オレンジをシンボル・カラーにしたデモや集会を開いて不正選挙を糾弾し, 再選挙を実現した結果, 一度は当選者とされた親露派のヤヌコビッチ前首相が落選して, 親欧米派のユーシェンコ[ユシチェンコ]政権が誕生した）

orbit 動 〈…の〉軌道を周回する, 軌道を回る, …の周りを回る, 軌道に乗る, 軌道に乗せる, 〈飛行機が〉旋回する

orbit 名 軌道, 軌跡, 行路, 活動[勢力]範囲, 効力範囲, 勢力圏, 引力圏, 圏内, 範囲, 影響力
- **circular orbit** 円軌道
- **elliptical orbit** 楕円軌道
- **orbit velocity** 軌道速度
- **stationary orbit** 静止軌道
- **within the orbit of** …の勢力圏内に

orbital 形 軌道の, 軌道を回る
- **orbital element** 軌道要素
- **orbital maneuvering system** オービター軌道操縦システム《略 OMS》

orbiter 名 探査機, 宇宙船, 軌道船, オービター
- **orbiter processing facility** オービター整備施設《略 OPF》
- **orbiter vehicle** オービター《略 OV》

orchestrate 動 調整する, 結集する, 画策する, 巧みに組織化する, 手はずを整える, 段取りをつける, お膳立てする

ordeal 名 辛い体験[経験], 恐ろしい経験, 恐怖体験, 苦難, 難儀, 辛い目, 辛い苦しみ, 厳しい試練, 試練
- **go through an ordeal** 辛い苦しみを経験する, 厳しい[恐ろしい]試練を切り抜ける
- **stand an ordeal** 厳しい試練に立ち向かう
- **survive the ordeal** 試練を乗り越える

order 動 命じる, 命令を出す, 指示する, 指図する, 注文する, 発注する, 並べる, 陳列する

order 名 注文, 注文書, 注文品, 受注品, 受注高, 命令, 順序, 秩序, オーダー
- **administrative order** 行政命令
- **blanket order** 一括注文, 包括注文
- **block order** 大口注文
- **bulk order** 大量注文, 一括注文
- **buy order** 買い注文
- **cash with order** 現金注文
- **court order** 裁判所命令
- **day order** 当日有効注文
- **factory orders** 製造業受注, 製造業受注残高
- **fill and kill order** 即時執行注文
- **fill or kill order** 即時執行注文, 即時一括執行注文
- **fill the order** 注文を執行する, 注文を処理する, 注文に応える
- **firm order** 確定注文, ファーム・オーダー

issue a purchase order of merchandise 商品注文書を発行する
job order 製造指図書, 作業票
mail order selling 通信販売
manufacture order 製造指図書, 生産指図書
manufacturing orders 製造業受注高, 製造業受注
market order 成り行き注文
money order 為替, 郵便為替, 送金為替
new orders 新規受注高
on order 注文中
Order of Culture 文化勲章
place a block order 大口注文を出す
place a limit order 指し値注文を出す
place a market order 成り行き注文を出す
production order 製造指図書
production to order 注文生産
sell order 売り注文
small order 小口注文
unfilled order 受注残高

orderly 形 整頓された, 整然とした, 規則的な, 規律正しい, 秩序正しい, 秩序ある, 系統的な
orderly exit 秩序ある撤退
orderly market 秩序ある市場
orderly marketing agreement 市場秩序維持協定

ordinance 名 法令, 法規, 条例, 地方条例, 規則, 規定, 定め, おきて, 命令, 布告, 儀式, 聖餐式
banking ordinance 銀行業務令
emergency ordinance 緊急令
Ministerial ordinance 省令
pollution prevention ordinance 公害防止条例
prefectural ordinance 県条例
stamp duty ordinance 印紙税法

ordinary 形 普通の, 通常の, 経常的
ordinary balance 経常収支
ordinary Diet session 通常国会
ordinary profit 経常利益
ordinary shareholder 普通株主 (=equity shareholder)

organ 名 臓器, 器官, 機関, 機関紙, パイプオルガン, オルガン
accounting organ 出納機関
advisory organ 諮問機関
digestive organs 消化器官
execution organ 執行機関, 実行機関
house organ 社内報 (=employee house organ)
official PR organ 政府広報誌
organ donation 臓器提供, 臓器の提供
organ donor 臓器提供者
organ systems 器官系, 臓器系
organ transplant [transplantation] 臓器移植
Organ Transplant Law 臓器移植法

organic 形 有機的な, 有機物の, 生物の, 組織的な, 有機栽培の, 有機農法の, 無農薬の, 自然の, 器官の, 〈身体の器官を冒す〉器質性の, 本質的な, 基本的な, 生来の, オーガニック
organic agriculture 有機農法
organic beer 有機ビール (殺虫剤や化学肥料を使わないで栽培したホップで醸造する)
organic body 有機体
organic chemicals 有機化学薬品
organic composition of capital 資本の有機的構成
organic compounds 有機化合物
organic disease [disorder] 器質性疾患
organic electroluminescent screen 有機ELディスプレー, エレクトロルミネッセンス・ディスプレー
organic farm products 有機農産物
organic farming 有機農業 (化学肥料や農薬を使わない農業)
organic fertilizer 有機肥料
organic food 自然食品, 有機食品, 無農薬食品
organic gardening 有機園芸
organic glass 有機ガラス
organic growth 有機的成長, 有機的成長率, 内部成長 (=organic：M&Aによる成長でなく, 自社内で新規事業を成長させること)
organic law 〈国家の〉基本法
organic life 生物
organic materials [matter] 有機物
organic mercury compound 有機水銀化合物
organic mercury poisoning 有機水銀中毒
organic produce 無農薬作物
organic society 有機社会
organic superconductor 有機超電導体
organic unity 有機的統一性
organic vegetables 有機野菜, 無農薬野菜
organic waste 有機性廃棄物
organic whole 有機的統一体

organization 名 組織, 機関, 機構, 団体, 組織体, 企業, 会社, 組織化, 企画, 企画力, 段取り, 構造, 構成

business organization 企業, 企業組織, 業務組織, 実業団体, 財界団体, 経済団体
divisional organization 事業部制, 事業部制組織
lateral organization 横断的組織
marketing organization マーケティング組織, 販売組織
nonprofit organization 非営利団体, 非営利組織 (=nonbusiness organization)
organization chart 組織図, 会社機構図
Organization for Economic Cooperation and Development 経済協力開発機構《略 OECD》
Organization for Security and Cooperation in Europe 欧州安保協力機構《略 OSCE》
Organization of African Unity アフリカ統一機構《略 OAU》
Organization of American States 米州機構《略 OAS》
Organization of Pacific Economic Cooperation 太平洋地域経済協力機構《略 OPEC》
Organization of Petroleum Exporting Countries 石油輸出国機構, オペック《略 OPEC》

organizational 形 組織的な, 組織上の, 組織全体の, 構造上の
organizational hierarchy 組織の階層, 組織の序列, 組織の上下関係
organizational interests 組織利益
organizational structure 組織形態

organize 動 組織化する, 系統立てる, 体系化する, まとめる, 編成する, 設立する, 結成する, 〈催しなどを〉準備する, 用意する, 手配する, 運営する, 開催する, 主催する
organize protests against a company 会社に対して抗議行動[運動]を組織する
organized activity 組織的活動
organized behavior 組織的行動, 組織された行動
organized boycott 組織的不買運動[行動]
organized decision making 組織的意思決定
organized financial market 組織金融市場
organized labor 組織労働, 組織労働者
organized market 規制市場
organized speculation 組織的投機
organized worker 組織労働者
organizing committee 組織委員会, 発起人会
right to organize 団結権

organized crime 組織犯罪
Organized Crime Control Act 〈米国の〉組織犯罪取締法
organized crime syndicate 暴力団

organizer 名 〈大会・イベントの〉組織者, 主催者, 運営者, 運営担当者, 開催団体, 興行主, 設立者, 〈労働組合の〉オルグ, 組織部員, オーガナイザー

–oriented 形 …志向の, …志向型, …集約型, …追求型の, …重視の, …に重点を置く, …中心の, …優先の, …偏重の (=-driven, -minded)
consumer–oriented 消費者志向
customer–oriented 顧客指向
export–oriented 輸出志向型
food–oriented supermarket 食品スーパー, 食品重視のスーパー
future–oriented 未来志向の
growth–oriented 成長指向型, 拡大志向型
labor–oriented 労働集約型
market–oriented 市場原理に基づく, 市場重視型
marketing–oriented マーケティング志向
needs–oriented ニーズ志向
personal–oriented 個人専用の, 個人重視の, 個人優先
problem–oriented language 問題向き言語
product–oriented 商品志向
production–oriented 生産志向
urban–oriented 都市型
user–oriented ユーザー志向, 顧客指向, 顧客第一主義
value–oriented investor 価値志向の投資家
value–oriented management 価値重視の経営
welfare–oriented 福祉的な, 福祉重視の

original 形 最初の, 初期の, 当初の, 初回の, 本来の, 原始の, 本源的, もとの, 原文の, 実物の, 原物[原作, 原画, 原型]の, 新作の, 独創的な, 独自の, 独特の, 新奇な, オリジナル
original copy 原本, 正本
original cost 取得原価
original insurance 元受け保険, 原保険
original investment 初期投資, 当初投資額
original margin 当初証拠金
original maturity 当初満期
original merchandise オリジナル商品 (=original goods)
original order 原注文, 初回注文
original purchasing power 本源的
original retail (price) 初回売価

original work of authorship 著作の原著作物
original write-down 当初評価額
original equipment manufacturing [manufacturer] 相手先ブランド製造業者, 相手先ブランドによる生産, 相手先ブランド販売, 相手先商標商品(製造), 委託生産方式《略 OEM》
originality 名 独自性, 独創力, 独創性, 創造力, 新機軸, 創意
originate 動 考案する, 発明する, 開発する, 創造する, 創設する, 実行する, 始める, スタートする, 起こす, 始まる, 生じる, 起こる, 発展する (＝create, develop, invent)
Oslo interim peace accords オスロ和平合意(イスラエルとPLOの直接対話によるパレスチナ暫定自治合意)
OTEC 海洋温度差発電 (ocean thermal energy conversionの略)
OTS 〈米〉貯蓄金融機関監督局[監督庁] (Office of Thrift Supervisionの略)
Ottawa 名 カナダ, 加政府, オタワ
oust 動 追放する, 追い出す, 更迭する, 駆逐する, 失脚させる, 放逐する, 排除する, 〈権利などを〉取り上げる
　be ousted from office 免職になる
　be ousted from one's post 地位を追われる
　be ousted from the premiership 首相の座を追われる
　oust management 経営者を更迭する
　oust one of [from] one's post …からその地位を奪う
　oust one of [from] one's right …からその権利を取り上げる
out-of-court settlement 示談による和解
out of the loop かやの外
outbreak 名 発生, 突発, 勃発, 突然の広がり, 爆発, 騒動, 暴動, 反乱
　massive outbreak of food poisoning 食中毒の集団発生
　outbreak of the economic crisis 経済危機の発生
outcome 名 結果, 成果, 行方, 成り行き
outcry 名 叫び, わめき, 悲鳴, どなり声, 怒りの声, 世間の非難, 激しい[強い]抗議, 強い要求, 厳しい批判, 大反発, せり売り(auction), 競売
　make one's outcry for …を強く要求する
　raise an outcry against …に対して強く抗議する
　without provoking outcry 世間の厳しい批判を呼び起こさないで
outfit 名 一団, グループ, 集団, 一行, 部隊, 関係団体, 活動団体, 旅行団体, 会社, 組織, 装備, 装備一式, …用品, 道具一式, 服装, 装い, 装束, 支度, 準備, 才能, 能力, 教養, 素養
　cooking outfit 料理用具, 調理道具一式
　engineering outfit 技術系の会社
　nonprofit making outfit 非営利組織
　regional terror outfit 地域テロ組織
　organized crime outfit 組織犯罪グループ
　ski outfit スキー用品
　spring outfit 春の装い
outflow 名 流出, 流出額, アウトフロー (⇒inflow)
　asset outflow 資産の流出, 資産流出額
　capital outflow 資本の流出
　cash outflow 支出, 支払い額, キャッシュ・アウトフロー
　investment outflow 投資支出額
　net inflow or outflow of capital 資本収支
　outflow of funds 資金の流出, 資金の海外流出
　outflow of wealth 富の流出
outgoing 形 辞職する, 退任する, 引退する (retiring), 引退間際の, 社交的な, 外向的な, 積極的な (extrovert), 発送用の, 出発の
　an outgoing message 留守番電話用メッセージ
　an outgoing personality 社交的な性格
　outgoing ministries 辞職する閣僚
outlaw 動 非合法化する, 禁止する, 法律による保護を奪う, 法的に無効とする
outlaw 名 無法者, 法の保護を奪われた者
　outlaw state 無法国家
outlay 名 支出, 経費, 出費 (＝outgo)
　budget outlays 財政支出
　capital outlay budget 資本支出予算
　cash outlay cost 現金支出原価
　consumer outlays 消費支出
　discretionary outlays 裁量的支出
　entitlement outlays 義務的経費
　federal [Federal] outlays 米連邦政府歳出
　government outlays 政府支出, 財政支出
　government outlays on defense 防衛予算
　initial cash outlay 当初支出額
　interest outlay 利払い
　investment outlays 設備投資 (＝outlays for capital equipment)
　national outlays 国民支出

outlays for national defense 国防支出
outlays for public works projects 公共事業関係費
personal outlays 個人支出
public works outlays 公共工事支出
real outlays 実質支出

outlet 名 店舗, …店, 販路, 小売店, 出店, 特約店, 系列販売店, 工場直売店, 支店, 出口, アウトレット
　affiliated outlet 系列販売店
　distribution outlet 販路
　fast-food outlet ファスト・フード店, ファスト・フード販売店
　investment outlet 投資先
　lending outlet 融資先, 貸付け先
　merchant outlet 加盟店店舗
　outlet mall アウトレット・モール
　outlet store 系列販売店
　network of outlets 店舗網
　retail outlet 小売店, 小売販売店
　sales outlet 販売店
　single outlet 単一店舗

outlook 名 見通し, 予測, 予想, 展望, 先行き, …観, 予報
　future demand outlook 需要の先行き, 今後の需要予測
　half-year earnings outlook 半期決算の業績予想［見通し］
　inflation outlook インフレの予想, インフレ見通し（＝outlook for inflation）
　production outlook 生産見通し, 生産の先行き
　strong earnings outlook 力強い増益見通し, 高収益見通し, 業績予想
　supply and demand outlook 需給見通し, 需給予測

outnumber 動 …より数が多い, …を上回る, …に勝る, …より多い

outpace 動 …を凌ぐ, …に優る, …を追い越す, …を超える［上回る］

outpatient 名 外来患者

outplacement 名 再就職先斡旋, 再就職斡旋, 再就職援助, 再就職支援, 転職斡旋, アウトプレースメント

output 名 生産, 生産量, 生産高, 製作, 産出量, 産出高, 出力, アウトプット
　aggregate output 総生産高, 総生産量, 総産出高
　capital-output ratio 資本・産出量比率, 資本産出高比率
　crude steel output 粗鋼生産量
　factory output 製造業生産高, 製造業の生産（＝manufacturing output）
　industrial output 工業生産, 鉱工業生産, 工業生産高
　input-output analysis 産業連関分析, 投入産出分析, インプット・アウトプット分析
　national output 国民産出量, GNP
　natural gas output 天然ガスの産出
　optimal output 最適生産量
　output capacity 生産能力, 生産設備（＝production capacity）
　output ceiling 生産枠
　output volume 生産量
　per capita output 1人当たり生産高, 1人当たりGDP
　per-worker output 従業員1人当たり生産高
　real output 実質生産高, 実質産出高, 実質GDP
　utility output 電力・ガスの生産高

outreach 名 出先機関, 出張, 派遣, 積極的救済, 貧困者救済, 福祉活動, 奉仕活動, 奉仕
　outreach program 積極的救済活動
　outreach service 出張サービス, 派遣サービス

outright 形 無条件の, 即座の, 徹底的な, 完全な, 絶対的な, 公然の, まぎれもない, はっきりした, あからさまな, アウトライト
　outright purchase 買切りオペレーション, 買切りオペ, 無条件購入（＝outright purchase operation）
　outright purchases of long-term government bonds 長期国債買切りオペレーション

outside director 社外取締役, 外部取締役（＝outside board director, outside board member）

outsider 名 部外者, 局外者, 第三者, よそ者, 門外漢, 勝ち目のない人, 穴馬, 本命でない馬

outsource 動 外部資源を活用する, 外部委託する, 外注する, 社外調達する, 業務委託する

outsourcing 名 外部資源の活用, 外部委託, 外注, 社外調達, 海外調達, 業務委託, アウトソーシング（企業が周辺業務を外部に委託すること）
　outsourcing deal 業務委託契約
　outsourcing of frozen food production 冷凍食品の生産委託

outspoken 形 無遠慮な, ずけずけ物を言う, 率直な（frank）, 歯に衣着せぬ（forthright）, 非常にあからさまな, 言いたいことを（正直に）言う

an outspoken person 率直な人
be outspoken in one's remarks 言うことに遠慮がない
deliver outspoken opinions 歯に衣着せぬ意見を述べる[物言いをする], 率直に意見を述べる

outstanding 形 傑出した, 際立った, 〈とくに〉目立った, 人目をひく, とくに優れた, 注目すべき, 明白な, 未解決の, 未払いの, 未納の, 未決済の, 未履行の, 未決定の, 未処理の, 発行済みの, すでに発生している
  a long outstanding problem 長い間懸案の問題
  an outstanding example 顕著な例, 好例
  loan outstanding 借入金残高, 融資残高
  long term debt outstanding 長期負債残高
  make an outstanding success 見事成功する
  make outstanding contributions to …に対して際立った貢献をする
  outstanding amount of bad loans 不良債権残高
  outstanding company 超優良企業
  outstanding current account target 当座預金残高目標
  outstanding debts 債務残高, 借入残高, 未払い負債額, 未償還負債
  outstanding government bonds 既発国債, 国債発行残高 (= outstanding balance of government bonds)
  outstanding issues 未解決の問題
  outstanding loan 融資残高, 貸出残高, 未決済貸付け金, 借入金残高
  outstanding loan extensions 融資残高
  outstanding long-term debts 長期債務残高
  outstanding nonperforming loans 不良債権残高 (= outstanding bad loans, outstanding balance of nonperforming loans)
  outstanding ordinary shares 発行済み普通株
  outstanding shares 発行済み株式, 社外株式, 社外発行株式, 流通株式数 (= outstanding capital stock)
  principal outstanding 残存元本額
  the outstanding balance of individual life insurance and annuity contracts 個人保険・年金の保有契約高
  warrant outstanding 発行済みワラント

outstanding balance 未払い残高, 残高
  outstanding balance of contracts 保有契約高, 保有契約, 保険の総額 (= outstanding contracts)
  outstanding balance of current accounts 当座預金残高
  outstanding balance of lending 銀行の貸出残高

outweigh 動 上回る, …より大きい, …より価値がある
▶ Increases in interest payments on deposits *outweighed* credit cost falls. 預金の利払い増加のほうが, 与信費用の低下より大きかった。

Oval Office 〈米ホワイトハウス内の〉大統領執務室, 大統領の職[地位], 大統領, 米国政府 (= Oval Room)

Oval Officer 米大統領補佐官, 米大統領側近

ovarian 形 卵巣の
  ovarian transplant 卵巣移植 (= ovarian transplantation)

over the counter 店頭, 店頭市場, 店頭売買, 店頭取引, 店頭銘柄《略 OTC》

over-the-counter 形 店頭の, 店頭市場の, 店頭売買の, 店頭取引の
  over-the-counter drug 〈薬局・薬店で購入できる〉一般用医薬品, 売薬
  over-the-counter market 店頭市場, 店頭株市場, 場外市場 (= OTC market, over-the-counter stock market)
  over-the-counter sale 店頭販売, 店頭売買, 窓口販売 (= OTC sale)
  over-the-counter services 窓口業務, 窓口サービス
  over-the-counter stock 店頭取引の株式

overall 形 総合的な, 全般的な, 全面的な, 全体的な, 全体の, 一切を含む, 総…
  overall balance (of payments) 〈国際収支の〉総合収支
  overall competitiveness 全体的な競争力
  overall consumption 総消費, 消費全体
  overall cooperation 全面協力, 全面的な協力
  overall demand 最終需要, 総需要
  overall domestic demand 国内需要全体, 内需全体
  overall efficiency 全効率, 全体的な効率性
  overall impact 全体的な影響
  overall index 総合指数
  overall industry 全産業, 産業全体
  overall leverage 総債務比率
  overall plan 全体計画

overall performance 性能全体, 全体的な性能
overall population 総人口
overall prices 物価全体
overall rate of return 総収益率《略 ORR》
overall sales 売上全体, 総売上
overall savings rate 総貯蓄率
overall score 総合成績
overall view 全景
overcapacity 名 過剰設備, 設備過剰, 過剰生産能力
overcharge 動 過剰請求する, 水増し請求する, 不当な[法外な]代金を請求する, 負荷をかけすぎる, 過剰に充電する, 情報を与えすぎる
overcome 動 克服する, 乗り越える, 打ち勝つ, 勝つ, 勝利する, 打ち負かす, 征服する, 圧倒する
  be overcome by liquor 酔いつぶれる
  be overcome with (by) …に打ちひしがれる, …に打ちのめされる, …にうろたえる
  be overcome with grief 悲しみに打ちひしがれる
  overcome adversity 逆境を乗り越える
  overcome injustice 不正を正す
  overcome losses 損失を補填する
  overcome obstacles 障害を克服する[乗り越える]
overconsumption 名 過剰消費
overdoses 名 〈薬の〉過剰投与, 定量超過
  overdoses of dangerous medicines 危険な薬剤の過剰投与
overdrive 動 酷使する, 名 過熱気味の活動, フル回転, オーバードライブ
  overdrive the economy 景気を過熱する
overdue 形 期限の経過した, 満期の経過した, 支払い遅延の, 支払い期限の過ぎた, 延滞の
  overdue tax 未納の税, 未納の税金
overemphasis 名 過度の強調, 偏重
overhaul 動 再編する, 抜本的に改革する, 見直す, 再検討する, 〈予算などを〉組み直す, 総点検する, 精密検査する, …を追い越す, …に追いつく
overhaul 名 再編, 改革, リストラ, 見直し, 総点検, 精密検査, リストラ, 分解修理, 解体修理, オーバーホール
  financial overhaul plan 金融改革案, 金融再編案, 金融監督の改革案
  overhaul of production processes 生産工程の見直し
  overhaul plan リストラ策, 再編策, 改革案
  radical overhaul 抜本的改革 （＝radical reform）

  structural overhaul 構造改革, 機構改革 （＝structural reform）
overheat 動 過熱する, 景気が過熱する
  overheated economy 過熱景気, 景気の過熱, 経済の過熱, 景気の過熱感
  overheating economy 経済の過熱, 景気の過熱
overheating 名 過熱, 景気過熱
  the overheating of the real economy 実体経済の過熱, 過熱した実体経済
  the signs of overheating 景気過熱の様相
overnight 形 翌日物の, 夜間の, 前夜の, 突然の
  overnight loan 翌日物, 翌日返済証券担保貸付け
  overnight repo 翌日物レポ取引, オーバーナイト現先, 翌日決済の買戻し条件付き証券売却
overnight call 翌日物コール
  overnight call rate 無担保コール翌日物金利
  unsecured overnight call money 無担保コール翌日物
overpass 名 歩道橋
overreact 動 過剰反応する
override 動 無視する, 拒否する, 無効にする, 取り消す, 〈決定を〉覆す, 踏みにじる, 蹂躙する, 優先する, 重視する, 名 拒否権の行使
overriding 形 最優先の, 最重要の, 第一の, 支配的な, はっきりした
overseas 形 海外の, 外国向けの, 外国からの, 副 海外に, 外国に
  overseas factors 海外要因
  overseas investment 対外投資, 海外への直接投資, 海外投資, 海外からの投資
  overseas market 海外市場
oversight 名 監視, 監督, 手落ち, 手抜かり, 見落とし, 失策
  by [through] oversight 手落ちで, 見落としで
  governing and oversight body 統制監督機関
  internal independent oversight board 社内独立監視委員会
  oversight agency 所轄官庁
  the Office of Federal Housing Enterprise Oversight 連邦住宅機関監督庁
  the oversight and regulatory powers of the bureaucracy 官僚の監視・監督権
overstate 動 過大表示する, 過大評価する
overstatement 名 過大表示, 過大評価, 過大計上
overstep the mark 度を越す, やり過ぎる

oversupply 名 過剰供給

overt act 外的行為, 顕示行為, オーバート・アクト(「オーバート・アクト」は, 共謀の参加者のうち1人でも犯行現場の下見など実行に向けた準備をすれば, 全体の共謀が成立するという考え方)

overthrow 名 〈政府などを〉転覆する, 倒す, 失脚させる, 〈制度などを〉打破する, 廃する
- **conspire to overthrow the government** 共謀して政府転覆を図る
- **plan to overthrow the government** 政府[政権]転覆を企てる

overtime 名 残業, 超過勤務, 時間外労働 (= overtime work; ⇒retain)
- **overtime allowance** 残業手当, 時間外勤務手当 (= overtime pay, overtime premium)
- **overtime hours** 残業時間
- **overtime pay** 残業手当, 超過勤務手当 (= overtime allowance, overtime premium)
- **overtime premium** 残業手当, 超過勤務手当, 時間外手当 (= overtime allowance)
- **overtime work** 残業, 超過勤務, 時間外労働
- **unpaid overtime** 無報酬の残業, サービス残業

overture 名 申し出, 申し入れ, 打診, 提案, 予備交渉[折衝], 序曲, 前奏曲, 序章
- **make overtures to** …に交渉の申し出をする, …に提案する, …と交渉を始める
- **reject one's overture(s)** …の提案を拒否する

overturn 動 ひっくり返す, 横倒しにする, 転覆させる, 倒す, 打倒す, 打ち負かす, 覆す, 翻す, 撤回する, 破棄する
- **overturn a not-guilty verdict** 無罪判決を破棄する
- **overturn district court sentences** 地裁判決を破棄する
- **overturn the government** 政府を倒す, 政府を打倒する
- **overturn the previous decision** 先の決定を撤回する[覆す, 翻す]

overvalue 動 過大評価する
- **overvalued dollar** ドル高, ドルの過大評価

overwork 名 過重労働, 過度の労働, 過労, 超過勤務, オーバーワーク
- **death from overwork** 過労死
- **illness as a result of overwork** 過労による病気

owe 動 …に負う, …に支払う[返済]義務がある, …する義務がある, …に借り[借金]がある, …を借りている, …を負担する
- **dividends owed** 未払いの配当
- **net amount owed** 正味負債額
- **owe debts** 債務を負担する, 債務を抱える
- **owe the bank interest on borrowings** 銀行に借入金の利子を支払う義務がある
- **the amount owing to ABC under this agreement** 本契約に基づいてABCに支払われる金額

own 動 所有する, 保有する, 持つ
- **equally owned by** …が折半出資している, …が共同所有している
- **owned capital** 自己資本 (= own capital)
- **state-owned company** 国有企業

own 形 自己の, 個人の, 独特の, 独自の, 特有の
- **own brand** 自社製品ブランド, 自主企画商品, PB(プライベート・ブランド)商品 (= private brand)
- **own capital** 自己資金 (= owned capital)
- **own effect** 自己効果
- **own fund** 自己資金, 自己資本
- **own stock** 自己株式

owner 名 所有者, 所有権者, 権利者, 株主, 出資者, 企業主, 荷主, 船主, プラント輸出契約の注文者, 発注者, 施主, オーナー
- **cargo owner** 荷主, 貨物所有者
- **factory owner** 工場主
- **joint owner** 共有者
- **majority owner** 過半数株主
- **managing owner** 経営所有者
- **stock owner** 株式所有者
- **virtual owner** 実質的な所有者, 実質的な保有者, 事実上の保有者

▶ Legally speaking, the shareholders are the *owners* of a joint stock company. 法律上は, 株主が株式会社の所有者だ。

ownership 名 所有, 所有権, 所有者, 保有株式, 所有比率, 出資比率, 持ち株比率, 経営権
- **capital ownership** 出資比率
- **foreign ownership** 外国人持ち株比率, 外国人保有比率

ox-walk tactic 牛歩戦術

ozone 名 オゾン, 新鮮な空気
- **ozone-depleting chlorofluorocarbon** オゾン層を破壊するフロン
- **ozone-depleting solvent** オゾン(層)を破壊する溶剤
- **ozone-friendly** オゾン層を破壊しない
- **ozone layer** オゾン層

P

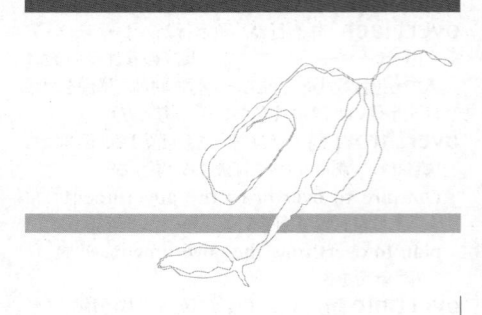

pace 名 速度, 速さ, スピード, 足並み, 足取り, テンポ, 歩調, ペース
  keep pace with inflation　インフレと足並みを揃える
  pace of business [economic] recovery　景気回復の足取り, 景気回復のピッチ
  pace of growth　成長のペース, 成長速度
  pace of rate reduction　利下げのテンポ
  pace of stockbuilding　在庫積上げのペース, 在庫増加のペース
  slow the pace of growth　景気が減速する

Pacific 形 太平洋の, 名 太平洋
  Asia-Pacific Economic Cooperation forum　アジア太平洋経済協力(APEC)会議
  Asia-Pacific region　アジア太平洋地域
  Economic and Social Commission for Asia and the Pacific　アジア太平洋経済社会委員会, エスカップ《略 ESCAP》
  Pacific Daylight Time　太平洋時間《略 PDT》(米国・カナダの太平洋岸の標準時で, 太平洋標準時の夏時間)
  Pacific Economic Cooperation Council　太平洋経済協力会議
  Pacific Ocean　太平洋
  Pacific Rim　環太平洋, 環太平洋諸国[地域], 太平洋周辺地域 (=Pacific Basin)
  Pacific Rim countries and territories　環太平洋の国と地域
  Pacific Standard Time　太平洋標準時 (=Pacific Time : グリニッジ標準時(GMT)より8時間遅い)
  Pan Pacific concept　環太平洋構想
  Trans-Asia-Pacific network　環太平洋ネットワーク

pacification 名　鎮圧, 平定, 鎮定, 和解

pacifist 名　平和主義者, 平和主義論者, 反戦主義者, 参戦拒否者

package 名　対策, 政策, 策, 案, 計画, プラン, 制度, 包括法案, 一括法案, 装置, 包装, 梱包, パッケージ
  aggressive stimulus package　大型の財政出動
  aid package　支援策, テコ入れ策 (=assistance package, rescue package)
  bailout package　救済策
  early retirement and buyout packages　早期退職優遇制度
  emergency employment package　緊急雇用対策
  package consolidating agency　小口運送業者 (=freight forwarder)
  package cost　包装費 (=packing cost)
  package deal　一括取引, 一括購入, セット販売, 抱き合わせ商品, 抱き合わせ契約, 包括案 (=packaged deal)
  package holiday [vacation]　パック旅行, パッケージ旅行
  package of business stimulating measures　総合景気刺激策
  package store　酒類小売店
  package tour　パッケージ・ツアー (=package holiday : 旅費, 宿泊費, 食費, 観光料など一切込みの周遊旅行)

pact

remuneration package 報酬, 給付, 謝礼, 代償, 報償
rescue package 支援策（＝aid package）

pact 图 国家間の協定, 条約, 協約, 契約, 取決め, 約束, 議定書（＝protocol, treaty）
alliance pact 提携契約
commercial pact 通商条約
free trade pact 自由貿易協定
nude pact 無償契約
peace pact 平和条約
sign a pact 条約に調印する, 条約を締結する
social pact 社会契約
trade pact 通商協定, 貿易協定
Washington Pact ワシントン条約

pad 動〈経費などを〉水増し請求する
pad accounts [books] 粉飾決算する
pad profits [earnings] 利益を水増しする
padded bills 水増し請求書
padded expense 経費の水増し

padding 图 水増し, 不正行為, 不正, 詰め物をすること, 余分な言葉, 不要な挿入句
padding of accounts 粉飾決算（＝window dressing）

paddy wagon 犯人護送車（＝patrol wagon）

Palestine 图 パレスチナ
Palestine Liberation Army パレスチナ解放軍
Palestine Liberation Front パレスチナ解放戦線《略 PLF》
Palestine Liberation Organization パレスチナ解放機構《略 PLO》
Palestine National Council パレスチナ民族評議会

Palestinian 图 パレスチナ人, 形 パレスチナの
Palestinian Authority パレスチナ自治政府
Palestinian National Authority パレスチナ自治政府《略 PNA》
Palestinian parliament パレスチナ評議会
Palestinian President パレスチナ自治政府議長

pall 图〈陰気な〉覆い, 陰, かげり, 幕, 棺,〈ベルベットの〉棺覆い, 棺衣
cast a pall over …に暗い影を落とす［暗い影を投げかける］, …を陰気にする

palm vein ID system 手のひら静脈認証システム

palm vein pattern recognition system 手のひらの静脈パターン認証システム

panacea 图 万能薬, 万能の解決策

pandemic 图 世界的［全国的］流行病, 世界的大流行, 大流行, パンデミック

panel 图 討論会, 座談会, 委員会, 小委員会, 審査会, 審議会, 委員団, 審査団, 調査団, 講師団, 専門家集団, 制御盤, 計器盤, パネル
blue ribbon panel ハイレベル委員会, そうそうたる顔ぶれの委員会
consumers' panel 消費者パネル, 消費者グループ
control panel 制御版
corporate reform panel 経営改革委員会
disciplinary panel 懲罰委員会
front panel 前面操作盤, フロント・パネル
government advisory panel 政府諮問委員会
independent panel 独立委員会
management reform panel 経営改革委員会
panel arbitrator 名簿仲裁人
panel conference 公開検討会, パネル・コンファレンス
panel discussion 公開討論会, 代表討論会, 討論会, パネル・ディスカッション
panel survey [research] パネル調査, パネル・サーベイ（マーケティング調査法の一つ）
tender panel method 競争入札制度
working-level panel 事務レベルの委員団

panic 图 動揺, 錯乱, 狼狽, あわてふためくこと, うろたえること, 臆病風, 恐怖心, 恐慌, 恐慌状態, パニック状態, 経済恐慌, 切羽詰まった状態, 窮地, パニック
a panic attack パニック発作
a state of panic パニック状態
be seized with panic 臆病風に吹かれる, 恐怖心にとらわれる
in (a) panic 動揺して, パニック状態で, 恐慌状態に陥って
panic buying 〈株価上昇を予測しての〉飛びつき買い,〈品不足を予測しての〉パニック買い, 恐慌買い, 熱狂相場
panic quotations 恐慌相場
panic selling 〈株価下落を予測しての〉狼狽売り,〈品余りを予測しての〉パニック売り, 恐慌売り
panic stations 緊急事態, パニック状態
press the panic button 非常ボタンを押す
semi-panic 半恐慌

paper 图 新聞, 文書, 書類, 資料, 論文, 手形, 証券, 債券, 紙, ペーパー
accommodation paper 融通手形（＝accommodation bill）
commercial paper 商業手形, 商業証券, コマー

シャル・ペーパー《略 CP》
financial paper 金融手形
government paper 国債, 政府発行有価証券
national paper 全国紙
on paper 名目上の, 書類の上では
short paper 短期証券
three-year paper 3年債
valuable paper 有価証券
white paper 白書
working paper 調査[研究]報告書

paper 形 架空の, 名目上の, 書面の, 帳簿上の
paper assets 金融資産
paper audit 書面監査
paper company 名目会社, 幽霊会社, ペーパー・カンパニー
paper gold ペーパー・ゴールド(国際通貨基金(IMF)の特別引出権(special drawing rights)の通称)
paper issuance CP発行
paper loss 含み損, 評価損, 架空損失
paper manufacturers 製紙業界
paper margin 帳簿上の利益
paper mill 製紙工場
paper money 紙幣 (＝paper currency)
paper profit 含み益, 評価益, 架空利益 (＝paper gain)
paper profit or loss 含み損益, 評価損益(証券類の取得価格と時価との差額)
paper work [paperwork] 文書業務, 文書事務, 書類事務, 事務処理, ペーパーワーク

paper over 取り繕う, 隠す, 糊塗する
paperless 形 紙を一切使わない, ペーパーレス, 副 紙を使用しないで
▶ Listed companies revised their articles of incorporation to make stock certificates *paperless* by holding shareholders meetings. 株券をペーパーレス化するため, 公開企業は, 株主総会を開いて会社の定款を変更した.

par excellence 優れた(superior), 優秀な, 卓越した, とくに優れた, 他より一段と優れている, とくに抜きん出た, 抜群の, 非常に腕のいい (＝by excellence:語源はフランス語で, 一般に名詞の後に置かれる。副詞として使われるときは「とくに, とりわけ(above all others), とくに抜きん出て(pre-eminently)」の意味を持つ)

paradigm 名 理論的枠組み, 枠組み, 構図, 模範, 範例, 典型, 例, 実例, パラダイム (＝example, framework, pattern, typical example)

conventional paradigm 従来の枠組, 従来のパターン
paradigm shift 根本的変化, 抜本的変革, 社会の価値観の移行, 社会全体の枠組の転換[変化], パラダイムの転換, パラダイム・シフト (＝paradigm change)

paragon 名 手本, 鑑(かがみ), 模範
paralysis 名 麻痺, 麻痺状態, 停滞, 行き詰まり, 無能力, 無気力
cerebral paralysis 脳性麻痺
policy paralysis 政策の行き詰まり
traffic paralysis 交通麻痺

paralyze 動 麻痺させる, 無力にする, …の活動を止める

paramedics 名 救急隊員, 医療補助員, 準医療活動従事者, パラメディック

parent 名 親会社, 母体, 根源, 単独ベース
at the parent base [basis] 単独ベースで
on a parent-only basis 単独ベースで
parent-basis earnings forecast 単独ベースの収益見通し
parent capex 単独ベースの設備投資 (＝parent capital spending)
parent company 親会社, 本体
parent operating profit 単独ベースの営業利益
parent recurring profit 単独経常利益
parent sales 単独ベースの売上高

parental leave 育児休業
Paris Club パリ・クラブ, 主要債権国会議(開発途上国の公的債務の救済策について非公式に話し合う日米欧19か国の提言会議。パリにある仏財務経済産業省で行われるため, パリ・クラブと呼ばれている)

park 名 公園, 遊園地, イベント広場, 駐車場, 団地, 競技場, 試合場, 軍需品置き場, 地域, パーク
amusement park 遊園地
ball park 球場
car park 駐車場
industrial park 工業団地, 工業用地 (＝industrial estate)
National Park Service 〈米国の〉国立公園局
park ranger 森林警備官
science park サイエンス・パーク(科学研究・科学産業の中心地域, ハイテク企業の集中地域)
theme park テーマ・パーク

Parliament [parliament] 名 〈英国やカナダ, 豪州の〉議会(英国議会は上院(the House of

Lords)と下院(the House of Commons)から成る。日本の議会はParliamentまたはDietという。⇒Congress, Diet)
- **a bill now before the Parliament** 議会に上程されている法案
- **European Parliament** 〈EU（欧州連合）の〉欧州議会
- **Member of Parliament** 〈英国の〉下院議員, 国会議員《略 MP》
- **reconvene Parliament** 国会［議会］を再開する
- **Taiwan's parliament** 台湾の立法院

parliamentarian 名 議会人, 議会通, 議会政治通,〈英国の〉国会議員,〈米〉下院議事主任［議事幹事補佐］, パーラメンタリアン

parliamentary 形 議会の, 国会の, 議会［国会］で制定された, 議院法による
- **parliamentary cabinet system** 議院内閣制（=the parliamentary system of government）
- **parliamentary candidate** 国会議員候補者
- **Parliamentary Commissioner (for Administration)** 英国の議会行政管理官［行政監察専門委員］（英国のオンブズマン（ombudsman）の正式名称）
- **parliamentary democracy** 議会制民主主義
- **parliamentary procedure** 議会運営手続き, 議員法
- **parliamentary secretary** 〈英国の〉政務次官,〈日本の〉政務官
- **parliamentary stenographer** 国会速記者
- **parliamentary usage** 議会のしきたり
- **parliamentary vice minister** 〈日本各省の〉政務次官 （=state minister）
- **win the parliamentary seat** 議席を獲得する

parole 名 仮釈放, 仮出獄, 仮出所, 仮入国許可権,〈捕虜の〉釈放宣誓, 誓言

parolee 名 仮釈放者, 仮出獄者

participant 名 参加者, 参加企業, 参加行, 参加国, 加入者, 受講者, 出席者, 関係者
- **market participant** 市場参加者, 市場参入企業, 市場関係者 （=market player）
- **transaction participant** 取引参加者

participate 動 参加する, 参入する, 関係する, 共にする
- **participate in a debate** 討論に加わる
- **participate in a market economy** 市場経済に参加する
- **participate in profits** 利益にあずかる
- **participate of** いくぶん…の性質がある

participating 形 参加している, 参加型の, 系列の, 受益権付きの
- **participating interests** 参加持ち分
- **participating preferred share [stock]** 利益配当優先株, 利益参加優先株
- **participating sponsorship** 〈テレビの〉共同提供

participation 名 参加, 参入, 進出, 加入, 関与 （=involvement）
- **capital participation** 資本参加
- **compulsory participation** 強制加入
- **employee participation** 従業員の経営参加
- **equity participation** 資本参加, 株式投資, 出資比率
- **female participation ratio** 女子有業率
- **individual participation** 個人参加
- **labor (force) participation ratio** 労働[労働力]参加率, 労働力化率
- **participation loan** 〈複数の銀行による〉協調融資, 共同融資, 参加融資
- **participation rate** 労働力率, 就業化率, 有業率
- **participation right** 参加権, 配当権
- **profit participation** 利益分配
- **worker participation** 労働者の経営参加, 経営参加, 共同所有

participatory 形 全員参加方式の
- **participatory democracy** 参加民主主義, 直接参加の民主政治
- **participatory theater** 観客参加劇場

particulate 名 微粒子, 形 微粒子の
- **particulate matter** 粒子状物質《略 PM》

partner 名 共同経営者, 共同出資者, 共同所有者, 提携者, 提携先, 提携企業, 組合員, 社員, パートナー
- **dormant partner** 匿名パートナー
- **equity partner** 出資者
- **executive partner** 理事
- **joint partner** 共同出資者, 共同パートナー
- **limited partner** 有限責任パートナー, リミテッド・パートナー
- **silent partner** 非執行パートナー, 匿名パートナー（経営や業務執行には参加しないが無限責任を負うパートナー）

partnership 名 共同出資, 共同所有, 共同経営, 提携, 連携, 協力, 組合, 合名会社, パートナー関係, パートナーシップ
- **equal partnership** 折半出資, 対等提携, 対等な協力関係

form a partnership 提携する
limited liability partnership 有限責任パートナーシップ
limited partnership 合資会社, 有限責任組合, リミテッド・パートナーシップ
Partnership for Peace 平和のためのパートナーシップ《略 PFP》
voluntary partnership 任意組合
parts maker 部品メーカー
parts per billion 10億分の1《略 ppb》
parts per million 100万分の1《略 ppm》
party 名 政党, 党派, 党派心, 派閥, 政治団体, 当事者, 契約当事者, 関係者, 団体, 一行, 一団, 宴会, 馬鹿騒ぎ, 祝賀会, 懇親会, (競争)相手, ライバル, 敵対者, 人, パーティ
accommodation party 融通当事者, 融通署名者
account party 発行依頼人
assigning party 譲渡する当事者, 譲渡人
be (a) party to …に関わる, …に加担する, …に加わる, …に参加する, …の一端を担う
each party 各当事者（＝each of the parties）
either of the parties hereto 本契約のいずれか一方の当事者（＝either party）
in a party mood お祭り気分で
interested party 利害関係者
party apparatus 政党機構, 政党組織, 派閥組織
party insuring 保険契約者
party line 〈政党の〉政策, 政策綱領, 〈政党の〉基本方針, 政治路線, 路線, 共同加入電話（party wire）
party machine 政党幹部
party organ 党機関紙
party piece 宴会用の芸, 十八番（おはこ）, 馬鹿の一つ覚え
party platform [program] 政党綱領
party political 党略の, 党に関連した
party to a suit [party in action] 訴訟当事者
ruling party 政権政党
search party 捜索隊
secured party 担保権者
surveying party 調査団, 測量団
the concerned parties 利害関係人
the disclosing party 開示当事者, 開示した当事者
the guilty party 犯人
the parties concerned 関係者, 当事者
the parties hereto 本契約当事者, 当事者
the party in default 不履行当事者
the party in question 当該当事者
the party whip 〈党の〉院内幹事長 （＝the chief whip）
the receiving party 受領当事者
the ruling party 与党, 政権政党
pass 動 〈法案などを〉可決する［通過させる］, 採択する, 〈判断・判決を〉下す, 伝える, 回す, 委ねる, 譲渡する, 〈範囲を〉越える
pass a bill 法案［議案］を可決する
pass along [on] to consumers 消費者に還元する, 価格に転嫁する
pass the Commons 下院を通過する
pass on to [onto] …に転嫁する, …に還元する
pass on the lower prices of crude oil to users 原油価格の低下をユーザーに還元する
pass on to consumers 消費者に転嫁する, 価格に転嫁する
pass on to customers 顧客に転嫁する
passage 名 通過, 通行, 通行権, 通行許可証, 移動, 空の旅, 船旅, 船賃, 通路, 出入り口, 〈時の〉経過, 〈事態の〉進展, 発展, 進歩, 成り行き, 推移, 〈議案の〉通過［可決］, 〈文章の〉一節, 殴り合い, 論争, 争論, 議論, 管, 便通（bowel movement）
a bird of passage 渡り鳥, 一時的滞在者
a rite of passage 通過儀礼
a ship in passage 航行中の船
have a rough passage to …へ行くのに難航する
have stormy passage with …と大いにやり合う
nasal passages 鼻腔
passage of a bill 法案の通過, 法案の可決
passage of arms 殴り合い, 言い合い, 口論
passage way 通路, 連絡通路, 廊下 （＝passageway）
the passage of time 時間の経過
passalong 名 消費者価格に上乗せする価格の引上げ
passenger 名 旅客
passenger transportation 旅客輸送
pass-fail 名 合否だけを決める方式, 合否判定方式
passive 形 受け身の, 受動的な, 消極的な, 人の言いなりになる, 間接的な, 無抵抗の, 服従的な, 危険のない, 活動的でない, 不活発な, 活気のない, 不活性の, 腐蝕しにくい, 受動型の, 反射用の, 単純

利用の, 無利子[無利息]の, 利益を生まない, パッシブ

passive balance 国際収支の赤字 (＝adverse balance, balance of payments deficit, unfavorable balance)
passive belt 自動シートベルト, 自動式安全ベルト (＝automatic seat belt)
passive bond 無利子債券, 無利子社債
passive damages 逸失利益
passive debt 無利子[無利息]の負債, 受動的公債
passive euthanasia 消極的安楽死(延命治療を停止して死期を早めること)
passive immunity 受動免疫
passive income 受動的所得(納税者が参加していない賃貸不動産や事業から生じる所得)
passive management パッシブ運用
passive obedience 黙従, 命令の絶対服従
passive protection 自動保護装置, 自動式の搭乗者保護装置
passive restraint 自動保護装置, 安全装置
passive smoking 受動喫煙, 間接的喫煙 (＝involuntary smoking)
passive solar design 太陽熱単純利用設計
passive trade 受動貿易 (＝passive commerce: 外国船による貿易)
passive trust 受動信託, 消極信託
passport 名 旅券, 海外渡航許可証, 確実な手段, パスポート
 a passport to success 製鋼へのパスポート
 multiple passport 数次旅券
 passport control 出国手続き, 出入国管理[管理局]
 passport inspection 旅券検査
password 名 暗証番号, 合言葉, パスワード
pat-down search 〈着衣の上からの〉身体検査
patent 名 特許, 特許権, 特許物件, 特許証, 特権, 権利, 公有地譲渡証書, パテント, 形 明白な, 公開の
 application for patent 特許出願, 特許申請 (＝patent application)
 dependent patent 従属特許
 design patent 意匠特許
 file for patent examination 特許審査を請求する, 特許の審査請求をする
 grant of a patent 特許付与
 improvement patent 改良特許
 independent patent 独立特許
 litigious patent 係争特許
 patent applicant 特許出願者
 patent application 特許出願 (＝application for patent)
 patent disputes 特許紛争
 patent infringement [violation] 特許侵害, 特許権侵害, 特許抵触
 Patent Law 特許法
 patent licensing 特許許諾, 特許実施許諾
 Patent Office 特許庁
 patent pending 特許出願中, 特許審査中
 patent protection 特許保護
 patent right 特許権
 pending patent 係属特許
 provisional (patent) application 仮特許出願, 仮出願
 share patents on basic techniques 基本技術に関する特許を相互利用する
patentable 形 特許取得可能な, 特許性のある
 patentable right 特許取得可能な権利, 特許が受けられる権利
paternalism 名 温情主義, 家族主義, 過度の規制, 干渉
paternity 名 父親であること, 父権, 父系, 父方の血筋, 起源(origin), 元祖, 作者であること
 false paternity 偽装認知
 paternity leave 男性の育児休業, 男性のための産休
 paternity suit 父親認知訴訟, 父権認知訴訟
 paternity test 父子鑑定検査
path 名 道, 道筋, 経路, 進路, 軌道, 方向, 動向, パス(指定したファイルやディレクトリまでの道筋), 方針, コース
 balanced [equilibrium] path 均衡経路, 均衡成長経路
 beat a path to …に押しかける
 consumption path 消費経路
 credit path 信用力の経路
 dynamic path 動態的経路
 efficient path 有効経路
 equilibrium path 均衡経路
 expansion [expanding, expansionary] path 拡張経路
 feasible path 実行可能経路, 実現可能経路
 golden rule path 黄金律, 黄金則経路
 growing path 成長経路, 成長軌道, 成長線
 marginal income [profit] path 限界利益線

modest upward path 穏やかな上昇軌道
path dependency 経路依存性, 経路依存型
path independency 経路独立性, 経路独立型
path planning 経路探索
path to profitability 利益への道筋《略 P2P》
random path 経路
recovery path 回復軌道, 景気回復軌道, 景気回復経路
short-term path 短期動向
stable path 安定経路
time path 時間経路
patient 名 患者, 形 辛抱強い
patient mix-up 患者の取り違え
patrimonial 形 世襲の, 先祖伝来の
patrimonial sea [waters] パトリモニアル水域（沿岸国が天然資源に主権を行使できる海域）
Patriot Advanced Capability-3 (PAC-3) surface-to-air missile system 地対空誘導弾パトリオット・ミサイル3 (PAC3)
Patriot missile パトリオット・ミサイル
patrol 名 巡回, 巡視, 偵察隊, 哨戒機, パトロール
patrol boat 巡視船艇
patrol bomber 偵察爆撃機
patrol plane 哨戒機
patrol wagon 囚人護送車（=paddy wagon）
patronage 名 ひいき, 愛顧, 引立て, 後援, 支援, 保護, 情実人事
under the patronage of …の後援[賛助, 支援]のもとに, …の庇護を受けて
pave the way for …に道を開く, …への道を開く, …を可能にする
Pax Americana 米国の力[主導, 支配]による平和
pay 動 支払う, 支出する, 負担する, 返済する, 弁済する, 利潤をもたらす, 利益になる, 採算が取れる, もうかる
pay 名 賃金, 給料, 手当, 報酬, 支払い, 形 有料の, ペイ
basic pay 基本給, 基本給与
daily pay 日給
dismissal pay 解雇手当
full pay 本給, 全給
merit-based pay plan 業績連動型の報酬制度
monthly pay 月給
overtime pay 超過勤務手当, 残業手当
pay cable 有線テレビ(放送), 有料ケーブルテレビ・サービス

pay channel 有料放送
pay check [cheque] 給料小切手, 給料支払い小切手, 俸給, 賃金, 後援者, 広告主（⇒paycheck）
pay day 給料日, 支払い日, 最良の日
pay dirt 採算の取れる採鉱地, 掘り出し物, 貴重な物, 金づる, 金もうけの種
pay per view [pay-per-view] 有料テレビ, 有料テレビ方式《略 PPV》
pay station 公衆電話, 公衆電話ボックス（= pay phone, pay telephone）
pay stub 給与明細票
pay toilet 有料トイレ
premium pay 奨励給
retirement pay 退職金, 退職手当
self pays 自己負担分
take-home pay 手取り給料, 可処分所得
time and a half pay 5割増し給[給与]
pay-as-you-go 形 現金払い方式の, 源泉課税方式の
pay-as-you-go basis 現金主義, 現金基準, 現金払い方式, 現金払い主義, 独立採算制
pay-as-you-go formula 賦課方式, 源泉課税方式, 現金払い方式
pay in 〈銀行口座に金を〉払い込む[振り込む], 預金する, 寄付する
pay off 〈借金を〉完済する, 〈債務を〉返済する, 償還する, 料金を支払う, …に口止め料を払う, 給料を支払って解雇する, よい結果[所期の成果]を生む, 実を結ぶ, うまく行く, 報われる, 引き合う, 効果がある, 成功する, …に仕返しをする, …に金をつかませる, 買収する
one's efforts pay off …の努力が報われる
pay off maturing commercial paper 満期が来た[満期を迎えた]コマーシャル・ペーパー (CP) を償還する
pay off old score 積年の恨みをはらす
pay off the loan ローン[借入金]を返済する
pay off the obligations 債務を返済する
pay off the public funds 公的資金を返済する
pay system 賃金制度, 賃金体系, 給与制度（=wage system）
performance-based [merit-based] pay system 能力給制度, 成果主義型給与制度, 成果主義型賃金体系
seniority-based pay system 年功序列賃金制度, 年功序列賃金体系, 年功序列型給与制度
paycheck 名 給料支払い小切手, 給料小切手,

給料, 賃金 (＝pay check)
average monthly paycheck 平均月収
cut paychecks 賃金をカットする
payload specialist 搭乗科学技術者, ペイロード・スペシャリスト《略 **PS**》
payment 图 支払い, 払込み, 振込み, 決済, 納入, 返済, 弁済, 支払い金額, 債権
payment transaction 支払い事務
payoff 图 〈給料などの〉支払い, 〈借金などの〉完済, 〈預金の〉払い戻し, 報酬, 利得, 利益, 利益供与, 賄賂, 回収, 成果
payoff of market reform 市場改革の成果
payoff period 回収期間
payoff scandal 贈収賄事件, 利益供与事件 (＝payoff case)
political payoffs 政治献金
payoff system ペイオフ制度 (＝payoff scheme)

> ペイオフ制度とは ⇒ 経営が破綻した金融機関の預金を, 預金保険機構を通じて預金者に払い戻す制度。払戻し額保証の上限は, 2001年4月から1人当たり1,000万円とされている。金融機関は毎年, 預金量の一定の割合を保険料として預金保険機構に納付しており, これがペイオフを行う際の原資となる。

payola 图 袖の下, 賄賂, 贈賄, 不正リベート
payout 图 支払い, 支出, 支出金, 〈株式などの〉配当[配当金], 〈保険金の〉支払い, 支払い保険金, 〈社会保障の〉給付費, 回収
dividend payout 配当性向, 配当金の支払い
expected payout ratio 期待配当性向
payout period 回収期間 (＝payout time)
pension payout 年金の支払い
payroll 图 給与表, 給与総額, 給与支払い簿, 人件費, 従業員名簿, 雇用者数, 総従業員数, 職員定数
PC パソコン, パーソナル・コンピュータ (**personal computer**の略)
P.C. 専門職法人, 職能法人, 知的職業法人 (**professional corporation**の略)
PCAOB 米上場企業会計監視委員会 (**Public Company Accounting Oversight Board**の略。民間の独立機関で, 2002年に制定された企業改革法に基づいて2003年に発足。米上場企業を扱う監査法人は, 国内外を問わずPCAOBへの登録を義務付けられている)
PCB ポリ塩化ビフェニール (**polychlorinated biphenyls**の略)
pct [pct.] パーセント (**percent**の略)

PDA 携帯情報端末 (**personal digital assistant**の略)
PDCA cycle PDCAサイクル(マネジメントの基礎サイクル。PDCAは, plan (計画), do (実行), check (検証)と action (改善)の頭文字)
peace 图 平和, 泰平, 和平, 和睦, 講和, 友好, 友好関係, 調和, 治安, 安定, 平穏, 安らぎ, 安楽, 静寂, 沈黙, 静けさ, 和解, 仲直り, ピース
be at peace with …と友好関係にある, …と和親の関係にある
breach of the peace 治安の妨害
disturb the peace 治安を乱す
Food for Peace 平和のための食糧
mailed-fist peace 武装平和 (＝armed peace)
make peace with …と仲直りする, …と和解する, …と折り合いをつける, …と和睦[講和] する
peace agreement [accord] 和平協定, 平和協定
peace and order 治安
peace at any price 絶対平和主義, 絶対平和論
peace conference 和平会議, 講和会議
Peace Corps 米平和部隊(米政府支援の民間ボランティア組織)
peace keeping [peace-keeping, peacekeeping] force 平和維持軍《略 **PKF**》(＝peace keeping troop)
peace-keeping operation PKO活動
peace offensive 平和攻勢
peace officer 治安官
Peace People 〈カトリックとプロテスタント両派から成る〉北アイルランドの平和運動
peace pill ピース・ピル(幻覚剤のフェンサイクリジン)
peace treaty 平和条約, 講和条約
separate peace 単独講和
UN [U.N.] peace cooperation law 国連平和協力法
peaceful 形 平和な, 平和的, 平和を好む, 泰平の, 平穏な, 静かな, 安らかな, 平時の
peaceful coexistence 平和共存, 平和的共存
peaceful uses of atomic energy 原子力の平和利用
peaceful utilization 平和利用
peacekeeper 图 和平監視者, 停戦監視者
Peacekeeper 图 〈国連の〉平和維持軍, 〈米国の〉主力大陸間弾道弾MXの愛称
peacekeeping [peace keeping] 图 平和維持

peacemaker / pension plan

peacekeeping activities 平和維持活動
peacekeeping force 平和維持軍, 平和維持部隊 (＝peacekeeping troop)
peacekeeping mission 国連軍の駐留期間, 平和維持活動
peacekeeping operations 平和維持活動《略 PKO》
U.N. peacekeeping [peace-keeping] operations 国連の平和維持活動《略 PKO》
peacemaker 名 調停者, 仲裁人
peacemaking 名 和平交渉, 仲裁, 調停
peak 動 〈最高潮・頂点に〉達する, 天井を打つ, ピークに達する, ピークを打つ, 峠を越す
economic activity has peaked 景気は峠を越した
peak out 〈景気が〉天井を打つ, ピークアウトする
peak 名 最高潮, 絶頂, 頂上, 頂点, 天井, 最高, 最高点, 最高限度, 最大限, 先端, ピーク
at one's peak 絶頂期に
be at the peak of …の頂点にある
cyclical peak 景気循環のピーク
first peak 一番天井
major peak 大天井
peak-hour traffic jam ピーク時の交通混雑
reach a peak ピークに達する
pedestrian 名 歩行者, 形 歩行者の, 歩行者専用の
pedestrian crossing 横断歩道
pedestrian overpass 歩道橋
peg 動 安定させる, 固定させる, 一定にさせる, 〈賃金・価格などを〉あるレベルに抑えておく, 釘付けにする, 連動させる, 凍結させる, リンクさせる, 裏付ける, 分類する, 識別する, 名 〈株価などの〉設定水準, 固定相場制, 等級, 位, ペッグ
adjustable peg rate system 調整可能な釘付け相場制
crawling peg 小刻みな為替変更, クローリング・ペッグ
dollar-pegged currency system 対ドル固定為替相場, 対ドル固定相場制
peg one's exchange rates to the dollar …の為替レートをドルに連動させる
peg point 基準点
pegged exchange 固定為替相場, 釘付け為替相場
pegged market 釘付け相場, 釘付け市場
penalty 名 処罰, 処分, 罰金, 違約金, 延滞金, 反則金, 制裁金, 制裁, 罰則, 刑罰, ペナルティ

increased penalties 罰則強化
newly installed penalty 罰則の新設
pecuniary penalty 罰金刑, 罰金
penalty charge 遅延損害金
penalty interest 遅延利息
penalty tax 追徴課税, 加算税
pencil in 予定に入れる, 〈予定を〉仮に入れる
pencil pusher 記者, 事務員, 書記
pending 形 未解決の, 懸案の, 未決定の, 〈訴訟などが〉係争中の, 係属中の, 審理[審査]中の, 差し迫った, 切迫した, 目前の
patent pending 特許出願中
pending action 係争中の事件, 係争中の訴訟
pending application 係属出願
pending issues 懸案問題, 未解決の問題, 懸案事項
pending lawsuit [suit] 係争中の訴訟
penetration 名 参入, 進出, 浸透, 浸透力, 浸透度, 普及率, 加入率, 市場進出普及度, 洞察力, 眼識, 看破, 侵害, 侵略, 勢力浸透, 〈敵陣の〉突破, 〈弾丸の〉貫通
cross penetration 相互浸透
external penetration 対外侵略
household penetration 家庭への普及率
market penetration 市場参入, 市場進出, 市場浸透[市場への浸透], 市場浸透度
mutual penetration of capital 資本の相互浸透
penetration price 浸透価格
penetration pricing (policy) 浸透価格政策
penetration rate 加入率, 普及率
penguin suit 宇宙服
pennant race 優勝争い
pension 名 年金
pension benefits 年金給付
pension defaulter 年金未納者
pension fund 年金基金
pension numbering system 年金番号システム
pension premium 年金保険料
pension scheme [plan, program, system] 年金制度
personal pension policy 個人年金
pension plan 年金制度 (＝pension program, pension scheme, pension system)
cost of pension plans 年金制度原価
defined benefit pension plan 給付建て年金制度
defined contribution pension plan 拠出建

て年金制度
employee pension plan 従業員年金制度

Pentagon 名 〈米国〉防総省（米陸海空3軍の最高軍事機構），米国軍当局，ペンタゴン（米バージニア（Virginia）州アーリントン（Arlington）にある国防総省（Department of Defense）の建物）

pentagon management ペンタゴン（五角形）経営，多角経営

pent-up demand 潜在需要，鬱積した需要，満たされない需要

people 名 人々，人，人材，世間，世間の人々，国民，民族，人間，身内，身内の者，社員，部下，家臣，臣民，ピープル
  a people without a country 祖国を持たない民族
  boat people ボート・ピープル（小船で祖国を脱出する難民・亡命者）
  feet people フィート・ピープル（陸地を歩いて祖国を脱出する難民・亡命者）
  one's faithful people …の忠実な部下
  people business 人材ビジネス
  people-generated risks 人為的災害リスク
  people-intensive 人手集約的な
  people mover 人員高速輸送機関，〈歩く歩道などの〉人間輸送手段，大型乗用車
  people with special needs 身体障害者，特別介護が必要な人々（hadicapped peopleやphysically disabled peopleに代わる表現）
  people-saving 人手を省く［節約する］
  People's Daily 人民日報（中国共産党機関紙）
  People's Liberation Army 人民解放軍
  people's life indicators 新国民生活指標《略 PLI》
  People's Republic of China 中華人民共和国（中国の正式名）
  People's Republic of Korea 朝鮮民主主義人民共和国，北朝鮮
  people's working uniform 〈中国の〉人民服

People's Bank of China 〈中国の中央銀行に当たる〉中国人民銀行，中国中央銀行《略 PBOC》

pep 名 元気，活気，気力（vigor），活力（pepperの短縮語）
  pep party 応援団
  pep pill 覚醒剤，興奮剤
  pep rally 決起集会，壮行会，激励会
  pep talk 激励の言葉，激励演説，檄（げき）をはっぱ

pepper gas 暴徒鎮圧用ガス

PER 株価収益率（＝P/E, P/E ratio：price earnings ratioの略。株式投資の主な投資指標の一つで，株価が1株当たり利益（税引き後利益）の何倍に相当するかを示す。PER（倍）は，株価を1株当たり利益（earnings per share）で割って算出する）

per annum 1年当たり，1年に付き，1年毎に，年，毎年，年間，年率
  five percent per annum GDP growth GDPの年成長率5％
  income per annum 年間所得
  ten percent per annum 年10％，年率10％

per capita 1人当たり，国民1人当たり
  per capita levy of residential tax 住民税の均等割り

per share 1株当たり

per worker 従業員［社員］1人当たり，労働者1人当たり

percentage 名 比率，割合，部分，分け前，歩合［歩合制］，百分率，利益，利点，得，パーセント
  annual percentage rate 実質年率
  as percentages of total revenues 総収益［総売上高］に対する比率［百分率］
  percentage achievement 達成率
  percentage basis 〈株式相場の〉100ドル建て
  percentage change 変化率，百分率変化
  percentage distribution 構成比
  percentage growth 百分率成長（パーセントで示した伸び率）
  percentage of capital structure 資本構成比率
  total debt as a percentage of total capitalization 資本総額に対する債務総額の比率

percentage point パーセント・ポイント，ポイント，パーセンテージ・ポイント（one percentage point＝1パーセント）

> **percentとpercentage pointの違い** ⇒ percentは比率のパーセントで，percentage pointは絶対数のパーセントを表す。例えば，年率10％の物価上昇率が10パーセント伸びた場合は，年率11％の伸び率になる。一方，年率10％の物価上昇率が10パーセント・ポイント伸びた場合は，年率20％の伸び率になる。

  a quarter percentage point 0.25％
  half a percentage point 0.5％

perennial 形 長く続く，永続的な（perpetual），永遠の，絶え間のない（constant），繰り返し起こる［現われる，持ち上がる］，〈植物が〉多年性の，〈川が〉年中流れる，1年中枯れない
  perennial complaints いつもの不平不満
  perennial issue [question] 懸案，繰り返し持ち

上がる問題, 永遠の問題
perennial plant 多年生植物, 多年草
perestroika 名 ペレストロイカ（改革, 改造を意味するロシア語）
performance 名 実績, 業績, 成果, 〈義務・債務の〉履行, 実行, 実施, 遂行, 運用, 運用成績, 実演, 上演, 動向, 値動き, 収益性, 性能, パフォーマンス
  export performance 輸出実績
  good performance 好調な業績, 好業績（＝ strong performance）
  performance-based fiscal budget system 成果主義の年度予算制度
  performance-based pay system 成果主義型給与制度
  performance test 性能テスト, 作業テスト, 業績テスト
  portfolio performance 資産運用実績, 資産運用成績, ポートフォリオの運用成績
  price performance 値動き, インフレ動向
  sales performance 販売実績
  sluggish performance 業績不振
perigee 名 近地点（月・人工衛星などの軌道上で地球に最も近い点）
perilune 名 近月点（月の周囲を回る人工衛星が最も月に近づく点）
perinatal medical care 周産期医療（妊娠28週以後から出生7日後までの出産前後期間の医療）
period 名 期間, 時局, 局面, …期, 年度, 年数, 会計期間, 会計年度, 事業年度, ピリオド
  accounting period 会計期間, 会計年度
  current period 当事業年度, 当期
  durable period 耐用年数
  during the period 期中
  employee's service period 従業員の勤務年数
  financing period 調達期間
  fiscal period 会計期間, 会計年度
  payback period 回収期間, 投資回収期間
  period average method 総平均法（＝ periodic average method）
  period income 期間利益
  period planning 期間計画
  prior period adjustment 過年度修正
  tender period 入札期間
  the same period 同期
  the year-ago period 前年同期
  throughout the period indicated 当該期間中に
perishables 名 生鮮食品, 生鮮食料品（＝ perishable food）
perjure oneself 偽証する
  perjure oneself at the ad hoc committee 特別委員会で偽証する
perjury 名 偽証, 偽証の陳述, 偽証罪, 誓約［約束］を破ること, 破約, 偽り
  be charged with [accused of] perjury 偽証罪に問われる
  commit perjury in the Diet testimony 国会の証言で偽証する, 国会の証言で偽証罪を犯す
permanent 形 永久の, 永久的, 恒久的, 長期的な, 常設の
  permanent employee 正社員
  permanent employment 終身雇用
  permanent members of the U.N. Security Council 国連安全保障理事会の常任理事国
  permanent neutral state 永世中立国
permissible 形 許容できる, 許される
  permissible standard 許容基準
permission 名 許可, 許し, 認可, 承認, 同意
permissive society 寛大な社会, 甘い社会, 自由放任の社会
permissivism 名 許容主義, 寛容主義, 放任主義, 許容的態度, 甘い態度
perpetrator 名 犯人, 犯行者, 犯罪人, 下手人, 加害者, 悪事を働く者
persecution 名 迫害, 虐待, 責め立て, 迫害［虐待］の事実
  persecution complex 被害妄想
  persecution mania 被害妄想狂
  suffer persecution 迫害される, 虐待される
  the persecution of the Jews ユダヤ人迫害
persona grata 〈駐在国, 受入れ国にとって〉好ましい人物［外交官］
persona non grata 〈駐在国, 受入れ国にとって〉好ましからざる［好ましくない］人物, 歓迎されない人物《略 PNG》（＝ person not acceptable）
personage 名 有名人, 著名人, 名士, 登場人物 (persona)
personal 形 個人の, 個人的, 私的な, 本人自らの, 人的な, 対人の, 動産の, 名 個人広告, 個人情報, 個人消息, パーソナル
  personal action 対人訴訟
  personal ad 個人広告欄
  personal allowance 〈英国の〉個人所得税控除

personal best　自己ベスト, 自己ベスト記録
personal [person-to-person] call　指名通話
personal consumption [spending]　個人消費 (=private consumption)
personal data [information]　個人情報
personal digital assistant　携帯情報端末, 携帯情報通信端末《略 PDA》
personal equation　〈解釈上の〉個人的傾向, 〈観測上の〉個人差, 個人誤差
personal identification number　暗証番号, 個人の識別番号 (=password, PIN number)
Personal Information Protection Law　個人情報保護法
personal physician　かかりつけの医者
personal service　個人サービス, 直接送達, 交付送達
personal spending　個人消費
personality 名　個性, 人柄, 人格, 性格, 名士, 有名人, タレント, 芸能人, 独特な雰囲気, 地勢, 地相
a TV personality　テレビ・タレント
double [dual] personality　二重人格
personalities　人身攻撃, 人のあら捜し, 人物批評
personality cult　個人崇拝, 英雄崇拝 (=cult of personality)
personality disorder　人格障害
personhood 名　個性
personkind 名　人類
personnel 名　人員, 要員, 従業員, 社員, 職員, 隊員, スタッフ, 人事
factory personnel　ブルー・カラー
key personnel　基幹人員, 主要人員
personnel administration　人事管理, 労務管理 (=labor management)
personnel affairs　人事, 人事問題
personnel agency　職業安定所
personnel allocation　人員配置, 要員配置, 人事配置
personnel carrier　兵員輸送車
personnel exchange　人事交流
personnel management　人事管理, 労務管理 (=labor management)
personnel manager [director]　人事担当重役 [取締役], 人事担当部長 (=staff manager)
perspective 名　視点, 観点, 見地, 総体的な見方, 大局, 大局観, 考え方, 見解, 全体像, 視野, 眺望, 遠景, 眺め, 見通し, 見込み, 予想, 展望, 釣り合い, 相関関係, 遠近画法, 遠近法, 透視図, 透視図法
broad perspective　広い観点, 大局
cyclical perspective　景気循環の観点
get the situation out of perspective　事態を正しく判断できない
historical perspective　歴史的視点, 過去の経緯
in perspective　大局的に, 正しい視点で, 遠近法で
out of perspective　不釣合いで
two-transaction perspective　2取引基準
persuadables 名　浮動投票者
persuasion 名　説得, 説得力, 確信, 信念, 派閥, グループ, 分派, 宗派, 流派, 種類, 部類, …タイプ, …風, …派, 性別
people of the same persuasion　同じ宗派 [流派] の人びと
art of persuasion　説得の技術
private persuasion　個人的信念
yield to persuasion　説得に屈する
pessimism 名　悲観主義, 悲観論, 厭世主義, ペシミズム
elasticity pessimism　弾力性悲観論
export [trade] pessimism　輸出悲観論, 輸出悲観主義
▶ The U.S. dollar briefly dipped below the ¥117 line in Tokyo on Monday on *pessimism* about the U.S. economy, but was boosted above it following market intervention by the Bank of Japan.　米ドルは, 月曜日の東京外為市場で, 米経済への悲観論から一時117円台を割り込んだが, 日銀の市場介入を受けて反発した。
pessimistic 形　悲観的な, 悲観主義の, 厭世的な
pessimistic conclusion　悲観的な結論
pessimistic views　悲観論, 悲観的な見方
pesticide 名　殺虫剤
PET　陽電子放射断層撮影装置, ポジトロン・エミッション・トモグラフィー (**positron emission tomography**の略)
PET bottle　ペット・ボトル
pet tactic　得意の戦術
peter out　徐々に [次第に] なくなる, 次第に消滅する [衰える, 尽きる], 先細りになる
petition 名　嘆願, 請願, 申請, 申立て, 陳情, 嘆願 [請願, 陳情] 書
bankruptcy petition　破産申請, 破産申立て, 破産申立書 (=petition in [of] bankruptcy)
deny a petition　請願書を却下する

petition for divorce 離婚の申立て
petition for liquidation 清算の申立て, 清算の申請書
petro bomb 火炎ビン
petrochemical 名 石油化学製品, 形 石油化学製品の
  petrochemical complex 石油化学コンビナート, 石油化学工場地帯
  petrochemical product 石油化学製品
petrochemistry 名 石油化学
petrocurrency 名 オイル通貨
petrodollars 名 オイル・ダラー, 石油ダラー (=oil dollars, oil money)
petroleum 名 石油
  International Petroleum Exchange (of London Limited) ロンドン国際石油取引所
  liquefied petroleum gas 液化石油ガス, LPガス
  National Petroleum Council 全米石油審議会
  petroleum refining 石油精製
  Petroleum Reserve Law 石油備蓄法
  petroleum reserves 原油埋蔵量
petropower 名 産油国の力, 産油国の影響力
PFI プライベート・ファイナンス・イニシアチブ, PFI方式, 民間資金による社会資本整備 (private finance initiativeの略。⇒PPP)
PFLP パレスチナ解放人民戦線 (Popular Front for the Liberation of Palestineの略)
PG [**PG-rated**] 保護者同伴映画 (PGはparental guidanceの略)
pharmaceutical disaster 薬害
pharmaceutical firm 製薬会社
pharmacokinetics 名 薬物に対する人体の反応
phase 動 段階的に実行する
  phase down 段階的に縮小する, 段階的に削減する
  phase in 段階的に導入する, 段階的に取り入れる, 段階的に投入する
  phase out 段階的に撤廃する, 段階的に廃止する, 段階的に削減する, 段階的に閉鎖する, 段階的に解消する
phase 名 段階, 局面, 様相, 相, 面, 方面, 部分, 状態, 時期, 期間
  adjustment phase 調整段階, 調整局面, 調整期間
  book-building phase 購入予約受付け期間
  early phase 初期の段階
  in phases 段階的に
  mature phase 成熟期, 成熟段階
  phase zero 〈政策, 計画などの〉準備段階
  pre-marketing phase 事前販売期間
phased 形 段階的な
  phased cutback 段階的な削減
  phased integration 段階的な統合, 段階的な統一
  phased withdrawal 段階的撤退
phase-down [**phasedown** 名 段階的縮小, 段階的削減
phase-in [**phasein**] 名 段階的の導入, 〈計画, 作戦などの〉段階的な利用化, 段階的の組込み
  phase-in period 経過期間
phase-out [**phaseout**] 名 段階的解消, 漸次解消, 段階的撤廃, 〈生産, 操業の〉漸次停止, 段階的撤退, 段階的の除去
phenomenon 名 現象, 事象, 逸材, 非凡な人, 天才, 奇才, 珍品
  a natural phenomenon 自然現象
  a social pathological phenomenon 社会病理
  a temporary phenomenon 一時的な現象
  an infant phenomenon 神童
Philadelphia lawyer 腕利きの弁護士 [法律家], 辣腕弁護士
philanthropy 名 慈善, 慈善行為, 慈善活動, 慈善事業, 慈善団体, 寄付活動, 企業の文化・社会への貢献, フィランソロピー活動, フィランソロピー
philosophy 名 理念, 方針, 主義, 哲学, 基本的な考え方
  financing philosophy 資金調達方針, 財務についての考え方
  investment philosophy 投資方針
  management philosophy 経営理念, 経営方針, 経営哲学, 経営思想, 経営者精神 (=management thought, managerial philosophy)
  nature philosophy 自然哲学
  operating philosophy 経営精神, 経営理念, 経営方針, 経営哲学
  positive philosophy 実証哲学
phishing 名 ウェブ偽装詐欺, フィッシング (fishingとsophisticatedの合成語で, 発音はfishingと同じ。銀行やクレジット・カード会社などの偽のホームページを使って, 口座番号やパスワードなどの個人情報を盗むこと)
  go phishing フィッシング詐欺をする
physics 名 物理学
  experimental physics 実験物理学

theoretical physics　理論物理学
phone-in 名　電話対談放送, 視聴者電話参加番組
phone number portability system　番号ポータビリティ（持ち運び）制度
photo finish　写真判定, 大接戦
photocall 名　宣伝用撮影会, 写真撮影だけの記者会見
photochemical smog　光化学スモッグ
　photochemical smog warning　光化学スモッグ警報
phototelegraph 名　電送写真, 写真電送［電送術］
photovoltaic power generation　太陽光発電
physically-handicapped people　身体障害者（健常者はable-bodied people）
pick up 動　景気づく,〈景気などが〉回復する, 持ち直す, 復調する, 勢い［はずみ］をつける, 増える, 増加する, 上昇する, 盛り上がる, 上向く, 改善する, 活況になる
pickup 名　景気の回復, 好転, 持ち直し, 上向くこと, 上昇, 向上, 改善, 増加, 増勢, 拡大, 伸び, 活発化
　economic pickup　景気回復, 景気拡大, 景気の勢いが増すこと, 景気の持ち直し（＝pickup in economic performance）
　equity pickup　株価の値上がり
　pickup in demand　需要の高まり, 需要の回復
　pickup in employment　雇用の回復
　pickup in inflation　インフレ率の上昇, インフレ昂進
　pickup in money supply growth　マネー・サプライ伸び率の上昇（＝pickup in monetary growth）
picturedom 名　映画界（＝filmdom）
pie 名　全体, 総額, わいろ, 不正利得, 理想郷, 簡単な仕事, 楽勝, 朝飯前, パイ
　a small share [piece, slice] of the pie　少ない分け前
　(as) nice as pie　見事な出来栄えの, まさに納得できる, とても行儀［愛想］がよい
　division of the economic pie　パイの分配
　easy as pie　朝飯前の, とても簡単な
　eat humble pie　非を認める, 甘んじて屈辱を受ける
　pie chart　円グラフ, パイ図表（＝circle graph）
pie in the sky [**pie-in-the-sky**]　絵に描いたモチ, 夢のような計画, あてにならない計画, 夢物語, 希望的観測, 未来の楽しみ, 見当違いの楽観主義, 天国, ユートピア
pigeonhole 動　整理する, 分類する, 仕分けする,〈計画や案を〉審議未了にする, 保留する, 保留事項にする, 棚上げする, 後回しにする, 頭の中に入れておく, 記憶にとどめておく, 握りつぶす, しまいこむ, 片づける
名〈ハト小屋などの〉出入り口, 仕切り棚, 整理棚, 分類棚
　pigeonhole it for later reference　後で取り上げるためそれを後回しにする［一時棚上げする］
　pigeonhole one's ideas　…の考えを整理［分類整理］する
　pigeonhole papers　書類を整理する, 書類を整理棚に納める
pigment 名　〈細胞の〉色素, 血色素, 顔料
pileup 名　山積み,〈車の〉玉突き衝突, 多重衝突
pill 名　経口避妊薬（oral contraceptives）, ピル, 錠剤, 丸薬, 覚せい剤, 扱いにくいもの, 不愉快な奴, 砲弾, 爆弾
　a bitter pill (to swallow)　不愉快なこと, 嫌なこと
　a vitamin pill　ビタミン剤
　be on the pill　ピルを常用している
　drop the pill　ピルの服用をやめる
　pep pill　覚せい剤
　sleeping pills　睡眠薬
　sugar [sugarcoat, sweeten] the pill　不快感を和らげる, 不愉快なことを受け入れやすくする, 嫌なものを魅力的［うまそうに］見せる
　take a (chill) pill　落ち着く, リラックスする
　take pain pills　鎮痛剤を飲む
pillar 動　柱で支える, …を柱とする, …に柱を付ける
pillar 名　柱, 支柱, 中心部分, 根幹部分, 礎（いしずえ）, 要所, 要（かなめ）, 中心となるもの, 中心人物, 重鎮, 大黒柱, 要所, 要点, ポイント, 眼目
　a pillar of the state　国家の礎, 国家の柱石
　the pillar of the emergency employment measures　緊急雇用対策の柱
　the pillar of the organization　組織の中心人物
pilot 形　試験的, 実験的, 予備の, 事前の, 先行的, 指標となる, 補助の, パイロット
　pilot experiment　先行的実験, 予備実験
　pilot plant　実験工場, 試験工場, 試験的の生産工場, 試験設備, パイロット・プラント
　pilot production　試験的生産, 試験生産, 試作, パイロット生産

pilot project [scheme] 予備計画, 先行的プロジェクト, パイロット・プロジェクト
pilot store 実験店
pilot test 事前調査, 予備テスト, 先行的試験, パイロット・テスト
PIN number 暗証番号, 個人識別番号 (= personal [private] identification number, PIN)
pink slip 解雇通知
pinnacle 名 高峰, 尖塔, 頂点, 絶頂
  ascend to the pinnacle of …の頂点に上り詰める
  at the pinnacle of one's fame …の名声が絶頂に達したときに, …の名声の絶頂期に
  at the pinnacle of one's profession 仕事[職業]で油の乗り切った時期に
pinpoint 動 正確に示す, 的確[正確]に指摘する, 特定する
pinstripe perpetrator ホワイトカラー犯罪者, ホワイトカラー犯
pioneer 名 草分け, 先駆者, 創始者, 首唱者, 率先者, 開拓者, 新規事業開発者, パイオニア
pipeline 名 〈原油や天然ガスなどの〉パイプライン, 供給ルート, 流通ルート, 情報ルート, 機密ルート, 入手経路, パイプ
  in the pipeline 輸送中, 準備中, 進行中
  play the role of a pipeline パイプの役割を果たす
piracy 名 海賊行為, 著作権侵害, 特許権侵害, 海賊版, 模造品, 模倣品
pirate 動 〈著作権などを〉侵害する, 海賊版を作る[用いる, 売る], 海賊行為を働く, 略奪する
  pirated designer goods 偽ブランド品 (= counterfeit brand product)
  pirated edition 海賊版
  pirated software 海賊版ソフト
pirate 名 海賊, 海賊船, 著作権[特許権]侵害者, 海賊版出版社, 無認可放送[放送局]
  pirate copy 侵害品, 模造品, 違法コピー, 著作権[特許権]侵害のコピー, 海賊版コピー (= pirate product, pirated copy)
PISA test 国際学習到達度調査 (PISA = Program for International Student Assessment)
PKO 価格維持策, 株価維持策 (**price-keeping operations** の略)
PKO 国連の平和維持活動 (= UN peacekeeping operations)
placate 動 なだめる, 和らげる, 静める, 懐柔する
  placate a population seething with anger 怒りで騒然としている住民をなだめる
  placate the opposition 反対派[反対者]を懐柔する
place 名 場所, 所, 地点, 部位, 空間, 職, 役職, 座席, 立場, 地位, 役割, 町, 村, 都市, 街, …通り, …街, 店, 飲食店, 料理店, …位, …番, 時期, 段階, 機会, 〈小数点以下の〉2桁
  get a place 3着までに入る
  get a place in …に就職する
  investment in place 投資実績
  meeting place 集合場所, 合流点
  place of origin 原産地
  place of work 職場, 仕事場, 会社, 事務所 (= place to work, workplace)
  put production facilities in place 生産拠点をつくる
  sense of place 土地勘
  take place 起こる, 発生する, 行なわれる, 開催される
  two decimal places 小数点以下2桁 (= the second decimal place)
  ▶Everything is in *place*. 万事順調だ。
placebo effect 偽薬効果
placement 名 株式[債券]の募集[販売], 売出し, 販売先, 職業紹介, 職業斡旋, 人員配置
  job placement 就職斡旋, 就職紹介 (job introduction), 労働者派遣
  placement agency [bureau] 職業紹介所, 職業安定所
  placement office [service] 〈大学などの〉就職課
  placement officer 就職担当者
  placement test 〈新入生の〉クラス分け試験
plagiarism 名 盗用, 盗作 (= plagiary)
plainclothesman 名 私服警官
plaintiff 名 原告, 告訴人
plan 名 計画, 構想, 提案, 案, 政策, 策, 制度, 方式, 方法, 予定, 段取り, 平面図, プラン
  capex plan 設備投資計画 (= capital spending plan)
  contributory plan 拠出型制度
  deferred compensation plan 報酬据え置き方式
  initial plan 当初の計画
  investment plan 投資計画
  operating plan 業務計画
  Plan B 代替案, 第二案, 代案
  tactical plan 戦術計画

plan to …する計画だ, …する方針だ, …する方向だ, …する考えだ, …する構えである (export control system)

planethood 图 地球社会, 地球市民 (地球の住人はすべて同胞, という意味)

planetocentric space 惑星中心の宇宙空間

planned 形 計画した, 立案した, 計画的な, 意図した
- **capitalist planned economy** 資本主義計画経済
- **planned demand** 計画需要
- **planned economic growth** 計画的成長率
- **planned investment** 計画投資, 意図した投資
- **planned parenthood** 〈産児制限による〉家族計画
- **planned target** 計画目標

planner 图 計画立案者, 企画者, 設計者, プランナー
- **financial planner** フィナンシャル・プランナー (=financial planning specialist)

planning 图 企画, 立案, 企画立案, 計画, 計画策定, プランニング
- **budget planning** 予算計画, 予算編成
- **computer-aided process planning** 自動工程設計《略 CAPP》
- **contingency planning** 緊急時対応計画
- **long-term planning** 長期計画, 長期経営計画 (=long-range planning)
- **management [managerial] planning** 経営計画
- **strategic planning** 戦略立案, 戦略計画, 戦略企画, 戦略策定
- **urban planning** 都市計画

plant 图 工場, 生産設備, 工場設備, 施設, プラント, 植物
- **chemical plant** 化学工場
- **idle plant** 遊休設備, 遊休施設
- **investment in plant and equipment** 設備投資
- **pilot plant** 試験工場, 実験工場, パイロット・プラント
- **subcontracting plant** 下請工場
- **utility plant** 公益設備

plasma 图 プラズマ, 粒子 (物質の原子核と電子が分離して, 激しく飛び回る状態をプラズマという)
- **plasma address liquid crystal** プラズマ・アドレス液晶
- **plasma duration time** プラズマの持続時間

plasma physics プラズマ物理学

plasma display panel プラズマ表示板, プラズマ・ディスプレー・パネル《略 PDP》(薄型テレビの中核部品)

plasma-display panel TV プラズマテレビ

plastic 形 可塑性の, 柔軟な, 合成樹脂製の, ビニール製の, プラスチック製の, 人工の, 形成の, 图 合成樹脂製品, ビニール, クレジット・カード, プラスチック
- **plastic tray** 食品用のトレー

plateau 图 踊り場, 横ばい状態, 安定状態, 安定水準, 安定期, 高水準, 停滞, 停滞期, 伸び悩み, 高原, 高原現象, 台地
- **climb out of a plateau** 踊り場から脱出する
- **economic plateau** 高原景気
- **reach a plateau** 横ばい状態[安定水準]に達する, 伸び悩む, 停滞期に入る
- **remain on a plateau** 高水準にとどまる

platform 图 〈政党の〉政策綱領, 綱領, 綱領発表, 〈米大統領選挙候補者選びでの〉綱領宣言, 政策綱領宣言, 政策方針, 公約, 場, ステージ, 演壇, 〈コンピュータの〉基盤, 〈ソフトウエアやハードウエアなど〉コンピュータの基盤となるシステム, 基本システム, 搭載機器とソフト, 業界標準, 共通基盤, 体制, 掘削の足場[海底油田のプラットフォーム], 足場, 足がかり, 土台, 駅のホーム, プラットフォーム
- **application platform** アプリケーション・プラットフォーム
- **election platform** 選挙綱領
- **foreign policy platform** 外交政策綱領
- **moving platform** 作業台
- **offshore drilling platform** 海底油田掘削プラットフォーム
- **platform plank** 政党綱領の項目
- **platform ticket** 〈駅の〉入場券
- **trading platform** 貿易体制

platinum 图 白金, プラチナ
- **platinum age** 黄金時代, 隆盛期

play 動 遊ぶ, 演奏する, 芝居をする, 振る舞う
- **be played out** 繰り広げられる, 疲れ切っている, 掘り尽くされる, 考えを出し尽くしている
- **play a part** 一員になる
- **play back** 再生する
- **play dirty** 不正を働く, 不正な手段を用いる, 詐欺的行為をする
- **play down** …を控え目に報道する[扱う], 目立たないように扱う, 軽く見る[軽視する], 重視しない, 調子を下げる, 〈感情などを〉抑える, 押し殺す

play fair 公平[公正]に振る舞う, 公正な態度を取る, インチキをしない
play false 欺く, 裏切る
play fast and loose with …をもてあそぶ, 無責任な行動を取る, 誠意がない, 信頼できない, …を軽んずる
play for time 時間を稼ぐ, 引き延ばして時間を稼ぐ, 裏をかく
play games とぼける
play games with …をいい加減に扱う
play hardball 強硬手段を取る, がめつくやる
play hell with …を台なしにする, …を壊す, …に大変迷惑をかける, …を非常に妨げる
play into the hands of …の術中[思うつぼ]にはまる, …を利する
play it cool 冷静に行動する, 冷ややかな態度を取る
play on words しゃれを言う
play opposite …と共演する
play out 演じきる, 表現する, 聴衆を前に演奏する, 終局を迎える, もう役に立たない, 選手生活を続ける, 最後までプレーする
play safe 安全第一に行動する
play the game ルールを守る, インチキをしない, 正直である
play to the gallery 俗受けを狙う
play up 大きく取りあげる, …を強調[誇張]する, 派手に宣伝する, ふざける, 問題を引き起こす, …を困らせる, 調子が悪くなる
play up to …のご機嫌を取る, …におべっかを使う, …に媚びる, …へつらう
player 名 選手, 参加者, 関係者, 投資家, トレーダー, 演奏家, 演者, 専門家, 要人, 主要国, 代表的企業, 企業, 主要団体, 俳優, 要因, 〈CDなどの〉再生機, プレーヤー (playersで「企業グループ」, 「勢力」を意味する場合もある)
become a player in …に参加する, …に参入する
central player 主役
emerging economic players 新興国 (= emerging economies)
key player 鍵を握る人物[国], キー・プレーヤー
local player 地場企業
market player 市場関係者, 市場参加者, 市場筋, マーケット・プレーヤー (= market participant)
minor player 二流選手, 中小企業
strong player 有力企業

yield players 高利回りねらい
playing field 事業環境, 競争条件
Plaza Accord [Agreement] プラザ合意 (1985年に日米英独仏の主要5か国(G5)の蔵相と中央銀行総裁がニューヨークのプラザ・ホテルで会議を開いて, 主にドル高是正のための政策協調(coordinated policy)を採択することで合意した。その結果, 当時1ドル=240円台の円相場が1988年には120円台にまで上昇した)
PLC 〈英国の〉公開有限会社, 公開有限責任会社 (= plc, p.l.c.: **public limited company**の略。株式会社(company limited by shares)と保証有限責任会社(company limited by guarantee)のうち, 公開会社(public company)として登録している会社の社名の末尾に表示することになっている)
plea 名 懇願, 嘆願, 請願, 弁解, 言い訳, 口実, 言い抜け, 〈被告の〉抗弁, 申し立て, 答弁, 訴訟 (被告の「抗弁」は, 被告が「有罪(guilty)」あるいは「無罪(not guilty)」と言うこと)
cop a plea 白状する, 口を割る
enter [make] a not guilty plea 無罪を申し立てる
enter a plea 罪状認否する
make a plea for help 援助を嘆願する
make [enter] a plea of not guilty 無罪を申し立てる, 無罪の申し立てをする
on [under] the plea of …を口実に
plea of guilty 〈罪状認否での〉有罪の答弁
plea of not guilty 〈罪状認否での〉無罪の答弁
refuse to enter a plea on 5 charges against …に対する5の罪状に申し立てることを拒否する
plea bargain [bargaining] 司法取引, 被告人の答弁の取引 (= plea bargaining)
make a plea bargain 司法取引をする
suggest a plea bargain 司法取引を示唆する
plead 動 弁護する, …に抗弁する, 主張する, 申し立てる, 答弁する, 嘆願する, 要請する
plead against wrong 不正に対して抗弁する
plead for …を要請する
plead guilty to …に対して罪を認める, …に対して有罪を認める
plead innocent [not guilty] to …に対して無罪を申し立てる, …に対して無罪を主張する
plead one's case …の事件を弁護する
plead with the jury to …するよう陪審に嘆願する
plebiscite 名 住民投票, 国民投票 (= public vote, referendum)

pledge 動 誓約する, 誓う, 約束する, 明言する, 抵当[担保]に入れる, 質に置く
pledge 名 誓約, 誓い, 公約, 担保, 抵当, 質物, 保証, 証(あかし)
  a campaign pledge　選挙公約
  an international pledge　国際公約
  the Pledge of Allegiance　〈国旗への〉忠誠の誓い
plight 名 窮状, 苦境, 深刻な状況, 悪状況
plug 名 栓, 詰め物, 充填材, 〈パソコンなどの〉コネクター, 売り込み, 宣伝, 広告, 推奨, 推薦, 売れ残り[店ざらし]の商品, プラグ
  fire plug　消火栓
  plug compatible　プラグ互換
  plug compatible machine　完全互換機《略 PCM》
  pull the plug on　…を止める[中止する], …を打ち切る, …を終わらせる, …への援助を打ち切る, …の生命維持装置を外す
  spark plug　点火プラグ
plug-in プラグイン・ソフト (=plug-in software: ブラウザ(ホームページ閲覧ソフト)に機能を追加するソフトウエア)
plum book 〈米〉連邦政府官職一覧, プラム・ブック(plumはappointmentの意。約5,000名の官職名が掲載され, 大統領が任命権をもつ)
plumbers 名 特別調査班, プラマーズ(Special Investigation Unit (特別調査班)の別称)
plumbing 名 秘密工作支援活動, 配管工事, 配管設備, 測深, 水深測量
plummet 動 急落する, 暴落する, 大幅に減少する
  plummeted operating profits　営業利益の大幅減少
  plummeting sales　販売の減少, 販売減, 売上の減少, 販売不振
plunge 動 減少する, 下落する, 低下する, 低迷する, 急落する, 安値を付ける, 転落する (=drop)
  plunge into loss　赤字に転落する
  plunge to a five month low　5か月来の安値を付ける
plunge 名 市場の低迷, 株価の急落, 下落, 激減, 減少, 急降下, 落ち込み, 突入
  plunge in demand　需要の落ち込み
  register a record plunge　過去最大の下げを記録する
  stock market's plunge　株式市場の低迷
  the sharp plunge in the dollar's value　急激なドル安
plus or minus 〈誤差の〉上下幅, 許容範囲, 〈数量の〉増減の幅, 変動幅, 範囲, プラスマイナス(±)
pluthermal 名 プルサーマル(プルトニウムとサーマル・リアクター(原発の軽水炉)を合わせて[プルサーマル]と呼ばれる。「プルサーマル」は, ウランと原子力発電所の使用済み核燃料を再処理して取り出したプトニウムとを混ぜて燃料を作り直し, 原発の軽水炉で再利用する仕組みをいう)
  pluthermal plan　プルサーマル計画
  pluthermal power generation　プルサーマル発電
plutocracy 名 金権政治, 財閥
plutocratic 形 金権の
  plutocratic democracy　民主主義的な金権政治
  plutocratic politics　金権政治
plutonium 名 プルトニウム
  plutonium stockpiles　プルトニウム抽出量
  plutonium-thermal power generation　プルサーマル発電
  plutonium-thermal project　プルサーマル計画 (=pluthermal plan)
  plutonium-uranium mixed oxide (MOX) fuel　プルトニウムとウランの混合酸化物(MOX)燃料
PM　粒子状物質 (particulate matterの略)
  PM emission control standards　PM排出防止基準, PM排出基準
  PM-grade emission filter　PM排ガス浄化装置
  PM regulation　PM規制, 粒子状物質規制
PM [P.M.] 首相 (Prime Ministerの略)
pneumoconiosis 名 塵肺(症)
  Pneumoconiosis Law　じん肺法 (=Black Lung Disease Law)
PNTR 恒久的最恵国待遇 (permanent normal trade relationsの略)
pocket book [pocketbook] 懐具合, 資力, 財源, 財布, 札入れ, 手帳, ハンドバッグ, 文庫本
point 名 〈為替相場などの〉騰落単位, 水準, 地点, 時点, 時期, 問題, 要点, 論点, 趣旨, 事項, 材料, ポイント
  ex point of origin　現地渡し
  point man　代表交渉人, 偵察隊の先頭に立つ兵士
  point of no return　帰還不能点, 引き返し不能地点, 引くに引けない状態

point system ポイント制
shipping point 出荷地渡し
tax point 課税時期
the two key points of contention 二つの主な争点

point-and-shoot 形 全自動の，シャッター［シャッター・ボタン］を押すだけの

point-of-sale 名 小売店，特約店，形 店頭の，販売時点の

point of sales 販売時点情報管理《略 POS》
  point-of-sales equipment POS機器
  point of sales system 販売時点情報管理システム，POSシステム（「POSシステム」は，スーパーなどで，バーコードで顧客の買い物の金額を出すと同時に顧客の特性や在庫の状態を把握するシステム。基本的に，レシート単位で販売情報を収集するシステムで，レシートには店舗名や販売時間，商品名，値段などが入力されている。また，ポイント・カードの場合は，購入者の氏名，職業，年齢，性別，購買履歴など顧客の属性が付け加えられる）

poised to …する用意［準備］ができている，…する覚悟だ，…する構えを見せている，…する方針だ，…しそうだ，…する見通しだ（＝ready to）
▶ The IAEA is *poised to* cut the frequency of inspections at the Japan's 50 or so light-water nuclear reactors from quarterly to once a year. 国際原子力機関（IAEA）が，日本の軽水炉約50基の査察回数を年4回から1回に削減する見通しとなった。

poison-pen 形 中傷を目的とした，中傷目的の，中傷の，毒舌の

poison pill 毒薬条項，敵対的買収に対する防衛手段，買収防衛策，ポイズン・ピル（敵対的買収に対する防衛策の一つ。「毒薬条項」は，既存株主に対して転換優先株式を株式配当の形で発行することを定めた条項を指す）
  poison pill defense [defence] ポイズン・ピル防衛，毒薬条項防衛，毒入り避妊薬

poisoning 名 中毒，毒を盛ること
  carbon monoxide poisoning 一酸化炭素中毒
  food poisoning 食中毒（＝poisoning from eating）
  lead poisoning 鉛中毒
  mercury poisoning 水銀中毒

pol 名 政治家（politicianの短縮形）
Pol Pot regime ポルポト政権
polar 形 南極［北極］の，極地の，極の，磁極の，正反対の，中枢の，中心の

polar flight 極地経由飛行
polar orbiting geophysical observatory 極軌道観測衛星《略 POGO》
the polar star 北極星（＝polestar）
Polaris 名 北極星，二段式弾道ミサイル
Polaris submarine ポラリス潜水艦
polarization 名 対立，分裂，2極化，分極化，多極化，両極分化，偏光
police 名 警察（通例the ～），警察官（policeman）
police action 〈国連などの〉軍事治安活動，治安活動
police brutality 警官による暴力
police commissioner 〈米国の市の〉警察部長
police constable 〈英国の〉巡査（＝police officer）
police cordon 非常線
police court 警察裁判所（軽犯罪の即決）
Police Duties Execution Law 警察官職務執行法
police inspector 〈米国の〉警部，〈英国の〉警部補
police officer 〈米国の〉巡査，警官（＝police constable, policeman, policewoman）
police sergeant 巡査部長
the military police 憲兵隊《略 M.P.》
the mounted police 騎馬警官隊
the New York Police Department ニューヨーク市警《略 NYPD》
the police emergency number 警察の緊急電話番号（米では911，英では999）
the riot police 機動隊
the security police 秘密警察（secret police），〈スパイ取締りの〉公安警察，〈空港などの〉警備隊

policy 名 政策，対策，施策，方策，策，手段，やり方，方法，方針，施政方針，経営方針，信条，主義，規定，保険証券，保険証書，保険契約，ポリシー
  acceptable use policy 〈ネットワークやコンピュータ・システムを利用する際の〉方針や約束事《略 AUP》
  accounting policy 会計方針，経理方針
  cancellation policy キャンセル規定
  credit underwriting policy 与信基準
  customs policy 通関規定
  dividend policy 配当政策，配当方針
  endowment policy 養老保険証券
  financial policy 金融政策，財政政策，財務政

策, 財務方針
financing policy 資金調達方針
fire policy 火災保険証券
insurance policy 保険証券
monetary policy 金融政策
open-door policy 開放政策
open policy 予定保険証券
policy conditions 保険約款
policy making 政策立案
policy mix ポリシー・ミックス, 経済政策ミックス
privacy policy プライバシー規定
pro-patent policy 特許重視政策, プロパテント政策
put [translate] policy into action 政策を実行に移す
take out a policy on …に保険をかける, …保険に入る
valued policy 確定保険証券

policyholder [**policy holder**] 名 保険契約者, 契約者, 保険加入者 (=insurance policyholder)
dividend to policyholders 契約者配当 (=policyholder dividend)
policyholder benefits 契約者給付金
policyholders' premiums 保険契約者の保険料
policyholders' representative meeting 〈保険会社の〉総代会 (=the meeting of representatives of policyholders; 株式会社の株主総会にあたる。総代は取引先などから選ばれることが多く, 経営へのチェック機能が乏しいとの批判がある)

policymaker 名 政策決定者
policymaking member 政策決定者
Politburo 名 〈中国の〉政治局常務委員会, 〈旧ソ連の〉共産党政治局, 政治局(中国, 旧ソ連, ベトナムなどの政策決定最高機関)
politic 名 政治力学, 力関係, 支配関係, 優劣関係
political 形 政治の, 政治上の, 政治的な, 政治に関する, 政治がらみの, 政治色の強い, 政略的な, 政党の, 派閥の, 政権の, ポリティカル
political agent 〈政府派遣の〉駐在官
political association 政治結社
political asylum 政治亡命, 政治的保護
political bargaining [bartering] 政治的駆け引き, 政治的取引
political calendar 政治日程
political climate [environment] 政治状況, 政治環境
political clout 政治力, 政治的影響力
political constituencies 支持者層
political correctness 政治的正当性, 政治的妥当性, 政治的公正, ポリティカル・コレクトネス《略 PC》
political donation [contribution] 政治献金
political economy 政治経済学 (=political economic science)
political efficacy 政治的有効性
Political Funds Control Law 政治資金規正法
political party 政党
political risk 政治的危険性, 政治的リスク (=country risk, sovereign risk)
political science 政治学
political task 政治課題 (=political agenda)
political vacuum 政治空白
political view 政見, 政治上の見解, 政治的意見
political action 政治活動, 政治行為
political action committee 〈企業の〉政治活動委員会《略 PAC》(選挙資金集めの団体)
political action groups 圧力団体
political power 政権(administration, administrative power, government), 政治権力, 政治力, 政治勢力
base for political power 政権基盤
change in political power 政権交代 (=the change of government)
politician 名 政治家, 政治屋, 策士, 策略家, 行政官, 出世主義者, ゴマすり
a party politician 党利を図る政治屋
opposition politicians 野党議員
politicization 名 政治問題にすること, 政治化
politicize 動 政治問題にする, 政治化する, 政治を論じる, 政治に携わる, 政治に関わる, 政治に関心を持つ, 政治に目覚める, 政治の世界に引き入れる
politick 動 政治活動をする, 遊説する
politicking 名 〈個人的利益のための〉政治活動, 政治運動, 政治工作, 政治的駆け引き
politico 名 政治屋, 政治家
politics 名 政治, 政務, 政界, 政治学, 策略, 策略, 駆け引き, 裏工作, 力関係, 抗争, 政治的意見, 政見, 政治観, 政綱, 政策
be engaged [involved] in politics 政治に携わる
enter [get into, go into] politics 政界に入る
not practical politics 〈現実離れしていて〉議論の価値のない, 論じる価値がない, 困難そうな

office politics　会社内での駆け引き
party politics　政党の駆け引き, 政党政治
play politics　裏工作をする, 政治的に画策する, 権謀[策]を弄する, 私利を図る, 他人を利用する
populist politics　大衆迎合政治, ポピュリズム政治
power politics　武力政策
run politics　政治活動をする
talk politics　政治を論じる
walk away from politics　政界から身を引く

poll 名　世論調査, 意識調査, 投票, 人気投票, 投票所, 投票数, 投票率, 選挙
- election poll　選挙の世論調査
- exit poll　出口調査
- Gallup poll [Poll]　ギャラップ調査, ギャラップ世論調査
- go to the polls　投票に行く[出かける]
- heavy poll　高い投票率
- light poll　低い投票率
- nationwide poll　全国世論調査
- poll watcher　投票立会人
- public opinion poll　世論調査 (＝opinion poll)
- respond to the poll　世論調査に応じる
- straw poll　非公式投票

pollen 名　花粉
- pollen allergy　花粉症 (＝hay fever, pollenosis, pollinosis)
- pollen count　花粉数, 花粉の飛散量, 花粉計測

polling 名　投票
- polling booth　投票用紙記入所 (＝voting booth)
- polling business　世論調査機関
- polling place [station]　投票所

pollster 名　世論調査員, 世論調査機関
polltaker 名　世論調査員, 世論調査専門家
pollutant 名　汚染物質, 汚染源
- air pollutants　大気汚染物質[汚染源]
- pollutant load　汚濁負荷
- Pollutant Standards Index　汚染基準指標

polluter 名　汚染者, 汚染企業, 汚染源, 公害犯人, 二酸化炭素(温室効果ガス)排出国
- carbon polluter　二酸化炭素(温室効果ガス)排出国
- polluter pays principle　汚染者負担の原則, 公害費用汚染者負担の原則《略 PPP [P.P.P]》

pollution 名　汚染, 公害, 汚染物質
- air pollution　大気汚染
- Air Pollution Control Law　大気汚染防止法, 大気汚染規制法
- atmospheric pollution control　地球環境保護
- cadmium pollution　カドミウム汚染
- Federal Air Pollution Regulations　連邦大気汚染防止規制
- heat pollution　熱汚染
- IMO pollution regulations　IMO(国際海事機関)の汚染規制
- pollution abatement　環境汚染低減, 環境汚染軽減
- pollution control　汚染防止, 公害防止, 公害管理, 環境保全, 環境保護
- pollution-free engine　無公害エンジン
- pollution litigation　公害訴訟, 汚染訴訟
- pollution loading amount　汚濁負荷量
- thermal pollution　熱公害
- water pollution　水質汚染
- Water Pollution Control Law　水質汚濁防止法

polycentric firm　現地指向型企業
polycentrism 名　多中心構造
polychlorinated biphenyl　ポリ塩化ビフェニール《略 PCB》
polyethylene 名　ポリエチレン
polygraph 名　うそ発見器(lie detector), 〈血圧, 呼吸, 脈拍などの〉多元同時記録計, ポリグラフ
polypolistic market　供給多占的市場
polypoly 名　売り手独占, 供給独占
polypropylene 名　ポリプロピレン
polypsonistic market　需要多占的市場
polypsony 名　買い手多占, 需要多占
polystyrene foam　発泡スチロール
polytechnic 名　科学技術専門学校, ポリテクニック
polyversity 名　マンモス大学
pontiff (the) 名　ローマ法王, 教皇
Ponzi 名　ポンジー式投資詐欺術
- Ponzi game　ネズミ講式仕組み, ネズミ講, マルチ商法, ポンジー講
- Ponzi scheme　ネズミ講, ポンジー講

pool 動　集めて置く, 〈共同で〉蓄える, 共同出資する, 共同管理する, 共同負担する, 共同計算にする, 共同の利権とする, プールする
- pool slush funds　裏金作りをする
- pooled fund　プール・ファンド

pool 名　蓄え, 備蓄, 予備の蓄え, 予備, ストック, 基金, 共同出資, 共同投資, 共同資金[基金], 共

同利用, 共同管理, 共同計算, カルテル, 企業連合, 共同施設要員, 共同役務要員 プール取材, 代表取材, プール制, プール
- **asset pool** 資産プール (＝pool of assets)
- **blind pool** 全権委任連合
- **bonus pool** 賞与基金, 賞与支給限度総額
- **dollar pool** ドル・プール制
- **indirect cost pool** 間接費集計額
- **labor pool** 労働要員
- **pool reporter** 代表取材記者
- **private pools** 私募ファンド
- **regional power pool** 地域電力共同機構
- **working-age population pool** 生産年齢人口
▶ This large *pool* of human resources is one reason there are so many talented young workers in China. この人材の層の厚さが, 中国に有能な若い社員が多くいる一因だ.

pooling of capital 資本の合同
pooling of interests 持ち分プーリング, プーリング法 (＝merger accounting, uniting-of-interests method：企業合併・買収の会計処理方式の一つで, 結合される会社の資産・負債を簿価のまま項目ごと合算して合併後の存続会社に継承される)

poor 形 不振の, 低迷した, 伸び悩みの, 不利な, 厳しい, 乏しい, 悪い
- **poor chance** 望み薄
- **poor demand** 需要減, 需要薄
- **poor economy** 景気低迷
- **poor family** 貧困世帯
- **poor harvest** 凶作
- **poor performance** 業績不振, 業績の伸び悩み
- **poor profitability** 収益性の低迷
- **poor sales** 販売低迷, 販売不振, 売上低迷, 業績不振, 業績悪化 (＝weak sales)
- **poor supply** 供給薄
- **poor tone of the market** 市場の地合いの悪さ

poorly 副 貧しく, へたに, まずく
- **poorly performing store** 業績不振の店舗

pop 形 大衆的な (popular), 通俗的な, ポピュラーな, ポピュラー音楽の, ポップ・アートの, ヤング向きの, 名 ポピュラー音楽, ポップ・ミュージック [ポップ音楽], ポップ・アート, ポップス界
- **pop industry** 文化産業
- **pop item** 文化商品 (＝cultural product)
- **pop music** ポップ音楽, ポップス, ポップ・ミュージック (＝popular music)
- **pop philosophy** 通俗的哲学

pop up 持ち上がる, 突然[突如]現われる, 突然起こる
▶ Two leaders will be opposed to moves toward protectionism that will *pop up* as governments try to weather economic turmoil. 両首脳は, 各国政府が経済の混乱を切り抜けようとする際に持ち上がる保護貿易主義への動きには反対する方針だ.

popular 形 人気がある, 評判の, 皆に喜ばれている, 一般的な, 一般通念の, 一般大衆向けの, 大衆[庶民]の, 大衆を巻き込んだ, 通俗的の, ポピュラーな
- **gain popular support** 大衆の支持を得る
- **popular base for political power** 民主的な政権基盤
- **popular front** 人民戦線
- **popular loan** 公募公債
- **popular subscription** 公募 (＝public offering)
- **popular suffrage** 普通選挙権
- **popular voice** 世論
- **popular vote** 〈米大統領選挙での〉一般投票 (選挙人ではなく一般有権者による投票のこと)

popularist 形 大衆受けのする, 大衆の関心を求める, 大衆の興味[参加]を得ようとする

popularity 名 人気, 評判, 支持, 普及
- **gain popularity among** …の間で好評を博する
- **lose popularity** 人気を失う, 支持を失う
- **popularity contest [poll, vote]** 人気投票

popularization 名 大衆化, 通俗化, 普及, 広めること

population 名 人口, 住民数, 全住民, 住民, 〈統計での〉母集団, 個体群, 集団, 〈動物の〉生息数
- **distribution of population** 人口分布
- **dynamic statistics of population** 人口動態統計
- **finite population** 有限母集団
- **population density** 人口密度
- **population explosion** 人口の爆発的増加, 人口爆発
- **population mean** 母平均
- **population mobility** 人口移動
- **static statistics of population** 人口静態統計
- **target population** 目標母集団, 対象グループ
- **working age population** 生産年齢人口

populism 名 大衆迎合主義, 人民主義, ポピュリズム

populist 形 大衆迎合的な
- **populist politics** 大衆迎合政治, ポピュリズム政治

populist protectionism 大衆迎合的な経済保護主義
populist style of politics ポピュリズム的な政治手法

pork 名 利権
pork barrel 政府の地方開発援助金,〈人気取りのため特定の地域・選挙区などにばらまかれる〉政府交付金[政府助成金], 人気取り政策
　election-year pork barrel 選挙の年に政府から出る地方開発援助金
　pork barrel add-ons 〈議員の人気取りのための〉法案の追加条項
　pork barrel project 〈特定の地域や選挙区の利益のために行われる〉政府事業計画[政府公共事業]
porn 名 好色文学, 春本, 春画, ポルノ映画[写真, 作家], ポルノ (＝pornography)
　child porn 児童ポルノ
　porn film [flick] ポルノ映画
　porn mag ポルノ雑誌
　porn shop [house] ポルノ専門店, ポルノ・ショップ
pornoflick 名 ポルノ映画 (＝porn flick, skin flick)
pornography 名 ポルノ (＝porn; ⇒child pornography)
port authority 港湾当局
port state control ポート・ステート・コントロール制度《略 PSC》(一般に老朽化した外国の船舶や新造船について, 入港を許可する寄港国がその監督を行う制度。検査の結果, 問題がある場合には, 寄港国が船舶の出港を差し止めることができるほか, 港から排除することができる)
portable 形 携帯用の, 持ち運びできる, 移動式, 移植可能な, 通算可能な年金制度の
　portable life support system 〈宇宙飛行士の〉携帯用生命維持装置《略 PLSS》
portal 名 ポータル・サイト, 玄関サイト, ポータル
　Internet portal ポータル・サイト
　portal site ポータル・サイト(インターネットに接続したとき最初にアクセスするホームページのこと。広告媒体として, 電子商取引を展開する企業が, バナー広告を出している)
portal-to-portal pay 拘束時間払い賃金
portfolio 名 所有有価証券, 保有株式, 有価証券明細書, 有価証券報告書, 資産内容, 資産構成, 資産管理, 金融資産, 投資資産, 品揃え, 大臣の職[地位], ポートフォリオ
　balanced portfolio 均衡のとれた資産内容
　brand portfolio 有価証券一覧表, ブランド・ポートフォリオ
　business portfolio 事業内容
　diversification of portfolio ポートフォリオの多様化, 製品の品揃えの多様化
　minister without portfolio 無任所大臣
　optimal portfolio selection 最適ポートフォリオ選択
　portfolio choice [selection] 資産選択, ポートフォリオ選択
　portfolio investment 有価証券投資, 証券投資, 株式・債券投資, 資産運用投資, 間接投資, ポートフォリオ投資, 投資有価証券
　portfolio management 最適資産管理, 資産管理, 金融資産管理, 資産運用, 資金運用, ポートフォリオ管理, ポートフォリオ運用, ポートフォリオ・マネジメント
　portfolio manager 資産管理担当者, 資産管理担当マネジャー
　win a ministerial portfolio 閣僚のポストを獲得する
position 動 位置につける, 据える,〈特定の場所に〉置く, 配置する
　be favorably positioned to …する上で有利な立場にある
　be positioned to …する体制を築く, …する態勢を整える
　be well positioned to …する上で有利な立場にある, …する好位置につける, …できる力がある
　position oneself to [for] …への準備を進める, …への対応を進める
position 名 〈有価証券の〉保有状態, 証券保有高, 持ち高, 経営基盤, 事業基盤, 位置, 地位, 役職, 状態, 地歩, 足場, 勤め口, 職, ポジション
　bear position 売り持ち, 投機的売り持ち, 空売り
　bedrock position 基本的立場
　bull position 買い持ち, 投機的買い持ち, 空買い
　cash position 現金持ち高, 現預金, 直物ポジション, キャッシュ・ポジション
　credit position 信用状態
　debt position 借入れ状況, 債務状況
　equity position 持ち株比率, 出資比率
　exchange position 為替持ち高, 為替ポジション
　long position 買い持ち, 買い建て, ロング・ポジション
　management position 管理職, 上級管理職
　market position 市場での地位, 市場での立場
　negotiating position 交渉力

operating position 営業状況, 事業基盤
overbought position 買い持ち
oversold position 売り持ち
position paper 〈特定の問題に関する〉方針説明書, 政策方針, 項目別政策集(国際会議などでの討議資料)
short position 売り持ち, 売り建て, ショート・ポジション

positive 形
プラスの, 正の, 黒字の, 強含みの, 強気の, 好影響を与える, 明るい, 上昇傾向にある, 積極的な, 明確な, 建設的な, 前向きの, 肯定的な, ポジティブ, 名 強気材料, 好材料, プラス要因
positive appraisal 好ましい評価
positive earnings 好業績, 好決算
positive euthanasia 積極的安楽死 (=active euthanasia)
positive factor 強気の材料, 好材料, 買い材料, プラス要因, 重要なポイント
positive goodwill 積極的のれん, 積極的営業権
positive growth プラス成長
positive impact [influence] 好影響, プラスの影響
positive implications 好材料, プラス要因, 格上げの方向
positive results 好業績, 好決算 (=good results, positive earnings, robust performance)
positive territory プラス, プラス基調
revise upward the rating outlook from negative to positive 格付け見通しを「ネガティブ(弱含み)」から「ポジティブ(強含み)」に上方修正する

positron 名 陽電子
positron emission tomography 陽電子放射断層撮影装置《略 PET》

possession 名 所有, 保有, 占有, 所持, 所有物, 所持品, 財産, 所有権, 支配権
possession of WMD 大量破壊兵器の保有 (WMD=weapons of mass destruction)

possible 形 可能な, 実現可能な, 可能性のある, 潜在的な, 起こりそうな, 想定される, …を視野に入れた, …候補の
a possible financial meltdown 想定される金融崩壊
possible merger 合併の可能性
possible new ventures 新事業の機会, 新規合弁事業の機会
possible transactions 実現可能取引, 発生可能な取引
possible war 想定される戦争
reserve for possible future loss 偶発損失準備金
reserve for possible loan losses 貸倒れ引当金

post 動
投函する, 郵送する, 〈メッセージを〉送る, 発表する, 公示する, 示す, 提示する, 記録する, 達成する, 〈赤字や黒字などを〉計上する, 〈担保や証拠金などを〉差し入れる, 担保を設定する, 配置する, 配属する, 任命する, 〈保釈金などを〉積む [支払う]
be posted to London ロンドンに配属となる
keep A posted on …についてAに逐一報告する
post A as Aを…と発表する
post a healthy advance [increase] 好調な伸びを示す
post additional margin 追加の証拠金を差し入れる
post bail [a bond, bond] 保釈金を積む, 保釈金を払う
post collateral 担保を差し入れる, 担保を設定する
post huge losses 巨額の赤字を計上する
post net gains 黒字を計上する
post net operating profits 〈金融機関が〉業務純益を計上する, 〈一般企業が〉営業純利益[純営業利益]を計上する
posted price 〈原油などの〉公示価格
posted prices of land 公示地価

post 名
郵便, 郵便制度, 郵便物, 職, 地位, 部署, 持ち場, 任務, 駐屯地, 駐屯部隊, 〈退役軍人会の〉地方支部, ポスト
be at one's post 持ち場についている, 任務についている
be relieved of one's post 解任される
beat [pip] A at the post Aを僅差[土壇場]で負かす
leave [deserve] one's post 持ち場を離れる
liquidation post 整理ポスト
post exchange 〈駐屯地, 基地などの〉購買部, 売店
retain one's post 留任する
trading post 取引ポスト, 交易所
wages attached to a post 職務給

post- 接頭 後の, 次の, ポスト…
post-bubble economy バブル後
post-bubble economy era バブル後の時期 (=postbubble era)
post-bubble low バブル後の最安値, バブル経

済崩壊後の最安値

post-Fordism 柔軟な多品種少量生産, ポスト・フォーディズム
post-fossil fuel 脱化石燃料
post-Kyoto Protocol ポスト京都議定書
post-traumatic stress disorder 心的外傷後ストレス障害《略 PTSD》

postal 形 郵便の, 郵便局の, 郵便による
　postal business [services] 郵政事業
　postal code [postalcode] 郵便番号（=zip code [Zip Code]）
　postal (money) order 郵便為替
　postal vote 郵送による投票
　U.S. Postal Service 米国郵政公社

posthumous 形 死後の, 死後に起こる, 父の死後に生まれた
　confer posthumous honors on a person 人を追叙する
　posthumous child 遺児
　posthumous recognition 死後認知
　posthumous reputation [fame] 死後の名声
　posthumous work 遺作, 遺著

postindustrialism 名 脱工業化, ポスト工業化

posting 名 書き込み, ニュースグループに送られるメッセージ（=online chat）

postpone 動 延期する, 延ばす

postretirement benefit 退職後給付（=benefit plan for retirees）
　postretirement benefit obligation 退職後給付債務
　postretirement health care benefit 退職後の健康管理給付, 退職後の健康保険給付金

pot 名 マリファナ (marijuana), インド大麻, 破滅, 悪化, 容器, 壺, なべ, 植木鉢, 基金, 皆で出し合った金, ポット
　a melting pot 〈人類, 文化の〉るつぼ, 多種多様な考えが話される状況
　a pot of gold 黄金の壺, 幻の宝物, 理想, 思いがけない収入
　go to pot 破滅する, 落ちぶれる, さびれる, 荒廃する, 駄目になる
　keep the pot boiling 何とか暮らしている, 順調に [景気よく] 行っている
　pot party マリファナ・パーティ, マリファナを吸う集い
　pots of 大量の…
　smoke pot マリファナを吸う
　the pot 共同出資総額

potent 形 説得力のある, 有力な, 強力な, 強い, よく効く, 強い効力 [効き目, 効果] がある

potential 名 可能性, 将来性, 見込み, 恐れ, 潜在能力, 潜在力, 〈潜在的な〉力, 潜在成長率, 成長力, 余力, 余地, 才能, 能力, 素質, 資質, ポテンシャル
　borrowing potential 借入余力, 借入能力
　cyclical potential 景気回復期待
　downside potential 下落する可能性, 値下りの可能性
　earnings potential 潜在収益力
　economic potential 経済の潜在力（=potential of the economy）
　growth potential 成長潜在力, 潜在成長力, 成長余地, 成長ポテンシャル
　industrial potential 潜在工業力
　investment potential 投資収益力
　potential for recovery 回復力
　upside potential 上昇する可能性, 値上りの可能性, 値上りの余地
　war potential 〈潜在的な〉戦力

potential 形 可能性がある, 潜在的な, 将来起こりそうな
　potential ability 潜在能力
　potential adversary 仮想敵国
　potential buyer 将来買ってくれそうな人, 買い手候補
　potential buying power 潜在購買力
　potential customers お客になってくれそうな人, 見込み顧客, 潜在顧客, 潜在的な顧客層, 潜在顧客層
　potential demand 潜在需要
　potential fraud 詐欺の可能性
　potential liability 潜在的債務額
　potential output 潜在生産力, 潜在的産出量, 潜在的生産量
　potential share [stock] 権利株, 潜在的株式

potentially 副 潜在的に, 可能性としては, もしかすると

pothead 名 マリファナ常用者

pottasium 名 カリウム（=potash）
　pottasium bromide 臭素酸カリウム
　pottasium chloride 塩化カリウム
　pottasium cyanide 青酸カリ

pour 動 注ぐ, 注入する, 流し込む, 大量に注ぎ込む [投入する], 打ち明ける, 洗いざらい話す, 自動 吹き出る, 広がる, 押し寄せる, 殺到する

pour cold water on [over] …に水を差す, ケチをつける, 冷ややかに反応する, …に冷たい態度を取る
pour down 激しく降る, 土砂降りになる, 豪雨になる, 〈大量に〉流れ落ちる
pour into [in] …になだれ込む, …に殺到する
pour it on 大げさに言う, 全力を注ぐ
pour money into …に大量の資金を投入する
pour oil on troubled waters けんかの仲裁をする, けんかを止めさせる, 騒ぎを鎮める
pour on to the black market 闇市場に大量に流出する
pour out money like water 湯水のように金を使う
pour out one's heart [soul] to …に心の内を打ち明ける
pour scorn on …を馬鹿げているという
poverty 名 貧困, 貧困ライン, 貧乏, 不足, 欠乏
  poverty line 貧困線, 最低生活水準
  poverty rate 貧困率
  poverty-stricken 貧乏に苦しむ, 非常に貧しい
  poverty trap 貧困の落とし穴
POW 捕虜 (prisoner of warの略)
powder 名 火薬, 粉, 粉末, パウダー
  keep one's powder dry 用意を怠らない, 万一に備える, 様子をうかがう
  not worth (the) powder and shot やってみる甲斐がない
  powder keg 火薬樽, 危険をはらむ状況, 危険な状態, 一触即発
  powder magazine 火薬庫
  powder monkey 爆薬取扱い者, 爆薬管理責任者 (=powderman)
  powder room 化粧室, 洗面所
  take a powder 雲隠れする, 逃げ去る, 中止する
power 動 …を動かす, …を牽引する, …の原動力になる, …に動力を供給する, …に動力源を与える, …を勢いよく進む [動く]
  be powered by …で動く
  power down 電源を切る [落とす], 〈宇宙船が〉出力消費を下げる
  power the economy 経済の原動力になる
  power the motor vehicle 自動車を動かす
  power up 〈機械などが〉始動する, 〈宇宙船が〉出力消費を上げる, 〈コンピュータが〉起動する
power 名 力, 能力, 体力, 電力, エネルギー, 動力, 支配力, 権力, 権限, 政治権力, 政権, 主権, 権限, 法的権限, 強国, 大国, 勢力, 影響力, 有力者, 有力組織, パワー
  assume [seize, take] power 政権を握る
  balance of power 勢力均衡
  bargaining power 交渉能力, 交渉力
  be in power 政権を握っている, 政権に就いている, 権力の座にある
  be kicked out of power 追われて政権を降りる
  black power 黒人解放運動, ブラック・パワー
  buying [purchasing] power 購買力
  cement one's grip on power 権力を掌握する
  come into [to] power 政権を握る, 政権に就く, 権力の座に就く, 権力を得る (=assume power, seize power)
  hand over power to …に権力の座を明け渡す
  hard power ハード・パワー(軍事力, 核戦力や経済力など他国を強制できる力のこと。とくに「核戦力」は, 米国のハード・パワーの象徴ともいわれている)
  in power 政権に就いている, 政権を握って, 権限のある
  military power 軍事力, 軍事大国
  power base 支持基盤, 支持母体, 支持組織
  power blackout [cut, failure] 停電
  power bloc パワー・ブロック(国際的政治力を構成する国家群)
  power breakfast 重役の朝食会
  power broker 〈政界の〉黒幕, パワー・ブローカー
  power center 大型ディスカウント・ショッピング・センター, パワー・センター (=power shopping center: ディスカウント店の集まり)
  power company 電力会社
  power crisis 電力危機
  power elite エリート権力者層, エリート支配者層, パワー・エリート
  power game 権力闘争, パワー・ゲーム
  power grid reform 配電網の改革
  power liberalization 電力自由化 (=liberalization of the electricity market)
  power line 送電線, 電線, 電源ケーブル
  power of appointment 指名権, 選任権
  power of attorney 委任状, 委任権 (=letter of attorney)
  power of attorney in litigation 訴訟委任状
  power operator 電力事業者
  power outage 停電 (=power blackout), 停電時間, 停電期間
  power play 実力行使, 攻勢的行動, 権力 [影響

力]誇示の戦略, パワー・プレー
power politics 権力政治, 力の政治, 武力外交, パワー・ポリティックス (軍事力や経済力をバックにした国際外交)
power producer and supplier 特定規模電気事業者《略 PPS》
power production capacity 発電能力
power reactor 動力炉
power recovery from LNG LNG冷熱発電
power-sharing 〈政党や連立政権内の〉権限分担, 権限分有, 権力の分担, 責任分担
power source 電源, 電力源
power station 発電所 (=power plant)
power strip 大型ディスカウント・ショッピング・センター (=power center)
power supply 電力供給
power tea 午後のお茶を飲みながらの実務会議
power tower 太陽エネルギー利用発電所
power train 伝動機構
power transfer 政権移譲
power transformer 変圧器
power transmission 送電
power user パワー・ユーザー (専門家に近い技術と能力のあるコンピュータ・ユーザー)
power utilities 電力会社, 電力各社
power vacuum 権力の空白, 力の空白
separation of powers 三権分立
smart power 賢い力, 賢いパワー, 賢く力を使うこと, スマート・パワー (ハード・パワー (軍事力や経済力) とソフト・パワー (文化や価値観による影響力) を柔軟に組み合わせた力のこと)
soft power ソフト・パワー (軍事力や経済力によらずに, 文化や政策などに対する支持や理解, 共感を得ることによって, 国際社会からの信頼や発言力を獲得できる力のこと)
staying power 持久力, 持続力
take (the reins of) power 政権を掌握する, 政権を握る
voting power 議決権
water power 水力
power generation 発電, 電力量
　combined-cycle power-generation system コンバインドサイクル発電システム (ガスタービンと蒸気タービンを組み合わせた複合発電方式)
　geothermal power generation 地熱発電 (=geothermal generation)
　magnetohydrodynamic power generation MHD発電, 電磁流体力学発電《略 MHD》
　nuclear power generation 原子力発電
　ocean current power generation 海流発電
　photovoltaic power generation 太陽光発電
　tidal power generation 潮流発電, 潮汐発電
　volcanic power generation 火山発電
　wind-power generation 風力発電
power plant 発電装置, 発電設備, 発電所, 〈自動車などの〉動力装置 (=power station, powerhouse)
　coal power plant 石炭火力発電
　power plant of an automobile 自動車の動力装置
powerful 形 強力な, 強い, 力強い, 影響力のある, 影響力を持った, 有力な, 権力のある, 人を動かす, 説得力のある, 大手の, 効力[効能]のある
　a powerful argument 説得力のある議論
　a powerful drug よく効く薬
　a powerful speech 説得力のある演説
　powerful muscles 強靭な筋肉
　powerful performers 演技の優れた人たち, 芸達者な役者
powerholder 名 実権派の人
powerhouse 名 発電所, 原動力, 強豪チーム, 強力なチーム[組織]
powermonger 名 権力主義者, 権力闘争家
powwow 名 会議, 会談, 話し合い, 協議, 作戦会議, 評定
ppb 10億分の1 (parts per billionの略)
ppm 100万分の1, 百万分率 (parts per millionの略)
PPP インターネット接続用プロトコル (point-to-point protocolの略)
PPP 汚染者負担の原則, 公害発生者負担の原則 (polluter pays principleの略)
PPP パブリック・プライベート・パートナーシップ (public private partnershipの略: 民間の資金とノウハウを導入して税金の効果的で効率的な活用を図るため, 企業や非営利組織が参加して公共サービスを提供する手法の総称。民間資金を利用した社会資本整備 (PFI) や公営企業の民営化, 政府資産の民間への売却, 官と民の合弁事業などが挙げられる。⇒PFI)
PPP 購買力平価 (purchasing power parityの略)
PR 広報, 広報活動, 広報宣伝活動, 宣伝, 渉外, ピーアール (⇒public relations)
　good PR 恰好の宣伝
　national PR strategy 国家PR戦略

practice 名 実行, 実践, 実務, 営業, 開業, 業務, 慣行, 慣習, 習俗, 手法, 仕組み, 法律事務, 訴訟実務, 訴訟手続き
- accounting practices 会計慣行, 会計実務, 会計処理
- best practice 最善の手法, 最良の方法, 卓越した事例, 最善の実施例[業務慣行], 最善の慣行
- business practice 商慣習, 商慣行, 企業慣行, 取引慣行, 取引方法, 営業手法, 業務
- collection practice 回収業務
- collusive practices 談合
- current practice 現行実務, 現行業務
- fair practice 公正慣行, 公正慣習
- lending practice 融資慣行
- management accounting practice 管理会計実務
- practice management 経営手法 (= operating management)
- present practice 現行業務, 現行実務 (= current practice)
- priority practice 優先交渉慣行
- Rules of Fair Practice 公正慣習規則, 公正慣行ルール (全米証券業協会の業界規則)

practitioner 名 実務家, 開業医, 開業者, 弁護士業務

pragmatism 名 実用[実利]主義, 現実[実際]主義, 実践主義, 実用的[実践的]な考え方, 現実

prank call いたずら電話

Pravda 名 プラウダ (ロシアの新聞)

prearrange 動 前もって取り決める
- prearranged formula 事前調整方式, 事前調整型

prebuttal 名 先手を打って述べておく反論,〈対立候補の発表文に対する〉先制反論

precautionary approach [measures] 予防措置

precedence 名 優位, 優先, 優先すること, 優先権, 重要であること, 先行, 上位, 席次, 序列, 上席権
- give precedence to …に上席を与える, …の優位[優先権]を認める
- have precedence over [of] …より重要である
- in order of precedence 優先順に
- take precedence over [of] …に[…よりも]優先する, …に先立つ, …に勝る, …より重要性がある
- the order of precedence 席次

precedent 名 先例, 判例

precensorship 名 事前検閲

precinct 名 選挙区, 警察管区, 境内

precipitation 名 降水, 降雨, 降水[降雨]量, 雨量, 急落下, 急落, 大急ぎ, 大あわて
- precipitation probability forecast 降水確率予報
- probability of precipitation 降水確率

precision 名 正確, 精密, 精度
- precision bombing 精密照準爆撃
- precision equipment manufacturer 精密機器メーカー
- precision-guided munitions 精密誘導兵器
- precision instrument [apparatus] 精密機器
- precision machinery 精密機械, 精密機器

precondition 名 前提条件, 必要条件

precut 形 あらかじめ切ってある[刻んである]
- precut salads 野菜サラダ・パック
- precut vegetables カット野菜

predecessor 名 前任者, 先任者, 先輩, 前身, 祖先
- predecessor firm 前身会社

predicament 名 困難な状況,〈特定の〉状況, 境遇, 窮状, 苦, 苦境, 窮地, 窮境
- a financial predicament 財政的苦境, 財政的に困難な状況
- a trio of predicaments 三重苦
- be placed in a predicament 苦境に置かれる
- come out of the predicament 苦境から脱出する, 苦境を抜け出す

predict 動 予測する, 予想する, 予知する, 予報する, 予言する
- predict future market moves 将来の市場動向を予測する
- predict price movement 価格変動を予測する
- predict (the direction of) interest rates 金利動向を予測する

prediction 名 予測, 予想, 予知, 予報, 予言
- intuitive prediction 直観的予測
- point prediction 点予測
- prediction error 予測誤差
- prediction region 予測域
- set prediction 集合予測
- statistical prediction 統計予測, 統計的予測

predominant 形 有力な, 優位な, 支配的な, 顕著な, 目立つ

pre-electioneering 名〈選挙の〉事前運動

preemptive 形 先買の, 先制の
- preemptive action 先制攻撃 (= preemptive attack)

preference 名 優先, 優遇, 特恵, 優先権, 先取権, 選好, 好み, 志向, 選択
  consumer's preference 消費者選好, 消費者選択
  credit preferences 信用優先権
  fiscal preference 財政選好
  give [show] preference to …に優先権を与える, …を優遇する
  in preference to …に優先して, …ではなく
  lender's preference 貸し手の選好
  occupational preference 職業選択
  preference dividend 優先配当
  preference index 選好指数
  preference ordering 選好順序
  preference share [stock] 優先株 (=preferred share [stock])
  preference treatment 特恵待遇
  preference treatment tariff 特恵関税 (=preferential duties)
  scale of preferences 選好の尺度
  special preference 特恵
  special tax preferences 優遇税制
  time preference 時間選好, 時差選好
  zone of preference for acceptance 合格域
  zone of preference for rejection 不合格域

preferential 形 優先的な, 優先する
  general preferential duties 一般特恵関税
  preferential duties [tariff] 特恵関税
  preferential interest rate for companies 企業向け融資の優遇金利
  preferential right 優先権, 先取特権
  preferential tax treatment 優遇税制措置, 税制優遇
  preferential tariff treatment 特恵関税の適用
  preferential trading agreement 特恵貿易協定
  preferential treatment 優遇措置
  preferential voting 順位指定連記投票

preferential tax system 優遇税制 (=preferential taxation system)
  preferential tax system for securities 証券優遇税制

preferred security 優先出資証券

preferred share [stock] 優先株式, 優先株 (利益の配当や会社解散時の残余財産の分配が普通株式に優先して与えられる株式で, 一般に議決権 (経営参加権:voting right) は与えられない。議決権がない代わりに普通株より配当を多く受け取れる)
  convertible preferred shares 転換型優先株
  nonconvertible preferred shares 非転換型優先株
  redeemable preferred shares 償還優先株

preimplantation 形 着床前の
  preimplantation genetic diagnosis 遺伝子の着床前診断

preliminary 形 予備の, 予備的な, 暫定的な, 仮の
  preliminary condition 予備的条件
  preliminary data 速報値
  preliminary election 予備選挙
  preliminary estimate 暫定推定値, 仮見積り
  preliminary examination 予備調査, 予備審査, 予備試験
  preliminary exploration 予備調査
  preliminary hearing 事前審理, 予審
  preliminary injunction 暫定的差止め命令
  preliminary negotiation 予備交渉
  preliminary notice 予告
  preliminary projections 暫定値
  preliminary prospectus 仮目論見書
  preliminary quotation 暫定見積り, 仮見積り
  preliminary rating 予備格付け
  preliminary report 速報, 速報値
  preliminary research 予備調査, 予備的調査
  preliminary review 予備調査, 予備審査
  preliminary stage 準備段階, 予備的段階
  preliminary statement 予備報告書
  preliminary study 予備調査, 事前調査
  preliminary survey 予備調査, 事前調査, 準備調査
  preliminary talks 予備会談, 事前協議, 事前の話し合い

prelude 名 前奏曲, 序曲, 前置き, 前触れ, 先駆け

premature 形 時期尚早の, 早計の, 早産の
  premature baby 未熟児
  premature death 早死
  premature decision 早まった決定

premeditated 形 計画的な, 前もって計画した, 前もって熟慮した
  premeditated attack 計画的な攻撃
  premeditated murder 計画的殺人, 謀殺

premier 名 〈仏・伊・中国などの〉首相 (prime minister), 総理大臣, 〈オーストラリアやカナダの〉州知事, 形 第一位の, 最上級の, 最上の, 優良な,

最も重要な
premier buyer 最大の買い手
premier supplier トップ・メーカー
provincial premier 〈カナダの〉州知事
state premier 〈オーストラリアの〉州知事

premiere 名 初演, 初公演, 初公演, 初興行, 封切り, プレミア, プレミア・ショー, 有料試写会, 花形女優, 主役女優

premiership 名 首相在任期間, 首相の任期, 首相の地位, 首相の職
assume the premiership 首相に就任する

premium 名 保険料, 保険金, 額面超過額, 割増価格, 割増金, 上乗せ, 手数料, 打歩, 権利金, 報奨金, 奨励金, 賞金, 景品, プレミアム, 形 とくに優れた, 高級な, 高品質の
additional premium 割増保険料
at a premium 高く評価されて, 額面以上で, プレミアム付きで, 割増金付きで, 手に入りにくい, 希少価値の, 通常より高い, 珍重されている, 大いに需要があって
bond premium 社債プレミアム, 社債発行差金
fixed-premium system 保険料固定方式
insurance premium 保険料
overtime premium 超過勤務手当
pension premium 年金保険料
place [put] a high premium on …を高く評価する, …を重んじる
premium beer 高級ビール, プレミアム・ビール
premium bond 〈英国の〉プレミアム付き国債[賞金付き無利子国債], 割増金付き債券, プレミアム債
premium borrower 優良発行体
premium on capital stock 株式発行差金
premium price 通常より高い値段
premium quality 最高の品質
premium revenue 〈保険会社の〉保険料収入（一般事業会社の売上高に相当）
premium sale 景品付き販売, プレミアム・セール
put a premium on …を高く評価する, …を奨励する, …にプレミアムを付ける

premonition 名 予感, 不安感, 虫の知らせ, 前兆

prepackaged bankruptcy 事前策定型破綻, プリパック, プリパッケージド・バンクラプトシー

prepaid 形 支払い済みの, 前払いの, プリペイド
prepaid book card プリペイド式図書カード
prepaid cell phone プリペイド式携帯電話, プリペイド携帯 (=prepaid mobile phone)

preparation 名 準備, 用意, 支度, 予習,〈書類の〉作成, 調理, 調理食品, 調合, 調合薬, 調剤薬
preparatory 形 予備の, 予備的な, 前もっての, 前置きの, 準備の
preparatory arrangement 予備協定
preparatory exercise 予備運動
preparatory measures 予備手段
preparatory negotiation 予備交渉
preparatory school 予備校
preparatory talks 予備会談, 予備交渉
preparatory to …の準備として, …の準備のために, …に先立って, …を見越して
preparatory training 予備訓練
preparatory work 準備作業
prepare 動 準備する, 用意する, 計画する, 段取りを整える, 覚悟させる, 心の準備をさせる,〈薬品などを〉調製する, 調合する, 作成する
be prepared to …の覚悟をしている, …することを予期[予想]している
prepare for …の準備[用意]をする, …に備える, …の覚悟をする
prepare pills 丸薬を調製する
preparedness 名 準備[用意]ができていること (readiness), 備え, 覚悟,〈軍備の〉充実
disaster preparedness 災害への備え
military preparedness 軍備, 軍備の充実
prepositioning 名 事前配置
prerequisite 名 前提条件, 必要条件, 先行条件
prerogative 名 特権, 特典, 下院議員の特典, 形 特権の, 大権を有する
prescription 名 処方箋, 提案, 構想, 命令, 規則, 時効
presence 名 存在, 存在感, 影響力, 地位, 立場, 事業基盤, 経営基盤, 拠点, 進出, 営業網, ポジション, 態度, 姿勢, プレゼンス
economic presence 経済的影響力, 経済力
establish a presence in the market 市場での地位を確立する
global presence 世界の営業網
market presence 市場での地位, 市場でのプレゼンス, 市場進出
present 動 表示する, 提示する, 示す, 作成する, 提出する, 提供する, 贈呈する, 口頭で説明する, 申し立てる
fairly present 適正に表示する (=present fairly)
present consolidated financial statements

連結財務書類[連結財務諸表]を作成する

presentation 名 公表, 発表, 表示, 説明, 説明会, 報告, 概要紹介, 提示, 提出, 贈呈, 授与, プレゼンテーション

- fair presentation 適正表示, 公正表示
- misleading presentation 不当表示
- presentation bill 一覧払い手形
- presentation ceremony 授与式, 贈呈式
- presentation copy 献本
- presentation paper 〈政党の〉政策方針書
- presentation period 提示期間

presenter 名 司会者, ニュース放送者, ニュース・キャスター, 贈呈者

preservative 名 食品防腐剤, 保存剤, 変色予防剤

presidency 名 大統領の職[地位, 任期], 大統領在任期間, 会長[社長, 総裁, 議長]の任期, 議長国

- the presidency of the EU EU議長国

president 名 社長, 会長, 会頭, 頭取, 総裁, 議長, 委員長, 学長, 総長, 大統領, 国家主席, 総統

米国大統領 ⊃ 米国の国家元首。行政府の長・最高責任者(Chief Executive)であると同時に, 陸・空・海軍と海兵隊(Marine Corps)の4軍のほか, 沿岸警備隊(Coast Guard)と州兵(National Guard)を統括する最高司令官(Commander in Chief)でもある。制度的には, 選挙人による間接選挙によって選出され, 538名の選挙人の過半数を得た者が当選する。これに該当する者がいないときは, 上位3名について連邦議会の下院の投票で選任される。任期は4年で再選も可能であるが, 1951年以降, 3選は禁止された。被選挙権は, 米国市民として生まれ, 選挙までの国内居住期間が14年以上で満35歳以上の男女(帰化市民は不可)となっている。大統領は国民に直接責任を負い, 議会には責任を負わず, 議会の解散権もない。ただし, 弾劾以外に辞任を強制されることもない。また, 法律執行の職務のほかに官吏任命権や条約締結権を持ち, 議会に教書(presidential message)を送って立法を勧告する一方, 法案への署名を拒否(veto)することによって立法を阻止することができる。なお, 大統領夫人はFirst Lady, 大統領一家はFirst Familyと呼ばれる。大統領が死亡, 辞職, 執務不能になったり解任されたりした場合, 大統領の残りの任期を務める大統領継承の順位(the order of presidential succession)は, 副大統領(the Vice President: 上院議長を兼任), 下院議長(Speaker of the House), 上院議長代行(President pro tempore of the Senate), 国務長官(Secretary of State), 財務長官(Secretary of the Treasury)の順となっている。

- be officially elected president 大統領に就任する
- be passed and signed by President 議会で可決後, 大統領が署名する
- deputy president 副社長, 副総裁, 副頭取
- EU's full time president EUの欧州理事会常任議長, EU大統領
- imperial president 尊大な大統領(行政の長としての権力が突出している大統領)
- president-designate 次期社長, 新任命社長
- president-elect 次期大統領, 大統領当選者, 会長[学長]当選者
- president emeritus 名誉会長
- president-for-life 終身大統領 (＝life president)
- president's day 〈米〉大統領誕生日
- the economic report of the president 〈米〉大統領経済報告, 経済教書
- the president of the European Union 欧州連合(EU)委員長
- the president's English アメリカ英語 (＝American English)

presidential 形 大統領の, 大統領選挙[大統領選挙戦]の, 大統領職の, 大統領の職務の

- presidential adviser 大統領顧問
- presidential assistant for national security affairs 〈米〉国家安全保障問題大統領補佐官
- presidential ball 大統領主催の晩餐会
- Presidential Medal of Freedom 自由勲章
- presidential nomination 大統領候補指名
- presidential nominee 大統領候補者
- presidential platform 党政策綱領
- presidential primary 〈米各政党の〉大統領予備選挙, 大統領選出予備選挙
- presidential secretary 大統領補佐官(presidential aide)
- presidential ticket 大統領公認候補者, 大統領公認候補者名簿, 全国党大会(National Convention)で選ばれた大統領と副大統領の組合せ(ticket＝政党などで指名された候補者のリスト)
- presidential veto 大統領拒否権, 法案署名拒否
- presidential year 大統領選挙の年(4で割り切れる西暦年に行われる)
- run for the Democratic presidential nomination 民主党の大統領候補者の指名選挙に出馬する

US Presidential Special Trade Representative 〈米〉大統領通商交渉代表
Weekly Compilation of Presidential Documents 週刊大統領公式文書
presidential election 大統領選挙, 大統領選挙戦, 大統領選, 総裁選挙 (＝presidential campaign, presidential race)
presidential election cycle theory 大統領選択循環理論
Presidential message 〈米〉大統領教書
(＝President's Message：代表的なものとして年頭の3大教書—Budget Message（予算教書）, Economic Report（経済報告書）, State of the Union Message（一般教書）, 必要に応じての特別教書がある)
Budget Message 〈米〉大統領の予算教書
Special Message 〈米〉大統領の特別教書
State of the Union Message [Address] 〈米〉大統領の一般教書
State of the World Message 〈米〉大統領の外交教書
the President's message to Congress 〈米〉大統領の議会への教書
presiding 形 議長を務める
presiding judge 裁判長
Presidium (of the Supreme Soviet) 旧ソ連最高会議幹部会
press 名 新聞, 雑誌, 定期刊行物, マスコミ, 新聞界, 報道, 報道機関, 報道陣, 報道関係者, 記者団, メディア, マスメディア, 出版社, 出版物, 印刷所, 印刷機, 圧迫, 押し, 印刷機, 切迫, 緊急, 多忙, プレス
be hot off the press 新聞で発表されたばかり
get a good press 新聞で評判が良い, マスコミで好意的に取り上げられる
get a negative [bad] press 新聞で評判が悪い, マスコミで批判的に取り上げられる
get extensive press coverage 多くの新聞で取り上げられる
go to press 印刷される, 印刷に回される
press agent 広報業者, 宣伝広報担当者, 宣伝[報道, 広報]係, プレス・エージェント《PA [p.a.]》
press aide 新聞補佐官
press attache 〈大使館の〉報道担当官
press box 新聞記者席, 報道記者席, 報道席
press briefing 記者団発表, 記者団への状況説明会
press conference 記者会見 (＝news conference)
press control 報道管制
press corps 新聞記者団, 報道関係者, 記者団
press gallery 〈議会・裁判所などの〉新聞記者席, 記者席
press kit 記者会見資料, 新聞記事見本
press office 〈政府などの〉広報部, 新聞報道課, 新聞関係局
press officer 〈政府の〉報道担当官, 〈企業の〉広報担当者
press pack 広報[広報用]パンフレット, 報道陣
press [media] packet PR素材一式, プレス・パケット (＝press kit, press book)
press pool 〈代表取材の〉代表記者, プール記者
press preview 報道関係者内覧, 報道関係者の下見
press release 新聞発表, 報道用公式発表, 報道関係者に対する発表, プレス・リリース (＝news release)
the freedom of the press 報道の自由
the gutter press 低俗紙
pressing 形 急を要する, 緊急の(urgent), 火急の, 差し迫った, 切迫した, 深刻な, 断りにくい, たっての
pressing bills 期限の迫った勘定
pressing business 緊急の用事
pressing demand 差し迫った要求, たっての要請, 切迫した需要
pressing invitation 熱心な誘い, たっての招待
pressing issue 緊急の課題, 緊急を要する問題
pressing need 差し迫った必要, 切迫した需要, 緊急の課題
pressure 動 圧力をかける, 強要する
pressure 名 圧力, 圧迫, 逼迫, 強い要請, 強要, 強制, 反発, 縮小, 減少, 低下, 悪化, 下落, 伸び悩み, ストレス
add to the upward pressure on prices 物価上昇圧力を強める
asset quality pressure 資産内容の悪化
be under pressure to …を迫られる
downward pressure 低下圧力, 引下げ圧力, 低下傾向, 低下要因
feel the pressure ストレスを感じる
give in to pressure 圧力に屈する
margin pressure 利益率低下, 利益率への圧力 (＝pressure on margins)
pile pressure on …に圧力をかける
pressure bulkhead 圧力隔壁

pressure group 圧力団体
pressure on pricing 価格圧力, 値下げ圧力 (=pricing pressure)
pressure suit 宇宙服, 与圧服, 気密服
put [exert, pile] pressure on …に圧力をかける (=bring pressure to bear on)
upward pressure 上昇圧力, 引上げ圧力, 上昇傾向, 上昇要因

prestige 名 名声, 評判, 信望, 威信, 威厳, 体面, 面子
prestige advertising 名声広告
prestige brand 有名ブランド, 高級品, 銘柄品
prestige paper 有力新聞
prestige price 名声価格, 威光価格
prestige pricing 名声価格設定
prestige retailer 有名小売業者
prestige school 名門校, 有名校, 一流校 (=prestigious school)
prestige store 有名店, 一流専門店, 老舗
the prestige of the nation 国家の威信, 国威

prestigious 形 名声[信望, 威信, 威厳]のある, 名門の, 有名な, 一流の, 評判の, 世評の高い, 高級の, 格式の高い, 老舗の

pretax [pre-tax] 形 税引き前の, 税込みの, 経常の

pretax loss 経常損失, 経常赤字, 課税前損失, 税引き前損失

pretax profit 経常利益, 経常収益(民間企業の税引き前利益に相当), 税込み利益, 課税前利益, 税引き前利益 (=current profit, recurring profit)

pretrial procedures 公判前整理手続き

pretrial summary procedures 公判前整理手続き (=pretrial procedures)

prevail 動 勝つ, まさる, 勝利を得る, 首尾よく行く, 成功する, 功を奏する, 効果がある, 一般に行われている, 一般に見られる, 広がる, 広まる, 広く行き渡る, 普及している, 流行している, はびこる, 説き伏せる, うまく説得する
prevail against all difficulties あらゆる困難に打ち勝つ
prevail upon [on] a person to do 人を…するよう説得する

prevailing 形 優勢な, 有力な, 卓越した, 優勢を占めている, 支配的な, 勢力がある, 広く受け入れられている, 広く行われている, 普及[流行]している, 実勢の, 現行の, ごく普通の, 世間一般の, 一般の
prevailing exchange rate 現在の為替レート
prevailing interest rate 現行金利[利子率], 実勢金利, 金利の実勢
prevailing market expectations 大方の市場の期待
prevailing market yield 市場実勢利回り
prevailing opinion 支配的な意見
prevailing price 一般価格, 時価
prevailing rate 市場の実勢金利, 市場金利, 実勢相場, 中心相場, 中心レート, 一般賃金, 一般賃率
prevailing wages 現行賃金, 一般賃金

prevalent 形 広く行われている, 広く認められる[見られる], 一般的な, 一般に行き渡った, 一般に流布している, 流行している, 普及している, 〈病気が〉蔓延している, 支配している, 優勢である, 主な

prevent 動 防ぐ, 防止する, 予防する, 中止させる, 邪魔する, 阻止する, …を妨げる

prevention 名 防止, 予防, 防止[予防]策
juvenile crime prevention 青少年犯罪の防止
prevention of cruelty to animals 動物虐待の防止
prevention of epidemics 流行病の予防
Prevention of Fraud (investment) Act 不正投資防止法
prevention of sea pollution 海洋汚染防止
prevention of suicide 自殺防止

preventive 形 防止するための, 予防するための
preventive custody 予備拘留
preventive detention 予防拘留, 予防拘束, 予防拘禁
preventive diplomacy 紛争の予防外交
preventive health care 予防的保険医療
preventive immunization 予防注射
preventive inoculation 予防接種
preventive maintenance 予防保守, 予防的保守, 定期点検
preventive measure 予防手段
preventive medicine 予防医学
preventive war 予防戦争

preview 名 試写, 試写会, 試演, 予告編, 下見, 内覧, 内見会, 予備知識, プレビュー

price 動 …の値段を付ける, …の値段を決める, 値決めする, 価格設定する, 値段を提示する
be fairly priced 適正価格が付けられている
be priced at current market rates 市場レートで値決めされる
be priced out of the market 価格の点で市場から脱落する

high-priced stock 値がさ株
well-priced issue 価格が適切な債券
price 名 価格, 値段, 物価, プライス
  acquisition price 取得価格
  aggregate demand price 総需要価格
  aggregate supply price 総供給価格
  agricultural price 農産物価格
  anticipated price 予想価格, 見込み価格
  asked price 言い値, 呼び値, 売り呼び値
  bedrock [bottom] price 底値
  best bid price 最高入札価格
  bid price 入札価格, 指し値, せり値, 買い呼び値
  closing price 終値, 引け値
  comparative price 相対価格
  competitive price 競争価格, 安い価格・値段
  consumer prices 消費者物価
  contract [contractual] price 契約価格, 協定価格
  conversion at market price 時価転換
  convertible price 転換価格
  current price 通り相場, 時価, 現行価格
  dip in price 価格の下落
  double price 二重価格
  effective price 実効価格
  list price 表示価格
  monopolistic [monopoly] price 独占価格
  offering price 売出価格, 公募価格, 申込み値段 (＝offer price)
  price cartel 価格カルテル, 価格協定 (＝price agreement)
  price index 物価指数
  price keeping operation 公的資金による株式の買い支え, 株価維持策, 株価維持活動 プライス・キーピング・オペレーション 《略 PKO》(国民年金や厚生年金などの公的資金による株式の買い支え)
  price leader 価格先導企業
  price markups 価格の上昇
  price mechanism 価格メカニズム
  redemption price 償還価格, 〈公社債の〉買入れ価格
  resale price 再販売価格
  ruling price 通り相場
  selling price 販売価格, 売却価格, 売価, 売り値
  share price on the first day 初値
  standard price 標準価格, 標準物価, 基準価格
  strike price 行使価格, 権利行使価格
price fixing 価格維持, 価格固定, 価格決定, 価格操作, 価格協定, 価格についての取り決め, 物価安定
  price-fixing agreement 価格維持協定, 価格カルテル, ヤミ価格協定
price increase 値上げ, 価格上昇, 物価上昇, 物価上昇率, インフレ率
  acceleration in monthly price increases 前月比インフレ率の上昇
  percentage price increase 価格上昇率
pricey 形 高価な, 金のかかる
pricing 名 価格設定, 価格決定, 価格計算, 価格政策, 値付け, 価格
  flat-rate pricing scheme 定額料金制
  option pricing オプションの値付け
  pricing behavior 価格方針
  pricing policy 価格決定方針, 価格政策
primacy 名 首位, 第一位, 最高, 卓越, 最も重要であること
  forfeit one's primacy 首位から転落する
  give primacy to …を最優先する, …を優先して考える, …を最重要視する
primary 名 米大統領候補予備選挙, 予備選挙 (＝primary election)
  closed primary 閉鎖的予備選挙(有権者が特定政党の支持者として登録した者に限られる場合)
  open primary 開放的予備選挙
primary 形 最初の, 第一次の, 一次的な, 第一順位の, 主要な, 最も重要な, 最大の, 中心的な, 有力な, 本来の, 根源的な, 初歩的な, 初期の, 初期段階の, 基本的な, 希薄化前, プライマリー
  primary activities 第一次産業活動
  primary beneficiary 第一順位保険金受取人
  primary bond 新発債
  primary budget deficit 基礎的財政収支の赤字, 基礎収支の赤字
  primary budget surplus 基礎的財政収支の黒字, 基礎収支の黒字
  primary capital 第一次資本, 本源的資本, 銀行の自己資本
  primary (health, medical) care 初期医療, 初期診療, プライマリー・ケア
  primary commodity 第一次産品, 一次産品, 基本財 (＝primary product)
  primary cooling water 一次冷却水 (＝primary coolant)
  primary data 一次的データ
  primary dealer 〈米国の〉公認政府証券ディーラー, プライマリー・ディーラー

primary deficit 基礎的赤字, 財政の基礎収支の赤字
primary demand 基礎的需要, 第一次需要, 基礎的需要, 基本的需要
primary distribution 募集, 第一次分売（＝primary offering）
primary duty 輸入付加税
primary earnings per common share 単純希薄化による普通株式1株当たり利益
primary earnings per share of common stock 普通株式1株当たり基本的利益
primary education 初等教育
primary election 予備選挙, 米大統領候補予備選挙（＝primary）
primary employment 第一次雇用
primary energy 一次エネルギー
primary evidence 一次的証拠
primary exports 一次産品輸出
primary financial statements 基本財務諸表, 基本財務書類, 第一次財務諸表［財務諸表］（第二次財務諸表＝secondary financial statements）
primary importing country 一次産品輸入国
primary industry 第一次産業, 一次産業（＝primary sectors：農業, 林業, 畜産, 漁業, 鉱業など）
primary jurisdiction 第一次的管轄, 第一次的管轄権
primary planet 惑星
primary processing 一次加工, 川上部門
primary production 一次生産
primary products 一次産品, 農産品, 主要製品
primary reason for …の最大の理由
primary resources 原産資源, 天然資源
primary surplus 基礎的黒字, 財政の基礎収支の黒字
primary trade 第一次産品貿易
primary wave 〈地震の〉縦波, P波

primary balance 基礎的財政収支, 財政の基礎的収支, プライマリー・バランス（国債発行による収入と国債の元利払い費を除いた基礎的収支。基礎的財政収支が赤字だと, 国の借金が増えるため, 財政再建には黒字化が必要になる）

primary market 発行市場, 新発債市場, プライマリー市場（新規株式公開や公募など, 企業や国が株や債券を新規発行して資金調達をする市場）

> 発行市場と流通市場との違い ⊃ 証券市場のうち, 有価証券を発行, 引受け, 募集する段階のことを有

価証券の発行市場（primary market, issue market）という。これに対して, 発行された証券を売買する段階を有価証券の流通市場（secondary market, trading market）という。

prime 形 主要な, 首位の, 最重要な, 優秀な, 優良な, 最優良な, 最高級の, 第一等の, 極上の, 信用等級が最高の, 素数の, 名 最上等, 素数
prime asset 優良資産
prime borrower [debtor, issuer] 優良発行体
prime commercial paper 一流商業手形
prime customer 優良顧客, 優良取引先
prime lending rate 一流企業向け最優遇貸出金利, プライム・レート（＝prime rate）
prime mover 主唱者, 原動力, 牽引力
prime name bank 超一流銀行
prime suspect 主犯容疑者
prime tenant 主要テナント
prime time 視聴率が最も高い［高視聴率の］時間帯, ゴールデン・アワー, プライム・タイム

prime minister 首相, 総理大臣, 総理《略 PM》

prime rate 一流企業向け最優遇貸出金利, 標準金利, プライム・レート（＝prime, prime bank rate, prime interest rate, prime lending rate, prime rate of interest）

long-term prime rate 長期プライム・レート, 長プラ（最も信用力がある銀行の顧客企業に対する1年超の貸付け金に適用される金利）
short-term prime rate 短期プライム・レート, 短プラ（優良企業向けに1年以内の短期資金を貸し出すときの基準金利）

Primorye 名 沿海州（日本海に面したロシアの行政区で, 州都はウラジオストク）

prince 名 王子, 皇子, 親王, …公, （…の）第一人者, 大御所, 大家, 大物, プリンス
a prince of the royal blood 王子, 親王
the Prince of Wales 英国皇太子, プリンス・オブ・ウェールズ《略 POW [P.O.W.]》
the prince royal 皇太子, 第一王子

princess 名 王女, 皇女, 内親王, 親王妃, 皇太子妃, 〈公国の〉王妃, 妃殿下, 貴族の婦人, 女性の第一人者, 女傑
the Princess of Monaco モナコ公国王妃
the Princess of Wales 英国皇太子妃, プリンセス・オブ・ウェールズ
the princess royal 第一王女

principal 名 元本, 元金, 基本財産, 株式の額面価額, 主債務者, 本人

collection of principal　元本回収
guaranteed principal　元本保証
original principal　元金, 元本
outstanding principal　残存元本
payment of principal and interest　元利の支払い, 元利払い, 元利の返済, 元利返済
principal and interest　元本と利息, 元利
repayment of principal　元本の償還, 元本の返済
trust principal　信託元本

principal 形　主な, 主要な, 第一の, 元金の
principal amount　元本
principal debtor [obligor]　主な債務者
principal guarantee　元本保証
principal repayment　元金返済
principal stockholder　主要株主

principle 名　原理, 原則, 法則, 主義, 信念, 信条, 根本方針, 方針, 〈基本的な〉考え方, 道義, 徳義, 節操, 本源, 本質, 原動力
a coloring principle　染色素
a conservative principle　保守的な考え方, 保守的な方針
a vital principle　活力, 精力
abandon [desert] one's principle　信念を捨てる
as a matter of principle　主義として
be against one's principles　…の信念[主義, 道義]に反する
benefit principle　受益者負担
economic principle　経済原則
guiding principles　指導原理
in principle　原則的に, 原則として, 全体としては, 大筋で, おおむね
lose one's moral principles from greed　欲に目がくらむ
market principles　市場原理
moral principles　道義
on principle　主義[信念]として, 主義に従って[に基づいて], 原則に則(のっと)って, 道義的見地から, 道義上
principles　〈料理などの〉基礎, 定石
priority principle　重点主義
satisfying principle　満足基準
stick [live up] to one's principles　信念に固執する, 信念を貫く
the first principle of all things　万物の根源
the fundamental principle of the universe　宇宙の根本原理
the principle of casualty　因果律
the principle of consistency　継続性の原則, 首尾一貫の原則
the principle of contradiction　矛盾律
the principle of relativity　相対性原理
the principle of the separation of religion from politics　政教分離の原則
the principle of the thing　ものの道理

prion 名　プリオン(たんぱく質の一種。狂牛病や人のヤコブ病, 羊のスクレイピーなど, 脳の神経組織が破壊されて死亡する一連のプリオン病は, プリオンの正常型が異常化することによって発病する)
abnormal prion　異常プリオン
normal prion　正常プリオン

prior 形　事前の, 前の, 先の, …より上の, 優先的な, …より重要な, 前歴のある
prior arrangement　事前の取決め
prior arrest　逮捕歴
prior consultation　事前協議 (＝preconsultation)
prior contact　事前の連絡
prior conviction　前科
prior engagement　先約
prior notice　事前通告
prior restraint　事前発表禁止命令
prior warning　事前警告

priority 名　優先, 優先事項, 優先権, 優先順位, 先取権
cost priority　コスト優先, コスト重視
export priority　輸出優先権, 輸出優先順位
first priority　最優先
give priority in negotiations for　…の優先交渉権を与える
investment priority　投資の優先順位
policy priority　政策の優先順位
priority country　優先交渉国
priority in budgetary discussion　予算先議権
priority items　重点品目
priority mail　優先郵便
priority of attachment　優先差押え権
priority practice　優先交渉慣行
priority production　傾斜生産
priority rate of duty　実行関税率
priority schedule　実行順位表
priority subscription period　優先割当期間
priority system principle]　重点主義
put priority on efficiency　効率を重視する
top priority　最優先課題, 最優先

prison 名 刑務所, 〈米国の〉州刑務所(State prison), 監獄, 牢獄, 拘置所, 留置所, 投獄, 収監, 監禁, 禁固, 拘置
- be [lie] in prison 服役している, 拘置中である
- be punishable with prison terms 懲役刑に当たる
- be sent to [put in] prison 刑務所に入れられる, 投獄される
- finish one's five years' prison term 5年の刑期[懲役]を終える
- give five-year suspended prison term to the man 男に5年の執行猶予の刑期を申し渡す
- leave prison on parole 仮出所する
- prison bird 囚人, 罪人
- prison breaker [escapee] 脱獄囚, 脱走犯
- prison-breaking 脱獄
- prison camp 捕虜収容所(prisoner-of-war camp), 政治犯収容所
- prison cell 独房, 収監房
- prison confession 獄中からの証言
- prison fever 発疹チフス
- prison garb 囚人服
- prison officer [guard] 刑務所看守
- prison sentence 懲役刑, 禁固刑
- prison term 刑期, 懲役 (＝term of imprisonment [penal servitude])
- prison visitor 刑務所面会人
- prison without bars 格子のない牢獄
- serve a prison term 刑期を勤める
- serve a ten-year prison sentence 10年の禁固刑に服する

prisoner 名 受刑者, 囚人, 刑事被告人
- innocent prisoner 無罪の囚人
- political prisoner 政治犯 (＝prisoner of conscience)
- prisoner at the bar 刑事被告人, 公判中の被告人
- prisoner in jail 収監された受刑者
- prisoner of conscience 良心の囚人, 政治犯
- prisoner of state 政治犯, 国事犯人 (＝state prisoner)
- prisoner of war 〈戦時中の〉捕虜 《略 POW [P.O.W., PW]》
- prisoner-of-war camp 捕虜収容所
- prisoner's base 陣取り遊び
- prisoner's [prisoners'] dilemma 囚人のジレンマ

privacy 名 私的自由, 個人的自由, 私生活, 秘密, プライバシー
- privacy enhanced mail 暗号化した電子メール 《略 PEM》
- privacy infringement プライバシーの侵害 (＝invasion of privacy)
- privacy policy プライバシー規定(ウェブ上の法的通知)
- privacy protection プライバシー保護, 個人情報保護
- privacy right プライバシー権
- privacy statement プライバシー規約
- violation of privacy rights プライバシー権の侵害, プライバシー侵害

private 形 私的な, 個人的な, 私有の, 私設の, 民営の, 民間の, 内密の, 一般に知られていない, 非公開の, 非公式の, 会員制の, 下位の, プライベート
- private affair 私事
- private apartment 私営アパート
- private banking 富裕層向け資産運用サービス業務, プライベート・バンキング(個人資産を管理・運用する銀行業務)
- private bill 個別法案
- private borrowing 民間借入れ
- private capital 民間投資
- private capital formation 民間資本形成(民間企業の投資)
- private capital investment 民間設備投資
- private car 自家用車, マイカー
- private citizen 民間人, 一市民, 平民
- private clothes 平服
- private company 民間企業, 民営会社, 私会社, 非公開会社, 閉鎖会社 (＝private corporation)
- private consumer spending [expenditure] 個人消費支出
- private consumption 個人消費, 民間消費支出, 民間最終支出 (＝personal consumption, personal spending, private spending)
- private contract 随意契約
- private debt 民間負債
- private demand 民需, 民間需要 (＝private-sector demand)
- private detective [eye, investigator] 私立探偵, 私服警官
- private donation 個人の寄付
- private education 私教育
- private economy 民間経済
- private external investment 民間対外投資

private first class 〈陸軍〉上等兵
private funeral (service) 密葬
private goods 私的財
private guard 民間警備員
private house 個人住宅
private income 不労所得
private initiative 民間の発意
private instruction 個人教授
private investment 民間投資, 民間設備投資, 民間企業による投資, 非公開投資
private investor 個人投資家
private jet 自家用ジェット機
private law 私法
private lending 民間貸付け
private letter 私信
private life 私生活
private marriage 内輪の結婚式
private means 事業所得, 給与[俸給]外所得
private medicine 〈国民健康保険の適用を受けない英国の〉個人負担医療制度
private member 平(ひら)の議員, 平議員
private monopoly 私的独占
private news 秘密情報
private offering 株式の直接募集, 縁故募集, 私募
private opinion 個人の見解, 私見
private organization 民間団体
private ownership 私的所有, 私有, 私有地
private parts 陰部, 性器
private patient 〈英国の〉個人負担の患者
private practice 〈英国の〉個人負担医療, 個人開業, 〈医師, 弁護士など〉個人営業の専門家
private productive investment 民間生産投資
private profit 私的利益, 私利
private property 私有財産, 私有地
private railway 私鉄
private room 個室
private savings 個人貯蓄
private secretary 私設秘書
private soldier 一兵卒, 兵卒
private talks 非公開の話し合い
private tender 指名入札
private trade 民間貿易
private TV station 民間テレビ局
private utility 民間公益事業
private view 個人的見解, 展示内覧, 内覧
private brand 自家商標, 商業者商標, 自主企画商品, プライベート・ブランド《略 PB》(=dealer brand, dealer's brand, private label)
private-brand items 自主企画商品
private brand product 自主開発(プライベート・ブランド)商品

private equity fund プライベート・エクイティ・ファンド(非上場企業に投資して株式公開で利益を得る投資ファンド)

private finance initiative 民間資金による社会資本整備, プライベート・ファイナンス・イニシアチブ《略 PFI》(道路や橋, ごみ処理施設などの社会資本整備で, 民間企業が資金調達から建設, 管理, 運営までを行い, 国や地方自治体, 利用者から施設使用料などを徴収する制度。⇒PFI, PPP)

private placement 私募発行, 私募, 私募債, 第三者割当て(公募=public offering:公募と違って, 私募は株主や取引先, 機関投資家など特定少数の投資家を対象に新株を発行, 募集するもの。⇒privately place [issue])

> 私募発行とは ⇒ 公募と違って, 私募は株主や取引先, 機関投資家など特定少数の投資家を対象に新株を発行, 募集するもの。米国では, 一定以上の資産・収入のある投資家(accredited investor)に私募発行する場合には, 証券取引委員会(SEC)に登録する必要がない。

private sector 民間部門, 民間セクター, 民間企業, 民間
private-sector businesses [firm] 民間企業
private-sector demand 民需 (=private demand)
private-sector economic diplomacy 民間経済外交
private-sector financial balance 民間セクターの資金需給
private-sector investment 民間部門の投資
private-sector mortgage rate 民間の住宅ローン金利

privately held 株式を公開していない, 株式非公開の, 非上場の

privately owned 民間所有の, 民有の, 民間の, 株式非公開の
privately owned bank 民間銀行
privately owned forests 民有林

privately place [issue] 私募発行する
privately-placed bond 私募債
privatization 名 民営化
privatize 動 民営化する, 非国有化する
PRO 広報担当官, 宣伝担当者 (public relations officerの略)

proactive 形 先のことを考えた，先を見越した，事前行動の，事前行動に訴えた，事前に対策を講じる，前向きの，積極的な，攻めの
- **proactive leverage of the branch network** 支店網の積極的利用
- **proactive management policies** 攻めの経営姿勢
- **proactive role** 積極的な役割

proactively 副 前向きに，先のことを考えて，事前に対策を講じて

probation 名 審査，試験，見習い期間，仮採用期間，保護観察，執行猶予

probationary 形 保護観察の，執行猶予中の
- **probationary supervision** 保護観察（＝supervised probation）

probe 動 徹底的に調べる(inspect)，調査する，探る，探り出す，探査する，探索する，検査する，立ち入り検査する
- **probe around the universe** 宇宙を探査する
- **probe for some way** 何か方法を探す
- **probe into** …を徹底的に調べる，…を精査する，…を検査する
- **probe the case to the bottom** 事件を徹底的に調査する

probe 名 厳密な調査，徹底的な調査，精査，探査，探索，〈疑惑の〉解明，宇宙探査機，探測機，探査用ロケット，宇宙探査機による調査，〈医療器具の〉探り針，プローブ
- **launch a probe into** …に対する調査を開始する
- **unmanned probe** 無人探査機

problem 名 問題，課題，難問，厄介な問題［事情］，悩みの種，支障，リスク，故障，障害，疾患，悪化，低迷，不振，トラブル
- **problem assets** 不良資産
- **problem bank** 〈財政上問題のある〉要注意銀行
- **problem child** 問題児
- **problem drinker** アルコール依存症患者
- **problem list** 問題銀行リスト，問題銀行
- **problem loans** 問題債権，不良債権，不良債権額（＝loans to questionable borrowers, problem debts）
- **problem oriented language** 問題指向言語
- **problem page** 読者相談コーナー
- **problem solving** 問題解決（＝problem solution）

problematic 形 問題のある，疑わしい
- **problematic borrower** 問題融資先

problematics 名 複雑な諸問題

problematique 名 複合矛盾
probusiness 形 親ビジネス派の，財界びいきの
procedure 名 手順，やり方，順序，プロセス，手続き，訴訟手続き，訴訟手続き，処置，手術，治療
- **analytical procedures** 分析的手続き
- **criminal procedure** 刑事訴訟
- **dispute settlement procedures** 紛争処理手続き
- **follow normal procedure** 普通のやり方に従う
- **freeze legal procedures** 法的手続きを凍結する
- **inspection procedures** 検査手続き，検収手続き
- **parliamentary procedure** 議会運営手続き，議会手続き
- **standardized procedures** 標準的な手続き

proceed with 進める，〈計画や政策などを〉推し進める，続ける，続行する

proceedings 名 議事進行，議事録，決議録，会議録，会報，訴訟手続き，法的手続き，手続き，措置，訴訟，弁論
- **administrative proceedings** 行政手続き，行政訴訟
- **bankruptcy proceedings** 破綻手続き
- **legal proceedings** 法律手続き，法的手続き，裁判手続き，法的手段
- **receivership proceedings** 破産手続き
- **take [bring, institute, start] proceedings against** …に対して訴訟を起こす

proceeds 名 代金，手取金，売上，売上高，売却収入，売却益，所得，収益，純利益，収入

process 動 処理する，加工する
- **processed food** 加工食品
- **processed goods** 加工財
- **processed product** 加工製品
- **processed tree carcass** 樹木形骸加工品(本，新聞，紙袋などの紙製品のこと)

process 名 過程，工程，流れ，段階，部門，製法，手続き，訴訟手続き，プロセス
- **business process reengineering** 業務革新
- **closing process** 決算手続き
- **decision process** 意思決定プロセス，意思決定の過程，決定過程（＝decision-making process）
- **initial goods in process** 期首仕掛品（＝beginning work in process）
- **legal process** 法的手続き，法手続き
- **manufacturing process** 製造工程，製造部門
- **production process** 生産工程，製造工程，生産過程，製造過程，製造部門（＝manufacturing

process)
quality processes 品質管理手続き
registration process 登録手続き
the Middle East peace process 中東和平プロセス
work in process 仕掛(しかけ・しかかり)品 (=goods in process)

processing 名 処理, 加工, 事務処理, 処理能力
advanced processing 二次加工
batch processing バッチ処理, 一括処理
export processing zone 輸出加工区
information processing 情報処理
inhouse processing 内製
primary processing 一次加工
processing industry 加工産業, 食品加工業

pro-choice 形 妊娠中絶に賛成の, 妊娠中絶擁護派の, 中絶権擁護派の (⇒pro-life)

pro-choicer 名 妊娠中絶賛成者, 妊娠中絶擁護者[擁護派]

procure 動 調達する, 購入する, 仕入れる, 取得する, 入手する, 獲得する, 引き起こす
procure funds 資金を調達する, 資金繰りをする
procuring funds 資金調達コスト

procurement 名 調達, 購入, 仕入れ, 機器調達, 取得, 入手, 獲得, プロキュアメント
competitive procurement 一般競争による調達
enterprise procurement automation software 企業調達オートメーション・ソフト
fund procurement 資金調達
local procurement 現地調達
noncompetitive procurement 非競争調達

prod 動 促す, 駆り立てる, 要請する, つつく, 突く, 刺激する

produce 動 生産する, 製造する, 製作する, 作成する, 提出する

producer 名 生産者, 生産国, 〈温室効果ガスなどの〉排出国, 製造業者, メーカー, 製作者, 制作者, プロデューサー
chemical producer 化学会社
industrial commodity producers 素材メーカー
low price producer 低価格品メーカー
oil producers 産油国
producer goods 生産財, 工業製品
producer of greenhouse gases 温室効果ガスの排出国
producer organization 生産者団体
producers' inventory of finished goods 生産者製品在庫

product 名 製品, 生産品, 産物, 商品, 結果, 成果, プロダクト
commodity product 汎用品
derivative product 派生商品
financial product 金融商品
fishery product 水産物, 海産物
food product 食料品
principal product 主力製品
processed product 加工製品, 調整品
product catalog 製品カタログ
product design 製品設計, 製品のデザイン, プロダクト・デザイン
product design management 製品設計管理
product development 製品開発
Product Liability Law 製造物責任法, PL法
product line 製品ライン, 商品ライン, 商品群, 製品系列, 製品種目, 製品品目, 製品構成, プロダクト・ライン
product price 製品価格
product range 製品の機種, 種類, 製品群, 品揃え, 製品の幅, 車種
variable product 変額商品

production 名 生産, 製造, 製作, 制作, プロダクション
assembly production 組立生産
batch production バッチ生産, 連続生産
class production 組別生産
commodity production 商品生産
contract production 委託生産
domestic production 国内生産
economics of production 生産効率
integrated production 一貫生産
joint production 共同生産
license production ライセンス生産
line production 直線生産, 流れ作業生産, 流れ作業
mass production 大量生産, 量産
offshore production 海外生産
optimum production 最適生産
production adjustment 生産調整
production base 生産拠点
production center 生産拠点, 製造拠点, 生産センター, 生産中心点, 生産の中核拠点
production cost 生産コスト, 製造コスト, 製造原価, 製品原価
production curtailment 生産削減, 生産カット
production cutback 生産削減, 操業短縮, 減産
production cycle 生産サイクル

production sharing contract 生産分与契約, 生産物分与契約
production volume 生産量, 製造高, 操業度
surplus production 余剰生産
total production 総生産

productive 形 生産的な, 生産力のある, 生産上の, 実りのある, 豊かな, 多作の, 建設的な, 有益な, 営利的な, 利益をもたらす, もたらす, 引き起こす
be productive of good results よい結果を生む
productive capacity 生産能力
productive facilities 生産設備
productive labor 生産的労働
productive of …を生み出す, …を生じる, …を輩出する
productive output 生産高
productive population 生産年齢人口
productive relationship 建設的な関係
productive skill 生産技能
productive soil 肥えた土地
productive writer 多作の作家

productivity 名 生産性, 生産力, 生産効率, 多様性, プロダクティビティ
capital productivity 資本生産性
comparative productivity 比較生産性
factor productivity 要素生産性
green productivity 環境にやさしい生産性, グリーン・プロダクティビティ
gross productivity 粗生産力, 粗生産性
hourly productivity 時間当たり生産性
improved productivity 生産性向上, 生産性の向上 (＝increased productivity)
labor productivity 労働生産性
land productivity 土地生産性
marginal productivity 限界生産力, 限界生産性
net productivity 純生産性, 純生産力
per capita productivity 1人当たり生産力
physical productivity 物的生産性
productivity agreement 生産協定
productivity behavior 生産性動向
productivity effect 生産力効果
productivity inflation 生産性格差インフレ
sales productivity 販売効率
total-factor productivity 全要素生産性
value productivity 価値生産性

profession 名 職業, 知的職業, 専門的職業, 専門職, 同業者集団, 公言, 宣言, 告白
enter the profession 職業に就く
make professions of loyalty 忠誠を誓う

professional 名 職業人, プロ, 専門家, 本職, 玄人, 熟練者, プロフェッショナル
credit professional 信用分析の専門家
highly-trained professional 高度の訓練を受けた専門家
money market professional 金融市場専門家
qualified professional 資格のある専門家, 有資格専門家
skilled professional 熟練労働者

professional 形 職業の, 職業上の, 業務上の, 専門職の, 本職の, プロの, 専門的な, 熟練した, 巧妙な
due professional care 職業上の正当な注意義務
professional dealer 〈株の〉玄人筋
professional education 専門教育, 職業教育
professional ethics 職業倫理
professional executive 専門経営者
professional income 勤労所得
professional investor 機関投資家
professional job 専門職
professional regulation 職業規則
professional secret 職業上の秘密
professional skill 専門技術, 特技
professional speculator 相場師, 玄人筋[プロ]の投機家
professional [vocational] skill 本職の腕
seek professional advice 専門家の意見を求める
unethical professional conduct 職業倫理違反行為

professional negligence 業務上過失
professional negligence resulting in a fire 業務上失火
professional negligence resulting in death 業務上過失致死
professional negligence resulting in death and injury 業務上過失致死障害

professionalism 名 プロ意識, プロ根性, 職人気質, 専門家気質, 優れた専門技術, 玄人芸

profile 名 構成, 構造, 輪郭, 概要, 外形, 知名度, 案内, 見通し, 予測, 特性, 地位, 方針, 横顔, 側面図, 縦断面図, 〈データの〉グラフ[図表], 人物紹介, 人物素描(sketch), プロフィール[プロファイル] (⇒high-profile)
adopt [take] a high profile 高姿勢をとる
business profile 事業構成

company profile 会社概要, 会社案内
credit profile 信用力, 信用情報
customer profile 顧客プロフィール, 顧客構成
earnings profile 収益見通し
financial profile 財務力見通し
high-profile 脚光を浴びる, 世間の注目を集める, 注目の, 著名な, 明確な, 鮮明な, 異彩を放つ, 大型の
in profile 側面から
investment profile 投資方針
keep a low profile 低姿勢を保つ, 目立った行動を控える
low-profile 目立たない, 控え目な, 低姿勢の
market profile 市場プロフィール, 市場特性, 市場情報
product profile 製品構成
risk profile リスク特性, リスク構造

profit 動 利益を得る, 利益になる, 役に立つ, 教訓を得る

profit 名 利益, 収益, 利得, 利潤, 黒字
excessive profit 超過利潤, 不当利得, 暴利
make a profit 利益を出す, 利益を上げる, 利益を得る
profit-at-any-price もうけ第一主義
profit decline 減益
profit-first principle 利益至上主義
profit forecast 利益予想, 収益見通し, 業績予想
profit making 利益を上げること, 利益を得ること, 収益, 営利
profit-making 利潤目当ての, 儲かる
profit-making capability 収益力
profit-seeking organization 営利組織
profit structure 収益構造
profit target 収益目標, 運用益の目標
profits for the term 当期利益金
profits from redemption 償還差益 (=gains from redemption)
rake in massive profits 巨額の収益を上げる, 大もうけする
realize a profit 利益を得る
return to profit 黒字に転換する, 黒字に戻る
take profits 利食い売りをする, 利食いに出る, 利食う

profit and [or] loss 損益
annual profit and loss 年次損益
consolidated profit and loss account 連結損益計算書
profit and loss for the preceding term 前期損益 (=profit and loss for the previous period)
profit and loss on securities sold 有価証券売却損益
profit and loss statement 損益計算書 (=profit and loss account, statement of earnings, statement of income, statement of operations)

profit margin 売上利益率, 売上純利益率, 利益率, 利ざや, 利幅(売上純利益率(%)＝(純利益÷純売上高)×100。「利ざや」は, 金融機関の資金の調達金利と貸出金利の差をいう)

profit sharing 利益分配, 利益分配, 利益配当, 利潤分配
profit sharing bond 利益配分社債
profit sharing cartel 利益配当カルテル
profit sharing fund 利益分配基金
profit sharing plan [scheme] 利益配分制度, 利益分配制度, 利益分配型退職金
profit sharing securities 利潤証券
profit sharing stock 利益分配株

profit taking 利食い, 利食い売り, 利益を確定するための売り, 利益確定売り (=profit taking sales)

profitability 名 収益性, 収益力, 営利性, 採算性, 利益率, 収益率 (=earning power)
achieve profitability 黒字転換を果たす, 黒字化する
core profitability コア収益性
increased profitability 収益性の改善, 収益性の向上, 収益力の高まり, 利益水準の向上 (=improved profitability)
investment profitability 投資収益性, 投資利益率, 投資収益率
profitability control 収益性管理
profitability ratio 収益性指標, 利益率, 収益率
random profitability 確率的収益性, 確率的利益性
rate of profitability 利益率, 収益率
regain profitability 収益力を回復する
return to profitability 黒字に転換する
social profitability 社会的有利性
weakened profitability 収益性の低下 (=decreased profitability)

profitable 形 儲かる, 利益を生む, 収益性[利益力]がある, 有利な, 有益な, ためになる, 役に立つ
profitable goods 利益率の高い商品, 収益性の高い商品, 収益商品

profitable investment 有利な投資［運用先］
turn profitable 黒字に転換する
profiteer 名 不当利得者, 暴利商人
profiteering 名 不当利得行為, 暴利行為
profiteering racket 暴利行為
proforma [pro forma] 形 仮定の, 仮の, 見積りの, 形式上の, 名 試算, 仮定計算, 見積り送り状, プロ・フォーマ
 pro forma amendment 形式的な修正案
 pro forma invoice 見積り送り状, 仮送り状, 試算用送り状
 pro forma motion 形式的な動議
 pro forma standard tax 外形標準課税(法人事業税(都道府県税)について, 現行の企業所得(黒字分)ではなく, 資本金や人件費, 売上高などの事業規模を基準に課税する方法。赤字企業にも課税できるため, 景気の影響を受けにくく, 税収の安定に役立つとされる)
program 名 計画, 予定, 政策, 対策, 策, 措置, 政党の綱領, 政治要項, 制度, 番組, コンピュータ・プログラム, プログラム
 aid program 援助計画
 career (development) program 経歴管理制度
 competition program 裏番組
 pension program 年金制度
 training program 研修計画, 研修制度, 研修プログラム, 研修内容, 教育訓練計画, 教育訓練制度
 World Food Program 世界食糧計画
progress 名 進歩, 発展, 足取り, 経過, 成長, 進捗状況, 未成工事
 earnings progress 増益
 long-term contract work in progress 長期請負契約
 product in progress 仕掛(しかけ・しかかり)品 (=goods in process, stock in process, work in process)
 progress control 製造工程の進度管理, 進度統制
 progress payment 分割払い, 分納
 progress payments 未成工事支出金, 未成工事の前受金
 progress report 経過報告, 経過報告書, 中間報告
 technical progress 技術進歩
 work in progress 仕掛品 (=product in progress, work in process)
progressive 形 進歩的な, 進歩主義の, リベラルな, 革新的な, 進取的な, 漸進的な, 〈病気が〉進行性の, 〈課税が〉累進的な, 名 進歩主義者, 革新主義者, 進歩党員(Progressive)
 Progressive Conservative Party 〈カナダの〉進歩保守党
 progressive form 進行形
 progressive muscular dystrophy 進行性筋ジストロフィー
 progressive nation 進取の国民
 progressive paralysis 進行性まひ
 progressive reform 漸進的な改革
 progressive tax 累進税, 累進課税
 progressive taxation 累進税, 累進所得税
prohibit 動 禁止する, …が…するのを妨げる
project 動 計画する, 企画する, 予測する, 予想する, 想定する, 見積もる
project 名 計画, 企画, もくろみ, 企て, 構想, 案, 考案, 工夫, 対策, 案件, 事業, 事業計画, 開発事業, 公共事業計画, 長期目標, 研究課題, 自主研究, プロジェクト
 drainage project 排水事業
 foreign invested project 外資プロジェクト
 high profile project 大型プロジェクト
 housing project 住宅建設事業, 〈低所得者層の〉公営住宅, 公営住宅団地
 improving management project 経営訓練のための開発プロジェクト《略 IMP》
 joint project 共同事業
 land readjustment project 土地区画整理事業
 Project Apollo 〈米国の〉アポロ計画(NASAの月着陸有人飛行計画)
 project finance [financing] プロジェクト金融, 特定事業に対する金融, プロジェクト・ファイナンス
 project loan プロジェクト・ローン(開発プロジェクトに対する国際的な融資)
 project management 計画管理, プロジェクト管理
 project plan [planning] 事業計画, 個別計画
 project planner 計画立案者
 project profit planning 個別利益計画
 project work プロジェクト作業
 urban development project 市街地再開発事業
 urban project 都市計画
projected 形 計画された, 予想される, 予測される, 見積りされた
 projected benefit obligation 予測給付債務, 見積り給付債務, 予定給付債務, 予測給付債務制

度, 退職給付債務
projected investment 計画投資
projected loss 赤字予想, 損失予想, 予想される赤字[損失], 赤字見通し
projected profit 黒字予想, 利益予想, 予想される黒字[利益], 黒字見通し

projectile 名 〈砲弾やミサイルの〉発射物, 飛翔体

projection 名 見積り, 予測, 推定, 予想, 想定, 見通し, 推計
- **cash flow projection** 資金繰りの見通し, キャッシュ・フロー予測
- **earlier projection** 当初予想 (＝earlier forecast, original projection)
- **earnings projection** 業績予想, 業績見通し, 収益予想, 収益見通し (＝earnings estimate, earnings forecast)
- **initial projection** 当初予想, 当初の想定, 当初見通し
- **operating loss projection** 営業損失予想, 営業赤字予想額
- **preliminary projections** 暫定値
- **profit projection** 利益予想
- **projection of future revenues** 将来の収益予想
- **projections on volume of auto traffic** 交通需要推計

pro-life 形 妊娠中絶に反対の, 妊娠中絶反対[反対派]の, 妊娠中絶合法化に反対の (⇒pro-choice)

pro-lifer 名 妊娠中絶反対者, 中絶反対者 (＝right-to-lifer)

proliferate 動 急増する, 増える, 増殖する, 繁殖する, はびこる, 拡散する

proliferation 名 急増, 増加, 増殖, 繁殖, 拡散
- **Nuclear Non-proliferation Treaty** 核拡散防止条約
- **proliferation of nuclear weapons** 核兵器の拡散, 核拡散
- **proliferation of weapons of mass destruction** 大量破壊兵器拡散 (＝proliferation of WMD)
- **Proliferation Security Initiative** 大量破壊兵器拡散阻止構想《略 PSI》

prolong 動 引き延ばす, 長引かせる, 延長する

prolonged 形 長引く, 長期の, 長期にわたる, 慢性的な

prolonged losses 慢性赤字, 慢性的な赤字
prolonged recession 長引く不況, 長期不況, 不況の長期化, 後退局面の長期化 (＝lingering recession)

pro-market 形 市場経済主義者の

promise 名 約束, 誓約, 公約, 契約, 契約事項, 将来性, 見込み, 有望, 希望, 望み, 可能性
- **afford [show] promise of success** 成功の見込みがある
- **campaign promises** 選挙公約
- **empty promise** 空手形
- **implied promise** 黙約, 黙示契約
- **strict [definite] promise** 確約
- **written promise** 約定書

promising 形 前途有望な, 有望な, 有力な, 前途を嘱望された, 将来見込みある, 将来を見込める, 将来のある, 明るい, 期待の持てる, 幸先のよい, 好転しそうな
- **promising business area** 期待できる事業分野
- **promising country for investment** 有望な投資先
- **promising market** 期待できる市場, 有望市場, 成長市場
- **promising option** 有力な選択肢
- **promising results** 期待の持てる結果, 期待の持てる業績
- **promising signs** 明るい展望
- **promising situation** 期待できる状況, 好転しそうな状況, うまくいきそうな情勢

promote 動 昇進させる, 昇格させる, 進級させる, 促進する, 推進する, 振興する, 増進する, 助長する, 育成する, 発展させる, 奨励する, 製品などを売り込む, 販売を促進する, 主催する, 〈事業などを〉発起する, …の発起人になる, 始める(launch), 〈議案・法案の〉通過に努める, 支持する
- **be promoted to** …に昇進する, …に昇格する, …に進級する
- **promote a new company** 新会社の発起人となる, 新会社を設立する
- **promote a new product** 新製品の販売を促進する, 新製品を売り込む
- **promote competition** 競争を促進する, 競争を促す
- **promote disorder** 混乱を助長する
- **promote employment** 雇用を促進する
- **promote equality of opportunity** 機会均等[機会の平等]を推進する
- **promote-from-within policy** 社内人材登用

の方針
- **promote health** 健康を増進する
- **promote ill will** 悪意を助長する
- **promote product segmentation** 商品［製品］の差別化を進める
- **promote productivity** 生産性を向上させる, 生産性の向上を図る
- **promote savings** 貯蓄を奨励する

promotion 名 昇進, 昇級, 昇格, 昇任, 促進, 推進, 増進, 助長, 振興, 奨励, 販売促進, 販売促進活動, 創設, 創立, 設立, 発起, プロモーション
- **job promotion** 職種内昇進
- **productivity promotion** 生産性向上
- **promotion expense** 販売促進費 (sales promotion cost), 創業費 (organization cost), 創立費, 設立費用
- **promotion shares** 発起人株
- **promotion system** 昇進制度
- **sales promotion** 販売促進, 販促, セールス・プロモーション

prompt 動 〈…するよう〉促す, 駆り立てる, 動かす, 起こさせる, …を刺激する, …を誘発する, 引き出す, きっかけを与える, ヒントを与える, せりふを思い出させる

prompt 名 支払い期限, 即時払い, 支払い期限付き契約, 刺激, 促進, せりふ付け, 入力促進記号, プロンプト

prompt 形 即時の, 即座の, 迅速な, 素早い, 早期の, 機敏な, 即時払いの, 即時渡しの, 直渡しの
- **for prompt cash** 即金で
- **prompt action** 素早い行動
- **prompt answer [reply]** 速答
- **prompt attention to** …に対する迅速な手配
- **prompt cash** 即金払い, 即時払い (4, 5日以内に支払う決済条件)
- **prompt cash discount** 直払い割引
- **prompt corrective action measures** 早期是正措置
- **prompt day** 支払い期日, 受渡し日
- **prompt delivery** 直渡し
- **prompt exchange** 直物為替
- **prompt first aid** 即座の応急手当て
- **prompt note** 買上票, 代金請求書, 支払い期日通知書, 即時払い手形
- **prompt payment** 即時払い
- **prompt response** 素早い対応, 素早い回答
- **prompt sale** 延べ取引
- **prompt shipment** 直積み, 即時船積み, 即船積み条件, 即時出荷 (= as soon as possible shipment, immediate shipment)

prop up 支える, 支持する, 買い支える, 後援する, 支援する, テコ入れをする
- **prop up the economy by fiscal means** 財政面でのテコ入れをする
- **prop up the sagging dollar** 下落するドルを買い支える

prop-up 名 支持, 支援, テコ入れ, 買い支え

propensity 名 性向, 傾向, 好み, 選好, 性癖, 性質
- **consumption propensity** 消費性向
- **dynamic marginal propensity to spend** 動学的限界支出性向
- **equilibrium propensity to save** 均衡貯蓄性向
- **expenditure propensity** 支出性向
- **have a propensity for** …の傾向がある, …の癖がある
- **investment propensity** 投資性向
- **marginal propensity to owe** 限界借入性向
- **private saving propensity** 民間貯蓄性向
- **propensity to exchange [truck]** 交換性向
- **propensity to expend [spend]** 支出性向 (所得に占める支出の割合. 支出には消費のほか, 投資や政府支出, 輸出などがある)
- **propensity to export** 輸出性向 (国民所得に占める輸出額の割合で, 輸出依存度のこと)
- **propensity to import** 輸入性向 (国民所得に占める輸入額の割合で, 輸入依存度のこと)
- **propensity to invest** 投資性向 (国民所得に占める投資額の割合で, 投資率ともいう)
- **propensity to save** 貯蓄性向 (国民所得に占める貯蓄の割合で, 貯蓄率ともいう)
- **propensity to tax** 租税性向 (国民所得に占める1国経済の租税額の割合)
- **propensity to withdraw** 控除性向
- **risk propensity** リスク選好
- **savings propensity** 貯蓄性向
- **schedule of propensity to consume** 消費性向表
- **unitary marginal propensity to consume** 限界消費性向

propensity to consume 消費性向 (消費者が消費すると予想される可処分所得に対する消費の割合)
- **average propensity to consume** 平均消費性向《略 APC》(消費者が所得のなかから消費する

割合）
equilibrium propensity to consume　均衡消費性向
marginal propensity to consume　限界消費性向《略 MPC》(所得増加分のうち消費に回される割合で，消費増加分を所得増加分で除して算出される）
▶ The average household's *propensity to consume* surpassed 1.　家計部門の平均消費性向が100％を超えた［消費性向が収入を上回った］．

property　❷　財産，有体財産，資産，固定資産，有形固定資産，所有，所有権，所有地，所有物，財産権，特性，属性，物件（「有体財産」には，営業用・製造業用の固定設備としての土地(land)，建物(buildings)，機械装置(machinery)および什器備品(furniture and fixtures)と，鉱山(mine)，山林(timber tract)，油井(oil well)などの天然資源が含まれる）
　after-acquired property　事後取得財産
　basic property　基本財産
　gain on property dividend　現物配当処分益
　immovable property　不動産（= immovables)
　investment property　投資不動産，投資資産
　leased property　リース資産
　movable property　動産（= movables)
　negative property　消極財産（負債や支払い勘定）
　personal property tax　動産税
　property and equipment　有形固定資産
　property market　不動産市場（= real estate market)
　property, plant and equipment　有形固定資産，土地，建物および設備，不動産・工場設備（= tangible fixed assets)
　property prices [values]　不動産価格
　property right　所有権，財産権，財産所有権，資産権利
　property values　不動産価格，資産価格（= property prices, real estate prices)
　total property　有形固定資産合計
proportion　❷　割合，比率，比例，釣り合い，均衡，バランス，大きさ，広さ，規模，部分，割当て，分け前
▶ It is our goal to increase the *proportion* of earnings contributed by the non-regulated business sector.　規制対象外の事業部門の利益貢献度拡大が，当社の目標です．

proportional-representative [proportional representation] system　比例代表制
proposal　❷　提案，案，企画，構想，計画，申込み，オファー
　merger or integration proposals　合併・経営統合の提案
　merger proposal　経営統合案，経営統合提案，経営統合の提案書（= business integration proposal)
　proposal for appropriation of retained earnings　利益処分案
　proposal for subscription　株式応募の申込み
　shareholders' proposals　株主提案
　stockholder's proposal right　株主の提案権
propose　❸　提案する，提唱する，企画する，打ち出す，申し出る，提出する，提示する，指名する，推薦する
　proposed dividend　予定配当
　proposed legislation　法案
　proposed management merger　経営統合案
　proposed purchase price　提示された買付け価格，予定買付け価格
proposition　❷　提案，提議，申し出，主張，陳述，説，命題，定理，〈提案された〉計画，企画，事柄，問題，仕事，事業，取引条件の提示，提供品，商品，住民提案（米州の住民投票にかけるために州民から一定の署名を集めた住民投票の提案），建議案，しろもの，相手，〈女性への〉みだらな誘い，誘惑，性交渉の誘いかけ
　a delicate proposition　微妙な問題
　a fundamental proposition　基本命題
　a negative proposition　否定的命題
　a paying proposition　儲かる仕事，採算の合う事業
　a tough [difficult] proposition　困難な問題，困難な仕事，厄介なしろもの
　not a proposition　成功の見込みがない
　vote on Proposition 50　建議案50号に関する投票，提案50号に関する投票
proprietary　❸　所有者の，所有権者の，独占の，専売の，特許の，財産的価値のある，❷　所有者，所有権
　exclusive proprietary　独占的所有権
　proprietary capital　自己資本
　proprietary drug　特許を取った薬
　proprietary estate　専有地
　proprietary product　特許製品

proprietary technique 特許技術, 特許技法（＝proprietary technology）
proprietary trading system 私設取引システム《略 PTS》(私設の株式市場)
proprietary wealth 所有財産
proprietor 名 事業主, 経営者, 所有者, 所有主, 出資者, 資本主, オーナー
proprietorship 名 自己資本, 出資者持ち分, 資本主, 資本主勘定, 正味財産, 個人企業, 自営業者
pro-reform 形 改革派の
pros and cons 良い点と悪い点, 賛否両論
prosecuting attorney 地方検事, 検察官
prosecution 名 起訴, 告発, 〈刑事〉訴追, 検察側, 検察官, 遂行, 実行
  a witness for the prosecution 検察側証人
  fully admit the facts presented by the prosecution in the indictment 検察側の起訴事実を全面的に認める
  fully agree with the prosecution charges 検察側の起訴事実に完全に同意する
  the prosecution and the defense 検察側と弁護側
prosecutor 名 検察官, 検事, 起訴者, 告発者, 〈刑事裁判所の〉訴追者, 遂行者, 実行者
  be sent to the prosecutor's office 送検される
  high prosecutor's office 高等検察庁
  public prosecutor 検察官, 検事
prosecutors 名 検察当局, 検察側（＝the prosecutory authorities）
  a district public prosecutors office 地方検察庁
  a public prosecutors office 検察庁
  the High Public Prosecutors Office 高等検察庁
  the Supreme Public Prosecutors Office 最高検察庁
  the Tokyo District Public Prosecutors Office 東京地検
prospect 名 見晴らし, 眺め, 景色, 見通し, 展望, 観測, 予想, 予測, 予期, 先行き, 目途, 行く末, 将来性, 見込み, 可能性, 期待, 買ってくれそうな人, 有望な候補者, 将来有望な計画[仕事], 探鉱有望地
  command a wide prospect 広々と見晴らせる
  demand prospects 需要見通し
  in prospect 予想されて, 期待されて, 考慮中で, 予想して

inflation prospects インフレ見通し（＝prospects for inflation）
production prospects 生産見通し, 生産予測
prospect for an improvement 好転の見込み
prospects for survival 生存の可能性
short-term prospects 短期見通し
prospective 形 未来の, 将来の, 今後の, 予想される, 予期される, 期待される, 見込みのある, …になる予定の
  prospective candidate 立候補予定者
  prospective customer 見込み客（＝prospective buyer）
  prospective retirees 退職予定者, 予想される退職者
prosperity 名 繁栄, 隆盛, 繁盛, 好景気, 好況, 景気拡大, 成功, 幸運, 富裕, 富
  artificial [false] prosperity から景気
  material prosperity 物質的繁栄
  recession and prosperity 景気後退期と景気拡大期
prostitution 名 売春, 買春, 悪用, 堕落
  child prostitution and pornography 児童買春と児童ポルノ, 児童買春・ポルノ
  licensed prostitution 公娼, 公娼制度
  prostitution ring 売春グループ
prosumer 名 生産消費者, プロシューマー (producer（生産者）とconsumer（消費者）の合成語。IT革命で, 消費者もプロシューマーとしてインターネットで商品開発に参加できるようになった)
prosumer development プロシューマー型開発（生産者と消費者が共同で商品やサービスを開発すること）
protagonist 名 主唱者, 指導者, 擁護者, 主人公, 主役, 〈スポーツ大会などの〉競技者
protect 動 保護する, 守る, 防ぐ, 保全する, 保証する, 補償する, 確保する
  be protected from …から保護される, …から守られる, …を免れる
  protect against cancer がんを防ぐ
  protect asset returns 資産の利回りを確保する
  protect investors from loses 投資家を損失から保護する
  protect jobs 雇用を確保する, 働く場を確保する
  protect oneself from crime 犯罪から身を守る
  protect the environment 環境を守る
protect 名 保護, データ保護 (data protection), プロテクト
  copy protect コピー・プロテクト

protection

file protect ファイル保護, ファイル・プロテクト (=file protection)
memory protect メモリ保護 (=storage protection)
write protect 書き込み禁止, ライト・プロテクト (=write protection)

protection 名 保護, 保全, 保証, 保障, 補償, 対策
　apply for protection from creditors 会社更生手続きを申請する, 資産保全を申請する
　blanket protection on bank deposits 銀行預金の全額保証, 銀行預金の全額保護
　Consumer Credit Protection Act 消費者信用保護法
　credit protection 信用保護
　debt protection 債権保護水準, 債権者保護, 債務返済能力
　debtholder [debt holder] protection 債権保有者保護
　economic protection 経済的保護
　effective protection 有効保護
　import protection 輸入保護, 輸入制限
　insurance protection 保険保障
　investment protection 投資保証
　investor protection 投資家保護
　protection from creditors 資産保全
　protection mechanism 保護機構
　protection of depositors 預金者保護
　protection of personal information 個人情報保護
　provide against liquidity protection 流動性リスクをカバーする
　Securities Investor Protection Act of 1970 1970年証券投資家保護法
　storage protection メモリ保護 (=memory protect, memory protection)
　tariff protection 関税による保護, 関税保護

protectionism 名 保護主義, 保護貿易主義

protectionist 名 保護貿易論者, 保護貿易主義者, 保護主義者, 野生動物保護論者, プロテクショニスト
　protectionist action 保護主義的行動
　protectionist policy 保護主義的な政策, 保護主義政策, 保護政策, 保護貿易政策, 貿易保護政策
　protectionist regionalism 保護主義的な地域主義
　protectionist sentiment 保護主義の高まり, 保護主義の高まり
　protectionist trade barriers 保護主義的な貿易障壁, 保護貿易障壁
　restrictive protectionist tariffs 制限的な保護貿易主義的関税
　▶ Politicians ignorant of basic economics tend in every country to be *protectionist* by nature. 経済の基礎知識にうとい政治家は, どこの国でもおのずと保護主義者になる傾向がある。(ポール・A・サミュエルソン)

protective 形 保護する, 保護用の, 保護を与える, 保護貿易の, 保護主義の, 保護貿易主義に基づく
　protective clothing 防護服, 保護服
　protective covenant 証券所有者保護条項, 所有者保護条項
　protective custody 保護拘置
　protective device 保護措置
　protective goggle 保護眼鏡
　protective inoculation 予防接種
　protective legislation 貿易保護法
　protective measures 保護策, 保護対策, 保護政策, 保護措置, 防衛策, 対応策
　protective reaction 報復[自衛]のための爆撃
　protective resemblance 保護擬態
　protective shield 防弾盾
　protective tariff [duties] 保護関税
　protective trade 保護貿易
　protective trust 保護信託

protein engineering たんぱく質工学, プロテイン・エンジニアリング

protest 動 〈…に〉抗議する, 〈…に〉異議を唱える, 〈…を〉主張する, 〈…と〉主張する, 〈…と〉言い張る
　officially protest against …に正式に抗議する
　protest strongly [vigorously] against …に強く抗議する, …に強硬に反対する
　protest vehemently against …に猛烈に抗議する, …に対して猛烈に異議を唱える

protest 名 抗議, 異議の申立て, 不平, 不満, 〈手形の〉拒絶証書, 抗議集会
　address a protest to …に抗議を申し込む
　antigovernment protests 反政府活動
　direct one's protest against 抗議のほこを…に向ける
　draw a protest from …からの抗議を招く
　enter a protest against …に対して異議を唱える

feeble protest 腰の弱い抗議
hold a protest 抗議集会を開く
in protest against …に抗議して, …に反対して
lodge [enter, make] a protest with …に抗議する, …に異議申立てを行う
massive protest 集団抗議
mild protest 穏当な抗議
protest march 抗議行進デモ, 抗議行進, 抗議デモ, デモ
protest rally 抗議集会
stage a protest demonstration 抗議デモを行う
stern protest 断固たる抗議
vehement protest 猛烈な抗議
voice a protest 異議を唱える

protocol 名 〈契約・条約などの〉原案[原本], 議定書, 条約議定書,〈協定・条約の〉付随書,〈国家間の〉補足協約,〈国家間の〉協定[協約],〈自治体などの〉規定, 議事録, 外交上の儀礼書, 外交文書, 外交慣習, 通信規約, 通信規則, 通信手順, プロトコル

authentication protocol 認証プロトコル
Internet Protocol インターネット・プロトコル《略 IP》
Kyoto Protocol to the U.N. Framework Convention on Climate Change 気候変動枠組み条約京都議定書
post–Kyoto Protocol international framework ポスト京都議定書の国際枠組み
Post Office Protocol 電子メールのプロトコル《略 POP》
protocol chief 儀典長
transmission protocol 転送プロトコル

protracted 形 長引く, 長引いた, 延長された, 遅延の, 遅延性の
protracted recession 長引く不況, 長期不況, 不況の長期化

proven oil reserves 原油確認埋蔵量

provide 動 提供する, 供給する, 与える, 付与する, 販売する, 創出する, 調達する, 発生する, 設定する, 定める, 規定する, 算定する, 計上する, 発表する
provide for …に備える, …に引き当てる, …を算定する, 定める, 規定する, 計上する
provide goods or services モノやサービスを販売する, モノやサービスを提供する
provide liquidity 流動性を提供する, 流動性を供給する
provide the required capital 必要資本を調達する
► The GPS system does not *provide* information on moving up and down. この全地球測位システム(GPS)を利用したシステムは, 上下移動に関する情報を提供できない。

provider 名 提供者, 請負業者, 業者, 企業, メーカー, インターネット接続業者, ネット接続会社, 一家の主, 扶養者, プロバイダー
application service provider アプリケーション・サービス・プロバイダー《略 ASP》
commercial access provider 商用アクセス・プロバイダー, インターネット接続業者・プロバイダー
health care provider 医療機関
information provider 情報提供者, 番組製作者《略 IP》
network (service) provider ネットワーク回線接続業者
provider responsibility law プロバイダー責任法
service provider サービス会社, サービス企業
solution provider ソリューション請負業者, ソリューション・サービス業者

province 名 〈カナダなどの〉州,〈中国の〉省, 地方, 管区
provincial government 地方政府, 省政府
provincialism 名 地方的偏見, 地方的偏狭, 地方的特色, 地方色, 地方的特質, 地方第一主義, 愛郷心, 愛党心, 方言, 田舎なまり, 田舎風, 粗野

proving ground 実験場

provision 名 提供, 供給, 供与, 支給, 用意, 準備, 備え, 蓄え, 貯蔵品, 準備金, 引当金, 引当金繰入額[充当額], 計上, 設備, 施設, 条項, 規定

> 準備金と引当金について ⇒「準備金」には, 一般に provisionよりreserveやallowanceが使用されることが多い。日本の場合,「準備金」は法定準備金(legal capital reserves, legal reserves, legally required reserves)である資本準備金(capital reserve), 利益準備金(profit reserve)や価格変動準備金(reserve for price fluctuation)などにだけ用いられている。これに対して「引当金」は, 将来の支出にあてるためにあらかじめ準備しておく資金のこと。

establish a provision for …の引当金を設定する
in provision for …の引当金として
income before provisions 引当金繰入れ前利益, 引当金前の利益
increase provisions 引当金を積み増す

life insurance provision 生命保険準備金
provision for bad debts 貸倒れ引当金（＝bad debts provision, provision for doubtful debts)
provision for losses 損失引当金
regulatory provision 法令
restrictive provision 制限条項
special provision 特別引当金
tax code provision 税法規定

provisional 形 臨時の, 一時的な, 仮の, 暫定的な, 予備の
apply for a provisional injunction 仮処分を申請する
provisional agreement 仮契約, 仮条約, 暫定協定
provisional attachment 仮差し押さえ
provisional asylum 一時庇護
provisional government 臨時政府, 暫定政府, 暫定政権
provisional license 仮免許
provisional rating 予備格付け
provisional registration 仮登録, 仮登記
provisional treaty 仮条約

provocation 名 挑発, 扇動, 誘発, 刺激, 誘因, 怒り, 立腹, 興奮

provocative 名 刺激物, 形 挑発的な, 腹立たしい
be provocative of sorrow 悲しみを誘う
provocative act 挑発行為

proxy 名 代理, 代理人(agent), 代理権, 代理資格, 名代, 替え玉
act as a proxy for …の名代として振舞う, …の代理人を務める
general proxy 総括的代理権
proxy authorization 代理委任
proxy fight [battle, contest] 委任状争奪戦, 委任状合戦, プロキシー・ファイト (＝proxy contest)
proxy form 代理人様式, 委任用紙, 委任状カード, 委任状 (＝form of proxy)
proxy marriage 代理結婚
proxy server 代理サーバー
proxy solicitation 委任状勧誘
proxy statement 代理勧誘状, 代理権勧誘状, 委任状, 委任状説明書, 議決権代理行使勧誘状, プロキシー・ステートメント
proxy voting [vote] 代理投票
proxy voting card 投票委任用紙, 代理投票用紙 (＝proxy card)
proxy war 代理戦争
stand proxy for …の代理になる

prudence 名 慎重, 慎重性, 冷静, 堅実, 保守主義, 賢明さ, 信用秩序維持, プルーデンス
financial prudence 堅実金融主義
macro prudence 信用秩序維持, マクロ・プルーデンス(金融システム全体の健全性重視)
macro prudence policy マクロ・プルーデンス政策(金融システム全体としての安全性・健全性確保のための政策)
macro prudence regulation マクロ・プルーデンス規制, 金融のマクロ規制
micro prudence 個別金融機関の監督
micro prudence policy ミクロ・プルーデンス政策(個々の金融機関の経営上の安全性・健全性確保のための政策)
prudence policy プルーデンス(信用秩序維持)政策
prudence principle 保守主義, 保守主義の原則

prudent 形 慎重な, 堅実な, 厳しい
prudent asset structure 堅実な資産構成
prudent investor 慎重な投資家
prudent macro-economic management 慎重なマクロ経済管理
prudent-man rule 堅実投資原則, プルーデントマン・ルール(とくに慎重な資産運用が要求される場合の投資基準原則で, 米国の多くの州で採用されている。年金基金や信託財産を管理する受託者(fiduciary)は, 投機に走らずにつねに堅実な投資に徹するよう義務付けるもの)

PSE mark PSEマーク(PSE＝product safety of electrical appliances and materialsの略)
PSE rule PSE法
pseudonym 名 仮名, 偽名, 筆名, ペンネーム
psychiatric 形 精神医学の, 精神病治療の
conduct psychiatric evaluations of the defendant 被告の精神鑑定を行う
psychiatric care [treatment] 精神病治療
psychiatric detention 精神病治療のための拘留
psychiatric hospital 精神病院
psychiatric nurse 精神病患者を扱う看護師
psychiatric specialist 精神医学の専門家

psychiatrist 名 精神科医, 精神病医, 精神医学者

psychic [**psychical**] 形 精神の, 心の, 精神的な, 心霊作用を受けやすい, 霊魂の, 超自然的な,

霊媒の
illness due to psychic causes 心因性の病気
illness with a psychic origin 精神の原因による病気
psychic healer 心霊治療者
psychic income 〈就労者の〉心理的収益, 精神的利得
psychic research 心霊研究, 心霊現象研究
psychic scar 精神的な傷跡

psychological 形 心理的な, 心理学の, 心理学的な, 精神的な(mental), 心の
- **psychological barrier** 心理的な壁
- **psychological effect** 心理効果
- **psychological element** 心理的要素
- **psychological factor** 心理的な要因, 心理的要因
- **psychological influence** 心理的影響
- **psychological laws** 心理的法則
- **psychological moment** 絶好の機会, 絶好の瞬間, 好機, 潮時, 心理的モメント
- **psychological segmentation** 心理学的市場細分化
- **psychological set** 心理的構え(各種ブランドに関する消費者のニーズ, 態度, 知覚など)
- **psychological stress** 精神的なストレス
- **psychological traits** 心理的特性
- **psychological test** 心理テスト, 心理検査, 心理学上の検査
- **psychological warfare** 心理戦争, 心理戦, 神経戦, 教化作戦
- **psychological welfare** 心のケア

psychological line サイコロジカル・ライン
サイコロジカル・ラインとは ○ある株が買われすぎか売られすぎかを短期的に判断する指数で, 株価の反落や反発時期などを予測して株を売買する参考になる。一般に, 12日の期間で, 株価の終値が前日から上がれば「勝ち」, 下がれば「負け」として, その勝率(何勝何敗か)を示す。勝率が100%に近いほど投資家心理が過熱していることを示し, 0%に近いほど売られすぎとされる。

psychology 名 心理, 心理状態, 心理学, 読心術, 人の心を見抜く力
- **applied psychology** 応用心理学
- **business psychology** 事業心理
- **buying psychology** 購買心理
- **child psychology** 児童心理学
- **consumer [consumer's] psychology** 消費者心理
- **criminal psychology** 犯罪心理学
- **deflationary psychology** デフレ心理
- **depth psychology** 深層心理
- **engineering psychology** 工学心理学
- **fiscal psychology** 財政心理学
- **group [mob] psychology** 群衆心理学
- **industrial psychology** 産業心理学
- **inflationary psychology** インフレ心理
- **management psychology** 経営心理学, 経営陣の心理
- **market [market's] psychology** 市場心理, 市場の地合い
- **social psychology** 社会心理学
- **sports psychology** スポーツ心理学
- **work psychology** 労働心理学

psychotherapy 名 精神療法

PTSD 心的外傷後ストレス障害(post-traumatic stress disorderの略。震災や暴力, 虐待, 大事故などで, 命の危険を感じる出来事を体験または目撃した人に起きる不眠, 怒りの爆発, フラッシュバックなどの障害)

public 名 大衆, 公衆, 一般の人々, 一般社会, …社会, …仲間, …界, …層
- **be open to the public** 一般に公開[一般公開]されている
- **in public** 人前で, 公衆の面前で, 公然と
- **the book-reading public** 読者層
- **the British public** 英国人, 英国民
- **the general public** 一般大衆
- **the public at large** 一般社会, 一般大衆, 大衆(= the general public)
- **the reading public** 一般読者層

public 形 公の, 公衆の, 公的の, 公共の, 公立の, 公営の, 民衆の, 大衆の, 庶民の, 社会的の, 広く知られた, 公然の, 有名な, パブリック
- **public acceptance** 社会受容性, 地域住民の合意を得ること
- **public access** 一般の立ち入り[閲覧権], 一般のアクセス
- **public access television** 視聴者制作テレビ
- **public accountant** 〈米国の州の認可を受ける〉公共会計士(PA), 公認会計士(certified public accountant)
- **public accounting firm** 会計事務所
- **public act** 〈一般国民に影響を与える〉立法行為, 公共関係の法律
- **public-address system** 拡声装置
- **public administration** 公務

public administrator 行政官, 遺産管理人
public affairs 公務, 公共の問題, 社会環境対策活動, 企業の広報活動《略 PA》
public affairs officer 広報官, 広報担当者
public analyst 〈食品の〉毒物検査官
public announcement 公表, 発表
public assistance 公的支援, 生活保護, 公的扶助
public attention 世間の注目, 世間の耳目
public auction 公売, 競売
public awareness 世間一般の認識
public bailout 公的資金の注入
public bill 公共関係法案, 公法案
public body 公共団体
Public Broadcasting Service 公共放送網, 公共テレビ放送《略 PBS》(=Public Television: コマーシャルなしの米国の教育・文化番組)
public burdens 国民負担
public choice 公共選択
public climate 世間の空気, 民衆の感じ方
public company 株式公開企業, 上場企業
public confidence 国民の信頼, 消費者の信頼
public convenience 公衆便所
public corporation 株式公開企業, 公開会社, 特殊法人, 公法人, 公社, 公団, 公共企業体, 公共団体, 公益法人, 地方自治体
public criticism 国民の批判, 社会の批判
public debates 公開討論
public defender 国選弁護人, 公選弁護人
public debts 公的債務
public display 一般公開
public distrust of politics 国民の政治不信
public document 公文書
public domain 公知, 公有, 公的資産, 公有地, 国有地, 州有地, 社会の共有財産, 著作権[特許権]消滅状態
public economic policy 公共経済政策, 公的経済政策
public education 公教育, 学校教育
public elderly care insurance service 公的高齢者介護保険制度, 介護保険
public elderly care service 公的高齢者介護サービス, 高齢者介護サービス (=publicly funded elderly care service)
public employee 公務員
public enemy 社会の敵, 民衆の敵, 公衆の敵, 公敵
public enterprise 公企業

public execution 公開処刑
public expenditure 公共支出, 財政支出, 公費 (=public spending)
public external debt 対外公的債務
public financing 公的融資
public foreign investment 対外公共投資
public funding [funds] 公債, 国債
public goods 公益, 公共の福祉, 公共財
public hearing 公聴会, 公開ヒアリング, 〈裁判の〉証人喚問, 公判
public holiday 祝日, 祭日, 公休日
public housing 〈低所得者用〉公営住宅
public income [revenue] 国の収入, 公共所得, 公収入
public indebtedness 公的債務
public information 公開情報, 広報《略 PI》
public inspection 公衆閲覧
public institution 公的機関
public interest law 公益法
public international law 国際法
public investment 公共投資
public issue 公募, 公募債, 公募証券, 直接発行 (新聞広告で応募を勧誘して行う証券発行)
public key cryptosystem 公開鍵暗号方式
public law 公法《略 PL》
public library 公立図書館
public loan 公債, 公的融資
Public Management Ministry 総務省
public market 公設市場, 公開市場, 大衆相場
public money 公的資金 (=public funds, taxpayers' money)
public monopoly 公的独占, 公共独占, 専売
public notice 公告
public nuisance 公的不法妨害, 公害, 〈世間の〉厄介者
public office 公職, 官公庁, 官公署, 官庁, 政界の要職
Public Offices Election Law 〈日本の〉公職選挙法
public official [officer] 公務員
public ownership 公的所有, 公有, 公有制, 国有, 産業の国有化, 国有権, 株式公開, 上場企業
public persona 公衆向けの顔
public policy 公益, 公の秩序, 公序良俗, 公共政策, 社会政策
public procurement 政府調達
public property 公有財産, 公共財産
public quotation 公定相場

Public Record Office 〈英国の〉公文書館
public responsibility 公的責任, 公共責任
public rights 公権
public sale 公売, 競売
public security 公安
public sentiment 国民意識, 国民の感情
public speaking 公の前で話すこと, 講演, 演説, 話術
Public Television 〈米国の〉公共テレビ放送
public transport 公共輸送機関
public trust 国民の信頼, 消費者の信頼, 慈善信託 (charitable trust)
public vocational training center 公共職業訓練施設, 公共職業訓練センター
public wants 公的欲求
Public Works Administration 〈米〉公共事業局
work for the public good 公共の福祉のために尽力する

public employment 政府雇用, 公務員雇用
  public employment security office 公共職業安定所
  public employment services 公共職業サービス

public entities 公益法人
▶ Public entities are those corporate bodies and foundations set up under Article 34 of the Civil Code to carry out business for the public interest such as those related to academic, charity and relief activities. 公益法人とは, 学術や慈善, 救済活動関連の事業など公益事業を行うために民法34条に基づいて設立される社団法人や財団法人のことである。

public facilities 公共施設
▶ Public facilities range from roads, ports, airports, parks and government buildings to cultural, educational, medical, welfare and waste-disposal facilities. 公共施設には, 道路, 港湾, 空港, 公園, 庁舎などから文化, 教育, 医療, 福祉, 廃棄物処理などの施設まで入る。

public finance 〈国家, 地方公共団体の〉財政
  public finance market 公募債市場
  public finance policy 財政政策
  public finance reform 財政改革

public funds 公的資金, 公金, 公費, 公債, 国債, 公募ファンド, 共同募金 (= public money, taxpayers' money)
  a huge amount of public funds 巨額の公的資金
  complete the repayment of public funds 公的資金を完済する
  inject public funds 公的資金を注入する (= use taxpayers' money)
  the public funds 公債, 国債 (= the Funds)
  use public funds to help [rescue] ... …を救済するために公的資金を使う

public health 公衆衛生, 公衆保健, 公共保健
  Public Health Service 〈米〉公衆保健局

public interest 公共の利益, 国民の利益, 公益, 公共の関心
  public interest corporation 公益法人

public investment 公共投資
  public investment spending 公共投資関係費

public nature 公益性
▶ Businesses that are recognized as having a highly public nature will be entitled to receive preferential tax treatment. 高い公益性を認められた事業は, 優遇税制措置を受けることができる。

public nursing care insurance system 国民介護保険制度, 国民介護保険, 公的介護保険制度

public offering 株式公開, 公募, 公募増資, 売出し (= primary offering, public stock offering: 一般投資家を対象に, 有価証券の取得の申込みを勧誘すること。有価証券が新規発行の場合はprimary offering (募集・公募), 既発行の場合はsecondary offering (売出し) と呼ばれる。私募= private placement; ⇒IPO)

public opinion 世論, 公論
  public opinion organ 社会の公器
  public opinion survey [poll, research] 世論調査

public pension 公的年金
  public pension benefits 公的年金給付
  public pension payments 公的年金の支給額
  public pension plan 公的年金制度, 公的年金 (= public-run pension system: 全国民を対象に国が運営している公的年金には, 自営業者や学生が中心の国民年金のほかに, 民間企業のサラリーマンが加入する厚生年金と公務員が加入する共済年金がある)
  public pension premium 公的年金保険料
  public pension reserves 公的年金積立金

public prosecutor 検察官, 検事
  the public prosecutor general 検事総長

public relations 広報, 広報活動, 広報宣伝活動, ピーアール, 宣伝, 渉外, 渉外事務, 企業と

社会との(良好な)関係, パブリック・リレーションズ 《略 PR》(企業や各種団体などの業務・活動内容や商品, サービスに関する情報を社会, 消費者に伝える仕事)
Cabinet Public Relations Office 〈日本の〉内閣広報室
public relations exercise 宣伝活動, 対外宣伝
public relations officer 広報担当者, 渉外担当者, 渉外係《略 PRO》
public relations outlay 広報費
public sector 政府部門, 公共部門, 公的部門, 公共セクター, 公営企業
　public-sector borrowing requirement 公的借入需要
　public sector debt 公共部門債権, 公共部門債務, 公共部門借入れ
　public sector finances 財政
　public-sector financial institutions 政府系金融機関
　public sector investments 公共投資
　public sector pay 公共部門[公務員]の賃金, 公共部門給与, 公務員給与
　public sector price increases 公共料金の引上げ
　public sector wage 公務員賃金
　public sector worker 公務員
　public sector workforce 公共部門従業員数
public servant 公務員, 公僕, 官公吏, 公益事業会社 (=government employee [personnel, public service personnel])
▶ *Public servants* have ranks according to their job categories and their base salaries are decided accordingly. 公務員は職務に応じて等級があり, 公務員の基本給はその等級別に定められている。
public service 公益事業, 公職, 公務員としての職務, 公務, 公共福祉, 社会奉仕
　public service advertising 公共奉仕広告
　public service announcement 公共広告
　Public Service Commission 〈米〉公益事業委員会, 公共サービス委員会
　public service corporation 公益事業会社, 公益法人, 公社
public spending 財政出動(政府の支出で景気浮揚策を講じること), 公共支出, 公共投資, 公共事業費
public stock offering 株式公募, 株式公開, 株式上場 (=public offering, stock offering)

public tender offer 株式公開買付け (=takeover bid, tender offer, TOB)
　public tender offer period 株式公開買付け期間, TOB期間 (=public tender period)
public utility 公共事業, 公益事業, 公益事業体, 公共施設, ライフライン
　public utilities 公益企業株
　Public Utilities Commission 〈米〉公共事業委員会
　public utility charges [fee, rates] 公共料金
　Public Utility Holding Company Act 〈米〉公益事業持ち株会社法
public welfare loans 福祉資金(都道府県などが, 国からの借入金を使って母子家庭などに修学資金, 生活資金, 住宅資金などを貸し付ける制度)
▶ The *public welfare loans* are extended to widows and single mothers to help them become economically independent by financing spending for education, living costs, housing costs and funds to start small businesses. 福祉資金は, 母子家庭や寡婦に対して教育費や生活費, 住宅費, 小規模事業の開始資金などを貸し付けて, その経済的自立を助けるために供与されている。
public works 公共工事, 公共土木工事, 公共事業, 公共建造物, 公共施設
　public works project 公共事業, 公共工事
　public works spending 公共投資, 公共投資関係費, 公共事業費 (=public spending)
publication 名 公表, 公開, 発表, 公示, 公布, 発行, 掲載, 出版, 刊行, 出版物, 刊行物, パブリケーション
　government publications 政府刊行物
　industry publications 業界紙
　internal publication 社内報
　periodical publication 定期刊行物
　publication of the invention 発明の公開
　suspension of publication 発行停止
　the publication of a person's death …の死亡公示, …の死亡公表
　the publication of personal background 個人の経歴の公表
　the publication of pictures without permission 写真の無断掲載
publicity 名 評判, 世間の注目, 世間に知れ渡ること, 公開, 周知, 知名性, 宣伝, 広告, ピーアール, 広報[宣伝]活動, パブリシティ(企業のPR活動の一環として行われるパブリシティの方法としては, 新製品, 人事や決算などの新聞発表による情報提

供, 記者会見による発表, 説明, 工場見学, 展示, VTRによる情報提供などが挙げられる)
  advance publicity 前宣伝
  bad publicity about …についての悪い評判
  manage publicity 広報を担当する
  negative publicity 悪評判
  publicity agent 広告代理業者
  publicity-available data 開示データ
  publicity campaign 宣伝活動
  publicity release パブリシティ・リリース (= news release)

publicity right パブリシティ権(有名人(スポーツ選手やタレントなど)の氏名や写真を使った商品が生み出す権益を, 本人やその契約者が独占的に得ることができる権利のこと)
  ▶ *Publicity rights* refer to the rights of celebrities to monopolize economic benefits resulting from their names or images. パブリシティ権とは, 有名人の氏名や映像から生じる経済的利益を, その本人が独占する権利のことをいう。

publicly held company 公開会社, 株式公開企業, 上場会社

publicly owned company [corporation] 株式公開企業, 公開会社, 上場企業 (= publicly held company, publicly quoted company, publicly traded company)

publicly traded 株式公開されている, 株式公開企業の
  publicly traded company [firm] 公開企業, 公開会社, 株式公開企業, 上場企業, 上場企業 (= publicly held company, publicly owned company, publicly quoted company, publicly traded enterprise)

publish 動 公表する, 発表する, 公開する, 発行する, 刊行する, 出版する, 掲載する
  a letter published in the newspaper 新聞に掲載された投書
  publish a financial report 有価証券報告書を公表する
  publish a law 法令を公布する
  publish or perish 書くか辞めるか(研究者に論文執筆, 研究発表, 出版活動を促すことば)
  ▶ Financial reports and other documents *published* by companies are the most fundamental sources of information for investors and creditors. 企業が公表する有価証券報告書などは, 投資家や債権者にとって最も基幹的な情報源だ。

Pulitzer Prize ピューリッツァー賞(報道, 文学, 音楽部門で功績を残した人に毎年贈られる賞)

pull date 店頭販売期限, 店頭販売期限日
pull money 金を引き出す, 資金を引き揚げる
pull out of …から手を引く, …から撤退する, …から脱退する, …から抜け出す (= withdraw from)
pull strings 陰で糸を引く, 糸を操る, 黒幕となる
pullback 名 撤退, 撤収, 後退, 引き揚げ, 引戻し, 障害, 障害物, 邪魔, 減少, 減速
  a significant pullback 相場の反落
  the troop pullback 軍隊の撤退

pump 動 注入する, 投入する, 出資する, 供給する, 大量に作り出す, もたらす, くみ上げる, ポンプでくみ出す, 上下に動かす, 〈汚染物質を〉排出する, 放出する
  pump and dump 株価をあおりたてた後に売り逃げる不法行為
  pump liquidity into the (banking) system 市中に流動性を供給する
  pump money into the (banking) system 市中に流動性を供給する
  pumped (hydroelectric) storage 揚水発電システム, 揚水貯蔵

pump 名 給油ポンプ, ガソリン・スタンド(filling station, gas station, service station), ポンプ
  petrol pump 石油ポンプ, ガソリン・ポンプ
  prime the pump 呼び水[誘い水]を入れる

pump-primer 名 景気刺激策

pump priming 呼び水, 誘い水, 予算ばらまき, 呼び水用の財政支出, 呼び水的支出政策, 呼び水経済政策, 呼び水[誘い水]式経済政策, 予算ばらまき, 大規模な財政投融資, 景気刺激策, 景気振興策
  pump-priming effect 呼び水効果, 誘い水効果, 刺激効果
  pump-priming measures 景気テコ入れ策, 景気刺激策, 景気振興策, 呼び水政策, 呼び水式景気浮揚策, 呼び水措置, 景気振興措置
  pump-priming money 呼び水用の資金
  pump-priming package 景気刺激策
  pump-priming policy 呼び水政策, 誘い水政策

pundit 名 権威者, 専門家, 学識者, 学者, 博識者, 賢者

punish 動 処分する, 処罰する, 罰する, 手荒く扱う, 酷使する

punishment 名 処分, 処罰, 刑罰, 罰, 手荒い扱い, 虐待, ひどい仕打ち, 強打
  capital punishment 極刑, 死刑
  corporal punishment 体刑, 体罰

disciplinary punishment 懲戒
harsh [severe] punishment 厳罰, 厳しい処罰
inflict a punishment on [upon] an offender 犯人[犯罪者, 違反者]を罰する, 犯人に刑を科す
pecuniary punishment 罰金刑
suffer [receive] a punishment 罰を受ける

punitive 形 刑罰の, 懲罰的な, 制裁の, 報復の (retaliatory), 報復的な, 因果応報の(retributive), 極めて厳しい, 過酷な
- punitive action 制裁措置, 対抗措置, 処罰行為
- punitive damage award 懲罰的損害賠償金
- punitive damages 懲罰的損害賠償, 懲罰的損害賠償金, 懲罰的賠償, 制裁的慰謝料
- punitive justice 因果応報, 当然の報い
- punitive laws 刑罰法規
- punitive measures 懲罰手段, 制裁措置, 厳しい措置
- punitive surcharge 課徴金
- punitive tariff 制裁関税, 報復関税
- take punitive measures [action, steps] against …に対して制裁措置を取る

purchase 動 買い取る, 買い付ける, 購入する, 引き受ける, 仕入れる, 調達する, 買収する, 取得する (=buy)
- purchase an indebted company 赤字企業を買収する
- purchase an insurance policy 保険をかける
- purchase receivables 債権を買い取る

purchase 名 買取り, 買付け, 買入れ, 購入, 購入品, 購買, 調達, 調達先, 引受け, 仕入れ, 買収, 取得, 獲得, パーチェス
- additional purchase 追加購入, 追加取得
- amount of purchase 仕入高
- basket purchase 一括購入
- cash purchase 現金購入, 現金仕入れ
- conservative purchase 買い控え
- corporate purchase 企業買収
- cost of purchase 購入原価, 仕入れ原価
- credit purchase 信用買い, 掛買い
- direct purchase of bank-held stocks 銀行保有株の直接買取り
- hire-purchase 買取り選択権付きリース, 買取権付きリース
- impulse purchase 衝動買い
- installment purchase 割賦購入, 月賦購入, 月賦買い, 分割払い購入方式 (=installment buying)
- joint purchase 共同仕入れ, 共同購入
- lump sum purchase 一括購入, 一時購入
- margin purchase 信用買い
- National Association of Purchasing Managers' survey 全米購買部協会景気総合指数
- personal purchase 個人購入
- purchase control 購買管理
- purchase price 購入価格, 買入れ価格, 買取り価格, 買付け価格, 取得価格, 買収価格仕入れ価格, 仕入れ値段 (=purchasing price)
- purchase right 購入権
- purchase tax 物品税
- purchases 仕入れ高, 購入品, 買ったもの, 購入量, 購買量
- redemption by purchase 買入れ償却
- small purchase 小口買付け
- speculative purchase 思惑買い
- stock purchase plan 株式購入精度

purport 名 趣旨, 意味, 主張, 意図, 目的
purported 形 …と名乗る, …と称する, …という評判のある, …と主張する, …を意味する
purportedly 副 噂によれば, その称するところでは

purse strings 財布のひも
- hold [control] the purse strings 財布のひもを握る, 財政上の権限を握る, 金銭の出納をつかさどる

push up 増加させる, 高める, 押し上げる
- push up consumer prices 消費者物価を押し上げる
- push up costs コストを押し上げる

put a brave face on しらを切る, 平然を装う
put another way その裏を返せば
put ... on hold …を棚上げする, …を保留する
put ... on the line …を危うくする, …を危険にさらす, …を賭ける
put up 掲示する, 掲げる, 出す, 売りに出す, 競売にする, 提出する, 〈資金を〉融通する, 出資する, 〈価格を〉上げる, 〈抵抗などを〉示す, 〈劇などを〉上演する, …を行う
- put up a candidate 候補者を立てる
- put up a flag 旗を掲げる
- put up for auction 競売にかける
- put up notices 掲示を出す
- put up tough resistance 頑強な抵抗を示す

Pyongyang 名 北朝鮮, 北朝鮮政府, 〈北朝鮮の首都の〉平壌, ピョンヤン
pyramid 名 ピラミッド型組織, 株式の買い乗せ

[売り乗せ], 利乗せ (pyramiding), ピラミッド式価格・賃金の決定, ピラミッド, **動**〈コストを〉価格に上乗せする, 徐々に上げる, 漸増する, 〈議論などを〉着々と進める[次第に高める], 取引を拡大して利ざやを稼ぐ, 〈株式を〉利乗せする, 〈信用取引で未実現利益を利用して〉買い乗せをする

pyramid control ピラミッド型管理
pyramid scam マルチ商法詐欺
pyramid selling マルチ商法, ネズミ講式販売[販売方式]
pyramid scheme ピラミッド型インチキ商法, ネズミ算式の無限連鎖講, ネズミ講, マルチ商法
pyramid [pyramidal] structure ピラミッド構造, ピラミッド型組織

Q q

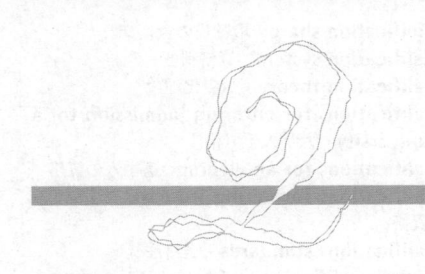

Q and A 質疑応答（＝questions and answers）
Q-clearance 名 厳重な身元調査
QDR 4年ごとの国防計画見直し（Quadrennial Defense Reviewsの略）
Q-fever Q熱
▶ *Q-fever* is caused by Coxiella burnetti, a type of rickettsia. Q熱の病原体は，リケッチアの一種の「コクシエラ・バーネッティ」である。
quadrennial 形 4年続く，4年ごとの，4年ごとに起こる，4年間の，4周年記念の
　a quadrennial period 4年間
　a quadrennial presidential election 4年に1回行われる大統領選挙，4年に1度の大統領選挙
　Quadrennial Defense Review 〈米国防省の〉4年ごとの国防計画見直し《略 **QDR**》（戦略目標や潜在的な軍事的脅威について分析した報告書）
　the quadrennial Olympic Games 4年に1度のオリンピック競技
　the quadrennial winter sports festival 4年毎に開催される冬のスポーツの祭典，冬季オリンピック
quadrilateral 形 4者の，4者間の，4極の，4角の，4辺形の
　quadrilateral trade ministers' meeting 4極通商閣僚会議，4極通商会議
　quadrilateral trade talks 4極通商会議
quadrillion 名 1,000兆，千兆
quadruple 動 4倍にする，4倍になる
quagmire 名 泥沼，沼地，湿地，〈抜け出せない〉苦境，窮地

a financial quagmire 財政難
a military quagmire 軍事的泥沼
a political quagmire 政治的苦境，政治的泥沼，政治的難局
a quagmire of debts [financial quagmire] 〈抜け出せない〉借金の泥沼
quake 名 地震（earthquake），震え，揺れ
quake-resistant technology 耐震技術
qualification 名 資格，資質，素質，適格，適性，能力，商品の品質検査，免許，免許証，免許状，資格証明書，制限（restriction），制約，条件，必要条件，留保条件，限定，限定事項，限定意見，手加減，修正（modification），手直し，数量化
　certificate of qualifications 資格証明書
　examination of the applicants' qualifications 資格審査
　form of qualification 限定意見の方式
　job qualification 職務資格要件
　medical qualification 医師免許状，医師免許証
　professional qualification 専門職としての資格
　promise without qualifications 無条件で約束する
　property qualification 財産資格，財産による選挙資格
　qualification for citizenship 市民権を得るための資格
　qualification for franchise 選挙資格
　qualification for success 成功する資質
　qualification for the application of a loan ローン審査
　qualification sales サムライ商法

qualification screening committee 資格審査委員会
qualification share 取締役の資格株
qualification system 資格制度
qualification theory 数量化理論
qualifications for entering [admission to] a university 大学入学資格
qualifications for an elector 選挙人の資格
qualifications for voting [to vote] 選挙する資格
qualifications standards 適格性基準
require qualification 手加減[限定]を要する
with certain qualifications 一定の条件を付けて, 一定の条件付きで, ある条件を付ければ

qualitative 形 質的な, 性質上の, 質に関わる, 定性的な
qualitative analysis 定性分析
qualitative change in society 社会の質的変化
qualitative credit control 金融の質的規制, 質的信用規制
qualitative difference 質的相違
qualitative economic growth 質的経済成長, 質的成長
qualitative economic policy 質的経済政策
qualitative economics 定性経済学
qualitative financial policy 質的金融政策
qualitative improvement 質的改善, 質的向上
qualitative interview 定性面接 (=depth interview)
qualitative parameters [factors] 質的要因
qualitative regulation [control, restriction] 質的規制
qualitative service 品質重視のサービス, 質的サービス

quality 名 質, 品質, 品位, 特質, 特性, 性格, 性質, 良質, 優良, 高級, 内容, 優良品, 社会的に高い地位, 上流階級, 音質, クオリティ
a man of quality 上流階級の人
acceptable quality 合格品, 合格品質
asset quality 資産内容, 資産の質
bad quality 粗悪品, 粗悪品質
best quality 最上品, 最高の品質, 最優良品質 (=top quality)
bond quality 債券格付け
credit quality 信用の質, 信用度, 信用力
debt quality 債券の質, 債券の信用力
fine quality 優良品質, 優良品

good merchantable quality 適商品質, 適商品質条件《略 GMQ》
good quality 上等品, 上等品質
high quality product 高品質製品, 優良品
high quality service 高品質サービス
higher quality 品質向上
management quality 経営の質
medium quality 中等品, 中等品質
merchantable quality 商品性
prime quality 上品, 上等品質
quality assurance 品質保証
quality improvement 品質改善, 品質向上
quality management 品質管理 (=quality control)
Quality Management Institute 品質管理協会《略 QMI》
quality movement QC運動 (=quality control activity)
quality of life 生活の質, 住みやすさ
quality of output 製品の品質
quality of the water 水質
quality paper 高級紙, 高級新聞
quality point 成績換算評点
quality standard 品質基準, 品質標準, 品質規格
quality stock 優良株, 優良銘柄
quality time かけがえのない時間, 上質の時間
service quality サービスの質
shipped quality terms 船積み品質条件
standard quality 標準品, 標準品質
uniform quality 均一品, 均一品質

quality control 品質管理《略 QC》 (=quality management)
companywide quality control 全社的品質管理
quality control chart 品質管理図
quality control circle QCサークル
quality control section 品質管理部門
quality control system 品質管理体制
quality control technique [technology] 品質管理技術, 品質管理手法
software quality control ソフトウエアの品質管理
Statement on Quality Control Standards 品質管理基準書
statistical quality control 統計的品質管理
total quality control 総合品質管理, 全社的品質管理《略 TQC》

quality controller 品質管理者
quantitative 形 量の, 数量の, 量的な, 定量的な
quantitative credit control 金融の量的規制, 量的信用規制
quantitative easy-money policy 量的金融緩和策, 量的緩和策 (＝quantitative easing policy)
quantitative economic policy 量的経済計画
quantitative expansion 量的拡大
quantitative goal 量的目標
quantitative guideline 量的指針
quantitative increase 量的増加
quantitative market expansion 量的市場拡大 (⇒market expansion)
quantitative model 数量化モデル, 数量的モデル
quantitative monetary easing 金融の量的緩和, 量的金融緩和 (＝quantitative easing)
quantitative monetary easing policy 量的緩和政策, 量的金融緩和政策 (＝quantitative easing policy)
quantitative monetary relaxation 量的金融緩和, 量的緩和
quantitative regulation policy 量的規制政策
quantitative relaxation of credit 量的金融緩和
quantitative requirements 数値基準
quantitative restriction [control, regulation] 量的規制
quantitative standards 量的基準, 物量標準
quantitative trade restriction 輸入数量制限
quantitative yardstick 量的尺度
quantitative easing 量的緩和, 量的金融緩和 (＝quantitative monetary easing:「金融の量的緩和政策」は, デフレ経済からの脱却をめざして, 日銀が2001年3月から2006年3月まで実施した異例の金融政策)
quantitative easing framework 量的金融緩和体制, 量的金融緩和策
quantitative easing measures 量的緩和策, 量的金融緩和策 (＝quantitative easing policy)
quantitative easing policy 量的緩和策, 量的金融緩和策, 量的緩和政策 (＝quantitative easing measures, quantitative monetary easing policy)
quantitative easing step 量的緩和策 (＝quantitative easing policy)
quantity 名 量, 数量, 大量
batch quantity バッチ数量, バッチ量
bill of quantities 数量説明書
economic batch quantity 経済バッチ数量, 経済的バッチ量《略 EBQ》
economic manufacturing quantity 経済的生産数量, 最適生産量《略 EMQ》
economic order quantity 経済的発注量, 最適発注量《略 EOQ》
labor quantity 労働量
output quantity 生産量
quantity adjustment 数量調整
quantity cartel 生産数量カルテル
quantity checking 数量検査
quantity delivered 受渡し数量
quantity demanded 需要量
quantity limit 数量制限
quantity of money 通貨供給量
quantity order 大量注文
quantity shipped 出荷数量, 積載数量, 積送数量
quantity supplied 供給量
quantity surveyor 積算士
small quantities 少量
unit quantity 単位量, 単位数
▶Labor is now evaluated only in terms of *quantity*, or how many hours a worker toils, by the homogenization of labor. 労働の均質化により, 労働は現在, 量によって, つまり労働時間の長さによってだけ評価されるようになった。
quarantine 名 検疫, 検疫期間, 検疫停船期間, 検疫所, 隔離, 隔離期間, 隔離所, 孤立化, 追放, 排斥
animal quarantine 動物検疫所
in quarantine 隔離中に, 隔離して
plant quarantine 植物防疫所
quarantine anchorage 検疫停泊
quarantine certificate 検疫証明書
quarantine depot 検疫所
quarantine fee 検疫料
quarantine inspection 検疫検査
quarantine office 検疫所
quarantine officer 検疫官, 防疫官
quarantine port 検疫港
quarantine regulation 検疫規則
quarantine station 検疫所
quarantining 名 検査, 検疫

quarter 名 四半期(1年の4分の1, つまり3か月を指す。暦年の第1四半期は,1月1日から3月31日までの3か月のこと)
- **for three consecutive quarters** 3四半期連続して, 3四半期連続
- **quarter of a percentage point** 0.25%, 0.25パーセント
- **quarter-on-quarter comparison** 前期比
- **quarter-point rate hike** 0.25%の利上げ
- **the accounts settlement for the first three quarters to September** 1－9月期決算
- **the April-June quarter** 4－6月期(日本の3月期決算企業の第1四半期にあたる)
- **the fifth straight quarter** 5四半期連続
- **the first quarter** 第1四半期
- **the first two quarters** 上半期の第1四半期と第2四半期
- **the fourth quarter** 第4四半期 (＝the last quarter)
- **the last quarter** 第4四半期, 前期
- **the preceding quarter** 前期 (＝the previous quarter)
- **the quarter ended Dec. 31** 10－12月期 (＝the October-December quarter)
- **the second quarter** 第2四半期
- **the second two quarters** 下半期の第3四半期と第4四半期
- **the third quarter** 第3四半期

quarterly 形 四半期の, 四半期ベースの, 四半期別, 四半期ごとの, 年4回の, 前期比, 副 年4回, 四半期ごとに, 3か月ごとに, 毎季に
- **quarterly basis** 四半期ベース
- **quarterly dividend** 四半期配当
- **quarterly loss** 四半期損失, 四半期の損失
- **quarterly net loss** 四半期純損失, 四半期税引き後損失, 税引き後四半期赤字
- **quarterly profit** 四半期利益

quarterly report 四半期報告書, 四季報 (quarterly statement)

> 四半期報告書とは ⇒ 四半期ごとの企業の決算報告書で, 米国の場合はSEC (米証券取引委員会) への提出が義務付けられている。提出期限は米国企業の場合, 各四半期以降35日以内(2002年7月に成立した企業改革法(サーベンス・オクスレー法：Sarbanes-Oxley Act)に基づくSECの措置として, 従来の45日以内が35日に短縮された)で, 報告書の様式はForm 10-Q (様式10-Q)となっている。ただし, 第4四半期については提出義務がなく, 提出する場合には記載する財務書類(財務諸表：financial statements)は要約版でよく, 一般に財務書類注記(notes to financial statements)も省略できる。また, この要約財務書類(summarized financial statements)は監査(audit, auditing)を受ける必要がなく, 未監査(unaudited)の状態で提出することができ, 年次報告書と違って株主への四半期ごとの財務情報(quarterly financial information)の通知は義務付けられていない。

quarterly results 四半期業績, 四半期決算 (＝quarterly business results, quarterly settlement of accounts)
▶ Toyota began announcing its *quarterly results* in fiscal 2002. トヨタは, 2002年度から四半期決算［業績］を発表している。

quartet [quartette] 名 四重奏団, 四重唱団, 4人組, 4人1組, 4つ1組, カルテット
- **a brass quartet** 金管四重奏団
- **a quartet of rescuers** 4人1組の救助隊, 4人組の救助隊
- **a string quartet** 弦楽四重奏団
- **a woodwind quartet** 木管四重奏団
- **Quartet of Middle East mediators** 中東和平4者協議
- **the Quartet of Middle East** 中東4か国

quasi-medicine 名 医薬部外品

quasi money 準通貨
▶ *Quasi money* refers to time deposits, including foreign currency deposits, and other types of savings at banks that cannot be immediately cashed. 準通貨とは, 定期性預金(外貨預金を含む)のほかに, 即時に換金できない銀行預金のことをいう。

quasi-public corporation 半官半民の企業

quasizenith satellite 準天頂衛星

quatlemma 四重苦, カトレンマ (⇒dilemma, trilemma)

queen bee 女王蜂, 女ボス, 女性リーダー

Queen's Counsel 〈英国の〉勅撰弁護士

Queer Street 経済的困難

quest 名 追求, 探求, 探索, 探究, 努力
- **in quest of** …を求めて, …を追求して
- **the quest for new treatments** 新治療法の探究［探求］
- **the quest for profit maximization** 利潤最大化の目標追求

question 動 質問する, 尋ねる, 尋問する, 事情聴取をする, 疑問を抱く, 異議を唱える

question 名 質問, 問い, 疑問, 疑惑, 疑い, 問題, 問題点, 論点, 可能性
- ask [put] a leading question　誘導尋問をする
- be not the question　無関係である
- be open to question　疑義がある
- beside the question　論点を外れて, 見当違いで
- beyond (all) question　何の疑いもなく, 疑いの余地もない, 確かに, 間違いなく
- call [bring, throw] ... in [into] question　…を問題視する, …に疑義を挟む, 異議を唱える
- come into question　論議される, 問題になる
- in question　問題の, 論議中の
- multiple-choice question　多項選択式問題
- no question of　…の可能性はない, …の疑問の余地はない
- open question　未解決の問題, 未決定の問題
- out of the question　話にならない, 問題にならない, 不可能な, 許されていない
- put the question　投票を求める
- question mark　疑問符, 未知数, 謎
- question master　クイズ番組司会者
- question sheet　問題用紙
- question time　質問時間, 答弁時間
- true-false question　マルバツ(○×)式問題

questioning 名 〈警察などの〉事情聴取, 尋問, 〈国会での〉証人喚問

quick 形 応急の, 当座の, 即効の
- quick fix　応急処置, 緊急措置, 応急の解決策, 当座の問題解決法, 当座の解決策, 即効薬, 即効

quick-fix 形 即効の, 即効性のある, 反応が早い, 緊急の, 応急の, 一時しのぎの, 安易な
- quick-fix fiscal measures　一時しのぎの財政出動, 安易な財政出動
- quick-fix program　即効性のある計画, 緊急の計画
- quick-fix remedies　応急対策

quid pro quo　見返り, 代償, 仕返し, しっぺ返し, 報酬, 代用品(ラテン語で, something for somethingの意味。複数形=quids pro quo)

quit 動 手放す, 放棄する, 止める, 中止する, 辞める, 辞する, 辞任する, 退く, 立ち去る, 退去する, 立ち退く, 〈借金などを〉返済する
- quit hold of　…を手放す
- quit office [a job]　辞職する
- quit school　退学する
- quit work　仕事をやめる

quizmaster 名 クイズ番組司会者

quorum 名 定足数, 定数

quota 名 割当て, 割当数量, 持ち分, 分担, 分担割当額
- catch quotas　漁獲割当て
- consumption quota　消費割当て
- import quota system　輸入割当制度
- marketing quota　販売割当て
- percentage quota　比例割当て
- quota restrictions　輸入割当制限
- tariff quota　関税割当て

quotation 名 相場, 時価, 建て値, 提示価格, 見積り, 見積り価格, 見積り額, 価格見積り書, 引用
- bid and asked quotations　買い呼び値と売り呼び値
- exchange quotations　外国為替表
- forced quotation　人為相場
- forward quotation　先物相場
- market quotation　市場相場, 相場表
- official quotation　公定相場
- split quotation　小刻み相場
- stock exchange quotation　株式相場, 株式市況

quote 動 値を付ける, 価格を提示する, 値段[相場]を言う, 見積もる, 上場する

R

R & D 研究開発（**research and development**の略）
R & R 保養休暇（**rest and recreation**の略）
rabbi 名 ラビ（ユダヤ教の聖職者，学者，教師）
rabble-rouser 名 民衆扇動家，デマゴーグ
race 名 競争，戦い，急務，競走，競馬，競技会，〈時の〉経過，〈天体の〉運行，人種，民族，種族，集団，仲間，一族，血統，人類，レース
  arms race 軍備競争，軍拡競争
  be in the race 成功の見込みがある
  be out of the race 成功の見込みがない
  discrimination based on [on the grounds of] race 人種差別（＝race [racial] discrimination）
  loan [lending] race 貸出競争，融資競争
  presidential [Presidential] race 大統領選挙戦
  race against time [the clock] 時間との競争
  race-baiting 人種攻撃
  race for governor 知事選挙戦
  race problem 人種問題
  race relations 人種関係，人種間の関係
  race riot 人種暴動，人種差別に対する暴動（＝racial riot）
racial 形 人種の，人種上の，民族の，民族間の，種族の
  racial bar 人種障壁，人種差別
  racial conflict 人種間の紛争
  racial diversity 人種の多様性
  racial discrimination 人種差別
  racial integration 人種差別の撤廃［廃止］，人種統合，人種融合
  racial prejudice 人種的偏見
  racial segregation 人種隔離，人種差別
  racial self-determination 民族自決
  racial slur 人種差別発言
  racial steering 人種差別的不当誘導
  racial tension 人種間の緊張
  racial unrest 人種騒動
racism 名 人種差別，人種差別主義，人種差別的行為，人種的偏見，人種の優越感，民族主義（＝racialism）
rack one's brains 知恵を絞る，懸命に考える，頭を悩ます，苦心する，工夫をこらす
racketeer 名 ゆすり，ゆすり屋，恐喝者，脅迫者，てき屋，暴力団員，詐欺師，ペテン師
  corporate racketeer 総会屋（＝corporate blackmailer, corporate extortionist）
  Racketeer-Influenced and Corrupt Organizations Statute 〈米国の〉組織犯罪規制法《略 RICO》
  Racketeers Influence and Corrupt Organizations Act 集団暴力腐敗組織法，強請と腐敗組織に関する法律
racketeering 名 ゆすり，密造［密売，密輸］，不正利得
radar 名 電波探知機，レーダー装置，レーダー
  airborne radar 機上レーダー
  altitude radar 高角測定レーダー
  be on the radar screen 世間の注目［関心］の的になっている，監視の対象となっている
  early warning radar 早期警戒レーダー
  guidance radar ミサイル誘導レーダー

perimeter acquisition radar　周辺捕捉レーダー
phased array radar　位相配列レーダー，フェーズド・アレイ・レーダー
radar approach control　レーダー進入管制
radar beacon　レーダー自動応答装置，レーダー・ビーコン
radar data processing system　航空路レーダー情報処理システム，航空監視レーダー
radar detector　自動車速度探知装置
radar dishes　〈皿状の〉レーダー・アンテナ
radar fence [screen]　レーダー網
radar gun　スピード・ガン
radar interferometry　レーダー干渉測定
radar trap　ねずみ取り，速度違反車取締り装置，自動車速度違反測定装置
radar warning system　電波警報システム
surveillance radar　捜索レーダー

radarscope 名　〈レーダーの〉写像スクリーン
radiation 名　放射，放射能，放射線，放射エネルギー，放射熱，放射能漏れ
　radiation amount　放射量
　radiation budget　放射収支（太陽から地球に入ってくる（短波）放射と地球から宇宙に出ていく赤外（長波）放射との収支を，地球の放射収支という）
　radiation chemistry　放射線化学
　radiation detector　放射線測定器（＝radiation measurement instrument）
　radiation dose　放射線量
　radiation exposure　放射線被曝，放射能被曝
　radiation hazards　放射線障害
　radiation therapy　放射線療法
　radiation utilization　放射線利用
radical 形　根本的な，基本的な，基礎の，抜本的な，徹底的な，過激な，急進的な，急進派の，本来の，生来の，病根を切除する，根治的な
　radical cure　完全治療
　radical element　過激分子
　radical error　根本的誤り
　radical faction　急進派，過激派
　radical formula　基礎公式
　radical improvements　徹底的な改良
　radical leftist group　急進的な左翼団体
　radical liberal　急進的進歩派，急進的進歩派の人（＝radic-lib）
　radical mastectomy　全乳房切除手術
　radical opinions　過激な意見
　radical reform　抜本的改革，徹底的な改革
　radical students　過激派学生
　undergo a radical change　根本的変化を受ける
radicalism 名　急進主義，過激主義，過激論
radio frequency heating　高周波加熱（電磁波を加えて加熱すること）
radioactive 形　放射性の，放射能のある，放射能による
　highly radioactive plutonium　放射能の高いプルトニウム
　radioactive contamination　放射能汚染
　radioactive dating　放射性炭素による年代測定，放射性炭素年代測定（＝carbon dating, carbon-14 dating, radiocarbon dating, radiometric dating）
　radioactive decay　放射性崩壊
　radioactive elements　放射性元素
　radioactive fallout　放射性降下物，死の灰
　radioactive gas　放射性ガス
　radioactive isotope　放射性同位元素（＝radioisotope）
　radioactive leak [leakage]　放射能漏れ
　radioactive noble gas　放射性貴ガス
　radioactive particle　放射性粒子
　radioactive substances [materials]　放射性物質
　radioactive waste [discharge]　放射性廃棄物（＝nuclear waste）
　radioactive waste disposal facility　放射性廃棄物埋設施設
radioactivity survey [measurement]　放射能検査
radiology 名　放射線医学
▶In *radiology* using heavy particles such as carbon, the National Institute of Radiological Sciences is a world leader.　炭素などの重粒子を使う放射線医学（重粒子線治療）では，放射線医学総合研究所が世界をリードしている。
rage 名　怒り，憤慨，憤怒，激怒，大荒れ，猛威，熱中，熱狂，大流行，ブーム，熱望，熱情
　be all the rage　大流行である
　fly [get, fall] into a rage　かっとなる，激怒する
　have a rage for　…を熱望する，…に熱中する
　the rage of the plague　疫病の猛威
rags-to-riches 形　赤貧[極貧]から大金持ちになった，貧困国から富裕国になった
raid 名　急襲，奇襲，襲撃，侵入，不法侵入，強盗，〈警察の〉強制捜査，手入れ，踏み込み，強行[武

力]突入，〈株式の〉売り崩し[買い崩し]，売り浴びせ，〈競争相手からの〉引き抜き工作，〈会社の〉乗っ取り行為
- **a bear raid** 売り崩し
- **a dawn raid** 早朝の踏み込み，暁の急襲
- **a police raid on** …への警察の手入れ
- **a raid on one's residence** …の家宅捜索，…の手入れ
- **an air raid** 空爆
- **make [carry out, launch] a raid on** …を襲撃する，…を急襲する，…の手入れをする

raider 名 侵入者，急襲者

railroad 動 強要する，〈法案の〉強行採決をする，〈法案，議案を〉一気に通過させる，〈証拠不十分のまま〉投獄する，鉄道で輸送する
- **be railroaded to prison without a fair trial** 公正な審理なしで投獄される
- **railroad a bill through a committee** 委員会で法案[議案]を一気に通過させる
- **railroad a bill through Congress** 議会で法案を強行通過させる[強引に通す]
- **railroad a person into hospital** 人を無理やり入院させる

rainmaker 名 人工降雨専門家，政界に顔のきく人物[会社役員，法律事務所の弁護士]

raise 動 〈資金などを〉調達する，〈料金・価格・資金などを〉引き上げる，上方修正する，増やす，増強する
- **raise capital** 資金を調達する，資本を調達する，資金を引き上げる，増資する，資金繰りをする
- **raise cash through a private placement** 第三者割当てで資金を調達する
- **raise equity** 増資する
- **raise external funds** 外部資金を調達する（=raise capital, raise money）
- **raise funds** 資金を調達する，資金を集める（=raise capital, raise money）
- **raise interest rates** 金利を引き上げる，利上げする
- **raise money** 資金を調達する（=raise capital, raise funds）
- **raise one's capital** 増資する（=increase one's capital）
- **raise one's stake in** …の持ち株比率を引き上げる，…の株式保有比率を高める，…への[…に対する]出資比率を引き上げる（=increase one's stake in）
- **raise tier-one capital** ティア1自己資本を調達する

- **raised costs** コスト高，コスト上昇

raison d'etre 存在理由

rake in 荒稼ぎする，大もうけする，〈大金を〉手にする，かき集める

rally 動 反騰する，回復する，盛り返す，上昇する，急騰する，急伸する，集まる，団結する，集会を開く（=rebound）
- **rally around [round]** …の支援のために集まる
- **rally on the good news** この好材料を受けて急伸する
- **rally sharply** 急反発する，急回復する
- **rally strongly** 大きく買われる，急騰する
- **rally through the old highs** 最高値を更新する
- **rallying cry** かけ声，決まり文句，標語，スローガン
- **rallying point** 集合場所，集結点，集結地，気力回復の契機

rally 名 〈株価の〉反騰，反発，〈景気などの〉持ち直し，回復，上昇，上昇局面，急騰，上げ相場，強気相場，大会，決起集会，示威運動，自動車レース，ラリー（=rebound）
- **bond rally** 債券相場の上昇，債券相場の急騰
- **mass rally** 集団決起集会
- **modest rally** 穏やかな上昇局面
- **sharp rally** 急騰
- **substantial rally** 大幅に買われること
- **sustainable rally** 本格的上げ相場
- **technical rally** アヤ戻し(とくに理由のない小幅上昇)

rampage 名 大暴れ，暴れ回り，怒り狂い，凶暴な行為，暴動，騒乱
- **go [be] on a [the] rampage** 暴れ回る，激怒する

rampant 形 過激な，激しい，はびこる，生い茂る，横行している，手のつけられない，猛威をふるう
- **rampant corruption** はびこる汚職
- **rampant violence** はびこる暴力

Ramsar Convention ラムサール条約，国際湿地条約，水鳥湿地保全条約(正式名称はThe Convention on Wetlands of International Importance, especially as Waterfowl Habitat「特に水鳥の生息地として国際的に重要な湿地に関する条約」で，1971年に採択された。締約国会議は，3年ごとに開催される)

random 形 無作為の，任意の，手当たり次第の，ランダム
- **random sampling (method)** 無作為抽出法，

任意抽出法
random-sample 動 無作為抽出する
range 名 範囲, 幅, 領域, 種類, 品揃え, 製品群, 限界, 射撃場, 射程, 射程距離, 等級, 階級, 山脈, 連山, レンジ
  agreed price range 協定価格帯
  full [broad, whole, wide] range of 広範な, 広範囲の, 多種多様な, 幅広い
  in the range of …の範囲内で
  long-range cash [fund] planning 長期資金計画
  out of one's range …の力が及ばない
  product range 製品構成, 製品の機種, 種類, 製品群, 品揃え, 製品の幅, 車種
  range finder 距離測定器, 距離計
  range of funding options 資金調達の選択の幅
  range of loss 損失の範囲, 損失の範囲額
  range rate 範囲職務給
  range trading もみ合い
  trading range 取引圏, 相場圏, ボックス圏, 取引レンジ
  within one's range …の力が及ぶ
rank 動 地位を占める, 並ぶ, 評価する, 位置づける, …の順位を決める, 等級をつける
  be ranked as …と位置づけされる, …と評価される
  be ranked top among …でトップにランクされる, …でトップを占める
  rank with …と肩を並べる
rank 名 地位, 身分, 階級, 等級, 順位, レベル, ランク
  break ranks 組織に刃向かう, 隊列を乱す
  rank correlation 順位相関
  ranks and honors 位階勲等
  the ranks 一般大衆
rank and file 平社員, 一般従業員, 一般職員, 一般労働者, 一般組合員, 一般大衆, 庶民
  rank-and-file employee 一般社員
ranking 名 順位, 番付, 序列, 格付け, ランキング
  global competitive ranking 国際競争力ランキング
  the Fortune ranking フォーチュン誌の番付
ranking 形 一流の, 上級の, 最高位の, 最高幹部の, …位の, …にランクされる
  a high-ranking officer 上級官吏
  a ranking official 幹部職員, 役職員, 幹部, 高官
ransom demand 身代金要求
rap 動 非難する, 酷評する, 批判する, 厳しく言う, 叩ぶ, こつんとたたく, ラップで歌う, しゃべるように歌う, 〈気軽に〉しゃべる, 雑談する, 告発する, 逮捕する, 刑を宣告する
rap 名 非難, 酷評, 叱責, 〈犯罪の〉告発, おしゃべり, 会話, 軽くたたくこと, 罰, 刑罰, 懲役刑, 容疑 (charge), ラップの曲 [音楽], ラップ・ミュージック
  beat the rap 罰 [刑罰] を免れる, 無罪になる (= escape punishment)
  get a bad rap 不当な扱いを受ける
  give a rap on [over] the knuckles 厳しく非難する
  murder rap 殺人容疑
  rap group 共通問題を討議するグループ, 討議グループ, ラップ・グループ
  rap on [over] the knuckles 叱りつけられること
  rap parlor 売春宿
  rap session ラップ・グループの討論会, グループ討論
  rap sheet 犯罪記録, 前科記録
  receive [get] a rap on [over] the knuckles 厳しく非難される
  take the rap for …で罰を受ける, …で責められる
rape 名 強姦, 強姦罪, 婦女暴行 (sexual assault [attack]), 強奪, 強奪行為, 略奪, レイプ
  a case of rape resulting in bodily injury 強姦致傷事件
  be convicted of rape 強姦 [強姦罪] で有罪となる
  commit a rape on …に暴行を働く
  rape charge 強姦罪での告訴
  rape resulting in injury 強姦致傷, 強姦致傷罪
  rape victim 暴行の被害者, 強姦の犠牲者
  statutory rape 制定法上の強姦 (承認年齢未満の女性との性交)
  unsuccessful rape attempt 暴行未遂
rapid 形 急激な, 急速な, 急な, 速い
  Rapid Deployment Forces 米国の緊急展開部隊《略 RDF》
  rapid economic growth 経済の急成長, 急速な経済成長, 高度経済成長
  rapid increase 急増, 急速な伸び
  rapid inflation 急激なインフレ

rapid reaction force 緊急対応部隊
rapid train 快速電車
rapid transit (system) 高速旅客輸送, 高速輸送体系, 高速移動システム, 高速輸送網
rapid transit railway 高速鉄道
rare breed 珍しい品種
rare metal 希少金属, レアメタル
rat-fucking 名 敵陣営の選挙運動に対する妨害工作
rat race 激しい生存競争, 過酷で無意味な競争, 際限のない競争, 手段を選ばない[愚かな]出世争い
ratchet [ratch] 動 徐々に上がる, 徐々に下がる, 〈物を〉かます, 入れる
　ratchet down 下げる, 下がる
　ratchet up 上げる, 高める, 上がる
ratchet effect 歯止め効果, 景気下降阻止効果, 断続的成長[拡大, 増加], 周期的成長[増加], ラチェット効果
rate 動 評価する, 格付けする, 見積もる
　G-rated (film) 一般向け映画 (Gはgeneralの略)
　newly-rated issuer 新規格付け発行体
　PG-rated (film) 保護者同伴映画 (PGはparental guidanceの略)
　R-rated action movie 準成人向けアクション映画 (Rはrestrictedの略)
　R-rated films with sexual content セックス・シーンがある準成人向け映画
　rated issue 格付け債券
　rated issuer 格付け取得済み発行体, 格付け取得発行体
　X-rated (film) 成人向け映画
rate 名 割合, 率, 金利, 歩合, 料金, 値段, 運賃, 相場, 等級, 速度, 進度, 程度, レート
　buying rate 買い相場
　fixed rate 固定相場
　flat rate 均一料金
　floating rate 自由変動相場
　keep interest rates unchanged 金利を据え置く
　lending rate 貸出金利
　market rate 市場金利, 市場相場, 市場レート, 銀行間相場
　open rate 基本料金
　opening rate 始値, 寄り付き
　operating rate 操業率, 設備稼働率
　per annum rate 年利
　per diem rate 日歩
　piece rate plan 出来高払い制
　prevailing rate 市場の実勢金利, 市場金利, 中心相場
　rate for unsecured overnight call 無担保コール翌日物金利 (=target rate for unsecured overnight call)
　rate of return on investment 投資収益率, 資本利益率, 投資の運用利回り
　rate of savings 貯蓄率
　rate of taxation 税率 (=tax rate)
　rates for international freight 国際線の貨物運賃
　real rate 実勢レート, 実効金利
　seasonal adjusted annual rate 季節調整済み年率
　single rate 単一相場
　U.S. rates 米国の金利(公定歩合とFF金利の誘導目標)
　vacancy rate 求人率
ratification 名 批准, 承認, 裁可, 〈契約などの〉追認
　await ratification 批准を待つ
　delay ratification 批准を遅らせる
　exchange of instruments of ratification 批准書の交換
ratify 動 〈条約などを〉批准する, 〈契約などを〉追認する, 承認する, 裁可する
rating 名 格付け, 評価, 信用度, 視聴率
　audience rating 視聴率
　bond rating 債券格付け, 社債格付け (=debt rating)
　efficiency rating system 勤務評定, 能率評定方式
　job rating 職務評価
　merit rating 人事考課
　performance rating 達成度考課, 職能考課, 職務考課
　personnel rating 人事考課, 人事考査 (=merit rating)
　rating agency 格付け機関, 信用格付け機関, 格付け会社
　rating downgrade 格下げ, 下方修正, 引下げ (=downgrading)
　rating scale 評価尺度, 測定尺度, 評定尺度
　rating upgrade 格上げ, 上方修正, 引上げ (=upgrading)
ratio 名 割合, 比率, 利益率, 収益率, 指標
　ratio of job offers to job seekers 有効求人

倍率

rationalization 名 合理化
- capacity rationalization　生産合理化, 設備合理化
- industrial rationalization　産業合理化
- rationalization of distribution　流通合理化
- rationalization of management　経営合理化

raw 形　生(なま)の, 未加工の, 未処理の, 精製していない, 未熟な, 不慣れな, 冷え冷えとした, むきだしの, ありのままの, 抑えきれない, 露骨な, 赤裸々な, 現実的な
- get a raw deal from　…からひどい扱いを受ける, …から不当な仕打ちにあう
- hit [touch] a raw nerve　怒らせる, 不愉快な思いをさせる
- raw data　生のデータ, 未処理のデータ, 未調整データ
- raw deal　不公平な扱い, ひどい扱い, 不当な仕打ち
- raw hostility　むきだしの敵意
- raw power [energy]　実力, ありのままの力
- raw product　〈食糧の〉原産物
- raw recruit　新参者, 未熟な進入社員
- raw silk　生糸
- raw steel　粗鋼

raw material　原料, 材料, 原材料, 素材
- raw material sourcing　原材料の供給源 (= raw material sources)
- raw material supply　原材料の供給 (= supply of imported raw materials)
- raw materials　原材料, 原料, 資材, 天然資源
- security of raw material imports　原材料の輸入確保

razor-edge 名　危機, 厳しい状況, 〈成功と失敗の〉きわどい分かれ目
- be on a razor-edge [the razor's edge]　危機[瀬戸際]に立っている, 厳しい状況にいる, 瀬戸際に瀕している

razor job　残忍な攻撃, 悪意に満ちたひどい批評

razor-thin 形　紙一重の, 僅差の, きわどい
- a razor-thin victory　辛勝
- razor-thin interest rates　超低金利
- win the election by a razor-thin margin　紙一重の差で選挙に勝つ

razzle-dazzle 名　大騒ぎ, ばか騒ぎ, 狂宴, 乱痴気パーティー, 混乱, 要領を得ない話しぶり, 派手な振る舞い
- be [go] on the razzle-dazzle　ばか騒ぎをする
- pyrotechnic razzle-dazzle　花火の狂宴

RDF　ごみ固形燃料, 固形化燃料 (refuse-derived fuelの略)

react 動　反応する, はね返る, 反作用する, 対応する, 反発する, 反抗する, 逆襲する, 〈株が〉反落する, 逆行する, 逆戻りする, 化学反応を起こす, 〈容態が〉悪くなる
- react against [to]　…に反発する, …に反対する
- react each other　相互に[互いに]作用しあう
- react favorably on　…に有利に作用する
- react in a positive way to　…に肯定的に反応する
- react to adverse situations　困難な状況に対応[対処]する
- react to the situation quickly [immediately]　事態に迅速に[速やかに]対応する

reaction 名　反応, 反響, はね返り, 対応, 反発, 反抗, 反動, 反作用, 影響, 逆襲, 〈株の〉反落, 反射能力, 保守的傾向, 化学反応, 容態悪化, 虚脱感, 疲労, 活力減退
- a reaction against　…への反発, …に対する反抗
- chain reaction　連鎖反応
- chain reaction bankruptcy　連鎖倒産
- chemical reaction　化学反応
- get a good reaction from　…から良い反応を得る
- have an adverse reaction to　…に対して拒絶反応がある
- have an allergic reaction to　…に対してアレルギー反応がある
- initial reaction　当初の対応, 当初の反応
- policy reaction function　政策反応関数
- reaction engine　反動推進エンジン
- reaction lag　反応ラグ
- reaction shot　〈演技者の表情の〉大写し
- reaction time　反応時間

reactionary 形　反動的な, 反動の, 逆コースの, 名　反動主義者, 保守主義者

reactor 名　原子炉, リアクター
- advanced boiling water reactor　改良沸騰水型炉《略 ABWR》
- advanced thermal reactor　新型転換炉《略 ATR》
- boiling water reactor　沸騰水型軽水炉《略 BWR》
- commercial reactor　実用炉
- corrosion of the reactors' cores　炉心崩壊

experimental reactor　実験炉
fast breeder reactor　高速増殖炉《略 FBR》
fast neutron reactor　高速中性子炉
fast reactor　高速炉
heavy water reactor　重水炉《略 HWR》
high temperature engineering test reactor　高温工学試験研究炉《略 HTTR》
high temperature gas-cooled reactor　高温ガス炉《略 HTGR》
light water reactor　軽水炉《略 LWR》
nuclear power reactor　原子炉
pressurized water reactor　加圧水型原子炉, 加圧水型軽水炉《略 PWR》
research reactor　研究炉
thermal neutron reactor　熱中性子炉

read 動　示す, 表示する, …と解釈[理解]する, …と書いてある, 読み取る, 研究する, 専攻する

reading 名　数値, 目盛り, 度数, 示度, 指標, 指数,〈議案の〉読会(議会での法令審議の段階), 読み方, 読書, 台本読み, 朗読, 文学的知識, 解釈
core inflation reading　基礎インフレ率の数値
first reading　第一読会, 第一回読会(全体の審議)
index reading for manufacturers' sentiment　製造業景況感判断指数
index reading for small companies' sentiment　中小企業景況判断指数
NAPM reading　全米購買部協会景気総合指数
negative reading　マイナスの数値
positive reading　プラスの数値
second reading　第二読会, 第二回読会(各条項の審議)
strength of the readings　景気指標の強弱
third reading　第三読会, 第三回読会(再度の全体審議)

readjustment 名　再調整, 再変更, 見直し,〈態勢などの〉立て直し, 整理, 再建, 整備, 不況(depressionの遠回し語),〈環境などへの〉再適応
administrative readjustment　行政整理
corporate readjustment　準更生, 会社の再建
downside readjustment　下方修正
financial readjustment　財政立て直し, 財政整理
land readjustment　土地区画整理

reaffirm 動　再確認する, 改めて確認する

real 形　実際の, 実体の, 現実の, 実質の, 実質上の, 重大な, 不動産の, リアル
real action　物的訴訟
real amount demanded　実質需要量
real amount supplied　実質供給量
real consumption　実質個人消費
real demand　実需, 実質需要
real disposable income　実質可処分所得
real dollar value　実質ドル価値
real economy　実体経済
real goods　実物財
real government financial wealth　実質政府金融資産
real gross domestic product　実質国内総生産(GDP), 実質GDP(国内総生産)(＝real GDP)
real growth　実質経済成長, 実質伸び率(＝real economic growth)
real import as a percent of GDP　実質輸入額のGDP比率
real income　実質所得
real interest rates　実質金利
real investment　実物投資, 実質投資
real market　実物市場
real national income　実質国民所得
real outlays　実質支出
real rate of exchange　実勢相場, 実勢為替レート
real resources　実物資源
real revenue　実質収入
real security　物的担保
real spending　実質個人消費
real stock　実株
real transaction　実物取引

real estate　不動産
real estate acquisition tax　不動産取得税
real estate appraiser　不動産鑑定士, 不動産鑑定者
real estate developer　不動産開発業者, 不動産開発会社, 不動産デベロッパー(＝property developer)
real estate investment fund　不動産投資ファンド, 不動産ファンド(投資家から資金を集めて, 不動産などへの投資事業で運用している投資ファンド)
real estate investment trust　不動産投資信託《略 REIT》

real terms　実質
capital in real terms　実質資本
in real terms　実質で, 実質ベースで
in real yen terms　円建て実質ベースで

real time [realtime]　実時間, 同時, 即時,

即時処理, 実時間処理, リアルタイム処理, リアルタイム

real–time [realtime] 形 実時間の, 同時の, 即時の, リアルタイム
- **real–time option trading** リアルタイム・オプション取引
- **real–time processing** 即時処理, 実時間処理, リアルタイム処理
- **real–time quotes** リアルタイム株価

realign 動 再編成する, 再編する, 再調整する, 再統合する, 再提携する, 〈資産などを〉整理する, 変更する

realignment 名 再編成, 再編, 再調整, 調整, 再統合, 再提携
- **currency realignment** 通貨調整, 通貨再調整 （＝realignment of currencies）
- **general realignment** 全面的再調整, 全面調整
- **the realignment of foreign exchange rates** 為替レートの調整

reality 名 現実, 現実のもの, 現実の世界, 真実, 実在, 迫真性, 事実, 実体, 実勢, 現実認識
- **economic reality** 経済実体, 経済の実勢
- **hard [stern] reality** 厳しい現実, 過酷な現実
- **objective reality** 客観的実在
- **subjective reality** 主観的実在

reap 動 刈り取る, 収穫する, 〈利益や報酬を〉得る, 手に入れる, 〈恩恵などを〉享受する
- **reap large profits** 大きな利益を上げる
- **reap the benefits of advanced technologies** 先進技術の恩恵を受ける［享受する］
- **reap the rewards of investment** 投資の成果を生かす, 投資の報酬を手に入れる

reappointment 名 再任, 再任命, 再指名

reapportionment 名 再配分, 再配当, 再割当て, 割当変更, 〈議員数の〉定数是正, 議席数再配分

rear–echelon logistic support 後方支援

reason 名 理由, わけ, 根拠, 拠り所, 道理, 理屈, 理性, 判断力, 要因, 材料, 事由
- **by reason of** …のために, …の理由により （＝due to, owing to）
- **cyclical reason** 循環要因
- **for whatever reason [reasons]** 理由は何であれ
- **good reason** 十分な根拠, 根拠が十分にあること
- **in [within] reason** 道理にかなって, 適当な
- **it stands to reason** 〈…は〉当然である, 道理に合っている
- **seasonal reason** 季節要因
- **secular reason** 構造要因
- **speculative reasons** 投機的な思惑
- **within reason** 無理のない範囲で

reassert 動 再主張する, 再断言する, 改めて強める, 再浮上する, 再び表面に出てくる

rebate 名 割戻し, 払戻し, 現金割戻し, 返金, 還付金, 奨励金, 報償金, 手数料, 戻し税, 割引, 控除, リベート
- **allowance for sales rebate** 売上割戻し引当金 （＝reserve for sales rebate）
- **cash rebate** 現金割戻し, 現金払戻し
- **income tax rebates** 所得税の還付, 戻し税
- **purchase rebate** 仕入割戻し
- **sales rebate** 売上割戻し, 販売奨励金, リベート （＝rebate on sales）
- **tax rebate** 税金の還付, 戻し減税, 戻し税

rebel 名 反逆者, 反乱兵士, 反主流, 反主流勢力, 反体制派, 反対者, へそ曲がり, 反抗的な人
- **rebel–held city** 反乱勢力支配下の都市
- **rebels in the party** 党内反主流派［反主流勢力］

rebound 動 回復する, 反発する, 持ち直す, 跳ね返る, 下落後に再び上昇する, 減少から増加に転じる

rebound 名 回復, 景気回復, 反発, 反転, 株価の持ち直し, 好転
- **modest rebound** 穏やかな回復, 穏やかな景気回復
- **rebound in profits** 収益の回復
- **small rebound** 小幅反発 （＝slight rebound）
- **strong rebound** 力強い回復, 大幅な回復
- **technical rebound** 自律反発

rebuild 動 再構築する, 再建する, 再興する, 再生する, 回復する, 〈在庫などを〉積み増す, 建て替える, 復元する, 立て直す

rebuilding 名 再構築, 再建, 再興, 再生, 建て替え, 復元, 立て直し

recall 動 リコール（無料回収・修理）する, 回収する, 撤回する, 取り消す, 召喚する, 呼び戻す, 解任［解職］する, 思い出す, 回想する

recall 名 欠陥車［欠陥品］の回収, リコール（無料回収・修理）, 撤回, 取消し, 召喚, 呼び戻し, 〈公職者の〉解任請求, 解任［解職］権, 回想
- **recall referendum** 解任の国民投票

recapitalization 名 資本再編, 資本の再構成, 資本変更, 資本組入れ

recapitalize 動 資本を再編する, 資本構成を修正 [変更] する, 〈法定準備金などを〉資本に組み入れる
recede 動 撤回する, 後退する, 低下する, 減退する, 弱まる
receipt 名 受領, 受取り, 領収書, 受領書, 売上, 収入, 売上金, レシート
receive 動 受け取る, 受領する, 受ける, 取得する, 歓迎する, 迎え入れる, 入れる, 収容する, 〈損害などを〉被る, 〈重みなどを〉支える, 受信する, 聴取する
  be received with cheers 喝采を受ける
  be well received by …に快く受け入れられる
  receive a fair return 適切な利益を得る
  receive a good education 立派な教育を受ける
  receive a new idea 新思想を受け入れる
  receive a weight on one's back 背で重いものを支える
  receive investment 出資を受ける
  receive less leverage テコ効果が薄くなる
  receive little attention ほとんど注目されない
  receive support from …から支持を受ける
  receive the blow on …に打撃を受ける, …を打たれる
recent 形 最近の, 近頃の, このところの, ついこの間の
  in recent years ここ数年, 近年
  recent highs 最近の高値
  recent indicators 最近発表された指標
  recent uptrend in the stock 最近の株価上昇
recession 名 景気後退, 不景気, 不況, リセッション (好況はboom, 不況はdepression)
> 景気後退について ⇒ 「景気後退」は, 景気の回復・拡大期が終わって底を打つまでの状態をいう。米国では, 一般に実質国内総生産 (GDP) が2四半期連続でマイナス成長になると, 景気後退と見なされる。日本の場合は, 鉱工業生産指数や有効求人倍率などの経済指標に基づいて, 景気動向指数研究会が判定している。

recessionary 形 景気後退の
  recessionary (economic) conditions 景気停滞, 景気低迷
  recessionary data 景気後退を示す指標
  recessionary impulses 景気後退の兆し
  recessionary pressures 景気後退の圧力, 不況圧力
  recessionary year 景気後退の年
reclusive 形 孤立した
  reclusive state 孤立国家

recipient 名 受領者, 受取人, 受賞者, 受給者, 情報開示を受けた者, 容器
  aid recipient 援助受入れ国, 援助受入れ側, 援助を受ける側
  ODA recipient 政府開発援助 (ODA) 受入れ国
  profit recipient 利潤取得者 [受領者]
  recipient country 受入れ国, 被援助国
  recipient of charity 慈善給付受給者
  recipient of the assistance 支援先
  recipient of the benefits 受益者
  recipient of the secret information 秘密情報の開示を受けた者
  recipients of heart transplants 心臓移植患者, 心臓移植を受けた人々
  social security recipient 社会保障受給者
recognize 動 認識する, 判別 [識別] する, わかる, 認める, 承認する, 認可する, 認定する, 認知する, 評価する, 表彰する, 計上する, 費用処理する
recombinant DNA 組換えDNA
reconnaissance plane 偵察機
reconstruct 動 再建する, 再構築する, 立て直す, 再現する, 復元する, 改築する
reconstruction 名 再建, 復興, 復元, 再現, 改築
  corporate reconstruction plan 企業再建計画, 再建計画
  economic reconstruction plan 経済再建計画
  fiscal reconstruction 財政再建
  reconstruction plan 再建計画, 再建策
  the reconstruction of business 事業再構築, 経営再建
record 動 記録する, 記帳する, 計上する, 登記 [登録] する, 表示する, 示す, …となる
  be recorded net 純額で表示される
  record a further increase さらに上昇する
  record a small gain 小幅上昇する
  record an all-time low 過去最低を記録する, 過去最低を更新する
  record as a long-term investment 長期投資として計上する
record 名 記録, 最高記録, 最低記録, 過去最高, 過去最低, 過去最悪, 成績, 登記, 登録, 経歴, 履歴, 業績, 成績, 動向, データ, レコード盤, レコード
  academic record 学歴
  all-time record 歴代最高記録
  break the record 記録を破る, 記録を更新する
  chronological record 年代順の記録
  credit record 信用履歴

criminal record 犯罪歴, 前科
driving record 運転歴
estoppel by record 記録による禁反言
for the record 事実は, 公式には, 念のために言うと
hold the record 記録を持っている
medical record 病歴
monthly record 月間過去最高
off the record 非公式の, 非公開の, オフレコの
on record 記録上の, 過去の
put [get, keep, set] the record straight 誤解を解く, 記録を正す
record of discussion 討議議事録
shareholder [stockholder] of record 登録株主, 株主名簿上の株主
stock record date 株式の名義書換え停止日
track record 実績

record 形 記録的な, 過去最高の, 空前の, 史上初めての [史上初の], レコードの
record crop 豊作, 記録的収穫
record date 配当基準日, 基準日, 名義書換え停止日, 登録日 (= date of record)
record earnings 過去最高益, 過去最高の利益
record high 記録的な高さ, 空前の高さ, 過去最高, 過去最悪, 過去最多, 史上最高, 最高値
record low 記録的な低さ, 記録的な低水準, 空前の低さ, 過去最低, 過去最悪, 史上最低
record net profit 過去最高の純利益, 過去最高の税引き後利益 (= record-high net profit)
record plunge 過去最大の下げ, 過去最大の下落, 過去最大の物価下落
record profit 過去最高益, 過去最高の利益
record sales 過去最高の売上高

recover 動 回復する, 〈貸出金などを〉回収する, 〈債権などを〉取り立てる
▶ None of the loans were *recovered*. 融資額は全額, 回収されなかった。

recoverable 形 回復可能な
recoverable reserves 可採埋蔵量

recovery 名 回復, 景気回復, 〈景気や市場の〉持ち直し, 相場の回復, 回収, 再建, 復興
choke off a global recovery 世界の景気回復を妨げる
cost recovery 原価回収
cyclical economic recovery 景気回復 (= cycle recovery, cyclical recovery, economic recovery)
early recovery 早期回復

fragile recovery 足取りが弱い回復, 景気回復の足取りが弱い
full-fledged recovery 本格復調, 本格回復
incipient recovery 景気回復の局面, 回復局面, 景気持ち直しの局面
recoveries of write-offs 償却債権取立益
self-sustaining recovery 自律回復

recreational vehicle レジャー・カー《略 RV》

recross-examination 再反対尋問

recruit 動 募集する, 募る, 新規採用する, 採用する, 新会員 [新党員] を入れる, 雇い入れる, 補充する, 徴兵する, 補給する, 強化する, 補強する, 〈健康・体力を〉回復する

recruit 名 新入社員, 新入生, 新入会員, 新会員, 新参者, 新兵, 補充兵, リクルート

recruiting 名 募集, 新規採用, 採用, 補充, 徴兵, 回復 (= recruitment)
campus recruiting 新卒者募集
midcareer recruiting 中途採用
recruiting agent 募集機関, 採用機関
recruiting expenses 従業員採用費
recruiting office 徴兵事務所
recruiting officer 徴兵事務官
recruiting station 志願者受付局

recruitment 名 新規採用, 求人, 新入社員募集, 人員補充, 人材登用, 人材開発, リクルートメント
campus recruitment 新卒者募集, 学内での新規採用活動
hold back on recruitment 新規採用を抑える
in-house staff recruitment system 社内公募制度
mass recruitment 大量採用
personnel recruitment 人事採用, 人員補充
post recruitment notices 求人広告を掲示する

rectify 動 修正する, 訂正する, 是正する, 正す, 改正する, 矯正する, 調整する, 純化する, 精留する

recurrence 名 再発, 再燃, 反復, 繰り返し
recurrence of deflation デフレの再燃

recurring loss 経常赤字
▶ In its semiannual settlement of accounts in September, the company incurred ¥2.3 billion of *recurring losses* and ¥2.6 billion of after-tax losses. 9月の中間決算で, 同社は経常赤字が23億円, 税引き後損失も26億円に達した。

recurring profit 経常利益 (= current profit, income before extraordinary items)
「経常利益について ⇒ 売上高から販売・管理費を差

し引いた営業利益に, 預金の受取利息や保有株式の配当収入を加えたり, 借入金の支払い利息などを差し引いたりして計算。ただし, メーカーの工場売却や保有株式の売却による利益, リストラのための割増退職金の費用などは特別利益または特別損失と呼ばれ, 経常利益には含まれない。経常利益は, 日本では, 企業の業績や中長期的な業況を知るのに最も適した指標とされている。

recycle 動 再利用する, 再生利用する, 循環処理する, 循環使用する, 〈資金などを〉還流する, 〈利益などを〉還元する, 修復する, リサイクル

recycling 名 資源循環, 再生利用, 再利用, 循環使用, 還流, 還元, リサイクリング
- **recycling environmental technology** リサイクル環境技術
- **recycling fee** リサイクル費用, リサイクル費, リサイクル料金 (＝recycling cost)

red 名 赤字 (＝red ink)
- **fall into the red** 赤字に転落する, 赤字に落ち込む
- **in the red** 赤字で
- **out of the red** 赤字を脱して

red-carpet 形 丁重な, 手厚い, 盛大な, 貴賓用の
- **red-carpet treatment** 丁重な扱い, 手厚い配慮
- **red-carpet welcome** 盛大な歓迎, 丁重な歓迎
- **roll out the red carpet for** …を丁重にもてなす

red cent 1セント銅貨, びた一文, 少しも(…ない)

red-handed 形副 現行犯の[で], 現場で
- **arrest a thief red-handed** どろぼうを現行犯で逮捕する
- **be caught red-handed** 現行犯で捕らえられる, 現場を見つけられる
- **catch a person red-handed** 人を現行犯で[その場で]捕らえる

red ink 赤字 (＝red figure, red-ink figure)
- **bleeding red ink** 巨額の赤字
- **red-ink firm** 赤字企業, 赤字会社 (＝company in the red, money-losing company)

redeem 動 買い戻す, 〈社債や株式を〉償還する, 〈株式などを〉現金と交換する, 現金化する, 補填する, 埋め合わせる, 〈債務を〉弁済する, 〈抵当物を〉受け戻す, 取り戻す, 約束を実行する, 〈義務・約束を〉履行する, 〈名誉などを〉回復する
- **pay a ransom to redeem the hostage** 身代金を払って人質を取り戻す
- **redeem a bond** 公社債を償還する
- **redeem mortgaged land** 抵当に入れた土地を取り戻す
- **redeem for cash** 現金で償還する
- **redeem one's rights** 権利を回復する

redemption 名 〈株式などの〉償還, 買戻し, 請戻し, 回復, 補償, 救済, 解放, 救出, 約束の履行, 解約, 贖罪 (＝refundment, repayment)
- **beyond [past] redemption** 救い難い, 回復の見込みがない
- **bond redemption** 社債償還, 発行済み社債の買戻し, 債券の償還 (＝redemption of bonds)
- **debt redemption** 債券償還, 負債償還
- **early redemption penalty** 早期償還罰則金
- **extension of redemption** 償還延長
- **in the year of our redemption 2010** 西暦2010年に
- **loan redemption** 借入金償還
- **national bonds with a 10-year period of redemption** 10年間償還付き国債
- **purchasing redemption** 買入れ償還 (＝redemption by purchase)
- **redemption date** 償還日
- **redemption gain** 償還差益
- **redemption sources** 償還財源
- **redemption yield** 償還利回り
- **stock redemption** 株式償還

redenomination 名 通貨単位の呼称変更, 券面額の変更, デノミ, デノミネーション (＝currency redenomination, renaming monetary units)
- **carry out [introduce] currency redenomination** デノミを実施する
- **downward redenomination** 呼称の下方変更, デノミ
- **upward redenomination** 呼称の上方変更

redeployment 名 配置転換, 再配備, 再配置, 配置替え, 〈工場施設の〉移動, 〈工場施設の〉改善, 有効利用, 移動, 転進

redlining 名 赤線引き, 〈米金融機関の〉貧民地区への融資拒否, 差別, 差別的慣行, 除外

redress 動 是正する, 〈不正などを〉正す, 改めさせる, 矯正する, 直す, 除く, 〈損害などを〉償う, 補償する, 救う, 救済する, 〈均衡などを〉取り戻す
- **redress grievances** 不平を取り除く[取り去る]
- **redress social evils** 社会悪を正す, 社会悪を取り除く, 社会悪を矯正する

redress the balance between A and B AとBの均衡を取り戻す

redress wrongs 不正を正す, 不正を直す

redress 名 賠償, 補償, 救済, 救済策, 矯正, 是正, 除去, 取戻し

redress of the bilateral trade imbalance 2国間の貿易不均衡の是正

seek redress at the district court 地方裁判所に賠償を請求する

reduce 動 減らす, 削減する, 低下させる, 押し下げる, 引き下げる, 下げる, 減少させる, 低減する, 緩和する, 軽減する, 解消する, 控除する, 短縮する

reduce capital 減資する

reduce gearing 負債比率を引き下げる

reduce inventories 在庫を圧縮する

reduce investment 投資を抑制する

reduce overhead costs 製造間接費を削減する, 経費を切り詰める

reduce the profitability 収益性を低下させる

reduced 形 減少した, 縮小した, 軽減した, 削減した, 落ち込んだ, 切り詰めた, 落ちぶれた, 還元した

reduced profit margins 利益率の低下

reduced reproduction 縮小再生産

reduced rate loan 低利融資

reduced sales 販売低下, 販売の落ち込み, 売上高の減少

reduced sampling inspection 緩和抜取り検査

reduction 名 削減, 軽減, 圧縮, 短縮, 引き下げ, 縮小, 低下

capital reduction 減資, 資本金の減額（＝capital decrease, reduction of [in] capital, reduction of capital stock）

reduction of operation 操業短縮

reduction of rates 金利引下げ, 利下げ

redundancy 名 解雇, 一時解雇, レイオフ, 余剰, 余剰人員, 人員過剰, 被解雇者, 割増退職金, 失業

reelect 動 再選する, 再任する

reelection 名 再選, 再任

run for reelection 再選をめざして出馬する

seek reelection 再選をめざす

win reelection 再選される, 再選を勝ち取る

reemergence 名 再来, 再出現, 再登場

the reemergence of economic deterioration 再度の経済悪化

the reemergence of large external imbalances 大幅な対外不均衡の再来

reemployment 名 再雇用, 再就職

Reemployment Act of 1994 1994年再雇用法

reemployment of retired workers 雇用延長, 退職した従業員の再雇用

reemployment opportunity 再雇用機会

reengineering 名 業務革新, 業務の根本的革新, リエンジニアリング（＝business process reengineering, business reengineering）

business process reengineering 業務革新, 業務改革

reentry 名 再入国, 再突入, 再入学［入社, 出場, 登場］, リエントリー

reentry vehicle 〈宇宙ロケットやミサイルの〉地球大気圏再突入部分, ミサイルの弾頭

reevaluate 動 再評価する, 再検討する, 見直す

reference 名 参考, 参照, 参照番号, 照会, 照会番号, 照会人, 身元保証, 問合せ, 問合せ先, 委託, 付託, 関連, 関係, 参考人, 参考文献, 言及, 論及

reference value for inflation インフレ参照値（＝an inflation guideline）

referendum 名 住民投票, 国民投票

by referendum 国民投票で

call a referendum 国民投票を求める

hold [have] a referendum on …について国民投票を実施する

referral sales plan ネズミ講式販売法, ネズミ講商法, マルチ商法, 連鎖配当組織

refinancing 名 借換え, 資金の再調達, 再融資, リファイナンス（＝refinance, refunding）

reflagging 名 船籍変更

reflate 動 〈通貨などを〉再膨張させる, 〈通貨供給量の増加により〉経済を活発にする, 通貨再膨張政策を取る

reflate the economy 景気浮揚を図る

reflation 名 通貨再膨張, 統制インフレ, リフレーション（インフレにもデフレにもならない程度に通貨を増やすこと）

reflation policy 景気浮揚策, リフレーション政策（不況打開策として, 減税や金利引下げ, 公共投資などにより景気の回復を図ること）

reflationary 形 通貨再膨張の, 統制インフレ的な, リフレ的な

reflationary impact 景気刺激効果

reflationary measures 景気浮揚策, 景気対策（＝reflation measures）

reflationary package 一連の景気刺激策, 一連のリフレーション政策

reflect 動 反映する, 表す, 示す, 記載する, 反映させる, 織り込む, 組み入れる, 適用する

be reflected in prices 価格に反映される
be reflected in the current share price 現在の株価に織り込まれている（=be reflected in the current valuation of the stock）

reform 動 改革する, 改正する, 改善する, 矯正する, 改心させる, 改める

reform 名 改革, 改正, 改善, 革新, 矯正, リフォーム
  health care reform 医療制度改革
  regulatory reform 規制改革

reformer 名 改革者, 改革派, 改革論者, 改革支持者, 改良者

reformist 名 革新主義者, 改革主義者, 形 革新主義の, 革新主義者の
  reformist and conservative camps 革新陣営と保守陣営

reformulated gasoline 組成変更ガソリン

refrain from 慎む, 差し控える, 自粛する, 遠慮する, 我慢する, 自制する, こらえる, 止める
  refrain from comment コメントを差し控える
  refrain from tears 涙をこらえる

refresh 動 元気づける, 活気づける, 活発にする, 元気を回復する, 再び元気づく, 新たにする, 一新する, 更新する

refueling activity 給油活動（=refueling mission）

refuge 名 避難, 逃避, 保護, 避難所, 隠れ家, 保護施設, 逃げ場, 逃げ道, 頼り, 手段, 方便,〈道路の〉安全地帯（safety island, traffic island）
  capital refuge 資本逃避
  give refuge to …を保護する
  house of refuge 養育院, 保護施設
  strong refuge 安定した拠り所
  take [seek] refuge in …に避難する, …して難を逃れる
  take refuge in books 本に安らぎを求める
  take refuge in telling lies 嘘をついてその場を逃れる
  wildlife refuge 野生動物保護区

refugee 名 難民, 避難民, 避難者, 亡命者, 逃亡者
  Convention Relating to the Status of Refugees 難民条約
  disguised refugees 偽装難民
  Office of the United Nations High Commissioner for Refugees 国連難民高等弁務官事務所
  Palestinian refugees パレスチナ難民
  port of refugee 避難港
  refugee capital 国外逃避資金（=hot money）
  refugees from political persecution 政治的迫害亡命者
  repatriation of Cambodian refugees カンボジア難民の本国送還
  U.N. High Commission on Refugees 国連難民高等弁務官事務所
  United Nations High Commissioner for Refugees 国連難民高等弁務官

refund 動 払い戻す, 返済する, 還付する, 弁済する, 借り換える, 償還する（=repay）
  advance-refunded issues 事前借換え債
  be refunded pro rata 一定比率払い戻される
  have one's money refunded 金を払い戻してもらう

refund 名 返済, 払戻し,〈税金の〉還付, 弁済, 弁償, 返済金, 弁済金, 借換え（=repayment）
  claim [demand] a full refund 全額払い戻しを請求する
  customs duty refund system 関税還付制度
  receive [get] a tax refund 税金の還付を受ける
  refund of duties 税の還付, 戻し税
  submit refund claims 還付請求書を提出する
  withholding tax refund 源泉税還付

refunding 名 借換え, 払戻し,〈税金などの〉還付, 償還, 国債入札
  advance refunding 期前償還
  bond refunding 社債借換え, 社債の借換え（発行済み社債の償還資金を得るため, 新規社債を発行して相互交換すること）
  debt refunding 債務借換え, 債務の借換え
  issuance of refunding bonds 借換え債の発行
  May refunding 5月の定例国債入札, 5月の定期国債入札
  quarterly refunding 米国債四半期入札, 米国債の四半期定例入札
  refunding bond 借換え債

refurbishment 名 改装, リフォーム, 一新

regain 動 取り戻す, 回復する, 奪い返す, 戻る
  regain confidence 自信を取り戻す
  regain credibility 信頼を回復する
  regain one's feet [footing, legs] 起き上がる, 立ち直る
  regain the upper hand of 再び…より優勢になる, 再び…に勝つ

regenerative medical techniques
再生医療
regime 名 政権, 政体, 政府, 体制, 制度, 食餌療法, 厳しい訓練, レジーム
  Communist [communist] regime 共産党政権
  financial regime 金融制度, 金融体系
  high tax regime 高率税制
  military regime 軍事政権, 軍事体制, 軍政
  monetary regime 金融体制
  regime change 体制転換, 制度的変化
regional 形 地域の, 地域的な, 地域全体の, 地方の, 局地の, 局所の, 局部的な
  be selected in regional preliminaries 地方予選で選出される
  regional distribution 地域的分布
  regional economic partnership 地域経済連携, 地域経済連携協定
  regional expansion policy 地域開発政策
  regional government 地方自治体
  regional imbalance 地域的不均衡
  regional integration 地域統合, 地域的統合, 域内統合
  regional monopoly 地域独占
  regional tax 地方税
regionwide agreement 地域協定
register 動 登録する, 登記する, 届け出る, 正式に記録する, 示す, 表す, 書留にする
regular 形 一定の, 不変の, 規則正しい, 秩序正しい, 正規の, 正式の, 本職の, 定期的な, 定期の, 定例の, 習慣的な, 常連の, 通常の, いつもの, 一般の, 並みの, 普通の, 標準サイズの, 完全な, まぎれもない, 感じのいい, 均整のとれた, 整った, 〈党の〉公認の, レギュラー
  regular army [forces] 正規軍
  regular candidate 公認候補
  regular checkup 定期健診
  regular customers 常連客, 顧客
  regular Diet session 通常国会
  regular habits 規則正しい習慣
  regular income 定期収入, 定期的な収入
  regular member 正会員
  regular solid 多面体
  regular staff 正社員
  regular students 一般の生徒
  regular worker 正規雇用者, 正社員 (=regular employee)
regulate 動 規制する, 取り締まる, 統制する, 調整する, 調節する

non-regulated company 規制対象外の企業
regulated company 規制対象企業
regulated industry 規制を受ける業界
regulated market 規制市場, 市場の規制
regulation 名 規則, 規定, 規程, 規制, 統制, 統括, 管理, 調節, 調整, 法規, 法令, 行政規則, 通達, レギュレーション
  automatic regulation 自動調節作用
  comprehensive regulation 包括規制
  financial regulations 金融規制
  fire regulations 火災防止規則
  organization regulation 組織規程
  regulation on exhaust gas and noise emission 排ガス騒音規制
  regulation on total emissions 排ガスの総量規制
  relaxed regulations 規制の緩和 (=relaxation of regulations)
  rules and regulations 規約
  safety regulations 安全規則
  SEC regulations SECの規制
  self-regulation 自主規制
  severance (benefit) regulation 退職手当規則
  temporary regulations 暫定通達
  traffic regulations 交通法規, 交通規則
regulators 名 規制当局, 規制機関, 規制責任者
  antitrust regulators 独占禁止規制当局, 反トラスト規制当局
  banking regulators 銀行規制当局
  federal and state regulators 連邦・州規制当局
  financial regulators 金融当局
  government regulators 規制当局
  securities regulators 証券業務規制当局, 証券規制機関
  self-regulators 自主規制機関
  U.S. federal antitrust regulators 米連邦反トラスト規制当局
regulatory 形 規制上の, 法規制の, 規制当局の, 監督当局の, 取り締まる
  minimum regulatory capital requirements 会社設立時の最低必要資本金規制
  regulatory agency [authority, body] 規制機関, 規制当局, 取締り機関, 監督機関, 調整機関
  regulatory approval 規制当局の認可
  regulatory barriers 規制の障壁, 規制上の障害
  regulatory capital adequacy 自己資本比率規制 (=regulatory capital adequacy require-

ments）
regulatory requirements 規制上の要件［条件］，規制基準
regulatory tax 経済活動調整税
self-regulatory organization 自主規制機関
rehabilitate 動 復帰させる，回復させる，復興させる，再生する，復興する，修復する，リハビリを施す，社会復帰させる，〈犯罪者などを〉更生させる
rehabilitation 名 〈信用などの〉回復，修復，再建，再興，復興，健全化，更生，復権，復職，復位，社会復帰，リハビリ
　Civil Rehabilitation Law 民事再生法
　corporate rehabilitation funds 企業再建ファンド
　Corporate Rehabilitation Law 会社更生法
　economic rehabilitation 経済復興
　file for court-protected rehabilitation 会社更生法の適用を申請する
　fiscal rehabilitation 財政再建 （＝fiscal reconstruction, fiscal restructuring）
　rehabilitation of juvenile delinquents 非行少年の更生
　rehabilitation of the physically handicapped 身体障害者の更生，身体障害者の社会復帰
　self-rehabilitation 自主再建
rehabilitation plan 再建計画，再生計画，経営健全化計画 （＝restructuring plan）
> **経営健全化計画とは** ⊃ 経営健全化計画とは，公的資金による資本注入を申請する金融機関が，金融庁に提出を義務付けられている経営計画のことをいう。これには，財務状況や収益の向上策，公的資金の返済原資確保の仕方などのほかに，役員数や従業員数，役員報酬，人件費などの合理化策を明示しなければならない。

rehire 動 再雇用する
reign 動 支配する，君臨する，優位を築く，優勢である，あたり一面に広がる，はびこる，みなぎる，名 統治，支配，時代，治世
reimburse 動 返済する，弁済する，償還する，払い戻す，返還する，補償する，弁償する，賠償する
rein 名 手綱，統率，統括，管理，制御，拘束，統率力，拘束力，支配権，指揮権，統制権，制御手段，統制手段
　assume [hold, retain] the reins of government 政権を握る，政権を取る
　be kept under a tight rein 厳しい統制の下に置かれる
　draw in the reins 手綱を引く，速力を弱める
　drop the reins of government 政権を失う，政権を捨てる
　gather the reins into one's hands 采配を振るう，きりもりする
　hold the reins of government for a long time 政権を長期間担当する
　loosen [let go] the reins 手綱を緩める
　pull up [gather up] one's reins 手綱を引き締める
　take the reins 支配権を取る
　take [pick] up the reins 主導権を握る
rein in 統括する，管理する，統制する，規制する，制御する，抑制する，抑える
reinforce 動 強化する，増強する，補強する，強固なものにする，強める，促進する
reinforcement 名 強化，増強，補強，促進，補強材，補給品，援軍，増援隊，増援部隊
　capital reinforcement 資本増強
　reinforcement of control 規制強化
reinventing government 行政革命
reinvention 名 再発明，作り直し，出直し
reinvigorate 動 …を再び元気づける，再び活力を与える，再活性化する
▶ Expanding cooperation among the sectors of agriculture, commerce and industry should *reinvigorate* these primary industries and boost tourism. 農商工間の連携拡大で，これらの一次産業は再活性化し，観光も活気づくはずだ。
REIT 不動産投資信託 （real estate investment trustの略）
reiterate 動 繰り返す，反復する，繰り返して主張する，主張を繰り返す，…と念を押す
reject 動 拒否する，拒絶する，否認する，否決する，否定する，棄却する
rejection 名 拒否，拒絶，否認，否決，否定，棄却，却下，拒絶反応，廃棄，廃棄物
　incorrect rejection 過誤棄却
　rejection or disposal 拒絶または処分
　rejection slip 〈原稿や論文の〉不採用通知
rejuvenate 動 若返らせる，若返りを図る，活気づける，活気づかせる，新品の状態に戻す
related 形 関係［関連］のある，関連した，同族の，同種の，…関連の
　related obligations 関連債務
　related papers 関係書類
　related parties 関連当事者，利害関係者
　related stories 関連記事

retirement-related benefits 退職関連給付
transaction-related contingencies 取引関連偶発債務, つて

relations 名 関係, 広報, リレーションズ
bilateral relations 両国関係, 二国間関係
capital and business relations with …との資本・業務関係
employer-employee relations 雇用者対従業員の関係
functional relations 職能関係, 関数関係
human relations 人間関係
interindustry relations table 産業連関表
investor relations 対投資家関係, 投資家向け広報, 財務広報, インベスター・リレーションズ《略 IR》
strategic and mutually beneficial relations 戦略的互恵関係

relationship 名 関係, 関連, 結びつき, 取引先
arm's length relationship 商業ベースの取引関係
build a better relationship 友好的な関係を築く, 関係を改善する
causal relationship 因果関係
collaborative relationship 協力関係
contractual relationship 契約関係
currency relationships 為替相場, 為替レート
debtor-creditor relationship 債権者・債務者関係, 債権債務関係
financial relationship 財務比率
functional relationship 関係関数
inter-industrial relationship 産業連関
interperiod relationship 期間相互の関係
invariant relationship 恒常的関係
legal relationship 法的関係
mutually beneficial strategic relationship 戦略的互恵関係
principal-agent relationship 本人と代理人の関係
relationship management 取引先総合管理, 関係性経営《略 RM》
relationship marketing リレーションシップ・マーケティング (データ・マイニング技術を駆使した分析で, 顧客戦略の策定を支援するもの)
symbiotic relationship 共生関係, もちつもたれつの関係
vertical and horizontal human relationships 縦と横の人間関係
▶ The growing stress is being felt by younger generations in relation to work and personal *relationships*. 若い世代では, 仕事や人間関係でストレスを抱えている人が増大している。

relax 動 緩める, 和らげる, 緩和する, …の力を抜く, くつろがせる, リラックスさせる
in a relaxed posture くつろいだ格好で
relax discipline 規律を緩める
relax one's muscles 筋肉の凝りをほぐす, 力を抜く
relax restrictions on exports 輸出規制を緩和する
relax the criteria 基準を緩める

relaxation 名 緩和, 軽減, 引下げ, 〈筋肉の〉弛緩, ゆるみ, 気晴らし, レクリエーション
credit relaxation 信用緩和, 利下げ
credit relaxation policy 信用緩和政策
monetary relaxation 金融緩和
qualified relaxation 条件付き緩和
quantitative monetary relaxation 量的金融緩和, 量的緩和
relaxation of import restrictions 輸入規制[制限]緩和
relaxation of underwriting standards 与信規準の緩和, 貸出審査基準の緩和
significant [substantial] relaxation 大幅緩和

release 動 発売する, 販売する, 公表する, 発表する, 公開する, 〈情報を〉開示する, 〈映画を〉封切る, 解放する, 放出する, 〈資金を〉捻出[調達]する, 〈借金などを〉免除する, 〈権利などを〉放棄する, 〈財産を〉譲渡する, 釈放する, 解放する, リリースする
release all claims to property 財産請求権をすべて放棄する
release funds 資金を捻出する, 資金を調達する
release one's liens on assets 資産に対する先取特権を解除する

release 名 発売, 販売, 公表, 発表, 公開, 〈情報の〉開示, 封切り, 解放, 放出, 〈資金の〉捻出[調達], 〈契約の〉解除, 〈借金・債務の〉免除, 免責, 責任免除, 〈権利の〉放棄, 〈財産の〉譲渡, 釈放, リリース
deed of release 権利放棄証書
economic releases 景気指標, 景気指標の発表
financial reporting release 財務報告通牒
legal release 法的免除
mutual release from liability 義務の相互免除
news release ニュース発表, ニュース・リリース
press release 新聞発表, 報道用公式発表, プレス・リリース

release copy 公表予告, 予告記事, 新刊見本
release from debts 債務免除
release of obligations 義務履行の免除
release of security 担保解除
release of the new job numbers 雇用統計の発表
release order 船積み命令, 引渡し指図書, リリース・オーダー
release permit 収容貨物解除許可
release price 放出価格
unemployment release 失業統計
reliability 名 信頼, 信頼性, 信頼度, 確実性
automobile reliability survey 自動車信頼度調査
product reliability 製品[商品]の信頼性
reliability survey 信頼度調査
reliable 形 信頼できる, 信用できる, 期待どおりの, 頼りになる, 安定した, 確かな
reliable source of information 確かな情報源
reliable sources 信頼できる筋, 信頼できる情報筋, 確かな情報源
reliance 名 依存, 依存度, 信頼, 信用, 頼り
act in reliance on …をあてにして行動する
put [have, place] reliance on …を信頼する, …に信頼を置く, …をあてにする, …に依存する
rate of reliance on bond issues 国債依存度
reliance on debt 借入依存
reliance on debt financing 外部負債に対する依存度
reliance on overseas markets 海外市場への依存
relief 名 安心, 安堵, 気晴らし, 息抜き, 救済, 救助, 救援, 緩和, 軽減, 除去, 控除, 救援金, 救援[救済]物資, 給付金, 生活保護手当, 〈職務からの〉解放, 職務の交代[交替要員], 更迭, 代行者, 浮き彫り, 浮き彫り細工, レリーフ, 鮮明さ, 明瞭さ, リリーフ
debt relief 債務救済, 債務削減 (＝debt forgiveness)
disaster relief 災害復旧, 災害復旧事業, 災害救援, 災害救援金
double taxation relief 外国税額控除
find relief 安堵する, ほっとする, 好感する
price relief 物価が落ち着くこと
provide some relief from stress ストレスをある程度和らげる[軽減する]
public relief 公共の救済基金
regulatory relief 規制の適用除外
relief agency 援助機関
relief loan 救済融資
relief road 迂回道路, 迂回路, バイパス
relief supplies 救援物資 (＝relief goods)
relief worker 救援[救出]活動家
relief works 失業対策事業
tax relief 免税, 減税, 税額免除, 税負担の軽減, 税金の減免
tax relief measures 税金の減免措置
temporary relief 一時救済
the hepatitis-relief law 肝炎対策法
U.K. stock relief 〈英国税法の〉棚卸し資産税額控除
reluctant 形 気が進まない, 気乗りしない, 二の足を踏む, 嫌々ながらの, …に消極的な, …には慎重な
rely on …に頼る, …に依存する, …をあてにする, …を信頼する
relocate 動 移す, 移動する, 移転する, 移設する, 再配置する, 配置転換する (＝deploy)
relocation 名 移動, 移転, 移住, 立地変更, 移設, 再配置, 配置転換 (＝redeployment)
employee relocation 従業員再配置, 従業員の配置転換
personnel relocation 人事配置転換
relocation allowance 引っ越し手当
relocation of production facilities 生産拠点の移設[移転]
remain 動 …のままである, まだ…されないままだ, 依然として…だ, …から抜け出していない, 引き続き…だ, 今後も…だ, …で推移する, 根強い
remain at high levels 高水準で推移している, 高水準で推移する
remain bullish 強気の見方を変えない
remain competitive 競争力を維持する
remaining 形 残りの, 残存する
remark 名 発言, 意見, 所信, 感想, 一言, 論評, 批評, 話, 注意, 注目
be worthy of remark 注目に値する
make the opening remarks 開会の言葉を述べる
pass [make] a remark about [on] …について所見を述べる, …について一言言う, …を批評する
remedy 名 対応策, 対策, 改善法, 薬, 治療, 治療法, 治療薬, 療法, 処方箋, 救済, 救済方法, 救済手段, 救済措置, 措置, 補償, 権利回復手段
civil remedy 民事上の救済手段

court remedies 訴訟による救済方法
effective remedy 特効薬
equitable remedy 衡平法上の救済, エクイティ上の救済
injunctive remedy 差止命令による救済, 差止めによる救済
legal remedy 法律上の救済方法, 法的救済, 法的救済手段, 法的救済措置
trade remedies 貿易救済措置

remind 動 思い出させる, 注意する, 念を押す

reminder 名 催促状, 記念品, 助言, 注意

remit 動 送達する, 納付する, 支払う, 送る, 送金する, 軽減する, 緩和する, 緩める, 免除する, 許す, 延ばす(put off), 延期する, 〈…まで〉持ち越す, 譲渡する, 元の状態に戻す[回復する], 差し戻す, 〈…の決定・判断に〉任せる
 remit all one's school fees …の授業料を全額免除する
 remit by post 郵便で送金する
 remit by return of post 折り返し送金する
 remit $5 million dollars to A Aに500万ドルを支払う
 remit one's efforts 努力を怠る
 remit one's watchfulness [vigilance] 警戒を緩める
 remit payment by check 小切手で支払い金を送る
 remit taxes to half the amount 税金を半額に軽減する[免じる], 税金を半減する
 remit the matter to the decision of 問題を…の判断[決定]に任せる

remittance 名 送金, 外国送金, 送金額, 送金高
 cash remittance 現金送金
 remittance advice 送金通知書
 remittance bill 送金為替
 remittance check 送金小切手
 remittance fees 送金手数料, 振込み手数料

remodel 動 改造する, 改装する, 改築する, 作り直す, 作り変える, 模様替えする, モデルチェンジする

remorse 名 深い後悔, 後悔の念, 悔恨, 良心の呵責, 自責の念, 罪悪感, 憐れみ, 同情
 express remorse 自責の念を表す
 feel remorse for [at] one's fault 過失を後悔する
 feelings of remorse 自責の念
 in remorse for …を後悔して
 show no signs of remorse 改悛の情がない
 without remorse 情け容赦なく, 冷酷に

remote 形 遠く離れた, 遠隔の, 遠い, 〈態度が〉よそよそしい
 remote access data processing system 遠隔アクセス・データ処理装置
 remote batch entry 遠隔一括入力, 遠隔バッチ入力
 remote communication 遠隔通信
 remote control 遠隔制御, 遠隔操作, 遠隔操縦, リモート・コントロール, リモコン
 remote manipulator system 遠隔操作用ロボット腕, 遠隔作業アーム, シャトル・ロボットアーム
 remote sensing 遠隔探知, 遠隔感知測定, リモート・センシング
 remote sensor 遠隔感知測定器, リモート・センサー
 remote work 遠隔勤務, 在宅勤務 (＝telecommuting, telework, teleworking)

remuneration 名 報酬, 給料, 代償, 報償, 謝礼, 対価
 monetary remuneration 金銭的報酬
 officers' remuneration 役員報酬
 remuneration package 報酬, 給付, 謝礼, 代償, 報償

renew 動 更新する, 継続する, 〈期間などを〉延長する, 〈手形や書類を〉書き換える, 再契約する, 再生する, 再開する, 繰り返す, 取り替える, 新たに補充する, 〈記憶や若さ, 力などを〉取り戻す[回復する]
 renew a subscription to a magazine 雑誌の購読期間を延長する, 雑誌購読の予約を継続する (＝renew a magazine subscription)
 renew an agreement 契約を更新する
 renew an attack 攻撃を再開する
 renew [resume] financial support to …に対する財政支援を再開する
 renew one's driving license [licence] 運転免許を更新する (＝renew one's driver's license)
 renew the memories of …の記憶をよみがえらせる
 renew the record low for the year 年初来の安値を更新する

renewable 形 更新できる, 再生できる
 renewable energy 再生可能エネルギー, 自然エネルギー
 renewable fuel 再生可能燃料

renewal 名 刷新, 更新, 書換え, 書換え継続, 期限延長, 自動継続, 再開, 再生, 復活, 回復, 再燃, 再開発, リニューアル

renewed 形 更新した, 新たになった, 回復した, 〈元気などを〉取り戻した, …の更新, …の再燃, …の再発, 再び…する
  come under renewed selling pressure 再び売り圧力を受ける
  make a renewed effort 新たな努力をする
  renewed bill 更新手形, 手形の更新
  renewed concern over …に対する懸念が再び高まること
  renewed recession 不況の再燃, 不況への逆戻り
  renewed slide in currency 再び通貨が下落すること, 通貨の下落トレンドへの逆戻り
  renewed tightening of monetary conditions 金融引締め[金融政策引締め]への転換
  with renewed enthusiasm 熱意を新たにして
renminbi 名 人民元, 人民幣《略 RMB [rmb]》
renovation 名 修理, 修復作業, 修復, 修繕, 改装, 更新, 刷新, 革新, 最新設備の導入
▶ Financial burdens are expected to sharply rise in the mid-to long-term due to rapid aging of the population and *renovation* of public facilities. 急速な高齢化や公共施設の更新で, 中長期的には, 財政負担の急増が見込まれる.
rental store レンタル店 (＝rental shop)
reorganization 名 再編成, 再編, 改造, 改組, 改革, 再生, 再建, 会社再建, 事業再編, 組織変更, 会社更生 (＝realignment, standardization)
  capital reorganization 資本再編
  corporate reorganization 会社更生, 企業再編
  debt reorganization 債務再構成
  financial reorganization 金融再編
  reorganization bond 整理社債
  reorganization of the industry 業界再編, 業界再編成
reorganize 動 再編成する, 再編する, 改造する, 改組する, 改革する, 再生する, 再建する, 組織変更する
repay 動 返済する, 払い戻す, 返金する, 返還する
repayment 名 返済, 払戻し, 返金
  repayment of debt 債務返済, 債務の支払い, 借入金返済額
repercussion 名 〈間接的な〉影響, 反動, 反響, 波及, 〈事件の〉余波, 跳ね返り, 反射, 反作用, 反撃, 撃退
  chain repercussion 連鎖的影響
  industrial repercussion 産業波及
  political repercussions 政治的影響
  repercussion effect 波及効果
  repercussion study 反作用研究
  suffer the repercussion of …の煽りを受ける
  technological repercussion 技術的波及
replace 動 取り替える, 置き換える, …と交替する, …の後を継ぐ, …の後任となる, …に取って代わる
replacement 名 取替え, 再調達, 再取得, 〈カードなどの〉再発行, 後任者, 後継者, 交換, 交換要員, 代替, 代替品, 返済, 返却, 復職
  card replacement カード再発行
  replacement demand 買換え需要, 設備更新需要
  replacement energy source 代替エネルギー, 代替エネルギー源
  replacement investment 更新投資, 取替え投資, 補填投資
  stock replacement 株式入れ替え
replanting 名 植林
report 動 報告する, 伝える, 報道する, 取材する, 公表する, 発表する, 通報する, 届け出る, 表示する, 計上する, 〈…の〉監督下にある, 直属する
  report back to …に(折り返し)報告する, 〈調査後に〉…に報告する
  report directly to …の直属である, …の監督下にある
  report for work [duty] 出社する, 出勤する
  report heavy losses 巨額の損失を計上する
  report out a bill 法案を修正条項付きで(討議と投票のため)本会議に戻す
  report the allowance for bad debts 貸倒れ引当金を設定する
  report to the police 警察に出頭する, 警察に通報する[届け出る]
report 名 報告, 報告書, 申告書, 報道, レポート
  annual report 年次報告書, 年報, アニュアル・レポート
  audit report 監査報告書
  business report 営業報告書, 事業報告書, ビジネス・レポート
  funding report 収支報告書
  half-year report 半期報告書, 中間事業報告書
  import and export report 輸出入申告書
  interim financial report 中間財務報告, 中間財務報告書
  management report 経営者報告, 経営者からのご報告
  midterm report 中間報告, 中間決算
  preliminary report 速報, 速報値

press report 新聞報道
quarterly report 四半期報告書, 四季報
report stage 〈英議会での〉報告審議
status report 現状報告, 現況報告

reportedly 副 報道によると, 伝えられるところによれば, 評判では, 噂によると, …という, …したそうだ, …と言われる
▶ In the past decade, the number of obstetricians and gynecologists *reportedly* has declined by 10 percent. 過去10年で, 産婦人科医の数は1割減ったと言われる.
▶ The ruling was *reportedly* the first ever to suspend ongoing merger talks between financial institutions. 継続中の金融機関の統合交渉を差し止める決定は, 前例がないという.

reporter 名 記者, 取材記者, 報道記者, ニュース・レポーター, 通信員, 通報者, 報告者, 情報提供者, 議事記録係, 速記係, レポーター
　a financial reporter 経済記者
　a newspaper reporter 新聞記者, ニュース・レポーター

reporting 名 報告, 表示
　reporting period 報告期間, 決算報告期間, 財務報告期間, 報告事業年度(文脈に応じて[当期]や「当四半期」を指す場合もある)
　reporting quarter 当四半期, 報告四半期

represent 動 表示する, 表明する, 意味する, 示す, …を表章する, …を表す, …の代理をつとめる, …を代表する, …を代行する, …に相当する, …に当たる
▶ An aggregate market value *represents* a corporate value in terms of stock price. 時価総額は, 株価による企業価値を示す.

representative 名 代表者, 代理人, 代行者, 国会議員, 〈米〉下院議員, 〈日本の〉衆議院議員, 事務所, 駐在員事務所, セールスマン, 販売員, 外務員, 駐在員, 担当者, 見本, 例, 典型, 形 代表的な, 典型的な, 代理の, 代表の
　account representative 証券会社のセールスマン
　act as one's representative at court 法廷で…の代理人を務める
　diplomatic representative 外交官
　duly authorized representative 正式に権限を与えられた代表[代表者, 代理人]
　House of Representatives 〈米〉下院, 〈日本の〉衆議院
　legal representative 法律上の代理者(法定代理人や遺言執行者など), 管財人, 遺産管理人
　Office of the United States Trade Representative 合衆国通商代表部, 米通商代表部
　registered representative 登録販売員, 登録取引会員
　representative action 株主の代表訴訟, 集団訴訟
　representative capacity 代表の資格
　representative company [firm] 幹事会社, 代表的企業
　representative democracy 代議民主制, 間接民主制
　representative for [of] the organization 組織の代表者
　representative government 代議政体, 代議政治
　representative of …を表す, 表現する, 象徴する
　representative office 駐在員事務所, 在外公館, 代表部
　representative rate for …の中心相場, 代表レート
　representative sample [example] 典型的な例
　representative sampling 代表標本抽出
　representative underwriter 代表引受会社
　sales representative 販売外交員, 販売担当者, 販売員
　the U.S. representative to the United Nations 国連への米国代表

representative director 代表取締役
> 代表取締役とは ⊃ 対外的に会社を代表する権限を与えられた取締役のことで, 取締役会で選任され, 株主総会や取締役会の決議を執行する. 人数に上限はないが, 1人以上必要. 他社との契約や訴訟行為の際には, 代表取締役の決済が不可欠となっている.

repression 名 抑圧, 弾圧, 抑止, 制止, 抑止, 〈暴動などの〉鎮圧

repressive 形 抑圧的な, 弾圧的な, 抑圧する, 抑制する
　repressive policy 抑圧的な政策
　repressive rule 弾圧統治

reprimand 動 懲戒する, 戒告する, 叱責する, 名 懲戒, 戒告, 叱責

reprocess 動 再処理する

reprocessing 名 再処理
> 再処理とは ⊃ 原子炉で燃焼させた使用済み燃料棒からプルトニウムを抽出する工程. 最初に, 短く切断した燃料棒を溶解槽に入れ, 硝酸溶液で溶かして被覆管を除去. 別の装置に移して核分裂生成物を

取り除いた後，ウランとプルトニウムを分離し，不純物を取り除く。こうして抽出されるプルトニウム含有量90％以上の兵器級プルトニウムは，核爆弾の原料として軍事利用できる。プルトニウムをウランと混ぜて原子力発電の燃料として再利用することも可能。（2003年7月12日付読売新聞から引用）

reprocessing plant 再処理工場
reproductive 形 生殖の, 再生産の
  reproductive medicine 生殖医療
  reproductive technology 生殖技術
republican 形 共和制の, 共和主義の, 〈米〉共和党の(Republican), 共和党支持の, 共和国の, 名 〈米〉共和党員 (⇒democratic)
  Republican 米共和党員 (＝Rep.)
  Republican administration 共和党政権
  Republican leadership 共和党指導部
  republican opinions 共和主義
  Republican Party 米共和党（GOP, G.O.P.は通称で Grand Old Partyの略）
Republicans 名 〈米〉共和党
  Republicans in Congress 議会共和党
repurchase 動 買い戻す, 再購入する （＝buy back）
  repurchasing government bonds 国債現先オペレーション
repurchase 名 買戻し, 再調達
reputation 名 評価, 名声, 地位, 信望, 知名度, 評判, 名誉, イメージ
▶ Courts have handed down decisions that emphasized the importance of an individual's *reputation* and privacy. 一連の裁判では，個人の名誉やプライバシーを重視する判断が示されている。
request 名 要求, 請求, 求め, 需要, 要望, 要請, 依頼, 頼みごと, 嘆願, 請託, 委任, 要求書, 要請書, 請願書, 依頼書［依頼文］, 委任, リクエスト
  at the request of …の請求により，…の要請を受けて
  be in great request 大いに需要がある, 引っ張りだこだ
  by request 要求に応じて, 依頼に応じて
  come into request 必要とされるようになる
  file a request with A for B AにおしてBを申請する
  on request 要求［申し込み］のあり次第, 申し込み次第, 請求次第
  request for proposal 入札要請書, 提案要請書 《略 RFP》
  request note 〈英国税関の〉有税貨物陸揚げ許可書
  yield to one's request …の要求に応じる
require 動 必要とする, 要求する, 義務付ける
required 形 必要な, 必修の, 義務付けられた, 法定の
  legal required reserve 法定準備金
  required capital 必要資本
  required course 必修課程
  required rate of return 予定投資収益率, 必要収益率 （＝required return）
  required reserves 所要準備
  required subject 必修科目
  required surplus 必要準備金
requirement 名 需要, 必需品, 入用品, 必要量, 需要, 要求, 要件, 条件, 必要条件, 基準, 規定, 制度, 資格
  BIS requirements BIS基準
  credit requirements 審査基準
  disclosure requirements 情報開示基準
  eligibility requirements 適性資格
  food requirements 食糧需要
  legal requirements 法的要件, 法的条件
  listing requirement 上場要件
  margin requirement 証拠金率
  meet the requirements 条件を満たす, 条件に合致する, 条件に適合する
  membership requirement 会員資格要件
  quality requirements 品質条件, 品質要件, 品質基準
  rating requirements 格付け基準
  reporting requirements 報告制度
  requirement fund 資金需要
rescind 動 〈規則などを〉廃止する, 無効にする, 〈命令などを〉撤回する, 取り消す, 〈上告などを〉取り下げる
rescue 動 救う, 救助［救出］する, 支援する, 救済する
rescue 名 救援, 支援, 救済, 救出, 救助, レスキュー
  rescue crew [squad, team, unit] 救助隊
  rescue dog 救助作業犬
  rescue ladder 救助はしご
  rescue mission 救助任務
  rescue operation 救助活動, 救助作業, 救出作戦 （＝rescue service, rescue work）
  rescue remedy 鎮静剤
  rescue work 救助作業
  rescue worker 救急隊員, 救助隊員, レスキュー

隊員

research 名 調査, 研究, 研究開発, リサーチ
  conduct [carry out] research 研究を行う
  Congressional Research Service 議会調査部
  credit research 信用調査
  media research 媒体調査
  panel research パネル調査
  pure [basic, fundamental] research 基礎研究
  research and development 研究開発
  research catch 調査捕鯨
  research example 調査事例
  research for facts 事実調査
  research institute 研究所
  research kitchen 食品関係の調査・開発研究所
  research of the continental shelf 大陸棚調査
  statistical research 統計調査
resell 動 転売する, 再販する, 再販売する
reserve 名 準備金, 積立金, 引当金, 充当金, 支払い準備, 予備品, 保存品, 保留, 留保, 保存, 制限, 条件
  bad debt reserves 貸倒れ引当金 (=reserve for dead loans)
  bank reserves 支払い準備, 銀行準備金, 準備預金
  capital reserve 資本準備金, 資本剰余金
  cash reserves 現金準備, 手元現金
  foreign currency reserves 外貨準備高
  forest reserves 保安林, 保有林
  hidden reserves 含み資産, 秘密積立金
  internal reserves 内部留保, 内部留保金
  latent reserves 含み益
  legal capital reserves 法定準備金 (=legal reserves, legally required reserves)
  liquidate legal reserves 法定準備金を取り崩す
  oil reserves 石油埋蔵量
  petroleum reserve 石油備蓄
  policy reserve 保険契約準備金
  provide reserves for …に対して引当金を設定する
  reserve bank 米連邦準備銀行 (=Federal Reserve Bank)
  reserve currency 準備通貨(米ドルなど国際間の決済に用いられる通貨)
  reserve funds 準備金, 準備資金, 積立金
  Reserve Officers Training Corps 〈米〉予備役将校訓練隊《略 RTC》
  reserve price 最低価格 (=floor price)
  reserve production ratio 可採年数《略 R/P》
  reserves-dedicated 売り先指定ガス埋蔵量
  reserves for potential costs 潜在費用に対する引当金
  set aside loan loss reserves 貸倒れ引当金を積み立てる
  valuation reserve 評価性引当金
reshuffle 動 〈人員を〉入れ替える, 〈閣僚を〉入れ替える, 〈内閣などを〉改造する, 刷新する, 更迭する, 改革する, 再編する
reshuffle 名 内閣改造, 〈人員の〉入れ替え, 人事刷新, 更迭, 〈構造などの〉改革, 再編
  cabinet reshuffle 内閣改造 (=reshuffle of the cabinet)
resident 名 居住者, 定住者, 住民, 市民, 医学実習生[研修生], 駐在官, 弁務官, レジデント
  foreign residents 在留外国人
  resident card 住民票
  resident identification number 住民コード番号
  resident registration 住民登録
  residents' association 自治会
residential mortgage-backed securities business 住宅融資証券事業
resign 動 辞職する, 辞任する, 退職する, 退任する, 〈権利などを〉譲り渡す (=step down)
resignation 名 辞任, 辞職, 退任, 退職, 退陣
  demand the resignation of the president 社長の退陣を要求する
  letter of resignation 辞表, 辞表願い (=resignation letter)
  tender one's resignation 辞表を提出する (=hand in one's notice [resignation])
resistance 名 抵抗, 反対, 反抗, 反撃, 妨害, 敵対, 抵抗力, 免疫力, 耐久性, 地下抵抗運動
  a piece pf resistance 主要作品, 圧巻, 一番重要な料理
  antibiotic resistance 抗生物質への抵抗力
  choose [follow, take] the line of least resistance 最も安易な方法[道]を選ぶ
  put up [make, offer] resistance to …に抵抗する, …を妨害する
  resistance movement 抵抗運動, 地下抵抗運動, レジスタンス
  resistance to fever 熱に対する抵抗力
  the line [path] of least resistance 最も楽な[安易な]方法, 最も安易な道

water resistance 耐水性
resolution 名 決議, 決議案, 決断, 決意, 決定, 裁決, 判定, 解決, 解答, 解明, 決着, 〈映像の〉鮮明度, 〈光の〉解像
- alternative dispute resolution 裁判外紛争解決手続き《略 ADR》
- ceasefire resolution 停戦決議
- concurrent resolution 一致決議案
- extraordinary resolution 特殊決議(議決権を持つ株主の半数以上, かつ議決権で3分の2以上の支持がなければ成立しない決議)
- Resolution 1546 決議1546, イラク新決議
- U.N. sanction resolution 国連の制裁決議
- U.N. Security Council resolution 国連安全保障理事会の決議, 安保理決議 (=UNSC resolution)

resort 名 手段, 頼みの綱, 頼ること, 訴えること, 保養地, 行楽地, 盛り場, リゾート
- a holiday resort 休日の行楽地
- a summer resort 避暑地, 夏の保養地
- a place of public [popular] resort 人手の多い場所, 盛り場
- as a [the] last resort 最後の手段として, 最後の頼みの綱として
- in the last resort 結局, 最終的に, 最後の手段として
- the best resort 最良の手段, 一番の手段
- without resort to the extreme measures 極端な手段に訴えることなく

resort to …を求める, …に頼る, …を利用する, …に訴える, …に行く[通う], …を訪れる
- resort to a dictionary 辞書を引く
- resort to violence [force] 暴力に訴える, 暴力に頼る

resource 名 資源, 財源, 資金, 源泉, 供給源, 教材, 資料, 手段, 方策, 兵力
- concentrate resources on best-selling products 経営資源を売れ筋商品に集中させる
- corporate resources 経営資源
- last resource 最後の手段
- managerial resources 経営資源
- resource-conserving product 省資源製品, 省資源を心がけた商品
- resource-conserving society 省資源社会
- resource-probing vessel 資源探査船
- scarce resource 希少資源

respiratory 形 呼吸器官の
- respiratory illness 呼吸性疾患

respond to …に答える, …に反応する[反応を示す], …に対応する, …に応じる, 効果を現わす
- respond to medical treatment 医療の効果が現れる
- respond to market forces 市場の力に任せる, 市場原理に反応する
- respond to medicine 薬が効く

response 名 対応, 対応策, 反応, 反響, 効果, 結果, 回答, 応答, 返答, レスポンス
- cost per response レスポンス1件当たりのキャンペーンのコスト
- crisis response 危機対応
- customer response 顧客の反応
- efficient customer response 効率的消費者反応
- gauge market responses 市場の反応を見極める
- in response to …に応じて, …に対応して, …に反応して, …に応えて, …を受けて, …に伴って, …を好感して
- joint response to …への共同対応, …への協調対応[協調対応策]
- quick response (system) 早期応答システム
- response error 回答の誤差
- supply response 供給反応
- survey responses 調査結果

responsibility 名 責任, 職責, 義務, 責務, 債務, 負担, 契約義務, 履行能力, 支払い能力
- clarify one's responsibility …の責任を明確化する
- collective responsibility 共同責任
- corporate social responsibility 企業の社会的責任《略 CSR》
- fiduciary responsibility 受託者責任
- responsibility accounting 責任会計
- responsibility audit 責任監査
- responsibility center 責任中心点, 責任センター
- responsibility costing 責任原価計算
- responsibility for financial reporting 財務報告に対する責任

responsible 形 責任がある, 責任を負うべき, 信頼できる, 責任能力がある
- hold [make] ... responsible for …に…の責任があるとする, …に…の責任を負わせる
- make oneself responsible for …の責任を引受ける
- responsible for …の責任がある, …に対して責

任がある, …の責任を負うべき

restoration 名 回復, 復活, 復帰, 復職, 修復, 立て直し, 再建, 復元, 復旧, 返還, 返却, 復元模型,〈英国の〉王政復古(the Restoration), 王政復古時代
- **be under restoration** 修復中である, 再建中である
- **restoration from sickness** 病気の全快
- **the restoration of a borrowed book** 借りた本の返却
- **the restoration of democracy** 民主主義の再建
- **the restoration of earnings momentum** 収益力の回復
- **the restoration of fiscal health** 財政健全化
- **the restoration of public order** 社会秩序の回復

restore 動 回復する, 復活させる, 復帰させる, 復職させる, 取り戻す, 修復する, 立て直す, 再建する, 復元する, 復旧する
- **restore consumer trust in** …に対する消費者[ユーザー]の信頼を回復する
- **restore the health of the financial system** 金融システムの健全性を回復する
- **restore the market's confidence** 市場の信認を回復する

restrain 動 抑える, 抑制する, 制止する, 禁止する, 制限する, 規制する, 拘置する, 監禁する
- **restrain inflation** インフレを抑える
- **restrain oneself from** …をこらえる, …を我慢する, …を抑える
- **restraining order** 現状変更差止め命令

restraint 名 抑え, 抑制, 制止, 制限, 規制, 引締め, 自制, 控え目
- **apply restraint** 緊縮政策をとる
- **capital restraints on banks** 銀行の自己資本比率規制
- **credit restraint** 信用引締め, 金融引締め, 信用規制
- **dividend restraint** 配当制約
- **price restraint** 価格抑制
- **quantitative export restraint** 輸出数量規制
- **restraint of trade** 取引制限, 営業制限, 貿易制限 (= trade restraint)
- **restraint on bank lending** 銀行貸出規制, 貸出規制, 融資規制
- **restraint on public spending** 公共投資の抑制
- **stock price restraint** 株価規制
- **voluntary restraint** 自主規制
- **wage restraint** 賃金抑制

restrict 動 制限する, 限定する, 規制する, 禁止する, 打ち切る
- **restricted competition** 競争制限
- **restricted fund** 限定資金
- **restricted item** 規制品目
- **restricted lending** 貸し渋り
- **restricted stock** 制限付き制限 (= letter stock, unregistered stock)

restriction 名 制限, 抑制, 規制, 制約
- **credit restriction** 信用規制, 信用制限
- **legal restrictions** 法的規制
- **quota restriction** 輸入割当制限
- **residual (quantitative) import restriction** 残存輸入制限
- **restriction on stock holding** 株式保有制限
- **restrictions on capital inflows** 資本流入規制
- **restrictions on capital movement** 資本移動規制
- **restrictions on share buyback** 自社株買戻しに対する規制
- **supply restriction** 供給制限
- **voluntary restriction of export** 輸出自主規制

restructure 動 再編成する, 再構築する, 再構成する, 再建する, 立て直す, 組織替えする, リストラする, 改編する

restructuring 名 〈事業の〉再構築,〈事業の〉再編成, 再構成, 再建, 再編, 改革, 解雇, リストラ, リストラクチャリング
- **capital restructuring** 資本再構成, 資本の再編成
- **debt restructuring** 債務再編, 債務再構成, 債務の特別条件変更 (= refinancing debt)

result 名 結果, 成果, 答え,〈立法機関などの〉決定, 決議 (⇒results)
- **as a result** その結果, その結果として
- **as a [the] result of** …の結果, …の末
- **get a result** 試合に勝つ, 勝利する
- **in result** その結果
- **in the result** 結局
- **the end [final, net] result** 最終結果
- **the result of a calculation** 計算結果
- **with the result that** その結果[そのため] …である, (…した)結果…である
- **without (much) result** 成果なく, 無駄に, むなしく

result in 〈…という〉結果に終わる, …に終わる,

…に帰着する, 〈…の結果に〉なる

results 名 成績, 業績, 決算, 決算内容, 実績, 成果, 結果, よい[素晴らしい]結果, 効果, 影響, 影響額, 統計
　achieve good results よい成績を収める
　bottom line results 純利益
　full year results 通期決算
　get results 成果を出す, よい結果を出す
　good results 好決算
　management by results 目標管理, 目標による管理 (＝result management)
　poll results 投票結果
　quarterly performance results 四半期決算の内容, 四半期業績の内容
　results announcement 決算発表
　successful results 好業績, 好結果, 上首尾
　test results 試験の成績, 検査結果

resume 動 再開する, 再び始める, 復活させる, 続行する, 取り戻す, 回復する, 要約する

resumption 名 再開, 続行, 取り返し, 回収, 回復

resuscitate 動 蘇生させる, 生き返らせる, 復活させる, 再興させる, 再生させる

resuscitation 名 蘇生, 生き返り, 意識の回復, 復活, 復興, 再興, 再生, 再建
　emergency resuscitation treatment 緊急蘇生治療

retail 名 小売り, 個人投資家, 小口投資家, 個人向け取引, リテール
　electric-power retail market 電力小売市場
　Large Scale Retail Store Law 大規模小売店舗法, 大店法
　retail and wholesale sector 流通
　retail driven 個人投資家主導の (＝retail-led)
　retail inventory method of accounting 売価還元法, 小売棚卸し法, 売価棚卸し法 (＝retail inventory method, retail method)
　retail sales 小売販売, 小売販売高, 小売売上高
　retail services 個人向け取引業務, リテール業務
　retail therapy ショッピング・セラピー (買い物をして憂うつな気分を治す治療法)

retail price 小売価格, 小売物価, 販売価格 (⇒diffusion index of retail prices)
　actual retail price 実売価格
　general index of retail prices 小売物価総合指数
　index of retail prices 小売物価指数
　retail price figure 小売物価指数 (＝retail price index)
　retail price index 小売物価指数
　retail price inflation 小売物価上昇率
　suggested retail price 小売希望価格

retailer 名 小売業, 小売企業, 小売業者, 小商, 小売店, 流通企業, スーパー, リテーラー

retain 動 保持する, 保有する, 維持する, 持ち続ける, つなぎとめる, …を失わない, 留保する, 確保する

retaliatory 形 報復的な
　retaliatory measures 報復措置
　retaliatory tariffs 報復関税 (＝punitive tariffs, tit-for-tat tariffs)

retire 動 退職する, 退任する, 〈株式を〉消却する, 〈株式を〉償還する, 〈債務[借入金]などを〉返済する
　retired employee 退職従業員, 退職後の従業員

retirement 名 退職, 引退, 〈株式の〉消却, 償還, 返済, 除却, 処分, 廃棄 (「除却」は, 耐用年数の到来や陳腐化などで使用に耐えられなくなった有形固定資産を, 処分して固定資産台帳から抹消すること)
　allowance for retirement and severance 退職給与引当金
　bond retirement 社債償還, 社債の買入れ消却 (＝retirement of bond)
　debt retirement 債務償還
　early retirement 早期退職, 期限前返済
　employee Retirement Income Security Act 従業員退職所得保障法
　extraordinary retirements 異常な除却
　mandatory retirement 強制退職, 定年退職
　ordinary retirements 通常の除却
　property retirement 有形固定資産の売却, 有形固定資産の廃棄
　regular retirement 正規退職, 自然減
　retirement allowance 退職金, 退職手当, 退職慰労金
　retirement of stock 株式の消却, 買入れ消却 (＝retirement of shares：発行済み自己株式を取得して消滅させること)
　retirement of treasury stock 自己株式の消却
　retirement pension 退職年金
　Social Security retirement benefits 社会保障退職給付
　voluntary retirement 希望退職, 任意退職

retool 動 再編成する, 再組織する, 改組する, 新しい機械設備を入れる

retreat 動 下落する, 反落する, 低下する, 下げる

continue to retreat 続落する
retreat across the board 全面安となる
retreat to the sidelines 手控える
retreat 名 相場の下落, 反落, 低下, 下げ, 縮小, 後退
fight a bitter retreat みじめな敗北を喫する
full retreat 本格的な下げ
market retreat 相場の下落, 相場の反落
progress and retreat 進歩と後退
retrench 動 節約する, 節減する, 〈経費などを〉切り詰める, 減らす(reduce), 削減する, 削除する, 除去する, 取り除く, 省く, 省略する (＝cut, downsize, reduce, trim)
retrench a paragraph 1節を削除する
retrench expenses 経費を切り詰める, 経費を節約[節減]する
retrenchment 名 緊縮, 節約, 節減, 削減, 縮小, 減少, 資産圧縮, 業務縮小, 削除除去, 省略
retrial 名 再審
retrial request 再審請求
return 名 帰還, 帰国, 再発, 復活, 復帰, 回復, 再開, 返却, 返送, 利益, 利益率, 収益, 収益率, 利回り, 運用成績, 運用収益, 戻り益, 還元, 申告, 申告書, 報告書, 投票結果, 往復切符, 改行キー, リターン
asset return 資産収益率, 資産利回り
census returns 国勢調査結果
current return 現行利回り
earn a return 利益を上げる, 利益率を上げる
enhance the returns on the portfolio ポートフォリオの運用成績を上げる
expected return 期待収益, 予想収益, 期待収益率
horizon return 所有期間利回り (＝holding period return)
in return for …の代わりに, …と引換えに, …の見返りに, …の返礼に
joint return 夫婦合算納税申告書
rate of return 収益率, 利益率
return on assets 資産利益率, 総資産利益率《略 ROA》
return on capital 資本利益率, 自己資本利益率
return on equity 株主資本利益率《略 ROE》(資本金などをどれほど有効に使って利益を生んだかを示す経営指標)
return to profit 利益回復, 黒字転換
revised return 修正申告 (＝amended return, amended tax return)

stock returns 株式総合利回り
traffic return 運輸統計表
return on investment 投下資本利益率, 使用総資本利益率, 投資収益, 投資利益率, 投資収益率, 投資利回り, 運用利回り, 運用, 投資リターン, 投下資本利益率《略 ROI》
return to …に戻る, …に復帰する, …に転じる, …に転換する
return to neutral 中立に戻る
return to positive growth プラス成長に転じる
rev up 回転速度を増す, スピード[速度]を上げる, 増加させる, 活性化する, 促進する, 開発する, 浮揚する
revaluation 名 再評価, 評価替え, 見直し, 平価切上げ
asset revaluation 資産再評価, 資産評価替え (＝revaluation of assets)
exchange revaluation 為替再評価 (＝revaluation of exchange)
revaluation method 再評価法
revaluation of the dollar ドルの平価切上げ, ドル高 (＝dollar revaluation)
revaluation surplus 再評価剰余金, 評価剰余金
revaluation surplus reserve 再評価積立金
stock revaluation 株式評価替え (＝equity revaluation)
revalue 動 再評価する, 〈平価を〉切り上げる
revamp 動 見直す, 立て直す, 再建する, 刷新する, 改良する, 改造する, 手直しをする, 修理する, 改訂する, 修正する, 改作する
revamp an ailing business 経営不振企業を再建する
revamp existing stores 既存店を改装する
revamp 名 改革, 改造, 刷新, 立て直し, 手直し, 改訂, 修正, 改作
management revamp plan 経営改革計画, 企業改革方針
sign a revamp 修正案件に調印[署名]する
reveal 動 発表する, 公表する, 明らかにする, 〈秘密などを〉漏らす, 示す, 開示する
revenue 名 収益, 営業収益, 売上, 売上高, 収入, 歳入

> 収益とは ⊃ 商品の販売, サービスの提供, その他企業の営業活動から生じる現金または現金等価物(cash equivalents：売掛金や受取手形などを含む)の流入額, 投資から得た利子, 配当ならびに固定資産の売却や交換に基づく利得, 負債の減少額をいう. 資本の払込みや借入金の受入れなどは,

収益とはならない。なお，会計上「現金」は，銀行預金のほかに小切手，手形，郵便為替証書などを含むが，流動資産に含まれるcashは手元現金と銀行の要求払い預金を指す。

annual revenue 年収，歳入，通期の［年間］売上高
casual revenue 臨時収入
commission revenue 手数料収入
consolidated revenues 連結売上高
cost of revenues 売上原価
current revenue 当期収益
earned revenue 実現収益
general revenue sharing 一般交付金
geographic revenues 地域別売上高
gross revenue 総収益
net revenue 純収入
operating revenue 営業収益，営業収入
public revenue 国庫収入，国の収入
real revenue 実質収入
realized revenue 実現利益
recognition of revenue 収益の認識（＝revenue recognition）
revenue base 収益基盤
revenue deficit [crunch, shortfall] 歳入欠陥
revenue loss 減収，収入減
revenue producer 収益源
revenue shortfall 歳入不足，歳入欠陥
revenue source 財源，収益源，収入源，歳入源
revenue tariff 収入関税，財政関税，歳入関税（＝financial duties, revenue duties）
sales revenues 売上収益，売上高
tax revenues 税収
total revenues 総収益，総売上高
unearned revenue 前受収益

reversal 名 逆転，反転，反発，どんでん返し，転換，政策変更，〈判決の〉破棄［取消し］
business-cyclical reversal 景気循環の反転
factor intensity reversal 要素集約度の逆転
factor reversal test 要素転逆テスト
reversal of the rate cut 引き下げた金利の引上げ
reversal of the transfer 復帰人事
reversal process 反転現象，リバーサル
reversal swap 反対スワップ
role reversal 立場［役割］の逆転（＝reversal of roles）
switch reversal 逆入替え

reverse 動 覆す，逆転させる，〈方向などを〉逆にする［反対にする］，置き換える，変える，〈判決などを〉破棄する，無効にする，取り消す，振り戻す，戻し入れる，入れ替える，取り崩す，再修正する，再整理する

reverse a car 車をバックさせる
reverse a court ruling 裁判所の判決を覆す
reverse a process 手順を逆［反対］にする
reverse one's position …の立場を逆転する
reverse oneself [one's previous statement] 前言を翻す，意見を変える
reverse the charges 〈電話料金を〉受信人払いにする，電話代を受信者に請求する
reverse the direction of …の方向を変える
reverse the order 順序を逆にする
reverse the position 状況を改善する
reverse the sentence [conviction] 原判決を破棄する

reverse 名 逆，反対，あべこべ，敗北，失敗，つまずき（setback），裏側，裏面，反対側，〈本の〉左［裏］ページ
a reverse in one's affairs …の身に降りかかった不幸
do the reverse 逆のことをする
go into [in] reverse 逆さまになる，反対になる
have [experience] reverses 打撃を受ける，失敗する，敗北する
in reverse 逆に，反対方向に，背面に，後陣に，バックで
put [get, shift] a car in reverse 車をバックさせる［後退させる］，車をバックギアに入れる
suffer a reverse 敗北を喫する，敗北する，ひどい目にあう
suffer [meet with] financial reverses 経済破綻の憂き目にあう

reverse 形 逆の，反対の，逆方向の，裏の，裏側の，裏面の
have a reverse effect 逆効果が出る
in reverse order 逆順で
reverse (annuity) mortgage （年金方式）逆住宅抵当貸付け
reverse bid 逆乗っ取り
reverse (charge) call コレクト・コール
reverse commuting 都市から郊外への逆方向通勤
reverse discrimination 逆差別
reverse engineering 逆行分析，分解工学，逆行分析工学，リバース・エンジニアリング（他社製品の分析・調査をとおして自社製品にその技術を

導入すること）
reverse fire 背面からの砲撃
reverse gear 逆進装置, 後退装置, バックギア
reverse income tax 逆所得税, 負の所得税 (＝negative income tax)
reverse note 逆変動利付き債
reverse racism 人種差別撤廃から生じる無意識の白人差別
reverse remittance 逆為替
reverse split 株式併合 (＝reverse split of stocks, reverse stock split, share split-down)
reverse takeover 逆買収, 逆乗っ取り（小企業による大企業の買収や非公開企業による上場企業の買収のこと）
review 動 見直す, 再考する, 再検討［再調査, 再吟味］する, 再審理する, 評価する, 検討する, 監査する, 調査する, 審査する, 査閲する, レビューする（監査が一般に公正妥当と認められる監査基準に従って実施されているかどうか, また所定の監査方針が遵守されているかどうかを確かめることを「査閲」という）
review 名 見直し, 再考, 再検討［再調査, 再吟味］, 再審理, 評価, 検討, 監査, 調査審査, 報告, 報告書, 評価, 監査調書の査閲, 監査技術としての閲覧, レビュー
revise 動 修正する, 改正する, 改定する, 改訂する, 校正する, 校閲する
revise downward 下方修正する (＝downgrade, revise down, slash)
revise upward 上方修正する (＝revise up, upgrade)
revision 名 修正, 改正, 改訂, 変更, 見直し
massive [large, substantial] upward revision 大幅な上方修正
slight downward revision 小幅な下方修正
revitalization 名 再生, 活性化, 再活性化, 健全化, 復興, 回復
revitalization of businesses 事業再生
revitalization of the economy 経済の活性化
revitalize 動 回復させる, 生き返らせる, 再生する, 復興させる, 活性化する, 活力を与える, 〈景気などを〉浮揚させる
revitalize the company 会社を再生する
revitalize the market 市場を活性化する, 市場の活性化を図る
revival 名 回復, 再生, 事業再生, 活性化, 再建, 復活, 更新, 再燃, 回復, 再上映, 再上演
economic revival 景気回復, 景気浮揚, 経済の再生, 経済復興
inflation revival インフレ再燃
revival account 再生勘定
revival in demand 需要の回復
revival plan 再生計画, 事業再生計画, 再建計画
revoke 取り消す (cancel), 無効にする (rescind), 廃止する
revolution 名 革命, 大革命, 大変革, 変革, 回転, 旋回, ひと巡り, 周期
Cultural Revolution 〈中国の〉文化大革命
industrial revolution 産業革命
the 1979 Islamic Revolution 〈イランの〉1979年のイスラム革命
reward 名 報酬, 報償, 報奨金, 褒賞金, 謝礼, 対価, 成果, リターン
cash reward 報奨金
pecuniary reward 金銭的報酬
reward based on merit 能力に基づく報酬, 能力に応じた報酬
reward power 報酬に基づく統制力
reward system 報酬体系
rewards system 報奨金制度
rhetoric 名 話術, 美辞麗句, 誇張した表現, 大げさな言い方［言葉］, 雄弁, 雄弁術, 発言, 作文法, 作文指導書
ribbon 名 飾りひも, リボン, リボン型記章, 略章, 授賞, インクリボン
a black ribbon 喪章, 黒いリボン
a Vietnam service ribbon ベトナム従軍略章
cut a ribbon テープカットをする
ribbon development 帯状宅地開発, 帯状開発 (＝sprawl, urban sprawl)
the blue ribbon ブルー・リボン賞, 最高賞 (the first prize), 1等賞, 最高の栄誉
ribbonsnipping 名 テープカット
rice policy コメ政策
Richter scale リクター震度計, リクター・スケール
rig 動 不正に操作する, 操る, 不正工作する, 不正をする
rig bids 入札談合する
right 名 権利, 権限, 所有権, 新株引受権, 正当, 公正 正義, 正道, 公平扱い, 真相, 実情, 本来の状態, 右翼, 右派 (Right), 保守党, 右翼団体
be in the right 道理がある, 誤りがない
business right 営業権
cum rights price 権利付き株価
dead to rights 現行犯で, 弁解の余地なく
deprivation of civil rights 公民権剥奪

do a person right 人を公平に扱う，正当に評価する
do right 正しいことをする
ex rights price 権利落ち株価
freedom of speech 言論の自由
give up [renounce] one's right 権利を放棄する
in the right 間違いなく，正確に
management rights 経営権
mining right 鉱業権，採掘権
minority stockholders' right 少数株主権
natural rights 生得権
right of abode 居住権
right of access アクセス権
right of appeal 上訴権
right of common 公有権，共有権，入会権
right of indemnity 求償権
right of search 捜索権
right of way 〈土地の〉通行権，〈車両の〉優先行権
right to collective self-defense 集団的自衛権
right to strike 争議権
right to sunlight [light, sunshine] 日照権
right to vote 投票権，選挙権
right-to-work law 労働権法(ユニオン・ショップ(union shop)を禁止する法律)
rights and duties 権利と義務
rights issue 株主割当発行，株主割当発行増資 (=rights offering)
rights of the case 事件の真相
shareholders' right 株主権 (=stockholders' right)
stand on one's rights 権利を主張する
stock right 新株引受権，株式引受権，株式買受権 (=subscription right)
the rights and wrongs 事の真相，実情
within one's rights …の権利の範囲内で，…をするのも当然のことで
right-of-center 形 保守寄りの，中道右派の
right-on 形 進歩的な，正しい，賛成できる，要領を得た，最新の，現代的な
right-to-die 形 死ぬ権利を支持する，延命医療拒否権を認める
right-to-life 形 妊娠中絶反対の，妊娠中絶禁止を支持する (=antiabortion, pro-life)
right-to-lifer 名 中絶禁止法支持者
right-wing [rightwing] 形 右派の，右翼の

right-wing radical [extremist] 右翼過激派
rightabout-face [turn] 名 回れ右，〈180度の〉方向転換
rightist 名 保守主義者，反動主義者，右翼[右派]の人，保守派，右派 (=right-winger)
rightsize 動 規模を縮小する
ringtone [ring-tone] 名 着信音
ringtone melody 着信メロディー
ringtone service distributor 着うた配信会社
riot 名 暴動，騒乱，騒動，混乱，騒擾，乱舞，多種多彩
bloody riots 流血の暴動
crime of riot 騒擾罪
put down a riot 暴動を鎮圧する[鎮める]
race riot 人種暴動
raise a riot 暴動を起こす
read the riot act to …に解散を命じる，…に問題行為を止めるよう戒告する
riot-equipped 暴動鎮圧用完全装備をした (=in full riot gear [garb])
riot gear [garb] 暴動鎮圧用装備
riot girl [girrl] 強硬派女権論者
riot police [squad] 警察機動隊，機動隊
riot policeman [trooper] 機動隊員
riot shield 防護盾，暴徒鎮圧用盾
run riot 騒ぎまわる，奔放に振る舞う，〈植物が〉はびこる，咲き乱れる
trigger a massive riot 大騒動を引き起こす，大暴動を引き起こす
Uygul riots ウイグル族暴動
Xinjiang riots 新疆(しんきょう)の暴動
rioter 名 暴徒
rip into 激しく非難する，激しく叱る，…に食ってかかる，…を襲う
riposte [ripost] 名 反撃，しっぺ返し，応酬，〈即座の〉受け答え，〔フェンシング〕迅速な[素早い]突き返し
ripple effect 波及効果
rise 動 増加する，上昇する，伸びる，拡大する，向上する，高まる
be expected to rise 上昇する見込みだ，上昇すると予想される
begin to rise 上昇に転じる
rise to one's responsibilities …の責任を果たす，…の責任を負う
rise 名 増加，増大，上昇，伸び，向上，高まり，値上り，物価の騰貴，昇給，賃上げ，出世，隆盛，台頭，出現

be on the rise 増加している, 上昇している, 上向いている, 上り調子だ
demand rise 需要の増加, 需要増
export rise 輸出の増加, 輸出増, 輸出の伸び
give rise to …を引き起こす, …を生む, …の原因となる
give rise to speculations 推測[臆測]を生む
pay rise 賃上げ
price rise 物価上昇, 価格引上げ, 値上げ (= rise of [in] prices)
rise and fall 盛衰, 浮沈, 興亡, 栄枯盛衰, 増減, 〈相場の〉騰落, 上下動

▶ Sharp *rises* in the price of crude oil and other commodity would push up consumer prices. 原油など市況商品の価格急騰が, 消費者物価を押し上げることになろう。

rising 形 増加する, 増大する, 上昇する, 向上する, 上り調子の, 出世している, 新進気鋭の, 伸び盛りの, 名 上昇, 昇進, 出世, 増水, 出現, 復活, 蜂起, 反乱, 隆起

risk 動 危険にさらす, …の危険を招く[冒す], 〈生命を〉賭ける, 覚悟してやる, 思い切ってやる, 一か八かやってみる, …する危険性[恐れ]がある, …の危機に陥る
risk a failure 失敗を覚悟してやる
risk life and limb 大きな危険を冒す
risk one's life 生命の危機に瀕する
risk one's life to save a person 身をもって[命をかけて]人を救う

risk 名 危険, 危険性, 危険負担, 〈価格などの〉値下がり確率, リスク
all risks 全危険担保, オール・リスク担保
an amount at risk 危険保険金額
bear the risk リスクを負う (=assume the risk)
business risk 事業リスク, 営業リスク
collection risk 回収リスク
country risk カントリー・リスク
currency risk 為替リスク
default risk 債務不履行リスク, 不履行リスク, デフォルト・リスク
diversification of risks リスク分散 (=diversity of risks)
diversify risks リスクを分散する
diversity of risk リスク分散 (=diversification of risk)
downside risks 下振れリスク, 業績悪化のリスク, 減益要因, 下値不安
financial risk 財務リスク, 金融リスク
financing risk 資金調達リスク
fire and usual marine risks 海上保険
foreign exchange risk 為替リスク
geopolitical risks 地政学的リスク
hedge risks リスクを相殺する, リスクをヘッジする
high risk 高リスク, ハイリスク
information technology risk IT (情報技術) リスク (=IT risk)
legal risk 法的リスク
liquidity risk 流動性リスク
passing of risk 危険負担の移転
prepayment risk 期限前償還リスク
rate risk 金利リスク (=interest rate risk)
reduce the default risk 不履行リスクを軽減する[低減する, 低下させる, 抑える]
risk assets リスク資産, リスク・アセット
risk-averse retail investors リスクを嫌う個人投資家, リスク回避型個人投資家
risk-bearing リスクを負担する
risk factor 危険要因, リスク要因, リスク・ファクター
risk management 危機管理, リスク管理, リスク・マネジメント
risk-taking 危険覚悟
risks and rewards approach リスク経済価値アプローチ
risks covered 担保危険
spreading of risk リスク分散
systematic risk システマティック・リスク(東京株価指数(TOPIX)の価格変動など, 分散投資では取り除けない金融市場全体に共通するリスクのこと)
uninsured risks 保険をかけていない危険
upside risk 上昇するリスク, 上昇リスク

法的リスク(legal risk)の種類:

illegal acts by employees	従業員による不法行為
infringement of intellectual property	知的財産権の侵害
litigation risk	訴訟リスク
sexual harassment	性的嫌がらせ, セクシャル・ハラスメント, セクハラ

▶ All financial instruments involve *risks* by their nature. 金融商品はすべて, その性質上, リスクを包含している。

▶ Downside *risks* to growth and the upside risks to inflation are both of significant concern. 景気が悪化する恐れとインフレが一段と進行する恐れの双

risky 形 危険な, 危険を伴う, 危険性の高い, リスクの高い, 高リスクの, 冒険的な, 一か八かの
 risky asset 高リスク資産, リスクの高い資産
 risky business 危険な仕事, 一か八かの商売
 risky investment 高リスク投資, リスクの高い投資
 risky operations リスクの高い業務
 risky shift phenomenon 冒険的転換現象
rival 動 …に劣らない, …に匹敵する, …と並ぶ, …と張り合う, …と競争する
rival 名 競争相手, 競争相手国, 同業他社, 好敵手, 対抗機種, ライバル
RMA 軍事における革命（Revolution in Military Affairsの略）
road map 行程表, 道路地図, 案内役, ロード・マップ
roadside land price 路線価 (=price of land facing main streets)
roaring 形 活発な, 活気がある, 活況の, 突然の活況にわく, 大繁盛の, 景気がよい, 騒々しい, 大荒れの
 do [drive] a roaring business [trade] 商売が大繁盛する, 商売が繁盛する
 roaring twenties 狂騒の1920年代
 ▶ The Tokyo stock market has recently been *roaring*, with record heavy trading seen. 東京株式市場が, 記録的な大商いを続けて, 活況を呈している。
robot 名 ロボット, 自動装置
 biped robot 歩行ロボット
 human care robot 介護ロボット
 humanoid robot 2足歩行ロボット
 industrial robot 産業ロボット, 産業用ロボット
 intelligent robot 知能ロボット
 robot-operated factory ロボット制御の工場
 robot skill ロボットの能力, ロボット・スキル
 robots for hazardous environment 極限作業ロボット
 surgical robot 手術ロボット, 手術支援ロボット
 welfare robot 福祉ロボット
robotic 形 ロボットの
 robotic rover 無人探査車
robotics 名 ロボット工学
robotization 名 無人化, ロボット化, 自動化, ロボットの導入
robust 形 好調な, 活発な, 活況の, 底堅い, 強力な, 力強い, 強靭な, 健全な, 目覚しい, 大幅な, 著しい, 際立った
 robust demand 需要の大幅な伸び
 robust economic recovery 目覚しい景気回復
 robust economy 好調な経済, 景気好調, 経済の活況
 robust growth 著しい伸び, 大幅な伸び
 robust performance 好業績, 好調な業績, 業績好調 (=robust earnings)
 robust sales 販売好調, 好調な販売
rock 動 激しく揺する, 揺さぶる, 動揺させる, 動転させる, 振り動かす, 振動させる
 be rocked by a scandal 不祥事に揺れる
 rock the boat 計画を揺さぶる, 問題を起こす
rock bottom [rock-bottom] 最低レベル, どん底, 大底, 大底圏
rock of Sisyphus シジフォスの岩, 無駄な努力
rocket 名 ロケット
 booster rocket 打上げロケット, 補助ロケット, 補助推進装置
 carrier rocket 運搬ロケット, 打上げロケット
 liquid-fuel rocket 液体燃料ロケット
 multistage rocket 多段式ロケット
 rocket astronomy ロケット天文学
 rocket base ロケット基地
 rocket bomb ロケット弾
 rocket gun ロケット砲
 rocket launcher ロケット発射台, 対戦車用ロケット砲
 rocket plane ロケット砲搭載機, ロケット機
 rocket propellant ロケット推進剤
 rocket range ロケット砲試射場
 rocket scientist ロケット工学者, プログラム売買 (program trading) による裁定取引 (arbitrage transaction) の専門家
 rocket ship [vehicle] 宇宙船, ロケット船
 rocket station ロケット架台
 rocket warhead ロケットの弾頭
 satellite-launch rocket 衛星打ち上げ用ロケット
 solid-fuel rocket 固体燃料ロケット, 固体燃料型ロケット
 supply rocket 補給機
rogue 名 ならず者
 rogue nation [state] ならず者国家
roil 動 かき乱す, 混乱させる, いらだたせる, 怒らせる
role 名 役, 役割, 任務, 立場
 a minor [small] role 端役
 a supporting role 脇役
 play a key [leading, major] role in …で重要な役割を果たす, …で主要な役割を果たす

play a leading role　牽引役を果たす, 主役を演じる
role model　手本, 理想像, 理想の姿, 雛型, 模範生, 優等生

roll 動　揺さぶる
　roll back　撃退する, 撤退させる, 押し返す, 後退させる, 以前の水準に下げる, …の勢力を減じる, 〈賃金や物価などを〉下げる, 引き下げる
　roll off the assembly line　〈完成して〉組立ラインを離れる, 流れ作業で完成する, 生産第1号が工場出荷される, 生産が開始される, 生産がスタートする
　roll out　大量生産する, 量産する, 生産する, 発表する, 公表する, 初公開する, 発売する
　roll over　繰越す, 借り換える, 乗り換える, 書き換える (＝carry over)

rollback 名　巻き返し, 巻き返し戦術,〈統制による〉物価引下げ政策
　rollback policy　巻き返し政策
　rollback strategy　巻き返し戦略

rollout 名　大量生産, 量産, 生産, 発表, 初公開, 発売, 新製品の紹介,〈事業などの〉展開

rollover 名　更新, 更改, 満期書替え, 資金の回転調達, 借りつなぎ, 借換え, 支払い繰延べ, ロールオーバー

root-and-branch reform　抜本改革

rope 名　縄, コツ, やり方, 秘訣, 絞首刑, ロープ
　a rope of sand　頼りにならないもの
　be at [come to, run to] the end of one's rope　万事休す, 力尽きる, 百計尽きる, 進退わまる,〈能力・体力などの〉限界にある
　be on the ropes　ロープに逃れる, 窮地に陥っている, 追い詰められている, ダウン寸前だ, 経営が悪化している
　know the ropes　コツを知っている
　learn the ropes　コツを覚える
　the rope　絞首刑

Rose Garden　〈ホワイトハウス(米大統領官邸)の〉ローズ・ガーデン

rotate 動　〈人を〉交替させる, 交替で勤務させる
　rotating EU presidency　輪番制のEU議長国, 輪番制のEU議長国の立場

rotation 名　転換, 回転, 輪番, 交替, 循環, ローテーション
　rotation system　輪番制

rotisserie 名　焼肉レストラン

round 名　一連の協議, 会議, 交渉, ラウンド
　ラウンド ⇒ 日本など, 世界貿易機関(WTO)に加盟する国々が行う貿易・投資の自由化に関する話し合い。二国間交渉でなく, 多くの国が参加して関税引下げなど世界の新しい貿易ルールを一括して取り決めるのが特徴。
　a fifth round of preliminary talks　第5回予備会談
　a round of calls　歴訪
　a round of talks　一連の会談
　a trade round　貿易交渉
　the daily round　日常の仕事
　the Doha Round　ドーハ・ラウンド
　the first round of tenders　第一次入札
　the first round of voting　1回目の投票
　the new round of multinational trade negotiations　新多角的貿易交渉, 新ラウンド
　the new round of WTO talks　新ラウンド(新多角的貿易交渉)
　the opening game of the women's curling round-robin preliminary round　女子カーリングの総当たり予選リーグ開幕戦
　the second round　第二弾, 決選投票
　the second round of repatriation　本国送還の第二陣

round-table conference 名　円卓会議

round-the-clock 形　24時間ぶっ通しで, 24時間連続で, 24時間態勢の, 24時間営業の (＝around-the-clock)

round up　一斉検挙する, 逮捕する, 捕まえる, 駆り集める, 寄せ集める, 集める

roundup 名　一斉検挙, 逮捕, …狩り, 駆り集め,〈情報の〉要約(summary), 総括, まとめ
　roundup of hoodlums　愚連隊狩り
　roundup of suspects　容疑者の一斉検挙[逮捕]
　roundup of the latest information　最新情報の総括, 最親情報の総まとめ
　roundup of the news　ニュースのまとめ

route 名　道筋, 経路, 行路, 道, 手順, 手段, 方法, 配達路, 配達区域, 郵便集配区域, 販売路, 路線, …号線, 航路, ルート
　commercial route　商路, 通商路
　delivery route　配達区域
　distribution routes　販売網
　go the route [distance]　完投する, 最後までやり通す
　marketing routes　販路, 配給経路
　newspaper route　新聞配達区域
　ocean route　遠洋航路
　overland route　陸路

route chart [sheet] 手順表, 工程表
route man 巡回販売員(route salesman), 特定区域[路線]担当者, 地域責任者(routeman), 作業配分担当者
route sales [selling] 巡回販売, ルート・セールス
route slips 送付票
trade route 通商路

rover 名 探査車
roving correspondent 移動特派員
row 名 列, 並び, 座席の列[ひと並びの座席], 〈表の〉横の欄, 横の列, …通り, 街路, 町
  a tough [hard, long] row to hoe 困難な状況, 困難な仕事, 大役, 扱いにくい問題
  at the end of one's row 切羽詰まって, 疲れ果てて
  death rows 死刑囚 (=death-row inmates)
  do not amount to a row of beans 何の役にも立たない, 何にもならない
  have a new [another] row to hoe 新しい仕事をしようとしている, 新しい企てがある
  hoe one's own row 独力で仕事をする, 独力で生きていく, 他からの援助なしにする, 自分の仕事をする, 自分のことだけに専心する
  in a row 続けて, 引き続いて, 連続して, 連続的に, 1列に, 1列になって
  in rows 列をなして, 幾列にもなって
  in the front row 最前列に, 1列目に
  row house 集合住宅, 長屋
  row upon row 幾重にも並んだ列
  stand in rows 幾重にも立ち並ぶ

row 名 騒々しい喧嘩, 騒々しい議論, 激論, 騒動, 騒音
  have a dreadful row over …をめぐってひどい喧嘩をする
  get into [in] a row for …のことでお目玉をくう
  make [kick up] a row about …のことで喧嘩する[騒ぎを起こす], …のことで強く抗議する, …について反対して騒ぐ, 不平をがなり立てる
  spark off [touch off] a row between A and B AとBの間に大喧嘩を引き起こす

royalty 名 〈著作権・特許権・鉱区などの〉使用料, 権利の実施料, 許諾料, 採掘料, 印税, ロイヤルティ
  copyright royalty 著作権料
  maximum royalty 最高実施料
  minimum royalty 最低実施料
  paid-up royalty ロイヤルティの一括払い
  royalty as to knowhow ノウハウ使用料
  royalty free ロイヤルティ無償の, ロイヤルティ支払い義務のない
  running royalty 継続的使用料, 継続的実施料, ランニング・ロイヤルティ

rubber-stamp 動 ゴム印を押す, 判を押す, 軽々と承認する, 十分考えずに賛成する

Rubicon 名 ルビコン川
  cross [pass] the Rubicon 背水の陣を敷く, 重大な決意をする, 断固たる手段をとる, (後退を許されない)思い切った処置をとる
  psychological Rubicon 心理的な壁

ruffle feathers いらいらさせる, いらだたせる, 怒らせる

rule 動 支配する, 統治する, 左右する, 判決[裁決]を下す, 裁定する, 決定する
  rule against …に不利な裁定[裁決]をする, …に反対の裁定を下す
  rule in favor of …に有利な裁定をする
  rule ... with an iron fist …を強権支配する, …を厳しく管理[支配]する

rule 名 規則, 規定, 法, 法規, 原則, 慣例, 通例, 支配, 〈裁判所の〉裁定[命令], 基準, 規準, ルール
  capital adequacy rule 自己資本規制, 自己資本比率規制
  client money rules 顧客資金ルール, 顧客資金規則
  compliance rules 法令[規則]の遵守規則
  general rule 総則
  listing rules 上場基準, 上場規則, 上場要件
  net capital rule 自己資本規制比率
  noise rules 騒音規制
  one-share/one-vote rule 1株=1議決権ルール
  Rule 415 shelf registration SEC規則415に基づく一括登録
  rules of engagement 交戦規定《略 ROE》
  standing rule 定款, 準用規則
  the Rules of American Arbitration Association 米国仲裁協会規則, アメリカ仲裁協会規則
  uniform rules 統一規則
  working rules 就業規則, 業務規定, 準則

rule of thumb 概算, 経験的[実際的]な目安, 過去の経験から見て, 経験法, 大ざっぱなやり方で, 目の子勘定で
  ▶The U.S. National Bureau of Economic Research does not define a recession as two consecutive quarters of decline in real GDP, as is the *rule of thumb* in many countries. 多くの国々で過去の経験的な目安としているように, 米経済研究所(NBER)は,

実質国内総生産(GDP)2四半期連続でマイナス成長になった場合を「リセッション(景気後退)」と定義しているわけではない。

ruling 名 判決, 裁定, 決定, 支配, 統治, 回答, 通達, 罫線
 court ruling　裁判所の裁定, 裁判所の判決
 ethics ruling　倫理通達
 final ruling　最終決定
 hand down a ruling on　…に判決を下す, …に判決を言い渡す
 IRS Revenue Ruling　内国歳入庁裁定(IRS＝Internal Revenue Service)
 letter ruling　書面回答
 provisional ruling　仮決定
 revenue ruling　米内国歳入庁細則税に関する個別通達, 内国歳入庁細則
 the WTO's ruling　世界貿易機関(WTO)の決定
 three bureau ruling　三極指導

ruling 形 支配的な, 支配[統治]している, 政権を担当する, 与党の, 第一党の, 現行の, 現在の, 目下の, 一般に行われている, 有力な, 優勢な, 主な
 ruling class　支配階級
 ruling coalition　連立政権, 連立与党, 与党連合
 ruling factors　主な諸要因
 ruling opinion　支配的な意見
 ruling party　与党, 政権政党, 政権党 (＝governing party)
 ruling passion　主情(行為を支配する主な動機)
 ruling precedent　確立した前例, 決定的な先例
 ruling prices　通り相場, 時価
 ruling spirit　首脳, 支配者, 主導者
 the ruling and opposition camps　与党・野党陣営, 与党と野党の陣営
 the ruling and opposition parties　与野党
 the ruling class　支配階級
 the ruling coalition parties　連立与党
 the ruling price　時価

rumor 名 噂, 評判, 風聞, 風説

run 他動 経営する, 指揮する, 管理する, 運用する, 運営する, 提供する, 操作する, 動かす, 実行する, 行う, 掲載する, 載せる, 〈党が候補者を〉立てる, 自動〈選挙に〉立候補する, 出馬する, …の状態になる, 〈契約などが〉有効である, 動く, 作動する, 稼働する, 進行する, 進む, 行われる, 上演される, 〈記事が〉掲載される, 〈編み物などが〉伝線する, 水を出す, 出場する, 走る
 run a cartel　カルテルを結ぶ
 run a country　国を動かす
 run a primary deficit　財政の基礎収支が赤字になる
 run a huge surplus　巨額の黒字になる, 大幅な黒字になる
 run a trade deficit　貿易赤字になる, 貿易赤字を出す
 run an ad in a paper　新聞に広告を載せる
 run an article on [about]　…に関する記事を掲載する
 run an investment trust fund　投資信託を運用する
 run for (a seat in) Congress　国会議員に立候補する
 run for President　大統領に立候補する (＝stand for President)
 run in the election and win　選挙に出て当選する
 run jointly　共同経営する, 共同管理する, 共同運営する
 run lean　無駄をなくす
 run low on　…が乏しくなる
 run on Microsoft Windows　マイクロソフトのウインドウズで動く
 run short of　…が不足する, …がなくなる
 run the gamut from ... to　…から…まで多岐にわたる
 the well runs dry　井戸が枯れる, 資金が底をつく

run 名 〈銀行などに対する〉取付け, 取付け騒ぎ, 〈証券価格の〉急上昇, 盛んな売行き, 注文殺到, 大量需要, 情勢, 趨勢, 成り行き, 流れ, 〈市場の〉気配, 気配値(「取付け」は, 経営破綻した銀行などに預金払戻しの請求者が殺到することをいう)
 bank run　銀行取付け, 取付け (＝a run on a bank)
 broker's run　ブローカーの気配値
 domino-like run on other banks　他行への連鎖的な取付け騒ぎ
 off-the-run issue　周辺銘柄
 on-the-run curve　新発債の利回り曲線
 on-the-run issue　指標銘柄
 run for the Oval Office　大統領の椅子をめぐる争い
 run of the market　市場の気配, 市場の成り行き, 市況の情勢
 run on a bank　銀行の取付け騒ぎ, 銀行に対する取付け (＝bank run)
 run on the dollar　ドルに対する大量需要

runaway 名 逃亡者, 脱走者, 家出人, 逃走, 駆け落ち, 楽勝, 一方的な勝利, 形 逃走した, 家出した, 駆け落ちの, 制御しきれない, 手に負えない, うなぎ上りの, 急騰する, けた外れの, 天井知らずの, とめどもない, 抑え[制御]のきかない, 野放しの, 楽勝の, 一方的な, 楽に得られた
runaway economy 過熱した景気
runaway inflation 天井知らずのインフレ, うなぎ上りのインフレ, とめどないインフレ, 悪性インフレ, 狂乱インフレ
runaway marriage 駆け落ち結婚
runaway success 楽な成功, 楽に得られた成功
runaway victory 楽勝, 一方的な勝利
runaway wage-price inflation 賃金・物価の急騰[天井知らずのインフレ]
rundown 名 要約, 概要, 詳しい報告, 項目別報告, 縮小, 削減, [野球]挟殺
running mate 〈米〉副大統領候補
runoff 名 優勝決定戦, 同点決勝, 決勝戦, 決選投票(runoff election), 製造過程で取り除かれる不良品, 地中に吸収されないで流れる排水
runoff election [vote] 決選投票
runoff primary 決選投票
▶ Both of the two top candidates are below the 50 percent needed to avoid going into a Nov. 21 *runoff*. 2人の上位候補は, 11月21日の決選投票に入るのを避けるために必要な50％（得票率）をいずれも下回っている。

runup [run-up] 名 助走, 準備期間, 〈選挙などの〉前哨戦, 〈株価などの〉高騰, 急騰
in the runup to …の準備期間に, …に向けて
the runup in oil prices 原油価格の高騰, 原油価格の上昇
the runup in the stock market 株式相場の上昇
the runup to the coming election 来たる選挙に向けての準備段階

rupture 名 決裂, 断絶, 断交, 仲たがい, 不和, 争い, 〈血管などの〉破裂, 破壊, ヘルニア
come to a rupture 決裂する, 仲たがいする
diplomatic rupture 外交断絶
rupture of a blood vessel 血管の破裂
rupture of diplomatic relations 外交関係の断絶[決裂], 国交断絶
rupture of friendly relations 友好関係の決裂

Russell 2000 index ラッセル2000指数, ラッセル2000種株価指数

rut 名 わだち, 溝, 決まりきった考え方, 型にはまったやり方
be in a deep rut 深い谷の中にある
get into a rut 型にはまる
get out of the rut マンネリな生活から抜け出す
move in a rut 型にはまったことをする

S

S & L 米貯蓄貸付け組合, 貯蓄金融機関 (savings and loan associationの略)
S & P 500 S&P500総合指数, S&P500株価指数, スタンダード＆プアーズ総合500種株価指数 (Standard & Poor's 500の略。ダウ平均（ダウ工業株30種）とともに, 米株式市場の動向を反映する標準的な経済指標)
saber rattling 軍事力による脅迫
saboteur 名 破壊工作員, 妨害活動をする人
sacred cow 聖牛, 批判［攻撃, 反対］できない神聖な人や組織・物, つねに大切に取り扱われる人［組織, 物］, 聖域
saddle 動 〈仕事や責任を〉負わせる, 課する, 〈馬に〉鞍を置く
 be saddled with …を背負っている, …を抱えている, …に縛りつけられる, …で手いっぱいである
 saddle a person with responsibility 人に責任を負わせる
saddle 名 鞍, 〈自転車などの〉腰かけ, サドル
 cast a person out of the saddle 人を免職する
 in the saddle 馬に乗って, 実権を握って, 仕事に取りかかって, 権力［権限, 責任］を持った
 lose the saddle 落馬する
 put [lay] the saddle on the wrong horse お門違いの人を責める
 take [get into] the saddle 馬に乗る, 権力を手に入れる, 実権を握る
safe 形 安全な, 危険がない, 危険な目にあわない, …しても大丈夫だ, …しても差し支えない, 無傷な, 無事な, リスクが少ない, 無難な, 当たり障りのない
 a safe bet かならず当たる賭け
 safe investment 安全な投資, リスクが少ない投資
 safe returns 安全な利回り
safe harbor rule 安全条項（規則や法律に抵触しないためのガイドライン), 避難条項, 安全港規則, 安全港ルール, セーフ・ハーバー・ルール（「セーフ・ハーバー・ルール」は, 会社が自社株を買い戻すときの規則を定めた米証券取引委員会(SEC)規則10-bの通称)
safe haven 安全な投資先, 資金の逃避先
 safe haven currency 有事に強い通貨
safeguard 動 保護する, 擁護する, 守る
safeguard 名 保護, 保全, 保護手段, 予防手段, 安全装置, 緊急輸入制限, 緊急輸入制限措置, セーフガード措置, 保障条項, 保障規約, セーフガード
 a safeguard against hostile takeovers 敵対的買収の防衛策
 a safeguard emergency import control measure 緊急輸入制限（セーフガード）措置
 environmental safeguard 環境保全
 impose safeguard on …に緊急輸入制限を課す
 multinational safeguard 多面的セーフガード
 safeguard clause [provision] 緊急輸入制限条項, 緊急避難条項, 例外条項, セーフガード・クローズ（＝escape clause）
 safeguard measure 緊急輸入制限措置, セーフガード措置, セーフガード（＝safeguard curbs）
 safeguard system 保障措置
 safeguard tariffs 緊急輸入制限のための関税, セーフガード関税

safeguards agreement 保障措置協定
selective safeguard 選択的セーフガード

safety 名 安全, 安定, 安全性, 安全装置, 安全確保, 保全, セーフティ
　margin of safety 安全余裕率, 安全余裕度, 安全比率, MS比率
　public safety 公安, 公共の安全, 治安, 国民の安全
　safety belt シート・ベルト
　safety criteria 安全基準
　safety net 安全網, 安全策, 安全装置, 救済, 救済策,〈政府の〉社会保障, 安全[安全用]ネット, セーフティ・ネット
　safety precautions 予防措置
　safety work 安全作業

sag 動 下落する, 低下する, 落ち込む, 低迷する, 鈍化する, 沈下する

salad bowl サラダ・ボウル(多民族国家アメリカの別称)

salaried 形 給料取りの, 月給取りの, 有給の
　salaried employee [worker] サラリーマン, 給料生活者
　salaried income 給与所得
　salaried manager 雇用経営者, 有給管理者
　salaried partner 定額給パートナー
　salaried position [post] 有給職

salary 名 給与, 給料, 月給, 俸給, 報酬, サラリー
　back salary 未払い給料
　commencing [initial, starting] salary 初任給
　fat salary 高い給与, 高給
　fixed [straight] salary 固定給
　net monthly salary 税引き後の月収
　salary scale 給与指数
　salary with tax 税込み給与
　small salary 少月給, 薄給

sale 名 販売, 売買, 売却,〈証券などの〉発行, セール
　cash sale 現金販売
　clearance sale 在庫一掃大売出し
　credit sale クレジット販売
　cut-price sale 大安売り
　discount sale 割引販売, 割引売出し, ディスカウント・セール
　forced sale 投げ売り
　funds gained from the sale of shares 株式売却で調達した資金, 株式発行で調達した資金
　gain on sale of bonds 社債売却益
　panic sale 出血大売出し

　proceeds from sale 売却額

sales 名 売上, 売上高, 取引高,〈航空会社などの〉営業利益, 販売, 売買, 売却, 商法, セールス
　approved sales 試用販売
　block sales 大量販売, 大量取引, 大量売付け
　consignment sales 委託販売
　demonstration sales 実演販売
　exclusive sales 独占販売
　exhibition sales 展示販売, 展示販売商法
　export sales 輸出販売, 輸出売上高
　gross sales 総売上高
　installment sales 割賦販売, 割賦売上高, 延べ払い
　premium sales 景品付き販売, プレミアム・セール
　sales agency 販売代理店
　sales base 営業拠点, 販売拠点
　sales force management 販売員管理
　sales projection 売上予想, 販売見通し, 予想売上
　sales resistance 販売拒否, 購買拒否, 需要鈍化傾向
　sales revenue 売上高, 売上収益, 総売上高
　sales task 販売業務, 販売の仕事

salvation 名 救い, 救済, 救助, 救い主, 救世主,〈危害, 損害などからの〉保護, 保存
　be the salvation of …の救い[救済者, 救済手段]となる
　find salvation 改宗する, これ幸いと[都合次第で]変節する, 変節に好都合の口実を見つける
　work out one's own salvation 独力で切り抜ける, 目標を達成する

same period last year 前年同期
▶Operating expenses in the third quarter of 2009 increase by $90 million compared with the *same period last year*. 当四半期[2009年第3四半期]の営業費用は, 前年同期比で9,000万ドル増加しました。

same store sales 既存店ベースの売上高, 既存店ベースの売上

sample 名 見本, 試供品, 標本, サンプル
　independent sample 独立標本
　random sample 無作為標本, 無作為抽出
　reference sample 参照標本
　sample book 見本帳
　sample mean 標本平均
　sample survey 標本調査, サンプル調査

sampler 名 見本検査係, 試食者, 試飲者, 見本集

sampling 名 標本[見本]抽出, 抽出, 抜取り, 見本配布, サンプル採取, サンプリング
　acceptance sampling inspection 受入れ抜取り検査
　cluster sampling 集団抽出(法), クラスター・サンプリング
　exact sampling 精密標本
　judgment sampling 有意抽出(法), 有意選出法
　multistage sampling 多段抽出法
　quota sampling 割当標本抽出法
　random sampling 無作為抽出(法), 任意標本抽出(法), 無作為標本抽出法, ランダム・サンプリング
　sampling rights 〈部下の仕事の〉再調査権
　sampling survey 標本調査 (＝sample survey)
　sequential sampling 逐次標本抽出
　simple random sampling 単純無作為標本, 単純無作為抽出
　stratified sampling 層別抽出(法), 層化抽出
　systematic sampling 系統的抽出(法), 等間隔抽出法
　two-stage sampling 2段抽出(法)
　variables sampling 変数サンプリング

sanctions 名 制裁, 処罰, 認可, 承認, 支持, 制裁措置, 経済制裁措置
　heighten sanctions against …に対する制裁を強化する
　implement economic sanction against …に対して経済制裁を実施する
　impose economic sanctions against …に対して経済制裁を課す, …に対して経済制裁に踏み切る, …に対して経済制裁措置を取る
　lift economic sanctions against …に対する経済制裁[経済制裁措置]を解除する

SAP 構造調整プログラム (structural adjustment programsの略)

SAPTA 南アジア特恵貿易協定 (South Asian Preferential Trade Agreementの略)

Sarbanes–Oxley Act 企業改革法(サーベンス・オクスレー法), 企業会計改革法, サーベンス・オクスレー法, SOX法 (＝Sarbanes-Oxley Act of 2002)
　▶ The *Sarbanes–Oxley Act* directed the SEC to implement some of the reporting changes in an attempt to force companies and their executives to be more honest with investors. 企業と企業経営者に投資家への一段と誠実な対応を義務付けるため, サーベンス・オクスレー法は, SEC (米証券取引委員会)に報告規則変更の一部実施を求めた。

SARS 重症急性呼吸器症候群, 新型肺炎 (severe acute respiratory syndromeの略)

SAT 〈米〉大学進学適性試験 (scholastic assessment testの略)

satellite 名 衛星, 人工衛星, 衛星都市, 近郊都市, 衛星国家, 従者, 家来
　anti-satellite (ASAT) weapons 対衛星兵器
　artificial satellite 人工衛星 (＝man-made satellite)
　application(s) satellite 実用衛星
　broadcasting satellite 放送衛星《略 BS》
　by [via] satellite 衛星を使って
　communication(s) satellite 通信衛星《略 CS》
　Data Relay Test Satellite データ中継技術衛星《略 DRTS》
　engineering test satellite 技術試験衛星《略 ETS》
　geodetic satellite 測地衛星
　Geostationary Operational Environmental Satellite 静止環境観測衛星, ゴーズ《略 GOES》(日本での愛称は「パシフィック・ゴーズ」)
　geostationary satellite 静止衛星
　Global Positioning System Satellite 全地球測位システム衛星, GPS衛星
　meteorological satellite 気象衛星
　Multifunctional Transport Satellite-1R 運輸多目的衛星新1号《略 MTSAT-1R》
　satellite communications 衛星通信
　satellite dish パラボナ・アンテナ
　satellite nation [country, state] 衛星国
　Tracking and Data Relay Satellite 追跡データ中継衛星《略 TDRS》

satisfaction 名 満足, 充足, 納得, 得心, 償い, 賠償, 返済, 弁済, 義務・債務の履行, 弁済証書
　customer satisfaction 顧客の満足, 顧客満足度《略 CS》
　full or partial satisfaction of previous debts 債務の全額または一部の弁済
　satisfaction of mortgage 譲渡抵当消滅証書
　satisfaction of senior obligations 優先債務の支払い
　satisfaction piece 償還履行証書
　▶ The emphasis on customer *satisfaction* emerged as a major business growth strategy in the 1980's. 顧客満足度を重視する考え方は, 1980年代に企業の重要な成長戦略として浮上した。

satisfy

satisfy 動 満足させる, 充足させる, 〈欲求などを〉満たす, 条件を満たす, 〈人を〉納得させる, 〈借金を〉支払う, 返済する, 〈義務を〉果たす[履行する], 〈損害などを〉賠償する, 償う, 〈疑いを〉晴らす
- **satisfy a creditor** 債権者に弁済する
- **satisfy a debt for a person** 人に負債を払う
- **satisfy one's doubts** 疑念[疑いの念]を晴らす, 疑念を解消する
- **satisfy oneself** 納得する, 確かめる
- **satisfy the convergence criteria** 収斂基準を達成する[クリア]する
- **satisfy the liability** 債務を履行する, 債務を返済する

saturate 動 〈商品を〉過剰供給する, だぶつかせる, 飽和状態にさせる, 一杯にする, 満たす, 没頭させる
- **be saturated with** …に没頭している, …で一杯だ, …が満ち溢れている
- **saturate oneself in** …に没頭する
- ▶ The market for these products is *saturated*. これらの製品の市場は, 供給過剰になっている[飽和状態だ]。

saturated 形 しみ込んだ, びしょぬれの, 飽和した, 飽和状態の, …の飽和, …を集中攻撃する

saturation 名 飽和, 飽和状態, 飽和感, 浸透, 浸透度, 普及率, 成熟, 成熟化
- **capital saturation** 資本の飽和点, 資本の飽和状態
- **saturation bombing** じゅうたん爆撃, 集中爆撃, 徹底的爆撃
- **saturation curve** 飽和曲線
- **saturation level** 普及率, 飽和水準
- **saturation point** 飽和点, 限界点
- **sign of saturation** 飽和感

Saturday night special 不意打ち[予告なし]の株式公開買付け, 土曜夜の特番

save 動 救う, 救助する, 救済する, 助ける, 救出する, 蓄える, 貯蓄する, 取っておく, 確保する, 節約する, 無駄[手間]を省く, 収集する, 保つ, 保護する, セーブする

savings 名 貯蓄, 貯金, 預金, 年金
- **callable savings deposits** 解約可能の貯蓄預金
- **Federal Savings and Loan Insurance Corporation** 米連邦貯蓄貸付保険公社
- **gross savings** 総貯蓄, 総貯蓄率
- **installment savings** 積立貯金
- **national savings** 国民貯蓄, 国内貯蓄
- **net savings** 純貯蓄
- **overall savings rate** 総貯蓄率
- **personal savings** 個人預金, 個人貯蓄, 個人貯蓄率, リテール貯蓄
- **retirement savings** 退職年金
- **savings account** 貯蓄預金, 貯蓄口座, 銀行預金, 普通預金
- **savings and loan association** 貯蓄金融機関, 〈米国の〉貯蓄貸付組合(S&L)
- **savings deposit** 貯蓄預金, 貯蓄性預金, 普通預金
- **savings from a debt waiver** 債務免除益
- **savings incentive plan** 貯蓄奨励制度
- **surplus savings** 余剰貯蓄
- **tax-exempt savings** 非課税貯蓄
- **thrift savings account** 積立預金口座
- **time savings** 定期預金

savvy 名 実際的な知識, 実務知識, 知識, 能力, 手腕, 理解力, 勘, 形 事情通の, 精通した, 物知りの, 博識の, 抜け目のない, やり手の, しっかりした, 経験[知識]の豊富な, ベテランの
- **computer savvy** コンピュータの知識を持った, コンピュータ通の
- **savvy businessman** やり手のビジネスマン
- **savvy investor** やり手の投資家
- **technological savvy** 技術通

say 名 発言権, 発言力
- ▶ The developing world wants a *say* in the Iraq crisis. 発展途上国も, イラク危機で発言権を求めている。

scale

scale 動 よじ登る, 削り取る, こすりとる, 秤にかける, 比べる
- **scale back** 縮小する, 削減する, 減額にする, 下方修正する
- **scale down** ある割合で減らす, 縮小する, 事業規模を縮小する
- **scale up** ある割合で増す, 拡大する
- ▶ Japanese electric machinery firms may accelerate moves to *scale* down or withdraw from unprofitable businesses. 電機メーカー各社は, 採算の合わない事業からの撤退や事業縮小の動きが加速する可能性がある。

scale 名 規模, 基準, 尺度, 段階, 金利体系, 発行条件, 目盛り, スケール
- **be in full scale recovery** 本格的に回復している
- **decimal scale** 十進法
- **economy of scale** 規模の経済, 規模の経済性, 規模の利益, 数量効果, スケール・メリット (= economies of scale, scale economies)

hold the scales even 公平に裁く
large-scale economic stimulus measures 大型の財政出動
manufacturing scale 生産規模
measurement of scale 測定尺度

scale-back [scaleback] 名 〈規模などの〉縮小, 削減, 小型化, 減額
scale merit 規模の利益, 規模拡大によるメリット［利益］, スケール・メリット
scaledown [scale-down] 名 規模縮小, 比率削減, 小型化（＝downsizing, scaleback）
　business scaledown 事業の規模縮小, 事業縮小
　debt scaledown 債務削減
　scaledown of flight services 運航路線［運航便］の縮小
　scaledown of loss-making businesses 不採算事業の縮小, 赤字事業の縮小
　substantial scaledown 大幅削減
scam 名 詐欺(fraud), 取り込み詐欺, ペテン, 不正, 噂, スキャンダル
　fake billing scam 架空請求詐欺
　insurance scam 保険詐欺
　marriage scam 結婚詐欺（＝marriage fraud）
　pull [carry out] a scam 詐欺を働く
　scam artist 詐欺師, ペテン師
scandal 名 醜聞, 流説, 疑惑, 不祥事, 不正行為, 汚職［疑獄］事件, 事件, 中傷, ひどいこと, 恥, 不名誉, スキャンダル
　corruption scandals 贈収賄スキャンダル
　cover up bribery scandals 贈収賄事件を隠す
　give rise to scandal 世間の反感を買う, 世間の物議をかもす
　scandal ridden スキャンダルに揺らぐ
　scandal sheet 〈興味本位の暴露記事を主とする〉赤新聞, スキャンダル雑誌
　to the scandal of …を憤慨させたことには
　uncover bribery scandals 贈収賄事件を暴く
scanlation 名 〈日本マンガなどのネットでの〉無断翻訳公開, スキャンレーション
scanner 名 読取り機, 映像走査機, 走査機, 走査装置, スキャナー
scanning 名 要点把握,〔監査技術〕通査, 走査
scapegoat 名 身代わり, 犠牲, スケープゴート
scenario 名 シナリオ, 台本, 筋書き, 事態, 状況, 脚本, 予測, 予定の計画, 行動計画, 計画案
　alternative scenario 代替プラン, 予備のプラン
　every possible scenario 想定されるあらゆる事態
　most likely scenario 最も実現しそうなシナリオ
　optimistic scenario 楽観的シナリオ
　worst case scenario 最悪の事態, 最悪のシナリオ（＝nightmare scenario）
scene 名 光景, 景色, 風景, 眺め, 舞台, 場面, 背景, 状況, 事情, 事態, 出来事, 現場, 現地, 場所, 場, 業界, 分野, …界, 大騒ぎ, 醜態, シーン
　be back on the scene 復活している
　behind the scenes 舞台裏で, 裏側で, 秘密裏に, ひそかに, 内密で, 陰で, 黒幕として, 内幕に通じて, 内情に詳しい
　come [appear] on the scene 現われる, 登場する, 姿を現わす
　make a scene 大騒ぎをする, 醜態を演じる, 口論する, 口喧嘩する
　make the scene 登場する, やってくる, 派手にやる, 人目を引く, 参加する, 加わる
　rush to the scene of …の現場に急行する
　set the scene 〈時や場所などの〉状況をくわしく述べる, 状況を話す
　set the scene for …の準備をする
　steal the scene 人気をさらう
schedule 動 予定する, 予定を立てる, 計画を立てる, 予定表を作る
　as scheduled 予定どおり
　be scheduled to …する予定だ, …する方針である
　scheduled flight [service] 定期便
　scheduled maintenance 定期保守
　scheduled payment 予定支払, 約定支払い
schedule 名 別表, 別紙, 付属書類, 明細表, 一覧表, 予定表,〈法律の〉付則, 予定, 計画, スケジュール
　aging schedule 年齢調べ表, 満期表
　attached schedule 付表, 添付の付属書類
　bank transfer schedule 銀行間振替明細表
　commission schedule 手数料明細表
　delivery schedule 納期
　demand schedule 需要表, 需要曲線
　maturity schedule 償還計画
　progressive schedule 付属明細表, 追加的明細表
　SEC schedules SEC付属明細表
　schedule control スケジュール管理, 進捗状況
　schedule maintenance 定期保守, 定期保全
　tariff schedule 関税表, 料金制度
scheduling 名 日程計画, 予定作成, スケジューリング

short interval scheduling ショート・インターバル・スケジューリング《略 **SIS**》(管理会計の手法。年次や決算期ではなく，月次や週次，日次など短い周期で損益を集計し，その都度，予算と実績のズレを監視することによって的確に予算の軌道修正をする手法)

scheme 名 事業，計画，企画，案，策，仕組み，制度，体系，方式，組織，機構，体制，概要
  collective investment scheme 集合投資計画，集合投資ファンド
  defined benefit scheme 確定給付年金
  employment training scheme 雇用訓練事業
  pension scheme 年金制度
  regulatory scheme 規制機構
  retirement benefit scheme 退職給与制度

SCHIP 州児童医療保険プログラム(低所得者層の子供を対象にした米国の公的医療保険で **State Children's Health Insurance Program** の略。「メディケード」の加入基準より所得は高いが，民間保険を購入する余裕がない低所得層が対象)

schizophrenia 名 統合失調症，精神分裂病 (＝dementia praecox, loss of coordination disorder, split mind disorder)

scholastic 形 学校の，学校教育の，教育の，学業の，研究の，中学・高校の，中等教育の，学者ぶった(pedantic)，学者風の，衒学的な，堅苦しい，スコラ哲学の
  scholastic ability 学力
  Scholastic Assessment Test 〈米国の〉大学進学適性検査，学力評価試験《略 **SAT**》
  scholastic performance 学業成績，学力 (＝scholastic ability, scholastic attainment)
  scholastic records 学業成績
  the scholastic post 教職

school 名 学校，大学，流派，学派，…流，…派，スクール
  school age 学齢，就学年齢
  school board 米教育委員会
  school career 学歴
  school meal [dinner, lunch] 学校給食
  school phobia 学校ぎらい，学校恐怖症
  school-rejection syndrome 登校拒否症
  school report 通知表，成績通知表
  school year 学年 (＝academic year：英米の学年度は9月～6月まで)

science and technology 科学技術
scientific community 科学界
scientific whaling 調査捕鯨

scion 名 御曹司
SCNT 体細胞核移植［転移］，体細胞クローン技術 (**somatic cell nuclear transfer** の略)
scope 名 範囲，領域，枠組み，構成，区分，余地，機会，可能性
scorn 名 軽蔑，侮辱，あざけり，嘲笑，軽蔑の的，笑いぐさ，物笑いの種，こきおろし
  become a scorn to [become the scorn of] …の物笑いになる
  have [feel] scorn for …に軽蔑の念を抱く，…を見下げる
  hold a person in scorn 人を軽蔑する
  laugh a person to scorn 人を一笑に付す，人を嘲笑する［嘲笑う］
  pour scorn on …をこきおろす，厳しく［強く］批判する
  show scorn for …を軽蔑する

scourge 名 苦しみのもと，悩みの種，天罰，災難，たたり，災厄
  the scourge of war 戦禍
  the white scourge 肺病

scrap 動 撤回する，撤廃する，打ち切る，中止する，止める，廃止する，廃案にする，捨てる，廃品にする，スクラップにする
  scrap flight services 運航を廃止する
  scrap the merger deal 合併協議を打ち切る，合併計画を撤回する

scratch 名 出発点，出発時間，なぐり書き，かすり傷，ひっかき傷，スクラッチ
  be [come] up to scratch 一定の水準［基準，標準］に達している，満足すべきだ，期待どおりだ，義務［約束］を果たす
  from [on] scratch 出発点［最初］から，始め［一］から，ゼロから，無一文から，何の蓄えもなしに
  scratch pad [paper] メモ用紙，メモ帳
  start on scratch 時間どおりに出発する

screeching halt 急ブレーキ
screen 動 ふるい分ける，ふるいにかける，選別する，審査する，選考する，検定する，上映する
▶Until last year, many start-up companies had to shelve planned listings when they were *screened* by securities firms. 昨年までは，新興企業の多くが，証券会社の審査段階で予定していた上場を見送らざるを得なかった。

screening 名 審査，検査，選別，選考，適格審査，適性検査，上映，放映，スクリーニング
  creditworthiness screening standard 与信審査基準

customer screening　顧客審査
lax screening　手薄な審査
scrutiny 名　綿密な調査, 調査, 検討, 監視, 再調査, 吟味, 詮索
　be under scrutiny　監視されている, 監視の目にさらされる, チェックされる
　give close [careful] scrutiny to　…を綿密に調査[検討]する
　make a scrutiny into　…を精査する
　undergo a careful scrutiny　入念な検査[チェック]を受ける
scuttle 動　止めさせる, 撤回させる, 台なしにする, だめにする, 廃棄する, 中止する
SDI　戦略防衛構想 (**Strategic Defense Initiative**の略)
SDR　〈IMFの〉特別引出し権 (**special drawing right(s)**の略)
sea 名　海, 海洋, 波, 大波, 海辺, 海岸
　North Sea Brent Spot　北海ブレント・スポット
　northern-sea fishery　北洋漁業
　sea bank　海岸堤防
　sea bed　海底
　sea change　大きな変化, 大変化, 大変革, 著しい変貌
　sea dumping operations　海洋投棄作業
　sea farming　海洋養殖, 海洋栽培 (= mariculture)
　sea-launched cruise missile　海上発射巡航ミサイル《略 SLCM》
　sea level　海面
　sea nation　海洋国
　sea power　海軍力, 海軍大国
　sea room　操船余地
　sea wall　防波堤, 護岸堤防
　sea well　海底油田
　sea wolf　海賊
　territorial sea　領海
　sea lane　海上交通路, 海上航路帯, 常設航路, 航路, シーレーン
　sea-lane defense　シーレーン防衛
seafloor hydrothermal deposits　海底熱水鉱床
▶ *Seafloor hydrothermal deposits* are formed with metals contained in hot water discharged from the seafloor.　海底熱水鉱床は, 海底から噴き出した熱水に含まれる金属が沈殿して作られる。
seal off　密封する, 包囲する, 立入りを禁じる, …を断つ

seam 名　継ぎ目, 縫い目, つなぎ目, ぎくしゃく感, しわ, 傷跡, 貴重な物
　an open seam　ほころび
　be bursting at the seams　あふれるばかりに一杯だ, あふれそうだ
　be coming [falling] apart at the seams　破綻しそうだ, 失敗しそうだ, 崩壊寸前にある, 服の縫い目からほつれかかっている
seamless 形　継ぎ目のない, 部位と部位との継ぎ目を感じさせない, ぎくしゃく感がない, 途切れない, 滑らかな, 円滑に, 完全に一体化した, 一貫した, シームレス
　seamless connections with　…とのシームレスな接続
　seamless pipe　継ぎ目なし鋼管
search 動　捜索する, 探求する, 追求する, 調査する, 精査する, 検索する
　search a ship　船を臨検する
　search for stolen goods　盗難品を捜す
　search into an accident　事故を調査する
　search the Internet for　…を求めてインターネットを検索する, …をインターネットで検索する
search 名　捜索, 探求, 調査, 精査, 分析, 検索, 情報検索, サーチ
　do [perform, run] a search on the Internet　インターネットで検索する
　job search　求職, 求職活動, 職探し, ジョブ・サーチ
　search and rescue system　捜索救難システム
　search and rescue transceiver　捜索救助用トランシーバー
　search engine　インターネット[ネット]検索エンジン, 検索エンジン, サーチ・エンジン
　search function　検索機能
　search goods　精査商品
　search party　捜索隊
　search warrant　〈家宅〉捜索令状
　title search　権原調査
season 名　季節, 時期, 最盛期, 活動期, …期, シーズン
　holiday season　〈米国の〉祝祭シーズン(感謝祭から正月までの休暇期間)
　most profitable season　書き入れどき
　off-demand season　需要減退期
　off season　閑散期, 商売の霜枯れ時, シーズンオフ (= dead season, dull season)
　results season　決算シーズン, 決算発表シーズン
　tourist season　観光シーズン

seasonal 形 季節の, 季節的な, 季節ごとの
 seasonal affective disorder 季節性うつ病, 季節性感情障害《略 **SAD**》
 seasonal credit 季節的信用(季節的資金需要の変化に応じて, 米連邦準備銀行が小規模預金受入れ機関に対して行う1か月以上の貸出)
 seasonal fluctuation 季節的変動, 季節変動
 seasonal influenza 季節性インフルエンザ
 seasonal moves [reasons] 季節要因
 seasonal swings 季節的なブレ
 seasonal worker 期間従業員, 季節労働者(＝seasonal laborer)

seasonally adjusted 季節調整済みの, 季節調整後の, 季節調整値
 in seasonally adjusted terms 季節調整済みで, 季節調整済みで見ると, 季節調整値で
 not seasonally adjusted 季節調整前[前の], 季節未調整
 seasonally adjusted basis 季節調整値, 季節調整済み, 季節調整ベース
 ▶ Industrial output fell a *seasonally adjusted* 1.1 percent in July from the previous month as demand for vehicles and machinery shrank. 7月の鉱工業生産高は, 自動車と機械の需要が減少したため, 前月比で1.1%(季節調整値)減少した。

seasonally unadjusted 季節未調整の, 季節調整前の, 季節未調整値

seasoned 形 経験豊かな, 老練な, 練達の, 年季の入った, 期間[年数]の経った, 期間が経過した, 適切な
 seasoned entrepreneur 経験豊かな経営者
 seasoned issue 既発銘柄, 既発債
 seasoned judgment 適切な判断
 seasoned loan 経過期間が長いローン
 seasoned new issue 公開済み証券の発行, 既存の証券の追加発行

seasoning 名 調味, 味付け, 調味料, 香辛料

seat 名 席, 座席, 座部, 〈ズボンの〉尻の部分, 中心部(center), 中心地, 中枢, 活動拠点, 場所(site, location), 所在地, 位置, 議席, 議員の地位, 議員権, 会員権(membership), 姿勢, 乗り方, シート
 a Diet seat 議席
 be in the driver's [driving] seat 責任者の立場にある
 be on [in] the hot seat 重責の立場にある
 contest a seat in the Congress 議会の議席を争う
 have [get] a seat on the board of directors 取締役会[理事会]の一員である, 取締役[理事]の1人である, 取締役会の一員になる
 keep one's congressional [parliamentary] seat 議席を維持する
 seat belt 安全ベルト, シートベルト
 seat turnover rate 客席回転率
 take a back seat to …の後部座席に座る, …より後回しになる, 二の次になる, 2番手につく
 take one's seat 議員活動を始める, 座る, 腰かける
 the (chief) seat of commerce 商業の中心地
 the seat of consciousness [mind] 意識の中枢
 win a seat (in Congress) 〈議会の〉議席を得る, 議員に当選する

SEATO 東南アジア条約機構(**Southeast Asia Treaty Organization**の略)

SEC 〈米〉証券取引委員会(**Securities and Exchange Commission**の略)

secession 名 分離, 離脱, 分離独立, 脱退, 脱党, 脱会

second 形 第二の, 二番目の, 従属的な, 補助の, 二流の, セカンド
 at second hand 間接的に, また聞きで
 be second only to …を除けば何にも劣らない, …を除けば1位だ
 second banana 脇役, ナンバー2
 second chamber 〈二院制議会(bicameral parliament)の〉上院(＝upper house)
 second half 下半期, 下期(＝the second half of the fiscal [business] year, the second half of the year)
 Second Lady 米副大統領夫人
 second mate [officer] 二等航海士
 second mortgage 二番抵当
 second nature 第二の天性, 深く身についた習慣
 second reading 〈議会での〉第二読会(議案の討議と修正を行って委員会に付託する)
 second shift 第二の勤務, 家事, 家事労働
 second thought 考え直し, 思い直し, 再考, 反省
 second-tiered 準大手の, 中堅の, 中位の, 二段目の
 second trial 〈裁判の〉2審
 second wind 気力[元気]の回復, 元気を取り戻すこと, 新たなエネルギー
 the second sex 第二の性, 女性

secondary 形 二次的な, 副次的な, 二流の

secondary flows 流通市場の取引
secondary infection 二次感染
secondary market 流通市場
secondary-market value 流通市場価格
secondary offering 売出し (＝secondary distribution：既発行の有価証券の取得申込みを勧誘すること)
secondary poisoning 二次的中毒
secondhand 形 中古の, 間接の, また聞きの, 受け売りの, 独創的でない
secondhand hand [second-hand] smoke 受動喫煙, 副流煙 (＝passive smoking)
secret 名 秘密, 機密, 内密, 秘訣, 秘伝, 形 秘密の, 機密の, シークレット
　be hardly a secret 周知の事実である
　secret ballot 無記名投票
　state secret 国家機密
　the secret of success 成功の秘訣
　the secret service 〈英の〉機密情報部 (intelligence service)
　the Secret Service シークレット・サービス, 米財務省秘密検察局
　trade secret 企業秘密, 営業秘密, 営業上の秘密, トレード・シークレット
secretary 名 秘書, 幹事, 書記官, 〈組合の〉書記長, 事務官, 〈米各省の〉長官, 〈英各省の〉大臣
　assistant secretary of U.S. State Department 〈米〉国務次官補
　diplomatic secretary 〈大使館などの〉書記官
　Foreign Secretary 〈英〉外務大臣
　General Secretary 〈国連や北大西洋条約機構の〉事務総長, 幹事長, 事務局長
　Home Secretary 〈英〉内務大臣
　Permanent Secretary 次官
　secretary firm 業務代行会社
　secretary general 事務総長, 事務局長, 官房長, 幹事長, 〈組合の〉書記長
　Secretary of Commerce 〈米〉商務長官
　Secretary of Defense 〈米〉国防長官
　secretary of state 〈米〉国務長官, 州務長官
　Secretary of State 〈米国の外務大臣に当たる首席閣僚の〉国務長官, 〈米州政府の〉州務長官, 〈英国の〉国務大臣
　Secretary of the Treasury 〈米〉財務長官
　U.S. Assistant Secretary of State 〈米〉国務省次官補
　U.S. secretary of state 〈米〉国務長官
　U.S. Treasury Secretary 〈米〉財務長官

sectarian 形 宗派の
　sectarian tensions 宗派間の緊張
section 名 区域, 地区, 区分, 区画, 地域, 地方, 階級, 階層, 部, 部門, 〈団体の〉党, 派, 切断, 断面, 断面図, 段落, 〈書物の〉節, 〈新聞などの〉欄, 〈法律, 契約書などの〉条, 条項, 切断, 切開, セクション
　conic section 円錐曲線
　cross [transverse] section 横断面, 社会の断面, クロス・セクション
　financial section 財務区分, 〈年次報告書の〉財務の部
　have a Caesarean section 帝王切開手術を受ける
　horizontal section 水平断面図
　opinion section 意見区分
　section steel 形鋼 (かたこう)
　Section 201 provision of the U.S. Omnibus Trade Act 米通商法201条, 米包括通商法201条
　surplus section 剰余金区分
　the document section 文書課
sectional 形 組立て式の, 特定集団のための, 特定区域に限定した, 派閥の, 派閥的な, 党派的な, 地方的な, 一地方偏重の, 断面の, 断面図の, 区分の, 部門の, 部分の, 部分的な
　sectional form 区分式
　sectional income statement 区分損益計算書
　sectional interests 地方的利害
　sectional quarrels 派閥争い
sectionalism 名 派閥主義, セクト主義, 縄張り主義, 地方主義, 地方偏重主義, 地方的偏見
sector 名 部門, 分野, 業界, 地域, 市場, 株, セクター
　banking sector 銀行業, 銀行業界, 銀行セクター, 金融機関
　corporate sector 企業部門, 法人部門, 企業セクター, 企業
　corporate sector's performance 企業業績
　domestic-demand dependent sectors 内需依存株
　household sector 家計部門
　labor-intensive sectors 労働集約型産業
　leasing sector リース部門
　life insurance sector 生命保険業界, 生保業界 (＝life insurance industry)
　manufacturing sector 製造業, 製造業セクター
　primary sectors 第一次産業
　private sector 民間部門, 民間セクター, 民間企業

public and private sector financial institutions　政府系金融機関と民間金融機関
public sector　政府部門, 公共部門, 公共セクター, 公営企業
T-bill sector　Tビル市場, 米財務省短期証券市場
technology sector　ハイテク株
transportation sector　運輸部門

secular 形　長期的な, 構造的な, 長年続く, 何世紀も続く, 現世の, この世の, 俗人の, 宗教とは関係ない
　cyclical and secular factors [reasons]　循環要因と構造要因
　secular affairs　俗事
　secular disequilibrium　長期的不均衡
　secular disturbance　長期的混乱
　secular education　普通教育
　secular expansion　長期拡大
　secular fluctuation　長期変動
　secular stagnation　長期停滞
　secular trend　長期的傾向, 長期趨勢, 長期トレンド, 構造的なトレンド

secularism 名　世俗主義, 政教分離論

secure 動　獲得する, 手に入れる, 得る, 確保する, 達成する, 実現する, 設定する, 固定する, 〈支払い を〉保証する, 請け合う, 〈…から〉守る, 安全にする, もたらす (bring about), 確実にする, 確固たるものにする, 〈…に〉保険を付ける, …に担保を付ける
　be secured by　…によって保証される, …で担保されている, …を担保にして, …を裏付けとする
　be secured on　…を担保とする
　secure against　…に備える
　secure bank financing　銀行融資を受ける
　secure oneself against accidents　損害保険を付ける
　secure human resources　人材を確保する
　secure the loan on mortgage　抵当を入れてローンを組む, 抵当を入れて融資を受ける

secure 形　安全な, 危険のない, 心配がない, 不安のない, 気苦労のない, 確実な, 確かな, 信頼できる, 安定した, しっかりした, 確立した, 揺ぎない, 落ち着いた, 自信に満ちた, 難攻不落の
　be secure of　…を確信する
　on secure ground　確信をもって
　secure base　確固たる基盤, 確かな基盤
　secure from [against]　…の恐れがない, …の心配[危険]がない, …から守られている

secured 形　確実な, 保証された, 担保付きの
　make secured loans　担保付き融資を行う

secured bond [debenture]　担保付き社債, 担保付き債券
secured credit　担保付き貸付け (secured loan), 担保付き信用状
secured debt　担保付き債務, 担保付き負債, 有担保債券
secured debt instrument　有担保債券
secured financing　担保付き資金調達
secured obligation　担保付き社債 (=secured bond)
secured party　担保権者

securities 名　有価証券, 証券, 債券, 証書, 権利証書
　available-for-sale securities　売却可能有価証券
　debt securities　債券, 債務証券, 債務証書
　equity securities　持ち分証券, 持ち分有価証券
　fixed income securities　確定利付き証券, 債務証券, 債券
　government securities　政府債
　held-to-maturity securities　償還期限まで保有する有価証券
　interest on securities　有価証券利息
　investment securities　投資証券, 投資有価証券
　listed securities　上場証券
　marketable securities　市場性ある有価証券, 市場性証券, 上場有価証券
　money market securities　短期金融証券
　municipal securities　地方債
　non-marketable securities　非市場性証券
　public debt securities　国債
　public market securities　公募証券
　securities account　有価証券勘定
　Securities Act of 1933　〈米国の〉1933年証券法
　Securities Acts Amendments of 1975　1975年証券改革法
　Securities and Exchange Law　証券取引法
　securities brokerage　証券仲介, 証券仲介業 (=stock brokerage : 株式や債券などの売買注文を取り次ぐ業務)
　securities brokering　証券仲介 (=securities brokerage business, stock brokerage business)
　securities company [firm, house]　証券会社 (=stock brokerage)
　securities exchange　証券取引所
　securities holdings　有価証券の保有, 保有有価

証券, 保有証券, 保有株
securities investment 証券投資, 有価証券投資
Securities Investor Protection Act of 1970 1970年証券投資家保護法
securities report 有価証券報告書
trading securities 売買目的有価証券, 商品有価証券
underlying securities 原証券, 対象証券
unlisted securities 非上場証券（＝unquoted securities)
unrealized gains on securities 証券含み益
yield on securities 有価証券利回り

Securities and Exchange Commission
米証券取引委員会《略 SEC》

> 米証券取引委員会(SEC) ⊃ 証券関連法の運用と公正な証券取引の維持および投資家保護を目的として、1934年証券取引法に基づいて創設された米国の独立した連邦政府機関。委員会は、上院の同意を得て大統領が任命する任期5年の委員5人で構成されている。

Securities and Exchange Surveillance Commission
証券取引等監視委員会《略 SESC》

securitization 名 証券化, 金融の証券化, セキュリタイゼーション
　asset securitization 資産の証券化（＝securitization of assets)
　bad loan securitization 不良債権の証券化（＝securitization of bad loans)
securitize 動 証券化する
　securitize borrowings 借入れを証券化する
　securitize housing loan claims 住宅ローンの債権を証券化する
securitized 形 証券化した, …の証券化
　securitized debt 証券化した債権, 債権の証券化
　securitized home mortgages 証券化した住宅モーゲージ, 住宅ローンの証券化
　securitized investment 証券化商品への投資
security 名 安全, 安全性, 安心, 無事, 安全保障, 公安, 保安, 警備, 保護, 防衛, 防衛手段, 警備対策, 保証, 保証人, 担保, 抵当, 証券, 銘柄, 保険, セキュリティ
　benefit security 給付保障
　collateral security 物的担保
　financial security 支払い能力, 財務上の安全性
　impersonal security 物的担保
　job security 雇用の安定, 雇用保障, 職務保証
　loan security 貸付け証券

national [state] security 国家の安全
on security of …を担保にして, …を抵当にして
real security 人的担保
risk security リスク証券
security camera 防犯カメラ
security check 身体検査, ボディチェック
security clearance 機密情報閲覧許可, 秘密事項取扱い許可
security credit 証券金融
security deposit 敷金
Security Force 国連軍
security forces 治安部隊, 警備隊, 治安維持勢力
security guard 警備員, 保安係, ガードマン（＝security man [woman], security officer)
security holes 安全対策の盲点, セキュリティ・ホール
security interest 担保権
security police 治安警察, 公安警察, 要人警護隊
security precaution 警備体制
security risk 危険な状況, 危険人物, 要注意人物
security taxation system 証券税制
security treaty [pact] 安全保障条約
social security 社会保障, 社会保険
unemployment security 失業保険

Security Council
〈国連〉安全保障理事会《略 SC》

Security Council resolution 安保理決議
see 動 見る, 理解する, 認める, 確かめる,〈…するように〉取り計らう, 予測する, 自動 見る, 見える, わかる, 気をつける
　see about …を取り計らう
　see eye to eye with …と意見［見解］が一致する, …と同意見である, …に同調している
　see into …を調査する
　see over …を調べる, 見分する
　see the back of …を追放する, …を追い払う, 厄介払いする
　see through …を見破る, 見抜く, 見通す
　see (to it) that …するように取り計らう, …するようにしておく
seek 動 求める, 追求する, 狙う, 要求する, 申請する, 探す, 探査する, 調査する, 手に入れようとする, 得ようとする, …に努める
　be (much) sought after 求められている, 需要がある, 引っ張りだこだ, もてはやされる
　be not far to seek 〈答えなどが〉すぐに見つか

る, すぐに分かる, 手元にある
seek a rating 格付けを申請する
seek advice from …に助言［アドバイス］を求める
seek compensation from …に補償を求める, …に賠償請求する（＝claim compensation from）
seek court protection 破産申請する
seek investments in …への出資を募る, …への投資を誘致する
seek out 探し出す
seek refuge in …に保護を求める
seek relief 減免を求める
seek to …しようとする, …に努力する, …に努める
seizure 名 差し押さえ, 押収, 没収, 接収, 監禁, 逮捕
select 動 選ぶ, 選択する, 選び出す, 選抜する, 抜粋する, 選出する, 選任する
select 形 特別の, 特別に選ばれた少数の, 選り抜きの, 極上の, 高級の, 上流階級限定の
  select committee 〈議会の〉特別委員会, 特別調査委員会
  select school 入学資格の厳しい学校
  select society 上流社会
  the select few 専門家, 目利き
selection 名 選択, 選出, 選任, 選抜, 選定, 抜粋, 選集, 精選品, 商品選択の幅, セレクション
  portfolio selection 資産選択, 資産選好, 資産管理, 株式銘柄選択, ポートフォリオ・セレクション
  risk selection リスクの選択, 危険選択
self 形 同じ, 同一の, 同一材料の, 同種の, 一様の, 単色の, 単一色の
self– 接頭 自己の, 自分で, 自らを, 自然の, 自動的な
  self–actualization 自己実現, 自己認識, 自己能力の発揮
  self assessment 自己査定, 自己評価, 申告納税
  self–control 自己管理, 自動制御
  self–criticism 自己批判, 反省
  Self–Defense Force 自衛隊《略 SDF》
  self–determination 民族自決
  self–development program 自己啓発計画《略 SDP》
  self–government 自治
  self–imposed ban [curb] 自主規制
  self–management 自主管理
  self–rehabilitation 自主再建, 自力再建
  self–service gas station セルフのガソリン・スタンド, セルフサービス方式のガソリン・スタンド
  self tender 株式の自己買付け
self–declared bankruptcy 自己破産（破産法に基づく債務整理の一つで, 債務者本人が裁判所に破産申立てを行う。破産宣告を受けると, 財産があれば管財人が選ばれて処分されるほか, 就くことのできる職業が限定されるとか, 裁判所の許可なく移転できなくなるなどの制限を受ける。その後, 裁判所から債務の免責が認められると, それ以上の支払い義務や職業などの制限はなくなる。）
self–employed 形 自営業の, 自家営業の, 自営の, 個人経営の（＝self–operated）
  the self–employed 自営業者
self–funding department 独立採算の事業部
▶ The company has expanded its business by encouraging competition between *self–funding departments* within the group. 同社はこれまで, 独立採算の事業部をグループ内で競争させて事業を拡大してきた。
self–help 名 自助
  self–help efforts 自助努力
self–sufficiency 名 自給自足, 自立, 自足, 自給, うぬぼれ
  food self–sufficiency 食糧自給率
  energy self–sufficiency エネルギー自給
self–supporting 形 自給の, 自営の, 自力の, 自活の
  self–supporting accounting system 独立採算制
self–sustainable growth 自律的な成長
self–sustaining 形 独力で維持できる, 自給の, 自活できる, 自立した, 〈核反応などが〉自動継続式の, 継続的な
  self–sustaining fund 自己調達資金
  self–sustaining growth 自律的成長
  self–sustaining recovery 自律回復
sell 動 販売する, 売る, 売却する, 売り渡す, 売り込む, 納入する, 〈電力などを〉供給する, 処分する, 〈債券などを〉発行する, 譲渡する
  sell by public tender 公開入札で売却する
  sell electricity to small–lot users 小口ユーザーに電力を供給［販売］する
  sell operating rights to …に営業権を譲渡する
sell off 売却する, 投げ売りする, 安く売り払う, 見切り品として処分する
sell–off 名 投げ売り, 売却, 売り, 売り局面, 売り抜け, 急落

accelerate sell-offs of stockholdings 保有株の売却を加速させる
spark a sell-off 売り進める
sell order 売り注文
seller 图 売り手, 売り主, 販売者, 売れる製品[商品]
　a bad seller 売れない商品
　a good [big, hot] seller ヒット商品, 売れ行きのよい商品
　a short seller 空売り筋, 相場師, 信用の売り手
　seller's inflation 売り手インフレーション, 費用圧力インフレ (=cost inflation, cost-push inflation)
　seller's monopoly 売り手独占, 販売独占
　seller's option 売り主の選択, 売り手オプション, 特約日決済取引, 特約日取引
selling 图 売り, 販売, 売込み, 売越し, 商法
　direct selling 直接販売, 直販, 無店舗販売
　distress selling 出血販売
　hard selling 強引な販売, 押売り, 強引な売込み
　selling by correspondence 通信販売
　selling commission 販売手数料
　selling expense [expenditure] 販売費
　selling order 売り注文
　selling point 売れ筋, セールス・ポイント, セリング・ポイント
　short selling 空売り
　soft selling 穏やかな商法, 低姿勢の売込み
　spot selling 現物売り
　switch selling おとり販売
selling pressure 売り圧力
　come under selling pressure across the board 軒並み売り圧力がかかる, 軒並み売られる, 軒並み売りを浴びせられる
　heavy selling pressure 強い売り圧力
semiconductor 图 半導体
semipublic 形 半官の, 半公共の, 半公共的な
　semipublic company 第三セクター (=joint public-private company, semipublic firm, semigovernmental company, semipublic joint venture company)
　semipublic consumption 半公共消費
　semipublic sector entities 第三セクター
Senate 图 〈米・豪・仏など2院制議会の〉上院, 上院議事堂, 上院議員（上院は立法権では下院と対等であるが, 条約批准権・弾劾裁判権・大統領任命の承認権などで下院より優位にある. ⇒House, House of Representatives）

engrossed Senate amendment 清書した上院の修正案
joint House/Senate conference 米上下両院協議会
message stating the action taken by the Senate 上院の採決を説明した文書
President Pro Tempore 上院議長代行
Secretary of the Senate 上院事務総長
Senate Appropriations Committee 〈米〉上院歳出委員会《略 SAC》
Senate Democrats 〈米〉上院の民主党
Senate Governmental Affairs subcommittee 〈米〉上院政府活動委員会の小委員会
Senate referred print 上院付託プリント, アクト・プリント（Act print）（清書された法案のコピー）
Senate Steering Committee 〈米〉上院運営委員会
the House and the Senate 〈米〉上下両院
Senate Standing Committees 上院の常任委員会

Agriculture, Nutrition and Forestry	農業・栄養・林業委員会
Appropriations	歳出委員会
Armed Services	軍事委員会
Banking, Housing and Urban Affairs	銀行・住宅・都市問題委員会
Budget	予算委員会
Commerce, Science and Transportation	商業・科学・運輸委員会
Energy and Natural Resources	エネルギー・天然資源委員会
Environment and Public Works	環境・公共事業委員会
Finance	金融[財政]委員会
Foreign Relations	外交委員会
Governmental Affairs	政府問題委員会
Judiciary	司法委員会
Labor and Human Resources	労働・人的資源委員会
Rules and Administration	議事運営委員会
Small Business	中小企業委員会
Veteran's Affairs	復員軍人委員会
Secretary	事務総長

Senator 图 〈米〉上院議員（米国の上院議員は, 任期が6年で各州2名計100名が選出され, 2年ごとに全上院議員の3分の1が改選される. 先に選出された議員を「先任上院議員(senior)」, 後任上院議員をjuniorという）
senile 形 老人性の, 老年の
　senile dementia 老人性痴呆症

senior 形 上級の, 上位の, トップクラスの, 優先の, 優先順位の, 首席の, 先輩の, 年上の, 古参の, 先任の, 経験豊かな, (大学) 4年生の, 最高学年の, シニア
 senior citizens 高齢者, 退職年金生活者
 senior company 親会社
 senior delegate 首席代表
 senior deposits 払戻しの優先順位の高い預金, 優先預金, 上位預金, 先順位預金
 senior executive 上級管理者, 上級執行役員, 上級幹部, 経営者, 〈党などの〉常任幹事
 senior issue 上位証券
 senior moment 度忘れ, 物忘れ
 senior officer 先任将校
 senior partner 〈合名会社などの〉社長, 代表社員
 senior unsecured debt rating 上位無担保債務格付け
 senior White House official 〈補佐官クラスの〉米政府高官
 Senior Service 〈英〉海軍
seniority 名 年功, 年功序列, 先任順, 先任権, 年長, 古参, 請求権の順位
 seniority allowance 勤続手当
 seniority-based 年功型の, 年功序列型の
 seniority of claim 請求権の順位
 seniority right 先任権制度
 seniority rule 古参制, シニオリティ・ルール (米議会の委員会などで, 多数党の委員のうち在任期間が最も長い者を委員長にすること)
 seniority system 年功序列, 年功序列制度, 年功序列賃金制度, 先任権制度
sense 名 感覚, 感じ, …感, 観念, 意識, 心持ち, 気持ち, …心, 良識, 分別, 思慮, 認識力, 判断力, 意味, 語義, 意図, 趣旨, 意義, 価値, 効果, センス
 abiding sense 固定観念
 common sense 常識
 have a strong sense of self 自意識が強い
 in a broad sense 広い意味では, 広義では
 in the sense that …という意味では
 latch the sense of shame 羞恥心がない
 make sense 意味がある, 筋が通る
 see sense 物の道理がわかる, 分別ある行動をする
 sense of humor ユーモアのセンス, ユーモアを解する心
 sense of occasion 正しい行動感覚, 状況を的確に見抜く力
 sense of perspective 大局観, 遠近感
 stand to sense 道理にかなう, もっともな言い分である
sensitive 形 敏感な, 左右されやすい, 影響を受けやすい, 不安定な, 動揺しやすい高感度の, 要注意の, 細心の注意を要する, 繊細な, 極秘の, 機密の, 重要な
 cost-sensitive コストに敏感な, コストに左右されやすい
 interest-sensitive instrument 金利感応商品 (=interest-rate sensitive instrument)
 market-sensitive 市場に敏感な, 市場に左右されやすい
 price-sensitive consumer 価格に敏感な消費者
 sensitive area 輸入要注意の分野
 sensitive film 高感度フイルム
 sensitive intelligence 機密情報
 sensitive item 輸入要注意品目, センシティブ品目 (=sensitive product: 輸入自由化によって多大な損害を受ける国内産品)
 sensitive list 輸入制限品目表
 sensitive sector センシティブ・セクター (外国製品の影響を受けやすい部門)
sentence 動 〈刑を〉宣告する, 申し渡す, 〈…に〉判決を下す, 刑に処する
 be sentenced for perjury 偽証罪の判決を受ける
 be sentenced to life imprisonment 終身刑の判決を受ける
 sentence a person to a five year prison term 人に5年の懲役刑の判決を下す
sentence 名 判決, 宣告, 刑, 刑罰, 処罰, 意見, 決定, 文, センテンス
 be given a three-year suspended sentence 執行猶予3年の判決を受ける
 pass [pronounce] sentence on …に判決を言い渡す, …に判決を下す
sentiment 名 景況感, 〈市場の〉地合い, 所感, 心理, 意見, 感情, 意識, 人気, マインド, 傾向
 bearish market sentiment 市場の弱気の地合い, 市場の弱気ムード
 bullish market sentiment 市場の強気の地合い, 市場の強気ムード
 consumer sentiment index 消費者マインド指数, 消費者態度指数
 express the same sentiments 同じ見方をする
 optimistic sentiment 楽観ムード, 楽観論
 sentiment index 業況判断指数

separate 動 分離する, 取り除く, 隔離する, 切り離す, 引き離す, 仲たがいさせる, 別居させる, 解雇する, 除隊させる, …を隔てる, …を分ける, 区分する, 区別する, 識別する, …の勝敗を決める, 別れる, 離れる, 離脱する, 離散する
　separate cause from effect 原因と結果を区別する
separate 形 別々の, 別個の, 個別の, 個々の, 独立した, …から離れている
　separate but equal 〈人種の〉分離平等政策の
　separate-but-equal principle [policy] 分離平等の原則
　separate estate 〈とくに妻の〉別有財産, 特有財産
　separate financial statements 個別財務諸表, 個別財務書類
　separate maintenance 〈別居中の夫が妻に与える〉別居手当, 生活手当, 別居扶養費
　separated taxation 分離課税
separation 名 分離, 分類, 隔離, 隔離状態, 〈ロケットの〉切り離し, 離脱, 別離, 別居, 別居状態, 離職, 退職, 休職, 解雇, 除隊, 除籍, 間隔, 隔たり, 距離, 分岐点, 境界線
　color separation 色分解
　employee separations and relocations 従業員の退職と配置転換
　judicial [legal] separation 〈法廷の判決に基づく〉夫婦別居
　separation center 〈米軍隊の〉復員本部, 復員事務取扱い本部
　separation from the service 離職
　separation of powers 三権分立
　separation of the accounts 勘定の分離, 勘定分離
　separation pay 退職金, 退職手当
　separation working unit 分離作業単位《略 SWU》
　the First Amendment's separation of church and state 合衆国憲法修正第1条の「政教分離」
separatist 名 分離独立主義者, 分離主義者, 政教分離主義者, 分裂主義者
▶ *Separatists* and independence movements have started to surface in Xinjiang, where many Muslim Uygurs live, since the collapse of the Soviet Union. イスラム教徒のウイグル族の多くが住む新疆（しんきょう）では, 旧ソ連の崩壊以降, 分離独立の動きが目立ち始めた.

Sept. 11 米同時テロ（2001年9月11日に起きた米同時テロのこと）
　Sept. 11 commission 9.11委員会（米同時テロに関する米国の独立調査委員会）
serious 形 深刻な, 重大な, 重要な, 危険な, 本格的な, 本気の, まじめな, 思慮深い, 堅い, 大量の, 大幅な, 値段が高い, 性能がよい
　make serious inroads 本格的に進出する
　serious downturn in business 深刻な業績悪化, 大幅な業績悪化
　Serious Fraud Office 重大詐欺特捜局
Serratia bacteria セラチア菌（＝Serratia enterobacteria）
▶ *Serratia bacteria* exist widely in nature, including soil, water and plants. セラチア菌は, 土壌や水, 植物などと自然界に広く存在する.
serve 動 務める, 勤務する, 働く, 仕事をする, 〈サービスなどを〉提供する, 供給する, 〈商品などを〉売る, 運航する, 文書を渡す, 送付する, …の役に立つ, 奉仕する, 貢献する, 利用できる, …の目的にかなう, …の要求などを満たす, …の機能を果たす, …の任務［職務］を果たす, …の手段として機能する, 助長する, 促進する, 推進する, 高める
　serve a customer 顧客に応対する
　serve a person with a summons 人に召喚状を送達する
　serve notice that …と言い渡す
　serve the community 地域社会に貢献する, 地域社会に奉仕する, 地域社会に尽くす
　serve the devil 悪事を行う, 悪魔に仕える
　serve three terms as mayor 市長を3期務める
　serve to …に役立つ, …する方向に働く, …する方向に動く
　serve as …を務める, として勤務する, …として機能する, …の機能を果たす, …としての役割を担う, …として役立つ, …に使える, …になる
　serve as a hedge against inflation インフレ・ヘッジの手段［インフレに対するヘッジ手段］として機能する
　serve as a role model 手本を示す
server 名 集配用コンピュータ, サーバー（ネットワークの中で特定のサービスを提供するコンピュータ）
service 名 事業, 業務, 役務, 労務, 勤務, 服務, 公務, 〈借入金の〉定期返済, 公債利子, 〈訴状や呼出状の〉送達, サービス
　employee's service period 従業員の勤務年数
　goods and services 財貨とサービス, 財貨・サー

ビス, モノとサービス, 財貨と役務, 財貨と用役
Internal Revenue Service 内国歳入庁
length of service 勤続年数
service [services] account 貿易外収支, サービス収支
service area 共用部分, 共益区域
service [services] balance サービス収支, 貿易外収支
service by mail 郵便送達
service of process 訴状や呼出し状の送達
service ordering サービスの発注
service sector サービス部門, サービス業, サービス産業
service station 給油所, ガソリン・スタンド
service-through-people 人を通じてのサービス
unattended service 無人サービス
session 名 開会, 会期, 開会期間, 議会, 会議, 会談, 会合, 集会, 集まり, 活動,〈証券取引所の〉立ち会い, 場, 開廷, 授業, 授業時間, 学期,〈1日の〉取引時間, セッション
 be in session 開会中である
 bull session 〈主に男同士の〉グループ討論, ざっくばらんな討論, 放談会
 call a session of the Diet 国会を召集する
 final session of a month 納会
 for the fourth straight session 4日連続で
 go into session 開会する
 in session 開会中に, 会議中[開廷中]の
 markup session (小委員会の会合で法案を審議する)マークアップ会議, 法案の最終審議
 petty sessions 簡易裁判所, 即決裁判所
 photo session 撮影会
 plenary session 〈国会の〉本会議, 総会
set aside 〈準備金などを〉積み立てる, 蓄えておく, 蓄える, 引き当てる, 設定する, 繰り入れる, 用意する,〈考えや問題を〉捨てる, 無視する, 棚上げする, 取り除く, 除外する
set out 言明する, 発表する, 提示する, 詳述する, 計画する, 企てる,〈仕事に〉着手する
set to …に取り掛かろうとしている, …する用意ができている, …する方針の, …する方針を固める, …する見通しの, …する見込みの, …する恐れがある
set up 〈建物などを〉立てる, 建てる, 築く, 組み立てる, 始める(start), 一本立ちする, 独立する, 設立する, 創設する, 開業する,〈ホームページなどを〉開設する,〈会合などを〉設定する, 設置する,〈…を〉掲げる, 用意する, 準備する, 供給する, 資金提供をする, 〈…の〉ふりをする,〈…を〉気取る,〈記録を〉樹立する(establish),〈原稿を〉活字に組む,〈策略で〉はめる, だます,〈連鎖反応などを〉引き起こす,〈ソフトウエアをコンピュータに〉インストールする, セットアップする
 be well set up with money 十分に資金提供を受ける, 十分に金をあてがわれている
 set up a joint venture 合弁会社[合弁事業]を設立する
 set up against …に対抗する
setback 名 後退, 景気後退, 下落, がた落ち, 落ち込み, 減少, 反落, 逆行, 逆風, 挫折, 失敗, 敗北, 調整局面
 a considerably severe economic setback かなり厳しい景気後退
 earnings setback 収益の落ち込み
 face setbacks 逆風にぶつかる
 the LDP's heavy setback 自民党の大敗北
set-top box セットトップ・ボックス(テレビ・セットの上に置いて利用する箱という意味で, 双方向テレビ向け家庭用通信端末がその代表)
settle 動 決済する, 清算する, 処分する, 処理する, 解決する, 決定する, 和解する
 ▶A labor-hearing system is designed to swiftly *settle* disputes, including dismissals and harassment at work, between workers and their employers. 労働審判制度の狙いは, 解雇や職場での嫌がらせなど, 労働者と使用者[会社]の間の紛争を迅速に解決することにある.
settlement 名 合意, 決着, 解決, 決定, 妥結, 処分, 決済, 清算,〈借金の〉支払い, 決算, 和解, 調停, 示談, 財産の譲渡, 贈与財産, 定款, 入植地,〈地盤などの〉沈下, 社会福祉事業団, 厚生施設
 a cash settlement 現金による返済
 agree to an out-of-court settlement 示談に応じる
 Bank of International Settlements 国際決済銀行《略 BIS》
 biannual settlement 半期決算, 半期決済
 in settlement of one's claim …の請求に対する支払いとして
 make an enormous settlement on …に莫大な財産を贈る
 reach [achieve, come to] a settlement with …と合意に達する
 semiannual settlement 半期決算, 半期決済
 settlement deposit 決済用預金 (=settlement account, settlement-specific deposit: 利子が付かない, 取引決済サービスを提供する,

要求払いに応じるの3条件を満たした預金口座のこと。銀行が破綻した場合に預金が全額保護される)
settlement fund 決済資金
settlement-specific deposit 決済用預金 (＝settlement deposit)
the settlement day 〈株式清算取引の〉決算日
the settlement duty 遺産相続税
settlement of accounts 決算, 決算報告
the deficit settlement of accounts 赤字決算
settler 名 植民者, 入植者, 移住者, 開拓者
setup 名 組立て, 配置(arrangement), 組織(organization), 機構, 構成, 編成, 体制, 仕組み, 装備, 設備, 装置, 容器一式, 姿勢, 身のこなし, 態勢, 態度, 計画, 行動方針, 準備, 段取り, 八百長試合, セットアップ
defense setup 防衛組織
setup cost 段取り費
setup time 始動時間, 段取り時間, 準備時間
severe 形 厳しい, 厳格な, 過酷な, 深刻な, ひどい, 地味な
sex 名 性, 性別, 性交, 性本能, 性欲, セックス
both sexes 男女, 両性
sex abuse 性的虐待 (＝sexual abuse)
sex drive 性衝動, 性的衝動, 性的能力
sex hormone 性ホルモン
sex offender 性犯罪者
sex test [check] 性検査, 性別判定テスト
sexual 形 性の, 性的な, 性欲の, 男女の, 性的魅力のある
make sexual advances 性的関係を迫る
sexual abuse 性的虐待
sexual assault 強制わいせつ, 強姦, 女性に対する暴行, 婦女暴行
sexual deviation 性倒錯, 性的逸脱
sexual orientation 性的志向, 性的関心を向ける方向(同性愛や異性愛などに対する志向性)
sexual relations [commerce, intercourse] 性交
shadow 名 影, 暗雲, 暗い影, 陰り, 悪影響, 悪い前兆, 〈野党内の〉影の大臣
beyond [without] a shadow of doubt 疑うまでもない
cast a shadow over [on] …に影を落とす, …に汚点を残す, 後ろ暗い点を残す, …の魅力を半減させる
under the shadow of …の脅威[危険]にさらされて, …の陰に隠れて, …の下に

shadow 形 影の, 非公式の, 潜在的な, シャドー
member of the shadow Cabinet 影の内閣の閣僚
shadow economy 地下経済
shady 形 いかがわしい, 怪しい, 不正な, 不正の疑いがある, 陰の多い, 日陰を作る
a shady business 虚業
shady dealings [deals] 不正取引, 不法取引, いかがわしい取引
shake 動 振る, 振り動かす, 振り回す, 揺さぶる, 動揺させる, ぐらつかせる, くじく, 感情をかき乱す
shake down 〈職場・場所などに〉慣れる, 〈組織として〉まとまる, 恐喝する, 徹底的に探す, 捜索する, …の所持品を検査する
shake off …から回復する, …を払拭する, …から逃れる, …を振りほどく
shake out 振り払う, 淘汰が進む, 〈在庫などを〉整理する, 再編する
shake up 再編する, 刷新する, 改造する, 活気づかせる
shake-up 名 再編, 大変革, 大刷新, 大改革, 大改造, 抜本的改革, 抜本的改組 (＝shakeout)
management shake-up 経営刷新, 経営陣の刷新, 役員交代 (＝management reshuffle)
shake-up within the house 機構改革
shakedown 名 調整, 調整期間, 試運転, 徹底的な捜索, 形 調整期間の, 試験の, 試験的な, 試験運転の
shakeout 名 企業合理化, 再編, 〈組織などの〉刷新, 改組, 大改造, 大改変, 立て直し, 再編成, 〈相場の〉急落, 〈インフレの〉沈静 (＝shake-up)
industry shakeout 業界再編 (＝shakeout in the industry)
inventory shakeout 在庫整理, 在庫削減
shallow 形 浅い, 浅はかな, 薄っぺらな, 軽微な, 軽度の, 穏やかな, 思慮の浅い
a shallow argument 奥行きのない議論
a shallow downturn 穏やかな景気後退, 軽微な景気後退
share 動 共有する, 相互利用する, 共同使用する, 分配する, 均等に分ける, 分け合う, 共にする, 共同負担する, 共同分担する, 分担する, 支持する, 参加する, 話やる
share a basic common interest 基本的に利害[共通の利益]が一致する
share in profits 利益の分配にあずかる
share one's view …の見方[意見, 考え]と同じ, …の見方を支持する

share 名 株, 株式, 株券, 持ち分株, 株価, 市場占有率, 市場占拠率, シェア
 active share 花形株
 authorized share capital 授権株式資本
 capital share 資本分配率, キャピタル・シェア
 common share 普通株式, 普通株
 deferred share 後配株
 inscribed share 記名株
 issued share 発行済み株式
 nonvoting share 無議決権株, 議決権のない株式
 potential share 権利株
 retirement of shares 株式消却
 share warrant 無記名株, 新株予約権

share allotment 株式割当て (=share allocation)
▶ In an attempt to recapitalize itself, the bank raised ¥15 billion through a third-party *share allotment*. 資本再編のため, 同行は第三者株式割当てで150億円を調達した。

share buyback 株式の買戻し, 自社株発行済み株式の買戻し, 自社株買戻し, 自社株買い, 自社株取得 (=share repurchase, stock buyback)
▶ The *share buyback* means a reduction in the company's shareholders to whom it has to pay dividends. 自社株買いは, 配当を支払わなければならない会社の株主数が減ることを意味する。

share price 株価
 share price outperformance 株価上昇 (=share price appreciation)
 the daily average for a month of the share prices 株価の月中平均

share purchase 株式購入, 株購入, 株式買取り, 株式の買入れ, 株式取得 (=stock purchase)
 share purchase unit 株式の購入単位

shared 形 共有の, 共同の, 共同利用の, 共通の, 〈費用を〉共同負担[共同分担]した, 等分した, 分割された, 合弁事業による
 shared appreciation mortgage 利益配分抵当, 価格上昇共有住宅担保貸付け《略 SAM》
 shared capital 株主資本金
 shared cost 共通原価
 shared equity mortgage 純資産共有[配分]抵当, 自己資本共有住宅担保貸付け
 shared ownership 共同所有
 shared revenue 地方交付金
 shared value 共有価値, 価値の共有

shareholder 名 株主 (=stockholder)
 create value for shareholders 株主の価値を高める, 株主の利益を高める, 株主に対する資産価値を創出する
 designated shareholder 指定株主
 individual shareholder 個人株主
 institutional shareholder 機関投資家
 majority shareholder 過半数株主, 多数株主, 支配株主
 minority shareholder 少数株主
 offers to existing shareholders 割当発行
 ordinary shareholder 普通株主 (=equity shareholder)
 preferred shareholder 優先株主
 shareholders' representative suit 株主代表訴訟 (=shareholders' lawsuit)
 shareholders' [shareholder] value 株主価値, 株主の資産価値, 株主利益 (=value for shareholders)
 stable [strong] shareholder 安定株主
 the largest [biggest] shareholder of the company 同社の筆頭株主

shareholders' assets 株主資本
▶ Stock buybacks and the resulting reduction in *shareholders' assets* can weaken a company's financial base and trigger a decline in performance. 自社株買いをして株主資本を減らすことは, 企業の財務基盤を悪化させ, 業績を落とす恐れもある。

shareholders' meeting 株主総会 (=shareholders meeting, stockholders' meeting)

shareholdings 名 持ち株, 保有株, 保有株式, 株式保有 (=stockholdings)

Sharia 名 シャリーア (アラビア語で「イスラム法」の意味)

sharing 名 分配, 配分, 分与, 分担, 共同分担, 共同負担, 共有, シェアリング
 bona fide cost sharing arrangement 真正な原価負担契約
 capital sharing system 資本分与法
 code sharing 共同運航, コード・シェアリング (=code-share)
 cost sharing 費用分担, 原価分担
 deferred profit-sharing plan 利益分配据え置き方式
 production sharing system [method] 生産分与方式, プロダクション・シェアリング方式, PS方式

time sharing (system) 時分割方式, 時分割処理方式, 機械の同時使用［共同使用］, 共有制, タイム・シェアリング・システム《略 TSS》 (= time shared system)

work sharing (system) ワークシェア, ワーク・シェアリング（1人当たりの労働時間を短縮して, 雇用を分かち合う制度）

sharp 形 急激な, 急速な, 急な, 大幅な
　a sharp increase 急増
　sharp rise 急増, 急騰, 急上昇

sharply 副 急激に, 急速に, 急に, 大幅に, 大きく
　appreciate sharply 急騰する
　decelerate sharply 急速に低下する, 急速に鈍化する
　spike sharply upward 急騰する, 大幅に上昇する

shed 動 落とす, 削減する, 押し下げる, 売却する, 取り除く, 捨て去る, 捨てる, 放棄する, 流す, 注ぐ, …から脱する, 減少する, 低下する, 下落する
　shed 5,000 jobs 人員を5,000人削減する, 5,000人を削減する
　shed [throw] light on …を照らす, …を明らかにする, 解明する, …に光［光明］を投じる
　shed oneself of …を取り除く, …を捨てる (= get shed of)

shelf life 賞味期間, 有効保存期間, 棚ざらし期間, 陳列許容期間

shell company 実態のない会社, 架空の会社, トンネル会社, ダミー会社, ペーパー・カンパニー, 弱小会社 (=dummy company, paper company)

shelter 名 避難, 避難所, 保護, 保護施設, 隠れ場, 救護所, 一時的収容施設, 一時的収容所, 住宅, 住居, シェルター
　a shelter for the homeless ホームレスの収容施設
　shelter loans 住宅関連貸付け
　take [find, seek] shelter from …から避難する, …から守る, …を避ける, …にさらされない
　take shelter under the umbrella of …の傘の下に隠れる［逃れる］, …の傘の下に逃げ込む
　tax shelter 税金天国, 税金逃れの隠れみの, 税金避難手段, 会計操作, タックス・シェルター (= tax haven)
　temporary shelter 仮設住宅

shelve 動 棚上げする, 見送る, 取り止める, 握りつぶす, 撤回する, お流れにする, 停止する, 延期する, 解雇する
　shelve the project for the time being 計画を当分の間棚上げにする

shield 名 盾, 保護者, 保護物, 遮蔽物
　human shields 人間の盾
　the other side of the shield 物事の裏面, 問題の他の一面

shift 動 移す, 移し替える, 振り向ける, 変更する, 変える, 転換する, 転嫁する, 入れ替える, 繰り上げる, シフトさせる, 移る, 移動する, 変わる, 変化する, シフトする
　shift money 資金を移動する, 資金を切り替える［移し替える］, 資金をシフトする
　shift production base overseas 生産拠点を海外に移す
　shift the raised costs of plastic parts onto product prices プラスチック部品のコスト高［コスト上昇分］を製品価格に転嫁する

shift 名 変化, 変動, 変更, 移動, 移行, 転換, 再構成, 交替勤務制, 交替制, シフト
　equity structure shift 資本再構成
　graveyard shift 深夜勤務
　night shift 夜勤, 宿直, 当直
　paradigm shift パラダイムの転換, 根本的変化, 社会の価値観の移行
　swing shift 半夜勤, 午後交代制
　work shift 作業の交代

Shiite Moslem [Muslem, Muslim] シーア派のイスラム教徒

shilly-shally 動 ぐずぐずする, 迷う, ためらう, 名 ためらい, 優柔不断, 形 優柔不断の, 及び腰の

ship 動 出荷する, 発送する, 発売する, 船で送る, 輸送する, 輸出する
▶ About 5.08 million cell phones were *shipped* domestically in June—a year-on-year increase of 2.1 percent.　携帯電話の6月の国内出荷台数は, 前年同月比2.1%増の約508万台だった。

shipment 名 出荷, 出荷量, 出荷台数, 発送, 輸出, 船積み, 船積み品, 船積み量, 積み荷, 船荷
　inventory to shipment ratio 在庫率, 在庫率指数
　orders and shipments of capital goods 資本財の受注と出荷
　shipment basis 出荷基準
　shipment in installment 分割船積み
　unfilled orders-shipments ratio 受注残高出荷比率

shipping agent 船舶代理店, 荷受業者
shipping industry 海運業界

shirk 動 ずるける, 怠ける, 怠る, さぼる, 避ける,

回避する, 責任逃れをする, 〈徴兵などを〉忌避する
shirk military service 徴兵を忌避する
shirk one's duty 義務を回避する (=shirk from one's duty)

shock 名 衝撃, 脅威, 精神的打撃, 電撃, 震動, 激突, ショック
shock absorber 緩衝装置, 緩衝器
shock loss 異常損害
shock tactics 急襲戦術, 突然の過激な行動
shock therapy [treatment] ショック療法, 荒療治
shock wave 衝撃波, 大きな反響

shoe 名 履き物, 靴, 蹄鉄, 〈車の〉変速装置
another pair of shoes まったく別の問題, まったく別なこと
fill [step into] one's shoes …に代わる, …の後がまに座る, …の後任となる
in one's shoes …の身になって, …に代わって, …の立場に立って, …の立場に身をおいて, …の視点から
put the shoe on the right [proper] foot 責めるべき人を責める, ほめるべき人をほめる
where the shoe pinches 悩みの種, 苦しみ[悩み, 困難]の真の原因

shoo-in 名 当選確実者, 本命
shootout 名 銃撃戦, 激しい銃の打ち合い
shoplifting 名 万引き, 万引き行為
shopper 名 買い物客, 顧客, 買い物代行者[代理人], 偵察員, 宣伝[広告]ビラ, ちらし, 大きい買い物袋, 無料新聞, 無料紙, 広告新聞, タウン紙, ショッパー
shopperholic 名 ショッピング中毒の人
shopping 名 買い物, 購買, 商戦, ショッピング
shopping bag 買い物袋
treaty shopping 租税回避, 節税行為, トリーティ・ショッピング
shopping mall 商店街, ショッピング・センター (=shopping center, shopping complex)
shore up 動 支える, 下支えする, 持ちこたえる, 防衛する, テコ入れをする, 強化する, 拡充する, 引き上げる, 高める

short 名 短い記事, 弱気, 強い酒, 漏電, 〈野球の〉ショート, 不足, 欠損, 空売り, 短期債券
capital short 資金不足 (=short of capital)
short of exchange 為替の空売り
short of hand 人手不足
shorts 短期社債, 短期債券, 短編映画, 半ズボン, 運動パンツ, 短パンツ

short 形 短い, 短期の, 短時間の, 短距離の, 低い, 不足の, 足りない, 不十分な, 乏しい, 品薄の, 空売りの, 空相場の, 売り方の, 弱気の, 簡単な, 簡潔な, 簡略の, 短縮形の
get [have] a person by the short hairs 人を完全に支配する, 人を手玉に取る
get [have] by the short and curlies 〈人の〉急所を握っている
short account 空売り勘定, 短期見越し売り勘定
short check 預金不足小切手
short covering 〈空売りの〉買戻し
short credit 短期信用貸し, 短期信用
short cut [shortcut] 〈…への〉近道, 手っ取り早い方法
short draft 短期為替手形
short drawing ショート・ドローイング(為替手形金額が信用状の金額を下回る状態のこと)
short drink 食前酒
short exchange 短期為替手形, 代金取立手形
short list 最終選抜候補者名簿
short notice 期限経過通知, 不十分な予告期間, 〈手形の〉短期通知
short odds ほぼ五分五分の賭け率
short order 即席料理
short range attack missile 短距離攻撃ミサイル《略 SRAM》
short-ranged 射程の短い, 短期間の
short-staffed 人員不足の, 人手不足の
short take-off and landing aircraft 短距離離着陸飛行機《略 STOL》
short-termism 〈目先の利益だけを考える〉短期計画集中
short time 操業短縮
short ton 米トン

short-dated 形 短期の
short-dated bill 短期手形
short-lived 形 短命の
short-lived upturn 薄命の景気回復
short loan 短期融資, 短期ローン, 短期貸付け資金
short loan fund 短期融資資金, 短期貸付け資金

short of 不足している, 足りない, 十分ない, …以外は, …を除いて, …は別問題として, …の手前で
be short of …が不足している, 十分ない, 足りない, …を切らしている, …に達しない, …に及ばない
fall [come] short of …に達しない, …に及ばな

い, …が不足する
go short of …なしでやって行く, …なしで済ませる, …に不自由する, …を切らす
little [nothing] short of ほとんど…の, まったく…の, …に近い, …以外の何物でもない, まったく…に他ならない
run short of …が不足する, …を切らす
stop short of 危うく…するところだ, …の手前で立ち止まる

short sale 空売り, 信用売り
short sale of futures 先物の売り建て

short selling 空売り (=selling short, short sale, short selling of stocks)

> 空売りとは ⊃ 証券取引法で認められた取引で, 投資家が保有していない株式を他から借り入れて市場で売る取引のこと。ただし, 空売りを意図的な株価引下げに利用すると, 違法となる。投資家が証券会社を通じて生命保険会社や信託銀行などの機関投資家から借りる場合と, 貸し株などを専門業務とする証券金融会社や証券会社から借りる(信用売り)場合がある。投資家が借りた株を市場で空売りすると, その後その株の値段が下がった時点で安く買い戻せるため, 株価下落の局面でも利益を確保できる。

short-term 形 短期の, 短期間の, 目先の
short-term capital 短期資本
short-term debt 短期債, 短期国債(short-term bond), 短期債務, 短期借入金
short-term money 短期資金 (=short-term funds: 1年以内に回収される資金の取引市場)
short term obligations to be refinanced 借換え予定の短期借入金

shortage 名 不足
inventory shortage 在庫不足, 棚卸し減耗費
labor shortages 労働力不足, 人手不足
shortages of supply 供給不足

shortfall 名 不足, 減少, 赤字, 赤字額, 不足額, 不足量, 短期投資利益
a profit shortfall 利益の減少, 減益
a revenue shortfall 歳入欠陥

shot 名 発砲, 射撃, 銃声, 銃弾, 射撃手, 辛らつな言葉, 試み, 企て, 一撃, 写真, 一画面, スナップ, 山勘, あてずっぽう, 勝ち目, ショット
a big shot 大物, 有力者, お偉方
a long shot 成功する見込みがない試み[企て], 当選の見込みがない候補者, ロング・シュート, ロング・ショット
a shot in the arm 刺激剤, カンフル剤, 景気づけ, 勇気づけ, 腕への麻薬注射
a shot in the dark あてずっぽう, 当て推量, 成功の見込みが薄い試み[企て]
by a long shot 断然, 並はずれて, まったく[全然]…でない
call the shots 采配を振る, 支配する, 支配権を握る[持つ], 牛耳る
have a shot (left) in one's locker 備え[蓄え, 所持金]がまだ残っている
make a parting shot 捨てぜりふを言う
shot across the bows 警告 (=warning)
take [have] a shot at …をやってみる, …を試みる

shoulder 動 肩にかつぐ, 背負う, 負担する,〈責任などを〉引き受ける, 負う, 肩代わりする, 前に進む
shoulder a task 仕事を引き受ける
shoulder great responsibilities 重大な責任を負う
shoulder the responsibility for …の責任を取る
shoulder one's way through [into] …を押し分けて進む[通る]

▶ Companies have been *shouldering* a large amount of labor costs as their employees grow older. 企業は, 従業員の高齢化に伴って多額の労務費を負担してきた。

shoulder 名 肩, 路肩
have broad shoulders 重荷[重責]に耐える
lay the blame on the right shoulders 当然負うべき人に責めを負わせる
put [set] one's shoulder to the wheel 全力を尽くす, 元気に仕事にとりかかる, 本腰で取り組む, …に協力する
shoulder to shoulder 肩を並べて, 協力[相協力]して, 連合して,〈建物が〉密集して

show 動 見せる, 示す, 表す, 明らかにする, 証明する, 指摘する, 教える, 案内する, 上映する, 上演する, 放送する, 公開する, 展示する,〈訴訟事由などを〉申し立てる
see and it shows 一見してすぐ分かる, 一目瞭然だ
have nothing to show for …の成果を得るものは何もない, …の成果は得られない
have something to show for …の成果を得る
show the way 手本を示す

show up 現れる, 姿[顔]を見せる, 姿を現す,〈ショーなどに〉出る, 見えるようになる, 目立つ

▶ The benefits of the U.S. financial bailout package will take time to *show up* in the U.S.

economy. 米国の金融救済策の効果が米国内経済に現れるのに、時間がかかるだろう。

showdown 名 対決, 決着 (=confrontation, face-off)

showing 名 成績, 業績, 出来, 出来栄え, 表示, 展示, 展示会, 展覧会, 上映, 上演, 外観, 体裁, 公表, 発表, 供述, 申立て
- **a good showing** 上々の成績, 上々の出来栄え
- **upturn in the business showing** 業績回復
- ▶ Japan's unemployment rate eased to 5.1 percent in August, the best *showing* in two years. 日本の8月の失業率は、過去2年で最も低い5.1%に改善した。

shrink 動 減少する, 低下する, 縮小する, マイナス成長になる, マイナスになる

shrinkage 名 縮小, 収縮, 減少, 下落, 縮小量, 収縮量, 減少量, 減耗, 減耗費, 減耗損, 減損

shrinking 形 減少している, 低下している, 縮小している, …の減少, …の低下, …の縮小
- **shrinking backlog** 受注残高の減少 (=shrinking backlog of unfilled orders)
- **shrinking balance sheet** バランス・シートの縮小

shutter 動 シャッターを閉める, 閉鎖する, 閉店する, 〈店を〉たたむ

shuttle 名 折り返し運転, 定期往復交通機関, シャトル
- **shuttle diplomacy** 往復外交, とんぼ返り外交, シャトル外交
- **shuttle project** 〈NASAの〉スペース・シャトル計画
- **shuttle service** 折り返し運転, 往復便

shy away from …を避ける, …を敬遠する, …にしり込みする

side 名 側, 側面, 〈問題の〉面, 〈血統の〉…系, サイド
- **credit side** 貸方
- **debit side** 借方
- **on the side** 副業として, 内職として
- **one-side preferential duties** 一方的特恵関税
- **side arms** 携帯武器
- **side effect** 副作用, 副次的効果
- **side issue** 派生的な問題, 枝葉の問題
- **side view** 側面の眺め, 横顔, プロフィール
- **take sides with** …に味方する, …を支持する

sideline 名 専門外取扱品, 副業, アルバイト, 内職, サイドビジネス, 側線, 様子見〔複数形〕, 模様眺め, サイドライン
- **on the sidelines** 〈参加しないで〉傍観して, 傍観者として, 控え選手として
- **on the sidelines of** …の際に
- **retreat to the sidelines** 手控える
- **stay on the sidelines** 圏外にいる

siege 名 包囲, 包囲作戦, 兵糧攻め, 〈人質を取っての〉立てこもり, 籠城, 〈病気などの〉長く苦しい期間
- **a regular siege** 正攻法
- **state of siege** 戒厳状態, 準戒厳令
- **under siege** 軍隊に包囲されて, 批判され続けて, 抑圧されて

sign 動 署名する, 署名調印する, 調印する, …と契約する
- **sign and seal** 署名・捺印する
- **sign on the dotted line** 文書に署名する, 無条件に同意する

sign 名 兆し, 兆候, 動き, 様相, 気味, 標識, 署名, サイン
- **clear [distinct] signs of recovery** はっきりした回復の兆し, 明らかな回復の兆し
- **positive signs** 好転の兆し

signal 動 信号〔合図〕を送る, 合図で知らせる, 示唆する, 示す, …の前兆〔証拠, しるし〕になる, …の兆しが見える

signatory 名 署名者, 調印者, 加盟国, 調印国, 調停国, 調停人, 調停機関
- **signatory country** 締約国
- **signatory power** 条約調印国

significant 形 重要な, 重大な, 重大な意味を持つ, かなりの, 大幅な, 相当な, 大きな, 巨額の, 本格的な, 著しい, 目立った, 際立った
- **have a significant effect on** …に大きな影響を及ぼす, …に大きな影響力がある
- **significant difference** 有意差
- **significant subsidiaries** 重要な子会社

silent 形 静かな, 音を立てない, 沈黙した, 無言の, 無口の, 寡黙な, 口に出して言わない, 言及しない, 沈黙を守る, 暗黙の, 活動しない, 休止した
- **Silent Majority [silent majority]** 声なき多数, 声なき大衆, 一般国民（政治的意見や活動をしない大多数の一般国民。ニクソン米大統領が, ベトナム戦争反対の声が高まるなか, 1969年11月3日の放送で国民の支持を訴えたときの言葉）
- **silent partner** 匿名社員, 匿名パートナー
- **the right to be [remain] silent** 黙秘権 (=the right to silence)
- **the Silent Spring** 『沈黙の春』（米国のレイチェル・カーソンの著作で, 農薬による自然環境破壊

を描いた作品）

silicon chip シリコンで作った半導体素子, シリコン・チップ（＝chip of silicon, microchip, semiconductor chip）
silicon cycle シリコン・サイクル（半導体産業に特有の現象で, 市況変動の繰り返しをさす）
simple majority 単独過半数
simplify 動 簡素化する, 簡略化[簡易化]する, 単純化する, 容易[平易]にする
　simplified report 簡易報告書
　simplified taxation system 簡易課税制度
simultaneous 形 同時の, 同時に起こる, 同時に行われる, 一斉の, 連立の
　simultaneous distribution 同時分布（＝joint distribution）
　simultaneous equations model 同時方程式[連立方程式]モデル
　simultaneous transmission and communication 同時送受信
single-family home [house] 1～4世帯住宅
single market 単一市場
single-minded 形 一心不乱の, 一途な, ひたむきな
sink 動 沈む, 沈下する, 傾く, 倒れる, 落ち込む, 下がる, 悪化する, 投下する, 投じる, つぎ込む, …を失う, 無視する, 不問に付す
　sink a large sum into an unprofitable business 大金を不採算事業につぎ込む
　sink one's identity 素性を隠す
　sink or swim のるかそるか, 成功するか失敗するか, 一か八か
　sink to nothing 価値がなくなる,〈在庫などが〉なくなる[ゼロになる]
　sinking land 地盤沈下
siphon off 吸い上げる, 吸収する,〈資金などを〉流用する, 搾取する
site 名 拠点, 施設, 事業所, 工場, 用地, 設置先, 現場, サイト, インターネット上の場所, ホームページ
　construction site 建設用地, 建設現場
　dating site 出会い系サイト（＝dating Web site, online dating site）
　investment site 投資先
　portal site ポータル・サイト
　production site 生産拠点, 生産施設, 生産先
　site leasing サイト・リース（ソフトウエア会社が手数料を取ってユーザー企業にプログラムの複製を認める契約）

sitting 名 座っている時間, 着席, ひと仕事,〈議会などの〉会期, 開会期間, 食事時間,〈法廷の〉開廷時間
　in [at] one sitting 一気に
sitting 形 現職の, 在職中の, 巣ごもりしている
　sitting tenant 借用中の入居者, 現借家[借地]人
　the sitting U.S. president 現職の米大統領
situation 名 状況, 状態, 情勢, 形勢, 時局, 局面, 事情, 事態, 境遇, 立場, 場面, 環境, 大詰め, 山場, クライマックス, 位置, 場所, 用地, 敷地, 立地条件, 勤め口, 就職口, 仕事, 職
　actual situation 実勢, 実態
　cash situation 資金繰り
　crop situation index 作況指数
　monetary situation 金融事情, 金融情勢, 金融状態
　no-win situation 勝ち目のない状況, 成功しそうにない状況, 絶望的状況
　over-borrowed situation 貸出過多の状態, オーバー・ローン（＝over-loaned situation）
　situation comedy 連続ホーム・コメディー, 連続ホームコメディー・ドラマ
　situation rent 好立地地代
　situation room 〈米ホワイトハウスの〉指揮センター,〈軍作戦本部の〉戦況報告質
　situation utility curve 状況効用曲線（＝utility frontier）
　situation vacant 欠員, 空位, 求人
　Situation Vacant 求人, 人を求む
　Situation Wanted 求職, 職を求む
six-nation talks 6か国協議（＝six-party forum）
six-party talks 6か国協議（＝six-nation talks, six-party forum）
six sigma シックス・シグマ（＝6σ：企業の製品, サービスのエラーやミスの発生確率が, 100万分の3.4回であること）
six-way meeting 6か国協議（＝six-party talks, six-way talks）
sizable [sizeable] 形 かなり大きい, 相当な大きさの, 大幅の, 大型の, 膨大な, 巨額の
　issue a sizable amount of new shares 新株を大量発行する
　sizable deferred tax assets 巨額の繰延べ税金資産
size 名 規模, 大きさ, 寸法, 大量, 大規模, 型, 番, サイズ

lot size 取引規模
offering size 入札総額
optimum size 最適規模
sample size 標本数, サンプル数
size effect 規模の効果
size of capacity 生産能力

skepticism 疑い, 疑念, 懐疑, 疑い深さ, 懐疑心, 懐疑的な見方, 懐疑論, 懐疑主義, 無神論, キリスト教不信
 express skepticism over …に疑念を表明する

skill 名 能力, 技術, 技能, 熟練, 職業能力, スキル
 skill test 技能検定 (=skills testing)
 skills assessment 技能評価
 skills center 技能センター
 skills development 職業能力開発

skilled 形 熟練の, 老練の, 上手な, 腕のたつ, 貴重な, 特殊技術[技能経験]を持った
 skilled employee 貴重な人材
 skilled hand [workman] 熟練工, 特殊技能者, 特殊技能工
 skilled labor 熟練労働
 skilled worker 熟練工, 熟練労働者 (= skilled hand, skilled labor)

skimming 名 スキミング(銀行の磁気キャッシュ・カードのデータ読取り)

skyrocket 動 急騰する, 高騰する, 急増する, 急上昇する, 跳ね上がる (=soar)

SkyTeam スカイチーム(米デルタ航空が率いる国際航空連合; ⇒Oneworld)

slack 名 不景気, 不振, 沈滞, 停滞, 低迷, 低調, 不況, 不況期, 余分, 余裕, だぶつき, たるみ, 緩み, スラック
 slack in business 事業不振, 商売の不振, 景気低迷[停滞, 停滞], 不況
 take up [pick up] the slack 活を入れる, たるみを引き締める, 不足分を補う, 是正する

slack 形 不景気な, 活気のない, 不活発な, 緩慢な, 不振な, 沈滞した, 弱含みの, いい加減の, 甘い, 怠慢な, 不注意な, 緩んだ, たるんだ
 slack capacity 遊休生産能力
 slack economy 景気低迷

slam 動 酷評する, こきおろす, 非難する, きびしく批判する, 〈戸や窓を〉ばたんと閉める, …に楽勝する, 〈ヒットを〉打つ, 自動 激突する, ばたんと閉まる, どすんとぶつかる
 slam into [against] …に激突する
 slam the door in a person's face 人の発言をはねつける

slander 名 名誉毀損, 悪口, 誹謗, 中傷
slanderous 形 中傷する
 slanderous leaflet 中傷ビラ, 中傷文書

slash 動 深く切り込む, 大幅に削減する, 減らす, 低減する, 縮小する, 引き下げる, 下方修正する, 名 大幅削減, 激減, 切り込み, 深い切り傷

slate 動 候補者の名簿に載せる, 候補に立てる, 候補に指名される[選ばれる], 予定を立てる, 酷評する, こきおろす
 be slated as …の候補になる
 be slated for …に予定されている, …候補に選ばれる
 be slated to …することになっている, …する予定である

slate 名 公認候補者名簿, 役員名簿, 予定表, 石板, スレート
 clean the slate 白紙に戻す, 行きがかり[過去]を水に流す, 過去を清算する (=wipe the slate clean)
 wipe the slate clean 過去を清算する, 一から出直す (=clean the slate)
 with a clean slate 白紙の状態で, 汚点のない経歴で, 一点の曇りもない状態で, 新規まき直しで

slaughterhouse 名 食肉処理場
sleep apnea syndrome 睡眠時無呼吸症候群
sleep-inducing agent 睡眠導入剤
sleeping partner 〈合名会社の〉匿名社員 (=silent partner：出資はするが経営には参加しない)

slew 名 多数, 多量, 大量, たくさん (=a great number, a lot)
 a slew of people 多数の人々, 多くの人々

slide 動 下がる, 低下する, 下落する, 減少する, 落ち込む, 悪化する, 滑る, 移動する, 変化する, スライドする
 slide into recession 景気後退に陥る
 slide to the floor of …の下限に達する

slide 名 低下, 下落, 減少, 落ち込み, 悪化, 滑走, 滑ること, 滑り込み, 滑り台, 滑走路, 地滑り, 山崩れ (landslide), 雪崩, 自在棚, スライド
 a downward slide in prices 物価の下落
 be on the slide 下落している, 悪化している
 go into a slide スリップする
 slide in confidence 信認の低下

sliding scale スライド制, 伸縮法, 順応率(経済状態に応じて賃金・物価や税などが上下する率), スライディング・スケール

sliding scale duties [tariff] スライド関税, 伸縮関税
sliding scale system 物価スライド制
sling mud 中傷する, 悪態をつく
slip 動 減少する, 縮小する, 低下する, 下落する, 滑り落ちる, ずり落ちる
  slip into …に陥る, …になる
  slip something over on …の裏をかく, 出し抜く, だます
  slip to …まで低下[減少]する
slipshod 形 だらしない, ずさんな, ぞんざいな
  slipshod accounting どんぶり勘定
  slipshod examination ずさんな審査
  slipshod investigation ずさんな調査
slogan 名 標語, モットー (motto, watchword), 宣伝[うたい]文句, キャッチフレーズ (catch phrase, catchword), スローガン
  phrase a slogan スローガンを作成する[作り出す]
  under the slogan of …というスローガン[標語]を掲げて, …のスローガンの下に
sloganeer 名 スローガンの作成者, スローガン使用者
slot 名 位置, 場所, 地位, ポスト, 〈放送番組の〉時間帯, 〈硬貨の〉差入れ口, 溝状の軌道スロット
  departure and arrival slots 発着枠
  in the slot 順番を待って
  the eight o'clock slot on the TV program テレビ番組の8時台の時間帯
slow 動 減速する, 弱まる, 鈍る, 鈍化する, 伸び悩む, 低迷する, 下降線をたどる, 落ち込む, 低下する, 鈍化させる, ブレーキをかける
  slow down 減速する, 後退する, 鈍化する, 停滞する, 低迷する
slowdown 名 〈景気などの〉減速, 失速, 鈍化, 後退, 沈滞, 低迷, 低下, 減産, 操業短縮, 怠業
  demand slowdown 需要の伸びの鈍化, 需要減速, 需要低迷
  slowdown in the decline of exports 輸出減少の鈍化
slow-growing economy 景気低迷
slowing 名 減速, 鈍化, 減少, 低迷, 落込み, 伸び悩み
  slowing of foreign demand 外需の伸びの低下, 外需拡大の鈍化, 外需の減少
slowing 形 減速している, 鈍化している, 低迷している, 落ち込んでいる, …の減速, …の鈍化, …の低迷
  slowing income growth 所得の伸び悩み, 所得の伸びの低迷 (=slowing in income growth)
sluggish 形 不振の, 低迷した, 低迷する, 不活発な, 不景気な, 動きが鈍い, 足どりが重い, 軟調な, 軟弱な
  sluggish liquidity 流動性の低さ
  sluggish market 市場低迷, 市況低迷, 軟弱市況, 軟調な市場, 活気のない市況
sluggishness 名 低迷, 停滞, 不振, 軟調, 軟弱, 不景気, 回復などの遅れ, 足取りが重いこと
  sluggishness in retail sales 小売り売上高の低迷
slump 動 暴落する, 急落する, 落ち込む, 減少する, 低迷する
slump 名 暴落, 急落, 落ち込み, 減少, 低迷, 不振, 不況, 不景気, 景気沈滞, スランプ (=sluggishness)
  prolonged slump in the real estate market 不動産市場の長期低迷
  slump-ridden industry 不況業種
slumpflation 名 不況下[不景気下]のインフレ, スランプフレーション (スタグフレーションより厳しい不況の状態をいう)
slumping 形 不振の, 低迷した, 落ち込んでいる, …の低迷[不振, 落ち込み, 減少]
  slumping economy 景気低迷, 不況
  slumping exports 輸出の減少, 輸出の落ち込み
slush fund 不正資金, 賄賂資金, 裏金
small 形 小さい, 狭い, 少ない, わずかな, 小幅な, 重要でない, ささいな, 二流の, 小規模の, 中小の, 小型の, 小口の, 少額の
  small and midsize 中小企業
  small balance sheet スモール・バランスシート (資産を極限まで小さくして, 効率よく大きな利益を生む体質を作り出すこと)
  Small Business Administration 〈米〉中小企業庁
  small capital 過小資本
  small claims court 少額請求裁判所
  small-lot user 小口ユーザー
  small profits and quick returns 薄利多売方式
smallpox vaccine 天然痘ワクチン
smart 形 情報処理機能を持つ, インテリジェントな, コンピュータ内蔵の, コンピュータで作動する, 高機能の, 高度な, 自動化された, センサー誘導の, スマート
  smart bomb スマート爆弾, 誘導爆弾, 誘導弾
  smart building スマート・ビル (=brain

building, intelligent building)
smart card ICカード
smart home 自動化住宅
smart money 相場師の投資金, ずる賢い投資家, 経験・知識が豊富な人, 負傷手当, 懲罰的損害賠償金
smart phone 高度自動機能電話
smart set 上流社会, 上流階級の人々, 新しがりの人々
smart grid [smart electric grid] 次世代送電網, スマート・グリッド(IT(情報技術)を利用してインテリジェントな送電網を構築して, 電力使用と配電を最適化するという構想・計画)
smart power 賢い力, 賢いパワー, 賢く力を使うこと, スマート・パワー(ハード・パワー(軍事力や経済力)とソフト・パワー(文化や価値観による影響力)を柔軟に組み合わせた力のこと。クリントン政権で国防次官補を務めたジョセフ・ナイ氏とアーミテージ元国務副長官を中心とする超党派集団が, 2007年に発表した安全保障報告で提案した概念)
smarts 名 良識, 知能, 知力, 頭脳, 知性, 実際的知識, 分別
smash hit 大ヒット
smokestack [smoke-stack] industry 重工業, 煙突型産業, 構造不況産業, 斜陽産業
smoking gun 動かぬ証拠, 決定的証拠 (= incontrovertible evidence)
smuggle 動 密輸する, 密輸入する, 密輸出する, 密入国させる, 密出国させる, …をこっそり運ぶ
  smuggle a pistol into the jail 拳銃をひそかに刑務所に持ち込む
  smuggle drugs into …に麻薬を密輸する
  smuggle oneself into …に密入国する
smuggling 名 密輸, 密航
snake 名 ヘビ, 陰険な人, 狡猾な人, 変動為替相場制, スネーク
  a snake in the grass 目に見えない敵
  have snakes in one's boots アル中になる (=see snakes)
  warm [cherish] a snake in one's bosom 恩をあだで返される, 飼い犬に手をかまれる
snap 形 急な, 即座の, 緊急の, 抜き打ちの, 不意の, 楽な, 名 容易なこと, 簡単にできること
  make a snap judgment 即断する
  snap election 抜き打ち選挙
snap up 先を争って買う, さっと買う[取る, 拾う]
snapshot of economic conditions 景況報告

snarl 名 混乱, 紛糾, 〈交通の〉渋滞, 麻痺, 〈毛髪, 糸などの〉もつれ
  be all in a snarl 混乱しきっている, 大混乱している, 大いに紛糾している
  snarl-up 〈事態の〉混乱, 交通渋滞
  traffic snarl 交通渋滞[麻痺] (=snarl-up, traffic jam)
soar 動 急騰する, 急増する, 大きく上回る
  ▶ Long-term interest rates have *soared* almost fourfold in the past three months as a result of plunges in the government bond market. 国債相場の急落で, 長期金利はこの3か月で4倍近くに急騰している。
soaring 形 急騰する, 高騰する, …の急増, …の急騰
  soaring oil prices 原油価格の高騰
social 形 社会の, 社会的な, 社会に関する, 社交の, 社交上の, ソーシャル
  a social gathering 懇親会
  social action 社会改革運動
  social activity 社会活動
  social audit 〈企業に対する〉社会監査
  Social Democratic Party 〈英国の〉社会民主党《略 SDP》
  social disease [plague] 社会病, 性病 (=venereal disease)
  social insurance labor consultant 社会保険労務士
  social insurance premium 社会保険料
  social marketing ソーシャル・マーケティング(企業の社会的責任(商品の安全性への配慮, 環境保全や地域社会への貢献など)を果たすために行う市場活動)
  social overhead capital 社会的間接資本, 社会共通資本, 社会資本 (=infrastructure)
  social register 社交界名士録, 名士録
  social responsibility 社会的責任
  social responsibility accounting 社会責任会計
  social safety net 〈米国の〉最低生活保障制度
  social science 社会科学
  social service 公共事業, 社会奉仕, 社会貢献, 社会事業, 社会福祉事業, 社会サービス
  social work 社会事業, 社会福祉事業
  social worker 社会福祉活動家, 社会福祉事業家, 民生委員, ソーシャル・ワーカー
social networking service ソーシャル・ネットワーキング・サービス《略 SNS》(日記や個人

情報などを，特定の仲間うちなどに限ってネット上で公開するサービス。原則としてお互いの名前や肩書などを公開して，意見交換や交流などを行うことができる）

social security 社会保障
  Social Security Act 〈米国の〉社会保障法
  Social Security Administration 〈米〉社会保障局
  social security benefits 社会保障給付
  social security insurance premium 社会保険料
  social security number 社会保障番号, 社会保障登録番号
  social security outlays 社会保障関係費
  social security services 社会保障事業, 社会保障サービス
  social security support 社会保障
  social security taxes payable 社会保険税預り金
social welfare 社会福祉
  social welfare indicator 社会生活指標, 総福祉指標
socialism 名 社会主義, 社会主義運動, 社会主義政策
▶ Under a system that can be termed "financial *socialism*," a government controls the massive amounts of money collected from the private sector. 「金融社会主義」ともいえる制度では，国が民間から集めた巨額の資金を管理する。
socialist 名 社会主義者, 社会党員
  socialist economy 社会主義経済
socially responsible investing 社会的責任投資《略 SRI》(法の遵守や社会貢献度などの社会性や環境問題への取組み姿勢などで投資先を判断する投資手法)
society 名 社会, 世間, 世間の人々, 共同体, 社会階層, 上流社会, 社交界, 協会, 団体, 組合, クラブ, …界, 交流, 交際
  a civil society 市民社会
  a cooperative society 協同組合
  seek the society of others 他人との交際を求める
  threat [menace] to society 社会に対する脅威
SoCs システム・オン・チップ, SoC (**systems-on-chips**の略)
soft 形 柔らかい, 滑らかな, 柔軟な, 穏やかな, 心地よい, 楽な, やさしい, 甘い, 寛大な, 敵の攻撃を受けやすい, 馬鹿な, 間抜けな, ソフト

be soft on [about] …に寛大である, …に惚れている
end on a soft note 引けにかけて相場が若干軟化する
have a soft [tender, warm] spot for …を好む, …が気に入っている
soft copy ソフト・コピー (ディスプレーの表示画面のこと)
soft currency 軟貨, 交換不能通貨, ソフト通貨, ソフト・カレンシー (金や他の通貨と交換できない通貨)
soft currency area 軟貨圏
soft demand 需要低迷, 需要の軟化
soft drug 習慣性の弱い麻薬
soft energy ソフト・エネルギー, 再生可能エネルギー
soft error 誤動作
soft goods 〈織物・衣服などの〉非耐久消費財, 繊維製品, ソフト・グッズ
soft information 未確認情報, 予測情報
soft landing 軟着陸
soft loan 長期低利貸付け, 条件の緩やかな融資 [貸出, 借款], ソフト・ローン
soft money 規制対象外の選挙運動資金, ソフト・マネー (政党活動費や意見広告など政党への献金)
soft patch 弱含みの時期
soft porn 露骨でないポルノ (=**soft-core porno [pornography]**)
soft power ソフト・パワー (軍事力や経済力によらずに，文化や政策などに対する支持や理解, 共感を得ることによって，国際社会からの信頼や発言力を獲得できる力のこと)
soft undertone 地合いが弱いこと
software 名 ソフトウエア, コンピュータ・プログラム, コンピュータの運用操作技術, 利用技術, 視聴覚教材, 〈ロケット・宇宙船の〉燃料, ソフト
  antivirus software ウイルス防止ソフト
  application software 応用ソフト
  proprietary software 専用ソフト
  software product license ソフトウエア使用許諾契約 [契約書] (=**software license agreement**)
  software tool ソフトウエア工具, テストや開発を支援するプログラム, ソフトウエア・メーカーが提供する補助的プログラム, ソフトウエア・ツール (=**utility program**)
  virus protection software ウイルス対策ソフト

software development ソフトウエア開発
  software development environment ソフトウエア開発環境
  software development process ソフトウエア開発工程
  software development support ソフトウエア開発支援
  software development tools ソフトウエア開発支援ツール

solar 形 太陽の, 太陽に関する, 太陽から生じる, 太陽熱を利用した, 太陽電池の
  solar battery 太陽電池, 太陽電池装置 (solar cellの集まったもの)
  solar breeder 太陽電池増殖工場, ソーラー・ブリーダー
  solar car ソーラー・カー (太陽電池を動力源とする車)
  solar collector 太陽熱集熱器, 太陽熱収集器
  solar cooling system 太陽熱冷凍機
  solar energy 太陽エネルギー, 太陽熱エネルギー (=solar power)
  solar flare 太陽面爆発, フレア
  solar furnace 太陽炉
  solar heating 太陽熱暖房, 太陽熱給湯
  solar market 太陽電池市場
  Solar Maximum Mission 米国の太陽活動観測衛星, ソーラー・マキシマム・ミッション (=Solar Max)
  solar observation satellite 太陽観測衛星
  Solar One 米国の太陽熱発電プロジェクト, ソーラー・ワン
  solar panel 太陽電池板, 太陽電池パネル
  solar pond 太陽蓄熱池, ソーラー・ポンド
  solar power house 太陽熱利用の発電所
  solar-powered plane 太陽力飛行機
  solar sail 太陽帆航法, ソーラー・セイル
  solar sailer 宇宙帆船, ソーラー・セーラー
  solar system 太陽系, 太陽熱利用システム, ソーラー・システム
  Solar System Exploration Committee 〈米国の〉太陽系探査委員会
  solar telescope 太陽望遠鏡
  solar water heater 太陽熱温水器
  solar wind 太陽風

solar cell 太陽電池
  CIS solar cell CIS太陽電池 (従来のシリコンではなく, 銅, インジウム, セレンの化合物を使うタイプの太陽電池. 人工衛星の電源としても注目されている)

solar power 太陽熱発電, 太陽光発電, 太陽光発電所, 太陽エネルギー
  solar power generation 太陽光発電
  solar power satellite 太陽発電衛星
  solar power station [plant] 太陽熱 [太陽光] 発電所, 太陽熱利用発電所
  solar thermal power station 太陽熱発電

solicit 動 勧誘する, 募集する, 募る, 強く求める, …するように要請する, 〈資金などを〉集める, 訪問販売する, 〈人を〉悪事に誘う
  solicit clients 顧客を勧誘する
  solicit funds from …に資金提供を要請する, …に出資を勧誘する, …から資金を集める
  solicit investors 出資者を募る [募集する], 投資家を募集する
  solicit opinions on …に関する意見を求める
  solicit proxies 委任状を取り付ける

solid 形 着実な, 堅実な, 底堅い, 強固な, 健全な, 安定した
  solid demand 堅実な需要, 需要の安定
  solid performance 底堅い業績, 堅調な値動き

solution 名 問題解決, 問題解決策, 問題解決手法, 解決法, 解決手段, コンピュータとアプリケーション, ネットワークの組合せによるシステム構築, ユーザーの要求に応じた情報システムの構築, ソリューション
  customized solution 顧客の要求に応じて特注化したソリューション, ソリューションの特注化
  solution provider ソリューション請負業者, ソリューション・サービス業者

solvency 名 支払い余力, 支払い能力, ソルベンシー (支払期日の到来時点で, 支払いできる状態にあること)
  solvency margin 支払い余力, 支払い余力比率, ソルベンシー・マージン比率, ソルベンシー・マージン
  solvency position 自己資本比率

somatic cell nuclear transfer 体細胞核移植 [転移], 体細胞クローン技術《略 SCNT》
▶The technology used to create genetically identical animals is called *somatic cell nuclear transfer*. 遺伝子がまったく同じ動物をつくる技術は, 「体細胞核転移」と呼ばれている.

soothe 動 落ち着かせる, なだめる, 静める, 和らげる, 慰める, 安心させる, 楽にする, 払拭する
  soothe market fears 市場不安を払拭する
  soothe pain 傷みを和らげる

soothe the opposition 反対派を静める

sophisticated 形 高度の, 高性能の, 最先端技術の, 最新式の, 最新装置の, 精巧な, 精密な, 巧みな, 複雑な, 手の込んだ, 凝った, 洗練された, あか抜けた, しゃれた, おしゃれな, 品のいい, 高級な, 超近代的な, 都会的な, 有能な, 優秀な, 効率的な, 無駄のない, 本格的な (=cutting-edge, leading edge, state-of-the-art, top of the line)
- financially sophisticated investor 金融知識を持ち合わせた投資家
- sophisticated drilling technology 高度な掘削技術

sophistication 名 技術の高度化, 発達, 高水準, 水準, 精密化, 複雑化, 精巧さ, 知的教養, 知識
- consumer sophistication 消費者の知識
- technological sophistication 技術の水準

soul-searching 名 自己分析, 反省, 猛省

sound 形 健康な, 健全な, 確かな, もっともな, 正しい, 理にかなった, 正当性のある, 安定した, 堅実な, 正常な, 正確な, 正統的な, 根拠の十分な, 頼りになる, 信頼できる, 思慮分別のある, 〈法律的に〉有効な
- a sound title to land 有効な土地所有権
- sound capitalization 自己資本の充実
- sound financial fundamentals 健全な財務体質
- sound loan 正常債権
- sound management 堅実な経営, 健全な経営 (放漫経営=lax [loose] management)
- sound policy 堅実な政策, 健全政策, 手堅い政策

soundness 名 健全性, 安定性, 確実性, 堅実性, 正当性
- Federal Housing Enterprises Financial Safety and Soundness Act of 1992 1992年連邦住宅機関財政安定健全法
- financial soundness 財務上の健全性, 財政の健全性, 経済的安定性, 経営の健全性 (=financial health)
- fiscal soundness 財務上の健全性, 財政の健全性, 財政の安定性

sour 動 悪くする, 悪化させる, 悪化する, 低迷する
- soured assets 不良資産 (=bad assets, non-performing assets, problem assets)
- soured loan 不良債権, 不良貸出, 貸倒れ (=bad loan, nonperforming loan, problem loan, troubled loan)

sour 形 不快な, 不愉快な, いやな, 気難しい, 厳しい, 過酷な, 標準以下の, へたな

be sour on …を嫌っている, …が嫌だ
come to a sour end 不愉快な結果に終わる
sour soil 酸性土壌
sour temper 気難しい気質
turn [go] sour 失敗する, 駄目になる, うまく行かなくなる, 酸っぱくなる

source 名 情報源, ニュースソース, 筋, 取材源, 関係筋, 関係筋, 資料, 出典, 出所, 水源, 源, 源泉, 種(たね), 〈利子・配当などの〉支払い者
- diplomatic sources 外交筋
- external sources of cash 外部流動性
- news source ニュースの出所
- official sources 公式筋
- reference sources 参考資料
- source and application of fund statement 資金運用表
- source of profit 収益源
- source of revenue 財源
- withholding at source 源泉徴収

sovereign 形 最高の, 最高権力を持つ, 主権のある, 〈国家が〉独立した, 特効のある, ソブリン
- British sovereign territory 英国主権の領土
- sovereign debt 国債, 公的債務
- sovereign immunity 主権免除
- sovereign loan ソブリン融資, ソブリン・ローン
- sovereign power 主権
- sovereign risk ソブリン・リスク (=country risk)
- sovereign state [country, nation] 独立国
- sovereign support 政府支援

sovereign wealth fund 政府系投資ファンド, 政府系ファンド, ソブリン・ウエルス・ファンド《略 SWF》(=government-affiliated investment fund, government-run investment fund: 政府が運用するファンドで, その原資の公的資金は主に中央銀行の外貨準備高や国有天然資源で得られる利益であることが多い)

世界の主な政府系ファンド:

アラブ首長国連邦	アブダビ投資庁
クウェート	クウェート投資銀行
サウジアラビア	サウジ通貨庁
シンガポール	シンガポール政府投資公社
中国	中国投資有限責任公司
ノルウェー	政府年金基金
ロシア	準備基金

sovereignty 名 主権, 統治権, 主権国, 独立国
Soyuz [soyuz] 名 ソユーズ宇宙船, ソユーズ

（Unionの意味。1967年以来，ロシアが打ち上げている有人宇宙船。国際宇宙ステーション（ISS）に長期滞在する宇宙飛行士の輸送は，退役する米スペース・シャトルに代わってソユーズで行なうことになっている）

space 名　宇宙，空間，宇宙空間，大気圏外，余地，余白，空き地，区域，場所，用地，面積，売場，船腹，紙面，広告欄，行間，スペース
　basic space law　宇宙基本法
　broken space　から荷，空き荷
　selling floor space　売場面積
　space-based antimissile system　対ミサイル用宇宙兵器システム
　space book　船腹原簿
　space carrier　宇宙ロケット
　space center　宇宙基地，宇宙センター
　space charter　共同配給，共同運航，スペース・チャーター
　space contract　船腹契約，広告のスペース契約
　space debris [junk]　宇宙廃棄物，宇宙ごみ
　space gear　宇宙装置（ロケットや人工衛星，宇宙船など）
　space industry　宇宙産業，宇宙ビジネス
　space lab　宇宙実験室，スペースラブ（＝spacelab）
　space outfit [suit]　宇宙服（＝spacesuit）
　space probe　宇宙探査機，宇宙探査用ロケット
　space shuttle　スペース・シャトル，宇宙連絡船，有人宇宙連絡船
　space tug　軌道間輸送機，スペースタグ
　space utilization　売場有効利用
　the U.N. Outer Space Treaty　国連宇宙条約
space use　宇宙利用
　▶The basic space law stipulates that the government formulates a basic plan for *space use*.　宇宙基本法には，政府が宇宙利用の基本計画を策定すると定めてある。

spacecraft 名　宇宙船，スペースシップ（＝spaceship）
spacefaring 名　宇宙旅行
Spacelab 名　有人宇宙実験室
spaceman 名　宇宙飛行士，宇宙研究者，宇宙人
spaceplane 名　宇宙飛行機，宇宙バス，宇宙連絡船，スペース・シャトル
spaceport 名　宇宙船基地
Spaceship Earth　宇宙船地球号
spacesickness 名　宇宙酔い
spacesuit 名　宇宙服

spacetrack 名　宇宙攻撃警戒網，スペーストラック
spacewalk 名　宇宙遊泳
spaceworthy 形　宇宙飛行できる
spam 名　迷惑メール，スパム・メール（＝spam e-mail）
span 名　長さ，期間，全期間，全長，全幅，全範囲，スパン
　a life span　寿命，一生
　the span of a bridge　橋の径間（わたりま）［支柱間の距離］
　the span of control　統制範囲，管理限界
　the whole span of a bridge　橋の全長
　wing span　〈飛行機の〉翼長
spanking 形　活発な，敏速な，きびきび動く，素晴らしい，素敵な，顕著な，著しい，とても速い，素早い，副 とても，極めて，非常に
　expand at a spanking clip　顕著なペースで拡大する，急速に拡大する
spare 動　〈費用などを〉惜しむ，節約する，…なしで済ます，…を手放す，…を容赦する，〈時間を〉割く，与える
　be spared from injury　負傷を免れる
　spare no effort　努力を惜しまない
　spare oneself　骨惜しみをする
　▶Firms should not *spare* any expense in enhancing the technical skills of young workers.　企業は，若い社員の技能を高めるのに，費用を惜しんではならない。
spark 動　引き起こす，誘発する，…の火付け役となる，かき立てる，奮起させる，鼓舞する（animate），刺激する（stimulate），活気づける，促進させる（stir up），火花を飛ばす，正気［意識］を失う，気を失う
　spark harsh criticism from　…から厳しい批判を招く，…からの厳しい批判を引き起こす
　spark off　…を起こす，…を引き起こす，…を誘発する，…のきっかけとなる，…の発端［直接原因］になる
　spark one's enthusiasm for A　Aに対する…の熱意をかき立てる
　spark one's interest in　…への関心に火を付ける
spark 名　火花，火の粉，火種，引き金，原因，ひらめき，きらめき，輝き，閃光，宝石，ダイヤモンド，生気，活気，刺激，電信技士，無線士，スパーク
　have the spark of life　活気がある，生気がある
　lack of (a) spark　活気がない，生気がない
　provide a spark for　…の原因を作る
spasm 名　突発的な行動

spate 名 大量, 多量, 多数, 多発, 続発, 連発, 殺到, 洪水, 氾濫, 豪雨
- **a spate of new issuances** 相次ぐ新規発行, 大量起債
- **a spate of inquiries** 相次ぐ問い合わせ, 殺到する問い合わせ, 問い合わせの殺到
- **be in (full) spate** 氾濫している

SPC 特定目的会社, 特別目的会社 (**special purpose company**の略)

speak [express, tell] volumes about …について［…を］雄弁に物語る, …を浮き彫りにする, …を強く支持する, …が明白である, …は大いに意味がある［意味深長である］

speaker 名 〈英米などの〉下院議長, 〈日本の〉衆議院議長
- **Speaker of the House** 〈米国の〉下院議長
- **Speaker of the House of Commons** 〈英国の〉下院議長
- **speaker of the House (of Representatives)** 〈日本の〉衆議院議長, 〈米国の〉下院議長 (米上院議長＝President of the Senate)

spearhead 動 先頭［陣頭, 先鋒］に立つ, 先陣を務める

SPEC 南太平洋経済協力機関 (**South Pacific Bureau for Economic Cooperation**の略)

special 形 特別の, 特定の, 特殊の, 専門の, 独特の, スペシャル
- **special adviser** 〈大統領などの〉特別補佐官
- **special agent** 特殊機関, 〈FBIの〉特別捜査権
- **special assault team** 特殊急襲部隊《略 SAT》
- **Special Branch** 〈英国の政治上の警備を担当する〉公安部
- **special drawing rights** 〈IMFの〉特別引出し権《略 SDR(s)》(＝paper gold)
- **special economic zone** 経済特区, 経済特別区
- **special envoy [emissary]** 特使
- **Special Forces** 米軍特殊部隊 (＝U.S. Army Special Forces)
- **Special Message** 〈米大統領の〉特別教書
- **Special Olympics** 〈知的障害者のための〉スペシャル・オリンピック
- **special pleading** 特別訴答, 特別弁論, 手前勝手な議論
- **special spousal exemptions** 配偶者特別控除
- **Special Weapons and Tactics** 特殊火器戦術部隊, スワット《略 SWAT》

special purpose company 特別目的会社, 特定目的会社《略 SPC》(＝special purpose corporation, special purpose entity: 不動産や債権の証券化など, 特別の目的を持って設立される会社. 有価証券を発行し, 小口化して広く資金を調達できるメリットがある)

specialty store 専門店 (＝speciality store)
▶ *Specialty stores* called category killers for home appliances and clothing providing unique items at low prices became more popular in the latter half of 1990s. 個性的な商品を手ごろな価格で提供する家電製品や衣料品の「カテゴリー・キラー」と呼ばれる専門店が, 1990年代後半から人気を集めるようになった。

species 名 種, 種類, 〈ミサ用の〉パンとぶどう酒, 形式, 体裁
- **a species of treason** 一種の裏切り (＝a kind of treason)
- **an endangered [threatened] species** 絶滅危惧種
- **the Endangered Species Act** 絶滅危惧種法《略 ESA》
- **the species** 人類 (＝our species, the human race, the human species)

specific 形 特定の, 特別の, 具体的な, 明確な, はっきりした, 個々の, 個別の, 特有の, 固有の, 独特の, 〈課税が〉重量の, 名 細部, 細目, 詳細, 特性, 特効薬
- **a specific medicine [remedy] for** …の特効薬
- **get down to specifics** 詳細を詰める
- **go [get [get]] into specifics** 細目に移る
- **specific duties** 従量税
- **specific gravity** 比重
- **specific performance** 特定履行 (契約どおりに債務を履行させること)
- **specific tariff** 従量税 (＝specific duties, specific tax)
- **the specifics of the requirements** 条件の細部

specification 名 明記, 詳述, 明細, 明細書, 仕様, 仕様書, 規格, 内訳, 加工, スペック
- **contract specifications** 契約仕様, 契約条件, 契約仕様書
- **job specifications** 職務明細書
- **production [manufacturing] specifications** 製造仕様書

specified account 特定口座 (株式投資を促進するための新証券税制で, 個人投資家の納税（税務）手続きを証券会社が代行する制度. 2003年1月から実施)

Specified [Specific] Commercial Transactions Law 特定商取引法（訪問販売法が2000年の改正で「特定商取引法」に変更された。その対象は訪問販売や通信販売，電話勧誘販売など六つの取引形態で，クーリングオフや違反があった場合の行政処分や刑事罰も規定されている）

specter [spectre] 图 怖いもの，恐ろしさ，不安のもと，不安材料，懸念，懸念材料，幽霊，亡霊，被害妄想の種
　raise the specter of …の観測を強める，…の懸念が高まる，…の脅威を騒ぎたてる
　the specter of a global downturn 世界不況の懸念，世界同時不況の観測

speculate 動 推測する，憶測する，考える，観測する，投機をする，相場に手を出す，思惑をやる，思惑買いをする，やまを張る
　speculate about one's future 将来をよく考える
　speculate for [on] a rise 騰貴を予想して投機をする
　speculate on interest rates 金利の思惑で投資する

speculation 图 投機，思惑，思惑買い，見越し売買，憶測，推測，観測，相場（「投機」とは，配当や株価の短期的な値上がりを期待して株式を売買することをいう）
　devaluation-speculation cycle 為替切下げ・投機循環
　on [for] speculation 投機で，思惑で
　speculation about [on] another rate [interest rate] hike 再値上げの観測，もう一段の利上げ観測，再利上げに関する思惑
　speculation stock 仕手株
　trade on speculation 値幅とり

speculative 形 投機的な，思惑による，推測に基づく，危険な，理論的な
　speculative dealing 仕手戦
　speculative demand 投機的需要，思惑需要，仮需要
　speculative grade 投機的格付け
　speculative importation 見越し輸入
　speculative interests 思惑筋，投機筋
　speculative name 仕手銘柄
　speculative operation 投機取引，投機的操作
　speculative transaction 投機性の高い取引，投機的取引，投機売買，思惑取引
　speculative venture 投機的事業，投機事業（＝speculative business, speculative enterprise）

speculator 图 相場師，投機筋，投機家，投機師，仕手，仕手筋，だふ屋　（＝speculative investor：短期勝負の株式売買を行う投資家のこと）
　land speculator 地上げ屋
　speculator buying 投機買い，思惑買い
　stock speculator 仕手筋

speech 图 話，演説，講演，談話，発言，あいさつ，陳述，話し方，話しぶり，話し言葉，話法，話す力[能力]，言語能力，〈役者の〉せりふ，スピーチ
　freedom of speech 言論の自由
　give [deliver, make] a speech on …について演説を行う
　speech clinic 言語障害矯正所
　speech community 言語共同体
　speech day 表彰日，終業式
　speech defect [impediment] 言語障害

speed up 速める，加速する，…のスピードを上げる，増進する，促進する，スピード違反をする

spell 動 …となる，…を意味する，…の結果を招く，…に導く，つづる
　explicitly spell out はっきり説明する
　spell a great danger 一大危機となる
　spell out 明確に［はっきり］説明する，詳細に［詳しく］説明する，〈計画や案を〉打ち出す，一字一字読み取る，判読する，略さないで書く
　spell ruin 破滅をもたらす，破滅を招く
　spell trouble 厄介なことになる

spend 動 支出する，投資する，〈金などを〉使う，消費する

spending 图 支出，歳出，予算，経費，投資，消費
　capital goods spending 資本財需要
　capital spending 設備投資，資本支出
　debt-servicing spending 国債費
　discretionary spending 裁量的経費
　mandatory spending 義務的経費
　spending habit 消費性向，消費習慣
　spending on inventories 在庫投資
　spending on plant and equipment 設備投資
　spending on public works projects 公共事業関係費
　spending policy 支出政策（有効需要を刺激して不況からの脱却を図る政策）
　spending spree 消費景気　（＝spending boom）
　spending unit 消費単位，支出単位
　U.S. defense spending 米国の防衛支出

spent fuel rod 使用済み燃料棒
spent nuclear fuel 使用済み核燃料
spent nuclear fuel rod 使用済み核燃料棒 (⇒krypton 85)
spike 名 急増, 急騰, 大幅な上昇, 高騰
 a spike in fuel prices 燃料価格の急騰, 燃料価格の高騰
 a spike in the dollar ドル急騰
spill over into …に流出する, …にあふれ出る, …に広がる, …に波及する, …に飛び火する
 ▶The financial crisis engulfing the United States and European nations has *spilled over into* Japan. 欧米諸国を巻き込んだ金融危機が, 日本にも波及［飛び火］した.
spin off 〈会社を〉分割する, 分社化する, 分離する, 切り離す
spinoff [**spin-off**] 名 分社化, 分社, 会社分割, 切り離し, スピンオフ（企業が事業の一部を切り離して別の会社に移すこと）
 establish [create, form] a new company by [through] spinoff 分社化で新会社を設立する
 spinoff of domestic sales operations 国内営業部門の分社化
 spinoff system 会社分割制度, 分社化制度 (=spin-off system)
 spinoff effects 波及効果 (=spin-off effects)
 ▶It is expected to create high added value and a wide range of *spinoff effects*. これは, 高い付加価値と幅広い波及効果を生むものと期待されている.
spiral 動 急騰する, 急増する, 急上昇［降下］する, らせん状に上昇［下降］する
spiral 名 悪循環, 連鎖的変動, 連鎖的上昇［低下］, 連鎖, 連続的変動, 急上昇, 急下降, 急増, らせん, 渦巻き線, スパイラル
 a deflationary spiral デフレの悪循環, デフレ的悪循環, デフレ・スパイラル
 a downward spiral 連鎖的急降下
split 動 分裂する, 離脱する, 解散する, 分離する, 分割する
split 名 分裂, 亀裂, 不和, 分割, 株式分割
 reverse split 株式併合
 share split 株式分割 (=stock split)
 share split-down 株式併合 (=stock split-down)
 share split-up 株式分割 (=stock split-up)
split up 分割する
 split up and privatize 分割・民営化する (=restructure and privatize)
split-up of stock 株式分割 (=share split-up, stock split-up)
spokesman 名 広報担当者, 報道官, スポークスマン (=spokesperson)
 company spokesman 広報担当者
sponsor 動 後援する, 主催する, 後押しする, 支持する, 支援する, 〈法案などを〉主唱する, 保証する, 保証人になる, 協力する, スポンサーになる
 federally sponsored agencies 連邦政府関連機関
 government sponsored agencies 政府系機関, 政府支援機関, 政府関連機関
sponsor 名 〈投資信託証券の〉引受人［引受業者］, 〈ベンチャー・ビジネスや慈善事業などへの〉出資者, 〈プロジェクト・ファイナンスの〉実質的推進者, 〈債務などの〉保証人, 原資産保有者, 後援者, 後援会, 主催者, 発起人, 支持者, 広告主, 番組提供者, スポンサー
 official sponsor 公式スポンサー
-sponsored 形 …後援の, …主催の, …主宰の, …が提唱［主唱］する, …が後押し［支持］する, …提出の, …をスポンサーとする
 government-sponsored agencies [enterprises, entities] 政府系機関
 government-sponsored bill 政府提出の法案
 lawmaker-sponsored bill 議員立法
 UN-sponsored activities 国連決議に基づく活動
spot 名 場所, 地点, 位置, 地位, 職, 現物, 現地品, スポット
 ad spot スポットCM
 merchandise on spot 現場渡し, 現物
 on the spot 即座に, その場で, 現場で, 現物で, 現金で
 price on spot 現物相場, 現金相場, 現金売価
spot 形 即座の, 現金の, 現金払いの, 現金取引の, 現物の
 spot basis 現物決済
 spot commodity 現物 (=cash commodity, spot goods)
 spot contract 現物即時渡し約定
 spot deal 直物取引, 現物取引, 直物為替取引
 spot market 現物市場, 直物市場, 現金取引市場, 当用買い市場, スポット市場, スポット・マーケット (=cash market: 現金の受け払いで商品が即時に受渡しされる市場)
 spot needs 急需要

spot next [spot/next] スポット・ネクスト（受渡し日が約定日から3日後となる取引。2営業日後（スポット）から翌日までの金利やスワップ・レートを意味することもある）

spot price 現物価格，直物価格，直物商品価格，スポット価格（＝cash price：スポット市場（現物市場）で取引される商品の現在価格）

spot purchase 当用買い，現金買い，即時買い

spot quotation 現物相場，現場渡し値段

spot start スワップの開始日（一般に約定日から2営業日後を開始日とする）

spot transaction 直物取引，現物取引，実物取引，直物為替取引，直物為替契約，直物契約

spread 動 広げる，広める，伸ばす，拡大する，蔓延させる，普及させる，拡散させる，分散させる，引き伸ばす，分布する，分担する，分配する，広がる，広まる，伝わる，及ぶ，蔓延する，普及する

spread the burden [load] 仕事を分担する

spread risks リスクを分散させる

▶ The recession in the United States has *spread* globally. 米国の景気後退は，世界中に広がっている[世界に波及している]。

spread 名 広がり，普及，〈病気などの〉蔓延，流行，見開きの記事，胴回りが太っていること，利幅，利ざや，上乗せ，金利差，開き，売り値と買い値の差，スプレッド，〈銀行の調達金利である〉預金金利と〈運用金利である〉貸出金利との差，〈株や債券，通貨取引などの〉買い呼び値(bid)と売り呼び値(offer)との差額，〈有価証券の発行者の引受業者への〉引渡し価格と〈引受業者の一般投資家への〉売出し価格との差額

bid-ask spread 呼び値スプレッド（＝bid-asked spread）

interest rate spread 金利スプレッド，利ざや

negative spread 逆ざや（＝negative yield）

profit spread 利ざや

two-to-30 year spread 2年物と30年物の利回り格差

underwriting spread 引受スプレッド

vertical spread バーティカル・スプレッド（＝money spread, price spread：オプション取引で，行使期間満了日は同じだが行使価格の異なるコール・オプションの売りと買い，またはプット・オプションの売りと買いを同時に実行すること）

yield spread 利回り格差，金利差

spring offensive 春闘，春季労使交渉（＝spring labor offensive, spring wage offensive）

spur 動 奮起させる，〈…するよう〉駆り立てる，せきたてる，…に拍車をかける，促進する，促す，…を活性化する，急ぐ

spur competition among …の間の競争を促す

spur technical [technological] innovation 技術革新を促す[促進する]

spur to investment 投資を促す

▶ China is *spurring* domestic-demand expansion policies by its own increased consumption. 中国は，消費拡大による内需拡大策を急いでいる。

spur 名 拍車，鼓舞，激励，刺激，誘因，動機，発奮材料，〈道路，鉄道の〉支線

earn [gain, get, win] one's spurs 名声を得る，名声をあげる，名をあげる，手柄をたてる，能力[価値]を実証する

on [upon] the spur 大急ぎで，全速力で

on the spur of the moment [occasion] 一時の思い付きで，その時のはずみで，出来心で，とっさに，即座に，突然に，思いつきで，衝動的に，前後の見境なく(without deliberation)，前後をわきまえないで

put [clap, give, set] spurs to …に拍車をかける，…に発破をかける，…を励ます

with whip and spur 即座に，直ちに（＝with spur and yard）

spy satellite 偵察衛星

spy ship 工作船

spyware 名 スパイウェア

▶ *Spyware* is computer software designed to allow information in a personal computer to be accessed through the Internet. スパイウェアは，インターネットを通じてパソコン内の情報にアクセスできる仕組みのコンピュータ・ソフトだ。

squad 名 隊，班，部隊，分隊，特捜班，別働隊，小集団，グループ，一団，〈スポーツの〉チーム

anti-terrorist squad テロ対策班，テロ対策部隊

flying squad 緊急機動隊

homicide squad 捜査第一課

riot squad 機動隊

special investigation squad 特捜部

squeeze 動 締め付ける，引き締める，〈予算や経費などを〉切り詰める，制限する，圧迫する，押し下げる，縮小する，低下する，減少する

▶ Before consumer spending could fully recover, oil prices began to rise in overseas markets, *squeezing* corporate profits. 個人消費が本格的に回復する前に，海外市場で原油価格が高騰し，企業利益を圧迫した。

SRI 社会的責任投資 (socially responsible investing)の略。法令順守や人権，労働など社会問題への企業の取組みで投資するかどうかを判断する)

SRI fund 社会的責任投資ファンド，SRIファンド
> SRIファンドとは ⇒ 社会に貢献する企業は消費者や投資家から信頼を得て，安定した利益が期待できることから，社会への貢献度の高い企業を選んで投資する投資信託。投資基準の社会への貢献度の要因としては，従業員の人権への配慮，社会活動への参加，消費者への対応，女性や障害者の雇用，消費者への対応などが挙げられる。

stability [名] 安定，安定性
  export stability 輸出安定性
  financial stability 金融システムの安定
  internal stability 国内の安定，国内安定性
  stability in the large 大範囲の安定
  stability in the small 小範囲の安定
  stability of the financial system 金融システムの安定性 (＝financial stability)

stabilization [名] 安定，安定化，安定操作，安定性，横ばいで推移すること
  currency stabilization loan 通貨安定借款 (＝stabilization loan)
  (exchange) stabilization fund 為替安定資金 (＝exchange equalization fund)
  monetary stabilization policy 通貨安定政策
  stabilization performance 安定化実績
  stabilization transaction 安定操作取引
  temporary stabilization 一時的安定

stabilize [動] 安定させる，固定させる，安定装置を施す，安定する，固定する，頭打ちになる
  stabilize financial markets 金融市場を安定させる
  stabilize the economy 経済を安定させる

stabilizing factor 安定要因
stabilizing transaction 安定操作

stable [形] 安定した，固定した，しっかりした，ぐらつかない，ぶれない，固い，不変の，一定の
  stable financial resource 安定財源
  stable growth path 安定成長の軌道，安定成長路線
  stable supplies 安定供給

staff [名] 社員，従業員，職員，人員，局員，幹部，スタッフ
  credit staff 与信担当者，与信担当スタッフ，審査担当者
  department of staff スタッフ部門

maintain staff 事務所を構える
managing staff 経営陣
staff benefits 従業員福利費
staff costs 人件費 (＝staff expenses)
staff department スタッフ部門 (＝department of staff：製造業では生産部門とマーケティング(販売)部門，販売業では仕入れ部門とマーケティング部門をスタッフ部門という)
staff reduction 人員削減 (＝reduction of staff numbers)

staffer [名] 職員，局員，記者，スタッフの一員，担当者

staffing agency 人材派遣会社 (＝temporary staffing agency [firm])
> The temporary workers are employed by *staffing agencies*, which dispatch them to the company. 派遣労働者は人材派遣会社が雇用し，雇用した労働者を同社に派遣している。

stagcession [名] 景気低迷 (stagnationとrecessionの合成語)

stage [動] 実行する，実施する，行う，開催する，上演する，企画する，〈ロケットを〉多段式にする
  stage a comeback 返り咲く，カムバックする，もうひと花咲かせる
  stage a sit-in 座り込み抗議を行う，座り込みを行う
  stage a strike ストを行う
  stage protests against …に対して抗議デモをする

stage [名] 段階，局面，時期，…期，舞台，活動の場所，ステージ
  closing stages 大詰めの段階
  early stages 初期の段階，初期 (＝initial stages)
  formative stage 草創期，試行錯誤の段階
  mature [maturity] stage 成熟期，成熟局面
  multi-stage sampling 多段抽出法
  set the stage for …のお膳立てをする，…の準備をする，…の態勢を整える
  stage of completion 作業進捗度，進捗度
  stages of financing 資金調達の段階
  stages of growth 成長段階 (＝growth stage)
  take center stage 衆目を集める，極めて重要になる (＝be at the center of the stage)

staggered board 任期別役員会，スタガー取締役会

staggered working [work] hours 時差出勤

staggerer 名 難問題, 大事件, よろめかす物, びっくりさせるもの

staggering 形 膨大な, 肝をつぶすほどの, 驚異的な, 驚くべき, 衝撃的な, 信じられないほどの, 信じがたいほどの, ふらふらする, よろめく
- **a staggering performance [achievement]** 驚異的な業績
- **a staggering result** 驚異的な業績, 信じがたい結果, 衝撃的な結果

staging 名 上演, 演出, 演出方法, 足場, 温室の棚, 多段式ロケットの切り離し[分離], ステージング
- **staging area** 〈部隊の〉中間集結基地, 部隊集結地, 宿営地
- **staging base** 中継基地
- **staging ground** 前進基地
- **staging post** 発進基地, 重要な準備段階, 一時着陸地, 一時寄港地, 途中停車[停泊]地

stagnancy 名 沈滞, 停滞, 頭打ちの状態, 不振, 不活発, 低迷, 悪化, 不景気, 不況
  ▶ The negative growth was due to the *stagnancy* of corporate capital investment as well as sluggish personal spending and other economy-slowing factors. マイナス成長は, 企業の設備投資が頭打ちの状態だったことと, 個人消費の伸び悩みや他の景気減速要因によるものだ.

stagnant 形 沈滞した, 停滞した, 進歩[発展, 発達, 成長, 向上]のない, 不振の, 低迷した, 活気のない, 動き[働き]の鈍い, 不活発な, 軟調の, 不景気な
- **stagnant domestic income** 国内所得の低迷
- **stagnant earnings** 収益悪化
- **stagnant economy** 沈滞[停滞]した経済, 景気低迷, 不景気, 経済の低迷[停滞], 不振の経済
- **stagnant industry** 停滞産業
- **stagnant market** 停滞する市場, 市場の低迷, 市場軟調, 沈滞市況, 軟調市況
- **stagnant results** 業績低迷, 業績不振, 業績悪化

stagnation 名 沈滞, 停滞, 景気沈滞, 不景気, 不況
- **fall into stagnation** 不景気[不況, 不振]に陥る
- **secular stagnation** 長期停滞
- **technical stagnation** 技術的停滞

stake 名 杭, 棒, 支柱, 出資, 出資比率, 投資, 投資金, 投資金額, 資本参加, 株式持ち分, 持ち株, 持ち株比率, 株, 株式, 関与, 利害関係, 関わり合い, 関心, 賭け金, 分配金, 賞金, …レース, リスクを伴う行為, ステークス(賞金付き競馬), 競争, 争い
- **a high-stakes bid** 大きな賭け
- **acquire a 30 percent stake in** …の株式の30％を取得する, …に30％出資する
- **be at stake** 危険な状態にある, 危険に瀕している, 危うくなっている, 争われている, 問題になっている, 賭けられている, 〈名誉などが〉かかっている
- **controlling stake** 支配持ち分, 経営支配権
- **drive [stick] one's stakes** 定住する
- **economic stake in** …への経済支援
- **equity stake** 持ち分
- **go [be prepared] to the stake for [over]** …のために大きなリスクを負う, (万難を排して)…を貫く
- **have a stake in** …に利害関係を持つ, …に関わり合い[関係]がある, …に関心がある, …に出資している
- **increase one's stake in** …の持ち株比率を引き上げる, …の出資比率を引き上げる (＝raise one's stake in)
- **majority stake** 過半数株式
- **make a stake** ひと儲けする, ひと財産作る
- **pull (up) stakes** 転居する, 転職する, 仕事をやめる, 立ち去る, 引き払う
- **raise one's stake in** …の持ち株比率を引き上げる, …の出資比率を引き上げる
- **reduce one's stake in** …の持ち株比率を引き下げる, …の出資比率を引き下げる
- **take a stake in** …へ出資する
- **the popularity stakes** 人気レース, 人気投票
- **win the stakes** 賞金を得る

stakeholder 名 利害関係者, 株主, ステークホルダー (「利害関係者」は, 企業の従業員, 取引先, 地域社会を指す)
  ▶ Any listed corporations must convince their customers, business partners and other *stakeholders* of their business philosophy and strategies. 上場企業は, 顧客や取引先などのステークホルダー(利害関係者)に対して, 経営理念と戦略をきちんと説明する必要がある.

stalemate 名 膠着状態, 手詰まり状態, 行き詰まりの状態, 停滞
- **result [end] in a stalemate** 手詰まり状態になる, 膠着状態[行き詰まり]に終わる

stalker 名 ストーカー(人をしつこくつけ回す人), 獲物をこっそり追う人

stalking 名 ストーカー行為

stall 動 止める, 遅らせる, 引き延ばす, …に水をさ

す, 〈人を〉待たせる, ごまかす, **自動** 止まる, 遅れる, 八百長試合をする
stall for time (on) (…の)時間を稼ぐ
stall to …まで落ち込む
stalling tactics 引延ばし戦術
stamp out 絶絶する, 鎮圧する, 撲滅する, 〈火などを〉踏み消す
stance **名** 姿勢, 態度, 立場, 構え, 政策, 策, …論, スタンス
  adhere to the stance of …の姿勢にこだわる
  basic stance 基本姿勢
  credit stance 金融政策のスタンス
  flexible stance 柔軟な姿勢
  hard-line stance 強硬姿勢, 強気な態度
  negative stance 消極的な態度, 弱気の構え
  populist-tinged stance 人気取りの姿勢, 大衆迎合的な色合いの姿勢
  pro-growth stance 成長重視の姿勢
  wait-and-see stance 模様眺めの展開, 模様眺めのスタンス
stand **名** 立場, 態度, 姿勢, 考え方, 見解, 論拠, 地位, 身分, 抵抗, 反撃, 防御, 固守, 擁護, 売店, 屋台, 露店, 展示台, 台, 観覧席, 証人席, 乗り場, 停車場, ステージ, 演壇, 興行, 興行地, スタンド
  hit the stands 店頭に並ぶ, 発売される
  newspaper stand 新聞の売店 (=newsstand)
  make one's last stand 最後の抵抗をする
  strengthen one's stand against terrorism 対テロ戦線を強化する
  take one's stand 態度を決める, 立てこもる
  take one's stand on …に立脚する
  take the stand 証言台[証人台]に立つ
  witness stand 証人席 (=witness box)
stand at …を示す, …である, …となる
▶The ratio of job offers to job seekers *stood at* a seasonally adjusted 0.42, the lowest on record. 有効求人倍率は, 過去最悪の0.42倍(季節調整値)だった。
stand defiant 一歩も引かない姿勢を示す
stand firm 断固として譲らない, 決然たる態度を保つ
stand squarely with …としっかり連帯する
▶The United States will *stand squarely with* Japan until all Japanese citizens kidnapped by North Korea are fully accounted for. 北朝鮮に拉致された日本人全員の行方が解明されるまで, 米国は日本としっかり連帯する方針だ。
stand shoulder to shoulder 一致協力する

stand-alone **形** 独立型の, 独立した形[形式]の, 自立型の, 単体の, スタンドアロン型の, 孤立した, スタンドアロン
  stand-alone entity 特別目的会社
  stand-alone information retrieval package 単体の情報検索パッケージ
  stand-alone meeting 独立した形式の会談[会議]
  stand-alone program スタンドアロン・プログラム
standard **名** 標準, 基準, 規格, スタンダード
  assessment standard 評価基準
  communications standard 通信規格
  de facto standard 事実上の標準, 事実上の国際標準, 事実上の世界標準, デファクト・スタンダード
  de jure standard 法による基準, 公的基準, デジュアリー・スタンダード
  disclosure standards 開示基準
  double standard 二重基準, ダブル・スタンダード
  environment standards 環境基準 (=environmental standards)
  highest standard of integrity 最高の倫理基準 (⇒integrity)
  international standard 国際標準, 国際規格
  Japanese Industrial Standards 日本工業規格《略 JIS》
  lending standard 貸出基準, 与信基準, 融資基準
  practice standards 業務基準
  quality control standard 品質管理基準
  standard accounts 一般投資家
  technical standard 技術標準
  universal standard ユニバーサル・スタンダード, 世界標準, 国際標準
  world [worldwide] standard 世界標準, ワールド・スタンダード
Standard & Poor's スタンダード&プアーズ, スタンダード・アンド・プアーズ
  Standard & Poor's 500 スタンダード・プアーズ株価指数, S&P500株価指数, SP株価指数 (=Standard & Poor's 500 index; ⇒Dow Jones industrial average [Industrial Average])
  Standard & Poor's index スタンダード&プアーズ株価指数, SP株価指数(通常は「総合500種株価指数」を指す。ダウ・ジョーンズ社の工業株30種平均(Dow Jones industrial average)と共に,

米国で最も広範に使用されている株価指数)
の, 決まり切った

standard-bearer 名　指導者, 主導者, 主唱者, 唱導者, 旗手, 旗頭, 首領

standardization 名　標準化, 規格化, 規格統一, 規格統一化, 共通化
▶ *Standardization* is aimed at providing a common framework such as in terminology, size and specification of industrial products.　標準化は, 工業製品の用語や大きさ, 仕様などの規格統一を目指している.

standardize 動　標準化する, 規格化する, 規格統一する, 共通化する
　standardize settlement [clearing] procedures　決済手続きを標準化する
　standardized distribution　標準分布
▶ Auto parts are increasingly becoming *standardized*, with the same part used in many different models.　自動車部品は共通化が進み, 同じ部品が多くの異なる車種に搭載されている.

standby commitment　銀行の保証, 信用供与枠, 株主割当ての際のスタンドバイ引受業者 (standby underwriter) による残額引受け, スタンドバイ引受け (「スタンドバイ引受け」は, 会社が株主割当てを行う際, 株主割当ての申込み期間が過ぎても株主からの応募額が予定の募集額に達しない場合, 引受業者 (スタンドバイ引受業者) がその残額分の買取りを約束すること)

standby credit　保証, 〈銀行による企業の〉借入金の保証, 資金引出し信用供与, 〈保証のための〉スタンドバイ信用状

standing 名　地位, 立場, 状態, 状況, 体質, 身分, 名声, 評判, 揺るがぬ地位, 順位, 持続, 存続, 存続期間, 期間, ランキング表, 信用評価
　a man of (good) standing　身分の高い人
　a rule of long standing　長く続いている規則
　a shop of long standing　老舗
　credit standing　信用状態, 信用度, 信用力 (=credit strength, credit worthiness)
　financial standing　財政状態, 財務状況, 財務体質
　have a high standing among　…の間で高い評判を得ている
　legal standing　法的地位, 法的な位置付け
　social standing　社会的地位
　standing of a firm　企業の信用評価

standing 形　常設の, 常置の, 常任の, 常備の, 永続的な, 不変の, 固定した, 立ったままの, 起立での, ずっと効力がある, 現在有効な, 現行の, いつもの, 決まり切った
　standing army　常備軍
　standing auditor　常任監査役
　standing authorization　自動引落し, 定期的支払い指図
　standing body　常設機関
　standing committee　常任委員会, 常設委員会
　standing cost　固定費
　standing credit　常設の信用枠
　standing expense　経常費
　standing order　継続注文, 〈口座からの〉自動引落し, 現行の規則, 〈議会の〉議事規則, 軍規
　standing ovation　起立喝采, スタンディング・オベーション
　standing room　立見席, 立つだけの余地
　standing rule　現在有効な規則
　standing [rising] vote　起立採決

standoff 名　孤立, 行き詰まり, 同点, 引き分け

standstill 名　行き詰まり, 停止, 休止, 運休, 立ち往生, 現状維持, ゼロ成長になること
　be at a standstill　行き詰まっている, 運休している, 停止している
　bring A to a standstill　Aを行き詰まらせる, Aを止める

standstill agreement　現状維持契約, 現状維持合意, 弁済の猶予 (「現状維持契約 (合意)」とは, 株式の発行会社と一定数以上の株式を保有する株主が, 株主の現保有株式の買い増しや処分をしないことで合意すること)

Star-Spangled Banner　星条旗 (Stars and Stripes), 米国国歌

star-studded 形　星のきらめく, 著名人 [スター] がずらりと並ぶ, 多くの有名スターが居並ぶ, 大物揃いの, 大物 [著名人, 有名人] が多数出席する, オールスターの
　a star-studded cast　オールスター・キャスト

star vehicle　スター出演番組

stark 形　殺風景な, さびれた, 荒涼とした, 陰気な, ありのままの, 正真正銘の, 完全な, まったくの, 丸裸の, 避けられない, 厳しい, こわばった, 硬直した, ごくじみの, きわめて簡素な
　be in stark contrast　著しい対照をなしている
　the stark fact　ありのままの事実, 赤裸々な事実
　the stark reality　厳しい現実, ありのままの現実

START　戦略兵器削減交渉, スタート (Strategic Arms Reduction Talksの略)

START　戦略兵器削減条約 (Strategic Arms Reduction Treatyの略)

start up 動 〈事業や会社などを〉起こす, 始める
▶ The new Corporate Law gives entrepreneurs more freedom to *start up* new companies. 新会社法では, 起業家にとってこれまでより自由に新会社を起こすことができる.

start-up 名 始動, 開始, 開業, 開業準備, ベンチャー企業, 新興企業, 新会社, 新規事業, 新規企業, 新企業, スタートアップ・カンパニー
 start-up business [company, corporation, firm] 新興企業, ベンチャー企業
 start-up costs 開業費, 開業準備費, 始動費, 運転開始費, 初期費用 (＝preoperating costs)

state 名 国, 国家, 〈米国の〉州, 状態, 状況, ステート, 形 国の, 国家の, 州の, 州立の, 州管理の, 儀式の, 儀式用の
 buffer state 緩衝国
 capitalist state 資本主義国, 資本主義国家
 declare a state of emergency 非常事態を宣言する
 flag state 旗国, 船籍国
 home state 本拠州
 Organization of American States 米州機構
 port state 港湾国(寄港を受け入れる国)
 secretary of state 米国の国務長官, 州務長官, 英国の国務大臣
 sovereign state 主権国家, 独立国家
 state aid 国家支援, 国家援助, 国庫補助[補助金], 国家補助
 state attorney 州地方検事 (＝district attorney), 国側の弁護士
 state bank 米州法銀行[ステート・バンク], 州免許銀行, 国営銀行, 国立銀行
 State Department 米国務省(他国の外務省(Foreign Office)に相当)
 state fair 州の農産物品評会, 州品評会, ステート・フェア
 state financed [state-financed] 政府出資の, 州が融資[出資]する, 政府系の
 state legislature 米州議会(米連邦議会＝Congress)
 state of business 業況
 State of the State address [Message] 〈州知事の〉施政方針演説
 State of the Union Message 〈米大統領の〉一般教書, 年頭教書
 State of the World Message 〈米大統領が議会に送る〉外交政策, 外交教書
 state of war 戦争状態, 交戦状態
 State Pen 〈米〉州刑務所 (＝State Penitentiary)
 state store 州営酒類販売店
 state's evidence 証拠物件
 states' rights 州権, 州の権利
 the States 米国
 totalitarian state 全体主義国家
 welfare state 福祉国家

state-backed 形 政府系の, 政府保証の

State Duma ロシア連邦議会の下院(Dumaの正式呼称. ロシアの最高議決機関である連邦議会(Federal Assembly)の下院. 定数450議席で, 議員の任期は4年. 上院はFederation Council)

state-of-the-art 形 最先端の, 最新式の, 最新鋭の, 最高級の, 高度の, 最高水準の, 最新技術の, 最高技術水準の, 技術水準 (＝cutting-edge, leading edge, sophisticated, top of the line, up-to-the-minute)

State of the Union address [speech] 一般教書演説 (＝State of the Union Address, State of the Union Message)

> **一般教書とは** ⇨ 米大統領が年頭に連邦議会上下両院合同本会議で表明する, 向こう1年間の施政方針. 大統領の演説中, 最も重要とされている. 内政・外交全般にわたる国家の情勢を要訳, 政府の基本政策のほか, 大統領の抱負や信念, 政治哲学なども織り込まれる. 予算教書(Budget Message), 経済報告(Economic Report of the President)とともに, 米大統領の三大年頭教書の一つ.

state-owned 形 国有の, 国営の
 state-owned property 国有財産
state ownership 国有, 国の所有, 国営, 国有制度
state-run 形 国営の, 国立の
statecraft 名 政治的手腕
Statehouse [statehouse] 名 〈米国の〉州議会議事堂
statement 名 声明, 声明書, 報告書, 届出書, 陳述, 申し立て, コメント, 計算書, 財務表, 規約, ステートメント
 annual statement 年次報告書
 bank statement 口座収支報告書
 distribution statement 分売届出書
 income statement 損益計算書
 mission statement 〈企業などの〉使命の宣言
 opening statement 冒頭陳述
 payment statement 支払い明細書
 policy statement 施政方針演説

profit and loss statement 損益計算書
quarterly statement 四半期報告書
statesman 名 政治家 （=statesperson）
statesmanlike 形 政治家にふさわしい，政治家らしい，政治家的な
statesmanship 名 政治的手腕，政治家の資質
stateswoman 名 女性政治家
statewide 形 州全体の，州全体にわたる，全州の
stationary orbit 静止軌道
statistics 名 統計，指標，統計学
  dynamic statistics 動態統計
  employment statistics 雇用統計
  export and import statistics 外国貿易統計
  import license statistics 輸入承認統計
  industrial statistics 業界統計
  labor statistics 労働統計
  national wealth statistics 国富統計
  official statistics 政府の統計
  static statistics of population 人口静態統計
  tourism statistics 観光統計
  vital [dynamic] statistics of population 人口動態統計
status 名 地位，状態，状況，情勢，事情，構造，身分，ランク，資格，信用，権威，ステータス
  immigration status 入国資格
  marital status 結婚の有無，婚姻状況
  social status 社会的地位
  status of forces agreement 地位協定《略 SOFA》
  status symbol 地位の象徴，身分の象徴，ステータス・シンボル
  the corporate status of a dormant company 休眠会社の法人格
status quo 現状，現状維持，情勢
statute of limitations 出訴期限，出訴期限法，出訴期限規則，消滅時効，公訴時効，時効（=statute limits）
statutory 形 法定の
  federal income tax at statutory rate 法定税率による連邦法人税
  statutory reserves 法定準備金
stave off …を辛うじて食い止める，…を未然に防ぐ，…を避ける，…を延ばす
stay-at-home worker 在宅労働者，在宅就労者（=home-based worker）
stay put 〈物価などが〉変わらないでいる，動かないでいる，1か所にじっとしている，定着している

steady 形 しっかり固定された，しっかりした，一様な，不変の，恒常的な，定常的な，着実な，堅実な，定まった，安定している
  maintain a steady hand 金融政策を据え置く
  steady accumulation of capital 恒常的な資本蓄積
  steady growth path 恒常的成長経路，安定した成長経路（=steady-state growth path）
  steady increase 着実な伸び，着実な増加，恒常的伸び[増加]
  steady job 定職
  steady market 堅調な市況，市況堅調
  steady money supply 通貨供給量の安定
  steady-state growth 恒常的成長，均斉成長，一様な成長
steam 名 推進力，駆動力，元気，力，勢い，蒸気，スチーム
  gather steam 勢いを増す，加速する（=build up steam, gain some steam, get up steam, pick up steam）
  go full steam ahead with …に全力で取り組む
  lose steam 勢いを失う，活力を失う，勢いが弱まる，勢いがなくなる，失速する（=lose some of the steam）
  pick up steam 上向く，景気が上向く，上昇傾向にある，上昇する，…の勢いが増す，勢いが強まる，次第に速度を上げる，次第に注目を浴びるようになる，次第に動きが出る（=get up [build up] steam）
  run out of steam 息切れする，元気がなくなる，気力[意欲]がなくなる，ブームなどが下火になる
steel 名 鉄鋼，鋼鉄，スチール
  steel mill 製鉄所，製鋼所（=steelworks）
  steel sheet 鋼板
steelworks 名 製鉄所，製鋼所（=steel mill）
steer 動 操縦する，〈…の〉舵を取る，運転する，導く，指導する，〈…に〉向ける，案内する
  steer a course of stability 安定の道を選ぶ
  steer a team to victory チームを勝利に導く
  steer between two extremes 中庸の道をとる
  steer the middle course 中立の立場をとる，極端な行動をとらない
  steer clear of …を避ける，…に近づかない，…に近寄らない
  steer one's way …の道を進む，進む，航行する
  steer the company to prosperity 会社を繁栄[成功，発展]に導く

steer to a growth path　成長軌道[成長経路]に向かう

steering 名　操舵, 操縦, ステアリング
- steering committee　運営委員会
- steering gear　操舵装置
- steering wheel　〈車の〉ハンドル, 〈船の〉操舵輪

stem 動　止める, せき止める, 食い止める, …に歯止めをかける, 抑える, 阻止する, 逆らって進む
- stem from　…から生じる[起こる, 始まる], …から発する, …に由来する, …に起因する, …による

step 名　措置, 手段, 対策, 足どり, 歩調, 歩み, 一歩, 段階, 足跡, ステップ
- a step backward [backwards]　後退, 悪影響をもたらすもの
- be [keep] in step　…と一致する, …と合う, 歩調を合わせて行進する
- be [keep] one step ahead of　…より一歩先んじている, …より一歩進んでいる
- in a person's step　…を見習って, …の例にならって
- in step　調子を合わせて, 歩調を揃えて
- in step with　…に伴って, …とともに, …に連動して, …と歩調[足並み]を合わせて
- take every step to　…に最善を尽くす
- take steps　処置[措置]を取る, 手段を講じる

step down　辞職する, 辞任する, 退任する, 身を引く, 引退する（=resign）
- step down as　…を辞職する
- step down from　…から身を引く, …から引退する, …を辞職する, …を辞任する
- step down in favor of a younger man　後進に道を譲る
- step down to take responsibility for　…の引責辞任をする, …に対して引責辞任をする

step in　…に乗り出す, …に介入する, …に干渉する, 割って入る, 援助を申し出る, 参加する, 立ち寄る
▶ The U.S. government *stepped in* to bail out Chrysler and GM in December 2008.　米政府は, 2008年12月にクライスラーとGMの救済に乗り出した。

step up　本格化させる, 活発化させる, 促進する, 強化する, 増大[拡大]させる, 高める, 〈調子を〉上げる, 作業を急ぐ, 昇進させる, 上がる, 向上する, 昇進する
- step up one's financial support　金融支援を強化する
- step up one's pace　歩調を速める
- step up support in economic areas　経済分野での支援を強化[促進]する

stepping stone [steppingstone]　踏み台, 足がかり, 手段, 方法, 飛び石, 踏み石

sterilization 名　殺菌, 消毒, 不妊, 不妊化, 不胎化, 断種
- gold sterilization policy　金不胎化政策
- sterilization of gold　金の不胎化

steroid 名　ステロイド（筋肉増強剤として用いられるが, スポーツ選手の使用禁止薬物となっている）
- anabolic steroids　蛋白同化ステロイド

stick to　〈約束などを〉守る, 実行する, …を固守する, 〈信念などを〉曲げない, …に執着する, …に固執する, …を固守する, …からそれない[外れない], …から離れないでいる
- stick to one's decision　決定を断固として実行する, 決心を守り抜く
- stick to the point　要点に沿って議論する
- stick to the rules　規則を厳守する

stiff 形　骨の折れる, 難しい, 困難な, 厄介な, 強い, 強気の, 激しい, 厳しい, 断固とした, 容赦ない, 法外な, 高価な, 堅い, 硬直した, ピンと張った, 堅苦しい, 形式的な
- a stiff demand　過度の要求
- stiff upper lip　断固とした態度
- take a stiff line　強硬な態度をとる

stiffen 動　緊張させる, 硬直させる, 強化する, 〈市況が〉強含みになる, 〈相場, 金利が多少〉上がる傾向にある[上がりそうである], 〈物価が〉騰貴する
- stiffen one's attitude　堅苦しい態度をとる

stimulant 名　刺激物, 刺激性飲料[食物], アルコール飲料, 興奮剤, 覚醒剤, シャブ, 誘因, 刺激
- Stimulant Control Law　覚せい剤取締り法
- stimulant drugs　覚醒剤（薬学的にはアンフェタミン（amphetamine）とメタンフェタミン（methamphetamine）の2種類）, 興奮剤
- stimulant effects　興奮作用, 興奮のある薬

stimulate 動　刺激する, 刺激して…させる, てこ入れする, 活気づける, 活性化させる, 浮揚させる, 励ます, 奨励する, 促す, 促進する, 喚起する, 刺激になる, 刺激剤になる
- stimulate domestic demand　内需を喚起する, 内需を拡大する
- stimulate monetary growth　通貨供給量の伸びを刺激する

stimulative 形　刺激的な, 刺激性の, 刺激型の, 景気刺激の, 景気刺激型の
- stimulative package　景気刺激策, 景気てこ入れ策, 景気刺激総合対策, 経済対策

stimulus 名　刺激, 刺激策, 刺激効果, 景気刺激

策, 景気対策, 励み
budgetary stimulus 財政出動
monetary stimulus 金融政策面での景気刺激策, 金融緩和
stimulus package 景気刺激策, 景気対策, 経済対策

sting operation おとり捜査 (=undercover operation [investigation, probe])
► *Sting operations* are currently conducted only for certain areas of investigations, such as those for uncovering illegal drug deals. おとり捜査は現在, 違法な薬物取引の摘発など一部の捜査で行われているだけだ.

stipulate 動 規定する, 定める, 明記する,〈条件として〉要求する, 合意する, 約定する, 保証する

stipulation 名 規定, 条項, 約定, 協定, 訴訟上の合意, 条件, 要求

stock 名 株, 株式, 株式資本, 在庫, 在庫品, ストック (=share)
　capital stock 株式資本, 株主資本, 総株数, 資本ストック, 資本金
　issue and payment of stock 株式の発行および払込み
　listed stock 上場株
　nonconvertible preferred stock 非転換優先株式
　stock at par 額面株
　stock brokerage 証券会社 (=stock brokerage firm)
　stock buyback 株式買戻し, 自社株発行済み株式の買戻し, 自社株買戻し, 自社株買い, 自社株取得, 自社株式の取得
　stock-buying limit 株式買入れ枠
　stock buyup scheme 株式買取り制度, 株式買入れ制度
　stock certificate 株券, 記名株券, 株式証券 (=share certificate)
　stock company 株式会社 (=stock corporation)
　stock deal 株式取引, 株の売買 (=stock dealing)
　stock holdings 保有株, 持ち株 (=stockholdings)
　stock index 株価指数
　stock issue 株式発行, 新株発行, 株式銘柄, 銘柄
　stock rally 株価の持ち直し, 株価回復, 株価急騰, 株価の反騰 (=rally in stocks)

stock-related gains 株式関連売却益
stock-related losses 株式関連損失, 株式等関連損失
tracking stock in a subsidiary 子会社連動株
transfer of stock 株式の名義書換え, 株式の譲渡
treasury stock 自己株式, 金庫株
unlisted stock 非上場株
voting stock 議決権株

stock exchange 証券取引所, 株式取引所, 株式交換
　American Stock Exchange アメリカン証券取引所, アメックス《略 AMEX》
　Chicago Stock Exchange シカゴ証券取引所《略 CSE》
　Financial Times-Stock Exchanges 100 Index FT100種総合株価指数
　New York Stock Exchange ニューヨーク証券取引所《略 NYSE》(=Big Board)
　Osaka Stock Exchange 大阪証券取引所《略 OSE》
　stock exchange ratio [rate] 株式交換比率 (=share exchange rate, stock-for-stock exchange rate)
　Tokyo Stock Exchange 東京証券取引所《略 TSE》

stock market 株式市場, 証券市場, 株式相場, 株式市況, 株式売買, 株価 (=equity market)
　domestic stock market 国内株式市場
　help the stock market 株式市場を活性化する
　sluggish stock market 株式相場の下落
　stock market gains 株式譲渡益 (=stock sale profits)
　stock market quotation [prices] 株式相場
　stock market turnover 株式出来高

stock offering 株式発行, 株式公開, 株式公募, 株式上場 (⇒public offering, public stock offering)

stock option 株式購入選択権, 株式買受権, 自社株購入権, 株式オプション, ストック・オプション (「ストック・オプション」は, 自社株をあらかじめ決められた権利行使価格で購入する権利. 報酬制度の一つで, 自社株の株価が権利行使価格を上回れば購入者が利益を上げることができる)
　stock option dealing 株式オプション取引, 個別株オプション取引
　stock option plan 株式購入選択権制度, 株式

選択権制度, 自社株購入権制度, 株式オプション制度, ストック・オプション制度（＝stock option program, stock option scheme, stock option system：「ストック・オプション制度」は, 企業が役員や従業員に, 前もって決めた価格で一定数の自社株を買う権利を与える制度）

stock price 株価（＝share price）
　stock price index 株価指数
　stock price restraint 株価規制
　year-end common stock price 1株当たり期末株価
stock purchase 株式購入, 株式取得, 株式買取り
stock purchase warrant 新株引受権, 新株予約権, 株式買付け権, 株式買取り権, 株式購入権, 新株引受権証書, 株式購入権証書（＝stock-purchasing warrant）
　convert bonds with stock purchase warrants into shares 新株引受権付き社債を株式に転換する
　exercise of stock purchase warrants ワラント権の行使, 新株引受権の行使
　redeem stock purchase warrants 新株予約権付き社債を償還する
stock split 株式分割, 株式の分割・併合, 無償交付（＝share split, share splitting, split-up of stock：「株式分割」は, 1株を分割して, 発行済み株式数を増やすこと。一般に, 投資家を増やして必要な事業資金を集めやすくするために行われる）
　stock split-down 株式併合（＝reverse split, reverse stock split, share split-down）
　stock split-up 株式分割（＝share split-up）
　two-for-one stock split 1対2の比率による株式分割
stock swap [swapping] 株式交換（＝share swap）
　stock swap deal 株式交換取引（＝share swap deal）
stock trading 株式取引, 株取引, 株式売買（＝equity trading, stock trade, stock transaction）
　stock trading via the Internet 株のインターネット取引, インターネットでの株取引
stock transaction 株式取引, 株取引, 株の売買（＝stock trading）
stockbroking commission revenues 株式売買手数料の収入
stockholder 名 株主（＝shareholder）
　corporate stockholder 法人株主（＝institutional stockholder）
　individual stockholder 個人株主
　issue to stockholders 株主割当て
　one-share stockholder 1株株主
　stockholders' meeting 株主総会（＝general meeting, stockholders meeting）
stockholdings 名 株式保有, 保有株式, 保有株, 持ち株（＝shareholdings, stock holdings）
▶ Most companies use the daily average for a month of the share prices in gauging the value of latent gains or losses in their *stockholdings*. 大半の企業は, 保有株式の含み損益を算出する際に株価の月中平均を使っている。
stop-and-desist administrative order 排除命令（＝stop-desist order）
stop short of (doing) …するまでには至らない, …する手前で止まる, …することを思いとどまる
stopgap 名 間に合わせ, 一時［当座］しのぎ, 一時しのぎの穴埋め, 穴埋め, 一時的な代理人, 形 間に合わせの, 一時しのぎの, 穴埋めの, 腰かけ的な, 暫定的な, 臨時の, 臨時雇いの, 代理の
　serve as a stopgap 一時［当座］しのぎになる, 間に合わせになる
　stopgap fund つなぎ資金, つなぎ融資
　stopgap loan つなぎ融資
　stopgap measures 対症療法, 一時しのぎの手段［対策］, 一時しのぎの策
　stopgap solutions 一時［当座］しのぎの解決策
store 動 蓄える, 貯蔵する, 蓄積する, 取っておく, しまっておく, 保管する, 供給する, 記憶する, 保存しておく, 格納する
　store a ship with provisions 船に食糧を積み込む
　store the mind with knowledge 頭に知識を詰める
　store up trouble 悩みの種をまく
store 名 店舗, 商店, 大型店, ストア
　chain store チェーン・ストア, 連鎖店
　directly operated store 直営店
　retail store 小売店
　specialty store 専門店
　store brand ストア・ブランド, 自社ブランド, 自店独自のブランド（＝private brand）
　store hours 営業時間
　store loyalty 店舗ロイヤルティ, ストア・ロイヤルティ
stowaway 名 密航者

straight 形 一直線の, 水平の, 直立した, 垂直の, 正直な, 隠し事をしない, 直接の無条件の, 単純な, 徹底した, 根っからの, 確かな, 信頼できる筋からの, 連続した, 1年前と比較した, 〈麻薬や酒など〉無関係な, 異性愛の, 副 連続して, 1年前と比較して, ぶっ通しで

straight bond 普通社債, 確定利付き社債(転換社債以外の普通の社債)

straight fight 2候補者間の争い, 一騎打ち

straight loan 通常のローン

straight salary system 固定給制

the fourth straight monthly decline 4か月連続の減少

vote a straight ticket 〈政党の〉公認候補だけに投票する

strain 名 緊張, 緊張状態, 緊迫, 圧迫, 逼迫, 逼迫状態, ストレス, 思い負担, 重圧, 悪化, 制約, 強要, 懸命の努力, 無理, 力み, 過労

capacity strain 生産設備の制約, 生産能力の制約

financial strain 金融逼迫, 金融負担, 財務上の負担, 財政面での圧迫

inflationary strain インフレ圧力の高まり

international monetary strain 国際通貨の緊張

strain between supply and demand 需給関係の逼迫

strain on cash flows 資金繰りの悪化

strain 名 血統, 家系, 家柄, 種族, 品種, 菌種, 特徴, 特質, 素質, 気質, 性向, 傾向, 気味, 旋律, 調子, 調べ, メロディー, 文体, 話し振り

a weak strain 虚弱体質

the familiar strains of songs よく耳にする歌

the new strain of influenza 新種のインフルエンザ, 新型インフルエンザ

straits 名 苦境, 困難, 難局, 窮乏, 貧窮, 困窮

be in dire [desperate] straits 窮乏している, ひどく困っている, 火の車, 資金繰りにひどく苦しんでいる, 金にひどく困っている, 財政事情が苦しい[苦しい財政事情にある]

financial straits 財政難, 財政逼迫, 財政的苦境, 財政危機

strapped 形 経済的に苦しい, 金欠の, 十分な資金がない, 文無しの

be strapped for …がとても不足している

cash-strapped 十分な資金がない

strategic 形 戦略的, 戦略上の, 戦略上重要な, 戦略上役に立つ, 戦略に必要な

strategic business unit 戦略的事業単位《略 SBU》(＝business center)

strategic diversity 戦略的多様性, 戦略的相違点

strategic framework 戦略的枠組み

strategic nuclear warhead 戦略核弾頭

Strategic Petroleum Reserve 〈米政府の〉戦略石油備蓄

strategic technology development program 戦略技術開発事業

Strategic Arms Reduction Treaty
戦略兵器削減条約《略 START》

a third round of Strategic Arms Reduction Talks 第三次戦略兵器削減条約《略 START3》

strategy 名 戦略, 策, 手法, 方針, ストラテジー

bottom-up strategy 意見上申戦略, 現場意見採用戦略

distribution strategy 流通戦略

downstream strategy 川下戦略

exit strategies 出口戦略

niche strategy すき間戦略, ニッチ戦略

product-market [product/market] strategy 製品・市場戦略

top-down strategy 上位下達戦略, 下降型戦略

upstream strategy 川上戦略

streak 名 傾向, 兆候, 気性, 性質, …気味, 調子, 閃光, 電光, 稲妻一時期, ひと続き, 一連, ひとしきり, 鉱脈, 層, 筋, 線, しま, 仕事の早い人, 足の速い人

a nervous streak 神経質

a pay streak 採算の取れる鉱脈

a streak of 一筋の…, 一連の, 一条の, …気味, 少々…なところ

a three-day losing streak 3日連続の値下がり

have a lucky streak しばらく幸運が続く (= have a streak of good luck)

hit [be on] a long winning streak 勝ち続ける, 連勝する, 値上がりを続ける

hit [be on] a long losing streak 負け続ける, 連敗する, 値下がりを続ける

like a streak (of lightning) 電光石火のごとく, 全速力で

stream 名 流れ, 傾向, 動向, 趨勢, 見通し, キャッシュ・フロー

come back on stream 生産・操業を再開する

come on stream 稼働する, 生産・操業を開始する

downstream 下流部門, 川下, 下流
earnings stream 収益見通し
fixed interest streams 固定金利のキャッシュ・フロー, 固定金利の流れ
floating interest streams 変動金利のキャッシュ・フロー, 変動金利の流れ
interest stream 金利の流れ
on stream 生産中の
production stream 生産の流れ
stream risk 趨勢リスク
upper stream industries 上流産業, 川上産業

streamline 動
合理化する, 能率化する, 効率化する, 簡素化する, スリム化する, リストラする
streamline development work on …の開発作業の効率化を進める
streamline management 経営を効率化する
streamline one's finances 財務をスリム化する

streamlining 名
合理化, 能率化, 効率化, 簡素化, スリム化, リストラ
streamlining of office work 事務の合理化

street 名
通り, 街路, ストリート
be [get] on easy street 裕福である, 安楽に暮す
be streets ahead of …よりずっと優れている, …よりはるかに優っている
by a street 大差で
lending street name 名義貸し
not in the same street with …とは比較にならない, …より能力が劣る, …にはとても及ばない
on [in] the street 末端価格で, ぶらぶらして, 無職で, 家がなくて, ウォール街で, 金融街で
street broker 場外取引人
street credibility [cred] 〈都会の若者の間での〉人気[流行], 都会の若者のファッション・センス, 若者受け
Street economist 市場エコノミスト
street name 証券業者名義, 仲買人名義, 名義貸し, ストリート・ネーム
street rally 街頭集会
street smarts 地元の事情に明るいこと
street value [price] 末端価格, 市価
take to the streets 街頭に繰り出す, 示威運動をする, 街頭デモ[街頭デモ行進]をする, 街頭行動に訴える
the man on [in] the street 一般市民
the Street ウォール街 (=Wall Street: ニューヨーク市の証券街)
up [right up] one's street 興味の範囲内で, 知識の範囲内で, …の好みに合って
win by a street 圧勝する

strength 名
力, 強さ, 強み, 力強さ, 体力, 勢い, 好調, 活況, 上昇, 伸び, 勢力, 兵力, 人数, 長所
be full strength 全員がそろっている, 勢ぞろいしている
from strength 強い立場から
gain [gather] strength 力強さ[力]を増す, 元気になる
in strength 大挙して, 大勢で
on the strength of …を根拠にして, …に基づいて, …を頼りにして, …の力で, …の影響で, …を背景に, …の勧めで
up to (full) strength 定員に達して

strengthen 動
強化する, 強める, 増強する, 補強する, 高める, 伸ばす, 活性化する, 拡大する, 充実させる, 〈規則などを〉厳しくする, 自動 上昇する, 向上する, 高まる, 伸びる, 改善する, 好転する
continue to strengthen 引き続き好調である, 〈円高, ドル高が〉続いている
intervention to strengthen the dollar ドル高誘導の介入
strengthen profitability 収益性を改善する
strengthen the balance sheet 財務基盤を強化する

strengthening 名
強化, 上昇, 伸び, 高まり, 充実, 改善, 持ち直し, 好転
strengthening in sales 販売の伸び
strengthening of capital base 資本基盤の強化
strengthening of capitalization 資本の充実
strengthening of credit criteria 与信基準の強化

strengthening 形
上昇している, 伸びている, 向上している, 改善している, 好転している
strengthening asset quality 資産内容の向上
strengthening demand 需要の伸び

stress 動
強調する, 力点を置く, …と強く言う, 圧力を加える, 緊張させる

stress 名
圧力, 圧迫, 困難, 困難な状況, 厳しい環境, 厳しい経営環境, 経営難, 強調, 重視, 力点, 重点, 応力, ストレス
lay stress on …に重きを置く
mechanical stress 機械的応力, 機械的応力
stress at work 仕事上[業務上]のストレス, 職場でのストレス
stress conditions [situations] 困難な状況
stress death 過労死 (=death from over-

stress evaluation chart ストレス評価表
stress interview 圧迫面接, ストレス・インタビュー (被面接者の状況打開能力を見るため, 敵対的・強圧的態度で行われる面接)
stress management 〈ストレス予防・治療などの〉ストレス対策
thermal stress 熱応力
under stress 困難な状況下で, 厳しい状況下で, 厳しい環境[経営環境]下で (=under stress conditions)
under the stress of …に迫られて, …にかられて
work stress 職場でのストレス
stress test 特別検査, 耐性試験, ストレス・テスト (=stress testing: 強い負荷や衝撃をかけても製品などが壊れないかを確かめるための検査で, パソコンなどの製品テストにも使われている)

> financial stress test (金融のストレス・テスト) つ米政府が, 金融機関の不良資産問題を抜本的に解決するため, 経済がさらに落ち込んだ場合やブラック・マンデー, アジア通貨危機など通常ではあまり考えられないケースを[負荷]として織り込んで, 2009年2月25日から大手19行に対して[ストレス・テスト]を行った。このテストで, 資本不足と認定された金融機関には, 市場からの資金調達を促す。市場で資金調達できなかった場合は, 政府が優先株を引き受ける形で公的資金を注入する。金融機関の経営がさらに悪化した場合は, 政府が優先株を普通株に転換して, 金融機関が事実上, 国有化される可能性もある。

stressor 名 ストレス要因
stricken 形 打ちひしがれた, 傷ついた, 〈病気に〉かかった, 打撃を受けた, 襲われた, 苦しめられた, 悩んでいる
cancer-stricken 癌にかかった
fire-stricken 火災で打撃を受けた
stricken area 被災地
stricken field 決戦, 決戦場
strict 形 厳しい, 厳重な, 厳密な(precise), 正確な, 几帳面な, 絶対の
in the strictest [strict] confidence 極秘で
strict liability 厳格責任, 無過失責任
strict warning 厳重注意
the strict interpretation of the constitution 憲法[規約, 規定]の厳密な解釈
strife 名 争い, 闘争, 紛争, 衝突, 争議, 不和, 反目, もめごと, 困難, 窮状
economic strife 経済の窮状, 経済的窮状
industrial strife 労使紛争
strike 動 打つ, 殴る, 攻撃する, 〈病気などが〉襲う, 感動させる, 〈…の心を〉打つ, …に気づく, …を表明する, …を表す, 掘り当てる, 自動 ストライキを行う, 当たる, ぶつかる, 〈地震や悲劇などが〉起こる
strike a deal [bargain] 取引をする, 売買する, 合意する
strike down 打ちのめす, 無効にする, 取り消す, 廃止する, 倒す
strike home 急所を突く, こたえる, 骨身にしみる, 命中する
strike in 口を出す, 入り込む, 邪魔をする
strike out 〈計画などを〉考えだす, 削除する, 消す, 三振に取る, 乗り出す
strike the right balance between A and B AとBのバランスをうまくとる
strike through 削除する, 抹消する
strike up 始める
strike 名 権利行使, スト, ストライキ, 〈鉱脈などの〉発見, 〈石油などの〉掘り当て, 突然の成功, 攻撃, 空襲, 〈野球やボウリングの〉ストライク
call [proceed with, stage] a strike ストを決行する
call off a strike ストを中止する
general strike ゼネスト, 総同盟罷業
strike price 〈オプション取引の〉権利行使価格, 行使価格
strikebreaker [strike breaker] 名 スト破り
string-pulling 名 陰で操ること, 陰で糸を引くこと, 黒幕として働くこと, 影響力を行使すること, 裏工作
stringency 名 厳しさ, 厳重さ, 引締め, 切迫, 逼迫, 金詰まり, 説得力
credit stringency 信用逼迫, 金融逼迫, 金融引締め
fiscal stringency 緊縮財政
monetary stringency 金融逼迫
stringent 形 厳格な, 厳しい, 厳重な, 過酷な, 緊急の(urgent), 引締めの, 緊縮の, 〈金融市場が〉切迫した, 逼迫した, 金詰まりの(tight), …の強化, 説得力のある, 有力な
stringent arguments 説得力のある議論
stringent budget 緊縮予算
stringent market 逼迫市場, 逼迫市況
stringent regulations 厳しい基準, 厳しい規制
strip-tease 名 ストリップショー
stroke 名 一撃, 発作, 脳卒中, 訪れ, 到来, 行

動, 努力, 手腕, 手柄, 業績, 手際, 説得力, 操作力
a great stroke of fortune まったく予期しなかった幸運, 突然の幸運
at a stroke 一気に, 一挙に, 一撃で (＝at one go)
with a stroke of the pen 署名することによって
with quick strokes 急ピッチで

strong 形 強い, 強力な, 力強い, 強固な, 堅調の, 好調な, 上昇基調の, 優良な
be in a strong position 優位に立っている, 優位に立つ
strong demand 需要の急増, 需要の旺盛, 需要が強いこと
strong outperformance 大幅なアウトパフォーマンス, パフォーマンスが市場平均を大幅に上回ること
strong shareholder 安定株主

stronghold 名 拠点, 本拠地, 要塞, 砦
▶ The company has a considerable share in the Asian market but has no *stronghold* in the European market. 同社は, アジア市場ではかなりのシェアを保持しているが, 欧州市場には拠点がない。

structural 形 構造的な, 構造上の, 構成状の, 組織上の
structural defects 構造上の欠陥
structural engineer 土木技師
structural engineering 土木工学
structural gene 構造遺伝子
structural impediments 構造障壁
structural impediments initiative 日米構造協議《略 SII》
structural safeguard 投資家保護の構造

structural adjustment 構造調整
structural adjustment facility 構造調整融資《略 SAF》
structural adjustment loans 構造調整借款
▶ *Structural adjustment* loans are often co-financed with multilateral financial institutions. 構造調整借款は, 国際金融機関との協調融資の形をとることが多い。

structural reform 構造改革
structural reform drive 構造改革路線
structural reforms of government finances 財政構造改革

structure 動 組織する, 組み立てる, 構築する, 構成する, 組成する, 体系化する, 仕組む
structured arbitrage transaction 仕組み裁定取引
structured equity product 株式仕組み商品
structured finance [financing] 仕組み金融, 仕組みファイナンス, ストラクチャード・ファイナンス
structured product 仕組み商品, 仕組み債, 仕組み案件
structured securities 仕組み証券, 証券化証券

structure 名 構造, 機構, 組織, 構成, 体系, 方式, 体制, 体質, 構築物, 構造物, 建造物, ストラクチャー
capital structure 資本構造, 資本構成
funding structure 資金調達の構成
vanilla structure 単純な方式
yield structure 利回り構造

struggle 動 奮闘[苦闘]する, 悪戦苦闘する, 苦戦する, 苦悩する, 戦う, 争う, …に取り組む

struggle 名 競争, 闘争, 戦い, もみ合い, 取っ組み合い, 攻防戦
internal struggle 内部闘争
law-abiding struggle 順法闘争
litigating struggle 法廷闘争
struggle for existence [life] 生存競争
struggle for power 権力闘争
work-to-rule struggle 順法闘争 (＝law-abiding struggle)

struggling 形 経営不振に陥っている, 経営再建中の, 生き残りに懸命の, 生き残りに必至になっている, もたついている, 苦境にあえぐ, 悪戦苦闘の

stuck 形 固定した, 動かなくなって, 動かなくて, 行き詰まって, にっちもさっちもいかなくなって, 困り果てて, 逃げ出せなくて, 離れられなくて, 名 困窮, 面倒, 厄介, 難儀
be in dead stuck 困ったことになる
be stuck on …に夢中になっている, …にのぼせている
be stuck on oneself うぬぼれる, 思い上がる
in stuck 困って, 困り果てて, 困窮して
out of stuck 難儀から逃れて

style 動 呼ぶ(call), 命名する, 称する, 〈流行に合わせて〉作る[デザインする, 設計する], 体裁を整える
a shop styled 'A&B' 「A&B」という店
style a dress 流行のドレスを作る[仕立てる]
style oneself (as) 自分を…と呼ぶ[称する], …と自称する, …と名のる

style 名 方法, 方式, 手法, 様式, …型, …式, …流, モデル, 名称, 商号, スタイル

subcontracting 名 丸投げ, 下請契約 (＝

farming out, subcontraction）

subcontractor 名 下請，下請企業，下請会社，下請業者，下請人，下請契約，サブコントラクター

subcritical nuclear test 未臨界実験（＝subcritical nuclear experiment）

subdivide 動 分割する，再分［再分割］する，細分する

subdued 形 控え目の，元気がない，活気がない，伸び悩みの，大きな動きがない，低迷している，低水準の，柔らかい，和らげられた，抑制された，抑えられた

　subdued economic growth 景気低迷，経済成長の低い伸び，経済成長率の低迷

subject to …に服する，…に従う，…の影響を受ける，…を必要とする，…を条件とする，…を条件として，…を前提として，…の場合に限って，…を免れない，…が適用される，…の適用を受ける，…次第で，…によって決まる，…を対象とする，ただし…

submission 名 提出，提示，提示案，提出物，報告書，服従，降伏，屈服，従順，送信，送信内容，考え，意見，付託，依頼，仲裁付託，仲裁付託合意，仲裁付託書

　in one's submission …の考え［意見］では
　in submission to …に服従して
　submission to …に対する服従
　the submission of a dispute to arbitration 争議の仲裁付託
　the submission of a report 報告書の提出
　▶ There were errors with your *submission*.　送信内容に，誤りがありました。

submit 動 提出する，提示する，提起する，付託する，付す，委ねる，従わせる，服従させる，意見を述べる，具申する，…と思う，自動 降伏する，服従する，屈服する

　resolve the questions submitted 付託された問題を解決する
　submit a case to a court 裁判所に提訴する
　submit bids for the deal 同案件の入札に応じる，同案件の入札条件を提示する
　submit one's resignation …の辞表を提出する
　submit oneself to …を甘んじて受ける，…を甘受する，…に服従する，…を付託する
　submit oneself to the jurisdiction of the court of …の裁判所にその裁判管轄を付託する
　submit to 〈検査，事情聴取などを〉受ける，甘受する，…に応じる，…に甘んじる，…に服従［屈服］する，…に服する，…に従う
　submit to one's fate 運命に甘んじる
　submit to a blood test 血液検査を受ける
　submit to an operation 手術を受ける
　submit to authority 権威に服従する
　submit to questioning 事情聴取に応じる，事情聴取を受ける
　submit to the decision 決定に従う
　submit to the government 政府に従う，政府に服従する
　submit to the nonexclusive jurisdiction of …の非専属管轄権に服する

subpoena [subpena] 動 召喚する，召喚状を出す，〈証拠の〉提出命令を行う

subpoena [subpena] 名 召喚状，呼び出し状，〈法廷への〉出頭命令
　issue a subpoena 召喚状を出す
　mail a subpoena 召喚状を送達する

subprime 形 金利がプライム・レート以上の，プライムより信用力が低い，信用力が低い，二級品の，サブプライム（米国の住宅ローン借入申請者の信用格付けは，prime（高所得者層），Alt-A（中間所得者層）とsubprime（低所得者層）に分けられている）

subprime lender サブプライム・ローンの融資行，信用力が比較的低い低所得者を対象にした住宅融資の融資銀行［融資行］，住宅ローン会社（＝subprime mortgage lender）

subprime loan 低所得者を対象にした住宅融資，低所得者層向け住宅ローン，サブプライム・ローン（＝subprime mortgage, subprime mortgage loan）

subprime mortgage 低所得者［低所得者層］向け住宅ローン，低所得者向け住宅融資，信用力が低い個人向け住宅融資，サブプライム・ローン（＝subprime loan, subprime mortgage loan）

subscribe 動 買い取る，〈株式を〉引き受ける，加入する，申し込む，予約する，予約購読する，署名する，調印する，寄付する，援助を与える，経済支援する，賛同する，同意する
　capital stock subscribed 引受済み資本金
　common stock subscribed 引受済み普通株式
　invitation to subscribe 直接募集
　subscribe a contract 契約書に署名する
　subscribe a petition 嘆願書に署名する
　subscribe for 500 (worth of) shares 500株申し込む
　subscribe ¥100 million to several charities 慈善事業に1億円寄付する
　subscribe one's name to the document 文

書に署名する
subscribe to an Internet service インターネット・サービスに登録する
subscribe to new shares 新株を引き受ける
subscribe to one's opinion …の意見に同意する, …の意見に賛同する
subscribe to the agreement 同意書に署名する, 契約書に署名する
subscribe to the Financial Times フィナンシャル・タイムズ紙を(定期)購読する
subscribe to 30 million shares at ¥250 per share 1株250円で3,000万株を引き受ける
subscribe to U.S. President Barack Obama's policy オバマ米大統領の政策に賛同する

subscriber 名 〈株式の〉引受人[購入者], 寄付者, 経済支援者, 出資者, 〈年金や電話などの〉加入者, 申込み者, 署名者, 賛同者, 支持者, 〈新聞や雑誌の予約・定期〉購読者, 予約者, 応募者
broadband subscribers 高速大容量通信の加入者
cell phone subscriber 携帯電話の加入者 (= mobile phone subscriber)
outside subscribers of new shares 新株の外部引受人
subscribers' cable network 加入者回線
subscribers' contributions 加入者の保険料
subscribers' lines 加入者回線
yield to subscribers 応募者利回り

subscription 名 〈株式の〉引受け, 応募, 加入, 出資, 寄付, 寄付金, 義捐金, 出資金, 予約, 予約金, (予約, 定期)購読, 購読料, 署名, 同意, 賛成, 賛同, 〈クラブなどの〉会費(「応募」とは, 株式などの有価証券が新規発行される場合に買付けの申込みをすること)
be available on subscription 予約購読で入手できる
mobile phone subscriptions 携帯電話の加入台数
pension subscription period 年金加入期間
raise [make] a subscription 寄付を募る
stock subscription 株式応募, 株式公募, 株式の引受け
subscription certificate 出資証券
subscription fee 加入費, 加入料金, (予約)購読料 (= subscription charge, subscription rate)
subscription for shares 株式申込み
subscription period 募集期間, 販売期間

subscription price 応募価格, 引受価格, 買取り価格
subscription renewal 予約更新
subscription to securities 証券応募
subscription to stockholders 株主優待
subscription to the fund 基金への寄付金
subscription warrant 新株引受権証書, 新株引受権, 新株予約権, ワラント

subsequent 形 その後の, それに続く, 次の
subside 動 沈下する, 沈む, 陥没する, 静まる, 収まる, 和らぐ, 沈静化する, 減る, 減少する, 衰退する, 弱まる
▶ The world economy will steer to a growth path again once the financial crisis *subsides*. 金融危機が沈静化したら, 世界経済はまた成長軌道[成長経路]に向かうだろう.

subsidiary 名 子会社 (= subsidiary company, subsidiary corporation)
consolidated subsidiary 連結子会社
majority owned subsidiary 過半数所有子会社
partially owned subsidiary 部分所有子会社
quasi-subsidiary 準子会社
unconsolidated subsidiary 非連結子会社
wholly owned subsidiary 完全所有子会社, 全額出資子会社, 100%所有子会社

subsidy 名 補助金, 助成金, 奨励金, 報奨金, 研究助成金 (= grant)
employment-adjustment subsidies 雇用調整助成金
government subsidies 政府補助金, 国庫補助金, 政府助成金
price subsidies 価格補助金

success 名 成功, 躍進, 成否, 立身, 出世, 成功した人, 発展, 勝利, 合格, 当選, 大当たり, ヒット, 上首尾, 上出来, 好結果, 盛会, サクセス
attain [achieve] a major success 大成功を収める, 大ヒットする
come off a huge success 大成功を収める
drink success to …の成功を祈って[祝して]乾杯する
drive one's success …の成功の原動力になる
economic success 経済発展, 経済の繁栄, 経済の成功, 経済成長
make a success of …を成功させる, …を首尾よくやる
make a success of life 出世する
make for success 成功をもたらす
score a success 成功する

successful

turn into an overnight success 一夜にして成功を収める

successful 形 成功した, うまくいった, 出世した, 立身出世した, 富を得た, 繁盛している, 上出来の, 上首尾の, 好結果の, 盛大な
- **be successful in** …に成功する, …することができる
- **successful bid** 落札
- **successful business** 商売繁盛の事業
- **successful candidate** 合格者, 当選者
- **successful cost-cutting efforts** コスト削減策の成功

succession 名 連続, 相続, 継承, 引き継ぎ, 相続権, 継承権, 継承順位
- **a succession of** 一連の…, 連続して起こる…, …の続発
- **by succession** 世襲で
- **claim the succession to** …の相続権を主張する
- **in quick [close, rapid] succession** 立て続けに, 矢継ぎ早に, 続々と
- **in succession** 連続して, 引き続いて
- **issues of succession to political leadership** 政治指導者の後継問題
- **succession duty** 相続税
- **succession issue [problem, question]** 後継者問題
- **succession state** 後継国家, 承継国家
- **three years in succession** 3年連続して

successive 形 歴代の, 継承した, 引き継いだ, 引き続く, 連続的な, 継続的な, 系統的な, 系列的な
- **for five successive days** 5日間連続で, 5日続けて
- **in successive generations** 代々続いて
- **on the second successive day** その2日目に
- **successive failures** 失敗の連続
- **win three successive games** 3連勝する

successively 副 引き続いて, 連続して, 続いて, 次々と, 連日

successor 名 後任者, 後継者, 承継者, 後継機種, …にとって代わるもの
- **successor bank** 受け皿銀行
- **universal successor** 全財産相続人

sue 動 訴える, 告訴する

suffer 動 〈損失などを〉受ける, 損失を計上する, 〈被害などを〉被る, 打撃を受ける, …に見舞われる, …に巻き込まれる, 耐える, 低迷する, 悪材料になる, 支障が生じる

suffer a loss 損失を被る, 損失を計上する
suffer a plunge in share prices 株価が下落する
suffer big [large] losses 大損害を受ける, 巨額の損失を被る, 多額の損失を計上する

suffer from …に苦しむ[悩む], 〈災害などに〉あう, …で打撃を受ける, …に見舞われる, 〈損害などを〉受ける, …が重荷になる

suffrage 名 投票権, 選挙権, 参政権, 賛成投票, 賛成, 同意, 一致した意見
- **suffrage for foreigners** 外国人参政権
- **universal suffrage** 普通選挙権
- **woman [female, woman's, women's] suffrage** 婦人参政権

sugar-bowl savings タンス預金 (=drawer savings)
▶ *Sugar-bowl savings* in the U.S. and European countries are a close equivalent of drawer savings in Japan. 欧米で使われる「シュガー・ボール(砂糖入れ)預金」は, だいたい日本の「タンス預金」に相当する.

suggested retail price 小売希望価格
suicide 名 自殺, 自殺行為, 自滅行為, 自殺者
- **suicide attack** 自爆テロ, 自爆攻撃
- **suicide bomber** 自爆テロリスト, 自爆犯
- **suicide bombing** 自爆テロ, 自爆 (=suicide bombing terrorism)

suit 名 訴訟(lawsuit), 民事訴訟, 請願, 嘆願, 要求, 服, スーツ
- **be at suit** 裁判中である
- **civil suit** 民事訴訟
- **criminal suit** 刑事訴訟
- **drop [discontinue] a suit** 訴訟を取り下げる
- **file [bring, start] a suit against** …を相手取って訴訟を起こす[訴えを起こす], …を告訴する, …を提訴する
- **file a suit against A for B** AをBで提訴する
- **file a suit against A with B** Aを相手取ってBに訴訟を起こす
- **go to suit** 起訴する
- **in suit with** …と一致する, …と調和する, …と釣り合う
- **lose one's suit** 敗訴する
- **one's strong suit** …の得意とするところ, …の強み
- **space suit** 宇宙服
- **suits** ビジネスマン, 重役, 長老, 高級官僚
- **win one's suit** 勝訴する

sulfuric pitch 硫酸ピッチ(タール状の硫酸混合物。軽油を密造する過程で生成される強酸性の有害廃油で，皮膚に触れるとやけどし，目に入ると失明の恐れがある)

sum 名 合計，総計，総額，総数，和(total)，金額，総和，全体，要旨，要約，概要，骨子，計算
  - **be good at sums** 計算がうまい
  - **come to a little sum** 少額に収まる
  - **do one's sum** 筋を通して考える，よく考える
  - **huge [enormous, large, vast] sum of money** 多額の金
  - **in sum** 要するに，つまり (＝in short)
  - **the sum and substance** 要旨，要点，概要
  - **the sum of things** 森羅万象，宇宙，全存在，公共の福祉，最高の公共の利益
  - **the total sum [the sum total]** 総計，要旨，大意，概要

sum up 要約する

summary 名 要約，概要，摘要，大要，まとめ，形 即座の，即時の，略式の，即決の，簡単な，概略的な，かいつまんだ，大まかな
  - **a brief summary** 簡単な要約，簡潔な要約
  - **a financial summary** 財務の要約
  - **a summary account** 略述，略記
  - **a summary budget** 概括予算
  - **a summary conviction** 〈有罪とする〉即決処分
  - **a summary court** 簡易裁判所
  - **a summary order** 略式命令
  - **a summary report** 簡単な報告，概略報告書
  - **a summary sheet** 集計表
  - **a summary statement** 総論，総括
  - **an executive summary** 概要
  - **file a summary indictment** 略式起訴する
  - **give a brief summary of** …の簡単な大要[要約]を述べる
  - **make a summary of** …を要約する
  - **summary judgment** 略式裁判，即決裁判
  - **summary justice** 即決裁判
  - **summary proceeding** 略式手続き
  - **summary statement of business** 事業説明書，財務情報

summit 名 サミット，首脳会議，主要国首脳会議，首脳会談，トップ会議，トップ会談
  - **APEC summit** アジア太平洋経済協力会議(APEC)首脳会議
  - **north-south summit** 南北サミット
  - **summit talks** 首脳会議，トップ会議，首脳協議，サミット会議 (＝summit conference, summit meeting)

summon 動 呼び出す，召集する，喚問[召喚]する，〈法廷に〉出頭させる，出廷を命じる，要求する，…するよう求める[命じる]，奮い立たせる，奮い起こす
  - **be summoned to a meeting** 会議に出席するよう求められる
  - **be summoned to appear in court** 出廷を命じられる
  - **be summoned (to appear) before the Diet** 国会に喚問される
  - **be summoned to appear before magistrates for assault** 暴行容疑で治安判事に出頭するよう命じられる
  - **summon a doctor** 医者を呼ぶ
  - **summon a conference [meeting]** 会議を招集する
  - **summon the Diet** 国会を召集する
  - **summon up all one's strength** ありったけの力を出す
  - **summon up one's courage** 勇気を奮い起こす

summons 名 呼び出し，召集，出廷命令，召喚，召喚状，呼び出し状
  - **in response to one's summons for help** …の援助要請に応えて
  - **receive a summons for tax evasion** 脱税の呼び出し状を受け取る
  - **serve a summons on** …に召喚状を送達する
  - **summons of a witness** 証人喚問

super-loose monetary policy 超金融緩和政策

Super Tuesday スーパー・チューズデイ(米国の民主・共和両党の全国党大会(National Convention)での大統領候補者を目指す予備選挙(presidential primary, primary)で，党員集会(caucus, presidential caucus)の山場となる決選の火曜日のこと)

super voting share 複数議決権株式 (＝super voting stock)

supermajority 名 圧倒的多数，大多数，超過半数，超過半数条項 (＝super-majority: 超過半数は一般に発行済み株式の80％以上の賛成投票を指し，株主総会で合併や買収などとくに重大な決議を行う場合には，株主の超過半数の賛成が必要と定めることがある)

supermarket sales スーパーの売上高

super-rotation system 総合診療方式

supervise 動 監督する，指揮する，管理する，監視する，査閲する，考査する

supervision 名 監督，指揮，管理，監視，観察，

査閲, 考査
administrative supervision 行政指導, 行政監督
audit supervision 会計監査上の査閲, 監査上の査閲
be under UN supervision 国連の管理下にある
credit supervision by the central bank 中央銀行の信用規制
price supervision 物価監視, 価格監視
probational supervision 保護観察
under the supervision of …の監督のもとに, …の指揮のもとに

supplementary 形 補足的, 補完的, 追加の, 補充の, 付属の, 増補の, 付遺の, 付録の
supplementary budget 補正予算, 追加予算 (＝additional budget, revised budget)

supplier 名 供給者, 供給会社, 供給業者, 供給下請業者, 供給源, 仕入先, 納入業者, 製造業者, メーカー, 供給国, 輸出国, 売り手, サプライヤー
capital goods supplier 資本財供給者
consumer goods supplier 消費財供給者
housing supplier 住宅メーカー
main supplier 主要輸入先, 主要供給者
telco supplier 通信機器メーカー
the largest supplier 最大の供給国

supplies 名 物資, 消耗品, 貯蔵品, 供給, 〈政府の〉歳出[経費], 〈個人の〉支出
construction supplies 建設資材 (＝building supplies)
factory supplies 工場消耗品
manufacturing supplies 製造用消耗品
office supplies オフィス用品費
operating supplies 作業用貯蔵品
product supplies 製品需給
productive material, work in process and supplies 原材料, 仕掛品と貯蔵品
supplies account 消耗品勘定

supply 動 供給する, 提供する, 与える, 〈不足などを〉埋め合わせる
supply funds 資金を供給する

supply 名 供給, 供給量, 供給品, 消耗品[複数形], 貯蔵品, 〈政府の〉歳出[経費][複数形], サプライ
commodity supply 商品供給
credit supply 信用供給
large supply 大口供給
moderate supply 供給薄
monopolist supply 独占的供給

power supply 電力供給 (＝electricity supply)
small supply 小口供給
stable supply 安定供給
supply capacity 供給能力, 供給余力
supply creating effect 供給創出効果
supply deficiency 供給不足
supply-demand balance 需給バランス
supply-demand gap 需給ギャップ (＝demand supply gap)
supply fluctuation 供給変動
supply line 補給線
supply network 供給ネットワーク
supply restriction 供給制限
supply chain management 供給連鎖管理, サプライ・チェーン・マネジメント《略 SCM》 (情報技術(IT)を利用して, 受注発注, 資材や部品の調達, 生産, 製品の配達, 在庫などを統合的に管理して, 企業収益を高めるための管理手法)
supply side 供給サイド, 供給側, 供給面, 供給重視, サプライサイド
supply-side economics 供給面重視の経済学, 供給重視経済学, サプライサイドの経済学, サプライサイド・エコノミックス
supply-side structural reform 供給サイドの構造改革

supplysider 名 供給重視論者

support 動 支援する, 援助する, 支援する, 賛成する, 支える, 支持する, 補強する, 補完する, 裏付ける, 保証する
be financially supported 資金援助を受ける, 資金面で支援を受ける
fully supported program 完全[100％]信用補完型プログラム
fully supported structure 信用補填構造, 完全保証構造
partially supported program 部分的信用補完型プログラム
support commercial interests 経済的利益を優先する
support growth 成長を支える
support the stock [stock price] 株価を支える, 株価の下支えする

support 名 支援, 援助, 支持, 賛成, 支柱, 補填, 補強, 保証, サポート
credit support 信用補填, 信用補強, 信用補完
customer support services 顧客支援サービス
fully supported structure 完全保証構造

official support 公的支援
price supports 価格維持
public support 国民の支持
support organization 支持団体
▶ A firm requires the *support* of more than two thirds of shareholders to decide on important matters, such as a merger, at shareholders meetings. 企業が株主総会で合併などの重要事項を決議するには，3分の2以上の賛成が必要だ。

supporter 名 支持者，支援者，後継者，援助者，援助者，〈スポーツ・チームの〉ファン，後ろ盾，取り巻き，助演者，サポーター
supporters' group 後援会，支援団体，支援組織

supranational 形 超国家的な，国家政府の権限［範囲］を超えた，国際機関の
supranational agencies 国際機関
supranational bond 国際機関債
supranational name 国際機関銘柄
supranational organization 超国家機構
supranationals 国際機関

suprapartisan diplomacy 超党派外交

supremacist 名 優越論者［主義者］，至上主義者
art supremacist 芸術至上主義者
white supremacist 白人優越主義者，白人至上主義者

supremo 名 最高指導者，最高司令官

surcharge 名 割増料金，追加料金，付加料金，上乗せ料金，追徴金，課徴金，不足金不当請求，〈荷物の〉積み過ぎ，過載，サーチャージ
export surcharge 輸出課徴金
fuel surcharge 燃油特別付加運賃
import surcharge 輸入課徴金
inflation surcharge インフレ課徴金
investment income surcharge 投資所得課徴金
optional surcharge 揚地割増量
out port surcharge 僻地割増運金
solidarity surcharge 統一割増税
tax surcharge 課徴金

surefire [sure-fire] 形 絶対確実な，成功確実の，成功間違いなしの，確実な

surge 動 急増する，急上昇する，急騰する，高まる，殺到する，押し寄せる，〈感情が〉込み上げてくる
briefly surge 短時間［短期間］急上昇する（＝ surge briefly）
surge to make a high of 急騰して…の高値を付ける
surge to record levels above 急騰して…の史上最高値を突破する，…を上回る史上最高値まで急騰する

surge 名 急増，急騰，急上昇，殺到，大波，うねり，高揚，〈感情の〉高ぶり，高まり，盛り上がり，ブーム
prepayment surge 期限前償還の急増
refinancing surge 借換えの急増，借換えブーム
sudden surge in demand 需要の急激な高騰，需要の急増
surge in capex [capital expenditure, capital investment, capital spending] 設備投資の急増
surge in consumer spending 消費支出の急増
surge in housing starts 住宅着工件数の急増

surgery 名 外科，外科医学，外科手術，手術，外科的処置，手術室，診察室，診療所，医院，診療時間
brain surgery 脳外科
clinical [clinic] surgery 臨床外科
cosmetic surgery 整形外科，美容整形外科
do [perform] surgery on the nose 鼻の手術を行う
have [undergo] surgery on the eye 目の手術を受ける
heart surgery 心臓外科
laser surgery レーザー手術
orthopedic surgery 整形外科
plastic surgery 形成外科
reconstructive surgery 再建外科
transplant [sparepart] surgery 臓器移植外科，移植外科

surging 形 急増する，急騰する，高騰する，…の急増［高騰］
surging dollar ドルの急騰
surging growth in imports 輸入の急増，輸入額の急増
surging prices 価格高騰，物価高騰［急増］，物価の上昇

surpass 動 超える，上回る，突破する，…を凌ぐ，…より優れている
▶ China *surpassed* the United States as Japan's major trading partner amid the continued U.S. economic slowdown. 中国は，米国の引き続く景気減速を受けて，日本の主要貿易相手国としての米国を追い越した。

surplus 名 余剰，過剰，余剰分，過剰分，余剰金，超過金，剰余金，積立金，黒字，歳入超過額，残額
appraisal surplus 再評価剰余金，評価替え剰

余金
balance of payments current account surplus 国際収支経常勘定黒字
balance of payments surplus 国際収支の黒字
be surplus to requirements 供給過剰である，もはや[もう]必要ない，必要以上に多い
budget [budgetary] surplus 予算の黒字，財政黒字
capital surplus 資本剰余金，資本積立金
cumulative [cumulated] surplus 累積黒字
current account surplus 経常黒字
export surplus 貿易収支の黒字
external surplus 経常海外余剰，貿易収支の黒字
financial surplus or [and] deficit 資金過不足
fiscal surplus 財政黒字，財政余剰
financing surplus 資金余剰，資金過剰
government current surplus 政府経常余剰
government surplus 公共部門の黒字
labor surplus 労働力過剰，労働余剰
liquidity surplus 流動性過剰
massive [huge] international payments surplus 巨額の国際収支の黒字
primary surpluses 基礎収支の黒字
producer's surplus 生産者余剰
seller's surplus 売り手余剰
surplus in the current account 経常収支の黒字，経常収支の黒字額（＝the current account surplus）
valuation surplus 評価剰余金
surplus 形 余剰の，過剰の，余分な，余剰的な，必要以上の(extra)，黒字の
surplus asset 余剰資産
surplus budget 黒字予算
surplus capacity 生産余力，過剰設備，設備過剰（＝excess capacity）
surplus country 黒字国，出超国
surplus equipment 遊休設備，過剰設備
surplus facilities 過剰設備
surplus labor 余剰労働[労働力]，過剰労働，剰余労働
surplus personnel 過剰人員，余剰人員（＝surplus worker）
surplus power 余剰電力
surplus production 過剰生産
surplus profit 超過利潤，剰余利益
surplus rice 余剰米

surplus savings 余剰貯蓄，純法人貯蓄
surplus stock 余剰在庫，過剰在庫
surplus value 余剰価値，剰余価値
surplus fund 余剰資金，剰余金（「剰余金」は，自己資本のうち資本金と資本準備金以外の部分のことで，過去の利益の蓄積を示す）
▶These *surplus funds* are moving into crude oil and grain markets in search of profitable investments. これらの余剰資金が，有利な運用先を求めて原油や穀物市場に向かっている。
surrogate 名 代理，代行，代理人，遺言検認判事
surrogate birth 代理出産（＝surrogate motherhood）
surrogate mother 代理母
surrogate motherhood 代理出産（＝surrogacy, surrogate birth）
surrogate wombs 代理母の代用の子宮
surround 動 取り巻く，取り囲む，包囲する，包み込む，包む，〈自分の周りを〉固める
surrounding 形 周りの，周囲の，近辺の，近くの
surrounding areas 周辺地域
surrounding nations 周辺諸国
the surrounding environment 取り巻く環境
surroundings 名 環境，状況，周囲，周囲の状況，周囲の事物，取巻き，側近
unfamiliar surroundings 不慣れな環境
surveillance 名 監視，監督，指揮，監察，査察，調査，捜索
aerial surveillance 空中査察
be under police surveillance as a suspect 容疑者として警察の監視下に置かれる
multilateral surveillance 多角的監視制度
price surveillance 価格監視，物価監視
Securities and Exchange Surveillance Commission 証券取引等監視委員会
surveillance camera 監視カメラ
surveillance radar 捜索レーダー
surveillance system for imports 輸入監視制度
survey 名 調査，意識調査，査察，査定，測量，概観，概説，サーベイ
business sentiment survey 企業景況感調査
establishment survey 事業所調査
fact-finding survey 実情調査，実態調査
geophysical survey 地球物理探査
household survey 家計調査
national purchasing managers survey 全米

購買部協会景気総合指数
nationwide survey 全国調査
ocean survey 海洋探査
public opinion survey 世論調査
sampling survey 標本調査, サンプル調査 (= sample survey)
telephone survey 電話による聞き取り調査, 電話調査法

▶ The latest *survey* points to a continued improvement in corporate earnings and capital investment. 今回の調査では，企業収益や設備投資の拡大が続いていることが示されている。

survival 名 生存, 存続, 残存, 生き残り, 生き延び, 生存者, 残存者, なごり, サバイバル
cooperation and coexistence for survival 生き残りのための協調と共存
survival guilt 〈戦争や災害の〉生存者が死者に対して感じる罪悪感 [後ろめたさ]
survival kit 非常用携帯品
survival of the fittest 適者生存
survival ratio 残存比率

survive 動 生き残る, 残存する, 存続する, 生き延びる, 生き抜く, 〈危機などを〉切り抜ける, 乗り切る

▶ It's not that those who are strong *survive*; it's those who succeed in adapting to a changing environment that will *survive*. 強いものが生き残るのではない，環境の変化に対応できるものが生き残るのだ。

susceptible to …に左右されやすい, …に影響されやすい, …にかかりやすい, 感染しやすい, …に敏感な, …に弱い

▶ The yen's stable rate at about ¥110 against the dollar serves as a stabilizing factor for importers, exporters and others doing business *susceptible to* exchange fluctuations. 円の対ドル為替相場が110円台(前後)で安定していることは，輸出入業者など為替変動に左右されやすい仕事をしている者にとって安定要因となる。

suspect 動 疑う, 疑いをかける, …ではないかと思う, 怪しいと思う, 感づく, 気づく

suspect 名 容疑者, 被疑者, 参考人, 嫌疑者, 感染容疑者
cholera suspect コレラ感染容疑者
murder suspect 殺人容疑者
prime suspect 重要参考人, 有力参考人

suspend 動 停止する, 一時停止する, 中止する, 中断する, 差し止める, 延期する, 一時見合わせる, 離脱する, 停職にする, 休職させる, 停学処分[出場停止処分]にする, 刑の執行を猶予する, 〈判決など

を〉保留する, 吊り下げる, ぶら下げる
be suspended from school 停学処分を受ける
suspend judgment 判断を保留する
suspend the prison term 禁固刑[懲役刑]に執行猶予を付ける, 禁固刑の執行を猶予する

▶ The company *suspended* operations at the factory for about three months. 同社は，約3か月間，同工場での操業を停止した。

suspended 形 停止した, 中止した, 一時停止した, 止まった, 停職[停学]になった, 執行猶予付きの, 空中に浮かんだ, 吊るした, ぶら下がった
suspended animation 仮死状態, 意識不明, 人事不省, 一時的活動停止, 休眠状態
suspended prison term 執行猶予付きの有罪判決, 執行猶予の刑期
suspended sentence 執行猶予付きの判決, 執行猶予

suspense 名 未決定, 未定, 停止, 一時停止, 未決算
suspense account 仮勘定, 未決算勘定
suspense payment of corporation tax 仮払い法人税
suspense payments 仮払い金, 仮渡し金
suspense receipt 仮受け, 仮受金
suspense receipts 仮受金
suspense receipts on capital subscriptions 新株式申込み証拠金

suspension 名 停止, 取引停止, 取引停止処分, 〈株式などの〉売買停止, 一時停止中止, 停職, 差し止め, 刑の執行猶予, 車体懸架装置
bank suspension 〈銀行の〉支払い停止
suspension of business order 業務停止命令, 取引停止命令, 営業停止命令
suspension of trade, capital transactions and remittances 貿易, 資本取引と送金の停止
suspension of works 工事中止
temporary suspension of trading 取引の一時停止

suspicion 名 疑い, 容疑, 嫌疑, 疑惑, 疑念, 猜疑心, 少量, 気味
above suspicion 嫌疑をかけられる余地がない
on suspicion of …の疑いで, …の容疑で
over cartel suspicions カルテルの疑い[容疑]で
suspicion is growing that …との疑念が広がっている
under suspicion of …の嫌疑をかけられて

sustain 動 持続させる, 維持する, 保持する, 存

続させる，支える，支持する，裏付ける，…に耐える，養う，扶養する，援助する，激励する，〈損失，負債，被害などを〉被る［受ける］，妥当［正当］と認める，是認する

sustain a competitive edge 競争力を維持する
sustain an injury 負傷する
sustain life 生命を維持する
sustain objection 異議を認める
sustain one's claim …の主張を認める
sustain organized efforts 組織的な取り組みを続ける
sustain overall economic growth マクロ経済の成長を維持する
sustain the interest of …の興味をずっと引きつける

sustainability 名 維持能力，持続可能性

sustainable 形 持続可能な，維持可能な，支持できる，持ちこたえられる，継続利用できる，長期的な，本格的な，立証可能な

sustainable growth 持続的成長，持続可能な経済成長（＝sustained growth, self-sustained growth）
sustainable rally 本格的な上げ相場
▶ The economic recovery is not *sustainable* if incomes do not rise. 所得が増えなければ，景気回復は続かない。

sustainable development 持続可能な開発，持続可能な発展，安定発展，環境維持開発

▶ Since the 1980s, when immense environmental issues such as global warming were recognized, the notion of "*sustainable development*" has become the governing concept in international development. 1980年代に地球温暖化などの地球規模の環境問題が認識されてから，「持続可能な開発」が国際開発の理念となった。

sustained 形 持続した，持続的な，長期的な，長期にわたる，維持された，保持された，不断の，一様の，支持された，是認された，確認された，認められた，立証された

fall on a sustained basis 下がり続ける
make sustained efforts たゆまず努力する
sustained efforts 不断の努力
sustained growth 持続的な［持続的］成長，持続的な経済成長，持続的な発展，長期的な成長，成長の維持（＝sustainable growth, self-sustained growth）
sustained low (interest) rates 低金利の定着
sustained reputation 定評

sustained-release capsule 徐法性カプセル，持続性カプセル（＝time-release capsule）

sustaining 形 支える，体力をつける，栄養になる
sustaining food 栄養になる食物，栄養食品
sustaining program 自主番組，サスプロ

sustainment 名 持続，維持，保持，支持

SUV スポーツ用多目的車（sport utility vehicleの略）

swap 動 交換する，切り替える，振り返る，取り替える，乗り換える，スワップする
swap A for B AをBと交換する
swap out of A into B AからBに乗り換える
swap some of the shares of the parent company for the target company's shares 親会社の株式の一部と買収標的企業の株式を交換する
swap the remaining debt of ¥200 billion into preferred shares 残りの債権2,000億円分を優先株に振り替える［切り替える］

swap 名 交換，スワップ（＝swapping）
amortization swap 分割償還型スワップ
asset-based swap 資産の交換スワップ，債権のキャッシュ・フローの交換
basis swap ベーシス・スワップ（同一通貨または異なる通貨間の変動金利と変動金利の交換）
cancelable [cancellable] swap 停止条件付きスワップ
conduct a debt-for-equity swap 債務の株式化を行う，債権の株式化を行う
currency swap 通貨スワップ
debt-bond swap 債務の債券化（＝debt-for-bond swap）
debt equity swap 債務の株式化，債権の株式化（＝debt-for-equity swap）
forward swap 先物スワップ
extendable swap 期限延長権付きスワップ
interest rate swap 金利スワップ（＝interest swap）
puttable swap 満期日の繰上げ可能性があるスワップ
share swap deal 株式交換取引（＝stock swap deal）
short swap 短期スワップ取引
stock swap deal 株式交換取引
swap ratio 株式の交換比率
swap transaction スワップ取引
total return swap トータル・リターン・スワップ（債券のクーポンと評価損益を短期金利などと交

換するスワップ)
yield curve swap イールド・カーブ・スワップ
sway 動 揺り動かす, 揺さぶる, 影響を与える, 感化する, 向かわせる, 変更させる, 左右する, 支配する, 統治する, 揺れる, 揺らぐ, 揺動する, 動く, 傾く
  be swayed by …に左右される, …の影響を受ける
  sway toward …に傾く
sway 名 揺れ, 動揺, 振動, 影響力, 支配, 支配力, 勢力, 支配権, 統治, 統治権
  be under the sway of …の支配下にある, …の勢力下にある
  exert one's full sway 権力を十分に振るう
  hold sway 支配する, 勢力を振るう
  hold sway over …を支配する
  wield sway on …に影響力を行使する
swear 動 誓う, 誓約する, 宣誓する, 断言する
  be sworn in as …に宣誓就任する
  swear on the Bible 聖書に手を置いて宣誓する, 聖書にかけて誓う
  swear out 宣誓して逮捕令状を取る
  swear to God 神に誓う
sweep 動 圧勝する, 大勝する, 掃除する, 一掃する, 徹底的に捜す, 押し流す [洗い流す], …を襲う, 席巻する, …に一帯に広がる, 自動 長く延びる, えんえんと続く, 吹きまくる, さっと吹き抜ける, 襲来する
  sweep away 払拭する (sweep aside), 押し流す, 吹きまくる, 完全に破壊する, 消し去る, …を夢中にさせる
  sweep the board 圧勝する, 楽勝する
  sweep the world [all, everything] before one 破竹の勢いで進む
  sweep to victory [power] 〈政党が選挙で〉圧勝する, 〈政党を〉政権に導く
sweep 名 圧勝, 全勝, 大勝, 掃討, 一掃, 長さ, 広さ, 範囲, 広がり, 視界
  a clean sweep of …の総なめ, …の完勝, …の圧勝
  a sweep of 一面の
  be in full sweep 最高潮に達する
  beyond the sweep of …の及ばないところに
  the sweep of influence 勢力範囲
  sweep aside 退ける, 〈意見などを〉一蹴する, 払拭する, 即座に払いのける
sweeping 形 破竹の勢いの, すさまじい, 強い, 猛烈な, 完全な, 圧倒的な, 決定的な, 徹底的な, 抜本的な, 大雑把な, 広範な, 広範囲にわたる, 広く見渡せる, 全面的な, 包括的な, 大々的な, ダイナミックな, 一掃する

a sweeping generalization 大雑把な概括, 大雑把な総括
a sweeping majority of votes 圧倒的多数票
a sweeping reshuffle 全面的入れ替え, 大規模な人事異動
score [win] a sweeping victory 圧勝する
sweeping changes 抜本的改革 (＝sweeping reforms)
sweeping plan 抜本的対策
sweeping reforms 抜本的改革, 広範囲に及ぶ改革
sweeping tax cuts 徹底的な減税
swell 動 膨張する, ふくれる, 大きくなる, ふくれ上がる, 増大する, 増加する
▶European countries and China have various kinds of bubbles and/or *swollen* monetary environments. 欧州や中国では, バブルや金融膨張の市場環境を抱えている。
swelling 名 膨張, ふくらみ, 増大, 増加, 腫れ物, こぶ
▶The IT bubble and the ensuing *swelling* of the financial market of late have stemmed from technology innovation coupled with the globalization of the economy. (1990年代後半の) ITバブルとそれに続く最近までの金融膨張を引き起こしたのは, 経済のグローバル化の動きと連動した技術革新だ。
swindle 動 だます, だまし取る, 詐取する
  be swindled out of …を詐取される, …を巻き上げられる
  swindle a person out of money 人をだまして金を詐取する
  swindle money out of a person 人から金をだまし取る
swing 名 動き, 情勢, 事情, 活動, 〈株価などの〉変動, 揺れ, 振動, 動揺, 振幅, 転換, 転向, 進行, はかどり, 旅行, 旅, 短期間の訪問, 〈候補者による〉遊説, スイング音楽, スイング
  a political swing to the right 政治的右傾化
  be in the swing 活況を呈している
  be on a downward swing 減少傾向にある
  be on an upward swing 上昇傾向にある
  be on the swing 揺れている
  be out of the swing of …の事情に暗い, …の事情にうとい
  catch the swing of affairs [things] 情勢をつかむ, 情勢を知る
  currency swings 為替変動 (＝currency changes [movements], forex swings)

cyclical swing 循環的波動
get into full swing 本格化する
get into the swing of …の流れに乗る, …の調子[情勢]をつかむ, …にすっかり慣れる
go with a swing 大成功する, 大盛況である, 調子よく行く, すらすら運ぶ, リズミカルで調子がよい
have [take] one's full swing 自由に行動する
large currency swings 過度の為替変動
leave for a 7-day swing through Latin America 7日間のラテン・アメリカ旅行に出かける[出発する]
long swing 〈景気循環の〉長期波動, 〈バットやゴルフ・クラブの〉大振り
major swing 大勢, 大波動
make a campaign swing through …を遊説する
small swing 小波動
swing of growth rate 成長率循環, 成長率変動
swings and roundabouts 利点もあれば欠点もあること, 一長一短, 損得が五分五分であること

swing 形 結果を左右する, 勝敗を決する, 決定的な, 移動式の, 可変型の
  swing line 信用供与枠
  swing shift 午後交代番, 半夜勤
  swing strategy スイング戦略（紛争時に, 兵力を他の地域から派遣する方策）
  swing vote 浮動票, 勝敗を決する票, 決定票, 決め手の一票
  swing voters 浮動票層, 浮動者層, 無党派, 支持政党のない人たち (=floating voters)
  swing-wing 可変翼, 可変翼機

switch 動 切り替える, 変更する, 変える, 転向する, すり替える, 交換する, 転職する
  be switched on 幻覚症状になっている, 流行の先端を行っている, 最新式である
  switch jobs [positions] 転職する
  switch off 〈電気の〉スイッチを切る, 注意を払わなくなる, 興味を示さなくなる
  switch on 〈電気の〉スイッチを入れる, 興味[活力]を起こさせる, 興奮させる

symptom 名 症状, 徴候, 現れ, 兆し
  symptoms of jaundice 黄疸症状

syndicate 名 〈証券発行の〉引受シンジケート団, 銀行の協調融資団, 銀行団, シンジケート, 動 シンジケートを組織する[組成する], シンジケートで管理する

syndicated loan 銀行団による協調融資, 国際協調融資, シ・ローン, シンジケート・ローン (=syndicated bank loan, syndicated lending)

syndrome 名 症候群, …現象, 行動様式, シンドローム
  acquired immune deficiency syndrome 後天性免疫不全症候群《略 AIDS》
  alpha syndrome アルファ・シンドローム（飼い犬が急に飼い主にかみついたり反抗したりする症状）
  blue bird syndrome ブルーバード・シンドローム（夢想的で地に足がついていないことをいう）
  economy class syndrome エコノミー・クラス症候群
  empty nest syndrome 空の巣症候群, エンプティ・ネスト・シンドローム
  Gulf War veteran's syndrome 湾岸戦争従軍者の精神的後遺症
  Maggie-Jiggs Syndrome マギー＝ジグス症候群（妻が夫に暴力を振るう病的傾向）
  metabolic syndrome 内臓脂肪症候群, 代謝症候群, メタボリック症候群, メタボリック・シンドローム
  night eating syndrome 夜食症候群
  Peter Pan syndrome ピーターパン・シンドローム（大人社会への仲間入りができない大人こどもの男性）
  premenstrual syndrome 月経前症候群
  sick-building syndrome オフィスビル症候群《略 SBS》
  survivor syndrome 生存者症候群
  syndrome syndrome シンドローム症候群, シンドローム・シンドローム（シンドロームという言葉を使いたがる症候群）
  "too" syndrome やり過ぎ症候群, やり過ぎの傾向, トゥー・シンドローム

synergy 名 相乗効果, 波及効果, シナジー
  synergy effect 相乗効果, 波及効果, 相互補完効果, シナジー効果 (=synergistic effect)
  ▶ Having sales and marketing, product, and research personnel working in close proximity should permit *synergy* and closer coordination between the functions. 営業・マーケティング, 製品部門と研究部門の従業員が近接して仕事に取り組むことにより, 部門間の相乗効果と協調関係が生まれるはずです。

system 名 組織, 器官, 機構, 体系, 系統, 方式, 方法, 合理的なやり方, 体制, 制度, 設備, 装置, 身体, 体, 五体, 仮説, 説, システム
  access signaling system アクセス信号方式
  accounting system 会計システム, 会計組織, 会計制度
  alarm system 警報装置
  be absorbed into the system 体内に吸収される

business system 企業体系, 事業体系, 事務機構, 企業システム, ビジネス組織, ビジネス・システム
crisis management system 危機管理システム, 危機管理体制
decision support system 意思決定支援システム
delivery system 配送システム
estimating systems costs システム原価見積り
executive age-limit system 役職定年制
expert system 専門家システム, エキスパート・システム (＝knowledge-based system)
flexible production system フレキシブル生産システム, フレキシブル生産ライン, 多品種少量自動車生産システム《略 FMS》(一般にNC工作機械, 産業用ロボット, 自動搬送システム, 自動倉庫システム, 自動保守・点検システム, コンピュータ中央管理システムで構成)
internship system インターンシップ制度
legal system 法律制度, 法制
logistics system 物流システム
open system 開放体制, 開放体系
pension, medical and welfare systems 年金・医療・福祉制度
position classification system 職階制
priority system 重点主義
procurement system 調達システム
quick response system 早期応答システム
railroad [railway] system 鉄道網, 鉄道系統
risk control system リスク管理システム (＝risk management system)
river system 河川系
seniority-order wage system 年功序列型賃金体系
specialist system 専門職制度
system architectures システム構成
system configuration システム構成, システムの機器構成
system crash システムの故障, システム障害, システムのトラブル
system development planning システム開発設計
system glitch システム障害
system installation システム導入
system LSI システムLSI (**system large-scale integrated-circuit**の略)
taxation system 税制 (tax system), 課税制度
the binary system 二進法
the decimal system 十進法
the digestive system 消化器系, 消化系

the metric system メートル法
the nervous system 神経系
the solar system 太陽系
work by a system 一定のやり方で仕事をする
world monetary system 国際通貨制度

systematic 形
組織的な, 系統的, 体系的, 計画的, 整然とした, 規則正しい, 几帳面な, 一貫した, 故意の, 計画的な, 分類上の, 分類学の, システマティック

highly systematic approach 高度に組織だったアプローチ
systematic bias [misleading] 故意にゆがんだ解釈をすること
systematic botany 植物分類学
systematic dumping 組織的ダンピング
systematic error 定誤差, 系統的誤差
systematic habits 規則正しい習慣
systematic intrigue 計画的陰謀
systematic management 組織的管理, 体系的管理
systematic risk 組織的危険
systematic sampling 系統的抽出法, 等間隔抽出法
systematic search 体系的調査
systematic violation 計画的な違反

systematization 名
組織化, 系列下, システム化

systematization of distributors 販売店の系列下
systematization strategy システム化戦略

systematize 動
組織化する, 体系化する, 系統立てる, 組織立てる, システム化する, 順序立てる 分類する

systematized 組織化した, システム化した
systematized product 制度品

systemic 形
組織の, 系統の, システム全体の, 〈病気が〉全身的な

systemic financial crisis 連鎖的な金融危機, 金融の連鎖的な危機
systemic risk 連鎖破綻リスク, 連鎖リスク, システム[システミック]・リスク(一つの銀行の破綻が, 連鎖的に他の金融機関に及び, 金融システム全体が機能不全に陥るリスク。これは, 個々の金融機関が各種取引や決済ネットワークを使った資金決済を通じて相互に結ばれているために起こる)

systems-on-chips
システム・オン・チップ《略 SoC》(複数のシステムLSI(大規模集積回路)の機能を一つのチップに収める半導体技術)

T t

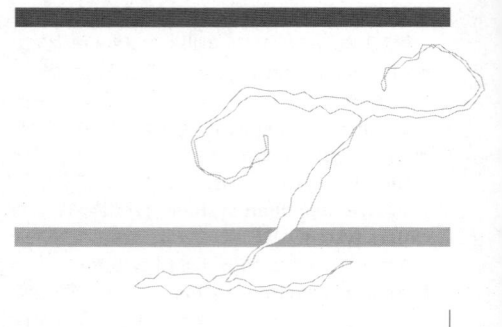

table 名 協議の場, 審議[討議]の場
  lay a thing on the table 〈英〉審議にかける, 審議に付す, 〈米〉審議を延期する, 棚上げする
  turn the tables on …に対して形勢を逆転させる
  under the table 正規のルートによらずに, ヤミで (=under the counter)
tackle 動 …に取り組む, …に立ち向かう, …に挑む, 論じ合う, 渡り合う, 組みつく, タックルする
  tackle a pressing issue 緊急課題[問題]に取り組む
  tackle crime 犯罪に立ち向かう
tactic [tactics] 名 作戦, 作戦行動, 手段, 方策, 策, 手, 策略, かけ引き, 戦術, 戦法
  adopt [use] the usual tactics いつもの手を用いる
  air tactics 航空戦術
  campaign tactics 運動の戦術, 選挙運動の戦術
  filibuster tactic 議事[議事進行]妨害戦術 (=stonewall)
  grand tactics 高等戦術
  guerrilla tactics ゲリラ戦術
  money tactics 買収戦術
  on-again, off-again tactics さみだれ戦術
  poison pill defense tactics ポイズン・ピル(毒薬条項)防衛策
  sabotage tactics 〈スト中の労働者による〉破壊戦術, 器物損壊戦術
  scorched earth tactics 焦土作戦
  steam-roller tactics 暴圧戦術
  struggle tactics 闘争戦術
  use strong-arm tactics 実力を行使する, 実力戦術を用いる
tailor 動 適応させる, 適合させる, …に合わせる, 組み立てる, 仕組む, 仕立てる, 調製する
  be tailored to the needs of …のニーズに合わせてある, …の需要に応じて…する
take a stake in …へ出資する
take-home pay 手取り賃金, 手取り給与, 可処分所得
take in 利益を上げる, 売上がある, 〈金を〉受け取る, 持ち込む, 吸収する, 吸い込む, 摂取する, 〈データを〉取り込む, 収容する, 泊める, 〈難民などを〉受け入れる, 〈容疑者などを〉連行する, …を扱う, 含む(include), …をだます
take issue with …に反論する, …に異議を唱える, …と論争する
take off 離陸する, 〈値段を〉割り引く, 値引きする, 差し引く, 控除する, 中止する, 削除する
  ▶Sales of suits have also *taken off*. 紳士服の販売も, 好調だ。
take on 〈仕事・責任を〉引き受ける, …と対決する, …と対戦する, …に対抗する, …の挑戦を受けて立つ, 雇う, 〈荷物を〉積み込む, 厳しく尋問する, 騒ぎ立てる
take out 〈ローンなどを〉組む, 保険に入る[加入する], 保険を付ける[かける], 契約する, 獲得する, 取得する, 取り出す, 持ち出す, 〈金を〉下ろす, 〈預金などを〉引き出す, 〈食事や散歩などに〉連れ出す, 出かける, 出発する(set out), 〈店で食べずに〉持ち帰る, 削除する, 取り除く, 除去する, 破壊する, 無力化する, 〈訴訟を〉起こす, 〈召喚状などを〉発行する
  take out a loan contract ローン契約を結ぶ

take out consumer loans 消費者金融から金を借りる

take out provisions against loan losses 貸倒れ損失に備えて準備金を引き当てる

take over 〈企業を〉買収する, 取得する, 乗っ取る, 〈資産・業務などを〉引き継ぐ, 継承する, 経営権を獲得する

take over the assets of …の資産を継承する, …の資産を引き継ぐ

take over the operations of …の営業譲渡を受ける

take … to task …を非難する
► The European Union (EU) *took* Israel *to task* over its killing of 10 Palestinians during a deadly raid in the Gaza Strip. イスラエルがガザ地区の猛襲でパレスチナ人10人を殺害したことで, 欧州連合(EU)はイスラエルを非難した。

takeover [take-over] 名 企業買収, 乗っ取り, 企業取得, 買収, 吸収合併, 〈債権などの〉譲り受け, 引継ぎ, テイクオーバー (＝acquisition, scuttle, tender offer)

bust-up takeover 解体買収
friendly takeover 友好的買収
hostile takeover 敵対的買収 (＝unsolicited takeover)
reverse takeover 逆買収
seek a takeover 営業譲渡先を探す
takeover attempt 買収劇, 買収攻勢, 買収の企て
takeover bidder 買収提案者, 買収者
takeover boom 買収ブーム, 企業買収ブーム
takeover defense 買収防衛手段, 防衛手段, 乗っ取り防衛手段, 買収防衛策

takeover bid 株式公開買付け, 株式公開買付けによる企業買収, 買収提案, テイクオーバー・ビッド《略 **TOB**》 (＝take-over bid, takeover offer, tender offer：主に経営権を支配するため, 株式の買取り業者が買付け期間と株数, 買付け価格を公表して不特定多数の株主から株を買い取る方法)

takeover bid period 株式公開買付けの期間, TOBの期間 (＝public tender offer period)

talent 名 才能, 才能のある人, 逸材, 人材, 適性, タレント

good [competent] talent 有能な人材
have a talent for …の才がある
hide one's talents in a napkin 自己の才能を埋もれさせる
homegrown managerial talent 生え抜きの経営幹部, 生え抜きの経営者

intellectual talents 知的人材
natural talent 生来の才能
talent scout 人材発掘者, 人材スカウト

talented 形 有能な, 才能のある

Taliban 名 タリバン(アフガニスタンのイスラム原理主義武装勢力)
Taliban militants タリバン兵士

talk through one's hat いい加減なことを言う, でまかせを言う, 大ぼらを吹く

talking book 〈盲人用の〉録音本
talking paper 討議資料
talking shop おしゃべりの場, 空論の場, 意見交換の場

talks 名 会談, 交渉, 協議, 話し合い, 講演
debt restructuring talks 債務再編交渉
multilateral talks 多国間協議
preparatory talks 準備協議
proximity talks 近接地往復外交交渉, 間接交渉(相対立する二者間を, 調停者が往復してまとめる外交交渉)
talks on normalizing relations 関係正常化協議
talk show 〈有名人との〉会見番組, トーク・ショー (＝chat show)
the latest round of multilateral trade liberalization talks 新多角的貿易交渉(新ラウンド) (＝the new round of WTO talks)
working-level talks 実務レベル協議, 実務協議, 実務者協議

tall order 無茶な注文, 無理な注文[仕事], 難しい仕事[注文], 難しい[無理な]こと(tallは「無茶な, 無理な, 難しい」という意味)

tandem 名 2人乗り自転車, タンデム
in tandem 縦に並んで, 縦1列になって, 縦並びで, 相前後して, 交代制で
in tandem with …と並んで, …と協力して, …と力を合わせて, …と提携して, …と一体で, 縦1列になって, …と相前後して, …と同時に
tandem currency タンデム通貨
tandem exchange 中継局
tandem plan 併設プラン

tantamount to …に等しい, …と同等の, …と同じ

tap 動 〈情報などを〉引き出す[求める], 開発[開拓]する, 利用する, 活用する, 選ぶ, 選出する, 盗聴する, 傍受する, 盗聴器を付ける

tap into dormant funds as drawer savings

tap | task force

タンス預金として眠っている資金を利用する
tap into the market 市場を利用する，…市場に乗り出す，市場で起債する
tap rising demand 需要増に応える
tap the market 市場を開発[開拓]する，市場に登場する，市場で起債する，市場で資金を調達する

tap 名 〈水道の〉蛇口，〈電話の〉盗聴，盗聴器[装置]，〈酒やビールの樽の〉栓，のみ口，〈樽仕込みの〉酒，特定醸造酒，居酒屋(taphouse)，いつでも買える国債[公債]，タップ，形 〈債券の〉発行期間[発行総額]に制限がない
on tap いつでも求めに応じられる，いつでも利用できる[使える]，用意されて，〈国債などが〉自由に買える
tap bond タップ債(遊休資金吸い上げのために発行される国債)
tap issue タップ発行(証券取引所や金融市場を通さないで，国債や政府証券券をイングランド銀行などの政府機関に直接売ること)，タップ債
tap stock タップ債

tape 動 テープに録音[録画]する，放映する，包帯を巻く
be taped よく理解されている，十分に[よく]把握されている
have [get] a thing taped 物事の決着をつける，物を十分に理解する

tape 名 磁気テープ，テープ録音[録画]，カセット・テープ，ビデオ・テープ，粘着テープ，テープ
adhesive tape 粘着テープ
breast the tape レースに勝つ
cassette tape カセット・テープ
magnetic tape 磁気テープ
red tape 官僚的形式主義，形式主義，お役所仕事，煩雑[煩瑣]な手続き，規制(公文書を縛る赤いヒモに由来)
tape measure 巻尺 (=tapeline)

target 動 …を目標に定める，目標にする，標的にする，…に的を絞る，対象にする，狙う，ターゲットにする

target 名 目標，標的，対象，的，〈物笑いの〉種，目標額，目標水準，買収目標企業，買収対象会社，買収標的会社，ターゲット
call target rate コール金利の誘導目標水準
off target 的を外れて，不正確で
on target 的を射て，正確で，目標どおり
soft [easy] target 狙われやすい人[物]，だまされやすい人，からかわれやすい人

target rate for unsecured overnight call money 無担保コール翌日物金利の誘導目標 (unsecured overnight call money = overnight unsecured call money)
target zone 目標相場圏，目標範囲，ターゲット・ゾーン
the Fed funds target フェデラル・ファンド(FF)金利の誘導目標[誘導目標水準]

targeted 形 目標とされる，目標とされている，標的の，…を対象とする
be targeted at …を対象にしている，…をターゲットにしている，…を狙っている
foreign-targeted issue 外国人投資家向け発行
retail-targeted deal 個人投資家を対象とする起債
targeted at …に向けられた，…対象の
targeted average yield 基準利回り
targeted company 買収の標的企業

tariff 名 関税，関税率，料金表，運賃表
ad valorem tariff 従価関税
antidumping tariffs 反ダンピング(不当廉売)関税
autonomous tariff 固定税率
concession of tariff 関税譲許
counter tariff 対抗関税
Customs Tariff Law 関税定率法
drug tariff 薬価基準
internal tariff 域内関税
non-discriminative tariff 無差別関税
preferential tariff treatment 特恵関税 (= preference treatment tariff)
protective tariff 保護関税
retaliatory tariffs 報復関税 (=punitive tariffs)
safeguard tariffs セーフガード関税
tariff autonomy 関税自主権
tariff barrier 関税障壁 (=tariff wall)
tariff cap 関税の上限 (=tariff ceiling)
tariff rate 関税率，表定運賃，許認可料金

task 名 仕事，任務，職務，業務，課業，作業，課題，問題，タスク
take [bring, call] a person to task …の責任を問う，…を(厳しく)非難する，…を叱る，…をとがめる
task and bonus system 課業賞与制度，課業賞与方式 (=task bonus system)

task force 対策委員会，対策本部，専門委員

会, 特別委員会, 作業部会, プロジェクト・チーム, 専門調査団, 特殊任務を持つ機動部隊, タスク・フォース
Presidential Task Force on Market Mechanisms 市場メカニズムに関する大統領特別委員会
task force on financial issues 金融問題委員会
task force on industrial structure changes and employment measures 産業構造転換・雇用対策本部
tax 動 〈…に〉課税する, 重い負担をかける, 重荷を負わせる, 酷使する, 責める, 非難する, 〈訴訟費用などを〉査定する, 〈会費などを〉徴収する, 割り当てる, 請求する
 be taxed at source 源泉徴収税が課される
 be taxed on …に課税される
 tax a person with a fault 人の過失を責める
 tax one's ingenuity 頭を絞る, 知恵を絞る, 苦心する, 創意工夫を凝らす
 tax the costs of an action in the suit 訴訟費用を査定する
 ▶ In Germany, individual investors' capital gains are not normally *taxed*. ドイツでは, 個人投資家の譲渡益については通常, 非課税となっている。
tax 名 税, 租税, タックス
 carbon tax 炭素税
 consumption tax 消費税
 corporate income tax 法人所得税, 法人税
 corporate tax 法人税
 enterprise tax 事業税
 extralegal taxes 法定外税
 federal income tax 連邦所得税, 連邦法人税
 foreign tax credit 外国税額控除
 gift tax 贈与税
 heavy penalty tax 重加算税
 income tax 所得税, 法人所得税
 income taxes 法人税等
 land transfer tax 土地譲渡益課税, 土地譲渡税
 Local Tax Law 地方税法
 net of tax 税引き後
 social security tax 社会保障税, 社会保険料
 state tax 州税
 state income tax 州法人所得税, 州税
 tax administration 納税事務
 tax assets 税金資産
 tax avoidance 租税回避, 課税逃れ, 税逃れ
 tax base 課税基準, 課税標準, 課税ベース, 税収基盤 (= tax basis)
 tax benefit 税務上の特典, 〈税額控除や所得控除などの〉税制上の優遇措置, 税効果, 節税益, 課税軽減額
 tax burden 租税負担, 税負担
 Tax Commission 税制調査会 (= Tax System Research Commission)
 tax declaration filing system 納税申告制度
 tax deduction 税額控除
 tax evasion 脱税, 税金逃れ
 tax-exempt 免税の, 非課税の, 無税の (= tax-free)
 tax-free disposal of bad loans 不良債権の無税償却 (= nontaxable write-off of bad loans)
 tax grants 交付税
 tax income 税収
 tax increase [hike] 増税
 tax investigation 税務調査 (= tax inspection)
 tax levies on capital gains 株式譲渡益課税
 tax liability 納税額
 tax on unreported income 無申告加算税
 tax preference 租税優遇, 優遇税制
 tax rebate 税金の還付, 戻し減税, 戻し税
 tax reform 税制改正, 税制改革
 tax refund 税金還付
 tax break 減税, 税額控除, 税率軽減措置, 租税優遇措置, 租税特別措置, 税務上の特典, 税制上の特典 (= tax cut, tax deduction, tax reduction)
  tax break for [on] capital gains 株式譲渡益, 株式売却益, キャピタル・ゲイン減税
 tax cut 減税 (= tax reduction)
  tax cuts and tax hikes 減税と増税, 減税措置と増税措置
 tax-deductible 形 所得から控除できる, 税額控除できる, 課税控除できる, 損金算入できる, 損金算入
 tax-free amortization 無税償却 (= nontaxable write-off, tax-free write-off)
 tax haven 租税回避地, 租税逃避地, 租税避難国, 税金天国, タックス・ヘイブン (= tax shelter: カリブ海のケイマン諸島や英領バージン諸島など, 法人税や所得税がかけられないか税率が著しく低い国や地域が多い。その特徴として, 各国の税務当局との情報交換を妨げる制度や慣行があり, 不正資金の洗浄(マネーロンダリング)に利用されることもある)

tax incentives 税制上の優遇措置, 減免税措置, 税制支援策 (=tax advantages, tax concessions)
▶The matter of deferred tax assets should be reviewed in tandem with such *tax incentives* as eased criteria on nontaxable write-off of bad loans and an expanded scope of refunds for banks to carry a loss back to the previous year. 繰延べ税金資産の問題は, 不良債権の無税償却基準の緩和や銀行の欠損金の前年度への繰戻し還付の大幅拡充などの税制支援策と一体で見直さなければならない。

tax rate 税率 (=rate of taxation)
  applicable tax rate 適用税率
  basic tax rate 基本税率
  corporate income tax rate 法人所得税率
  effective tax rate 実効税率
tax reduction 減税 (=tax cut)
  tax reductions for corporations 企業減税
  tax reductions for part-timers パート減税
tax resources 税源
tax return 納税申告(書), 税務申告(書), 租税申告(書)
tax revenue 税収
  tax revenue allocations 地方交付税
  tax revenue shortfall [shortage] 税収不足
tax shelter 租税回避地, 租税回避国, 税金天国, 税金逃れの隠れみの, 会計操作, タックス・シェルター (=tax haven)
tax system 税制, 租税体系 (=system of taxation, taxation system)
  tax system reform 税制改正, 税制改革
  Tax System Research Commission 税制調査会
tax treaty 租税条約 (=tax agreement, tax convention)
taxable 形 課税対象となる, 課税できる
  taxable income 課税所得, 申告所得, 課税対象所得
taxation 名 課税, 徴税, 税収
  taxation system 税制, 課税制度 (=tax system)
taxpayer 名 納税者, 納税義務者
  high-income taxpayer 高所得納税者
  self-assessed taxpayer 申告納税者
  taxpayer identification number 納税者番号
TB 結核 (tuberculosisの略)
TCOG 日米韓3か国調整会合 (Trilateral Coordination and Oversight Groupの略。1999年4月から数か月に1度の割合で開かれている日米韓3か国の北朝鮮政策に関する局長級事務レベル協議)
teachware 名 視聴覚教材
team 名 団, 組, 班, 隊, チーム
  cross-functional team 機能横断チーム, クロス・ファンクショナル・チーム
  go team 〈航空機事故の際に出動する〉緊急派遣団
  self-directed team 自主管理チーム, セルフ・ディレクテッド・チーム
  team game 団体スポーツ
  team medical care チーム医療
  team player チームのために働く人, 団結を乱さない人, チームの一員, 協調主義者, 連帯主義者, チーム・プレーヤー
  team spirit 団体精神, 団結心, 共同精神, チーム精神
  transition team 米政権移行チーム
  U.N. weapons inspection team 国連の兵器査察団
team up with …と協力する, …と提携する, …とチームを組む (=join forces)
Teamsters Union 国際トラック運転手組合 (米最大の労働組合)
technical 形 技術の, 技術的な, 工業技術の, 科学技術の, 専門的な, 技巧的な, 実務上の, 実用の, 市場の内部要因による, 人為的な, 操作的な, テクニカル
  technical advisor 技術顧問, 技術アドバイザー
  technical assistance 技術協力, 技術援助, 技術支援, 技術指導 (=technical aid, technical cooperation)
  technical balance of trade 技術貿易収支
  technical change 技術変化, 技術革新, アヤ (やや長期的な相場のなかでの特に理由のない小さい変動のことを「アヤ」という)
  technical cooperation [collaboration] 技術提携, 技術協力
  technical conditions テクニカル要因 (=technical factors, technical forces)
  technical density 技術密度
  technical environment 市場の内部環境
  technical external effect 技術的外部効果
  technical factors テクニカル要因, 市場内部要因 (=technical conditions, technical forces：信用取引残高, 投資家の売買動向, 新株発行による資金調達状況, 株価規制など, 動向株

価を動かす要因のうち株式の需給に直接かかわる要因を「市場内部要因」や「内部要因」という）
technical guidance 技術指導, 専門的指導
technical improvement 技術革新(technical innovation), 技術的改良, 技術の改良, 改良技術
technical innovation 技術革新（＝technological innovation）
technical invention 技術的革命, 技術革新
technical learning 技術の習得
technical monopoly 技術の独占
technical picture 需給関係
technical position 取組み, 内部要因, 内部要因相場, 不自然な人為相場
technical problem 実務上の問題
technical rebound 自立反発
technical reserves 総責任準備金
technical recession 2四半期連続のマイナス成長, 景気後退, テクニカル・リセッション
technical review 技術調査
technical stagnation 経済的停滞
technical support 技術援助, 技術サポート, テクニカル面からの下支え, テクニカル・サポート

technicality 名 手続き上の問題, 技術上の問題, 専門事項, 学術的事項, 専門用語, 専門用語の使用
　legal technicality 法律上の専門的事項
　on a technicality 法律上では

technique 名 技術, 技法, 手法, 技巧, 技量, テクニック
　attitude measurement technique 態度評定法
　audit [auditing] technique 監査技術, 監査技法
　capital-intensive technique 資本集約的技術
　cash management technique 現金管理技法
　clinical interview technique 臨床的面接法
　hedging techniques ヘッジ手法, ヘッジ技術
　Monte Carlo technique モンテカルロ法
　panel technique パネル調査
　production-line technique 生産の流れ作業法
　projective technique 投影法, 投影技法
　quality control technique 品質管理技法, 品質管理手法
　reswitching of technique 技術の再転換
　sampling technique サンプリング技法

technocracy 名 技術主義, 技術家政治, 技術専門家による社会支配, 技術家支配国, 技術家集団, テクノクラシー

technocrat 名 政治力を持つ技術家, 技術家政治の主張者, 技術系出身の管理職, 技術畑出の高級官僚［高級行政官］, 実務型官僚, テクノクラート

technological 形 科学技術の, 技術的な, 工芸の, テクノロジカル
　technological assessment 技術評価, 技術の事前評価, 技術開発事前評価, 技術の再点検, テクノロジー・アセスメント《略 TA》（＝technology assessment）
　technological backlog 技術の蓄積, 技術的蓄積
　technological change 技術の変化, 技術革新（＝technical change, technological innovation, technological renovation）
　technological differential 技術格差
　technological diffusion 技術的拡散
　technological edge 技術的な優位
　technological fluidity 技術の変化
　technological followership 技術追随戦略
　technological industry 技術集約型産業
　technological innovation 技術革新（＝technological revolution）

technology 名 技術, 科学技術, 工業技術, テクノロジー
　alternative technology 代替技術
　capital-intensive technology 資本集約的技術
　commercialization of technologies 技術の製品化
　encryption technology 暗号技術, 暗号化技術
　financial technology 金融技術, 金融テクノロジー, 財テク
　imported technology 輸入技術, 導入技術, 技術の導入
　intellectual technology 知的技術
　licensing of technology 技術供与
　military technology 軍事技術
　processing technology 処理技術
　sources of technology 技術の供給源, 技術の導入先
　technology choice 技術選択
　technology commercialization 技術商品化
　technology diffusion 技術の普及
　technology licensing organization 技術移転機関《略 TLO》
　technology transfer 技術移転
　transfer of technology 技術移転（＝technology transfer）

tech-savvy 形 技術通の, 技術に精通した, 技術知識のある

teeter on the brisk of …の瀬戸際に瀕する

teetering 形 経営破綻の危機に瀕している, 破綻の危機に陥っている, 破綻の瀬戸際[危機]にある

Tehran [Teheran] 名 イランの首都テヘラン, イラン政府

telco 名 電気通信事業者, 遠距離通信会社, 情報通信会社, 通信株, 通信機器
 telco supplier 通信機器メーカー

telecom 名 通信, 電気通信, 通信事業, 通信会社, テレコム (=telecommunication, telecommunications)
 telecom and broadcasting facilities 通信・放送設備
 telecom carrier 通信事業者
 telecoms services 通信サービス, 通信業務

telecommunication 名 電気通信, 遠隔通信, 通信, テレコム (=telecom)
 telecommunications business 通信事業
 Telecommunications Business Law 電気通信事業法
 telecommunications network 通信網, 電気通信網, 通信ネットワーク

telemarketing 名 テレマーケティング (= telephone shopping, teleshopping：電話での商品販売法, または電話での各種調査や案内, コールセンター構築のサポートなどを行う会社のこと)

telematics 名 テレマティックス, 情報通信, 高度情報社会 (telecommunication（電気通信）とinformatics（情報工学）の造語。車に搭載した端末で交通渋滞や娯楽施設などの情報を入手したり, 駐車場やレストランなどを探したりすることができるシステム)

telephone conversation 電話会談
temp workers 派遣労働者
temperature 名 温度, 気温, 体温
temporal method 属性法, テンポラル法 (=temporal approach：外貨で評価されているものは現金で, 債権・債務と時価で評価されているものは決算日レートで, 取引日の評価額で評価されているものは取引日レートで換算する外貨換算方法)

temporary 形 一時的な, 臨時の, 暫定的, 仮の
 temporary employee 期間従業員, 派遣社員
 temporary staffing agency [firm, company] 人材派遣会社
 temporary worker 派遣社員, 派遣労働者

tendency 名 傾向, 風潮, 趨勢, 動向, 性向, 性癖, 向き, 〈文学作品の〉意図, 目的, 趣向, 才能, 素質, 〈党内の〉急進派, 反対勢力
 a downward tendency 下向き, 下げ足
 a falling tendency 下向き, 下降傾向
 a rising tendency 上向き, 上昇傾向
 an expansionary tendency 拡大傾向
 an exclusive tendency 排他的傾向
 an upward tendency 上向き, 上げ足
 secretive tendencies 秘密主義

tender 名 入札, 応募入札, 入札書, 申込み, 提出, 提供, 提出物, 提供物, テンダー
 alternative tender 代案入札
 approved tender 指名入札
 cost of preparing tender 入札の準備費用
 estimated tender value 予定入札価格
 form of tender 入札書様式, 入札書式
 limited tender 指名入札
 open tender 一般入札, 公開入札, 一般競争入札
 private tender 指名入札
 public tender 競争入札
 sealed tender 競争入札
 specified tender 指名入札

tender offer 株式公開買付け, テンダー・オファー (=public tender offer, takeover bid, takeover offer, TOB：一般の証券取引市場の外で行われる大口証券購入の申込みのこと)
 cash tender offer 現金公開買付け, 現金による株式公開買付け, キャッシュ・テンダー・オファー (買収先の会社の株式を現金で公開買付けする方法)
 proposed tender offer price 提示された株式公開買付け(TOB)価格, 株式公開買付け(TOB)の予定価格

tense 形 緊張した, 緊迫した, 張りつめた, 神経質な
 a tense atmosphere 張りつめた空気, 緊張した空気, 緊張感
 a tense meeting [session] 緊張した会議
 look tense 緊張の色を示す

tension 名 緊張, 不安, 緊迫, 緊張関係, 緊迫状態, 均衡, 拮抗, 張り, 張力, 電圧
 a state of tension 緊張状態
 heighten [raise] tensions 緊張を高める
 the surface tension of water 水の表面張力

tenure 名 在職期間, 任期(term of office), 終身在職権, 保有, 所有, 保有期間, 保有条件, 保有権
 expired tenure 任期満了

free tenure 自由保有条件
job tenure 在職期間
tenure for life 永代［終身，生涯］土地保有権
tenure of office 在職，在職期間，任期
unfree tenure 不自由保有条件

term 名 期間，契約期間，専門用語，用語，言葉づかい，言い方，表現，定期不動産権，条件（複数形で用いられることが多い），条項，規定，約定，合意，間柄，関係，仲
  be on familiar terms 親しい間柄だ
  bring to term 条件を受け入れさせる
  come to terms with …と合意に達する，…と折り合いをつける，…を甘受する
  credit terms 支払い条件
  general terms 一般条項
  in concrete terms 具体的に
  in dollar terms ドル・ベースで，ドル表示で（＝in dollar-denominated terms）
  in nominal terms 名目ベースで，名目で
  in real terms 実質ベースで，実質で，実勢価格で
  in terms of …の点から，…に関して，…の言葉［表現］で
  in terms of value 金額ベースで
  medical terms 医学用語
  on one's own terms …の出した条件で，…の言い値で
  payment terms 支払い条件
  principal terms 主要条項
  remaining terms 残りの条項，残存条項，残存規定
  term of office 任期
  terms of reference 考慮すべき事柄
  terms of trade 貿易条件

terminal 形 期末の，最終の，終点の，末期の，末端の，一定期間の，定期の，毎期の
  terminal demand 最終需要
  terminal equipment 端末機器，端末装置
  terminal medical care 終末期医療（＝terminal care）

terminate 動 〈契約を〉終了させる，解除する，解約する，解消する，打ち切る，終了する
  automatically terminate 自動終了する，自動的に解約し終了する
  terminate this agreement or any part thereof 本契約またはその一部を解除する
  unconditionally terminate 無条件で終了する，無条件で終了させる，無条件で解除する
  unless earlier terminated as provided for in this agreement 本契約に定めるとおり早期終了しないかぎり，本契約に規定するとおり中途終了する場合を除いて

termination 名 〈契約の〉終了，〈期間の〉満了，解約，解除，解消，打ち切り，〈権利の〉消滅，解散

terrestrial digital television broadcasting 地上デジタル・テレビ放送，地上デジタル放送（＝terrestrial digital broadcasting）

territory 名 領土，領地，領域，分野，区域，範囲，ゾーン，販売区域，販売地域，販売領域，担当区域，〈商標やソフトウェア・プログラムなど知的財産権の〉使用許諾地域，許諾地域，契約地域，レベル，テリトリー
  business territory 商圏，商勢圏
  distribution territory 販売区域
  junk territory 投資不適格のレベル
  manufacturing territory 製造地域
  negative territory マイナス，マイナス基調
  neutral territory 中立ゾーン
  positive territory プラス，プラス基調
  sales territory 販売領域，販売区域，販売地域
  service territory サービス区域，サービス・エリア
  Territory 〈米・加・豪の〉準州

terror 名 恐怖，恐ろしさ，恐怖の的，暴力行為，テロ行為，テロ

terrorism 名 暴力行為，恐怖政治，テロ行為，テロ
  anthrax terrorism 炭疽菌テロ（＝anthrax terror）
  eco-terrorism 環境テロ，エコ・テロリズム
  electronic terrorism 電子テロ
  suicide bombing terrorism 自爆テロ
  terrorism using nuclear, biological and chemical weapons NBCテロ
  the Antiterrorism Law テロ対策特別措置法

terrorist 名 テロ行為者，暴力主義者，恐怖政治家，テロリスト
  a terrorist attack テロ攻撃
  protective measures against possible terrorist activities テロ対策
  the International Convention for the Suppression of Terrorists Bombings 爆弾テロ防止条約

tertiary industry 第三次産業（サービス産業とほぼ同義で，商業，運輸・通信業，金融業，公務・自由業，有給の家事サービス業などのこと）
  tertiary industry activity index 第三次産業

活動指数（=tertiary industry index）
the index of tertiary industry activity 第三次産業活動指数
test 動 試験する, 実験する, 検査する, 調べる, 分析する, 試す, テストする, 試験[実験, 検査]結果が…である
　test for …の検査を受ける
　test out …を実際に試してみる
　test positive for …に陽性となる, …に陽性反応を示す
test 名 試験, 実験, 試査, 検査, チェック, 試金石, 検査用器具, 試薬, テスト
　sample test サンプル検査
　test delivery テスト配信
　test drilling 試掘
　test flight テスト飛行
　test production 試験生産
　written test 筆記試験
test-fire 動 発射実験を行う, 試射する, テスト発射する
test-firing 名 発射実験, 試射, テスト発射
testify 動 証言する, 宣誓証言する, 証明する, 立証する, 保証する, 示す, 表明する, 公言する
　testify against …に不利な証言をする
　testify as a sworn witness 参考人として証言する
　testify before …で宣誓して証言する
　testify for [on behalf of, in favor of] …に有利な証言をする
　testify to …の証拠となる, …を証明する, …を立証する
testimony 名 証言, 証拠, 証明, 言明, 表明, 供述書, 陳述書
　bear testimony to …を証言する, …の証となる, …を立証[証明]する
　call a person in testimony 人を証言[証人]に立たせる
　give false testimony 偽証をする
　give testimony that …という証言をする, …と証言する
　in testimony of …の印に
　produce testimony to [of] …の証拠を提出する, …の証拠をあげる, …を証明する
　testimony of witnesses 目撃者の証言
testing 名 試査, 検査, 検定, 実験, 試験, テスト
　audit testing 試査, 監査テスト
　compliance testing 準拠性テスト (=compliance test)
　sampling testing 試査
　testing period 対象期間
THAAD ターミナル段階高高度地域防衛システム, 戦域高高度空域防衛, サード (Theater High Altitude Area Defenseの略)
theme 名 主題, 論題, 題, 題材, テーマ
　dominant theme 最大のテーマ
　forecast themes 予想の大枠
　guiding theme 指針
　theme paper 〈大学の〉レポート
　theme park テーマ・パーク
　theme pavilion テーマ館
therapy 名 療法, 治療, 治療法, 理学[物理]療法, セラピー
　aromatherapy 芳香療法, アロマセラピー［アロマテラピー］
　gene therapy 遺伝子治療
　heavy particle beam therapy 重粒子線治療
　physical therapy 物理療法
　proton beam therapy 陽子線治療
　shock therapy ショック療法
　speech therapy 言語矯正療法, 言語療法
thermal 形 熱の, 火力発電の, 保温用の
　thermal efficiency 熱効率
　thermal generator 火力発電所 (=thermal power plant)
　thermal power 火力発電
thin 形 薄い, 希薄な, 薄手の, 細い, 水っぽい, 〈アルコール度が〉弱い, 手薄な, 閑散とした, まばらな, 茂っていない, 不景気の, 振るわない, 不振の, 乏しい, 低い, 説得力がない, 内容の薄い, 内容のない, 実質のない, 通り一ぺんの, 見え透いた
　be (as) thin as a knife's edge 紙一重だ
　have a thin time (of it) みじめな[不愉快な]時を過ごす, 不愉快な思いをする, 〈金銭問題で〉嫌な思いをする, 嫌な目にあう, 困ったことになる
　on thin ice 薄氷を踏んで, 危険な状態で
　the thin end of the wedge 将来重大な結果を引き起こしそうなこと, 重大事に発展するささいなこと
　thin applause まばらな拍手
　thin evidence 乏しい根拠
　thin liquidity 乏しい流動性, 流動性が乏しい状況
　thin market 不景気な市況, 薄商い市場, 閑散市場, 手薄な市場, 市場低迷, 閑散(活況市場=active market)
　thin on the ground 数が少ない, 乏しい

think 動 考える，…と思う，思案する，思索する，判断する，期待[予期]する，想像する
　think a lot of …を高く評価する
　think better of 考え直す，思いとどまる，考え直して止める，考えを改める，…を見直す，…をもっと高く評価する
　think highly of 高く評価する
　think out of the box 型にはまらず考える，既存の枠組みにとらわれずに考える，独創的な考え方をする
think piece 社説，論説文
think tank [factory] 頭脳集団，頭脳会社，総合研究所，シンクタンク
thinking 名 考え，考え方，思考，発想，意見，判断，観測，思想
　lateral thinking 水平思考，側面思考（常識や既成概念にとらわれずに直感や論理の飛躍などさまざまな角度から物事をとらえる自由な考え方）
　vertical thinking 垂直思考，常識的思考
　way of thinking 考え方，思考法，発想法
　wishful thinking 希望的観測
thinner sniffing シンナー遊び
thinning work 間伐作業
third 形 第三の，3番目の，3分の1の
　third-class matter 第三種郵便物
　Third Conference of Parties (COP3) 第三回締約国会議
　third country 第三国
　third degree 拷問，厳しい尋問，根掘り葉掘りの質問
　third market 第三市場，場外市場，上場株の店頭取引（over-the-counter trading）市場（fourth market（第四市場）＝非上場株の投資家間の直接取引）
　third person 第三人称，第三者
　third reading 第三読会（米法案の最終審議）
　Third World 第三世界（主にアジア，アフリカ，中南米の発展途上国）
third party 第三者，当事者以外の人，〈米民主党，共和党以外の〉第三政党，第三党
　third-party allocation 第三者割当て（＝third-party allotment：業務提携先や金融機関など特定の相手に新株を引き受けてもらう形の第三者割当増資に対して，一般投資家を引受先として新株を発行することを公募増資という）
　third-party insurance 第三者保険（被保険者以外の第三者の傷害に対する保険）
　third-party support 第三者支援

threat 名 脅威，兆し，前兆，恐れ，懸念，可能性，阻害要因，脅迫，威嚇，脅し
　competitive threat 競争圧力，競争力で後れをとること
　external threat 外部からの脅威
　pose financial threats to …の財政負担になる
　recessionary threat 景気後退の恐れ
threaten 動 脅す，脅迫する，威嚇する，…するといって脅す，〈安全などを〉おびやかす，危うくする，危険にさらす，…の兆候がある，…しそうだ
　be threatened with …の危機に瀕している，…の危機にさらされている
　threaten to …すると脅す，…する恐れがある
threatening 形 脅しの，脅すような，脅迫的な，荒れ模様の，荒れる気配の
　a threatening letter 脅迫状
　a threatening sky 怪しい空模様
three-cornered trade conference 三極通商会議
three-dimensional [3-D] 形 3次元の，立体の，立体的，立体感のある，生きているような，説得力のある，陸海空からの（＝three-D）
　three-dimensional computer-aided design 3次元コンピュータ支援設計，3次元CAD（＝three-dimensional CAD）
　three-dimensional electron devices 3次元素子
　three-dimensional integrated circuit 3次元集積回路（＝3D IC）
　three-dimensional model 立体構造
three minutes' silence 死者の霊に捧げる黙とう
three non-nuclear principles 非核3原則
three-pillar reform 三位一体の改革
three R's 〈資源を有効活用するための〉スリーアール，3R
▶The G-8 environment ministerial meeting discussed global warming, biodiversity and the *three R's*—reduce, reuse and recycle. G-8（主要8か国）環境相会合では，地球温暖化と生物多様性のほか，ゴミの減量（リデュース）や製品の再利用（リユース），資源の再生利用（リサイクル）により資源を有効活用するための「3R（スリーアール）」も討議された。
three Rs 読み・書き・算数［算術］，基礎学科（reading, writingとarithmeticを指す）
three-way 形 三者による，三方向からの
　three-way cooperation 産官学の連携，3者

協力
three-way intervention　三極の市場介入
three-way reform　三位一体の改革
threshold 名　敷居, 戸口, 出発点, 門出, 発端, 閾(いき), 境界, 限界点, 〈賃金の〉物価スライド制
boom-or-bust threshold of 50 percent　50％の景気判断の分かれ目, 50％の景気判断分岐点
dive [drop] below the threshold of　…の水準を割り込む
thrift 名　倹約, 節約, 貯蓄金融機関(S&L), 貯蓄銀行
Office of Thrift Supervision　貯蓄金融機関監督局
thrift and savings plans　貯蓄制度
thrift industry　貯蓄金融業界, S&L業界
thrift shop [store]　〈慈善目的の〉中古品店 (=charity shop)
thrifts　米貯蓄金融機関 (=thrift institutions: 相互貯蓄銀行(mutual savings bank), 貯蓄貸付組合(savings and loan association), 信用組合(credit union)の総称)
thriving 形　盛況な, 好況の, 好調な, 繁盛する, 繁栄する, 栄える, 成功する, 成長[生長]する
throw 動　投げる, 〈水を〉かける, 〈ミサイルなどを〉発射する, 〈手足などを〉突然動かす, 〈視線などを〉向ける, 〈質問などを〉浴びせる, 〈パーティなどを〉開く, 〈スイッチを〉入れる, 〈試合に〉わざと負ける, 八百長で負ける
be thrown back on　…に頼らざるをえない
be thrown into　…に投げ出される, …に陥る
be thrown into the state of　…の状態に陥る
throw a party for　…のためにパーティを開く
throw aside a plan　計画を放棄する, 計画を捨てる
throw away　処分する, 捨てる, 使い捨てる, 〈機会などを〉ふいにする, 無駄にするまき散らす, 何度もうるさく言う, さりげなく言う
throw cold water on　…に水を差す, けちをつける
throw doubt on　…に疑問を投げかける
throw down　はねつける, 拒否する, 放り出す, 〈武器などを〉捨てる, 敵に屈する
throw down one's tools　働くのを拒否する
throw in　投げ込む, 投入する, 差し向ける, 〈言葉などを〉差しはさむ, 挿入する, おまけに付ける[添える]
throw in the towel [sponge]　敗北を認める,

負けを認める
throw off　…を脱ぎ捨てる, …から脱する, …から逃れる[自由になる], …から免れる, 〈病気が〉治る
throw on　あわてて着る, 〈ブレーキを〉急にかける
throw one's head and laugh　頭をのけぞらせて笑う
throw one's weight about [around]　威張り散らす, にらみをきかす
throw oneself at　…に媚を売る
throw oneself into　…に身を投げ出す, …に飛び込む, …に専念する, …に没頭する, …に打ち込む
throw oneself on [upon]　…に頼る, …にすがる, …に襲いかかる, …を攻撃する, …に飛びつく
throw open　開放する, 公開する, 自由参加にする
throw out　捨てる, 追い出す, 追放する, 失業させる, 〈議案を〉否決する, 〈案, 計画などを〉拒否する, 〈訴訟などを〉却下する, さりげなく言う, ほのめかす
throw up　投げ上げる, 断念する(give up), 辞職する, 急造する, 指摘する, 批判する
throwaway 形　使い捨ての, 使い捨て偏重の, さりげない〈しぐさ, 一言〉, 名　使い捨てのもの, 〈使い捨てられる〉広告ビラ, ちらし
throwaway product　使い捨て製品
the throwaway age of mass consumption　大量消費の使い捨て時代
thumb 動　親指でめくる, ヒッチハイクする, 名　〈手の〉親指
a rule of thumb　大体の目安, 概算, 大雑把な計算
have one's thumb in a pie　事業に参加する
stick [stand] out like a sore thumb　ひどく目立つ
thumb a ride　ヒッチハイクする
thumb one's nose at　…を馬鹿にする
thumb through　パラパラめくる, さっと読む, 目を通す
turn down the [one's] thumb　不満の意を示す[表す], けなす
turn up the [one's] thumb　満足の意を示す[表す], ほめる
thumbs-down [thumbs down] 名　反対, 拒否, 拒絶, 不賛成, 不満足
give the thumbs-down on　…に反対する
thumbs-up [thumbs up] 名　賛成, 承諾, OK
thumbs-up sign　承諾の印
two thumbs up　大賛成

thwart 動 〈計画などを〉妨害する, 邪魔する, 阻止する, 阻む, 妨げる, くじく, 失敗させる, 挫折させる, 〈見通しなどを〉台なしにする, …の裏をかく
  thwart a coup attempt クーデター計画を失敗させる
  thwart aid activities 支援活動を妨げる
Tiananmen [Tian An Men] Square 〈中国の〉天安門広場(中国北京市にある旧清朝の皇城「紫禁城」(現在の博物館「故宮」)の正門にあたる天安門前の広場)
TIBOR [Tibor] 東京銀行間取引金利, 東京銀行間貸し手金利, タイボー (Tokyo interbank offered rateの略)
TICAD アフリカ開発会議 (Tokyo International Conference on African Development の略。アフリカの経済・社会開発問題を協議する国際会議で, 日本や国連などの主催で1993年から5年ごとに東京で開催。アフリカ諸国に対する経済援助のほかに, アフリカ諸国のオーナーシップ(自助努力)を提唱している)
ticker 名 株式相場表, 相場速報機, 心臓, 時計
  ticker tape 〈歓迎のための〉色テープ, 紙吹雪, 受信用紙テープ, チッカー・テープ(相場表示機から出てくるテープ)
  ticker-tape parade 紙吹雪の舞うパレード
ticket 名 伝票, 報告書, 取引, 取引額, 割当額, 券, 札, 交通違反カード, チケット, 党公認候補者, 党公認候補者名簿
  big-ticket item 高額商品, 高価格商品
  deposit ticket 預金伝票
  make the ticket 公認する
  piece work tickets 出来高報告書
  put candidates on the party ticket 党の公認候補を立てる
  sales ticket クレジット・カード
  ticket-day ロンドン証券取引所の規約規定の伝票回付日
  tickets at the colead level 共同主幹事の割当額
  write tickets 取引をまとめる
tide 名 潮流, 流れ, 時流, 傾向, 動向, 風潮, 形勢, 潮, 潮の干満, 〈季節などの〉移り変わり, 栄枯盛衰, 盛衰, 増減, 浮沈, 時期, 季節
  a neap tide 小潮
  a spring tide 大潮
  against the tide 時勢に逆らって, 時勢に抗して
  go with the tide 時勢に従う
  high [flood, full] tide 満潮
  low [ebb] tide 干潮
  the tide turns against 形勢が…に不利になる
  the tide turns in one's favor 形勢が…に有利になる
  wait for the favorable tide 潮時を待つ
  work double tides 昼夜兼行で働く, 大車輪で働く
tie 動 つなぐ, 結びつける, 連動させる, リンクさせる, 縛る, 結ぶ, 束縛する, 拘束する
  be tied to …に連動する, …と結びついている, …とリンクしている, …に関連する
  tied aid ひも付き援助, タイド・エイド
  tied crude oil ひも付き原油
  tied loan ひも付き援助, ひも付き融資, タイド・ローン
  tied store [shop] 連鎖店 (=chained store)
  tied transaction ひも付き取引, 連結取引
tie 名 つながり, 結びつき, 絆, 縁, 関係, ひも, 結び目, コード, ネクタイ, 足手まとい, 重荷, 同点, 引き分け, 再試合
  close ties to …と親しい間柄[関係]
  friendly ties 友好関係
tie up 動 提携する, 連携する, 協力する, 束縛する, 拘束する, 縛り上げる, 不通にする, 立ち往生させる
  be tied up in …につぎ込まれる
  be tied up with …と関連がある, …と関係[つながり]がある, …と結びついている, …と提携[合併]する, …で忙しい
  tie up a loan deal ローン契約を結ぶ
  tie up loose ends 残務整理をする, すっかり仕上げる, 解決をつける
tie-up 名 提携, 合併, 統合, 協力, 結びつき, 業務の一時停止, 業務停滞, 〈交通などの〉不通, 途絶, 停滞, ストライキ, タイアップ
  comprehensive tie-up 包括提携
  cross-sectoral tie-up 業態を超えての統合, 業態超え統合
  equity tie-up 資本提携
  sales tie-up 販売提携
  technical tie-up 技術提携
  tie-up agreement 提携契約, 業務提携契約
tier 名 段, 段階, 層, 階層, ティア
  first-tier bank 大手行, 上位行
  second-tier securities firm [house] 準大手の証券会社
  tier-one own funds 自己資本の基本的項目
  tier-two capital 補完的自己資本, 自己資本の

補完的項目, 二次資本（= secondary capital, Tier 2 capital）
top-tier stock 高業績株
two tier price 二重価格
tier-one capital ratio [**rate**] 中核的自己資本比率, ティア1自己資本比率（= core capital ratio, Tier 1 capital ratio）
TIFA 貿易投資枠組み協定, TIFA協定（**trade and investment framework agreement**の略）
tight 形 厳しい, きつい, 身動きできない, 狭い, 厄介な, 困難な, 厳重な, 厳格な, 徹底した, 緊張した,〈金融市場が〉逼迫した, 金詰まりの, 高利で金を借りにくい, 余裕がない, 品薄の, 入手しにくい,〈物が〉不足している, 接戦の, 勢力伯仲の, 互角の, …を通さない, 防[耐]…の
  be in a tight corner [**place, spot, squeeze**] 困難な状況にある, 進退きわまっている, 窮地に陥っている
  maintain short-term money rates at a tight level 短期市場金利を高めに維持する
  tight budget きつい予算, 緊縮予算, 予算の引締め, 予算不足
  tight credit 信用逼迫, 金融逼迫
  tight election 伯仲した選挙戦
  tight lending 貸し渋り, 貸出の抑制（= credit crunch）
  tight monetary policy 金融引締め政策, 金融緊縮政策, 高金利政策（= monetary restraint policy, monetary tightening policy, tight money policy）
  tight terms きつい条件, 厳しい条件
  water tight 防水の
tight money 金融引締め, 金融引締めの状態, 金融逼迫, 資金需要の逼迫, 高金利の金（= monetary restraint, monetary tightening）
  tight money policy 金融引締め政策, 高金利政策（= credit squeeze, monetary restraint policy, monetary tightening policy, tight monetary policy）
  tight money times 金融引締め期
tighten 動 強化する, 厳しくする, 厳格化する, 引き締める,〈金融を〉引き締める, 利上げする, 縮小する, 低下する, 硬直する
  tighten regulations on investment funds 投資ファンドの規制を強化する
  tighten security along the border 国境の安全を強化する
  tighten underwriting standards 引受け基準を強化する
  tighten up 厳しくする, 強化する, 固く[しっかり]締める, ぴんと張る
  tightened cash flow 資金繰りの悪化（= tightened liquidity）
  tightened sampling inspection 厳格抜取り検査
tightening 名 引締め, 金融引締め, 硬直, 緊張, 形（金融）引締めの, …の引締め
  credit tightening 信用引締め, 金融引締め
  financial tightening 金融引締め
  monetary tightening 金融引締め
  tightening bias 引締めのスタンス
tighter 形 一段と厳しい, 一段と逼迫した, 悪化した, …の強化[逼迫, 悪化]
  tighter lending standards 貸出基準の強化
  tighter liquidity 資金繰りの悪化, 資金需給の逼迫
  tighter regulations 規制強化
tightrope 名 ピンと張った綱, 綱渡り, 危ない橋, 難しい状況, タイトロープ
  tightrope diplomacy 綱渡り外交
  walk (on) a tightrope 綱渡りをする, 危ないことをする
time 名 時, 時間, 期間, 時期, 時代, 時勢, 機会, 期限, タイム
  access time アクセス時間
  closing time 閉店時間
  core time コア・タイム（フレックスタイム制で, 必ず勤務しなければならない時間帯）
  delivery time 納期
  do time 服役する, 刑期を務める
  down time [**downtime**] 故障時間, 機械停止時間, 使用不能時間
  fault time 故障時間
  in one's time 若いころ, 全盛期
  keep abreast with [**of**] **the times** 時代遅れにならないようにする
  keep up [**pace**] **with the times** 時勢について行く, 時勢に歩調を合わせる
  latency time 待ち時間
  local time 現地時間
  on [**in**] **one's own time** 勤務時間外に
  over time 長期にわたって
  reference time 基準時間
  time and a half 残業手当,〈時間外労働に対する〉5割増し賃金, 5割増し給
  time and motion study 時間作業研究,〈作業

効率向上の研究〉
time bomb 時限爆弾, 危険な状態, 不安な政情
time book 就業時間記録簿, 勤務時間記録簿
time clock タイム・レコーダー
time deposit 定期性預金, 定期預金, 貯蓄性預金（期限付き預金の総称）
time difference 時差
time lag [lapse] 時間的ずれ, 時間のずれ, タイムラグ
time of completion 完了期限
time scale 時間の尺度, 期間 (＝time frame)
time shared input/output system 時分割入出力システム
time shared system 時分割システム (＝time sharing system)
time to market 製品化までの時間
time zone 〈標準〉時間帯
times interest covered 利子補償率, 支払い利息負担能力倍率 (＝times interest earned ratio)
transfer time 転送時間
turnaround time 業績回復, 応答時間, 往復所要時間, ターンアラウンド・タイム
▶ When *times* get tough, the first things to get cut are advertising, expense accounts and travel expenses. 景気が悪くなるとまず削られるのは, 広告宣伝費と交際費, 交通費だ。

time frame [timeframe] 表示期間, 時間の制限, 時間枠, 時期, 期間, タイムリミット (＝time scale)
time horizon 運用期間, 将来展望, タイム・ホライゾン
  investors with a time horizon of 10 years 10年の運用期間を設定している投資家
time off [out] 休暇, 休憩, 休息時間, レクリエーションの時間 (＝time-out)
  get [have, take] time off from work 仕事を休んで休暇を取る
  take (the) time off to do 時間を割いて…する, …するのに時間を割く
  time off for good behavior 素行良好による（刑務所からの）仮出所
timeline 名 工程表, 日程, 期限 (＝time line)
  envisaged timeline 目標期限
  tentative timeline for …の暫定的な日程, …の暫定期限
timing 名 時期, 時間[時期・速度]の調整[選択], 好機の選択, 潮時, 頃合い, タイミング

tin ear 音痴
  tin ear for politics 政治音痴
tip 動 情報を伝える, 内報する, 密告する, 予想する, 有力候補として挙げる, 下馬評に挙げる, 折り紙をつけるる, チップをやる
  be tipped as …として取り沙汰される, …として折り紙をつけられる
  be tipped for …になると予想される, …になると見られている, …を得ると予想される
  tip off 内報する, 密告する, 警告する
tip 名 内部情報, 内報, 秘密情報, 未公開の重要情報, インサイド情報, 情報, たれ込み, 密告, 助言, ヒント, 秘訣, 方法, 妙計, よい思いつき, 〈競馬の〉予想
  get a tip that …というたれ込みがある
  miss one's tip 予想が外れる, 失敗する
  saving tips 節約の秘訣
  tips on …に関する情報
tipoff [tip-off] 名 秘密情報, 事前通報, 事前漏洩, 通報, 内部[事前]情報, 警告, 予想, ヒント
  in exchange for tipoffs on …に関する情報の事前漏洩
  obtain a tipoff from …から通報を受ける
  on a tipoff from an anonymous caller 匿名の人からの電話による通報を受けて
tippee trading 〈会社の株価などの〉内部情報の不正使用
tipster 名 内報者, 密告者, 情報提供者, たれ込み屋, 〈競馬などの〉予想屋
tit-for-tat 形 しっぺ返しの, 相互依存的な
TOB 株式公開買付け (take-over bid [take-over bid]の略)
  TOBとは ⊃ 自社株の消却のほか, 上場企業などが経営の支配権を強化したり子会社化したりする目的で, 証券取引所の市場外で3分の1超の株式（新株予約権や新株予約権付き社債などを含む）を買い付ける場合, あらかじめ買付け価格や買付け期間, 株数などを提示して, 株主に対して平等に売却の機会を与える制度。応募が取得目標の株式数に達しない場合, TOBは不成立となり, 応募された株式を返さなければならない。
TOEFL トーフル, 外国語としての英語学力テスト[英語能力検定試験] (Test [Testing] of English as a Foreign Languageの略)
TOEIC トーイック, 国際コミュニケーション英語能力テスト (Test of English for International Communicationの略)
Tokyo 名 日本, 日本政府, 東京

Tokyo Metropolitan Assembly　都議会
Tokyo metropolitan government　東京都
Tokyo Regional Taxation Office　東京国税局
Tokyo Stock Exchange　東京証券取引所, 東証《略 TSE》
Tokyo Stock Price Index　東証株価指数, TOPIX（＝Tokyo stock price index, Tokyo stock price index and average）

tolerance 名　寛大, 寛容, 許容, 許容誤差［限度］, 容認, 抵抗力, 忍耐, 忍耐力, 耐性
　constant risk tolerance　不変リスク許容度
　have a high tolerance to [for] stress　ストレスに強い
　loss tolerance percentage　損失受容率
　set tolerance limits　許容限度［許容水準］を設定する
　tolerance level of income　許容所得水準

toll 名　〈道路や橋の〉通行料, 通行料金,〈港などの〉使用料, 長距離電話料金, 犠牲, 犠牲者, 死傷者, 死傷者数, 損害, 損失
　take a heavy toll among　…の間に多数の犠牲を出す
　take a heavy toll on　…に大きな影響を及ぼす, …に大きな損害［打撃］を与える
　take its toll　損失をもたらす, 障害をもたらす
　toll booth [plaza]　料金所
　toll call　長距離電話, 長距離通話
　toll revenue　有料道路料金収入
　toll road　有料道路（＝tollway）

toll-free 形　無料電話の, フリーダイヤルの
　toll-free telephone inquiries　フリーダイヤルでの問い合わせ

tone 名　調子, 明暗, 濃淡, 傾向, 風潮, 気風, 基調, ムード, 地合い, 論調, 口調, 格調, 気品, 品位, 高低, トーン
　hesitant tone　様子見気分
　improved tone of the market　市場の地合いの好転
　in sharp tones　鋭い口調で
　lower the tone　その場の品位を下げる
　underlying tone　基調
　weak tone　弱含み

Tony (Awards) 名　トニー賞（米ブロードウェーで上演される演劇やミュージカルの中から優れた演技・演出をした者に毎年与えられる賞）

too big to fail　大き過ぎてつぶせない

too close to call　〈選挙が〉接戦で予測がつかない

tool 名　道具, 用具, 工具, 工作機械, 手段, 方法, 手法, ツール
　automatic operating tool　自動運用ツール
　debt management tool　負債管理の手法
　machine tool　工作機械
　management tool　管理手法, 管理の手段, 経営手法
　productivity tool　生産性向上の手段（＝tool for improving productivity）
　project management tool　プロジェクト管理ツール
　trade policy tool　通商政策の道具, 通商政策の手段

tooth 名　歯, 刃向かい, 反抗, 猛威, 威力, 鋭さ, 効力, 効果, 実効性, 好み, 嗜好, 食欲
　cut one's teeth on [in]　…の最初の経験を積む, …の仕事を学ぶ, …をしっかりと学ぶ
　fight tooth and nail against　…に対して全力で［力一杯, あらゆる手段を尽くして］戦う
　get [sink] one's teeth into　…に真剣［熱心］に取り組む, …に打ち込む, …を夢中でやる
　have teeth　効力がある, 効果を発揮する
　in the teeth of　…に逆らって, …を物ともしないで
　lack teeth　実効性を欠く
　put teeth in [into]　…の効力を強める
　set one's teeth against　…に対して抵抗［断固反対］する
　show one's teeth　敵意を示す, 威嚇する
　to the teeth　完全に, 十分に

toothless 形　鋭さに欠ける, 効果がない, 実効性がない, 決定的拘束力に欠けた

top 動　上回る, 突破する, …を越える, 首位になる, 首位を占める, トップになる, …を負かす［破る］

top 名　最高位, 最高点, 頂上, 首位, 首席, 最優先課題, 最優先事項, トップ
　be (at the) top of the agenda [list]　議題［表］の最優先事項, 最優先課題
　come to the top　名声を博する
　double top　2番天井
　from top to toe　すっかり, 徹底的に
　on top of　…の上に, …に加えて
　the top of the ... tree　…界の最高峰, …の世界の第一人者
　top-to-bottom communication　上［上位の者］から下［下位の者］への意思疎通

top 形　最高の, 最高位の, 最上位の, 首位の, 筆頭の, 最上の, 最高級の, 最大の, 最大限の, 上位

の, 上部の, 頂上の, 大手の, 最重要な, 最優先の, トップの

top banana 最重要人物, 主演喜劇役者[スター・コメディアン], 第一人者
top brass 幹部, 最高幹部, 高級幹部, 高級将校
top cadre 最高幹部
top copy 原本
top dog 勝利者, 勝者, 主要人物, 権力者, 最高実力者
top dollar 最高金額
top drawer 上流階級
top echelon 最高幹部, 上層部
top eliminator 最優秀選手, 最有望選手
top executive 最高経営者, 最高執行部, 最高経営幹部, 経営幹部, 経営首脳, 経営者, 経営トップ (top executivesは「首脳陣, 経営幹部」の意)
top machine 首脳陣, 最高幹部
top management 最高経営者, 最高管理層, 最高経営管理者層, 経営首脳陣, 首脳陣, 首脳部, トップ・マネジメント
top priority 最優先課題, 最優先事項, 最優先権
top secret 極秘, 極秘事項
top-tier stock 高業績株

top-down 形 上から下への, 上から下へ組織された, 天下りの, 中央集権的な, 上位下達の, 上位下達方式の, トップダウンの

top-down approach 天下り方式, 中央集権的な管理方法, トップダウン方式
top-down approach to investment [investing] 投資のトップダウン方式, トップダウン式投資 (景気判断から投資対象の産業部門の決定, 企業の選択の順で銘柄を決める投資戦略)

top-of-the-line 形 最高級の, 最新式の, 最新鋭の, 高性能の (=state-of-the-art)

topic 名 話題, 論題, テーマ, 要旨, 総論, 見出し, 項目, 事項, トピック

current topics 時事問題, 最新の話題, 今日の話題, 現在の話題
topic A 最大の話題, 本日の重要ニュース, 第一面に載せる連載物
topics of the day 時事問題

topicalities 名 時事問題

TOPIX 東証株価指数, トピックス (Tokyo Stock Price Indexの略)

> **東証株価指数** ⊃ 東証一部の時価総額を加重平均して算出する. 日経平均がハイテク株の組入れ比重が高いためにハイテク株の動きに左右されやすいのに対して, 東証株価指数 (TOPIX) は銀行株など時価総

額の大きい株価の動きに敏感.

topple 動 〈政府を〉倒す, 転覆させる, 追放する, 放逐する, 〈権力の座などから〉引き下ろす

be toppled from the dictator's position 独裁者の地位から引きずり落とされる
topple the government by a coup クーデターで政府を倒す

topsider 名 高官, 首脳部, 上層部の人
White House topsiders ホワイトハウスの上層部

Tory 名 〈英〉保守党員
Tory party 保守党

tossup 名 五分五分の見込み

total 名 総額, 総量, 総計, 合計, 全部
a total of 合計…, 総額…
actual total 実際の累計額
balance sheet total 貸借対照表合計, 総資産
control total 照合合計
cumulative total 累計
grand total 累計, 総計
ground total 単純集計
in total 合計して, 全部で
intermediate total 中間合計, 小計
minor total 小計
net total 純計
running total 現在合計高
spending totals 歳出
sum total 総計

total 形 全体の, 全部の, 総計の, 合計の, 全体的な, 完全な, まったくの
total capitalization 総資本
total compensation 給与総額
total cost of ownership 企業情報システムの総保有コスト, 総合保有コスト《略 **TCO**》(TCO=システム部門や各社員のハード, ソフト購入費用+情報システムの維持管理費, 運用費, 教育・研修費など)
total emissions volume 排出総量
total income 総収入, 総所得
total loss 全損
total management 総合管理
total net assets 純資産総額
total production 総生産
total turnover 総売上高
total war 総力戦, 全面戦争

totalitarian 名 全体主義者, 形 全体主義の
totalitarian dictatorship 全体主義的独裁国家

touch 動 〈…に〉触れる, 〈…と〉接触する, 〈…に〉言及する, 〈…を〉取り上げる, 〈…に〉影響を及ぼす,

touch 〈…にまで〉達する, 寄港する
- **touch at** …に寄港する, 〈船が〉…に立ち寄る
- **touch bottom** 底に届く, 底入れする, 底を打つ, 最悪［最低］の状態になる
- **touch close the historical high** 過去最高に近づく
- **touch down** 着陸する, タッチダウンする
- **touch off** 誘発する, 触発する, 引き起こす, 爆発させる
- **touch on [upon]** …に触れる, 簡単に言及する［述べる］, …に関係する
- **touch up** 最後の仕上げをする, …を修正する, …を直す

touch 名 連絡, 接触, 感覚, 感触, 感じ, 手ごたえ, 筆致, 手法, 技法, 仕上がり, 仕上げ, 少量, 簡単に金を出す人, 触診, タッチ
- **be [keep, stay] in touch with** …に通じている, …をよく知っている
- **be out of [lose] touch with** …と連絡が途切れる, …と連絡していない, …に通じていない
- **get in touch with** …と連絡をとる
- **lose touch with** …と接触がなくなる, …と接触を失う, …との交流がなくなる, …に関心を持たなくなる

touch and go 不安定な状態, 一触即発の状態, 不安な［危ない, きわどい］状況, きわどさ, 生死の瀬戸際

touch-and-go 形 不安定な, 不安な, 一触即発の, 危ない, 危険な, きわどい, 生死の瀬戸際の, 大雑把な, ぞんざいな

tough 形 ひどい, つらい, 苦しい, 耐えがたい, 嫌な, 困難な, 骨の折れる, 難しい, 厳しい, 手ごわい, 粘り強い, 頑丈な, 丈夫な, たくましい, 強硬な, 激しい, 激烈な, 乱暴な, 粗野な, 物騒な, 犯罪の多い, 凶悪な, 堅い, 固い, 折れない, 信じがたい, 理解しがたい, タフな, タフ
- **get tough with** …に厳しくする［厳しく対処する］, …に強硬な態度を取る, …に強硬姿勢で臨む, …に食い下がる, 〈人に〉つらく当たる
- **have a tough time** 苦しい時を過ごす, 苦境に立つ
- **make a tough break** ひどい失態［へま, 失策］をしでかす, 大失態を演じる
- **take a tough line** 強硬路線を取る
- **tough line on** …に対する強硬姿勢

toughen 動 強くする, 強化する, 頑丈にする, 困難にする
- **toughen restrictions on** …に対する規制を強化する
- **toughening competition** 熾烈な競争

tourism 名 観光, 観光旅行, 観光事業, ツーリズム

tout 動 勧誘する, うるさく勧める, しつこく求める, 大げさに宣伝する, 〈主義, 主張を〉掲げる, 標榜する, 情報を提供する［探る］, 〈製品などを〉売り込む, 持ち上げる, 大いにほめる, ほめそやす
- **tout for business** 商売の宣伝をする
- **tout for orders** うるさく［しつこく］注文を求める
- **tout one's attractiveness** …の魅力を売り込む
- **tout one's power** …の力を誇示する

tout ensemble 全体的効果

toxic assets 不良資産

TPA 通商一括交渉権 (Trade Promotion Authorityの略。ファスト・トラック(fast track：速い道筋)と呼ばれ, ブッシュ政権は2002年にTPA法を成立させたが, 07年6月末に期限切れとなった。「通商一括交渉権」は米大統領権限で, 外国政府と結んだ通商合意を, 大統領は議会に対して無修正で承認するよう要求できる)

traceability 名 追跡可能性, 生産履歴管理, 履歴管理, 〈測定器の〉標準追遡性, トレーサビリティ (商品の生産情報から製造, 加工, 流通などの過程をさかのぼって参照できる仕組み)

traceable 形 追跡可能な

track 動 調べる, 調査する, 〈原因などを〉突き止める, 追う, 追跡する, 追求する, 跡を残す, 跡をつける, 能力別にクラス分けする

track 名 進路, 行路, 線路, 走路, 軌道, 足跡, 痕跡, 航跡, 跡, 能力別クラス編成, トラック
- **be on the inside track** 有利である, 有利な立場［地位］を得る, インコースを走る (＝have [get] the inside track)
- **be on the right track [lines]** 思ったとおりに行っている［進んでいる］, 間違いなく［正しく］進んでいる
- **fast track** 突貫工事, 速い道筋, ファスト・トラック (⇒fast-track, TPA)
- **full-fledged recovery track** 本格回復の軌道
- **have a one-track [single-track] mind** いつも同じように考える, いつも同じ考え方をする, ワンパターン思考である
- **in the track of** …の例にならって, …の途中で
- **keep track of** …の跡をつける, …の経過を追う, …の状態を把握する, …を見失わない
- **the right side of the (railroad) tracks** 富裕地区

track record 業績記録, 競技場での記録, 実績, 業績
track [tracking] system 能力別クラス編成方式 [制度] (＝ability grouping, streaming)
trade 動 売買する, 取引する, 商う, 商売する, 交易する, 交換する, 〈冗談などを〉交わす, 〈砲火を〉応酬する, 〈選手を〉トレードする
trade above par 額面以上で取引される
trade away 売り払う, 売る, 〈権利などを〉手放す
trade down 〈下取りに出して〉買い換える, 値を下げる
trade fire with …と交戦する
trade in 下取りに出す
trade off …と交換する, …と相殺する
trade on [upon] …に付け込む, …を利用する, …を売り物にする
trade up 高い物と買い換える[交換する]
trade within a narrow range もみ合いが続く
trade 名 貿易, 交易, 通商, 取引, 商売, 売買, 職業, 同業者, 顧客(customers), 得意先, 取引先, 〈政党間の〉取引, 妥協, 談合 下取り, 交換, トレード
bilateral trade 二国間貿易
block trade 大口取引
Board of Trade 〈英〉商務省, 〈米国の〉商工会議所
Committee For a National Trade-Policy 〈米〉国家貿易政策委員会
commodity terms of trade 商品交易条件
Comprehensive Trade Act 包括通商法
directional trade 方向性取引
domestic [home] trade 国内商業
execute a large trade 大口取引を執行する
external trade 対外貿易
fair trade 公正取引
international trade fair 国際見本市
International Trade Organization 国際貿易機構《略 ITO》
market-neutral trade 市場中立取引
merchandise trade モノの貿易, 財の貿易, 財の輸出入, 貿易取引
multilateral trade 多角貿易
new global trade rules 新たな国際貿易ルール
registered trade mark 登録商標 (＝registered trademark)
trade account 貿易収支
trade agreement [accord] 通商協定, 通商条約, 貿易協定, 取引契約, 〈労使の〉団体協約, 労働契約, 労働協約

trade association 同業者団体, 同業組合, 産業団体, 事業者団体, 商工団体
trade balance 貿易収支 (＝balance of trade)
trade ban 国際取引禁止, 取引禁止, 禁輸
trade barrier 貿易障壁
trade book 一般書, 大衆本, 大衆版, 流布版
trade conflict 貿易摩擦, 通商摩擦 (＝trade friction)
trade cycle 景気変動, 景気循環 (＝business cycle)
trade deficit 貿易赤字, 貿易収支の赤字 (＝trade gap)
trade dispute 通商摩擦, 貿易摩擦, 貿易紛争 (＝trade friction)
trade edition 普及版, 市販版, 大衆版
trade expansion 貿易拡大
trade fair 見本市
trade friction 貿易摩擦, 通商摩擦 (＝trade conflict, trade dispute)
trade gap 貿易赤字, 貿易収支の赤字, 貿易欠損, 輸入超過 (＝trade deficit)
trade imbalance 貿易不均衡, 輸出入不均衡
trade journal [magazine] 業界誌
trade management agreement 貿易管理協定
trade name 商号, 屋号, 社名, 商標, 商標名 (brand name)
trade organization 同業者組織
trade pact 貿易協定, 通商協定
trade paper 業界紙, 業界新聞
trade partner 貿易相手国 (＝trading partner)
trade policy 通商政策
trade price 卸値
Trade Representative 〈米〉通商代表
trade round 貿易交渉
trade route 通商航路
trade sanctions 貿易制裁, 貿易制裁措置, 制裁措置
trade show 封切映画試写会
trade terms 貿易条件, 取引条件, 貿易用語
trade troubleshooter 貿易問題対策特使
trade union 労働組合 (＝labor union)
trade usage 取引慣行, 商慣習 (＝usage of trade)
trade war 貿易戦争
Trades Union Congress 労働組合会議《略 TUC》(英最大の労働組合の中央組織)

yen-denominated trade　円建て貿易
trade surplus　貿易黒字, 貿易収支の黒字
（＝merchandise trade surplus：輸出額－輸入額＝貿易黒字）
　chronic trade surplus　慢性的な貿易黒字, 貿易黒字の慢性化
　current account and trade surpluses　貿易黒字と経常黒字
　dollar-based customs-cleared trade surplus　ドル表示の通関ベース貿易黒字
　FOB trade surplus　貿易黒字（FOBベース）
　invisible trade surplus　貿易外取引の黒字
　massive [considerable, large] trade surplus　大幅貿易黒字, 巨額の貿易黒字
　merchandise trade surplus　財の貿易黒字
　recycle trade surpluses　貿易黒字を還流させる
　visible trade surplus　貿易収支の黒字
　yen-denominated trade surplus　円表示の貿易黒字
trader 名　証券業者, 売買担当者, ディーラー, 貿易業者, 取引業者, 同業者, 業者, 市場関係者, トレーダー
　bearish traders　弱気筋
　bullish traders　強気筋
　commodity trader　商品取引業者
　contraband trader　密輸商
　export trader　輸出業者
　forex trader　為替トレーダー（＝forex dealer）
　free trader　自由貿易主義者
　general trader　一般貿易業者
　individual trader　個人トレーダー
　international speculative traders　海外投機筋
　online trader　オンライン・トレーダー, ネット・トレーダー
　retail trader　小売業者
　wholesale trader　卸売業者
trading 名　取引, 売買, 商業, 貿易, 営業, トレーディング
　day trading　デイ・トレーディング
　insider trading　インサイダー取引
　margin trading　信用取引, 証拠金取引
　online trading　オンライン取引
　option trading　オプション取引
　proprietary trading system　私設取引システム
　public trading　公募取引
　real time option trading　リアルタイム・オプション取引
　stock trading　株式売買, 株式取引, 株取引
　regulation of trading　売買規制
　trading area　商圏
　trading asset　事業資産, 販売資産
　trading day　営業日
　trading firm [house]　商社, 商事会社
　trading hours　取引時間, 取引途中
　trading market　流通市場
　trading network　取引ネットワーク
　trading partner　取引先, 貿易相手国, 貿易のパートナー（＝trade partner）
　trading volume　売買高, 売買額, 出来高, 売買株数, 売上高, 取引量
trading limit　取引制限
　daily trading limit　日々の取引制限, 値幅制限（＝daily limit, daily price limit）
>値幅制限 ⊃ 日本の株式市場では, 予想外の暴騰, 暴落で市場が混乱するのを防ぐため, 個別銘柄の1日の株価変動幅が, 株価水準（前日の終値）から上下一定の範囲に制限されている。買い注文が殺到して値幅制限の上限まで達すれば「ストップ高」となり, 逆に売り注文が殺到して値幅制限の下限まで下落すれば「ストップ安」となる。

traffic 動　不正に取引する, 違法取引する, 密売を行う
traffic 名　交通, 通行, 交通量, 車の流れ, 往来, 人通り,〈不正・不法の〉取引, 密売買, 売買, 輸送,〈意見の〉交換, 意見交換, 情報の量, 通信量, 記事の量, データ量, 接続者数, トラヒック［トラフィック］
　freight traffic　貨物輸送
　long-distance traffic　長距離輸送
　traffic accident [smashup]　交通事故
　traffic calming　スピード制限策, 徐行補助装置
　traffic circle　環状交差点, ロータリー（roundabout）
　traffic court　交通裁判所
　traffic island　〈道路の〉安全地帯, 分離帯
　traffic pattern　離着陸コース,〈人や車の〉交通パターン
　traffic volume　交通量, 通信量, トラヒック量
　traffic warden　交通監視員, 駐車［交通］違反取締官
trafficking 名　不正取引, 密売買
trail 動　〈人に〉負けている［遅れをとる］, …を予告編で宣伝する, 次第に小さくなる［弱くなる］
training 名　訓練, 教育, 研修, トレーニング
　career-focused training　職業訓練

field training　現場訓練, 実地訓練, 現場研修
public vocational training　公共職業訓練
retraining　再研修, 再教育
training at hospitals　臨床研修
training camp　研修キャンプ
training expense　研修費, 訓練費
workplace training　現場訓練, 現場教育, 現場研修, 企業実習

trans fats　トランス脂肪酸

transaction 名　取引, 取扱い, 処理, 業務処理, 業務, 商取引, 売買, 和解, 示談, 法律行為
　capital transaction　資本取引
　circular sales transaction　循環取引
　encrypted transaction　暗号化された取引
　financial transaction　金融取引, 財務取引
　foreign currency transaction　外貨建て取引
　invisible current transaction　貿易外経常取引
　invisible transaction　貿易外取引, サービス取引
　speculative transaction　投機的取引
　spot transaction　直物取引, 現物取引, 直物為替取引
　swap transaction　スワップ取引
　visible current transaction　貿易経常取引
　visible transaction　貿易取引, 商品取引

transfer 動　移転する, 移す, 移管する, 転送する, 配置転換する, 譲渡する, 名義を書き換える, 振り込む, 送金する, 繰り入れる
▶ If golden shares held by a friendly company are *transferred* to another party, such shares could be *transferred* again to a hostile bidder.　友好的な企業が保有する黄金株を第三者に譲渡した場合, その黄金株はまた敵対的買収者に譲渡される可能性もある.

transfer 名　〈財産などの〉譲渡, 移転, 〈権限などの〉委譲, 継承, 〈名義の〉書換え, 転送, 転任, 配属, 配置転換, 出向, 振替, 振込み, 送金, 繰入れ
　account transfer　口座振替
　business transfer　営業譲渡, 企業移転 (＝transfer of business)
　ownership transfer　所有移転
　private transfers　民間移転収支
　reversal of the transfer　復帰人事
　stock [share] transfer　株式の名義書換, 株式譲渡
　technology transfer　技術移転 (＝transfer of technology)
　telegraphic transfer　電信送金, 電信為替
　transfer of sovereignty　主権移譲 (＝transfer of power)
　transfer of technical skills　技能継承
　transfer pricing taxation system　移転価格税制
　transfer tax　譲渡税, 財産移転税

transform 動　変える, 変換する, 変形させる, 変質させる, 変化を起こさせる, 変身する, 変化する, 変貌する, 〈電流を〉変圧する
▶ Machine-tool techniques are used to *transform* metal, ceramics and other raw materials into products with various shapes.　工作機械の技術は, 金属やセラミックなどの原材料を(用途に応じて)さまざまな形状の製品に作り上げるのに用いられている.

transformation 名　変化, 変形, 変貌, 変質, 変換, 転換, 転化, 移行, 変革, 改革, 事業再編
　transformation into a holding company　持ち株会社への移行
　transformation of the markets　市場の変質
　transformation of value　価値の転換

transition 名　移行, 推移, 変遷, 経過, 移行時, 移行期間, 過渡期
　be in transition　過渡期にある
　generational transitions　世代交代 (＝transitions to the next generation)
　make the transition from A to B　AからBに移行させる
　transition period　過渡期, 移行期, 移行期間, 米政権移行期間(11月上旬の大統領選挙日から翌年1月20日の大統領就任式までの政権交代の引継ぎ期間)
　transition team　米政権移行チーム

translate 動　換算する, 翻訳する, 変換する, 移行する

translation 名　換算, 変換, 調整, 解釈, 翻訳
　automatic language translation　自動翻訳, 機械翻訳 (＝machine translation, mechanical translation)
　currency translation　外貨換算
　translation adjustment　換算調整, 換算調整勘定, 外貨換算調整勘定 (＝foreign currency translation adjustment)
　translation gain or loss　為替差損益, 換算差損益 (＝translation gains and losses)

transmission 名　伝送, 送信, 伝達, 伝導, 伝染, 送電, 放送, 放送番組, 伝動装置, 変速機, トランスミッション
　automatic transmission　自動伝動装置, 自動変速機

data transmission　データ伝送, データ通信
growth transmission　成長伝達, 成長伝播
transmission capacity　伝送容量
transmission facility　送電施設
transmission gear　伝動装置
transmission mechanism　〈政策の〉効果波及経路
transmission right on a cabled line　有線送信権
transmission speed [rate]　伝送速度, 通信速度

transmit 動　送信する, 伝送する, 送る, 伝える, 放送する, 知らせる
▶ Some information is *transmitted* in real time globally.　情報の一部は, リアルタイムでグローバルに伝達される.

transparency [transparence] 名　透明, 透明性, 透明度, 透かし模様, 明白なこと
cost structure transparency　コスト構造の透明性
▶ *Transparency* and accountability became key words for business operations.　透明性と説明責任が, 企業経営のキーワードになった.

transparent 形　透明な, 透き通る, 透き通るような, 透き通って見える, 透けて見える, 薄い, 澄んだ, 見え透いた, すぐ見抜ける, 明らかな, 明白な, 平明な, 分かりやすい, 明快な, 率直な, 正直な, 気取らない
transparent decision　理解できる決定 [判断]
transparent discourse　明快な論文
transparent excuses　見え透いた言い訳 [口実]
transparent (writing) style　平明な文体

transplant 動　移植する, 移住させる
transplant 名　移植, 海外現地生産工場
a bone-marrow transplant　骨髄移植
the Organ Transplant Law　臓器移植法
undergo transplants of cells　細胞の移植を受ける

transportation 名　輸送, 運送, 運輸, 輸送機関, 輸送手段, 交通機関, 交通手段, 輸送料金, 輸送料, 運賃, 輸送許可書
a means of transportation　移動手段
intermodal transportation　複合一貫輸送
ocean transportation　海上輸送
public transportation　公共交通機関
transportation authority　交通局
transportation cost　運送費, 輸送費用, 輸送コスト, 運賃（＝transportation charge, transportation expense）

Transportation Department　〈米〉運輸省
transportation equipment　輸送機器, 運送設備
transportation facility　輸送施設
transportation information system　運輸情報システム
transportation route　輸送ルート
transportation strike　交通機関のスト

transsexual 名　性転換者
transsexual athlete　性転換選手
undergo transsexual operation [surgery]　性転換手術を受ける

trap 動　罠に掛ける, 閉じ込める, 動けなくする, 抜け出せなくする, 身動きがとれなくする

trap 名　罠, 落とし穴, 策略, 計略, 窮地, 難局, スピード違反車監視所, 〈ゴルフの〉バンカー, トラップ
fall into the trap of　…の罠に陥る
fall right [straight] into one's trap　…の策略にはまってしまう
walk into a trap　罠に掛かる

trapped 形　捕われの, 閉じ込められる, 抜け出せない

treadmill 名　足踏みマシーン

treasury 名　金庫, 国庫, 資金, 基金, 財源, 歳入, 財務
government treasury bills　短期国債
government treasury charge　国庫負担金
national treasury　国庫
national treasury disbursement　国庫支出金
treasury bill　〈米〉財務省短期証券 [政府短期証券, 短期国債, Tビル], 〈英〉大蔵省証券
treasury bond market　国債市場
treasury investment and loan　財政投融資
treasury operation　財務運用
treasury purchases　自己株式購入
treasury surplus　国庫余裕金

Treasury 名　〈米〉財務省, 〈英〉大蔵省, 米国債《略 T》
Lords of the Treasury　〈英〉大蔵委員会委員
the First Lord of the Treasury　〈英〉大蔵委員会委員長
Treasuries　〈米〉財務省証券, 米国債, 米国債相場（＝Treasury securities）
Treasury Bench　〈英下院の〉大臣席
Treasury bill　〈米〉財務省短期証券, Tビル
Treasury Board　〈英〉大蔵委員会
Treasury bond　〈米〉政府長期証券, 財務省長期証券, 財務省証券, 米国債

Treasury bond yield 〈米〉財務省長期証券の利回り
Treasury Department 〈米〉財務省
Treasury market 〈米〉国債市場, 米国債相場, 米債券相場
Treasury note 〈米〉財務省証券, 財務省中期証券, 中期国債, Tノート(「米財務省中期証券」は, 利息が年2回支払われる利付き証券(coupon issues)のこと)
Treasury official 財務省高官
treasury secretary [Treasury Secretary] 〈米〉財務長官
treasury stock 金庫株, 自社株, 自己株式, 社内株 (＝reacquired shares, reacquired stock, repurchased shares, repurchased stock, treasury shares:「金庫株」は, 株価の低迷や乱高下を防ぐため, 企業が自社株を買い戻して, 買い取った株を保有し, 相場が持ち直したときに売ることができる株のこと. 自己株式に議決権と配当受取権はない)
U.S. Treasuries 〈米〉国債, 米財務省証券 (＝U.S. Treasury securities；⇒status)
treat oneself to …を楽しむ
treatment 名 処理, 取扱い, 扱い方, 待遇, 措置, 治療, 治療法, 処置, 手当て, トリートメント
equal national treatment 内国民待遇 (＝national treatment)
favorable treatment to foreign companies 外資優遇策
most favored-nation treatment 最恵国待遇
preference treatment tariff 特恵関税
sewage treatment 下水処理, 下水の浄化
special treatment 特別待遇
surgical treatment 外科治療
tax treatment of transactions 取引の税務上の扱い
treaty 名 条約, 条約議定書, 盟約, 盟約書, 協約, 協定, 取決め, 約束, 契約, 約定, 交渉, 協議
be in treaty with …と交渉中である
climate change treaty 気候変動条約
commercial treaty 通商条約 (＝treaty of commerce)
double taxation treaty 二重課税防止条約
Japan-China Peace and Friendship Treaty 日中平和友好条約
Lisbon Treaty 〈EUの〉リスボン条約
Maastricht Treaty マーストリヒト条約
make a treaty with …と条約を結ぶ

nuclear nonproliferation treaty 核拡散防止条約
Patent Cooperation Treaty 特許協力条約
peace treaty 平和条約, 講和条約
ratify the treaty 条約を批准する
security treaty 安全保障条約
tax treaty 租税条約
trend 名 傾向, 動向, 基調, 趨勢, 大勢, 地合い, 市場の足取り, 推移, 流れ, 潮流, 波, 現象, 流行, トレンド
be above trend トレンドを上回る
bear trend 弱気トレンド
deflationary trend デフレ傾向, 物価下落傾向
demographic trend 人口動態
earnings trend 収益動向
secular trend 長期的な傾向, 長期傾向, 長期トレンド
trend analysis 趨勢分析, 時系列分析, トレンド分析
trend effect 趨勢効果
trend model 傾向型モデル
trend (percentage) method 趨勢法
trend rate 潜在成長率, 傾向率, 傾向値, トレンドの水準
trend toward service economy サービス経済化, サービス化
trendsetting [trend-setting] 形 流行の先端を行く, 流行を作る, 流行の傾向を決める, 時代の流れを決める, 方向[趨勢]を決める, …の誘導目標
trendsetter 名 先導役, トレンドセッター
trial 名 試み, 試験, 試用, 試運転, 試験期間, 試用期間, 試練, 苦しみ, 頭痛の種, 苦難, 裁判, 公判, 正式事実審理, 審理, レース, 競技会, 予選, トライアル, 形 裁判の, 公判の, 予審の, 試しの, 試験的な, 予選の
civil trial 民事裁判
clinical trials 臨床実験
closed trial 非公開裁判
court trial 裁判 (＝court actions)
criminal trial 刑事裁判
field trials 実地試験
on a trial basis 試験的に, 実験的に
open trial 公開裁判
pretrial (summary) procedures 公判前整理手続き
stand [go on] trial for …のかどで裁判を受ける, …の罪で裁判を受ける

trial and error 試行錯誤
trial balance 試算表
trial balloon 気象観測気球
trial by jury 陪審裁判, 陪審審理
trial calendar 開廷予定表
trial court 事実審判所, 第一審裁判所
trial deliberations 審理
trial judge 事実審判官, 第一審裁判官
trial jury 審理陪審, 公判陪審,〈12名で構成される〉小陪審 （＝petit jury）
trial kit 試供品, 試供品セット
trial lawyer 法廷弁護士
trial rate 当初使用率
trial run 試験, 実験, 試運転, 試乗, 試行, 試行テスト, 予行演習, テスト・ラン （＝test run）
trial session 公判
trial value 試算価値
trials and tribulations 苦難, 困難

triangle merger 三角合併 （＝triangular merger：買収する企業が, その子会社と被買収企業と合併させて傘下に収めるM&Aの手法。会社法制定で, 2007年度から合併の対価として, 買収側の親会社の株式を被買収企業の株主に渡すこと（株式交換）になっている）

trickle 名 しずく, したたり, 細流, 少量, 少数, わずかの動き, まばらの状態
  trickle charger 細流充電装置
  trickle irrigation 点滴灌漑, 細流灌漑

trickle-down 形 浸透理論に関する, おこぼれ理論式の, 浸透の
  trickle-down effect 通貨浸透効果, トリクル効果
  trickle-down strategy 浸透戦略
  trickle-down theory 通貨浸透説, おこぼれ理論

trickle-up 形 トリクルアップ理論の, トリクルアップ理論に基づく, 吸い上げの, 逆浸透の

trigger 動 引き起こす, …のきっかけを作る, …のきっかけとなる, …の引き金となる, …を誘発する, 触発する, …を促す, 発射する, 発する, 発砲する, 発動する, 動かす
  a financial sector-triggered recession 金融不況
  a triggered transaction 起因となる取引
  trigger a flight to quality 質への逃避のきっかけとなる

trigger 名 起爆装置, 引き金, きっかけ, 誘因, 起爆剤,〈コンピュータがある処理をする前の〉同期信号, トリガー回路, トリガー
  be quick on the trigger 〈反応が〉素早い, すばしこい, 抜け目がない
  trigger effect 引き金効果
  trigger price 指標価格, 輸入最低基準価格, 発動価格, 引き金価格, トリガー価格（「トリガー価格」は, ダンピングに基づく鉄鋼の大量流入を防ぐため, 米政府が1978年に採用した価格のこと。このトリガー価格を下回る価格の鉄鋼輸入に対しては, 即座にダンピング調査が実施される）
  trigger price mechanism トリガー価格方式, トリガー価格制《略 TPM》
  trigger pricing トリガー価格
  trigger system 〈ミサイル弾頭の〉起爆装置

trilateral 形 3者間の, 3者構成の, 3極の, 3角形の, 3角の
  Trilateral Commission 3極委員会, 3者委員会, 日米欧委員会
  trilateral cooperation 3角協力
  Trilateral Coordination and Oversight Group meeting 〈日米韓の〉3国政策調整会合《略 TCOG》
  trilateral meeting 3者会議, 3か国会談
  trilateral relations 3者間の関係, 3者協力, 3者間協力
  trilateral trade 3角貿易, 3極貿易 （＝triangular trade）
  trilateral trade negotiation 3極貿易交渉

trilateralism 名 3者相互協力, 相互経済協力促進政策

trilemma 名 三重苦, トリレンマ （⇒dilemma, quatlemma）
  the trilemma of inflation, recession and balance of payments problems インフレ, 不況, 国際収支問題の三重苦

trim 動 削減する, 縮小する, 切り詰める,〈人員などを〉整理する, 引き下げる, 減額する
  trim affiliates 関連会社を整理する
  trim costs 費用を削減する
  trim down debt 債務を削減する
  trim the number of employees 従業員を削減する, 従業員の人員整理をする
  trim three excesses of debt, workforces and facilities 債務, 人員, 設備という三つの過剰を削減する

trinity reform plan 三位一体改革案 （＝a three-part reform package）

trip 名 旅行, 旅, 外出, 往復, 移動, 交通, 過ち,

つまずき, 強烈な経験, 幻覚経験, 幻覚症状［期間］, 妄想, トリップ
business trip 商用旅行
daily trip 毎日の通勤
day trip 日帰り旅行
delivery trip 配達回り
ego trip 自己満足の行為, 自己中心的な振る舞い, 独善的な考え, 自己陶酔
trip distribution 分布交通量
trip generation 発生交通量, トリップ発生量
trip restraint 交通抑制
trip through bankruptcy court 破産手続き
trip of the tongue 失言, 言い間違い（＝slip of the tongue）

trip up つまずく, 間違い［へま］をする, 失敗する, つまずかせる, 失敗させる,〈…の〉揚げ足をとる
trip ... up …をつまずかせる, …に間違い［へま, 失敗］をさせる
trip up over [on] …で間違いをする, …で失敗する

tripartite 形 3者間の, 3社間の, 3国間の, 3者［3国］から成る, 三位一体の
tripartite coalition government 3者連立政権
tripartite contribution 3者負担
tripartite division 3分割
tripartite partnership 3国間パートナーシップ
tripartite reforms 三位一体改革
tripartite treaty 3国間条約

triple 動 3倍になる, 3倍増となる, 3倍にする
triple 形 三つの, 3位の, 3重の, 3倍の, 3部から成る, 3国間の, トリプル
triple A issuer トリプルA格の発行体
triple alliance 3者同盟, 3国同盟
triple bill 〈映画などの〉3本立て
triple digits 3桁
triple equilibrium 3重均衡
triple nine 99.9, 純度99.9%の金

troika 名 3巨頭, 3頭制, 3頭政治, トロイカ方式, トロイカ

troop 名 部隊, 兵隊, 軍隊

tropical 形 熱帯の
tropical cyclones 熱帯性サイクロン

trouble 名 困難, 苦悩, 労苦, 悩み, 悩み事, 心配, 経営不振, 経営破綻, 経営難, 経営危機, 迷惑, 厄介, 骨折り, 苦心, 問題点, 欠点, 短所,〈体や機械の〉不調, 故障, 騒ぎ, もめごと, 内紛, 紛争, 動乱, 争議, トラブル

be in trouble 経営不振［経営難, 経営破綻］に陥っている, 経営破綻の可能性がある, 経営が行き詰まる, 危ない［危険な］状況にある, 困っている, もめている, 検挙されている,〈未婚女性が〉妊娠している
borrow trouble 取り越し苦労をする
domestic troubles 家庭のいざこざ
get [run] into trouble 苦しい事態に追い込まれる, 経営難に陥る, 困難に陥る, 面倒なことになる, ごたごたを引き起こす, しかられる, 罰せられる
get out of trouble いざこざから抜け出る, 罰を免れる
give a person trouble 人に迷惑をかける（＝get a person into trouble）
give oneself trouble 骨を折る, 尽力する
go to the trouble of doing わざわざ…する
have trouble in …が困難だ
labor trouble 労働紛争, 労働争議
look [ask] for trouble 軽率なことをして災難を招く, 自ら災難を招く, 余計なことをする
make trouble 騒ぎを起こす, 紛争を起こす
make trouble for …を困らせる, …を苦しめる
meet trouble halfway 取り越し苦労をする
share trouble 株式事故
social trouble 社会問題
trouble shooter 仲介役, 紛争仲裁者, 修理係
trouble spot 紛争地域, 問題のよく起こる場所

troubled 形 経営不振の, 経営破綻した, 経営難の, 経営難に陥った, 経営危機に陥った, 問題のある, 問題の多い, もめごとの多い, 荒れた, 騒然とした, 不安［心配］そうな
be troubled with …で困っている
troubled debt 不良債権
troubled state-backed mortgage firms 経営不振の政府系住宅金融会社

trough 名 景気の谷, 景気の底, 最悪期
cyclical trough 景気の底, 景気サイクル［景気循環］の底, 景気の谷
fall to a trough 底を打つ
get out of a trough 底から抜け出る, 最悪期を脱出する
Juglar trough ジュグラー循環の谷
Kitchin trough キチン循環の谷
reach a trough 底を打つ（＝reach the recession trough）
the peak and trough of the business cycle 景気の山と谷

truancy 名 不登校, 無断欠席, ずる休み

truce 名 休戦, 停戦, 休戦[停戦]協定, 中断, 一時的中止,〈苦痛などの〉軽減, 緩和
  a general truce 全面停戦
  break a truce 停戦を破る
  call [announce, declare] a truce 休戦を宣言する
  conclude a truce with …と停戦協定を結ぶ
  make [arrange] a truce with …と停戦する, …と停戦[休戦]協定を結ぶ
  truce observers 国連の停戦監視要員
  truce to one's pain 苦痛の軽減[緩和]

trump 名 切り札, 奥の手, 最後の手段, 立派な[素晴らしい]人, 役に立つ[頼りになる]人, 当てになる人, 好漢, トランプ
  a call for trumps 切り札を出せという合図
  keep [have] a trump up one's sleeve 最後の切り札を用意している
  call no trumps 切り札なしを宣する
  play a trump 切り札を出す, 奥の手を使う
  put a person to his trumps 人に切り札を出させる, 人を窮地に追い込む
  turn [come] up trumps とんとん拍子に行く, 予想以上にうまく行く, 思いがけなくよい, 幸運に恵まれる

trumped-up accusation 言いがかり

trumpet 動 大声で知らせる, 公言する, 公に示す, 誇示する, 吹聴する, アピールする

trunk call 長距離電話

trunk line 幹線, 本線,〈油田と精油所, 輸出港を結ぶ〉主要油送管

trust 名 信頼, 信用, 信託, 委託, トラスト
  信託とは ⊃ 財産所有者が金融機関などに財産権を移して, 特定の第三者の利益のために財産を管理・保全するよう依頼すること. 財産の信託設定者を委託者(settlor)といい, 委託を受けた財産(信託財産:trust property)を管理・保全する者を受託者(trustee), 信託の利益を受ける者を受益者(beneficiary)という.
  be indicted on charges of aggravated breach of trust 特別背任罪で起訴される
  breach-of-trust charges 背任の罪
  charitable trust 公益信託, 慈善信託 (= public trust)
  investment trust 投資信託
  trust bank 信託銀行
  trust business 信託業, 信託業務 (=fiduciary business)
  trust fund 信託基金, 信託資金, 投資信託, トラスト・ファンド
  trust services 信託業務
  trust territory 〈国連の〉信託統治地域
  un-incorporated investment trust 非会社型投資信託
  unit investment trust 単位型投資信託, ユニット型投資信託
  unit trust 契約型投資信託, ユニット・トラスト
  voting trust 議決権信託

trustee 名 信託機関, 幹事会社, 受託者, 受託会社, 被託者, 管財人, 破産管財人, 金融整理管財人, 理事, 評議員, 信託統治管理国
  bankruptcy trustee 破産管財人
  board of trustees 理事会
  fund amounts for postretirement benefits with an independent trustee 退職後給付額を独立した信託機関に積み立てる
  trustee fee 受託手数料
  trustee in bankruptcy 破産管財人
  trustee process 管財人手続き, 債権差押え手続き
  under the trustee's management 管財人の管理下で, 金融整理管財人の管理下で
  voting trustee 議決権受託者

TSE 東証, 東京証券取引所 (Tokyo Stock Exchangeの略)
  list shares on the TSE 東証に上場する
  TSE-listed companies 東証上場企業
  TSE's First Section 東証一部
  TSE's Mothers market 東証マザーズ

tsunami 名 津波

tug of war [tug-of-war] 綱引き, 決戦, 主導権争い, 互角の争い, 激突

tumble 動 〈物価・株価が〉下落する, 暴落する, 急落する, 急減する, 減少する, 上下動を繰り返す
  tumble across the board 全面安となる, 全銘柄にわたって急落[暴落]する
  tumble against major currencies 主要通貨に対して下落する
  tumble into a deflationary spiral デフレの悪循環に落ち込む

tumble 名 下落, 暴落, 減少, 混乱, 転落, 転倒, とんぼ返り, 宙返り
  rough-and-tumble market [marketplace] 浮き沈みの激しい市場
  take a serious tumble 深刻な危機に陥る
  take a tumble 大きく下落する

tumbling 形 下落する, 急減する, 暴落する, …

の下落［急減，減少，悪化］
- **tumbling dollar**　ドルの下落
- **tumbling sales**　販売の急減

turbulence 名　大荒れ，混乱，激動，動乱，騒乱，不安，乱気流
- **currency turbulence**　通貨危機，通貨不安，為替市場の波乱
- **economic turbulence**　経済的混乱
- **financial turbulence**　金融危機，金融不安，金融［金融市場］の混乱

turbulent 形　荒れ狂う，大荒れの，混乱した，激動の，動乱の，不穏な，騒然とした，騒がしい，不安な，暴風雨の，乱気流の

turmoil 名　混乱，波乱，動揺，騒動，騒ぎ，不安，危機
- **credit market turmoil**　金融市場の混乱（= turmoil in the financial markets）
- **credit turmoil**　信用不安
- **currency turmoil**　通貨危機，通貨不安，為替市場の混乱

turn 動　回す，向き［進路，方向］を変える，曲がる，迂回する，裏返す，流れを変える，好転させる，自動　回る，開店する，振り返る，向く，変わる，転じる，変質する，…になる
- **turn for good**　好転する
- **turn professional**　プロに転向する
- **turn the heat on**　…への圧力を強める
- **turn the tables**　立場を逆転させる，形勢［局面］を一変する

turn 名　回転，転回，順番，番，機会，交替，曲がり角，変わり目，節目，転機，転換期，方向転換，転換，折り返し，変化，新発展，成り行き，才能，素質，性質行為，行い，出し物，演目，言い回し，スタイル，表現，ちょっとしたドライブ［散歩］，売買，利益，利ざや，ターン
- **a [the] turn of events**　事態の変化，〈予期しない〉一連の出来事［変化］，転換点
- **a turn of mind**　〈人の〉物事に対する考え方
- **a turn of work**　一仕事
- **at every turn**　絶えず，つねに，事あるごとに，あらゆる場合に
- **make a turn**　利ざやを稼ぐ
- **round turn**　反対売買
- **serve one's turn**　…の役に立つ

turn around　好転する，改善する，回復する，持ち直す，方向転換する，方針を変える，考えを変える，企業［事業］を再生する，再建する
- **turn around the struggling manufacturer**　この経営不振のメーカーの事業を再生する

turn down　断る，拒絶［拒否，否決］する，〈訴えなどを〉却下する，折りたたむ，折り返す，〈音などを〉小さくする［弱くする，細くする］

turn oneself in　自首する，出頭する，投降する

turn out　〈製品などを〉生産する，製造する，作り出す，〈有能な人材などを〉輩出する，〈電灯などを〉消す，追い出す，首にする，…と判明する，結局…になる
- **as it turned out**　結果的に，結局は，後で分かったことではあるが
- **turn out goods**　商品［製品］を生産する，商品［製品］を製造する
- **turn out to be**　…になる，…だと分かる［判明する］

▶ An increasing number of loans *turn out* to be nonperforming because of a deterioration in the business situation of the borrower or because the value of the real estate used as collateral has fallen.　融資先の経営悪化や担保不動産の目減りなどによって，不良債権化する貸出が増えている。

turnabout 名　向きを変えること，方向転換，180度の転換，〈主義，主張，思想の〉転向，変節，寝返り，裏切り，〈役割，趨勢などの〉変化，変動，会社の再建，転回，回転木馬，仕返し，返報
- **in a turnabout from**　…から一転して

turnaround 名　転換，好転，〈経営戦略や営業・販売，財務などの〉改善，企業再生，事業再生，〈会社の〉再建，ターンアラウンド
- **Enterprise Turnaround Initiative Corporation of Japan**　企業再生支援機構
- **turnaround in the stock market**　株式市場の持ち直し
- **turnaround management company**　企業再生専門会社，事業再生専門会社
- **turnaround manager**　ターンアラウンド・マネージャー（経営不振企業に経営責任者などとして入って，企業再生を図る人のこと）
- **turnaround specialist**　企業再生請負人，再生請負人，再生専門家，ターンアラウンド・スペシャリスト

turnout 名　生産高，産出額，人手，出足，出席者，観客数，投票者数，ストライキ参加者，分岐点，待避所，待避線

turnover 名　売上，売上高，総売上高，取引高，出来高，売買高，回転，回転率，就労率，転職率

TVA　付加価値税（**tax on value-added**の略）

twin attacks 連続テロ
twin deficits 双子の赤字
twist 名 歪み, ねじれ, 湾曲, 〈意味などの〉歪曲, 回転, 旋回, 〈物語などの〉意外な展開, 〈事態の〉急変, 急転回, 〈政策などの〉予期しない転換, 新しい試み, 取扱い, 工夫, 考案, 方式, 傾向, 性向, 不正, 詐欺, らせん状, らせん運動
  a new twist 新しい試み, 新しい工夫, 新案, 新機軸, 新展開
  take a strange twist 意外な急展開を見せる, 意外な方向に発展する
  the twist of the wrist 腕前, 手際のよさ
  twists and turns 紆余曲折, 迷走
twitter 名 ツイッター
  ▶ *Twitter* is a free microblogging service that lets users send and read "tweets" which are messages up to 140 characters long. ツイッターは, 無料で使えるミニブログ・サービスで, ユーザー (利用者) が「ツイート (つぶやき)」(140字以内の短いメッセージ) を投稿 [発信] して閲覧者 (フォロワー) がそれを読む仕組みになっている.
two-horse race 一騎打ちのレース, 一騎打ち
two-income family 夫婦共働き家族
two-plus-two meeting 日米安保協議委員会
two-pronged 形 二方面の, 両方向からの, 両面の, 両面からの

two quarters 2四半期
  the first two quarters 上半期の第1四半期と第2四半期
  the second two quarters 下半期の第3四半期と第4四半期
two sides of the same coin 表裏一体
two-track 形 二重の, 両面の, 二元的な
  two-track decision 二重決定
  two-track income taxation system 二元的所得課税方式
two-way 形 両面の, 双方向の, 相互的な, 対面交通の, 往復両方向の
  two-way cable 双方向ケーブル
  two-way market 双方向市場 (＝two-sided market)
  two-way quotation 外国為替で買い値と売り値の両建て建値のこと
  two-way traffic 両面交通 (＝two-way street)
  two-way voice and data communications 双方向の音声・データ通信
tycoon 名 実力者, 重鎮, …王, 大御所, 大立者, 実業界の巨頭, 〈資産や権力のある〉実業家, 経営者, 大君
  drug tycoon 麻薬王
  oil tycoon 石油王

U

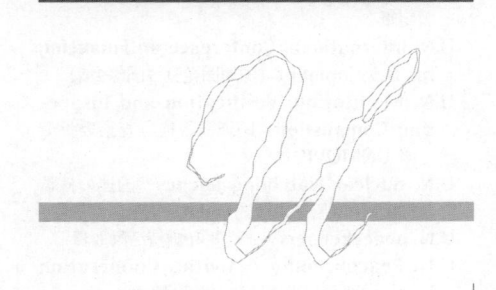

UAW 全米自動車労働組合, 全米自動車労組（United Auto Workersの略）
ubiquitous 形 遍在する, ユビキタス
  ubiquitous computing ユビキタス・コンピューティング（あらゆる所にコンピュータやコンピュータ機器が設置される環境）
  ubiquitous computing society ユビキタス社会
  ubiquitous information networks ユビキタス情報ネットワーク, ユビキタス情報通信ネットワーク
UFO 未確認飛行物体, 空飛ぶ円盤, ユーフォー（＝flying saucer : unidentified flying objectの略）
  UFO flaps ユーフォー騒動
ufologist 名 UFO研究家
ufology 名 UFO研究
ultimate 形 究極の, 究極的な, 最終の, 最後の, 決定的な, 根本の, 根本的な, 根源的な, 第一の, 第一義的な, 最高の, 極限の, 最大限の
  the ultimate analysis 元素分析
  the ultimate authority 最高権威
  the ultimate consumer 最終消費者
  the ultimate customer エンド・ユーザー
  the ultimate demand 最終需要
  the ultimate deterrent 究極的戦争抑止力
  the ultimate end [aim, goal] 究極の目的, 最終目的, 最終目標
  the ultimate destination 最終仕向地
  the ultimate principles [causes] 根本原理
  the ultimate purchaser 最終消費者, 最終購入者, エンド・ユーザー
  the ultimate weapon 最終兵器, 究極兵器

ultimatum 名 最後通告, 最後通牒, 最後の申し出［条件］, 最終提案, 最終的な提案, 最終結論, 究極点, 根本原理
  deliver an ultimatum to …に最後通牒を出す
  issue an ultimatum 最後通牒を発する
ultra-easy [ultraeasy] money policy 超低金利政策, 超金融緩和政策, 金融の量的緩和政策（＝ultra-easy monetary policy, ultra-loose monetary policy）
ultra-loose monetary policy 超金融緩和政策（＝super-loose monetary policy, ultra-loose money policy）
ultralow interest rates 超低金利
umbrella 名 傘, 傘下, 保護, 包括的組織, 形 包括的な（＝wing）
  place ... under one's umbrella …を…の傘下に置く, …を…の傘下に収める
  umbrella agreement 包括契約, 包括契約書
  umbrella group 包括団体
  umbrella master agreement 包括標準契約書
  umbrella payments 包括支払い, 包括支払い制
  under the umbrella of …傘下の, …に保護［援護］されている
U.N. [UN] 国連（⇒United Nations）
  U.N. Commission on the Limits of the Continental Shelf 国連大陸棚限界委員会
  U.N. Convention against Transnational Organized Crime 国際組織犯罪防止条約
  U.N. General Assembly 国連総会
  U.N. High Commissioner for Refugees 国連難民担当高等弁務官《略 UNHCR》

U.N. Interim Force in Lebanon　国連レバノン暫定軍
U.N. International Conference on Financing for Development　国連開発資金国際会議
U.N. Monitoring, Verification and Inspection Commission　国連監視検証査察委員会《略 UNMOVIC》
U.N. nuclear watchdog agency　国連の核監視機関, 国際原子力機関(IAEA)
U.N. peacekeepers　国連平和維持活動要員
U.N. Peacekeeping Activities Cooperation Law　国連平和維持活動(PKO)協力法
U.N. Secretary General　国連事務総長
U.N. Security Council　国連安全保障理事会, 国連安保理《略 UNSC》
U.N.-brokered 形　国連調停による
unabated 形　衰えない, 弱まらない, 弱まる気配[様子]がない, 一向に減らない, 低下しない
unanimous 形　満場[全員]一致の, 異議のない, 意見が一致している, 同意見である, 同意の, 合意の
　be unanimous for　満場一致で…に賛成である, …に全員賛成である, …に賛成である, …に異議はない
　unanimous action　全会一致の決議, 満場一致の決議
　unanimous applause　満場の拍手
　unanimous decision　満場一致の決定, 全会一致による決定
　unanimous vote　満場一致の票決
unanimously 副　満場一致で, 全会一致で, 全員一致して, 全員異議なく
unauthorized 形　非正規の, 不正の, 無許可の
　unauthorized export　不正輸出
　unauthorized moneylending business　ヤミ金融
　unauthorized use　不正使用, 無権限使用, 無断使用
　unauthorized vaccine　未承認ワクチン
unbundling 名　独占企業の強制分轄, 価格分離, 〈ハードウエアの価格とソフトウエアの価格の〉切り離し販売, バンドリング
uncertain 形　不確かな, 不透明な, 不確定な, 不確実な, 不安定な
　uncertain factor　不確定要因
　uncertain market conditions　不透明な市場環境, 市場環境の不安定性
　uncertain outlook　先行きの不透明感

uncertainty 名　不確実性, 不確定, 不確定要因, 波乱要因, 不透明, 不透明性, 不透明要因, 先行き不透明感, 先行き不安, 不安, 不安要因
　increase the uncertainty about future profitability　将来の収益性に対する不確実性を高める
　remove the uncertainty　不確実性を払拭[排除]する, 不透明感を払拭する
　uncertainties in the market　市場の不確定要因, 市場の波乱要因
unchanged 形　据え置かれた, 変わらない
　be left unchanged　据え置かれる, 据え置きになる
　keep monetary [credit] policy unchanged　金融政策を据え置く, 金融政策を維持する
　leave ... unchanged at　…を…に据え置く
uncollateralized overnight call rate　無担保コール翌日物
uncollectible 形　回収不能の, 貸付け金の取立てができない, 焦げ付いた (=uncollectable)
　uncollectible loans　不良債権, 不良貸付け, 貸倒れ, 回収不能の融資 (=bad loans, non-performing loans)
unconsolidated 形　連結から除外された, 連結の範囲に含まれない, 連結対象外の, 連結されていない, 非連結の, 単独ベースの, 単独決算の
　unconsolidated basis　単独ベース, 非連結ベース, 単独決算
uncontested reelection　無投票での再選
UNCTAD　国連貿易開発会議 (United Nations Conference on Trade and Developmentの略)
undeclared income　申告漏れの所得, 所得の申告漏れ
underemployment 名　不完全雇用, 不完全就業
undergo 動　経験する, 体験する, 味わう, 経る (go through), 〈治療などを〉受ける, 被る, 〈困難などに〉遇う[遭遇する], 耐える, 忍ぶ
　undergo a DNA test　DNA検査を受ける
　undergo a sudden change　急激な変化を受ける[経る], 急激に[急に]変化する, 急に変貌する
　undergo drug treatment　薬物治療を受ける
　undergo great hardships　大辛苦をなめる, 多大な苦難に耐える
underground bank　地下銀行
underground nuclear test　地下核実験
underline 動　…に下線を引く, アンダーラインを引く, …を強調する, 目立たせる, 明示する(under-

score), 示す, 明らかにする

undermine 動 損なう, 蝕む, 傷つける, 害する, 弱める, 悪化させる, 低下させる, …に水をさす, 浸食する
  undermine one's centripetal force …の求心力を低下させる
  undermine morale 士気を損なう
  undermine public confidence in the securities market 証券市場に対する国民の信認を低下させる

underperforming loans 不良債権

underperforming operations 不採算事業

underpin 動 下から支える, 下支えする, 支持する, 補強する, 実証する, 立証する
  underpin prices 価格に下限を設ける[設定する]
  underpin the short end 短期債を下支えする, 短期債市場を下支えする
  ▶For the time being, the government must resort to monetary measures to *underpin* the economy. 当面, 政府は景気を下支えするような金融政策を取らなければならない。

underpinning 名 支え, 下支え, 支持, 補強, 裏付け, 根拠, 基礎, 土台, 実証, 立証, 〈女性の〉下着(underpinnings)

underreport 動 過少申告する (=understate)

undersea mining right 海底資源の採掘権

undertake 動 引き受ける, 請け負う, 〈義務や責任を〉負う, 請け合う, 約束する, …を保証する, 断言する, …することに同意する, …を企てる, 始める, 着手する, 乗り出す, …の世話をする, …の面倒を見る
  undertake a task 仕事を引き受ける, 仕事を始める
  undertake an air clean-up campaign 大気清浄化キャンペーン[運動]を始める
  undertake an enterprise 事業を企てる
  undertake an initial public offering 株式を新規公開する
  undertake responsibility 責任を負う

undervaluation 名 過小評価, 割安な株価評価

undervalue 動 過小評価する

underwrite 動 〈株式や社債, 保険などを〉引き受ける

underwriter 名 証券引受人, 引受業者, 引受証券会社, 引受行, 保険業者, 保険会社, 保険代理業者

underwriting 名 〈保険や証券の〉引受け

unemployed 形 失業した, 失業[失職]中の, 仕事[職]のない, 現在使用されていない, 遊休の
  ratio of wholly unemployed 完全失業率
  the latent unemployed 潜在失業者
  the long-term unemployed 長期失業者
  unemployed capital 遊休資本
  unemployed worker 失業者

unemployment 名 失業, 失職, 失業者, 失業率
  cyclic unemployment 循環的失業, 周期的失業
  disguised unemployment 偽装失業
  heavy [mass] unemployment 大量失業
  invisible [latent, potential] unemployment 潜在失業
  natural rate of unemployment 自然失業率
  temporary unemployment 一時的失業
  unemployment benefits 失業手当, 失業給付
  unemployment compensation 失業補償, 失業給付, 失業手当
  Unemployment Insurance Law 雇用保険法
  unemployment insurance system 失業保険制度, 雇用保険制度
  unemployment relief 失業救済, 失業対策

unemployment rate 失業率, 完全失業率 (=jobless rate)
> 完全失業率とは ⊃ 労働力人口に占める完全失業者の割合のこと。完全失業者とは, 「仕事をまったくしていない, 仕事があればすぐに仕事ができる, 求職活動をしている」の三つの条件を満たす者を指す。

  blue-collar unemployment rate ブルーカラー失業率
  insured unemployment rate 被保険失業率
  natural unemployment rate 自然失業率
  seasonally adjusted unemployment rate 完全失業率(季節調整値)
  structural unemployment rate 構造的失業率

unfair 形 不当な, 不正な, 不公平な
  unfair advertising 不正広告, 不当広告
  unfair competition 不正競争, 不当競争, 不公正競争, 不正競業
  Unfair Competition Prevention Act 不正競争防止法
  unfair dismissal 不当解雇
  unfair labor practice 不当労働行為

unfavorable 形 不利な, 好ましくない, 悪い, マイナスの

unfavorable balance 支払い超過
unfavorable developments 不利な展開, 好ましくない展開, 逆風
unfavorable effects on earnings per share 普通株式1株当たり利益に対する不利な影響額
unfavorable factor 不利な材料, マイナス要因, 悪材料
unfold 動 開く, 広げる, 明かす, 打ち明ける, 明らかにする, 示す, 繰り広げる, 展開する, 発展する, 明らかになる, 見えてくる, 広がる
unfriendly takeover 非友好的買収, 敵対的買収
unheated blood products 非加熱製剤
unidentified vessel 不審船
unification 名 統一, 統合, 一本化
　German unification ドイツ統一
　unification by stages 段階的統一
　Unification Ministry 〈韓国の〉統一省
　unification of account settlement 決済処理の一本化
　unification of the two Koreas 朝鮮半島の統一
uniform 形 一定の, 規則正しい, 均等な, 均一の, 同一の, 一律の, 一様な, 統一的な, 画一的な, 同一標準の, 変動のない, ユニフォーム
　at a uniform pace 一定のペースで
　be uniform with …と同じである, …と変わらない
　uniform accounting standards 統一会計基準
　uniform charge 均一料金, 統一料金
　uniform distribution 一様分布
　uniform exchange rate 単一為替レート (= single general foreign exchange rate)
　uniform size 同じ大きさ, 同一サイズ
　uniform tariff 統一関税
　uniform wage 同一賃金, 均一賃金
unify 動 統一する, 統合する, 一本化する, 一体化する, 一様にする
　unified market 統一市場, 市場統合
　unified modeling language モデル作成言語 《略 UML》(モデル設計用の標準言語)
　unified price 統一価格
unilateral 形 片側だけの, 一方的な, 片務的な, 単独の, 一国主義の
　net unilateral transfers 純移転収支
　unilateral benefit 一方的利益
　unilateral causal relationship 一方の因果関係

unilateral ceasefire 一方的休戦, 一方的な停戦
unilateral commercial transaction 単独商行為
unilateral contract [agreement] 片務契約 (契約当事者の一方だけが債務を負う契約)
unilateral deployment [use] of military forces 単独派兵, 単独での派兵
unilateral disarmament 一方的軍備縮小
unilateral dismissal notice 一方的解雇通知
unilateral distribution 一方的分布
unilateral foreign policy 一国主義の外交政策, 一国主義の外交方針
unilateral mistake 契約当事者の一方の錯誤
unilateral transaction 一方的取引
unilateral transfer 一方的取引
unilateralism 名 一国主義, 単独主義, 一方的軍縮論
uninvited spam e-mail 迷惑なスパム・メール, 勝手に送られてくる迷惑な電子メール
union 名 労働組合, 組合, 合衆国, 連邦, 結合, 合体, 合併, 一致, 団結, 調和, 結婚, 結びつき, 夫婦仲, 学生会館, ユニオン
　craft union 職業別組合
　credit union 信用組合
　enterprise union 企業組合, 企業別組合
　general trade union 一般労働組合
　horizontal union 職業別労働組合
　in union 共同で
　industrial union 産業別組合
　in-house union 企業別組合
　Japan Federation of Basic Industry Workers' Unions 基幹労連
　Japanese Electrical, Electronic and Information Union 電機連合
　Japanese Federation of Iron and Steel Workers' Unions 鉄鋼労連
　Japanese Trade Union Confederation 連合
　join a union 労働組合に加入する
　labor union 労働組合, 労組
　teachers [teachers'] union 教職員組合
　trade union 労働組合, 同業組合 (= labor union)
　union agreement 労働協約 (= union contract)
　union catalog 総合図書目録, 総合目録
　union charter 組合規約 (= union constitution)
　union density 労働組合の組織率

union dues 組合費 （=union fee）
Union Jack [Flag] 英国国旗, ユニオン・ジャック
union shop ユニオン・ショップ（就職後の一定期間内に組合への加入を義務付けられる企業）
Universal Postal Union 万国郵便連合
vertical union 産業別労働組合
workers union 労働組合, 労組 （=labor union, trade union）

unipolar domination 一極支配
unison 名 一致, 調和, 協調, 斉唱, ユニゾン
　act in unison with …と一致した行動を取る, …と一致して行動する
　in unison 一致して, 調和して, 同時に, 異口同音に, 一斉に
▶ World's central banks cut interest rates in unison in a joint response to the global financial crisis. 世界の中央銀行は, 世界の金融危機への協調対応策として金利 [政策金利] を同時に引き下げた。
unit 名 単位, 構成単位, 部門, 事業部門, 会社, 支社, 支店, 子会社, 設備一式, 台, 基, 装置, 部隊, セット, ユニット
　business unit 事業部, 事業単位
　cash surplus units (savers) 資金余剰主体（貯蓄者）
　condominium unit マンション
　deficit spending units (borrowers) 資金不足主体（借り手）
　economic unit 経済主体
　European Currency Unit 欧州通貨単位
　export unit value 輸出単価
　government unit 政府機関
　operating unit 事業体
　property unit trust 財産契約型投資信託
　rental units starts 賃貸住宅の着工戸数
　starts of built-for-sale units 分譲住宅の着工戸数
　unit kilometers 走行台キロ
　unit of GDP [gross domestic product] 国内総生産 (GDP) 単位
　unit of measurement 測定単位
　unit price 単位価格, 単価
　unit pricing 単位価格表示
　unit sales 販売数量, 販売台数
　unit sales price 販売単価
　unit trust オープン型投資信託
　unprofitable unit 不採算部門
unite 動 結びつける, 統合する, まとめる, 一本化する, 結合させる, 団結させる, 力を合わせる, 協力する, 団結する, まとまる, 一つになる, 結合する
united 形 団結した, 連合した, 共同の, 全員の, 統一の
　United Arab Emirates アラブ首長国連邦
　United Automobile Workers 全米自動車労働組合, 全米自動車労組
　united declaration 共同宣言
　united Europe 統合欧州, 欧州統合
　United Farm Workers 全米農業労働組合
　United Kingdom 英国, 連合王国
United Nations 国際連合, 国連 (1945年10月24日創立。⇒U.N. [UN])
　United Nations [U.N.] Capital Development Fund 国連資本開発基金《略 UNCDF》
　United Nations Charter 国連憲章
　United Nations Children's Fund 国連児童基金, ユニセフ
　United Nations Conference on Environment and Development 国連環境開発会議, 地球サミット
　United Nations Conference on Science and Technology for Development 国連科学技術開発会議《略 UNCSTD》
　United Nations Conference on Trade and Development 国連貿易開発会議, アンクタッド《略 UNCTAD》
　United Nations Day 国連創立記念日
　United Nations Development Program 国連開発計画《略 UNDP》
　United Nations Educational, Scientific, and Cultural Organization 国連教育科学文化機関, ユネスコ《略 UNESCO》
　United Nations Environment Program 国連環境計画《略 UNEP》
　United Nations Fund for Population Activities 国連人口基金
　United Nations General Assembly 国連総会《略 UNGA》
　United Nations High Commissioner for Refugees 国連難民高等弁務官
　United Nations Industrial Development Organization 国連工業開発機関《略 UNIDO》
　United Nations International Children's Emergency Fund 国連国際児童緊急基金, ユニセフ
　United Nations Protection Force 国連保護軍《略 UNPROFOR》
　United Nations Relief and Works Agency

for Palestine Refugees in the Near East 国連パレスチナ難民救済事業機関《略 UNRWA》
United Nations Secretariat 国連事務局
United Nations Security Council 国連安全保障理事会《略 UNSC》
United Nations University 国連大学《略 UNU》

United States アメリカ合衆国, 米国 (⇒U.S. [US])
United States Air Force 米国空軍《略 USAF》
United States Army 米国陸軍
United States Information Agency 米国海外情報局《略 USIA》
United States Information Service 米国広報文化局《略 USIS》
United States International Trade Commission 米国国際貿易委員会
United States Marine Corps 米国海兵隊
United States Navy 米国海軍《略 USN》
United States of America アメリカ合衆国, 米国《略 USA》
Unites States Postal Service 米国郵政公社
United States Ship 米国船《略 USS》
United States Trade Representative 米通商代表部
United States Travel Service 米国政府観光局《略 USTS》

universal 形 全体の, 全員の, 万人の, 普遍的な, 万国の, 世界の, 共通の, 一般的な, 総合的, 万能の, 博識の, 多方面にわたる, ユニバーサル
by universal request 全員の要請で
receive universal approval 全員の賛同を得る
universal agent 総代理店
universal coverage 国民皆保険
universal custom 一般的な習慣
universal gravitation 万有引力
universal language 世界共通言語, 世界共通語, 万国共通語
universal measure 普遍的尺度
universal practice 一般的慣習
universal rule 普遍的規則
universal service ユニバーサル・サービス(郵便事業の場合は, 全国同一料金でサービスを提供すること)
universal suffrage 普通選挙権
universal time coordinated 協定世界時

unlawful 形 不法な, 違法な
unlawful act 不法行為, 違法行為
unlawful business practice 違法な営業手法
unlawful moneylending ヤミ金融

unlikely 形 …しそうにない, ありそうもない, 起こりそうもない, 見込みのない, 成功しそうにない, 気に入らない, 好ましくない
an unlikely scenario うまくいきそうにない筋書き［シナリオ］
be unlikely to …しそうにない
in the unlikely event of 万一…が起こったら
▶The Bank of Japan is *unlikely* to change its quantitative easing policy this year. 日銀が今年度中に量的緩和政策を変えるようなことは, ないだろう.

unlisted joint-stock company (株式を上場していない)非公開会社 (＝unlisted stock company)

unlisted stock company 非公開会社
▶Many *unlisted stock companies*—the majority of them small and midsize companies— do not issue stock certificates. 中小企業を中心とする非公開会社の多くは, 株券を発行していない.

unload 動 処分する, 売り払う, 売却する

unmanned reconnaissance plane 無人偵察機
▶Information on enemy forces obtained by spy satellites and *unmanned reconnaissance planes* was transmitted through digital communication systems. 偵察衛星や無人偵察機が集めた敵軍の情報は, デジタル通信システムで伝送された.

UNMIS 国連スーダン派遣団, 国連スーダン・ミッション (United Nations Mission In Sudanの略. 難民帰還支援や停戦監視に従事)

UNMOVIC 国連監視検証査察委員会 (U.N. Monitoring, Verification and Inspection Commissionの略)

unpaid 形 未払いの, 不払いの
unpaid balance 未払い額, 未払い残高
unpaid bill 代金の踏み倒し, 不渡り手形
unpaid dividend 未払い配当金, 配当金未払い高
unpaid interest 未払い利息
unpaid invoice 未払い請求書
unpaid overtime allowance 不払い時間外手当, サービス残業代
unpaid tax 税金滞納
unpaid wages due 未払い賃金

unprecedented 形 前例［先例］のない, かつてない, 例をみない, 無類の, 前代未聞の, 空前の, 未曾有の, 過去最高［最悪, 最低］の, 新奇の, 新しい

an unprecedented event 空前の出来事
the unprecedented economic crisis 前例のない経済危機, かつてない経済危機

unprofitable 形 採算の合わない, 不採算な, 儲からない, 利益を生じない, 無駄な
unprofitable division 不採算の事業部門, 不採算部門 （＝unprofitable operation）
unprofitable operation [business] 不採算事業, 採算の取れない事業［業務］, 不採算事業部門
unprofitable outlet [store] 不採算店舗

unreasonable 形 道理をわきまえない, 道理に合わない, 無分別な, 不合理な, 常軌を逸した, 不当な, 法外な, べらぼうな, 過度の, 無茶な, 無理な, 理性のない, 非理性的な
be unreasonable to do …するのは道理に合わない
make unreasonable demands 法外な［不当な］要求をする, 過度の要求をする

unrest 名 不安, 不穏な状況, 心配, 不満, 動揺, 紛争, 争議, 暴動
labor [labour] unrest 労働争議, 労働不安
political unrest 政情不安, 政治的不安
social unrest 社会不安
student unrest 学生紛争

UNRWA 国連パレスチナ難民救済事業機関 (United Nations Relief and Works Agency for Palestine Refugees in the Near Eastの略)

UNSC 国連安全保障理事会 (U.N. Security Councilの略)

unsecured 形 安全でない, 無担保の, 抵当のない, 無保証の, 保証のない
unsecured loan 無担保融資, 無担保貸付け, 無担保ローン, 無担保債権 （＝unsecured credit）
unsecured overnight call rate 無担保コール翌日物の金利 （＝rate for unsecured overnight call money）

unsettle 動 不安定にする, 不安にする, 動揺させる, 不安定になる, 動揺する
be unsettled by …で動揺する

unsettled 形 不安定な, 不安な, 変わりやすい, 定まらない, 不穏な, 不順な, 未解決の, 決着していない, 未決定の, 未定の, 未決済の, 未払いの, 支払いが済まない, 法的処分をされていない, 人が暮らしていない
unsettled account 未決済勘定
unsettled bill 未決済の勘定書, 未払い請求
unsettled conflict 未決済の紛争

unsettled weather 不順な天候

unsolicited 形 一方的な, 頼みもしない, 懇請された訳でもない, おせっかいな, 敵対的な
unsolicited bidding 直接入札
unsolicited e-mail 迷惑メール
unsolicited takeover offer 敵対的買収提案, 敵対的買収, 一方的な企業買収

unstinting 形 気前の良い, 惜しまない (lavish), 無条件の, 不退転の
unstinting support for …を無条件に支持すること

untapped 形 未開発の, 未開拓の, 利用されていない, 未利用の, 栓を開けていない, 口を切ってない
untapped crude oil 未開発の原油
untapped resources 利用されていない資源, 開発されていない資源

unveil 動 発表する, 明らかにする, 打ち明ける, 公表する, 公にする, 初公開する, 公開する, 序幕する, ベールを外す

up-and-comer 名 前途有望な人, 将来性のある人, 頭角を現わしてきた人, 活動家, やり手

up-and-coming 形 前途［将来］有望な, 上昇株の, 売出し中の, 積極的な, 精力的な, 進取的な

up the ante 賭けに出る, 賭け金をつり上げる, 分担金を引き上げる

up to 最高…まで, …まで, 最高…, 最大…, …の義務［責任］で, …次第で, …が決めることで, …をしていて, …を計画して
be up to no good 悪事をたくらんでいる
up to a thing or two 抜け目がない, 利口な
up to now 今まで, 今までずっと

upbeat 形 楽観的な, 快活な, 楽しい, 陽気な, 〈見通しが〉明るい, 盛り上がりのある, 景気がよい, 上昇傾向の （⇒downbeat）
show an upbeat trend 上昇傾向を示す
upbeat endings 楽しい結末, ハッピーエンド
upbeat outlook 明るい見通し, 見通しの明るさ

upcoming 形 近く発表される, 近々発売［公開］の, 近く予定されている, 近く上映［放映］予定の, 近刊の, 将来型の, 予想される, 当面の, やがて起ころうとしている, 近づく, 今回の
upcoming economic data 近く発表される景気指標
upcoming capital requirements 予想される必要資本, 当面の資金需要
upcoming financing needs 当面の資金調達のニーズ

update 動 更新する, 更新処理する, 更改する, 最

upfront 形 正直な, 率直な, 重要な, 最前列の, 前もっての(advance), 当初の, 前払いの, 前金の, 先行投資の, 管理[経営]部門の, 外交的な, 外交性の, 積極的な
  upfront capital 初期資本
  upfront fee 前払い手数料
  upfront payment 前払い
upgrade 動 昇格させる, 高める, 向上させる, 強化する, 底上げする, 等級を上げる, 格上げする, 格付けを引き上げる, 上方修正する, 改善する, 改良する, グレードアップする, グレードアップを図る
  upgrade economic relationship 経済関係を改善する, 経済関係を強化する
  upgrade features 機能を拡張する
  upgrade the long-term ratings for …の長期格付けを引き上げる[格上げする]
  upgrade one's economic outlook …の経済見通しを上方修正する
upgrade 名 昇格, 向上, 強化, 格上げ, 上方修正, 改善, 高度化, 機能拡張, グレードアップ (⇒downgrade)
  be on the upgrade 向上している, 進歩している, 上昇している, 増加している
  rating upgrade 格付けの引上げ, 格上げ
upgrading 名 昇進, 昇格, 格上げ(rating upgrade), 上方修正, 引上げ, 品質改良高度化, 機能拡張, イメージ・アップ
  upgrading and diversification 高度化と多様化
upheaval 名 激変, 激動, 大変動, 革命, 混乱, 不安, 〈地殻の〉隆起
  distribution upheaval 流通革命
  political upheavals 政治的激変, 政治の変動, 政治的混乱, 政情不安
  social upheavals 社会の激変, 社会改革
uphill 形 困難な, 苦しい, 骨の折れる, 上りの, 上り坂の
  fight uphill battles 苦戦する
  uphill struggle 困難, 困難な戦い, 苦戦
  uphill work 骨の折れる仕事
upload 動 データを送信する, 転送する, アップロードする
upmarket supermarket 高級スーパー (=upscale supermarket)
upper 形 上の, 上方の, 上位[上層, 上級, 上流]の, 高地方の, 北部の, 後期の

  get [gain, have] the upper hand (of) 台頭する, 〈…を〉支配する, 〈権力を〉掌中に収める, 〈…に〉勝つ, 〈…より〉優勢になる, 優位に立つ
  the upper chamber 上院
  the upper crust 貴族社会
  the upper echelons of the company 会社の上層部
  the upper end of the band レンジの上限
  the upper end of the market 高級市場
  the upper hand 優勢, 優越(dominance), 支配
  the upper Jurassic 後期ジュラ紀
  the upper middle class 上流中産階級
  the upper reaches of the Amazon アマゾン川上流
Upper House [upper house] 〈2院制議会の〉上院, 〈日本の〉参議院(House of Councillors) (=英国のthe House of Lords, 米国のthe Senate)
  upper house poll 参院選
upper limit 上限
  upper limit money rate 上限金利
  upper limit of a loan 融資限度額, 貸付け限度額
uproar 名 大騒ぎ, 騒動, 騒乱, 大論争
  be in an uproar 大騒ぎする, 大騒動になる
  cause an uproar 大騒ぎを引き起こす
upscale 形 高級な, 上流指向の, 富裕消費者向けの
upside 名 上昇, 上昇傾向, 上昇気味, 上値の余地, 上昇余地, 有利, 有利な点, メリット, 良い面 (⇒downside)
  further upside 相場の一層の上昇, 一層の上値余地
  upside potential 上値余地, 株価上昇の可能性, 上昇の余地, 値上りの余地(上値は「現在の株価より高い株価」のこと)
  upside risk 上昇のリスク, 上振れリスク
upstream 名 川上産業, 上流部門, 石油採掘部門, 子会社から親会社への販売, 上り, アップストリーム(「アップストリーム(上り)」は, 回線の信号の流れが利用者から電話局の方向のこと)
uptrend 名 上昇, 上昇傾向, 上昇基調
  an economic uptrend 景気上昇, 景気の上昇傾向, 経済的好況
  the current uptrend in the stock market 現在の株高, 現在の株価上昇
upturn 名 上昇, 上昇傾向, 上向き, 向上, 好転, 増加に転じること, 回復, 景気回復, 景気拡大局面

cyclical upturn 景気回復
upturn in business barometers 景気指標の回復
upturn in IPOs 株式公開の増加
upvalue 動 〈通貨の〉平価を切り上げる
upward 形 上向きの, 上昇する, 副 上方へ, さかのぼって, …以上, …以来 （⇒downward）
　upward adjustment 上方修正, 増額修正
　upward mobility 昇進, 昇級, 出世, 立身出世, 栄達, 上方志向［志向性］
　upward of …以上
　upward path 上昇基調, 増加傾向, 増加基調
　upward revision 上方修正
　upward trajectory 上昇軌道
　upward trend 上昇傾向, 上昇基調, 増大傾向
uranium 名 ウラニウム, ウラン（天然ウランは, 核分裂するウラン235を0.7％しか含んでいない。この比率を遠心分離器などで高める作業がウラン濃縮。濃縮度5％以下が低濃縮ウランで, 通常の原子力発電所で燃料として使われる。濃縮度が70％以上の高濃縮ウランは, 核兵器に使用される）
　depleted uranium 劣化ウラン
　low-enriched uranium 低濃縮ウラン
　mixed uranium-plutonium oxide (MOX) fuel プルトニウムとウランの混合酸化物（MOX）燃料
　natural uranium 天然ウラン
　uranium-based nuclear development program ウラン濃縮型の核開発計画
urban 形 都会の, 都市の, 都会的な, 都市特有の, アーバン
　urban crime 都市犯罪
　urban decline 〈人口流出に伴う〉都市の衰退
　urban design 都市設計
　urban development 都市開発, 市街地開発
　urban homesteading 都市定住奨励策
　urban landscape 都市景観
　urban ore 都会の鉱石（都会のごみ捨て場の空き缶やビンなど）
　urban oriented industry 都市型産業
　urban planning 都市計画
　urban redevelopment project 都市［市街地］再開発事業, 市街地再開発プロジェクト
　urban renewal 都市再開発, 都市改造, アーバン・リニューアル
　urban sprawl 都市のスプロール現象, 都市の郊外への拡散現象, スプロール化現象
urge 動 強く迫る, 強く要望する, 求める, 強く勧める, 促す, 催促する, 力説する

urine 名 尿
　urine test 尿検査
U.S. [US] アメリカ合衆国, 米国 （Unites States の略。正式名はthe United States of America）
　surplus with the U.S. 対米貿易黒字 （＝trade surplus with the U.S.）
　trade with the U.S. 対米貿易
　U.S. Bankruptcy Reform Act 米連邦改正破産法
　U.S. bond market 米国債市場, 米国の債券市場
　U.S. bond yields 米国債利回り
　U.S.-Canada Free Trade Agreement 米加自由貿易協定
　U.S. Constitution 合衆国憲法
　U.S. Council of Economic Advisers 米大統領経済諮問委員会
　U.S.-destined exports 米国向け輸出, 対米輸出
　U.S. dollars 米ドル
　U.S. economic indicators 米国の景気指標
　U.S. International Trade Commission 米国際貿易委員会
　U.S.-Japan Framework Talks on Bilateral Trade 日米包括経済協議
　U.S. Labor Department 米労働省
　U.S. military draft 米国の徴兵制
　U.S.-North Korea bilateral framework accord 米朝の枠組み合意
　U.S. Secretary of State 米国務長官
　U.S. Senate Finance Committee 米上院財政委員会
　U.S. slowdown 米国の景気減速
　U.S.-style board structure 米国型の取締役会制度
　U.S. Supreme Court 合衆国最高裁判所
　U.S. Trade Representative 米通商代表 （⇒USTR）
　U.S. Treasury Department 米財務省
U.S. Treasuries 米国債 （＝Treasuries, U.S. Treasury securities）

　米国債について ⊃ 米国の財務省（U.S. Treasury）が発行する市場性証券（marketable securities）で, 償還期限が1年以内の財務省短期証券（Treasury bill, T-bill）と1年超10年以内の財務省中期証券（Treasury note, T-note）, 10年超の財務省長期証券（Treasury bond, T-bond）の3種類がある。こ

のうち短期証券は割引発行，中期証券と長期証券は利付き発行となっている。発行方法としては競争入札と非競争入札があり，入札者は公示で募集する。

usage 名 慣習，使用，扱いかた，慣習法
usage history data 〈パソコンなどの〉利用履歴データ
USAMRID 米国陸軍伝染病医学研究所 (United States Army Medical Research Institute of Infectious Diseasesの略)
use 名 使用，使用量，使用法，利用，活用，運用，採用，使途，用途，効用，有用，収益権，ユース
  capital in use 使用資本
  consumer use 消費者使用
  economic use 経済的利用，経済的用途
  exclusive use 専用
  fictitious use 仮需要
  final [end] use 最終用途
  home use 自家消費，家庭用
used 形 中古の，使用された，使い古しの
  used electric appliances 中古電化製品
user 名 使用者，利用者，消費者，顧客，加入者，会員，投資家，ユーザー
  active service user 使用頻度の高いユーザー
  actual user 実需筋
  end user 最終使用者，一般使用者，最終利用者，最終投資家，エンド・ユーザー
  high-end user ハイエンド・ユーザー（自分でシステムを構築するユーザー）
  unauthorized user 不正使用者
  power user パワー・ユーザー（専門家に近い技術と能力のあるコンピュータ・ユーザー）
  spectrum user fee 電波利用料
  user account ユーザー識別符号，ユーザー・アカウント（ユーザーのパスワードやユーザー ID，所属するグループなどの情報）
  user authentication ユーザー認証
  user charge 利用者料金
  user cost 使用者費用 (＝user charge)
  user fee 受益者負担金
  user-friendly ユーザーに使いやすい，使いやすい，使い勝手がよい，操作が簡単な，ユーザーに親しみやすい，ユーザーに分かりやすい，利用者に親切
  user-hostile 使いにくい，使いづらい，ユーザーに親しみにくい，不便
  user identification ユーザー登録名，ユーザー識別コード，ユーザー ID
  user-oriented ユーザー志向の
  user [user's] registration ユーザー登録
  user-unfriendly 使いにくい，ユーザーに親しみにくい (＝user-hostile)
username [user name] 名 ユーザー名 (＝log-in ID, log-in name, user ID)
USTR 米国通商代表 (＝U.S. Trade Representative)
usurp 動 不法行使する，強奪する
  usurp office 職権を乱用する
uterine 形 子宮の，同母異父の
  uterine cancer 子宮がん
  uterine wall 子宮壁
utility 名 効用，有用，実用，実用性，実用品，公益事業，公共事業，公共事業体，公共事業株
  cost utility analysis 費用効果分析
  expected utility 期待効用
  privatized utilities 民営化された公益事業，公益事業の民営化
  the utility of a disarmament conference 軍縮会議の効果
  total utility 全体効用
  utility bill ガス電気水道代
  utility charges 公共料金 (＝utilities, utility rates)
  utility [utilities] company 公益企業
  utility creation 効用創造
  utility goods 実用品
  utility vehicle 多目的車，多用途車，ユーティリティ・ビークル
utilization [utilisation] 名 利用，使用，活用，運用，稼動率
  asset utilization 資産の活用
  capacity utilization 生産能力利用，生産設備の稼働状況，設備稼動率
  capacity utilization rate 設備稼動率，稼動率 (＝utilization rate)
  capital utilization 資本運用，資本稼動率
  full utilization 完全利用
  labor utilization 労働力利用
  land utilization 土地利用
  resource utilization 資源利用，設備と労働力の稼動率
  storage utilization 備蓄使用
  utilization of plant and equipment 設備稼動率
utilize 動 利用する，活用する

V

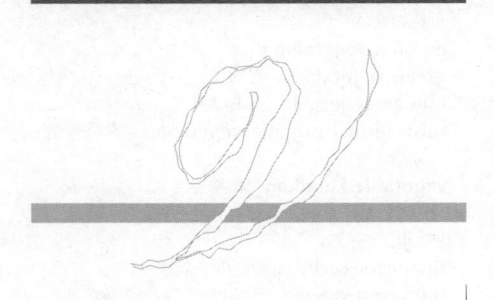

vacancies-to-applications ratio 有効求人倍率
vaccine 名 ワクチン
 live polio vaccine ポリオ生ワクチン
 smallpox vaccine 天然痘ワクチン
 vaccine bank ワクチン・バンク(コンピュータ・ウイルス対策の組織)
 vaccine program ワクチン・プログラム (= vaccine, virus protection software：コンピュータ・ウイルスの感染発見と治療を目的とするプログラム)
vacillate 動 揺れる(waver), 揺らぐ, ぐらつく, 動揺する, 迷う, 二の足を踏む
vacuum 名 空白
 a political vacuum 政治空白, 政治的空白
 a vacuum in foreign policy 外交空白
valuation 名 評価, 査定, 見積り, 評価価格, 査定価格
 valuation losses 評価損, 保有株の評価損を損失として計上する減損処理額 (=appraisal losses, evaluation losses)
value 名 価値, 価格, 評価, 評価額, 金額, 相場, バリュー
 the value of exports 輸出額
 the yen's value against the dollar 円の対米ドル相場
 value analysis 価値分析, バリュー・アナリシス《略 VA》
 value-creative economy 価値創造経済
 value for shareholders 株主価値
 value innovation バリュー・イノベーション《略 VI》
 value of oil imports 原油輸入額
 values of shares 株価
 value-oriented management 価値重視の経営
value-added 形 付加価値の, 付加価値のある, 付加価値の高い, 高付加価値の
 value-added per person 1人当たり付加価値
 value-added tax 付加価値税, 付加価値割《略 VAT》
 value-added technology 付加価値の高い技術, 高付加価値技術
vandalism 名 文化芸術破壊,〈公共施設などの〉破壊行為
vanguard 名 先鋒, 先陣, 前衛, 先駆者
variant 名 変種, 変形, 別形, 異形, 異文, 異本
variety 名 種類, 品種, 変種, 銘柄, 変化, 多様性, 相違, 差異, 寄席演芸, バラエティ
 a wide [large] variety of 種々さまざまな, 各種さまざまな, 多種多様な, 多岐にわたる
 for the sake of variety 目先を変えるため, 変化をつけるため (=for variety's sake)
 give variety to …に変化をもたせる
 variety reduction 品種削減, 品種整理
 variety store 雑貨店, バラエティ・ストア (=dime store)
vCJD 変異型クロイツフェルト・ヤコブ病 (variant Creutzfeldt-Jakob diseaseの略)
veep 名 副大統領, 副会長, 副総裁, 副頭取, 副社長
vegetable 名 野菜, 植物, 植物人間(cabbage)

無気力人間, 形 野菜の, 植物性の, 植物人間の, 反応のない
go on a vegetable diet 菜食をとる
green vegetables 青物類
human vegetable 植物人間
raise [grow] organic vegetables 有機野菜を栽培する
vegetable kingdom 植物界

vehicle 名 手段, 媒体, 会社, 子会社, 商品, 銘柄, 車, ビークル
finance vehicle 金融会社, 金融子会社
financing vehicle 資金調達手段, 金融商品
funding vehicle 資金調達手段, 資金調達の場
hedging vehicle ヘッジ手段
investment vehicle 投資会社, 投資子会社, 投資商品
issuing vehicle 起債子会社
retirement savings vehicle 退職年金商品
savings vehicle 貯蓄商品
special purpose vehicle 特別目的会社
vehicle currency 取引通貨, 貿易通貨 (=trading currency)

velvet-glove approach to politics ソフトタッチ外交 (=velvet-glove diplomacy)

vending machine 自動販売機

venture 名 冒険的事業, 投機的事業, 危険性の高い事業, 事業, 合弁事業, 業務, ベンチャー
venture business ベンチャー企業, 新ビジネス, 投機的事業, 研究開発型企業, 開拓型新興小規模企業, ベンチャー・ビジネス《略 **VB**》 (=start-up business, venture company)
venture capital 危険資本, 危険負担資本, ベンチャー資本, リスク資金, ベンチャー企業に投資する会社, ベンチャー・キャピタル投資会社, ベンチャー・キャピタル《略 **VC**》 (=risk capital)
venture capitalist ベンチャー・ビジネスへの出資者[投資家], 危険資本家, 危険投資家, 危険負担資本家, ベンチャー・キャピタリスト
venture company [firm] ベンチャー企業 (=start-up, start-up business, start-up company, venture)
venture fund ベンチャー・ファンド(投資ファンドの一種で, 創業間もない企業の未上場株式に投資して, 売却益を狙う)

verdict 名 〈陪審員の〉評決, 答申, 判決, 判定, 判断, 裁断, 決定, 決議, 意見
a guilty verdict 有罪評決
a verdict against the plaintiff 原告に不利な評決 [判決]
a verdict for the plaintiff 原告に有利な評決, 原告勝訴の評決
accept the verdict of the majority 多数の意見に従う
bring in [return] a verdict of not guilty 無罪の評決を下す
reach a verdict 評決を決定する
return [bring in] a unanimous verdict of guilty 全員一致で有罪の評決を下す
return [bring in] a verdict of guilty 有罪の評決を下す
the verdict of the public 世評, 世間の批判
wait for the verdict of time 後世の裁断を待つ
win favorable verdicts 有利な判定を勝ち取る

verification 名 立証, 検証, 証明, 確認, 確証, 証拠
▶The enriched uranium and nuclear proliferation *verification* of the issues has been incorporated into the main document's appendix. 濃縮ウランと核拡散問題の検証は, 本文書の付帯文書に盛り込まれている。

verify 名 立証する, 検証する, 証明する, 実証する, 確認する

version 名 説明, 見解, 意見, 説, 翻訳, 訳文, 変形, 別形, 異形, 異説, 改作, 脚色, …版

vessel 名 容器, 船, 大型ボート, 艦船, 人

vested 形 確定した, 受給権の発生した, 既得の
vested interest 既得権, 既得権益, 確定権利 (=vested right)

veteran 名 功労者, 老練者, 経験豊富な人, 従軍兵, 退役軍人, 復員軍人, ベテラン, 形 復員[退役]軍人の, 老練な, 老巧な, 経験豊富な, 長い経験を積んだ, ベテランの
a veteran politician 老練な政治家
a veteran soldier 老練兵
army veteran 復員帰還兵
veteran car クラシック・カー
Veterans Administration 復員軍人援護局
Veterans Day 復員軍人記念日, 復員軍人の日
Veterans of Foreign Wars 米国海外派兵戦士団《略 **VFW**》
Vietnam veterans ベトナム戦争の従軍兵, ベトナム帰りの軍人

veto 動 拒否権を行使する, 拒否する, 差し止める, 禁止する, 同意[承諾]を拒む
veto 名 拒否権, 否認権, 拒否権の行使[発動],

拒否, 否認, 禁止, 禁止命令
exercise a veto 拒否権を行使する
override a veto 拒否権を覆す
pocket veto 法案［議案］の握りつぶし, 法案［議案］の拒否権, ポケット拒否（米議会から閉会前10日以内に送付された法案を大統領が署名しないで放置して, 法案を成立させない（廃案とする）こと）
put [place, set] one's veto on [upon] …を禁止する
put one's veto on a proposal 提案を拒否する
veto message 〈米大統領の〉拒否教書, 拒否理由書, 拒否通告書
veto power 拒否権 （＝veto right, the power of a veto）

viable 形 有望な, 成長［発展］可能な, 実行可能な, 実行できる(practicable), うまくいきそうな, 立派に存続できる, 生存できる, 生育可能な, 如実の, 迫真の
economically viable 経済的にやっていける
viable candidate 当選見込みの候補者
viable idea 有望なアイデア

vice 名 悪, 悪徳, 悪徳行為, 不道徳, 悪習, 悪行, 悪癖, 欠陥, 欠点, 傷
vice raid 風紀取締り
vice ring 犯行グループ, 悪の集団
vice squad 風俗犯罪取締り班

vice-chairman [vice chairman] 名
副会長, 副議長, 副委員長, 副主席

vice minister for international affairs 国際担当次官, 財務官（事務次官と同格で財務省官僚組織のトップ。仕事は, 国際会議で財務相に代わり政府代表を務めたり, 円売り・ドル買いなどの市場介入を実質的に指揮する権限などを与えられている）

vice president [vice-president] 副大統領, 副総裁, 副理事長, 副会長, 副社長, 副頭取, 副総長, 副学長《略 VP》（＝veep）
executive vice-president 執行副社長, 業務執行副社長, 副社長, 副理事長
financial vice-president 財務担当副社長
senior vice president 上級副社長, 上席副社長

vicious 形 悪意のある, 意地の悪い, 悪性の, 激しい, ひどい, 残虐な, 残忍な, 不道徳な, 正しくない, 不完全な, 欠点のある
vicious call-sales merchant 悪質訪問販売者, 悪質訪問販売業者
vicious cycle 悪循環 （＝vicious circle）
vicious inflation 悪性インフレーション （＝inflationary spiral）
vicious reasoning 不完全な推論
vicious spiral of wages and prices 物価と賃金の悪循環

vicious circle 悪循環, 循環論法 （＝vicious cycle, vicious spiral)
be trapped [be caught, get caught up] in a vicious circle 悪循環に陥る
fall into a vicious circle of a progressive deflationary trend, deteriorating business performance and deepening unemployment デフレの進行, 企業業績の悪化と深刻化する雇用情勢という悪循環に陥る
vicious circle of poverty 貧困の悪循環

victim 名 犠牲, 犠牲者, 被害者, 被害者企業, 被災者, 遭難者, 罹病者, えじき, いけにえ
a victim of domestic violence 家庭内暴力（DV）に苦しむ人
a victim to the axe 人員削減の犠牲
earthquake victims 震災被災者, 地震の被害者
fall (a) victim to …の犠牲となる, …によって傷つけられる［殺される］,〈魅力などの〉とりこになる, …に敗れる
fashion [style] victim つねに最新のファッションを身につける人
the victim of malice 悪意のえじき
victims of a flood 洪水の犠牲者
victims of defamation on the Internet ネットでの中傷被害者
war victims 戦争の犠牲者 （＝victims of war）

victory 名 勝利, 勝ち, 戦勝, 克服, 征服
a big [great, resounding] victory 大勝利
a victory over difficulty 困難の克服
a victory over fear 恐怖の克服
an easy victory 楽勝

vie 動 競う, 張り合う, 争う

view 名 見方, 考え, 考え方, 意見, 見解, …観, 視野, 視界, 眺望, 眺め, 概観, 概説, …図, 見通し, 見込み, 意図, 目的, 意向, ビュー
a bird's eye view 俯瞰図, 概説
bill of view 仮輸入届け, 仮陸揚げ申告書
economic view 経済見通し
exchange views frankly 率直に意見を交換する
optimistic view 楽観的な見方, 楽観的な考え, 楽観的な見通し
positive view 明るい見通し
share one's view …の見方を支持する
take a dim view of …に対して懐疑的な見方を

示す, …を疑う

vigilance 名 警戒, 用心, 寝ずの番
- **exercise vigilance** 用心する
- **watch with vigilance** 監視する
- ▶ Continued *vigilance* is needed. 引き続き[まだ]警戒が必要である。

violate 動 〈約束などを〉破る, 裏切る, 〈法律, 契約, 規則などに〉違反する, 侵害する, 侵犯する, 犯す, 汚す, 冒涜する, 〈条項などに〉触れる, 〈睡眠などを〉妨げる, 乱す, 〈女性を〉レイプする, 暴行する, 強姦する
- **violate exchange controls** 外為規制に触れる
- **violate freedom of the press** 報道の自由を犯す
- **violate human rights** 人権を侵害する, 人権を抑圧する
- **violate one's privacy** …のプライバシーを侵害する
- **violate the airspace [territorial skies]** 領空を侵犯する
- **violate the law** 法律を破る, 法律に違反する, 法律違反をする
- **violate the sanctuary** 神聖を犯す, 神聖を汚す
- **violate the territorial waters** 領海に侵入する
- **violate the treaty** 条約に違反する

violation 名 違反, 違反行為, 侵害, 妨害, 侵犯, 冒涜, レイプ, 〈婦女〉暴行, 〈意味の〉曲解
- **in violation of** …に違反して
- **serious violation of one's obligations** …の義務の重大違反
- **the problem of patent violation** 特許侵害問題
- **violation of covenant** 契約違反
- **violation of law** 法律違反
- **violation of one's territorial skies** …の領空侵犯
- **violation of privacy rights** プライバシー[プライバシー権]の侵害
- **violation of sovereignty** 主権侵害
- **violation of the Minor Offenses Law** 軽犯罪法違反

violence 名 暴力, 暴力行為, 乱暴, 婦女暴行, 強姦, 害, 損害, 激しさ, 猛威
- **attack with violence** 猛烈に抗議する
- **do violence to** …に暴行を加える, …を犯す, …に違反する, …に反する, …を損なう, …を害する, …を冒涜する, 〈事実などを〉曲げる, 曲解する
- **domestic violence** 家庭内暴力, 配偶者による暴力, ドメスティック・バイオレンス《略 DV》
- **resort to violence** 暴力に訴える
- **sexual violence** 性暴力
- **use violence on** …に暴力を振るう
- **violence against women** 女性に対する暴力, 婦女暴行
- **violence on campus** 校内暴力 (=school violence)
- **violence organization** 暴力組織

violent 形 乱暴な, 暴力的な, 暴力による, 激しい, 猛烈な, 乱暴な, 凶暴な, 著しい, 極端な, 無理な, 不自然な, 非業な
- **be in a violent mood [temper]** 激怒している
- **die [meet] a violent death** 変死する, 事故死する, 不慮の死を遂げる, 非業の最期を遂げる
- **lay violent hands on [upon]** …に暴力を振るう, …に暴行を加える
- **violent colors** 極彩色
- **violent contrast** 著しい対照, 極端な対象
- **violent controversy** 激しい議論, 猛烈な論争
- **violent crime** 暴力犯罪
- **violent deeds** 暴行
- **violent fluctuation** 乱高下
- **violent interpretation** こじつけの解釈, 曲解した解釈
- **violent pain** 激痛
- **violent passions** 激情

viral 形 ウイルスの, ウイルス性の, ウイルスによる
- **viral hepatitis** ウイルス性肝炎
- **viral infection** ウイルス感染
- **viral marketing** バイラル・マーケティング(利用者の口コミによる販売促進手段のこと)

virtual 形 事実上の, 実質的な, 仮想の, 物理的に存在しない, バーチャル
- **virtual bank** 仮想銀行, バーチャル・バンク (=web bank：インターネット上で金融取引を専門に行う銀行)
- **virtual community** 仮想現実社会, ネットワーク上の社会, ネットワーク上の社交界バーチャル・コミュニティ
- **virtual engineering** 仮想エンジニアリング, バーチャル・エンジニアリング (⇒popularity)
- **virtual marketplace** 仮想電子取引市場, 電子商取引市場, バーチャル市場
- **virtual owner** 実質的な所有者[保有者], 事実上の所有者
- **virtual reality** 仮想現実, 仮想現実感, 仮想世界, 人工現実感, バーチャル・リアリティ《略 VR》

（=artificial reality）
virtual (shopping) mall 仮想商店街, 仮想モール, バーチャル・モール
virtuous 形 徳の高い, 有徳な, 高潔な
virtuous cycle [circle] 好循環, 良循環
virus 名 ウイルス, コンピュータ・ウイルス
  computer virus コンピュータ・ウイルス
  macro virus [macrovirus] マクロウイルス
  remove a virus from the infected files 感染したファイルからコンピュータ・ウイルスを取り除く
  virus-infected personal computer ウイルス感染のパソコン
  virus disease ウイルス性疾患
  virus infection ウイルス性伝染病
  virus penetration ウイルス侵入
  virus protection software ウイルス対策ソフト（=vaccine）
vis-à-vis [vis-a-vis] 前 …と比較して, …に関して, …に対する, …と向かい合って, …に相対して, 形 向かい合っている, 相対している
  vis-à-vis the U.S. dollar 対米ドルで, 米ドルに対する
visible 形 目に見える, 見える, 有形の, 明らかな, はっきりした, 目立った, よく目にする, よく登場する, 出演する, 面会できる, 会う気のある
  balance of visible trade 貿易収支（=trade balance, visible balance, visible trade balance）
  highly visible speech 大きな注目を集める演説
  visible asset 有形資産
  visible current item 貿易経常項目
  visible current transaction 貿易経常取引
  visible evidence 可視証拠
  visible goods 有形財
  visible imports 有形品輸入
  visible payment 貿易支払い
  visible receipt 貿易受取り
  visible stock 市場在庫
  visible trade 貿易取引, 商品貿易, 有形品貿易
  visible trade deficit 貿易収支の赤字
  visible trade surplus 貿易収支の黒字
vision 名 展望, 見通し, 未来像, 想像力, 先見の明, 先見性, 洞察力, 予見力, 構想, 視野, 視力, 視覚, 視線, 夢, 空想, 光景, 映像, 画像, ビジョン
  clear-cut vision 明確なビジョン
  management vision 経営者の展望, 経営的視野, 経営陣のビジョン
visionary 形 見通す力のある, 構想力のある, 先見的な, 名 先見者, ビジョンのある経営者
  visionary company 未来志向型企業, 先見的な企業, ビジョンを持っている企業, ビジョナリー・カンパニー
  visionary product 先見的商品, ビジョンのある商品
visitor 名 サイト来訪者, サイト閲覧者, ビジター
visual 形 視覚の, 視力による, 目視による
  visual aid 視覚教具, 視覚資料, 視覚教材
  visual display unit 表示端末装置, 表示装置, ディスプレー装置《略 VDU》
  visual effects 視覚効果
  visual flight 有視界飛行
  visual impairment 視力障害
  visual instruction [education] 視覚教育
  visual literacy 視覚理解力
  visual perception 視覚認知
  visual pollution 視覚公害, 風致公害
  visual presentation 視覚的演出, ビジュアル・プレゼンテーション
vitality 名 元気, 活力, 活気, 体力, 生命力, 持続力, 持久力, 存続力, バイタリティ
  economic vitality 経済の活力
  the private sector's vitality 民間の活力
vocational 形 職業上の, 就職指導の
  vocational court 職業裁判所
voice 動 表明する, 言葉に言い表わす, 言葉にする, 言う
voice 名 音声, 音質, 声, 表明, 発言, 発言力, 発言権, 影響力, 投票権, ボイス
  dominant voice 圧倒的な発言権
  voice mail 留守番電話, 音声メール, ボイスメール（=voicemail）
  voice recognition 音声認識
  voice vote 発声投票
volatile 形 変わりやすい, 乱高下する, 変動が激しい, 変動が大きい, 変動性が高い, 不安定な, 左右されやすい
  volatile market 変わりやすい市場, 乱高下する市場, 変動が激しい市場
  volatile pricing 価格変動, 価格の変動（=volatile prices）
volatility 名 変動, 乱高下, 変動性, 変動率, 将来の価格変動性, 価格変動率, 予測変動率, ボラティリティ
  excess volatility 過度の変動
  exchange rate volatility 為替の乱高下, 為替相場の変動, 為替変動（=forex volatility）

expected income volatility 予想収益変動幅
historical volatility 過去の変動性, ヒストリカル・ボラティリティ
implied volatility 予想変動率, インプライド・ボラティリティ
stem volatility 極端な変動を阻止する

volume 名 出来高, 取引高, 売上高, 販売高, 操業度, 数量, 量(「出来高」は株式市場全体の売買株数を示し, 売買高ともいう。一般に, 株価が上昇して出来高も多いときは, 相場が強いとされている)
   actual volume 実際操業度
   cost-volume-profit analysis 原価・営業量・利益分析, CVP分析
   in volume terms 実質ベースで, 台数ベースで, 数量ベースで (＝in terms of volume)
   normal volume 正常操業度
   optimum volume 最適生産量 (＝volume optimum)
   profit-volume chart [graph] 損益分岐点図表
   retail sales volume 小売売上数量
   traffic volume 交通量, 通話量 (＝volume of traffic)
   unit of volume 容積単位
   volume budget 製造高予算
   volume business 大量取引
   volume index 数量指数
   volume of orders placed 注文量
   volume production 量産
   volume quotation system 外国通貨建て相場制
   work volume 作業量, 仕事量

voluntary 形 任意の, 自主的な, 自発的な, 自由意志による, 無償の
   voluntary retirement 希望退職, 任意退職

vote 動 投票する, 票決する, 投票で決める, 議決する, 株式の議決権を行使する, 提案する
   vote against …に反対の投票をする, …に反対票を入れる
   vote down 否決する, 投票で否決する
   vote for …に賛成の投票をする, …に賛成票を入れる, …を提案する
   vote in 投票で選出する
   vote in favor of …に賛成票を入れる
   vote off [out] 投票で解任する
   vote on …に投票を行う, …に投票する
   vote one's share 議決権を行使する
   vote the bill down 法案を否決する
   vote with one's feet 〈出席あるいは欠席によって〉自分の意見を示す
   vote yes 賛成の票を投じる

vote 名 投票, 投票用紙, 投票[採決]の結果, 投票数, 投票方法, 票, 得票, 得票数, 票田, 票決, 採決, 決議, 投票権, 議決権, 票決権, 選挙権, 参政権
   affirmative vote 賛成投票
   buy a [one's] vote 票を買収する
   by a standing vote 起立採決により
   by the vote of …の票決により
   cast [give] a vote 投票する, 議決権を行使する
   close vote 僅差の投票結果
   come [go, proceed] to the vote 投票で決められる
   count [tally] the votes 票を数える, 票を集計する
   electoral vote 選挙人投票
   floating vote 浮動票
   get one's vote …の支持を得る
   give one's vote to …に投票する
   large vote 大量票
   light vote 少数票
   limited vote 制限投票
   majority vote 多数投票
   one man [person] one vote 1人1票制
   one vote for each share 1株につき1議決権
   open vote 記名投票
   pass a vote of …を議決する
   popular vote 一般投票
   postal vote 郵送投票
   propose a vote of thanks 感謝のスピーチをする
   put ... to the vote …を票決する, …を票決に付する, …を票決にかける
   recorded vote 記録投票
   roll-call vote 発声による採決
   secret vote 無記名投票
   simple majority vote 単純過半数
   single vote 単記投票
   spoilt vote 無効票
   take [have] a vote on …について採決する, …について投票を行う
   teller vote 集計人投票
   viva voce vote 発声投票
   voice vote 口頭投票, 発声投票
   vote by a show of hands 挙手による採決
   vote by acclamation 発声による採決
   vote by rising 起立による採決

vote of censure　譴責決議
vote of confidence　信任投票, 信任決議, 賛成［支持］の態度表明
vote of no confidence　不信任投票, 不信任決議, 不賛成［不支持］の態度表明
vote-rigging allegations　投票操作疑惑, 不正開票疑惑
vote station　投票機器
write-in vote　書き込み投票, 書き込み票
yea-and-nay vote　口頭賛否投票（=yeas and nays）

voter 名　投票者, 選挙人, 有権者
buy voter support　有権者の支持を獲得する
eligible voters　有資格の投票者
voter approval　有権者の承認, 住民投票による承認
voter registration　投票人登記
voter turnout　投票率, 有権者の出足, 投票者数

voting 名　投票, 投票権行使, 議決権行使
abstain from the voting　投票［採決］を棄権する
audience response voting　聴衆反応投票
by voting in the aggregate　単純合計の投票により
cross voting　交差投票
cumulative voting　累積投票
electronic voting　電子投票
multiple choice voting　マルチ選択投票
nonvoting delegate　投票権を持たない代表者
parliamentary voting　議会式投票
plural voting　連記投票
proxy voting　代理投票
single voting　単記投票
super voting share　複数議決権株式
voting age　選挙年齢
voting agreement　議決権契約, 票決契約
voting bond　議決権付き社債
voting by ballot　秘密投票, 無記名投票
voting by proxy　代理人による議決権の行使
voting list　投票名簿
voting power　議決権, 投票権（=voting right：株主が会社の総会で各種の重要な決議に参加できる権利のこと。一般に, 普通株式1株につき1個の議決権が与えられている）
voting register　選挙人名簿
voting right　議決権, 投票権, 選挙権
voting stock [share]　議決権株式, 議決権株, 議決権付き株式
voting stock authorized　授権された議決権付き株式
voting trust　議決権信託
voting trust arrangement　議決権信託契約
voting upon stocks　株式に基づく投票

vow 動　誓う, 制約する, 明言する, 断言する

vulnerable 形　傷つきやすい, 攻撃されやすい,〈病気などに〉かかりやすい, 影響されやすい, 弱い, もろい, 脆弱な, 危険にさらされている, 無防備な

vulnerable to …の影響を受けやすい, …に弱い, …になりやすい, …にもろい, …に無防備な, …の攻撃を受けやすい
be vulnerable to a hostile takeover bid　敵対的TOBに狙われやすい
be vulnerable to attacks　攻撃を受けやすい
be vulnerable to an economic downturn　景気後退の影響を受けやすい

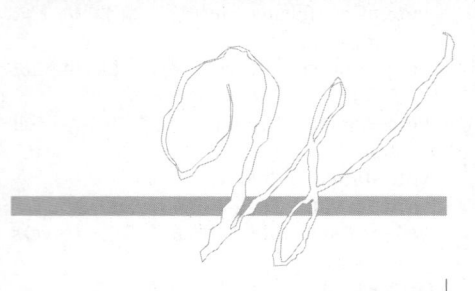

W

wafer 名　ウエハ［ウエハー］（集積回路を作るためのシリコンなどからなる半導体の円板）
　gallium arsenide wafer　ガリウムひ素ウエハ
　wafer fab　ウエハ組立工場　（＝wafer fabrication plant）
wage 動　〈戦争や運動などを〉行う，する，遂行する，起こす
　wage a war against [on, with] poverty　貧困撲滅運動をする
　wage an internal power struggle　内部抗争をする
　wage an opposition campaign against　…に対して反対運動を起こす
wage 名　賃金，給料，労賃
　average wage　平均賃金
　basic wage　基本給
　dismissal wage　解雇手当
　efficiency wage　能率給
　external wage structure　企業間賃金構造
　fixed wage　固定賃金，固定給
　floor [minimum] wage　最低賃金
　incentive wage　奨励給
　job wage　職務給
　living wage　生活給
　standard wages　基準賃金
　wage agreement　賃金協定
　wage and benefit costs　雇用コスト
　wage bill　賃金総額
　wage boost [hike, increase, gains]　賃上げ，昇給
　wage claim　賃上げ要求
　wage cuts　賃金引下げ，賃下げ，賃金カット
　wage data　雇用統計
　wage deal　賃金協約
　wage disparity [differential, dispersion, gap]　賃金格差
　wage earners' average overtime pay　賃金労働者の平均残業手当（所得動向の指標）
　wage-earning households　サラリーマン世帯　（＝households of salaried workers）
　wage growth　賃金上昇率，賃金の伸び［伸び率］
　wage index　賃金指数
　wage inflation　賃金上昇率，賃上げ率，賃金インフレ
　wage on job classification　職階給，職階制賃金，資格給
　wage negotiation　賃金交渉，賃上げ交渉　（＝wage talks）
　wage on job evaluation　職能給　（＝wage based on job evaluation）
　wage rates [levels]　賃金水準
　wage restraint　賃金抑制
　wage rise　賃金引上げ，賃上げ，ベア　（＝wage increase）
　wage round　春闘，賃上げ交渉
　wage settlement　賃上げ妥結，賃上げ妥結内容，賃上げ妥結額
　wage stop　社会保険給付の支給制限
　wage system　賃金体系
　wage talks　賃金交渉，賃上げ交渉　（＝wage negotiation）
　wages and salaries　賃金・俸給，賃金・給与，賃

金給与所得
wait-and-see 形 様子見の, 模様眺めの, 静観, 見送り
  wait-and-see attitude [stance] 様子見の構え, 模様眺めの姿勢
  wait-and-see outlook 模様眺め
waive 動 〈権利などを〉放棄する, 〈問題などを〉見送る, 延ばす, 〈権利などの行使を〉差し控える
waiver 名 権利の放棄, 債務の免除, 権利放棄の意思表示, 権利放棄証書
  a waiver of debt 債権放棄, 債務免除
  loan waiver 債権放棄, 債務免除
  waiver of obligation 債務免除
  seek debt waivers from the creditor banks 取引銀行に債権放棄を求める
wake 名 航跡, 波の跡, 通った跡
  in one's wake [in the wake of] …に引き続いて, …に続いて, …の後, …を受けて, …の結果(として), …に従って, …に倣って, …として, …によって
  the wake of the tornado 竜巻の通った跡
wake-up call 警鐘, モーニング・コール
wall 名 壁, 城壁, 内壁, 内面, 邪魔, 障害, ウォール
  go to the wall 破産する, 倒産する, 負ける, 失敗する, 没落する, わきへ押しやられる, 無用扱いされる
  hit the wall くたくたになる, 〈肉体的に〉限界に達する
  see through a brick wall 洞察力に富む
  the Berlin Wall ベルリンの壁
  the Great Wall of China 万里の長城
  up against a [the] wall 八方ふさがりで, 打つ手がなくて
  with one's back to the wall 追い詰められて, 窮地に陥って, 後がなくなって
Wall Street 米国の証券市場, 米ニューヨークの株式市場, ニューヨーク株, ウォール街の証券市場, 米ニューヨークの株式中心街, 米金融街, 米金融市場, 米金融業界, 米金融界, ウォール・ストリート
  a Wall Street economist 市場エコノミスト
  Wall Street watchers 米証券市場関係者
Wall Streeters 米証券市場関係者 (＝Wall Street watchers)
wallop 動 手で激しくたたく, 打つ, 強打する, 大勝する, 圧勝する
wane 動 弱まる, 徐々に弱まる, 希薄化する, 衰える, 衰退[衰微]する, 消えようとしている, 〈月が〉欠けている, 新月に近づいている
wane 名 弱体, 弱体化, 希薄化, 衰退, 衰微, 落ち目, 衰退期
  on the wane 衰えかけて, 衰退して, 落ち目になって
wanted 形 指名手配されている, 指名手配中の, 必要とされている, 〈電話などで〉呼ばれている, 〈子どもが〉愛されている, かわいがられている
  a wanted man 指名手配の男, おたずね者
  be put [placed] on a nationwide wanted list 全国に指名手配されている
  wanted ad 求人広告, 求職広告
war 名 戦争, 紛争, 争い, 戦い, 競争, 運動, 活動
  aggressive war 侵略戦争
  at war with …と交戦中, …と不和で, …と相いれないで
  civil war 内戦, 内乱
  drug war 麻薬戦争
  holy war 聖戦
  nuclear war 核戦争
  prisoners of war 捕虜
  the Civil War 〈米国の〉南北戦争 (＝the War between the States, the War of Secession)
  the Cold War [cold war] 冷戦
  the sinews of war 軍資金, 活動資金, お金
  war chest 運動資金, 活動資金, 軍資金
  war clouds 戦雲, 戦争直前の気配
  war correspondent 従軍記者
  war crimes trial 戦犯法廷
  war crimes tribunal 戦争犯罪裁判所
  war criminal 戦犯, 戦争犯罪人
  war cry 〈政党などの〉標語, スローガン, ときの声
  war damage 戦禍, 戦災
  war footing 戦時体制
  war game 軍事作戦演習, 模擬演習, 戦争ゲーム
  war hawk 主戦論者, タカ派の人, タカ派
  war memorial 戦没者慰霊碑
  war of attrition 消耗戦
  war of nerves 神経戦
  war of the elements 自然災害, 嵐
  war of words 舌戦, 論戦
  war on terror [terrorism] 対テロ戦争
  war orphan 戦争孤児
  war pension 軍人恩給
  war potential 戦力
  war powers resolution 武力行使容認決議
  war situation 戦況
  war trophy 戦利品
  war veteran 退役軍人, 元兵士
  war zone 交戦地帯

ward off 避ける, 防ぐ, かわす
warhead 名 弾頭
　nuclear warhead　核弾頭
　warhead missile　核弾頭装着ミサイル
warmonger 名　戦争屋, 戦争挑発者
warn 動　警告する, 注意する, 予告する
warning 名　警告, 呼びかけ, 注意, 予告, 通告, 通知, 警戒, 警報, 戒め
　advance warning　事前の注意, 事前の警告
　discharge warning　解雇予告
　early warning　早期の注意, 早期警告
　early warning system　早期警告制度, 早期警告システム
　issue warnings against photochemical smog　光化学スモッグ警報を出す
　warning lamp　警告灯, ウォーニング・ライト
　warning sales　「危険です」販売
warplane 名　戦闘機, 軍用機
warrant 名　令状, 許可書, 証明書, 論拠, 根拠, 権限, 新株引受権, 新株予約権, 株式買取り請求権, 倉荷証券, 権利証券, 権利証書, 権限証書, ワラント
　bond with warrant　ワラント付き社債, ワラント債
　bond with warrants attached　新株引受権付き社債 (＝warrant bond)
　by warrant　令状により, 許可により
　detachable warrant　分離型ワラント, 分離型新株引受権付き証書
　dividend warrant　配当金領収書
　equity warrant　新株予約権
　exercise of warrant　新株引受権の行使, ワラントの行使
　issue warrants for new shares to　…への新株予約権を発行する
　search warrant　捜査令状
　stock [share] warrant　新株引受権, 新株予約権, 株式引受権, 新株引受権付き証券[証書], 新株引受保証書, 株式ワラント
　warrant bond　ワラント債, 新株引受権付き社債《略 WB》
　warrant of arrest　逮捕令状, 逮捕状 (＝arrest warrant)
wartime mobilization　戦時動員
wary 形　注意深い, 用心深い, 警戒する, 慎重な, 財布の紐を引き締めている, 手控えている
wash 動　〈考えなどが〉信じられない, 受け入れられない, 洗う
　wash away　洗い流す, 破壊する

wash out　中断する, 中止にする, きれいに洗う
Washington 名　米国, 米国政府, ワシントン
waste 名　無駄, 浪費, 廃棄, 廃棄物, 老廃物, 荒れ地, 砂漠, 〈家屋などの〉毀損
　go [run] to waste　無駄になる
　sandy wastes　砂漠
　the wastes of war　戦争による廃墟
　waste ground　空き地
　waste of opportunity　機会を逃す[逸する]こと, 逸機
　waste pipe　排水管
　wastes of the Sahara　サハラ砂漠
watch 動　用心する, 気をつける, 注目する, 監視する, 見張る, 警戒する
　most closely watched gauge　特に注目される指標
watchdog 名　番犬, 見張り, お目付け人, 監視人, 監視機関
　a watchdog organization　監視団体
　the U.N. nuclear watchdog agency　(国連)核監視機関
watcher 名　観察者, 観測筋, 観察者, …問題研究家・専門家, …情勢分析家, …通, 関係者, 選挙立会人, ウォッチャー
　market watcher　市場関係者
　Peking watcher　中国情勢分析家, 中国問題専門家, 中国通
　poll watcher　選挙立会人
wave 名　波, 波動, ウェーブ
wax and wane　盛衰する, 増減する, 消長する
way 名　方法, 手段, 方策, 仕方, やり方, 流儀, 様式, 方向, 方角, 方面, 方針, 行く末, 路線, 進路, 道筋, 規模, 要領, 点, 観点, 要因, 余地, 機会, 慣習, 風習, 慣例
　be already under way　すでに始まっている, すでに進行している
　be on the way down　減速軌道に乗る
　clear the way for　…を承認する, …を許可する
　get under way　始まる
　go a long way　大いに役立つ, 出世する, 成功する
　have it both ways　二股をかける, どっちに転んでも得するようにする
　in a major way　本格的に
　make way for　…に道を譲る, …に道をあける
　one-way option　一方的選択権
　one-way trade　片貿易
　right of way　通行権

seek ways to …する手段を講じる
the way things are 現状, 現状を見ると, 状況から判断して
3-way talks 3か国協議, 3社間協議
three-way intervention 3極の市場介入
two-way account 相互勘定
way of thinking 考え方, 思考法, 発想法

ways and means 歳入財源, 財源, 手段・方法, 手段, 方法
committee of ways and means 〈議会の〉財政委員会, 歳入委員会
the House Ways and Means Committee 〈米〉下院歳入委員会
ways-and-means advances 〈英国の〉財源貸出金

weak 形 弱い, 弱小の, 中小の, 低迷する, 軟調の, 落ち込んだ, 低下した, 減少した, 冷え込んだ, 厳しい, 悪化した
weak climate deal 緩やかな気候変動の取決め
weak confidence 消費者マインドの冷え込み
weaker asset 不良資産
weaker operating income 営業収益[営業利益]の減少[低下, 落ち込み]

weaken 他動 悪化させる, 低下させる, 軟化させる, 弱める, 抑える, 自動 弱くなる, 弱まる, 軟化する, 弱化する, 弱体化する, 低迷する, 悪化する, 下落する, 低下する, 低迷する, 減少する
weaken the balance sheet 財務内容[バランス・シート]を悪化させる
weakening demand 需要の減退, 需要の軟化, 需要低迷

weakened 形 弱まった, 軟化した, 弱体化した, 低迷した, 悪化した, 下落[低下, 減少]した, …の軟化[弱体化], …の低迷[悪化], …の下落[低下, 減少]
weakened asset quality 資産の質の悪化
weakened immune systems 弱化した免疫系

weakness 名 弱み, 短所, 弱点, 弱含み, 低下, 落ち込み, 減少, 軟化, 下落, 低迷
cyclical weakness 景気後退による低迷
weakness in output 生産低下, 生産の低迷

wealth 名 富, 資産, 財産, 富裕, 資源, 価値のある産物
expected wealth 期待資産
financial wealth 金融資産
income and wealth 所得と資産, 所得と富
maximize shareholder wealth 株主の富を極大化する, 株主の富を最大限に増やす
mineral wealth 鉱物資源
national wealth statistics 国富統計
negative wealth effect 逆資産効果
real wealth 実質資産
wealth effect 資産効果, 富効果
wealth management 資産管理, 資産運用
wealth maximization 資産の極大化, 富の極大化

wealthiest nation 最富裕国
wean self off …から脱却する, …を捨てる, …を止める (＝wean oneself (away) from)
weapon 名 武器, 兵器, 凶器, 攻撃手段, 対抗手段
biological weapons 生物兵器
chemical weapons 化学兵器
Chemical Weapons Convention 化学兵器禁止条約
nuclear weapons 核兵器
small weapons 小火器
Treaty on the Nonproliferation of Nuclear Weapons 核兵器拡散防止条約
weapons of mass destruction 大量破壊兵器《略 WMD》

weaponize 動 兵器化する
weapons-grade 形 兵器級の
weapons-grade enriched uranium 兵器級濃縮ウラン
weapons-grade plutonium 兵器級プルトニウム

wearable technology ウエアラブル技術
weather 動 〈困難などを〉切り抜ける, 乗り切る, しのぐ, 克服する, …に耐える, 風化させる, 変色させる
weather a recession 不況を乗り切る
weather tough times 困難な[厳しい]時期を切り抜ける

weather 名 天気, 天候, 気象, 天気情報, 天気予報
abnormal weather 天候不順
foul [bad] weather 悪天候
go [fly, run] into heavy weather 苦境に陥る, 暗い状況になる
keep a weather eye on …を警戒する
keep one's weather eye open [awake, lifted] 絶えず注意している, 抜け目がない
keep the weather of …を牛耳る, …の風上にいる
make heavy weather of …を難儀に思う, …を

大げさに考える
make heavy weather with …で四苦八苦する
the National Weather Service 米国気象課
the Weather Bureau 気象庁, 気象局
the weather forecast [report] 天気予報
weather damage 風雨による損傷
weather eye 警戒, 用心, 天気を予想する眼力, 気象衛星
weather map [chart] 天気図
weather merchandising 天気管理経営, ウェザー・マーチャンダイジング
weather observation 気象観測
weather radar 気象レーダー
weather satellite 気象衛星
weather station 気象台, 測候所
weather vane 風見鶏, 風向計
weatherman 気象予報士, 天気予報官, 気象学者
weathers 浮き沈み, 栄枯盛衰
Web [web] 名 ネット上の情報通信網, ホームページ, ウェブ
  Web donations ネット献金 (＝donations via Internet, online donations)
  Web marketing ウェブ・マーケティング (＝Internet marketing)
  Web portal ポータル(玄関)サイト
  Web ratings インターネット視聴率
Web site ホームページ, ウェブ・サイト, サイト (＝homepage, Web page, website)
  dating Web site 出会い系サイト
  incorporate the anti-spyware program into the homepage of one's Web site …のウェブ・サイトのホームページにスパイウエア防止プログラムを組み込む
  subscription Web site 有料サイト, 有料ウェブ・サイト
  Web site operator サイト運営業者
wedged between 板ばさみの
Weekly Compilation of Presidential Documents 〈米国の〉週刊大統領公式文書
weigh on …の足を引っ張る, …を圧迫する
weight 名 重さ, 重量, 体重, 重荷, 負担, 圧迫, 重圧, 重要性, 有力, 勢力, 加重値, 厚み, 重み, 構成比率, ウェート
  add weight to …を促進する, …に拍車をかける
  carry weight 効果がある, 影響力がある
  credit risk weight 与信リスクのウェート
  dead weight ton 重量トン

gross weight 総重量
net weight 純重量, 正味重量
security weights 証券の組入れ比率
throw one's weight about [around] 権威をちらつかせる, 権威を盾に威張り散らす, 権力や地位を乱用する, 威張り散らす, でしゃばりすぎる
throw one's weight behind …を後押しする, 権威[地位]を利用して…を支援する
under the weight of …の重圧のもとで
weights and measures 度量衡
welfare 名 福祉, 厚生, 福利厚生, 福祉事業
  community welfare 地域福祉
  employee welfare fund 従業員福利厚生基金
  public welfare 公共福祉
  social welfare 社会福祉
  welfare expense 福利厚生費
  welfare facilities for workers 勤労者福祉施設
  welfare pension 福祉年金
well-placed 形 地位の高い, 実力者の, 信頼できる
  well-placed official 信頼できる当局筋, 高官
  well-placed person 実力者
West Texas Intermediate ウェスト・テキサス・インターミディエート《略 WTI》
whaling 名 捕鯨, 捕鯨業
  aboriginal whaling 先住民生存捕鯨
  antiwhaling nation 反捕鯨国
  coastal whaling 沿岸捕鯨
  commercial whaling 商業捕鯨
  International Convention for the Regulation of Whaling 国際捕鯨取締条約
  International Whaling Commission 国際捕鯨委員会《略 IWC》
  pro-whaling nation 捕鯨容認国
  research whaling 調査捕鯨
  whaling nation 捕鯨国
  whaling resources 捕鯨資源
whichever is lower principle 低価主義
whip 動 むちで打つ, 激しく打つ, 打ち負かす, 勝つ
  whip on …を行動に駆り立てる
  whip the rebels 反逆者を打ち負かす
  whip up あおり立てる, かき立てる, 刺激する, …を手早く用意する
  whip up feelings against …への反感をかき立てる
whip 名 むち, 御者, 院内幹事, 院内総務, 〈自党議員の出席を求める〉登院命令, 登院命令書, しな

	やかさ, 弾力性
a fair crack of the whip	公平な機会, フェアなやり方
a three-line whip	〈英政党が自党の国会議員に出す〉緊急登院令, 緊急登院命令, 緊急登院命令書
crack the whip	厳しく監督する, 厳しく指導する
have the whip hand	権限を持っている, 人を支配する, 操る
send [issue] a whip round	党員命令を出す[発する]
the government whip	与党の院内幹事
the majority whip	多数党副院内総務[幹事]
the minority whip	少数党副院内総務[幹事]
the opposition whip	野党の院内幹事
the party [chief] whip	党の院内幹事長, 首席院内幹事
the whip hand	支配, 優位
whistle 名	笛, 口笛, 警笛
blow the whistle on	…を告発する, …を密告する, たれこむ, 〈スキャンダルなどを〉暴く, ばらす, 〈人を〉裏切る, 〈計画などを〉止めさせる, 中止させる, 取り締まる
not worth the whistle	まったくつまらない, まったく無益な
pay [dear] for one's whistle	ひどい目にあう, つまらないものを高く買う
wet one's whistle	酒でのどを潤す, 酒を一杯やる
whistle-blower 名	内部告発者, 密告者
whistle-blowing 名	内部告発, 密告
White House	米国大統領官邸, 米国政府, ホワイトハウス (=the Executive Mansion)

ホワイトハウス関連語句

Assistant	大統領補佐官
Assistant, Chief of Staff	大統領首席補佐官
Assistant, Deputy Chief of Staff	大統領次席補佐官
Blue Room	青の間
Cabinet Room	閣議の間
China Room	陶器の間
Counselor	大統領顧問
Deputy Assistant to the President and Director of White House Operations	大統領補佐官・ホワイトハウス運営担当主任
diplomatic reception room	外交使節接見の間, 外交使節レセプション・ルーム
East Room	東の間
East Wing	東館, イースト・ウイング
entrance hall	玄関ホール
First Lady's office	大統領夫人執務室
Green Room	緑の間
library	図書館
Lincoln Suite	リンカーンの間
Monroe Room	モンローの間
North Portico	北玄関
Oval Office [Room]	大統領執務室
Oval Officer	大統領側近
President's living quarters	大統領の居室
President's Study	大統領の書斎
Press Secretary	大統領報道官
Red Room	赤の間
Roosevelt Room	ルーズベルト会議室
Rose Garden	ローズ・ガーデン
Rose Room	バラの間
Secretary	秘書
Special Assistant to Counselor	大統領顧問の特別補佐官
State dining room	公式晩餐会室, 公式晩餐室
West Wing	西館, ウエスト・ウイング
White House Chief of Staff	米大統領首席補佐官
White House Hostess	ホワイトハウス・ホステス (大統領夫人に代わって客を接待する女性)
White House Military Office	ホワイトハウス軍務局
White House spokesman	ホワイトハウスの報道官, 米大統領補佐官
Vermail Room	朱の間

White House Office ホワイトハウス事務局

ホワイトハウス事務局 (the White House Office)
スタッフの役職名:

Chief of Staff to the President	大統領首席補佐官
Counsel to the President	大統領法律顧問
Physician to the President	大統領医務官
Assistant to the President and Deputy Chief of Staff	大統領補佐官・副首席補佐官
Assistant to the President and Deputy for National Security Affairs	大統領補佐官・国家安全保障問題担当副官

Assistant to the President and Director, Office of National Service	大統領補佐官・国家的サービス活動室長
Assistant to the President and Press Secretary	大統領補佐官・報道官
Assistant to the President and Secretary of the Cabinet	大統領補佐官・内閣書記官
Assistant to the President and Staff Secretary	大統領補佐官・スタッフ秘書官
Assistant to the President for Communications	通信[広報]担当大統領補佐官
Assistant to the President for Economic and Domestic Policy	経済・内政政策担当大統領補佐官
Assistant to the President for Intergovernmental Affairs	州・地方自治体・政府間問題担当大統領補佐官
Assistant to the President for Legislative Affairs	議会担当大統領補佐官
Assistant to the President for Media Affairs	メディア問題担当大統領補佐官
Assistant to the President for National Security Affairs	国家安全保障問題担当大統領補佐官
Assistant to the President for Policy Development	政策立案担当大統領補佐官
Assistant to the President for Political Affairs	政治問題担当大統領補佐官
Assistant to the President for Presidential Personnel	大統領人事担当大統領補佐官
Assistant to the President for Public Events and Initiatives	公的行事・イニシアティブ担当大統領補佐官
Assistant to the President for Public Liaison	民間団体連絡[一般公衆渉外]担当大統領補佐官
Assistant to the President for Science and Technology	科学技術政策担当大統領補佐官
Deputy Assistant to the President and Director, Office of Intergovernmental Affairs	大統領副補佐官・政府間問題担当室長
Deputy Assistant to the President and Executive Assistant to the Chief of Staff	大統領副補佐官・首席補佐官事務補佐官
Deputy Assistant to the President for Appointments and Scheduling	会見日程調整・スケジュール担当大統領副補佐官
Deputy Assistant to the President for Cabinet Liaison	内閣連絡担当大統領副補佐官
Deputy Assistant to the President for Communications and Director of Speechwriting	通信[広報]担当大統領副補佐官・演説原稿作成主任
Deputy Assistant to the President for Legislative Affairs (House)	議会担当大統領副補佐官(下院担当)
Deputy Assistant to the President for Legislative Affairs (Senate)	議会担当大統領副補佐官(上院担当)
Deputy Assistant to the President for Policy Planning	政策企画担当大統領副補佐官
Deputy Chief of Staff and Assistant to the President	大統領次席補佐官
Deputy Counsel to the President	大統領副法律顧問
Special Assistant to the President and Executive secretary, Economic Policy Council	大統領特別補佐官・経済政策委員会事務秘書官
Special Assistant to the President for Presidential Messages and Correspondence	大統領教書・書簡担当大統領特別補佐官

white knight 白馬の騎士, 友好的買収者, 善意の買収者, 友好的な支援者, 友好的な第三者, 友好的企業, 友好的株主, ホワイト・ナイト(ホワイト・ナイトは, 敵対的買収を防ぐ手法として, 敵対的なM&A(企業の合併・買収)にさらされている企業が, 友好的な関係にある別の企業に自社を買収してもらうこと)

white paper 白書
　White Paper on Commerce 通商白書
　white paper on national defense 国防白書
　white paper on science and technology 科学技術白書

Whitehall 名 英国首相官邸, 英国政府, ホワイトホール街(英国の政府官庁街)

WHO 世界保健機関 (World Health Organizationの略)

who was who 故人人名録, 物故録

who's who 紳士録, 人名録, 名士録, 名士, フーズフー

whole-hearted support 最大級の賛意

wholesale 名 卸売り, 大企業向け, 機関投資家向け, 大口, ホールセール
　retail and wholesale sector 流通業
　wholesale bank 法人向け銀行, 大企業向け銀

行, ホールセール・バンク
- **wholesale business** 卸売業
- **wholesale house** 卸売問屋
- **wholesale inflation** 卸売物価指数 (＝wholesale price inflation)
- **wholesale investor** 機関投資家
- **wholesale market** 卸売市場
- **wholesale storage** 大量保管
- **wholesale trading** 卸売業

wholesale price 卸売価格, 卸値, 卸売物価, 企業物価
- **wholesale price inflation** 卸売物価指数上昇率
- **wholesale price index** 企業物価指数(旧卸売物価指数)
- **wholesale price index number** 卸売物価指数
- **wholesale price report** 卸売物価指数
- **wholesale prices** 卸売物価, 卸売物価指数, 日本の企業物価(旧卸売物価), 企業物価指数

wholly capitalized domestically 純国内資本の

wholly owned subsidiary [affiliate] 完全所有子会社, 全額出資子会社, 100％出資子会社, 100％子会社 (＝fully owned subsidiary [unit], totally held subsidiary)

whopping 形 でっかい, 途方もなく大きい, 莫大な, 巨大な, 巨額の
- **a whopping lie** 大うそ

wide-awake 形 目を大きく見開いた, 油断のない, 抜け目のない, つけ込まれる隙のない

widen 動 拡大する, 広げる, 規模拡大する, 大きくする, 自動 広がる, 広くなる, 大きくなる

wield 動 振り回す, 使う, 使いこなす, 巧みに使う, 操る, 行使する, 振るう, 握る, 持つ, 支配する, 統治する
- **wield influence over [upon]** …に影響を与える, …に影響を及ぼす
- **wield authority [power, the scepter]** 権限[権力]を行使する, 権力を振るう
- **wield several languages** 数か国語を操る, 数か国語を使いこなす
- **wield the [a facile] pen** 健筆を振るう

win 動 勝つ, 勝ち取る, 勝ち抜く, 勝利を得る, 獲得する, 得る, もたらす
- **win a bidding competition for** …を競争入札で落札する
- **win a contract** 契約を獲得する, 受注する
- **win back** 取り戻す
- **win come-from-behind victory over** …に対して逆転優勝する
- **win hands down** 楽勝する
- **win or lose** 勝っても負けても, 結果はどうあれ
- **win out [through]** 〈苦労の末に〉成功する, 勝ち抜く, 勝利を収める, やり遂げる, 勝る
- **win out over** …に勝つ, 勝利を収める
- **win over [around, round]** 説得する, 説き伏せる, 首尾よく[まんまと]味方に引き入れる
- **win the day** 〈議論などに〉勝つ, 成功する

win 名 勝ち, 勝利, 勝つこと
- **come-from-behind win** 逆転勝ち
- **surprise win over** …に対する予想外の勝利
- **win-win-win solution** 三方一両得の解決策

wind 名 風, 強風, 風力, 破壊力, 影響力, 兆し, 気配, 動き, 傾向, 大勢, 世論, 呼吸, 息, ほら, 空言(そらごと), 管楽器部
- **a wind [the winds] of change** 変化の兆し, 改革の影響[影響力]
- **against the wind** 風に逆らって, 大勢[世論]に逆らって
- **deregulatory winds** 規制緩和の動き
- **get wind of** …をかぎ付ける, …を[…の気配を]察知する, …を知る, …に気がつく
- **hang in the wind** 未決定の状態にある
- **how [which way] the wind is blowing [blows]** 世間の情勢[動向], 形勢, 風向き
- **raise the wind** 〈借りて〉現金を調達する
- **see [find out] which way [how] the wind blows [lies]** 風向きを見る, 形勢を察知する
- **the wind of war** 戦争の破壊力
- **wind energy** 風力エネルギー
- **wind farm** 発電用風車の列, 風力発電施設
- **wind-generated electricity** 風力発電
- **wind-generating potential** 風力発電能力
- **wind generation** 風力発電
- **wind power** 風力
- **wind resource** 風力資源
- **wind shear** 青天乱流, ウインドシアー
- **wind tunnel** 風洞
- **wind turbine** 風力タービン,〈風力発電用の〉風車
- **World Wind Energy Association** 世界風力エネルギー協会《略 WWEA》

wind-riched 形 風力の豊かな
▶ The three most *wind-riched* states of the United States have enough harnessable wind energy to satisfy national electricity needs. 米国で最も

風力が豊かな3州(ノースダコタ, カンザスとテキサスの3州)には, 合わせて全米の電力需要を満たすだけの利用可能な風力エネルギーがある.

wind up 解散する, 清算する, 整理する, 中止する, 切り上げる, 終える, 事業停止する,〈企業を〉閉鎖する, …で終わる, 結局…することになる, 結局…する羽目になる, 最後には…に行き着く
　be wound up 緊張する, 興奮する, 閉鎖される, 中止される
　wind up an account 口座を清算する
　wind up the meeting 会議を切り上げる
wind-down [wind down] 名 〈段階的な〉規模縮小, 段階的縮小, 縮小的解消, 徐々に収束すること, 元利払い
windfall 名 タナボタ利益, 思わぬ利益, 思いがけない利益, 望外の利益, 臨時利益, 偶発利益, 過剰利得, タナボタ[棚ぼた], 思いがけない幸運, 追い風, 形 意外の, 一時的な, 一回かぎりの, 臨時の
　windfall effect 偶発的効果
　windfall gains 思いがけない利益, 意外な利益, 偶発利益
　windfall loss 思いがけない損失, 意外な損失, 偶発損失
　windfall profit tax 超過所得税, 過剰所得税[利得税]
window-dress 動 粉飾する, 粉飾決算する
window dressing 粉飾, 粉飾決算 (= window-dressed accounts)
window period ウインドー期間, 空白期間(ウイルスに感染してからウイルスを検知できる時点までの期間)
wing 名 一翼, 分派, 保護, 活動力
　spread [stretch] one's wings 能力を十分に発揮する
　under one's wing …の保護下に, …の傘下に
winner 名 勝ち組, 勝ち組企業, 成功企業, 勝者, 値上がり銘柄
　election winner 当選者
　the winner of a contract 契約獲得企業, 受注者, 施工業者, 元請業者, 落札者 (= contract winner)
　the winner of the bidding 落札業者, 受注者, 受注業者
winning price 落札価格
winning product ヒット商品
WIPO 世界知的所有権機関 (World Intellectual Property Organizationの略)
Wire Telecommunications Law 有線電気通信法

wireless 名 無線, 無線通信, 無線業務, 形 電線を用いない, 無線の, 無線通信の
　wireless communication(s) 無線通信
　wireless GSM 無線GSM (GSM＝グローバル移動通信システム)
　wireless in-building network 構内無線通信網, 構内無線ネットワーク
　wireless local area network 無線LAN (構内情報通信網) (＝ wireless LAN : 電波を使ってデータをやりとりする通信形態で, 配線不要, 高速でインターネットを利用できる)
　wireless market 無線通信市場
　wireless remote control 無線遠隔操作
　wireless telecommunications 無線通信
　wireless telegraphy 無線電信, 無線電信術
wiretap 動 盗聴する
wiretapping 名 盗聴
wishful thinking 希望的観測
withdraw 動 〈預金などを〉引き出す,〈預金などを〉引き揚げる,〈通貨などを〉回収する,〈市場などから〉撤退する, 取り消す, 打ち切る, 撤回する
　withdraw cash from the account 口座から預金を引き出す
　withdraw deposits 預金を引き出す, 預金を引き揚げる
　withdraw from the market 市場から撤退する (＝ pull out of the market)
　withdraw money 金を引き出す, 金を下ろす, 払い戻す, 通貨などを回収する, 解約する
withdrawal 名 撤退, 脱退, 離脱, 撤回, 回収, 預金の引出し, 引落し, 払戻し, 取消し, 解約,〈出資者や株主に対する〉利益の分配, 資本の減少
　compulsory withdrawal 強制退会
　double withdrawal 二重引落し
　early withdrawal 期限前払戻し, 期限前解約
　employee withdrawal 従業員の脱退
　profit withdrawal 利益控除
　social withdrawal 引きこもり
　withdrawal from a company 退社, 退職
　withdrawal of charges 公訴の取下げ
　withdrawal rate 撤退率
　withdrawal slip for a savings account 普通預金払戻し票
withholding tax 源泉徴収税, 源泉課税, 源泉所得税, 源泉税
　separate withholding tax system 源泉分離課税方式

withholding tax rate 源泉徴収税率
withholding tax refund 源泉税還付
withstand 動 反対する, 抵抗する, 〈…に〉耐える, 持ちこたえる, 逆らう
WMD 大量破壊兵器 (weapons of mass destructionの略)
woes 名 苦難, 災難, 災い, 危機, 悩み, 苦悩, 苦境, 悲哀, 問題
  financial woes 財政難, 経営難, 経営危機, 金融危機 (= financial troubles)
won 名 ウォン (韓国と北朝鮮の通貨単位)
word 名 語, 単語, ことば, 約束, 指図, 命令, 知らせ, 連絡, 便り, 音信, 伝言, うわさ, 言い争い, けんか
  a battle of words 論戦
  at a word 〈求められたら〉すぐに, 〈…からの〉一言で
  be as good as [better than] one's word 約束を果たす
  beyond words ことばでは言い表せない, 筆舌に尽くし難い
  by [through] word of mouth 口コミで, 口伝えで, 口頭で
  choose one's words ことばを選ぶ, 吟味して発言する
  eat one's words 前言を取り消す
  four-letter word 四文字ことば, 卑猥なことば [表現]
  get into a battle of words 論戦を始める
  have a word with …とちょっと話し合う
  have no words for …を表現できない
  have words 口論する
  keep one's word 約束を守る
  pass the word 命令[指示]を出す, 伝言を伝える
  take a person's word for it 人のことばを信用する
  the last [final] word on …についての決定権 [最終決定権], 最終発言, まとめの意見 [一言]
  word blindness 失語症
  word order 語順
  words and deeds 言動
  words of one syllable 平易なことば
work 動 働く, 仕事をする, …を担当する, …を仕事場とする, 動かす, 操作する, 加工する, 効果がある, 影響する, 作動する
  work at …で働く, …で仕事をする, …で作業をする, …に取り組む
  work out 〈問題などを〉解く, 計算する, 解決する, 〈人を〉理解する, 〈計画などを〉立てる, 打ち出す, つめる, 工夫する, 作り上げる, 成し遂げる, 練る, よく考える, 手はずを整える, 練習[トレーニング]をする, 結局…になる
  work to rule 順法闘争をする
  work [band, join] together 協力する, 協調する, 提携する
work 名 仕事, 事業, 作業, 工事, 労働, 職, 研究, 勉強, 作品, 作用, 働き, 行為, しわざ, ワーク
  a work in progress 執筆中の作品
  be dismissed from work 解雇される
  be in the works 計画されている
  engineering works 土木工事
  field work 現場作業
  good works 慈善活動
  in work 就職して
  irrigation works 灌漑工事
  legal work 法律業務
  life's work [lifework] ライフワーク
  mighty works 奇跡
  off work 仕事を休んで, 休暇を取って
  out of work 失業して
  population at work 就業人口
  return to work 復職する
  right to work 労働権
  social work 社会事業, ソーシャル・ワーク
  the works of nature 自然
  voluntary work ボランティア活動
  work camp 作業刑務所
  work contract 労働契約
  work environment 労働環境
  work ethic 労働倫理, 労働観, 仕事至上主義, 労働意欲
  work flat out 全力で取り組む, 全力をあげて取り組む
  work force 労働力, 労働人口, 全従業員, 全社員 (= labor force, workforce)
  work hazard 労働災害の原因となるもの
  work hours 勤務時間
  work practices 労働慣習
  work record 勤務成績, 作業記録
  work release 労働釈放
  works council 工場協議会
work off 〈不満や怒りを〉晴らす, 発散する, 解消する, …を取り除く, 片付ける, 仕上げる, 消化する, 〈借金を〉働いて返す, 刺激する, …を装う, 〈疲労などが〉徐々にとれる
work on [upon] …に取り組む, …に精を出す,

…を手がける, …に影響を及ぼす, …に作用する, …を説得する

work sharing [**work-sharing**] 雇用分割, ワークシェア, ワーク・シェアリング（＝work sharing system）
  work sharing system 雇用分割, 仕事［雇用］の分かち合い, ワーク・シェアリング方式, ワークシェア, ワーク・シェアリング・システム（企業の雇用維持対策として, 1人当たりの労働時間を短縮して雇用を分かち合う制度。失業が社会問題化したオランダなど欧州を中心に, 1980年代から普及した）

workable 形 運用できる, 活用できる, 実行可能な（feasible）, 実行できる, 採掘可能な, 耕作可能な, 加工できる, 実際的な

worker 名 労働者, 勤労者, 就労者, 就業者, 働き手, 従業員, 人材
  blue-collar worker 肉体労働者, 労働者, 工員, ブルー・カラー
  commitment of workers 社員の帰属意識
  excess workers 余剰人員
  extra worker 臨時雇い労務者
  full time worker フルタイム従業員
  gray-collar worker 技術関係労働者, グレー・カラー
  green-collar worker グリーン・カラー
  illegal worker 不法就労者
  lower skilled worker 未熟練労働者
  non-union workers 未組織労働者
  part-time worker パート, パート従業員, パート社員, パートタイマー
  public sector worker 公務員
  regular worker 常用労働者
  semi-skilled worker 半熟練労働者
  skilled worker 熟練労働者
  time worker 時間給労働者
  white-collar worker サラリーマン, 事務職員, 頭脳労働者, ホワイト・カラー
  worker buyout 従業員の経営権買取り
  Worker Dispatching Law 人材派遣法
  Worker Profiling and Reemployment Services 労働者選別・再就職支援サービス《略 WPRS》
  workers compensation 労災
  workers compensation insurance system 労災保険制度, 労災保険
  workers household 勤労者世帯, サラリーマン世帯
  workers with limited-term contract 期間従業員

workforce 名 就業者, 労働力, 労働人口, 従業員, 社員, 人員, 全従業員, 全社員（＝labor force, resort to, work force）
  early workforce retirement 早期退職
  foreign workforce 外国人労働力, 外国人労働人口
  global workforce 全世界の従業員
  total group workforce グループ全体の人員, グループ全体の従業員
  total workforce 労働力人口, 総労働人口
  workforce development 労働力開発
  workforce in employment 雇用者数
  Workforce Investment Act of 1998 1998年労働力投資法

working 名 労働, 働き, 作業, 作業現場, 運転, 動き, 動作, 作用
  behind-the-scenes workings 舞台裏の動き
  off-line working オフライン動作
  online working オンライン動作
  overtime working 時間外労働
  percentage working 就労率
  real time working 実時間動作, リアルタイム動作
  time working 作業時間
  wood working 木材加工
  working from home 在宅就労, 在宅勤務（＝remote work, telecommuting, telework, teleworking）

working 形 経営の, 運転する, 運用している, 営業の, 仕事上の, 作業の, 労働の, 職場での, 実用の, 実際の役に立つ, 機能している, 実動の
  working area 作業領域（＝work area）
  working assets 運用資産
  working capital 運転資本, 運転資金, 経営資本, 資金（＝operating capital）
  working class 労働者階級
  working committee 作業部会, 作業委員会, 運営委員会
  working conditions 労働条件, 労働環境, 職場環境
  working day 営業日, 勤務日, 就業日, 平日, 〈1日の〉労働時間（＝workday）
  working days 労働日数, 作業日数, 稼動日数
  working diagram 施工図
  working director 常勤取締役
  working drawing 作業図, 設計図, 工作図

working environment 労働環境, 作業環境
working expense 作業費, 経費
working fund 運転資金, 運転資本, 経営資本
working generation 現役世代
working group 作業部会, 作業グループ, 作業班, 専門調査委員会
working holiday ワーキング・ホリデー（就労ビザなしで外国人が働ける制度）
working hours 就業時間, 勤務時間, 作業時間, 労働時間
working knowledge 実用知識, 実際に役立つ知識
working life 耐用年数, 仕事をしている期間
working lunch 実務昼食会, 昼食を取りながらの会議
working majority 議会の決議に必要な多数
working model 実用模型
working office 作業事務所
working order 〈機械の〉稼動状態
working partner 業務執行社員, 労務出資社員（＝acting partner, managing partner）
working party 特別調査委員会, 作業部会, 作業委員会
working paper 監査調書, 調書, 精算表, 計算書類《略 W/P》
working profit ratio 経営利益率
working reserve 〈米連邦準備加盟銀行の〉運転準備金
working rules 就業規則, 業務規定, 準則
working session 会議
working standards 労働基準
working storage 作業用記憶領域, 作業用記憶域
working week 週当たり労働時間
working year 営業年度, 会計年度
working-level 形 事務レベルの, 実務レベルの
working-level meeting [talks, conference] 実務レベル協議, 実務協議, 実務者協議
working-level negotiation 事務レベルの折衝, 事務レベルの交渉
working-level panel 事務レベルの委員団
workload [work load] 名 仕事量, 作業量, 作業負担量, 作業負荷, 標準作業量, 標準作業時間
carry one's usual workload いつもの仕事量をこなす
heavy workload 過重労働
workload imbalance 作業負担量［仕事量］の不均衡, 労働力の不均衡

workout 名 〈事業部ごとの〉問題点の改善, 訓練, 処理, 整理, 体調調整, 〈機械などの〉点検, 適性試験, ワークアウト
bankruptcy workouts 破産関連業務
workplace 名 職場, 仕事場
workplace bullying 職場のいじめ, 職場でのいじめ（＝bullying in the workplace）
world 名 世界, 世間, 世の中, この世, あの世, …界, ワールド
business world 経済界, 財界, 産業界, 実業界, 業界（＝business circles, business community）
World Administrative Radio Conference 世界無線通信主管庁会議《略 WARC》
World Bank 世界銀行（国際復興開発銀行（IBRD）の通称）
World Bank Group 世界銀行グループ（第一世銀（IBRD）, 第二世銀（国際開発協会：IDA）, 第三世銀（国際金融公社：IFC）の国際金融機関のほか, 多国間投資保証機関（MIGA）, 国際投資紛争調停機関（ICSSI）を指す）
world class 世界一流の, 国際レベル, 世界クラス
World Conservation Union 国際自然保護連合（IUCN）
world debt problem 累積債務問題
World Economic Forum 世界経済フォーラム《略 WEF》（世界各国の政財界人や学識経験者が集まって, 毎年1月にスイスのリゾート地ダボスで開かれる世界経済フォーラム年次総会は, ダボス会議（Davos Conference）と呼ばれる）
World Energy Council 世界エネルギー会議《略 WEC》
World Environment Day 世界環境デー
world exposition 世界万国博覧会
World Food Program 世界食糧計画
World Health Organization 世界保健機関《略 WHO》
World Heritage 〈ユネスコの〉世界遺産
World Heritage Convention 世界遺産条約
World Intellectual Property Organization 世界知的所有権機関, 世界知的所有権機構《略 WIPO》
World Meteorological Organization 世界気象機関《略 WMO》
World Natural Heritage Site 世界自然遺産
World Partners ワールド・パートナーズ（メガキャリアの米AT&T社とKDD, シンガポール・テレコムの国際企業連合）

World Product Code 国際製品コード, 世界製品コード《略 WPC》
world standard 世界標準, ワールド・スタンダード (=global standard)
World Summit on Sustainable Development 持続可能な開発に関する世界首脳会議, 環境開発サミット
World Trade Organization 世界貿易機関《略 WTO》
World Wide Web [WWW] ワールド・ワイド・ウェブ, スリー・ダブリュー (=W3, Web)
worm 名 コンピュータ・ワーム, ワーム (=computer worm：コンピュータに忍び込んで, ネットワークを通じて他のコンピュータに侵入するプログラムのこと)
worry 動 心配する, 気をもむ, 悩む, 苦労する
 worry about …を心配する
 worry out 〈問題の〉答えを得る
 worry through 根気強い努力で問題を解決する
worry 名 懸念, 懸念材料, 不安, 不安材料, 心配, 心配事, 心配の種, 気苦労, 悩み
 inflation worries インフレ懸念
 worries about cash burn 資金枯渇への懸念, 手持ち資金涸渇に対する不安
worsen 動 悪化する, 低下する, 拡大する, 増大する, 悪化させる
worsening 名 悪化, 拡大
 the worsening of the massive trade deficit of the United States 米国の膨大な貿易赤字の拡大
worsening 形 悪化している, 低下している, 拡大している, …の悪化[低下, 拡大, 増大]
 worsening employment situation 雇用情勢の悪化, 雇用の悪化
 worsening fiscal conditions 財政の悪化
 worsening job market 雇用情勢の悪化
worst 形 最低の, 最悪の, 最も深刻な, 名 最悪, 最悪の状態, 最悪期
 be past the worst 最悪期を過ぎた
 come off worst 〈競争などに〉負ける
 if the worst comes to the worst いよいよ最悪の場合になったら
 in the worst way とても, 非常に
 the worst-case scenario 最悪のシナリオ
worth 名 価値, 価額, 自己資本, …に相当する量, …分, 有用性, 重要性
 bushiness worth 企業価値
 fixed assets to net worth ratio 固定比率

 net asset worth 純資産額
 present worth 現在価値, 割引現価 (=present value)
 profit ratio of net worth 株主資本利益率
 total liabilities and net worth 総資本
 worth of …相当のもの, …分の…
 worth (to) current debt ratio 資本対流動負債比率, 資本流動負債比率
 worth (to) fixed debt ratio 資本対固定負債比率, 資本固定負債比率
 worth (to) fixed ratio 資本対固定資産比率, 資本固定[固定資本]比率, 固定比率
would-be 形 …志望の, …志願の, …希望の, 自称…の, …のつもりでいる, …予備軍, …側, …未遂の
 would-be acquirer 買収側, 買収希望者
 would-be legal practitioner 法律家志望者
 would-be rape 暴行未遂
 would-be refugee 亡命志願者
 would-be terrorist テロリスト志願者, テロリスト予備軍
wrack 動 悩ます, 苦しめる (=rack)
wrap up 〈協議などを〉上首尾に終える, …をうまくまとめ上げる, …に隠して表現する
 be wrapped up 没頭している
 wrap up a week of meetings 1週間の協議を上首尾に終える
wreak 動 〈被害などを〉与える, 〈罰などを〉加える, 〈怒りを〉ぶちまける, 浴びせる, 〈損害などを〉引き起こす
 wreak one's anger on …に怒りをぶちまける
 wreak havoc in …で大被害を与える, …で大混乱を招く
 wreak revenge on [upon] …に恨みを晴らす, …に復讐する
 wreak vengeance on …に復讐する
wriggle out of …から何とか逃れる, …をすり抜ける, …を巧みに避ける
write an option オプションを売る, オプションを売り建てる
write-down [writedown] 名 評価減, 評価損, 評価引下げ, 減損
write off 〈債権を〉帳消しにする[処理する], 償却する, 放棄する, 〈評価額・価格を〉引き下げる, 減価償却する
write-off 名 〈債権の〉帳消し[処理, 放棄], 消却, 評価減, 評価引下げ, 貸倒れ償却, 減価償却, 削除, 〈帳簿の〉締切り

written 形 文書にした, 書面にした, 文書による, 書面による, 成文の, 筆記の
- written agreement 契約書, 合意文書, 合意書, 書面契約
- written approval 書面による承認, 書面による認可
- written assignment 譲渡証書
- written assurance 保証書
- written consent 同意書, 承諾書, 書面による同意［承諾］
- written decision 裁決書
- written demand 要求書
- written estimate 見積り書, 予測書
- written guarantee 保証書
- written instrument 書面, 文書, 証書
- written law 成文法
- written notice [notification] 書面による通知, 書面通知, 通知書
- written opinion 意見書
- written order 注文書
- written permission 許可証, 承諾書
- written premiums 計上収入保険料
- written program 書面計画
- written record 文書, 書面
- written representation 陳述書
- written representation 証明書
- written request 書面による要求［請求］, 要求書, 請求書, 要請, 要請書
- written stipulation 明文規定
- written waiver or renunciation 書面による放棄

written-off bad debts 貸倒れ償却, 貸倒償却費, 不良債権の償却, 不良債権の処理

wrongdoing 名 犯罪, 罪, 悪事, 悪行, 非行, 不正, 罪悪

WTI ウェスト・テキサス・インターミディエート (West Texas Intermediateの略。米テキサス州西部とニューメキシコ州東南部で産出される軽質の原油。米国の市況動向を示す代表銘柄)

WTO 世界貿易機関 (World Trade Organizationの略)
- the new round of WTO talks 新ラウンド, 新多角的貿易交渉
- WTO General Council WTO一般理事会
- WTO panel WTO紛争処理小委員会(パネル)

WWEA 世界風力エネルギー協会 (World Wind Energy Associationの略)

X

x 形 未知の, 未知数の, 不確定の, X字形の, 動 …にX印をつける
X 名 成人向け映画 (X film [movie])
X car 米GMの低燃費車
X chromosome X染色体
X terminal X端末, Xターミナル
x-axis 名 X軸, 横軸（縦軸＝y-axis）
X-C skiing クロスカントリー・スキー
x-Digital Subscriber Line デジタル加入者線 （＝x-DSL）
x-dividend 配当落ち （＝ex dividend. [ex div.]）
X-rate 動 成人向け映画に指定する
X-rated 形 成人向けの, 成人用の, わいせつな, みだらな, 扇情的な, ポルノの
  X-rated film [movie] 成人向け映画
  X-rated shop ポルノ店, ポルノ・ショップ
X-rating 名 成人向け映画指定
X-ray X線
  X-ray astronomy エックス線天文学
  X-ray laser X線レーザー
  X-ray lithography X線露光装置
  X-ray nova X線新星
  X-ray pulsar X線を放射する電波天体
  X-ray scanning X線精査
  X-ray spectrometer X線分光計
  X-ray telescope X線望遠鏡
  X-ray television X線テレビジョン
x-warr. ワラント落ち （＝ex warrants)
Xanadu 名 桃源郷
xenobiology 名 宇宙生物学
xenocurrency 名 本国外流通通貨, ゼノカレンシー（本国以外でも流通する通貨）
xenocurrency market ゼノカレンシー市場
xenophobic 形 外国人嫌いの
xero-radiography 名 X線電子写真
xerox 動 ゼロックスで複写［コピー］する
Xi'an 名 （中国陝西（せんせい）省の首都）西安
Xinhua News Agency 新華通信, 新華社 （＝Xinhuashe：中国の国営通信社）
Xinjiang 名 新疆（しんきょう）, シンチャン
Xinjiang Uygur Autonomous Region 新疆（しんきょう）ウイグル自治区
xor 接 二者のうちどちらか一方の
Xu （ベトナムの通貨単位）スー, スー硬貨
XXX 名 本格的ポルノ, 最も強いビールの記号, 形 わいせつな, 性表現を多く含む

Y

yardstick 名 基準, 尺度, 物差し, 指標
year 名 年,〈会計営業報告書〉年度, 期
  accounting year 会計年度
  base year 基準年, 基準年度
  business year 事業年度, 営業年度, 会計年度 (＝financial year)
  calendar year 暦年
  current year 今期, 今年度, 当期 (＝current fiscal year)
  financial year 会計年度, 事業年度 (＝business year, fiscal year)
  full-year earnings forecast 通期業績予想
  full year results 通期決算
  half year 半期
  half year point 年央
  over a year ago 前年同期比, 前年同月比
  prior year adjustment 過年度損益修正
  profit or loss for the financial year 当期損益
  tax year 税務年度, 課税年度, 事業年度, 会計年度 (＝fiscal year, taxable year)
  taxable year 課税年度 (＝tax year)
  year high 年間最高値
  year-to-date highs 今年最高値, 今年の最高値
  years in business 業歴
year-on-year 名形副 前年同期比, 前年同月比, 前年比 (＝year-over-year)
year-over-year 名形副 前年同期比, 前年同月比, 前年比 (＝over a year ago, year-on-year)
year through next March 来年3月期, 来年3月までの事業年度
year to March 31 3月期決算
  ▶The company fell into negative net worth of ¥357.6 billion on a consolidated basis in the *year to March 31*. 3月期連結決算で, 同社は3,576億円の債務超過に陥った[赤字だった]。
yellow sand 黄砂
yen 名 円, 円相場
  yen-buying, dollar-selling operation 円買い・ドル売り操作, 円買い・ドル売りオペ, 円買い・ドル売りの動き (＝yen-buying and dollar-selling operation)
  yen credits 円借款
  yen-selling, dollar-buying operation 円売り・ドル買い, 円売り・ドル買い操作, 円売り・ドル買いオペ, 円売り・ドル買いの動き (＝yen-selling and dollar-buying operations)
  yen's appreciation against the dollar 円高ドル安
  yen's value 円相場, 円価値
  yen's value against the dollar 円の対米ドル相場
yen loan 円借款, 円貨貸付け (＝yen-based loan, yen-denominated loan)
  provide [extend, offer] a yen loan to …に円借款を供与[貸与]する
  untied yen loans ひも付きでない円借款
yield 名〈株式・債券などの〉利回り, 歩留まり, 収益, イールド
  yield rate 歩留まり, 利率
yuan 〈中国の〉人民元 (＝the Chinese yuan)

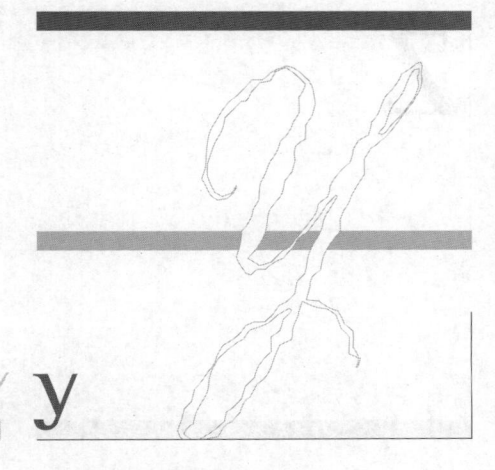

Z

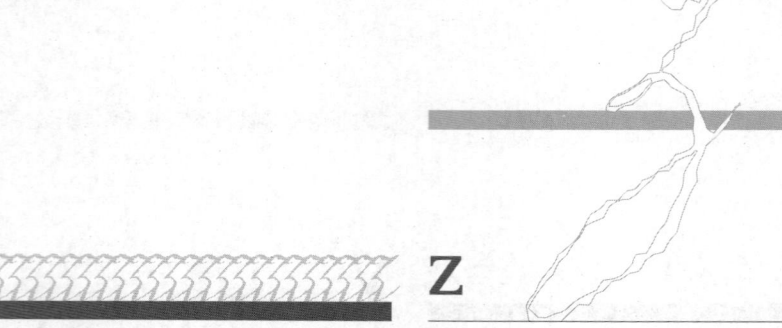

zero 名 ゼロ, 零度
　zero coupon bond　ゼロ・クーポン債
　zero defects movement　無欠陥運動, 無欠点運動, ZD運動
　zero economic growth　経済のゼロ成長, ゼロ経済成長
　zero emission vehicle　排気ガス・ゼロの車, ゼロ・エミッション車
　zero gravity　無重力状態
　zero growth　ゼロ成長
　zero hour　〈ロケットなどの〉発射予定時刻, 予定行動作戦, 攻撃開始時刻, 決定的瞬間, 重大な決断を下す時
　zero-interest rate policy　ゼロ金利政策 (= zero-interest policy)
　zero-interest tax-free (government) bonds　無利子非課税国債（利子が付かないかわりに相続税がかからない国債）
　zero population growth　人口のゼロ成長, 静止人口《略 ZPG》
　zero tillage　ゼロ耕作
zero in on　…に照準を合わせる, …に狙いを定める, …に的を絞る, …に努力[注意]を集中する
zero tolerance　不寛容主義, 例外なしの法規適用, 厳しい態度で臨むこと
zone delivered pricing　地域別輸送価格

和英索引

あ

アイアール　IR
相容れない考え　competing ideas
愛顧　patronage
合言葉　password
アイコン　icon
合図で知らせる　signal
間にある　intervene
相手　opponent
相手先ブランド製造業者　OEM
相手先ブランドによる生産　original equipment manufacturing
相反する　clash
相反する　conflicting
iPS細胞　induced pluripotent stem cell
隘路　bottleneck
青写真　blueprint
青図　blueprint
赤字　deficit
赤字　red
赤字　shortfall
赤字に悩む　deficit-ridden
赤字の　loss-making
赤字を抱えた　debt-saddled
赤字を出す　lose
明かす　unfold
アカデミー賞　Academy Awards
上がり気味の　bullish
上がる　appreciate
上がる　mount
商う　trade
明らかにする　clarify
明らかにする　reveal
明らかにする　unveil
悪　vice
悪意のある　vicious
悪事　wrongdoing
悪循環　spiral
悪循環　vicious circle
悪性の　vicious
悪戦苦闘する　struggle
悪徳　vice
悪徳行為　vice
悪の枢軸　axis of evil
…をあくまで主張する　hold out for
悪夢　nightmare
悪用　prostitution
悪用する　abuse
悪用する　misuse
アグリビジネス　agribusiness
上げ相場　bull market
挙げる　cite
上げる　hike
浅い　shallow

あざけり　scorn
足　foot
アジア欧州会議　ASEM
アジア開発銀行　ADB
アジア太平洋経済協力会議　APEC
アジア太平洋地域　Asia-Pacific region
足跡　footstep
足がかり　stepping stone
味付け　seasoning
足取り　progress
足踏みマシーン　treadmill
味わう　undergo
…の足を引っ張る　weigh on
アスファルト舗装道路　blacktop street
アスベスト　asbestos
アセット　asset
遊ぶ　play
値入れ　markon
値入れ　markup
…に値を付ける　bid for
値を付ける　quote
与えられた　given
与える　award
与える　feed
与える　grant
与える　inflict
与える　supply
与える　wreak
あだ名を付ける　dub
頭打ちの状態　stagnancy
新しい　fresh
新しい　new
新しく　newly
悪化　deterioration
悪化　downturn
悪化　exacerbation
悪化　worsening
扱い方　treatment
扱いかた　usage
悪化させる　aggravate
悪化させる　exacerbate
悪化させる　sour
悪化させる　weaken
悪化した　contractionary
悪化した　cooled
悪化した　tighter
悪化している　worsening
悪化する　deteriorate
悪化する　sour
悪化する　worsen
熱くなる　heat up
圧縮　cutback
圧縮　reduction
圧勝　grand slam
圧勝　landslide victory
圧勝　sweep

圧勝する　sweep
斡旋業者　agent
圧倒する　devastate
圧倒的多数　supermajority
圧迫　constraint
圧迫　pressure
圧迫　stress
…を圧迫する　bear down on
…を圧迫する　weigh on
アップロードする　upload
集まり　basket
集まる　center
集めて置く　pool
集める　accumulate
集める　amass
集める　collect
集める　garner
あつらえの　custom-made
あつらえの　made-to-order
圧力　muscle
圧力　pressure
圧力　stress
圧力団体　lobby
圧力をかける　pressure
…をあてにする　rely on
あてはめる　apply
…の後　in the wake of
後押し　boost
後押しする　help
後押しする　sponsor
…の後に　following
後の　post-
後回し　backburner
…の穴埋めをする　make up for
…に穴を開ける　hollow out
アパルトヘイト　apartheid
暴れ回り　rampage
アパレル　apparel
アフガニスタンの　Afghan
危ない橋　tightrope
アフリカ開発会議　TICAD
アフリカ統一機構　OAU
アベンド　abend
天下りの　top-down
アメリカ合衆国　U.S.
アメリカ合衆国　United States
アメリカ合衆国の　federal
危うくする　jeopardize
…を危うくする　put ... on the line
怪しい　shady
操る　rig
過ち　mistake
誤った　errant
粗い　crude
洗う　wash
あらかじめ切ってある　precut
荒稼ぎする　rake in

争い conflict	安定化 stabilization	異議を唱える protest
争い contention	安定させる stabilize	…に異議を唱える take issue with
争い dispute	安定した stable	異議を申し立てる appeal
争い fight	安定状態 plateau	行く fare
争い strife	安定性 soundness	育児休業 child care leave
争い war	安定性 stability	育児休業 parental leave
争う combat	安定操作 stabilizing transaction	イケイケの go-go
争う fight	安定装置を施す stabilize	意見 bet
争う vie	安定要因 stabilizing factor	意見 comment
新たに newly	安堵 relief	意見 idea
新たになった renewed	案内 guidance	意見 opinion
改めさせる redress	案内役 road map	意見 remark
改める change	アンバランス imbalance	意見 version
アラブ石油輸出国機構 OAPEC	案文策定 drafting	意見が一致している unanimous
粗利益 gross margin	安楽 comfort	意見交換 dialogue
粗利益 gross profit	安楽死 euthanasia	意見交換 exchange
…を表す mark	安楽死 mercy killing	意見交換の場 talking shop
表す mean		意見聴取 hearing
表す reflect		意見の相違 dispute
表す show	**い**	意見を異にする dissident
現れ symptom		憩いの時[場] oasis
現われる emerge	ES細胞 embryonic stem cells	意向 intention
現われる show up	ES細胞 ES cells	移行 transition
ありそうもない unlikely	言いがかり trumped-up accusation	…する意向である intend to
有体財産 property	イージス艦 Aegis-equipped destroyer	いさかい bickering
ありのままの bare	言い抜け dodge	遺産 inheritance
ありふれた ho-hum	EU憲法 EU constitution	意志 intention
アル・カーイダ Al-Qaida	EU大統領 EU president	意思 intention
アルバイト sideline	委員会 committee	維持 maintenance
荒れ狂う turbulent	委員会 panel	維持 sustainment
アレルギー allergies	委員長の地位 chairmanship	維持可能な sustainable
…に合わせる tailor	家柄 strain	…を意識した -conscious
暗雲 shadow	家出人 runaway	意識調査 poll
暗殺 assassination	家のない homeless	意識調査 survey
暗示 hint	いかがわしい shady	意識の回復 resuscitation
案出する forge	威嚇 duress	意思決定 decision
暗証番号 password	威嚇する threaten	意思決定 decision making
暗証番号 PIN number	医学の medical	維持する maintain
安心 comfort	生かす capitalize on	維持する retain
安心 relief	怒り rage	維持する sustain
安心 security	怒り狂う rampage	意思疎通 communication
安全 safety	移管する transfer	維持能力 sustainability
安全 security	勢い momentum	意地の悪い vicious
安全条項 safe harbor rule	勢いづかせる fuel	いじめ bullying
安全性 safety	勢いよく飛び出す catapult	医師免許 doctor's license
安全性 security	生き返らせる resuscitate	移住 immigration
安全装置 backstop	生き返らせる revitalize	移住 relocation
安全でない unsecured	生き返り resuscitation	移住させる transplant
安全な safe	意気消沈させる choke off	移住者 settler
安全な secure	行き詰まり impasse	異常 abnormality
安全な投資先 safe haven	行き詰まり logjam	異常 glitch
安全保障理事会 Security Council	行き詰まり standoff	委譲 transfer
アンダーラインを引く underline	行き詰まり standstill	異常終了 abend
暗たんとした downbeat	生き残る survive	異常な abnormal
安定 safety	異議のない unanimous	異常な extraordinary
安定 stability	異議の申立て protest	移植 transplant
安定 stabilization	異議申立て appeal	移植する implant

移植する	transplant
石綿	asbestos
イスラム化	Islamization
イスラム教徒	Muslim
イスラム教の	Muslim
イスラムの	Islamic
いずれにせよ	one way or the other
威勢がよい	high-spirited
依然として…だ	remain
以前の	former
急ぐ	expedite
依存	dependence
依存	reliance
依存関係	dependence
…に依存する	rely on
委託する	commission
委託する	entrust
いたずら電話	prank call
板挟み	dilemma
板ばさみの	wedged between
痛めつける	buffet
位置	location
位置	slot
位置	spot
一員にする	enroll
一区画	block
一撃	stroke
一元化	integration
一元化した	consolidated
一元化する	coordinate
一件書類	dossier
一時帰休	furlough
一時帰休させる	furlough
一時しのぎ	stopgap
一時しのぎの	makeshift
一時停止した	suspended
一時停止する	suspend
一時的な	casual
一次的な	primary
一時的な	provisional
一時的な	temporary
一時的な現象	blip
一途な	single-minded
一団	outfit
一段と厳しい	tighter
位置につける	position
1年当たり	per annum
一番手の	leadoff
…に一歩先んじる	one-up
一枚岩	monolith
一枚岩の	monolithic
一様な	steady
一翼	wing
一里塚	milestone
一律の	across-the-board
一律の	flat
一流の	ranking
一連の協議	round
…の位置を示す	mark
1か所ですべて揃う	one-stop
一括の	across-the-board
一括払い	lump sum
…と一貫性がある	consistent with
一貫生産する	integrate
一騎打ち	two-horse race
一極支配	unipolar domination
一国主義	unilateralism
逸材	phenomenon
逸材	talent
一切を白状する	come clean about
一酸化炭素	carbon monoxide
一笑に付す	laugh off
一触即発の	touch-and-go
一触即発の状態	touch and go
一新する	houseclean
一心不乱の	single-minded
一斉検挙	roundup
一斉検挙する	round up
一斉摘発	blanket action
1対1	one on one
一体型の	all-in-one
逸脱	divergence
一致	concert
一致	unison
一致協力する	stand shoulder to shoulder
一致した	concerted
…と一致して	in line with
…と一致する	consistent with
一致する	corresponding
一直線	beeline
一直線の	straight
一定にさせる	peg
一定の	given
一定の	regular
一定の	uniform
一般教書演説	State of the Union address
一般社員	nonmanagerial employee
一般従業員	rank and file
一般使用者	end user
一般庶民	grass roots
一般人	grass roots
一般的な	broad
一般的な	general
一般的な	prevalent
一般に認められている	acceptable
一般の	general
一般の人々	public
一般用医薬品	nonprescription drugs
一方的軍縮論	unilateralism
一方的な	lopsided
一方的な	unilateral
一方的な	unsolicited
…の一歩先を行く	one-up
一歩も引かない姿勢を示す	stand defiant
一本化	unification
一本化する	unify
移転	relocation
移転	transfer
遺伝子	gene
遺伝子組換え食品	genetically altered food
遺伝子の	genetic
移転する	relocate
移転する	transfer
意図	aim
緯度	latitude
移動	flow
移動	mobility
移動	relocation
移動させる	move
移動式	portable
移動式の	mobile
移動する	relocate
移動性	mobility
移動特派員	roving correspondent
意図する	mean
…に挑む	tackle
稲妻	bolt
委任	commission
委任	delegation
委任する	commission
委任する	entrust
違反	violation
違反する	violate
衣服	apparel
違法行為	malfeasance
違法行為	misconduct
違法行為	offense
違法取引する	traffic
違法な	illegal
違法な	unlawful
違法の	illicit
戒め	lesson
意味	purport
意味する	mean
意味する	represent
…を意味する	spell
移民	immigration
移民労働者	migrant worker
イメージ・チェンジ	makeover
嫌がらせ	harassment
違約金	fine
医薬部外品	quasi-medicine
いやな	sour
医用の	medical
意欲	motivation
意欲的な	aggressive

意欲を起こさせる	motivate
意欲をそそる	challenging
依頼する	invite
依頼人	client
イラク政府	Baghdad
イラク戦争	Iraq war
イラクの	Iraqi
いらだたせる	roil
苛立ち	frustration
イラン政府	Tehran
医療	medical care
医療の	medical
医療保険	medical insurance
医療補助員	paramedics
威力	force
入れ替える	reshuffle
異論のある	contentious
異論の多い	controversial
祝い	celebration
院内活動	lobbyism
院外工作者	lobbyist
陰気な	gloomy
イングランド銀行	BoE
陰険な人	snake
インサイダー	insider
因子	factor
飲酒運転	DUI
飲酒検知器	breathalyzer
インターネット	Internet
インターネット・プロトコル	IP
インターンシップ	internship
引退	retirement
引退する	outgoing
インティファーダ	intifada
インデックス	index
インテリジェントな	smart
院内幹事	whip
院内感染	nosocomial (hospital) infection
インフラ	infrastructure
インフルエンザ	flu
インフルエンザ	influenza
インフレ	inflation
インフレ圧力	inflationary pressures
インフレ・ターゲット	inflation target
インフレの	inflationary
インフレ目標	inflation target
インフレ抑制	anti-inflation
インフレ率	inflation rate
インフレを誘発する	inflationary
隠蔽	cover-up
隠蔽する	cover up
インベスター・リレーションズ	IR
陰謀	conspiracy
陰謀	machination
陰謀の	cloak-and-dagger
引用する	cite

う

ウイルス	virus
ウイルス対策ソフト	antivirus software
ウイルスの	viral
ウインドー期間	window period
ウエアラブル技術	wearable technology
上から下へ組織された	top-down
上から下への	top-down
ウエスト・テキサス・インターミディエート	WTI
植え付ける	implant
飢えに苦しむ	hunger-stricken
上の	upper
ウエハ	wafer
ウェブ	Web
ウェブ・サイト	Web site
ウェブ偽装詐欺	phishing
ウォン	won
受け入れられない	wash
受け入れる	accept
請負	contract
請負業者	provider
請け負う	contract
請け負う	undertake
受け継ぐ	inherit
受取り	receipt
受取人	beneficiary
受取人	recipient
受け取る	receive
受け取る	take in
受け身の	passive
受ける	receive
受ける	submit to
受ける	suffer
動かす	move
…を動かす	power
動かす	prompt
動かないでいる	stay put
動かなくて	stuck
動かぬ証拠	smoking gun
動き	activity
動き	campaign
動き	move
動き	movement
動き	sign
動き	swing
動き出す	kick in
動く	act
動く	function
動かなくする	trap
牛海綿状脳症	BSE
失う	hemorrhage
失う	lose
後ろ	back

薄い	thin
薄型テレビ	flat screen TV
薄手の	thin
うそ発見器	polygraph
疑い	skepticism
疑い	suspicion
疑いをかける	suspect
疑う	suspect
疑わしい	problematic
打上げ	blastoff
打上げ	liftoff
打ち明ける	unveil
打合せ	arrangement
打合せ	conference
打ち勝つ	overcome
打ち切る	scrap
打ち出す	come out with
打ち出す	come up with
打ちひしがれた	stricken
打ち負かす	whip
宇宙	space
宇宙基地	cosmodrome
宇宙空間	space
宇宙攻撃警戒網	spacetrack
宇宙人	spaceman
宇宙生物学	xenobiology
宇宙船	orbiter
宇宙船	spacecraft
宇宙船基地	spaceport
宇宙バス	spaceplane
宇宙飛行	astrogation
宇宙飛行士	astronaut
宇宙飛行士	spaceman
宇宙飛行できる	spaceworthy
宇宙服	penguin suit
宇宙服	spacesuit
宇宙遊泳	spacewalk
宇宙酔い	spacesickness
宇宙利用	space use
宇宙旅行	spacefaring
宇宙連絡船	spaceplane
宇宙ロケット発射基地	cosmodrome
打つ	strike
打つ	wallop
移し替える	shift
映し出す	mirror
映す	mirror
移す	move
移す	relocate
移す	shift
移す	transfer
訴える	appeal
訴える	call for
訴える	invoke
訴える	lodge
訴える	sue
促す	prod

促す	prompt	売り手独占	polypoly	営業活動を行う	do business
奪い返す	regain	売り主	seller	…に影響されやすい	susceptible to
奪い取る	hijack	売り払う	unload	営業収益	revenue
右派の	right-wing	売る	sell	営業純利益	net operating profit
うまくいった	successful	うるさく勧める	tout	営業所	office
うまく処理する	field	噂	rumor	営業上の	operating
うまく逃げる	elusive	うわさ好き	newsmonger	…に影響する	affect
…をうまくまとめ上げる	wrap up	噂によれば	purportedly	営業する	do business
馬跳び	leapfrog	上回る	exceed	営業免許権	license
海	ocean	…を上回る	outnumber	影響力	presence
海	sea	上回る	outweigh	影響力の大きい	influential
生み出す	generate	上回る	surpass	影響力の強い	influential
…を生み出す	make for	上回る	top	影響を与える	concern
海の	maritime	上向く	upturn	影響を与える	sway
生む	draw	上向きの	bull	影響を受けやすい	sensitive
…を埋め合わせる	make up for	上向きの	upward	…の影響を受けやすい	vulnerable to
埋め合わせをする	offset	運営	conduct	…の影響を受ける	subject to
埋め込む	implant	運営者	operator	影響を及ぼす	affect
埋め立て地	landfill site	運営者	organizer	英国首相官邸	No. 10 Downing Street
埋める	bridge	運営上の	administrative		
右翼の	right-wing	運営する	operate	英国政府	Whitehall
裏	back	運営能力	governability	英才	meritocrat
裏書き	endorsement	運送	transportation	エイズ	AIDS
裏方の	backstage	運送業者	carrier	エイズウイルス	HIV
裏切る	belie	運賃	fare	衛星	moon
裏切る	violate	運転する	drive	衛星	satellite
裏付ける	back	運転する	steer	衛星都市	satellite
ウラニウム	uranium	運転する	working	映像	footage
恨み	animosity	運転免許	driver's license	映像	image
裏目に出る	backfire	運命を左右する	make or break	映像走査機	scanner
裏ルートの	backchannel	運輸	transportation	永続的な	perennial
ウラン	uranium	運用	investment	英保守党員	Tory
売り	selling	運用	management	栄養になる	sustaining
売り	sell-off	運用期間	time horizon	栄養のバランス	nutritional balance
売上	proceeds	運用している	working	営利化する	commercialize
売上	revenue	運用する	invest	営利主義	mercantilism
売上	sales	運用できる	workable	営利性	profitability
売上	turnover	運用の	operational	鋭利な	acute
売上がある	take in	運用の誤り	maladministration	営利の	commercial
売上純利益率	profit margin			役	role
売上総利益	gross margin	**え**		液化	liquefaction
売上総利益	gross profit			液化天然ガス	liquefied natural gas
売上高	sales	永遠の	perennial	液化天然ガス	LNG
売上高	turnover	映画界	picturedom	液晶	liquid crystal
売上高	volume	永久的	permanent	液状化現象	liquefaction
売上利益率	profit margin	永久の	permanent	液晶ディスプレー	LCD
売り圧力	selling pressure	影響	aftermath	液晶表示装置	LCD
売り一色	freefall	影響	bearing	役務	service
売込み	selling	影響	effect	エクササイズ狂	exercise nut
売出し	flotation	影響	grip	エコツーリズム	ecotourism
売出し	offering	影響	impact	エコノミスト	economist
売出し	placement	影響	implication	X軸	x-axis
売出し中の	up-and-coming	影響	influence	X線	X-ray
売り出す	issue	影響	repercussion	X染色体	X chromosome
売り出す	market	営業	operation	X線電子写真	xero-radiography
売り注文	sell order	影響額	effect	X端末	X terminal
売り手	seller	営業活動	operation	閲覧	browsing

閲覧する browse
絵に描いたモチ pie in the sky
エネルギー源 energy source
エネルギー源 fuel
エネルギー節約 energy saving
絵文字 icon
選ばれた人々 elite
選び出す select
選ぶ elect
選ぶ name
選ぶ select
選ぶべき方法 option
エリート意識 elitism
得る earn
得る gain
得る garner
得る reap
得る secure
エル・ニーニョ現象 El Niño
エレクトロニクス electronics
エレクトロルミネッセンス electroluminescence
円 circle
円 yen
沿海州 Primorye
円貨貸付け yen loan
遠隔通信 telecommunication
遠隔の remote
沿岸警備隊 Coast Guard
延期 delay
延期する adjourn
延期する extend
延期する postpone
遠距離通信会社 telco
縁故主義 cronyism
縁故主義 nepotism
縁故募集 private offering
演算 computing
エンジェル angel
円借款 yen loan
演出 staging
演出する engineer
演出方法 staging
炎暑 heat wave
援助 aid
援助 assistance
援助 auspices
援助 help
援助 support
炎上 flaming
援助機関 relief agency
援助交際 compensated dating
援助する help
援助する support
エンジン engine
遠心分離機 centrifugal separator
遠心分離機 centrifuge

厭世主義 pessimism
厭世的な pessimistic
演説 speech
演奏する play
円相場 yen
延滞 arrears
円卓会議 round-table conference
延長された protracted
延長する prolong
延長する renew
延命医療拒否権を認める right-to-die
延命措置 life-sustaining measures
遠慮する abstain (from)
遠慮する forgo

お

オアシス oasis
オアペック OAPEC
追い討ち follow-up
…を追い越す outpace
追い出す oust
追い詰める box in
オイル oil
オイル・ダラー petrodollars
オイル・タンカー oiler
オイル通貨 petrocurrency
お色直し makeover
…王 tycoon
負う undertake
応援 aid
応急の quick
黄金株 golden share
王子 prince
応酬 riposte
押収 seizure
欧州委員会 European Commission
押収する confiscate
欧州中央銀行 ECB
欧州中央銀行 European Central Bank
欧州通貨協力基金 EMCF
欧州連合 Brussels
欧州連合 EU
欧州連合 European Union
欧州連合統計局 Eurostat
王女 princess
応じる meet
…に応じる submit to
応募 subscription
応募者 applicant
応募入札 tender
応用する apply
応用できる applicable
横領事件 embezzlement scandal
終える close

大当たり blockbuster
大暴れ rampage
大荒れ turbulence
大荒れの turbulent
覆い pall
覆う cap
大型の big-ticket
大型爆弾 blockbuster
大型ボート vessel
大きく上回る soar
大きく取り上げる feature
大きくなる swell
大きさ magnitude
大きさ size
大きな成果 breakthrough
オークション auction
オークション業者 auctioneer
多くの問題を抱えた embattled
大蔵省 Treasury
OK thumbs-up
大声で知らせる trumpet
大騒ぎ razzle-dazzle
大騒ぎ uproar
大底 rock bottom
大手の leading
大手の major
大通り avenue
大ばくち high-stakes
大幅な dramatic
大幅な上昇 spike
大幅に削減する slash
大幅の sizable
大もうけする rake in
オール・イン・ワン all-in-one
置き換える replace
置く position
憶測する speculate
億単位の nine-figure
奥の far
奥の手 trump
奥行き depth
遅らせる stall
送る feed
送る post
送る transmit
…に遅れないでついて行く keep up with
遅れる fall behind
遅れる lagging
起こす initiate
起こす start up
…を怠る fail
怠る shirk
起こっている afoot
行う commit
行う stage
行う wage

怒らせる	irk	踊り場	leveling off	温室	greenhouse
起こりそうもない	unlikely	踊り場	plateau	音質	voice
起こる	eventuate	衰えている	flagging	温情主義	paternalism
抑え	restraint	衰えない	unabated	音声	audio
抑える	choke off	衰える	dwindle	音声	voice
抑える	curb	音を立てない	silent	音声多重放送	multiplex broadcasting
抑える	dampen	同じ	self		
抑える	restrain	…と同じ	tantamount to	御曹司	scion
治める	govern	お膝元	heartland	音痴	tin ear
収める	notch	オプションを売る	write an option	温度	temperature
押し上げ	boost	汚名を着せる	brand	オンライン	online
押し上げる	push up	重い	heavy	温和な	benign
押し下げ要因	drag	思い描く	envisage		
押し下げる	lower	思いがけない利益	windfall		
押し下げる	shed	思い切った	drastic	**か**	
推し進める	proceed with	思い出させる	remind	カーシェアリング制度	car-share scheme
押し付ける	inflict	思いつき	brainstorm	カード	card
惜しまない	unstinting	重い負担をかける	tax	カード会員	cardholder
惜しむ	spare	…と思う	think	カーボンナノチューブ	carbon nanotube
汚職	bribery	重苦しい	downbeat		
汚職	corruption	重さ	weight	買い	buying
汚職の	corrupt	表看板	front man	買上げ	buyback
押し寄せる	deluge	表向きの	front	会員	member
押し寄せる	inundate	表向きの人物	front man	会員の資格	membership
オスロ和平合意	Oslo interim peace accords	主な	principal	会員の地位	membership
		重荷	burden	海運業界	shipping industry
お節介	meddling	…に重荷を負わせる	burden	外貨	foreign currency
汚染	infection	重荷を負わせる	tax	開会	opening
汚染	pollution	思惑	speculation	開会	session
汚染源	pollutant	思惑買い	speculation	海外移住者	expatriate
汚染者	polluter	思惑による	speculative	開会期間	session
汚染者負担の原則	PPP	思わぬ利益	windfall	海外現地生産工場	transplant
遅い	lagging	親会社	parent	開会式	opening
恐ろしい経験	nightmare	親会社専用の	captive	開会式を行う	inaugurate
恐ろしい経験	ordeal	親ビジネス派の	probusiness	海外資産	foreign assets
恐ろしさ	specter	親指	thumb	海外駐在員	expatriate
恐ろしさ	terror	親指でめくる	thumb	海外渡航許可証	passport
オゾン	ozone	折り返し運転	shuttle	海外の	foreign
穏やかな	modest	オレンジ革命	Orange Revolution	海外の	overseas
穏やかにする	calm down	オレンジ・ブック	Orange Book	改革	innovation
オタワ	Ottawa	卸売り	wholesale	改革	overhaul
落ち込み	slump	卸売り価格	wholesale price	改革	reform
落ち込む	sag	卸値	wholesale price	改革	revamp
落ち込む	slump	降ろす	drop	改革者	reformer
落ち込んでいる	slumping	下す	pass	改革主義者	reformist
落ち着かせる	soothe	負わせる	impose	改革する	houseclean
落ちる	falling	負わせる	saddle	改革する	reform
音	audio	終値	close	改革派	reformer
落とし穴	trap	終値	closing price	改革派の	pro-reform
脅しの	threatening	終わる	end	買い方	bull
落とす	drop	…に終わる	result in	快活な	upbeat
落とす	shed	音楽配信	music distribution	下位から上位への	bottom-up
脅す	threaten	音響	audio	外観	appearance
脅すような	threatening	音響効果を加える	dub	会期	session
…に劣らない	rival	恩恵	accommodation	会議	conference
おとり商法	bait-and-switch	恩恵を受ける	benefit	会議	forum
おとり捜査	sting operation	穏健派	centrist		

会議	meeting
会議	powwow
会議	round
懐疑	skepticism
会議の	congressional
階級	grade
階級	rank
開業	start-up
開業医	practitioner
概況を説明する	brief
会計	accounting
会計監査	auditing
会計期間	accounting period
会計検査	audit
会計士	accountant
会計責任	accountability
会計年度	accounting period
会計年度	budget year
会計年度	business year
会計年度	fiscal year
会計年度	FY
解決	settlement
解決策	fix
解決する	deal with
解決する	iron out
会見	interview
外見	appearance
戒厳令	martial law
解雇	dismissal
解雇	layoff
解雇	redundancy
介護	nursing care
外交	diplomacy
外交官	diplomat
外交関係	diplomatic relations
外交政策	foreign policy
外交の	diplomatic
外国からの	overseas
外国為替	foreign exchange
外国為替	forex
外国為替	FX
外国人嫌いの	xenophobic
外国人投資家	nonresident investor
外国人登録制度	alien registration system
戒告する	reprimand
外国送金	remittance
外国の	foreign
外国向けの	overseas
解雇する	ax
解雇する	dismiss
解雇する	fire
解雇する	lay off
解雇通知	pink slip
悔恨	remorse
開催国	host
開催する	host
介在する	intervene
買い支える	prop up
解散	dissolution
概算	rule of thumb
解散する	disband
解散する	dissolve
解散する	split
解散する	wind up
概算の	estimated
開始	leadoff
開始	opening
開始	start-up
開示	disclosure
開始する	kick off
開示する	disclose
買占め	buyout
会社	company
会社	corporation
会社	house
会社	office
会社	vehicle
…と解釈する	deem
…と解釈する	read
会社更生手続き	Chapter 11
会社の設立	incorporation
会社分割	spinoff
回収	collection
回収する	call in
回収する	collect
回収する	recall
回収する	recover
回収する	withdraw
回収不能の	uncollectible
外出	trip
解除	dissolution
解消する	dissolve
解消する	work off
海上の	maritime
外食業界	fast food providers
解除する	lift
解除する	terminate
改正	amendment
改正	reform
改正	revision
改正する	amend
改正する	reform
改正する	revise
解説記事欄	op-ed
解説者	analyst
開設する	open
改善	improvement
改善	reform
改善	turnaround
改善する	develop
改善する	improve
改善する	reform
改善する	turn around
改善法	remedy
階層	bracket
階層	ladder
改装	refurbishment
改造	reorganization
改造	revamp
改装する	remodel
改造する	reorganize
階層制度	hierarchy
買い相場	bull market
海賊	pirate
海賊行為	piracy
海賊対処法案	antipiracy bill
海賊版を作る	pirate
改組する	retool
解体する	disband
開拓する	carve out
会談	powwow
会談	talks
改築する	remodel
外注	outsourcing
害虫駆除業者	exterminator
外注する	outsource
買い注文	buy order
買付け	buying
買付け	purchase
改訂	revision
改定する	revise
快適	comfort
外的行為	overt act
買い手多占	polypsony
回転	rotation
回転	turn
外電受信者	monitor
回転速度を増す	rev up
解読する	decode
買取り	acquisition
買取り	buyback
買取り	purchase
買い取る	buy back
買い取る	purchase
買い取る	subscribe
介入	interference
介入	intervention
…に介入する	step in
解任	dismissal
解任する	dismiss
懐妊の証明書	conception certificate
開発	development
開発	exploitation
海抜	altitude
開発する	develop
開発する	exploit
開発する	originate
開発する	tap
開発途上の	developing
開発の	developing

外販の	merchant	
回避	evasion	
回避する	avert	
回避する	dodge	
回避する	evade	
…を回避する	forestall	
外部委託する	outsource	
回復	rebound	
回復	recovery	
回復	rehabilitation	
回復	restoration	
回復	revival	
回復可能な	recoverable	
回復局面	incipient recovery	
回復させる	rehabilitate	
回復させる	revitalize	
回復した	renewed	
回復する	pick up	
回復する	rally	
回復する	rebound	
回復する	recover	
回復する	regain	
回復する	restore	
回復する	turn around	
外部資源の活用	outsourcing	
外部調査委員会	external investigation committee	
外部の	external	
回報	newsletter	
開放式の	open-end	
解放する	free	
解放戦線	liberation front	
開放的な	open	
開幕	curtain	
壊滅的打撃を与える	devastate	
買い持ちの	long	
買戻し	buyback	
買戻し	redemption	
買戻し	repurchase	
買い戻す	buy back	
買い戻す	redeem	
買い戻す	repurchase	
買い物	shopping	
買い物客	shopper	
解約	cancelation	
解約	termination	
解約する	terminate	
海洋	ocean	
海洋	sea	
概要	brief	
概要	rundown	
概要	summary	
外洋域の	oceanic	
海洋温度差発電	OTEC	
海洋資源	marine resources	
海洋の	oceanic	
外来患者	outpatient	
外来語	loanword	
改良	improvement	
改良する	improve	
街路	street	
回廊	corridor	
会話	dialogue	
下院	House	
下院	House of Representatives	
下院	lower house	
下院議員	assemblyman	
下院議員	Congressman	
下院議員	Congressperson	
下院議長	speaker	
買う	buy	
カウンターカルチャー	counterculture	
変える	convert	
変える	switch	
変える	transform	
火炎ビン	petro bomb	
顔ぶれ	lineup	
顔を立てる	face-saving	
顔をつき合わせた	face-to-face	
加害企業	offending enterprise	
価格	price	
価格	value	
価額	worth	
価格維持	price fixing	
価格維持策	PKO	
科学技術	technology	
科学技術専門学校	polytechnic	
科学技術の	technological	
価格競争力が高い	cost-competitive	
価格計算	pricing	
価格決定	price fixing	
価格修正因子	deflator	
価格上昇	price increase	
化学製品	chemical product	
価格設定	pricing	
価格分離	unbundling	
化学兵器	chemical weapons	
化学療法	chemotherapy	
価格を提示する	quote	
掲げる	put up	
かかった	stricken	
かかと	heel	
鏡	mirror	
鑑	paragon	
輝かしい成果	breakthrough	
…にかかりやすい	susceptible to	
かかりやすい	vulnerable	
かかわり合い	implication	
鍵	key	
書換え	renewal	
書き込み	posting	
垣根	fence	
かき乱す	roil	
火急の	pressing	
核	core	
格上げ	upgrading	
架空の	fictitious	
架空の	nonexistent	
架空の	paper	
核開発計画	N-program	
核拡散防止条約	NPT	
学業の	academic	
覚悟	preparedness	
覚悟する	brace	
…する覚悟だ	poised to	
格差	differential	
格差	disparity	
格差	divide	
格差	gap	
画策する	orchestrate	
格下げ	downgrade	
格下げする	downgrade	
隠された	covert	
核酸増幅検査	nucleic acid amplification test	
拡散防止	nonproliferation	
学士	graduate	
学識	education	
学識者	pundit	
確実性	soundness	
確実な	secured	
確実な手段	passport	
確実にする	ensure	
…を隠しておく	keep ... under wraps	
…に隠して表現する	wrap up	
学習曲線	learning curve	
学習率	learning rate	
確信	conviction	
核心	crux	
革新	innovation	
核心	nitty-gritty	
確信	persuasion	
革新主義の	reformist	
確信する	bet	
革新的な	innovative	
隠す	cover up	
隠す	paper over	
拡大	expansion	
拡大	worsening	
拡大している	worsening	
拡大する	climb	
拡大する	expand	
拡大する	grow	
拡大する	increase	
拡大する	widen	
拡大する	worsen	
拡大の	expansionary	
拡張	expansion	
拡張する	expand	
拡張する	extend	
拡張の	expansionary	

格付け	credit rating	
格付け	rating	
格付けする	rate	
確定した	defined	
確定した	fixed	
確定した	vested	
確定申告	final income tax return	
確定する	lock in	
獲得する	clinch	
獲得する	collect	
獲得する	earn	
獲得する	gain	
獲得する	garner	
獲得する	secure	
核となる	core	
確認する	identify	
核燃料	nuclear fuel	
核の	N-	
核の	nuclear	
核のない	nuclear-free	
核武装を解除する	denuclearize	
核分裂	nuclear fission	
核兵器	nuclear weapon	
核兵器	nuke	
核兵器ぬきの	nonnuclear	
核兵器の	nuclear	
核兵器を使わない	nonnuclear	
核兵器を撤去する	denuclearize	
確保する	ensure	
確保する	lock in	
革命	revolution	
額面金額	denomination	
額面超過額	premium	
学問の	academic	
格安航空会社	LCC	
格安の	budget	
隔離	separation	
隔離する	separate	
閣僚	minister	
閣僚の	ministerial	
隠れた	invisible	
隠れる	hunker down	
陰	pall	
影	shadow	
家系	family	
家計	household	
家系	strain	
家計部門の支出	consumer spending	
過激な	rampant	
掛け金	annuity	
可決する	pass	
崖っぷち	jaws	
…が欠乏する	fall short of	
陰で操ること	string-pulling	
陰で糸を引く	pull strings	
陰で指ғ揮する	mastermind	
賭けに出る	up the ante	
影	shadow	
駆け引き	game	
駆け引き	gamesmanship	
駆け引き	maneuver	
かげり	pall	
賭ける	bet	
かける	cover	
…を賭ける	put ... on the line	
賭ける	risk	
かける	throw	
下限	bottom	
かご	basket	
下降	dip	
加工	manufacturing	
加工	processing	
下降傾向	downside	
下降する	dip	
加工する	process	
化合物	compound	
過酷な	severe	
過去最高	all-time high	
過去最低	all-time low	
傘	umbrella	
かさ上げする	inflate	
かさ上げする	make up	
火災	fire	
ガザ地区	Gaza Strip	
かさむ	balloon	
飾りひも	ribbon	
加算する	add	
瑕疵	defect	
瑕疵	fault	
瑕疵	flaw	
舵	helm	
貸金	moneylending	
貸金業者	moneylender	
貸倒れ	bad debt	
貸倒れ	bad loan	
貸倒れ	default	
貸倒れ	nonperforming loans	
貸倒償却	written-off bad debts	
貸倒れ引当金	loan loss provisions	
貸倒れ引当金	loan loss reserves	
貸出	lending	
貸出行	lender	
貸し出す	lease	
貸し出す	lend	
過失	negligence	
果実	fruit	
貸付け	lending	
貸付け	loan	
貸付け金の取立てができない	uncollectible	
貸付け先	borrower	
貸し付ける	lend	
貸し手	lender	
瑕疵のない	clean	
カジュアル衣料品	casual clothing	
過重労働	overwork	
過剰	excess	
過剰	surplus	
過剰供給	oversupply	
過剰供給する	saturate	
過剰消費	overconsumption	
過少申告する	underreport	
過剰請求する	overcharge	
過剰生産能力	overcapacity	
過剰摂取	abuse	
過剰設備	overcapacity	
過剰投与	overdoses	
過剰の	surplus	
過剰反応する	overreact	
過小評価する	undervalue	
可処分所得	disposable income	
可処分所得	take-home pay	
舵を取る	steer	
課す	inflict	
数	number	
ガス	gas	
ガス・ツー・リキッド	GTL	
数に関する	numerical	
数の	numerical	
課する	charge	
課する	impose	
課する	saddle	
風	wind	
課税	levy	
課税	taxation	
課税控除できる	tax-deductible	
課税する	impose	
課税する	levy	
課税する	tax	
課税対象外の	nontaxable	
課税対象となる	taxable	
稼ぎ手	earner	
化石燃料	fossil fuels	
稼ぐ	bank	
稼ぐ	earn	
…に下線を引く	underline	
仮想…	cyber-	
画像	image	
仮想移動体通信事業者	MVNO	
下層から上層への	bottom-up	
仮想の	virtual	
仮想の情報空間	cyberspace	
家族	family	
家族経営の	mom-and-pop	
加速した	accelerated	
家族主義	paternalism	
加速する	accelerate	
加速する	speed up	
可塑性のある	plastic	
ガソリン	gas	
ガソリン	gasoline	

ガソリン・スタンド	pump	活性化	revitalization	加入	enrollment
型	model	活性化する	activate	加入	subscription
肩	shoulder	かつてない	unprecedented	加入する	enroll
課題	agenda	活動	action	加入する	enter
課題	challenge	活動	activity	加入する	subscribe
課題	problem	活動	behavior	金	money
固い	hard	活動	campaign	金貸し	moneylender
過大評価	overstatement	活動	movement	金貸し	moneylending
過大評価する	overstate	活動休止中の	dormant	過熱	frenzy
過大評価する	overvalue	活動的な	active	過熱	overheating
過大表示	overstatement	活動的な	dynamic	過熱気味の活動	overdrive
過大表示する	overstate	活動の一時停止	moratorium	過熱する	overheat
片側だけの	unilateral	活動の場	arena	…に金などを融通する	accommodate
肩代わりする	assume	活動領域	department	鐘の音	knell
肩にかつぐ	shoulder	…の活動を止める	paralyze	金儲け	moneymaking
型にはまった	cookie-cutter	活発な	active	金を引き出す	pull money
型にはまったやり方	lockstep	活発な	brisk	可能性	capability
塊	block	活発な	dynamic	可能性	potential
傾き	lurch	活発な	roaring	可能性がある	potential
傾く	declining	活発な	robust	可能性としては	potentially
傾く	sink	活発な	spanking	可能性のある	possible
偏った	biased	活発にする	activate	可能な	possible
加担させる	implicate	合併	combination	…を可能にする	pave the way for
価値	value	合併	merger	過半数	majority
勝ち	victory	合併	tie-up	株	share
勝ち	win	合併・買収	M & A	株	stock
価値	worth	合併させる	fuse	株価	share price
勝ち組	winner	合併する	affiliate	株価	stock price
勝ち組企業	winner	合併する	consolidate	株価維持策	PKO
勝ち取る	clinch	合併する	fuse	株価収益率	PER
勝ち抜く	win	合併する	merge	株価つり上げ	ballooning
勝つ	prevail	活用	exploitation	株価の急落	plunge
勝つ	win	活用	utilization	株券	share
学会	congress	活用する	capitalize on	株券	stock certificate
活気	pep	活用する	exploit	株式	equity
活気	vitality	活用する	utilize	株式	share
活気がある	roaring	活用できる	workable	株式	stock
活気がない	subdued	活力	energy	株式会社	stock company
活気づかせる	buoy	活力	vitality	株式公開	flotation
活気づかせる	fuel	…に活を入れる	jump-start	株式公開	IPO
活気づける	refresh	家庭	household	株式公開	public offering
活気づける	rejuvenate	過程	process	株式公開買付け	public tender offer
画期的な	innovative	家庭教育	home education	株式公開買付け	takeover bid
画期的な出来事	breakthrough	…と仮定すると	given	株式公開買付け	tender offer
活気のある	brisk	仮定の	proforma	株式公開買付け	TOB
活気のない	anemic	家電	electrical appliance	株式公開企業	publicly held company
活気のない	slack	家電	home appliance	株式公開企業	publicly owned company
活況の	buoyant	稼働しない	dead		
活況の	roaring	稼得者	earner		
活況の	robust	過度の	excessive	株式公開されている	publicly traded
活況を呈している	active	過度の規制	paternalism	株式公開する	go public
学校	school	過度の強調	overemphasis	株式交換	stock swap
学校の	scholastic	かどわかす	abduct	株式購入	share purchase
勝つこと	win	金型	molding	株式購入	stock purchase
合算する	combine	要	linchpin	株式購入選択権	stock option
合衆国	union	かなり大きい	sizable	株式公募	public stock offering
活性化	activation	加入	access	株式市況	bourse

株式市場	stock market
株式資本	stock
株式相場表	ticker
株式取引	stock trading
株式取引	stock transaction
株式の買い乗せ	pyramid
株式の時価総額	market capitalization
株式の大量買取り	greenmail
株式の募集	placement
株式の割当て	allotment
株式発行	stock issue
株式発行	stock offering
株式非公開の	privately held
株式分割	stock split
株式保有	stockholdings
株式持ち合い	cross shareholding
株式割当て	share allotment
株式を上場する	go public
株式を大量に買い取る	greenmail
株式を非公開化する	go private
…が不足する	fall short of
…が不足する	run short of
株主	shareholder
株主	stockholder
株主資本	shareholders' assets
株主総会	shareholders' meeting
下部の	lower
株の買戻し	greenmail
花粉	pollen
花粉症	hay fever
壁	wall
貨幣の	monetary
貨幣流通高	cash in circulation
下方修正する	downgrade
下方への	downward
…の構えをとる	hunker down
…にかみ合う	bite
紙一重の	razor-thin
紙を使用しないで	paperless
かむ	bite
仮名	alias
仮名	pseudonym
加盟国	signatory
加盟している	affiliated
加盟する	enter
加盟する	join
カメラの前で	on-camera
火薬	powder
かやの外	out of the loop
通った跡	wake
空売り	short
空売り	short selling
体細胞核移転	SCNT
体細胞核移転	somatic cell nuclear transfer
借り上げる	lease

借入れ	borrowing
借入れ	debt
借入れ	leverage
借入金	borrowing
借入金で投機をする	leverage
借入金の保証	standby credit
借入資金による企業買収	LBO
借り入れる	borrow
カリウム	pottasium
借換え	refinancing
借換え	refunding
仮釈放	parole
仮釈放者	parolee
仮出獄	parole
仮出獄者	parolee
仮出所	parole
カリスマ的指導者	guru
駆り立てる	drive
駆り立てる	prod
駆り立てる	prompt
駆り立てる	spur
借り手	borrower
刈り取る	reap
仮に入れる	pencil in
仮の	proforma
仮の	provisional
カリブ共同体	CARICOM
火力発電の	thermal
加齢	aging
枯れた	dead
過労	overwork
…を辛うじて食い止める	stave off
側	side
乾いた	dry
川上産業	upstream
かわす	ward off
為替	forex
為替先物予約	forward exchange contract
為替市場	currency market
為替相場	currency exchange rate
為替相場	exchange rate
変わらない	unchanged
変わりやすい	unsettled
変わりやすい	volatile
刊	edition
…感	sense
がん	cancer
肝炎	hepatitis
考え	idea
考え	opinion
考え	thinking
考え	view
考え方	attitude
考え方	mindset
考え方	opinion
考え方	thinking

考え方	view
考え出す	hammer
…と考える	deem
考える	speculate
考える	think
…を考えると	in the face of
感覚	sense
感覚	touch
…に鑑みて	in the face of
カンガルー	kangaroo
肝機能障害	hepatic disorder
観客	audience
環境	climate
環境	ecology
環境	environment
環境	surroundings
環境維持開発	ecodevelopment
環境共生住宅	ecohouse
環境共生都市	ecocity
環境中心経営	ecocentric management
環境にやさしい	ecological
環境にやさしい	environmentally friendly
環境にやさしい	green
環境の	eco-
環境の	environmental
環境の	green
環境の質	environmental quality
環境破壊	ecocide
環境保護	environmental protection
環境保護狂	ecofreak
環境保護に関する	environmental
環境保護の	eco-
環境保護の	green
監禁	lock-in
監禁	lockup
元金	capital
元金	principal
換金する	cash
監禁する	detain
換金性が高い	liquid
関係	bearing
関係	concern
関係	connection
関係	relations
関係	relationship
関係会社	associated company
関係者	insider
関係者	player
関係する	participate
…を歓迎する	favor
関係のある	related
完結させる	finanize
簡潔に報告する	brief
…に還元する	pass on to
看護	nursing

刊行　issuance	管制業務　control-tower procedures	管理　custody
観光　tourism	関節炎　arthritis	管理　governance
勧告　encouragement	間接の　secondhand	管理　hand
監獄　prison	間接費　burden	管理　management
韓国政府　Blue House	感染　infection	監理　monitoring
監査　audit	幹線　trunk line	管理　supervision
監査　examination	感染症　infection	管理者　manager
監査　inspection	感染症の　infectious	管理職　executive
完済　payoff	完全所有子会社　wholly owned subsidiary	管理する　control
完済する　pay off		管理する　manage
監査人　accountant	感染する　contract	管理する　monitor
監査人　auditor	完全性　integrity	管理する　rein in
監査する　audit	感染性の　infectious	管理する　run
観察者　watcher	完全な　absolute	管理する　supervise
監査法人　auditor	完全な　integrate	管理人　caretaker
監査役　auditor	乾燥した　dry	管理の誤り　mismanagement
換算　translation	簡素化する　simplify	簡略化する　simplify
換算する　convert	観測者　watcher	官僚　bureaucrat
換算する　translate	観測筋　observer	完了　completion
監視　guard	観測筋　watcher	顔料　pigment
監視　monitoring	歓待　entertainment	完了する　end
監視　oversight	寛大　tolerance	官僚制度　bureaucracy
監視　surveillance	寛大な　liberal	官僚的な　bureaucratic
幹事　secretary	寛大な社会　permissive society	…の管理を任せる　entrust
感じ　sense	簡単な　easy	関連　connection
幹事会社　trustee	姦通　adultery	関連　relationship
監視者　monitor	鑑定　appraisal	関連会社　affiliate
監視する　monitor	観点　light	関連会社　associated company
…に関して　in terms of	観点　perspective	関連した　related
…に関して　vis-a-vis	監督　oversight	緩和　alleviation
監視モニター　monitor	監督　supervision	緩和　easing
患者　inmate	監督　surveillance	緩和　relaxation
患者　patient	監督する　supervise	緩和策　cushion
観衆　audience	カンヌ映画祭　Canne film festival	緩和する　abate
慣習　usage	観念論　ideology	緩和する　alleviate
甘受する　submit to	間伐作業　thinning work	緩和する　assuage
完勝　grand slam	幹部　cadre	緩和する　ease
干渉　interference	幹部　elite	緩和する　relax
干渉　intervention	幹部　manager	
干渉　meddling	還付　refunding	
勘定　account	幹部会　caucus	**き**
緩衝材　buffer	還付する　refund	
緩衝材　cushion	カンフル剤の注入　camphor injection	議員　lawmaker
勘定残高　account balance	陥没する　subside	議員　legislator
干渉しない　hands-off	元本　principal	…に起因する　attributable to
干渉する　interfere	喚問する　summon	議員立法の　lawmaker-sponsored
…に干渉する　step in	勧誘する　lure	気温　temperature
緩衝装置　buffer	勧誘する　solicit	機械　machine
頑丈にする　toughen	勧誘する　tout	機械　machinery
関心　attention	関与　commitment	機会　opportunity
関心　concern	関与　input	議会　assembly
…の歓心を買う　curry favor with	関与　involvement	議会　chamber
冠水　inundation	寛容　tolerance	議会　Congress
関数　function	寛容主義　permissivism	議会　Diet
完成　completion	関与させる　involve	議会　Parliament
関税　customs	管理　administration	機械運転者　machinist
関税　tariff	管理　control	機械可読式の　machine-readable

機会均等	equal opportunity
機械工	machinist
議会工作	lobbyism
機械受注	machinery orders
議会人	parliamentarian
機械装置	machinery
議会で制定された	parliamentary
議会の	parliamentary
機会平等	equal opportunity
企画	design
企画	planning
企画	project
企画	proposal
企画	scheme
規格	standard
規格化	normalization
規格化	standardization
規格化する	standardize
企画者	planner
企画する	design
企画する	project
企画する	propose
規格統一	standardization
規格統一する	standardize
気が進まない	reluctant
旗艦	flagship
機関	institution
器官	organ
機関	organization
期間	period
帰還	return
期間	span
器官	system
期間	term
期間	time
機関投資家向け	wholesale
危機	crisis
危機	crunch
機器	equipment
機器	machine
危機	razor-edge
危機経路	critical path
危機に陥れる	jeopardize
危機の	critical
気球	balloon
危急の事態	juncture
企業	company
企業	corporate
企業	enterprise
起業	entrepreneurship
企業家	entrepreneur
企業会計改革法	Sarbanes-Oxley Act
企業家精神	entrepreneurship
企業家の	entrepreneurial
企業合理化	shakeout
企業取得	takeover
企業取得と合併	merger and acquisition
企業体	entity
企業の合併・買収	mergers and acquisitions
企業の吸収合併	M & A
企業の系列化	integration
企業の社会的責任	CSR
企業買収	takeover
企業連合	cartel
基金	foundation
基金	fund
器具	appliance
偽薬効果	placebo effect
議決権行使	voting
危険	risk
期限	deadline
機嫌	mood
期限	timeline
危険がない	safe
棄権する	abstain (from)
危険性	risk
危険性の高い	risky
危険性の高い事業	venture
危険な	risky
危険な目にあわない	safe
危険にさらす	jeopardize
…を危険にさらす	put ... on the line
危険にさらす	risk
期限の経過した	overdue
危険のない	secure
危険負担	risk
危険を伴う	risky
…の機嫌をとる	curry favor with
…の危険を招く	risk
気候	climate
機構	machine
機構	mechanism
機構	organization
機構	structure
機構	system
技巧的手腕のある	diplomatic
機甲部隊	armored cavalry
気候変動	climate change
気候変動に関する政府間パネル	IPCC
帰国	return
期近物	front month
記載	entry
起債する	issue
記載する	list
兆し	sign
兆し	threat
記事	article
儀式	ceremony
儀式	formality
議事進行	proceedings
議事妨害	obstructionism
記者	pencil pusher
記者	reporter
記者	staffer
機種	line
奇襲	raid
奇襲攻撃	ambushes
技術	ability
技術	skill
技術	technique
技術	technology
技術主義	technocracy
技術上の問題	technicality
技術知識のある	tech-savvy
技術的な	technical
技術的な	technological
技術に精通した	tech-savvy
技術の	technical
技術の高度化	sophistication
期首の	initial
基準	base
基準	baseline
基準	basis
基準	benchmark
基準	gauge
基準	norm
基準	scale
基準	standard
基準	yardstick
基準金利	key rate
基準線	baseline
基準値	benchmark
…基準の	based
気性	streak
気象	weather
偽証	perjury
議場	chamber
希少金属	rare metal
偽証罪	perjury
偽証する	perjure oneself
議事録	proceedings
傷	flaw
築く	set up
傷ついた	stricken
傷つきやすい	vulnerable
傷つける	undermine
絆	tie
…に帰する	attribute
規制	restriction
犠牲	scapegoat
犠牲	victim
規制上の	regulatory
規制緩和	deregulation
規制緩和する	liberalize
既成事実	fait accompli
犠牲者	victim
規制する	regulate
規制する	restrict

規制当局　regulators	鍛える　forge	機能不全　dysfunction
規制当局の　regulatory	北大西洋条約機構　NATO	機能不全　malfunction
規制を緩和する　deregulate	北大西洋条約機構　North Atlantic Treaty Organization	気乗りしない　reluctant
軌跡　locus		希薄化　wane
軌跡　orbit	北朝鮮　DPRK	希薄化する　wane
議席　bench	北朝鮮政府　Pyongyang	起爆装置　trigger
季節　season	帰着　eventuation	希薄な　thin
季節調整値　seasonally adjusted	帰着する　eventuate	奇抜な　novel
季節の　seasonal	…に帰着する　result in	揮発油　gasoline
季節労働者　migration worker	期中の　interim	揮発油　naphtha
基礎　base	基調　baseline	気晴らし　relief
基礎　cornerstone	基調　keynote	規範　norm
起訴　indictment	基調　trend	基盤　bedrock
起訴　prosecution	記帳する　book	基盤　infrastructure
競う　compete	記帳する　carry	…を基盤とする　based
起草　drafting	記帳する　record	忌避　evasion
競う　vie	議長を務める　presiding	きびきび動く　spanking
偽装　falsification	きつい　tight	厳しい　prudent
寄贈された　donated	きっかけ　trigger	厳しい　severe
偽造した　forged	…のきっかけとなる　trigger	厳しい　strict
起草する　draft	ぎっしり詰まった　chock-full	厳しい　stringent
起草する　draw	キット食品　meal kits	厳しい　tight
起草する　draw up	切符売り場　box office	厳しい検査　acid test
偽装する　falsify	詰問する　grill	厳しい批判　bashing
偽造する　counterfeit	規定　clause	厳しく尋問する　grill
偽造する　fabricate	規程　regulation	厳しくする　tighten
偽造する　fake	規定　rule	厳しく問い詰める　grill
偽造する　falsify	規定　stipulation	…を厳しく取り締まる　crack down on
偽造の　fake	議定書　protocol	厳しさ　stringency
偽造の　false	規定する　define	機敏な　agile
偽装表示　mislabeling	規定する　stipulate	寄付　donation
偽造品　counterfeit	機転　intelligence	基部　foot
基礎学科　three Rs	軌道　locus	寄付された　donated
規則　regulation	軌道　orbit	寄付者　donor
規則　rule	機動性　mobility	寄付者　subscriber
…に帰属する　attributable to	機動的な　flexible	寄付する　donate
規則正しい　regular	軌道に乗って　on track	寄付する　pay in
規則正しい　uniform	軌道に乗る時間　injection	気分　mood
規則的な　orderly	軌道の　orbital	規模　dimension
起訴状　indictment	既得の　vested	規模　extent
起訴する　accuse	記入　entry	規模　magnitude
起訴する　indict	記入する　book	規模　scale
基礎的財政収支　primary balance	記入する　enroll	規模　size
基礎的条件　fundamentals	疑念　skepticism	技法　technique
基礎年金　basic pension	記念日　anniversary	希望的観測　wishful thinking
基礎の　radical	偽の　bogus	…希望の　would-be
既存店ベースの　like-for-like	偽の　fake	規模拡大する　widen
既存店ベースの売上　same store sales	偽の　fictitious	規模縮小　scaledown
既存の　existing	偽の　forged	規模縮小　wind-down
期待　expectation	機能　function	規模の利益　scale merit
気体　gas	技能　ability	規模を縮小する　downsize
議題　agenda	技能　skill	規模を縮小する　rightsize
…を期待して　in anticipation of	機能障害　dysfunction	基本　base
期待する　expect	機能障害　malfunction	基本　fundamentals
期待にそむく　frustrate	機能障害の　dysfunctional	基本　nuts and bolts
期待外れに終わる　backfire	機能する　function	基本契約　basic agreement
…の期待を裏切る　disappointing	機能不全　breakdown	基本合意書　memorandum of

	understanding	
基本的な	net	
基本的な	nuts-and-bolts	
基本的な	radical	
基本方針	keynote	
気前の良い	unstinting	
期末の	terminal	
欺瞞的な	fraudulent	
機密	secret	
機密の	classified	
義務	duty	
義務	responsibility	
…する義務がある	owe	
義務付けられた	required	
義務付ける	mandate	
義務付ける	require	
義務的な	mandatory	
義務として課される	incumbent	
義務の免除	exemption	
偽名	alias	
偽名	pseudonym	
決める	decide	
気持ち	mood	
疑問	question	
逆	reverse	
客観的な	objective	
逆効果になる	backfire	
逆効果の	counterproductive	
虐待	abuse	
虐待	persecution	
逆転	contradiction	
逆転	flip-flop	
逆転	reversal	
逆転させる	reverse	
逆転の	come-from-behind	
逆に	counter	
逆の	adverse	
逆の	counter	
逆の	negative	
逆の	reverse	
逆方向の	reverse	
逆戻り	backsliding	
却下する	turn down	
脚光を浴びる	high-profile	
キャッチオール規制	Catch-all or End-use Controls	
キャップ・アンド・トレード	cap and trade	
キャリー取引	carry trade	
級	notch	
救援	rescue	
休暇	furlough	
休暇	time off	
休会とする	adjourn	
休暇を与える	furlough	
救急隊員	paramedics	
救急治療室	ER	

究極的な	ultimate	
究極の	ultimate	
休憩	time off	
急激な	dramatic	
急激な	explosive	
急激な	rapid	
急激な	sharp	
急激に	sharply	
急減する	nosedive	
急減する	tumbling	
急降下する	dive	
救済	bailout	
救済	redress	
救済	rescue	
救済	salvation	
救済する	bail out	
救済する	save	
休止	standstill	
休日の行楽客	holidaymakers	
急襲	assault	
急襲	raid	
吸収合併する	merge	
急襲者	raider	
吸収する	absorb	
吸収する	siphon off	
急所	crux	
救助	salvation	
窮状	plight	
急上昇	run	
急上昇	surge	
急上昇する	jump	
急上昇する	surge	
求職者	jobseeker	
救助する	rescue	
救助する	save	
求人	job offer	
求人	job opening	
求人	recruitment	
急進主義	extremism	
急進主義	radicalism	
急進主義者	extremist	
求心力	centripetal force	
急成長	boom	
急成長する	go-go	
急成長の	burgeoning	
急性の	acute	
休戦	ceasefire	
休戦協定	truce	
急増	ballooning	
急増	buildup	
急増	jump	
急増	proliferation	
急増	spike	
急増	surge	
…の急増	soaring	
急増する	bolt	
急増する	bulge	

急増する	jump	
急増する	skyrocket	
急増する	soar	
急速な	rapid	
急速な	sharp	
急速に	sharply	
急速に広がる	burgeoning	
窮地	dilemma	
窮地	distress	
窮地	ditch	
窮地	fix	
窮地に追い込まれた	beleaguered	
急転換	about-face	
急騰	boom	
急騰	jump	
急騰	spike	
急騰	surge	
急騰する	skyrocket	
急騰する	soar	
急騰する	surge	
急な	abrupt	
急な	sharp	
急な	snap	
急に	sharply	
牛肉買上げ制度	beef buyback scheme	
牛肉製品	beef products	
急に景気づく	boom	
吸入	intake	
急に沸く	boom	
Q熱	Q-fever	
急場しのぎの	makeshift	
急発進させる	jump-start	
急発展の	burgeoning	
牛歩戦術	ox-walk tactic	
休眠している	dormant	
休眠中の	dormant	
急務	race	
究明する	investigate	
給油活動	refueling activity	
給油する	fuel	
給油ポンプ	pump	
給与	salary	
給与制度	pay system	
給与総額	payroll	
給与表	payroll	
急落	downfall	
急落	free fall	
急落	meltdown	
急落	slump	
急落する	dive	
急落する	free-fall	
急落する	nosedive	
急落する	plummet	
急落する	slump	
急落する	tumble	
給料	pay	

給料	paycheck	供給独占	monopoly	競争する	compete
給料	remuneration	供給独占	polypoly	競争力	competitiveness
給料	salary	供給の停止	cutoff	競争力のある	competitive
給料	wage	狂牛病	bovine spongiform	強打	bashing
給料小切手	paycheck		encephalopathy	強打する	wallop
急を要する	dire	狂牛病	BSE	協調	concert
急を要する	pressing	狂牛病	mad cow disease	協調	cooperation
寄与	contribution	供給面	supply side	協調	coordination
凶悪な	atrocious	供給量	supply	凶兆	knell
凶悪な	heinous	供給ルート	pipeline	協調	unison
脅威	shock	業況	business conditions	協調した	concerted
脅威	threat	業況判断指数	DI	協調する	coordinate
教育	education	業況判断指数	diffusion index	強調する	accentuate
教育	training	境遇	predicament	強調する	highlight
「教育に新聞を」	NIE	教訓	lesson	強調する	stress
教育の	scholastic	狂言	hoax	…を強調する	underline
驚異的な	staggering	教皇	pontiff	協調融資する	co-finance
強化	beef-up	競合	competition	協調融資団	consortium
強化	buildup	強行採決をする	railroad	協調融資団	syndicate
強化	reinforcement	強行する	bulldoze through	共通の	mutual
強化	strengthening	競合する	compete	協定	accord
強化	upgrade	競合他社	competitor	協定価格	contract price
協会	association	強行着陸	hard landing	強度	intensity
業界	sector	強硬派	hard-liner	共同開催する	co-host
境界線のない	borderless	強硬路線	hard line	共同企業体	joint venture
強化する	beef up	共産主義	communism	共同経営	partnership
強化する	buttress	共産主義者	communist	共同経営者	partner
強化する	enhance	共産党政治局	Politburo	共同事業体	consortium
強化する	intensify	行事日程表	calendar	共同出資	partnership
強化する	reinforce	業者	provider	共同出資者	partner
強化する	stiffen	行事予定	calendar	共同出資する	pool
強化する	strengthen	強制	coercion	共同使用する	share
強化する	tighten	強制	constraint	共同所有	partnership
強化する	toughen	強制	duress	共同正犯	co-principal
恐喝	blackmail	行政	government	共同体	community
恐喝者	racketeer	行政改革する	houseclean	共同で	jointly
凶器	weapon	強制する	force	共同による	concerted
協議	consultation	強制する	mandate	共同の	joint
教義	doctrine	強制的思想改造	brainwashing	共同の	mutual
協議	negotiation	強制的な	mandatory	共同の	shared
協議	talks	業績	exploit	共同の	united
協議会	committee	業績	financial results	共同利用の	shared
協議事項	agenda	業績	performance	京都議定書	Kyoto Protocol
協議する	negotiate	業績	results	競売	auction
協議の場	table	業績	showing	競売人	auctioneer
供給	injection	業績悪化	downside	強迫観念	obsession
供給	provision	業績が悪化している	ailing	脅迫する	threaten
供給	supply	競争	competition	強迫的な買い物症候群	oniomania
供給過剰	glut	競争	emulation	脅迫的な	threatening
供給側	supply side	競争	race	恐怖	terror
供給業者	supplier	競争	struggle	恐怖政治	terrorism
供給重視論者	supplysider	競争相手	competition	恐怖体験	ordeal
供給する	feed	競争相手	competitor	恐怖の的	terror
供給する	inject	競争相手	contender	共謀	collusion
供給する	provide	競争相手	rival	共謀	conspiracy
供給する	supply	競争条件	playing field	共謀罪	conspiracy charges
供給多占的市場	polypolistic market	競争上の	competitive	共謀の	collusive

興味をかきたてる	challenging
業務	affair
業務	business
業務	job
業務	service
業務粗利益	gross operating profit
業務革新	reengineering
業務執行役員	executive officer
業務上過失	professional negligence
業務上の	professional
業務提携	business tie-up
業務の	operating
協約	convention
協約	pact
共有する	share
共有の	shared
供与	provision
強要	coercion
強要	duress
強要する	force
強要する	pressure
強要する	railroad
教養の	cultural
狂乱	frenzy
協力	concert
協力	cooperation
協力関係	cooperative relationship
…と協力して	in conjunction with
…と協力して	in tandem with
…と協力する	team up with
協力する	tie up
強力な	potent
強力な	powerful
強力な	strong
共和主義の	republican
共和制の	republican
共和党	Republicans
共和党の	republican
許可	authorization
許可	permission
巨額の	massive
漁獲枠	catch quota
許可書	warrant
虚偽記載	falsification
虚偽記載	misstatement
虚偽の	bogus
虚偽の	false
虚偽の	misleading
虚偽表示	misstatement
曲射砲	howitzer
局員	staffer
極右政党	far-right party
極右民族主義者	far-right nationalist
極左の	leftmost
極小化	minimization
局所的な	localized
極大化	maximization
極端な	excessive
極端な	far
局地化	localization
局地的送電停止	load-shedding
局地的に	localized
極地の	polar
極度に	highly
極の	polar
局部的な	local
局面	period
局面	phase
局面	stage
虚構の	fictitious
巨視的分析	macroanalysis
御者	whip
虚弱性	fragility
虚弱な	fragile
居住者	resident
拠出	contribution
拠出する	contribute
拠出する	donate
拒食症	anorexia
拒食症患者	anorectic
寄与する	contribute
拒絶	rejection
拒絶	thumbs-down
拒絶する	reject
拒絶する	turn down
巨大銀行	megabank
巨大な	enormous
巨大な	giant
巨大な	huge
巨大な	massive
許諾する	grant
許諾料	royalty
曲解報道	mediamorphosis
拠点	center
拠点	site
拠点	stronghold
拒否	boycott
拒否	rejection
拒否	thumbs-down
拒否権	veto
拒否する	boycott
拒否する	override
拒否する	reject
拒否する	veto
許容	tolerance
許容主義	permissivism
許容できる	acceptable
許容できる	permissible
許容範囲	latitude
許容範囲	plus or minus
許容範囲の	acceptable
切り上げる	revalue
切り替える	swap
切り替える	switch
ぎりぎりのところ	eleventh hour
切下げ	cut
切り詰めた	austere
切り詰める	cut back
切り詰める	retrench
切り詰める	squeeze
切り詰める	trim
切り抜ける	weather
切り離し販売	unbundling
切り開く	carve out
切り札	trump
気力	energy
気力	pep
儀礼的な	formal
亀裂	split
記録	file
記録	log
記録	record
記録された	on-the-record
記録されていない	off-the-book
…を記録する	chalk up
記録する	hit
記録する	log
記録する	notch
記録する	record
記録的な	record
記録にとどめない	off-the-record
キロバイト	kilobyte
議論	contention
議論	controversy
議論	debate
議論されている	disputed
議論の余地のある	moot
疑惑	distrust
疑惑	scandal
…疑惑の	alleged
際立たせる	highlight
際立った	outstanding
際立った特徴	highlight
きわどい	razor-thin
きわどいジョーク	off-color jokes
きわどい戦術	gamesmanship
きわどい分かれ目	razor-edge
極めて	highly
気をつける	watch
気をもむ	worry
気をもんで	on tenterhooks
均一の	flat
緊急	emergency
緊急援助	bailout
緊急援助する	bail out
緊急の	dire
緊急の	pressing
緊急の	snap
緊急輸入制限	emergency import restrictions

キングメーカー　kingmaker
金欠の　strapped
金権政治　plutocracy
金権の　plutocratic
金庫　coffers
金庫　treasury
均衡　equilibrium
銀行業　banking
…を均衡させる　balance
銀行に預ける　bank
僅差の　razor-thin
禁止　ban
禁止する　ban
禁止する　outlaw
禁止する　prohibit
均質の　homogeneous
禁止薬物使用　doping
金種　denomination
緊縮　austerity
緊縮　retrenchment
緊縮政策　belt-tightening policy
緊縮の　austere
禁制品　contraband
金銭　money
金銭的　financial
近代化する　modernize
緊張　strain
緊張　tension
緊張させる　stiffen
緊張した　tense
緊張状態　strain
均等　equality
均等な　uniform
緊迫　strain
緊迫　tension
緊迫した　tense
近辺の　surrounding
勤務する　serve
禁輸　embargo
金融　banking
金融　finance
金融　financing
金融安定化　financial stability
金融安定化フォーラム　FSF
金融安定化理事会　FSB
金融以外の　nonfinancial
金融活動　financing operations
金融緩和　easy money
金融緩和政策　easy monetary policy
金融機関　financial institution
金融危機　financial crisis
金融規制　financial regulation(s)
金融恐慌　financial crisis
金融業者　financier
金融業者　moneylender
金融サービス　financial services
金融支援　bailout

金融支援　financial assistance
金融市場　money market
金融システムの安定　financial stability
金融政策　monetary policy
金融制度　financial system
金融の　financial
金融の　monetary
金融の証券化　securitization
金融派生商品　derivative
金融引締め　tight money
金融引締め　tightening
金融逼迫　tight money
金融保証会社　monoline
金利　interest rate
金利　rate
金利入札証券　ARS
金利入札証券　auction-rate security
金利入札証券市場　auction-rate market
金利の誘導目標　key interest rate
近隣の　adjacent
勤労意識　morale
勤労意欲　morale
勤労者　worker

く

区域　block
区域　locality
区域　section
クイズ番組司会者　quizmaster
食い止める　stem
空間　space
空気　air
空気の　aerial
空気を抜く　deflate
空港　airport
空前の　record
空中の　aerial
クーデター　coup
空洞化　hollowing-out
空洞化　hollowization
…に空洞をつくる　hollow out
空白　vacuum
空白期間　window period
偶発事故　casualty
偶発事象　contingency
偶発の　casual
クーリング・オフ　cooling off
苦境　difficulties
苦境　distress
苦境　fix
苦境　plight
苦境　straits
草分け　pioneer

苦情　complaint
苦情調査官　ombudsman
薬　drug
苦戦する　struggle
具体的な　specific
駆逐艦　destroyer
口コミで　by word of mouth
口止め料　hush money
口笛　whistle
靴　shoe
覆す　reverse
掘削技術　drilling technology
…に屈する　give in to
…に食ってかかる　rip into
駆動力　steam
苦難　hardship
苦難　woes
苦難の時代　locust years
国　nation
国　state
クネセト　Knesset
苦悩　trouble
区分　bracket
区分　section
区別　difference
区別の　differential
組　team
組合　union
…と組み合う　grapple with
組み合わせ　matchup
組合せ　mix
組み入れる　include
組込みデリバティブ　embedded derivative
組み込む　incorporate
組立て　assembly
組立て　setup
組立工程　line
組立て式の　sectional
組立方式の　knockdown
組み立てる　assemble
組み立てる　structure
組む　take out
鞍　saddle
暗い　gloomy
暗い影　shadow
暮らす　fare
ぐらつく　vacillate
…と比べて　compared with
鞍を置く　saddle
繰り上げる　bring forward
グリーンメール　greenmail
繰り返して主張する　reiterate
繰り返す　reiterate
繰り越す　carry over
クリティカル・パス　critical path
…をくり抜く　hollow out

け

繰延べ税金資産	deferred tax assets
苦しい	tough
苦しい	uphill
苦しみのもと	scourge
…に苦しむ	suffer from
苦しめる	beset
苦しめる	buffet
…を苦しめる	burden
苦しめる	haunt
苦しめる	wrack
クレジット・カード	credit card
クロイツフェルト・ヤコブ病	CJD
クロイツフェルト・ヤコブ病	Creutzfeldt–Jakob Disease
グローカル	glocal
クローニズム	cronyism
グローバリズム	globalism
グローバリゼーション	globalization
グローバル移動通信システム	GSM
クローン作製術	cloning
黒字	black
黒字の	positive
クロス・ライセンス契約	cross licensing contract
クロスカントリー・スキー	X-C skiing
黒肺病	black lung disease
黒幕	backroom fixer
黒幕	kingmaker
黒幕	mastermind
黒幕として働くこと	string-pulling
黒幕となる	pull strings
クロマグロ	bluefin tuna
…に加えて	on the back of
加える	add
加える	wreak
詳しい報告	rundown
企て	attempt
…群	bloc
軍	military
軍事政権	junta
軍縮	disarmament
軍需品	munition
軍事力	military force
軍隊	military
軍隊	troop
軍の	military
軍の警報	alert
軍備縮小	disarmament
軍法会議	courtmartial
軍民両用物資	dual-use items
軍用機	gunship
軍用機	warplane
軍用資材	munition
軍用品	munition
君臨する	reign
訓練	discipline
訓練	training
訓練	workout
経営	administration
経営	management
経営が行き詰まった	ailing
経営管理上の	administrative
経営管理学修士	MBA
経営危機に直面している	financially troubled
経営再建中の	struggling
経営者	entrepreneur
経営者	executive
経営者	manager
経営者	official
経営者	operator
経営者	proprietor
経営者による自社買収	management buyout
経営上の	administrative
経営上の	operating
経営陣と従業員による企業買収	MEBO
経営する	manage
経営する	operate
経営する	run
経営統合	merger
経営統合する	merge
経営難の	troubled
経営の	managerial
経営の	operational
経営の	working
経営破綻	bankruptcy
経営破綻した	bankrupt
経営破綻した	troubled
経営破綻する	go belly-up
経営判断	decision making
経営不振に陥っている	struggling
経営不振の	ailing
経営不振の	embattled
経営不振の	troubled
…を敬遠する	shy away from
警戒	vigilance
警戒感	fear
警戒警報	alert
警戒させる	alert
…を警戒する	guard against
警戒する	wary
経過期間	age
計画	plan
計画	program
計画	project
計画	scheme
計画された	projected
計画されている	afoot
計画した	planned
計画する	design
計画する	eye
計画する	map out
計画する	prepare
計画する	project
…する計画だ	plan to
計画的な	planned
計画的な	premeditated
計画立案	drafting
計画立案者	planner
計画を立てる	schedule
経過報告	briefing
経過報告する	brief
桂冠詩人	laureate
景気	business conditions
景気	business cycle
景気	economic performance
景気一致指数	coincident indicator
景気回復	economic expansion
景気回復	economic recovery
景気回復の局面	incipient recovery
景気拡大	economic expansion
景気後退	economic downturn
景気後退	recession
景気後退	setback
景気後退の	recessionary
景気刺激策	pump-primer
景気循環	business cycle
景気循環	economic cycle
景気対策	anti-cyclical measures
景気沈滞	stagnation
景気づく	pick up
景気低迷	stagcession
景気動向指数	DI
景気の回復	pickup
景気の底	trough
景気の谷	trough
景気の二番底	double dip recession
景気持ち直しの局面	incipient recovery
景況感	business sentiment
景況感	confidence
景況感	sentiment
景況報告	snapshot of economic conditions
迎撃	interception
迎撃戦闘機	interceptor
迎撃ミサイル	interceptor
軽減	alleviation
軽減	easing
軽減	minimization
軽減	reduction
軽減	relaxation
軽減した	reduced
軽減事由	extenuating circumstances
経験する	go through

経験する	undergo	形式的行為	formality	軽微の	mini
軽減する	abate	形式的な	formal	景品	freebies
軽減する	alleviate	刑事上の	criminal	軽蔑	scorn
軽減する	ease	掲示する	put up	警報	alarm
経験豊富な人	veteran	継承	inheritance	警報機	alarm
経験豊かな	seasoned	継承	succession	警報を出す	alert
傾向	propensity	警鐘	wake-up call	警報を発する	alarm
傾向	streak	経常赤字	pretax loss	刑務所	prison
傾向	stream	経常赤字	recurring loss	契約	agreement
傾向	tendency	経常勘定	current account	契約	contract
傾向	trend	継承した	successive	契約違反	infringement
軽工業	light industry	継承者	successor	契約価格	contract price
経口避妊薬	oral contraceptive	経常収益	pretax profit	契約期間	term
経口避妊薬	pill	経常収支	current account	契約者	policyholder
警告	warning	継承する	inherit	契約する	contract
警告する	warn	計上する	carry	経理	accounting
経済	economies	計上する	charge	経理担当者	accountant
経済	economy	計上する	declare	計略	game
経済学者	economist	計上する	earmark	経歴	career
経済活動	economic activity	計上する	record	系列	affiliation
経済協力開発機構	OECD	経常損失	pretax loss	系列下	systematization
経済協力機構	ECO	経常的	ordinary	系列会社	affiliate
経済支援者	subscriber	経常の	pretax	系列会社	associated company
経済実績	economic performance	経常利益	pretax profit	系列化する	integrate
経済諮問委員会	Council of Economic Advisers	経常利益	recurring profit	系列の	affiliated
		軽水炉	LWR	経路	course
経済主義	economism	形成	formation	経路	path
経済循環	economic cycle	形成	formulation	経路	route
経済状況	economic conditions	形成	making	外科	surgery
経済上の	economic	形成する	formulate	外科手術	surgery
経済性	economies	形勢を立て直す	bounce back	激化	exacerbation
経済成長	economic expansion	係争中の	contentious	激化させる	aggravate
経済成長	economic growth	係争中の	disputed	激化させる	exacerbate
経済全体の	macroeconomic	継続して…する	continue to	激化する	heat up
経済大国	economic power	継続する	renew	劇的な	dramatic
経済地域	economies	珪素の記憶素子	chip	激動	turbulence
経済的困難	Queer Street	携帯情報端末	PDA	激動	upheaval
経済的に苦しい	strapped	携帯電話	cell phone	激変	breakneck changes
経済動向	economic activity	携帯電話	mobile phone	激変	upheaval
経済の	economic	携帯用の	handheld	激励	spur
経済白書	economic report	携帯用の	mobile	激烈な	cutthroat
経済発展	economic development	携帯用の	portable	激論	row
経済発展	economic growth	警笛	whistle	景色	prospect
経済封鎖	blockade	軽電機	light electrical equipment	景色	scene
経済不快指数	misery index	系統	chain	削り取る	scale
経済報告	economic report	系統立てる	organize	桁	digit
経済力	economic power	系統立てる	systematize	桁外れの	exceptional
経済連携	economic partnership	系統的	systematic	血液製剤	blood product
経済連携協定	EPA	系統の	systemic	血液法	Blood Law
警察	police	刑罰	punishment	結果	implication
警察管区	precinct	刑罰の	punitive	結果	outcome
計算	accounting	経費	cost	結果	result
計算	computing	経費	outlay	結核	TB
計算書類	accounts	警備	guard	結果に終わる	result in
軽視	cold shoulder	経費削減	cost cutting	…の結果になる	eventuate
形式	form	経費削減	cost reduction	結果を左右する	swing
形式	format	…を警備する	guard against	…の結果を招く	spell

…の結果を招く　　検査

欠陥　defect	report	限界　limit
欠陥　fault	月例の　monthly	限界質量　critical mass
欠陥　flaw	決裂　breakdown	減額　deduction
決議　resolution	決裂　breakup	厳格化する　tighten
血気盛んな　high-spirited	決裂　rupture	厳格な　severe
月給　salary	懸念　concern	厳格な　stringent
月給取りの　salaried	懸念　fear	原価削減　cost reduction
結局の　net	懸念　misgiving	減価償却する　write off
欠勤　absence	懸念　worry	玄関サイト　portal
欠勤　absentee	懸念材料　worry	嫌疑　suspicion
結合　blending	気配　hint	元気　pep
結合　combination	気配　indication	元気　steam
結合　linkage	下落　depreciation	元気　vitality
結婚　marriage	下落　dip	元気がいい　high-spirited
結婚仲介　matchmaking	下落　drop	元気がない　subdued
決済する　settle	下落　drop-off	元気づけられる　heartening
決算　account settlement	下落　erosion	元気づける　encouraging
決算　results	下落　fall	元気づける　refresh
決算期　business term	下落　meltdown	元気のない　dull
結集する　mobilize	下落　plunge	研究　research
結集する　orchestrate	下落　setback	研究開発　R & D
傑出した　outstanding	下落　slide	研究開発　research
欠如　absence	下落　tumble	研究する　investigate
欠如　lack	下落気味の　bearish	言及する　cite
決勝戦　runoff	下落する　decline	言及する　touch
決然たる態度を保つ　stand firm	下落する　depreciate	検挙　arrest
決然とした　decisive	下落する　deteriorate	検挙する　arrest
欠損　deficiency	下落する　dip	現金　cash
欠損金　deficit	下落する　fall	現金公開買付け　cash tender offer
結託　collusion	下落する　plunge	現金自動預け払い機　ATM
結託の　collusive	下落する　retreat	献金集金人　bundler
決断　decision	下落する　sag	現金収支　cash flow
決断　resolution	下落する　slide	現金通貨　cash in circulation
決着　settlement	下落する　tumble	現金の　spot
決着　showdown	下落する　tumbling	現金払いの　spot
決着をつける　finalize	ゲリラ兵　guerrilla	現金払い方式の　pay-as-you-go
決定　decision	…圏　bloc	権限　authority
決定　ruling	原案　draft	権限　mandate
決定機関　arbiter	原案　protocol	権限　right
決定者　arbiter	懸案の　pending	権限を与える　commission
決定する　decide	権威　czar	権限を付与する　empower
決定的証拠　smoking gun	権威者　pundit	健康　fitness
決定的な　decisive	原因　cause	健康　health
決定的な　swing	原因　culprit	健康管理　health care
…を決定的にする　clinch	…を牽引する　power	健康状態　health
欠点　fault	牽引役　driver	健康診断　checkup
血統　strain	牽引役　locomotive	健康的な　healthy
欠乏　lack	検疫　quarantine	健康な　sound
結末　eventuation	検疫　quarantining	現行の　existing
月面車　moonwalker	現役　downside	現行犯の　red-handed
月面作業　moonwork	検閲　censorship	健康保険　health insurance
月面写真　moonscape	原価　cost	原告　plaintiff
月面風景　moonscape	減価　depreciation	堅固な　hard
月面歩行　moonstroll	見解　comment	検査　checkup
月面歩行　moonwalk	見解　judgment	検査　examination
月面歩行者　moonwalker	見解　version	検査　inspection
月例経済報告　monthly economic	限界　ceiling	検査　investigation

検査	quarantining
検査	screening
検査	testing
…現在で	as of
…現在の	as of
現在の	current
現在の	existing
原材料	material
検索	browsing
検査する	examine
検査する	test
検察官	prosecuting attorney
検察官	prosecutor
検察官	public prosecutor
検事	prosecutor
顕示行為	overt act
現実	reality
現実主義	pragmatism
現実的	actual
堅実な	prudent
堅実な	solid
現実の	real
現実の所有	occupancy
原子の	A–
検収	acceptance
研修	training
厳重さ	stringency
厳重取締り	crackdown
厳重な	strict
厳重な	stringent
憲章	charter
検証	verification
減少	contraction
減少	deterioration
減少	drop
減少	drop-off
減少	erosion
減少	fall
現象	phenomenon
減少	shortfall
減少	shrinkage
減少	slide
減少	slowing
…現象	syndrome
減少	tumble
現状	status quo
現状維持	status quo
減少させる	decrease
減少させる	erode
減少した	reduced
減少している	dwindling
減少している	shrinking
検証する	verify
減少する	decline
減少する	fall
減少する	plunge
減少する	shrink

減少する	slip
減少の	downward
現職の	incumbent
現職の	sitting
原子力の	A–
原子力の	N–
原子力発電所	nuke
原子力を利用した	nuclear powered
減じる	impair
原子炉	reactor
献身	dedication
減税	tax break
減税	tax cut
減税	tax reduction
建設	construction
源泉課税	withholding tax
源泉課税方式の	pay-as-you-go
健全性	health
健全性	soundness
源泉徴収税	withholding tax
健全な	healthy
健全な	sound
建造物	construction
減速	deceleration
減速	downturn
原則	principle
減速	slowdown
減速	slowing
減速効果	drag
減速している	slowing
減速する	slow
減損	loss
現代化する	modernize
倦怠感	lassitude
減退する	languish
現代風にする	modernize
見地	perspective
現地	locality
建築家	architect
現地指向型企業	polycentric firm
現地調達	local content
現地の	local
堅調な	good
検定	testing
限定	exception
限定された	defined
…に限定する	narrow down
限定する	restrict
限度	limit
検討	discussion
検討	scrutiny
検討する	go through
検討する	mull
原動力	driver
原動力	driving force
原動力	engine
原動力	locomotive

原動力	powerhouse
…の原動力になる	drive
…の原動力になる	power
限度のない	open-end
兼任重役	interlocking directorate
権能	authority
権能	mandate
現場	field
現場で	red-handed
現物供与	in-kind donation
見聞の広い	informed
憲法	constitution
厳密な	strict
言明する	set out
懸命に考える	rack one's brains
券面額の変更	redenomination
減耗	consumption
倹約	thrift
倹約家	economist
原油	crude
原油	crude oil
原油	oil
原油価格	oil price
原油確認埋蔵量	proven oil reserves
原油タンカー	oiler
権利	concession
権利	right
原理	fundamentals
原理	principle
権利行使	strike
権利者	owner
原理主義	fundamentalism
権利の実施料	royalty
権利の侵害	infringement
権利の付与	empowerment
権利の放棄	waiver
権利放棄の意思表示	waiver
原料	raw material
権力	authority
権力者	czar
権力闘争家	powermonger

こ

号	edition
考案	invention
考案する	invent
考案する	originate
行為	behavior
行為	conduct
好意	favor
好意	goodwill
厚意	goodwill
合意	accord
合意	agreement
合意	consensus

合意	consent
合意	engagement
合意	settlement
高位高官の	high-level
合意する	agree
好意的な	friendly
強引に通す	bulldoze through
降雨	precipitation
豪雨	deluge
公益	public goods
公益	public interest
交易	trade
公益事業	public service
公益事業	public utility
公益性	public nature
公益法人	nonprofit foundation
公益法人	public entities
後援	auspices
公園	park
講演	speech
講演行脚	lecture circuit
後援者	moneyman
後援する	sponsor
…後援の	-sponsored
効果	impact
公開	disclosure
航海	navigation
公開	publication
更改	rollover
公害	pollution
公開会社	public corporation
公開会社	publicly held company
公開価格	opening price
航海術	navigation
公開する	disclose
公開する	publish
更改する	update
高解像度の	high-definition
公開討論会	forum
後悔の念	remorse
公害発生者負担の原則	PPP
公開有限会社	PLC
効果が出始める	kick in
効果がない	toothless
工学機器メーカー	engineering machinery maker
高額な	big-ticket
狡猾な人	snake
効果的な	effective
高価な	big-ticket
高価な	pricey
交換	exchange
交換	swap
高官	topsider
強姦	rape
抗がん剤	anticancer drug
交換する	exchange
交換する	swap
交換できる	convertible
交換比率	exchange rate
後期	latter term
好機	opportunity
抗議	complaint
抗議	protest
抗議する	appeal
抗議する	protest
好機の選択	timing
高級志向の	high-end
高級スーパー	upmarket supermarket
恒久的	permanent
恒久的最恵国待遇	PNTR
高級な	upscale
高級の	high-end
高級ブランド	luxury brand
工業	industry
工業化	industrialization
工業技術	technology
工業技術の	technical
公共工事	public works
公共事業	public works
公共支出	public spending
公共施設	public facilities
興行収入	box office
工業生産	industrial output
工業生産高	industrial output
公共投資	public investment
公共投資	public spending
好況になる	boom
好況の	thriving
工業の	industrial
公共の福祉	public goods
公共の利益	public interest
公共部門	public sector
公金	public funds
工具	tool
航空会社	carrier
航空機	aircraft
航空の	aerial
航空路	airline
航空路線	airline
光景	scene
合計	footing
合計	gross
合計	sum
合計金額	lump sum
後継者	heir apparent
後継者	successor
後継者	supporter
攻撃	attack
攻撃	fire
攻撃	offensive
攻撃されやすい	vulnerable
攻撃する	strike
攻撃の	offensive
攻撃物体の自動追跡	lock-on
高潔な	virtuous
貢献	contribution
抗原	antigen
…に貢献する	benefit
貢献する	contribute
公言する	trumpet
後見人	guardian
航行	navigation
広告	ads
広告	advertisement
広告	advertising
広告放送	commercial
交互実施許諾	cross licensing contract
交互躍進	leapfrog
黄砂	yellow sand
口座	account
交際	entertainment
口座残高	account balance
鉱山業	mining
降参する	give oneself up
公使	minister
工事	construction
公式の	formal
公式の	official
公式の	on-the-record
公式発表	communique
公社債	bond
公衆	public
公衆衛生	public health
高収益	high return
高周波	high frequency
高周波加熱	radio frequency heating
好循環	virtuous cycle
控除	deduction
控除	exemption
公証	attestation
交渉	negotiation
交渉	round
交渉	talks
工場	factory
工場	mill
工場	plant
向上	upgrade
交渉員	negotiator
向上させる	bolster
向上させる	upgrade
向上している	strengthening
交渉者	negotiator
交渉する	negotiate
交渉担当者	negotiator
交渉の切り札	bargaining chip
工場閉鎖	lockout
交渉力	bargaining power

公職	public service
好色文学	porn
控除する	deduct
更新	renewal
更新	rollover
更新した	renewed
更新処理する	update
更新する	renew
更新する	update
更新できる	renewable
構図	paradigm
降水	precipitation
洪水	flood
高水準	sophistication
高水準の	high
構成	makeup
構成	mix
攻勢	offensive
構成	profile
厚生	welfare
構成員	member
更生施設	halfway house
合成樹脂製の	plastic
構成状の	structural
公正妥当と認められている	acceptable
構成単位	unit
公正取引委員会	FTC
公正な	arm's length
公正な	clean
公正な	judicial
攻勢の	offensive
高性能の	sophisticated
合成の誤謬	fallacy of composition
構成比率	basket
合成物	compound
功績	exploit
航跡	wake
…を公然と無視する	fly in the face of
高鮮明度の	high-definition
構想	design
構想	idea
構想	plan
構想	prescription
構造	constitution
構造	makeup
構造	mechanism
構造	profile
構造	structure
高層建築	high rise
構造上の	structural
構想中の	on the drawing board
構造調整プログラム	SAP
構造的な	secular
構造的な	structural
構想力のある	visionary
拘束時間払い賃金	portal-to-portal pay
拘束する	handcuff
高速増殖炉	fast breeder nuclear reactor
高速大容量通信	broadband communication
高速大容量通信網	broadband network
高速道路	expressway
高速度の	high-speed
高速の	high-speed
拘束力のある	binding
抗体	antibody
後退	fallback
後退	pullback
後退	setback
広帯域通信	broadband communication
広帯域ネットワーク	broadband network
交替させる	rotate
後退する	recede
…と交替する	replace
交替で勤務させる	rotate
強奪	hijack
強奪する	hijack
強奪する	usurp
拘置	arrest
構築	development
構築する	structure
拘置する	arrest
拘置する	detain
膠着状態	stalemate
好調	kilter
公聴会	hearing
好調な	brisk
好調な	good
好調な	healthy
好調な	robust
好調な	thriving
好調の	buoyant
硬直	tightening
硬直させる	stiffen
交通	traffic
交通渋滞	gridlock
交通量	traffic
好都合な	favorable
工程	process
行程表	road map
工程表	timeline
公定歩合	official discount rate
公的	public
公的介護保険制度	public nursing care insurance system
公的資金	public funds
公的な	official
公的年金	public pension
鋼鉄	steel
更迭する	oust
好転	pickup
好転	turnaround
好転する	turn around
後天性免疫不全症候群	AIDS
高度	altitude
高騰	boom
行動	action
行動	behavior
行動	campaign
行動	conduct
行動	movement
合同	coalition
行動計画	deadline
高騰する	skyrocket
高騰する	soaring
高騰する	surging
行動する	act
合同で	jointly
行動の規範	ethics
行動様式	syndrome
行動を起こす	act
高度技術	high-tech
高度情報社会	telematics
高度先端技術	high technology
高度に	highly
高度の	sophisticated
構内通信網	LAN
購入	acquisition
購入	buying
購入	procurement
購入する	acquire
購入する	buy
購入する	procure
購入する	purchase
公認	authorization
公認候補者	nominee
公認候補者名簿	slate
後任者	successor
後任の	incoming
購買	shopping
購買拒否	boycott
光背効果	halo effect
荒廃させる	devastate
購買力平価	PPP
後発	latecomer
後発医薬品	generic drug
後発開発途上国	least developed countries
公判	court
後半	heel
広範な	broad
公判前整理手続き	pretrial procedures
公費	public funds

合否判定方式			国内情勢

合否判定方式	pass-fail	効率的に情報[情報源]にアクセスする	inforsize	極悪な	heinous
公表	announcement			国営	nationalization
公表	presentation	効率の悪い	inefficiency	国営	state ownership
公表	publication	小売店	point-of-sale	国営化	nationalization
公表	release	高利回り	high yield	国営の	state-owned
公表する	announce	交流	exchange	国営の	state-run
公表する	come out with	合流する	join	黒鉛減速炉	graphite-moderated nuclear reactor
公表する	disclose	考慮	consideration		
公表する	publish	綱領	charter	国王擁立者	kingmaker
公表する	release	綱領	platform	国外退去命令	deportation order
公表する	reveal	荒涼とした	stark	国外に追放する	expatriate
高品位の	high-definition	効力	availability	国外の	external
交付	issue	効力	effect	国際化	globalization
交付する	deliver	高齢化	aging	国際会計基準審議会	IASB
合弁会社	joint venture	高齢化	graying	国際開発協会	IDA
合弁事業	joint venture	高齢者	senior citizens	国際開発局	AID
…に抗弁する	plead	高齢者医療保障制度	Medicare	国際学習到達度調査	PISA test
合弁の	joint	高齢の	aging	国際化する	internationalise
公募	public offering	行路	orbit	国際間の協定	pact
公報	newsletter	行路	route	国際管理下に置く	internationalise
広報	PR	行路	track	国際機関の	supranational
高峰	pinnacle	功労者	veteran	国際刑事警察機構	Interpol
後方支援	logistic support	口論	bickering	国際刑事裁判所	ICC
合法性	legality	港湾当局	port authority	国際決済銀行	Bank for International Settlements
合法性	legitimacy	声	voice	国際決済銀行	BIS
広報担当官	PRO	越える	exceed	国際原子力機関	IAEA
広報担当者	spokesman	超える	exceed	国際財務報告基準	IFRS
合法的に偽装する	launder	超える	surpass	国際収支	balance of payments
候補者	candidate	…を越える	top	国際上の	international
候補者	hopeful	コール市場	call market	国際治安支援部隊	ISAF
候補者の名簿に載せる	slate	誤解	mistake	国際通貨基金	IMF
公募増資	public offering	子会社	affiliate	国際的	international
候補に指名される	slate	子会社	arm	国際電気通信連合	ITU
候補に立てる	slate	子会社	subsidiary	国際電気標準会議	IEC
公務員	officer	誤解を招く	misleading	国際トラック運転手組合	Teamsters Union
公務員	official	互角で	nip and tuck		
公務員	public servant	互角に	neck-and-neck	国際熱核融合実験炉	ITER
公務員雇用	public employment	互角の勝負の	head-to-head	国際標準化機構	ISO
被る	suffer	小型化	downsizing	国際捕鯨委員会	IWC
項目	item	小型化	miniaturization	国際民間航空機関	ICAO
公約	pledge	小型化	scale-back	国際連合	United Nations
効用	utility	小型化	scaledown	酷使	abuse
小売り	retail	小型化する	downsize	酷使する	overdrive
合理化	rationalization	小型集積回路	chip	国籍法	Nationality Law
合理化	streamlining	小型の	mini	国籍離脱者	expatriate
合理化する	streamline	小型補正予算	minibudget	告訴人	plaintiff
小売企業	retailer	枯渇	exhaustion	告訴する	accuse
小売希望価格	suggested retail price	枯渇した	dry	告訴する	lodge
小売業	retailer	互換性	compatibility	告訴する	sue
小売業者	retailer	互換性がある	compatible	告知	disclosure
小売商	merchant	こきおろす	slam	告知	herald
小売商人	merchant	小切手外交	checkbook diplomacy	告知する	herald
効率	efficiency	顧客	client	小口投資家	retail
効率化	streamlining	顧客	customer	小口ユーザー	small-lot user
効率化する	streamline	顧客	shopper	国内志向型企業	ethnocentric firm
効率的な	effective	顧客記録	CIF	国内情勢	internal affairs
効率的な	efficient	呼吸器官の	respiratory		

国内総生産	GDP
国内の	domestic
告発	indictment
告発する	accuse
告発する	indict
極秘の	classified
酷評	rap
酷評する	rap
酷評する	slam
克服する	overcome
国防	defense
国民	nation
国民医療扶助	Medicaid
国民所得	national income
国民総生産	gross national product
国民投票	plebiscite
国民投票	referendum
国民の	national
国民の利益	public interest
国有	state ownership
国有化	nationalization
国有化する	nationalize
国有の	state-owned
国立の	state-run
国連	U.N.
国連安全保障理事会	UNSC
国連監視検証査察委員会	UNMOVIC
国連スーダン派遣団	UNMIS
国連調停による	U.N.-brokered
国連の平和維持軍	Peacekeeper
国連パレスチナ難民救済事業機関	UNRWA
国連貿易開発会議	UNCTAD
固形化燃料	RDF
焦げ付いた	uncollectible
焦げ付き	bad debt
護憲評議会	Guardian Council
後光効果	halo effect
小言を言う	chide
試査	test
試査	testing
心強い	heartening
心の	mental
心の	psychic
試み	attempt
試み	effort
試み	trial
心を和ませる	melting
腰かけ	saddle
ゴシップ屋	newsmonger
…を固守する	stick to
故障	breakdown
故障	bug
故障	malfunction
呼称	name
故障する	break down
…の腰を折る	nip
誤審	miscarriage of justice
個人識別番号	PIN number
個人識別法	biometrics
個人消費	consumer spending
個人消費	private consumption
故人人名録	who was who
個人的	personal
個人的な	private
個人投資家	retail
個人の	individual
個人の	own
個人の	personal
コスト効率	cost effectiveness
コスト効率がよい	cost-efficient
コスト削減	cost reduction
コスプレ	cosplay
こすりとる	scale
個性	personality
個性	personhood
固体	object
答え	result
応える	meet
…に答える	respond to
誇張した表現	rhetoric
コツ	rope
国家	nation
国家	state
国家安全保障会議	NSC
国会	Diet
国会の	congressional
国会の	parliamentary
国家政府の権限を超えた	supranational
国家の	national
国境のない	borderless
国庫	treasury
国交	diplomatic relations
国庫の	fiscal
固定観念	obsession
固定させる	peg
固定させる	stabilize
固定式の	fixed
固定した	stable
固定した	stuck
固定する	lock in
固定電話	landline
糊塗する	paper over
言付け	message
ことば	word
言葉に言い表わす	voice
言葉にする	voice
断る	turn down
…することを怠る	fail to
粉	powder
好ましい	favorable
好ましい人物	persona grata
好ましからざる人物	persona non grata
好ましくない	detrimental
好ましくない	unfavorable
好み	propensity
…を好む	favor
小幅の	modest
コバルトリッチ・クラスト	cobalt-rich crusts
コピー生物	clone
コピー生物を作る	clone
鼓舞	spur
五分五分で	nip and tuck
五分五分の見込み	tossup
個別化	customizing
個別の	individual
個別の	separate
ごまかし	dodge
困らせる	irk
ごみ固形燃料	RDF
顧問	adviser
顧問	aide
顧問の	advisory
コモンロー	common law
雇用	employment
雇用	hiring
雇用	job
雇用機会均等法	Equal Employment Opportunity Law
雇用者	employer
雇用	employ
雇用する	hire
誤用する	misuse
雇用適性	employability
雇用主	employer
雇用の安定	job security
雇用分割	work sharing
雇用保障	job security
暦	calendar
孤立	standoff
孤立した	reclusive
これを受けて	in response
怖いもの	specter
壊す	destroy
壊れやすい	fragile
壊れやすさ	fragility
婚姻	marriage
懇願	plea
困窮	distress
根拠	evidence
根拠	reason
…を根拠にして	on the strength of
困苦	hardship
コングロマリット	conglomerate
根源	parent
混合	blending
混合	mix
混合経済	mixed economy

混合物　compound	在外資産　foreign assets	最高のもの　best
今後の　prospective	再開する　resume	最後通告　ultimatum
コンサルタント会社　consulting firm	災害予測地図　hazard map	最後通牒　ultimatum
コンサルタント業　consultancy	再確認する　reaffirm	最後の手段　trump
根性　gut	再活性化　revitalization	最後の申し出　ultimatum
懇請された訳でもない　unsolicited	再活性化する　reinvigorate	再雇用　reemployment
根絶する　stamp out	最近　newly	再雇用する　rehire
近地点　perigee	最近の　recent	財産　asset
近月点　perilune	採掘　mining	財産　property
根底　bedrock	債券　bond	財産　wealth
困難　difficulties	債権　claim	財産権　property right
困難　hardship	債権　credit	財産所有権　property right
困難　hurdle	債務　debt security	採算性　feasibility
困難　morass	再建　rebuilding	採算性調査　feasibility study
困難　straits	再建　reconstruction	採算の合わない　unprofitable
困難　stress	再建　rehabilitation	採算の取れる規模　critical mass
困難　trouble	債券　securities	財産目録　inventory
困難な　stiff	財source　coffers	材質　material
困難な　uphill	財源　pocket book	再指名　reappointment
コンパクト・ディスク　CD	財源　resource	最終使用者　end user
コンピュータ・ワーム　worm	債権者　creditor	再就職　reemployment
コンピュータ処理　computing	再建する　rebuild	再就職斡旋　outplacement
根本　bedrock	再建する　reconstruct	再就職援助　outplacement
根本原理　basis	再建する　revamp	再就職先斡旋　outplacement
根本的な　radical	再検討　review	最終処理をする　finalize
混乱　confusion	再検討　review	最終段階　countdown
混乱　disarray	再検討する　reevaluate	最終的な　net
混乱　dislocation	債権保有者　creditor	最終的な厳しい考査　acid test
混乱　disorder	在庫　backlog	最重点項目　centerpiece
混乱　disruption	在庫　inventory	最終の　terminal
混乱　disturbance	最高　high	最終の　ultimate
混乱　mess	採鉱　mining	最重要な　prime
混乱　snarl	最高　primacy	再主張する　reassert
混乱　turbulence	再興　rebuilding	歳出　spending
混乱　turmoil	再考　review	再取得　replacement
混乱させる　roil	最高…　up to	最小　minimum
混乱した　turbulent	最高位　top	最上位の　top
混乱状態　confusion	最高位の　top	最小化　minimization
混乱状態　mess	最高級の　top-of-the-line	最小限　minimum
	最高経営責任者　CEO	最小限に抑える　minimize
さ	最高指導者　supremo	最小限にする　minimize
	再興する　rebuild	最小限に減らす　minimize
差　imbalance	再考する　review	在職期間　tenure
差　margin	再構成　restructuring	在職中　sitting
サード　THAAD	再構成する　restructure	在職の　incumbent
サーバー　server	再構築　rebuilding	最初の　initial
差異　difference	再構築　restructuring	最初の　original
財　commodity	再構築する　rebuild	最初の　primary
罪悪感がある　guilty	再構築する　reconstruct	再処理　reprocessing
最悪期　trough	再構築する　restructure	再処理する　reprocess
最悪の　worst	最高潮　peak	再審　retrial
最大手　leader	最高潮に達した　in full swing	最新鋭の　state-of-the-art
裁可　ratification	最高点　top	最新鋭の　top-of-the-line
最下位　foot	再購入する　repurchase	最新式　cutting edge
再開　resumption	最高の　sovereign	最新式の　cutting-edge
災害　casualty	最高の　top	最新式の　new-fangled
災害　disaster	最高の状態　best	最新式の　state-of-the-art

最新式の	top-of-the-line
最新の	emerging
最新の	latest
最新流行の	mega-trendy
再生	revitalization
再生	revival
財政	public finance
財政赤字	budget deficit
再生医療	regenerative medical techniques
最盛期	season
最盛期の	in full swing
再生産の	reproductive
財政状況	financial condition
財政状態	financial condition
財政上の	economic
再生する	revitalize
財政政策	fiscal policy
再生できる	renewable
財政難	crunch
財政難の	cash-strapped
財政難の	financially troubled
財政の	fiscal
再生利用	recycling
再生利用する	recycle
再選	reelection
再選する	reelect
最前線	cutting edge
最前線	forefront
最前線	front line
最前線	leading edge
最前線の	cutting-edge
最先端	cutting edge
最先端	leading edge
最先端技術の	sophisticated
最先端の	cutting-edge
最先端の	latest
最先端の	state-of-the-art
最先端を行く	mega-trendy
催促状	reminder
再組織する	retool
最大化	maximization
最大級の賛意	whole-hearted support
最限に増やす	maximize
最大にする	maximize
最大の競争相手	archrival
最大の敵	archenemy
在宅介護	at-home care
採択可能な	acceptable
在宅就労者	home-based worker
在宅就労者	stay-at-home worker
採択する	adopt
採択する	pass
財団	foundation
再断言する	reassert
最長時間経路	critical path

再調整	readjustment
再調整	realignment
再調整する	realign
再調達	replacement
再調達	repurchase
最低	bottom
最低	minimum
裁定	ruling
裁定する	award
最低の	worst
最低レベル	rock bottom
再登場	reemergence
サイト閲覧者	visitor
再突入	reentry
サイト来訪者	visitor
災難	calamity
災難	catastrophe
災難	disaster
災難	woes
再入学	reentry
再入国	reentry
再任	reappointment
再任	reelection
再任する	reelect
再燃	recurrence
才能	talent
才能のある	talented
サイバー	cyber
サイバー空間	cyberspace
サイバー攻撃	cyber attack
サイバー作戦	cyber-tactics
サイバー資本主義	cybercapitalism
サイバーテロ	cyber attack
サイバーテロ	cyberterrorism
サイバーテロ	cyberterrorist attack
栽培する	cultivate
再配置	redeployment
再配備	redeployment
再配分	reapportionment
再発	recurrence
再発	return
財閥	plutocracy
再発明	reinvention
裁判	justice
裁判員	lay judge
裁判官	bench
裁判官	judge
裁判管轄権	jurisdiction
裁判官の	judicial
裁判所	court
再販する	resell
再反対尋問	recross-examination
裁判長	presiding judge
裁判の	judicial
裁判の	judiciary
再評価	revaluation
再評価する	reevaluate

再評価する	revalue
最貧国	least less-developed country
財布のひも	purse strings
細分する	subdivide
再編	consolidation
再編	overhaul
再編	realignment
再編	reorganization
再編	shakeout
再編	shake-up
再変更	readjustment
再編する	overhaul
再編する	realign
再編する	reorganize
再編成	reorganization
再編成	restructuring
再編成する	reorganize
再編成する	restructure
再編成する	retool
再膨張させる	reflate
債務	debt
債務	liabilities
債務	obligation
財務	finance
財務活動	financing operations
債務株式化	debt-for-equity swap
財務官	financier
財務官	vice minister for international affairs
財務広報	IR
財務省	Treasury
債務証書	debt security
債務証書	debt security
財務状態	financial condition
財務諸表	accounts
財務書類	accounts
財務成績	financial results
財務体質	financial health
債務担保証券	CDO
債務超過	deficiency
債務超過額	negative net worth
財務の	financial
債務の株式化	conversion of debt to equity
財務の健全性	financial health
債務の支払い	debt servicing
債務の免除	waiver
債務負担	obligation
債務不履行	default
債務返済	debt servicing
財務報告	financial report
財務報告書	financial statement
財務レバレッジ	leverage
債務を抱えた	debt-saddled
細目	item
最優遇貸出金利	prime rate

再融資 refinancing	削減する trim	座席 seat
最優先事項 front burner	策士 politician	座席の列 row
最優先の overriding	搾取 exploitation	挫折 defeat
最優良資産 crown jewel	搾取する exploit	誘い水 pump priming
最有力候補 front-runner	作成する compile	定める stipulate
採用 hiring	作成する draw up	座談会 panel
採用 recruiting	作戦 tactic	殺菌 sterilization
採用する adopt	作戦行動 tactic	雑誌 journal
採用する hire	作付け面積 acreage	雑誌 press
再来 reemergence	策定 formulation	雑種 hybrid
裁量 discretion	策定する craft	殺傷までには至らない武器 nonlethal weapon
裁量 latitude	策定する formulate	
材料 material	策謀 machination	刷新 innovation
材料 raw material	錯乱 destabilization	刷新 renewal
さえないもの clunker	錯乱 panic	刷新 revamp
差額 balance	錯乱する destabilize	刷新 shakeout
差額 difference	探り feeler	殺人 homicide
下がる falling	策略 game	殺虫剤 pesticide
下がる moderate	策略 trap	殺到 deluge
下がる slide	探る probe	殺到 flood
詐欺 fraud	下げ相場 bear market	殺到 influx
詐欺 scam	下げ止まり bottoming out	殺到する deluge
先の prior	叫び outcry	殺到する flood
詐欺の fraudulent	避ける avert	殺到する inundate
先買の preemptive	…を避ける shy away from	殺風景な stark
先細になる peter out	…を避ける stave off	査定 appraisal
先回りの anticipatory	避ける ward off	査定 assessment
先物 futures	下げる cut into	査定 valuation
先物為替予約 forward exchange contract	支え mainstay	査定する assess
	支え underpinning	作動 activation
先物取引 futures	支える brace	作動し始める kick in
先物取引所 futures exchange	支える buttress	作動する function
先行き direction	支える prop up	サドル saddle
作業 work	支える shore up	左派 leftist
作業 working	支える sustaining	左派 left-winger
作業負担量 workload	査察 inspection	左派の left-wing
作業量 workload	査察 survey	さびれた stark
先を争って買う snap up	差し押さえ foreclosure	座部 seat
先を見越した proactive	差し押さえ seizure	サブプライム subprime
策 attempt	差し押さえる confiscate	差別 discrimination
策 package	指図 directive	差別 redlining
策 strategy	差し迫った dire	サマータイム daylight saving time
索引 index	差止請求 injunction	妨げ obstruction
削減 curtailment	差止命令 injunction	妨げる choke off
削減 cutback	差し止める clamp down on	妨げる impede
削減 layoff	差し止める veto	妨げる nip
削減 reduction	差し伸べる extend	さまよう hover
削減 scale-back	差し控える forgo	サミット summit
削減する ax	…を差し控える hold back on	左右されやすい sensitive
削減する curtail	差し控える refrain from	…に左右されやすい susceptible to
削減する cut	差引 deduction	左右する governing
削減する cut back	差引勘定 offset	左右する rule
…を削減する cut back on	差引残高 account balance	左翼 left-winger
削減する downsize	差し引く balance	左翼思想 leftism
削減する lay off	差し引く deduct	左翼の left-wing
削減する reduce	詐取する defraud	さらす expose
削減する shed	詐取する swindle	さりげない throwaway

去る	exit
騒ぎ	disturbance
賛意	favor
3位の	triple
参加	commitment
参加	involvement
参加	participation
傘下	umbrella
産科医院	obstetric hospital
散会する	adjourn
傘下入りする	affiliate
参加型の	participating
参加企業	participant
参加拒否	boycott
三角合併	triangle merger
参加させる	involve
参加している	participating
参加者	participant
参加者	player
参加する	join
参加する	participate
傘下に…がある	group
酸化防止剤	antioxidant
参議院	Upper House
残虐な	atrocious
産業	industry
残業	overtime
産業化	industrialization
産業資本家	industrialist
産業相互協力	trilateralism
産業の	industrial
3極の	trilateral
3巨頭	troika
参考	reference
参考人	suspect
惨事	calamity
惨事	disaster
3次元の	three-dimensional
3者間の	trilateral
3者間の	tripartite
3者構成の	trilateral
3者相互協力	trilateralism
三者による	three-way
三重苦	trilemma
3重の	triple
産出額	turnout
参照	reference
斬新な	innovative
斬新な	novel
賛成	thumbs-up
酸性雨	acid rain
参政権	suffrage
賛成する	approve
賛成できる	right-on
残存	survival
残存する	remaining
残存する	survive
残高	balance

残高	outstanding balance
算定する	carry
暫定政府	junta
暫定的	temporary
暫定的な	interim
暫定的な	preliminary
3頭制	troika
3頭政治	troika
参入	access
参入	entry
参入	influx
参入	participation
参入	penetration
参入する	enter
算入する	include
参入する	participate
残忍な	atrocious
残忍な	inhuman
残忍な攻撃	razor job
残念賞	consolation prize
3倍増となる	triple
3倍にする	triple
3倍になる	triple
3番目の	third
賛否両論	pros and cons
賛否両論のある	controversial
産物	product
3分の1の	third
三方向からの	three-way
三位一体の改革	three-pillar reform
残務	backlog
産油国の影響力	petropower
産油国の力	petropower
散乱	mess

し

死	death
地合い	sentiment
思案する	think
シーア派のイスラム教徒	Shiite Moslem
示威運動	demonstration
飼育する	cultivate
GTL製品	GTL products
強いる	force
仕入れ	procurement
仕入れる	procure
シーン	footage
試飲する	sampler
試運転	shakedown
自営業の	self-employed
自営の	self-employed
自営の	self-supporting
ジェネリック医薬品	generic drug
ジェノサイド	genocide
ジェマア・イスラミア	Jemaah Islami-yah

支援	aid
支援	assistance
支援	auspices
支援	help
支援	prop-up
支援	rescue
支援	support
支援者	advocate
支援者	supporter
支援する	back
支援する	help
支援する	rescue
支援する	support
支援する	support
市価	market price
市価	market value
時価	market price
時価	quotation
司会者	broadcaster
司会者	emcee
司会者	presenter
司会する	emcee
司会をする	host
仕返し	quid pro quo
時価会計制度	mark-to-market accounting system
資格	qualification
視覚の	visual
資格を与える	empower
時価総額	market valuation
時価で評価する	mark to market
自家発電装置	auxiliary generator
しかる	chide
時間	time
時間外取引	after-hours trading
時間外取引	Moon Trade
時間外取引	off-hours trading
時間外労働	overtime
時間稼ぎ	buy time
志願者	hopeful
…志願の	would-be
時間の制限	time frame
時間の調整	timing
時間枠	time frame
指揮	supervision
指揮	surveillance
次期…	-elect
時期	period
時期	season
時期	stage
時期	timing
敷居	threshold
磁気共鳴映像法	MRI
指揮権	helm
時期尚早の	premature
磁気情報	magnetic information

指揮する run	資金の流れ money flow	事後の ex post fact
指揮する supervise	資金引出し信用供与 standby credit	自己破産 self-declared bankruptcy
色素 pigment	資金を調達する borrow	自己批判 self-criticism
磁気ディスク disk	資金を調達する finance	自己分析 soul-searching
磁気テープ tape	資金を調達する fund	施策 policy
式典 ceremony	資金を引き揚げる pull money	時差出勤 staggered working hours
次期の incoming	しくじり blunder	示唆する signal
磁気浮上式超高速列車 maglev	試掘権 exploratory right	自殺 suicide
識別 discrimination	軸となる core	資産 asset
識別符号 ID	仕組み mechanism	資産 coffers
支給 issuance	刺激 incentive	資産 property
支給する dole	刺激 stimulus	資産 wealth
子宮の uterine	刺激して…させる stimulate	資産価格 property values
自給の self-supporting	刺激する stimulate	資産化する capitalize
事業 business	刺激性飲料 stimulant	資産査定 due diligence investiga-
事業 enterprise	刺激性の stimulative	tion
事業 operation	刺激となる encouraging	資産譲渡益 capital gain
事業 scheme	刺激物 provocative	試算する estimate
事業 service	刺激物 stimulant	資産に計上する capitalize
事業 work	刺激誘因 motivation	資産売却益 capital gain
事業家 industrialist	試験 probation	指示 instruction
事業環境 playing field	試験 test	支持 advocacy
事業機会 opportunity	試験 trial	支持 championship
事業期間 business term	資源 resource	支持 favor
事業再生 revival	次元 dimension	支持 popularity
事業主 operator	資源循環 recycling	支持 prop-up
事業主 proprietor	試験する test	支持 support
事業所 site	試験的 pilot	支持 underpinning
事業体 entity	施行 enforcement	支持者 advocate
事業統合 merger	思考 thinking	支持者 loyalist
事業年度 accounting period	…志向の -driven	支持者 supporter
事業年度 business year	…志向の -minded	時事週刊誌 newsmagazine
事業年度 fiscal year	…志向の -oriented	指示する order
事業の提携 business tie-up	思考力 brainpower	支持する adhere
試供品 sample	自己最高の career-high	支持する back
事業部 division	自己資金 net worth	支持する buttress
事業モデル business model	自己資本 capital base	支持する prop up
事業を行う do business	自己資本 net worth	支持する underpin
資金 fund	自己資本 proprietorship	…を支持する favor
資金 resource	自己資本 worth	資質 qualification
資金 treasury	自己資本比率 capital adequacy ratio	事実上 effectively
資金援助 financial assistance	自己資本比率 capital position	事実上の de facto
資金管理手段 moneykeeping tool	自己資本比率 capital standards	事実上の virtual
資金供給 money supply	自己中心的な考え方 me-ism	支持できる sustainable
資金供給者 financier	仕事 affair	時事問題 topicalities
資金供与者 creditor	仕事 labor	使者 envoy
資金繰り cash flow	仕事 occupation	試写 preview
資金繰り liquidity	仕事 task	試射 test-firing
資金循環 money flow	仕事 work	自社株買戻し share buyback
紫禁城 Forbidden City	仕事のない unemployed	試射する test-fire
資金洗浄 laundering	仕事場 workplace	自主 freedom
資金調達 borrowing	仕事量 workload	四重奏団 quartet
資金調達 finance	仕事をする work	自主企画商品 private brand
資金調達 financing	仕事を任せる farm out	自粛する refrain from
資金調達 funding	死後の posthumous	自主再建 self-rehabilitation
資金の借り手 borrower	自己の own	自首する give oneself up
資金の再調達 refinancing	自己の self-	自首する turn oneself in

自主性	independence
自主性	initiative
支出	outlay
支出	payout
支出	spending
支出金	payout
支出する	defray
支出する	pay
支出する	spend
自主的な	voluntary
自主能力	governability
自助	self-help
市場	market
市場	mart
事象	event
事象	phenomenon
事情	backdrop
事情	circumstances
事情	swing
市場アクセス	access
市場外取引	off-market trading
市場開放	deregulation
市場開放する	deregulate
市場価格	market price
市場価値	market value
市場経済	market economy
市場経済主義者の	pro-market
市場原理に基づく	market-based
市場原理に基づく	market-oriented
史上最高値	all-time high
市場シェア	market share
市場志向型	market-oriented
至上主義者	supremacist
市場諸力	market forces
市場占有率	market share
市場操作	manipulation
事情聴取	questioning
市場取引	marketing
市場に出す	market
市場に基づく	market-based
市場の力	market forces
市場の低迷	plunge
市場の冷え込み	chilled market
市場要因	market forces
辞職	resignation
辞職させる	force out
試食者	sampler
辞職する	outgoing
辞職する	resign
辞職する	step down
指針	direction
地震	earthquake
地震	quake
指数化方式にする	index
静かな	silent
しずく	trickle
システム・オン・チップ	systems-on-chips
システム化	systematization
システム全体の	systemic
沈む	sink
沈む	subside
鎮める	assuage
…を静める	calm down
静める	placate
静める	soothe
姿勢	attitude
姿勢	commitment
姿勢	stance
姿勢	stand
私生活	privacy
私生活の	off-camera
市政の	municipal
次世代	next generation
次世代送電線網	smart grid
使節	ambassador
使節	envoy
施設	institution
施設	site
施設群	complex
施設の	institutional
慈善	philanthropy
事前運動	pre-electioneering
自然界の	natural
事前検閲	precensorship
事前行動の	proactive
事前策定型破綻	prepackaged bankruptcy
事前精査	due diligence investigation
事前調査	feeler
事前通報	tipoff
事前に対策を講じて	proactively
自然の	natural
事前の	prior
次善の策	lesser of two evils
事前配置	prepositioning
事前漏洩	tipoff
…しそうにない	unlikely
自足	self-sufficiency
持続	sustainment
持続可能性	sustainability
持続可能な	sustainable
持続させる	sustain
持続した	sustained
持続する	maintain
持続的な	sustained
事態	circumstances
事態	event
事態	juncture
次第に消滅する	peter out
次第に迫ってくる	loom
次第に小さくなる	trail
次第に減る	dwindle
下請	subcontractor
下請企業	subcontractor
下請に出す	farm out
下押し効果	depressing effect
…に従う	subject to
下書き	draft
…に従って	in compliance with
下から支える	underpin
支度	preparation
下支え	underpinning
下支えする	shore up
下支えする	underpin
したたり	trickle
下の	lower
…を下回る	fall short of
下回る	lag
下向きの	downward
示談	compromise
示談による和解	out-of-court settlement
自治	autonomy
自治体	municipality
市中	market
支柱	pillar
支柱	stake
視聴覚教材	teachware
視聴者電話参加番組	phone-in
質	quality
実演	demonstration
実演者	demonstrator
しっかり固定された	steady
しっかりした	stable
しっかりした	steady
しっかりつかむ	grip
…としっかり連帯する	stand squarely with
疾患	disability
質疑応答	Q and A
湿気のない	arid
失脚させる	overthrow
失業	job loss
失業	joblessness
失業	unemployment
実業家	industrialist
失業した	unemployed
失業中	jobless
失業者	unemployment
失業中の	jobless
失業中の	unemployed
失業率	unemployment rate
実験	test
実現	fruition
実現可能性	feasibility
実現可能性調査	feasibility study
実現可能な	possible
実験場	proving ground
実験する	test

実験台　guinea pig	失敗　defeat	児童相談所　child counseling center
実験的　pilot	失敗　failure	自動装置　robot
実権派の人　powerholder	失敗　gaffe	指導的地位　helm
実行　action	失敗させる　defeat	自動的　knee-jerk
実行　enforcement	失敗する　break down	自動販売機　vending machine
実行　implementation	失敗する　fail	児童ポルノ　child pornography
実行　practice	失敗する　go sour	…しない　fail to
実行可能な　viable	失敗する　trip up	…しないよう警告する　caution against
実行可能な　workable	実物宣伝　demonstration	….ing
実行しない　default	実物大の　full-scale	シナジー　synergy
実行する　implement	しっぺ返し　riposte	品物　merchandise
…を実行する　live up to	しっぺ返しの　tit-for-tat	シナリオ　scenario
実行する　stage	失望　frustration	死にかけている　moribund
実行する　stick to	失望させる　frustrate	ジニ係数　Gini Index
実効性がない　toothless	実務　practice	死に体　lame duck
執行部　administration	実務家　practitioner	辞任　resignation
執行猶予中の　probationary	実務知識　savvy	辞任する　resign
実際　effectively	実務レベルの　working-level	辞任する　step down
実在しない　nonexistent	質問　question	死ぬ権利を支持する　right-to-die
実際的な　hands-on	質問する　question	…を凌ぐ　outpace
実際に　effectively	実用　utility	しのぐ　weather
実際の　actual	実用化する　commercialize	支配　control
実際の　real	実用主義　pragmatism	支配　dominance
実際の居住　occupancy	実力者　bigwig	支配　domination
実施　enforcement	実力者　meritocrat	支配　governance
実施　implementation	実力者　tycoon	支配　grip
実時間　real time	実力者の　well-placed	支配　hand
実時間の　real-time	実力主義　meritocracy	支配　hegemony
実施される　come into force	指定　appointment	支配関係　politic
実施する　implement	指定する　assign	支配する　control
実施する　invoke	私的自由　privacy	支配する　dominate
実施する　stage	私的な　personal	支配する　govern
実質　real terms	私的な　private	支配する　governing
実質的な　de facto	…として機能する　serve as	支配する　reign
実質的な　virtual	視点　perspective	支配する　rule
実質ベースで　on a real-term basis	…の時点で　as of	支配的な　predominant
失職　unemployment	指導　guidance	支配的な　ruling
失政　maladministration	指導　leadership	支配力　influence
失政　mismanagement	始動　start-up	芝居をする　play
実勢市場　free market	自動化　automation	自発的な　voluntary
叱責　rap	自動化　robotization	支払い　payment
実績　performance	児童買春　child prostitution	支払い　payoff
叱責する　reprimand	児童虐待　child abuse	支払い　payout
実践　practice	始動させる　jump-start	支払い期限　prompt
実践的な　hands-on	指導者　bellwether	支払い期日　due date
失速　slowdown	指導者　head	支払い期日のきた　due
質素倹約　austerity	指導者　leader	支払い残高　balance of payments
質素な　austere	指導者　mastermind	支払い手段　instrument
実体経済　economic activity	指導者　protagonist	支払い済みの　prepaid
実体の　real	指導者　standard-bearer	支払い遅延の　overdue
湿地　quagmire	自動車　car	支払い停止　default
実地の　actual	指導者グループ　cadre	支払い停止　moratorium
実地の　hands-on	自動車重量税　automobile weight tax	支払い猶予期間　moratorium
失墜　eclipse		支払い余力　solvency
質的な　qualitative	自動車製造業者　automaker	支払う　defray
失敗　blunder	指導性　leadership	支払う　foot
失敗　clunker	自動操作　automation	支払う　pay

支払う remit	資本変更 recapitalization	社会保障 social security
…に支払う義務がある owe	資本ポジション capital position	弱小の weak
縛る handcuff	資本利得 capital gain	弱体 wane
市販 marketing	資本を再編する recapitalize	弱体化 destabilization
地盤 footing	市民の civil	弱体化 wane
市販可能性 merchantability	事務 affair	弱体化させる debilitate
四半期 quarter	事務員 pencil pusher	弱体化させる destabilize
四半期の quarterly	事務所 office	弱体化した weakened
四半期報告書 quarterly report	事務処理 processing	弱体化する enfeeble
市販薬 nonprescription drugs	事務レベルの working-level	蛇口 tap
慈悲深い benign	指名 appointment	弱点 weakness
指標 barometer	指名された designate	尺度 barometer
指標 gauge	指名する adopt	尺度 benchmark
指標 index	指名する anoint	尺度 gauge
指標 indication	指名する appoint	尺度 scale
指標 key gauge	指名する name	尺度 yardstick
指標 statistics	指名する nominate	釈放する free
支部 local	指名手配されている wanted	借用語 loanword
私服警官 plainclothesman	指名手配中の wanted	射撃 shot
自分主義 me-ism	締切り deadline	社債 bond
自分で self-	締め切る close	車載AV用品 in-car audiovisual product
司法 justice	…を示す make for	
死亡記事 obituary	示す present	写真電送 phototelegraph
司法権 jurisdiction	示す read	写真判定 photo finish
司法取引 plea bargain	示す reflect	社説 editorial
司法の judicial	示す show	社説 think piece
司法の judiciary	…を示す stand at	写像スクリーン radarscope
…志望の would-be	締め出し crowding-out	社団 association
司法の場での legal	締め出し lockout	社団 company
私募債 privately-placed bond	…を締め出す keep out	遮断 cutoff
しぼませる deflate	締め付ける squeeze	遮断 interception
絞る narrow down	占める dominate	遮断する intercept
資本 capacity	占める occupy	社長 president
資本 capital	地面 ground	借金がない afloat
資本 net worth	下期 latter term	…の借金返済を猶予する accommodate
資本家 capitalist	地元住民 local	
資本化 capitalization	地元の local	シャッターを押すだけの point-and-shoot
資本額固定の closed-end	下半期 latter term	
資本化する capitalize	諮問 adviser	シャッターを閉める shutter
資本基盤 capital base	諮問 consultation	シャトル shuttle
資本金 capital base	諮問の advisory	社内の in-house
資本金 common share	ジャーナリズム journalism	社内の inside
資本構成 capitalization	社員 hire	社報 newsletter
資本再編 recapitalization	社員 member	じゃま obstruction
資本支出 capex	社員 staff	邪魔する impede
資本市場 capital market	社会 society	邪魔する thwart
資本主義 capitalism	社会主義 socialism	シャリーア Sharia
資本主義 capitalist	社会主義者 socialist	謝礼金 gratitude money
資本総額 capitalization	社会的生産基盤 infrastructure	ジャンク junk
資本増強 capital increase	社会的責任投資 SRI	首位 lead
資本提携 capital tie-up	社会的な social	首位 primacy
資本的支出 capex	社会党員 socialist	首位の first
資本的支出 capital spending	社外取締役 outside director	首位の prime
資本投下 capital investment	社会に関する social	主因 driving force
資本投資 capital investment	社会の social	州 province
資本に組み入れる recapitalize	社会福祉 social welfare	州 state
資本の合同 pooling of capital	社会復帰施設 halfway house	自由 freedom

周囲	surroundings
周囲の	environmental
周囲の	surrounding
収益	earnings
収益	income
収益	profit
収益	revenue
収益	yield
収益性	profitability
収益性がある	profitable
収益力	profitability
収益をあげる	chalk up
10億分の1	ppb
自由化	deregulation
自由化	liberalization
集会	assembly
収穫する	reap
就学前児童の保育	day care
自由化する	deregulate
自由化する	liberalize
周期	circle
周期	cycle
衆議院	House of Representatives
従業員	employee
従業員	personnel
従業員	staff
従業員1人当たり	per worker
就業者	workforce
就業不能	disability
集金	collection
襲撃	attack
襲撃	raid
銃撃戦	shootout
重工業	smokestack industry
集合体	complex
重債務貧困国	HIPCs
自由裁量の	discretionary
周産期医療	perinatal medical care
集産主義の	collective
収支	balance
…を重視した	-conscious
自由市場	free market
自由市場主義者	free-marketer
…を重視する	focus on
州児童医療保険プログラム	SCHIP
収集	collection
自由主義	liberalism
自由主義市場	free market
自由主義の	liberal
収縮	contraction
収縮	shrinkage
収縮させる	deflate
習熟曲線	learning curve
習熟率	learning rate
重症急性呼吸器症候群	SARS
就職指導の	vocational
囚人	prisoner
終身雇用制度	lifetime employment system
終身在職権	tenure
修正	adjustment
修正	amendment
修正	correction
修正	revision
銃声	shot
修正する	adjust
修正する	amend
修正する	correct
修正する	rectify
修正する	revise
州全体にわたる	statewide
州全体の	statewide
重層的な	multitiered
充足	satisfaction
充足させる	satisfy
従属的な	second
渋滞	snarl
重大局面	crisis
重大な	critical
重大な	major
重大な	serious
重大な	significant
重大な局面	juncture
住宅	housing
住宅金融	housing loan
住宅市場	housing
住宅着工件数	housing starts
住宅の差し押さえ	home foreclosure
住宅ローン	home mortgage
住宅ローン	housing loan
住宅ローン担保証券	MBS
住宅ローンの焦げ付き	home foreclosure
集団	family
集団	group
集団	mafia
集団	outfit
集団虐殺	genocide
集団座り込み	lie-down
集団代表訴訟	class action suit
集団の	collective
米国の州知事	chief executive
州知事	premier
周知の	known
集中	concentration
集中作戦	blitz
集中させる	center
集中する	concentrate
集中治療室	ICU
重鎮	tycoon
充填材	plug
終点の	terminal
充当	appropriation
柔軟性	flexibility
柔軟な	flexible
柔軟な	plastic
柔軟な	soft
自由にする	free
自由に使える	disposable
収入	earnings
収入と支出	incomings and outgoings
就任	inauguration
就任させる	inaugurate
就任式	inaugural
私有の	private
集配用コンピュータ	server
宗派の	sectarian
修復	rehabilitation
修復	renovation
修復作業	renovation
醜聞	scandal
十分な資金がない	strapped
州兵	militia
周辺機器	device
自由貿易	free trade
自由貿易協定	FTA
自由放任の社会	permissive society
終末	death
終末期医療施設	hospice
住民	resident
住民数	population
自由民主党	Lib Dems
住民投票	plebiscite
住民投票	referendum
重役	board member
重役	executive
重役会	board of directors
…集約型	-oriented
集約する	consolidate
集約度	intensity
修養	discipline
充用	appropriation
収容者	inmate
重要人物	bigwig
重要人物	key
重要性	import
重要である	concern
重要な	key
重要な	serious
重要な	significant
重要な	upfront
従来の	conventional
自由落下	free fall
修理	renovation
修理工	machinist
終了	close
終了	end
終了	termination
重量	weight
終了させる	terminate

終了する end	首相 PM	出訴期限 statute of limitations
終了する expire	首相 premier	出張 outreach
就労 employment	首相 prime minister	出廷命令 summons
就労者 worker	首相在任期間 premiership	出頭する turn oneself in
就労体験 internship	主唱者 protagonist	出頭命令 subpoena
受益者 beneficiary	主唱者 standard-bearer	出入国管理業務 immigration
主演させる feature	受賞者 laureate	出入港停止命令 embargo
主義 approach	首相の地位 premiership	出発時間 scratch
主義 cause	守勢の defensive	出発点 scratch
主義 doctrine	主題 matter	出発点 threshold
主義 philosophy	主題 theme	出費 outlay
受給権の発生した vested	受諾 compliance	主導 drive
受給資格がある eligible	受託者 trustee	主導権 dominance
受給者 beneficiary	受諾する accept	主導者 bellwether
需給の demand-supply	手段 facility	主導者 standard-bearer
授業 lesson	手段 instrument	主導する head
塾 cramming school	手段 resort	主導的 leading
祝賀 celebration	手段 step	主導的地位 leading edge
縮小 contraction	手段 stepping stone	受動的な passive
縮小 curtailment	手段 tactic	…主導の -driven
縮小 cutback	手段 vehicle	…主導の -led
縮小 downsizing	手段 way	取得 acquisition
縮小 scale-back	受注生産 make-to-order	取得価格 book value
縮小 shrinkage	主張 allegation	取得者 acquirer
縮小させる narrow	主張 assertion	取得する acquire
縮小した contractionary	主潮 mainstream	取得する buy
縮小した reduced	主張 purport	取得する obtain
縮小している dwindling	主張する allege	取得する take over
縮小している shrinking	主張する claim	首脳 leader
縮小する curtail	主張する plead	首脳会議 summit
縮小する cut	出荷 shipment	首脳部 topsider
…を縮小する cut back on	出荷する ship	主婦 homemaker
縮小する dwindle	出荷台数 shipment	手法 approach
縮小する moderate	出荷量 shipment	手法 method
縮小する shrink	出願 application	手法 strategy
縮小する slip	出願者 applicant	手法 style
縮小する trim	出血 hemorrhage	手法 technique
縮小的解消 wind-down	出血する hemorrhage	首謀者 mastermind
祝典 celebration	出現 advent	樹木 greenery
熟慮 deliberation	出現 emergence	需要 demand
熟練者 expert	出現する emerge	需要 requirement
熟練の skilled	熟考する mull	主要経済国フォーラム MEF
受刑者 prisoner	出産前の休暇 blow-out holiday	主要債権国会議 Paris Club
主権 sovereignty	出資 investment	主要成功要因 CSF
主権のある sovereign	出資金 annuity	需要多占 polypsony
取材 coverage	出資金 capital	需要多占的市場 polypsonistic market
取材記者 reporter	出資者 investor	
主催者 host	出資者持ち分 proprietorship	主要な key
主催者 organizer	出資する finance	主要な leading
主催する host	出資する fund	主要な main
主催する sponsor	出資する invest in	主要な major
取材担当区域 newsbeat	出資する pump	主要な nuts-and-bolts
…主催の -sponsored	出場しない default	主要な prime
主旨 gist	出生届け birth registration	主要な principal
趣旨 purport	出生率 fertility rate	主要な基準 key gauge
主軸 linchpin	出世が速い fast-track	授与する award
首席 chancellor	出世した successful	樹立する notch

主流 mainstream	上院議員 Senator	証言 deposition
受領 acceptance	小衛星 moonlet	証言 evidence
受領 receipt	省エネルギー energy saving	証言 testimony
受領者 recipient	上演 staging	条件 condition
受領する receive	上演する enact	上限 ceiling
主力 mainstay	紹介 introduction	上限 upper limit
主力機種 flagship	障害 barrier	証券化 securitization
主力商品 flagship	障害 bottleneck	…の証券化 securitized
主力商品 mainstay	障害 disability	証券会社 investment bank
主力の main	障害 glitch	証券化した securitized
種類 species	障害 hurdle	証券化する securitize
種類 variety	渉外 liaison	証券業 brokerage
準安定性 metastability	生涯教育 lifelong education	証券業者 trader
順位 ranking	場外市場 curb	証券市場関係者 Wall Streeters
準医療活動従事者 paramedics	紹介する introduce	証言する testify
純営業利益 net operating profit	昇格 promotion	証券取引委員会 SEC
春画 porn	昇格 upgrade	証券取引所 bourse
巡回 patrol	昇格 upgrading	証券取引所 stock exchange
瞬間 moment	昇格させる promote	証券引受人 underwriter
循環 circle	昇格させる upgrade	証券保有高 position
循環 cycle	償還 redemption	上限を設ける cap
循環させる circulate	召喚状 subpoena	証拠 evidence
循環処理する recycle	召喚状を出す subpoena	証拠 testimony
循環論法 vicious circle	償還する pay off	照合 adjustment
殉教 martyrdom	償還する redeem	条項 article
…に準拠して in compliance with	償還する reimburse	条項 clause
殉死 martyrdom	召喚する subpoena	条項 stipulation
巡視 patrol	小規模な minor	症候群 syndrome
遵守 compliance	小規模の mom-and-pop	錠剤 pill
順序 procedure	償却 cancelation	詳細な計画 blueprint
潤沢な ample	消却 retirement	詳細な計画を立てる map out
順調に進んで on track	消却 write-off	小冊子 booklet
準通貨 quasi money	償却する depreciate	使用された used
殉難 martyrdom	消却する retire	正直な upfront
順応不良 maladaptation	上級の ranking	商社 house
順応率 sliding scale	上級の senior	使用者 employer
順番 turn	商業 commerce	使用者 user
準備 arrangement	商業 trading	成就 completion
準備 preparation	状況 circumstances	成就 fruition
準備期間 runup	状況 condition	召集 summons
準備金 reserve	商業化 commercialization	招集する call
準備する prepare	商業化する commercialize	召集する summon
準備なしの off-the-cuff	商業主義 mercantilism	常習犯 hardened criminal
順法精神 law-abiding spirit	商業取引所 mercantile exchange	詳述 specification
純利益 bottom line	商業の commercial	上首尾に終える wrap up
省 ministry	商業の mercantile	照準を合わせる gear
省 province	消極的な passive	…に照準を合わせる zero in on
試用 trial	常勤 full-time employee	証書 instrument
使用 usage	常勤従業員 full-time employee	症状 symptom
使用 use	使用契約 charter	上昇 appreciation
使用 utilization	衝撃 blow	上昇 rise
掌握 hold	衝撃 shock	上昇 strengthening
掌握する control	上下幅 plus or minus	上昇 upside
上位の senior	証券 bill	上昇 uptrend
上位の upper	証券 issue	上昇 upturn
上院 Senate	証券 note	上場 listing
上院 Upper House	証券 securities	上場会社 publicly held company

上昇株の	up-and-coming	承諾　thumbs-up
上場企業　publicly owned company	承諾する　accept
上昇基調　uptrend	商談　negotiation
上昇気味　upside	常置の　standing
上昇傾向　upside	消長する　wax and wane
上昇傾向　uptrend	焦点　focal point
上昇傾向　upturn	焦点　focus
上昇傾向の　buoyant	焦点　highlight
上昇させる　inflate	商店　house
上場された　listed	商店　store
上昇している　strengthening	…に焦点を当てる　focus on
上昇する　appreciate	譲渡　assignment
上昇する　climb	譲渡　handout
上昇する　rise	譲渡　transfer
上昇する　rising	小島嶼国連合　AOSIS
上昇する　upward	消毒　sterilization
上場する　list	衝突　clash
上場投資信託　exchange-traded fund	衝突　conflict
上場廃止　delisting	衝突する　clash
上場を廃止する　delist	衝突する　conflicting
昇進　promotion	商取引　commerce
昇進　upgrading	承認　acceptance
昇進させる　promote	承認　approval
昇進停滞の　mid-career	承認　endorsement
少数　minority	商人　merchant
少数株主持ち分　minority interest	承認　ratification
少数集団　minority	承認する　agree
少数派　minority	承認する　approve
少数民族　minority	承認する　ratify
上手な　skilled	商人の　mercantile
…と称する　purported	商人の　merchant
称する　style	常任の　standing
使用する　employ	生の　raw
情勢　environment	商売　business
情勢　situation	商売　deal
情勢　swing	商売の　mercantile
情勢分析家　analyst	商売の　merchant
常設の　standing	勝敗を決する　swing
商戦　shopping	消費　consumption
上訴　appeal	消費財　consumer goods
上層部による　high-level	消費財　consumer product
上層部の人　topsider	消費者　consumer
消息　information	消費者　user
消息筋　observer	消費者心理　consumer confidence
消息通の　informed	消費者物価指数　CPI
状態　condition	消費する　consume
状態　going	消費税　consumption tax
状態　kilter	消費性向　propensity to consume
状態　situation	商標　brand
状態　standing	商品　commodity
状態　status	商品　goods
招待する　invite	商品　merchandise
承諾　acceptance	商品化　commercialization
承諾　approval	商品先物取引委員会　CFTC
承諾　compliance	商品性　merchantability
承諾　consent	商品取引　mercantile exchange
	商品貿易　merchandise trade

障壁　bar
障壁　barrier
障壁　bulwark
城壁　wall
譲歩　climb-down
使用法　use
情報　content
情報　data
情報　information
情報　intelligence
情報　knowledge
情報　news
情報隔壁　firewall
情報技術　information technology
情報技術　infotech
情報源　deep throat
情報源　source
上方修正する　raise
情報処理機能を持つ　smart
情報通信　telematics
情報通信会社　telco
情報通信技術　ICT
情報提供者　informant
情報提供者　informer
情報提供者　tipster
…の情報に通じている　keep up with
上方の　upper
上方へ　upward
情報を伝える　tip
賞味期間　shelf life
商務省　Commerce Department
証明　attestation
証明　certification
照明　light
証明　testimony
証明　verification
証明書　warrant
証明する　certify
証明する　testify
証明する　verify
消滅　death
消滅しかけている　moribund
正面の　front
消耗　consumption
消耗　exhaustion
消耗する　consume
消耗品　supplies
条約　pact
条約　treaty
条約議定書　treaty
条約締約国会議　COP
賞与　bonus
乗用車　car
剰余金　surplus fund
将来起こりそうな　potential
将来性　capability
将来性　potential

将来性のある人	up-and-comer
将来展望	time horizon
将来の	prospective
将来を見越した	forward-looking
勝利	victory
勝利	win
上陸	landfall
上陸する	make landfall
上流指向の	upscale
上流部門	upstream
使用料	hire
使用料	royalty
使用料	toll
使用量	use
省力化	automation
奨励	encouragement
奨励金	subsidy
奨励する	encourage
奨励報酬	incentive award
初演	premiere
除外	exception
初回の	maiden
所感	sentiment
書記	pencil pusher
書記官	secretary
初期の	early
初期の	initial
初期の	original
除却	disposal
序曲	prelude
食	eclipse
職	job
職	occupation
職員	officer
職員	staff
職員	staffer
職業	career
職業	occupation
職業	profession
職業訓練	job training
職業上の	vocational
職業人	professional
職業の	occupational
職業の	professional
職責	responsibility
食肉加工業者	meat processor
食肉加工工場	meatpacking plant
食肉処理場	slaughterhouse
職人気質	professionalism
食の安全	food safety
職能	function
職能法人	P.C.
職場	workplace
職場研修	on the job training
食品	food
食品スーパー	grocery store
食品防腐剤	preservative
植物	vegetable
植物人間	vegetable
植民者	settler
職務	task
職務代行者	caretaker
職務保証	job security
食物	food
食欲	appetite
食欲抑制剤	anorectic
食料	food
植林	replanting
助言	reminder
助言者	adviser
助言の	advisory
所産	fruit
書式	form
書式	format
徐々に上がる	ratchet
徐々に動く	inch
徐々に下がる	ratchet
徐々になくなる	peter out
…を徐々に止める	get out of
徐々に弱まる	wane
所信	remark
助成金	bonus
助成金	subsidy
女性政治家	stateswoman
書籍	book
助走	runup
所帯	household
助長する	facilitate
ショック	blow
職権乱用	misconduct
ショッピング・センター	shopping mall
所得	earnings
所得	income
所得	melon
所得隠し	concealing income
所得から控除できる	tax-deductible
所得税	income tax
所得の申告漏れ	undeclared income
処罰	penalty
処罰	punishment
処罰	sanctions
処罰する	punish
処分	deep six
処分	disposal
処分	liquidation
処分	punishment
処分可能な	disposable
処分する	destroy
処分する	liquidate
処分する	punish
処分する	settle
処分する	unload
処方箋	prescription
除幕	inauguration
署名者	signatory
署名する	sign
署名調印する	sign
書面にした	written
書面の	paper
所有	holding
所有	ownership
所有	possession
所有権	property right
所有権者	owner
所有者	holder
所有者	owner
所有者の	proprietary
所有する	own
所有地	land
所有有価証券	portfolio
処理	address
処理	disposal
処理	processing
処理	transaction
処理	treatment
処理	workout
処理する	address
…を処理する	cope with
…を処理する	deal with
処理する	process
処理の誤り	maladministration
助力	assistance
助力	help
書類	document
書類	paper
書類一式	dossier
序列	ranking
序論	introduction
地雷撤去作業	mine-clearing work
知らせ	news
調べによると	allegedly
調べる	examine
調べる	track
しらを切る	put a brave face on
自力での	bootstrap
自力の	self-supporting
…にり込みする	shy away from
自立	autonomy
自立	independence
自立	self-sufficiency
自立型の	stand-alone
自立した	independent
自律性	autonomy
自律的成長	self-sustainable growth
時流	tide
資料	data
資料	file
資力	pocket book
視力による	visual
思慮分別	discretion

…に印をつける	mark	人工知能	cyber	身体障害者	physically-handicapped people
指令	directive	進行中の	afoot	信託	trust
事例	case	進行中の	ongoing	信託機関	trustee
熾烈な	cutthroat	人口統計上の	demographic	信託市場	fiduciary market
熾烈な競争	fierce competition	人工透析	dialysis	新着の	fresh
白物	home appliance	人口動態に関する	demographic	慎重	deliberation
仕訳	journal	新興の	emerging	慎重	prudence
仕分けする	pigeonhole	信号を送る	signal	慎重な	cautious
芯	core	申告書	report	慎重な	prudent
新案	invention	申告する	declare	心的外傷後ストレス障害	PTSD
腎移植	kidney transplant	深刻な	deep	人的資源	human resources
人員	personnel	深刻な	serious	人的資源	manpower
陣営	camp	深刻な状況	plight	人的損害	casualty
震央	epicenter	申告漏れの所得	undeclared income	進展	advance
侵害	violation	審査	assessment	進展中の	ongoing
…を侵害する	encroach on	審査	investigation	深度	depth
侵害する	infringe on	審査	probation	浸透	penetration
侵害する	pirate	審査	screening	震動	jolt
人格	personality	人材	people	振動	sway
新華社	Xinhua News Agency	人材派遣会社	staffing agency	震動させる	jolt
新型の	new-fangled	審査する	assess	人道主義的な	humanitarian
新型肺炎	SARS	診察	interview	浸透の	trickle-down
新株引受権	stock purchase warrant	人事部	human resources	浸透理論に関する	trickle-down
新株割当抽選	ballot	新自由主義	neoliberalism	シンナー遊び	thinner sniffing
審議	discussion	人種隔離政策	apartheid	侵入者	raider
新規株式公募	IPO	伸縮法	sliding scale	新入社員	recruit
新規採用	recruiting	人種差別	racism	新入社員募集	recruitment
新規採用	recruitment	進出	participation	信認	credibility
新規採用する	recruit	進出	penetration	信念	conviction
新規参入企業	newcomer	人種の	ethnic	心配	misgiving
新規参入者	newcomer	人種の	racial	心配	unrest
新機軸の	innovative	進取の気性	enterprise	塵肺	black lung disease
新規住宅着工件数	housing starts	信条	doctrine	塵肺	pneumoconiosis
新規上場	debut	侵食する	encroach on	心配がない	secure
新規上場する	debut	浸食する	erode	心配する	worry
新規な	novel	紳士録	who's who	新発債市場	primary market
新規の	fresh	新人	freshman	侵犯	infringement
新規の	new	新人議員	backbencher	審判者	arbiter
真偽の疑わしい	alleged	浸水	inundation	侵犯する	encroach on
審議の場	table	浸水させる	inundate	人物	figure
新規発行	flotation	申請	application	新聞	newspaper
新疆	Xinjiang	申請	petition	新聞	paper
神経ガス	nerve agent	新生児集中治療室	NICU	新聞	press
神経伝達物質	neurotransmitter	申請者	applicant	新聞記者	newsman
神経毒	neurotoxin	申請する	file	新聞紙	newspaper
人権	human rights	親善	affiliation	新聞社	newspaper
震源地	epicenter	新鮮凍結血漿	fresh frozen plasmas	新聞売店	newsstand
人件費	labor cost	新鮮な空気	ozone	新聞販売業者	newsagent
進行	course	心臓	ticker	新聞販売業者	newsdealer
人口	population	深層の	deep	新聞編集者	newspaperman
人工衛星	satellite	心臓の	cardiac	新聞用紙	newsprint
人口減少社会	age of people decline	心臓の	cardiac	進歩	advance
新興工業経済地域	NIEs	心臓病の	cardiac	進歩	progress
新興工業国	NICs	心臓部	heartland	信望	prestige
進行している	ongoing	迅速な	prompt	信奉者	following
人工多能性幹細胞	induced pluripotent stem cell	死んだ	dead	辛抱強い	patient
		身体言語	body language		
		身体検査	pat-down search		

す

進歩した	advanced
進歩主義の	progressive
進歩する	advance
進歩的な	liberal
進歩的な	progressive
進歩的な	right-on
進歩のない	stagnant
親密	affiliation
人民元	renminbi
人民元	yuan
人民主義	populism
人民大会堂	Great Hall of the People
人民幣	renminbi
人名録	who's who
信用	claim
信用	credit
信用	trust
陣容	lineup
信用売り	short sale
信用格付け	credit rating
信用供与	facility
信用供与枠	standby commitment
信用できる	reliable
信用度	creditworthiness
信用度	rating
信用の質	creditworthiness
信用リスク	credit risk
信用リスク移転商品	CRT product
信用力	credibility
信用力	creditworthiness
信用力が低い	subprime
信頼	confidence
信頼	credibility
信頼	dependence
信頼	integrity
信頼	reliability
信頼	reliance
信頼	trust
信頼性	reliability
信頼できる	reliable
信頼できる	responsible
信頼できる	well-placed
信頼度	reliability
心理	psychology
心理学	psychology
心理学の	psychological
審理する	judge
心理的な	psychological
尽力	effort
森林伐採	deforestation
森林伐採	logging
人類	personkind
進路	course
進路	track
吸い上げの	trickle-up
吸い上げる	siphon off
推移	transition
随意契約	noncompetitive contract
随意選択の	elective
随意の	discretionary
随意の	option
水銀中毒症	Mad Hatter's disease
遂行	implementation
遂行する	implement
遂行する	make good
遂行する	wage
衰弱させる	debilitate
衰弱させる	enfeeble
水準	level
水準	mark
水準	point
水上に不時着する	ditch
推進する	accelerate
推進する	boost
推進する	further
推進力	driver
推進力	driving force
推進力	locomotive
推進力	steam
水生の	aquatic
推薦する	nominate
水素	hydrogen
推測する	speculate
推測に基づく	speculative
衰退	eclipse
衰退している	dwindling
水中の	aquatic
推定	estimate
推定	projection
推定する	estimate
推定の	estimated
水平の	level
水平の	straight
水平飛行をする	level off
水平飛行をする	level out
睡眠時無呼吸症候群	sleep apnea syndrome
睡眠導入剤	sleep-inducing agent
水面下の	backchannel
水面下の	behind-the-scenes
水路	ditch
数字	digit
数字	number
趨勢	tendency
数値	figure
数値	level
数値	number
数値	reading
スーパー・チューズデイ	Super Tuesday
スーパーの売上高	supermarket sales
枢要な	key
数量	quantity
数量の	quantitative
据え置かれた	unchanged
据え置き	freeze
据え置く	freeze
据える	position
スカイチーム	SkyTeam
スギ花粉	cedar pollen
透き通る	transparent
透き通るような	transparent
…好きの	-minded
スキミング	skimming
救い	salvation
救う	bail out
救う	rescue
救う	save
少ない	small
優れた	excellent
優れた	par excellence
図形	figure
スケープゴート	scapegoat
スケール・メリット	scale merit
スケジューリング	scheduling
すさまじい	sweeping
ずさんな	slipshod
ずさんな管理	mismanagement
筋	source
筋書き	scenario
筋金入りの	hard-core
素性	identity
進み具合	going
勧める	encourage
進める	facilitate
進める	proceed with
進んだ	advanced
スタンダード＆プアーズ	Standard & Poor's
ステアリング	steering
…を捨てる	wean self off
ステロイド	steroid
スト	strike
ストーカー	stalker
ストーカー行為	stalking
スト破り	strikebreaker
ストライキ	strike
ストレス要因	stressor
頭脳	brain
頭脳作業	brainwork
頭脳集団	think tank
頭脳労働	brainwork
頭脳労働者	brainworker
スパイウエア	spyware
スパイ行為の	cloak-and-dagger

スパム・メール	spam	
素早い	agile	
スピードを上げる	rev up	
スペーストラック	spacetrack	
スポークスマン	spokesman	
スポーツ用多目的車	SUV	
スマート・グリッド	smart grid	
スライド制	sliding scale	
スライド方式にする	index	
すりつぶした	ground	
…をすり抜ける	wriggle out of	
する	wage	
…とすると	given	
鋭い	acute	
鋭さに欠ける	toothless	
ずる休み	truancy	
座っている時間	sitting	
スワップ	swap	
寸評	one-liner	
寸法	dimension	
寸法	size	
寸法をとる	measure	

せ

背	back	
性	sex	
税	tax	
西安	Xi'an	
精鋭	elite	
成果	fruit	
成果	outcome	
成果	performance	
成果	result	
政界	politics	
政界に顔のきく人物	rainmaker	
正確	precision	
税額控除	tax break	
税額控除できる	tax-deductible	
正確に示す	pinpoint	
青瓦台	Blue House	
生活妨害	nuisance	
生活様式	lifestyle	
成果のある	fruitful	
静観	wait-and-see	
請願	petition	
請願	plea	
請願	suit	
税関	customs	
正義	justice	
正規雇用	full time payroll	
生気のない	anemic	
請求	claim	
請求	demand	
請求	request	
請求書	bill	
請求書を送る	bill	
請求する	charge	
請求する	claim	
請求する	demand	
盛況な	thriving	
政教分離論	secularism	
制御する	curb	
税金の還付	refund	
政権	government	
政権	political power	
政権	regime	
制限	restriction	
税源	tax resources	
制限する	infringe on	
制限する	restrict	
制限なしの	all-in	
制限のない	no-holds-barred	
制限のない	open	
政権を担当する	ruling	
性向	propensity	
性交	sex	
成功	success	
成功確実の	surefire	
成功企業	winner	
成功した	successful	
製鋼所	steelworks	
…と整合する	consistent with	
税込みの	pretax	
税込み利益	pretax profit	
精査	probe	
制裁	sanctions	
精彩がない	lackluster	
制裁金	fine	
制裁の	punitive	
製作	making	
製作	manufacture	
政策	policy	
製作	production	
政策	program	
政策金利	key interest rate	
政策金利	key rate	
政策決定	decision making	
政策決定者	policymaker	
政策綱領	platform	
製作された	manufactured	
製作所	mill	
製作する	fabricate	
製作する	manufacture	
製作する	produce	
清算	liquidation	
生産	manufacture	
生産	manufacturing	
生産	output	
生産	production	
生産	rollout	
生産効率	productivity	
生産国	producer	
生産された	manufactured	
生産者	producer	
生産消費者	prosumer	
生産する	assemble	
生産する	manufacture	
生産する	produce	
生産する	turn out	
清算する	liquidate	
清算する	settle	
清算する	wind up	
生産性	productivity	
生産設備	factory	
生産設備	plant	
生産高	output	
生産高	turnout	
生産的な	productive	
生産の	manufacturing	
生産品	product	
生産量	output	
生産力	productivity	
生産力のある	productive	
生産履歴管理	traceability	
制止	restraint	
政治	government	
政治	politics	
政治運動	politicking	
政治家	pol	
政治家	politician	
政治家	politico	
政治家	statesman	
政治化	politicization	
政治化する	politicize	
政治活動	political action	
政治活動	politicking	
政治活動をする	politick	
政治家の資質	statesmanship	
政治家らしい	statesmanlike	
政治局	Politburo	
政治局常務委員会	Politburo	
政治工作	politicking	
政治資金	barrel	
制止する	restrain	
誠実	integrity	
性質上の	qualitative	
政治的手腕	statecraft	
政治的手腕	statesmanship	
政治的な	political	
政治の	political	
政治犯保護	asylum	
政治亡命	asylum	
政治問題にする	politicize	
政治屋	politician	
政治屋	politico	
正社員	full-time employee	
脆弱性	fragility	
脆弱な	fragile	
税収	tax revenue	
税収	taxation	

| 正常化 normalization
| 正常化する normalize
| 星条旗 Star-Spangled Banner
| 正常通商関係 normal trade relations
| 聖職者 cleric
| 生殖の reproductive
| 政治力学 politic
| 政治を論じる politicize
| 成人 major
| 精神医学の psychiatric
| 精神科医 psychiatrist
| 精神的打撃 shock
| 精神的な psychic
| 成人年齢 age of majority
| 精神の mental
| 精神の psychic
| 成人向け映画に指定する X-rate
| 成人向けの X-rated
| 精神療法 psychotherapy
| 精神労働 brainwork
| 精神労働者 brainworker
| 盛衰する wax and wane
| 生成 formation
| 生成 generation
| 税制 tax system
| 生成する generate
| 成績 results
| 成績 showing
| 聖戦 Jihad
| 生鮮食品 perishables
| 整然とした orderly
| 製造 making
| 製造 manufacture
| 製造 manufacturing
| 製造 production
| 製造過程の manufacturing
| 製造技術 knowhow
| 製造業 factory
| 製造業者 manufacturer
| 製造された manufactured
| 製造する manufacture
| 製造する produce
| 製造する turn out
| 製造の manufacturing
| 生存 survival
| 生態 ecology
| 政体 regime
| 生態学 ecology
| 生態学の ecological
| 生態環境 ecotop
| 生態系 ecosystem
| 盛大 red-carpet
| 生態の eco-
| 生態の ecological
| 聖地 holy city
| 成長 expansion

成長 growth
成長可能な viable
成長軌道 growth path
成長する growing
性的いたずら molestation
性的虐待 molestation
性的少数者 LGBT
性的な sexual
製鉄所 mill
製鉄所 steelworks
性転換者 transsexual
聖都 holy city
制度 institution
精度 precision
政党 party
性同一性障害 gender identity disorder
正統性 legitimacy
制動装置 brake
正当な due
制度の institutional
整頓された orderly
整頓する marshal
成年者 major
正の positive
性の sexual
成否 success
整備 development
税引き後 after tax
税引き後所得 disposable income
税引き後で after tax
税引き後利益の赤字 negative net worth
税引き前の pretax
整備する develop
整備する improve
成否をかけた make or break
…の成否を決める make or break
製品 commodity
製品 goods
製品 product
製品化 commercialization
政府 government
政府系の government-affiliated
政府系ファンド sovereign wealth fund
政府交付金 pork barrel
政府雇用 public employment
政府支援機関 GSE
生物 bio-
生物・化学兵器 biological and chemical weapons
生物資源 biomass
生物テロ攻撃 bioterrorist attack
生物統計 biometrics
生物毒性 biotoxin

生物に関する bio-
生物量 biomass
政府部門 public sector
政府保証の state-backed
成分 element
性別 sex
精密 precision
政務 politics
税務申告 tax return
生命 bio-
声明 communique
声明 declaration
声明 manifesto
声明 statement
生命維持装置 life support
生命環境科学 life and environmental science
声明書 statement
生命線 lifeline
生命保険 life insurance
生命保険会社 life insurer
制約 barrier
誓約 pledge
誓約 promise
製薬会社 pharmaceutical firm
誓約する pledge
誓約する swear
制約する vow
性欲の sexual
整理 divestiture
整理 divestment
整理する divest
整理する marshal
整理する pigeonhole
整理する wind up
税率 tax rate
整理統合する consolidate
精力 energy
勢力 force
精力的な aggressive
精力的な dynamic
…に精を出す work on
背負う shoulder
世界 world
世界化 globalization
世界知的所有権機関 WIPO
世界的規模の global
席 seat
せきたてる spur
石炭ガス化複合発電 IGCC
石炭消費量 coal burning
せき止める stem
責任 duty
責任 responsibility
責任がある accountable
責任がある responsible
責任者 head

責任能力がある	accountable
…の責任を負う	foot
石油	oil
石油	petroleum
石油汚染	oiling
石油価格	oil price
石油化学	petrochemistry
石油化学製品	petrochemical
石油企業家	oilman
石油業者	oilman
石油採掘部門	upstream
石油ダラー	petrodollars
石油輸出国機構	OPEC
セキュリタイゼーション	securitization
赤裸々な	bare
セクト主義	sectionalism
世間	society
世間	world
世間に知れ渡ること	publicity
世間の注目	publicity
世間の注目を集める	high-profile
世間の人々	society
世襲の	patrimonial
是正	correction
是正する	correct
是正する	rectify
是正する	redress
世俗主義	secularism
世帯	household
世代	generation
世代間の資産移転	intergenerational transfer of assets
積極的な	aggressive
積極的な	forward-looking
積極的な	offensive
接近戦	infighting
設計	design
設計者	planner
設計する	design
設計する	draft
節減	retrenchment
節減する	cut
節減する	retrench
接種	inoculation
摂取	intake
接触	liaison
接触	touch
接触する	touch
接戦で	neck-and-neck
接戦の	head-to-head
接続する	access
接待	entertainment
絶対安全性	fail safe
絶対確かな	surefire
絶体絶命の	last-ditch
絶対的な	hard-core
絶対の	absolute
絶調	peak
説得	persuasion
説得力	persuasion
説得力のある	potent
設備	capacity
設備	equipment
設備過剰	overcapacity
設備投資	capex
設備投資	capital investment
設備投資	capital spending
説明	version
説明会	briefing
説明責任	accountability
絶滅危惧種	endangered species
絶滅の恐れのある動植物の国際取引に関する条約	CITIES
節約	retrenchment
節約	thrift
節約する	retrench
節約する	spare
設立	foundation
設立者	founder
設立する	form
設立する	incorporate
瀬戸際	jaws
瀬戸際外交	brinkmanship
瀬戸際政策	brinkmanship
…の瀬戸際に瀕する	teeter on the brisk of
是認	approval
是認	endorsement
ゼノカレンシー	xenocurrency
狭める	narrow
狭い	small
責める	condemn
セラチア菌	Serratia bacteria
競り	bidding
競り手	bidder
ゼロ	zero
ゼロックスで複写する	xerox
世論	public opinion
世論調査機関	pollster
世話人	caretaker
栓	plug
全頭検査	blanket testing
繊維	fiber
善意	goodwill
全域	gamut
戦域高高度空域防衛	THAAD
全員一致して	unanimously
全員参加方式の	participatory
全員の	universal
前衛	vanguard
全会一致で	unanimously
全額引出し	full withdrawal
全期間	span
全機種	full line
選挙	election
占拠	lock-in
選挙運動	electioneering
選挙区	precinct
選挙権	suffrage
選挙する	elect
選挙戦	campaigning
選挙人	elector
選挙人	voter
選挙の	elective
選挙の	electoral
先駆	forerunner
先駆者	pioneer
前月比	month-on-month
宣言	declaration
宣言	manifesto
宣言書	manifesto
宣言する	allege
宣言する	declare
先見的な	visionary
選好	appetite
…先行型	–led
専攻科目	major
先行条件	prerequisite
先行の	anticipatory
宣告	sentence
全国規模の	nationwide
宣告する	condemn
宣告する	sentence
全国的な	national
全国的な	nationwide
全国店頭銘柄気配自動通報システム	NASDAQ
全国に拡大する	nationalize
全国の	nationwide
潜在意識抑圧力	censorship
潜在需要	pent-up demand
潜在的な	latent
潜在的な	potential
潜在的な	shadow
潜在的に	potentially
戦士	militant
漸次解消	phase-out
漸次的移行	gradation
戦時動員	wartime mobilization
全自動の	point-and-shoot
選手	player
全州の	statewide
選手権	championship
選手権保持者	champion
選出	selection
選出された	–elect
選出する	elect
戦勝	victory
戦場	battlefield
全勝	sweep
前哨戦	runup

専心	dedication
先陣	vanguard
前身	forerunner
漸進主義	incrementalism
前進する	advance
先陣を務める	spearhead
潜水	dive
宣誓	oath
専制君主	czar
宣誓証言	deposition
宣誓証言する	testify
宣誓証書	deposition
宣誓する	swear
専制政治	autocracy
専制的な	dictatorial
先制の	preemptive
先制反論	prebuttal
船籍変更	reflagging
前線	front
戦争	war
前奏曲	prelude
戦争挑発者	warmonger
漸増の	graduated
戦争屋	warmonger
喘息	asthma
専属の	captive
先祖伝来の	patrimonial
全体	pie
全体主義者	totalitarian
全体主義の	totalitarian
全体的効果	tout ensemble
全体の	total
全体の	universal
選択	option
選択	selection
選択肢	alternative
選択する	select
選択の	elective
選択の	option
先端	edge
先端	end
先端技術	high-tech
先端的な	emerging
全地球測位システム	GPS
千兆	quadrillion
全長	footage
前兆	herald
前兆	threat
前提条件	precondition
前提条件	prerequisite
選定する	anoint
宣伝	commercial
宣伝担当者	PRO
宣伝による説得	brainwashing
宣伝用撮影会	photocall
戦闘	battle
先頭	forefront
先頭	lead
尖塔	pinnacle
扇動	provocation
戦闘機	warplane
戦闘区域	battlefield
先導者	bellwether
扇動者	firebrand
先導する	lead
戦闘中止	ceasefire
戦闘中の行方不明兵	missing in action
先頭に立つ	spearhead
先頭の	leadoff
先導役	trendsetter
前途有望な	promising
前途有望な	up-and-coming
前途有望な人	hopeful
前途有望な人	up-and-comer
先入観	bias
選任	selection
先任者	predecessor
前任者	predecessor
先任順	seniority
選任する	appoint
専念	concentration
専念	dedication
…に専念する	committed to
前年同期比	same period last year
前年同期比	year-on-year
前年同期比	year-over-year
前年同期比で	compared to a year earlier
前年比	from a year ago
前年比	year-on-year
前年比	year-over-year
洗脳	brainwashing
専売	monopolization
船舶代理店	shipping agent
全範囲	gamut
全般的な	overall
全般的に	across the board
全費用込みの	all-in
全品種	full line
潜伏期間	incubation period
潜伏性の	latent
全部の	total
選別	screening
選別する	screen
千変万化	kaleidoscope
先鋒	vanguard
全方位外交	omnidirectional diplomacy
前方の	front
全面回復	full recovery
全面禁止	blanket ban
全面的	across-the-board
全面的な	comprehensive
全面的な	full-blown
全面的な	full-scale
全面的に	across the board
全面撤退	full withdrawal
専門委員会	task force
専門家	expert
専門家	professional
専門家	pundit
専門外取扱品	sideline
専門技術	expertise
専門技術	knowhow
専門事項	technicality
専門職法人	P.C.
専門知識	expertise
専門的意見	consultancy
専門的職業	profession
専門店	specialty store
専門用語	term
前夜の	overnight
占有	occupancy
占有	possession
占有する	occupy
戦略	strategy
戦略上の	strategic
戦略的	strategic
戦略兵器削減交渉	START
戦略兵器削減条約	START
戦略防衛構想	SDI
全領域	gamut
占領する	occupy
占領の	occupational
全力を傾ける	concentrate
先例	footstep
先例	precedent
先例に従う	follow suit
前例に倣う	follow suit
前例のない	unprecedented
線路	track

そ

訴因	count
層	bracket
沿う	live up to
層	tier
総意	consensus
相違	disparity
躁うつ病	manic depression
総売上高	turnover
増加	appreciation
増加	buildup
増加	enhancement
増加	gain
増加	growth
増加	increase
増加	proliferation
増加	rise

総会 meeting	操作 handling	送達する remit
総額 gross	操作 manipulation	相談 conference
総額 pie	走査 scanning	相談 consultancy
総額 sum	相殺 offset	相談 consultation
総額 total	相殺額 offset	装置 appliance
増加させる boost	相殺関税 countervailing tariff	装置 device
増加させる push up	相殺する average	装置 equipment
増加させる rev up	相殺する offset	想定 anticipation
増加する climb	走査機 scanner	送電網 grid
増加する grow	捜索 manhunt	送電線網 grid
増加する increase	捜索 search	騒動 confusion
増加する rise	捜索する search	騒動 riot
増加する rising	操作上の operational	騒動 uproar
総括的な omnibus	操作する operate	相当額 equivalent
送還 extradition	捜査当局 investigators	掃討作戦 mop-up operations
臓器 organ	操作能力 literacy	相当する corresponding
早期の early	早産の premature	…に相当する equivalent to
増強 beef-up	増資 capital increase	相当な大きさの sizable
増強 boost	創始者 pioneer	相場 market
増強 reinforcement	創始する initiate	相場 quotation
創業家 founding family	掃除する sweep	相場師 speculator
創業者 founder	操縦 handling	相場速報機 ticker
増強する beef up	操縦 maneuver	相場の下落 retreat
増強する intensify	操縦 steering	装備 gear
増強する reinforce	操縦する steer	総飛行マイル数 mileage
増強する strengthen	贈収賄 bribery	増幅させる aggravate
送金 money flow	贈収賄 corruption	双方向の interactive
送金 remittance	創出する invent	双方向の two-way
送金額 remittance	送受話器 handset	双方の bilateral
総計 sum	相乗効果 synergy	相補的な complementary
総計 total	増殖 proliferation	総マイル数 mileage
早計の premature	増殖する proliferate	双務主義 bilateralism
総計の total	送信 transmission	双務的な bilateral
増減する wax and wane	増進 enhancement	贈与 donation
増減の幅 plus or minus	送信する transmit	贈与された donated
相互依存 interdependence	増進する further	騒乱 disturbance
相互依存的な tit-for-tat	増水させる flood	騒乱 riot
草稿 draft	創設する form	騒乱 uproar
総合株価指数 broader stock indicators	創造する create	総理大臣 premier
	想像する envisage	総理大臣 prime minister
走行距離 mileage	創造的集団思考法 brainstorming	総量 total
総合研究所 think tank	相続 inheritance	贈賄 payola
総合司会者 anchor	相続 succession	ソーシャル・ネットワーキング・サービス social networking service
総合診療方式 super-rotation system	操舵 steering	
	増大 enhancement	疎開者 evacuee
総合スーパー GMS	増大 increase	阻害する impede
総合的 general	増大 rise	阻害要因 bottleneck
総合的 integrate	増大 swelling	遡及的な ex post fact
総合的な comprehensive	増大させる exacerbate	即座の outright
総合的な overall	増大した bloated	即座の prompt
相互経済協力促進政策 trilateralism	増大する augment	即座の snap
相互作用 interactive	増大する balloon	即座の spot
相互的な two-way	増大する grow	即時 real time
相互の bilateral	増大する growing	即時の prompt
相互の mutual	増大する rising	即時の real-time
相互補完性 complementarity	壮大な墓 mausoleum	即時払い prompt
相互利用する share	送達 delivery	促進 activation

促進	encouragement
促進計画	incentive program
促進された	accelerated
促進する	accelerate
促進する	activate
促進する	bolster
促進する	encourage
促進する	expedite
促進する	facilitate
促進する	further
促進する	step up
属性法	temporal method
測定された	measured
測定する	gauge
測定する	measure
速度	pace
束縛	constraint
束縛のない	no-holds-barred
側面	side
底	bottom
底入れ	bottoming out
底入れする	bottom out
底打ち	bottoming out
底堅い	solid
損なう	hurt
損なう	impair
損なう	undermine
底値	low
底割れ	freefall
底を打つ	bottom out
底をつく	bottom out
阻止	interception
組織	constitution
組織	makeup
組織	organization
組織	setup
組織	structure
組織	system
組織化	systematization
組織化する	organize
組織化する	systematize
組織者	organizer
組織する	form
組織する	structure
組織体	entity
組織的な	organizational
組織的な	systematic
組織の	institutional
組織の	systemic
組織犯罪	organized crime
阻止する	deterrent
…を阻止する	forestall
阻止する	nip
阻止する	thwart
訴訟	lawsuit
訴訟	legal action
訴訟	litigation

訴訟	suit
組成	formation
蘇生	resuscitation
租税	tax
租税回避地	tax haven
租税回避地	tax shelter
粗製ガソリン	naphtha
蘇生させる	resuscitate
租税条約	tax treaty
租税体系	tax system
組成変更ガソリン	reformulated gasoline
礎石	cornerstone
塑造	molding
注ぐ	pour
育てる	nurture
措置	measure
措置	step
訴追	impeachment
訴追	prosecution
卒業生	graduate
側近	aide
素っ気なく拒絶する	brush off
続行	resumption
即効性のある	quick-fix
即効の	quick
即効の	quick-fix
率直な	outspoken
率直な	upfront
…に沿って	in line with
そつのない	button-down
袖の下	payola
備え	preparedness
備える	brace
その裏を返せば	put another way
その後の	subsequent
ソフトウエア	software
粗末な	meager
ソユーズ	Soyuz
ソルベンシー	solvency
それに続く	subsequent
損益	profit and loss
損害	damage
損害賠償	damage
損害保険	nonlife insurance policy
損害保険会社	nonlife insurance company
損害保険会社	nonlife insurer
損害保険証券	nonlife insurance policy
損害を与える	hurt
存在	presence
存在感	presence
ぞんざいな	slipshod
存在理由	raison d'etre
損失	deficit
損失	hemorrhage

損失	loss
損失を計上する	suffer
損失を被る	lose
損失を出す	hemorrhage
存続	survival
存続する	survive

た

ターミナル段階高度地域防衛システム	THAAD
隊	squad
…台	mark
題	theme
代案	alternative
第一位	primacy
第一次の	primary
第一の	first
第一の	overriding
第一の	principal
第一面	front
第一線	forefront
第一線	front line
退役航空母艦	decommissioned aircraft carrier
ダイエット食品	diet aid
対応	measure
対応	response
対応策	countermeasure
対応策	remedy
対応策	response
…に対応する	cope with
…に対応する	corresponding
…に対応する	respond to
…対応の	compatible
体温	temperature
対価	compensation
対価	consideration
大会	convention
体外受精	in vitro fertilization
対外直接投資	FDI
対外的な	external
大学	school
大学院生	graduate
大学進学適性試験	SAT
大学の	academic
大革命	revolution
代価を請求する	bill
大気	air
大企業	giant
大企業向け	wholesale
大規模環境破壊	ecodoom
大規模機械化	megatechnics
大規模な	heavy
大規模の	huge
耐久財	durable goods
大恐慌	Great Depression

大金 bundle	対象 matter	退任する retire
代金 proceeds	対象 object	退任する step down
代金を請求する bill	対象 objective	耐熱材 heat-resistant material
退屈な ho-hum	大勝 sweep	大破壊 havoc
体系化する organize	対象 target	代表 ambassador
体系化する systematize	退場 exit	代表 envoy
体系的 systematic	大小 magnitude	代表者 representative
対決 matchup	代償 quid pro quo	代表団 contingent
対決 showdown	代償 remuneration	代表団 delegation
…と対決する take on	対象者 case	大不況 Great Recession
体験する undergo	大勝する sweep	太平洋 Pacific
代行 surrogate	代償の compensatory	大変革 revolution
代行者 representative	退職 retirement	大変革 shake-up
対抗手段 countermeasure	退職後給付 postretirement benefit	大変動 upheaval
対抗処置 countermeasure	退職する resign	逮捕 arrest
対抗する counter	退職する retire	逮捕 roundup
対抗馬 contender	…に対処する cope with	逮捕されていない at large
対抗文化 counterculture	大臣 minister	逮捕する arrest
大国 giant	耐震技術 quake-resistant technology	逮捕する round up
太鼓をたたく drum	対審制度 adversary system	台本 scenario
大混乱 havoc	耐震設計 earthquake-proof design	大麻 cannabis
体細胞クローン技術 somatic cell nuclear transfer	大臣の ministerial	怠慢 negligence
対策 countermeasure	…に対する vis-a-vis	対ミサイルの antimissile
対策 cushion	大成功 blockbuster	代役 double
対策 measure	大成功 coup	太陽から生じる solar
対策 package	耐性試験 stress test	太陽光発電 photovoltaic power generation
対策 policy	体制擁護者 loyalist	太陽光発電 solar power
対策 remedy	大接戦 photo finish	太陽光発電 solar power generation
対策 step	大宣伝 blitz	太陽電池 solar cell
大惨事 debacle	大損害 havoc	太陽に関する solar
第三次産業 tertiary industry	代替策 alternative	太陽熱発電 solar power
第三者 outsider	代替 fallback	大洋の oceanic
第三者 third party	代替品 fallback	太陽の solar
第三の third	大打撃を与える hammer	代理 proxy
大使 ambassador	大多数 majority	代理 surrogate
大事件 staggerer	大多数 supermajority	大陸棚 continental shelf
体質 culture	大胆な drastic	代理出産契約 birth contract
大失態 fiasco	大腸菌 E. coli	対立 clash
大失敗 catastrophe	大敵 archfoe	対立 opposition
大失敗 debacle	大敵 archrival	対立 polarization
大失敗 fiasco	態度 attitude	対立する clash
貸借 lending	態度 stance	代理店 distributor
貸借対照表 balance sheet	態度 stand	代理人 agent
大衆 grass roots	台頭する emerge	代理人 attorney
大衆 public	大統領官邸 Executive Office	代理人 proxy
体重 weight	大統領教書 Presidential message	代理人 representative
大衆受けのする popularist	大統領顧問団 cabinet	代理人 surrogate
大衆化 popularization	大統領在任期間 presidency	大流行 pandemic
大衆迎合主義 populism	大統領執務室 Oval Office	大量 slew
大衆迎合的な populist	大統領の presidential	大量 spate
大衆的な pop	大統領の職 presidency	大量生産 rollout
大衆の mass	大統領補佐官 Oval Officer	大量生産する mass-produce
大衆の関心を求める popularist	対内直接投資 FDI	大量の ample
退出 exit	台なしにする scuttle	大量の heavy
退出する exit	退任 resignation	大量の mass
対処 emulation	退任する outgoing	大量破壊兵器 WMD

体力 power	多国籍の multinational	立て直す reconstruct
体力をつける sustaining	他国の foreign	立て直す revamp
対話 dialogue	確かな sound	…建ての –denominated
対話型 interactive	…を出し抜く one-up	立てる draw up
ダウ工業株平均 Dow	出し物 fare	立てる set up
ダウ平均 Dow	多重債務者 heavily indebted people	多動性障害 hyperactivity disorder
ダウンロードする download	多重衝突 pileup	…を棚上げする put ... on hold
絶えずつきまとう haunt	打診 feeler	棚上げする shelve
耐える withstand	打診 overture	棚上げにした backburner
倒す overthrow	出す put up	棚上げにする mothball
倒す topple	多数 majority	棚卸し inventory
高い運用益 high return	多数 slew	種 species
高い収益率 high return	多数 spate	楽しい upbeat
多角化 diversification	助け合い interdependence	頼みの綱 resort
多角化 multilateralization	尋ねる question	頼みもしない unsolicited
多角化する diversify	堕胎 abortion	束 bundle
多角経営 pentagon management	戦い battle	束ねる bundle
多角主義 multilateralism	戦い fight	旅 trip
多額の massive	戦い race	だぶつかせる saturate
高値 high	戦い struggle	ダボス会議 Davos Conference
高める buoy	戦う battle	だまし取る defraud
高める enhance	…と戦う combat	だまし取る swindle
高める heighten	戦う fight	だます swindle
高める push up	たたきのめす batter	だめになる go sour
高める upgrade	たたく drum	ためらう shilly-shally
兌換できる convertible	正しい right-on	ためる amass
抱き合わせ販売 bundle	正しくない incorrect	多目的の multipurpose
妥協 compromise	正す redress	保つ maintain
多極化 multipolarity	立ち上げる launch	多様化 diversification
多極の multipolar	立入り検査 on-the-spot inspection	多様化する diversify
多極分散 decentralization	立入を禁じる seal off	多用途の multipurpose
卓越 excellence	立ち退かせる force out	便り news
卓越した par excellence	立場 camp	…に頼る rely on
卓越した prevailing	立場 stance	…に頼る resort to
卓上型 desktop	立場 stand	頼ること resort
卓上の desktop	立場 standing	堕落した corrupt
宅配サービス home delivery service	立ちはだかる loom	だらしない slipshod
巧みな誘導 maneuver	…に立ち向かう face	足りない short of
巧みに処理する engineer	立ち向かう fight	タリバン Taliban
巧みにそらす dodge	…に立ち向かう tackle	多量 barrel
企み machination	多中心構造 polycentrism	多量 slew
蓄え pool	…から脱却する wean self off	多量 spate
蓄えておく set aside	脱臼 dislocation	多量の mass
蓄える amass	タックス tax	団 team
蓄える pool	脱工業化 postindustrialism	段 tier
蓄える set aside	脱出 get-out	弾圧 crackdown
蓄える store	…に達する hit	弾圧 repression
打撃 blow	達する peak	弾圧する clamp down on
打撃 impact	達成 fruition	…を弾圧する crack down on
…に打撃を与える deal a blow to	脱線 divergence	弾圧的な repressive
打撃を与える hit	脱走者 runaway	単位 unit
…だけれども albeit	脱退 withdrawal	単一市場 single market
多元同時記録計 polygraph	脱同調化 decoupling	単一の事業 monoline
多項選択式の closed-end	手綱 rein	段階 grade
多項目の omnibus	脱落 fallout	段階 notch
多国間主義 multilateralism	盾 shield	段階 phase
多国間の multilateral	建て値 quotation	段階 stage

段階 tier	弾頭 warhead	力強い strong
弾劾 impeachment	…を担当する work	痴漢行為 molestation
弾劾する blast	弾道ミサイル ballistic missile	地球温暖化 global warming
段階的移行 gradation	単独過半数 simple majority	地球市民 planethood
段階的解消 phase-out	単独主義 unilateralism	地球社会 planethood
段階的縮小 phase-down	たんぱく質工学 protein engineering	地球的規模にする globalize
段階的撤廃 phase-out	ダンピング防止 antidumping	地区 section
段階的導入 phase-in	担保 collateral	畜産業界 livestock industry
段階的な graduated	担保 mortgage	蓄積 accumulation
段階的な phased	担保権実行 foreclosure	蓄積する accumulate
段階的に実行する phase	担保付きの secured	蓄積する store
団塊の世代 baby boomers	端末 end to end	地区連銀景況報告 Beige Book
嘆願 petition	端末機 handset	治験 clinical test
嘆願 plea	端末同士 end to end	遅行指標 lagging indicator
短期貸付け資金 short loan	端末利用者 end user	遅行する lag
短期間の short-term	短命の short-lived	知識 information
短期金融市場 money market	弾力性 flexibility	知識 knowledge
短期市場 call market	鍛練 discipline	知識 savvy
短期の short		血色素 pigment
短期の short-dated		地上に配備された ground-based
短期の short-term	**ち**	地政学的リスク geopolitical risks
探求 quest	地位 rank	遅滞 arrears
探求 search	地位 reputation	遅滞 delay
短期融資 short loan	地位 slot	父親であること paternity
探求する search	地位 standing	縮める narrow
団結した united	地位 status	窒素酸化物 nitrogen oxides
探検 exploration	地域 community	知的エリート meritocrat
断言 assertion	地域協定 regionwide agreement	知的資産 intellectual asset
断言する allege	地域全体の regional	知的所有権 intellectual property
断言する bet	地域特化 localization	知的な mental
単語 word	地域の regional	地点 place
断交 rupture	地域別輸送価格 zone delivered pricing	地点 point
談合 bid-rigging		地点 spot
談合行為 bid-fixing	小さい small	知能 brainpower
断固たる decisive	地位の高い high-ranking	知能 intelligence
探査 exploration	…とチームを組む team up with	知能 smarts
探査機 orbiter	地位を占める rank	地方 local government
探索 quest	チェーン店 chain	地方 province
探査車 rover	知恵を絞る rack one's brains	地方開発援助金 pork barrel
短時間 moment	遅延 delay	地方行政 local government
短時間の short	地価 land price	地方検事 prosecuting attorney
短縮 curtailment	誓い oath	地方自治体 municipality
短縮した contractionary	誓い pledge	地方自治の municipal
短縮する curtail	治外法権区域 extraterritorial area	地方支部会 caucus
単純化する simplify	誓う pledge	地方政府 local government
短所 weakness	誓う swear	地方政府 provincial government
断絶 divide	誓う vow	地方分権 decentralization
断絶 rupture	近くの adjacent	着実な solid
炭素 carbon	近く発表される upcoming	着手 launch
断層 dislocation	近く予定されている upcoming	着手する launch
断続的に on and off	近頃の recent	着床させる implant
団体 association	力 force	着床前の preimplantation
団体 bloc	力 muscle	着信音 ringtone
団体 community	力 power	着席 sitting
団体 corporation	力 strength	着服事件 embezzlement scandal
団体 collective	力関係 politic	着目する eye
タンデム tandem	力強い powerful	チャット chat

チャットする chat	中傷 assassination	超大型小売店 megastore
チャットルーム chatroom	中傷 defamation	超過 excess
注意 attention	中小企業 small and midsize	懲戒 disciplinary action
注意 care	中傷する slanderous	懲戒する reprimand
注意 warning	抽象的思考 ideology	超過勤務 overtime
注意する remind	中傷の poison-pen	超過半数 supermajority
注意する warn	中小の weak	長期 long range
中位の median	中傷目的の poison-pen	長期金融市場 capital market
注意深い cautious	中心 center	長期金利 long-term interest rate
注意深い wary	中心 core	長期契約 long-term contract
中央銀行 central bank	中心 focal point	長期国債 long-term government bonds
中央市場 emporium	中心 focus	
中央の median	中心 hub	長期債務 long-term debt
中央舞台 arena	中進工業国 NICs	長期的な secular
仲介 brokerage	中心に置く center	長期的な sustained
仲介業者 agent	…中心の –driven	長期の long
仲介者 intermediary	…中心の –led	長期の long-run
仲介者 middleman	中心部 heartland	長期の prolonged
中核 cadre	中心部分 pillar	長距離 long range
中核 centerpiece	虫垂炎 appendicitis	長距離電話 trunk call
中核 hub	中枢 center	帳消し write-off
中核的自己資本比率 tier-one capital ratio	忠誠心 loyalty	帳消しにする offset
	中性の neutral	帳消しにする write off
中核の hard-core	中絶禁止法支持者 right-to-lifer	兆候 barometer
中間 half	中絶擁護派の pro-choice	兆候 sign
中間 half year	中絶胎児 aborted fetus	兆候 streak
中間 midterm	中絶反対者 pro-lifer	徴候 symptom
中間管理職 middle manager	鋳造 molding	超高速の high-end
中間選挙 midterm election	中断 abandonment	超国家的な supranational
中間選挙 off-year election	中断 cut	調査 examination
中間の interim	中断 disruption	調査 investigation
中間の median	中断する abandon	調査 research
中期 midterm	中東危機 Middle East crisis	調査 scrutiny
中規模の midsize	中道主義 centrism	調査 search
中堅幹部 middle manager	中道派 centrist	調査 survey
中国人民銀行 People's Bank of China	中毒 poisoning	調査する examine
	中途の mid-career	調査する investigate
中国政府 Beijing	中途半端な half-baked	調査する monitor
中国本土 Mainland China	注入 injection	調査する probe
中古の secondhand	注入する inject	調査する track
中古の used	注入する pour	調子 kilter
仲裁 interference	注入する pump	調子 tone
仲裁 mediation	注目 attention	長時間に及ぶ会談 marathon talks
仲裁 peacemaking	注目する eye	聴衆 audience
仲裁する intervene	注目する watch	徴収 levy
仲裁する mediate	注目の的 focal point	徴収する levy
仲裁人 intermediary	注文 order	長所 merit
仲裁人 peacemaker	注文仕立ての custom-made	頂上 peak
中止 abandonment	注文生産 make-to-order	頂上 top
中止 cutoff	注文生産した customized	調整 adjustment
中軸 hub	注文生産する customize	調整 coordination
中止した suspended	中立の neutral	調整 mediation
中止する abandon	中立の nonaligned	調整 shakedown
中止する suspend	腸 gut	調整 translation
忠実さ loyalty	調印者 signatory	徴税 levy
忠実になぞる clone	調印する sign	徴税 taxation
抽出 sampling	超大型合併 megamerger	調整期間 shakedown

調整する adjust	著作権侵害 piracy	追跡 follow-up
調整する coordinate	著作権侵害者 pirate	追跡可能な traceable
調整する discount	著作権を取得する copyright	追徴課税 back tax
調整する gear	貯蔵施設 depot	ツイッター twitter
調整する iron out	貯蔵所 depot	追認する ratify
調整する orchestrate	貯蔵する store	追放する oust
調節する adjust	貯蔵品 supplies	追放する topple
挑戦 challenge	貯蓄 savings	通貨 currency
朝鮮人参 ginseng root	貯蓄貸付け組合 S & L	通貨 money
朝鮮半島エネルギー開発機構 KEDO	貯蓄金融機関 thrift	通過 passage
調達 funding	貯蓄金融機関監督局 OTS	通貨供給量 M
調達 procurement	直近の月 front month	通貨供給量 money supply
調達手段 funding	直結 online	通貨再膨張 reflation
調達する obtain	著名人 personage	通貨再膨張の reflationary
調達する procure	著名人がずらりと並ぶ star-studded	通貨収縮 deflation
調達する raise	著名な known	通貨収縮の deflationary
調停 accommodation	治療 therapy	通貨主義 monetarism
調停 mediation	治療する doctor	通貨政策 monetary policy
調停 peacemaking	治療不能の宣告 condemnation	通貨単位の呼称変更 redenomina-
超低金利 ultralow interest rates	治療法 therapy	tion
超低金利政策 ultra-easy money	知力 brain	通貨の monetary
policy	知力 brainpower	通貨膨張 inflation
調停者 peacemaker	知力 smarts	通期 entire fiscal year
調停する accommodate	鎮圧 pacification	通期 full business year
調停する interfere	鎮圧する stamp out	通期の annual
調停する mediate	沈下する sink	通期の full-year
頂点 pinnacle	沈下する subside	通勤者 commuter
超党派 nonpartisan	賃金 pay	通行 passage
超党派外交 suprapartisan diplo-	賃金 wage	通行 traffic
macy	賃金体系 pay system	通行権 passage
超党派立法 bipartisan law	賃借料 hire	通行料金 toll
挑発 provocation	陳情運動 lobbying	通告 notice
挑発的な provocative	陳情者 lobbyist	通査 scanning
懲罰的な punitive	陳情する lobby	通商 commerce
超微細加工技術 nanotechnology	沈滞 doldrums	通商 trade
重複上場する dual-list	沈滞 slack	通商一括交渉権 TPA
帳簿 book	沈滞 stagnancy	通商禁止 embargo
超法規措置 extralegal measure	沈滞 stagnation	通商の commercial
帳簿外の off-the-book	沈滞した stagnant	通常の conventional
徴募する draft	賃貸借 lease	通常の ordinary
超マンモス・タンカー oilberg	鎮定 pacification	通信 communication
調味 seasoning	沈黙した silent	通信 telecom
調味料 seasoning	陳列する expose	通信 telecommunication
聴聞会 hearing		通信員 correspondent
調理済み食品販売店 delicatessen	つ	通信員 mediaman
潮流 tide		通信業者 carrier
調和 unison	追加 add-on	通信記録 log
…と調和して in line with	追加する add	通信事業 telecom
直後 aftermath	追加性 additionality	通信の秘密 communications
…を直視する face	追加的措置 follow-up	privacy
直接投資 direct investment	追加的な additional	通信販売 mail order
直接募集 private offering	追加の supplementary	通信文 message
勅撰弁護士 Queen's Counsel	追加料金 surcharge	通俗的な pop
…に直面して in the face of	追求 quest	通達 instruction
…に直面する face	追求する search	通知 notice
直立した straight	追求する seek	通知 notification
著作権 copyright	追随する follow suit	通販 mail order

通報	
通報	notification
通報者	informer
痛烈な	blistering
通路	corridor
使い勝手がよい	user-friendly
使いこなす	wield
使い捨ての	throwaway
使い捨て偏重の	throwaway
使い古しの	used
使いやすい	user-friendly
使う	wield
捕まえる	round up
捕まっていない	at large
月	moon
突合せ	footing
月ステーション	moonstation
月探測船	moonship
突き止める	track
月並みな	cookie-cutter
月の	lunar
次の	following
次の	incoming
次の	post-
次の	subsequent
月飛行	moonflight
月への打上げ	moonshot
継ぎ目	seam
継ぎ目のない	seamless
月旅行宇宙船	mooncraft
月ロケット	moonik
月ロケット	moonshot
作り上げる	carve out
作り上げる	make up
作り出す	create
作り出す	forge
作り出す	turn out
作り直し	reinvention
作る	craft
付ける	cover
告げる	herald
伝える	report
槌	hammer
…に続いて	in the wake of
…に続いて	on the heels of
続いて	successively
突っ込んだ議論	in-depth discussions
慎む	abstain (from)
慎む	refrain from
包む	bundle
勤め	employment
務める	serve
…を務める	serve as
つながり	link
つながり	tie
つなぎ目	seam
つなぐ	bridge
つなぐ	link
つなぐ	tie
綱引き	tug of war
津波	tsunami
綱渡り	tightrope
募る	recruit
募る	solicit
つまずき	misstep
つまずく	trip up
つまらない	ho-hum
罪	crime
罪	offense
罪	wrongdoing
積立て	accumulation
積立金	fund
積み立てる	set aside
罪の	criminal
罪の意識がある	guilty
積み増す	hike
詰め込み教育	cram education
詰め物	plug
強い	powerful
強い	strong
強い	sweeping
強い酒	short
強いはね返り	backlash
強い反発	backlash
強い批判	blast
強気市場	bull market
強気筋	bull
強気筋の	bull
強気の	bullish
強気の	long
…と強く言う	stress
強くする	toughen
強く迫る	urge
強く批判する	blast
強く要望する	urge
強さ	strength
強み	advantage
強み	strength
強める	heighten
強める	intensify
強める	strengthen
つらい	tough
辛い体験	ordeal
…の釣合いをとる	balance
連れてくる	bring

て

手	hand
出会い系サイト	dating Web site
手当たり次第の	random
手厚い	red-carpet
手当	pay
提案	motion
提案	prescription
提案	proposal
提案	proposition
提案する	come up with
提案する	float
提案する	propose
ディーゼル排気微粒子	DEPs
ディーラー	trader
帝王切開	Cesarean section
低下	deceleration
低下	depreciation
低下	deterioration
低下	dip
低下	drop
低下	drop-off
低下	erosion
低下	fall
低下	retreat
低下	slide
低価格品	cheaper product
低下させる	decrease
低下させる	erode
低下させる	reduce
低下させる	weaken
低下する	decline
低下する	depreciate
低下する	dip
低下する	fall
低下する	falling
低下する	falter
低下する	moderate
低下する	plunge
低下する	recede
低下する	retreat
低下する	sag
低下する	shrink
低下する	slide
低下する	slip
低下する	worsen
提議	proposition
定期往復交通機関	shuttle
定期刊行物	journal
定期刊行物	press
定期航空便	flight
提起する	submit
定義する	define
提供	donation
提供	provision
提供者	donor
提供者	provider
提供する	offer
提供する	provide
提供する	supply
提携	alliance
提携	cooperation
提携	tie-up
…と提携して	in tandem with

提携している	affiliated	停滞した	stagnant	敵対的買収	unfriendly takeover
提携する	affiliate	停滞している	lackluster	出来高	volume
…と提携する	team up with	停滞する	flounder	適度な	moderate
提携する	tie up	停滞する	languish	…できない	fail to
低減	layoff	丁重な	red-carpet	摘発	exposure
低原価	low cost	蹄鉄	shoe	…の摘発を強化する	crack down on
低減する	lay off	停電	blackout	摘要	summary
低減する	lower	程度	extent	適用される	applicable
抵抗	opposition	程度	level	適用する	apply
抵抗	resistance	程度	notch	適用範囲	coverage
抵抗する	withstand	抵当	mortgage	テコ	leverage
低コスト	low cost	抵当のない	unsecured	てこ入れ	prop-up
デイサービス	day service	低燃費の	fuel-efficient	てこ入れする	stimulate
偵察衛星	spy satellite	低費用	low cost	手頃な	moderate
偵察隊	patrol	低迷	doldrums	出先機関	outreach
停止	ban	低迷	downturn	デジタルの	digital
停止	disruption	低迷	sluggishness	手順	procedure
停止	logjam	低迷させる	depress	手錠をかける	handcuff
停止	standstill	低迷した	depressed	手数料	charge
停止	suspense	低迷した	dull	手数料	commission
停止	suspension	低迷した	poor	手数料	fee
提示	submission	低迷した	sluggish	テスト発射	test-firing
提示案	submission	低迷した	slumping	テスト発射する	test-fire
停止した	suspended	低迷している	slowing	鉄	iron
停止する	ban	定率	fixed rate	撤回	climb-down
停止する	suspend	定量超過	overdoses	撤回	recall
提示する	float	手入れをする	doctor	でっかい	whopping
提示する	present	データ中継技術衛星	DRTS	撤回させる	scuttle
提示する	set out	データ保護	protect	撤回する	recall
提示する	submit	データを検索する	access	撤回する	recede
定住者	resident	データを送信する	upload	撤回する	rescind
提出	submission	テープカット	ribbonsnipping	撤回する	scrap
…を提出する	come up with	テープに録音する	tape	鉄鋼	steel
提出する	file	テープ録音	tape	撤収	pullback
提出する	file for	テーマ	topic	鉄製器具	iron
提出する	lodge	デオキシリボ核酸	DNA	撤退	exit
提出する	submit	出遅れる	lag	撤退	pullback
提出命令を行う	subpoena	手落ち	oversight	撤退	withdrawal
提唱する	propose	手斧	hatchet	…から撤退する	exit
低所得者向け住宅融資	subprime mortgage	…を手がける	work on	…から撤退する	pull out of
		出稼ぎ労働者	migration worker	でっちあげる	make up
低水準の	benign	手形	bill	手続き	formality
低水準の	low	手形	note	手続き上の問題	technicality
定数	quorum	デカップリング	decoupling	徹底的な	outright
ディスク	disc	出来	showing	徹底的な調査	probe
訂正	correction	敵意	animosity	徹底的に捜索する	comb
訂正する	correct	適応させる	tailor	撤廃	elimination
訂正する	rectify	的確に指摘する	pinpoint	撤廃	jettison
停戦	ceasefire	適格の	eligible	撤廃する	abolish
停戦	truce	適合	fitness	撤廃する	eliminate
停戦監視者	peacekeeper	適合させる	gear	撤廃する	jettison
定足数	quorum	適合させる	tailor	撤廃する	scrap
停滞	logjam	適合性	compatibility	手詰まり状態	stalemate
停滞	paralysis	適切でない	incorrect	手で激しくたたく	wallop
停滞	sluggishness	適切な	due	手で持てる	handheld
停滞	stagnancy	敵対者	opponent	手取り給与	disposable income
停滞	stagnation	敵対的な	hostile	手取り賃金	take-home pay

出直し reinvention	伝言 message	電力会社 genco
手に入れる jockey	電子… cyber-	電力の electric
手に入れる secure	電子化する go electronic	電力量 power generation
手のひら静脈認証システム palm vein ID system	電子機器 electronics	電話会談 telephone conversation
	電子計算機 computer	電話対談放送 phone-in
…では in terms of	電子工学 electronics	
手配 arrangement	電子工学の electronic	**と**
手配する arrange	電子取材 ENG	
手はずを整える arrange	電子の electronic	問い question
…ではないかと思う suspect	天井 ceiling	同意 accord
手放す divest	天井を打つ peak	同意 agreement
手放す quit	…に転じる return to	同意 consensus
手引き guidance	伝染 infection	同意 consent
デフレーション deflation	伝染病 epidemic	同意する accept
デフレーター deflator	伝送 transmission	同意する agree
デフレの deflationary	電送写真 phototelegraph	統一 unification
テヘラン Tehran	転送する import	同一材料の self
手本 paragon	転送する upload	同一条件の like-for-like
デメリット diseconomy	伝送する transmit	統一する unify
デモ参加者 demonstrator	伝達 communication	同一の self
デリバティブ derivative	伝達 transmission	動因 drive
テレビ画面で on-camera	…の点で in terms of	党員集会 caucus
テレビ通販 home shopping	店頭 over the counter	動員する mobilize
テレマーケティング telemarketing	店頭株式市場 NASDAQ	灯火管制 blackout
テレマティックス telematics	店頭市場 over the counter	投下資本利益率 return on investment
テロ行為 terrorism	店頭市場の over-the-counter	
テロ対策 antiterrorism	伝動装置 gear	統括 rein
…から手を引く pull out of	伝統的な conventional	統括する manage
天安門広場 Tiananmen Square	店頭の over-the-counter	統括する rein in
展開 deployment	店頭の point-of-sale	等価物 equivalent
転回 turn	電動の electrical	投函する post
展開する deploy	店頭販売期限 pull date	投棄 deep six
電界発光 electroluminescence	天然ガス natural gas	投機 speculation
…に点火する ignite	天然ガス・ハイドレート NGH	討議 debate
…に転嫁する pass on to	天然痘ワクチン smallpox vaccine	討議 deliberation
転換 rotation	天然の crude	討議 discussion
転換 turnaround	天然の natural	動機 cause
転換可能な convertible	電脳… cyber-	動機 incentive
転換する convert	電脳空間 cyber	道義 morality
天気 weather	電脳空間 cyberspace	動議 motion
電機 electrical machinery	転売する resell	投機家 speculator
電気 electricity	電波探知機 radar	道義上の moral
電気機械 electrical machinery	天罰 scourge	討議資料 talking paper
電気器具 electrical appliance	伝票 ticket	投機筋 speculator
電気製品 appliance	転覆させる overturn	騰貴する appreciate
電気通信 telecom	転覆させる topple	投棄する deep six
電気通信 telecommunication	転覆する overthrow	登記する register
電気通信事業者 telco	添付する attach	討議する mull
電気の electric	店舗 outlet	動機づけ motivation
電気の electrical	店舗 store	動機づける motivate
電気部品 device	展望 vision	動議提出者 mover
電撃作戦 blitz	埋補する absorb	投機的事業 venture
電撃的な electrical	テンポラル法 temporal method	投機的な speculative
点検 checkup	転落 downfall	当期の current
電源 electric power	電流 electricity	当期分 current
天候 weather	電力 electric power	等級 grade
電光 bolt	電力 electricity	東京 Tokyo

東京銀行間取引金利	TIBOR
同業組合	fraternity
同業者	competitor
同業者	counterpart
東京証券取引所	TSE
同業他社	rival
当局	authorities
当期利益	bottom line
動機を与える	motivate
道具	gear
道具	tool
統計	statistics
統計学	statistics
凍結	freeze
凍結した	frozen
凍結する	block
凍結する	freeze
桃源郷	Xanadu
統合	consolidation
統合	integration
統合	tie-up
統合	unification
動向	cycle
動向	environment
動向	event
動向	move
動向	stream
動向	trend
統合した	combined
統合した	consolidated
統合失調症	schizophrenia
投降する	turn oneself in
統合する	combine
統合する	consolidate
統合する	integrate
統合する	unify
統合する	unite
党公認候補者	ticket
同梱する	bundle
踏査	exploration
盗作	plagiarism
当座の	current
当座の	quick
当座預金	current account
倒産	bankruptcy
倒産	collapse
倒産した	bankrupt
倒産する	collapse
倒産する	go bankrupt
倒産する	go belly-up
倒産する	go under
投資	investment
闘士	militant
導師	guru
同時	real time
投資家	investor
投資家	moneyman
投資家説明会	briefing
投資家向け広報	IR
投資銀行	investment bank
投資収益	return on investment
投資する	invest
…に投資する	invest in
投資する	spend
同時の	simultaneous
投資不適格	junk
同種の	homogeneous
東証	TSE
東証株価指数	TOPIX
搭乗率	load factor
同情をさそう	melting
当初の	early
当初の	original
答申	verdict
統制	control
統制インフレ	reflation
統制する	regulate
統制する	rein in
透析	dialysis
当選確実者	shoo-in
当然のこと	given
闘争	battle
闘争	fight
闘争	strife
闘争	struggle
闘争する	battle
逃走中の	at large
同族の	related
統率	rein
統率力	leadership
統治	domination
統治	governance
統治権	sovereignty
統治している	ruling
統治する	govern
統治する	rule
統治能力	governability
盗聴	tap
盗聴	wiretapping
盗聴器	tap
盗聴する	wiretap
同点	standoff
同点決勝	runoff
同等	equality
…と同等	equivalent to
…と同等の	level
…と同等の	tantamount to
同等物	counterpart
同等物	equivalent
道徳	ethics
道徳	moral
道徳	morality
道徳の	moral
党内抗争	intraparty conflict
党内紛争	factionalism
東南アジア条約機構	SEATO
東南アジア諸国連合	ASEAN
東南アジア諸国連合地域フォーラム	ARF
投入	injection
投入	input
導入	import
導入	intake
導入	introduction
導入	launch
投入する	earmark
投入する	inject
投入する	invest
投入する	pump
導入する	import
導入する	introduce
糖尿病	diabetes
党派	party
党派に属さない人	nonpartisan
同母異父の	uterine
党派連合	cartel
逃避	evasion
逃避	flight
投票	ballot
投票	election
投票	poll
投票	polling
投票	vote
投票権行使	voting
投票者	voter
投票する	vote
動物実験規範	GLP
逃亡	bolt
東方拡大	eastward expansion
逃亡者	runaway
透明	transparency
透明な	transparent
盗用	hijack
盗用	plagiarism
動揺	instability
動揺	jolt
動揺	panic
動揺	sway
動揺	turmoil
動揺させる	rock
動揺させる	unsettle
動揺する	fluctuate
…に動揺を与える	jolt
到来	advent
騰落単位	point
道理に合わない	unreasonable
道理をわきまえない	unreasonable
登録	enrollment
登録する	enroll
登録する	register
道路地図	road map

討論			
討論 debate	特別検査 stress test	とっさの knee-jerk	
討論会 panel	特別損失 one-off losses	とっさの off-the-cuff	
遠い far	特別注文の custom-made	突然現われる pop up	
遠い remote	特別調査班 plumbers	突然起こる pop up	
遠く離れた remote	特別に選ばれた少数の select	突然…になる catapult	
通しの consecutive	特別の additional	突然の abrupt	
ドーピング doping	特別の exceptional	突然の故障 glitch	
通り street	特別の extraordinary	突破する surpass	
都会的な urban	特別の select	突破する top	
都会の urban	特別の special	突発 outbreak	
都会風の button-down	特別の specific	突発的な行動 spasm	
とがめる chide	特別の目的のための ad hoc	突風 blast	
時 moment	特別引出し権 SDR	届け出る file for	
時 occasion	特別目的会社 SPC	届ける deliver	
時 time	匿名 anonymity	整える marshal	
時の人 newsmaker	匿名社員 sleeping partner	とどまる hover	
得意先 customer	匿名の anonymous	ドナー donor	
得意の戦術 pet tactic	毒薬条項 poison pill	トニー賞 Tony (Awards)	
独裁権 autocracy	徳用の economy	飛び出す bolt	
独裁国家 autocratic state	独立 freedom	途方もなく大きい whopping	
独裁者の dictatorial	独立 independence	富 wealth	
独裁政治 autocracy	独立型の stand-alone	ドミノ domino	
独自性 initiative	独立行政機関 independent agency	弔いの鐘 knell	
独自性 originality	独立した arm's length	ドメスティック・バイオレンス DV	
特質 hallmark	独立した independent	…に伴って on the back of	
特集する feature	独立当事者間の arm's length	共働き世帯 dual-income family	
特殊の special	独力で維持できる self-sustaining	とらえ所のない elusive	
特色 feature	独力での bootstrap	捕われの trapped	
独占 monopolization	毒を盛ること poisoning	トランス脂肪酸 trans fats	
独占 monopoly	所 place	取扱い address	
独占企業の強制分轄 unbundling	年 year	取扱い handling	
独占禁止の antitrust	年老いた aging	取扱い transaction	
独占禁止法の適用外 ATI	年換算の annualized	取扱い treatment	
独占する monopolize	閉じ込められる trapped	取扱い説明書 instruction	
独占の proprietary	閉じ込める box in	取り扱う address	
独創性 originality	閉じ込める trap	取り扱う deal with	
独創力 initiative	都市の urban	鳥インフルエンザ avian flu	
戸口 threshold	戸締り lockup	鳥インフルエンザ avian influenza	
特注化 customizing	都心部 downtown	鳥インフルエンザ bird flu	
特注化する customize	度数 reading	とりえ merit	
特注の customized	土台 cornerstone	取替え replacement	
特徴 feature	土壇場 eleventh hour	取り返し resumption	
特徴 hallmark	土壇場の last-ditch	取り替える exchange	
特定区域に限定した sectional	土地 land	取り替える replace	
特定口座 specified account	途中で切り上げる cut short	取り囲む engulf	
特定集団のための sectional	…に特化する concentrate	取り囲む surround	
特定する identify	特価の knockdown	取決める engagement	
特定する pinpoint	特許 patent	取り決める arrange	
特定の special	特許 patent	取り決める close	
特定の specific	特許権侵害 piracy	取り決める negotiate	
特定目的会社 SPC	特許取得可能 patentable	取組み address	
特定領域 niche	特許物件 patent	取組み approach	
特典 prerogative	特恵 preference	取り組む address	
独特の own	特権 concession	…に取り組む battle	
徳の高い virtuous	特権 prerogative	取り組む commit	
特派員 correspondent	特権意識 elitism	…に取り組む committed to	
特別扱いする lionize	特権株 golden share	…に取り組む grapple with	

…に取り組む	tackle			投げ売り	sell-off
…に取り組む	work on			投げ売りする	dump
トリクルアップ理論の	trickle-up	**な**		投げ売りする	sell off
取り消す	cancel	…のない	-free	投げる	throw
取り消す	dissolve	内閣	cabinet	…なしで済ます	spare
取り消す	revoke	内閣	ministry	ナスダック	NASDAQ
取り込み詐欺	scam	内閣改造	reshuffle	なだめる	calm down
取り込む	attract	内閣の	ministerial	なだめる	placate
取り込む	download	内閣府	Cabinet Office	なだめる	soothe
取締役	board member	内勤の	inside	納得	satisfaction
取締役	director	内国歳入庁	Internal Revenue Service	ナノ・メートル	nanometer
取締役会	board			ナノテク製品	nanotech product
取締役会	board of directors	内視鏡	endoscope	…と名乗る	purported
…を取り締まる	clamp down on	内需	domestic demand	ナフサ	naphtha
鳥衝突	bird strike	内政	internal affairs	怠ける	shirk
取り立てる	call in	内製の	captive	生ワクチン	live-virus vaccine
取り立てる	recover	内臓	gut	波	sea
取り繕う	paper over	内定の	designate	波	wave
取付け	run	内部抗争	infighting	並木道	avenue
取付け騒ぎ	run	内部告発	whistle-blowing	波の跡	wake
取り付ける	attach	内部告発者	whistle-blower	滑らかな	soft
取り除く	iron out	内部事情	internal affairs	悩ます	beset
取り除く	separate	内部者	insider	…を悩ます	burden
取引	deal	内部情報	tip	悩ます	irk
取引	ticket	内部統制	internal control	悩ます	wrack
取引	trading	内部の	in-house	悩ませる	beset
取引	transaction	内部の	inside	悩ませる	haunt
取引先	client	内紛	bickering	悩みの種	scourge
取引先	correspondent	内紛	faction	悩む	worry
取引先	customer	内紛	infighting	ならず者	rogue
取引時間中の取引	intraday trading	内壁	wall	並び	row
取引所	bourse	内報	tip	並ぶ	rank
取引する	trade	内報者	tipster	…と並ぶ	rival
取引制限	trading limit	内報する	tip	…と並んで	in tandem with
取引高	sales	内密	secret	鳴り物入りの	much-heralded
取引高	volume	内密の	off-the-record	…となる	make for
取引停止	suspension	内容	content	…となる	spell
取引停止処分	suspension	仲卸業者	middleman	縄	rope
取巻き	crony	仲買	brokerage	縄張り主義	sectionalism
取り巻く	beset	仲買人	middleman	…の名をもつ	-name
取り巻く	surround	長く続く	perennial	軟化させる	weaken
取り乱す	break down	長さ	span	軟化した	weakened
取り戻す	regain	流し込む	pour	難関	hurdle
取り止める	shelve	長年続く	secular	難局	crisis
努力	effort	長引かせる	prolong	難局	dilemma
ドル	dlrs	長引く	lingering	難局	morass
ドル	dollar	長引く	prolonged	難局	straits
取るべき道	option	長引く	protracted	南極大陸	Antarctica
トレンドセッター	trendsetter	仲間	crony	難航する	flounder
ドロップシッピング	drop shipping	眺め	prospect	難題	challenge
泥沼	quagmire	流れ	flow	…から何とか逃れる	wriggle out of
度を越す	overstep the mark	流れ	process	難民	refugee
鈍化	deceleration	流れ	stream	難問	problem
鈍化	slowdown	流れ	tide	難問題	staggerer
鈍化	slowing	なぐり書き	scratch		
鈍化している	slowing	殴る	strike		
鈍化する	falter	投げ売り	dumping		

に

ニート NEET
ニールセン調査 Nielsen research
荷受業者 shipping agent
二極化 polarization
肉骨粉 MBM
憎しみ animosity
逃げ出す bolt
二元的な two-track
二国間交渉主義 bilateralism
二酸化炭素 carbon dioxide
二酸化炭素の回収・貯留 CCS
二次的な secondary
二者のうちどちらか一方の xor
二重の two-track
24時間態勢の round-the-clock
二段式弾道ミサイル Polaris
日常生活の off-camera
日常の daily
二地点間の最短距離 beeline
日量…バレル bpd
日経平均 Nikkei index
日経平均株価 Nikkei Stock Average
日程 timeline
日程計画 scheduling
日本政府 Tokyo
二等分する halve
二の次 backburner
二番目の second
…を鈍くする deactivate
鈍る slow
二方面の two-pronged
日本銀行 Bank of Japan
日本たたき Japan-bashing
ニュー・ディール政策 New Deal
入院患者 inmate
入会 enrollment
入会させる enroll
入札 auction
入札 bid
入札 bidding
入札 tender
入札者 bidder
入札書 tender
…に入札する bid for
入札の付け値 bid
入手する gain
入手する obtain
入植者 settler
ニュース・キャスター anchor
ニュース・バリューのある newsworthy
ニュース映画 newsreel
ニュースグループ newsgroup
ニュース雑誌 newsmagazine
ニュース時間 newstime

ニュースソース source
ニュース速報 newsflash
ニュース種になる人 newsmaker
ニュース短信 newsbrief
ニュースの豊富な newsy
ニュース編集室 newsroom
ニュートリノ neutrino
ニューヨーク株 Wall Street
ニューヨーク市 New York
ニューヨーク商業取引所 NYMEX
ニューヨーク証券取引所 NYSE
入力 input
尿 urine
任意の discretionary
任意の option
任意の random
任意の voluntary
認可 authorization
認可 certification
認可 license
認可 licensing
認可 permission
認可 sanctions
認可する certify
人気 popularity
任期 tenure
人気がある popular
任期別役員会 staggered board
人間機械系 man-machine system
人間の human
認識 knowledge
認識する recognize
認証 authentication
妊娠中絶 abortion
妊娠中絶禁止を支持する right-to-life
妊娠中絶合法化に反対の pro-life
妊娠中絶反対者 pro-lifer
妊娠中絶擁護者 pro-choicer
妊娠中絶擁護派の pro-choice
認知症 dementia
認定する identify
任務 duty
任務 mission
任務 role
任務 task
任命 appointment
任命する appoint
任命する assign
任命する name

ぬ

縫い目 seam
抜取り sampling
抜け穴 loophole
…から抜け出す get out of

抜け出せない trapped
抜け道 loophole
抜け目のない wide-awake
沼地 quagmire
ヌメロニム numeronym

ね

値上りした higher-priced
値上げ hike
値上げ markup
値上げ price increase
値決めする price
値下がり銘柄 loser
値下げ markdown
値下げ markoff
ねじれ contradiction
ねじれ distortion
ねじれ twist
ねじれた awry
寝ずの番 vigilance
値段 price
値段を言う quote
…の値段を付ける price
熱狂 frenzy
…に熱心な –minded
捏造 hoax
捏造する fabricate
捏造する falsify
熱帯の tropical
熱中症 heat-related ailments
ネット Internet
ネット Net
ネットブック netbook
熱の thermal
熱波 heat wave
値引き cut
値引きする take off
…に狙いを定める zero in on
ねらう aim
狙う seek
念入りに調べる go through
年間の annual
年金 annuity
年金 pension
年金制度 pension plan
年功 seniority
年次の annual
年数 age
年度 FY
年度 year
燃費がよい fuel-efficient
年率換算の annualized
年率換算の成長率 annualized growth rate
燃料 fuel
燃料効率がよい fuel-efficient

燃料電池	fuel cell
年齢	age
年齢層	age bracket
念を押す	remind

の

脳	brain
農園	farm
農業	agriculture
農業	farming
農業関連産業	agribusiness
農業の	agricultural
農産物に関する	agricultural
濃縮	concentration
濃縮ウラン	enriched uranium
農場	farm
農場経営	farming
納税義務者	taxpayer
納税者	taxpayer
納税申告	tax return
脳卒中	stroke
濃淡	tone
農地	farm
ノウハウ	knowhow
納付する	remit
能率	efficiency
能率化	streamlining
能率化する	streamline
能力	ability
能力	capability
能力	capacity
能力	power
能力	skill
能力向上	empowerment
能力主義	meritocracy
能力を高める	empower
ノーベル賞	Nobel
ノーベル賞受賞者	Nobelist
逃れる	dodge
逃れる	evade
…から逃れる	get out of
軒並み	across the board
残りの	remaining
乗っ取り	buyout
乗っ取り	hijack
乗っ取り	takeover
乗っ取り犯	hijacker
乗っ取る	hijack
乗っ取る	take over
伸ばす	bolster
延ばす	postpone
延ばす	spread
延ばす	waive
伸び	growth
伸び	increase
伸び	strengthening

伸びている	strengthening
伸び悩みの	flat-lined
伸び悩みの	poor
伸び悩む	level out
伸びる	rise
登る	mount
…をのみ込む	bear down on
飲み込む	engulf
乗り切る	weather
乗組員を乗せた	manned
乗り越える	bridge
乗り越える	overcome
…に乗り出す	step in
乗る	mount
ノロウイルス	norovirus

は

歯	tooth
バー	bar
場合	occasion
把握	hold
把握する	grip
バーゼル協定	Basel Accord
パーセンテージ・ポイント	percentage point
パーセント	pct
パーセント・ポイント	percentage point
バード・ストライク	bird strike
ハードディスク駆動装置	hard-disk drive
バード法	Byrd Amendment
灰色の	neutral
バイオエタノール車	bioethanol vehicle
バイオマス	biomass
バイオメトリクス	biometrics
媒介物	intermediary
倍加する	double
配管工事	plumbing
配管設備	plumbing
廃棄	deep six
排気	emission
廃棄	jettison
廃棄	waste
廃棄する	deep six
廃棄する	jettison
売却	divestiture
売却	divestment
売却	sale
売却	sell-off
売却する	divest
売却する	sell
売却する	sell off
売却する	unload
配給	distribution

背景	backdrop
背景説明	backgrounder
背景説明資料	backgrounder
配合	blending
背後で操る	mastermind
廃止	abandonment
廃止	elimination
廃止する	abandon
廃止する	abolish
廃止する	eliminate
廃止する	rescind
廃止する	revoke
敗者	loser
ハイジャック犯	hijacker
買収	buyout
買収会社	acquirer
買収者	acquirer
買収する	bribe
買収する	take over
買収提案	takeover bid
買収防衛策	antitakeover measure
買収防衛策	poison pill
排出	emission
排出国	producer
排出量取引	emission trading
売春	prostitution
排除	elimination
賠償	redress
賠償責任	liabilities
賠償の	compensatory
排除する	eliminate
…を排除する	keep out
陪審	jury
排水管	drain
排水溝	drain
倍数	multiple
胚性幹細胞	embryonic stem cells
胚性幹細胞	ES cells
排斥する	boycott
廃絶	ban
廃絶する	abolish
配送	delivery
倍増する	double
媒体	media
媒体	vehicle
配達	delivery
配達する	deliver
排他的経済水域	EEZ
配置	deployment
配置	setup
配置する	deploy
配置する	field
配置転換	redeployment
バイト	byte
配当	dividend
配当落ち	x-dividend
背任行為	malfeasance

排熱	exhaust heat
売買	deal
売買	sale
売買	trading
売買する	trade
売買担当者	trader
配備	deployment
配備する	deploy
配賦	allocation
配布	circulation
配布	handout
配賦可能な	applicable
配賦する	absorb
配賦する	allocate
配布する	circulate
配布する	dole
パイプライン	pipeline
ハイブリッド車	hybrid
配分	allocation
配分	appropriation
配分	sharing
配分する	allocate
敗北	defeat
売申込み	offer
倍率	multiple
配慮	care
破壊行為	vandalism
破壊工作員	saboteur
破壊者	destroyer
破壊する	deep six
破壊する	destroy
破壊するもの	destroyer
ばか騒ぎ	razzle-dazzle
測った	measured
計る	measure
破棄する	cancel
履き物	shoe
波及	influence
波及効果	ripple effect
波及効果	spinoff effects
波及効果	synergy
バグ	bug
迫害	persecution
育む	nurture
博識な	informed
白紙撤回する	cancel
拍車	spur
拍車がかかった	accelerated
白書	white paper
爆心地	epicenter
莫大な	enormous
莫大な	huge
莫大な	whopping
バグダッド	Baghdad
爆発性の	explosive
爆発的な	explosive
白馬の騎士	white knight
暴露	exposure
暴露する	expose
激しい	cutthroat
激しい	rampant
激しい銃の打ち合い	shootout
激しい反動	backlash
激しい非難	blast
激しく打つ	batter
激しく打つ	lash out at
激しく打つ	whip
激しく叱る	rip into
…と激しく衝突する	lock horns with
激しくなる	heat up
激しく非難する	blast
激しく非難する	lash out at
激しく非難する	rip into
激しく揺する	rock
激しさ	intensity
励まされる	heartening
励みとなる	encouraging
派遣	dispatch
覇権	hegemony
派遣	outreach
覇権主義	hegemonism
派遣する	dispatch
派遣団	contingent
派遣団	delegation
派遣部隊	contingent
派遣労働者	temp workers
ハザード・マップ	hazard map
破産	bankruptcy
破産した	bankrupt
破産する	go bankrupt
破産する	go under
破産防止手段	buffer
把持	hold
はしご	ladder
初めての	maiden
始める	inaugurate
始める	initiate
始める	kick off
始める	start up
場所	ground
場所	location
場所	locus
場所	place
場所	slot
場所	spot
柱	pillar
柱で支える	pillar
…を柱とする	pillar
はずみ	bounce
はずみ	momentum
…から外れる	break away from
パスワード	password
派生商品	derivative
派生物	offshoot
パソコン	PC
裸の	bare
果たす	make good
働き	activity
働き	working
働く	serve
働く	work
破綻	collapse
破綻	failure
破綻する	collapse
破綻する	fail
破綻する	go bankrupt
破綻する	go belly-up
破綻する	go under
破綻の瀬戸際にある	teetering
破竹の勢いの	sweeping
発案する	engineer
ハッカー	hacker
発覚	exposure
発火させる	ignite
発火点	flashpoint
発がん物質	carcinogen
発議者	mover
はっきりさせる	clarify
はっきり説明する	articulate
白金	platinum
罰金	fine
罰金	penalty
ハッキング	hacking
バックエンド費用	back-end cost
バックネット	backstop
白血病	leukemia
発言	remark
発言権	say
発言力	say
発行	issuance
発行	issue
発行	offering
初公開	premiere
発光技術	lighting technology
発行市場	primary market
発行済み株式	issued shares
発効する	come into force
発行する	float
発行する	issue
発光ダイオード	LED
発光ダイオード	light-emitting diode
発行部数	circulation
発散する	work off
発射	blastoff
発射	liftoff
発射実験	test-firing
発射実験を行う	test-fire
発射する	throw
発射物	projectile
発信者番号	ID
罰する	punish

発生	emergence	話好きな	newsy	繁華街	downtown
発生	generation	…から離れる	break away from	半官半民の企業	quasi-public corporation
発生	outbreak	跳ね上がる	jump		
発生学的な	genetic	はね返り	bounce	半期	half
発生源	generator	はね返り	reaction	半期	half year
発生させる	incur	はね返る	react	半旗の位置	half-mast
発生装置	generator	幅	margin	反逆者	rebel
発想	mindset	幅	range	反響	feedback
発送する	dispatch	派閥	faction	反響	reaction
発送する	ship	派閥争い	factionalism	反響	repercussion
発達	sophistication	派閥主義	sectionalism	番組制作	broadcasting
発展	advance	派閥の	factional	番組に出演する	broadcast
発展	progress	母の	maternal	反撃	riposte
発電	power generation	はびこる	rampant	反撃する	counter
発電機	generator	パブリシティ権	publicity right	判決	judgment
発展した	advanced	バブル	bubble	判決	ruling
発電所	power plant	ハマス	Hamas	判決	sentence
発電所	powerhouse	はまり込ませる	bog	判決	verdict
発展する	advance	刃向かい	tooth	判決を下す	sentence
発展途上の	developing	破滅	pot	版権	copyright
発電の	electric	速さ	pace	番犬	watchdog
初登場	debut	早める	bring forward	版権を取得する	copyright
初登場する	debut	早める	expedite	反抗	resistance
発動する	invoke	速める	speed up	反抗	tooth
発売	debut	払込み	payment	半公共の	semipublic
発売	release	払い込む	pay in	犯行者	perpetrator
発売する	debut	払い戻し	payoff	反国家分裂法	anti-secession law
発売する	launch	払戻し	rebate	犯罪	crime
発売する	release	払戻し	refund	犯罪	offense
発売する	ship	払戻し	refunding	犯罪	wrongdoing
発表	announcement	払戻し	repayment	犯罪者	criminal
発表	launch	払い戻す	refund	犯罪秘密結社	Mafia
発表	presentation	払い戻す	repay	反作用する	react
発表	publication	晴らす	work off	判事	judge
発表する	announce	ハラスメント	harassment	判事席	bench
発表する	come out with	波乱	turmoil	反射鏡	mirror
発表する	publish	バランス・シート	balance sheet	反射的な	knee-jerk
発表する	reveal	張り合う	vie	反主流	rebel
発表する	set out	張りつめた	tense	…に反する	belie
発表する	unveil	バルーン融資	balloon	反省	self-criticism
発砲	shot	春本	porn	反省	soul-searching
発泡スチロール	polystyrene foam	パレスチナ	Palestine	反政府暴動	insurgency
抜本的な	drastic	パレスチナ解放人民戦線	PFLP	反戦主義者	pacifist
抜本的に改革する	overhaul	パレスチナの	Palestinian	反対	opposition
発明	invention	バレル	barrel	反対	resistance
発明する	invent	ハロー効果	halo effect	反対	reverse
発明する	originate	版	edition	反対	thumbs-down
波動	wave	班	squad	反対者	opponent
歯止め	brake	班	team	…に反対する	combat
歯止め効果	ratchet effect	範囲	extent	反対する	withstand
歯止め効果	ratchet effect	範囲	range	反体制派	dissident
パトリオット・ミサイル	Patriot missile	範囲	scope	反体制派	nonconformist
パトリモニアル水域	patrimonial sea	反インフレ	anti-inflation	反対に	counter
パトロン	moneyman	繁栄	prosperity	反対の	adverse
花形	lion	反映する	mirror	反対の	counter
話	speech	反映する	reflect	反対の	reverse
話し合い	powwow	汎欧州デジタル携帯電話規格	GSM	反対分子	insurgent

ハンタウイルス	Hantaan virus
判断	discretion
判断	judgment
判断する	gauge
判断する	judge
反ダンピング	antidumping
汎地球主義	globalism
反デフレ政策	anti-deflation policy
反デフレ戦略	anti-deflationary strategy
反テロ行為	antiterrorism
反転	reversal
反騰	rally
反動	repercussion
反動主義者	rightist
反騰する	rally
半導体	chip
半導体	semiconductor
半導体製造業者	chipmaker
反動的な	reactionary
反動の	reactionary
反トラストの	antitrust
犯人	perpetrator
犯人護送車	paddy wagon
犯人捜査	manhunt
犯人追跡	manhunt
万人の	universal
反応	feedback
反応	reaction
反応	response
反応が早い	quick-fix
万能細胞	embryonic stem cells
万能細胞	iPS cell
反応する	react
…に反応する	respond to
万能の解決策	panacea
万能薬	panacea
販売	marketing
販売	release
販売	sale
販売	selling
販売先	placement
販売時点情報管理	point of sales
販売者	seller
販売する	distribute
販売する	market
販売する	offer
販売する	release
販売する	sell
販売店	distributor
反発	bounce
反発	rally
反発	rebound
反発	reversal
反発する	bounce back
反発する	rebound
反復	recurrence
反復する	reiterate
パンフレット	booklet
半分	half
半分に分ける	halve
判別する	recognize
反保護主義	antiprotectionism
ハンマー	hammer
反ユダヤ主義	anti-Semitism
反落	retreat
反落する	retreat
氾濫	deluge
氾濫	flood
反乱	insurgency
氾濫させる	flood
反乱者	insurgent
反乱兵士	rebel
判例	precedent
販路	outlet
…に反論する	take issue with
判を押す	rubber-stamp

ひ

ひいき	bias
ひいき	patronage
ピークに達する	peak
PDCAサイクル	PDCA cycle
秀でた	excellent
ヒート・アイランド現象	heat island phenomenon
非営利法人	nonprofit corporation
冷え込んだ	cooled
被害	damage
被害者	victim
非階層的な	bottom-up
控え目な	subdued
日帰り介護	day service
控える	forgo
比較	matchup
非核化	denuclearization
非核化する	denuclearize
比較可能数値	comparable figures
…と比較して	vis-a-vis
比較的重要でない	minor
非核の	nonnuclear
比較優位	competitive advantage
東アジア共同体	East Asian community
東アジア自由貿易圏	East Asia free trade area
非課税の	nontaxable
非加熱製剤	unheated blood products
光	light
光ファイバー	fiber optics
光ファイバー	optical fiber
光ファイバー網	fiber optic (cable) network
悲観主義	pessimism
悲観主義の	pessimistic
非関税の	nontariff
悲観的な	gloomy
悲観的な	pessimistic
悲観的な暗い	downbeat
非管理職	nonmanagerial employee
悲観論	pessimism
引上げ	hike
引き上げる	boost
引き上げる	hike
引き上げる	raise
引き揚げる	withdraw
引当金	reserve
…を率いる	head
引受け	subscription
引受け	underwriting
引受証券会社	underwriter
引受シンジケート団	syndicate
引受人	subscriber
引き受ける	accept
引き受ける	acquire
引き受ける	assume
引き受ける	subscribe
引き受ける	take on
引き受ける	undertake
引き受ける	underwrite
引き起こす	generate
引き起こす	incur
…を引き起こす	lead to
引き起こす	spark
引き起こす	trigger
引き落とす	deduct
引き金	trigger
引下げ	cut
引下げ	easing
引下げ	relaxation
引き下げる	decrease
引き下げる	lower
引き下げる	write off
引締め	austerity
引締め	crunch
引締め	stringency
引締め	tightening
引き締める	squeeze
被疑者	suspect
引き出す	draw
引き出す	tap
引き出す	withdraw
引き継いだ	successive
引き継ぐ	carry over
引き継ぐ	inherit
引きつける	attract
…に引き続いて	in the wake of
…に引き続いて	on the back of
引き続いて	successively

引き続き…する	continue to
引き延ばす	prolong
引き延ばす	stall
非協力者	nonconformist
引渡し	extradition
非金融	nonfinancial
低い	low
非軍事化	demilitarization
否決する	nix
引け値	close
引け値	closing price
飛行	flight
非公開会社	unlisted stock company
非公開会社にする	go private
…を非公開にする	keep ... under wraps
非公開の会談	behind-closed-doors session
非公式記者会見	backgrounder
非公式の	off-the-record
非公式の	shadow
飛行場	airport
非合法化する	outlaw
非合法な	illegal
非効率	inefficiency
被告人	culprit
被告人	defendant
日毎に	by the day
被雇用者	employee
膝を交えての	face-to-face
ビジター	visitor
微視的経済学	microeconomics
微視的経済の	microeconomic
微視的分析	microanalysis
ビジネス・モデル特許	business model patent
ビジネス手法	business model
ビジネスピープル	businesspeople
ビジネスマン	businesspeople
非主力事業	noncore business
批准	ratification
批准する	ratify
秘書	secretary
飛翔体	projectile
非常事態	contingency
非常事態	emergency
非上場の	privately held
びしょぬれの	saturated
聖牛	sacred cow
美辞麗句	rhetoric
非人道的な	inhuman
ヒズボラ	Hizbollah guerrillas
非正規雇用者	nonregular employee
非正規の	unauthorized
非正規労働者	nonregular worker
非製造業	nonmanufacturing business
非製造業者	nonmanufacturer
非製造部門	nonmanufacturing sector
非政府機関	NGO
微生物	microorganism
非戦闘員	noncombatant
非戦闘部隊	noncombat troop
非対称デジタル加入者回線	ADSL
びた一文	red cent
火種	spark
ひた向きな	single-minded
備蓄	pool
非中核事業	noncore business
ひっくり返す	overturn
…の火付け役となる	spark
必修の	mandatory
必修の	required
必需品	requirement
必須の条件	must
ヒッチハイクする	thumb
ヒット商品	winning product
逼迫	pressure
筆名	pseudonym
必要	needs
必要条件	precondition
必要条件	prerequisite
必要性	needs
必要とされている	wanted
必要とする	demand
必要とする	require
必要な	required
必要量	needs
否定する	nix
美点	merit
人扱いがうまい	diplomatic
ひどい	tough
ひどい打撃	bashing
ひどい打撃を受けた	hard-hit
非道な	heinous
非同盟	nonalignment
非同盟の	nonaligned
1株当たり	per share
人柄	personality
…に等しい	tantamount to
ひと仕事	sitting
人質	hostage
人手	turnout
人に知られていない	new
ヒト胚性幹細胞	embryonic human stem cells
ヒトパピローマウイルス	HPV
人々	people
人目につかない	covert
人目を引く	high-profile
人目を引く	noticeable
ヒト免疫不全ウイルス	HIV
1人当たり	per capita
一人っ子政策	one-child policy
非難	condemnation
非難	criticism
非難	rap
避難	refuge
避難	shelter
避難勧告	evacuation recommendations
避難所	asylum
避難所	shelter
非難する	condemn
非難する	rap
非難する	slam
…を非難する	take ... to task
避難民	evacuee
避難民	refugee
否認	rejection
否認権	veto
否認する	nix
否認する	reject
非農産品	nonagricultural products
火の粉	spark
火花	spark
批判	criticism
日々の	daily
批評	criticism
批評的な	critical
非武装化	demilitarization
非武装地帯	Demilitarised Zone
非不胎化	nonsterilization
被扶養者	dependent
微分の	differential
疲弊	exhaustion
誹謗	defamation
誹謗	slander
肥満	obesity
秘密	confidence
秘密	secret
秘密工作支援活動	plumbing
秘密情報	tip
秘密情報	tipoff
秘密情報を公開する	go public
…を秘密にしておく	keep ... under wraps
秘密の	backstage
秘密の	covert
秘密裏の	behind-the-scenes
悲鳴	outcry
罷免する	dismiss
100万分の1	ppm
ピューリツァー賞	Pulitzer Prize
表	list
表	listing
費用	charge
費用	cost

評価　appraisal	標本抽出　sampling	品質管理者　quality controller
評価　assessment	表明　announcement	品質保持期限　freshness date
評価　reputation	表明する　announce	瀕死の　moribund
評価　valuation	表明する　represent	貧弱な　meager
評価　value	表明する　voice	品種　variety
評価替え　revaluation	秒読み　clock ticking	敏捷な　agile
評価替えする　mark to market	秒読み　countdown	敏速な　spanking
評価減　write-down	兵糧攻め　siege	ピント　focus
評価する　assess	平壌　Pyongyang	ピンと張った綱　tightrope
評価する　gauge	開かれた　open	貧乏　poverty
評価する　judge	開き　gap	貧民地区への融資拒否　redlining
評価する　rank	開き　margin	品目　item
評価する　rate	平議員　backbencher	
評価損　write-down	開く　open	**ふ**
評価引下げ　write-down	開く　unfold	
病気　ailment	開ける　open	ファイバー　fiber
評議員会　board meeting	平社員　rank and file	ファスト・トラック　fast-track
票決　election	平然を装う　put a brave face on	不安　fear
評決　verdict	ピラミッド型組織　pyramid	不安　instability
票決する　vote	ピラミッドの底辺　BOP	不安　misgiving
標語　slogan	ひらめき　brainstorm	不安　tension
標高　altitude	比率　percentage	不安　unrest
費用効率　cost effectiveness	比率　proportion	不安　worry
費用効率が高い　cost-efficient	比率　ratio	不安感　premonition
費用削減　cost reduction	比率削減　scaledown	不安定　instability
表示　indication	微粒子　particulate	不安定化　destabilization
表示　labeling	非臨床試験基準　GLP	不安定な　touch-and-go
表示　presentation	ピル　pill	不安定な　unsettled
表示　reporting	非礼　gaffe	不安定にする　destabilize
標識　landmark	比例　proportion	不安定にする　unsettle
表示期間　time frame	…に比例する　keep pace with	不安定になっている　afloat
表示する　present	比例代表制　proportional-representative system	不安定の弧　crescent of instability
表示する　read		不安な　unsettled
表示する　represent	非連動　decoupling	不安にする　unsettle
…表示の　-denominated	広い　broad	不安のもと　specter
標準　mark	拾い読み　browsing	フィージビリティ　feasibility
標準　standard	拾い読みする　browse	フィッシング　phishing
標準化　normalization	疲労感　lassitude	不一致　clash
標準化　standardization	非労働力人口　nonworking labor force	部位と部位との継ぎ目を感じさせない　seamless
標準化する　standardize		
表題　headline	非労働力人口　nonworking population	フィブリノゲン　fibrinogen
標的　bull		風景　scene
標的　target	広がり　spread	封鎖　blockade
標的にする　target	広く行われている　prevalent	封鎖　closure
標的の　targeted	広く認められる　prevalent	封鎖する　block
平等　equality	広げる　expand	風船　balloon
平等　equilibrium	広げる　spread	風潮　tendency
平等機会　equal opportunity	広げる　unfold	風土　climate
表に記載された　listed	広げる　widen	風土　culture
費用のかからない　inexpensive	広場　forum	夫婦共働き家族　two-income family
評判　popularity	広める　spread	風聞　rumor
評判　prestige	火をつける　ignite	フーリガン　hooligan
評判　publicity	敏感な　sensitive	風力　wind
評判　rumor	品行　moral	風力の豊かな　wind-riched
評判では　reportedly	貧困　poverty	プーリング法　pooling of interests
評判の　popular	品質　quality	不運　catastrophe
標本　sample	品質管理　quality control	笛　whistle

フェール・セーフ	fail safe	不均衡	disparity	父権	paternity
フェデラル・ファンド金利	Federal funds rate	不均衡	imbalance	不幸	calamity
増える	proliferate	不均衡な	lopsided	不幸	catastrophe
フェンス	fence	不均等	odds	不公平な	unfair
フェンフルラミン	fenfluramine	不具合	defect	布告	declaration
無遠慮な	outspoken	副会長	veep	負債	debt
不穏な状況	unrest	副会長	vice-chairman	負債	liabilities
深い	deep	副業	sideline	負債	obligation
不快	malaise	復元	reconstruction	不在	absence
部会	committee	複合映画館	cinema complex	不在	absentee
深い後悔	remorse	複合企業	conglomerate	不採算事業	underperforming operations
部外者	outsider	復号する	decode		
不快な	sour	複合体	complex	不採算な	unprofitable
付加価値	added value	複合の	multiple	負債を抱えた	debt-saddled
付加価値税	TVA	複合矛盾	problematique	不支持率	disapproval rating
付加価値税	value-added tax	複合メディア	multimedia	不時着水させる	ditch
付加価値の	value-added	複雑な諸問題	problematics	不十分な	half-baked
不覚	blunder	副作用	side effect	不十分な	meager
深く切り込む	slash	福祉	welfare	不出場	noncandidacy
不拡散	nonproliferation	複式の	double	不出馬表明	noncandidacy
不確実性	uncertainty	複式の	multiple	不首尾	fiasco
不確定	uncertainty	福祉資金	public welfare loans	浮上	emergence
不確定な	uncertain	副次的効果	side effect	不祥事	irregularity
不可欠のもの	linchpin	副次的な	collateral	侮辱	libel
深さ	depth	副次的な	secondary	侮辱	scorn
不可侵条約	nonaggression treaty	腹心の部下	Mafia	腐食する	bite
賦課する	levy	複数議決権株式	super voting share	婦女暴行	rape
付加装置	add-on	…に服する	subject to	不信	distrust
不活化処理	deactivation processing	複製品	clone	不振	doldrums
		副総裁	veep	不振	slack
不活化ワクチン	inactivated polio vaccine	副総裁	vice president	不振	sluggishness
不恰好な頭	loggerhead	副大統領	veep	婦人科医	gynecologist
不活性化する	deactivate	副大統領	vice president	不審船	unidentified vessel
不活発な	dull	副知事	lieutenant governor	不振な年	off year
不活発な	lethargic	腹部の	abdominal	不振にする	depress
不活発な	slack	副本	counterpart	不信任	nonconfidence
不活発にする	deactivate	…を含まない	-free	不振の	lackluster
付加的な	additional	含みを持つ	latent	不振の	lethargic
深まる	deepen	含む	include	不振の	poor
深める	deepen	膨らませる	inflate	不振の	sluggish
不干渉の	hands-off	ふくらみ	swelling	不振の	slumping
不完全雇用	underemployment	膨らむ	balloon	不正	collusion
不完全な	half-baked	ふくらむ	bulge	不正	fraud
不寛容主義	zero tolerance	福利厚生	welfare	不正	malpractice
武器	arms	副理事長	vice president	不正	padding
武器	weapon	膨れ上がった	bloated	不正アクセス	hacking
不規則性	irregularity	膨れた	bloated	不正確な	incorrect
吹き付ける	implant	ふくれる	swell	不正規兵	guerrilla
普及	popularization	袋小路	impasse	不正行為	irregularity
普及	spread	父系	paternity	不正行為	misconduct
不況	depression	不景気	depression	不正工作する	rig
不況	recession	不景気	recession	不正資金の洗浄	laundering
不況期	depression	不景気	slack	不正資金を洗浄する	launder
不況の	depressed	不景気な	slack	不正使用する	abuse
部局	arm	不景気にする	depress	不正侵入防止機能	firewall
武器を持った	armed	不景気の	depressed	不正操作	manipulation
		不経済	diseconomy	不正取引	trafficking

不正な	false	普通株式	common share	不平等	odds
不正な	fraudulent	普通の	ordinary	部品メーカー	parts maker
不正な	shady	物価	price	不服の申立て	appeal
不正な	unfair	物価下落	deflation	部分	percentage
不正にアクセスする	hack	物価下落の	deflationary	不平	complaint
不正に操作する	rig	物価上昇	inflation	不返特約	nonrefundable agreement
不正に取引する	traffic	物価上昇圧力	inflationary pressures		
不正に変更する	doctor	物価上昇率	inflation rate	不変の	regular
不正入札	bid-rigging	復活	restoration	訃報	obituary
不正の	corrupt	復活させる	restore	不法行為	malfeasance
不正の	unauthorized	復活させる	resume	不法行使する	usurp
不正表示	mislabeling	復活させる	resuscitate	不法な	illegal
不正目的使用	misappropriation	物価引下げ政策	rollback	不法な	unlawful
不正流用	misappropriation	復帰	restoration	不法の	illicit
防ぐ	avert	復帰させる	rehabilitate	付保する	insure
防ぐ	prevent	復帰させる	restore	不満	frustration
防ぐ	protect	…に復帰する	return to	踏み誤り	misstep
防ぐ	ward off	復興	reconstruction	踏み台	stepping stone
敷設網	grid	復興させる	rehabilitate	踏み外し	misstep
武装解除	disarmament	不都合な	adverse	不毛な	arid
武装解除する	disarm	物故録	who was who	不毛な	fruitless
武装した	armed	物資	supplies	部門	arm
武装ヘリ	gunship	物資補給路	lifeline	部門	department
不足	deficiency	物体	object	部門	division
不足	lack	ぶっつけ本番の	off-the-cuff	部門	sector
不足	shortage	物品	goods	部門	unit
不足	shortfall	物品	merchandise	増やす	increase
付属させる	attach	物理学	physics	富裕消費者向けの	upscale
不足している	short of	物流	distribution	不愉快な	sour
付属書類	schedule	不貞	adultery	扶養家族	dependent
不測の事態	contingency	不定愁訴	malaise	浮揚させる	buoy
付属品	add-on	不貞の	errant	扶養親族	dependent
付属文書	appendix	不適応	maladaptation	付与する	grant
舞台	arena	不手際	gaffe	プライベート・ファイナンス・イニシアチブ	PFI
部隊	squad	不登校	truancy		
部隊	troop	不動産	real estate	プライマリー・バランス	primary balance
舞台裏の	backstage	不動産価格	property values		
舞台裏の	behind-the-scenes	不動産投資信託	REIT	プライム・レート	prime rate
舞台裏の論争	backroom bickering	浮動投票者	persuadables	プラウダ	Pravda
付帯的な	collateral	不当な	unfair	プラグイン・ソフト	plug-in
2桁	double digit	不当な代金を請求する	overcharge	プラザ合意	Plaza Accord
双子の赤字	twin deficits	不当な手数料	kickback	プラスの	positive
不確かな	uncertain	不当表示	mislabeling	プラズマ	plasma
再び活力を与える	reinvigorate	不透明な	uncertain	プラチナ	platinum
再び始める	resume	不当利得行為	profiteering	ブラックメール	blackmail
2人乗り自転車	tandem	不当利得者	profiteer	プラム・ブック	plum book
負担	burden	不当廉売	dumping	不利	disadvantage
負担する	assume	不当廉売する	dump	不利	downside
負担する	defray	不当廉売防止	antidumping	フリースタイルの	all-in
負担する	foot	懐具合	pocket book	フリーダイヤル	toll-free
負担する	pay	歩留まり	yield	ブリーチーズ	brie
負担する	shoulder	歩留まり	yield rate	フリート街	Fleet Street
ぶちまける	wreak	不妊	sterilization	振り動かす	shake
付着する	adhere	船	vessel	プリオン	prion
不注意	negligence	負の	negative	振り返る	swap
不調	malaise	腐敗	corruption	不履行	failure
不調に終わる	go sour	不払いの	unpaid	ブリック&モルタル	bricks & mortar

不利な	unfavorable
振り回す	shake
振り回す	wield
振り向ける	shift
ブリュッセル	Brussels
不良[欠陥]箇所	bug
不良貸出	bad loan
不良貸付け	nonperforming loans
不良債権	bad debt
不良債権	bad loan
不良債権	nonperforming loans
不良債権	underperforming loans
不良債権の償却	written-off bad debts
不良資産	bad assets
不良資産	toxic assets
不良融資	bad loan
武力	arms
武力	military force
武力政変	coup
武力による	armed
不倫	adultery
振る	shake
ふるいにかける	screen
ふるい分ける	screen
ブルームバーグ通信	Bloomberg news agency
ブルーレイ規格	Blu-ray standard
震え	quake
フル回転	overdrive
フルサービス証券会社	full-service brokerage
プルサーマル	pluthermal
プルトニウム	plutonium
ブレーンストーミング	brainstorming
フレキシブル生産システム	FMS
フレディ・マック	Freddie Mac
触れる	touch
プロ	professional
プロ意識	professionalism
ブロードバンド通信	broadband communication
ブログ	blog
ブログの書き手	blogger
プロシューマー	prosumer
不和	split
文化	culture
憤慨	rage
文化芸術破壊	vandalism
文化支援	mecenat
文化大革命	Great Cultural Revolution
分割	divestiture
分割する	spin off
分割する	split up
分割する	subdivide
文化の	cultural
分岐	divergence
奮起させる	spur
紛糾	snarl
憤激	exacerbation
文献	document
分権化	decentralization
分散	diversification
分散する	diversify
分子	molecular
分社化	spinoff
文書	data
文書	document
文書	paper
粉飾	window dressing
粉飾決算する	window-dress
粉飾する	window-dress
粉飾の	bogus
文書にした	written
文書による	written
分身	double
分水嶺	divide
分析家	analyst
紛争	dispute
紛争	litigation
紛争	strife
紛争	war
分担	contingent
奮闘する	struggle
憤怒	rage
分派	faction
分派	offshoot
分派	wing
分配	handout
分配	sharing
分配金	dividend
分売する	distribute
分配する	distribute
分配する	dole
分派の	factional
文筆業	journalism
粉末	powder
分野	field
分野	niche
分野	sector
分与	sharing
分離	secession
分離	separation
分離主義者	separatist
分離する	separate
分離する	spin off
分離独立	secession
分離独立主義者	separatist
分類	labeling
分類	separation
分類する	pigeonhole
分裂	breakup
分裂	division
分裂	polarization
分裂	split
分裂する	split

へ

ペイオフ制度	payoff system
閉会	closure
弊害	abuse
平価切上げ	appreciation
平価を切り上げる	upvalue
兵器	arms
兵器	weapon
兵器化する	weaponize
兵器級の	weapons-grade
平均化する	level off
平均化する	level out
平均寿命	life expectancy
…の平均値を出す	average
平衡	equilibrium
米航空宇宙局	NASA
米国	U.S.
米国	United States
米国	Washington
米国議会の	congressional
米国国歌	Star-Spangled Banner
米国債	Treasury
米国債	U.S. Treasuries
米国再生・再投資法	American Recovery and Reinvestment Act
米国政府	Washington
米国大統領官邸	White House
米国の力による平和	Pax Americana
閉鎖	closure
閉鎖式の	closed-end
閉鎖する	block
閉鎖する	shutter
兵士	militant
米州機構	OAS
平常化する	normalize
米製品の優先購入	Buy American
閉塞	blockade
兵隊	troop
平定	pacification
閉店する	shutter
米ドル	greenback
兵力	military force
平和	peace
平和維持	peacekeeping
平和維持活動	PKO
平和主義者	pacifist
平和な	peaceful
ベーシス・ポイント	basis point
ベーシス・ポイント	bp
ベージュ・ブック	Beige Book
…ベースの	-denominated
ペーパーレス	paperless

北京					
北京	Beijing	変更	shift	棒	stake
隔たり	gap	偏向した	biased	包囲	siege
下手な人	clunker	変更する	amend	法域	jurisdiction
へたに	poorly	変更する	change	包囲作戦	siege
別形	variant	変更する	switch	包囲された	beleaguered
別個の	separate	弁護士	attorney	包囲する	seal off
別紙	appendix	弁護士	bar	包囲する	surround
別紙	schedule	弁護士	lawyer	放映	broadcasting
ペット・ボトル	PET bottle	弁護する	plead	防衛	defense
別表	schedule	返済	refund	防衛策	defensive measure
別々の	separate	返済	repayment	放映する	tape
別名	alias	返済期日	due date	防衛する	defend
…にへつらう	curry favor with	返済する	pay off	貿易	trade
ペテン	scam	返済する	refund	貿易黒字	trade surplus
…への関心が高い	-conscious	返済する	reimburse	貿易投資枠組み協定	TIFA
…への道を開く	pave the way for	返済する	repay	崩壊	breakup
ヘビ	snake	遍在する	ubiquitous	崩壊	collapse
ベビー・ブーマー	baby boomers	弁済する	liquidate	妨害	interception
ベビームーン	babymoon	弁済する	reimburse	妨害	obstruction
…を減らす	cut back on	編纂者	editor	妨害活動をする人	saboteur
…を減らす	cut into	編纂する	compile	妨害する	impede
減らす	drop	変種	variant	妨害する	intercept
減らす	reduce	変種	variety	妨害する	interfere
減らす	slash	編集者	editor	妨害する	thwart
ヘラルド	herald	編集する	compile	妨害戦術	obstructive tactics
ヘリコバクター・ピロリ菌	Helicobacter pylori	編集の	editorial	法外な	excessive
ペルシャ湾岸諸国	Gulf States	編集プログラム	editor	法外な価格で株を買い戻す	green-mail
ベルトコンベヤー方式	conveyer belt system	偏頭痛	migraine	包括的	global
ペレストロイカ	perestroika	編成	lineup	包括的核実験禁止条約	CTBT
変異型クロイツフェルト・ヤコブ病	vCJD	変遷	transition	包括的取引	grand bargain
便益	benefit	変造した	forged	包括的な	comprehensive
変化	change	変造する	customize	包括的な	omnibus
変化	fluctuation	変造する	fake	傍観の	hands-off
変化	gradation	変則な	abnormal	放棄	jettison
変化	shift	偏重	overemphasis	法規	ordinance
変化	transformation	変動	change	放棄	write-off
変革	change	変動	fluctuation	謀議	conspiracy
変化させる	change	変動	move	放棄する	abolish
変化をもたらす	affect	変動	shift	放棄する	jettison
変換	translation	変動	volatility	放棄する	quit
変換する	transform	変動が激しい	volatile	放棄する	waive
変換する	translate	変動する	fluctuate	法規制の	regulatory
便宜	accommodation	変動性	volatility	防御壁	bulwark
便宜	convenience	変動相場制	float	防禦壁	firewall
返金	repayment	変貌	transformation	防御措置	defensive measure
返金する	repay	片務的な	unilateral	防御の	defensive
変形	transformation	弁明	allegation	冒険的事業	venture
変形	variant	便利	convenience	防護	guard
変形させる	transform	遍歴する	errant	方向	direction
偏見	bias			暴行	assault
偏見を抱いた	biased	**ほ**		方向転換	about-face
弁護	advocacy	補遺	appendix	方向転換	flip-flop
変更	amendment	保育休暇	child care leave	方向転換	rightabout-face
偏向	distortion	ボイコットする	boycott	方向転換	turnabout
		ホイヘンス	Heugens	方向転換する	flip-flop
		法	rule	報告	report

和英

報告 reporting	防虫剤の玉 mothball	暴落する free-fall
報告書 report	膨張 swelling	暴落する nosedive
報告書 statement	膨張する bulge	暴落する plummet
報告書 ticket	膨張する swell	暴落する slump
報告する report	膨張性の expansionary	暴落する tumble
報告責任 accountability	法廷 court	暴落する tumbling
方策 way	法定準備金 legally required reserves	暴利行為 profiteering
防止 prevention	法定の statutory	法律 law
方式 method	法的措置 legal action	法律 legislation
方式 mode	法的な legal	法律違反 crime
方式 style	法的実体を持つ come into force	法律家 attorney
防止策 prevention	法的に拘束力のある binding	法律家 lawyer
防止する prevent	暴徒 insurgent	法律制定者 legislator
防止するための preventive	暴徒 rioter	法律による保護を奪う outlaw
法執行のための通信援助法 CALEA	報道 coverage	法律の legal
放射 radiation	暴騰 jump	法律の制定 enactment
放射性の radioactive	暴動 riot	法律を制定する enact
放射線医学 radiology	報道価値のある newsworthy	暴力 attack
放射能 radiation	報道官 spokesman	暴力 violence
放射能検査 radioactivity survey	報道関係者 mediaman	暴力行為 terrorism
放射能による radioactive	報道管制 blackout	暴力行為 violence
報酬 commission	報道機関 journalism	暴力組織 mafia
報酬 compensation	報道記者 newscaster	暴力団 organized crime syndicate
報酬 fee	報道記者 newshound	暴力的な violent
報酬 remuneration	報道記者 newsman	暴力による violent
報酬 reward	報道記者 newsperson	法令 enactment
放出 emission	報道記者 reporter	法令 ordinance
報償 compensation	報道娯楽番組 infotainment	飽和 saturation
報償 reward	報道する broadcast	飽和した saturated
報奨金 incentive award	報道する report	飽和状態にさせる saturate
報奨金 reward	報道によると reportedly	ポータル portal
報奨金制度 incentive program	報道によれば allegedly	ボーダレス borderless
方針 basis	冒頭部分 front	ボーナス bonus
方針 philosophy	暴徒鎮圧用ガス pepper gas	ホーム・エクイティ・ローン home equity loan
法人 corporate	放任主義 permissivism	ホームページ homepage
法人 corporation	防波堤 bulwark	ホームレスの homeless
法人格の付与 incorporation	防備 defense	保温用の thermal
法人化する incorporate	防備の defensive	簿価 book value
法人事業税 corporate tax	報復的な retaliatory	簿外の off-the-book
法人税 corporate tax	豊富な affluent	保管 custody
法人税 income tax	豊富な ample	補完的 supplementary
法人組織 incorporation	砲兵隊 artillery	補完的な complementary
…する方針だ plan to	方法 method	補給所 depot
…する方針である intend to	方法 mode	補強 beef-up
方針を固める decide	方法 style	補強 reinforcement
放送 air	方法 way	補強材 backstop
放送 broadcast	泡沫 bubble	補強する beef up
放送 broadcasting	亡命者 defector	補強する enhance
放送局 broadcaster	訪問販売 door-to-door sales	補強する reinforce
放送事業者 broadcaster	暴落 debacle	保菌者 carrier
放送する broadcast	暴落 dive	牧師 cleric
暴走族 one percenter	暴落 free fall	北米自由貿易協定 NAFTA
法則 law	暴落 meltdown	撲滅する stamp out
法則 principle	暴落 slump	捕鯨 whaling
膨大な enormous	暴落 tumble	保険 insurance
膨大な staggering	暴落する collapse	
包帯を巻く tape	暴落する dive	保健医療 medical care

保険会社 insurer	保証 certification	保有株 stockholdings
保険加入者 policyholder	保証 protection	保有株式 portfolio
保険監督者国際機構 IAIS	補償 redress	保有株式 shareholdings
保険業者 insurer	保証 standby credit	保有株式 stockholdings
保険金の不払い nonpayment of insurance benefits	保証された secured	保有者 holder
保険契約者 policyholder	保証する certify	保有状態 position
保険に入る take out	保証する ensure	保有する own
保険料 premium	保証人 insurer	保有する retain
保険をかける insure	補償の compensatory	保有高 holdings
保護 care	補助金 subsidy	保養休暇 R & R
保護 conservation	補助的な auxiliary	ポリエチレン polyethylene
保護 custody	補助の auxiliary	ポリ塩化ビフェニール PCB
保護 protect	ポスト… post-	ポリオ不活化ワクチン inactivated polio vaccine
保護 protection	ホスト・コンピュータ host computer	ポリグラフ polygraph
保護 refuge	ホスト計算機 host computer	掘り下げた論議 in-depth discussions
保護 safeguard	ホスピス hospice	ポリプロピレン polypropylene
保護 shelter	保全 conservation	…を保留する put ... on hold
保護 umbrella	保全 integrity	捕虜 POW
保護 wing	保全 maintenance	ポルノ pornography
歩行者 pedestrian	保全 protection	ポルノ映画 pornoflick
歩行者専用の pedestrian	保全 safeguard	ポルポト政権 Pol Pot regime
保護観察 probationary supervision	捕捉しがたい elusive	ホログラム hologram
保護観察の probationary	補足的 supplementary	ホワイトカラー犯罪者 pinstripe perpetrator
保護者 guardian	細流 trickle	
保護者 shield	保存剤 preservative	ホワイトハウス White House
保護者同伴映画 PG	保存する mothball	ホワイトハウス事務局 White House Office
保護主義 protectionism	母体 parent	
保護主義者 protectionist	母体の maternal	ホワイトホール街 Whitehall
保護手段 safeguard	母体の maternal	本 book
保護する defend	…と歩調を合わせる keep pace with	本格回復 full recovery
保護する protect	…と歩調を合わせる keep up with	本格化させる step up
保護する protective	発起人 founder	本格的な full-blown
保護する safeguard	発起人 mover	本格的な full-fledged
保護物 shield	北極星 Polaris	本格的な full-scale
保護貿易論者 protectionist	没個性 anonymity	本格的ポルノ XXX
保護用の protective	発作 stroke	本業の core
保護を与える protective	没収 seizure	本拠地 stronghold
補佐官 aide	没収する confiscate	本国外流通通貨 xenocurrency
保持 holding	発足に当たっての inaugural	本腰を入れた full-fledged
保持 sustainment	ボットネット Botnet	ポンジー式投資詐欺術 Ponzi
保持者 holder	勃発 outbreak	本質 crux
保持する retain	没落 downfall	本質 nitty-gritty
保持する sustain	ボツリヌス毒素 botulinum toxin	本質 nuts and bolts
星のきらめく star-studded	ボディ・ランゲージ body language	…に本社を置く headquartered
保釈 bail	…を補填する make up for	本線 trunk line
保釈金 bail	歩道橋 overpass	本人確認 identification
保守 maintenance	程よい moderate	…に本部を置く based
募集 offering	骨組み framework	本命 shoo-in
募集 recruiting	骨の折れる stiff	翻訳する translate
募集する recruit	骨の折れる uphill	ぼんやりと現われる loom
募集する solicit	骨太の方針 big-boned policy	本流 mainstream
保守主義者 conservative	ポピュラーな pop	
保守主義者 rightist	ポピュリズム populism	**ま**
保守党員 conservative	保有 holding	
保守反動主義 hardhattism	保有 possession	マーケット同士の取引 m to m EC
保守寄りの right-of-center	保有株 holdings	マイクロチップ microchip
	保有株 shareholdings	

マイクロプロセッサー microprocessor	貧しく poorly	マンツーマン one on one
毎月の monthly	また聞きの secondhand	万引き shoplifting
マイナス基調 minus territory	まだ…されないままだ remain	マンマシン・インターフェース man-machine interface
マイナスの negative	間違い mistake	
マイナス要因 drag	間違いをする trip up	マンマシン・システム man-machine system
毎日の daily	真っ最中の in full swing	
マイル標石 milestone	マッチング方式 matching system	マンモス大学 polyversity
前置き prelude	…まで up to	満了 end
前倒しする bring forward	まとめる hammer	満了 termination
前倒しする front-load	まとめる unite	満了する expire
前の ex-	…に的を絞る focus on	
前の prior	…に的を絞る zero in on	**み**
前払いの prepaid	間に合わせ stopgap	
前評判の高い much-heralded	間に合わせの makeshift	身動きできない tight
前向きに proactively	免れる evade	身動きをとれなくする bog
前向きの forward-looking	間抜け loggerhead	身内びいき nepotism
前もって計画した premeditated	マネー・サプライ money supply	見える visible
前もって熟慮した premeditated	マネー・マーケット money market	見送る shelve
前もって取り決める prearrange	マネー・ロンダリング laundering	見送る waive
負かす defeat	招く incur	未解決の disputed
曲がった awry	…を招く lead to	未解決の pending
賄う cover	マネタリズム monetarism	磨いた ground
曲がる turn	麻痺 paralysis	未開拓の untapped
巻き上げる defraud	麻痺させる paralyze	未開発の untapped
巻き上げる jockey	マフィア Mafia	見返り consolation prize
巻き返し rollback	マフィアの構成員 Mafioso	見返り quid pro quo
巻き返し戦術 rollback	…のままである remain	未確認飛行物体 UFO
巻き込む engulf	守る defend	未加工の raw
巻き込む implicate	守る protect	見方 view
紛らわしい misleading	守る safeguard	身柄拘束者 detainee
幕 curtain	守る stick to	身代わり scapegoat
幕状のもの curtain	麻薬 drug	ミクロ経済学 microeconomics
マグニチュードで on the Richter scale	迷う shilly-shally	ミクロ経済的 microeconomic
	マリファナ pot	ミクロ分析 microanalysis
マクロ経済学 macroeconomics	マリファナ常用者 pothead	未決済小切手 float
マクロ経済的 macroeconomic	丸1日ぶっ通しの around-the-clock	未決定 suspense
マクロ工学技術 macroengineering	マルチ商法 referral sales plan	未決定の moot
マクロ政策 macro policy	マルチメディア multimedia	…を見越して in anticipation of
マクロファージ活性化因子 macrophage activating factor	丸投げ subcontracting	見越す anticipate
	回す turn	見込み potential
マクロ分析 macroanalysis	周りの surrounding	見込みのある likely
マクロ予測 macroforecasting	…の周りを回る orbit	見込む anticipate
負けず劣らず neck-and-neck	回れ右 about-face	見込む expect
負けている trail	回れ右 rightabout-face	未婚の maiden
曲げる distort	マン・マシン通信 man-machine communication	ミサイル missile
マザーズ Mothers		ミサイル迎撃の antimissile
…に勝る outnumber	蔓延 spread	短い short
…に優る outpace	満開の full-blown	短い記事 short
まさる prevail	満期書替え rollover	短い冗談 one-liner
増す augment	満期になる expire	未就任の designate
増す deepen	満期日 due date	未処理 backlog
増す heighten	万華鏡 kaleidoscope	未処理の raw
まずく poorly	満場一致で unanimously	自らの self-
マスコミ media	満場一致の unanimous	見捨てる ditch
マスコミ受けのする mediagenic	慢性の chronic	水の aquatic
マスコミの世界 medialand	満足 satisfaction	水浸しにする deluge
マスコミ向きの mediagenic	満足させる satisfy	水増し padding

水増し請求する	overcharge
水増し請求する	pad
ミスマッチ	mismatch
…店	outlet
見せる	show
…を未然に防ぐ	stave off
溝	ditch
溝	rut
満たされない需要	pent-up demand
見出し	headline
満たす	meet
満たす	satisfy
見た目	appearance
道	path
満ち溢れている	chock-full
未知数の	x
道筋	path
道筋	route
未知の	x
導く	lead
密航	smuggling
密航者	stowaway
密告	whistle-blowing
密告者	deep throat
密告者	informer
密告者	tipster
密告者	whistle-blower
密告する	tip
密接行進法	lockstep
密造	racketeering
三つの	triple
密売買	trafficking
密売を行う	traffic
密封する	seal off
見積り	estimate
見積り	projection
見積り	valuation
見積りの	estimated
見積りの	proforma
見積もる	estimate
密輸	smuggling
密輸する	smuggle
密輸による	contraband
未定	suspense
見通し	bet
見通し	expectation
見通し	forecast
見通し	outlook
見通し	vision
見通しが明るい	bullish
見通す力のある	visionary
認められている	acceptable
認める	accept
認める	approve
認める	see
見直し	readjustment
見直し	revaluation
見直し	review
見直す	overhaul
見直す	reevaluate
見直す	revamp
見直す	review
…と見なす	deem
南アジア特恵貿易協定	SAPTA
南太平洋経済協力機関	SPEC
身代金要求	ransom demand
実りの多い	fruitful
未払い金	arrears
未払い残高	outstanding balance
未払いの	unpaid
見晴らし	prospect
見張り	watchdog
身びいき	cronyism
身分	rank
身分証明	identification
身分証明	identity
身分の高い	high-ranking
見本	sample
見本検査係	sampler
身元	identity
身元確認	identification
脈絡	connection
ミラー	mirror
未来像	vision
未来の	prospective
ミリシア	militia
見る	see
実を結ばない	fruitless
民営化	privatization
民営化する	privatize
民間企業	private sector
民間最終支出	private consumption
民間資金による社会資本整備	PFI
民間消費支出	private consumption
民間所有の	privately owned
民間の	civil
民間部門	private sector
民事訴訟	suit
民事の	civil
民需	private demand
民衆扇動家	rabble-rouser
民主化	democratization
民主主義者	democrat
民主主義の	democratic
民主政治の	democratic
民主制の	democratic
民主党	Democrats
民主党員	democrat
民生機器	consumer product
民生支援	civilian assistance
民族の	ethnic
民族の	racial
民兵	militia
民有の	privately owned

む

ムーアの法則	Moore's Law
ムーディーズ	Moody's Investors Service Inc.
ムーンウォーク	moonwalk
無害薬剤	magic bullet
…に向かう	head
無傷の状態	integrity
無許可の	unauthorized
無気力な	lethargic
向きを変える	turn
向きを変えること	turnabout
無形の	invisible
無血クーデター	bloodless coup
向ける	aim
無効にする	abate
無効にする	override
無効にする	rescind
無効にする	revoke
無作為抽出する	random-sample
無作為の	random
無視する	brush off
無視する	override
蝕む	undermine
矛盾	contradiction
…と矛盾する	belie
矛盾する	conflicting
無条件の	absolute
無条件の	clean
無条件の	outright
無条件の	unstinting
無人化	robotization
無人偵察機	unmanned reconnaissance plane
難しい	stiff
結びつき	link
結びつき	relationship
結びつき	tie
結びつける	link
結びつける	tie
結びつける	unite
ムスリム	Muslim
ムスリムの	Islamic
無制限の	no-holds-barred
無制限の	open-end
無税償却	tax-free amortization
無性的に繁殖させる	clone
無線	wireless
無線業務	wireless
無線通信	wireless
無駄	waste
無断欠席	truancy
無担保コール翌日物	uncollateralized overnight call rate
無担保の	unsecured

無断翻訳公開　scanlation	メガストア　megastore	申込み　bidding
むち　whip	目利き　judge	申込み　offer
無秩序　disarray	メキシコ湾岸諸州　Gulf States	申し込む　offer
無秩序　disorder	目先の　short-term	申立て　allegation
むちで打つ　whip	めざす　aim	申し立てられた　alleged
無投票での再選　uncontested reelection	目印　hallmark	申し立てる　file
無能力　inefficiency	目印　landmark	申し出　offer
無分別な　unreasonable	珍しい品種　rare breed	申し出　overture
無法者　outlaw	目立たせる　accentuate	申し出　proposition
無名　anonymity	目立たせる　highlight	網状組織　network
無銘品　off-brand	目立つ　noticeable	申し渡す　sentence
無料電話　toll-free	目立った　outstanding	猛スピード　breakneck speed
無力にする　paralyze	メタボリック症候群　metabolic syndrome	猛省　soul-searching
		猛烈な　blistering
め	目玉　centerpiece	モーニング・コール　wake-up call
	目玉商品　highlight	…にもかかわらず　albeit
名案　brainstorm	メタンガス　methane gas	目視による　visual
明暗　tone	メタンハイドレート　methane hydrate	目的　aim
明確化した　defined	メディケア　Medicare	目的　goal
明確にする　define	メディケイド　Medicaid	目的　objective
明確に述べる　articulate	目に付く　noticeable	目的地　goal
明確に表明する　articulate	目に見えない　invisible	黙秘権　Fifth (Amendment)
銘柄　brand	目に見える　visible	目標　aim
明記　specification	目盛り　reading	目標　goal
名義　name	目を大きく見開いた　wide-awake	目標　objective
明記する　stipulate	目を通す　browse	目標　target
明言する　vow	面　side	目標とされている　targeted
明細　specification	免疫体を含む　immune	目標とされる　targeted
名士　best	免疫性の　immune	…を目標に定める　target
名士　celebrity	免疫の　immune	目標にする　target
名士　personage	免許　concession	もくろみ　project
名称　denomination	免許　license	模型　model
名称　name	免除　cancelation	モサド　Mossad
命じる　mandate	免職　dismissal	モスクワ　Moscow
命じる　order	免除する　forgive	模造する　counterfeit
名士録　who's who	面積　acreage	模造する　fake
名声　celebrity	免責　exemption	模造品　counterfeit
名声　prestige	面接　interview	模造品　dummy
名声　reputation	メンター　mentor	模造品　knockoff
名声のある　prestigious	メンター制度　mentoring	もたらす　bring
…の名声を持つ　-name	メンターによる支援　mentoring	…をもたらす　lead to
名簿　listing	メンターの支援の受け手　mentee	持ち合い株　crossheld stocks
命名する　style	メンツを立てる　face-saving	持ち合い株式　crossheld stocks
名目　nominal terms	メンティー　mentee	持ち上がる　pop up
名目上の　paper	面と向かっての　face-to-face	持ち上げる　lift
名目の　nominal	綿密な調査　scrutiny	持ち株　holdings
名目ベース　nominal terms	綿密に計画する　map out	持ち株　shareholdings
盟約　treaty		持ち株会社　holding company
盟友　crony	**も**	持ち越す　carry over
名誉毀損　assassination		持ちこたえる　shore up
名誉毀損　slander	儲からない　unprofitable	持ち込む　introduce
名誉毀損罪　libel	儲かる　lucrative	持ち高　position
命令　directive	儲かる　profitable	持ち直し　pickup
命令を出す　order	猛攻撃　assault	持ち直し　rally
迷惑　nuisance	申し入れ　overture	持ち直し　recovery
迷惑メール　spam	申込み　application	持ち直す　pick up
	申込み　bid	持ち直す　rebound

持ち場　newsbeat	躍進　success	優位　hegemony
持ち運びできる　portable	約束　engagement	優位　precedence
持ち分　equity	約束　promise	優位な　predominant
持ち分　interest	約束事　convention	優位に立つ　dominate
持ち分　quota	約束する　commit	優位を築く　reign
持ち分権　equity	約束する　pledge	誘因　culprit
持ち分プーリング　pooling of interests	約束手形　note	誘因　incentive
持つ　own	約定　stipulation	誘引する　attract
持ってくる　bring	役に立つ　available	優越　excellence
モットー　slogan	…に役に立つ　–friendly	優越論者　supremacist
最も深刻な　worst	役に立つ　profit	遊園地　park
最も強いビールの記号　XXX	薬物　drug	誘拐する　abduct
最も左の　leftmost	薬物に対する人体の反応　pharmaco-kinetics	誘拐する　kidnap
モデル　model		有害な　detrimental
元の　ex-	役割　role	有価証券　securities
元の　former	焼き付くような　blistering	有価証券報告書　financial statement
求め　request	野菜　vegetable	有価証券明細表　portfolio
求める　call for	…にやさしい　–friendly	勇気づけられる　heartening
求める　call in	安い　competitive	有機的な　organic
…を求める　resort to	安い　inexpensive	有給の　salaried
求める　seek	安く売り払う　sell off	遊休不動産　idle real estate
求める　urge	安値　low	優遇　discrimination
…に戻る　return to	厄介　nuisance	優遇　preference
物差し　yardstick	約款　clause	優遇税制　preferential tax system
物の見方　mindset	雇う　employ	有形の　visible
模範　paragon	雇う　hire	遊撃兵　guerrilla
模倣　emulation	宿なしの　homeless	有権者　elector
もみ消し　cover-up	…に雇われた　in the pay of	有権者　voter
もみ消す　cover up	…に雇われている　in the pay of	友好　olive branch
模様替え　makeover	破る　defeat	融合する　fuse
模様眺めの　wait-and-see	破る　violate	有効性　availability
漏らす　leak	山火事　bushfire	有効性　efficiency
盛り返す　rally	山積み　pileup	友好的な　friendly
モルモット　guinea pig	ヤミ市場　black market	友好的買収者　white knight
漏れ　leakage	ヤミ専従　on-the-job union work	融合動物　hybrid
問責決議案　censure motion	ヤミ取引　black market	有効な　available
問題　difficulties	止めさせる　scuttle	有効な　effective
問題　matter	止める　ax	有効保存期間　shelf life
問題　problem	止める　quit	ユーザー同士　end to end
問題解決　solution	止める　stall	ユーザー名　username
問題点　count	止める　stem	有罪宣告　condemnation
問題点の改善　workout	…を止める　wean self off	有罪の　guilty
問題のある　problematic	やりがいのある　challenging	有罪の判決を下す　convict
	やり方　mode	有罪判決　conviction
や	やり方　rope	有罪を宣告する　convict
	柔らかい　soft	融資　lending
野営　camp	和らげる　alleviate	融資　loan
八百長疑惑　match-fixing scandal	和らげる　assuage	有事　emergency
夜間　night	和らげる　ease	有識者　expert
夜間外出禁止令　curfew	和らげる　placate	融資者　lender
夜間の　overnight	和らげる　relax	融資する　finance
焼肉レストラン　rotisserie		融資する　lend
約因　consideration	**ゆ**	融資する　loan
役員　director		有刺鉄線　barbed wire
役員　official	友愛　fraternity	勇者　lion
役員名簿　slate	優位　advantage	優秀　excellence
薬害　pharmaceutical disaster	優位　edge	優秀な　excellent

優秀な　par excellence	有力な　influential	養育する　nurture
優勝争い　pennant race	有力な　potent	用意する　prepare
優勝決定戦　runoff	有力な　predominant	容易な　easy
優勝者　champion	有力な　prevailing	要因　backdrop
融資枠　facility	優劣　odds	要因　element
融資を受ける　borrow	ユーロ　euro	要因　factor
有人宇宙実験室　Spacelab	ユーロ圏　eurozone	要員　personnel
有人の　manned	歪み　distortion	容器　vessel
優勢　dominance	歪み　twist	容疑　suspicion
優勢　domination	歪める　distort	容疑者　suspect
遊説する　politick	床面積　floor space	要求　demand
優勢な　prevailing	歪んだ　awry	要求　mandate
優先　precedence	輸血　blood transfusion	要求　request
優先　preference	揺さぶる　buffet	要求する　call for
優先　priority	揺さぶる　rock	要求する　claim
優先株　preferred share	揺さぶる　roll	要求する　demand
優先権　priority	揺さぶる　sway	要求する　require
優先出資証券　preferred security	輸出　export	用具　tool
優先する　preferential	輸出関連企業　export-related businesses	擁護　advocacy
優先すること　precedence		擁護　championship
優先的な　preferential	輸出企業　exporting company	養護　day care
郵送する　post	輸出業者　exporters	擁護者　advocate
誘致する　lure	輸出国　exporters	擁護者　champion
融通のきく　flexible	輸出される　exported	擁護者　protagonist
誘導する　lead	輸出重視の　export-oriented	擁護する　safeguard
有徳な　virtuous	輸出主導の　export-driven	要塞　stronghold
有能な　efficient	輸出主導の　export-led	要旨　gist
有能な　talented	輸出入禁止の　contraband	要旨　keynote
誘発　provocation	輸出品　export	様式　form
誘発する　spark	ゆすり　blackmail	様式　format
郵便　post	ゆすり　racketeer	容赦する　forgive
郵便局の　postal	ゆすり　racketeering	要所　key
郵便の　postal	輸送　transportation	養殖する　cultivate
郵便物　post	油送船　oiler	用心　vigilance
郵便法　Mail Law	豊かな　affluent	用心する　watch
UFO研究　ufology	油断なく気を配っている　alert	用心深い　cautious
UFO研究家　ufologist	油断のない　wide-awake	用心深い　wary
裕福な　affluent	癒着した　collusive	様子見　wait-and-see
有望な　likely	輸入　import	要請する　invite
有望な　promising	輸入する　import	要請する　prod
有望な　viable	ユビキタス　ubiquitous	要素　element
有名人　celebrity	揺らぐ　vacillate	要素　factor
有名人　personage	揺り動かす　jolt	様相　phase
有名な　known	揺り動かす　sway	用地　land
有用　utility	許される　permissible	要点　gist
有用性　availability	許す　forgive	陽電子　positron
猶予期間　grace period	緩める　relax	要点把握　scanning
有利　advantage	緩やかな　modest	容認する　accept
有利子負債　interest bearing debt	揺れ　jolt	容認できる　acceptable
有利な　favorable	揺れ　quake	要約　brief
…に有利な　-friendly	揺れ　sway	要約　rundown
有利な　lucrative	揺れる　vacillate	要約　summary
有利取引材料　bargaining chip		要約する　sum up
優良株　blue chip	**よ**	容量　content
優良の　good		要領書　brief
有力者　bigwig	用意　preparation	予感　premonition
有力新興国　BRICs	…する用意ができている　poised to	良き指導者　mentor

預金　account	予想　bet	…と呼ぶ　dub
預金　banking	予想　expectation	呼ぶ　style
預金　cash	予想　outlook	余分な　surplus
預金　savings	予想　prediction	予防　prevention
預金する　bank	予想される　projected	…を予防する　forestall
預金する　pay in	予想する　anticipate	予防する　prevent
預金保険機構　DIC	予想する　envisage	予防するための　preventive
抑圧　coercion	予想する　expect	予防接種　inoculation
抑圧　repression	予想する　forecast	予防措置　precautionary approach
抑圧的な　repressive	予想する　predict	読み書き能力　literacy
抑止　deterrence	予想の　anticipatory	読取り機　scanner
翌日物コール　overnight call	予想を裏切った　disappointing	予約する　book
翌日物の　overnight	予測　anticipation	…より大きい　outweigh
抑止力　deterrent	予測　estimate	…より数が多い　outnumber
抑制　brake	予測　forecast	…より価値がある　outweigh
抑制　restraint	予測　outlook	寄り付き価格　opening price
抑制　restriction	予測　prediction	選り抜きの　select
抑制効果　depressing effect	予測　projection	…による　attributable to
抑制する　cap	予測される　projected	夜　night
抑制する　curb	予測する　forecast	世論調査　poll
抑制する　dampen	予測する　predict	世論調査員　pollster
抑制する　restrain	予測する　project	世論調査員　polltaker
欲望　appetite	予測できる　foreseeable	…に弱い　vulnerable to
抑留者　detainee	余地　flexibility	弱い　weak
予見する　forecast	予知　forecast	弱いものいじめ　bullying
予見できる　foreseeable	予兆　forerunner	弱気　short
予告　herald	欲求不満にさせる　frustrate	弱気市場　bear market
予告　notice	予定作成　scheduling	弱気の　bearish
予告する　herald	予定されている　due	弱気含みの　bearish
予告する　warn	予定する　schedule	弱まった　weakened
…を予告編で宣伝する　trail	…する予定である　intend to	弱まらない　unabated
横軸　x-axis	予定に入れる　pencil in	弱まる　falter
横ばい　flat	予定表　slate	弱まる　slow
横ばい　leveling off	予定利率　guaranteed yield	弱まる　wane
横ばい状態　plateau	予定を立てる　schedule	弱まる気配がない　unabated
横ばい状態になる　level off	夜中　night	弱み　weakness
横ばい状態になる　level out	4人組　quartet	弱める　dampen
予算　budget	4年ごとの　quadrennial	弱める　enfeeble
予算　spending	世の中　world	弱める　impair
予算案の　budgetary	余波　aftermath	弱々しい　anemic
予算外支出　off-budget spending	余波　momentum	弱らせる　debilitate
予算教書　Budget Message	呼びかけ　warning	4者の　quadrilateral
予算上の　budgetary	予備選挙　primary	四重苦　quatlemma
予算に計上する　budget	呼び出し　summons	4倍にする　quadruple
予算の　budgetary	呼び出し状　subpoena	
予算ばらまき　pump priming	呼び出す　summon	**ら**
予算を組む　earmark	予備的合意書　memorandum of	
予算を立てる　budget	understanding	来期　coming year
よじ登る　scale	予備的な　preliminary	ライセンス供与　licensing
余剰　excess	予備の　auxiliary	来年度　coming year
余剰　surplus	予備の　pilot	烙印を押す　brand
余剰資金　surplus fund	予備の　preliminary	落伍　fallout
余剰の　surplus	予備の　preparatory	落札価格　winning price
余剰分　surplus	予備の蓄え　pool	落成　inauguration
余剰利益　melon	呼水　pump priming	落成式を行う　inaugurate
与信　credit	呼び寄せる　call	楽天的な　optimistic
予想　anticipation	呼ぶ　call	楽な　easy

拉致	abduct
ラチェット効果	ratchet effect
拉致する	kidnap
楽観的な	optimistic
楽観的な	upbeat
楽観的な見通し	optimism
ラッセル2000指数	Russell 2000 index
ラ・ニーニャ現象	La Niña
ラビ	rabbi
ラムサール条約	Ramsar Convention
ラン	LAN
乱獲	indiscriminate fishing
乱高下	volatility
乱高下する	fluctuate
乱高下する	volatile
乱雑	disarray
卵巣の	ovarian
乱打する	batter
乱暴	violence
乱暴な	violent
乱用する	abuse
乱用する	misuse

り

リース契約	lease
リーダー	guru
リードをひっくり返しての	come-from-behind
利益	benefit
利益	gain
利益	income
利益	interest
利益	melon
利益	profit
利益になる	profit
利益の大きい	lucrative
利益の出ない	fruitless
利益配当	profit sharing
利益分配	profit sharing
利益率	profit margin
利益率	ratio
利益をあげる	chalk up
利益を上げる	take in
利益を上げること	moneymaking
利益を与える	benefit
利益を生む	profitable
利益を得る	profit
リエンジニアリング	reengineering
利害関係がある	concern
利害関係者	stakeholder
理解する	grip
理解する	see
力点を置く	stress
利食い	profit taking
陸上回線	landline
リクター震度計	Richter scale
利権	pork
履行しない	default
履行する	make good
リコール	recall
利子	interest
理事	director
理事会	board
理事会	board meeting
利潤	gain
利殖	moneymaking
リスボン条約	Lisbon Treaty
利息払い	debt servicing
離脱	fallout
離脱	secession
離脱	withdrawal
…から離脱する	break away from
離脱する	split
リチウムイオン電池	lithium-ion battery
率	rate
立案	formulation
立案	planning
立案した	planned
立案する	formulate
立憲君主	constitutional monarch
立証	attestation
立証	verification
立証者	demonstrator
立証する	verify
立証責任	burden of proof
立体の	three-dimensional
立地	location
立法	enactment
立法	legislation
立法化する	enact
立法機関	legislature
立法権のある	legislative
立法者	lawmaker
立法者	legislator
立法の	legislative
立法府	legislature
里程標	milestone
利点	advantage
離党者	defector
利得	benefit
利得	profit
理念	philosophy
理念主義	ideology
利乗せ	pyramid
リフォーム	refurbishment
リフレーション	reflation
リフレ的な	reflationary
リベート	kickback
利便性	convenience
リボン	ribbon
利回り	yield
略式の	casual
理由	occasion
理由	reason
流行の傾向を決める	trendsetting
流行病	epidemic
流行を作る	trendsetting
硫酸ピッチ	sulfuric pitch
粒子	plasma
粒子状物質	PM
流出	flow
流出	hemorrhage
流出	leakage
流出	outflow
流出額	outflow
流出する	leak
…に流出する	spill over into
隆盛	prosperity
流説	scandal
りゅう弾砲	howitzer
留置する	detain
流通	circulation
流通	currency
流通	distribution
流通業者	distributor
流通させる	circulate
流通している	afloat
流通量	float
流通ルート	pipeline
流動資産の換金性	liquidity
流動性	current
流動性	liquidation
流動性	liquidity
流動性の高い	liquid
流動性の罠	liquidity trap
流入	influx
流派	school
流用	misappropriation
量	quantity
利用	utilization
領域	field
領域	ground
領域	niche
領域	range
領域	scope
領域	territory
両替する	exchange
料金	charge
料金	fare
料金	fee
利用されていない	untapped
量産	rollout
量産する	mass-produce
良識	smarts
利用者	user
領収書	receipt
良循環	virtuous cycle
利用する	access

利用する　capitalize on
…を利用する　leverage
…を利用する　resort to
利用する　tap
利用する　utilize
領地　territory
量的緩和　quantitative easing
量的な　quantitative
利用できる　available
利用できる　disposable
領土　territory
量の　quantitative
療法　therapy
両方向からの　two-pronged
両面の　two-pronged
両面の　two-track
両面の　two-way
利用率　load factor
両立性　compatibility
旅客　passenger
緑樹　greenery
旅券　passport
旅行　trip
離陸する　take off
利率　interest rate
利率　yield rate
履歴　career
履歴管理　traceability
理論的枠組み　paradigm
臨界　critical mass
臨界　criticality
輪郭　profile
臨機応変的経営　ad hocracy
臨機応変の　ad hoc
林業　forestry industry
林業経営　forestry business
臨時総会　extraordinary meeting
臨時の　ad hoc
臨時の　extraordinary
臨時の　provisional
臨時の　temporary
臨床研修病院　clinical training hospital
隣接する　adjacent
輪番　rotation
倫理　ethics
倫理　moral
倫理　morality

る

類似製品　me-too product
累進的な　graduated
累積　accumulation
累積する　accumulate
ルビコン川　Rubicon

れ

レアメタル　rare metal
レイオフ　redundancy
例外　exception
例外の　exceptional
冷却期間　cooling off
冷遇　cold shoulder
零細小売店　mama and papa store
零細の　mom-and-pop
令状　warrant
冷静　prudence
冷戦　Cold War
零度　zero
冷凍の　frozen
霊廟　mausoleum
例をみない　unprecedented
レーザー　laser
レーザー写真　hologram
レーダー　radar
レームダック　lame duck
歴史の古い　long-established
歴代の　successive
レジャー・カー　recreational vehicle
列　row
劣位　disadvantage
劣化する　deteriorate
レバレッジ　leverage
レポーター　newsperson
廉価な　knockdown
連携　alliance
連携　coordination
…と連携して　in conjunction with
連携する　tie up
連結　combination
連結　consolidation
連結　group
連結　linkage
連結から除外された　unconsolidated
連結した　combined
連結する　combine
連結する　link
連結対象外の　unconsolidated
連結の範囲に含まれない　unconsolidated
連合　alliance
連合　coalition
連合国暫定当局　CPA
連合した　united
連合して　jointly
連鎖　chain
連鎖　linkage
連座させる　implicate
連鎖的変動　spiral
連鎖反応　chain reaction
連鎖反応　knock-on effect
連続　succession
連続した　consecutive
連続して　successively
連続自爆テロ　back-to-back suicide bombings
連続テロ　twin attacks
連帯感　fraternity
練達の　seasoned
連動させる　tie
連邦議会議事堂　Capitol
連邦公開市場委員会　Federal Open Market Committee
連邦航空局　FAA
連邦住宅公社監督局　OFHEO
連邦住宅抵当公庫　Fannie Mae
連邦準備制度理事会　Fed
連邦政府官職一覧　plum book
連邦取引委員会　FTC
連邦の　federal
連絡　liaison
連絡　touch
連絡網　network
連立　coalition

ろ

漏洩　leak
漏洩　leakage
老化　aging
廊下　corridor
労苦　trouble
労使　labor management
老人性の　senile
労賃　wage
漏電　leak
労働　labor
労働　working
労働意欲　morale
労働組合　union
労働市場　labor market
労働者　worker
労働人口　workforce
労働力　labor
労働力　manpower
労働力　workforce
老年の　senile
狼狽　panic
浪費　waste
浪費する　consume
労務管理　labor management
労務費　labor cost
労力　manpower
老齢の　aging
老練者　veteran
老練な　seasoned
老練の　skilled
ローカル・エリア・ネットワーク　LAN

ローマ法王 pontiff	論評 comment	わだち rut
路肩 shoulder	論理の一貫した consecutive	罠 trap
録音テープ audiotape		罠に掛ける trap
録音本 talking book	**わ**	和平 olive branch
ロケット rocket		和平 peace
ロシア政府 Moscow	ワーク・シェアリング work sharing	和平監視者 peacekeeper
ロシア連邦会議下院 Duma	ワーム worm	和平交渉 peacemaking
ロシア連邦議会の下院 State Duma	歪曲する distort	笑い飛ばす laugh off
路線 drive	歪曲報道 mediamorphosis	ワラント落ち x-warr.
路線 line	わいせつな X-rated	割合 percentage
ロックアウト lockout	わいせつな XXX	割合 proportion
ロハス Lohas	賄賂 bribe	割合 rate
ロビー活動 lobbying	賄賂 payola	割合 ratio
ロビー活動をする lobby	賄賂の授受 bribery	割当て allocation
ロビイスト lobbyist	賄賂を贈る bribe	割当て assignment
ロボット robot	和解 compromise	割当て quota
ロボット化 robotization	和解 olive branch	割当量 assignment
ロボット工学 robotics	和解させる mediate	割り当てる allocate
ロボットの robotic	若返らせる rejuvenate	割り当てる assign
ロヤ・ジルガ Loya Jirga	若返りを図る rejuvenate	…に割り込む cut into
論議 controversy	枠組み framework	割引 discount
論議の的となっている controversial	枠組み paradigm	割り引く discount
論拠 case	枠組み scope	割り引く take off
論説 article	惑星中心の宇宙空間 planetocentric space	割増料金 surcharge
論説 editorial		割戻し rebate
論説文 think piece	ワクチン vaccine	割戻し金 kickback
論争 contention	わけ reason	割安な株価評価 undervaluation
論争 controversy	災い woes	悪い unfavorable
…と論争する take issue with	話術 rhetoric	悪くする sour
論争中の moot	ワシントン Washington	悪口 defamation
論争の的 battlefield	ワシントン条約 CITIES	悪口 slander
論争を引き起こす contentious	話題 topic	湾岸協力会議 GCC
論題 theme	話題の newsworthy	湾岸戦争 Gulf War
論題 topic	話題の豊富な newsy	湾曲 twist
論点 contention	私募 private offering	ワンストップ one-stop
論点 count	私募 private placement	ワンセグ One Seg
ロンドン株式取引所 House	私募発行 private placement	腕力 muscle
ロンドン国際石油取引所 IPE	私募発行する privately place	ワンワールド Oneworld

2010年7月10日　初版発行

ビジネス時事英和辞典

2010年7月10日　第1刷発行

著者	菊地義明（きくち・よしあき）
発行者	株式会社三省堂　代表者八幡統厚
印刷者	三省堂印刷株式会社
発行所	株式会社三省堂

〒101-8371
東京都千代田区三崎町二丁目22番14号

電話　編集　（03）3230-9411
　　　営業　（03）3230-9412

振替口座　00160-5-54300
http://www.sanseido.co.jp

〈ビジネス時事英和・640pp.〉

落丁本・乱丁本はお取替えいたします

ISBN 978-4-385-11032-5

Ⓡ本書を無断で複写複製（コピー）することは，著作権法上の例外を除き，禁じられています。
本書をコピーされる場合は，事前に日本複写権センター（JRRC）の許諾を受けてください。
http://www.jrrc.or.jp　　　　eメール: info@jrrc.or.jp　　　電話: 03-3401-2382